# 독자의 1초를 아껴주는 정성!

세상이 아무리 바쁘게 돌아가더라도

책까지 아무렇게나 빨리 만들 수는 없습니다.

인스턴트 식품 같은 책보다는

오래 익힌 술이나 장맛이 밴 책을 만들고 싶습니다.

길벗이지톡은 독자여러분이 우리를 믿는다고 할 때 가장 행복합니다.

나를 아껴주는 어학도서, 길벗이지톡의 책을 만나보십시오.

독자의 1초를 아껴주는 정성을 만나보십시오.

―――

미리 책을 읽고 따라해본 2만 베타테스터 여러분과
무따기 체험단, 길벗스쿨 엄마 2% 기획단,
시나공 평가단, 토익 배틀, 대학생 기자단까지!
믿을 수 있는 책을 함께 만들어주신 독자 여러분께 감사드립니다.

(주)도서출판길벗 www.gilbut.co.kr
길벗이지톡 www.gilbut.co.kr
길벗스쿨 www.gilbutschool.co.kr

## 동영상 강의 보는 방법

**1** 길벗/이지톡 홈페이지(gilbut.co.kr)에서 로그인한 다음 검색창에 '시나공 토익 850 실전 모의고사' 를 검색합니다.

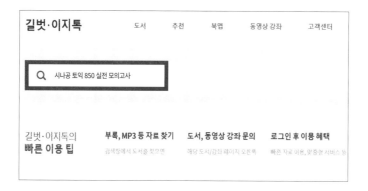

**2** 해당 책을 클릭한 다음 상세 페이지로 들어가 '동영상 강좌'를 클릭합니다.

**3** 무료(0원)로 표시된 동영상 강좌를 '수강 신청'한 후 수강할 수 있습니다. 무료 강좌이기 때문에 결제하지 않습니다.

# 목표 달성 계획표

Actual Test 01을 푼 후 대략적인 점수환산표 점수에 따라 자신의 수준에 맞는 학습 플랜을 선택하세요. 점수환산표는 정답 및 번역 끝부분(번역 및 정답 p.117)에 있습니다.

- [800점 이상]　10일 완성 플랜
- [550~800점]　20일 완성 플랜
- [550점 이하]　40일 완성 플랜

## Listening & Reading

점수 환산표는 정답 및 번역 앞 부분을 참조하세요.

|  | Actual Test 01 | Actual Test 02 | Actual Test 03 | Actual Test 04 | Actual Test 05 |
|---|---|---|---|---|---|
| 맞은 개수 |  |  |  |  |  |
| 틀린 개수 |  |  |  |  |  |
| 환산 점수 |  |  |  |  |  |

|  | Actual Test 06 | Actual Test 07 | Actual Test 08 | Actual Test 09 | Actual Test 10 |
|---|---|---|---|---|---|
| 맞은 개수 |  |  |  |  |  |
| 틀린 개수 |  |  |  |  |  |
| 환산 점수 |  |  |  |  |  |

| 점수 / 회차 | Actual Test 01 | Actual Test 02 | Actual Test 03 | Actual Test 04 | Actual Test 05 | Actual Test 06 | Actual Test 07 | Actual Test 08 | Actual Test 09 | Actual Test 10 |
|---|---|---|---|---|---|---|---|---|---|---|
| 900 |  |  |  |  |  |  |  |  |  |  |
| 800 |  |  |  |  |  |  |  |  |  |  |
| 700 |  |  |  |  |  |  |  |  |  |  |
| 600 |  |  |  |  |  |  |  |  |  |  |
| 500 |  |  |  |  |  |  |  |  |  |  |
| 400 |  |  |  |  |  |  |  |  |  |  |
| 300 |  |  |  |  |  |  |  |  |  |  |

▲ 위 그래프에 자신의 환산 점수를 표시해 보세요.

# 부가 자료 다운로드 방법

**1** | 길벗이지톡 홈페이지(gilbut.co.kr)에서 로그인한 다음 검색창에 '시나공 토익 850 실전 모의고사'를 검색합니다.

**2** | 해당 책을 클릭한 다음 상세 페이지로 들어가 '자료실'을 클릭합니다.

**3** | '자료실'에서 MP3나 학습자료를 선택해 다운로드 할 수 있습니다. (MP3는 실시간 듣기 가능)

시험에 나오는 것만 공부한다!

시나공 토익

## 850

## 실전
## 모의고사

김병기 지음

**문제집**

Actual Test 01~05

길벗
이지:톡

**시나공 토익**

# 850 실전 모의고사

**초판 1쇄 발행** · 2020년 7월 10일
**초판 2쇄 발행** · 2021년 2월 10일

**지은이** · 김병기
**발행인** · 이종원
**발행처** · ㈜도서출판 길벗
**출판사 등록일** · 1990년 12월 24일
**주소** · 서울시 마포구 월드컵로 10길 56(서교동)
**대표전화** · 02) 332-0931 | **팩스** · 02) 322-6766
**홈페이지** · www.gilbut.co.kr | **이메일** · eztok@gilbut.co.kr

**기획 및 책임편집** · 고경환 (kkh@gilbut.co.kr) | **디자인** · 황애라 | **제작** · 이준호, 손일순, 이진혁
**영업마케팅** · 김학흥, 장봉석 | **웹마케팅** · 이수미, 최소영 | **영업관리** · 심선숙 | **독자지원** · 송혜란, 윤정아

**CTP 출력 및 인쇄** · 예림인쇄 | **제본** · 예림바인딩

- 이 도서의 국립중앙도서관 출판예정도서목록(CIP)은 서지정보유통지원시스템 홈페이지(http://seoji.nl.go.kr)와
  국가자료공동목록시스템(http://www.nl.go.kr/kolisnet)에서 이용하실 수 있습니다.(CIP제어번호: CIP2020025709)

**ISBN** 979-11-6521-213-1 03740
(이지톡 도서번호 300993)

**정가 19,500원**

· · · · · · · · · · · · · · · · · · · · · · · · · · · · · · · · · · · · · · · · · · · · · · · · · · · · · · · · · · · · · · · · · · · · · · · · · · · · · · · ·

**독자의 1초까지 아껴주는 정성 길벗출판사**

**(주)도서출판 길벗** | IT실용, IT/일반 수험서, 경제경영, 취미실용, 인문교양(더퀘스트) www.gilbut.co.kr
**길벗이지톡** | 어학단행본, 어학수험서 www.eztok.co.kr
**길벗스쿨** | 국어학습, 수학학습, 어린이교양, 주니어 어학학습, 교과서 www.gilbutschool.co.kr

# 시간에 쫓기는 수험생을 위한
# 효율적인 850점 맞춤 학습!

토익 점수가 급히 필요한 수험생들에겐 최근의 상황은 '좋지 않다'라는 말로 표현할 수 없을 만큼 힘들다. 그리고 학원에 가는 것도 걱정이 되는 이런 상황일수록 효율적인 학습의 중요도는 더 높아진다. 이런 상황에 조금이나마 도움이 되고자 저자는 이 책을 기획하고 집필했다. 이 책의 가장 큰 특징은 효율적으로 목표점수 850점을 달성할 수 있는 맞춤 학습 방법을 제시했다는 것이다.

## 850점 달성을 위한 10세트, 2,000문제 훈련! 친절하고 자세한 해설집!

이 책에는 총 10회분으로 구성된 2,000문제가 실려있다. 이 책에 실린 모든 문제는 억지로 꼬아놓은 문제가 아니라 실제 출제 유형에 기반을 두고 있다. 미묘한 함정까지도 파헤치기 위해 노력했고 850점에 맞춰 난도를 조정했다. 문제 학습과 함께 이 책의 해설집은 시중 어떤 책보다 자세히 풀어서 설명해준다. 정답과 함께 오답도 자세히 설명해주며 고득점을 위한 팁도 아낌없이 알려준다.

## 기본 실력을 더 견고하게 해주는 'LC+RC' 학습 자료!

이 책은 10회분 문제뿐만 아니라 다양한 학습자료도 같이 제공한다. LC는 기출 표현과 듣기력을 모두 잡을 수 있는 850점 맞춤 듣기 훈련집을 제공하며, RC는 고득점의 기본인 핵심 문법집을 제공한다. 이 학습 자료만 다 학습해도 단기간 850점을 얻고 싶은 수험생들이 기본 문제를 틀리는 실수를 절대 하지 않게 된다.

## 20일에 맞춘 850점 달성 학습 커리큘럼 및 문제 풀이 동영상 강의 제공

이 책은 20일에 맞춰서 학습하도록 학습커리큘럼을 제공한다. 자기 수준에 맞는 커리큘럼을 선택해서 맞춤 학습을 할 수 있게 학습커리큘럼을 제공했고 다양한 학습 자료와 함께 학습할 수 있도록 했다. 또한 고득점의 핵심인 파트 5 문제 전체 동영상 강의를 제공하여 짧은 시간에 효율적으로 학습할 수 있도록 했다.

이 책이 850점을 목표로 하는 수험생들에게 조금이라도 도움이 된다면 더 바랄게 없다. 온 힘을 다해 이 책을 썼다. 끝으로 이 책이 나오는 데 도움을 준 길벗 편집부와 독자들에게 감사드린다.

2020년 여름

저자 김병기

# 이 책의 특징 및 활용 방법

## 1 'LC+RC' 실전 모의고사 10회분으로 1개월 안에 850점을 달성하세요!

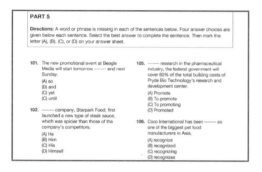

### 최신경향을 반영한 10회분 실전 모의고사

최근 실제 토익 출제 경향을 반영한 실전 모의고사 10회분을 수록했습니다. 이 책에 실린 문제만다 풀어도 실전은 완벽하게 대비할 수 있습니다.

### 20일 안에 850점을 달성하는 커리큘럼 제공!!

10회분 2000제와 함께 20일 안에 850점을 달성할 수 있게 해주는 20일 완성 커리큘럼을 제공합니다. 다양한 학습자료와 동영상 강의를 통해 학습한 내용을 더 깊이 이해하고 학습 효율을 높일 수 있게 구성했습니다.

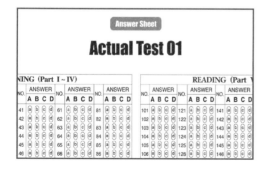

### 정답표 제공

교재 뒤에 수록된 정답표를 활용해서 실전처럼 답안지 마킹을 연습해 볼 수 있게 했습니다. 실전처럼 정해진 시간에 마킹하는 연습을 하며 실전에 익숙해지세요.

# 2 상세하고 명쾌한 해석과 해설로 핵심을 파악하세요!

**108.** With the purchase of any new cosmetic product from CoCo, a stylish gift bag will be ------- for free.

(A) you
(B) your
(C) yours
(D) yourself

------------------------------------

**해석** CoCo 사의 새로운 화장품을 구입하시면 멋진 선물 가방이 무료로 제공됩니다.

**표현 정리** purchase 구매, 구입, 구매하다 cosmetic 화장품 for free 무료로, 공짜로

**유형 파악** 소유대명사 ★★★

**해설** be 동사 뒤에는 위치해야 하는 인칭대명사를 선택하는 문제로 무엇보다 be 동사 뒤에 명사 보어가 위치하려면 앞에 오는 주어와 동일 대상(동격 관계)이 형성되어야 한다는 전제 조건을 충족시켜야 한다. 그러므로 선물 가방이 당신하고 동격일 수 없으니 주격 혹은 목적격 대명사로 쓰이는 you와 재귀대명사 yourself는 동사 뒤에서 목적어로 쓰이거나 혹은 완전한 절의 구조에서 수식어인 부사로 쓰이는 만큼 이들 모두 오답이라고 할 수 있다. 아울러 소유격 대명사 your 역시 단독으로 사용이 불가하니 이 또한 오답이다. 따라서 빈칸에는 선물 가방이 무료로 당신의 것이 될 것이란 문맥을 만들 수 있는 소유대명사 yours가 와야 한다.

**정답** (C)

## 해석
영문의 의미를 명확하게 전달한 해석을 제공하여 해석이 잘 되지 않는 문장의 구조를 파악하는데 도움이 될 수 있게 구성했습니다.

## 표현 정리-온라인 무료 다운로드
본문에서 나온 어휘중 실제 토익에서 출제율이 높거나 어려운 단어만을 선별해서 정확한 의미와 함께 실었습니다.

## 유형 파악 및 해설 -온라인 무료 다운로드
정답뿐만 아니라 오답도 정확히 이해되도록 상세한 해설과 용법을 쉽게 풀어냈습니다. 저자가 수업시간에만 알려주는 풀이 노하우도 추가해 읽기만 해도 점수가 오를 수 있게 구성했습니다.

# 3 다양한 부가 학습자료로 고득점을 완성하세요!

## 저자 직강 문제 풀이 동영상 강의

토익 전체 파트 중에 풀이 노하우가 가장 중요한 파트인 파트 5 문제 전체를 저자가 직접 강의 해 줍니다. 풀이 시간을 줄일 수 있는 노하우와 함께 비슷한 문제가 나와도 풀 수 있는 응용력까지 길러주며 효율적으로 학습할 수 있게 해줍니다.

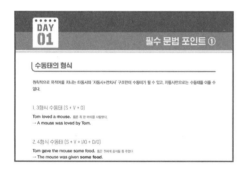

## 20일 안에 정리하는 핵심 문법집과 듣기 훈련집

본문에 나오는 핵심 문법과 듣기 표현을 복습하며 20일 안에 정리 할 수 있게 해줍니다. 본문 문제 풀이 후에 해설집을 확인한 후 커리큘럼에 맞춰 20일동안 학습할 수 있게 구성했습니다. 이 것만 학습해도 기본문제에서는 절대 실수를 하지 않습니다.

## 복습용 어휘 쪽지 시험 & MP3 4종 무료 제공!

본문에 나온 어휘에서 출제율이 높은 어휘만 선별해서 쪽지 시험을 제공합니다. 복습용 또는 스터디용으로 홈페이지에서 다운로드해서 사용할 수 있습니다. MP3파일도 실전용, 복습용, 1.2배속, 고사장 소음버전 4종을 홈페이지에서 무료로 제공합니다.

# 4 추가 자료 다운로드 방법

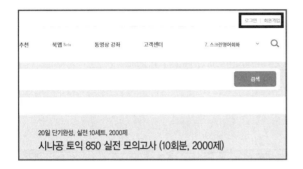

❶
홈페이지(www.gilbut.co.kr)에 접속해 로그인합니다.
(비회원은 회원 가입 권장)

❷
상단 메뉴의 파일 찾기 검색창에
《시나공 토익 850 실전 모의고사》를 입력합니다.

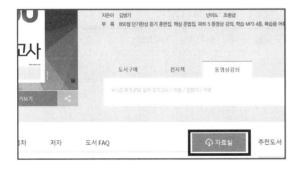

❸
《시나공 토익 850 실전 모의고사》가 검색되면 선택한 후
'자료실'을 클릭하고 자료를 다운로드합니다.

# 토익 시험 소개

## TOEIC이란?

TOEIC은 Test Of English for International Communication의 앞 글자들을 따서 만든 용어로서, 영어가 모국어가 아닌 사람들을 대상으로 하여 언어의 주 기능인 의사소통 능력을 평가하는 시험입니다. 주로 비즈니스와 일상생활 같은 실용적인 주제들을 주로 다루고 있으며, 듣고 이해하는 Listening 분야와 읽고 파악하는 Reading 분야로 나뉩니다. 이 두 부분은 각각 495점의 배점이 주어지며, 총 만점은 990점입니다. 특히 Listening은 미국뿐만 아니라 영국, 호주의 영어발음까지 섞여 나오기도 합니다.

## 시험의 구성

| 구성 | Part | 내용 | 문항 수 | 시간 | 배점 |
|---|---|---|---|---|---|
| Listening Comprehension | 1 | 올바른 사진 설명 찾기 | 6 | 45분 | 495점 |
| | 2 | 질문에 알맞은 대답 찾기 | 25 | | |
| | 3 | 짧은 대화 내용 찾기 | 39 | | |
| | 4 | 긴 연설문 내용 찾기 | 30 | | |
| Reading Comprehension | 5 | 문법 / 어휘 빈칸 채우기(문장) | 30 | 75분 | 495점 |
| | 6 | 문법 / 어휘 빈칸 채우기(지문) | 16 | | |
| | 7 | 1개 장문의 주제와 세부사항 찾기 | 29 | | |
| | | 2개 장문의 주제와 세부사항 찾기 | 10 | | |
| | | 3개 장문의 주제와 세부사항 찾기 | 15 | | |
| Total | | 7 Part | 200 | 120분 | 990점 |

## 토익 출제분야

토익은 국제적으로 통용되는 비즈니스와 특정 문화에 국한되지 않는 일상생활에 관한 내용을 다룹니다.

| | | |
|---|---|---|
| 비즈니스 | 일반업무 | 구매, 영업/판매, 광고, 서비스, 계약, 연구/개발, 인수/합병 |
| | 제조 | 생산 공정, 품질/공장 관리 |
| | 인사 | 채용, 지원, 승진, 퇴직, 급여 |
| | 통신 | 공지, 안내, 회의, 전화, 이메일, 팩스, 회람, 인트라넷, 협조 |
| | 재무/회계 | 투자, 세금 신고, 환급/청구, 은행 |
| | 행사 | 기념일, 행사, 파티, 시상식 |
| 일상생활 | 문화/레저 | 영화, 공연, 박물관, 여행, 쇼핑, 외식, 캠핑, 스포츠 |
| | 구매 | 주문/예약, 변경/취소, 교환/환불, 배송 |
| | 건강 | 병원 예약, 진료, 의료보험 |
| | 생활 | 고장, 보수, 생활 요금, 일정 |

# 토익 접수 및 응시, 성적 확인

## 토익 접수

**접수기간 및 접수처 확인:** TOEIC 위원회 홈페이지 / 응시료 : 44,500원

① **방문 접수**
- 해당 회 접수기간에 지정된 접수처에서 응시료를 납부하고, 신청서를 작성한 후 접수합니다.
- 사진(반명함판, 3x4cm) 한 장을 지참합니다.
- 원서 접수시간: 09:00 ~ 18:00(점심시간 12:00 ~ 13:00)

② **인터넷 접수**

해당 회 접수기간에 TOEIC 위원회 홈페이지(www.toeic.co.kr)에서 언제든 등록이 가능합니다. 사진은 jpg 파일로 준비하면 됩니다.

③ **특별 추가 접수**

특별 접수기간 내에 인터넷 접수로만 가능하며 응시료가 48,900원입니다.

## 토익 응시 준비물

규정 신분증     연필과 지우개     시계     수험번호

＊성적은 정해진 성적 발표일 오전 6시부터 토익위원회 홈페이지와 ARS 060-800-0515를 통해 조회할 수 있습니다. 성적표는 선택한 신분증은 주민등록증, 운전면허증, 공무원증, 기간 만료 전의 여권, 만 17세 미만의 중고생에 한 해 학생증 등도 인정됩니다. 수험번호는 수험장에서도 확인할 수 있습니다. 필기도구는 연필 종류면 다 되지만 사인펜은 사용할 수 없습니다.

## 시험 시간 안내

| 시간 | 내용 |
| --- | --- |
| 09:30 ~ 09:45 | 답안지 배부 및 작성 오리엔테이션 |
| 09:45 ~ 09:50 | 휴식 시간 |
| 09:50 ~ 10:05 | 1차 신분증 검사 |
| 10:05 ~ 10:10 | 문제지 배부 및 파본 확인 |
| 10:10 ~ 10:55 | LC 시험 진행 |
| 10:55 ~ 12:10 | RC 시험 진행(2차 신분 확인) |

＊아무리 늦어도 9시 50분까지는 입실해야 하며, 고사장의 상황에 따라 위의 시간은 약간 변할 수 있습니다.

## 성적 확인 및 성적표 수령

성적은 정해진 성적 발표일 오전 6시부터 토익위원회 홈페이지와 ARS 060-800-0515를 통해 조회할 수 있습니다. 성적표는 선택한 방법으로 수령이 가능하며 최초 발급만 무료입니다.

# 파트별 유형 및 전략

 **Part 1**

## 사진 묘사 (6문제)
사진을 보고 가장 알맞은 문장을 고르는 유형

**Example**

| 문제지 | 음성 |
|---|---|
|  | **1.** Look at the picture marked number 1 in your test book.<br><br>(A) She is raking some leaves.<br>(B) She is washing her shorts.<br>(C) She is watering some plants.<br>(D) She is selecting vegetables.<br><br>정답 (C) |

### 출제 경향

❶ 파트 1에서 1인/2인 이상 등장하는 사람들의 행동 및 상태를 묘사하는 문제는 평균 3~4문항(전체 60%)이 출제되고 있으며 주로 현재 시제 및 현재 진행형으로 구성된 문장이 정답으로 제시됩니다

❷ 사물/정경을 묘사하는 사진 및 사람과 사물 또는 정경의 복합 사진 문제가 평균 2~3문항(전체 40%)이 출제되고 있으며 이들은 사물의 위치나 배열형태 그리고 정경 묘사에 치중하는 정답이 제시되는 만큼 주로 현재시제, 현재완료 수동태, 현재 수동태 및 There 구문으로 구성된 문장이 정답으로 등장하고 있습니다.

### 풀이 전략

❶ **사진을 최대한 적절하게 묘사한 사진을 골라야 합니다.**
자주 출제되는 오답유형을 알고 있어야 합니다. 보기를 들으며 o/x를 표시해 가며 확실히 오답을 제거합니다.

• 사진에서 확인이 불가한 행동/대상을 지칭하는 동사/명사가 등장하는 선택지는 오답
• 사진에 인물이 등장하지 않는 상황에서 being이 들리면 선택지는 거의 오답
• 선택지에서 All, Every, Each, Both가 등장하는 경우 거의 대부분 오답

❷ **사진을 보기 전에 나올 단어를 예상 할 수 있어야 합니다.**
보기를 듣기 전에 사진을 보고 나올 동사나 명사를 미리 연상해봅니다. 거의 나오는 어휘가 정해져 있으므로 내용을 파악하는데 큰 도움이 됩니다.

## Part 2 — 질의 응답 (25문제)

질문을 듣고 보기 세 개중 가장 적절한 답을 고르는 유형

### Example

| 문제지 | 음성 |
|---|---|
| **8.** Mark your Answer on your answer sheet. | **8.** Where do you usually go for computer repairs?<br><br>(A) Last Thursday.<br>(B) I think I can fix it.<br>(C) Do you have a problem?<br><br>정답 (C) |

### 출제 경향

❶ 파트 2에서 출제되는 문제 유형의 비중을 살펴보면 '의문사의문문 – 일반/긍정의문문 – 평서문 및 부가의문문 – 일반/부정의문문 – 선택의문문 – 간접의문문' 순이며 이전에 비해 일반의문문과 평서문 및 부가의문문의 출제 비중이 높아졌다고 할 수 있습니다.

❷ 질문에 따른 단서를 우회적으로 제시하는 간접적 답변의 비중이 단서를 직접적으로 제시하는 직접적 답변에 버금갈 정도로 상당히 증가했습니다.

### 풀이 전략

❶ 의문사의문문에서 자주 출제되는 기본 문형을 바탕으로 초반 의문사를 비롯하여 주어와 동사/형용사로 이어지는 연속적인 3~4 단어, 즉 핵심어(키워드)의 의미를 파악하는 것이 관건입니다.
  • 의문사 + 조동사[do/does/did/will/would/can/could/should] + 주어 + 동사원형~?
  • 의문사 + 조동사[be/has/have] + 주어 + 형용사/현재 및 과거분사~?

❷ 질문에 따른 단서를 우회적으로 제시하는 간접적 답변의 비중이 단서를 직접적으로 제시하는 직접적 답변에 버금갈 정도로 상당히 증가했습니다.

❸ 정형화된 오답 유형을 사전에 충실히 익히고 이를 적극적으로 활용하여 정답을 선별하도록 합니다. 대표적으로 의문문에서 등장한 특정 단어를 선택지에서 반복하여 들려주는 동일어휘 오답, 특정 단어와 유사한 발음의 단어를 선택지에서 들려주는 유사발음 어휘 오답, 그리고 특정 단어를 통해 연상할 수 있는 단어를 들려주는 연상어휘 오답은 수시로 접하는 정형화된 오답 유형이므로 이를 적극적으로 활용하면 오답을 수월하게 소거할 수 있습니다.

❹ 절대 정답을 선택함에 시간을 끌지 않도록 합니다. 세 번째 선택지를 다 듣고 난 직후에도 답을 선택하지 못한 상태라면 과감히 찍고 미련을 버린 후 바로 다음 문제를 풀 수 있도록 대비해야 합니다. 파트 2는 문제 사이 간격이 4초 밖에 되지 않으므로 정답 선택을 머뭇거릴수록 이어지는 질문 내용을 파악하는 것에 집중하지 못하여 연이어 문제를 틀리게 되는 도미노 현상이 유독 심하다는 점에 주의하도록 합니다.

# 짧은 대화 (39문제)

2명 또는 3명이 나누는 대화를 듣고 문제지에 있는 질문을 보고 알맞은 보기를 고르는 유형

## Example

| 문제지 | 음성 |
|---|---|
| **32.** Where most likely does the conversation take place?<br><br>(A) At a restaurant<br>(B) At a hotel<br>(C) At an airport<br>(D) At a food processing company<br><br>**33.** Why is the man complaining?<br><br>(A) He did not get a receipt.<br>(B) He was served the dish he didn't order.<br>(C) A bill is higher than he expected.<br>(D) Some food has gone bad.<br><br>**33.** What does the woman suggest the man do?<br><br>(A) Speak to a manager<br>(B) Place a new order<br>(C) Check a menu<br>(D) Wait for a replacement<br><br><div align="right">정답 32. (B) 33. (D) 34. (D)</div> | **Questions 32 through 34 refer to the following conversation.**<br><br>W: Reception. How may I help you?<br>M: This is Wesley White in room 101. I ordered some tuna sandwiches from your restaurant and would like to return them. They smell weird. I think the tuna is not fresh.<br>W: Oh, I'm sorry to hear that. I'll call the chef immediately and ask him to bring you a replacement soon.<br>M: Um... Could you please give me a few minutes to have a look at the menu? I don't want to try the same thing again.<br><br>**32.** Where most likely does the conversation take place?<br><br>**33.** Why is the man complaining?<br><br>**33.** What does the woman suggest the man do? |

### 출제 경향

❶ 파트 3 대화들은 주로 회사 업무, 회사 출장 및 여행, 회사 회의, 공사와 같이 회사에서 겪는 다양한 비즈니스 활동 및 일상 생활에 관한 내용이 주류를 이루고 있습니다. 따라서 해당 주제를 다루는 대화 내용을 학습하며 주제별 주요 어휘와 표현을 익히는 것이 매우 중요합니다.

❷ 파트 3 대화의 전반적인 주제 및 대화에서 언급하는 문제점, 대화 장소 및 대화자의 직업, 그리고 세부적인 대화의 내용을 묻는 문제들의 출제 비중이 높습니다. 그러므로 문제 유형별로 대화 내에서 주로 단서가 등장하는 위치를 알아두고 이를 활용하여 효율적으로 단서를 파악하는 문제풀이 방식에 익숙해져야 합니다.

### 풀이 전략

❶ 대화 지문을 듣기에 앞서 문제와 선택지의 내용을 먼저 파악해야 합니다. 문제와 선택지의 내용을 사전에 알아두는 것만으로도 정답률이 높아진다. 만약 시간이 없을 경우에는 문제만이라도 읽어봅니다.

❷ 문제 유형에 따른 정답의 위치가 어느 정도 정해져 있으므로 대화 지문을 듣기에 앞서 미리 문제의 유형과 해당 내용을 파악해야 합니다. 각 문제의 유형을 파악한 후에는 이들의 단서가 지문 어디쯤에서 제시될 것이라 예상하며 청해하는, 소위 노려 듣기를 해야 합니다.

❸ 첫 번째 대화 내용과 마지막 대화 내용은 절대 놓치지 말아야 합니다. 첫 번째 대화 내용과 마지막 대화 내용에는 대부분 해당 대화 지문의 첫 번째 문제와 마지막 문제의 단서가 들어가 있습니다.

# Part 4

## 짧은 담화 (39문제)
짧은 담화를 듣고 문제지에 있는 질문을 보고 알맞은 보기를 고르는 유형

### Example

| 문제지 | 음성 |
|---|---|
| **71.** What is the message mainly about?<br><br>(A) A new library policy<br>(B) An upgraded computer room<br>(C) A special reading program<br>(D) A temporary location<br><br>**72.** According to the speaker, what can be accessed on a Web site?<br><br>(A) A new location<br>(B) A moving schedule<br>(C) Specific directions<br>(D) Discount coupons<br><br>**73.** What should the listeners do to borrow a laptop computer?<br><br>(A) Complete a form<br>(B) Show a membership card<br>(C) Pay a security deposit<br>(D) Join a free rental service<br><br>정답 71. (D) 72. (C) 73. (B) | **Questions 71 through 73 refer to the following recorded message.**<br><br>Thank you for calling the Warren Public Library. The Warren Public Library will be closed at the end of August for six months for upgrades and remodeling. For your convenience, we are going to open a temporary library facility located at 911 Harder Street next Monday. Please be advised that we will not provide computer rooms at all for library patrons due to limited space. However, you can borrow library laptop computers as usual if you present your library card to any of our librarians. If you need to get step by step directions for your drive or walk to the temporary library, please visit our Web site, www.warrenpl.org. Thank you.<br><br>**71.** What is the message mainly about?<br>**72.** According to the speaker, what can be accessed on a Web site?<br>**73.** What should the listeners do to borrow a laptop computer? |

### 출제 경향

❶ 파트 4에선 주로 안내(사내, 행사, 관광), 담화/소개, 녹음 메시지, 광고, 일기 예보, 뉴스 등 여러 가지 다양한 소재의 지문이 등장합니다.

❷ 파트 4에서는 전반적인 주제 및 문제점, 장소 및 화자/청자의 정체(직업/직장), 지문 내 세부적인 특정 내용을 묻는 문제, 그리고 화자의 의도/시각 정보 연계 문제들이 비교적 균형있게 출제되고 있습니다.

### 풀이 전략

❶ 지문을 듣기에 앞서 문제와 선택지의 내용을 먼저 파악해야 한다. 문제와 선택지의 내용을 사전에 알아두는 것만으로도 정답률이 높아집니다. 시간이 없을 경우에는 문제만이라도 먼저 읽어봅니다.

❷ 문제 유형에 따른 정답의 위치가 어느 정도 정해져 있으므로 지문을 듣기에 앞서 미리 문제의 유형과 해당 내용을 파악해야 합니다. 각 문제의 유형을 파악한 후에는 이들의 단서가 지문 어디쯤에서 제시될 것이라 예상하며 청해하는, 소위 노려 듣기를 해야 합니다.

❸ 지문 초반 2문장의 내용과 지문 후반 마지막 2문장의 내용은 절대 놓치지 않도록 합니다. 이 부분에는 해당 지문의 첫 번째 문제와 마지막 문제의 단서가 포함되어 있습니다. 따라서 지문 초반 2문장의 내용과 지문 후반 마지막 2문장의 내용을 놓치지 않는다면 최소한 두 문제는 상대적으로 수월하게 정답을 확보할 수 있습니다.

 **Part 5**

## 단문 빈칸 채우기 (30문제)

문장의 빈칸에 알맞은 보기를 골라 채우는 유형. 늦어도 12~15분 안에 다 풀어야 파트 7에 시간을 더 할애할 수 있습니다. 문법(어형)과 어휘 문제로 구성되어 있습니다.

### Example

---

**105.** ------- research in the pharmaceutical industry, the federal government will cover 60% of the total building costs of Pryde Bio Technology's research and development center.

(A) The quality of some new products
(B) The improvement in customer satisfaction
(C) The variety of service options
(D) The willingness of the attendees

정답 105. (B)

---

**Part 6**

## 장문 빈칸 채우기 (16문제)

파트 6는 지문에 있는 4개의 빈칸에 알맞은 보기를 골라 채우는 유형. 늦어도 8~10분 안에 다 풀어야 파트 7에 시간을 더 할애할 수 있습니다.

### Example

---

**Questions 135-138 refer to the following notice.**

If your baggage was damaged while being carried or supported by airport employees or by the airport baggage handling system, please ------- it to the airport baggage office on Level
**135.**
1. According to regulations, domestic travelers must report damage within 48 hours of their actual time of arrival. International travelers must submit a damage report within seven days of a(n) ------- baggage incident. -------. Office personnel will review reports and evaluate all
**136.** **137.**
damage claims. Please be advised that the airport baggage office is only responsible for damaged baggage ------- by the airport staff and the airport baggage handling system.
**135.**

---

**135.** (A) bring
(B) bringing
(C) brought
(D) brings

**136.** (A) overweight
(B) unattended
(C) forgotten
(D) mishandled

**137.** (A) Please fill out a baggage damage claim form as directed.
(B) The new baggage handling system is innovative and efficient
(C) The airport will expand next year to accommodate the increasing demand for air travel.
(D) The airport baggage office will be temporarily closed to travelers while it is renovated.

**138.** (A) cause
(B) caused
(C) will cause
(D) causing

정답 135. (A) 136. (D) 137. (A) 138. (B)

❶ 파트 5/6은 전체적으로는 문법과 어휘, 그리고 파트 6에서 문장 삽입을 묻는 문제들이 추가되어 있습니다. '문법'과 '어휘'부분은 신토익 실시 이후에도 변화가 거의 없습니다. 간혹 어휘 문제로 새로 등장하는 단어들이 보일 뿐, 특이점들은 많이 발견되지 않습니다. 따라서, 토익이 시작된 시점으로부터 변하지 않고 출제되는 기존의 유형들을 확실하게 다짐과 동시에, 드물지만 새로 추가되는 유형들을 익혀 둔다면 충분한 대비가 될 것입니다.

❷ 전체적인 비율은 바뀐 TOEIC 유형이 나오게 된 2006년 5월이래 사실 크게 달라진 것은 없습니다. 다만, 문법 출제 패턴들 중에 2006년 5월 이전에 강조되었던 명사 부분의 가산/불가산 구분, 수일치, 문제를 읽지 않아도 답이 나오는 숙어 및 관용 표현, 가정법, 생략, 도치 등의 유형들이 많이 사라지고, 질문 내용을 다 읽어야 풀 수 있는 세련된 형태들이 많이 등장하고 있다는 점이 특이점입니다.

**꾸준히 출제되는 문법 유형 중에 최근에도 자주 나오는 유형들을 정리하면 다음과 같습니다.**
• 관계사나 접속사/부사/전치사 혼합형 문제
• 자동사/타동사를 구분하는 문제
• 문맥을 통해 대명사의 격을 고르는 파트 6문제
• 문맥을 통해 특정 시제를 고르는 파트 6문제
• 부사절접속사들 사이의 차이점 구분 문제
• 사람/사물 또는 수식/보어로 형용사를 구분하는 문제
• 복합어이나 하나인 명사 앞의 형용사나 소유격을 고르는 문제
• 생활영어와 접목된 약간 까다로운 전치사 문제
• 재귀대명사의 강조용법 문제
• 관계사/의문사를 구분하고 들어가야 하는 wh- 문제
• 보기들 중에 동의어가 많이 제시되는 부사 어휘/연결사 문제

❶ 파트 5/6은 항상 보기를 먼저 읽고 문제 유형을 예상 및 파악합니다.

❷ 보기가 같은 어원으로 품사만 달리 나온 어형 문제의 경우, 자리를 묻는 경우가 많으므로 빈칸 주변이나 문장 전체의 [주/목/보어]구조를 따져 봅니다.

❸ 보기가 모두 다른 어휘 문제의 경우 반드시 해석을 해야 합니다.

❹ 보기에 접속사류(wh-로 시작하는 의문사/관계사, 부사절접속사 등)가 보이면 절(주어+동사)의 개수를 파악하고, '하나의 접속사는 두 개의 절을 연결한다'는 내용을 적용하여 접속사의 부족하고 넘침, 빈칸 뒤 문장의 완전/불완전 등을 따져야 합니다.

❺ 보기에 같은 동사가 형태만 달리 나올 때는 (1) 능/수동 (2) 수일치 (3) 시제의 순으로 따져서 풀어야 합니다.

❻ 명사 어휘 문제의 경우, 빈칸 앞의 관사관계를 먼저 살피고, 빈칸 앞이 무관사인 경우는 가산/불가산을 따져 풀어야 하는 문제입니다.

❼ 파트 6에 새로 추가된 유형은 문장 삽입인데, 바로 앞이나 뒤에 제시된 문장과의 연결성을 묻는 것이므로 그 점에 유의해야 합니다.

 **장문 독해 (54문제)**

지문을 읽고 질문에서 가장 적절한 보기를 정답으로 고르는 유형. 4개의 빈칸에 알맞은 보기를 골라 채우는 유형. 단일 지문 29문제, 이중 지문 10문제, 삼중 지문 15문제로 구성되어 있다.

**Example 단일 지문**

Questions 164-167 refer to the following notice.

## Kamon Financial Solutions

Yesterday, management and the owners held a meeting to discuss the future of the company. We have seen a great rise in profits during the last two years and also a large increase in our number of clients. So there are many customers that we are unable to serve from our current office. As such, it has been decided that in order to enable the business to grow, we will move to a much larger new office, which will open on October 2. —[1]—.

To make the relocation to the new office as smooth as possible, we have decided to move the majority of our equipment on September 29. —[2]—. On behalf of management, I would like to request that all staff members come to work that Saturday to help us move to the new location. You will be paid for your time at an overtime rate of $50 per/hour. —[3]—. You will be working from 11 A.M. until 3 P.M. In addition, the day before the move, Friday, September 28, management requests that you pack all of your folders and documents into cardboard boxes so that they can be easily loaded into the truck. —[4]—. You will find spare boxes located in the storeroom.

If you have any questions, feel free to contact me directly. My extension is #303. Thank you for your cooperation. Together, we can help Kamon Financial Solutions become a market leader.

164. What is the main purpose of the notice?
(A) To announce a relocation to a new office
(B) To advertise a new product offered by the company
(C) To provide a list of new contact details of clients
(D) To invite employees to attend a conference

165. The word "majority" in paragraph 2, line 2, is closest in meaning to
(A) least
(B) most
(C) absolute
(D) nearly

166. What are employees requested to do on September 29?
(A) Complete some sales reports
(B) Phone some new clients
(C) Come to the office
(D) Park their cars in a different parking lot

167. In which of the positions marked [1], [2], [3], and [4] does the following sentence best belong?

"This day is a Saturday, and our office is usually closed on weekends, so there will be a minimum amount of disruption to our business."

(A) [1]
(B) [2]
(C) [3]
(D) [4]

정답 164. (A) 165. (B) 166. (C) 167. (B)

**Example** 이중 지문

# Wallace Zoo Volunteer Program

**Requirements:**
- 18+ years of age
- High school diploma
- Satisfactory recommendation from previous or current employers
- Ability to commit to one full shift each week
- A clean, professional appearance
- Reliable transportation to the zoo
- The ability to attend employee training

**Attendance:**
Volunteers will work one full shift each week during the season they are hired. Fall and winter volunteers work shifts from 10 A.M. to 2 P.M. on weekends. Spring and summer volunteers have weekday shifts from 10 A.M. to 4 P.M. However, they might have to work on a weekend shift, which runs from 10 A.M. to 6 P.M. Shifts are assigned by the zoo's assistant manager.

If you are interested in volunteering at the city's best zoo, visit our Web site at wz.org for an application. If you have any questions, contact Kate Kensington at 703-221-8923 or katek@ wz.org. Applications for the spring program must be submitted by the end of the business day on March 18. Training for the spring program begins on March 28.

---

To: katek@wz.org
From: stevel@pgh.com
Date: March 20
Subject: Volunteer work
Attached: Application; Recommendation Letter

Dear Ms. Kensington;

I'm responding to your advertisement for volunteers at the zoo. I saw the advertisement ten days ago; however, I had an illness that put me in the hospital for the past week. So I was unable to respond until now. I understand that the deadline for the spring program has passed. But I hope that you can understand my situation and let me still apply for it. I have attached a completed application and recommendation letter from my current employer.

Only on weekdays am I available for work. I work at a cinema and must work a full shift on both Saturdays and Sundays. I hope this won't be a problem as I would love to work at the zoo. I am a consummate professional, and I am certain I can do great work at the zoo.

Thank you,
Steve Lionsgate

**181.** What is NOT a requirement of the volunteer position?

(A) Completion of high school
(B) Attendance at staff training
(C) A recommendation letter
(D) Experience at a zoo

**182.** On what date were applications due for spring positions?

(A) March 10
(B) March 18
(C) March 20
(D) March 28

**183.** What does Mr. Lionsgate request in his email?

(A) Consideration for her late application
(B) An extra weekend shift at the aquarium
(C) Information about employee training
(D) More time to submit her high school diploma

**184.** How many hours will Mr. Lionsgate likely volunteer per day at the time he is available?

(A) 4
(B) 6
(C) 8
(D) 16

**184.** In the email message, the word "consummate" in paragraph 2, line 3, is closest in meaning to

(A) determined
(B) absolute
(C) independent
(D) meticulous

정답 181. (D) 182. (B) 183. (A) 184. (B) 185. (B)

## Example 삼중 지문

**Questions 196-200 refer to the following Web page, Web search results, and advertisement.**

http://www.amityoldtown.com

Old Town in Amity is the perfect place to spend the day with your friends, family, or tour group. You'll love the experience of going on foot through the streets of Amity, which have been preserved to look exactly as they appeared in the 1700s. Go back in time as you tour Old Town.

Discounts are available for groups of 12 or more. In addition, for groups of 15 or more arriving by bus, the driver will get a complimentary ticket. Advance reservations are not required but are recommended for summer weekends. Contact 849-3894 to reserve your tickets today. Group discounts only apply to reservations made at least 24 hours in advance.

### Restaurants in Amity

**Seascape** Features some of the finest dining in the city. Expect to pay high prices, but you'll love the service and the quality of the meals. The specialties are seafood, especially lobster and crab. Located down by the pier.

**Hilltop** Decorated like an old-style ranch, you'll get some of the finest steaks and ribs in the region. Don't be distracted by the loud music and casual atmosphere. The food here is incredible. About 400 meters from Old Town.

**Green Table** Enjoy hearty food that takes you back to the 1800s. All the meats and vegetables come from local farmers. Reservations at least a week in advance are a must. Located in the city's center.

**Romano's** Get a taste of Italian food here. Giuseppe Romano, the owner, has been running this establishment for the past 12 years. It's located just 200 meters from the entrance to Old Town.

---

Visit Old Town in Amity with the Galway Travel Agency. Enjoy spending a day at Old Town and then dining down by the waterfront. You can do this for the low price of $175.

Your group will depart from the Galway Travel Agency at 9:00 A.M. on August 20. You'll return to the same place sometime around 8:00 P.M. Call 830-1911 for more information. The trip will not be made unless at least 18 people sign up for it.

**196.** What is indicated about Old Town?

(A) It requires reservations in summer.
(B) It has reduced its admission fees.
(C) It has historical reenactment shows.
(D) It is designed for people to walk through.

**197.** How can a group get a discount to Old Town?

(A) By purchasing tickets a day in advance
(B) By paying with a credit card
(C) By having 10 or more people
(D) By downloading a coupon from a Web site

**198.** What is mentioned about Green Table?

(A) It serves vegetarian meals.
(B) Its food is locally produced.
(C) It was established in the 1800s.
(D) It does not require reservations.

**199.** Where most likely will the excursion organized by the Galway Travel Agency have dinner?

(A) At Seascape
(B) At Hilltop
(C) At Green Table
(D) At Romano's

**200.** What is suggested about the excursion to Old Town?

(A) It will involve an overnight stay.
(B) It must be paid for in advance.
(C) It may receive a complimentary ticket.
(D) It includes three meals that are paid for.

정답 196. (D) 197. (A) 198. (B) 199. (A) 200. (C)

## 출제 경향

❶ 파트 7은 신유형이 추가되면서 예전보다 비중이 더 커졌습니다. (1) text-message chain (2) online chat discussion (3) 삼중 지문 (4) 문장 삽입 (5) 특정문구 내용 파악 등이 새로 추가된 유형인데, 삼중지문이 버겁기는 하지만, 이전 토익에 비해 난이도가 전체적으로 높아지지는 않았습니다. 그리고, 유념할 것은 파트 7 전체가 다 어려운 것이 아니라 3-4개의 지문, 그리고 그 지문들 중에서도 특정한 몇 개의 문제들이 어렵다는 것입니다. 주로 (most) likely/probably와 같은 유추/추론의 문제 유형입니다. 논란의 대상이 되는 유형들은 대부분 이 유형으로, 지문에 근거가 100퍼센트 명확히 제시되지 않는 경우가 있어 정답을 골라 내기 쉽지 않습니다. 이외에는 마치 '숨은 그림 찾기'하는 것과 같이 단서를 찾기 어려운 문제들이 대부분인데, 이는 정독을 통해서만 해결할 수 있으므로, 적절한 요령의 숙지와 더불어 정독을 하더라도 시간이 많이 걸리지 않을 정도의 진짜 '독해력'이 필요합니다.

## 풀이 전략

❶ 해당 문제의 키워드를 찾으며 지문을 정독합니다. 어차피 각 지문당 문제를 다 풀려면, 지문 하나당 3~4번 정도를 읽게 되는데, 읽을 때마다 전에 읽었던 내용들이 머리 속에 남게 되므로 읽는 속도는 빨라지게 되니 읽는 회수가 늘어나는 것에 그리 신경 쓰지 않아도 됩니다. 또한, 가끔 학생들 중에 문제마다 키워드를 미리 다 찾아서 한꺼번에 빈 공간 한 켠에 표시해 두고 풀이하는 사람들이 있는데 이것도 괜찮은 방법입니다.

❷ 독해가 된다는 것은 머리 속에 상황이 그려지는 것이니, 단순히 단어만 읽히고 내용이 머리 속에 들어오지 않는다면, 글 전체의 분위기를 전하는 지문의 제목과 초반부를 다시 한 번 정독합니다.

❸ 이중 지문의 경우, 두 지문 모두에서 부분적인 단서를 찾는 연계문제는 많아야 두 개입니다. 이 말은 다섯 문제 중에 3~4문제는 특정 한 지문만 읽어도 답이 나온다는 것입니다.

❹ 이중/삼중 지문의 경우 꾸준히 출제되는 반복되는 유형들이 있습니다.
- 한 지문에 일정이 나오면, 다른 지문에는 그것이 변경된 내용이 나옵니다.
- 한 지문에 교환/할인/반품에 대한 규정이 나오고, 다른 지문에 특정한 인물이 나오면, 그 인물이 교환/할인/반품의 대상이 되는가와, 또는 되지 않는 이유를 묻는 문제가 나옵니다.
- 특이한 성격의 지문, 예를 들면, draft, invoice, 예약확인 메일 등과 같은 것들은 그 지문의 내용이 아닌 형식이나 성격이 주제로 제시되는 경우가 많습니다.
- 특정 인물에 관한 사실관계, 유추문제가 질문으로 나오면, 그 인물이 발신자인 글을 먼저 읽는 것이 빠릅니다.
- 회사가 여러 개 언급되는 문제의 경우, 지문 맨위 수신자/발신자 이메일 부분의 회사 이름을 반드시 숙지하고 풀어야 합니다.

❺ 평소에 학습할 때 풀고 답을 맞추고 해설 등을 참조한 후에, 반드시 여러 번 정독해야 합니다. 이때, 문제 풀 때는 보이지 않던 많은 단서들이 눈에 들어오게 됩니다.

❻ 파트 7은 오답노트를 만들지 않아도 되지만, 나중에 복습할 때 대략적인 내용을 알 수 있도록 각 문단마다 내용을 한 두 줄로 요약해서 적어 두는 방법도 좋습니다.

# 목차

*자세한 해설을 확인하고 싶으시면 홈페이지에서 해설집을 다운로드하세요.(www.gilbut.co.kr)

# 수준별 학습 일정표

Actual Test 01을 풀어본 후 이 책에 같이 수록된 점수 환산표(번역 및 정답 P.117)에서 자신의 대략적인 환산 점수를 확인하고 맞는 학습 일정을 선택하세요. 매일 본문과 해설집 그리고 문법 정리와 듣기 학습 자료를 활용해 학습한 내용을 복습합니다.

## 800점 이상
## 10일 완성 일정

- 첫 날 Actual Test 01 전체를 풀어 본 뒤. 자신의 환산점수에 맞는 일정을 선택합니다.
- 하루에 한 세트씩 풀고, 해설집을 참고해 리뷰합니다.
- 테스트 리뷰를 한 뒤 꼭 문법과 듣기 훈련 하루 분량을 학습합니다.
- 다음 세트 문제를 풀기 전 전날 문제의 주요 어휘를 쪽지 시험으로 복습합니다. 마지막 날 분은 같은 날에 복습합니다.

|      | 월요일 | 화요일 | 수요일 | 목요일 | 금요일 |
|------|--------|--------|--------|--------|--------|
| 1주 차 | Actual Test 01<br>풀이 및 리뷰<br>문법, 듣기 훈련 1일 차 | Actual Test 02<br>풀이 및 리뷰<br>문법, 듣기 훈련 2일 차 | Actual Test 03<br>풀이 및 리뷰<br>문법, 듣기 훈련 3일 차 | Actual Test 04<br>풀이 및 리뷰<br>문법, 듣기 훈련 4일 차 | Actual Test 05<br>풀이 및 리뷰<br>문법, 듣기 훈련 5일 차 |
| 2주 차 | Actual Test 06<br>풀이 및 리뷰<br>문법, 듣기 훈련 6일 차 | Actual Test 07<br>풀이 및 리뷰<br>문법, 듣기 훈련 7일 차 | Actual Test 08<br>풀이 및 리뷰<br>문법, 듣기 훈련 8일 차 | Actual Test 09<br>풀이 및 리뷰<br>문법, 듣기 훈련 9일 차 | Actual Test 10<br>풀이 및 리뷰<br>문법, 듣기 훈련 10일 차 |

## 550~800점
## 20일 완성 일정

- 첫 날 Actual Test 01 전체를 풀어 본 뒤. 자신의 환산점수에 맞는 일정을 선택합니다.
- 하루에 한 세트씩 풀고, 해설집을 참고해 리뷰합니다. 리뷰를 할 때 꼭 동영상 강의를 같이 학습합니다.
- 문법과 듣기 훈련 하루 분량을 학습하고 전날 틀렸던 문제를 리뷰한 후 모르는 것은 홈페이지에서 질문합니다.
- 문법, 듣기 훈련을 하기 전에 꼭 전 날 풀이한 문제의 주요 어휘를 쪽지 시험으로 복습합니다.

|      | 월요일 | 화요일 | 수요일 | 목요일 | 금요일 |
|------|--------|--------|--------|--------|--------|
| 1주 차 | Actual Test 01<br>풀이 및 리뷰<br>(동영상 강의 학습) | 문법, 듣기 훈련 1일 차 | Actual Test 02<br>풀이 및 리뷰<br>(동영상 강의 학습) | 문법, 듣기 훈련 2일 차 | Actual Test 03<br>풀이 및 리뷰<br>(동영상 강의 학습) |
| 2주 차 | 문법, 듣기 훈련 3일 차 | Actual Test 04<br>풀이 및 리뷰<br>(동영상 강의 학습) | 문법, 듣기 훈련 4일 차 | Actual Test 05<br>풀이 및 리뷰<br>(동영상 강의 학습) | 문법, 듣기 훈련 5일 차 |
| 3주 차 | Actual Test 06<br>풀이 및 리뷰<br>(동영상 강의 학습) | 문법, 듣기 훈련 6일 차 | Actual Test 07<br>풀이 및 리뷰<br>(동영상 강의 학습) | 문법, 듣기 훈련 7일 차 | Actual Test 08<br>풀이 및 리뷰<br>(동영상 강의 학습) |
| 4주 차 | 문법, 듣기 훈련 8일 차 | Actual Test 09<br>풀이 및 리뷰<br>(동영상 강의 학습) | 문법, 듣기 훈련 9일 차 | Actual Test 10<br>풀이 및 리뷰<br>(동영상 강의 학습) | 문법, 듣기 훈련 10일 차 |

# 40일 완성 일정

- 첫 날 Actual Test 01 전체를 풀어 본 뒤, 자신의 환산점수에 맞는 일정을 선택합니다.
- 하루에 한 세트씩 풀고, 해설집을 참고해 리뷰합니다.
- 전날 분의 쪽지시험으로 어휘를 복습한 후, 동영상 강의를 학습합니다.
- 문법 정리집을 학습하고 본문에서 틀렸던 문제를 다시 리뷰해 봅니다. 모르는 문제는 홈페이지에서 질문합니다.
- 듣기 훈련집을 학습하고 본문에서 틀렸던 문제를 다시 듣고 리뷰해 봅니다. 모르는 문제는 홈페이지에서 질문합니다.

| | 월요일 | 화요일 | 수요일 | 목요일 | 금요일 |
|---|---|---|---|---|---|
| 1주 차 | Actual Test 01<br>풀이 및 리뷰 | Actual Test 01<br>동영상 강의 학습 | 문법 정리집 학습 1일 차,<br>틀린 문제 리뷰 및 질문 | 듣기 훈련집 학습 1일 차,<br>틀린 문제 리뷰 및 질문 | Actual Test 02<br>풀이 및 리뷰 |
| 2주 차 | Actual Test 02<br>동영상 강의 학습 | 문법 정리집 학습 2일 차,<br>틀린 문제 리뷰 및 질문 | 듣기 훈련집 학습 2일 차,<br>틀린 문제 리뷰 및 질문 | Actual Test 03<br>풀이 및 리뷰 | Actual Test 03<br>동영상 강의 학습 |
| 3주 차 | 문법 정리집 학습 3일 차,<br>틀린 문제 리뷰 및 질문 | 듣기 훈련집 학습 3일 차,<br>틀린 문제 리뷰 및 질문 | Actual Test 04<br>풀이 및 리뷰 | Actual Test 04<br>동영상 강의 학습 | 문법 정리집 학습 4일 차,<br>틀린 문제 리뷰 및 질문 |
| 4주 차 | 듣기 훈련집 학습 4일 차,<br>틀린 문제 리뷰 및 질문 | Actual Test 05<br>풀이 및 리뷰 | Actual Test 05<br>동영상 강의 학습 | 문법 정리집 학습 5일 차,<br>틀린 문제 리뷰 및 질문 | 듣기 훈련집 학습 5일 차,<br>틀린 문제 리뷰 및 질문 |
| 5주 차 | Actual Test 06<br>풀이 및 리뷰 | Actual Test 06<br>동영상 강의 학습 | 문법 정리집 학습 6일 차,<br>틀린 문제 리뷰 및 질문 | 듣기 훈련집 학습 6일 차,<br>틀린 문제 리뷰 및 질문 | Actual Test 07<br>풀이 및 리뷰 |
| 6주 차 | Actual Test 07<br>동영상 강의 학습 | 문법 정리집 학습 7일 차,<br>틀린 문제 리뷰 및 질문 | 듣기 훈련집 학습 7일 차,<br>틀린 문제 리뷰 및 질문 | Actual Test 08<br>풀이 및 리뷰 | Actual Test 08<br>동영상 강의 학습 |
| 7주 차 | 문법 정리집 학습 8일 차,<br>틀린 문제 리뷰 및 질문 | 듣기 훈련집 학습 8일 차,<br>틀린 문제 리뷰 및 질문 | Actual Test 09<br>풀이 및 리뷰 | Actual Test 09<br>동영상 강의 학습 | 문법 정리집 학습 9일 차,<br>틀린 문제 리뷰 및 질문 |
| 8주 차 | 듣기 훈련집 학습 9일 차,<br>틀린 문제 리뷰 및 질문 | Actual Test 10<br>풀이 및 리뷰 | Actual Test 10<br>동영상 강의 학습 | 문법 정리집 학습 10일 차,<br>틀린 문제 리뷰 및 질문 | 듣기 훈련집 학습 10일 차,<br>틀린 문제 리뷰 및 질문 |

# Actual Test 01

MP3

해설집

적정 풀이 시간 120분

**120 min**

시작 시간 ___시 ___분

종료 시간 ___시 ___분

중간에 멈추지 말고 처음부터 끝까지 풀어보세요.
문제를 풀 때에는 실전처럼 답안지에 마킹하세요.

목표 개수 _____ / 200    실제 개수 _____ / 200

예상 점수는 번역 및 정답에 있는 점수 환산표를 참조하세요.

# LISTENING TEST

In the Listening test, you will be asked to demonstrate how well you understand spoken English. The entire Listening test will last approximately 45 minutes. There are four parts, and directions are given for each part. You must mark your answers on the separate answer sheet. Do not write your answers in your test book.

## PART 1

**Directions:** For each question in this part, you will hear four statements about a picture in your test book. When you hear the statements, you must select the one statement that best describes what you see in the picture. Then find the number of the question on your answer sheet and mark your answer. The statements will not be printed in your test book and will be spoken only one time.

Statement (B), "They are sitting at a table," is the best description of the picture. So you should select answer (B) and mark it on your answer sheet.

**1.**

**2.**

**3.**

**4.**

**5.**

**6.**

▶ ▶ ▶GO ON TO THE NEXT PAGE

## PART 2

**Directions:** You will hear a question or statement and three responses spoken in English. They will not be printed in your test book and will be spoken only one time. Select the best response to the question or statement and mark the letter (A), (B), or (C) on your answer sheet.

7. Mark your answer on your answer sheet.

8. Mark your answer on your answer sheet.

9. Mark your answer on your answer sheet.

10. Mark your answer on your answer sheet.

11. Mark your answer on your answer sheet.

12. Mark your answer on your answer sheet.

13. Mark your answer on your answer sheet.

14. Mark your answer on your answer sheet.

15. Mark your answer on your answer sheet.

16. Mark your answer on your answer sheet.

17. Mark your answer on your answer sheet.

18. Mark your answer on your answer sheet.

19. Mark your answer on your answer sheet.

20. Mark your answer on your answer sheet.

21. Mark your answer on your answer sheet.

22. Mark your answer on your answer sheet.

23. Mark your answer on your answer sheet.

24. Mark your answer on your answer sheet.

25. Mark your answer on your answer sheet.

26. Mark your answer on your answer sheet.

27. Mark your answer on your answer sheet.

28. Mark your answer on your answer sheet.

29. Mark your answer on your answer sheet.

30. Mark your answer on your answer sheet.

31. Mark your answer on your answer sheet.

## PART 3

**Directions:** You will hear some conversations between two or three people. You will be asked to answer three questions about what the speakers say in each conversation. Select the best response to each question and mark the letter (A), (B), (C), or (D) on your answer sheet. The conversations will not be printed in your test book and will be spoken only one time.

32. Where most likely does the conversation take place?

(A) At a restaurant
(B) At a hotel
(C) At an airport
(D) At a food processing company

33. Why is the man complaining?

(A) He did not get a receipt.
(B) He was served the dish he didn't order.
(C) A bill is higher than he expected.
(D) Some food has gone bad.

34. What does the woman suggest the man do?

(A) Speak to a manager
(B) Place a new order
(C) Check a menu
(D) Wait for a replacement

35. Where did the men come from?

(A) A cafeteria
(B) A coffee shop
(C) A new office room
(D) A breakroom

36. What is Mr. Finley going to order?

(A) Office supplies
(B) Black ink cartridges
(C) Refreshments
(D) Cleaning products

37. What will the speakers probably do next?

(A) Make some coffee
(B) Photocopy some documents
(C) Report a problem
(D) Make a list of things

38. What kind of company does the woman work for?

(A) An accounting firm
(B) A security company
(C) A financial institution
(D) A cleaning company

39. What will happen tomorrow evening?

(A) A big contract will be signed.
(B) Some renovations will be completed.
(C) Some workers will visit the man's company.
(D) Some money will be transferred to Ms. Winston.

40. What should Ms. Porter do tomorrow?

(A) Buy some cleaning supplies
(B) Meet with Mr. King
(C) Deliver a payment
(D) Confirm a work order

41. What kind of business does the woman probably work for?

(A) A florist
(B) A business consulting firm
(C) A restaurant
(D) A real estate agency

42. What is the purpose of the man's call?

(A) To modify a reservation
(B) To ask about a menu
(C) To reserve a conference room
(D) To arrange airline tickets

43. What does the woman suggest?

(A) Choosing another venue
(B) Canceling a meeting
(C) Changing rooms
(D) Dining at a different time

44. What problem does the man mention?

(A) A waiting time is long.
(B) A cashier is unavailable.
(C) Some food is out of stock.
(D) Some street signs were removed.

45. What does the man ask the woman about?

(A) Contact details
(B) Menu prices
(C) Opening times
(D) Payment methods

46. Why does the woman say, "I doubt it"?

(A) To ask a question
(B) To request an explanation
(C) To indicate suspicion of the man
(D) To give a negative answer

47. Which department needs a new manager?

(A) Personnel
(B) Maintenance
(C) Accounting
(D) Customer Service

48. According to the man, what is one qualification for the job?

(A) A license in accounting
(B) A bachelor's degree
(C) Management ability
(D) Communication skills

49. What will the woman probably do next?

(A) Contact a possible candidate
(B) Relocate to a different place
(C) Place an advertisement online
(D) Arrange some interviews

50. When is the party?

(A) On Monday
(B) On Tuesday
(C) On Wednesday
(D) On Thursday

51. Why is the man unsure about attending the party?

(A) He is scheduled to attend a seminar.
(B) He has to do very much work.
(C) He has to make business travel arrangements.
(D) He has to sign up for an evening course in time.

52. What does the woman offer to do?

(A) Prepare some food for an outing
(B) Give the man a raise
(C) Give the man a ride to the banquet
(D) Help the man finish his reports

53. What is the purpose of the man's call?

(A) To check on the status of an order
(B) To change the color of an item
(C) To increase the quantity of an order
(D) To confirm a reference number

54. Why does the man say, "I can't believe it"?

(A) He doesn't trust the quality of the products the woman sells.
(B) He feels very satisfied with a lot of orders.
(C) He is unhappy with the woman's comment.
(D) He just heard about some good news from the woman.

55. Why is the package being delivered late?

(A) Some delivery trucks have broken down.
(B) It was delivered to the wrong address.
(C) It went missing during shipping.
(D) There was a day that people did not work.

**56.** What are the speakers talking about?

(A) A discount sale
(B) A new chocolate store
(C) A fundraising event
(D) A social volunteering service

**57.** What does the man say about the chocolates?

(A) They are made with organic ingredients.
(B) They are selling really well at his company.
(C) They are surprisingly easy to create at home.
(D) They will be donated to children who live locally.

**58.** What will the speakers probably do this afternoon?

(A) Attend a local charity event
(B) Sign a contract with a new client
(C) Visit the Sales Department
(D) Buy some chocolates for their outing

**59.** Who most likely is the man?

(A) An interior decorator
(B) An apartment manager
(C) A travel agent
(D) A repairman

**60.** What does the man ask about?

(A) Renting an apartment
(B) Making a reservation
(C) Repainting a wall
(D) Arranging a time to meet

**61.** Why is the woman unavailable for the property inspection on September 9?

(A) She is going out of town.
(B) She is going on vacation.
(C) She doesn't have a key.
(D) She is working late.

| Spreadsheet Software Package | Price |
|---|---|
| Expert Package | $300 |
| Semi-Pro Package | $250 |
| Regular Package | $200 |
| Basic Package | $100 |

**62.** Why does the man call?

(A) To recommend some new products
(B) To complain about some poor service
(C) To ask for some help
(D) To enroll in a computer course

**63.** What information does the woman ask the man for?

(A) His order number
(B) His contact information
(C) His work address
(D) The size of his company

**64.** Look at the graphic. How much will the man probably pay for his purchase?

(A) $100
(B) $200
(C) $250
(D) $300

# Discount Coupon

(Valid until 4/5)

0110  0105

**AAA Size Batteries**

12 Pack ········· $1 Value (1 PACK)
24 Pack ········· $2 Value (1 PACK)
36 Pack ········· $4 Value (1 PACK)
48 Pack ········· $6 Value (1 PACK)

## MIMI POWER BATTERIES

**65.** Look at the graphic. What discount will the man most likely receive?

(A) $1
(B) $2
(C) $4
(D) $6

**66.** What does the woman offer to do for the man?

(A) Order more items
(B) Bring him some batteries
(C) Dispose of some waste material
(D) Show him the location of a new warehouse

**67.** What is the man asked to do?

(A) Wait in a seating area
(B) Fill out an order form
(C) Get a new coupon printed
(D) Speak to a cashier

---

PLEASE JOIN US FOR THE WEDDING OF
# KAY & BLAINE

Saturday, July 4
St. Joseph's Cathedral, Harder Road

**2:00 P.M.**
Pre-ceremony photographs

**3:00 P.M**
Guests seated in preparation for ceremony

**4:00 P.M**
Wedding ceremony

**5:00 P.M**
Dinner & Drinks

Please respond to confirm your attendance.

**68.** Where most likely are the speakers?

(A) At a gym
(B) At a cathedral
(C) In a photo studio
(D) At a department store

**69.** What does the man recommend that the woman do?

(A) Attend a local event
(B) Change her work schedule
(C) Visit a place early in the day
(D) Take some photographs

**70.** Look at the graphic. When does the woman expect to arrive at the wedding?

(A) At 2 P.M.
(B) At 3 P.M.
(C) At 4 P.M.
(D) At 5 P.M.

---

# PART 4

**Directions:** You will hear some short talks given by a single speaker. You will be asked to answer three questions about what the speaker says in each short talk. Select the best response to each question and mark the letter (A), (B), (C), or (D) on your answer sheet. The talks will not be printed in your test book and will be spoken only one time.

71. What is being advertised?

    (A) Home appliances
    (B) Computer software
    (C) Office equipment
    (D) Mobile devices

72. What service is being offered to customers?

    (A) Free repairs
    (B) Same-day delivery
    (C) An additional discount
    (D) Free extended warranties

73. When does the sale begin?

    (A) On Friday
    (B) On Saturday
    (C) On Sunday
    (D) On Monday

74. Where most likely is this announcement being made?

    (A) At a radio station
    (B) At an art gallery opening
    (C) In a concert hall
    (D) In a television studio

75. What has caused the delay?

    (A) Technical difficulties
    (B) The closing of a facility
    (C) Unfavorable weather
    (D) Road repairs

76. What are the listeners asked to do?

    (A) Watch a performance
    (B) Proceed to their assigned seats
    (C) Wait for assistance
    (D) Turn off all the lights

77. What product is the speaker talking about?

    (A) Cake
    (B) Sandwiches
    (C) Coffee
    (D) Fruit juice

78. What did the Starpark View Café recently do?

    (A) It released a new beverage.
    (B) It changed its logo.
    (C) It moved its headquarters.
    (D) It increased an order.

79. What does the speaker mean when he says, "I'd like to hear from all of you"?

    (A) Some coffee machines are broken.
    (B) Customer feedback should be considered.
    (C) Informal meetings will be held more often.
    (D) Comments are needed to make a decision.

80. Where does the speaker most likely work?

    (A) At a bus terminal
    (B) At an electronics store
    (C) At an airport
    (D) At a magazine company

81. What does the speaker mean when she says, "At this time, we have our best air mechanics working on it"?

    (A) All passengers should wait in a lobby.
    (B) A problem will not last long.
    (C) Repair team members don't need more training.
    (D) The company has outstanding employees.

82. What does the speaker say she will do?

    (A) Wait near Gate 53
    (B) Request a full refund
    (C) Provide updates
    (D) Issue a boarding pass

**83.** Who most likely is the speaker?

(A) A job applicant
(B) An accounting manager
(C) A recruiter
(D) A vendor

**84.** What occurred with the speaker today?

(A) She submitted an application.
(B) She received a reference letter.
(C) She got a professional designation.
(D) She started a company with her family.

**85.** What does the speaker want to do?

(A) Update her job application
(B) Negotiate a salary and benefits
(C) Change a previous order
(D) Prepare for an interview

---

**86.** What does the speaker mean when he says, "Few people are capable of such an innovative design"?

(A) He wants more powerful cars.
(B) He is commending some employees.
(C) He is proud of his achievement.
(D) He suggests recruiting more designers.

**87.** According to the speaker, what will the company do in October?

(A) Acquire another company
(B) Participate in an event
(C) Modify existing designs
(D) Announce an award winner

**88.** What does the speaker suggest the listeners do?

(A) Come up with new designs
(B) Submit request forms
(C) Test-drive a new car
(D) Organize a corporate event

---

**89.** Who most likely is the audience?

(A) Electricians
(B) Software developers
(C) Graphic professionals
(D) Photography experts

**90.** What did the company recently purchase?

(A) Some accounting software
(B) A fully furnished apartment
(C) A movie camera
(D) A computer graphic program

**91.** What will the speaker probably do next?

(A) Offer a pay raise
(B) Give a demonstration
(C) Hire new designers
(D) Lead a tour of a manufacturing plant

---

**92.** According to the speaker, what was announced today?

(A) A sporting event
(B) The expansion of a road
(C) A new traffic policy
(D) A major construction project

**93.** According to the speaker, why is the project necessary for local residents?

(A) To create more job opportunities
(B) To attract more tourists from around the world
(C) To improve the local economic conditions
(D) To provide chances for people to participate in sports

**94.** Why are some people opposed to the new project?

(A) There are not enough funds.
(B) It will cause bad traffic.
(C) A lot of noise will occur.
(D) Property prices will depreciate sharply.

---

| TRAINING SESSIONS | DATE |
|---|---|
| Time Management | July 24 |
| Communication Skills | August 27 |
| E-mail Policies | September 13 |
| How to Write a Report | October 9 |

**95.** What does the speaker say he is pleased about?

(A) The quality of some new products
(B) The improvement in customer satisfaction
(C) The variety of service options
(D) The willingness of the attendees

**96.** Look at the graphic. Which training session has been postponed?

(A) Communication Skills
(B) Time Management
(C) How to Write a Report
(D) E-mail Policies

**97.** According to the speaker, what will happen after the morning session?

(A) Lunch will be served.
(B) A coffee break will be held.
(C) A monetary reward will be given.
(D) A staff meeting will be held.

# Beltran Car Repair Shop

| Service | Charge |
|---|---|
| Engine Oil Change | $50 |
| Side-View / Rear-View Mirror Replacement | $60 |
| Front / Rear Tire Change | $110 |
| Front / Rear Bumper Repair | $270 |

**98.** What is the purpose of the call?

(A) To place an order
(B) To give directions
(C) To make an appointment
(D) To report the completion of a job

**99.** What did the speaker find while working?

(A) A mirror was broken.
(B) A tire was flat.
(C) A bill was not fully paid.
(D) Some replacement parts were out of stock.

**100.** Look at the graphic. How much will Mr. Wilson save?

(A) $50
(B) $60
(C) $110
(D) $270

This is the end of the Listening test. Turn to Part 5 in your test book.

▶ ▶ ▶ GO ON TO THE NEXT PAGE

# READING TEST

In the Reading test, you will read a variety of texts and answer several different types of reading comprehension questions. The entire Reading test will last 75 minutes. There are three parts, and directions are given for each part. You are encouraged to answer as many questions as possible within the time allowed.

You must mark your answers on the separate answer sheet. Do not write your answers in your test book.

## PART 5

**Directions**: A word or phrase is missing in each of the sentences below. Four answer choices are given below each sentence. Select the best answer to complete the sentence. Then mark the letter (A), (B), (C), or (D) on your answer sheet.

**101.** The new promotional event at Beagle Media will start tomorrow ------- end next Sunday.
(A) so
(B) and
(C) yet
(C) until

**102.** ------- company, Starpark Food, first launched a new type of steak sauce, which was spicier than those of the company's competitors.
(A) He
(B) Him
(C) His
(D) Himself

**103.** The floor manager is responsible for keeping the selling area ------- and for making customers satisfied.
(A) clean
(B) cleanly
(C) cleaning
(D) cleanness

**104.** Park Library offers a writing class for ------- on every Monday night.
(A) begin
(B) began
(C) beginning
(D) beginners

**105.** ------- research in the pharmaceutical industry, the federal government will cover 60% of the total building costs of Pryde Bio Technology's research and development center.
(A) Promote
(B) To promote
(C) To promoting
(D) Promoted

**106.** Coco International has been ------- as one of the biggest pet food manufacturers in Asia.
(A) recognize
(B) recognized
(C) recognizing
(D) recognizes

**107.** All visitors must ------- the speed limit that is posted in the underground parking lot at the research center.
(A) obey
(B) protect
(C) lower
(D) refuse

**108.** According to the new schedule, the training session for our new employees will be ------- on November 23.
(A) recruited
(B) held
(C) notified
(D) promoted

**109.** The ------- way to get to the New York Municipal Museum is to park at a New Jersey station and to take the bus into the city.

(A) easiest
(B) more easily
(C) most easily
(D) easy

**110.** Ace Web Designs ------- by two friends who started working together on a similar project in college.

(A) have been establishing
(B) was established
(C) has established
(D) establishing

**111.** For a period of three years from the original date of purchase, the company will repair defective products or ------- them with new ones.

(A) generate
(B) verify
(C) replace
(D) assist

**112.** Graduate students usually try to find a boarding house that is ------- walking distance of their school.

(A) through
(B) nearby
(C) in front of
(D) within

**113.** The board of directors will ------- plan many benefits that the company offers for new employees.

(A) compatibly
(B) meticulously
(C) considerably
(D) enormously

**114.** Foreign companies must ------- with the laws and regulations to launch new businesses in South Korea.

(A) comply
(B) achieve
(C) authorize
(D) create

**115.** The new computer battery charger is ------- with almost all types of laptop computers sold on the domestic market.

(A) technical
(B) compatible
(C) innovative
(D) satisfactory

**116.** ------- the new business plan is not cost effective and environmentally friendly, there should be problems approving it.

(A) Since
(B) While
(C) Although
(D) Unless

**117.** The plant manager could not receive the replacement parts for some broken conveyor belts because all of the component suppliers have ------- in stock.

(A) none
(B) every
(C) them
(D) little

**118.** The new warehouse in Walnut County, ------- is mostly rural, will serve as a regional logistics center of our company.

(A) where
(B) much
(C) which
(D) itself

**119.** Some economists predicted that the pace of economic recovery will slow down without any ------- improvements in the fourth quarter.

(A) marked
(B) slight
(C) intensive
(D) respective

**120.** Even though Haru Catering Service has lower rates, Andrew Catering Service ------- our overall business needs.

(A) suit
(B) suits
(C) is suited
(D) have suited

▶▶▶GO ON TO THE NEXT PAGE

**121.** Mr. Williams, the ------- head of the personnel department, left some reference materials to share his work knowledge with his replacement.

(A) capable
(B) previous
(C) equal
(D) collaborative

**122.** ------- department must complete an internal audit and submit plans for quality improvement by March 1.

(A) Even
(B) Other
(C) Most
(D) Each

**123.** Cheeze Energy announced an ------- to establish a chain of filling stations for cars powered by electricity in Europe early next year.

(A) initiative
(B) alert
(C) admission
(D) expertise

**124.** The lease with the local shopping mall ------- if the renovation work is completed successfully next week.

(A) will be renewed
(B) was renewed
(C) have renewed
(D) is renewed

**125.** *World Business Monthly Review* appealed to its members to renew their subscriptions ------- to avoid missing any issues.

(A) enough
(B) seldom
(C) early
(D) helpfully

**126.** ------- hiring someone from within the firm to take over the Hayward branch, the board has decided to look outside the company.

(A) In case
(B) Instead of
(C) Because
(D) Even so

**127.** Some countries ------- are highly dependent on trade taxes as a source of revenue are likely to be affected by the reduction in tariffs.

(A) that
(B) whose
(C) what
(D) these

**128.** Most banks usually open checking accounts for people 18 or older ------- they have an identification card such as a driver's license or passport.

(A) once
(B) since
(C) although
(D) as long as

**129.** The strike for better wages at BK Heavy Industries ------- as soon as formal negotiations begin.

(A) ends
(B) ended
(C) has ended
(D) will end

**130.** The International Cat Video Film Festival accepts entries only from cat owners who have not ------- made their own videos.

(A) barely
(B) currently
(C) previously
(D) timely

# PART 6

**Directions:** Read the texts that follow. A word, phrase, or sentence is missing in parts of each text. Four answer choices for each question are given below the text. Select the best answer to complete the text. Then mark the letter (A), (B), (C), or (D) on your answer sheet.

**Questions 131-134** refer to the following e-mail.

To all housekeeping staff,

Hotel management decided last week to start a new policy ------- the daily laundering of
**131.**
bedsheets and towels. As usual, we collect all the towels and bedsheets left on the floor by

customers and wash them every day. But this is not the case for any towels used once or

twice and hung up on hooks or racks in rooms. They will be left for guests to reuse. The new

policy will ------- water usage, energy consumption, and daily laundry loads. -------, it will
**132.** **133.**
increase awareness of energy conservation and environmental protection. The staff in the

management office will post notices in every room informing guests of the implementation of

this policy. -------.
**134.**

**131.** (A) concern
(B) concerning
(C) concerned
(D) concerns

**132.** (A) eliminate
(B) require
(C) measure
(D) minimize

**133.** (A) Nevertheless
(B) On the other hand
(C) Moreover
(D) In spite of this

**134.** (A) They think that installing showers is a
waste of resources.
(B) I hope all of you suggest many
creative ideas at the regular meeting.
(C) Please let me know if you need any
maintenance support.
(D) We would greatly appreciate your
cooperation with this effort.

---

## NOTICE

### FOR TRAVELERS AT SAN FRANCISCO INTERNATIONAL AIRPORT

If your baggage was damaged while being carried or supported by airport employees or by

the airport baggage handling system, please ------- it to the airport baggage office on Level
               **135.**

1. According to regulations, domestic travelers must report damage within 48 hours of their

actual time of arrival. International travelers must submit a damage report within seven

days of a(n) ------- baggage incident. -------. Office personnel will review reports and
      **136.**              **137.**

evaluate all damage claims. Please be advised that the airport baggage office is only

responsible for damaged baggage ------- by the airport staff and the airport baggage
             **138.**

handling system.

---

**135.** (A) bring
(B) bringing
(C) brought
(D) brings

**136.** (A) overweight
(B) unattended
(C) forgotten
(D) mishandled

**137.** (A) Please fill out a baggage damage claim form as directed.
(B) The new baggage handling system is innovative and efficient.
(C) The airport will expand next year to accommodate the increasing demand for air travel.
(D) The airport baggage office will be temporarily closed to travelers while it is renovated.

**138.** (A) cause
(B) caused
(C) will cause
(D) causing

**MEMORANDUM**

WALNUT CREEK PUBLIC LIBRARY

To: Walnut Creek Public Library Staff
From: Amy Jordan
Re: New Study Rooms
Date: April 5

I am very pleased to announce that the construction of our new study rooms, which started six months ago, will be completed by the end of the week. The seven study rooms will be ------- starting next Monday.
**139.**

The new study rooms can accommodate from 10 to 30 people and are intended for small book clubs and study groups in the community. -------. Jack Grant will be temporarily
**140.**
responsible for the management of the new study rooms until the end of May. -------, he will
**141.**
return to his role as administrative support manager.

A job advertisement for a permanent reservations supervisor will be posted sooner or later. The person in this position will be in charge of ------- all reservations and administrative
**142.**
control for the new study rooms. Thank you.

Sincerely yours,

Amy Jordan
Library Director

---

**139.** (A) approachable
(B) appropriate
(C) acceptable
(D) available

**140.** (A) Parking will be available to all library visitors.
(B) All the new study rooms must be reserved before use.
(C) Jack Grant has already contributed to the library financially.
(D) Job interviews will be conducted in the middle of June.

**141.** (A) Therefore
(B) Simultaneously
(C) After that time
(D) In other words

**142.** (A) overseeing
(B) oversee
(C) oversaw
(D) overseen

▶ ▶ ▶ GO ON TO THE NEXT PAGE

Dear Mr. Hong:

Thank you for asking about the 400-square-meter space at 1123 Grand Street. But I'm afraid to tell you that this property has already been taken off the market.

You told me on the phone you have been looking for a site for your second manufacturing plant for over six months. Why don't you give me an idea of what ------- you are searching
**143.**
for? -------. All you have to do is e-mail me back with your preferred size, price, and any other
**144.**
important requirements.

You may want to register for app alerts. You can receive free instant text message notifications to your mobile phone ------- new properties are put up for sale. It provides you
**145.**
with the ability to check detailed information on ------- property on the list and quickly reply to
**146.**
incoming notifications right away.

I'm looking forward to hearing back from you.

143. (A) specifically
(B) significantly
(C) promptly
(D) apparently

144. (A) Real estate agents negotiate transactions related to properties.
(B) Some owners have open houses and show their properties to prospective buyers.
(C) It is one of the recent interesting trends in the real estate industry.
(D) I will search for some good sites in Castro Valley that meet your criteria.

145. (A) and
(B) whenever
(C) even though
(D) since

146. (A) all
(B) other
(C) each
(D) another

# PART 7

**Directions:** In this part you will read a selection of texts, such as magazine and newspaper articles, e-mails, and instant messages. Each text or set of texts is followed by several questions. Select the best answer for each question and mark the letter (A), (B), (C), or (D) on your answer sheet.

**Questions 147-148** refer to the following notice.

# NOTICE

## Woodbridge News

We have been proud to deliver the free newsletter, the *Woodbridge News*, to residents every other Tuesday for the last twenty years. Unfortunately, the mayor recently decided that the newsletter should only be delivered once a month to save the town money.

As such, the *Woodbridge News* will no longer be delivered every other week. Instead, you will receive the newsletter on the 20th of each month. Thank you for your understanding.

**Woodbridge News**
**Your Community Newsletter**

**147.** What is the purpose of the notice?

(A) To announce a change in a newspaper delivery schedule
(B) To inform readers of changes in the content of a newspaper
(C) To publicize changes in the price of a newspaper
(D) To announce changes in the staff of a newspaper company

**148.** Who made the decision to make the change?

(A) The editor-in-chief
(B) The publishing company
(C) The town mayor
(D) The town council

Finalnet provides an extensive searchable database of over 10,000 Web-based documents, which include research on economies and product markets as well as investment-related laws. These resources, catalogued by country, economic area and topic, are obtained primarily from the World Bank Group, investment promotion agencies, and privatization agencies. The Finalnet business directories comprise contact information for over 30,000 organizations and individuals involved in foreign investment. The online service also provides links to a large number of other diverse sources of investment highlights and particulars, including links to its subsidiary Web sites. Finalnet has approximately 79,000 registered users and receives approximately 20,000 visitors per month. The information service has been in the prestigious position of finalist for the Financial Times' Business Web Site of the Year award.

**149.** Who most likely would be interested in the advertisement?

(A) Auditors
(B) Computer technicians
(C) Environmentalists
(D) Company executives

**150.** Which information does Finalnet provide?

(A) Public international law
(B) Contact numbers of investors
(C) Methods of online stock investment
(D) Information on trends in business-to-business commerce

**Questions 151-152** refer to the following text message chain.

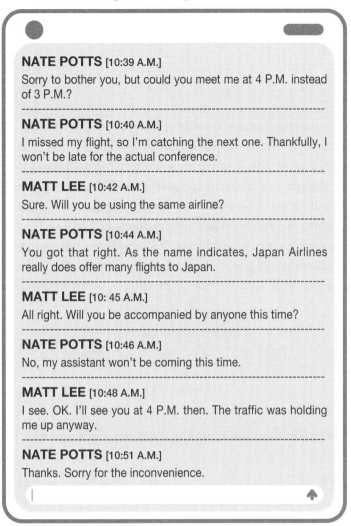

**NATE POTTS** [10:39 A.M.]
Sorry to bother you, but could you meet me at 4 P.M. instead of 3 P.M.?

**NATE POTTS** [10:40 A.M.]
I missed my flight, so I'm catching the next one. Thankfully, I won't be late for the actual conference.

**MATT LEE** [10:42 A.M.]
Sure. Will you be using the same airline?

**NATE POTTS** [10:44 A.M.]
You got that right. As the name indicates, Japan Airlines really does offer many flights to Japan.

**MATT LEE** [10: 45 A.M.]
All right. Will you be accompanied by anyone this time?

**NATE POTTS** [10:46 A.M.]
No, my assistant won't be coming this time.

**MATT LEE** [10:48 A.M.]
I see. OK. I'll see you at 4 P.M. then. The traffic was holding me up anyway.

**NATE POTTS** [10:51 A.M.]
Thanks. Sorry for the inconvenience.

**151.** What is suggested about Mr. Potts?

(A) He is Mr. Lee's assistant.
(B) He is leaving Japan.
(C) He has visited Japan before.
(D) He will be escorted by his assistant.

**152.** At 10:44, what does Mr. Potts mean when he writes, "You got that right"?

(A) He was held up by traffic.
(B) He can fix mechanical problems.
(C) He will be flying on Japan Airlines.
(D) He has never met Mr. Lee before.

▶ ▶ ▶GO ON TO THE NEXT PAGE

Fine Art Institute

January 23

Dear Faculty Members,

I regret to inform you that I have accepted a teaching position at Oakland College. This means that I have to resign my current position by the end of June. Without question, my years here at the Fine Art Institute have been some of the most fulfilling in my life. It has been a fantastic experience all around. So making a decision to leave here was certainly not an easy one. However, as many of you know, I have been searching for a tenure-track opportunity for quite some time now. Please understand my decision to move on to the next stage of my career. I believe the position at Oakland College will help me achieve some of the career goals I've set for myself. During my twelve years at this institute, I have had the privilege of working with many talented artists such as yourselves. I am very grateful for your hard work and dedication, and I wish you continued success in all of your endeavors.

Sincerely,

Grace Park
Fine Art Institute
San Francisco, California

---

**153.** What is the main purpose of the letter?

(A) To state a job description
(B) To accept a job offer
(C) To apply for a transfer
(D) To announce a resignation

**154.** According to the letter, what is true about Grace Park?

(A) She is one of students of Fine Art Institute.
(B) She started her career in Fine Art Institute.
(C) She has worked in Fine Art Institute for more than 10 years.
(D) She is planning to retire in a few years.

**155.** What does Ms. Park mention about the position at Oakland College?

(A) It requires some teaching experience.
(B) It mostly involves art projects.
(C) It will advance her career.
(D) It is a prerequisite to becoming an art expert.

**Questions 156-157** refer to the following e-mail.

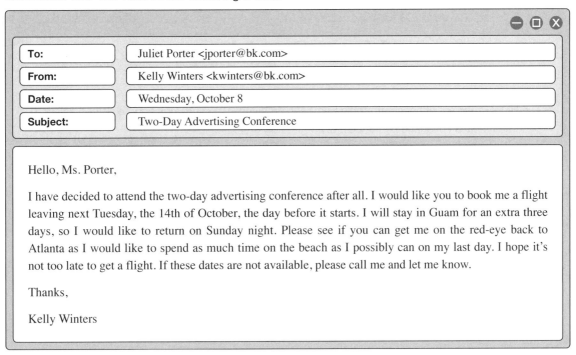

To: Juliet Porter <jporter@bk.com>

From: Kelly Winters <kwinters@bk.com>

Date: Wednesday, October 8

Subject: Two-Day Advertising Conference

Hello, Ms. Porter,

I have decided to attend the two-day advertising conference after all. I would like you to book me a flight leaving next Tuesday, the 14th of October, the day before it starts. I will stay in Guam for an extra three days, so I would like to return on Sunday night. Please see if you can get me on the red-eye back to Atlanta as I would like to spend as much time on the beach as I possibly can on my last day. I hope it's not too late to get a flight. If these dates are not available, please call me and let me know.

Thanks,

Kelly Winters

**156.** What is the purpose of the e-mail?

(A) To propose changes to a budget
(B) To inquire about an advertisement
(C) To make travel arrangements
(D) To postpone a meeting

**157.** When will the conference start?

(A) On Monday
(B) On Tuesday
(C) On Wednesday
(D) On Thursday

▶ ▶ ▶GO ON TO THE NEXT PAGE

# Hotel President
## Directory of services

The Hotel President offers comfortable European ambience with spacious and beautifully decorated suites enhanced by the helpful and friendly staff.

Throughout your stay, relax and enjoy various services and amenities.

**BREAKFAST** Available in your room between 7:30 A.M. and 8:30 A.M.

**BABYSITTING** A reputable service is available.

**BUSINESS FACILITIES** Facsimile machine $1.00 per page (local area). Photocopying 20 cents per page. Available during normal reception hours only.

**COTS** Available free of charge.

**DRY-CLEANING** Same-day dry-cleaning service is available Monday to Friday (except on public holidays). Please leave at reception before 9:30 A.M. daily.

**TAXIS** 24-hour service is available with a free telephone located in the foyer near the reception desk.

**CHECKOUT** Checkout time is 10:00 A.M. Should you require a later checkout time, prior arrangements are necessary. Half rates apply.

**PAYMENT** Payment is due upon the completion of your stay and may be made either in cash or by credit card. Personal checks are not accepted unless previous arrangements have been made with the manager.

**RECEPTION HOURS** The normal reception hours are 7:00 A.M. to 9:00 P.M.

• Complimentary daily morning newspapers, early-riser coffee service, and a fitness center are all available.

---

**158.** When are business services available?

(A) 7:30 A.M. to 8:30 A.M.
(B) 7:00 A.M. to 9:00 P.M.
(C) 9:00 A.M. to 5:00 P.M.
(D) 9:30 A.M. to 5:30 P.M.

**159.** What is required for customers to use personal checks for payment?

(A) Notice three days before checkout
(B) A social security number
(C) The prior approval of the manager
(D) An identification card

**160.** What is available to guests free of charge?

(A) The weekend newspaper
(B) Afternoon tea
(C) The health club
(D) Babysitting services

**161.** What is NOT a service provided by the hotel?

(A) Room service
(B) Extra cots
(C) Conference facilities
(D) Free telephone calls

# MEMORANDUM

To: All staff
From: James Brady, General Affairs Manager (EXT. 5493)
Date: September 11

This week, we will install backup power units in our building. They will provide reliable short-term backup power in the event of a blackout and will protect our information and equipment. We will connect the units to the computer's power source with a special cable. When a power outage takes place, the units will instantly switch computers to emergency battery backup power and signal the outage by making beeping sounds for 10 minutes. We encourage all of you to make comments about this plan at any time.

**162.** What will be done this week?

(A) Electrical fire alarms will be installed.
(B) Extra computer units will be purchased.
(C) An auxiliary power system will be installed.
(D) A network of online systems will be constructed.

**163.** When will the units give a signal?

(A) When the generator is broken
(B) When the backup power unit is down
(C) When the electricity used by computers is down
(D) When the security device turns off suddenly

# NOTICE

## Kamon Financial Solutions

Yesterday, management and the owners held a meeting to discuss the future of the company. We have seen a great rise in profits during the last two years and also a large increase in our number of clients. So there are many customers that we are unable to serve from our current office. As such, it has been decided that in order to enable the business to grow, we will move to a much larger new office, which will open on October 2. —[1]—.

To make the relocation to the new office as smooth as possible, we have decided to move the majority of our equipment on September 29. —[2]—. On behalf of management, I would like to request that all staff members come to work that Saturday to help us move to the new location. You will be paid for your time at an overtime rate of $50 per/hour. —[3]—. You will be working from 11 A.M. until 3 P.M. In addition, the day before the move, Friday, September 28, management requests that you pack all of your folders and documents into cardboard boxes so that they can be easily loaded into the truck. —[4]—. You will find spare boxes located in the storeroom.

If you have any questions, feel free to contact me directly. My extension is #303. Thank you for your cooperation. Together, we can help Kamon Financial Solutions become a market leader.

Andrew Lee
Chief Executive Officer

---

**164.** What is the main purpose of the notice?

(A) To announce a relocation to a new office
(B) To advertise a new product offered by the company
(C) To provide a list of new contact details of clients
(D) To invite employees to attend a conference

**165.** The word "majority" in paragraph 2, line 2, is closest in meaning to

(A) least
(B) most
(C) absolute
(D) nearly

**166.** What are employees requested to do on September 29?

(A) Complete some sales reports
(B) Phone some new clients
(C) Come to the office
(D) Park their cars in a different parking lot

**167.** In which of the positions marked [1], [2], [3], and [4] does the following sentence best belong?

"This day is a Saturday, and our office is usually closed on weekends, so there will be a minimum amount of disruption to our business."

(A) [1]
(B) [2]
(C) [3]
(D) [4]

**Questions 168-171** refer to the following article.

**January 10**

# *Soda Company to Unveil Its Latest Soda Soon*

Chicago – The Lite Soda Company, an international brand, is set to unveil its latest diet soda. —[1]—. Its new soda, called Mountain Spring, will hit markets on June 25, the start of the summer season. Mountain Spring's aggressive advertising campaign will be launched on May 15 with TV and print advertisements, first in major markets like New York, Chicago, Los Angeles, San Francisco, and Miami. Billboards along highways will be put up at the end of May. These will be seen in long stretches of highways in Ohio, Michigan and the Carolinas. —[2]—.

—[3]—. Unlike the company's other two diet sodas, which have only 10 calories each, Mountain Spring is said to have 0 calories and is sweetened with fruit juice, not artificial sweeteners. The Lite Soda Company is said to be following the market trend where consumers are demanding more natural food consumption and fewer artificial materials in their foods. —[4]—. This is the company's first all-natural soda.

**168.** When will the new soda be available nationally?

(A) May 15
(B) May 31
(C) June 21
(D) June 25

**169.** What is an advantage of Mountain Spring?

(A) It is less expensive.
(B) It is more familiar to the public.
(C) It includes natural sugar.
(D) It has only 10 calories.

**170.** What is mentioned as a reason for developing the new soda?

(A) Consumer demand
(B) Competition from other soda companies
(C) Employee surveys
(D) New health guidelines

**171.** In which of the positions marked [1], [2], [3], and [4] does the following sentence best belong?

"The Lite Soda Company has introduced three new sodas in the past five years."

(A) [1]
(B) [2]
(C) [3]
(D) [4]

**Questions 172-175** refer to the following online chat discussion.

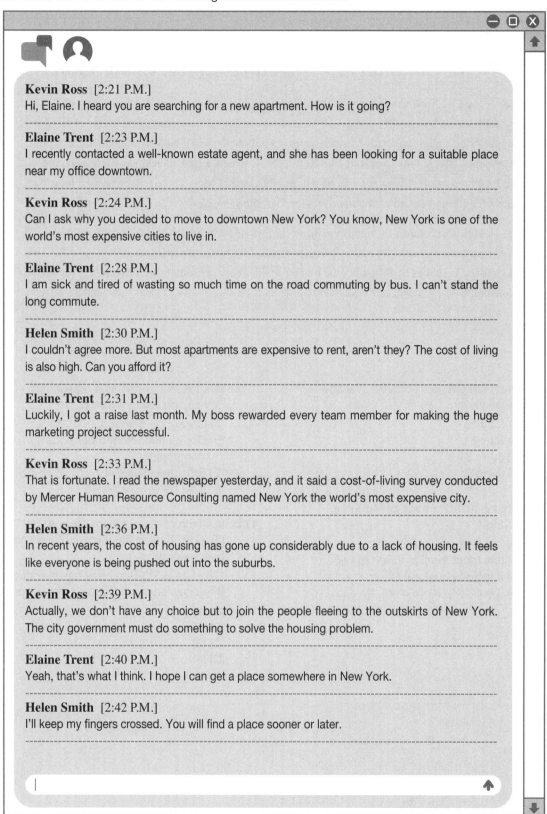

**Kevin Ross** [2:21 P.M.]
Hi, Elaine. I heard you are searching for a new apartment. How is it going?

**Elaine Trent** [2:23 P.M.]
I recently contacted a well-known estate agent, and she has been looking for a suitable place near my office downtown.

**Kevin Ross** [2:24 P.M.]
Can I ask why you decided to move to downtown New York? You know, New York is one of the world's most expensive cities to live in.

**Elaine Trent** [2:28 P.M.]
I am sick and tired of wasting so much time on the road commuting by bus. I can't stand the long commute.

**Helen Smith** [2:30 P.M.]
I couldn't agree more. But most apartments are expensive to rent, aren't they? The cost of living is also high. Can you afford it?

**Elaine Trent** [2:31 P.M.]
Luckily, I got a raise last month. My boss rewarded every team member for making the huge marketing project successful.

**Kevin Ross** [2:33 P.M.]
That is fortunate. I read the newspaper yesterday, and it said a cost-of-living survey conducted by Mercer Human Resource Consulting named New York the world's most expensive city.

**Helen Smith** [2:36 P.M.]
In recent years, the cost of housing has gone up considerably due to a lack of housing. It feels like everyone is being pushed out into the suburbs.

**Kevin Ross** [2:39 P.M.]
Actually, we don't have any choice but to join the people fleeing to the outskirts of New York. The city government must do something to solve the housing problem.

**Elaine Trent** [2:40 P.M.]
Yeah, that's what I think. I hope I can get a place somewhere in New York.

**Helen Smith** [2:42 P.M.]
I'll keep my fingers crossed. You will find a place sooner or later.

**172.** At what kind of company does Ms. Trent most likely work?

(A) A real estate company
(B) A design company
(C) An accounting firm
(D) A marketing firm

**173.** What is mentioned about New York in the article?

(A) Housing prices are still falling there.
(B) Living there is very costly.
(C) It has become less attractive to foreigners.
(D) It is packed with upscale shops.

**174.** What is implied about the city government?

(A) It is doing very well these days.
(B) It plans to build more housing facilities.
(C) It should be blamed for the housing crisis.
(D) It has begun to take heed of the popular outcry.

**175.** At 2:42 P.M., what does Ms. Smith mean when she writes, "I'll keep my fingers crossed"?

(A) She has a problem with her fingers.
(B) She agrees with Ms. Trent's opinion about the new policy.
(C) She wants Ms. Trent to find a suitable place.
(D) She thinks environmental pollution is an urgent issue.

**Questions 176-180** refer to the following memorandum and form.

# MEMORANDUM

To all employees:

This is a reminder of our travel reimbursement policies as outlined in the Ace Technology employee handbook.

Under our travel reimbursement policy, expenses are categorized under three different headings:

### Category 1:
- Air travel
- Accommodations
(Please note that Category 1 expenses are prepaid and arranged in advance by the accounting department.)

### Category 2:
- Local travel
- Meals
- Client entertainment

### Category 3:
- Incidental expenses
(Please note that for both Category 2 and Category 3 expenses, the employee will pay out of pocket at the time of purchase and will be reimbursed upon submitting the relevant itemized receipts.)

**Travel:** Local travel must have direct relevance to Ace Technology business in order to qualify for reimbursement. Travel via rail, privately-owned vehicles, taxicabs, and rental cars for business purposes is permitted. Receipts for private and rental automobile use must include the amount of fuel used and the distance driven. Employees must provide itemized receipts for all methods of transportation used during a trip in order to receive reimbursement for the related expenses.

**Client Entertainment Allowances:** Costs for entertaining clients will be reimbursed only if entertainment is clearly work-related. Itemized receipts must be provided for each transaction.

All employees must complete a travel expense report form that notes the required information on any work-related travel expenses. This form is to be signed by the employee and the employee's immediate supervisor. Employees must submit the completed travel expense report form and all receipts together within 60 days of returning from a business trip.

# Ace Technology

Los Angeles, California
Travel Expense Report Form

**Name:** George Parker
**Date:** Aug 3
**Department:** Advertising
**Code number:** X6425
**Departing Date:** Jul 20                                  **Returning Date:** Jul 26

| Date | Jul 22-Jul 23 | Jul 24-Jul 25 | Jul 26 |
|---|---|---|---|
| Place | Sydney | Auckland | Melbourne |
| Meals and Tips | $100 | $120 | $35 |
| Entertainment | $0 | $0 | $0 |
| Transportation(Taxi, rail etc.) | $35 | $45 | $32 |
| Other expenses | $80 | $0 | $0 |
| | $215 | $165 | $67 |
| Total | | $447 | |

Explanation for other expenses
Jul 22 – Outgoing Faxes

**Employee Signature:** George Parker *George Parker*

**Supervisor Signature:** Linda Wilson *Linda Wilson*

---

**176.** What is the purpose of the memo?

(A) To explain why some expenses are
not reimbursable
(B) To inform employees of expense
report requirements
(C) To announce revisions to the
employee handbook
(D) To extend the deadline for submitting
reimbursement requests

**177.** What type of expense is NOT mentioned
in the memo?

(A) Fax fees
(B) Client entertainment
(C) Fuel costs
(D) Rental car fees

**178.** When did Mr. Parker incur a Category 3
expense?

(A) on July 20
(B) on July 22
(C) on July 25
(D) on July 29

**179.** Where was Mr. Parker on July 25?

(A) Los Angeles
(B) Auckland
(C) Sydney
(D) Melbourne

**180.** What is suggested about Mr. Parker?

(A) He has requested some airline tickets.
(B) He made his own hotel reservations.
(C) He took a client to dinner in Auckland.
(D) He sent some faxes while in Sydney.

# Wallace Zoo Volunteer Program

**Requirements:**

- 18+ years of age
- High school diploma
- Satisfactory recommendation from previous or current employers
- Ability to commit to one full shift each week
- A clean, professional appearance
- Reliable transportation to the zoo
- The ability to attend employee training

**Attendance:**

Volunteers will work one full shift each week during the season they are hired. Fall and winter volunteers work shifts from 10 A.M. to 2 P.M. on weekends. Spring and summer volunteers have weekday shifts from 10 A.M. to 4 P.M. However, they might have to work on a weekend shift, which runs from 10 A.M. to 6 P.M. Shifts are assigned by the zoo's assistant manager.

If you are interested in volunteering at the city's best zoo, visit our Web site at wz.org for an application. If you have any questions, contact Kate Kensington at 703-221-8923 or katek@ wz.org. Applications for the spring program must be submitted by the end of the business day on March 18. Training for the spring program begins on March 28.

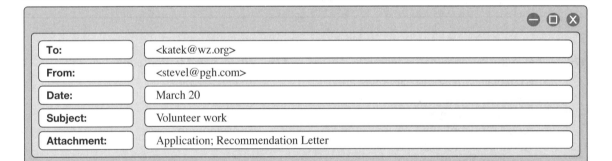

| To: | <katek@wz.org> |
| --- | --- |
| From: | <stevel@pgh.com> |
| Date: | March 20 |
| Subject: | Volunteer work |
| Attachment: | Application; Recommendation Letter |

Dear Ms. Kensington;

I'm responding to your advertisement for volunteers at the zoo. I saw the advertisement ten days ago; however, I had an illness that put me in the hospital for the past week. So I was unable to respond until now. I understand that the deadline for the spring program has passed. But I hope that you can understand my situation and let me still apply for it. I have attached a completed application and recommendation letter from my current employer.

Only on weekdays am I available for work. I work at a cinema and must work a full shift on both Saturdays and Sundays. I hope this won't be a problem as I would love to work at the zoo. I am a consummate professional, and I am certain I can do great work at the zoo.

Thank you,

Steve Lionsgate

181. What is NOT a requirement of the volunteer position?

(A) Completion of high school
(B) Attendance at staff training
(C) A recommendation letter
(D) Experience at a zoo

182. On what date were applications due for spring positions?

(A) March 10
(B) March 18
(C) March 20
(D) March 28

183. What does Mr. Lionsgate request in his e-mail?

(A) Consideration for his late application
(B) An extra weekend shift at the zoo
(C) Information about employee training
(D) More time to submit his high school diploma

184. How many hours will Mr. Lionsgate likely volunteer per day at the time he is available?

(A) 4
(B) 6
(C) 8
(D) 16

185. In the e-mail message, the word "consummate" in paragraph 2, line 3, is closest in meaning to

(A) determined
(B) absolute
(C) independent
(D) meticulous

# New Horizons
## *Family Townhouses Now Available!*

I am so pleased to announce the completion of the new development of luxury family townhouses in the Napa Valley area. The new townhomes have been constructed with the modern family in mind. The townhouses are ideally located near all main transit routes and are also surrounded by greenery.

The units also boast ecofriendly building practices combined with modern designs. There are plenty of schools and entertainment options in the neighborhood. The homes are right for families of differing sizes and budgets.

To discuss your dream rental home, please don't hesitate to get in touch with me at 707-926-7399.

Susan Kang
New Horizon Developer

# New Horizons
### Available Properties

### Family-Sized Townhouses

| Property Number | Property Code | Size | Monthly Rent | Deposit |
|---|---|---|---|---|
| Townhouse 12 | #MS986 | 1,200ft² | $1,200 | $600 |
| Townhouse 14 | #MS304 | 1,500ft² | $1,500 | $750 |
| Townhouse 23 | #MS230 | 2,000ft² | $1,800 | $900 |
| Townhouse 26 | #MS129 | 2,500ft² | $2,000 | $1,000 |

All deposits must be paid in full prior to the move-in date.

| To: | Rental Office <rentals@newhorizons.com> |
| From: | Jenna Marshall <j.marshall@sws.net> |
| Date: | March 23 |
| Subject: | Apartment rental |

Dear Ms. Kang,

New Horizons sounds like a great fit for my family of 4. We are the most interested in viewing the property with the monthly rent of $2,000. The size and the price are good for us. The pictures that were posted online are lovely! Could we schedule an appointment to view the property? I work at a general hospital in San Francisco, but I'm currently on maternity leave, so I am free during the day. Would sometime this week work for you? Is there anything I should bring with me? I know that great rentals at this price will go quickly!

Jenna Marshall

**186.** In the advertisement, the word "boast" in paragraph 2, line 1, is closest in meaning to

(A) boost
(B) feature
(C) create
(D) ensure

**187.** What is indicated about the townhouses of New Horizons?

(A) They are all fully furnished.
(B) They are near public transportation.
(C) They are pet friendly.
(D) Their rental rates are subsidized.

**188.** Who most likely is Ms. Marshall?

(A) A product developer
(B) A health professional
(C) A real estate agent
(D) A constructor

**189.** Which property does Ms. Marshall most likely desire to rent?

(A) Townhouse 12
(B) Townhouse 14
(C) Townhouse 23
(D) Townhouse 26

**190.** When is a good time for the appointment for Ms. Marshall?

(A) Anytime
(B) Only in the evenings
(C) Only on the weekend
(D) Only today

Speed Pass would like to reward its loyal customers by offering superb online discounts on all rail tickets valid for travel between October and January. Gold rail card holders can take advantage of a huge 30% saving on all services and routes, and customers with a Silver rail card will save 20% on all off-peak journeys. You can purchase an unlimited number of tickets for travel at these amazing discounted rates. Our Web site contains information about all of our routes and services.

As a bonus, if you upgrade your rail card to our Platinum service, we will see that you receive exclusive offers directly to your inbox every month, and your first journey will be absolutely free. Please note that once confirmed, tickets are nonrefundable but can be exchanged for a $10.00 administrative fee.

# Speed Pass Booking Confirmation

**Customer Name:** Diane Portland
**Date:** September 13

## Your Journey Details

| Service Number | Date | Departure Time | Leaving From | Arrival Time | Arriving At | Journey Time | Price |
|---|---|---|---|---|---|---|---|
| SP2581 | October 1 | 10:05 | Hunter's Mill | 12:31 | Pockelfields | 2h26m | $27.00 |
| SP2582 | October 1 | 19:12 | Pockelfields | 21:42 | Hunter's Mill | 2h30m | $29.00 |
| SP5665 | November 15 | 10:22 | Lincoln Stadium | 13:50 | Saltsburgh Road | 3h28m | $36.50 |
| SP5433 | November 17 | 15:02 | Saltsburgh Road | 18:27 | Lincoln Stadium | 3h25m | $33.00 |
| | | | | | | Total Before Discount | $125.50 |
| | | | | | | Discount | 20% |
| | | | | | | Balance Due | $100.40 |

<table>
<tr><td>**To:**</td><td>Customer Services &lt;cservices@sp.net&gt;</td></tr>
<tr><td>**From:**</td><td>Diane Portland &lt;dp07@coolmail.net&gt;</td></tr>
<tr><td>**Date:**</td><td>September 14</td></tr>
<tr><td>**Subject:**</td><td>Booking Confirmation</td></tr>
</table>

Dear Sir/Madam,

I'm contacting you regarding a booking I recently made with you via your Web site. According to your latest offer, my rail card subscription means that I should have received a 30% discount on my travel tickets. However, the discount I received was actually only 20%. As a loyal customer, I would appreciate it if you could arrange to refund me the difference.

Additionally, I would like to exchange one of my tickets. I am no longer able to make the 15:02 departure time for the SP5433 service and would like to change my ticket to the 16:02 departure time. I would be grateful if this could be arranged.

Regards,
Diane Portland

---

**191.** In the advertisement, the word "note" in paragraph 2, line 3, is closest in meaning to

(A) sign up
(B) log on
(C) be aware
(D) find out

**192.** What are Speed Pass customers encouraged to do?

(A) Book cheaper travel tickets through their rail card subscription
(B) Recommend Speed Pass to their friends and family members
(C) Contact Speed Pass to ask for a full overview of its services
(D) Renew their rail card for another two years

**193.** What can be inferred about Ms. Portland?

(A) She is a Gold rail card holder.
(B) She would like to upgrade to a Platinum Rail card.
(C) She wants to cancel all of the tickets she has purchased.
(D) She has never used the Speed Pass services before.

**194.** Which journey does Ms. Portland indicate she wishes to change?

(A) Hunter's Mill to Pockelfields
(B) Pockelfields to Hunter's Mill
(C) Lincoln Stadium to Saltsburgh Road
(D) Saltsburgh Road to Lincoln Stadium

**195.** What is Ms. Portland's problem?

(A) She was overcharged for her train tickets.
(B) She has not received her train tickets.
(C) She could not access the Speed Pass Web site.
(D) She was charged for a ticket she did not reserve.

▶ ▶ ▶GO ON TO THE NEXT PAGE

# MK Corporation Training Course

The MK Corporation would like to bring your attention to the fantastic program of training courses we have coming up next quarter. We urge you to take the opportunity to research what each module has to offer and how it could contribute to your own professional development as well as take responsibility for ensuring that you achieve your professional competencies. For those of you who have not yet completed your yearly mandatory training, you will be required to book a place in each of the courses marked with an asterisk as these modules are a yearly requirement for all staff members. You will also find a list of modules that you are required to complete as part of your own personal job role on the intranet. We will cover the cost of these courses. If you would like to attend any courses that are not part of your job specification but you feel they would help expand your skill set going forward, we would be happy for you to do this, but you will be personally responsible for the enrollment fee.

If you have any questions about any of the training modules, or you would like to book a place, please feel free to e-mail Brian McGowan (b.mcgowan@mk.net).

# MK Corporation Training Course

| Course Code | Course Title | Dates/Times | |
|---|---|---|---|
| MK94091 | Performance-Management Skills Workshop | November 13 | 10:00 |
| | | November 20 | 10:00 |
| | | November 27 | 13:00 |
| MK73112 | Effective Communication Master Class | November 10 | 14:30 |
| | | November 17 | 11:00 |
| | | November 24 | 10:30 |
| MK92035 | Time-Management Skills Workshop | December 1 | 09:30 |
| | | December 8 | 15:00 |
| | | December 17 | 14:30 |
| MK74011 | Interpersonal Skills Workshop | November 30 | 10:00 |
| | | December 3 | 14:30 |
| | | December 5 | 16:00 |

**To:** Brian McGowan <b.mcgowan@mk.net>

**From:** Linda Wilson <lw@mk.net>

**Date:** October 10

**Subject:** Training Courses

Dear Mr. McGowan,

I would like to book a place in course MK92035 on December 1 at 09:30. I also wonder how much this course will cost to attend. I am also interested in course MK74011, but I will be on my annual leave during that period. Do you know if this course will be held at any point in the future? Finally, I am not sure whether I am up to date with my performance-management skills competencies; I know I attended course MK94091 twice previously, but I am not sure of the exact date of the last one. I would be grateful if you could look into this for me.

Many thanks,

Linda Wilson

**196.** In the advertisement, the word "take" in paragraph 1, line 2, is closest in meaning to

(A) remove
(B) bring
(C) use
(D) capture

**197.** What are the employees encouraged to do?

(A) Reserve a place in all four of the training courses as soon as possible
(B) Give the course enrollment fee to Mr. McGowan
(C) Make suggestions for training courses they would like to add to the program
(D) Take some time to look at which courses would best suit their professional growth

**198.** What is implied about the time-management skills workshop?

(A) It is not a required module for Ms. Wilson's job.
(B) It is a new module that has been added to the program this year.
(C) It has the highest enrollment fee.
(D) It is compulsory for all staff members.

**199.** What is suggested about Ms. Wilson?

(A) She is unsure about what the courses entail.
(B) She is leaving the company and will not complete her mandatory training.
(C) She has been working at the company for over a year.
(D) She does not wish to attend any courses she has to pay for herself.

**200.** What problem did Ms. Wilson mention in her e-mail?

(A) She cannot access the intranet.
(B) She will be on vacation during one of the courses she wishes to attend.
(C) She cannot afford the enrollment fee for a course.
(D) She does not wish to attend the mandatory training.

STOP! This is the end of the test. If you finish before time is called, you may go back to Parts 5, 6, and 7 and check your work.

# Actual Test 02

MP3 해설집

적정 풀이 시간 120분

**120 min**

시작 시간 ___시 ___분

종료 시간 ___시 ___분

중간에 멈추지 말고 처음부터 끝까지 풀어보세요.
문제를 풀 때에는 실전처럼 답안지에 마킹하세요.

**목표 개수** _____ / 200 **실제 개수** _____ / 200

예상 점수는 번역 및 정답에 있는 점수 환산표를 참조하세요.

# LISTENING TEST

In the Listening test, you will be asked to demonstrate how well you understand spoken English. The entire Listening test will last approximately 45 minutes. There are four parts, and directions are given for each part. You must mark your answers on the separate answer sheet. Do not write your answers in your test book.

## PART 1

**Directions:** For each question in this part, you will hear four statements about a picture in your test book. When you hear the statements, you must select the one statement that best describes what you see in the picture. Then find the number of the question on your answer sheet and mark your answer. The statements will not be printed in your test book and will be spoken only one time.

Statement (B), "They are sitting at a table," is the best description of the picture. So you should select answer (B) and mark it on your answer sheet.

**1.**

**2.**

▶ ▶ ▶GO ON TO THE NEXT PAGE

**3.**

**4.**

**5.**

**6.**

▶ ▶ ▶GO ON TO THE NEXT PAGE

# PART 2

**Directions:** You will hear a question or statement and three responses spoken in English. They will not be printed in your test book and will be spoken only one time. Select the best response to the question or statement and mark the letter (A), (B), or (C) on your answer sheet.

7. Mark your answer on your answer sheet.

8. Mark your answer on your answer sheet.

9. Mark your answer on your answer sheet.

10. Mark your answer on your answer sheet.

11. Mark your answer on your answer sheet.

12. Mark your answer on your answer sheet.

13. Mark your answer on your answer sheet.

14. Mark your answer on your answer sheet.

15. Mark your answer on your answer sheet.

16. Mark your answer on your answer sheet.

17. Mark your answer on your answer sheet.

18. Mark your answer on your answer sheet.

19. Mark your answer on your answer sheet.

20. Mark your answer on your answer sheet.

21. Mark your answer on your answer sheet.

22. Mark your answer on your answer sheet.

23. Mark your answer on your answer sheet.

24. Mark your answer on your answer sheet.

25. Mark your answer on your answer sheet.

26. Mark your answer on your answer sheet.

27. Mark your answer on your answer sheet.

28. Mark your answer on your answer sheet.

29. Mark your answer on your answer sheet.

30. Mark your answer on your answer sheet.

31. Mark your answer on your answer sheet.

## PART 3

**Directions:** You will hear some conversations between two or three people. You will be asked to answer three questions about what the speakers say in each conversation. Select the best response to each question and mark the letter (A), (B), (C), or (D) on your answer sheet. The conversations will not be printed in your test book and will be spoken only one time.

**32.** Who most likely is the woman?

(A) An accountant
(B) A lawyer
(C) A receptionist
(D) A hotel employee

**33.** What does the woman say about Mr. Watson?

(A) He is awaiting a trial.
(B) He is attending a conference.
(C) He owns a hotel in London.
(D) He works as a marketing manager.

**34.** What does the woman suggest the man do?

(A) Leave a message
(B) Contact a hotel
(C) Send an e-mail
(D) File a lawsuit

**35.** What is the conversation mainly about?

(A) A change to an advertising strategy
(B) The release of a new product
(C) A recently installed machine
(D) The development of a security system

**36.** Why does the woman say, "Tell me about it"?

(A) She didn't hear what one of the men just said.
(B) She joined the discussion late.
(C) She strongly agrees with the man.
(D) She already knows what happened this morning.

**37.** What does the woman say about the new system?

(A) It needs repairing.
(B) It doesn't perform properly.
(C) It has resulted in more sales.
(D) It provides better security.

**38.** What are the speakers mainly discussing?

(A) A focus group study
(B) An advertising strategy
(C) A print layout
(D) A TV commercial

**39.** What part of the commercial does the man say must be changed?

(A) The layout of the product
(B) The size of the brand logo
(C) The method of communication
(D) The length of the clip

**40.** According to the man, what will happen in November?

(A) A meeting with the marking team will be held.
(B) A new product will be launched.
(C) A shopping season will begin.
(D) A decision will be made by the executives.

**41.** What is the woman calling about?

(A) A refund
(B) A change in her schedule
(C) A missing paycheck
(D) An electrical problem

**42.** What department does the man most likely work in?

(A) Payroll
(B) Customer Service
(C) Personnel
(D) Sales

**43.** What does the man offer to do?

(A) Print a related document
(B) Make a payment immediately
(C) Deliver some samples to the woman
(D) Issue a new check to her

▶ ▶ ▶ **GO ON TO THE NEXT PAGE**

44. Why does the man congratulate the woman?

(A) She started a new job.
(B) She received a promotion.
(C) She got a raise.
(D) She passed an examination.

45. What problem does the woman mention?

(A) A new supervisor is inexperienced.
(B) Her salary was paid late.
(C) Sales are lower than expected.
(D) Some products were recalled.

46. Why does the man say, "Oh, you don't say"?

(A) He would like to discuss something in more detail.
(B) He is surprised by some information.
(C) He thinks the woman is exaggerating.
(D) He doesn't want to hear what the woman is saying.

47. Where does the man most likely work?

(A) At a shipping company
(B) At an online store
(C) At a computer software company
(D) At a travel agency

48. Why does the woman contact the man?

(A) To inquire about shipping charges
(B) To make an address change
(C) To ask for a new catalogue
(D) To complain about the company's poor service

49. What will the woman probably do later?

(A) Ask for a refund
(B) File a lawsuit
(C) Ship a product
(D) Pay an additional charge

50. What are the speakers talking about?

(A) A new hiring plan
(B) A business luncheon
(C) A success in the job market
(D) A proposal for relocation

51. What is the man asked to do this weekend?

(A) Reserve a table for lunch
(B) Attend an orientation
(C) Hold a job interview
(D) Meet some researchers

52. What will the speakers probably do later?

(A) Spend some time together
(B) Fill out job applications
(C) Visit a main office
(D) Start a new project

53. What problem does the woman mention?

(A) An incorrect item was delivered.
(B) A document is missing.
(C) An office closed early.
(D) A printer is not working correctly.

54. What does the man ask the woman for?

(A) Technical support
(B) An order number
(C) A product's serial number
(D) Her personal contact information

55. Why does the man say, "No problem at all"?

(A) He is very good at operating a machine.
(B) He doesn't have any problems with the woman.
(C) He is satisfied with all the details on a warranty certificate.
(D) He can transfer the woman's call to the right person.

**56.** What will happen at the beginning of September?

(A) A new product will be released.
(B) Job seekers will submit applications.
(C) Some employees will be at a trade fair.
(D) The company will export its products to the U.S.

**57.** What does the man suggest changing?

(A) The requirements for job applicants
(B) The date some interns arrive
(C) The export price of a new product
(D) The venues of some job fairs

**58.** What will the woman do later in the day?

(A) Contact a colleague
(B) Conduct some interviews
(C) Attend a college career fair
(D) Prepare some materials

---

**59.** What is the problem?

(A) There is a shortage of manpower.
(B) The speakers' productivity is getting low.
(C) There is a lack of office furniture.
(D) A company's advertising costs are too high.

**60.** What temporary solution is discussed?

(A) Purchasing some desks
(B) Sharing furniture
(C) Giving a big pay raise
(D) Hiring more employees

**61.** What will the man probably do next?

(A) Place an order
(B) Post an advertisement
(C) Work overtime
(D) Check his calendar

---

## ROAD MAP

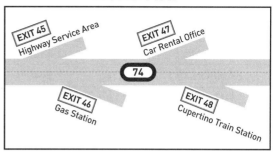

**62.** What are the speakers worried about?

(A) Missing a train
(B) Getting stuck in a traffic jam
(C) Spending too much on gas
(D) Arriving at work late

**63.** Look at the graphic. Which exit will the speakers take?

(A) EXIT 45
(B) EXIT 46
(C) EXIT 47
(D) EXIT 48

**64.** What will the speakers probably do later?

(A) Buy something to eat
(B) Check a seating chart
(C) Confirm a schedule
(D) Order tickets online

---

# COMPUTER SECTION

| Model | Weight | Price |
|-------|--------|-------|
| YUMI 115 | 1.8kg | $380 |
| SAMSON X5 | 2.7kg | $440 |
| HARU 4K | 1.4kg | $580 |
| GABY SUPER | 3.0kg | $590 |

**65.** Where does the man most likely work?

(A) At a publishing company
(B) At a travel agency
(C) At a laboratory
(D) At an electronics store

**66.** What does the woman say about her job?

(A) It is well compensated.
(B) It is physically demanding.
(C) It requires frequent business trips.
(D) It needs expert knowledge with machines.

**67.** Look at the graphic. What computer model will the woman probably select?

(A) YUMI 115
(B) SAMSON X5
(C) HARU 4K
(D) GABY SUPER

## List of Dates and Times

| Day | Time |
|-----|------|
| Monday | 10 A.M. |
| Tuesday | 2 P.M. |
| Wednesday | 5 P.M. |
| Thursday | 1 P.M. |

**68.** What is the woman's occupation?

(A) Journalist
(B) Chef
(C) Restaurant manager
(D) Photographer

**69.** What does the woman want to do?

(A) Cancel an order
(B) Recommend a dish
(C) Review an article
(D) Interview the man

**70.** Look at the graphic. When will the woman probably visit the restaurant?

(A) Monday
(B) Tuesday
(C) Wednesday
(D) Thursday

# PART 4

**Directions:** You will hear some short talks given by a single speaker. You will be asked to answer three questions about what the speaker says in each short talk. Select the best response to each question and mark the letter (A), (B), (C), or (D) on your answer sheet. The talks will not be printed in your test book and will be spoken only one time.

**71.** Where does the caller work?

(A) At a hotel
(B) At a restaurant
(C) At a travel agency
(D) At a bakery

**72.** What problem does the speaker mention?

(A) The serving staff is not big enough.
(B) A room was booked twice for the same date.
(C) A price was quoted inaccurately.
(D) A flight schedule has been changed.

**73.** What is the listener asked to do?

(A) Check e-mail
(B) Cancel a reservation
(C) Pick up a coupon
(D) Contact the caller

**74.** What is the talk about?

(A) A guided tour
(B) An ice cream brand
(C) A jewelry item
(D) A cruise line

**75.** What benefit will buyers of two Family Voyages get?

(A) Souvenirs made of gold
(B) Free excursions
(C) Automatic membership
(D) Special dining privileges

**76.** What should the listeners do if they need more information?

(A) Attend a presentation
(B) Complete a form
(C) Contact a shop manager
(D) Speak with a representative

**77.** What type of business does the speaker probably work for?

(A) A department store
(B) A furniture store
(C) A fabric shop
(D) A shipping company

**78.** What problem does the speaker mention?

(A) A shipping delay
(B) A scheduling conflict
(C) The damaging of a product
(D) The recording of wrong contact information

**79.** What does the speaker offer Mr. Stanford?

(A) A catalog of new furniture
(B) A gift certificate
(C) A discount on a future order
(D) Free delivery

**80.** Who most likely are the listeners?

(A) Event organizers
(B) Financial planner
(C) Educators
(D) Entrepreneurs

**81.** Why does the speaker say, "Now, she is the owner of the largest pet shop in the country"?

(A) To congratulate a person on her business success
(B) To emphasize a speaker's qualifications
(C) To suggest a topic for his next speech
(D) To give an example of responsibility and teamwork

**82.** What will the listeners probably do after the speech?

(A) Ask some questions
(B) Attend a reception
(C) Review some printouts
(D) Look at some products

83. Why is the speaker calling?

(A) To call in sick
(B) To report a mistake
(C) To ask for more information
(D) To explain a personnel plan

84. What does the speaker imply when he says, "But he had a car accident this morning"?

(A) An employee will take sick leave.
(B) An employee cannot train his replacement.
(C) An employee will not be able to attend an orientation.
(D) An employee has recently worked a lot of overtime.

85. What will the speaker do tomorrow?

(A) Meet with an employee
(B) Leave the company
(C) Manage a new project
(D) Review a proposal

86. Why does the speaker thank Mr. Wright?

(A) He made a generous donation.
(B) He gave an impressive presentation.
(C) He contributed to health improvements.
(D) He planned a conference in New York.

87. Who does the speaker work for?

(A) A pharmaceutical company
(B) A business consulting firm
(C) A local charity
(D) A general hospital

88. What does the speaker ask Mr. Wright to do next month?

(A) Reimburse her travel expenses
(B) Make a speech at a conference
(C) Postpone an appointment
(D) Train her new sales representatives

89. What does the speaker say will take place in an hour?

(A) A safety inspection
(B) A training session
(C) An evacuation drill
(D) A performance evaluation

90. What does the speaker imply when she says, "I know you might be a little annoyed by this inspection"?

(A) Some equipment is not working properly.
(B) The inspection usually interrupts customers.
(C) The inspection is being unexpectedly conducted.
(D) Employees are not interested in workplace safety.

91. According to the speaker, what will the employees do next?

(A) Conduct an evaluation
(B) Learn evacuation routes
(C) Go on a factory tour
(D) Discuss work assignments

92. What type of business does the man work for?

(A) A cosmetics company
(B) A marketing firm
(C) A design firm
(D) A packaging company

93. What did the company recently do?

(A) Sent some samples to clients
(B) Released new cosmetics
(C) Obtained a new client
(D) Moved to another location

94. What new task will the company complete in the coming weeks?

(A) Creating new samples
(B) Advertising new cosmetics
(C) Developing a new product
(D) Analyzing the French market

| Monday | Tuesday | Wednesday | Thursday |
|--------|---------|-----------|----------|
| 🌧️ | 🌧️ | ⛅ | ☀️ |

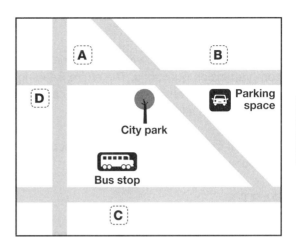

**95.** Who most likely is the speaker?

(A) A weather forecaster
(B) A caterer
(C) An event organizer
(D) A radio show host

**96.** Look at the graphic. What day was the corporate event originally scheduled to be held?

(A) Monday
(B) Tuesday
(C) Wednesday
(D) Thursday

**97.** What does the speaker ask the listener to do?

(A) Search for other venues
(B) Cancel a corporate event
(C) Provide an order number
(D) Contact a service provider

**98.** What is the speaker mainly discussing?

(A) Renovating a property
(B) Choosing a business location
(C) Having a special promotion
(D) Advertising a sporting competition

**99.** Look at the graphic. Which location does the speaker prefer?

(A) Location A
(B) Location B
(C) Location C
(D) Location D

**100.** What does the speaker say he will pass out?

(A) A construction timetable
(B) A market analysis report
(C) Some printouts
(D) Some photographs

This is the end of the Listening test. Turn to Part 5 in your test book.

▶ ▶ ▶GO ON TO THE NEXT PAGE

# READING TEST

In the Reading test, you will read a variety of texts and answer several different types of reading comprehension questions. The entire Reading test will last 75 minutes. There are three parts, and directions are given for each part. You are encouraged to answer as many questions as possible within the time allowed.

You must mark your answers on the separate answer sheet. Do not write your answers in your test book.

## PART 5

**Directions**: A word or phrase is missing in each of the sentences below. Four answer choices are given below each sentence. Select the best answer to complete the sentence. Then mark the letter (A), (B), (C), or (D) on your answer sheet.

**101.** Ms. Banks attended a business certificate program at a local college to learn how to manage ------- company.

(A) she
(B) herself
(C) her
(D) hers

**102.** Wonderful Flowers offers ------- of various flower arrangements and balloon bouquets to the city of Fremont.

(A) delivery
(B) deliverable
(C) to deliver
(D) delivered

**103.** The annual report released during the seminar showed significant improvement in labor ------- and cost reduction.

(A) product
(B) produce
(C) production
(D) productivity

**104.** Making an extra effort to be kind to people can create a friendly atmosphere and help us ------- new customers.

(A) attract
(B) attraction
(C) attractive
(D) attracted

**105.** Customers must pay an additional $3 shipping fee so as to ------- the same-day delivery of their online purchases.

(A) afford
(B) inform
(C) charge
(D) guarantee

**106.** With such rapid rates of growth, one of the ------- problems the company faces is a shortage of computer graphic designers.

(A) collaborative
(B) major
(C) favorable
(D) effective

**107.** The chairman of the BK Financial Group planned his congratulatory speech at a reception ------- the event.

(A) following
(B) behind
(C) prior
(D) until

**108.** The merger of One International and Komi Ltd. is expected to be completed ------- the next three weeks.

(A) along
(B) until
(C) within
(D) about

**109.** ------- overwhelming demand for tickets, the Syracuse Philharmonic Orchestra has added four performances dates to its regular schedule.

(A) As a result
(B) In addition to
(C) In place of
(D) In response to

**110.** The infectious disease is prevailing throughout the country, but there is no ------- vaccination method for patients.

(A) competitive
(B) extensive
(C) adequate
(D) inexpensive

**111.** ------- his experience in North America, Mr. Chan understands Americans' working style better than other employees at his company.

(A) Owing to
(B) In spite of
(C) Regardless of
(D) Nevertheless

**112.** Several business magazines reported that Hachi Technology ------- a huge investment proposal from a Chinese company.

(A) receive
(B) will be received
(C) had received
(D) have received

**113.** Thanks to his remarkable talent at advanced management and his knowledge of technology, Mr. Baker has shown ------- to be an outstanding CEO.

(A) he
(B) him
(C) himself
(D) his

**114.** Any questions regarding obtaining ------- to be a computer graphic specialist should be forwarded to the head of the Technical Education Department.

(A) certify
(B) certification
(C) certified
(D) certificate

**115.** ------- interested in purchasing property overseas should be aware that their actions have the potential to hurt the domestic economy.

(A) Which
(B) We
(C) Those
(D) Themselves

**116.** The board of directors ------- selected Ms. Beckinsale, the head of Marketing, as the employee of the year.

(A) unanimously
(B) locally
(C) securely
(D) shortly

**117.** The new corporate headquarters is strategically ------- near some global giant banks and prominent securities firms.

(A) locate
(B) location
(C) locating
(D) located

**118.** ------- participants are required to put their name tags on their desks before the conference starts.

(A) Each
(B) All
(C) Much
(D) Every

**119.** Some people pointed out that Mr. Winston's marketing strategy is very similar to ------- of our new marketing head.

(A) it
(B) them
(C) one
(D) that

**120.** Cheese Technology's new accounting software makes it much ------- than before for companies to create financial statements.

(A) easy
(B) easier
(C) ease
(D) more easily

▶ ▶ ▶GO ON TO THE NEXT PAGE

121. According to our new policy, ------- leaves last is responsible for turning off all the lights in the office.
(A) some
(B) whoever
(C) which
(D) they

122. ------- working on his new task, James struggled to gather information scattered here and there in the company database.
(A) While
(B) Although
(C) Over
(D) Along with

123. To stay on top, we must invent new products, services, and businesses that ------- customers nor competitors have imagined.
(A) both
(B) neither
(C) but
(D) not only

124. The application process to get a loan from West California Bank will be much faster and easier than ever ------- the elimination of most of the paperwork.
(A) as of
(B) instead of
(C) with regard to
(D) thanks to

125. If you would like to reserve several rooms, you need to use a different name for each room. -------, the duplicate booking will be canceled by the hotel.
(A) Otherwise
(B) As if
(C) Therefore
(D) So that

126. The use of fossil fuels such as coal, natural gas, and oil ------- steadily over the past 100 years.
(A) increase
(B) increases
(C) will be increased
(D) has increased

127. The tsunami that brought chaos to the northern coast left ------- 10,000 people dead or missing.
(A) urgently
(B) considerably
(C) approximately
(D) simultaneously

128. Energy Companies need to develop different forms of alternative energy that can reduce pollution and ------- scarce resources.
(A) conserve
(B) supply
(C) produce
(D) specialize

129. ------- figure out how customers feel about a particular product, the company conducts surveys twice a year.
(A) In order to
(B) As to
(C) Furthermore
(D) As a result of

130. ------- Ms. Armitage was elected as mayor, she has been actively involved in many local economic issues.
(A) For
(B) Because
(C) Since
(D) Although

# PART 6

**Directions:** Read the texts that follow. A word, phrase, or sentence is missing in parts of each text. Four answer choices for each question are given below the text. Select the best answer to complete the text. Then mark the letter (A), (B), (C), or (D) on your answer sheet.

**Questions 131-134** refer to the following e-mail.

Dear Mr. Finley,

Thank you for your recent ------- with World Auction. We have your message regarding your
           **131.**

refund request on the product CK vacuum. Our records indicate that you ordered two

products, a CK vacuum and a Speed microwave, on our Web page on July 7, but you are

requesting a refund only for the vacuum.

-------. For your convenience, we ------- a return shipping label for you to download and then
**132.**                    **133.**

place on the package. You will receive a refund in the form of the payment method that you

used.

Please ------- that refunds can take 7-15 days to process. We apologize for any
      **134.**

inconvenience caused. Do not hesitate to contact us with additional questions.

---

**131.** (A) inquiry
    (B) application
    (C) compliment
    (D) transaction

**132.** (A) We sincerely appreciate your
        informative feedback.
    (B) We have processed your refund
        request for that product.
    (C) Your order has been placed and will
        be shipped to your address in a week.
    (D) Please provide an explanation for your
        request so we can determine if you
        are eligible for a refund.

**133.** (A) attached
    (B) have attached
    (C) were attached
    (D) will attach

**134.** (A) note
    (B) warn
    (C) remind
    (D) assure

Coco Heating Systems
160 Pine Ave
Syracuse, NY 13244

October 1

Stacy Nguyen
310 Main Street
Syracuse, NY 13244

Dear Ms. Nguyen,

I'm writing to let you know that your year-long boiler maintenance plan comes to an end on

November 12. -------.
**135.**

Before winter comes, protecting your boiler ------- breakdown is a key consideration for
**136.**
keeping you and your family safe and warm. Our low-cost maintenance plan means that you

don't have to worry about pricy repairs ------- your boiler break down.
**137.**

Please give us a call today and let us ------- bringing peace of mind to your household
**138.**
through the long winter.

Sincerely,

Customer Care Division
Coco Heating Systems

---

**135.** (A) You must receive specialized training from some boiler experts.
(B) You need to verify your identity and protect yourself from being defrauded.
(C) You are required to purchase a new boiler as soon as possible.
(D) You should call us to renew your plan before the end of the month.

**136.** (A) for
(B) into
(C) by
(D) against

**137.** (A) while
(B) now that
(C) should
(D) in spite of the fact

**138.** (A) keep
(B) be kept
(C) to keep
(D) keeping

---

Dear Ms. Jenkins,

Thank you again for attending the interview with us at Joshua Securities last week. The managers were all greatly impressed by your previous work experience and potential and are ------- to offer you the role of senior trader at our Los Angeles headquarters. We would like to
**139.**
ask you, if possible, to start on April 15.

-------. I am enclosing a summary of them for your reference. Also ------- is an employment
**140.**                                                                                            **141.**
agreement that we will require you to sign on your first day of work with us. It lists the duties involved in your position, which we also outlined during the interview. Please let me know if anything needs -------.
**142.**

I would be grateful if you could telephone me to confirm that you would like to accept the position and to confirm start date. I look forward to hearing from you and to welcoming you to the company.

---

**139.** (A) delighted
(B) preferred
(C) specified
(D) requested

**140.** (A) We talked about how to survive in the rapidly changing market.
(B) Please decide what types of jobs you are qualified for.
(C) We were very impressed with your market analysis report.
(D) Your employment terms and benefits will be as discussed at interview.

**141.** (A) enclose
(B) enclosed
(C) enclosure
(D) enclosing

**142.** (A) clarify
(B) clarifying
(C) clarified
(D) to clarify

ACTUAL TEST... **02**

**Questions 143-146** refer to the following memorandum.

---

**MEMORANDUM**

From: Thomas Lee, Chief Executive Officer
To: All employees
Date: June 6
Subject: Overtime for two weeks

Please be aware that all employees will need to put in extra hours ------- the end of this
                                                                    **143.**
year's tax season. We have a large number of clients who are demanding more hard work

this year.

However, your efforts will be rewarded once the tax season -------. Any requests for leave
                                                            **144.**
during this tax season must be approved ------- by me. Your supervisor or team leader
                                         **145.**
cannot approve requests during this critical time.

-------. We will also give everyone extra time off in appreciation of your hard work.
**146.**

Thank you for your understanding and cooperation in advance.


Thomas Lee
Chief Executive Officer

---

**143.** (A) by
(B) through
(C) since
(D) within

**144.** (A) finishes
(B) has finished
(C) is finished
(D) will be finished

**145.** (A) exactly
(B) easily
(C) uniquely
(D) directly

**146.** (A) Becoming a global accounting
company is the top priority.
(B) The city is a popular place for
corporations because of its low tax
rates.
(C) We are going to have a company
banquet after the busy period is over.
(D) Several employees were rewarded by
their company with a vacation abroad.

## PART 7

**Directions:** In this part you will read a selection of texts, such as magazine and newspaper articles, e-mails, and instant messages. Each text or set of texts is followed by several questions. Select the best answer for each question and mark the letter (A), (B), (C), or (D) on your answer sheet.

**Questions 147-148** refer to the following advertisement.

# Max Interior Design

## Cutting-edge design tailored to each homeowner's tastes

Award-winning design team with decades of experience
### Quick turnaround
### Free quotes
### Project management
### References available

Please visit our expansive showroom on Main Street in Pleasant City, or visit us on-line at www.maxinteriordesign.com.

**147.** For whom is this advertisement intended?

(A) Homeowners
(B) Shop managers
(C) Architects
(D) Fashion designers

**148.** What is indicated about Max Interior Design?

(A) It will soon open an additional store.
(B) It matches the prices of its competitors.
(C) It displays examples of its work.
(D) It acquires its materials from local producers.

# FAX

**Recipient:** Chan Hong (510-575-4332)
**Sender:** Andrew Kim (525-412-9267)
**Re:** Reshipment

**Message:**

Thank you for your letter informing us that the external hard disk drives you ordered had not arrived. We are sorry for the inconvenience this has caused and have arranged to have another one sent to you today.

In the event that the original order is delivered to you, please call the toll-free number listed on our Web site.

We have notified our shipping agent in an attempt to discover why this problem occurred. Please accept our apology and thanks for placing your order with us.

Sincerely,

Andrew Kim

---

**149.** What does Mr. Kim send Mr. Hong?

(A) A business contract
(B) An order sheet
(C) A new software program
(D) A storage device

**150.** What should Mr. Hong do if the first order is delivered?

(A) Send it back to Mr. Kim
(B) Cancel his second order
(C) Call the company to tell it has arrived
(D) Visit a new Web site to download a coupon

Questions 151-152 refer to the following text message chain.

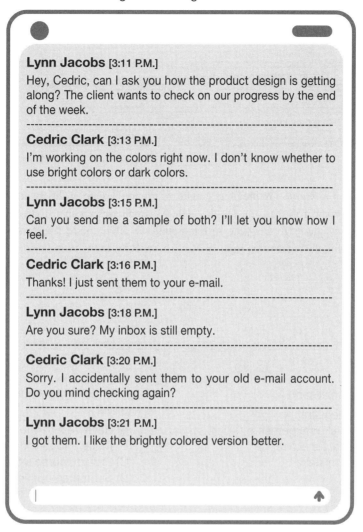

**Lynn Jacobs** [3:11 P.M.]

Hey, Cedric, can I ask you how the product design is getting along? The client wants to check on our progress by the end of the week.

**Cedric Clark** [3:13 P.M.]

I'm working on the colors right now. I don't know whether to use bright colors or dark colors.

**Lynn Jacobs** [3:15 P.M.]

Can you send me a sample of both? I'll let you know how I feel.

**Cedric Clark** [3:16 P.M.]

Thanks! I just sent them to your e-mail.

**Lynn Jacobs** [3:18 P.M.]

Are you sure? My inbox is still empty.

**Cedric Clark** [3:20 P.M.]

Sorry. I accidentally sent them to your old e-mail account. Do you mind checking again?

**Lynn Jacobs** [3:21 P.M.]

I got them. I like the brightly colored version better.

**151.** What type of business does Mr. Clark most likely work for?

(A) An art college
(B) An auto manufacturer
(C) An accounting firm
(D) A design agency

**152.** At 3:18 P.M., what does Ms. Jacobs most likely mean when she writes, "Are you sure"?

(A) She is questioning Mr. Clark's choice of colors.
(B) She is asking if Mr. Clark sent an e-mail.
(C) She is wondering if Mr. Clark can start a product design project.
(D) She is asking Mr. Clark to send his portfolio files online now.

**Questions 153-155** refer to the following e-mail.

| To: | Ellen Smith <es@sheba.com> |
|---|---|
| From: | Tiffany Anderson <ta@sheba.com> |
| Date: | May 10 |
| Subject: | A typing error |

Dear Ms. Smith:

I wanted to point out a typo in my previous e-mail regarding the date of the marketing workshop. It's supposed to be the 20th of this month, not the 29th. My apologies for that. I also heard that they are allowing two more people to go this year, so ask around the office to see if anyone else would like to attend. I have to submit the registration form on May 16, so let me know before then.

Thanks,

Tiffany Anderson
Personnel

**153.** Why was the e-mail sent?

(A) To cancel a registration
(B) To make travel arrangements
(C) To congratulate a colleague
(D) To correct a mistake

**154.** When will the marketing workshop take place?

(A) On May 11
(B) On May 16
(C) On May 20
(D) On May 29

**155.** What does Ms. Anderson ask Ms. Smith to do?

(A) Reserve a venue
(B) Place a food order
(C) Provide some information
(D) Submit an application

# MEMO

**From:** Brianna Palmer
**To:** All staff
**Date:** Tuesday, January 10
**Subject:** Notice

Our office printer will be unavailable for about an hour this Thursday, January 12, beginning at 1:00 P.M. A new printer will be installed during this time and will need to be tested several times. Afterward, the installer will bring the old one and discard it.

If you need to print on Thursday, please do your printing either before 1 P.M. or after 3 P.M. You can also use the print shop right across the street.

Please pardon any inconvenience this may cause you. Thank you for your understanding and cooperation in advance.

**156.** What does Ms. Palmer indicate in her memo?

(A) The safety inspection will be performed.
(B) A new machine will be installed.
(C) A new policy will be implemented.
(D) The office will be closed on Thursday.

**157.** What is suggested by the memo?

(A) Ms. Palmer works in an electronics store.
(B) A printer shop has recently opened.
(C) There is only one printer in the office.
(D) Some employees are in need for large copies.

# New Restaurant Set to Open Soon

## By John Wilson – *New Jersey Daily Telegraph*

Jersey City – The Soul Food Café will be opening its doors this Friday for breakfast at 8:00 A.M. The Soul Food Café will be a welcome addition to the area's Main Street restaurants.

The owner of the Soul Food Café, Linda Hamilton, said, "Soul Food will specialize in down-home country-style meals. We are different from other restaurants in that we will offer low-calorie, healthier versions of good country cooking by using healthier oils and cooking practices. We want our customers to enjoy high-quality entrées which are not high in fat and cholesterol. Our goal is to make the customers want to come back and maybe even become a little healthier in the meantime."

Ms. Hamilton, the former head chef at Creole's Home Cooking, started her plans for her own restaurant over two years ago. After looking at several spaces around the city, she bought a former carpet store on Main Street and had it fully restored and renovated. Ms. Hamilton stated, "I personally worked with the designers to get this place looking exactly like how I remember some of the southern restaurants I went to as a kid in Alabama."

The Soul Food Café is beautiful both inside and outside. We will soon see if many residents will patronize the restaurant like Linda and her eager staff hope. The Soul Food Café will be open for breakfast starting at 8:00 A.M. and will close at 9:00 P.M. On Sundays, it will open for brunch starting at 10:00 in the morning.

158. What is the purpose of the article?

(A) To explain food-preparation techniques
(B) To review local restaurants
(C) To describe an entrepreneur's business strategy
(D) To publicize the opening of a new restaurant

159. What is NOT mentioned about the Soul Food Café?

(A) It is owned by Creole's Home Cooking.
(B) It will serve low-calorie meals.
(C) It is located close to downtown.
(D) It will open at 8:00 A.M. almost every day.

160. What is suggested about Ms. Hamilton?

(A) She enjoys all kinds of cuisine.
(B) She is new to the industry.
(C) She helped design the interior.
(D) She specializes in architecture.

We appreciate that you chose to purchase a Pegasus Electronics mobile phone. If you made your purchase between July 1 and 31, you are entitled to claim a gift pack containing some Pegasus Electronics accessories, including a case, a set of earphones, and a protective screen cover.

Once you have completed this form by entering the requested details below, send it, along with the original proof of purchase, to Pegasus Electronics Head Office, Johnson Technology Park, Edmonton, Alberta T5A 0FH. Should you have any questions, please do not hesitate to contact Pegasus Electronics' Customer Service Department at customerservice@pegasus.ca.

I confirm that I would like to be sent a free gift of Pegasus Electronics mobile phone accessories. ☑

**Name:** Brendan Baker
**Address:** 5 Joseph Street
**City/Province/Postal Code:** Bracebridge, ON P1L 5JY
**Phone Number:** 555-9231
**\*E-mail Address:** _____
**Mobile Phone Model Purchased:** ☐ S350      ☐ S400   ☑ S450

Delivery of your items may take up to two weeks. This is a limited-time offer that ends on August 30. The offer does not extend to purchases made outside of Canada or to purchases made on our Web site. In addition, individuals currently employed by Pegasus Electronics are not permitted to take advantage of this offer.

\* By supplying your e-mail address, you indicate that you wish to receive Pegasus Electronics' monthly newsletter, which contains information about forthcoming phone models and special discounts.

---

**161.** What is suggested about Pegasus Electronics?

(A) It is headquartered in Edmonton.
(B) It will discontinue the production of mobile phones on August 30.
(C) It has created a store membership plan for customers.
(D) It recently launched a new model of mobile phone.

**162.** Why did Mr. Baker fill out the form?

(A) To ask that a product be exchanged
(B) To give feedback on a service
(C) To request a refund on a product
(D) To receive some complimentary items

**163.** What is implied about Mr. Baker?

(A) He is a former employee of Pegasus Electronics.
(B) He ordered a mobile phone from Pegasus Electronics' Web site.
(C) He would like to receive Pegasus Electronics' monthly newsletter.
(D) He bought a Pegasus Electronics mobile phone in July.

# MEMORANDUM

To: All Office Personnel
From: Anthony Jackson
Date: Dec 15
Subject: A contract with Cradle Technologies

Fellow Employees,

In an effort to conserve energy consumed by our offices, the management has decided to introduce a new automated system from Cradle Technologies. —[1]—. For example, 8 p.m. each weekday, all office lights will be turned off and dimmed (except for hallway and stairwell lights). —[2]—. Likewise, the temperature will be maintained at a steady 18°C instead of the usual 22°C during the week. This new system should help reduce our monthly utility bills by at least 13% and help us meet our goal of conserving electricity. —[3]—.

We realize that some of you will be affected by this change more than others, particularly those whose schedules do not conform to our regular working hours. —[4]—. If this situation applies to you, please feel free to contact the maintenance department to request the office change, as some sections of buildings will be set to a later schedule.

Thank you.

Sincerely,

Anthony Jackson
Maintenance Head

**164.** What is the purpose of the memo?

(A) To encourage employees to leave work on time

(B) To announce a new environmental law

(C) To offer employees some financial benefits

(D) To explain a new change in workplace conditions

**165.** What is mentioned as a benefit of the Cradle Technologies product?

(A) It will reduce employee workloads.

(B) It has the best quality among all products.

(C) It can be used in any work environment.

(D) It will help reduce the company energy expense.

**166.** What are employees who typically work late advised to do?

(A) Change their work schedule

(B) Talk to their supervisor

(C) Ask to change offices

(D) Consider working from home

**167.** In which of the positions marked [1], [2], [3], and [4] does the following sentence best belong?

"The system will automatically regulate thermostats and overhead lights according to all personnel schedules."

(A) [1]

(B) [2]

(C) [3]

(D) [4]

## *Transit Council Approves Construction of Walkways*

CASTRO VALLEY (July 14) – The Transit Council of Castro Valley has voted in favor of using $300,000 to build pedestrian walkways over ten of the busiest streets in the city. —[1]—. The approval comes after the city conducted a safety audit following complaints by pedestrians living in Castro Valley about dangerous traffic conditions and long waiting times at pedestrian crosswalks. The conductors of the audit agreed that the issues brought up by pedestrians should be addressed within the next year. —[2]—. The walkways will allow pedestrians to cross roads without hindering the flow of traffic, which will also make drivers happy, especially during the tourist season, when traffic in the riverside district can be very congested.

Simon Livingston, the mayor of Castro Valley, suggested the construction of the walkways to the transit council on March 12. Mr. Livingston related the outcome of a study of residents of Castro Valley that was conducted in November. —[3]—. The study shows that only 10 percent of the population in Castro Valley enjoyed jogging or walking in the city. Based on events when similar walkways were constructed in surrounding cities, Mr. Livingston believes that the number of people who walk or jog recreationally or for exercise could triple.

The initial phase for the construction will include temporarily closing down lanes on the road when necessary. Detours will be marked at these times. After the initial construction, the walkways will be painted and have lights added to make them accessible to residents at night. —[4]—.

**168.** What is a purpose of the article?

(A) To report on some plans to attract tourists

(B) To give details about a new commuter expressway

(C) To describe a project that could increase pedestrian numbers

(D) To recruit workers to renovate council offices

**169.** What is suggested about Castro Valley?

(A) There are many problems with traffic near the riverside district year-round.

(B) More than 10,000 people enjoy walking recreationally in the city.

(C) The number of residents there has tripled in the last few years.

(D) Its riverside district is popular with tourists.

**170.** What is scheduled to be done as part of the construction?

(A) The streetlights on roads will be replaced.

(B) Some parking facilities near the construction areas will be unavailable.

(C) The walkways will be painted to be more noticeable to pedestrians.

(D) Lanes will be made to separate people walking and jogging.

**171.** In which of the positions marked [1], [2], [3], and [4] does the following sentence best belong?

"Construction on the first walkway will begin on August 3, and all ten will be completed within 4 months."

(A) [1]

(B) [2]

(C) [3]

(D) [4]

**Questions 172-175** refer to the following online chat discussion.

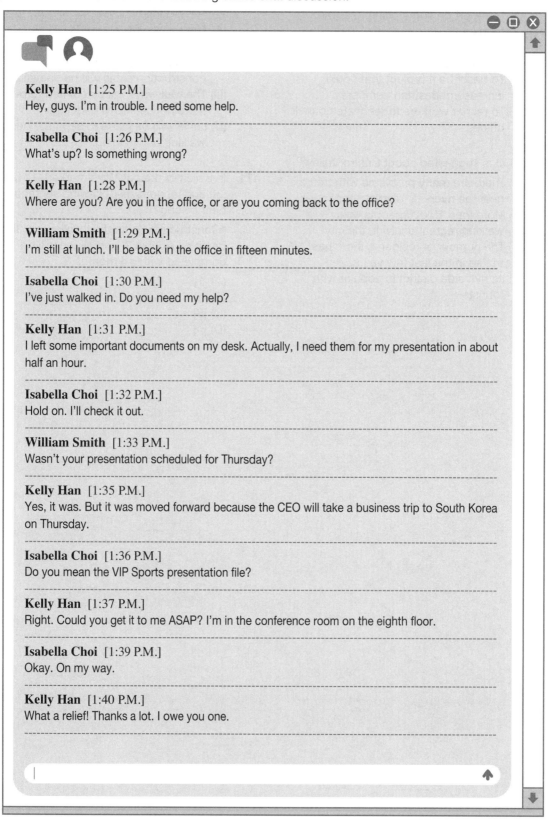

**Kelly Han** [1:25 P.M.]
Hey, guys. I'm in trouble. I need some help.

---

**Isabella Choi** [1:26 P.M.]
What's up? Is something wrong?

---

**Kelly Han** [1:28 P.M.]
Where are you? Are you in the office, or are you coming back to the office?

---

**William Smith** [1:29 P.M.]
I'm still at lunch. I'll be back in the office in fifteen minutes.

---

**Isabella Choi** [1:30 P.M.]
I've just walked in. Do you need my help?

---

**Kelly Han** [1:31 P.M.]
I left some important documents on my desk. Actually, I need them for my presentation in about half an hour.

---

**Isabella Choi** [1:32 P.M.]
Hold on. I'll check it out.

---

**William Smith** [1:33 P.M.]
Wasn't your presentation scheduled for Thursday?

---

**Kelly Han** [1:35 P.M.]
Yes, it was. But it was moved forward because the CEO will take a business trip to South Korea on Thursday.

---

**Isabella Choi** [1:36 P.M.]
Do you mean the VIP Sports presentation file?

---

**Kelly Han** [1:37 P.M.]
Right. Could you get it to me ASAP? I'm in the conference room on the eighth floor.

---

**Isabella Choi** [1:39 P.M.]
Okay. On my way.

---

**Kelly Han** [1:40 P.M.]
What a relief! Thanks a lot. I owe you one.

---

**172.** What is Ms. Han's problem?

    (A) She has no ride to work.
    (B) Her laptop computer broke down.
    (C) She does not have some documents.
    (D) She may not be able to meet a
         deadline.

**173.** At 1:29 P.M., what does Mr. Smith imply when he writes, "I'm still at lunch"?

    (A) He can't help Ms. Han.
    (B) He will not make a presentation today.
    (C) He can't start working right now.
    (D) He is currently enjoying a very
         delicious lunch.

**174.** What is suggested about Mr. Smith?

    (A) He will be making a presentation on
         Thursday.
    (B) He currently works at the VIP Sports
         Corporation.
    (C) He will meet with one of his biggest
         clients this afternoon.
    (D) He was not informed the presentation
         schedule had changed.

**175.** What will Ms. Choi most likely do next?

    (A) Go on a business trip
    (B) Bring some important papers to
         Ms. Han
    (C) Prepare to do some research
    (D) Send an e-mail to Mr. Smith

**Questions 176-180** refer to the following e-mail and order form.

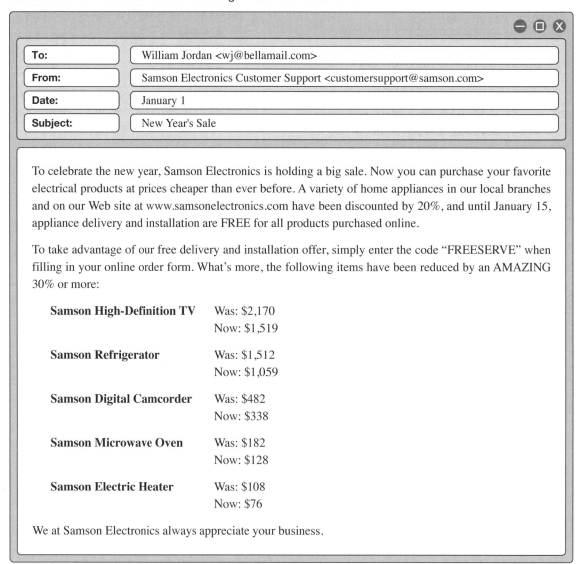

To: William Jordan <wj@bellamail.com>

From: Samson Electronics Customer Support <customersupport@samson.com>

Date: January 1

Subject: New Year's Sale

To celebrate the new year, Samson Electronics is holding a big sale. Now you can purchase your favorite electrical products at prices cheaper than ever before. A variety of home appliances in our local branches and on our Web site at www.samsonelectronics.com have been discounted by 20%, and until January 15, appliance delivery and installation are FREE for all products purchased online.

To take advantage of our free delivery and installation offer, simply enter the code "FREESERVE" when filling in your online order form. What's more, the following items have been reduced by an AMAZING 30% or more:

| | |
|---|---|
| **Samson High-Definition TV** | Was: $2,170<br>Now: $1,519 |
| **Samson Refrigerator** | Was: $1,512<br>Now: $1,059 |
| **Samson Digital Camcorder** | Was: $482<br>Now: $338 |
| **Samson Microwave Oven** | Was: $182<br>Now: $128 |
| **Samson Electric Heater** | Was: $108<br>Now: $76 |

We at Samson Electronics always appreciate your business.

# SAMSON ELETRONICS
## "We change your life style!"
721 Barton Springs Rd.
Austin, TX 78704

## ORDER FORM

**Order Number:** X4949393      **Date:** January 4
**Name:** William Jordan
**Home Address:** 25836 Hayward Blvd, Hayward, CA 94542
**Phone number:** (510) 857-7399      **E-mail:** wj@bellamail.com

## ORDER DETAILS

| | |
|---|---|
| Samson High-Definition TV | $1,519 |
| Samson Microwave Oven | $128 |
| Sales tax | $131.76 |
| Shipping charge / FREESERVE | $0 |
| Installation charge / FREESERVE | $0 |
| **GRAND TOTAL** | **$1,778.76** |

**CREDIT CARD:** **** **** **** 0603

YOUR ORDER HAS BEEN PROCESSED. THANK YOU VERY MUCH.
YOUR ORDER WILL BE DELIVERED TO YOUR HOME ON JANUARY 5.

**176.** Why was the e-mail sent to Mr. Jordan?

(A) To advertise a job opening
(B) To announce that a new store will open shortly
(C) To publicize a change in a store's opening hours
(D) To advertise a range of discounted products

**177.** According to the e-mail, when does the free delivery offer expire?

(A) January 1
(B) January 4
(C) January 5
(D) January 15

**178.** According to the order form, what product did Mr. Jordan order?

(A) A high-definition TV
(B) A refrigerator
(C) A digital camcorder
(D) An electric heater

**179.** How much money did Mr. Jordan save by ordering the products on sale?

(A) $128
(B) $651
(C) $705
(D) $1,778

**180.** What is stated about Mr. Jordan's order?

(A) It will be delivered on January 15.
(B) It will be delivered to his work address.
(C) He received the free installation service.
(D) He paid for the order with cash.

▶ ▶ ▶GO ON TO THE NEXT PAGE

To: Arizona Realty <luxury@arizonarealty.com>

From: Derrick McGuire <derrickmac@nsumail.com>

Date: June 25

Subject: More information

Dear Mr. Joseph Lowe,

I have heard that you have several apartments for rent in Southern Arizona. I'll be starting work at the Indigo Heights General Hospital in March and will need a two-bedroom apartment. As we don't own a car and my wife plans to rely on public transportation, I hope you have a nice apartment in the downtown area. Please contact me and let me know what you have available.

We will be in Arizona next week and hope to see available and suitable apartments at that time. You can e-mail the relevant information to this address, or fax me at 345-555-2490.

Sincerely,
Derrick McGuire

# ARIZONA REALTY

25 Grove Street
Mohave Valley, AZ 86440

# *APARTMENTS FOR RENT*

Arizona Realty proudly proclaims the GRAND OPENING of four housing developments located throughout the state of Arizona.

### SANDSTONE GARDENS

Perfectly situated in downtown Silicon Fields, these brand-new apartments have one bedroom and one bathroom and have easy access to the local swimming pool. From $800 a month.

### WILLOUGHBY VILLAS

Located in downtown Indigo Heights, these spacious two-bedroom, one-bathroom villas have private balconies and peaceful views in all directions. From $950 a month.

### LENTON APARTMENTS

Conveniently located in bustling Wellington Village, these completely renovated three-bedroom apartments are wired for cable TV. Prices start at $650 a month.

### EMBER HALL

Located within walking distance of downtown Ember Park, these gorgeous three-bedroom, two-bathroom apartments are very spacious. Rent starts at $1500 a month.

Caught your attention?

Please e-mail us at luxury@arizonarealty.com for more information, call us at 818-555-2837. You may also visit our office.

181. What is Mr. McGuire's primary concern?

(A) The availability of health-care facilities
(B) The location of the housing
(C) The rental rate of the apartments
(D) The price of the transportation

182. Why is Mr. McGuire moving?

(A) He is going to start a new job.
(B) He will study in a graduate school.
(C) He wants to live in a quiet place.
(D) He will open his private hospital.

183. What housing in the advertisement will Mr. McGuire most likely be interested in?

(A) Sandstone Garden
(B) Willoughby Villas
(C) Lenton Apartments
(D) Ember Hall

184. What can be suggested about Ember Hall?

(A) It is renovated.
(B) It is isolated.
(C) It is crowded.
(D) It is near a park.

185. What is NOT mentioned as a method of contacting Arizona Realty?

(A) Telephone
(B) Visiting in person
(C) E-mail
(D) Fax

▶ ▶ ▶ GO ON TO THE NEXT PAGE

# Lake Tahoe Resort

As the manager of the Lake Tahoe Resort, it is my pleasure to announce that we have just made four new cabins available for rent. Unlike our other cabins, which are located deep in the forest, these new cabins have been built right on the edge of Tahoe Lake. These luxurious accommodations were designed and furnished by the renowned interior designer Selena Vasquez, and they are spacious enough to easily accommodate large families. Our resort is only a 25-minute drive from the airport, and a 15-minute drive from downtown Clarkedale, and complimentary shuttle buses run between the city and the resort on a regular schedule. Our activities manager, Colin Painter, is always on hand to recommend fun things for our guests to do, and he can sign up interested individuals for water skiing, jet skiing, windsurfing, kayaking, archery, and hiking expeditions. To reserve a cabin at Lake Tahoe Resort, please contact Brigitte Maltin on 555-0104.

Brandon Knight
General Manager
Lake Tahoe Resort

# Lake Tahoe Resort

### Accommodation Type B: Lakeside Cabins

| Cabin Name | Bedrooms | Daily Rental Rate | Booking Deposit |
|------------|----------|-------------------|-----------------|
| Pine Cone | 2 | $300 | $350 |
| Forest Glen | 3 | $350 | $400 |
| Green Meadow | 2 | $275 | $300 |
| Sandy Shore | 3 | $325 | $350 |

Booking deposits should be paid at the time of reservation.

| To: | Lake Tahoe Resort <rentals@ltr.com> |
|---|---|
| From: | Edward Parker <eparker@hanamail.com> |
| Date: | June 25 |
| Subject: | Renting a Cabin |

Dear sir/madam,

I am writing in the hope that you can assist me with a small issue regarding my booking at the Lake Tahoe Resort. I called your booking agent on June 20th and arranged for my family to stay in one of your new 3-bedroom lakeside cabins for a week-long vacation. We plan to stay in the cabin from July 3rd to July 10th, and we are very much looking forward to it. As per your policy, I paid the booking deposit by credit card over the phone while finalizing my cabin reservation with your booking agent. However, although I authorized a payment of $350, I have just noticed that $400 was debited from my account. I assume this was just a simple misunderstanding, but I would appreciate it if you could credit the 50 dollars to my account at your earliest possible convenience. Please inform me once this has been done. Thank you, and I look forward to arriving at your resort on July 3rd.

Best regards,

Edward Parker

---

**186.** In the advertisement, the phrase "on hand" in paragraph 1, line 9, is closest in meaning to

(A) experienced
(B) integral
(C) available
(D) useful

**187.** What is NOT indicated about Lake Tahoe Resort?

(A) It is equipped for various watersports.
(B) It is situated in a convenient area.
(C) It runs a downtown business location.
(D) It provides free transportation for guests.

**188.** Who did Mr. Parker most likely speak with on June 20th?

(A) Selena Vasquez
(B) Colin Painter
(C) Brigitte Maltin
(D) Brandon Knight

**189.** Which cabin does Mr. Parker most likely wish to rent?

(A) Pine Cone
(B) Forest Glen
(C) Green Meadow
(D) Sandy Shore

**190.** What problem did Mr. Parker describe in his e-mail?

(A) He was quoted the wrong daily rental rate.
(B) He failed to pay a booking deposit in time.
(C) He needs to change the dates of his stay.
(D) He was charged an erroneous amount.

▶ ▶ ▶GO ON TO THE NEXT PAGE

# Modern Art Gallery of Austin
## Scheduled Exhibitions

| Dates | Exhibition Titles | Descriptions |
| --- | --- | --- |
| May 7 – October 5 | The Moon and the Sea | This outstanding collection of drawings and photographs from various regions, including several Caribbean nations, describes the importance of the moon and the sea, which have affected humankind for centuries. |
| May 28 – October 5 | Furniture Is Art | We think that furniture is just a tool, but it is also art. This collection shows an array of distinctive antique and modern furniture from across Europe. |
| July 3 – December 18 | Dance: Art by Movement | With sculptures, paintings, photographs, and digital recordings, this exhibition features performing art from countries from Albania to Zambia. |
| July 24 – August 22 | The Photography of Animals | This exhibition is a collection of fascinating pieces, which features photographs of a variety of wild animals around the world. |

For more information about tickets, visit our Web site or send an e-mail to cedlecon@magob.org. We will provide two free tickets to all members. To become a member, visit the membership page.

| To: | Charlie Deleon <Blan@cdelion.margob.org> |
| --- | --- |
| From: | Molly Hudson <mhudson@mason.inet> |
| Date: | May 1 |
| Subject: | Tickets |

Dear sir,

I have two complimentary tickets for the Dance: Art by Movement exhibition, but I wish to purchase two more tickets. I'm sure my credit card information is in your database. So could you charge the tickets to my credit card and then send them to me via mail? I've been waiting to see Furniture Is Art. Thank you for putting on these gorgeous exhibits.

Molly Hudson

May 3

Molly Hudson
P.O. Box N-123
NASSAU N.P.

Dear Ms. Hudson,

Thank you for being a patron of the Modern Art Gallery of Austin. I regret to inform you that the exhibition you've been waiting for has been canceled. I have enclosed two additional tickets. These are substitutes for the canceled exhibition. The new exhibition is called Indigenous Cultures of the Americas. It is a traveling exhibition and will be held in our gallery until December 18. It features several pieces of famous paintings including Barry Gilpin's. Your JPax credit card has been charged $24.

Sincerely,

Charlie Deleon
Modern Art Gallery of Austin

Enclosures

**191.** According to the schedule, what do all of the exhibitions have in common?

(A) They include photographs.
(B) They include live performances.
(C) They feature works by artists from the Caribbean.
(D) They feature works from multiple countries.

**192.** What is indicated about Ms. Hudson?

(A) She is requesting a refund.
(B) She has a membership to the museum.
(C) She is a contemporary artist.
(D) She has already seen the exhibits.

**193.** Which exhibit has been canceled?

(A) The Moon and the Sea
(B) Furniture Is Art
(C) Dance: Art in Movement
(D) The Photography of Animals

**194.** In the letter, the word "features" in paragraph 1, line 4, is closest in meaning to

(A) shows
(B) manages
(C) moves
(D) covers

**195.** What did Mr. Deleon do for Ms. Hudson?

(A) Mail a list of upcoming events
(B) Change the date of an exhibition
(C) Confirm a reservation
(D) Charge her credit card

▶ ▶ ▶ GO ON TO THE NEXT PAGE

| To: | Mary Benson; Ramona Taylor; James Porter |
| --- | --- |
| From: | Tim Rolland |
| Date: | June 12, 7:54 A.M. |
| Subject: | Office Space |
| Attachment: | Properties |

Hi, all,

I tremendously enjoyed our luncheon at Manke Grill last Monday. As an AHG Consultants employee, I am excited to be a part of the team to have our first branch in Alamo. During the meeting, I felt our effort to get our first customer and to begin giving advice to entrepreneurs in Alamo about how using information technology is helpful to achieve their aims.

I would appreciate it if you could give me your opinions about the types of office space that will be suitable. I have explored Syeogain.ca to find well-conditioned ones that can fit our basic criteria and budget and have summarized the information so that you can decide. Please read the attached document and reply to me with your opinions.

Tim Rolland
AHG Consultants

### 3874 Thunderland Hilltop
Open concept office/retail space in a well-developed rural area of Alamo with a lot of pedestrians. The building has a remarkable appearance and enough space for a signboard for company use. The energy-efficient heating system will reduce your expenditures every winter.
Monthly lease: $1,000

### 29485 Clearance Path
First-floor office. Elegantly decorated. Surrounded onsite parking with security fence. Located near Gasi Browse Park in the vicinity of the train station. 20 minutes from downtown. Joo Park's path is very popular with people exercising. Vodafone phone system is already installed for use.
Monthly lease: $950

### 4991 Commercial Park Lot
Not communal, single-floor building. Equipped with furniture made by famous designers. Safe parking lot near the street and a discount for renters. Fast Internet access can be installed if you want. Located west of the city center in the shopping district.
Monthly lease: $875

### 1432 Timothy Street
Fourth-floor office suite. Covered garage for vehicles with security system and guards. Located outside Alamo's main commercial zone. Business equipment such as color copier, scanner, printer, and fax are ready for use. Video conferencing studio renovated with latest technology and free high-speed wireless Internet.
Monthly lease: $1,000

| To: | Mary Benson; Tim Rolland; Ramona Taylor |
|---|---|
| From: | James Porter |
| Date: | June 15, 4:39 P.M. |
| Subject: | Re: Office Space |

Dear all,

Thank you, Tim, for narrowing down the options that we had to look over. I guess last Monday's team meeting went very well. I wish I had been there, but my trip to Toronto was unavoidable. I guess I am the last person to provide comments by e-mail. Thank you for your patience.

Ramona, I like the office with roomy space, but I feel we'd better not be located in the middle of downtown. Is anyone familiar with Alamo's public transit systems? It would be helpful to know if we can use them to commute.

I also agree with Tim's opinions that we should attend the technology fair in Alamo. I'm going to visit it next weekend because I have an appointment at a place nearby for my housing options. I will also be having lunch with an Alamo delegate who used to work for AHG Consultants. I will let you know when I have any news.

James Porter
AHG Consultants

**196.** Who most likely is Mr. Rolland?

(A) A technology consultant
(B) A worker at Manke Grill
(C) A conference organizer
(D) A real estate agent

**197.** What is one property feature mentioned in the attachment?

(A) A shower room for employees
(B) A popular restaurant in the building
(C) An electricity bill paid by its owner
(D) A location close to an exercise trail

**198.** What is suggested about Mr. Porter?

(A) He missed the gathering at Manke Grill.
(B) He is considering selling his car.
(C) He plans to attend a performance.
(D) He will tour Alamo City by bus.

**199.** What is indicated about Ms. Taylor?

(A) She just relocated to a new home.
(B) She will meet her former client.
(C) She sent an e-mail to her colleagues.
(D) She used to live in Alamo.

**200.** Which property does Mr. Porter most likely prefer?

(A) 3874 Thunderland Hilltop
(B) 29485 Clearance Path
(C) 4991 Commercial Park Lot
(D) 1432 Timothy Street

STOP! This is the end of the test. If you finish before time is called,
you may go back to Parts 5, 6, and 7 and check your work.

# Actual Test

MP3

해설집

적정 풀이 시간 120분

120 min

시작 시간 ___시 ___분

종료 시간 ___시 ___분

중간에 멈추지 말고 처음부터 끝까지 풀어보세요.
문제를 풀 때에는 실전처럼 답안지에 마킹하세요.

목표 개수 _____ / 200    실제 개수 _____ / 200

예상 점수는 번역 및 정답에 있는 점수 환산표를 참조하세요.

# LISTENING TEST

In the Listening test, you will be asked to demonstrate how well you understand spoken English. The entire Listening test will last approximately 45 minutes. There are four parts, and directions are given for each part. You must mark your answers on the separate answer sheet. Do not write your answers in your test book.

## PART 1

**Directions:** For each question in this part, you will hear four statements about a picture in your test book. When you hear the statements, you must select the one statement that best describes what you see in the picture. Then find the number of the question on your answer sheet and mark your answer. The statements will not be printed in your test book and will be spoken only one time.

Statement (B), "They are sitting at a table," is the best description of the picture. So you should select answer (B) and mark it on your answer sheet.

**1.**

**2.**

▶ ▶ ▶GO ON TO THE NEXT PAGE

**3.**

**4.**

**5.**

**6.**

▶ ▶ ▶ GO ON TO THE NEXT PAGE

## PART 2

**Directions:** You will hear a question or statement and three responses spoken in English. They will not be printed in your test book and will be spoken only one time. Select the best response to the question or statement and mark the letter (A), (B), or (C) on your answer sheet.

7. Mark your answer on your answer sheet.

8. Mark your answer on your answer sheet.

9. Mark your answer on your answer sheet.

10. Mark your answer on your answer sheet.

11. Mark your answer on your answer sheet.

12. Mark your answer on your answer sheet.

13. Mark your answer on your answer sheet.

14. Mark your answer on your answer sheet.

15. Mark your answer on your answer sheet.

16. Mark your answer on your answer sheet.

17. Mark your answer on your answer sheet.

18. Mark your answer on your answer sheet.

19. Mark your answer on your answer sheet.

20. Mark your answer on your answer sheet.

21. Mark your answer on your answer sheet.

22. Mark your answer on your answer sheet.

23. Mark your answer on your answer sheet.

24. Mark your answer on your answer sheet.

25. Mark your answer on your answer sheet.

26. Mark your answer on your answer sheet.

27. Mark your answer on your answer sheet.

28. Mark your answer on your answer sheet.

29. Mark your answer on your answer sheet.

30. Mark your answer on your answer sheet.

31. Mark your answer on your answer sheet.

## PART 3

**Directions:** You will hear some conversations between two or three people. You will be asked to answer three questions about what the speakers say in each conversation. Select the best response to each question and mark the letter (A), (B), (C), or (D) on your answer sheet. The conversations will not be printed in your test book and will be spoken only one time.

**32.** Who most likely is the woman?

(A) A customer
(B) A store manager
(C) A marketing agent
(D) A seasonal employee

**33.** Why are the business's hours changing?

(A) Sales have decreased sharply.
(B) There is a shortage of workers.
(C) The holiday season will start soon.
(D) An annual sale will be held.

**34.** What will the woman probably do next?

(A) Hire some new employees
(B) Visit a store
(C) Set a new goal
(D) Return some merchandise

**35.** Who most likely are the speakers?

(A) Television reporters
(B) Sales representatives
(C) Marketing experts
(D) Restaurant chefs

**36.** What is the main problem?

(A) Supplies of a new product are running low.
(B) The advertising effects did not lead to profit.
(C) The cost of a new marketing campaign is too high.
(D) Some broadcast equipment is not working properly.

**37.** What will the man do later in the day?

(A) Conduct a survey
(B) Meet with some customers
(C) Use a new shampoo
(D) Share some ideas

**38.** According to the woman, what was recently bought?

(A) A photocopier
(B) A mobile phone
(C) A camera
(D) A laptop computer

**39.** What does the woman tell the man to do?

(A) Give her a discount
(B) Send her a photo
(C) Check his e-mail
(D) Turn off his computer

**40.** What will the woman most likely do later?

(A) Buy some ink cartridges
(B) Repair a copy machine
(C) Purchase a similar product
(D) Help the man make copies

**41.** Why did the woman call?

(A) To request a refund
(B) To cancel an order
(C) To check on a delivery
(D) To change a shipping address

**42.** When did the woman place the order?

(A) On January 5
(B) On January 10
(C) On January 13
(D) On January 15

**43.** What does the man say will happen tomorrow?

(A) A copy machine will be repaired.
(B) A document will be mailed.
(C) A shipment will be delivered.
(D) A recent order will be canceled.

▶ ▶ ▶ GO ON TO THE NEXT PAGE

44. What are the speakers talking about?

(A) Renovating a theater
(B) Attending a local event
(C) Arranging a meeting
(D) Seeing a performance

45. What does the man imply when he says, "But today is Wednesday"?

(A) The board members have made hasty decisions.
(B) Some colleagues confuse what day it is today.
(C) The deadline is approaching very soon.
(D) The tickets to a Friday night show may have been sold out.

46. What will the speakers probably do next?

(A) Watch another movie
(B) Purchase some chairs
(C) Book some tickets
(D) Come back another time

47. Where does the man work?

(A) At an employing agency
(B) At a newspaper company
(C) At an art gallery
(D) At an advertising agency

48. Why should the woman speak to Mr. Thompson?

(A) To talk about a vacant position
(B) To complain about a service
(C) To interview him for a magazine
(D) To request a document

49. What will the man probably do next?

(A) Submit a résumé
(B) Change an appointment time
(C) Arrange an interview
(D) Contact his colleague

50. Where most likely are the speakers?

(A) At a warehouse
(B) At a clothing store
(C) At a restaurant
(D) At a bank

51. What does the man say the problem is?

(A) A product is in the wrong color.
(B) A product is missing.
(C) A product is poor in quality.
(D) A product is not available in the right size.

52. What will the woman do next?

(A) Look for another size
(B) Check the inventory in her store
(C) Give the man a full refund
(D) Call another store location

53. What does the woman need to rent?

(A) Large boxes
(B) Office furniture
(C) Construction equipment
(D) Storage space

54. What does the woman say about her office?

(A) It is very large.
(B) It is too old.
(C) It is far from downtown.
(D) It is being renovated.

55. What does the man mean when he says, "No problem"?

(A) He can renovate the woman's office building.
(B) He can satisfy the woman's specific demands.
(C) He thinks everything is under control.
(D) He has no problem moving to a different location.

**56.** What does the woman ask the man to do later?

(A) Make a plane reservation
(B) Analyze a new market
(C) Give her a ride to the airport
(D) Help her catch up with some information

**57.** According to the woman, where is the head office located?

(A) In Germany
(B) In China
(C) In South Korea
(D) In Scotland

**58.** What is the woman advised to do?

(A) Create a new sales strategy
(B) Leave the office quickly
(C) Cancel a meeting
(D) Gather some data

---

**59.** What is the conversation mainly about?

(A) A new branch office
(B) Some imported products
(C) A company reorganization
(D) An upcoming meeting

**60.** Who most likely is the woman?

(A) A banker
(B) An accounting manager
(C) An architect
(D) A fashion designer

**61.** According to the woman, what will Ms. Kellogg do this afternoon?

(A) Leave for San Francisco
(B) Make a speech
(C) Sign a new contract
(D) Hold a board meeting

---

| Origin | Status | Expected Time of Arrival |
|--------|--------|--------------------------|
| New York | Landed | 11:00 A.M. |
| Manchester | On Time | 12:45 P.M. |
| Glasgow | Canceled | 2:00 P.M. |
| Chicago | Delayed | 4:30 P.M. |

**62.** Look at the graphic. Which city is Ms. Travis flying from?

(A) New York
(B) Manchester
(C) Glasgow
(D) Chicago

**63.** What does the woman suggest?

(A) Canceling a business trip
(B) Leaving early to avoid heavy traffic
(C) Using an alternate parking area
(D) Reserving a table for dinner

**64.** What will the speakers most likely do when they meet with Ms. Travis?

(A) Go to the airport
(B) Discuss some issues
(C) Check a seating chart
(D) Have a meal together

---

## Meeting Room 101

| Time | Event |
|------|-------|
| 10:00 A.M. | Accounting Meeting |
| 1:00 P.M. | Marketing Presentation |
| 2:00 P.M. | |
| 3:00 P.M. | Staff Meeting |

| Studio Name | Ceiling Height | Monthly Rent |
|-------------|----------------|--------------|
| Regus | 3 meters | $200 |
| Heron | 4 meters | $300 |
| Shard | 5 meters | $400 |
| Union | 6 meters | $600 |

**65.** What are the speakers talking about?

(A) Postponing a meeting
(B) Publishing a yearly report
(C) Reserving a room
(D) Preparing for a presentation

**66.** Look at the graphic. What department does Ms. Lane probably work in?

(A) Accounting
(B) Marketing
(C) Human Resources
(D) Maintenance

**67.** What does the man say he will do?

(A) Cancel a presentation
(B) Call a colleague
(C) Hire new employees
(D) Attend a meeting

**68.** Who most likely is the woman?

(A) A realtor
(B) An artist
(C) An architect
(D) A curator

**69.** According to the woman, what is the problem?

(A) She wants to cancel her contract.
(B) She doesn't have enough funds.
(C) She can't complete some of her work.
(D) She is unable to attend a local event.

**70.** Look at the graphic. Which place will the woman probably contact?

(A) Regus
(B) Heron
(C) Shard
(D) Union

## PART 4

**Directions:** You will hear some short talks given by a single speaker. You will be asked to answer three questions about what the speaker says in each short talk. Select the best response to each question and mark the letter (A), (B), (C), or (D) on your answer sheet. The talks will not be printed in your test book and will be spoken only one time.

71. What is the announcement mainly about?
    (A) A job opportunity
    (B) A new software program
    (C) The installation of a machine
    (D) Preparations for a trial

72. What most likely is the speaker's occupation?
    (A) Instructor
    (B) Accountant
    (C) Legal expert
    (D) Computer programmer

73. What does the speaker ask the listeners to do?
    (A) File a legal action
    (B) Attend a demonstration
    (C) Buy a new laptop computer
    (D) Send some documents to a client

74. What type of store is Patterson's?
    (A) A bookstore
    (B) A furniture store
    (C) A clothing store
    (D) A sporting goods store

75. What does Patterson's provide for children and their parents?
    (A) A free ride
    (B) A safe fun zone
    (C) A reading class
    (D) A discount coupon

76. What does the speaker say about Web site orders?
    (A) The shipping fee is waived.
    (B) Some items are not available.
    (C) Fast delivery is guaranteed.
    (D) Special discounts are offered.

77. Where does the speaker work?
    (A) At a dental office
    (B) At a cleaning company
    (C) At an automobile dealership
    (D) At an Internet service provider

78. Why does the speaker ask Mr. Miller to visit a Web site?
    (A) To learn about some services
    (B) To receive driving directions
    (C) To set up an appointment
    (D) To read some useful information

79. What does the speaker mean when she says, "You can't miss it"?
    (A) A special offer is very attractive.
    (B) The listener must take a flight today.
    (C) Reservation changes are not permitted.
    (D) The listener won't have difficulty finding something.

80. What is the main purpose of the speech?
    (A) To present an award
    (B) To say farewell to some colleagues
    (C) To describe a type of renewable energy
    (D) To announce an increase in sales

81. According to the speaker, what did Brandon White recently do?
    (A) Created some stylish designs
    (B) Made some new corporate policies
    (C) Developed a new engine
    (D) Donated to a local charity

82. Why does the speaker say, "He is really amazing"?
    (A) Brandon White made an impressive speech.
    (B) Brandon White is all dressed up.
    (C) Brandon White returned his profits to society.
    (D) Brandon White made a great achievement.

▶ ▶ ▶GO ON TO THE NEXT PAGE

83. What is the speaker mainly discussing?

(A) A new work schedule
(B) A new sales goal
(C) An upcoming event
(D) A productivity improvement plan

84. According to the speaker, what change has occurred?

(A) There is little room for storage.
(B) There are more participants.
(C) There are a series of flight delays.
(D) There are new arrival dates.

85. What are the listeners instructed to do this week?

(A) Search for some venues
(B) Install some wide screens
(C) Prepare some training material
(D) Raise the morale of employees

86. What did the speaker do last Thursday?

(A) She quit her job.
(B) She signed a lease.
(C) She met with her customer.
(D) She worked late at night.

87. What does the speaker say about parking spaces?

(A) They are currently available.
(B) They are located downtown.
(C) They are only for customers.
(D) They are offered for a small fee.

88. Why does the speaker say, "This is a very popular apartment building"?

(A) To promote a new apartment
(B) To emphasize a place's superior quality
(C) To request a prompt decision
(D) To explain some advantages

89. Where is the talk taking place?

(A) At a winery
(B) At a restaurant
(C) At a culinary school
(D) At a supermarket

90. What does the speaker emphasize about the place?

(A) The affordable prices
(B) The timely service
(C) The fresh ingredients
(D) The free delivery

91. What does the speaker say about the house wines?

(A) They are all imported.
(B) They have an excellent reputation.
(C) They are exported internationally.
(D) They are good for people's health.

92. What type of industry is the news report mainly about?

(A) The computer industry
(B) The automobile industry
(C) The manufacturing industry
(D) The food processing industry

93. According to the speaker, what is the goal of the acquisition?

(A) To reduce production costs
(B) To expand internationally
(C) To manufacture innovative products
(D) To help protect the environment

94. According to the news report, what happened last week?

(A) Stock prices rose sharply.
(B) New computer products were released.
(C) Negotiations were conducted.
(D) Some companies went bankrupt.

## Feedback Survey

| Cleanliness | ★★★★ |
|---|---|
| Location | ★★★★ |
| Staff friendliness | ★★★★★ |
| Cost | ★★★ |

**95.** Who most likely is Lena Park?

(A) A hotel manager
(B) A fitness instructor
(C) A marketing expert
(D) An entrepreneur

**96.** What does the speaker say she is giving the listener?

(A) A gift certificate
(B) A discount coupon
(C) A skincare product
(D) Two nights' free accommodations

**97.** Look at the graphic. Which category does the speaker ask for additional information about?

(A) Cleanliness
(B) Location
(C) Staff friendliness
(D) Cost

## Speech Schedule
### for Annual Video Game Convention

June 3 - June 6
Seoul Convention Center

| June 3 Afternoon | Speaker |
|---|---|
| Session 1 | Kelly McKenzie |
| Session 2 | Sangkyu Kim |
| Session 3 | Brian Joo |
| Session 4 | Soona Ha |

**98.** Who most likely is attending the convention?

(A) Medical experts
(B) Professional photographers
(C) Video game developers
(D) Computer engineers

**99.** Look at the graphics. Which session has been changed?

(A) Session 1
(B) Session 2
(C) Session 3
(D) Session 4

**100.** According to the speaker, how can participants win a prize?

(A) By attending some presentations
(B) By subscribing to a game magazine
(C) By providing their opinions
(D) By purchasing some software

This is the end of the Listening test. Turn to Part 5 in your test book.

▶ ▶ ▶ GO ON TO THE NEXT PAGE

# READING TEST

In the Reading test, you will read a variety of texts and answer several different types of reading comprehension questions. The entire Reading test will last 75 minutes. There are three parts, and directions are given for each part. You are encouraged to answer as many questions as possible within the time allowed.

You must mark your answers on the separate answer sheet. Do not write your answers in your test book.

## PART 5

**Directions**: A word or phrase is missing in each of the sentences below. Four answer choices are given below each sentence. Select the best answer to complete the sentence. Then mark the letter (A), (B), (C), or (D) on your answer sheet.

**101.** Mr. Chandler said during ------- press briefing that the market deserves freedom but companies should respect its responsibility.

(A) he
(B) his
(C) him
(D) himself

**102.** Customers may speak with one of our customer service representatives ------- calling the toll-free number below.

(A) of
(B) by
(C) during
(D) to

**103.** Sunhill Apartment is very popular with people because of its ------- to several city parks.

(A) route
(B) distance
(C) proximity
(D) similarity

**104.** The government is currently trying hard to find ------- ways to carry out more effective residential welfare policies.

(A) practice
(B) practical
(C) practicing
(D) practically

**105.** *World Economy* is the second ------- distributed magazine in the United States and Canada.

(A) wide
(B) wider
(C) more widely
(D) most widely

**106.** Some employers make the erroneous assumption that ------- wages don't lead to high efficiencies.

(A) tangible
(B) competitive
(C) indicative
(D) favorable

**107.** Some domestic analysts said the recent increase in oil prices in the Middle East is a key ------- that will determine the future economic growth of the country.

(A) series
(B) factor
(C) system
(D) basis

**108.** Next week, the state government ------- a set of measures to stimulate the sluggish economy and to create jobs in the short term.

(A) announcing
(B) will announce
(C) announced
(D) is announced

**109.** According to some biologists, human beings have a tremendous ------- to analyze visual information.

(A) amount
(B) capability
(C) appreciation
(D) opportunity

**110.** To improve the quality of our customer service, every inquiry should be -------.

(A) monitor
(B) monitored
(C) monitors
(D) monitoring

**111.** Many people have ------- become accustomed to shopping at large department stores in big cities.

(A) concisely
(B) recently
(C) severely
(D) diligently

**112.** Please be aware ------- before employees begin to operate the new printing machine, it is essential that they thoroughly review the operating manual.

(A) of
(B) whether
(C) that
(D) from

**113.** Any foreigner who wants to work at our new factory for over a month must apply for the ------- work permit.

(A) relevance
(B) relevancies
(C) relevant
(D) relevantly

**114.** Every employee must follow security procedures when sending ------- documents or files electronically to clients.

(A) confident
(B) confidentiality
(C) confidential
(D) confidentially

**115.** The city's annual summer festival ------- swimming, surfing, rafting, and many other fun events.

(A) include
(B) including
(C) includes
(D) is included

**116.** The water supply was too inadequate to support the ------- population due to the serious drought.

(A) sizable
(B) numerous
(C) wide
(D) plenty

**117.** The ------- of a high fruit and vegetable intake and a low saturated fat intake usually helps reduce the risk of obesity, diabetes, and heart disease.

(A) possibility
(B) cooperation
(C) combination
(D) admiration

**118.** According to the newspaper, the bill to ------- the implementation of the free trade agreement with the EU was passed yesterday.

(A) sign
(B) import
(C) conclude
(D) authorize

**119.** ------- takes the chief executive officer job should not expect a quick improvement in the business situation facing the company.

(A) Whichever
(B) Whoever
(C) Since
(D) Even though

**120.** Drivers over 60 should not be allowed to renew their licenses through the mail, ------- is the standard practice in many states.

(A) whose
(B) when
(C) which
(D) that

121. Our city's tour bus routes operate ------- for the areas north of the river and south of the river.

(A) separate
(B) separating
(C) separation
(D) separately

122. The board of directors is going to reward some ------- employees who have been with the company for over 10 years.

(A) dedicated
(B) satisfied
(C) temporary
(D) promotional

123. Mr. Kamang established his own style of Post-Impressionism after he was ------- by many Impressionist artists in Europe.

(A) presented
(B) reminded
(C) influenced
(D) determined

124. About 200 flights to the southern resort island of Cayo Costa ------- through to August 15 due to the strike by pilots.

(A) canceling
(B) cancels
(C) will be canceled
(D) have canceled

125. Our board members ------- planned to set out for New York on Wednesday but were held up by the inclement weather.

(A) inadvertently
(B) precisely
(C) knowingly
(D) initially

126. The city government must ban plastic bags at markets ------- people want to live on a landfill sooner or later.

(A) whether
(B) where
(C) unless
(D) how

127. ------- our new laptop computer model is much more expensive than other ones, customers are hesitating to purchase it.

(A) In order for
(B) Even though
(C) While
(D) Now that

128. ------- who are interested in participating in the marketing seminar should contact Ms. Maya Cruise in the Marketing Department.

(A) Someone
(B) Everyone
(C) Anyone
(D) Those

129. Brilliant artistry is one of the ------- reasons why Asian culture is currently identified as unique in the world.

(A) chief
(B) straight
(C) reliable
(D) adept

130. Mr. Thompson's sales results were far below average in September, ------- he decided to put in a lot of hours meeting with potential clients in October.

(A) when
(B) so
(C) for
(D) until

## PART 6

**Directions:** Read the texts that follow. A word, phrase, or sentence is missing in parts of each text. Four answer choices for each question are given below the text. Select the best answer to complete the text. Then mark the letter (A), (B), (C), or (D) on your answer sheet.

**Questions 131-134** refer to the following notice.

### RENOVATION NOTICE

The New York Central Library will ------- a major renovation project from early August until
   **131.**

late December. The renovation will bring greatly extended ------- space to library users who
                                                   **132.**

choose to spend time at the library reading or studying.

We will be making every effort to ensure that the renovation work causes as little ------- as
                                                                          **133.**

possible to the library's operations. However, it is possible that some areas of the library will

be closed for short periods during this time.

A schedule of the planned closures will be posted on library notice boards and on the library

Web site during the course of the renovations. -------.
                                      **134.**

We greatly appreciate your patience and support.

---

**131.** (A) undergo
   (B) notify
   (C) consult
   (D) monitor

**132.** (A) seat
   (B) seats
   (C) seating
   (D) seated

**133.** (A) expansion
   (B) organization
   (C) disruption
   (D) coordination

**134.** (A) The library is scheduled to reopen in the fall of this year.
   (B) You must not leave your personal possessions unattended.
   (C) Over 20,000 books will be housed in the renovated library.
   (D) Please check the schedule in order to avoid any inconveniences.

**Questions 135-138** refer to the following letter.

Dear Mr. Lee,

As our new letterhead indicates, we have ------- changed the name of our business from
**135.**
Washington Machine to Washington Manufacturing.

There has been no change in management, and we will be providing the same products and

fine service upon which we ------- our reputation in the industry. We would appreciate it if
**136.**
you would bring this announcement to the attention of your Accounting Department and

direct them -------.
**137.**

-------. We appreciate your cooperation in this matter.
**138.**

Sincerely,

Cindy Walker
Chief Executive Officer
Washington Manufacturing

135. (A) rapidly
(B) periodically
(C) increasingly
(D) recently

136. (A) build
(B) will build
(C) have built
(D) had built

137. (A) aggressively
(B) accurately
(C) attentively
(D) accordingly

138. (A) Thank you for being one of our valued
customers.
(B) We successfully developed a new,
innovative device.
(C) Many naming customs are still
followed today.
(D) I think this is the best example of
value creation.

From: Yvette Chen <yc@klpfreight.com>
To: Komi Kellogg <kk@bellapetfactory.com>
Date: March 10
Subject: Price Changes

Dear Mr. Kellogg,

Please accept this e-mail as notification of a slight rate adjustment, ------- April 1. The
**139.**

adjustment is a result of increased transportation costs ------- the last twelve months.
**140.**

A summary of rate changes is located at the bottom of this e-mail. We anticipate no

additional rate adjustments for the next three years.

Should you have any questions regarding our services, please contact us at 692-9815. -------.
**141.**

Thank you for understanding that this price increase means that we can continue to -------
**142.**

the superior quality standards of our freight services for the coming year.

Cordially yours,

Yvette Chen
Chief Executive Officer
KLP Freight Services, Inc.

---

**139.** (A) acute
(B) good
(C) effective
(D) entitled

**140.** (A) with
(B) until
(C) over
(D) following

**141.** (A) We have great difficulty
communicating with overseas clients.
(B) Marketing is concerned with customer
needs and customer satisfaction.
(C) Our customer service representatives
will be happy to assist you.
(D) Better service for all customers should
be a priority for every store and
restaurant.

**142.** (A) examine
(B) maintain
(C) organize
(D) accomplish

▶ ▶ ▶ GO ON TO THE NEXT PAGE

Hello, Ms. Hamilton,

Thank you for your recent application for the position of chief of legal affairs.

We have had a large number of applications and have been able to identify candidates whose backgrounds and experiences closely match our requirements.

-------, you were not selected for this position. We know ------- hard you worked to improve
**143.**                                                                **144.**
your abilities. Therefore, we are sure that you will make yourself stronger than ever and will

become a great lawyer. -------.
**145.**

Many thanks for your interest and for the time you took in ------- your application. If you have
**146.**
any questions, please do not hesitate to call me at 776-7323.

Sincerely yours,

Stacy Park
Personnel Manager
Modern Education

---

143. (A) Additionally
     (B) Consequently
     (C) Regrettably
     (D) Previously

144. (A) that
     (B) either
     (C) who
     (D) how

145. (A) There are some skills and qualities employers seek in all their employees.
     (B) I have reviewed your proposal and have decided to sign with another vender.
     (C) We wish you the best of luck in all of your future endeavors.
     (D) We always acknowledge our staff members for their outstanding performances.

146. (A) forwarding
     (B) delivering
     (C) including
     (D) concentrating

## PART 7

**Directions:** In this part you will read a selection of texts, such as magazine and newspaper articles, e-mails, and instant messages. Each text or set of texts is followed by several questions. Select the best answer for each question and mark the letter (A), (B), (C), or (D) on your answer sheet.

**Questions 147-148** refer to the following notice.

# RYAN FABRIC
## NOTICE

From September 1 to September 8, our store will be closed for business. The reason is that the state gas company, Pacific Gas, is digging up the main road outside our store to install some new gas pipes for our city. The road will be closed to both vehicles and pedestrians during this time.

During this temporary closure, our online and telephone order service will be fully operational. You can order goods through our secure Web site at www.ryanfabric.com or by calling this toll-free number 1-800-741-0110. If you want to receive a catalogue of our merchandise, please call us at 1-800-870-0603.

Our store will be open for business on September 9. We look forward to serving you again once the roadwork outside the store is complete.

Thank you for your patience and understanding.

Thomas Ryan
Store Manager

147. What is the purpose of this notice?
    (A) To introduce some policy changes of the store
    (B) To inform customers of a temporary closure
    (C) To announce a new business plan for expansion
    (D) To provide new construction guideline to residents

148. According to the notice, how can customers place orders between September 1 and September 8?
    (A) By sending an e-mail
    (B) By calling a toll-free number
    (C) By visiting the store in person
    (D) By submitting an order form

▶ ▶ ▶ GO ON TO THE NEXT PAGE

# MEMORANDUM

To: All Kitchen Staff
From: Alley Goodroad
Date: September 9
Subject: New guidelines

Dear Staff,

New guidelines have been set forth by the City Food Safety Commission regarding the proper handling of food in a business establishment. Whether you work with food or not, you are required to adhere to the following standards:

1. All employees must wash their hands a minimum of once every two hours.
2. Shirts with sleeves shorter than 4 inches are not permitted.
3. Hair cannot touch the shoulders (this applies to long ponytails).
4. Fingernails cannot extend beyond the tips of the fingers.

Additional guidelines will be announced next month and they will apply to staff that come in direct contact with raw meat for cooking. A mandatory training seminar has been scheduled for Saturday, September 15, at 10 A.M.

Thank you for your attention to these matters.

Alley Goodroad
Kitchen Staff Supervisor

---

**149.** What is the purpose of the memo?
(A) To announce Ms. Goodroad as the new supervisor
(B) To provide emergency tips to kitchen staff
(C) To explain changes to some business practices
(D) To inform employees of an upcoming special event

**150.** According to the memo, what should all employees do?
(A) Wear an apron while cooking
(B) Sign up for a training session
(C) Take shower before going to work
(D) Wash their hands at least every two hours

**151.** Who would follow the additional guidelines?
(A) Restaurant servers
(B) Culinary experts
(C) Health workers
(D) Hotel employees

**Questions 152-153** refer to the following receipt.

# *Target Tech Store*

4893 Dresden St.
Orient, OH 40359
Phone: 3983-7651
Open Monday to Saturday from 7 A.M. to 10 P.M.

-------------------------------------------------------------------

12 APRIL 3:12 P.M.

LINE 4
SERVER: Mark Farrow

-------------------------------------------------------------------

| | |
|---|---|
| 128GB of RAM by FX Electronics | $210.00 |
| Drum machine | $57.25 |
| Mobile phone charger | $16.00 |
| Tax | $30.52 |

**Total Due** **$313.77**

-------------------------------------------------------------------

**After-sales service also included.**

Please retain this receipt in case you need to process a refund or an exchange in any of our stores across Ohio.

Please enter the code underneath this receipt to receive a 10% off coupon when you shop online at www.targettech.com/coupon.

**152.** What is indicated about Target Tech Store?

(A) It offers a membership discount.
(B) It is open on Sundays.
(C) It specializes in musical instruments.
(D) It operates other branches in Ohio.

**153.** Why should customers visit the Web site of Target Tech Store?

(A) To request a refund or exchange
(B) To sign up for a membership
(C) To provide customer feedback
(D) To obtain a discount coupon

▶ ▶ ▶ GO ON TO THE NEXT PAGE

# United Health Group
## Now hiring for the following positions!

**Certified Dietitian:** We currently have two openings for the position of certified dietitian. Candidates should have a current certification by a state board. A minimum of two years of experience working as a certified dietitian is also required. The job requires working with doctors to provide nutrition support for patients. The schedule for the full-time position is Monday through Thursday from 8 A.M. to 4 P.M. and Saturdays from 9 A.M. to 12 P.M.

**Administrative assistant:** One position is currently available for a full-time administrative assistant. The position should be able to send out and process bills, sort mail, take calls from clients, and organize all billing records. The assistant is also responsible for all patient scheduling. Work hours for this position are Monday through Thursday from 7:30 A.M. to 5 P.M. The job candidate must have at least two years of experience as an administrative assistant.

All applicants should visit www.unitedhealth.com and select the human resources department link. There you will find more information about these jobs. Click on the job desired to submit a cover letter, a resume, copies of all certifications, and a list of professional references.

**154.** What most likely is United Health Group?

(A) A dental office
(B) A diet company
(C) A medical center
(D) A health insurance provider

**155.** What is NOT required as a responsibility of the administrative assistant?

(A) Scheduling appointments
(B) Speaking on the phone
(C) Sending mail to other branches
(D) Keeping track of payment information

**Questions 156-157** refer to the following job text message chain.

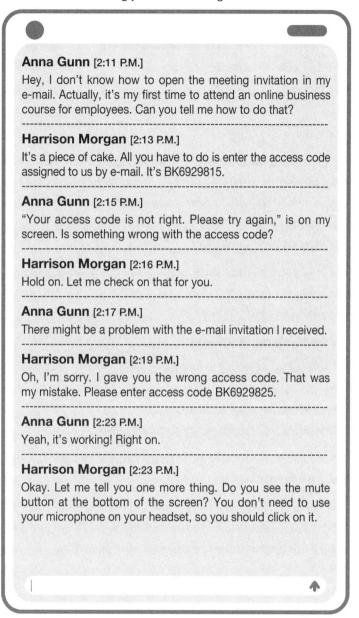

**Anna Gunn** [2:11 P.M.]

Hey, I don't know how to open the meeting invitation in my e-mail. Actually, it's my first time to attend an online business course for employees. Can you tell me how to do that?

------------------------------------------------

**Harrison Morgan** [2:13 P.M.]

It's a piece of cake. All you have to do is enter the access code assigned to us by e-mail. It's BK6929815.

------------------------------------------------

**Anna Gunn** [2:15 P.M.]

"Your access code is not right. Please try again," is on my screen. Is something wrong with the access code?

------------------------------------------------

**Harrison Morgan** [2:16 P.M.]

Hold on. Let me check on that for you.

------------------------------------------------

**Anna Gunn** [2:17 P.M.]

There might be a problem with the e-mail invitation I received.

------------------------------------------------

**Harrison Morgan** [2:19 P.M.]

Oh, I'm sorry. I gave you the wrong access code. That was my mistake. Please enter access code BK6929825.

------------------------------------------------

**Anna Gunn** [2:23 P.M.]

Yeah, it's working! Right on.

------------------------------------------------

**Harrison Morgan** [2:23 P.M.]

Okay. Let me tell you one more thing. Do you see the mute button at the bottom of the screen? You don't need to use your microphone on your headset, so you should click on it.

---

**156.** At 2:19 P.M., what does Mr. Morgan most likely mean when he writes, "Oh, I'm sorry"?

(A) He needs to start a business workshop without Ms. Gunn.

(B) He gave Ms. Gunn some wrong information.

(C) He hasn't found the cause of a problem yet.

(D) He will not register for the business course.

**157.** What is probably true about Ms. Gunn?

(A) She recently bought a new headset.

(B) She will lead a business seminar tomorrow.

(C) She doesn't need to speak during the online course.

(D) She hasn't received an e-mail invitation.

▶ ▶ ▶GO ON TO THE NEXT PAGE

# MEMORANDUM

To: Best Motors Mechanics
From: Richard Redford
Date: March 8
Subject: Course Registration

Best Motors is happy to announce that we have once again contracted the National Automobile Institute (NAI) to train our team of mechanics through a series of hands-on classes covering a number of areas. All Best Motors mechanics will complete the training by the end of next month. —[1]—. You are responsible for registering for the courses on your own. Reimbursement for the registration fees will be provided upon completion of the course.

The courses will take place at the National Automobile Institute's two campuses in Dearborn, one located on Eight Mile Drive and the other on 4th Avenue. —[2]—. They will each last six weeks, meeting on select weekdays from 4:00 P.M. to 6:00 P.M.

The courses that you should take are as follows:

• Fuel System Installation: Mondays, Eight Mile Drive campus
• Production Tolerances: Tuesdays, Eight Mile Drive campus
• Vehicle Safety Systems: Thursdays, 4th Avenue campus
• Techniques for minimizing injuries: Fridays, 4th Avenue campus

—[3]—. Some of the content covered is specific to Best Motors automobiles, with some of our engineers assisting with the instruction.

—[4]—. However, we strongly recommend staying up-to-date in the field. Your performance is reviewed yearly, and the training can help you move on to higher positions in our organization. If you have any questions about this program, please speak with your supervisor.

Thank you.

Sincerely,

Richard Redford
Director of Production
Best Motors

**158.** What is the purpose of the memo?

(A) To ask for feedback on some classes

(B) To discuss training for certain employees

(C) To provide instructions for company trainers

(D) To announce job openings for local car mechanics

**159.** Why would employees most likely take an interest in the memo?

(A) Their company has been losing money due to manufacturing issues.

(B) Their participation can influence their position within the company.

(C) They will get a raise after completing the courses.

(D) They can learn ways to decrease production time.

**160.** In which of the positions marked [1], [2], [3], and [4] does the following sentence best belong?

"Please be aware that participation is not mandatory."

(A) [1]

(B) [2]

(C) [3]

(D) [4]

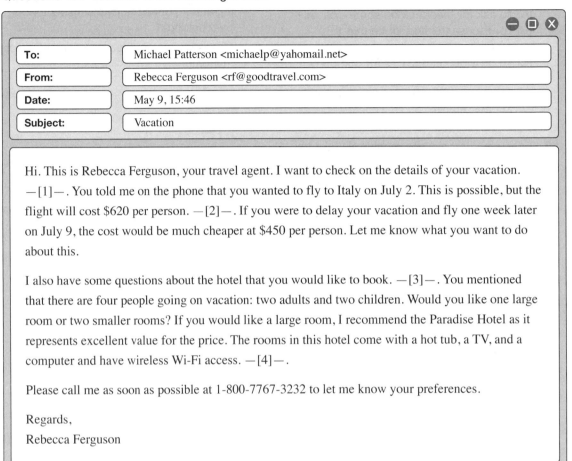

To: Michael Patterson <michaelp@yahomail.net>

From: Rebecca Ferguson <rf@goodtravel.com>

Date: May 9, 15:46

Subject: Vacation

Hi. This is Rebecca Ferguson, your travel agent. I want to check on the details of your vacation. —[1]—. You told me on the phone that you wanted to fly to Italy on July 2. This is possible, but the flight will cost $620 per person. —[2]—. If you were to delay your vacation and fly one week later on July 9, the cost would be much cheaper at $450 per person. Let me know what you want to do about this.

I also have some questions about the hotel that you would like to book. —[3]—. You mentioned that there are four people going on vacation: two adults and two children. Would you like one large room or two smaller rooms? If you would like a large room, I recommend the Paradise Hotel as it represents excellent value for the price. The rooms in this hotel come with a hot tub, a TV, and a computer and have wireless Wi-Fi access. —[4]—.

Please call me as soon as possible at 1-800-7767-3232 to let me know your preferences.

Regards,
Rebecca Ferguson

**161.** What is the purpose of the e-mail?

(A) To offer Mr. Patterson a discounted vacation

(B) To inform Mr. Patterson that his vacation has been canceled

(C) To promote a travel insurance package to Mr. Patterson

(D) To ask Mr. Patterson some questions about his vacation arrangements

**162.** In which of the positions marked [1], [2], [3], and [4] does the following sentence best belong?

"Could you be more flexible with your vacation dates?"

(A) [1]

(B) [2]

(C) [3]

(D) [4]

**163.** What does Ms. Ferguson NOT mention about the Paradise Hotel?

(A) It represents excellent value for the price.

(B) Each of its rooms is fitted with a hot tub.

(C) Suites are available at the hotel.

(D) Every room has free Internet access.

Pramerica Insurance
193 Lake Street
Austin, TX 49302
(800) 2020-5830

July 3

Dear Ms. Anderson,

I am writing with regard to our telephone conversation held on July 1, during which you requested further information on our insurance packages. Please find enclosed a company brochure.

In the brochure, the various types of insurance packages that are currently offered have been outlined. I would like to take this opportunity to recommend the Life Term Cover policy, which would cover both you and your husband in the event of an accident or emergency. This policy is priced at just $1,200 per year (or $100 per month) and is the most popular program with our clients in your region.

I understand that choosing an appropriate insurance policy can often be a stressful and overwhelming business. That is why we have recently set up some insurance seminars. These are held one Saturday a month at the Austin town hall and last for approximately one hour. These seminars are designed to help you decide which insurance package is right for you. At these sessions, you can also have the chance to speak to one of our dedicated advisers about your own personal situation.

For further information on our insurance seminars and for detailed information on our terms and conditions, please visit our Web site at www.pramericainsurance.com.

Thank you for choosing Pramerica Insurance. I wish you a pleasant day.

Sincerely,

Linda Bush
Insurance Development Head
Pramerica Insurance

**164.** What is the purpose of the letter?

(A) To outline the terms and conditions of an insurance policy

(B) To provide further product information as requested by a client

(C) To offer the reader a position at the company

(D) To announce the opening of a new store

**165.** What is the purpose of the seminar sessions?

(A) To train new employees in sales techniques

(B) To provide education in the area of Web site design

(C) To discuss the company's sales figures with board members

(D) To help customers choose the appropriate insurance policy

**166.** What is NOT mentioned about the Life Term Cover policy?

(A) It costs twelve hundred dollars a year.

(B) It would be valid for both Ms. Anderson and her spouse.

(C) Ms. Anderson's children would be covered by the policy.

(D) It is the company's most popular insurance program in the local area.

**167.** What is Mr. Anderson encouraged to do?

(A) Choose an insurance over $1,500

(B) Participate in the seminar every week

(C) Consult with the advisor online

(D) Visit the Web site for more information

▶ ▶ ▶ GO ON TO THE NEXT PAGE

May 10 - Scolan Construction's president, Lyle Vines, stated at a press conference that the company would donate 1.5 million dollars to the Canton Parks Restoration Initiative over the next year.

With the initiative's financial support having decreased over the last two years, the funding is greatly needed. "Our organization couldn't be happier with Scolan's generous donation," said Canton Parks Commissioner Betty Judge. "It will certainly help us maintain and improve the parks in Canton.

The Canton Parks Restoration Initiative was established five years ago by the Canton Parks Commission (CPC) to help improve park and playground facilities around Canton. When it was first started, the local government provided funding for the initiative, but two years ago, the Canton City Council voted to use the revenue for the CPC to fund a new commercial district. The initiative has had difficulties finding funding since then.

Finally, the CPC began asking for donations from companies in the area six months ago. "We sent out letters to many companies with a pamphlet showing the beauty of our parks," Ms. Judge stated. The photographs in the pamphlets showed the parks throughout the years, and many had children playing in them. "We had no idea that Mr. Vines is a former resident until he called and asked about making a contribution to the initiative," Ms. Judge said.

Citizens and community leaders of Canton are pleased about the increased funding the initiative will receive. Councilman Carl Nesmith lauded Mr. Vines for his company's donation. The city council has talked about placing honorary plaques in the parks. "Canton has a number of beautiful parks that are highly beneficial to everyone in the community," said Mr. Vines when announcing the donation, "My fascination with building actually began when I would play at these parks. If it weren't for the time I spent making little cities in the sandboxes on playgrounds, I may have chosen a different career. I just hope this donation helps the community continue to enjoy the parks."

Michael Pyke, Local Reporter

**168.** When was the Canton Parks Restoration Initiative started?

(A) Six months ago
(B) One year ago
(C) Two years ago
(D) Five years ago

**169.** According to the article, why did the initiative lose financial support?

(A) Funding from the local government was redistributed.
(B) The cost of maintenance increased too much.
(C) Many residents of Canton moved away from the city.
(D) Further maintenance work was no longer needed.

**170.** Who is currently NOT a resident of Canton?

(A) Lyle Vines
(B) Betty Judge
(C) Carl Nesmith
(D) Michael Pyke

**171.** What does Mr. Vines suggest about the parks in Canton?

(A) They are not used by members of the community.
(B) They guided him toward a career in construction.
(C) Companies in the area should provide support for them.
(D) All parks should have plaques giving information about donors.

▶ ▶ ▶ GO ON TO THE NEXT PAGE

**Questions 172-175** refer to the following online chat discussion.

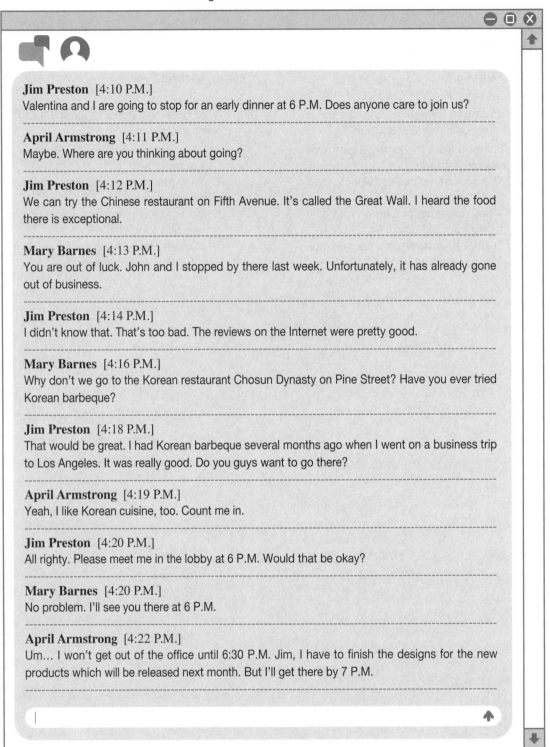

**Jim Preston** [4:10 P.M.]
Valentina and I are going to stop for an early dinner at 6 P.M. Does anyone care to join us?

-------------------------------------------------------------------------------

**April Armstrong** [4:11 P.M.]
Maybe. Where are you thinking about going?

-------------------------------------------------------------------------------

**Jim Preston** [4:12 P.M.]
We can try the Chinese restaurant on Fifth Avenue. It's called the Great Wall. I heard the food there is exceptional.

-------------------------------------------------------------------------------

**Mary Barnes** [4:13 P.M.]
You are out of luck. John and I stopped by there last week. Unfortunately, it has already gone out of business.

-------------------------------------------------------------------------------

**Jim Preston** [4:14 P.M.]
I didn't know that. That's too bad. The reviews on the Internet were pretty good.

-------------------------------------------------------------------------------

**Mary Barnes** [4:16 P.M.]
Why don't we go to the Korean restaurant Chosun Dynasty on Pine Street? Have you ever tried Korean barbeque?

-------------------------------------------------------------------------------

**Jim Preston** [4:18 P.M.]
That would be great. I had Korean barbeque several months ago when I went on a business trip to Los Angeles. It was really good. Do you guys want to go there?

-------------------------------------------------------------------------------

**April Armstrong** [4:19 P.M.]
Yeah, I like Korean cuisine, too. Count me in.

-------------------------------------------------------------------------------

**Jim Preston** [4:20 P.M.]
All righty. Please meet me in the lobby at 6 P.M. Would that be okay?

-------------------------------------------------------------------------------

**Mary Barnes** [4:20 P.M.]
No problem. I'll see you there at 6 P.M.

-------------------------------------------------------------------------------

**April Armstrong** [4:22 P.M.]
Um… I won't get out of the office until 6:30 P.M. Jim, I have to finish the designs for the new products which will be released next month. But I'll get there by 7 P.M.

**172.** What are the writers talking about?

(A) Where to host a corporate event
(B) Whom to go with
(C) Where to go for dinner
(D) Which restaurant serves delicious food

**173.** What is indicated about a Chinese restaurant?

(A) It has moved to a new location.
(B) It received very poor reviews.
(C) It is not in business anymore.
(D) It offers a special menu after 6 P.M.

**174.** At 4:14 P.M., what does Mr. Preston mean when he writes, "That's too bad"?

(A) He has a prior engagement.
(B) He cannot meet a deadline for his project.
(C) He wanted to try Chinese food.
(D) He thinks a new restaurant is too far away.

**175.** What will Ms. Armstrong do next?

(A) Join her colleagues a little late
(B) Work overtime
(C) Go to a new restaurant
(D) Go on a business trip to China

▶ ▶ ▶ GO ON TO THE NEXT PAGE

**Questions 176-180** refer to the following Web page and online form.

HOME | ABOUT SBRG | REGISTER | CONNECT

# Maximize your small businesses' profits

Is your small business busy but still struggling to turn a profit? Subscribe to the Small Business Resource Guide (SBRG) and learn how to better manage the financial aspects of your small business! For over two decades, we have been helping small business owners all over the country achieve financial success. Here are just a few of the things we offer:

Informational Resources – Get access to a wide variety of articles, reports, and reviews created by successful small business owners. These materials provide realistic, practical advice that will help your business achieve long-term profitability. Every month, we add many new resources to the site, with topics covering everything small business owners need to know.

Downloadable Forms, Worksheets, and Templates – We offer a large database of downloadable worksheets, forms, and templates, all for free. It is easy to adapt these materials to suit your businesses' needs.

Small Business Forums – Our online forum allows members to share ideas and insights into the details of running a small business. Interact with thousands of members who understand the unique challenges of running a small business.

Online and In-person Seminars – Take part in a variety of online classes given by experts. We also frequently hold in-person seminars in major cities, and a gold-level membership allows you to attend these events for free! Please note that silver-level members can attend these events, but they are required to pay $80 per event.

Get immediate access to SBRG now! You simply need to pay a one-time fee of $100 and $30 per month (for silver-level membership) or $45 per month (for gold-level membership).

HOME | ABOUT SBRG | REGISTER | CONNECT

## SBRG Inductee Information

**First Name:** Thomas
**Last Name:** Dekker
**Company Name:** Garmon Clothing
**Phone Number:** 800-555-8209

**Street:** 7891 Fields St.
**City:** Winston
**State:** North Carolina
**Postal Code:** 61771

**E-mail Address:** thomas.dekker@garmonclothing.com
**Create Username:** t.de

**Create Password:** *******

**Verify Password:** *******

**Select Payment Type:** $100 registration fee

**plus:** ● Silver Level ($30 a month)　　　　● Gold Level ($45 a month)

SBRG guarantees results with our memberships, and if your business' finances fail to improve within the first year that you are a member, we will reimburse half of the cost of your membership fees for the year.

**176.** What is the purpose of the Web page information?

(A) To announce a new forum on a Web site
(B) To explain the benefits of being an SBRG member
(C) To promote the opening of a new small business
(D) To describe some ways for a small business to save money

**177.** What is true about the SBRG?

(A) It charges a fee to all members at in-person events.
(B) It specializes in helping restaurant owners.
(C) It is based in Winston, North Carolina.
(D) It has existed for over 20 years.

**178.** According to the Web page, what is updated monthly?

(A) Its informational resources
(B) Its downloadable materials
(C) Its business plans
(D) Its forum layout

**179.** What is suggested about Mr. Dekker?

(A) He has been a member of the SBRG for several years.
(B) He is interested in attending in-person seminars.
(C) He recently changed the location of his business.
(D) He has taken some of the online classes.

**180.** When does the SBRG provide a refund?

(A) When a small business cannot get financing
(B) When a small business does not turn a profit
(C) When a seminar has already been paid for
(D) When a payment is made after a deadline

**Questions 181-185** refer to the following e-mails.

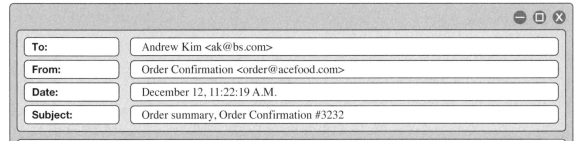

| To: | Andrew Kim <ak@bs.com> |
| From: | Order Confirmation <order@acefood.com> |
| Date: | December 12, 11:22:19 A.M. |
| Subject: | Order summary, Order Confirmation #3232 |

Dear Mr. Kim,

Thank you for choosing Ace Food Supply. This e-mail is a confirmation of your order, which is as follows:

| Order # | Description | Quantity |
|---------|-------------|----------|
| E390 | Napa Avocados | 100 lbs |
| C932 | Chicken Breasts | 50 lbs |
| B820 | Wild Cranberries | 80 lbs |
| O400 | Sweet Potatoes | 125 lbs |

All orders are delivered on the same day of their receipt. The exact time the shipment arrives is based on your restaurant's proximity to our headquarters.

An invoice for this order will be sent to your restaurant within the next three business days.

If you have any questions, contact us either by telephone or e-mail. Please note that we cannot change orders once they are en route for delivery.

Thank you for your order.

Ace Food Supply

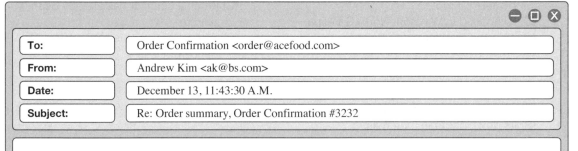

| To: | Order Confirmation <order@acefood.com> |
| From: | Andrew Kim <ak@bs.com> |
| Date: | December 13, 11:43:30 A.M. |
| Subject: | Re: Order summary, Order Confirmation #3232 |

I'm contacting you regarding order number 3232. Although the copy of the order is correct, I would like to make a few changes if possible. I originally ordered 100 of item E390. However, I would like the quantity to be changed to 250. Plus, we will only be needing 30 lbs of chicken breasts (item #C932). By the way, I noticed your Web site no longer lists the 30-lb bags of strawberries anymore. They were excellent. Have they been discontinued? If not, when will you be getting them in?

Thank you.

Andrew Kim
Blue Sky Restaurant

**181.** What is the purpose of the first e-mail?

(A) To detail some discounts on a bulk order
(B) To announce some items that are out of stock
(C) To confirm that an order has been shipped
(D) To provide the details of a recent order

**182.** What is mentioned about shipping in the first e-mail?

(A) It is provided free of charge with all items.
(B) It occurs on the same day of the order.
(C) Items cannot be returned after they are shipped.
(D) It is limited to smaller items.

**183.** In the first e-mail, the word "proximity" in paragraph 2, line 2, is closest in meaning to

(A) closeness
(B) direction
(C) shortage
(D) range

**184.** What item does Mr. Kim want to increase the quantity of in the order?

(A) Napa Avocadoes
(B) Chicken Breasts
(C) Wild Cranberries
(D) Sweet Potatoes

**185.** What is implied about Mr. Kim?

(A) He wants to cancel his order.
(B) He added a different item to his original order.
(C) He is a new customer of Ace Food Supply.
(D) He would like to order some strawberries.

▶ ▶ ▶ GO ON TO THE NEXT PAGE

Audiofile Online is a brand new British company that provides a music download service that is sure to be adored by music fans all over the world. We provide our subscribers with the newest tracks from the world's top artists at the most affordable rates! When you subscribe to Audiofile Online, you will have no limit to the number of tracks you can download per month, and you'll automatically be signed up to receive our free monthly magazine by e-mail. Spend more than $100 on music tracks and receive a free gift! In our 'Featured Artists' section, we allow our subscribers to "try before they buy." You can order one free track from each of our featured artists, and if you like what you hear, you can go ahead and download the full albums. Standard subscribers receive MP3 tracks encoded at a crisp 128 kbit/s, while Audiofile Max and Audiofile Pro subscribers get access to 192 kbit/s and 320 kbit/s tracks, respectively.

**Visit www.audiofile.co.uk for more details!**

www.audiofileonline.co.uk/shoppingcart

Audiofile Online
Subscriber Name: Chris Boyd

Downloads (Featured Artists)

| Artist | Track/ Album Title | Details | Number of Tracks | Bit Rate (kbit/s) | Price |
|---|---|---|---|---|---|
| Justin Haynes | All My Friends | Free Track | 1 | 320 | $0.00 |
| One Promise | From the Heart | Free Track | 1 | 320 | $0.00 |
| Digital Dreamz | Full Evolution | Full Album | 14 | 320 | $18.06 |
| The Black Days | In Your Head | Free Track | 1 | 320 | $0.00 |
| | | | | **Payment Due:** | **$18.06** |

**Proceed to Checkout**

| To: | Audiofile online customer service <helpdesk@audiofile.co.uk> |
| --- | --- |
| From: | Chris Boyd <chrisboyd@digimail.net> |
| Date: | April 16 |
| Subject: | Recent purchase |

Hi,

I'm contacting you regarding the tracks I recently ordered from your Web site. First of all, I'd like to say that I am a huge fan of your service, and I especially like having a chance to try free tracks from your featured artists. In fact, I ordered some free MP3 tracks a few days ago. I also purchased "Full Evolution" by Digital Dreamz, but I actually received the album "Nine Lives" by Digital Dreamz instead. I already own this one, so I'm hoping you can rectify the situation for me. Based on the free tracks I listened to, I plan to purchase One Promise's album. I can't stand "All My Friends," but "In Your Head" isn't as bad as I first thought, so I may consider buying that artist's album, too. Thanks for the great service, and I hope to hear from you soon.

Regards,

Chris Boyd

186. In the advertisement, the word "top" in paragraph 1, line 3, is closest in meaning to

(A) highest
(B) advanced
(C) excessive
(D) leading

187. What is true about Audiofile Online according to the advertisement?

(A) It is a long-established company.
(B) It enforces a monthly download limit.
(C) It issues an electronic publication.
(D) It has offices in several countries.

188. What is indicated about Mr. Boyd?

(A) He recently upgraded his subscription.
(B) He downloaded four full albums.
(C) He is an Audiofile Pro subscriber.
(D) He received a complimentary gift.

189. Which artist's music was Mr. Boyd most disappointed with?

(A) Justin Haynes
(B) One Promise
(C) Digital Dreamz
(D) The Black Days

190. What problem did Mr. Boyd describe in his e-mail?

(A) He received a track from the wrong artist.
(B) He received MP3 files that were poor quality.
(C) He received an album he did not request.
(D) He received fewer tracks than expected.

▶ ▶ ▶GO ON TO THE NEXT PAGE

# American Elite Inc.

We are pleased to announce our business skills workshops for the month of September. The workshops listed below will run every Saturday throughout the month. The cities in which the workshops will be available are indicated below. Full venue and schedule details are available on our Web site.

**Workshop #091 – (CH, LA, CI, PH, SA) – 'Better Customer Communication Skills'**

**Workshop #092 – (CH, NY, LA, CI, CL) – 'Creating Spreadsheets with SmartSuite 6'**

**Workshop #093 – (CH, NY, LA, SA, DE) – 'Succeeding in the Pharmaceutical Field'**

**Workshop #094 – (LA, HO, PH, SA, DE) –'Web Site Design: The Key to Winning Clients'**

Location Key: Chicago (CH), New York City (NY), Los Angeles (LA), Houston (HO), Cincinnati (CI), Philadelphia (PH), San Antonio (SA), Cleveland (CL), Detroit (DE)

Please visit www.americaneliteinc.com/workshops/ to view detailed information about all the above-listed events and to fill out an electronic registration form.

www.americaneliteinc.com/workshops/registration

## Event Registration Form – September Workshops

| | |
|---|---|
| **Applicant's Name:** | Veronica Lamb |
| **Applicant's E-mail:** | veronicalamb@blitzco.com |
| **Workshop Number:** | 092 |
| **Location Code:** | CH |
| **Workshop Date:** | ■ September 3 ☐ September 10 |
| | ☐ September 17 ☐ September 24 |
| **Name of Employer**: | Blitzco Corporation |
| **Position Held**: | Advertising Executive |

Registration must be completed at least 7 days prior to the selected workshop date.

**Continue to Payment Screen**

| To: | Registration Services <registration@americanelite.org> |
| From: | Veronica Lamb <veronicalamb@blitzco.com > |
| Date: | September 1 |
| Subject: | Workshop Registration |

Hello,

I'm contacting you concerning the registration form I submitted yesterday. I wasn't concentrating when I was filling it out and I made a mistake. When I clicked on the date, I chose the wrong one. The payment for the workshop has already been taken out of my account, so I'd be very grateful if you could change the date on my registration form to the following Saturday. If it is impossible to push my date back by one week, please refund the registration fee to me and I will register a second time using the correct details. I hope to hear from you soon.

Best regards,

Veronica Lamb

---

**191.** What type of business most likely is American Elite Inc.?

(A) An advertising corporation
(B) An executive recruitment agency
(C) A professional development firm
(D) A publisher of business journals

**192.** Which city will host all of the listed workshops?

(A) Chicago
(B) New York
(C) Los Angeles
(D) Detroit

**193.** What is indicated about Ms. Lamb?

(A) She has experience in Web site design.
(B) She currently works for a pharmaceutical firm.
(C) She wants to improve her communication skills.
(D) She hopes to learn how to use some software.

**194.** When does Ms. Lamb want to attend a workshop?

(A) On September 3rd
(B) On September 10th
(C) On September 17th
(D) On September 24th

**195.** In the e-mail, the word "concerning" in paragraph 1, line 1, is closest in meaning to

(A) assuming
(B) including
(C) pending
(D) regarding

# San Diego Convention Center

1201 North Harbor Drive
San Diego, CA 92093
(858) 534-1123

## "We always care your business."

Set overlooking the Pacific Ocean, the San Diego Convention Center is more than just a convention center. We offer outstanding resort and various conference services to meet all your business needs. The San Diego Convention Center provides fax machines, computers, printers, and Internet access in every conference room and has an upscale bar as well as formal restaurants and amenities facilities such as spacious spas and saunas with joining men's and women's areas. Besides, the Pacific Ocean view will have you enjoying your stay at the San Diego Convention Center.

To make a reservation or to get more information, check out our Web site at www.sdccenter.com and click on "MAKE A RESERVATION."

The San Diego Convention Center is the best place where business and people meet. Here you can find everything you need for your conference.

---

www.sdccenter.com/reservation

| HOME | MEETING ROOM LIST | ACCOMMODATION | OUTDOOR SPORTS | CONTACT US |

**NAME / CAPACITY / RATES**

1. ORION MEETING ROOM / 30 PEOPLE / $200 PER DAY

2. GALAXY MEETING ROOM / 45 PEOPLE / $320 PER DAY

3. ANDROMEDA MEETING ROOM / 70 PEOPLE / $480 PER DAY

4. UNIVERSE MEETING ROOM / 100 PEOPLE / $630 PER DAY

**To:** Jason Green <jasongreen@pacificenergy.com>

**From:** Belle Borden <bborden@sdccenter.com>

**Date:** September 11

**Subject:** Reservation

Dear Mr. Green,

We received your initial deposit of $500.00 for a two-bedroom grand suite for October 8 and 9. The Orion room has been booked for your meeting on October 8. We need an additional deposit of $250.00 one week prior to your arrival for the reservation of the meeting room.

If there are any pieces of electronic equipment you need ready in the Orion room for your presentation, please let us know in advance so that we may prepare them for you.

Furthermore, if you have any questions about our catering service for the meeting, please call our kitchen manager, Ms. Joanna Spencer, at (213) 767-3232, ext. 7311.

We wish you the very best in your business.

Sincerely,

Belle Borden
Reservations Coordinator
San Diego Convention Center

**196.** For whom is the advertisement most likely intended?

(A) Realtors
(B) Business professionals
(C) Tourists
(D) Employees at a convention company

**197.** What is NOT offered by the San Diego Convention Center?

(A) Accommodations
(B) Food service
(C) Office equipment
(D) Beach tours

**198.** What is implied about Mr. Green?

(A) He will make a presentation.
(B) He is a company president.
(C) He has contacted Ms. Borden before.
(D) He is pleased with the quality of Ms. Borden's work.

**199.** What can be inferred about Mr. Green's meeting?

(A) It will take place on October 9.
(B) The participants will bring their own electronic equipment.
(C) No more than thirty people will attend.
(D) Partial payment for the conference room has been made.

**200.** What does Ms. Borden ask Mr. Green to do?

(A) Process a full refund
(B) Sign a rental agreement
(C) Make a deposit before arriving
(D) Contact Ms. Spencer for catering service

STOP! This is the end of the test. If you finish before time is called,
you may go back to Parts 5, 6, and 7 and check your work.

# Actual Test 04

MP3 해설집

적정 풀이 시간 120분

**120 min**

시작 시간 ___시 ___분

종료 시간 ___시 ___분

중간에 멈추지 말고 처음부터 끝까지 풀어보세요.
문제를 풀 때에는 실전처럼 답안지에 마킹하세요.

목표 개수 _____ / 200    실제 개수 _____ / 200

예상 점수는 번역 및 정답에 있는 점수 환산표를 참조하세요.

# LISTENING TEST

In the Listening test, you will be asked to demonstrate how well you understand spoken English. The entire Listening test will last approximately 45 minutes. There are four parts, and directions are given for each part. You must mark your answers on the separate answer sheet. Do not write your answers in your test book.

## PART 1

**Directions:** For each question in this part, you will hear four statements about a picture in your test book. When you hear the statements, you must select the one statement that best describes what you see in the picture. Then find the number of the question on your answer sheet and mark your answer. The statements will not be printed in your test book and will be spoken only one time.

Statement (B), "They are sitting at a table," is the best description of the picture. So you should select answer (B) and mark it on your answer sheet.

**1.**

**2.**

▶ ▶ ▶ GO ON TO THE NEXT PAGE

**3.**

**4.**

**5.**

**6.**

## PART 2

**Directions:** You will hear a question or statement and three responses spoken in English. They will not be printed in your test book and will be spoken only one time. Select the best response to the question or statement and mark the letter (A), (B), or (C) on your answer sheet.

7. Mark your answer on your answer sheet.

8. Mark your answer on your answer sheet.

9. Mark your answer on your answer sheet.

10. Mark your answer on your answer sheet.

11. Mark your answer on your answer sheet.

12. Mark your answer on your answer sheet.

13. Mark your answer on your answer sheet.

14. Mark your answer on your answer sheet.

15. Mark your answer on your answer sheet.

16. Mark your answer on your answer sheet.

17. Mark your answer on your answer sheet.

18. Mark your answer on your answer sheet.

19. Mark your answer on your answer sheet.

20. Mark your answer on your answer sheet.

21. Mark your answer on your answer sheet.

22. Mark your answer on your answer sheet.

23. Mark your answer on your answer sheet.

24. Mark your answer on your answer sheet.

25. Mark your answer on your answer sheet.

26. Mark your answer on your answer sheet.

27. Mark your answer on your answer sheet.

28. Mark your answer on your answer sheet.

29. Mark your answer on your answer sheet.

30. Mark your answer on your answer sheet.

31. Mark your answer on your answer sheet.

## PART 3

**Directions:** You will hear some conversations between two or three people. You will be asked to answer three questions about what the speakers say in each conversation. Select the best response to each question and mark the letter (A), (B), (C), or (D) on your answer sheet. The conversations will not be printed in your test book and will be spoken only one time.

**32.** What are the speakers talking about?

(A) A regular vacation
(B) A renovation project
(C) A new subway line
(D) A delayed bus

**33.** Where most likely are the speakers?

(A) On a bus
(B) In an auto repair shop
(C) At the side of a road
(D) At a construction site

**34.** What problem does the woman mention?

(A) People often use mobile phones while driving.
(B) The bus engine stopped working.
(C) Car accidents are happening more frequently.
(D) Energy is being used inefficiently.

**35.** Who most likely is the woman?

(A) A café owner
(B) A sales representative
(C) A technician
(D) A packaging designer

**36.** What does the woman offer the man?

(A) Free home delivery
(B) A free room upgrade
(C) An amended contract
(D) Free installation

**37.** How can the man qualify for the promotion?

(A) By making a significant purchase
(B) By recommending two customers
(C) By attending a sales meeting
(D) By subscribing to a new magazine

**38.** What task does the man need to complete?

(A) Budget projections
(B) An annual report
(C) Data recovery
(D) A donor listing

**39.** Why is Kate unable to find the information immediately?

(A) She is not in the office.
(B) She does not have time.
(C) She needs more information.
(D) She does not know how.

**40.** What will the man probably do next?

(A) Call his supervisor
(B) Submit a report
(C) Attend an event
(D) Consult a database

**41.** What does the woman ask about?

(A) A product return
(B) A discounted price
(C) An equipment upgrade
(D) Phone repair services

**42.** What does the woman mean when she says, "Oh, that's good"?

(A) Some new items are of fine quality.
(B) An exchange offer is worth accepting.
(C) Various discounts will be offered.
(D) Her current mobile phone can be fixed for free

**43.** What does the man offer to do?

(A) Recommend the woman's business
(B) Transfer some data
(C) Repair the woman's cellular phone
(D) Print some photographs

▶ ▶ ▶ GO ON TO THE NEXT PAGE

44. Where is the conversation taking place?

(A) At a bank
(B) At an electronics store
(C) At an office furniture store
(D) At a stationery store

45. Why does the woman ask Mr. Goodroad for help?

(A) A machine is broken.
(B) A receipt has been lost.
(C) Some documents are missing.
(D) Some products are out of stock.

46. What does the man say he can do for the customer?

(A) Give the customer a full refund
(B) Allow the customer to exchange products
(C) Send the customer a discount coupon
(D) Contact another store

47. What are the speakers discussing?

(A) Changing a product's packaging
(B) Redesigning some business processes
(C) Simplifying current investment regulations
(D) Replacing an old slogan

48. How did the woman find out about the change?

(A) From a memo
(B) From a press conference
(C) From a meeting
(D) From a monthly newsletter

49. According to the woman, why did the company make the change?

(A) To market new value-added services
(B) To attract younger customers
(C) To refurbish the company's image
(D) To launch differentiated marketing strategies

50. What does the man need?

(A) To find the packing materials
(B) To have his mail forwarded
(C) To locate the post office
(D) To find someone help him fill out a form

51. What does the woman say the man should do?

(A) Contact his mailman
(B) Visit the post office
(C) Call again after he moves
(D) Register electronically

52. How long will it take to process the form?

(A) Two days
(B) Three days
(C) Five days
(D) Seven days

53. What problem does the man mention?

(A) More storage space is needed.
(B) His card has been misplaced.
(C) A new security system is malfunctioning.
(D) His application form has not been processed yet.

54. What department does Ms. McDonald probably work in?

(A) Technical Support
(B) Personnel
(C) Security
(D) Maintenance

55. What does the man mean when he says, "Right on time"?

(A) He is not late for a meeting.
(B) He thinks his watch tells the exact time.
(C) His colleagues leave work at 6 P.M.
(D) His card has arrived right when he needs it.

**56.** What will take place next weekend?

(A) A marketing conference
(B) A concert
(C) A fundraiser
(D) A software demonstration

**57.** What is the man concerned about?

(A) Repairing his mobile phone
(B) Purchasing tickets
(C) Exceeding a budget
(D) Making a presentation

**58.** What is the man asked to do?

(A) Reserve some tickets
(B) Visit a new Web site
(C) Call a technician
(D) Tell the woman whether he will attend an event

---

**59.** Why did the woman contact the company?

(A) To reserve a vehicle
(B) To file a complaint
(C) To dispute a bill
(D) To ask about rates

**60.** According to the man, why was the charge made?

(A) A vehicle was returned late.
(B) A gas tank was not full.
(C) There was some damage to a vehicle.
(D) A payment was not made on time.

**61.** Why will the branch manager call the woman?

(A) To confirm a reservation
(B) To finalize the terms of a contract
(C) To complete a payment
(D) To cancel some charges

---

| Name | Capacity | Cost |
|------|----------|------|
| Central Hall | 30 people | $800 |
| Ruby Hall | 40 people | $1,200 |
| Warren Hall | 50 people | $1,700 |
| Emerald Hall | 60 people | $2,000 |

**62.** What will happen next month?

(A) An international conference
(B) An exhibition
(C) A reception
(D) A corporate event

**63.** According to the woman, what did the hotel recently do?

(A) Held a year-end event
(B) Opened a new hall
(C) Expanded its accommodations
(D) Installed wireless Internet

**64.** Look at the graphic. Which place would be the best for the event?

(A) Central Hall
(B) Ruby Hall
(C) Warren Hall
(D) Emerald Hall

▶ ▶ ▶ GO ON TO THE NEXT PAGE

| Hotel | Room / Price |
|---|---|
| Castro Valley Inn | Single Room / $75 |
| | Special Single Room / $100 |
| Bay Hotel | Single Room / $125 |
| | Special Single Room / $200 |

65. What does the woman ask the man to do?

(A) Make a reservation
(B) Identify the source of a problem
(C) Communicate with a client
(D) Compare hotels

66. What is the difference between the two hotels?

(A) The number of bedrooms
(B) The availability of free services
(C) The sizes of the rooms
(D) The quality of customer service

67. Look at the graphic. Which room will the man probably reserve?

(A) Castro Valley Inn - Single Room
(B) Castro Valley Inn – Special Single Room
(C) Bay Hotel – Single Room
(D) Bay Hotel – Special Single Room

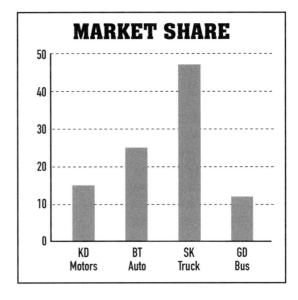

68. What are the speakers talking about?

(A) A new car model
(B) An acquisition plan
(C) A financial crisis
(D) A new marketing strategy

69. Look at the graphic. Where do the speakers probably work?

(A) KD Motors
(B) BT Auto
(C) SK Truck
(D) GD Bus

70. What does the woman say about GD Bus?

(A) It is in financial trouble.
(B) It has overseas branches.
(C) It was founded last year.
(D) Its profits have decreased.

## PART 4

**Directions:** You will hear some short talks given by a single speaker. You will be asked to answer three questions about what the speaker says in each short talk. Select the best response to each question and mark the letter (A), (B), (C), or (D) on your answer sheet. The talks will not be printed in your test book and will be spoken only one time.

**71.** What product is being advertised?

(A) A blender
(B) A food scale
(C) A coffee machine
(D) A professional knife set

**72.** What does the speaker say about the Perfect Balance 46?

(A) It is small.
(B) It is affordable.
(C) It is durable.
(D) It is easy to use.

**73.** According to the speaker, what is being offered?

(A) A cookbook
(B) A special discount
(C) An extended warranty
(D) A free shipping

**74.** What is the purpose of the talk?

(A) To propose several trips
(B) To advertise a travel agency
(C) To introduce a policy
(D) To suggest hiring new employees

**75.** What must employees do before departing on a trip?

(A) Obtain approval
(B) Reserve a flight
(C) Submit a travel report
(D) Reimburse all expenses

**76.** According to the speaker, what should employees keep while traveling?

(A) Order forms
(B) Product samples
(C) Receipts
(D) Boarding passes

**77.** Where do the listeners work?

(A) At a restaurant
(B) At a supermarket
(C) At a travel agency
(D) At a department store

**78.** What does the speaker imply when she says, "We're getting close to the peak travel season"?

(A) Some prices will increase.
(B) There will be more tourists.
(C) Traffic will be getting worse.
(D) A business will have more customers.

**79.** What does the speaker ask the listeners to do?

(A) Work additional hours
(B) Buy some cleaning supplies
(C) Update a work calendar
(D) Turn off their cell phones while working

**80.** What is the purpose of the message?

(A) To apply for a job
(B) To schedule a meeting
(C) To discuss a company merger
(D) To order from another store

**81.** What does the speaker imply when she says, "The grand opening is in two weeks"?

(A) She wants to reserve a table.
(B) A new restaurant should be redesigned.
(C) A hiring decision should be made quickly.
(D) Construction must be completed within two weeks.

**82.** What will the speaker probably do next?

(A) Visit Ms. Lane's office
(B) Fill out a survey form
(C) Interview some applicants
(D) Send a list electronically

▶▶▶GO ON TO THE NEXT PAGE

83. What industry does the speaker most likely work in?

(A) Advertising
(B) Publishing
(C) Hotel and lodging
(D) Retail

84. Why does the speaker say, "They are not what the client is expecting"?

(A) To indicate surprise at a decrease in sales
(B) To express disapproval of a design
(C) To break a contract with a client
(D) To ask employees to keep up with the latest trends

85. What does the speaker recommend the listeners do?

(A) Work overtime tonight
(B) Apply to an advertising company
(C) Attend a marketing seminar
(D) Consult with a colleague

86. When is the news report being broadcast?

(A) In the morning
(B) At noon
(C) In the evening
(D) At midnight

87. According to the speaker, what is causing traffic delays?

(A) Wet roads
(B) Fallen branches
(C) Building construction
(D) Bridge repair

88. What will happen on Tuesday?

(A) Trees will be cut down.
(B) An athletic event will occur.
(C) There will be heavy rainfall.
(D) A road will be closed.

89. What type of business does the speaker probably work in?

(A) Advertising
(B) Nutrition
(C) Journalism
(D) Mental health

90. According to the speaker, why was the listener chosen as an interviewee?

(A) He can speak other languages.
(B) He knows traditional food well.
(C) He has managed his own business.
(D) He has published research papers.

91. What does the speaker ask the listener to do?

(A) E-mail some feedback
(B) Visit a research facility
(C) Sign a publishing contract
(D) Allow an interview

92. Who is the announcement for?

(A) Auto mechanics
(B) Production workers
(C) Maintenance staff members
(D) Safety inspectors

93. According to the speaker, what will begin tomorrow morning?

(A) A regular audit
(B) A plant tour
(C) Maintenance work
(D) A safety inspection

94. What are the listeners asked to do before 10 A.M. tomorrow?

(A) Use different equipment
(B) Report test results
(C) Stop using machines
(D) Complete a form

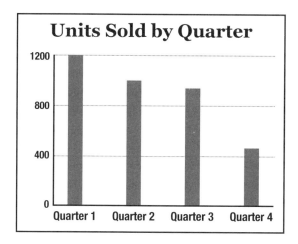

## Units Sold by Quarter

95. What does the company sell?

    (A) Portable music devices
    (B) Mobile devices
    (C) Chemical products
    (D) Office supplies

96. Look at the graphic. When is the meeting taking place?

    (A) Quarter 1
    (B) Quarter 2
    (C) Quarter 3
    (D) Quarter 4

97. What does the speaker want to discuss next?

    (A) Ways to increase sales
    (B) Web site design
    (C) Client complaints
    (D) Business expansion plans

## Franklin Fresh Market
### 30% Discount This Weekend!

| Sale Item | Store Location |
|---|---|
| Fresh Produce | Fremont |
| Dairy Products | San Jose |
| Beverages | Cupertino |
| Baked Goods | Oakland |

98. What is Franklin Fresh Market celebrating?

    (A) Its anniversary
    (B) The opening of a new store
    (C) A national holiday
    (D) A profitable quarter

99. Look at the graphic. At which store location is the announcement being made?

    (A) Fremont
    (B) San Jose
    (C) Cupertino
    (D) Oakland

100. Why should the listeners visit a Web site?

    (A) To vote for the employee of the week
    (B) To check for job openings
    (C) To sign up for a membership program
    (D) To write a customer review

This is the end of the Listening test. Turn to Part 5 in your test book.

▶▶▶GO ON TO THE NEXT PAGE

# READING TEST

In the Reading test, you will read a variety of texts and answer several different types of reading comprehension questions. The entire Reading test will last 75 minutes. There are three parts, and directions are given for each part. You are encouraged to answer as many questions as possible within the time allowed.

You must mark your answers on the separate answer sheet. Do not write your answers in your test book.

## PART 5

**Directions**: A word or phrase is missing in each of the sentences below. Four answer choices are given below each sentence. Select the best answer to complete the sentence. Then mark the letter (A), (B), (C), or (D) on your answer sheet.

---

**101.** Ms. Keller usually attends trade fairs by -------, but she will take some colleagues to the one in Tokyo.

(A) she
(B) her
(C) hers
(D) herself

**102.** Because of the bad weather conditions, there was a small ------- at the local film festival yesterday.

(A) crowd
(B) crowds
(C) crowding
(D) crowded

**103.** The refund request form must be put in writing and delivered ------- hand to the customer service desk.

(A) on
(B) by
(C) through
(D) with

**104.** Ms. Ryan is ------- to meet with our important client at 10 o'clock tomorrow morning.

(A) available
(B) prospective
(C) possible
(D) critical

**105.** Tickets for the new musical were ------- sold out, so the theater decided to add more shows next week.

(A) completion
(B) completing
(C) complete
(D) completely

**106.** Among the applicants, Ms. Reagan is the ------- one for the head accountant position.

(A) qualified
(B) more qualified
(C) most qualified
(D) qualification

**107.** Most marketing departments ------- searchable databases to collect marketing data.

(A) user
(B) using
(C) uses
(D) use

**108.** With the purchase of any new cosmetic product from CoCo, a stylish gift bag will be ------- for free.

(A) you
(B) your
(C) yours
(D) yourself

**109.** ------- an online portfolio is highly recommended for job seekers on the graphic design career path.

(A) Creating
(B) Creation
(C) Create
(D) Creative

**110.** Most financial institutions advise their customers to change their passwords regularly to make sure their personal information is kept ------- at all times.

(A) imperative
(B) confident
(C) secure
(D) adjusted

**111.** A recent study indicates ------- nine out of ten office workers enjoy the freedom to wear casual clothing occasionally.

(A) when
(B) that
(C) whether
(D) although

**112.** Accountants at the JH Accounting Firm must complete at least 40 hours ------- training annually.

(A) of
(B) during
(C) from
(D) before

**113.** ------- of the analysts in London predict the size of the online marketing industry will explode as social commerce companies grow rapidly.

(A) Every
(B) Most
(C) Each
(D) Other

**114.** Our stocks usually benefit ------- so-called January effect that causes the prices of some stocks to rise between December and January.

(A) of
(B) since
(C) from
(D) within

**115.** Countless devoted fans responded ------- throughout the new musical *Romantic Cats*.

(A) enthusiasm
(B) enthusiast
(C) enthusiastic
(D) enthusiastically

**116.** The BK Corporation offers special language courses to teach employees the proper way ------- foreign languages.

(A) speak
(B) to speak
(C) speaking
(D) spoken

**117.** Although Dr. Roberts has retired from the general hospital in New York, he ------- provides voluntary medical services.

(A) ever
(B) already
(C) enough
(D) still

**118.** Mr. Nguyen will receive an award next week for his exceptional ------- in the fashion industry.

(A) achieve
(B) achieves
(C) achievable
(D) achievement

**119.** The breakable items must be fully wrapped so as to ------- damage during delivery.

(A) disrupt
(B) prevent
(C) cause
(D) claim

**120.** The Quick Shave is a rechargeable electric razor that does not need ------- standard batteries.

(A) much
(B) frequent
(C) any
(D) either

121. ------- Mr. Lee has been transferred to the new branch in Manchester, our branch is currently selecting his replacement.

(A) Even though
(B) In addition to
(C) If not
(D) Now that

122. Audient Power ------- the brand power of major foreign companies based on their global market shares and export volumes.

(A) built
(B) evaluated
(C) decided
(D) attracted

123. According to our personnel director, several experienced employees ------- at the job fair in Seoul next month.

(A) to recruit
(B) recruiting
(C) recruited
(D) will be recruited

124. ------- completion of the accounting courses offered by Oakland Community College, diplomas will be issued to graduates.

(A) Of
(B) For
(C) Until
(D) Upon

125. All of the board members expect employees to respond to customers ------- lodge complaints about our products within two business days.

(A) they
(B) who
(C) whose
(D) what

126. The sales tax rate was set at 3.3% ten years ago, but it has since been ------- increased by the government.

(A) intensely
(B) extensively
(C) shortly
(D) incrementally

127. Many experts say that solving customer problems ------- is one of the most crucial key elements for business success.

(A) increasingly
(B) entirely
(C) consistently
(D) simultaneously

128. By the time the chief executive officer returns to the office from his vacation, the sales director ------- several new clients who want to import our new mobile devices.

(A) meets
(B) has met
(C) had met
(D) will have met

129. ------- much the company earns, the analysis report underlines the difficulty of making ends meet at our current profit levels.

(A) Whoever
(B) When
(C) Whether
(D) However

130. ------- gas prices are becoming stable now, many people are choosing to take the subway or bus throughout the city instead of driving their own cars.

(A) Provided that
(B) Even though
(C) Seeing that
(D) Despite

# PART 6

**Directions:** Read the texts that follow. A word, phrase, or sentence is missing in parts of each text. Four answer choices for each question are given below the text. Select the best answer to complete the text. Then mark the letter (A), (B), (C), or (D) on your answer sheet.

**Questions 131-134** refer to the following memorandum.

To: All employees
From: David Kisling, Store Manager
Date: September 9
Subject: Reminders

It has come to my attention that many customers who recently visited our store have complained about the attitudes of some staff members.

Please be reminded that our objective is to bring our customers the best service at all times, and the quality of the service we provide is dependent on each store staff member who ------- serves customers.
    **131.**

Let us get back to basics and start by greeting customers with a smile and asking if they need help with anything. -------, please do not just walk away after you are done assisting
        **132.**
customers. Instead, ask them once more if they need further -------.
            **133.**

-------. I will be expecting better attitudes from all store staff members and, hopefully,
**134.**
greater satisfaction from our customers as well.

---

**131.** (A) direct
(B) direction
(C) directs
(D) directly

**132.** (A) Otherwise
(B) Even so
(C) In addition
(D) As soon as

**133.** (A) improvement
(B) notice
(C) question
(D) assistance

**134.** (A) This will help you better assist our customers for the following reasons.
(B) In spite of the promotional event we held, our sales remained the same.
(C) A simple favor you do today may change our store's image for a lifetime.
(D) Keep up the good work to maintain the current customer satisfaction level.

▶ ▶ ▶GO ON TO THE NEXT PAGE

**MEMORANDUM**

To: All employees
From: Daniel Blake, Head of Personnel
Date: September 9
Subject: A new mailing policy

To help ------- our mailing system work more efficiently, Jambo Computer has decided to
**135.**

change our current mailing policy.

All of our internal mail will change to use unique envelopes that will be provided in the

mailroom on the ground floor. These new envelopes will not cost our employees anything

and will be marked with a special insignia to differentiate them from ------- used for customer
**136.**

postal mail.

Any internal mail that is ready to be picked up for delivery should ------- in the bin at the end
**137.**

of every hallway by the end of the afternoon.

-------. Please be aware that this new mailing policy is to protect employees as well as the
**138.**

company.

135. (A) make
(B) makes
(C) made
(D) making

136. (A) what
(B) which
(C) those
(D) them

137. (A) place
(B) be placed
(C) have placed
(D) placing

138. (A) Recently, many items have been
stolen from parcels.
(B) An unhealthy mailing policy reduces
productivity.
(C) Postal rates have recently climbed at
a fast pace.
(D) We have suffered from leaks of our
corporate secrets to our competitors.

BK Office Machinery, Inc.
128 South Street
Queens, New York 10111

May 5

Preston Manufacturing, Inc.
888 Grand Avenue
Los Angeles, CA 90037

To Whom It May Concern:

We intend ------- a new office copier before the end of the fiscal year. We would like to
    **139.**
consider your copier and wonder if you have a model that would suit our needs.

Our company is small, and the copier would generally be used by twenty employees. We

make ------- 7,800 copies a month and prefer a machine that uses regular paper. -------.
    **140.**                                                                        **141.**

Since our fiscal year ------- on June 30, we hope to hear from you as soon as possible.
                      **142.**

Sincerely yours,

Brandon Parker
Personnel Manager
BK Office Machinery, Inc.

**139.** (A) purchase
(B) purchasing
(C) having purchased
(D) to purchase

**140.** (A) approximate
(B) approximating
(C) approximately
(D) approximation

**141.** (A) We would also like to know about your warranty and repair service.
(B) A printer which is combined with a scanner can function as a kind of photocopier.
(C) We are happy to supply you with the estimate you requested.
(D) The company expressed disappointment at the deadline being missed.

**142.** (A) end
(B) ends
(C) has ended
(D) ended

**Questions 143-146** refer to the following article.

### Moto Electronics is now set to rebuild itself as a global electronics leader

By Kate Thompson
Sept. 24 Updated 7:48 p.m. ET

Moto Electronics announced today that it ------- Green Computer in a deal valued at 20
**143.**
million dollars.

Andrew Kim, a spokesperson for Moto Electronics, said this morning the company had

purchased Green Computer to bolster its overseas operations to improve its global -------.
**144.**

He also said Moto Electronics aims to double its global sales by the end of next year.

-------. Therefore, most industry experts strongly believe this acquisition will make Moto
**145.**
Electronics the leading producer and vendor of memory chips and computer parts since

Green Computer is expected to offset the weakest points of Moto Electronics.

Moto Electronics plans to ------- Green Computer's current workforce and to hire additional
**146.**
employees over the next two years.

143. (A) organized
(B) merged
(C) sold
(D) acquired

144. (A) compete
(B) competitor
(C) competitiveness
(D) competition

145. (A) Green Computer has a strong sales network and marketshare.
(B) It is regarded as one of the best-managed large corporations in North America.
(C) The board of Moto Electronics made a big decision to recruit foreign employees next year.
(D) We will accomplish this goal by making use of our recently updated production facilities.

146. (A) encourage
(B) seek
(C) maintain
(D) protect

## PART 7

**Directions:** In this part you will read a selection of texts, such as magazine and newspaper articles, e-mails, and instant messages. Each text or set of texts is followed by several questions. Select the best answer for each question and mark the letter (A), (B), (C), or (D) on your answer sheet.

Questions 147-148 refer to the following e-mail.

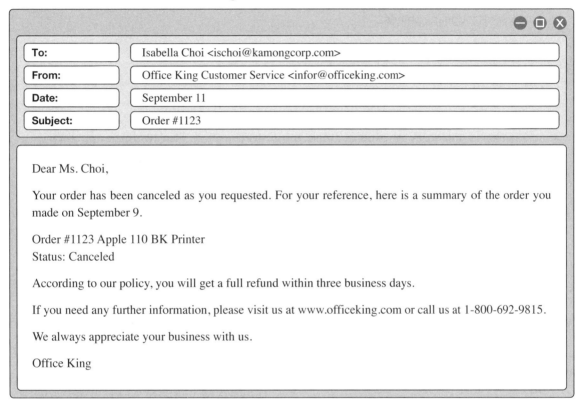

To: Isabella Choi <ischoi@kamongcorp.com>
From: Office King Customer Service <infor@officeking.com>
Date: September 11
Subject: Order #1123

Dear Ms. Choi,

Your order has been canceled as you requested. For your reference, here is a summary of the order you made on September 9.

Order #1123 Apple 110 BK Printer
Status: Canceled

According to our policy, you will get a full refund within three business days.

If you need any further information, please visit us at www.officeking.com or call us at 1-800-692-9815.

We always appreciate your business with us.

Office King

**147.** Why was the e-mail sent?
(A) To inquire about a refund policy
(B) To inform a customer of a sales promotion
(C) To confirm an order cancelation
(D) To correct a mistake

**148.** What is suggested about Ms. Choi?
(A) She already paid for the item.
(B) She will get a full refund next week.
(C) She will receive a printer in three days.
(D) She has been offered a special discount.

▶ ▶ ▶ GO ON TO THE NEXT PAGE

## Attention, Creative Writing Students!

The annual Sandstone Short Story Writing Contest has begun.

Entries are now being accepted until the deadline of October 30. All short stories should be between 1,000 and 4,000 words in length and can be on any topic. A panel of noted authors – horror novelist Samuel J. Kingston, mystery writer Janice Bonderman, and essayist Diana Jacobi – will judge the entries.

**There will be numerous prizes awarded in two different age categories:**
• Ages 16 and under
• Ages 17-19

The winner of the major prize of Most Promising Writer will receive a $1,000 university scholarship, a three-day all-expenses-paid trip to New York to visit two major publishing houses, and the publication of the winner's short story in the Sandstone Beacon Gazette.

**Registration forms are available from English teachers at all local area schools. Send the forms in by mail to:**
Sandstone Short Story Writing Contest
P.O. Box 50
Sandstone, VA 65455

Best of luck to all budding writers out there!

149. What date must all entries be received by?
(A) October 3
(B) October 16
(C) October 19
(D) October 30

150 Where should registration forms be sent?
(A) To Samuel J. Kingston
(B) To the local newspaper
(C) To a post office box
(D) To the local community center

151. What will the top prizewinner get?
(A) A full four-year university scholarship
(B) A week's stay in New York with all expenses paid
(C) A chance to meet top publishers
(D) A position at a popular magazine

Questions 152-153 refer to the following text message chain.

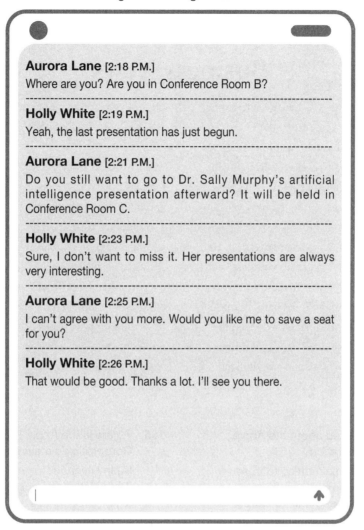

**Aurora Lane** [2:18 P.M.]
Where are you? Are you in Conference Room B?

------------------------------------------------------------

**Holly White** [2:19 P.M.]
Yeah, the last presentation has just begun.

------------------------------------------------------------

**Aurora Lane** [2:21 P.M.]
Do you still want to go to Dr. Sally Murphy's artificial intelligence presentation afterward? It will be held in Conference Room C.

------------------------------------------------------------

**Holly White** [2:23 P.M.]
Sure, I don't want to miss it. Her presentations are always very interesting.

------------------------------------------------------------

**Aurora Lane** [2:25 P.M.]
I can't agree with you more. Would you like me to save a seat for you?

------------------------------------------------------------

**Holly White** [2:26 P.M.]
That would be good. Thanks a lot. I'll see you there.

**152.** At 2:25 P.M., what does Ms. Lane most likely mean when she writes, "I can't agree with you more"?

(A) She thinks there is no evidence to support Dr. Murphy's theory.
(B) She is certain Ms. White's opinion is not as good as hers.
(C) She is very impressed with Ms. White's presentation.
(D) She agrees with Ms. White's opinion of Dr. Murphy's speech.

**153.** What is probably true about Ms. Lane?

(A) She will go to Conference Room C before Ms. White.
(B) She will make a presentation after Dr. Murphy.
(C) She has already reserved a conference room for an event.
(D) She wants to write a thesis on artificial intelligence with Ms. White.

▶ ▶ ▶GO ON TO THE NEXT PAGE

**Questions 154-155** refer to the following article.

# World Economy Leader
## Business News

September 9, Los Angeles - Lance Merrier, the vice president of the Apple Republic Corporation, released a statement on Tuesday stating that the company is going through with plans to open stores in Chicago, Atlanta, New York, and New Orleans within the next year.

Mr. Merrier admitted a mistake on his part. He confessed that the main problem with last year's unsuccessful expansion was that the company was not yet strong enough financially to make that kind of move then. He acknowledged that the company had misjudged its value. With a strong marketing campaign and a revitalized mission, the company maintains that expansion will be far easier this time.

The Los Angeles-based Apple Republic Corporation was founded by Christopher Lee and maintains a clean and classic style marketed at middle-aged adults. The company will begin adding a new line of clothing for youths in the spring at all of its stores. The company will keep a close watch on how well its first foray into children's clothing starts out. Early projections have the four new stores bringing in record numbers, but no one at the company is going to believe that until they see it.

154. What is suggested about the Apple Republic Corporation?

(A) It moved its main office to Los Angeles.
(B) It recently closed half its stores.
(C) It carries children's clothing.
(D) Its merchandise is currently limited to adults.

155. Where is the Apple Republic Corporation's main office?

(A) In Chicago
(B) In New York
(C) In Los Angeles
(D) In New Orleans

**Questions 156-157** refer to the following memorandum.

To: Dr. Harvey Davis, Chief Resident
From: Dr. Dana Kamon, Head of Pediatrics
Subject: Nursing shortage

As you know from the buzz around the wards, the staff shortages are becoming too much of a distraction. We all know we need more nurses, but the budget is tight. I propose job sharing because that might at least provide a temporary solution to the crisis.

Of course, in the long term, we need to hire full-time nurses, but here in Pediatrics, where we have had job sharing for over a year, we feel it works well. I'm not saying it's a perfect situation, but to cover shortages of staff, it has worked.

**156.** What is the memo mainly about?

(A) A shortage of hospital beds
(B) Doctors working too many long shifts
(C) Patient care in the pediatric ward
(D) A nurse staffing problem

**157.** What solution is offered by Dr. Kamon?

(A) Job sharing by nurses
(B) Hiring more full-time doctors
(C) Cutting the nursing staff
(D) Rotating doctors from ward to ward

# Sea World
# The Pacific Ocean Hotel

Welcome to the Pacific Ocean Hotel. We hope you thoroughly enjoy your stay. If you are looking for a restaurant with delicious food and the best view in town, look no further than Sea World, the restaurant located on the 1st floor. Chef Albert Cardoza serves up the freshest food of the day all evening long, and there is a table waiting just for you.

Sea World is open from Tuesday through Sunday from 11:00 A.M. until 11:30 P.M. If you are in your room and would like to order room service, there is a menu in every room. You can order anything from the Sea World menu during regular restaurant hours.

Hotel guests can come and visit this Sunday from 1:00 P.M. until 3:00 P.M. You can enjoy a shrimp and crab feast. All you need to do is bring this advertisement with you to the restaurant, and you can enjoy an unlimited amount of succulent crab legs and giant shrimp at absolutely no cost to you.

**158.** At what time does the restaurant open on Wednesdays?

(A) 11:00 A.M.
(B) 11:30 A.M.
(C) 1:00 P.M.
(D) 3:00 P.M.

**159.** What is NOT indicated about room service?

(A) It includes the full menu.
(B) Items can be bought for low prices.
(C) It is available during business hours.
(D) The food comes from Sea World.

**160.** What will the Pacific Ocean Hotel provide its guests with?

(A) A discount coupon for the restaurant
(B) Complimentary room service
(C) Free seafood meals for certain customers
(D) Special water ballet shows

**Questions 161-163** refer to the following memorandum.

From: Wesley Kim, Personnel Manager

To: All employees

Date: September 15

Subject: Maintenance Work

Dear colleagues:

Please be advised that our underground parking lot will be unavailable from October 2 through October 5 due to some maintenance work that will be done then. —[1]—. It is scheduled to reopen on Monday, October 6. Those of you who drive to work are encouraged to use nearby parking lots such as the Downtown Public Parking Lot. The company will reimburse you any parking costs incurred. —[2]—. You can also discuss with your department heads the possibility of working from home if you have a long commute. —[3]—.

We will have ten additional parking spaces once the maintenance work is complete. —[4]—. If you are a full-time employee and have worked here for over three years, you qualify to enter the lottery to be granted one. Please call me at ext. 1123 to enter the lottery.

Thank you for your understanding and cooperation in advance.

Wesley Kim

Personnel Manager

Hayward Accounting Firm

**161.** According to the personnel manager, what can employees talk about with their supervisors?

(A) Transitioning to permanent employment
(B) A lottery drawing for a parking space
(C) The possibility of telecommuting
(D) The reimbursement of their travel expenses

**162.** What is probably true about the Downtown Public Parking Lot?

(A) It will reopen on October 6.
(B) It charges people to park their vehicles there.
(C) It is far from the Hayward Accounting Firm.
(D) It was recently expanded.

**163.** In which of the positions marked [1], [2], [3], and [4] does the following sentence best belong?

"We have decided to expand the underground parking lot to provide room for more vehicles."

(A) [1]
(B) [2]
(C) [3]
(D) [4]

To: Chris Bundy <cbundy@dahmercorp.com>

From: Yuliana Lim <ylim@trentonhotel.com>

Date: August 19

Subject: Trenton Hotel Reservation Inquiry

Dear Mr. Bundy,

I just received your e-mail regarding your reservation at our hotel. You are correct that your September stay will be eligible for our Reward Points Plan for frequent guests. —[1]—.

In your e-mail, you mentioned that you would like to check in earlier than usual on September 1. As you are probably aware, our normal check-in time is not until 2 P.M., but we will do our best to have your room ready by noon. —[2]—. You may call the front desk in advance to ask about this. If you choose to turn up early and your assigned room is still being prepared, you may leave your luggage with the front desk staff, and they will store it securely while you relax or walk around town.

You are also correct about the issue regarding your July stay here. Due to a computer error, we failed to refund the $100 security deposit after you checked out. I personally made sure that the amount was refunded to your credit card this morning. —[3]—. To make amends for this mistake, I have arranged for you to receive a gift certificate that can be exchanged for two tickets to see any film at the nearby Odeon Cinema.

If you have any further questions, please contact me directly at 555-5674. —[4]—.

Regards,

Yuliana Lim
Trenton Hotel Reservations Manager

**164.** What is the purpose of the e-mail?

(A) To inform a guest that a checkout time has been changed

(B) To request that a guest send an advance payment

(C) To notify a guest that a room is unavailable on a certain date

(D) To confirm that a guest is eligible for a special program

**165.** What is mentioned about the Trenton Hotel?

(A) It is situated next to a fitness center.

(B) It recently renovated some of its rooms.

(C) It allows guests to store their bags there.

(D) It notified Mr. Bundy about reduced room rates.

**166.** What problem did Mr. Bundy experience when he last stayed at the Trenton Hotel?

(A) He was overcharged for room service.

(B) He did not receive his security deposit.

(C) He lost some of his personal belongings.

(D) He arrived after the standard check-in time.

**167.** In which of the positions marked [1], [2], [3], and [4] does the following sentence best belong?

"I apologize for this oversight and any inconvenience it may have caused you."

(A) [1]

(B) [2]

(C) [3]

(D) [4]

▶ ▶ ▶ GO ON TO THE NEXT PAGE

Calvert City News

# A Chance to Escape the City

### By Kelly McGowan

MAY 23 – Rather than focusing on activities and restaurants here in Calvert City, I decided to make this week's column a little different by discussing the beautiful town of Greybridge, just 20 kilometers north of the city limits. Greybridge is a quaint, peaceful little town that offers people the chance to escape the noise and chaos of the city. It also boasts a surprising number of things to do and places to eat. Below, you can read my suggestions for planning an enjoyable day-trip to Greybridge.

(8:30 A.M.) When you arrive, you should head straight for Dale Bakery. Although it is primarily a bakery, selling various breads and pastries, it also has a dining area and has a limited, yet delicious, menu. It is a long-time fixture in Greybridge, and it has become particularly well-known for its delicious breakfast offerings. Try the full English breakfast with some freshly brewed coffee.

(9:45 A.M.) After gaining energy from your delicious breakfast, I recommend taking a walk along the nearby Glenford River. Not only is the entire area picturesque, but it also contains several sites of interest. During your walk, stop to check out the many sculptures and murals at Balgay Art Park, and don't miss the Alton Farm Petting Zoo, which will be of particular interest to young children.

(1:30 P.M.) Once you've worked up an appetite walking along the river, head back into town and visit Alma's Country Kitchen for lunch. Although it has not been open long, it has already established itself as one of the town's premier eateries. Alma's serves dishes that are made using only produce from nearby farms and suppliers, and I would like to single out its expertly cooked grilled salmon and chopped salad for special praise. Its menu can be viewed online at www.almascountrykitchen.co.uk. Be warned, however, that you may face a long wait if you go there on the weekend. It's also possible to take out certain foods, such as baguettes and baked potatoes, which means you can enjoy them in nearby Meadow Park if you choose. This is a great choice when the weather is nice.

(3:00 P.M.) For the remainder of your day in Greybridge, try taking a guided tour of Greybridge Cathedral. This stunning building was built in the late-15th century and is preserved and maintained by the Greybridge Cultural Heritage Society. One wing of the cathedral has been converted into an art gallery, which features various works of art made by local painters and sculptors. Admission to both the cathedral and the gallery is free from Monday to Thursday. At all other times, a ticket can be purchased at the main entrance. Check www.greybridgecathedral.org for current rates.

Do you have any of your own suggestions regarding what to do on day-trips to Greybridge? If so, please send your thoughts to kmcgowan@calvertnews.org.

186

**168.** The word "boasts" in paragraph 1, line 8, is closest in meaning to

(A) awards
(B) announces
(C) equips
(D) offers

**169.** What is suggested about Ms. McGowan's column?

(A) It often focuses on Greybridge.
(B) It ordinarily includes interviews.
(C) It is a weekly feature in a publication.
(D) It is the publication's newest column.

**170.** According to the article, what is true about Alma's Country Kitchen?

(A) It offers a wide variety of baked goods.
(B) It opens for business at 1:30 P.M. every day.
(C) It uses only locally sourced ingredients.
(D) It is generally less busy on weekends.

**171.** What is NOT a recommendation made by Ms. McGowan?

(A) Purchasing a ticket for the cathedral in advance
(B) Taking restaurant food to a local park
(C) Visiting an exhibition of paintings
(D) Submitting ideas for things to do in Greybridge

**Questions 172-175** refer to the following online chat discussion.

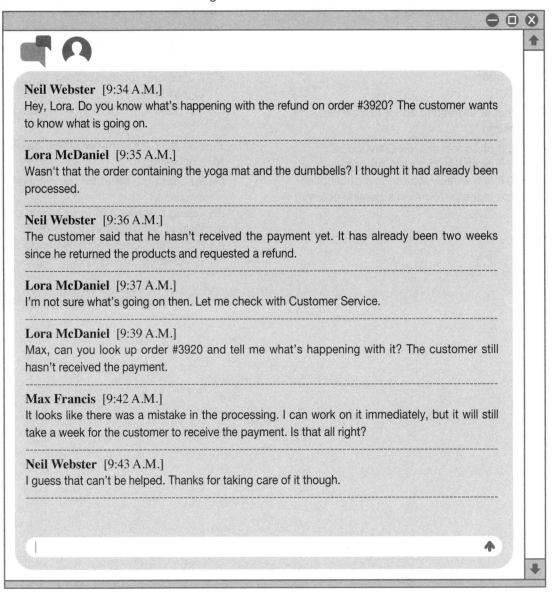

**Neil Webster** [9:34 A.M.]
Hey, Lora. Do you know what's happening with the refund on order #3920? The customer wants to know what is going on.

---

**Lora McDaniel** [9:35 A.M.]
Wasn't that the order containing the yoga mat and the dumbbells? I thought it had already been processed.

---

**Neil Webster** [9:36 A.M.]
The customer said that he hasn't received the payment yet. It has already been two weeks since he returned the products and requested a refund.

---

**Lora McDaniel** [9:37 A.M.]
I'm not sure what's going on then. Let me check with Customer Service.

---

**Lora McDaniel** [9:39 A.M.]
Max, can you look up order #3920 and tell me what's happening with it? The customer still hasn't received the payment.

---

**Max Francis** [9:42 A.M.]
It looks like there was a mistake in the processing. I can work on it immediately, but it will still take a week for the customer to receive the payment. Is that all right?

---

**Neil Webster** [9:43 A.M.]
I guess that can't be helped. Thanks for taking care of it though.

---

**172.** What type of business do the writers work for?

(A) A real estate agency
(B) An exercise equipment store
(C) An accounting firm
(D) A fitness center

**173.** What did the customer ask for?

(A) A refund on a previous order
(B) A change in a shipping address
(C) An addition on an order
(D) An update on the delivery of an order

**174.** Why does Ms. McDaniel contact Mr. Francis?

(A) To ask for advice on the delivery of a product
(B) To look up where a returned package is
(C) To find out if she can get a refund on her order
(D) To know why a refund has not been processed yet

**175.** At 9:43 A.M, what does Mr. Webster most likely mean when he writes, "I guess that can't be helped"?

(A) He wants Mr. Francis to handle a problem immediately.
(B) He accepts the fact that it will take time to fix a problem.
(C) He does not understand why a process will take so long.
(D) He is asking for additional help from Customer Service.

▶ ▶ ▶ GO ON TO THE NEXT PAGE

# SIMMONS HEAT & AIR

April 2
Jessie Spano
Dunder Miflin Corp.
9923 Swanson Street
Nashville, TN 92929

Dear Ms. Spano,

We were going through our records during the past few days and found that the heating unit you installed at your company was purchased almost a year ago. This message is a recommendation to have your system examined. As noted in your contract, your purchase comes with a five-year warranty, so you can have any defective parts replaced for free. Just send us an e-mail to schedule a convenient time for us to come by to check the unit out.

Even if you think the unit is working fine right now, it is never a bad thing to have it checked to make sure nothing is close to wearing out or breaking. It will save you lots of money in the long run. In addition, do not hesitate to schedule a service call immediately because the winter months can get very busy with requests, house calls, and service repairs.

Get in touch with us as soon as you can to ensure that you are cozy and warm throughout the winter months. You can call us at 606-555-0994 or e-mail us at customerservice@simmonshna.com.

Sincerely,

J. K. Simmons *J. K. Simmons*
President
Simmons Heat & Air

To: &lt;customerservice@simmonshna.com&gt;

From: &lt;jspano@dundermif.com&gt;

Date: April 5

Subject: Heating Unit Inspection

Dear Mr. Simmons,

I received your letter about inspecting my current heating system. You are correct in your assessment that our unit has not been examined since we purchased it. I do think it is time we get a proper inspection to ensure that it is running efficiently. Would it be possible to send someone out next week?

I would also like the service technician to check out our current air-conditioning system. We are looking into getting a new one because our current one is old and unreliable. We are in the office from 9 A.M. until 6 P.M., so you can send a service technician any time we are here. Just e-mail and inform me when your technician will be coming by.

Thank you.

Jessie Spano
Director of Operations
Dunder Miflin Corp.

ACTUAL TEST... 04

**176.** What is the purpose of the letter?

(A) To recommend a service
(B) To report test retake days
(C) To cancel an appointment
(D) To inquire about a replacement part

**177.** According to Mr. Simmons, why should an inspection be scheduled promptly?

(A) The winter weather damaged some components.
(B) A manufacturing error has been detected.
(C) The warranty will expire at the end of the fall.
(D) It will be difficult to schedule an inspection in winter.

**178.** When was the heating system at the Dunder Miflin Corp. inspected?

(A) One week ago
(B) One month ago
(C) One year ago
(D) Two years ago

**179.** What is suggested about the Dunder Miflin Corp.'s air-conditioning system?

(A) It is broken.
(B) It is not in good working order.
(C) It has never been inspected.
(D) It was installed recently.

**180.** In the e-mail, the phrase "looking into" in paragraph 2, line 1, is closest in meaning to

(A) expecting
(B) investigating
(C) observing
(D) researching

▶ ▶ ▶ GO ON TO THE NEXT PAGE

# MEMO

From: Nancy Palosi, Executive Assistant, Office of the Vice President
To: Carmina Falcone, Chief Financial Officer
Date: September 13
Subject: Bixby, Inc. Tour

The itinerary has unfortunately been changed for next month's Bixby, Inc. facilities tour starting in El Paso and ending in San Antonio. I have listed the new dates and times of your flights from Seattle to El Paso as well as from El Paso to San Antonio below. Your flight from San Antonio to Seattle has not been determined yet. I will give that information to you as soon as I have it.

| | |
|---|---|
| **Flight E443** | Departing Seattle 10:00 A.M., September 19 |
| | Arrive El Paso 12:50 P.M., September 19 |
| **Flight F559** | Departing El Paso 2:40 P.M., September 21 |
| | Arrive San Antonio 4:30 P.M., September 21 |

Mr. Stern's flight arrives in El Paso a few hours before you, so he has asked if you could contact him once you have landed. The two of you will then proceed to Bixby, Inc.'s El Paso plant, and the tour will then commence. Because of the arrival time of your flight, the meeting has been moved back to 2:00 P.M.

---

| | |
|---|---|
| **To:** | Nancy Palosi <npalosi@millerco.com> |
| **From:** | David Thornbush <guestservice@grandritz.com> |
| **Date:** | September 11 |
| **Subject:** | Your requests for Ms. Falcone and Mr. Stern |

This is a confirmation of the reservation you made over the phone last week for Carmina Falcone and Daniel Stern at the Grand Ritz Hotel. Two single rooms have been booked on the executive floor. All their business needs will be met inside their rooms. Each room is equipped with a computer with Internet access, a printer, and a fax machine. I received the package that was sent by courier from your company in Seattle. It will be placed in Ms. Falcone's room when she arrives.

As Mr. Stern is arriving around 10:00 A.M., I have arranged for him to have an early check-in time of 10:30 A.M. free of charge. Mr. Stern and Ms. Falcone can make full use of Conference Room C at 2:00 P.M. on the day of their arrival. Conference Room C is located on basement level one. We have also included a special dinner for our two guests at our hotel restaurant, the Olive. The meals will be charged to the guests' account. If you have any questions at all about their stay, please contact us before their arrival, and I am sure we can assist you. Thank you.

Mina Sohn
Service Manager
Grand Ritz Hotel, El Paso

**181.** What is the main purpose of Ms. Palosi's memo?

(A) To request a new date for a trip
(B) To determine who is going on a trip
(C) To confirm a change in travel plans
(D) To cancel a planned meeting

**182.** Where will the facilities tour take place?

(A) In El Paso
(B) In San Antonio
(C) In Seattle and El Paso
(D) In El Paso and San Antonio

**183.** Where will the two guests hold their meeting?

(A) In a hotel conference room
(B) In the San Antonio office
(C) At the El Paso facility
(D) In Ms. Falcone's office

**184.** What is mentioned about Mr. Stern's arrival?

(A) It will be delayed because his flight was canceled.
(B) It will take place before the documents from the office arrive.
(C) It will be earlier than the standard hotel check-in time.
(D) It will be after Ms. Falcone has arrived.

**185.** What is NOT mentioned about the guest rooms that have been reserved?

(A) They are single rooms.
(B) They have office equipment.
(C) They are on the same floor.
(D) They are adjacent to the dining room.

▶ ▶ ▶ GO ON TO THE NEXT PAGE

Questions 186-190 refer to the following letter, schedule, and e-mail.

# NOBLE BOOKSTORE

741 Piccailly Avenue
Dundee, UK
DD4 8TW

Mr. Frank Peterson
42 Mitchell Avenue
Dundee, UK
DD4 8TW

May 23

Dear Mr. Peterson,

Thank you for your interest in our upcoming book signing events. At Noble Bookstore, we work hard to connect our customers with their favorite authors through these exciting events. I have enclosed a schedule for our June and July book signings. However, this schedule has been changed. Please note that the book signing on June 22 has now been moved from its original 3:15 p.m.-5:00 p.m. time slot to a new 10:30 a.m.-12:00 p.m. time slot. Similarly, the book signing on July 22 will now begin at 2:15 p.m. instead of 10:30 a.m. All other details on the enclosed schedule are precise. There is no admission fee or registration required for our book signings; simply turn up on the day with something for the author to sign. The authors will each be promoting their latest novel, so you should buy a copy if you haven't done so already. If you have any further questions, please e-mail me at ghopkins@noblebooks.com.

Regards,

Gerald Hopkins

## Noble Bookstore
### Book Signing Schedule - June/July

| Date | Time | Author | Book Title |
|------|------|--------|-----------|
| June 5 | 10:30 a.m. – 12:00 p.m. | Casey Bakke | Forest of Echoes |
| June 13 | 2:00 p.m. – 3:30 p.m. | Rachel Durst | Safe From Harm |
| June 22 | 3:15 p.m. – 5:00 p.m. | Karim Benzia | A Drop In the Ocean |
| June 27 | 4:15 p.m. – 6:00 p.m. | Elsa Aronson | Story of Your Life |
| July 5 | 2:15 p.m. – 4:00 p.m. | Viktor Fischer | Cave of Forgotten Dreams |
| July 11 | 10:00 a.m. – 11:30 a.m. | Lisa Kimberly | Ghosts of Meliora |
| July 22 | 10:30 a.m. – 12:15 p.m. | Yuri Utsugi | The Happy House |
| July 25 | 5:15 p.m. – 7:00 p.m. | Amanda Davis | Blackened Feathers |

| To: | Gerald Hopkins <ghopkins@noblebooks.com> |
| From: | Frank Peterson <fpeterson@dunhillco.com> |
| Date: | May 24 |
| Subject: | Summer Book Signings |

Dear Mr. Hopkins,

Thank you for responding to my letter and sending me the book signing schedule. As an avid reader, I'm pleased to see that one of my favorite authors will be visiting your store this summer to participate in a book signing event. Given how close I live to your store, I'm surprised that I have never attended one of your signing events before. If I hadn't heard about your book signings from my coworker, I would never have known about them. Perhaps you should consider advertising them more aggressively in your store. I assume there is probably book signing information on your Web site, but I rarely buy books online. I'm really looking forward to meeting my favorite author, and I'll bring along my new copy of *Ghosts of Meliora* to be signed. Thanks once again for your reply.

Best wishes,

Frank Peterson

**186.** Whose book signing has been moved to an afternoon time slot?

(A) Casey Bakke
(B) Karim Benzia
(C) Viktor Fischer
(D) Yuri Utsugi

**187.** In the letter, the word "precise" in paragraph 1, line 6, is closest in meaning to

(A) punctual
(B) early
(C) calculated
(D) accurate

**188.** What does Mr. Hopkins encourage Mr. Peterson to do?

(A) Register in advance for a book signing
(B) Confirm his intention to attend an event
(C) Purchase a recently-released publication
(D) Prepare an extra copy of a document

**189.** When is Mr. Peterson planning to attend a book signing?

(A) On June 13
(B) On June 27
(C) On July 11
(D) On July 25

**190.** What can be inferred about Mr. Peterson from his e-mail?

(A) He has attended an event at Noble Bookstore in the past.
(B) He will accompany a coworker to an upcoming event.
(C) He saw an advertisement for the book signings online.
(D) He does not live very far from Noble Bookstore.

# *Sherman Tours*

Sherman Tours proudly presents our special one-day trip to the Grand Canyon. You can enjoy a memorable and comfortable trip to the South Rim of the Grand Canyon in a small group of 6. Our expert guide will drive you to the Grand Canyon and other major local tourist attractions in a spacious van and tell you about the history of, as well as tales about, each place. Note that only members of Sherman Tours can take advantage of this very reasonably priced tour. To register and for further information about our trip to the Grand Canyon, please refer to our Web site at www.shermantours.com.

http://www.shermantours.com/tourinfo

# *Sherman Tours*

| HOME | ABOUT US | TOUR INFO | TESTIMONIALS | BOOK A TOUR |
|------|----------|-----------|--------------|-------------|

## Sherman Tours

### Special One-Day Trip to the Grand Canyon

**When:** 10:00 A.M. – 8:00 P.M.
Available Sunday – Friday (Not available on Saturday)

**Where:** From the Flagstaff Airport to the South Rim of the Grand Canyon (pickup and drop-off services included). Lunch at Olivares' Italian and dinner at Mitchell's Diner or All about French on Thursdays.

**How much:** $145 per adult
$80 per child under the age of 16

**Other:** A helicopter ride at the Grand Canyon for sightseeing is available for an additional $200. Dietary preference must be reported in advance.
**Click Here** to view pictures of the Grand Canyon and other tourist attractions.

# *Sherman Tours*

| HOME | ABOUT US | TOUR INFO | TESTIMONIALS | BOOK A TOUR |
|------|----------|-----------|--------------|-------------|

## "Great Trip to the Grand Canyon"

Reviewed by Samantha Watts
Reviewed on October 10

This was such a wonderful and well-organized tour provided by Sherman Tours. I especially liked the fact that I was never rushed, which enabled me to take in the view and appreciate the nature of the beautiful Grand Canyon. Our guide Joshua O'Neil was very informative, knowledgeable, and entertaining. I greatly enjoyed the delicious dinner I had at All about French as well. I would recommend this trip package to all those who want to have an unforgettable experience at the Grand Canyon in a relatively short time.

**191.** What is true about Sherman Tours?

(A) It is offering its members an exclusive deal.
(B) It consists of six employees.
(C) It issues a newsletter monthly.
(D) It has a long history.

**192.** What is mentioned about the helicopter ride?

(A) It must be requested in advance.
(B) It will be given to returning guests.
(C) It is offered for an extra fee.
(D) It is currently available for a reduced price.

**193.** What is included in the one-day trip to the Grand Canyon?

(A) An airline ticket
(B) Meals
(C) A souvenir
(D) Picture-taking service

**194.** When did Ms. Watts most likely go on a tour to the Grand Canyon?

(A) On a Thursday
(B) On a Friday
(C) On a Saturday
(D) On a Sunday

**195.** What can be inferred about Mr. O'Neil?

(A) He is a professional entertainer.
(B) He paid $145 for his tour of the Grand Canyon.
(C) He is a new employee at Sherman Tours.
(D) He gave Ms. Watts a ride to the Grand Canyon.

https://www.josestexmexfiesta.com/employment/

| OUR HISTORY | MENU | OUR TEAMS | BRANCH FINDER | JOB VACANCIES |
| OUR PHILOSOPHY | EVENT CATERING | MONTHLY DEALS | HOME DELIVERY | CONTACT US |

**We are currently seeking crew members and managers at several of our branches:**

**Job #012 – Crew Member (Kitchen) (All branches) –** Must be enthusiastic and a good team player. Must have good personal hygiene and be able to lift heavy boxes, sweep/mop, and use grills, toasters, etc.

**Job #034 – Shift Running Manager (TH/NS/IP/IN) –** Must have at least 12 months of experience supervising employees in any area of the service industry. Must be able to complete paperwork on time

**Job #042 – Payroll Assistant (AH/TH/NS/LV) –** Must have 1 year (preferably 2) of experience in a financial/accounting role. Preference given to holders of degrees or diplomas in accounting

**Job #024 – Restaurant Manager (NS/IP/WC/IN) –** Must have at least 3 years of experience as a restaurant manager. Must be proficient at delegating tasks and motivating lower management and crew

**Branch Key:** Alamo Heights (AH), Terrell Hills (TH), North Star Mall (NS), Leon Valley (LV), Ingram Park Mall (IP), Wind Crest (WC), Inglewood Park (IN)

Please **click here** to download an application form. Fill this out completely and mail it to: HR Services, José's Tex-Mex Fiesta, PO BOX 348, San Antonio, TX 78205

---

# José's Tex-Mex Fiesta

### Job Application (Page 1)

Where applicable, enter the job or branch codes used in our Web site job listings. Thank you.

**Name of Applicant:** Casey Grillo

**Position Applying For:** Job #034

**Branch Applying For:** NS

**Home Address:** 1007 West Heenan Street, Alamo Heights, San Antonio

**Date of Birth:** 25th July 1984

**E-mail Address:** cgrillo@ace.com

**Telephone Number:** 010-555-8761

Please include the following supporting documents: Copy of passport or social security card, résumé, cover letter, at least one letter of reference, copy of driver's license (delivery driver positions only), work portfolio (advertising/marketing/Web design positions only).

| To: | HR Services <recruitment@josestexmex.org> |
| From: | Casey Grillo <cgrillo@ace.com> |
| Date: | January 23 |
| Subject: | Recent application |

Dear sir/madam,

I am contacting you regarding the job application I sent yesterday. I just realized that I made a mistake while filling out the form. I currently live in Alamo Heights, and I often visit North Star Mall to eat at the José's Tex-Mex Fiesta there. That's the location I put down on my application form, but I wasn't thinking straight at the time. My family and I are moving across town at the start of February, so I should have indicated branch "IP" on my application form. I'd greatly appreciate it if you could amend this for me once you receive my documents. I included my résumé, a letter from my former employer, and a copy of my passport with my application form. Please let me know if I forgot to include anything.

Sincerely,

Casey Grillo

**196.** What information is NOT indicated as being available on the Web site?

(A) A business location search function
(B) Details about the company's founding
(C) Comments from satisfied customers
(D) Information about special offers

**197.** How should interested individuals apply for one of the listed jobs?

(A) By filling out a form online
(B) By visiting a business location
(C) By e-mailing human resources
(D) By mailing some documents

**198.** What is most likely true about Mr. Grillo?

(A) He has a strong background in the restaurant industry.
(B) He has an academic qualification in a financial field.
(C) He has experience in using kitchen tools and appliances.
(D) He has at least one year of managerial experience.

**199.** At which location does Mr. Grillo hope to be employed?

(A) Alamo Heights
(B) North Star Mall
(C) Ingram Park Mall
(D) Inglewood Park

**200.** What required item did Mr. Grillo forget to include with his application?

(A) A copy of his driver's license
(B) A work portfolio
(C) A cover letter
(D) A letter of reference

STOP! This is the end of the test. If you finish before time is called, you may go back to Parts 5, 6, and 7 and check your work.

# Actual Test

MP3

해설집

적정 풀이 시간 120분

**120 min**

시작 시간 ___시 ___분

종료 시간 ___시 ___분

중간에 멈추지 말고 처음부터 끝까지 풀어보세요.
문제를 풀 때에는 실전처럼 답안지에 마킹하세요.

목표 개수 _____ / 200    실제 개수 _____ / 200

예상 점수는 번역 및 정답에 있는 점수 환산표를 참조하세요.

# LISTENING TEST

In the Listening test, you will be asked to demonstrate how well you understand spoken English. The entire Listening test will last approximately 45 minutes. There are four parts, and directions are given for each part. You must mark your answers on the separate answer sheet. Do not write your answers in your test book.

## PART 1

**Directions:** For each question in this part, you will hear four statements about a picture in your test book. When you hear the statements, you must select the one statement that best describes what you see in the picture. Then find the number of the question on your answer sheet and mark your answer. The statements will not be printed in your test book and will be spoken only one time.

Statement (B), "They are sitting at a table," is the best description of the picture. So you should select answer (B) and mark it on your answer sheet.

**1.**

**2.**

▶ ▶ ▶ GO ON TO THE NEXT PAGE

**3.**

**4.**

**5.**

**6.**

## PART 2

**Directions:** You will hear a question or statement and three responses spoken in English. They will not be printed in your test book and will be spoken only one time. Select the best response to the question or statement and mark the letter (A), (B), or (C) on your answer sheet.

7. Mark your answer on your answer sheet.

8. Mark your answer on your answer sheet.

9. Mark your answer on your answer sheet.

10. Mark your answer on your answer sheet.

11. Mark your answer on your answer sheet.

12. Mark your answer on your answer sheet.

13. Mark your answer on your answer sheet.

14. Mark your answer on your answer sheet.

15. Mark your answer on your answer sheet.

16. Mark your answer on your answer sheet.

17. Mark your answer on your answer sheet.

18. Mark your answer on your answer sheet.

19. Mark your answer on your answer sheet.

20. Mark your answer on your answer sheet.

21. Mark your answer on your answer sheet.

22. Mark your answer on your answer sheet.

23. Mark your answer on your answer sheet.

24. Mark your answer on your answer sheet.

25. Mark your answer on your answer sheet.

26. Mark your answer on your answer sheet.

27. Mark your answer on your answer sheet.

28. Mark your answer on your answer sheet.

29. Mark your answer on your answer sheet.

30. Mark your answer on your answer sheet.

31. Mark your answer on your answer sheet.

## PART 3

**Directions:** You will hear some conversations between two or three people. You will be asked to answer three questions about what the speakers say in each conversation. Select the best response to each question and mark the letter (A), (B), (C), or (D) on your answer sheet. The conversations will not be printed in your test book and will be spoken only one time.

**32.** What does the man ask for?

(A) Direction to an office
(B) Building plans
(C) The engineering manager
(D) A change in a schedule

**33.** When will the man meet the team from the construction company?

(A) Tomorrow morning
(B) Tomorrow afternoon
(C) In two weeks
(D) Later today

**34.** What does the woman suggest that the man do?

(A) Talk to an engineer
(B) Plan a presentation
(C) Start a meeting later
(D) Use a previous draft

**35.** According to the man, what made the flight delayed?

(A) A mechanical problem
(B) Inclement weather
(C) Overbooking
(D) A change in the flight deck crew

**36.** What time will the speakers arrive in Toronto?

(A) At 7 A.M.
(B) At 10 A.M.
(C) At 2 P.M.
(D) At 3 P.M.

**37.** Why is the woman worried?

(A) She may lose a reservation.
(B) She doesn't like the weather in Toronto.
(C) There aren't any seats left on the plane.
(D) There is a lack of time to practice.

**38.** Why is Mr. Turner going to London?

(A) To take up a new position
(B) To meet with a client
(C) To do some market research
(D) To enjoy his vacation

**39.** According to the man, what makes Mr. Turner qualified for his new job?

(A) Extensive knowledge of products
(B) Excellent customer service skills
(C) Previous experience in a region
(D) Knowledge of foreign languages

**40.** Why does the woman say Mr. Turner will be busy?

(A) A major project will begin soon.
(B) New employees need extensive training.
(C) He has to prepare for his presentation.
(D) The company is growing its business.

**41.** Where do the speakers most likely work?

(A) At a public library
(B) At a city council building
(C) At an architectural firm
(D) At a pizza restaurant

**42.** What does the man mean when he says, "I've been meaning to send them"?

(A) He has forgotten to send some blueprints.
(B) He is waiting to receive feedback from clients.
(C) He is not satisfied with his work.
(D) He wants the woman to pick up some pizzas.

**43.** What does the woman intend to do tomorrow?

(A) Reschedule a delivery
(B) Take a tour of a building
(C) Submit some documents
(D) Participate in a meeting

▶ ▶ ▶ GO ON TO THE NEXT PAGE

44. Where is the man probably calling?

(A) A hotel
(B) An airport
(C) A tourism agency
(D) A real estate agency

45. What does the man say is important for him?

(A) Living near an airport
(B) Saving money for a vehicle
(C) Finding a better workplace
(D) Getting discounts on tickets

46. Why does the woman say she will call back later?

(A) The information is not available now.
(B) It will take time to make some listings.
(C) She must consult with some other clients first.
(D) The man's travel arrangements have changed.

47. Where does the woman probably work?

(A) At a travel agency
(B) At a performance venue
(C) At a movie theater
(D) At a publishing company

48. What does the man request?

(A) A revised schedule
(B) An additional ticket
(C) Expedited delivery
(D) A product in a smaller size

49. What might the man do before calling the woman back?

(A) Get a refund on his ticket
(B) Request a brochure
(C) Talk to a coworker
(D) Deliver a package

50. Why did the man call the woman?

(A) To get directions to a park
(B) To gather information
(C) To plan a sporting event
(D) To offer new designs

51. What does the woman like about Dawson Park?

(A) It has beautiful scenery.
(B) It offers classes for senior citizens.
(C) She is able to play a sport there.
(D) It is conveniently located in the heart of a city.

52. What does the woman suggest?

(A) Adding sports facilities
(B) Parking in a different place
(C) Visiting her office tomorrow
(D) Improving a certain area

53. What is the man going to do next week?

(A) Rent a car
(B) Open a clothing store
(C) Pay a late fee
(D) Participate in a corporate event

54. How long is the current rental period?

(A) Two days
(B) Three days
(C) Four days
(D) Five days

55. Why was the man confused about the rental period?

(A) A late fee wasn't paid.
(B) A product is unavailable.
(C) A membership was canceled.
(D) A policy has been changed.

**56.** Where most likely do the speakers work?

(A) At a hotel
(B) At a travel agency
(C) At a magazine
(D) At a photography studio

**57.** What does the man mean when he says, "That sounds good"?

(A) He wants to hear more options.
(B) He thinks the sound quality is great.
(C) He is willing to work together with the woman.
(D) He wants to hire a professional photographer.

**58.** What will the speakers probably do after lunch?

(A) Watch another movie
(B) Confirm a schedule
(C) Have an interview
(D) Hold a meeting

---

**59.** Who most likely is the woman?

(A) A market analyst
(B) A treasurer
(C) A product developer
(D) A human resources manager

**60.** What are the speakers mainly discussing?

(A) A swimming suit
(B) A sports center
(C) A marketing survey
(D) A digital device

**61.** What does Celine say will occur this month?

(A) A sports complex will be renovated.
(B) People will try out a new product.
(C) A new album will be released.
(D) Different packaging designs will be provided.

---

## NO PARKING

| Monday | 5 A.M. - 9 A.M. |
|--------|-----------------|
| Tuesday | 5 P.M. - 8 P.M. |
| Saturday | 8 A.M. - 4 P.M. |
| Sunday | 8 A.M. - 1 P.M. |

THE CITY OF HAYWARD

**62.** Why does the man want to park on the street?

(A) He doesn't have a parking permit.
(B) His car is running out of gas.
(C) He thinks he can save money.
(D) The parking garage is far from a theater.

**63.** Look at the graphic. What day is it?

(A) Monday
(B) Tuesday
(C) Saturday
(D) Sunday

**64.** What will the woman probably do next?

(A) Talk with the parking manager
(B) Buy some tickets
(C) Tell the guests about a delay
(D) Ask for driving directions

▶ ▶ ▶GO ON TO THE NEXT PAGE

## EAST BAY REAL ESTATE
### (TWO-BEDROOM APARTMENT)

| Room Number | Address | Rent (per month) |
|---|---|---|
| 1A | 1123 Pine Street | $400 |
| 3B | 603 Rumi Avenue | $550 |
| 4B | 909 Sunhill Boulevard | $700 |
| 8C | 911 Harbor Road | $900 |

65. What does the woman want to do?

(A) Find a place to live
(B) Visit her friend's place
(C) Get a job
(D) Purchase an apartment

66. According to the man, what is the problem?

(A) All the rooms have already been reserved.
(B) Every option exceeds the woman's budget.
(C) Public transportation in an area is poor.
(D) The woman's preferred choice is not available.

67. Look at the graphic. Which apartment will the woman probably choose?

(A) 1A
(B) 3B
(C) 4B
(D) 8C

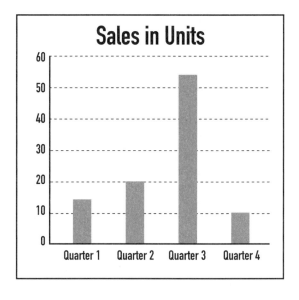

68. Where do the speakers probably work?

(A) At an auto repair shop
(B) At a game manufacturer
(C) At an advertising agency
(D) At a car manufacturer

69. Look at the graphic. Which quarter's sales figure is the man surprised about?

(A) Quarter 1
(B) Quarter 2
(C) Quarter 3
(D) Quarter 4

70. Who most likely is Ms. Witherspoon?

(A) An accountant
(B) An auto mechanic
(C) An event planner
(D) A marketing professional

## PART 4

**Directions:** You will hear some short talks given by a single speaker. You will be asked to answer three questions about what the speaker says in each short talk. Select the best response to each question and mark the letter (A), (B), (C), or (D) on your answer sheet. The talks will not be printed in your test book and will be spoken only one time.

**71.** What is the main topic of the message?

(A) A damaged product
(B) A contract renewal
(C) A late delivery
(D) An upcoming event

**72.** What did the speaker do last Saturday?

(A) She held a party.
(B) She read some recipe books.
(C) She attended a reception
(D) She registered for a course.

**73.** What does the speaker want to do?

(A) Correct an advertisement
(B) Get a full refund
(C) Schedule a delivery
(D) Cancel an order

---

**74.** What business is being advertised?

(A) A travel agency
(B) A city zoo
(C) A cruise line
(D) An amusement park

**75.** How long has the business been operating?

(A) 10 years
(B) 20 years
(C) 30 years
(D) 40 years

**76.** According to the speaker, what is the business best known for?

(A) Designing the most exciting rides
(B) Donating to local charities
(C) Protecting the environment
(D) Attracting visitors to the area

---

**77.** Who is being introduced?

(A) A keynote speaker
(B) A company researcher
(C) A pharmacist
(D) An award committee chairperson

**78.** What is suggested about the vaccines developed by Ms. Campbell?

(A) They are affordably priced.
(B) They are used worldwide.
(C) They will be released next month.
(D) They have passed clinical tests.

**79.** Why does the speaker say, "I know her achievements are very important to the company"?

(A) To praise a person for her achievements
(B) To encourage the listeners to be patient
(C) To place a large emphasis on a person's personality
(D) To complain about the company's management policy

---

**80.** Where does the speaker most likely work?

(A) At a wireless carrier
(B) At a department store
(C) At an electronics company
(D) At a market research firm

**81.** What problem does the speaker mention?

(A) A shortage of goods in stock
(B) A high level of customer dissatisfaction
(C) Sudden rises in some prices
(D) An increasing loss of market share

**82.** What does the man imply when he says, "So here's the plan"?

(A) He wants to hear other opinions.
(B) He wants to change a meeting date.
(C) He wants to give some instructions.
(D) He wants to develop another battery.

---

▶ ▶ ▶ GO ON TO THE NEXT PAGE

83. What type of business does the speaker work for?

(A) A camera store
(B) A photo studio
(C) A print shop
(D) A department store

84. Why is the new service most likely being introduced?

(A) To reduce expenses
(B) To attract new clients
(C) To offer unique items
(D) To attract attention from the media

85. What does the speaker say she will do tomorrow?

(A) Visit some relatives
(B) Evaluate job applicants
(C) Schedule an interview
(D) Purchase photography equipment

86. What is the speaker planning?

(A) A company awards banquet
(B) A job change
(C) A vacation trip
(D) An office visit

87. Who most likely is the listener?

(A) A hotel receptionist
(B) A travel agent
(C) A train driver
(D) A conference organizer

88. What does the speaker imply when she says, "But I heard I can see beautiful scenes in Europe during that time of the year"?

(A) She regrets canceling her vacation trip.
(B) She wants to take a trip with the listener.
(C) She disagrees with the listener's opinion.
(D) She thinks the purchase will be worth the fare.

89. Who is the announcement intended for?

(A) Library users
(B) Airplane passengers
(C) Department store customers
(D) Conference attendees

90. What are the listeners instructed to do?

(A) Present identification
(B) Take a shuttle bus
(C) Go to the registration desk
(D) Get information booklets

91. According to the speaker, what will happen next week?

(A) The normal hours will change.
(B) An exhibition will take place.
(C) Another workshop will be held.
(D) A new library will open.

92. What is the news report mostly discussing?

(A) The opening of a plant
(B) An upcoming election
(C) A serious air pollution problem
(D) A reduction in the tax rate

93. According to the speaker, what are local citizens concerned about?

(A) A lack of money in the city's budget
(B) A decline in air quality
(C) The closure of a school
(D) The effects of traffic congestion

94. What are residents asked to do?

(A) Complete a questionnaire
(B) Refer to an annual report
(C) Attend a job training course
(D) Use public transportation

| **Sedell International Office Building** |  |
|---|---|
| **Information** |  |
| **1F** | Lobby / Cafeteria / Bank / Info Desk |
| **2F** | Mailroom / PR / Accounting / Finance |
| **3F** | Sales(Domestic) / Sales(International) / Personnel |
| **4F** | Marketing / Product Development / R&D Conference Room / Auditorium |

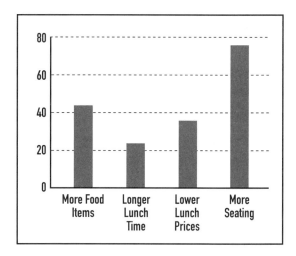

95. What is the speaker calling about?

(A) A furniture delivery
(B) An interview arrangement
(C) A request for elevator repairs
(D) A regular checkup

96. What does the speaker request the listener do?

(A) Look at a catalog
(B) Schedule an interview
(C) Complete some renovation work
(D) Use the stairs

97. Look at the graphic. On which floor will the speaker probably meet with Ms. Moore?

(A) The first floor
(B) The second floor
(C) The third floor
(D) The fourth floor

98. Where does the announcement probably take place?

(A) In a cafeteria
(B) At a department store
(C) At a manufacturing plant
(D) At a cooking school

99. Look at the graphic. Which suggestion will the company act on?

(A) More Food Items
(B) Longer Lunch Time
(C) Lower Lunch Prices
(D) More Seating

100. According to the speaker, what will the respondents receive?

(A) A discount coupon
(B) A free T-shirt
(C) A complimentary lunch
(D) A gift certificate

This is the end of the Listening test. Turn to Part 5 in your test book.

▶ ▶ ▶ GO ON TO THE NEXT PAGE

# READING TEST

In the Reading test, you will read a variety of texts and answer several different types of reading comprehension questions. The entire Reading test will last 75 minutes. There are three parts, and directions are given for each part. You are encouraged to answer as many questions as possible within the time allowed.

You must mark your answers on the separate answer sheet. Do not write your answers in your test book.

## PART 5

**Directions**: A word or phrase is missing in each of the sentences below. Four answer choices are given below each sentence. Select the best answer to complete the sentence. Then mark the letter (A), (B), (C), or (D) on your answer sheet.

**101.** As Kamon Machines discontinued producing replacement parts for old fax machine models, we can't purchase ------- anymore.

(A) they
(B) them
(C) their
(D) theirs

**102.** Mr. Jones has been ------- recommended by most of his former employers.

(A) high
(B) higher
(C) highest
(D) highly

**103.** ------- at the city festival was significantly lower because the date of the parade was changed with little advance notice.

(A) Attend
(B) Attendance
(C) Attendees
(D) Attendants

**104.** Tang Toys increased its second-quarter revenue thanks to the continued ------- of sales in Japan and America.

(A) assets
(B) expansion
(C) decline
(D) compensation

**105.** The shipping manager is worried about making the ------- date because of the record snowfall yesterday.

(A) deliver
(B) delivers
(C) delivery
(D) delivered

**106.** Komi Motors has overcome the global economic crisis by ------- its manufacturing plant in Eastern Europe.

(A) close
(B) closing
(C) closed
(D) closes

**107.** The design school in New York called the Fashion Academy has produced ------- professional designers to the competitive fashion industry.

(A) create
(B) creation
(C) creative
(D) creatively

**108.** ------- it was snowing heavily, many people decided to walk to work to avoid the traffic in town.

(A) Besides
(B) Instead of
(C) Apart from
(D) Even though

**109.** According to the yearly sales report, the Genelec Factory's revenue showed a ------- improvement after the company's rigorous restructuring.

(A) wealthy
(B) significant
(C) comparing
(D) worsening

**110.** In the early 20th century, it was quite an ------- experience to travel about 50 miles due to the inadequate transportation infrastructure.

(A) excite
(B) exciting
(C) excited
(D) excitedly

**111.** Smoking is not allowed inside the petroleum storage area, ------- is it allowed near the petrochemical plant.

(A) unless
(B) whether
(C) nor
(D) besides

**112.** All the residents without exception are ------- to evacuate the building during a fire drill.

(A) spoken
(B) described
(C) asked
(D) realized

**113.** ------- located in the business district, the duty-free shops will open their doors to international tourists.

(A) Strategy
(B) Strategize
(C) Strategic
(D) Strategically

**114.** Even though Jason Heavy Industries received many job applications for the accounting manager position, few individuals were -------.

(A) qualify
(B) qualifies
(C) qualified
(D) qualifications

**115.** From casinos, fantastic shows, shopping malls, and incredible tourist attractions to fine dining, Las Vegas ------- a world-class vacation destination for families and couples alike.

(A) remains
(B) stays
(C) locates
(D) appears

**116.** Please be ------- that international bank processing times vary depending on the local banking system.

(A) advise
(B) advised
(C) advisable
(D) advisory

**117.** The old industrial park and the ------- property have been redeveloped into a new apartment complex.

(A) surround
(B) surrounds
(C) surrounded
(D) surrounding

**118.** Please make sure to list the results of Mr. Watson's market analysis research on the final slide ------- the marketing presentation.

(A) within
(B) of
(C) through
(D) except

**119.** According to the results of the new survey, most people usually think art is for the highly gifted or for the ------- trained.

(A) profession
(B) professional
(C) professionals
(D) professionally

**120.** To help prevent workplace accidents, it is ------- that all employees take part in our free workplace health and safety training program every year.

(A) ambiguous
(B) mandatory
(C) preventive
(D) appreciative

▶ ▶ ▶ GO ON TO THE NEXT PAGE

121. At the regular marketing meetings, Mr. Thompson ------- offers some innovative marketing strategies that can help expand its market share.

(A) frequently
(B) enormously
(C) considerably
(D) promptly

122. ------- she quit her job last week, Ms. Parker has time to take a management course at a college in Palo Alto.

(A) Since
(B) When
(C) Despite
(D) Therefore

123. Once our employees have successfully completed this month's training, they will be ------- at doing their accounting work.

(A) flexible
(B) aware
(C) proficient
(D) economical

124. Our survey indicated that most consumers ------- mint-flavored chocolate chips very appetizing.

(A) take
(B) find
(C) expect
(D) feel

125. According to the recently revised regulations, ------- of the member nations must undergo periodic audits of their trade policies and practices.

(A) all
(B) another
(C) every
(D) few

126. The insurance company attempted to ------- the fire damage to the office building as accurately as it could.

(A) avoid
(B) cover
(C) appraise
(D) claim

127. If we cannot locate your bag within 21 days, it will be considered lost, and we will ------- you for any fee charged to transport your luggage.

(A) provide
(B) reimburse
(C) transfer
(D) allocate

128. Some of the reasons for the decrease in housing sales across the country are not ------- clear.

(A) apparently
(B) usually
(C) meticulously
(D) immediately

129. Regardless of ------- an applicant is offered a business loan, all applications must be kept for a whole year.

(A) whereas
(B) even though
(C) instead
(D) whether

130. If the company ------- to our demands in a reasonable manner, the labor union will resume salary negotiations.

(A) respond
(B) responds
(C) will respond
(D) was responding

# PART 6

**Directions:** Read the texts that follow. A word, phrase, or sentence is missing in parts of each text. Four answer choices for each question are given below the text. Select the best answer to complete the text. Then mark the letter (A), (B), (C), or (D) on your answer sheet.

**Questions 131-134** refer to the following memorandum.

**MEMORANDUM**

TO: All employees
FROM: Eric Haller, Head of Public Relations
DATE: June 25
SUBJECT: Warren Hall Tour

John Baker, a renowned theatrical dance performance director in New York, ------- us a
                                                                      **131.**
guided tour of the new municipal performance theater, Warren Hall.

This guided tour includes a sit-in during a dry rehearsal for the most recent musical to play

at Warren Hall next Saturday, *Jungle Fever*. I think it must be a good chance for us to see

Warren Hall, a new state-of-the-art facility with a capacity of 3,000 people. -------.
                                                                        **132.**

------- there is no charge for it, every employee must reserve a spot on the tour before
**133.**

going. Please be ------- that tickets are limited and that the final day to sign up is June 30.
                **134.**
Don't miss registering for this remarkable tour.

If you need more information about this tour, please visit the Web site at www.warrenhall.

com.

**131.** (A) giving
(B) will be giving
(C) was given
(D) give

**132.** (A) All employees are advised to attend.
(B) Small amount of money was spent for donations.
(C) It has been praised by many critics for its beautiful sets and costumes.
(D) Many of this year's films will be shown at the recently constructed theater.

**133.** (A) Even if
(B) Since
(C) When
(D) Although

**134.** (A) reluctant
(B) possible
(C) willing
(D) aware

**Taylor & Murphy Accounting**
110 Pine Street, San Francisco, CA 94137

To Whom It May Concern,

Taylor & Murphy Accounting is soliciting bids for the management of its information technology needs. Starting in January, we ------- all our computer maintenance and data
                                                        **135.**
management operations. Please see the technical information below for the details of our requirements on data system management policies and technical standards.

We currently expect to have our employees from our potential outsourcing partner on site for continuity's sake. -------, we understand that this may not always be possible.
                     **136.**

We anticipate that there will be some extra work needed at the start ------- upgrade our
                                                                    **137.**
copper-based telecommunications networks to ones that use fiber optics via Broadband Transport Technologies, and we would like that work to be included in the bid. -------.
                                                                                    **138.**

Thank you.

Sally Murphy
Vice President
Taylor & Murphy Accounting

---

**135.** (A) outsourcing
(B) outsourced
(C) have been outsourced
(D) will be outsourcing

**136.** (A) While
(B) Even
(C) Furthermore
(D) However

**137.** (A) so that
(B) in order to
(C) which
(D) in case

**138.** (A) All proposals and bids must be received at our head office by August 31.
(B) We expect many bidders will compete with one another to win the contract.
(C) You should be aware of the importance of paperwork and document accuracy.
(D) Our experienced personnel and technical infrastructure can help your company improve efficiency.

Questions 139-142 refer to the following notice.

## Renovation Effort
### Regency Apartment Complex

Management is preparing to renovate apartment interiors beginning in October.

After renovating a few vacant units ------- the building, the main renovation effort will begin
                                         **139.**

on the 10th floor and will include four to six units at a time. ------- set of units under
                                                                    **140.**

renovation will require at least two or three weeks to complete.

Affected residents will need to move prior to the renovations beginning in their current unit.

Their units will be available again after the renovation work -------.
                                                                  **141.**

-------. Your questions may be directed to the management office.
 **142.**

Thank you for your kind understanding and full cooperation in advance.

Regency Apartment Complex
Management Office

139. (A) for
     (B) near
     (C) into
     (D) throughout

140. (A) All
     (B) Some
     (C) Each
     (D) Almost

141. (A) completes
     (B) completed
     (C) is complete
     (D) will be completed

142. (A) Notices will be posted in each unit
         informing our residents of this policy.
     (B) The management office will be
         temporarily closed this week.
     (C) Please pardon the appearance of
         the apartment complex during the
         renovations.
     (D) We hope that the renovation project
         will bring better life for the residents.

March 10

Ms. Allie Goodroad
1123 5th Avenue
Houston, TX 79038

Dear Ms. Goodroad,

We are pleased to inform you that the KABI Recycling Program will commence in your area

on April 1. Residents who would like to participate in the ------- will be issued a wheeled
                                                                143.

green container. To ------- a container, please call 1-800-575-4331.
                     144.

Curbside recycling will take place twice a month rather than once a week as was initially

proposed. -------, trips into neighborhoods will be less frequent, which will lower fuel costs
          145.
and emissions.

A list of recyclable materials can be found in the enclosed brochure. For more information on

the schedules of citywide recycling programs, visit www.kabirecycling.org. -------.
                                                                            146.

Sincerely yours,

Brandon Lee
Manager of KABI Recycling Program

143. (A) initiative
     (B) hearing
     (C) competition
     (D) exhibition

144. (A) prepare
     (B) return
     (C) repair
     (D) request

145. (A) After all
     (B) Furthermore
     (C) As a result
     (D) In fact

146. (A) We hope that you take part in this
         important program.
     (B) Your container will arrive at your door
         within seven days.
     (C) Please make sure not to put broken
         glass into your container.
     (D) The city has invested an enormous
         sum of money in this project.

# PART 7

**Directions:** In this part you will read a selection of texts, such as magazine and newspaper articles, e-mails, and instant messages. Each text or set of texts is followed by several questions. Select the best answer for each question and mark the letter (A), (B), (C), or (D) on your answer sheet.

**Questions 147-148** refer to the following receipt.

## CASH ALLOWANCE RECEIPT

**DATE** November 23
**NAME (IN BLOCK LETTER)** HANK SHREDDER

| DETAILED INFORMATION | AMOUNT |
|---|---|
| To pay for all business travel and meal expenses associated with the accounting conference I will attend in Manhattan, New York, on November 25 and 26 | $1,974 |

**I confirm receipt of the above sum.**

**Signature** *Hank Shredder*

ACTUAL TEST··· 05

**147.** What will Mr. Shredder do in New York in November?

(A) Sign a new contract
(B) Go on vacation
(C) Hire some accountants
(D) Participate in an event

**148.** What does Mr. Shredder confirm?

(A) Purchasing some accounting software
(B) Submitting original receipts
(C) Paying hotel costs
(D) Receiving some funds

Questions 149-150 refer to the following invoice.

# New Line Office Supply Warehouse

25200 Carlos Bee Blvd, Hayward, CA 94542, 510-212-6313

## Delivery Invoice

**Date:** January 10
**Invoice No:** 941796
**Purchased by:** Anna Gunn
**Delivery Address:** 540 Pine Street, Daly City, CA 94015

| | |
|---|---|
| Prima Silver Work Desk / Workstation | $209.95 |
| Support System 10 Desk Chair | $109.95 |
| Samson 19-inch Monitor | $149.95 |
| Samson Computer (Model #: Andromeda X110) | $909.90 |
| Subtotal | $1,559.75 |
| Frequent Shopper Discount | - $100.00 |
| Tax | $86.99 |
| **Total** | **$1,546.74** |

Thank you for shopping at New Line Office Supply Warehouse.

**149.** What is suggested about Ms. Gunn?

(A) She will pick up her order.
(B) She works for an office supply company.
(C) She often shops at the New Line Office Supply Warehouse.
(D) She will purchase a desk next week.

**150.** What is the total amount paid on this invoice?

(A) $1,559.75
(B) $1,546.74
(C) $909.90
(D) $86.99

**Questions 151-152** refer to the following text message chain.

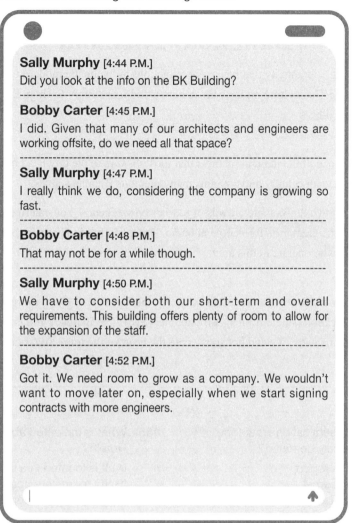

**Sally Murphy** [4:44 P.M.]
Did you look at the info on the BK Building?

---

**Bobby Carter** [4:45 P.M.]
I did. Given that many of our architects and engineers are working offsite, do we need all that space?

---

**Sally Murphy** [4:47 P.M.]
I really think we do, considering the company is growing so fast.

---

**Bobby Carter** [4:48 P.M.]
That may not be for a while though.

---

**Sally Murphy** [4:50 P.M.]
We have to consider both our short-term and overall requirements. This building offers plenty of room to allow for the expansion of the staff.

---

**Bobby Carter** [4:52 P.M.]
Got it. We need room to grow as a company. We wouldn't want to move later on, especially when we start signing contracts with more engineers.

**151.** Where do Ms. Murphy and Mr. Carter work?

(A) At an architectural firm
(B) At a moving company
(C) At a real estate agency
(D) At an interior design firm

**152.** At 4:52 P.M., what does Mr. Carter most likely mean when he writes, "Got it"?

(A) The company needs to improve its existing office space.
(B) A new office space will be too expensive.
(C) The building may accommodate plans for future growth.
(D) The property needs structural improvements.

# Bangkok, Thailand

Bangkok is a thrilling, vibrant city that has many attractions to excite the modern traveler. Whether you are here to sample the Thai culture, to taste the delicious food, or simply to shop, Bangkok has something for everybody.

**Things to See:**

The Grand Palace is one of the main attractions that most visitors to the city head to first. This palace was built in the eighteenth century and contains many precious Buddha statues.

The market in Chinatown draws huge crowds of tourists on weekends. You can find some fantastic bargains that will make great gifts for people at home. Don't be afraid to bargain, but be polite. Watch out for pickpockets, who operate in this area.

**Accommodations:**

There are many great budget hotels around the city. Try the Royal Thai Hotel for reasonably priced rooms in a central location (single rooms - $10, double - $18). The Bangkok Inn is also popular with tourists. It offers rooms with TVs and hot showers in the heart of the tourist district (single rooms - $12, double - $20).

**153.** In what type of publication would the article mostly likely be found?

(A) An economic report
(B) A business journal
(C) A hotel magazine
(D) A travel guidebook

**154.** Why must tourists be cautious when visiting the market in Chinatown?

(A) There is a lot of traffic on the roads.
(B) There are some thieves at the market.
(C) Taxis charge high prices to go to the market.
(D) Lots of pirated goods are sold at the market.

**155.** What is indicated about the Royal Thai Hotel?

(A) It is located in a central area.
(B) Its rooms are spacious and clean.
(C) Its restaurant serves fantastic Thai cuisine.
(D) It has a swimming pool for guests to use.

# Roseville Community Center

Located just a short 10-minute drive from downtown Roseville in a scenic mountain setting, the Roseville Community Center (RCC) is the community's new center for leisure, exercise, and relaxation. The RCC is a great place for families and singles to get a massage, to play sports, to swim, and even to take a nap in our sunroom.

With a variety of things to keep you busy and a variety of ways to relax, the RCC is an ideal place for family get-togethers and short business meetings as well as a comfortable spot to meet other singles. Our onsite coordinator will help you create the perfect plan for your day. For an additional charge, we will provide a personal bath accessory package.

For memberships, please call the front desk at 404-555-3242 or send us an e-mail at members@rcc.com. To contact our onsite coordinator, please call 404-575-4331. For more information, photos, directions, and feedback from other members, please visit us at www.rcc.org.

ACTUAL TEST... 05

**156.** What is indicated about the Roseville Community Center?

(A) It is located in the heart of town.
(B) It provides massages.
(C) It has a catering service.
(D) It has a café.

**157.** What is available for an extra charge?

(A) Transportation from downtown
(B) A large meeting room
(C) Use of the exercise facility
(D) Bath accessories

**158.** According to the advertisement, how can people get directions to the Roseville Community Center?

(A) By visiting the center's Web site
(B) By calling the coordinator
(C) By contacting the front desk
(D) By e-mailing the manager

# Superfit Sportswear

490 Over Street
London, England

November 23

Jeremiah Osterland
490 Rinke Strata
Vienna, Austria

Dear Mr. Osterland,

Thank you for your e-mail inquiring about our sportswear products. We are a dynamic, growing company, and we are excited about the prospect of supplying our sportswear to your stores all over Austria.

Superfit Sportswear is a family business established in 1992. Currently, our company has over thirty stores serving the needs of over one million customers throughout England every year. We manufacture and sell a range of products from footwear to sports therapy products.

Please find enclosed our trade catalogue for you to look at. This catalogue contains a list of all of our current products and descriptions of them.

I have arranged for our sales director, Mr. Rhodes, to fly to Vienna to meet with you on December 12. He will be able to negotiate the terms and conditions of the sales contract with you to create a deal profitable for both parties.

We look forward to doing business with you.

Sincerely,

*Saul Goodman*

Saul Goodman
Superfit Sportswear

159. To what kind of communication is Mr. Goodman replying?

(A) A magazine article
(B) A shareholder's letter
(C) An e-mail inquiry
(D) A telephone message

160. What does Mr. Goodman send along with his letter?

(A) A flight ticket
(B) A trade catalogue
(C) A booklet of discount vouchers
(D) A list of business contacts

161. Why is Mr. Rhodes going to fly to Vienna?

(A) To examine one of Mr. Osterland's stores
(B) To take a vacation with Mr. Osterland
(C) To discuss the details of a contract
(D) To establish a branch of the company

**Questions 162-164** refer to the following e-mail.

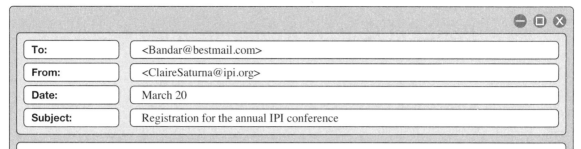

To: &lt;Bandar@bestmail.com&gt;

From: &lt;ClaireSaturna@ipi.org&gt;

Date: March 20

Subject: Registration for the annual IPI conference

Dear Mr. Bandar,

I'm writing to thank you for your considerable support of the International Petroleum Institute. As a reminder, please keep in mind that the deadline for registration for the annual IPI Conference in Sao Paulo is October 15. —[1]—. There are exciting things in store for this conference, including over 200 vendors, displays, and lectures, and all in a state-of-the-art convention facility right in the heart of downtown. —[2]—.

As a preferred contributor to the programs at the International Petroleum Institute, we are offering you a voucher for 20% off your hotel and complimentary shuttle service to the convention hall. —[3]—. Visit our Web site to register online. —[4]—. Otherwise, you may want to reach us by phone at 512-555-8760. Please have your membership number ready.

Sincerely,

Claire Saturna
Membership Coordinator

ACTUAL TEST... 05

**162.** Who most likely is Mr. Bandar?

(A) An oil company executive
(B) A conference organizer
(C) A journalist
(D) A teacher

**163.** What is NOT a benefit being offered?

(A) A reduced hotel rate
(B) A hotel room upgrade
(C) Hundreds of vendors' booths
(D) Complimentary transportation to the event

**164.** In which of the positions marked [1], [2], [3], and [4] does the following sentence best belong?

"You will also find a detailed conference program there, including maps for the vendor booths."

(A) [1]
(B) [2]
(C) [3]
(D) [4]

# President Hotel to Reopen in Santa Fe

### By Jesse Pinkman – Santa Fe Weekly

Santa Fe – After being closed for six months while much-needed renovations were carried out, the President Hotel reopened for business this Monday at 9 A.M.

The manager of the hotel, Janice Ha, claims that the hotel is better than ever before. "Everybody loved the old hotel," she claimed. "But the work done on it was essential in allowing us to keep up with modern trends. We were experiencing a lot of demand from tourists that we couldn't cope with before. As such, we have installed a state-of-the-art swimming pool and a gym, upgraded our restaurant, and added a movie theater for our guests to enjoy. Everybody here is excited about the reopening and can't wait to get back to work."

Designer and owner Chan Hong spoke of his inspiration for the new design. "I wanted to create a memorable experience for our guests," he said. "I wanted people of all ages to be able to enjoy the hotel, whether it be for business or pleasure." When asked if he believed the new hotel is equipped to meet the needs of the ever-demanding travel community, Mr. Hong said that he was, "Extremely confident that we will be able to cater to even the most discriminating of tastes."

One of the first to sample the delights of the new hotel was Jim Gomez, who works out four times a week. "The new gym is great," said Mr. Gomez. "It has everything you need to keep yourself in shape on your vacation. I loved the swimming pool and restaurant, too. I would definitely stay here again."

The President Hotel certainly looks regal both inside and out. Each room is now equipped with a wide-screen TV, a king-sized bed, and wireless Internet access. And if you're feeling like you want to splurge, the luxurious emperor suites offer exceptional value for money. Priced at $220, these exclusive rooms are certainly fit for royalty.

**165.** What is the purpose of the article?

(A) To publicize the reopening of a hotel
(B) To compare several different hotels
(C) To offer free use of some facilities to the local community
(D) To advertise some job vacancies at a hotel

**166.** What is NOT mentioned about the President Hotel?

(A) It will be open on Christmas Day.
(B) It has a swimming pool.
(C) It was closed for six months.
(D) It is owned by Mr. Hong.

**167.** What is suggested about Jim Gomez?

(A) He stayed at the hotel with his wife and children.
(B) He works in the hotel industry.
(C) He is passionate about exercising.
(D) He helped plan the improvements to the fitness center.

▶ ▶ ▶ GO ON TO THE NEXT PAGE

**Questions 168-171** refer to the following online chat discussion.

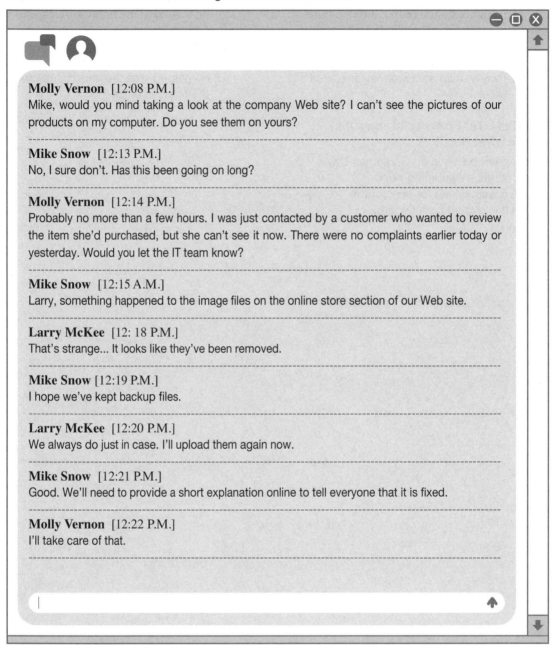

**Molly Vernon** [12:08 P.M.]
Mike, would you mind taking a look at the company Web site? I can't see the pictures of our products on my computer. Do you see them on yours?

**Mike Snow** [12:13 P.M.]
No, I sure don't. Has this been going on long?

**Molly Vernon** [12:14 P.M.]
Probably no more than a few hours. I was just contacted by a customer who wanted to review the item she'd purchased, but she can't see it now. There were no complaints earlier today or yesterday. Would you let the IT team know?

**Mike Snow** [12:15 A.M.]
Larry, something happened to the image files on the online store section of our Web site.

**Larry McKee** [12: 18 P.M.]
That's strange... It looks like they've been removed.

**Mike Snow** [12:19 P.M.]
I hope we've kept backup files.

**Larry McKee** [12:20 P.M.]
We always do just in case. I'll upload them again now.

**Mike Snow** [12:21 P.M.]
Good. We'll need to provide a short explanation online to tell everyone that it is fixed.

**Molly Vernon** [12:22 P.M.]
I'll take care of that.

**168.** What problem does Ms. Vernon report?

(A) Online purchases are not being processed.

(B) Some contact information is listed on the company's Web site.

(C) The company's Web site appears to have been hacked.

(D) Product photos cannot be viewed in the online store section.

**169.** From whom did Ms. Vernon learn about the problem?

(A) An accountant

(B) An IT coworker

(C) A customer

(D) The company president

**170.** At 12:19 P.M., what does Mr. Snow most likely mean when he writes, "I hope we've kept backup files"?

(A) He is afraid that the company has lost a lot of money.

(B) He wants his coworker to explain the procedure for handling files.

(C) He is looking for some clients' financial transaction records.

(D) He hopes that all of the pictures are still available.

**171.** What will Ms. Vernon most like do next?

(A) Update her personal profile

(B) Contact the safety office

(C) Contact the IT team

(D) Post a note online

# *Sweetwater Lake State Park*
## Things to Do

At Sweetwater Lake State Park, you can fish, paddle, hike, picnic, camp or stay in a cabin, and go boating. Rent our group hall for your next reunion!

Alligators live in the park; read our alligator safety tips before your visit. —[1]—.

**Fish:** Sweetwater Lake State Park is 26,810-acres, and the lake itself harbors more than 70 species of fish. We have a fishing pier and a boat ramp. You do not need a fishing license to fish from shore in a state park. —[2]—. Ask about borrowing fishing equipment to use in the park.

**Paddle:** Explore Sweetwater Lake's twists and turns. Rent a canoe in the park or bring your own canoe or kayak. —[3]—.

**Stay:**
• Choose from 46 campsites, ranging from water-only to full hookup sites.
• Stay at a screened shelter.
• Rent one of our historic cabins. These range from two- to six-person cabins, and several are handicapped accessible.

**Hike:** Explore the forest afoot. One-quarter mile of the Sweetwater Forest Trail is handicapped accessible. Learn more on our Interactive Map page. —[4]—.

**Volunteers:** Visit our Volunteer page to see how you can help.

**172.** What is indicated about Sweetwater Lake State Park?

(A) It is difficult to get to from the highway.
(B) It is a relatively new manmade lake.
(C) A variety of activities are provided.
(D) The entry fee is affordable.

**173.** What is indicated about camping at the park?

(A) There are many options available.
(B) There is no electricity at any of the campsites.
(C) There is no camping allowed this year.
(D) Many additional campsites are being constructed.

**174.** What is NOT suggested about Sweetwater Lake State Park?

(A) It is only for in-state residents.
(B) It has options for the handicapped.
(C) It has many forms of wildlife.
(D) It is currently recruiting volunteers.

**175.** In which of the positions marked [1], [2], [3], and [4] does the following sentence best belong?

"Click on the link for Handicapped Trail."

(A) [1]
(B) [2]
(C) [3]
(D) [4]

▶ ▶ ▶GO ON TO THE NEXT PAGE

**Questions 176-180** refer to the following e-mails.

| To: | Eric Woodhouse, AZA Medical Supplies |
| From: | Ryan Taylor, Manager, Ivy Hotel |
| Date: | November 29 |
| Subject: | Your stay at the Ivy Hotel |
| Attachment: | AZAinvoice.txt |

Dear Mr. Woodhouse,

We were pleased that you and your colleagues chose to stay at the Ivy Hotel during your visit to Montreal for the medical conference. We hope that you enjoyed your stay on November 26. I have attached your final bill to this e-mail. It includes tax and room service charges. Please call me soon at 992-9599 to make a prompt payment by credit card.

As the Ivy Hotel is quite new, we are always keen to receive feedback from our customers on ways that we can improve our service. If you or anyone on your staff have any comments about any aspect of your stay, please let us know so that we can better serve you in the future.

It was a pleasure to have you stay with us. If you choose the Ivy Hotel again for the next conference, we will give you a 20% discount.

Sincerely,

Ryan Taylor
General Manager
The Ivy Hotel

To: Ryan Taylor, Manager, Ivy Hotel
From: Eric Woodhouse, AZA Medical Supplies
Date: December 1
Subject: Re: Your stay at the Ivy Hotel

Dear Mr. Taylor,

Thank you for your e-mail. My staffers and I thoroughly enjoyed our stay at your hotel. The staff was very helpful, and the rooms were spacious and a pleasure to stay in. You made us very feel welcome.

My staffers and I are actually returning to Montreal to attend a sales workshop next month. We would like to book four rooms to stay at your hotel if possible. Would it be possible to stay in the same rooms as the last time? They were all fantastic although the bathroom in the Oak Room was a little dirty.

In addition, we would like to hold our next conference on March 1 at your hotel.

I will call you on Friday to make the payment.

Sincerely,

Eric Woodhouse
Sales Consultant
AZA Medical Supplies

---

**176.** What is one purpose of the first e-mail?

(A) To advertise a job opening at a hotel
(B) To promote the opening of a new hotel
(C) To request comments on a hotel stay
(D) To place an order for medical supplies

**177.** In the first e-mail, the word "prompt" in paragraph 1, line 4, is closest in meaning to

(A) delayed
(B) late
(C) financial
(D) punctual

**178.** How does Mr. Taylor want Mr. Woodhouse to pay?

(A) With cash
(B) By credit card
(C) By check
(D) By bank transfer

**179.** What comment does Mr. Woodhouse make about the Oak Room?

(A) The toilet was unclean.
(B) The window was broken.
(C) The bathroom was messy.
(D) The room was fantastic.

**180.** When will Mr. Woodhouse most likely receive a special discount?

(A) On November 26
(B) On November 29
(C) On December 1
(D) On March 1

## The Daily News

December 1

# For a "Pick-me-up"

Aaron Milton's days revolve around coffee beans, sugary syrups, and cream with a variety of unique flavors added. His recently opened shop, the Daily Perk, serves a nice selection of deli sandwiches and sugary sweets, but it is the custom coffee drinks that really stand out. By combining homegrown and roasted coffee beans with a creative flair for flavor combinations, Mr. Milton has become famous as "Mr. Coffee" among store patrons. Mr. Milton, a former school teacher, now produces the best caffeinated beverages in town. Because his drink concoctions are often inspired by the seasons – for example, pumpkin spiced pie during the fall and candy cane delight during the winter holidays – the selections of flavors change frequently. Even the staff members are encouraged to put their own personal touches to the menu and have created several staple items available year-round.

Mr. Milton started the Daily Perk with a loan from his parents, which he was able to repay after his first year in business.

If you haven't been there yet, the Daily Perk is conveniently located at the corner of Weems Lane and Elm Street. It opens every morning at 6:30. For more information, visit its Web site at www.perkup.com.

| To: | Aaron Milton <amilton@mail.com> |
| --- | --- |
| From: | Peter Vickers <Pvickers@mail.com> |
| Date: | December 3 |
| Subject: | Article |

Dear Aaron,

I saw the story about you in the *Daily News*, and it reminded me that I haven't been to your coffee shop yet. It sounds great, and I hope to stop by soon. We miss you at Crown Pointe Academy. Several students still ask about you. Things are going well here. We're renovating the science lab this summer, which I know you had been begging for, for years! You'll have to come see it when all the work is done.

I'll be seeing you soon!

Peter

**181.** What is suggested about Mr. Milton?

(A) He joined the family business.
(B) He owes his parents money.
(C) He is a sort of farmer.
(D) He plans to change careers.

**182.** In the article, the word "revolve" in paragraph 1, line 1, is closest in meaning to

(A) resign
(B) design
(C) repeat
(D) postpone

**183.** What is NOT indicated about the Daily Perk?

(A) It is only open in the evening.
(B) Its menu changes often.
(C) It has experienced quick success.
(D) It offers a variety of products.

**184.** Why did Mr. Vickers send the e-mail?

(A) To ask Mr. Milton to come to a party
(B) To ask Mr. Milton for a job
(C) To determine Mr. Milton's interest in an investment opportunity
(D) To tell Mr. Milton he read an article about his business

**185.** Where most likely did Mr. Vickers and Mr. Milton work together?

(A) At a coffee shop
(B) At a school
(C) At an advertising agency
(D) At a charity event

▶ ▶ ▶ GO ON TO THE NEXT PAGE

# A New Sponsor for the Upcoming Barrington Children's Hospital Marathon

It has been confirmed that the Pueblo Corporation will be the biggest sponsor of the upcoming Barrington Children's Hospital Marathon. Details regarding the sponsorship are to be announced in the near future. The corporation is the third largest pharmaceutical company in the country.

The Barrington Children's Hospital Marathon has been held annually for the past 15 years. Over the years, more than $15 million has been raised to help children suffering from rare diseases. The event consists of a marathon (26 miles) and a half marathon (13 miles). All profits and contributions will be donated to the Barrington Children's Hospital. Participants are encouraged to make their own fundraising efforts.

The event will take place next month on Saturday, June 16. The Barrington Children's Hospital Marathon is the 20th largest marathon in the nation with over 10,000 participants in the half marathon and about 5,000 participants in the marathon.

| To: | Jim Douglas <jimdouglas@pueblo.net> |
| --- | --- |
| From: | Teresa Martinez <teresamartinez@pueblo.net> |
| Date: | May 10 |
| Subject: | Interview with *Social Interests News* |

Dear Mr. Douglas,

Following the recent press release on the Barrington Children's Hospital Marathon, multiple news media agencies have requested interviews. They want to hear someone from the Public Relations Department make a statement about our sponsorship decision. I decided to go with the most reputable agency, *Social Interest News*. A writer from *Social Interest News* will contact you soon to schedule an interview. Considering your schedule, it seems like you will be free on May 12, 14, 15, and 20. I hope one of these days works.

Sincerely,

Teresa Martinez
Secretary
Pueblo Corporation

| To: | Jim Douglas <jimdouglas@pueblo.net> |
| From: | Matthew Stokes <mstokes12@socialinterestnews.com> |
| Date: | May 10 |
| Subject: | Interview Request to the Pueblo Corporation |

Dear Mr. Douglas,

My name is Matthew, and I am a writer at *Social Interest News*. I already contacted your secretary, Teresa Martinez, regarding an interview. I heard about your company's decision to become a sponsor of the upcoming Barrington Children's Hospital Marathon. Our newspaper thought it would be a great opportunity for us to introduce a major sponsor to the public. We have no doubt that the interview will also be beneficial to your company by giving it good publicity. Are you available on any of the following dates: May 13, 14, or 16? If not, I can try to fit another day in my schedule.

Best regards,

Matthew Stokes
Social Interest News

**186.** What is NOT indicated about the Barrington Children's Hospital Marathon?

(A) It has happened every year for 15 years.
(B) It is a fundraising event for children with illnesses.
(C) It consists of only a 26-mile marathon.
(D) It will be held in mid-June this year.

**187.** Who most likely is Mr. Douglas?

(A) The director in Pueblo's Public Relations Department
(B) A secretary at the Pueblo Corporation
(C) The chief editor at *Social Interest News*
(D) A representative of the Barrington Children's Hospital

**188.** What is suggested about the Pueblo Corporation?

(A) Its employees are participating in the marathon.
(B) It has always been a sponsor of the marathon.
(C) It is the biggest pharmaceutical company in the country.
(D) It specializes in producing medicinal drugs.

**189.** In the second e-mail, the word "beneficial" in paragraph 1, line 5, is closest in meaning to

(A) helpful
(B) favorable
(C) profitable
(D) publicized

**190.** When will the interview most likely be held?

(A) On May 13
(B) On May 14
(C) On May 16
(D) On June 16

**Questions 191-195** refer to the following Web pages and e-mail.

## Visiting Professor Seeking Downtown Apartment

**Topic:** Six-Month Sublease
**Date:** September 12

I will be in London from January to June on a teaching assignment at Coleridge College.
I am looking for a six-month lease or sublease for the upcoming year.

I am not looking for anything luxurious. I'm in the market for a nice, clean one- or two-bedroom apartment with basic amenities like a stove and a refrigerator. Anything else would be an added bonus. A patio or open balcony would be ideal as I like to entertain friends and colleagues. I am looking to live near the college, however, as I will not be bringing my car from the United States. My budget is 1,600 American dollars, including water, gas, and electricity. I am a nonsmoker.

## Apartment for Rent in London

**Topic:** Real Estate and Housing
**Date:** September 13

Enjoy this great one-bedroom apartment that is going through a major renovation. This clean and simple yet modern apartment will be move-in ready on December 15. It will feature a lovely balcony, new floors throughout, and all new appliances. The apartment is just outside downtown London but close to major public transportation hubs. It is an ideal option for students and staff members at Coleridge College as well as employees at the post office and other government buildings. It is less than a kilometer from a major municipal park. £.1,000 pays for water, sewer, garbage pickup, and general upkeep of the property. The electricity and natural gas bills will be the responsibility of the tenant. Nonsmokers only. A one-time security deposit equal to one month's rent should be paid upon signing the rental agreement.

| To: | Martha Turner <turnerproperties@hmail.net> |
|---|---|
| From: | Dr. Reed McMahon <reed.mc@talkmail.com> |
| Date: | September 14 |
| Subject: | Apartment |

Dear Ms. Turner,

I am responding to your listing for the recently renovated one-bedroom apartment just outside downtown. It is very appealing to me and definitely fits my budget. Unfortunately, I won't be able to see the apartment first hand, so I was hoping you had some pictures of the property. Obviously, it is still being renovated, but I'm sure I can fill in the blanks. Please use this e-mail address to respond or if you wish, feel free to call me anytime.

Thank you.

Dr. Reed McMahon
512.578.6090

**191.** Why is Dr. McMahon moving?

(A) To teach
(B) To return home
(C) To study part time
(D) To coach

**192.** What aspect of the property does NOT match Dr. McMahon's preferences?

(A) The monthly cost
(B) The size
(C) The location
(D) The smoking rules

**193.** What additional information does Dr. McMahon require?

(A) When the apartment will be available
(B) A conversion from U.S. dollars to pounds
(C) Who to call about repairs
(D) Photos of the apartment

**194.** Why did Dr. McMahon send the e-mail?

(A) To find out about the layout of the apartment
(B) To change the details of a residential advertisement.
(C) To inquire about transportation options
(B) To inquire about local businesses

**195.** When will Dr. McMahon most likely be moving?

(A) In February
(B) In December
(C) In January
(D) In September

# AMERICAN AIR
## Late Arrival Baggage Form

Dear American Air Customers,

We are sorry to inform you about the late arrival of your luggage. Please write down the details below to help us track your belongings and return them to you as soon as possible. An American Air clerk will inform you by phone as soon as we find your luggage. Most bags are traced and returned to their owners within a couple of days. Should your luggage not be found, it still won't be classed as "lost" until it's been missing for 21 days – until then, it's "delayed."

**Date:** November 16
**Name:** Raymond Walker
**Local Address:** Hotel Forest, Downtown, 984-2 Auckland, New Zealand
**Tel:** +62 185 0253
**Flight No.:** K53GC6

## Delayed Luggage Information

|          | Quantity | Descriptions |
|----------|----------|--------------|
| Suitcase | 1        | Small red suitcase with 2 wheels; "Raymond Walker" written on the name tag |
| Backpack |          |              |
| Handbag  |          |              |
| Box      | 1        | Small plastic box with "Raymond Walker, Samion Foods" written on it |
| Other    |          |              |

| To: | Raymond Walker <rwalker@samionfood.com> |
|-----|------------------------------------------|
| From: | Harry Hernandez <hh@samionfood.com> |
| Date: | November 16, 5:23 P.M. |
| Subject: | Re: Food Samples |

Dear Mr. Walker

Since we do not know when your luggage will be found and returned, I sent sauce samples by overnight shipping. Therefore, you will be able to take the goods to tomorrow's meeting. There are five flavors packed in the box as well as two small sauce bottles with labels. I sent the items by TWS Shipping to your lodging. The package will arrive by 9:30 A.M., so you can show them when you speak at the meeting at 11:00.

Sincerely,

Harry Hernandez
Samion Foods

# TWS SHIPPING

## Your Shipment Information

**Ship from:** Samion Foods, 27 Earot Street, Archeis 1, 1UE, AU

**Ship to**: Hotel Forest, Downtown, 984-2 Auckland, New Zealand

**Weight:** 0.68kg

☐ Enclosed   ■ Box   ☐ Custom packaging

## Your Overnight Shipment Options

**TWS Early morning:** Deliver by 9:30 A.M. tomorrow [$62 Ship Now]

**TWS morning:** Deliver by 11:30 A.M. tomorrow [$49 Ship Now]

**TWS afternoon:** Deliver by 3:00 P.M. tomorrow [$31 Ship Now]

**TWS evening:** Deliver by 8:30 P.M. tomorrow [$35 Ship Now]

**196.** What is indicated about American Air?

(A) It requires customers to include name tags on all pieces of luggage.

(B) It guarantees that missing luggage will be returned in three days.

(C) It will notify Mr. Walker when his luggage is found.

(D) It will reimburse Mr. Walker for his lost luggage.

**197.** Where did Mr. Walker most likely pack his samples?

(A) In a box

(B) In a refrigerator

(C) In a briefcase

(D) In a backpack

**198.** What is implied about Mr. Hernandez?

(A) He is meeting with clients in New Zealand.

(B) He travels frequently for Samion Foods.

(C) He is an American Air customer service agent.

(D) He wants his customers to sample some products.

**199.** According to the e-mail, what will Mr. Walker do tomorrow at 11 A.M.?

(A) Accept a delivery

(B) Make a presentation

(C) Check out of his hotel

(D) Confirm his return flight

**200.** How much was Mr. Hernandez charged for shipping?

(A) $35.00

(B) $31.00

(C) $49.00

(D) $62.00

STOP! This is the end of the test. If you finish before time is called, you may go back to Parts 5, 6, and 7 and check your work.

# 900점은 기본, 만점까지 가능한 고득점용 실전 1000제!

# 토익 실전서는 이 책 한 권이면 충분합니다!

**시나공 토익**

## 950 실전 모의고사

고경희, 이관우 지음 | 816쪽 | 22,000원

---

## 900은 기본, 만점까지 가능한 12회분, 2400제 수록!

**❶ 최신 경향을 반영한 12회분, 2400제 수록!**
최근 출제 경향을 완벽하게 반영한 2400제를 수록했습니다.

**❷ 친절한 해설집 온라인 무료 다운로드!**
필요한 문제만 간편하게 확인할 수 있게 해설집을 PDF로 제공합니다.

**❸ 만점 대비용 '독학용 복습 노트' 제공!**
저자들의 강의 노하우가 담긴 '만점 훈련용' 독학용 학습노트를 제공합니다.

> **LC** 저자의 수업 방식을 그대로 가져온 소리 통암기 훈련 및 MP3 제공
> **RC** 고득점을 좌우하는 어휘 문제를 통해 고난도 어휘 학습

**❹ 실전용, 복습용, 1.2배속, 고사장 소음버전 MP3 무료 다운로드!**
www.gilbut.co.kr에서 무료로 다운로드 하세요.

---

| 권장하는 점수대 | 400 | 500 | 600 | 700 | 800 | 900 |
|---|---|---|---|---|---|---|

| 이 책의 난이도 | 쉬움 | 비슷함 | 어려움 |
|---|---|---|---|

길벗
이지:톡

**시나공 토익**

# 850 실전 모의고사

**초판 1쇄 발행** · 2020년 7월 10일
**초판 2쇄 발행** · 2021년 2월 10일

**지은이** · 김병기
**발행인** · 이종원
**발행처** · ㈜도서출판 길벗
**출판사 등록일** · 1990년 12월 24일
**주소** · 서울시 마포구 월드컵로 10길 56(서교동)
**대표전화** · 02) 332–0931 | **팩스** · 02) 322–6766
**홈페이지** · www.gilbut.co.kr | **이메일** · eztok@gilbut.co.kr

**기획 및 책임편집** · 고경환 (kkh@gilbut.co.kr) | **디자인** · 황애라 | **제작** · 이준호, 손일순, 이진혁
**영업마케팅** · 김학흥, 장봉석 | **웹마케팅** · 이수미, 최소영 | **영업관리** · 심선숙 | **독자지원** · 송혜란, 윤정아

**CTP 출력 및 인쇄** · 예림인쇄 | **제본** · 예림바인딩

• 이 도서의 국립중앙도서관 출판예정도서목록(CIP)은 서지정보유통지원시스템 홈페이지(http://seoji.nl.go.kr)와
  국가자료공동목록시스템(http://www.nl.go.kr/kolisnet)에서 이용하실 수 있습니다.(CIP제어번호: CIP2020025709)

ISBN 979-11-6521-213-1 03740
(이지톡 도서번호 300993)

정가 19,500원

· · · · · · · · · · · · · · · · · · · · · · · · · · · · · · · · · · · · · · · · · · · · · · · · · · · · ·

**독자의 1초까지 아껴주는 정성 길벗출판사**

**(주)도서출판 길벗** | IT실용, IT/일반 수험서, 경제경영, 취미실용, 인문교양(더퀘스트) www.gilbut.co.kr
**길벗이지톡** | 어학단행본, 어학수험서 www.eztok.co.kr
**길벗스쿨** | 국어학습, 수학학습, 어린이교양, 주니어 어학학습, 교과서 www.gilbutschool.co.kr

# 목차

*자세한 해설을 확인하고 싶으시면 홈페이지에서 해설집을 다운로드하세요.(www.gilbut.co.kr)

# Actual Test 정답표

**Listening Comprehension**  **Reading Comprehension**

## 01

| | | | | | | | | | |
|---|---|---|---|---|---|---|---|---|---|
| 1. (D) | 2. (A) | 3. (C) | 4. (D) | 5. (B) | 101. (B) | 102. (C) | 103. (A) | 104. (D) | 105. (B) |
| 6. (D) | 7. (A) | 8. (C) | 9. (C) | 10. (C) | 106. (B) | 107. (A) | 108. (B) | 109. (A) | 110. (B) |
| 11. (B) | 12. (B) | 13. (A) | 14. (C) | 15. (C) | 111. (C) | 112. (D) | 113. (B) | 114. (A) | 115. (B) |
| 16. (B) | 17. (A) | 18. (C) | 19. (C) | 20. (A) | 116. (A) | 117. (C) | 118. (C) | 119. (A) | 120. (B) |
| 21. (B) | 22. (C) | 23. (B) | 24. (B) | 25. (C) | 121. (B) | 122. (D) | 123. (A) | 124. (A) | 125. (C) |
| 26. (B) | 27. (B) | 28. (C) | 29. (A) | 30. (C) | 126. (B) | 127. (A) | 128. (D) | 129. (D) | 130. (C) |
| 31. (C) | 32. (B) | 33. (D) | 34. (D) | 35. (D) | 131. (B) | 132. (D) | 133. (C) | 134. (D) | 135. (A) |
| 36. (C) | 37. (B) | 38. (D) | 39. (C) | 40. (C) | 136. (D) | 137. (A) | 138. (B) | 139. (D) | 140. (B) |
| 41. (C) | 42. (A) | 43. (C) | 44. (A) | 45. (D) | 141. (C) | 142. (A) | 143. (A) | 144. (D) | 145. (B) |
| 46. (D) | 47. (C) | 48. (C) | 49. (A) | 50. (C) | 146. (C) | 147. (A) | 148. (C) | 149. (D) | 150. (B) |
| 51. (B) | 52. (D) | 53. (A) | 54. (C) | 55. (D) | 151. (C) | 152. (C) | 153. (D) | 154. (C) | 155. (C) |
| 56. (C) | 57. (B) | 58. (C) | 59. (B) | 60. (D) | 156. (C) | 157. (C) | 158. (B) | 159. (C) | 160. (C) |
| 61. (A) | 62. (C) | 63. (D) | 64. (B) | 65. (C) | 161. (C) | 162. (B) | 163. (C) | 164. (A) | 165. (B) |
| 66. (B) | 67. (D) | 68. (A) | 69. (C) | 70. (C) | 166. (C) | 167. (B) | 168. (D) | 169. (C) | 170. (A) |
| 71. (A) | 72. (B) | 73. (B) | 74. (C) | 75. (A) | 171. (C) | 172. (D) | 173. (B) | 174. (C) | 175. (C) |
| 76. (B) | 77. (C) | 78. (D) | 79. (D) | 80. (C) | 176. (B) | 177. (A) | 178. (B) | 179. (B) | 180. (D) |
| 81. (B) | 82. (C) | 83. (A) | 84. (C) | 85. (A) | 181. (D) | 182. (B) | 183. (A) | 184. (B) | 185. (B) |
| 86. (B) | 87. (B) | 88. (B) | 89. (C) | 90. (D) | 186. (B) | 187. (B) | 188. (B) | 189. (D) | 190. (A) |
| 91. (B) | 92. (D) | 93. (D) | 94. (B) | 95. (D) | 191. (C) | 192. (A) | 193. (A) | 194. (D) | 195. (A) |
| 96. (C) | 97. (A) | 98. (D) | 99. (A) | 100. (B) | 196. (C) | 197. (D) | 198. (A) | 199. (C) | 200. (B) |

## 02

| | | | | | | | | | |
|---|---|---|---|---|---|---|---|---|---|
| 1. (C) | 2. (D) | 3. (B) | 4. (D) | 5. (A) | 101. (C) | 102. (A) | 103. (D) | 104. (A) | 105. (D) |
| 6. (D) | 7. (A) | 8. (C) | 9. (B) | 10. (B) | 106. (B) | 107. (A) | 108. (C) | 109. (D) | 110. (C) |
| 11. (C) | 12. (A) | 13. (A) | 14. (B) | 15. (B) | 111. (A) | 112. (C) | 113. (C) | 114. (B) | 115. (B) |
| 16. (C) | 17. (B) | 18. (B) | 19. (A) | 20. (B) | 116. (A) | 117. (D) | 118. (B) | 119. (D) | 120. (B) |
| 21. (A) | 22. (C) | 23. (B) | 24. (A) | 25. (C) | 121. (B) | 122. (A) | 123. (B) | 124. (D) | 125. (A) |
| 26. (C) | 27. (A) | 28. (B) | 29. (A) | 30. (B) | 126. (D) | 127. (C) | 128. (A) | 129. (A) | 130. (C) |
| 31. (A) | 32. (C) | 33. (B) | 34. (B) | 35. (C) | 131. (D) | 132. (B) | 133. (B) | 134. (A) | 135. (D) |
| 36. (C) | 37. (B) | 38. (B) | 39. (C) | 40. (C) | 136. (D) | 137. (C) | 138. (B) | 139. (A) | 140. (D) |
| 41. (C) | 42. (A) | 43. (D) | 44. (A) | 45. (B) | 141. (B) | 142. (B) | 143. (B) | 144. (C) | 145. (D) |
| 46. (B) | 47. (B) | 48. (B) | 49. (D) | 50. (C) | 146. (C) | 147. (A) | 148. (C) | 149. (D) | 150. (C) |
| 51. (B) | 52. (A) | 53. (B) | 54. (B) | 55. (D) | 151. (D) | 152. (B) | 153. (D) | 154. (C) | 155. (C) |
| 56. (C) | 57. (B) | 58. (A) | 59. (C) | 60. (B) | 156. (B) | 157. (C) | 158. (D) | 159. (A) | 160. (C) |
| 61. (A) | 62. (C) | 63. (B) | 64. (A) | 65. (D) | 161. (A) | 162. (D) | 163. (D) | 164. (D) | 165. (D) |
| 66. (C) | 67. (A) | 68. (A) | 69. (D) | 70. (C) | 166. (C) | 167. (A) | 168. (C) | 169. (D) | 170. (C) |
| 71. (A) | 72. (B) | 73. (D) | 74. (D) | 75. (C) | 171. (D) | 172. (C) | 173. (A) | 174. (D) | 175. (B) |
| 76. (D) | 77. (B) | 78. (C) | 79. (D) | 80. (D) | 176. (D) | 177. (D) | 178. (A) | 179. (C) | 180. (C) |
| 81. (B) | 82. (A) | 83. (D) | 84. (B) | 85. (A) | 181. (B) | 182. (A) | 183. (B) | 184. (D) | 185. (D) |
| 86. (B) | 87. (A) | 88. (B) | 89. (C) | 90. (C) | 186. (C) | 187. (B) | 188. (C) | 189. (D) | 190. (D) |
| 91. (B) | 92. (D) | 93. (C) | 94. (A) | 95. (C) | 191. (D) | 192. (B) | 193. (B) | 194. (A) | 195. (D) |
| 96. (C) | 97. (D) | 98. (B) | 99. (C) | 100. (C) | 196. (A) | 197. (D) | 198. (A) | 199. (C) | 200. (D) |

# Actual Test 정답표

**Listening Comprehension**        **Reading Comprehension**

## 03

| | | | | | | | | | |
|---|---|---|---|---|---|---|---|---|---|
| 1. (B) | 2. (C) | 3. (C) | 4. (B) | 5. (D) | 101. (B) | 102. (B) | 103. (C) | 104. (B) | 105. (D) |
| 6. (A) | 7. (B) | 8. (B) | 9. (B) | 10. (B) | 106. (B) | 107. (B) | 108. (B) | 109. (B) | 110. (B) |
| 11. (B) | 12. (B) | 13. (C) | 14. (C) | 15. (B) | 111. (B) | 112. (C) | 113. (C) | 114. (C) | 115. (C) |
| 16. (C) | 17. (C) | 18. (C) | 19. (A) | 20. (B) | 116. (A) | 117. (C) | 118. (D) | 119. (B) | 120. (C) |
| 21. (B) | 22. (C) | 23. (C) | 24. (B) | 25. (C) | 121. (D) | 122. (A) | 123. (C) | 124. (C) | 125. (D) |
| 26. (C) | 27. (A) | 28. (C) | 29. (B) | 30. (B) | 126. (C) | 127. (D) | 128. (D) | 129. (A) | 130. (B) |
| 31. (A) | 32. (B) | 33. (C) | 34. (A) | 35. (C) | 131. (A) | 132. (C) | 133. (C) | 134. (D) | 135. (D) |
| 36. (B) | 37. (D) | 38. (A) | 39. (C) | 40. (D) | 136. (C) | 137. (D) | 138. (A) | 139. (C) | 140. (C) |
| 41. (C) | 42. (B) | 43. (C) | 44. (D) | 45. (D) | 141. (C) | 142. (B) | 143. (C) | 144. (D) | 145. (C) |
| 46. (C) | 47. (B) | 48. (A) | 49. (D) | 50. (B) | 146. (A) | 147. (B) | 148. (B) | 149. (C) | 150. (D) |
| 51. (D) | 52. (D) | 53. (D) | 54. (D) | 55. (B) | 151. (B) | 152. (D) | 153. (C) | 154. (C) | 155. (C) |
| 56. (D) | 57. (D) | 58. (B) | 59. (D) | 60. (C) | 156. (B) | 157. (C) | 158. (D) | 159. (B) | 160. (D) |
| 61. (B) | 62. (D) | 63. (B) | 64. (D) | 65. (C) | 161. (D) | 162. (B) | 163. (D) | 164. (B) | 165. (D) |
| 66. (A) | 67. (B) | 68. (B) | 69. (B) | 70. (C) | 166. (C) | 167. (D) | 168. (D) | 169. (A) | 170. (A) |
| 71. (B) | 72. (C) | 73. (B) | 74. (A) | 75. (B) | 171. (B) | 172. (C) | 173. (C) | 174. (C) | 175. (A) |
| 76. (C) | 77. (A) | 78. (C) | 79. (D) | 80. (A) | 176. (B) | 177. (D) | 178. (A) | 179. (B) | 180. (B) |
| 81. (B) | 82. (D) | 83. (B) | 84. (B) | 85. (B) | 181. (D) | 182. (B) | 183. (A) | 184. (A) | 185. (D) |
| 86. (C) | 87. (A) | 88. (C) | 89. (B) | 90. (C) | 186. (D) | 187. (B) | 188. (C) | 189. (A) | 190. (C) |
| 91. (B) | 92. (A) | 93. (C) | 94. (C) | 95. (D) | 191. (C) | 192. (C) | 193. (D) | 194. (B) | 195. (D) |
| 96. (A) | 97. (C) | 98. (C) | 99. (C) | 100. (C) | 196. (B) | 197. (D) | 198. (A) | 199. (C) | 200. (C) |

## 04

| | | | | | | | | | |
|---|---|---|---|---|---|---|---|---|---|
| 1. (C) | 2. (D) | 3. (D) | 4. (B) | 5. (D) | 101. (D) | 102. (A) | 103. (B) | 104. (A) | 105. (D) |
| 6. (A) | 7. (A) | 8. (B) | 9. (A) | 10. (A) | 106. (C) | 107. (D) | 108. (C) | 109. (A) | 110. (C) |
| 11. (A) | 12. (B) | 13. (C) | 14. (B) | 15. (B) | 111. (B) | 112. (A) | 113. (B) | 114. (C) | 115. (D) |
| 16. (C) | 17. (B) | 18. (C) | 19. (C) | 20. (A) | 116. (B) | 117. (D) | 118. (D) | 119. (B) | 120. (C) |
| 21. (A) | 22. (B) | 23. (B) | 24. (C) | 25. (C) | 121. (D) | 122. (B) | 123. (D) | 124. (D) | 125. (B) |
| 26. (B) | 27. (A) | 28. (C) | 29. (C) | 30. (C) | 126. (D) | 127. (C) | 128. (D) | 129. (D) | 130. (B) |
| 31. (A) | 32. (D) | 33. (C) | 34. (C) | 35. (B) | 131. (D) | 132. (C) | 133. (D) | 134. (C) | 135. (A) |
| 36. (D) | 37. (A) | 38. (A) | 39. (B) | 40. (D) | 136. (C) | 137. (B) | 138. (B) | 139. (D) | 140. (C) |
| 41. (C) | 42. (B) | 43. (B) | 44. (D) | 45. (B) | 141. (A) | 142. (B) | 143. (D) | 144. (C) | 145. (A) |
| 46. (B) | 47. (A) | 48. (C) | 49. (B) | 50. (B) | 146. (C) | 147. (C) | 148. (A) | 149. (D) | 150. (C) |
| 51. (D) | 52. (B) | 53. (B) | 54. (C) | 55. (D) | 151. (C) | 152. (D) | 153. (A) | 154. (D) | 155. (C) |
| 56. (B) | 57. (B) | 58. (D) | 59. (C) | 60. (B) | 156. (D) | 157. (A) | 158. (A) | 159. (B) | 160. (C) |
| 61. (D) | 62. (D) | 63. (B) | 64. (B) | 65. (A) | 161. (C) | 162. (B) | 163. (A) | 164. (D) | 165. (C) |
| 66. (B) | 67. (C) | 68. (B) | 69. (C) | 70. (D) | 166. (B) | 167. (C) | 168. (D) | 169. (C) | 170. (C) |
| 71. (B) | 72. (C) | 73. (C) | 74. (C) | 75. (A) | 171. (A) | 172. (B) | 173. (A) | 174. (D) | 175. (B) |
| 76. (C) | 77. (A) | 78. (D) | 79. (C) | 80. (B) | 176. (A) | 177. (D) | 178. (C) | 179. (B) | 180. (B) |
| 81. (C) | 82. (D) | 83. (A) | 84. (B) | 85. (D) | 181. (C) | 182. (B) | 183. (A) | 184. (C) | 185. (D) |
| 86. (A) | 87. (B) | 88. (D) | 89. (C) | 90. (D) | 186. (D) | 187. (D) | 188. (C) | 189. (C) | 190. (D) |
| 91. (D) | 92. (B) | 93. (C) | 94. (C) | 95. (B) | 191. (A) | 192. (C) | 193. (B) | 194. (A) | 195. (D) |
| 96. (D) | 97. (A) | 98. (A) | 99. (C) | 100. (C) | 196. (C) | 197. (D) | 198. (D) | 199. (C) | 200. (C) |

# Actual Test 정답표

## 05

| | | | | |
|---|---|---|---|---|
| **1.** (D) | **2.** (C) | **3.** (D) | **4.** (C) | **5.** (A) |
| **6.** (B) | **7.** (A) | **8.** (B) | **9.** (A) | **10.** (B) |
| **11.** (B) | **12.** (A) | **13.** (A) | **14.** (B) | **15.** (B) |
| **16.** (C) | **17.** (B) | **18.** (B) | **19.** (A) | **20.** (B) |
| **21.** (C) | **22.** (C) | **23.** (B) | **24.** (C) | **25.** (A) |
| **26.** (B) | **27.** (B) | **28.** (C) | **29.** (B) | **30.** (C) |
| **31.** (C) | **32.** (B) | **33.** (B) | **34.** (D) | **35.** (B) |
| **36.** (A) | **37.** (D) | **38.** (A) | **39.** (C) | **40.** (D) |
| **41.** (C) | **42.** (C) | **43.** (D) | **44.** (D) | **45.** (A) |
| **46.** (A) | **47.** (B) | **48.** (B) | **49.** (C) | **50.** (B) |
| **51.** (C) | **52.** (D) | **53.** (D) | **54.** (D) | **55.** (D) |
| **56.** (C) | **57.** (C) | **58.** (D) | **59.** (C) | **60.** (D) |
| **61.** (B) | **62.** (C) | **63.** (B) | **64.** (B) | **65.** (A) |
| **66.** (D) | **67.** (C) | **68.** (D) | **69.** (D) | **70.** (D) |
| **71.** (C) | **72.** (A) | **73.** (B) | **74.** (D) | **75.** (C) |
| **76.** (D) | **77.** (B) | **78.** (B) | **79.** (C) | **80.** (C) |
| **81.** (B) | **82.** (C) | **83.** (B) | **84.** (C) | **85.** (B) |
| **86.** (C) | **87.** (B) | **88.** (D) | **89.** (A) | **90.** (D) |
| **91.** (B) | **92.** (A) | **93.** (B) | **94.** (B) | **95.** (B) |
| **96.** (D) | **97.** (C) | **98.** (C) | **99.** (A) | **100.** (C) |

| | | | | |
|---|---|---|---|---|
| **101.** (B) | **102.** (D) | **103.** (B) | **104.** (B) | **105.** (C) |
| **106.** (B) | **107.** (C) | **108.** (D) | **109.** (B) | **110.** (B) |
| **111.** (C) | **112.** (C) | **113.** (D) | **114.** (C) | **115.** (A) |
| **116.** (B) | **117.** (D) | **118.** (B) | **119.** (D) | **120.** (B) |
| **121.** (A) | **122.** (A) | **123.** (C) | **124.** (B) | **125.** (A) |
| **126.** (C) | **127.** (B) | **128.** (A) | **129.** (D) | **130.** (B) |
| **131.** (B) | **132.** (A) | **133.** (D) | **134.** (D) | **135.** (D) |
| **136.** (D) | **137.** (B) | **138.** (A) | **139.** (D) | **140.** (C) |
| **141.** (C) | **142.** (D) | **143.** (A) | **144.** (D) | **145.** (C) |
| **146.** (A) | **147.** (D) | **148.** (D) | **149.** (C) | **150.** (B) |
| **151.** (A) | **152.** (C) | **153.** (D) | **154.** (B) | **155.** (A) |
| **156.** (B) | **157.** (D) | **158.** (A) | **159.** (C) | **160.** (B) |
| **161.** (C) | **162.** (A) | **163.** (B) | **164.** (D) | **165.** (A) |
| **166.** (A) | **167.** (C) | **168.** (D) | **169.** (C) | **170.** (D) |
| **171.** (D) | **172.** (C) | **173.** (A) | **174.** (A) | **175.** (D) |
| **176.** (C) | **177.** (D) | **178.** (B) | **179.** (C) | **180.** (D) |
| **181.** (C) | **182.** (C) | **183.** (A) | **184.** (D) | **185.** (B) |
| **186.** (C) | **187.** (A) | **188.** (D) | **189.** (A) | **190.** (B) |
| **191.** (A) | **192.** (C) | **193.** (D) | **194.** (A) | **195.** (B) |
| **196.** (C) | **197.** (A) | **198.** (D) | **199.** (B) | **200.** (D) |

# Actual Test

01
02
03
04
05

## 번역 및 정답

**1.** 미W

(A) The woman is installing a computer monitor.

(B) The woman is reviewing a document.

(C) The woman is staring out the window.

(D) The woman is doing some work at the computer.

(A) 여자는 컴퓨터 모니터를 설치하고 있다.

(B) 여자는 서류를 검토하고 있다.

(C) 여자는 창문 밖을 응시하고 있다.

(D) 여자는 컴퓨터로 작업을 하고 있다.　　　　정답 (D)

**2.** 영W

(A) The man is walking down a staircase.

(B) The man is holding onto a railing.

(C) The man is standing near an archway.

(D) The man is taking a bicycle up some steps.

(A) 남자는 계단을 걸어서 내려가고 있다.

(B) 남자는 난간을 잡고 있다.

(C) 남자는 아치 형태의 통로 근처에 서있다.

(D) 남자는 자전거를 들고 계단을 오르고 있다.　　정답 (A)

**3.** 호M

(A) She is raking some leaves.

(B) She is washing her shorts.

(C) She is watering some plants.

(D) She is selecting vegetables.

(A) 그녀는 갈퀴로 나뭇잎을 긁어 모으고 있다.

(B) 그녀는 반바지를 세탁하고 있다.

(C) 그녀는 화초에 물을 주고 있다.

(D) 그녀는 야채를 고르고 있다.　　　　　　정답 (C)

**4.** 미M

(A) Some people are talking in small groups.

(B) Some performers are entertaining an audience.

(C) Some chairs are being set up in an auditorium.

(D) A presentation is being shown on both screens.

(A) 몇몇 사람들이 소규모 집단으로 나뉘어 이야기를 하고 있다.

(B) 몇몇 공연자들이 청중을 즐겁게 하고 있다.

(C) 몇몇 의자들이 강당에 설치되고 있다.

(D) 발표 내용이 양쪽 화면을 통해 제공되고 있다.　정답 (D)

**5.** 미W

(A) Salespeople are arranging merchandise on the shelves.

(B) Rows of caps are displayed on the rack.

(C) Price tags have been placed on each item.

(D) An awning has been stretched across the store entrance.

(A) 판매사원들이 선반에 상품을 배열하고 있다.

(B) 여러 줄의 야구 모자들이 진열대에 전시되어 있다.

(C) 가격표가 각 제품에 부착되어 있다.

(D) 상점 입구를 가로지르는 차양이 곧게 뻗어 있다.　정답 (B)

**6.** 영W

(A) Some guests are being shown to their seats.

(B) A large flower centerpiece is on the table.

(C) Several candles are being lit by a waitress.

(D) A dining table has been set for a meal.

(A) 몇몇 손님들이 자리로 안내되고 있다.

(B) 큰 꽃장식이 테이블 위에 놓여 있다.

(C) 여종업원이 몇몇 양초들에 불을 붙이고 있다.

(D) 테이블이 식사를 할 수 있는 준비가 되어 있다.　정답 (D)

### Part 2

**7.** 미W 호M

When does the express bus leave?

(A) In half an hour.

(B) To Los Angeles.

(C) I'll take a week off.

고속버스는 언제 출발합니까?

(A) 30분 후에요.

(B) Los Angeles로 가요.

(C) 저는 일주일 휴가를 낼 겁니다.　　　　　정답 (A)

**8.** 영W 미M

Where do you usually go for computer repairs?

(A) Last Thursday.

(B) I think I can fix it.

(C) Do you have a problem?

대개 컴퓨터 수리를 하러 어디로 가세요?

(A) 지난주 목요일에요.

(B) 제가 그걸 수리할 수 있을 거예요.

(C) 무슨 문제가 있으세요?　　　　　　　　정답 (C)

**9.** 미W 호M

Who developed the new product?

(A) Well, Mr. Wilson will.

(B) It's very expensive.

(C) Let me check.

신제품은 누가 개발했나요?

(A) Wilson 씨가 할 겁니다.

(B) 그건 너무 비싸요.

(C) 제가 확인해 볼게요.　　　　　　　　　정답 (C)

**10.** 호M 영W

Why was Ms. Williams late for the staff meeting?

(A) The meeting will be held in room 201.

(B) Yes, I usually commute to work by subway.

(C) She thought that it had been canceled.

Williams 씨가 직원 회의에 늦은 이유가 뭔가요?

(A) 회의는 201호에서 열릴 겁니다.

(B) 네, 저는 대개 지하철을 이용하여 통근해요.

(C) 그녀는 회의가 취소된 것으로 알고 있더군요.　정답 (C)

**11.** 미M 영W

Isn't it time to advertise our new product?

(A) Yes, take it twice a day.

(B) Why don't we wait until next month?

(C) It took a year to develop.

우리 신제품을 광고할 때가 되지 않았나요?

(A) 네, 하루에 두 번 복용하세요.

(B) 다음달까지 기다려 보는 게 어때요?

(C) 그것을 개발하는 데 1년 걸렸어요.      정답 (B)

**12.** 미W 미M
Where are the fabric samples Mr. Baker received yesterday?
(A) I've already sampled the wine.
(B) Ms. Franklin might know.
(C) There was a welcome party yesterday.

Baker 씨가 어제 수령한 직물 견본품은 어디에 있나요?
(A) 저는 이미 그 포도주를 시음했어요.
(B) Franklin 씨가 알 겁니다.
(C) 어제 환영 파티가 있었어요.      정답 (B)

**13.** 호M 영W
How are customers responding to our new product?
(A) It's been favorably reviewed.
(B) Customs is not open yet.
(C) By e-mail.

우리 신제품에 대한 고객들의 반응은 어떤가요?
(A) 긍정적인 평가를 받고 있어요.
(B) 세관은 아직 열지 않았어요.
(C) 이메일을 통해서요.      정답 (A)

**14.** 미W 호M
Can I make a dental appointment for a regular checkup?
(A) Yes, I have a serious toothache.
(B) Weekdays from 9:00 to 5:00.
(C) No problem. What time would work best for you?

정기 검진을 위한 치과 진료 예약을 할 수 있을까요?
(A) 네, 심한 치통이 있어요.
(B) 주중에 9시부터 5시까지요.
(C) 물론입니다. 언제가 가장 좋으신가요?      정답 (C)

**15.** 미M 영W
We don't think you can drive to Seoul in this weather.
(A) We can drive you there.
(B) Yes, I used to work in Seoul.
(C) I just heard it will stop snowing soon.

당신이 이런 날씨에 서울까지 운전해서 갈 수는 없을 것 같아요.
(A) 우리가 그곳까지 차로 데려다 줄 수 있어요.
(B) 네, 저는 서울에서 일했어요.
(C) 눈이 곧 그친다고 들었어요.      정답 (C)

**16.** 영W 호M
Do you need some help with the market report, or can you do it yourself?
(A) We'll market a new cellular phone next week.
(B) Well, I'm almost done.
(C) Thanks. I think that was very helpful.

시장 보고서 작성에 도움이 필요하신가요, 아니면 혼자서 하실 수 있나요?
(A) 우리는 새로운 휴대전화를 다음주에 출시할 겁니다.
(B) 음, 거의 다 마무리했어요.
(C) 고맙습니다. 큰 도움이 된 것 같아요.      정답 (B)

**17.** 미M 미W
Hasn't Ms. Choi returned from vacation yet?
(A) I think she already has.
(B) Yes, she left for San Francisco yesterday.
(C) No, she will return it soon.

Choi 씨는 휴가에서 복귀했나요?
(A) 이미 복귀한 걸로 알고 있어요.
(B) 네, 그녀는 어제 San Francisco로 떠났어요.
(C) 아니오, 그녀는 그걸 곧 반납할 겁니다.      정답 (A)

**18.** 미W 호M
Doesn't your company offer free shipping for online purchasing?
(A) Some duty-free shops.
(B) No, here's your receipt.
(C) Yes, but only on orders over 150 dollars.

귀사에서는 온라인 구매에 대해 무료 배송을 제공하지 않습니까?
(A) 몇몇 면세점들이요.
(B) 아니오, 여기 영수증이에요.
(C) 네, 하지만 주문이 150달러 이상에만요.      정답 (C)

**19.** 미M 영W
When will the sales projections for the next quarter be ready?
(A) About 25,000 dollars, I guess.
(B) Yes, it will be ready.
(C) In about a week.

다음 분기 매출 예상 자료가 언제 준비될까요?
(A) 대략 25,000달러로 생각해요.
(B) 네, 준비될 거예요.
(C) 대략 일주일 후에요.      정답 (C)

**20.** 영W 미M
Who's taking care of the new construction project?
(A) I heard Mr. Moore is handling it.
(B) It's a ten-story building.
(C) We have a new projector.

새로운 건설 공사는 누가 담당하나요?
(A) Moore 씨가 담당하고 있다고 들었어요.
(B) 그건 10층 건물이에요.
(C) 우리는 새로운 영사기를 보유하고 있어요.      정답 (A)

**21.** 미W 미M
I think my cargo truck needs an oil change.
(A) Up to 3 tons in weight.
(B) It'll take about 40 minutes.
(C) Oil prices are expected to remain high.

제 화물 트럭의 오일을 교환해야 할 것 같습니다.
(A) 최대 3톤 무게까지요.
(B) 40분 정도 소요될 겁니다.
(C) 유가는 계속 높은 수준을 유지할 것으로 예상됩니다.      정답 (B)

**22.** 호M 미W
Can I see you in your office on Wednesday or Thursday?
(A) I think she is free on Wednesday.
(B) It won't last long.
(C) Let me check my schedule.

당신 사무실에서 수요일에 볼까요, 아니면 목요일에 볼까요?
(A) 그녀는 수요일에 시간이 있는 것으로 알고 있어요.
(B) 오래 걸리지 않을 겁니다.
(C) 제 일정을 확인해 볼게요.      정답 (C)

**23.** 영W 미M

You hired another tax accountant, didn't you?
(A) I'd like to open a bank account.
(B) Yes, she starts next Monday.
(C) No, please call me a taxi.

또 다른 세무사를 채용하셨죠, 그렇지 않나요?
(A) 은행 계좌를 열고 싶어요.
(B) 네, 그녀는 다음주 월요일에 근무를 시작해요.
(C) 아니오, 택시를 불러주세요. 　　　　정답 (B)

**24.** 미M 미W

Didn't you think the presentation was boring?
(A) That's my birthday present.
(B) No, I thought it was quite informative.
(C) Yes, it'll be held next Friday.

발표가 지루했다고 생각하지 않아요?
(A) 그건 제 생일 선물이에요.
(B) 아니오, 저는 꽤 유익했던 것 같아요.
(C) 네, 다음주 금요일에 열릴 겁니다. 　　정답 (B)

**25.** 미M 호M

Should I contact Ms. Parker directly?
(A) Well, I've been trying to call you.
(B) Yes, they changed the terms of the contract.
(C) No, I would talk to her assistant first.

제가 Parker 씨에게 직접 연락을 해야 할까요?
(A) 음, 계속 당신에게 연락을 취하려고 했어요.
(B) 네, 그들은 계약조건을 변경했어요.
(C) 아니오, 나라면 그녀의 비서한테 먼저 연락하겠어요. 　정답 (C)

**26.** 미W 영W

Which logo design should be sent to the printer?
(A) It has a very distinctive design.
(B) Let me check on that for you.
(C) Yes, every board member likes it.

어떤 로고 디자인이 인쇄업자에게 전달되어야 하나요?
(A) 그건 굉장히 독특한 디자인이에요.
(B) 제가 확인해 볼게요.
(C) 네, 모든 이사진이 그걸 좋아해요. 　　정답 (B)

**27.** 미M 영W

How would you like to join us for dinner tonight?
(A) A Chinese restaurant.
(B) Sure, what time should I come?
(C) Yes, I had spaghetti for dinner.

오늘밤에 우리와 함께 저녁식사를 하시는 게 어때요?
(A) 중국 식당이요.
(B) 좋아요, 몇 시에 가면 될까요?
(C) 네, 저는 저녁으로 스파게티를 먹었어요. 　정답 (B)

**28.** 호M 미W

Why haven't the brochures been sent?
(A) Please e-mail them to me.
(B) We have some apartments for rent.
(C) They're still being printed.

안내책자들이 발송되지 않은 이유가 무엇인가요?

(A) 이메일로 제게 보내주세요.
(B) 우리는 몇몇 임대용 아파트를 보유하고 있어요.
(C) 아직 인쇄되는 중이에요. 　　　　정답 (C)

**29.** 미M 영W

The new photocopier model we released last month is doing great, isn't it?
(A) Well, I haven't read the recent sales data yet.
(B) Yes, we leased an office last month.
(C) The performance starts at 6:00.

지난달에 출시한 새로운 복사기의 매출이 좋다고 하던데요, 그렇지 않나요?
(A) 음, 저는 최근 매출 자료를 읽어보지 못했어요.
(B) 네, 우리는 지난달에 사무실을 임대했어요.
(C) 공연은 6시에 시작해요. 　　　　정답 (A)

**30.** 호M 미W

It's a two-day international marketing conference held in California.
(A) Put it on my hotel bill, please.
(B) He delivered the keynote speech.
(C) Do you know what's on the agenda?

California에서 열리는 이틀 간의 국제 마케팅 회의예요.
(A) 제 호텔 숙박료에 포함시키세요.
(B) 그는 기조연설을 했어요.
(C) 의제가 무엇인지 아세요? 　　　　정답 (C)

**31.** 영W 미M

You handle all matters related to imports and exports, don't you?
(A) Yes, Mr. Baker usually takes care of it.
(B) Sorry. We can't import them right now.
(C) Yes, but I'm quitting my job next week.

수출입 관련 업무를 모두 담당하고 계시죠, 그렇지 않나요?
(A) 네, 대개 Baker 씨가 그 부분을 담당하고 있어요.
(B) 미안합니다만 지금 당장은 그것들을 수입할 수 없어요.
(C) 네, 하지만 저는 다음주에 퇴사합니다. 　정답 (C)

## Part 3

문제 32-34번은 다음 대화를 참조하시오. 영W 호M

W: (32) **Reception.** How may I help you?
M: (32) **This is Wesley White in room 101.** I ordered some tuna sandwiches from your restaurant and would like to return them. (33) **They smell weird. I think the tuna is not fresh.**
W: Oh, I'm sorry to hear that. (34) **I'll call the chef immediately and ask him to bring you a replacement soon.**
M: Um... Could you please give me a few minutes to have a look at the menu? I don't want to try the same thing again.

------

W: 프런트 데스크입니다. 어떻게 도와드릴까요?
M: 저는 101호실의 Wesley White입니다. 호텔 식당에서 참치 샌드위치를 주문했는데, 가져온 음식을 반품하고 싶어서요. 냄새가 이상해요. 참치가 신선한 것 같지 않아요.
W: 아, 죄송합니다. 제가 바로 요리사에게 전화해서 곧 새 것으로 가져다 드리라고 하겠습니다.
M: 음… 메뉴를 살펴보게 잠시 시간을 주시겠어요? 같은 음식을 다시 먹고 싶진 않네요.

**32.** 대화가 발생하는 장소는 어디겠는가?
(A) 음식점
(B) 호텔
(C) 공항
(D) 식품 가공업체 　　　　　　　　정답 (B)

**33.** 남자가 불만을 제기하는 이유는 무엇인가?
(A) 그는 영수증을 받지 못했다.
(B) 그가 주문하지 않은 요리를 제공받았다.
(C) 청구액이 예상보다 높다.
(D) 음식이 상했다. 　　　　　　　　정답 (D)

**34.** 여자가 남자에게 제안하는 것은 무엇인가?
(A) 매니저에게 이야기한다.
(B) 새로 주문한다.
(C) 메뉴를 살펴본다.
(D) 대체 요리를 기다린다. 　　　　　정답 (D)

**문제 35-37번은 다음의 3자 대화를 참조하시오.** [미M] [호M] [미W]

M1: Hi, Ms. Ryan. Do you have any coffee? (35) **We just went to the employee lounge to make a cup of coffee, but there's none left in there.**
M2: (35) **Yeah, there's no tea or sugar either.**
W: I don't have any, but (36) **I think that Mr. Finley is going to order some snacks and drinks for the breakroom this afternoon.**
M1: Good. (37) **We should make a list of the things we need and give it to him.**
W: Good idea. (37) **I know he's really busy, so he would probably appreciate it if we gave him a list so that he doesn't have to check everything himself.**

- - - - - - - - - - - - - - - - - - - - - - - - - - - - - - - -

M1: 안녕하세요, Ryan 씨. 혹시 커피 좀 있어요? 커피 한 잔 마시려고 직원 휴게실에 갔는데 남은 것이 없네요.
M2: 네, 차나 설탕도 남은 것이 없더라고요.
W: 저도 없어요. 하지만 Finley 씨가 오늘 오후에 휴게실에 둘 간식과 음료를 주문할 거예요.
M1: 잘됐네요. 그러면 우리가 필요한 것들의 목록을 만들어 그에게 줘야겠어요.
W: 좋은 생각이에요. 그가 매우 바쁘니 우리가 목록을 만들어서 그에게 주면 고마워할 거예요. 그가 모든 것을 직접 확인해 볼 필요가 없을 테니까요.

**35.** 남자들은 방금 어느 곳을 다녀왔는가?
(A) 구내식당
(B) 커피숍
(C) 새로운 사무실
(D) 휴게실 　　　　　　　　　　　정답 (D)

**36.** Finley 씨는 무엇을 주문할 예정인가?
(A) 사무용품
(B) 검은색 잉크 카트리지
(C) 다과
(D) 세제 　　　　　　　　　　　　정답 (C)

**37.** 화자들은 이후에 무엇을 할 것 같은가?
(A) 커피를 만든다.
(B) 서류를 복사한다.

(C) 문제점을 보고한다.
(D) 물품 목록을 만든다. 　　　　　정답 (D)

**문제 38-40번은 다음 대화를 참조하시오.** [미W] [미M]

W: Hello, Mr. King. (38) **My name is Kelly Winston, and I'm calling from Wesley Office Cleaning Service to confirm your work order.** (39) **We will arrive at your workplace tomorrow evening at 6 to check on and care for all of your offices.**
M: That's what I want, Ms. Winston, (39) **I already told the night guards and my personal secretary that they should expect you and your crew tomorrow evening.**
W: Thank you, Mr. King. There's one more thing to discuss. We need to collect payment before leaving as requested in our contract.
M: That's right. (40) **I'll leave a check with my personal secretary, Ms. Porter, tomorrow. Please don't forget to sign the receipt when you receive the check from her.** If you have any problems, do not hesitate to call me.

- - - - - - - - - - - - - - - - - - - - - - - - - - - - - - - -

W: 안녕하세요, King 씨. 제 이름은 Kelly Winston이라고 하고요, Wesley Office Cleaning Service에서 귀하의 작업 주문에 대해 확인차 연락을 드립니다. 저희는 내일 오후 6시에 귀하의 사무실에 도착하여 모든 사무실들을 살펴보고 관리해 드리려고 합니다.
M: 제가 원하는 바예요, Winston 씨, 저는 이미 야간 경비원들과 제 개인 비서에게 내일 저녁에 작업할 분들이 방문하실 것이라고 말했습니다.
W: 감사합니다, King 씨. 한 가지 더 논의해야 할 사항이 있습니다. 저희 계약서에서 요청된 바와 같이 저희는 작업이 끝나고 복귀하기 전에 작업 비용을 받아야 합니다.
M: 맞습니다. 내일 제 개인 비서인 Porter 씨에게 수표를 남겨 놓겠습니다. 그녀에게서 수표를 수령할 때 영수증에 서명하는 부분 잊지 않으셨으면 합니다. 그리고 문제가 발생하면 언제든 제게 연락을 주시고요.

**38.** 여자는 어떤 업종의 회사에서 근무하는가?
(A) 회계 사무소
(B) 보안 회사
(C) 금융 기관
(D) 청소 회사 　　　　　　　　　정답 (D)

**39.** 내일 저녁에는 어떤 일이 발생할 것인가?
(A) 큰 계약이 체결될 것이다.
(B) 보수공사가 완료될 것이다.
(C) 몇몇 직원들이 남자의 회사를 방문할 것이다.
(D) 돈이 Winston 씨에게 송금될 것이다. 　정답 (C)

**40.** Porter 씨는 내일 무엇을 해야 하는가?
(A) 청소용품을 구매한다.
(B) King 씨와 만난다.
(C) 지불 금액을 전달한다.
(D) 작업 주문을 확인한다. 　　　　정답 (C)

**문제 41-43번은 다음 대화를 참조하시오.** [미M] [미W]

M: Hi. My name is Barry Jones. (41) **I have a reservation for lunch on Tuesday.**
W: Yes, sir. We have you down for eight people in the private room at one o'clock. Do you need to make any changes?

M: Yes, actually. (42) **Some colleagues from Tampa will be joining us, so there will be a total of twelve people.**

W: I'm sorry, sir. The private room only has enough space for ten people. (43) **However, we could seat you upstairs, and that would be rather private.** Would that work?

---

M: 안녕하세요. 제 이름은 Barry Jones입니다. 화요일 점심으로 예약을 해놨어요.

W: 네, 고객님. 여덟 분을 위한 개인실이 1시로 예약이 되어 있습니다. 변경하셔야 할 내용이 있나요?

M: 네, 그렇습니다. Tampa에서 동료들이 더 올 거라서 총 12명이 될 것 같네요.

W: 죄송합니다, 고객님. 개인실은 열 분을 모실 수 있는 규모입니다. 하지만 고객님 일행을 위층으로 모실 수 있는데, 더 조용하고 방해를 받지 않을 겁니다. 괜찮으시겠습니까?

**41.** 여자는 어떤 사업체에서 근무할 것 같은가?
(A) 꽃집
(B) 비즈니스 컨설팅 회사
(C) 레스토랑
(D) 부동산 중개업체　　　　　　　　　　정답 (C)

**42.** 남자가 전화한 목적은 무엇인가?
(A) 예약을 변경하기 위해서
(B) 메뉴에 대해 문의하기 위해서
(C) 회의실을 예약하기 위해서
(D) 항공권을 예약하기 위해서　　　　　정답 (A)

**43.** 여자가 제안하는 것은 무엇인가?
(A) 다른 장소를 선택할 것
(B) 회의를 취소할 것
(C) 방을 변경할 것
(D) 다른 시간대에 식사를 할 것　　　　정답 (C)

---

문제 44-46번은 다음 대화를 참조하시오. 호M 영W

M: Lisa, have you seen the length of the line in the cafeteria? There is only one cashier working today. (44) **We'll have to wait a long time to buy our lunch.**

W: I don't really want to wait a long time. Do you? How about going to the fast-food cart down the street instead?

M: That's a good idea. That cart is quite cheap, too. (45) **Oh, I forgot. I don't have any cash on me today. Do you think I can use my card there?**

W: (46) **I doubt it. Don't worry about it though. I can lend you some money.** You can give me my money back tomorrow morning.

---

M: Lisa, 구내식당의 줄 길이 봤어요? 오늘 일하는 계산원이 딱 한 명밖에 없네요. 점심을 사려면 오래 기다려야 할 거예요.

W: 저는 정말 오래 기다리고 싶지 않은데요. 당신은 어때요? 대신에 거리의 패스트푸드 노점에 가는 게 어떨까요?

M: 좋은 생각이네요. 그 노점은 꽤 저렴하기도 하니까요. 아, 잊고 있었네요. 오늘 제가 현금이 없어요. 거기서 신용카드도 받을까요?

W: 그렇지 않을 걸요. 하지만 걱정하지 마세요. 제가 돈을 빌려줄 수 있어요. 빌린 돈은 내일 오전에 주세요.

**44.** 남자는 어떤 문제점을 언급하고 있는가?
(A) 대기시간이 길다.
(B) 계산원이 없다.
(C) 일부 음식이 품절되었다.
(D) 일부 도로 표지판이 없어졌다.　　　정답 (A)

**45.** 남자는 여자에게 무엇에 관해 물어보는가?
(A) 연락처
(B) 메뉴 가격
(C) 개점 시간
(D) 지불 방법　　　　　　　　　　　　정답 (D)

**46.** 여자가 "I doubt it."이라고 말하는 이유는 무엇인가?
(A) 질문을 하기 위해
(B) 설명을 요청하기 위해
(C) 남자의 말을 믿을 수 없다는 것을 나타내기 위해
(D) 부정적인 답변을 하기 위해　　　　정답 (D)

---

문제 47-49번은 다음 대화를 참조하시오. 미W 호M

W: Hi, Mr. Morris. (47) **What's the latest news regarding the accounting manager position? Have you found anyone suitable yet?**

M: Unfortunately, no, Ms. Keller. The personnel manager has shown me numerous applications, but I've yet to find anyone who has enough experience. (48) **The successful candidate will be in charge of a large group of accountants, so we need someone with excellent management skills.**

W: (49) **I have a friend from my previous job who would be perfect.** He's been managing an accounting department for many years now, so he has lots of leadership experience. He is currently based in Boston, but he may be willing to relocate to New York. (49) **Would you like me to call him to ask if he'd be interested?**

---

W: 안녕하세요, Morris 씨. 회계부장 직에 대한 최근 진행 상황은 어떤가요? 그 자리에 적합한 사람을 찾았나요?

M: 유감스럽게도 아직이에요, Keller 씨. 인사부장이 많은 지원 서류들을 보여줬지만 충분한 경험을 가진 사람을 아직 찾지 못했어요. 채용될 후보자는 많은 회계사들을 관리해야 해서 훌륭한 관리 능력을 갖춘 사람이 필요합니다.

W: 전 직장의 한 친구가 완벽할 것 같은데요. 그는 몇 년간 회계 부서를 관리해 왔기 때문에 많은 통솔 경험이 있어요. 현재 Boston에 상주해 있지만 기꺼이 New York으로 이주할 거예요. 그가 관심이 있는지 전화해 볼까요?

**47.** 어떤 부서에 새 부장이 필요한가?
(A) 인사부
(B) 관리부
(C) 회계부
(D) 고객 관리부　　　　　　　　　　　정답 (C)

**48.** 남자에 따르면 그 직책에 필요한 자격요건은 무엇인가?
(A) 회계사 자격증
(B) 학사 학위
(C) 관리 능력
(D) 의사소통 능력　　　　　　　　　　정답 (C)

**49.** 여자는 이후에 무엇을 할 것 같은가?
(A) 가능한 후보자에게 연락한다.
(B) 다른 사무실로 전이한다.
(C) 온라인 광고를 낸다.
(D) 면접 일정을 정한다.　　　　　　　　정답 (A)

**문제 50-52번은 다음 대화를 참조하시오.** 미W 호M

W: (50) **Are you going to the firm's Christmas party on Wednesday?** It sounds like it will be a lot of fun.
M: (51) **I hope I can make it, but I have so many reports to finish this week.** I have several items of work to finish by Thursday, and some for Friday too. I might have to work all day on Wednesday.
W: Well, most of my work is due on Tuesday, and I'm nearly done already. (52) **I could give you a hand with some of your reports if you'd like.**
M: You'd really do that? Thanks! Maybe I'll make it to the party after all.

------------------------------------------------

W: 수요일에 있을 회사의 크리스마스 파티에 갈 건가요? 아주 재미있을 것 같던데요.
M: 저도 갈 수 있으면 좋겠지만, 이번주에 끝쳐야 할 보고서들이 너무 많아서요. 목요일까지 마쳐야 할 작업이 몇 개 있고 금요일까지 마쳐야 할 것도 몇 개 있어요. 아마도 수요일에는 온종일 일해야만 할 것 같아요.
W: 음, 제가 할 일의 대부분은 화요일까지 마감이고 이미 거의 마쳤어요. 원한다면 보고서 몇 개를 제가 좀 도와드릴 수도 있을 것 같은데요.
M: 정말 그렇게 해주시겠어요? 고마워요! 그럼 아마 파티에 갈 수 있겠네요.

**50.** 파티는 언제인가?
(A) 월요일
(B) 화요일
(C) 수요일
(D) 목요일　　　　　　　　정답 (C)

**51.** 남자가 파티 참석을 확신하지 못하는 이유는 무엇인가?
(A) 그는 세미나에 참석할 예정이다.
(B) 그는 해야 할 일이 너무 많다.
(C) 그는 출장 준비를 해야 한다.
(D) 그는 야간 강좌 등록을 제시간에 해야 한다.　　정답 (B)

**52.** 여자는 남자에게 무엇을 제안하는가?
(A) 야유회를 위한 음식을 준비한다.
(B) 월급을 인상해 준다.
(C) 연회장까지 태워 준다.
(D) 보고서 작성을 마칠 수 있도록 도와준다.　　정답 (D)

**문제 53-55번은 다음 대화를 참조하시오.** 호M 영W

M: Good morning. I bought some shoes on your Web site last Friday, but I still haven't received them. (53) **Could you update me on the status of my order?** The reference number is 73041796.
W: Okay, let me take a look. I see you ordered the Black Cat model shoes. (54) **Um... they were shipped to you on Tuesday.**
M: (54) **What? I can't believe it. They should have arrived by now then.** They're actually a birthday present for my brother. I

want to give them to him at his party this Saturday.
W: (55) **As this Monday was a public holiday, it's normal for mail to take a little longer than usual to be delivered.**

------------------------------------------------

M: 안녕하세요. 지난주 금요일에 귀사의 홈페이지에서 신발을 구매했는데 아직 못 받았어요. 제 주문 상태를 알려주실 수 있나요? 조회번호는 73041796입니다.
W: 네, 제가 볼게요. Black Cat 모델 신발을 주문하셨군요. 음… 화요일에 배송됐네요.
M: 뭐라고요? 믿을 수가 없네요. 그럼 지금쯤이면 도착했어야 하는데요. 사실 제 형의 생일 선물이라서요. 이번 토요일에 그의 파티에서 선물하고 싶어요.
W: 이번 월요일이 공휴일이었으니 배송에 시간이 조금 더 걸리는 것이 정상이에요.

**53.** 남자가 전화한 목적은 무엇인가?
(A) 주문품의 현재 상황을 확인하기 위해서
(B) 제품의 색상을 변경하기 위해서
(C) 주문 수량을 늘리기 위해서
(D) 조회번호를 확인하기 위해서　　　　정답 (A)

**54.** 남자가 "I can't believe it."이라고 언급한 이유는 무엇인가?
(A) 그는 여자가 판매하는 제품들의 품질을 신뢰할 수 없다.
(B) 그는 많은 주문량에 매우 만족하고 있다.
(C) 그는 그녀가 언급한 말에 불만족스럽다.
(D) 그는 방금 그녀에게서 좋은 소식을 들었다.　정답 (C)

**55.** 주문한 제품의 배송이 늦어지고 있는 이유는 무엇인가?
(A) 몇몇 배송트럭들이 고장 났다.
(B) 주문한 제품이 잘못된 주소로 배달이 되었다.
(C) 주문한 제품이 배송 도중 분실됐다.
(D) 직원들이 근무하지 않는 날이 하루 있었다.　정답 (D)

**문제 56-58번은 다음의 3자 대화를 참조하시오.** 미W 영W 미M

W1: (56) **Have you heard the Sales Department is doing a fundraiser for charity this year?** The employees there are selling chocolates to raise $2,000, which is about 50 percent more than last year.
W2: Wow! I think they're doing a good thing again. We should think about how we can help make the world better. There are many things we can do to help people in need. Do you know what? We should buy some.
M: That's right. (57) **Their chocolates are selling like hotcakes among our employees. I think they will be sold out soon.**
W1: How much are they charging for a box of chocolate? I would pay $5 for one.
W2: It is $3 with $2 of the sale going to a local charity organization. (58) **Why don't you go to the Sales Department office with me right after lunch?**

------------------------------------------------

W1: 영업부에서 올해 자선기금 마련 행사를 진행하고 있다는 소식을 들었어요? 지금 영업부에서 2천 달러를 모으기 위해서 초콜릿을 판매하고 있다는데요, 이 목표액이 작년에 비해 50퍼센트나 증가한 것이라고 하네요.
W2: 와! 좋은 일을 또 하고 있네요. 우리도 세상을 위해 어떻게 더 좋은 일을 할 수 있는지 고민해봐야 해요. 도움을 필요로 하는 사람들을 위해 우리가 할 수 있는 일들이 많이 있어요. 그래서 말인데, 우리가 그 초콜릿을 좀 사야 해요.

M: 맞는 말이에요. 그들의 초콜릿이 불티나게 팔리고 있어요. 금방 다 팔릴 것 같아요.

W1: 초콜릿 한 박스가 얼마에 판매되나요? 5달러라면 살 용의가 있는데 말이에요.

W2: 개당 3달러인데, 그 중 2달러가 이 지역에 있는 자선 단체에게 기부된다고 하네요. 그럼 점심식사 바로 후에 저와 같이 영업부 사무실로 가는 건 어떨까요?

**56.** 화자들은 무엇에 대해 이야기하는가?
(A) 할인 판매
(B) 새로운 초콜릿 가게
(C) 기금 마련 행사
(D) 사회 봉사 서비스 　　　　　　　　정답 (C)

**57.** 남자는 초콜릿에 대해 무엇이라고 언급하는가?
(A) 유기농 재료로 만들어졌다.
(B) 사내에서 불티나게 팔리고 있다.
(C) 집에서 만들기가 놀라울 정도로 쉽다.
(D) 지역 아이들에게 기증될 것이다. 　　　정답 (B)

**58.** 화자들은 오늘 오후에 무엇을 할 것 같은가?
(A) 지역 자선 행사에 참여한다.
(B) 새로운 고객과 계약을 체결한다.
(C) 영업부를 방문한다.
(D) 야유회에 필요한 초콜릿을 구매한다. 　정답 (C)

**문제 59–61번은 다음 대화를 참조하시오.** ⓜW ⓗM

W: Good afternoon. (59) **This is Isabella Choi from apartment 48. I wonder what I need to do when my lease comes to an end on September 9.**

M: Well, on the day that your lease expires, we will send someone over to inspect the property and to take final readings of the gas and electricity meters. After that, you just need to drop off the keys when you move out.

W: I see. Well, (61) **I'm actually going away on a two-week business trip on September 9, so would it be possible to hand in the keys and to move out on the 7th?**

M: Of course. That's no problem. We can arrange to have your apartment inspected and your meters read before you leave. (60) **Just let me know when a suitable time to come over is.**

--------------------------------------------

W: 안녕하세요. 저는 48호에 살고 있는 Isabella Choi입니다. 제 임대 계약이 9월 9일에 끝나면 어떻게 해야 하나 궁금해서요.

M: 음, 귀하의 임대가 만료되는 날에 저희가 사람을 보내서 아파트를 점검하고 가스와 전기 계량기를 최종 확인하도록 하겠습니다. 그 후에 이사 갈 때 열쇠를 주고 가시면 됩니다.

W: 알겠습니다. 음, 사실 제가 9월 9일에 2주간 출장을 떠나는데요, 7일에 열쇠를 드리고 이사 가도 될까요?

M: 물론, 괜찮습니다. 나가시기 전에 저희가 아파트와 계량기 점검 일정을 잡으면 됩니다. 언제 방문하는 것이 적절할지 알려만 주세요.

**59.** 남자는 누구일 것 같은가?
(A) 실내 장식가
(B) 아파트 관리인
(C) 여행사 직원
(D) 수리공 　　　　　　　　　　　　정답 (B)

**60.** 남자가 묻는 것은 무엇인가?
(A) 아파트를 임대하는 것
(B) 예약하는 것
(C) 벽을 다시 칠하는 것
(D) 만날 시간을 정하는 것 　　　　　정답 (D)

**61.** 여자가 9월 9일에 아파트 점검을 받을 수 없는 이유는 무엇인가?
(A) 출장을 간다.
(B) 휴가를 간다.
(C) 열쇠가 없다.
(D) 야근을 한다. 　　　　　　　　　정답 (A)

**문제 62–64번은 다음 대화와 목록을 참조하시오.** ⓗM ⓔW

M: Hello. This is James Parker. I recently saw an advertisement for your spreadsheet software. (62) **I'm interested in purchasing it, but I don't know which version is suitable for me.**

W: We provide four packages to our customers. (63) **It usually depends on what kind of business your company is engaged in and how many employees your company has.**

M: Um... I'm running a manufacturing company with about 80 employees.

W: Oh, I see. (64) **In that case, I'd recommend the Regular Package.**

--------------------------------------------

M: 안녕하세요. 저는 James Parker입니다. 최근에 귀사의 스프레드시트 소프트웨어 프로그램에 대한 광고를 봤습니다. 그 제품을 구매하는 것에 관심이 많지만 어떤 상품이 제게 적절한지 모르겠어요.

W: 저희는 네 가지 종류의 패키지 제품을 고객분들에게 제공하고 있습니다. 일반적으로 제품 선택은 고객님의 회사가 어떤 사업 분야에 종사하는지 그리고 몇 명의 직원을 보유한 회사인지에 따라 다릅니다.

M: 음… 저희는 80명 정도의 직원을 보유하고 있는 제조업체입니다.

W: 아, 알겠습니다. 그렇다면 저는 일반 패키지를 추천해 드리고 싶습니다.

| 스프레드시트 소프트웨어 패키지 | 가격 |
|---|---|
| 전문가용 패키지 | $300 |
| 준전문가용 패키지 | $250 |
| **(64) 일반 패키지** | **$200** |
| 기본 패키지 | $100 |

**62.** 남자가 전화한 이유는 무엇인가?
(A) 신제품을 추천하기 위해서
(B) 부실한 서비스에 대한 불만을 제기하기 위해서
(C) 도움을 요청하기 위해서
(D) 컴퓨터 강좌에 등록하기 위해서 　　정답 (C)

**63.** 여자는 남자에게 어떠한 정보를 요청하고 있는가?
(A) 그의 주문 번호
(B) 그의 연락처
(C) 그의 회사 주소
(D) 그의 회사의 규모 　　　　　　　정답 (D)

**64.** 그래픽을 보시오. 남자가 제품 구매를 위해 지불할 비용은 얼마일 것 같은가?
(A) $100
(B) $200
(C) $250
(D) $300 　　　　　　　　　　　　정답 (B)

문제 65-67번은 다음 대화와 쿠폰을 참조하시오. 미M 영W

M: Excuse me. (65) **I'm looking for a 36-pack of Mimi power batteries**, but I see only packs of 24 on the display rack. Did you stop stocking the 36-packs?

W: No, we just sold out of them this morning, but you'll be pleased to hear that more have just been delivered. (66) **I'll go and grab some from the backroom for you.**

M: Thanks a lot. One pack will be fine. Oh, and I'd just like to make sure of something… (65) **I can use this coupon here, right?**

W: Yes, of course. (67) **Make sure the cashier knows that you want to use it to buy your batteries, and she'll scan the bar code for you.**

-------------------------------------------------------

M: 실례합니다. 36개의 건전지가 들어 있는 Mimi 파워 건전지 한 상자를 찾고 있는데요. 진열대에는 24개가 들어 있는 제품뿐이네요. 36개가 들어 있는 제품은 입고하지 않나요?

W: 아닙니다. 오늘 오전에 모두 판매가 되었어요. 하지만 방금 더 많은 제품이 입고되었다는 소식을 들으셔서 다행입니다. 제가 창고에 가서 제품을 가지고 오겠습니다.

M: 감사합니다. 한 상자면 됩니다. 아, 그리고 한 가지 확인하고 싶은 것이 있는데요… 이 곳에서 이 쿠폰을 사용해도 되죠, 그렇죠?

W: 네, 물론이에요. 건전지를 구매할 때 계산원에게 이 쿠폰을 사용하고 싶다는 것을 알려주시면 계산원이 바코드를 스캔할 겁니다.

---

## 할인 쿠폰
### (4월 5일까지 유효)

0110  0105

### AAA 규격 건전지

12팩 · · · · · · $1 할인 혜택 (1팩)
24팩 · · · · · · $2 할인 혜택 (1팩)
(65) **36팩** · · · **$4 할인 혜택 (1팩)**
48팩 · · · · · · $6 할인 혜택 (1팩)

**MIMI POWER BATTERIES**

---

**65.** 그래픽을 보시오. 남자는 얼마나 할인을 받겠는가?
(A) $1
(B) $2
(C) $4
(D) $6    정답 (C)

**66.** 여자는 남자에게 무엇을 해주겠다고 제안하는가?
(A) 더 많은 제품을 주문한다.
(B) 그에게 건전지를 갖다 준다.
(C) 폐기물을 처리한다.
(D) 새로운 창고의 위치를 알려준다.    정답 (B)

**67.** 남자는 무엇을 하도록 요청받는가?
(A) 대기 장소에 앉아 기다린다.
(B) 주문서를 작성한다.
(C) 새로운 쿠폰을 프린트한다.
(D) 계산원에게 이야기한다.    정답 (D)

---

문제 68-70번은 다음 대화와 초대장을 참조하시오. 미M 영W

M: Oh, look who's here! Jessica, what a nice surprise! You are a member here.

W: Oh, what's up, Robert? Good to see you here! Yes, I'm a member. You know, (68) **I really need to get in shape. My office is in this building, so it's easy for me to have a quick workout on my lunch break.**

M: (69) **You should try to come here early in the morning before you start work. It's less busy then.**

W: Thanks for the tip. Oh, by the way, did you get an invitation for Kay and Blaine's wedding on July 4?

M: I did, and Kay and Blaine asked me to take some photographs at 2 P.M. on their big day. Are you planning to go?

W: Yes, but I have a tight schedule on that day. (70) **With a little luck, I'll get there right when the ceremony is starting.**

-------------------------------------------------------

M: 아, 이게 누구인지! Jessica, 너무 반갑네요. 이 곳의 회원이셨군요.

W: 아, 안녕하세요, Robert? 여기서 만나다니 반갑네요! 네, 이 곳 회원이에요. 아시다시피 저도 건강관리를 해야 해요. 제 사무실이 이 건물에 있어서, 점심시간을 활용해서 서둘러 운동하기가 쉽거든요.

M: 출근 전에 아침에 일찍 와보세요. 그 때는 덜 붐벼요.

W: 좋은 정보 고마워요. 아, 그런데 7월 4일에 있을 Kay와 Blaine의 결혼식 청첩장은 받으셨어요?

M: 받았어요. 그리고 Kay와 Blaine의 결혼식 당일 오후 2시에 사진을 찍어 달라고 요청하더군요. 당신도 가실 계획인가요?

W: 네, 하지만 그날 일정이 바쁜가 해요. 약간의 운만 따라준다면 결혼식이 시작하는 시간에 딱 맞춰 갈 수 있을 것 같아요.

---

## KAY과 BLAINE의
## 결혼식에 참석해 주세요

7월 4일 토요일
St. Joseph's Cathedral, Harder Road

오후 2시
식전 사진 촬영

오후 3시
결혼식 손님 착석

**(70) 오후 4시**
**결혼식**

오후 5시
저녁식사&음료

귀하의 참석 여부를 답해 주세요.

---

**68.** 화자들은 어디에 있을 것 같은가?
(A) 헬스 클럽
(B) 성당
(C) 사진 스튜디오
(D) 백화점    정답 (A)

**69.** 남자가 여자에게 권고하는 것은 무엇인가?
(A) 지역 행사에 참석한다.
(B) 그녀의 업무 일정을 변경한다.
(C) 시설을 좀 더 일찍 방문한다.
(D) 사진을 찍는다.    정답 (C)

**70.** 그래픽을 보시오. 여자는 언제 결혼식에 도착할 예정인가?

(A) 오후 2시

(B) 오후 3시

(C) 오후 4시

(D) 오후 5시 ........................... 정답 (C)

## Part 4

문제 71-73번은 다음 광고를 참조하시오. ㅁW

Who doesn't need to upgrade their home appliances? (71) **Best Deals is having an incredible sale! We have flat-screen TVs, computers, refrigerators, and much more.** We even have someone here who can help you choose the right size equipment for your home and for your personal entertainment needs. (72) **On top of that, we will deliver your new appliance to your home on the same day you purchase it!** (73) **This sale is for two days only this coming Saturday and Sunday.** Don't miss it.

----

새로운 가전제품을 원하지 않는 사람이 어디 있을까요? Best Deals가 놀라운 세일을 진행하고 있습니다! 저희는 평면 TV와 컴퓨터, 냉장고를 비롯한 많은 전자제품을 취급합니다. 고객 여러분의 가정에, 그리고 여러분의 개인적인 필요에 딱 알맞은 제품을 고르실 수 있도록 저희 직원이 도와드립니다. 이에 더하여 새로운 가전제품을 구매한 당일에 가정으로 배송해 드립니다! 이번 세일은 토요일과 일요일, 단 이틀 동안만 진행됩니다. 놓치지 마세요.

**71.** 무엇이 광고되고 있는가?

(A) 가전제품

(B) 컴퓨터 소프트웨어

(C) 사무용 장비

(D) 모바일 기기 ........................... 정답 (A)

**72.** 고객에게 어떠한 서비스가 제공되는가?

(A) 무상 수리

(B) 당일 배송

(C) 추가 할인

(D) 무료 보증기간 연장 ........................... 정답 (B)

**73.** 할인 행사는 언제 시작하는가?

(A) 금요일

(B) 토요일

(C) 일요일

(D) 월요일 ........................... 정답 (B)

문제 74-76번은 다음 안내문을 참조하시오. 호M

Good evening, ladies and gentlemen! (74) **Welcome to the first performance of the London Symphony this Christmas holiday season.** To celebrate the first performance, Celina Watson will sing "Brindisi" from the opera "La Traviata" by Giuseppe Verdi, a famous Italian Romantic composer. (75) **Now, the light engineers are working on getting the stage lights functioning properly due to low light conditions, and that has caused a little delay in getting started.** (74) **The concert should commence in exactly 30 minutes.** (76) **Please finish your conversations and make your way to your seats.** Thank

you and enjoy the show!

----

안녕하세요, 신사 숙녀 여러분! 올해 Christmas 연휴 기간을 맞이하여 열리는 London Symphony의 첫 번째 공연에 와 주신 여러분을 환영합니다. 첫 공연을 축하하기 위해서 Celina Watson 씨가 이탈리아의 낭만파 작곡가인 Giuseppe Verdi의 오페라 "La Traviata" 중 "Brindisi"를 불러드릴 것입니다. 현재 낮은 조도 문제로 인해 조명 전문가들이 조명이 적절하게 작동할 수 있도록 작업 중이며, 이로 인해 공연 시작이 약간 지연되었습니다. 콘서트는 정확히 30분 후에 시작될 예정입니다. 담화를 마치고 여러분의 좌석으로 가주시기 바랍니다. 감사드리고 즐거운 공연 되십시오!

**74.** 이 안내문은 어디에서 이루어지는 것 같은가?

(A) 라디오 방송국

(B) 미술관 개관식

(C) 콘서트 홀

(D) 텔레비전 스튜디오 ........................... 정답 (C)

**75.** 지연을 초래한 이유는 무엇인가?

(A) 기술적인 문제

(B) 시설 폐쇄

(C) 악천후

(D) 도로 보수 ........................... 정답 (A)

**76.** 청자들에게 요청되는 것은 무엇인가?

(A) 공연을 관람한다.

(B) 지정 좌석으로 간다.

(C) 도움을 받기 위해 대기한다.

(D) 모든 불을 끈다. ........................... 정답 (B)

문제 77-79번은 다음 담화를 참조하시오. ㅁM

Good morning, everyone. Um... before we start our work today, I want to share some good news with you. (78) **I got a phone call yesterday from the sales director of the Starpark View Café**, one of the largest café chains in the country. (77) **Due to high demand for our coffee beans,** (78) **the company has decided to increase its order by 30% starting next quarter.** However, you know, every coin has two sides. (79) **We will enjoy an increase in sales, which means we will have to work a lot of overtime.** So... before we accept the order, (79) **I'd like to hear from all of you.** As this is an informal meeting, please speak freely.

----

좋은 아침입니다, 여러분. 음... 오늘 우리가 업무를 시작하기에 앞서 저는 여러분과 좋은 소식 하나를 공유하고자 합니다. 국내에서 가장 규모가 큰 카페 체인 중 하나인 Starpark View Café의 영업 이사로부터 어제 연락을 받았습니다. 그 회사는 우리 커피 원두에 대한 수요가 높은 관계로 다음 분기부터 주문량을 30% 늘리기로 결정을 했다고 합니다. 그렇지만 여러분도 아시다시피, 모든 동전에는 양면이 있습니다. 우리는 매출 증가란 성과를 누리겠지만, 이는 곧 더 많은 잔업을 해야 한다는 걸 의미합니다. 그래서... 그들의 주문을 받아들이기에 앞서, 저는 여러분 모두의 의견을 듣고 싶습니다. 이건 비공식적인 자리인 만큼 허심탄회하게 이야기를 하셔도 좋습니다.

**77.** 화자는 어떠한 제품에 대해 언급하고 있는가?

(A) 케이크

(B) 샌드위치

(C) 커피

(D) 과일 주스 ........................... 정답 (C)

**78.** Starpark View Café가 최근에 한 일은 무엇인가?

(A) 새로운 음료를 출시했다.

(B) 회사의 로고를 변경했다.

(C) 본사의 위치를 이전했다.

(D) 주문량을 늘렸다.                   정답 (D)

**79.** 화자가 "I'd like to hear from all of you."라고 말했을 때 의미하는 바는 무엇인가?

(A) 일부 커피 기계가 고장 났다.

(B) 고객 의견을 고려해야 한다.

(C) 비공식적인 회의가 좀 더 자주 열릴 것이다.

(D) 결정하는 데 의견이 필요하다.                   정답 (D)

**문제 80-82번은 다음 안내방송을 참조하시오.** ⓜⓦ

(80) **Attention, all passengers on Redhouse Airline Flight 124 to Boston.** Unfortunately, we are not currently able to issue boarding passes at Gate 53 due to a technical problem with the electronic reservation system. We just completed an emergency inspection of the system and discovered that some computer chips were malfunctioning due to overheating. (81) **At this time, we have our best air mechanics working on it. We will begin the boarding process as soon as the repairs are finished.** (82) **We'll keep you informed of our progress.** We sincerely apologize for the inconvenience we have caused. Thank you for your patience.

--------------------------------

Boston 행 Redhouse 항공 124편의 탑승객 여러분은 모두 주목해 주십시오. 안타깝게도 현재 전자 예약 시스템의 기술적인 문제로 인해 53번 탑승구에서 탑승권을 발급해 드리지 못하고 있습니다. 저희는 시스템에 대한 긴급 점검을 방금 완료했으며 과열로 인한 컴퓨터 칩이 오작동한 것으로 파악했습니다. 현재 저희 회사 최고의 항공 기술자들이 작업 중에 있습니다. 수리가 완료되는 대로 바로 탑승 수속을 시작하겠습니다. 이후 상황에 대한 소식은 계속 전해 드리도록 하겠습니다. 불편을 초래한 점에 대해 진심으로 사과드립니다. 기다려 주셔서 감사합니다.

**80.** 화자는 어디에서 근무할 것 같은가?

(A) 버스 터미널

(B) 전자제품 매장

(C) 공항

(D) 잡지사                   정답 (C)

**81.** 화자가 "At this time, we have our best air mechanics working on it."이라고 말할 때 의미하는 바는 무엇인가?

(A) 모든 탑승객들은 로비에서 대기해야 한다.

(B) 문제가 오래 지속되지는 않을 것이다.

(C) 수리팀원들은 더 많은 훈련이 필요하지 않다.

(D) 회사는 우수한 직원들을 보유하고 있다.                   정답 (B)

**82.** 화자는 무엇을 할 것이라고 언급하는가?

(A) 53번 탑승구 근처에서 대기한다.

(B) 전액 환불을 요구한다.

(C) 새로운 소식을 전달한다.

(D) 탑승권을 발급한다.                   정답 (C)

**문제 83-85번은 다음 녹음 메시지를 참조하시오.** ⓔⓦ

Hello, Mr. Brown. (83) **This is Emily Marsh. I'm calling about the senior accountant position I applied for through your company's Web site.** (84) Today, I received an e-mail from **the state board of accountancy stating that I had just been certified as a certified public accountant**, so I'd like to add that certification to my application. But since I've already submitted the form, I don't know how to do that. (85) **Please give me a call at 692-9815 and let me know how to update my application.** I look forward to hearing from you soon. Thanks.

--------------------------------

안녕하세요, Brown 씨. 저는 Emily Marsh입니다. 제가 귀사의 홈페이지를 통해서 지원한 수석 회계사 직과 관련하여 전화 드립니다. 오늘 제가 주회계 심의회에서 제게 공인 회계사 자격을 수여한다는 이메일을 받은 관계로, 제 이력에 공인 회계사 자격을 추가하고 싶습니다. 하지만 제가 이미 지원서를 제출한 상황인지라 이력을 추가하고 싶을 때 어떻게 해야 하는지 모릅니다. 692-9815로 전화해 주셔서 지원서를 갱신하는 방법에 대해 알려주셨으면 합니다. 빠른 답신을 기대하고 있겠습니다. 감사합니다.

**83.** 화자는 누구일 것 같은가?

(A) 취업 지원자

(B) 회계부장

(C) 채용자

(D) 판매업자                   정답 (A)

**84.** 오늘 화자에게 발생한 일은 무엇인가?

(A) 그녀는 지원서를 제출했다.

(B) 그녀는 추천서를 받았다.

(C) 그녀는 전문 자격을 취득했다.

(D) 그녀는 가족과 함께 창업을 했다.                   정답 (C)

**85.** 화자가 원하는 것은 무엇인가?

(A) 취업 지원서를 갱신한다.

(B) 연봉과 복리후생 혜택에 대해 협상한다.

(C) 이전 주문을 변경한다.

(D) 면접 준비를 한다.                   정답 (A)

**문제 86-88번은 다음 회의 내용을 참조하시오.** ⓗⓜ

Electric vehicles are the future of transportation. (86) **Our Elecgreen SUV is the bestselling SUV in the electric vehicle market. I'm very proud of all of you, the product innovation team in particular. Few people are capable of such an innovative design.** And on that note, I'm pleased to announce that the latest vehicle in our lineup, (87) **the new Jambo SUV, is ready to launch!** Since we are now ready to present it to the public, we'll take it with us to the Los Angeles Auto Show in October. If any of you wants to go to the auto show with us, (88) **please fill out a business travel request form and submit it to the personnel manager by the end of the month.**

--------------------------------

전기 자동차는 운송의 미래입니다. 우리의 Elecgreen SUV는 전기 자동차 시장에서 가장 많이 판매되는 SUV 차량입니다. 저는 여러분 모두, 특히 제품 혁신 팀을 자랑스럽게 여기고 있습니다. 그러한 혁신적인 디자인을 개발할 수 있는 사람은 극소수입니다. 그런 맥락에서 우리 자동차 라인업의 최신 차량을 발표하게 되어 기쁘게 생각합니다. 우리의 새로운 Jambo SUV가 출

시 준비를 마쳤습니다! 이제 일반 대중에게 Jambo SUV를 공개할 준비가 되었기 때문에 우리는 이를 10월에 있을 Los Angeles 자동차 전시회에 출품하려고 합니다. 여러분 중 저희와 함께 자동차 전시회에 참여하길 원하시는 분이 있으면 출장 신청서를 작성하여 이달 말까지 인사부장에게 제출해 주시기 바랍니다.

**86.** 화자가 "Few people are capable of such an innovative design."이라고 말할 때 의미하는 바는 무엇인가?
(A) 그는 더 힘이 좋은 자동차를 원한다.
(B) 그는 몇몇 직원들을 칭찬하고 있다.
(C) 그는 자신의 성과를 자랑스럽게 생각한다.
(D) 그는 더 많은 디자이너의 채용을 제안하고 있다. 정답 (B)

**87.** 화자에 따르면 회사는 10월에 무엇을 할 것인가?
(A) 다른 회사를 인수한다.
(B) 행사에 참여한다.
(C) 기존 디자인을 변경한다.
(D) 수상자를 발표한다. 정답 (B)

**88.** 화자가 청자들에게 제안하는 것은 무엇인가?
(A) 새로운 디자인을 고안한다.
(B) 신청서를 제출한다.
(C) 새로운 자동차를 시험 운전한다.
(D) 회사 행사를 준비한다. 정답 (B)

문제 89-91번은 다음 회의 내용을 참조하시오. 호M

Good morning, everyone. I am very glad you could make it to this important seminar on the new revolutionary computer software, Final Cutting, we will be using to do computer graphic work. (89) **I would like for employees in computer-related positions, especially the graphic designers** who are responsible for creating optimal design solutions that have a visual impact for people, to know how to use it. What Final Cutting does is it allows you to manipulate visual images and to create professional and realistic 3D computer-generated imagery you can be proud of. (90) **That's why this top-end computer graphic software easily cost our company thousands of dollars last week.** With Final Cutting, it is possible to build entire worlds and realities. (91) **If you all look at the monitor in front of you, I will demonstrate how to do that.**

------------------------------------------------

안녕하세요, 여러분. 향후 우리가 컴퓨터 그래픽 작업을 하는 데 사용하게 될 새로운 혁신적인 컴퓨터 소프트웨어 Final Cutting에 대한 중요한 세미나에 참석해 주셔서 매우 기쁩니다. 저는 컴퓨터와 관련된 직책을 맡고 있는 직원들이 이 프로그램을 어떻게 사용하는지 알고 계시길 바라며, 특히 사람들에게 시각적 영향을 주는 최적의 디자인 해결안을 창출하는 그래픽 디자이너들은 더욱 그렇습니다. Final Cutting이 하는 것은 여러분이 시각적 이미지를 다루고, 3D 컴퓨터를 이용하여 자랑할 만한 수준의 전문적이고 실제적인 이미지를 창작할 수 있도록 해줍니다. 그것이 바로 지난주에 이 최고급 컴퓨터 그래픽 소프트웨어를 구매하는 데 우리 회사가 수천 달러의 비용을 들인 이유이기도 합니다. Final Cutting이 있으면 온세상과 현실을 창조하는 것이 가능합니다. 여러분 모두 앞에 있는 모니터를 보시면 제가 어떻게 그럴 수 있는지 보여드리겠습니다.

**89.** 이 담화를 듣는 청중은 누구인가?
(A) 전기 기사
(B) 소프트웨어 개발자

(C) 그래픽 전문가
(D) 사진 전문가 정답 (C)

**90.** 회사가 최근에 구입한 것은 무엇인가?
(A) 회계 소프트웨어
(B) 가구가 완비된 아파트
(C) 영화 촬영용 카메라
(D) 컴퓨터 그래픽 프로그램 정답 (D)

**91.** 화자는 이후에 무엇을 할 것인가?
(A) 연봉 인상을 제공한다.
(B) 시연을 한다.
(C) 새로운 디자이너를 채용한다.
(D) 제조 공장 견학을 이끈다. 정답 (B)

문제 92-94번은 다음 뉴스를 참조하시오. 영W

This is Judy Foster with your local community news for today. (92) **The city of Oakland announced a new construction project today. It will build a new multisport complex which includes a soccer stadium, indoor volleyball courts, Olympic-sized swimming pools, and a state-of-the-art ice rink.** The new structure will be built on the east side of the old city sports center and will be able to accommodate approximately 70,000 people. (93) **Supporters say it is absolutely necessary to increase the opportunities for city residents to enjoy a variety of sports.** (94) **But some local residents have expressed opposition to the construction project by explaining that a new, large sports facility will increase the already high-volume of traffic within the city.** The city will hold a public hearing to provide an opportunity for broad public participation so that people can comment on the new sports complex next Thursday.

------------------------------------------------

저는 오늘의 지역뉴스를 담당하고 있는 Judy Foster입니다. Oakland 시에서는 오늘 새로운 건설 계획을 발표했습니다. 시는 축구장, 실내 배구장, 올림픽 규격의 수영장, 최첨단 빙상 경기장을 포함하는 새로운 다목적 스포츠 종합 경기장을 건설할 것입니다. 새로운 스포츠 종합 경기장은 구 시립 스포츠 센터의 동쪽에 건설될 것이며, 약 7만 명의 관중을 수용할 수 있을 것입니다. 스포츠 종합 경기장 신축안 지지자들은 시민들이 다양한 스포츠를 즐길 수 있도록 기회를 확대한다는 면에서 꼭 필요하다고 이야기하고 있습니다. 하지만 일부 시민들은 새로운 대형 스포츠 시설은 안 그래도 심한 시내 교통체증을 더 악화시킬 것이라며 신축 계획에 대한 반대의사를 표명해왔습니다. 시에서는 새로운 스포츠 종합 경기장의 건설에 대해 시민들이 의견을 전달할 수 있는 폭넓은 참여와 기회를 제공하고자 다음주 목요일에 공청회를 개최합니다.

**92.** 화자에 따르면 오늘 무엇이 발표되었는가?
(A) 스포츠 행사
(B) 도로 확장
(C) 새로운 교통 정책
(D) 큰 건설 계획 정답 (D)

**93.** 화자에 따르면 이 계획이 시민들에게 필요한 이유는 무엇인가?
(A) 더 많은 일자리를 창출하기 위해서
(B) 전세계에서 더 많은 관광객을 유치하기 위해서
(C) 지역 경제 상황을 개선시키기 위해서
(D) 스포츠를 즐길 수 있는 기회를 제공하기 위해서 정답 (D)

**94.** 일부 사람들이 새로운 계획에 반대하는 이유는 무엇인가?
(A) 충분한 기금이 없다.
(B) 심각한 교통체증을 초래할 것이다.
(C) 많은 소음이 발생할 것이다.
(D) 부동산 가격이 급락할 것이다. 　　　　　정답 (B)

---

문제 95-97번은 다음 담화와 일정표를 참조하시오. 호M

(95) We're so happy you are willing to join us for one of the employee enhancement training sessions. I know that many of you are excited about the new opportunities for growth at our company and in the entire industry. This first session deals with professional e-mail rules and regulations, but first, I'd like to point out a change in the schedule. There will be a workshop next month in September. (96) But, unfortunately, the October session has been postponed until November due to the staff meeting on the ninth. (97) Remember that all workshops include lunch, which is catered by the sandwich shop next door. We'll break for lunch after the morning session.

---

여러분이 다양한 직원 능력 강화 교육에 기꺼이 참여해주신 점에 대해 기쁘게 생각합니다. 저는 많은 분들이 우리 회사와 업계 전체에서의 성장을 도모할 수 있는 새로운 기회에 설레고 있다고 알고 있습니다. 첫 번째 교육에서는 전문적인 이메일 작성 규칙 및 규정을 다룰 것이지만, 우선 일정 변경에 대한 알려드리고자 합니다. 다음달인 9월에 워크숍을 개최합니다. 그러나 안타깝게도 10월 교육은 9일로 예정된 직원 회의로 인해 11월까지 연기되었습니다. 모든 워크숍에는 점심식사가 포함되며 이는 옆에 있는 샌드위치 가게에서 제공됩니다. 우리는 오전 교육 후에 점심식사를 위한 휴식을 취할 것입니다.

| 교육 | 날짜 |
|---|---|
| 시간 관리 | 7월 24일 |
| 의사소통 기술 | 8월 27일 |
| 이메일 방침 | 9월 13일 |
| (96) 보고서 작성법 | 10월 9일 |

**95.** 화자는 무엇에 관해 기뻐하고 있다고 말하는가?
(A) 신제품의 품질
(B) 고객 만족도의 향상
(C) 서비스 선택사항의 다양함
(D) 참석자들의 의지 　　　　　정답 (D)

**96.** 그래픽을 보시오. 어떤 교육이 연기되었는가?
(A) 의사소통 기술
(B) 시간 관리
(C) 보고서 작성법
(D) 이메일 방침 　　　　　정답 (C)

**97.** 화자에 따르면 오전 교육이 끝난 후에 무슨 일이 발생할 것인가?
(A) 점심식사가 제공될 것이다.
(B) 커피 시간이 주어질 것이다.
(C) 금전적인 보상이 주어질 것이다.
(D) 직원 회의가 열릴 것이다. 　　　　　정답 (A)

---

문제 98-100번은 다음 전화 메시지와 정보를 참조하시오. 미M

Good morning, Mr. Wilson. This is Donald Datcher at the Beltran Car Repair Shop. It's 11 o'clock in the morning. (98) I just finished changing your flat tires and engine oil. I think you can pick your vehicle up any time after you leave the office. Ah, I have one more thing to tell you. (99/100) While changing the tires, I noticed that your right side-view mirror was broken, so I replaced it for you. I won't charge you for that. Mr. Wilson, if you have any questions, please give me a call at 974-0110. All right. I'll see you later when you come in to get your truck.

---

안녕하세요, Wilson 씨. 저는 Beltran 자동차 정비소의 Donald Datcher 입니다. 지금은 오전 11시입니다. 방금 펑크 난 타이어와 엔진 오일을 교체했습니다. 퇴근하면서 언제라도 차를 가지고 가셔도 될 것 같습니다. 아, 한 가지 더 말씀드리겠습니다. 타이어를 교체하는 동안 오른쪽 사이드 미러가 깨진 것을 파악하고 교체했습니다. 고객님께 이를 청구하지는 않을 것입니다. Wilson 씨, 질문이 있으시면 제게 974-0110으로 전화해 주십시오. 좋습니다. 그럼 트럭을 가지러 오실 때 뵙겠습니다.

## Beltran 자동차 정비소

| 서비스 | 비용 |
|---|---|
| 엔진 오일 교체 | $50 |
| (100) 사이드 미러 / 백 미러 교체 | $60 |
| 앞/뒤 타이어 교체 | $110 |
| 전후 범퍼 수리 | $270 |

**98.** 화자가 전화한 목적은 무엇인가?
(A) 주문을 하기 위해서
(B) 길안내를 하기 위해서
(C) 예약을 하기 위해서
(D) 작업 완료를 알리기 위해서 　　　　　정답 (D)

**99.** 화자는 작업 중에 무엇을 발견했는가?
(A) 거울이 깨졌다.
(B) 타이어가 펑크 났다.
(C) 청구액이 전액 지불되지 않았다.
(D) 일부 교체용 부품의 재고가 동이 났다. 　　　　　정답 (A)

**100.** 그래픽을 보시오. Wilson 씨는 얼마를 절약하겠는가?
(A) $50
(B) $60
(C) $110
(D) $270 　　　　　정답 (B)

---

**Part 5**

**101.** Beagle Media의 새로운 판촉 행사는 내일 시작해서 다음주 일요일에 끝날 것이다. 　　　　　정답 (B)

**102.** 그의 회사인 Starpark Food 사는 경쟁사의 제품들에 비해 더 매운 새로운 종류의 스테이크 소스를 최초로 출시하였다. 　　　　　정답 (C)

**103.** 매장 관리자는 판매 구역을 깨끗이 유지하고 고객을 만족시키는 것에 대한 책임을 지고 있다. 　　　　　정답 (A)

**104.** Park 도서관은 매주 월요일 저녁에 초보자를 위한 작문 강좌를 제공한다. 정답 (D)

**105.** 제약 산업의 연구를 촉진시키고자 연방 정부는 Pryde Bio Technology 사의 연구 개발 센터의 전체 건설 비용의 60%를 부담할 것이다. 정답 (B)

**106.** Coco International 사는 아시아에서 반려동물용 식품을 제조하는 가장 큰 회사들 중 하나로 인정받아 왔다. 정답 (B)

**107.** 모든 방문객들은 연구 센터의 지하 주차장에 붙어 있는 속도 제한을 준수해야 한다. 정답 (A)

**108.** 새로운 일정에 따르면 우리 신입사원들을 위한 연수 과정은 11월 23일에 개최될 것이다. 정답 (B)

**109.** New York 시립 박물관에 가장 쉽게 가는 방법은 New Jersey 역에 주차한 후 버스를 타고 시내로 가는 것이다. 정답 (A)

**110.** Ace Web Designs 사는 대학 시절에 유사한 프로젝트에서 함께 일하기 시작했던 두 친구에 의해 설립되었다. 정답 (B)

**111.** 구입일로부터 3년의 기간 동안 그 회사는 결함이 있는 제품을 수리하거나 새로운 상품으로 교체해줄 것이다. 정답 (C)

**112.** 대학원생들은 보통 학교에서 도보 거리에 있는 기숙사를 찾으려고 시도한다. 정답 (D)

**113.** 이사회는 회사가 신입사원들에게 제공할 많은 복리후생 혜택들을 꼼꼼하게 계획할 것이다. 정답 (B)

**114.** 외국계 기업들이 한국에서 신규 사업을 시작하기 위해서는 법과 규정을 준수해야만 한다. 정답 (A)

**115.** 새로운 컴퓨터 충전기는 국내 시장에서 판매되는 거의 모든 노트북 컴퓨터와 호환된다. 정답 (B)

**116.** 새로운 사업 계획안은 비용 효율이 좋지 않고 친환경적이지 않기 때문에 이를 승인하는 데 문제가 발생할 수밖에 없다. 정답 (A)

**117.** 모든 부품 제공업체들의 재고가 동이 난 상태라서 공장장은 고장 난 컨베이어 벨트에 대한 교체용 부품을 수령하지 못했다. 정답 (A)

**118.** Walnut County는 대부분 시골지역이지만 이 곳에 건립된 새로운 창고는 우리 회사의 지역 물류 중심지로서의 역할을 하게 될 것이다. 정답 (C)

**119.** 일부 경제학자들은 4분기에서 두드러지는 경기 향상이 없다면 경제 회복의 속도가 느려질 것으로 예측했다. 정답 (A)

**120.** Haru Catering Service 사는 비용이 더 저렴하지만 Andrew Catering Service 사가 전반적으로 우리 회사의 사업상 필요한 부분을 충족시켜 준다. 정답 (B)

**121.** 전 인사부장인 Williams 씨는 후임자와 자신의 업무 지식을 공유하기 위해 몇몇 업무 참고 자료들을 남겨두었다. 정답 (B)

**122.** 각 부서는 필히 내부 감사를 완료하고 품질 개선을 위한 계획안을 3월 1일까지 제출해야 한다. 정답 (D)

**123.** Cheeze Energy 사는 내년 초에 전기 자동차들을 위한 일련의 충전소들을 유럽 지역에 설립하겠다는 계획을 발표했다. 정답 (A)

**124.** 만약 보수 공사가 다음주에 성공적으로 마무리된다면 지역 쇼핑몰의 임대는 재개될 것이다. 정답 (A)

**125.** 〈World Business Monthly Review〉는 잡지를 한 달이라도 놓치지 않도록 회원들에게 일찍 구독 갱신할 것을 요청했다. 정답 (C)

**126.** 이사회는 Hayward 지점을 맡을 인물을 회사 내부에서 물색하는 대신 회사 외부에서 충원하기로 결정했다. 정답 (B)

**127.** 무역 관련된 세금을 수입원으로 크게 의존하고 있는 일부 나라들은 관세 감소에 영향을 받는 경향이 있다. 정답 (A)

**128.** 대부분의 은행들은 일반적으로 18세 이상으로 운전면허증 또는 여권과 같은 신분증을 보유하고 있다면 그들에게 예금 계좌를 개설해 준다. 정답 (D)

**129.** 임금 인상을 위한 BK Heavy Industries 사에서의 파업은 공식 협상이 시작하자마자 종료할 것이다. 정답 (D)

**130.** 국제 고양이 영화제는 이전에 영상물을 한 번도 제작해보지 않은 고양이 소유주들의 참가만 받는다. 정답 (C)

## Part 6

**문제 131-134번은 다음 이메일을 참조하시오.**

> 모든 객실 관리 직원에게
>
> 우리 호텔 경영진은 지난주 매일 침대보와 수건을 세탁하는 것에 관련하여 새로운 방침을 시행하기로 결정했습니다. 늘 그랬듯이, 우리는 고객에 의해 바닥에 놓인 모든 수건과 침대보를 매일 세탁합니다. 그러나 객실 안에 있는 걸쇠나 거치대에 걸려있는 한 번 혹은 두 번 정도 사용한 수건들은 이에 해당되지 않습니다. 이는 고객들이 재사용하도록 그대로 두어야 합니다. 새로운 방침은 물의 사용량, 에너지 소비량 그리고 매일의 세탁 양을 최소화할 것입니다. 더구나 이는 에너지 절약과 환경 보호에 대한 인식을 향상시켜 줄 것입니다. 경영 지원부의 직원들이 이 방침의 시행을 고객들에게 전달하는 공지를 모든 객실에 부착할 것입니다. 이러한 노력에 대한 여러분의 협조에 큰 감사드립니다.

**131.** 정답 (B)

**132.** 정답 (D)

**133.** 정답 (C)

**134.** (A) 그들은 샤워기를 설치하는 것이 자원 낭비라고 생각합니다.
(B) 여러분 모두가 정기 회의에서 많은 창의적인 아이디어를 제안해주길 바랍니다.
(C) 수리 보수가 필요하면 제게 알려주세요.
(D) 이러한 노력에 대한 여러분의 협조에 큰 감사드립니다. 정답 (D)

**문제 135-138번은 다음 공지를 참조하시오.**

> 공지
>
> SAN FRANCISCO 국제공항의 여행객

만약 귀하의 수하물이 공항 직원에 의해, 또는 공항 수하물 처리 시스템에 의해 운반 혹은 도움을 받다가 파손되었다면 수하물을 가지고 공항 1층에 위치한 공항 수하물 사무소를 방문해 주십시오. 규정에 따르면, 국내선 여행객은 수하물 파손을 실제 도착시간에서 48시간 이내에 보고하셔야 합니다. 국제선 여행객은 수하물을 잘못 처리한 사고가 발생한 지 7일 이내에 파손에 대해 보고해야 합니다. <u>수하물 파손 보고서를 지시대로 작성해 주시기 바랍니다.</u> 사무소 직원이 보고서를 검토하고 모든 파손 주장에 대해 평가를 할 것입니다. 공항 수하물 사무소는 오직 공항 직원과 공항 수하물 처리 시스템에 의해 파손이 발생한 수하물에 대해서만 책임을 진다는 점을 알아두시기 바랍니다.

**135.** 정답 (A)

**136.** 정답 (D)

**137.** (A) 수하물 파손 보고서를 지시대로 작성해 주시기 바랍니다.
(B) 새로운 수하물 처리 시스템은 혁신적이며 효율적입니다.
(C) 내년에 공항은 증가하는 항공 수요를 수용할 수 있도록 확장될 것입니다.
(D) 공항 수하물 사무소는 보수 기간 동안 일시적으로 여행객들에게 폐쇄됩니다. 정답 (A)

**138.** 정답 (B)

---

문제 139-142번은 다음 회람을 참조하시오.

**회람**

WALNUT CREEK 공립 도서관

수신: Walnut Creek 공립 도서관 직원
발신: Amy Jordan
회신: 새로운 스터디 룸
날짜: 4월 5일

6개월 전에 시작된 새로운 스터디 룸의 공사가 이번주 말까지 완공될 것이란 점을 발표하게 되어 기쁘게 생각합니다. 일곱 개의 스터디 룸은 다음 주 월요일부터 사용이 가능할 것입니다.
새로운 스터디 룸은 10명에서 30명까지 수용이 가능하며 지역의 소규모 독서 클럽과 스터디 그룹을 목적으로 만들어졌습니다. <u>모든 스터디 룸은 사용 전에 필히 예약이 되어야 합니다.</u> Jack Grant 씨가 임시로 5월 말까지 새로운 스터디 룸의 관리를 담당할 예정입니다. 그 이후에 그는 다시 본래의 역할이었던 행정 지원 담당으로 복귀하게 될 것입니다.
정규 예약 관리직에 대한 구인 광고는 조만간에 게재될 것입니다. 이 직책을 맡은 사람은 새로운 스터디 룸에 대한 모든 예약 및 행정 관리를 감독하는 직무를 담당하게 될 것입니다. 감사합니다.

Amy Jordan
도서관장

**139.** 정답 (D)

**140.** (A) 모든 도서관 방문객들의 주차가 가능해질 것입니다.
(B) 모든 스터디 룸은 사용 전에 필히 예약이 되어야 합니다.
(C) Jack Grant 씨는 이미 재정적으로 도서관에 기여했습니다.
(D) 취업 면접은 6월 중순에 시행될 것입니다. 정답 (B)

**141.** 정답 (C)

**142.** 정답 (A)

---

문제 143-146번은 다음 이메일을 참조하시오.

Hong 씨께:

Grand가 1123번지에 위치한 400평방미터에 달하는 부지에 대한 문의에 감사드립니다. 하지만 그 부동산은 이미 회수되었다는 점을 말씀드리게 되어 아쉽게 생각합니다.

귀하는 전화 통화에서 두 번째 공장 부지를 6개월 넘게 물색 중이시라고 말씀하셨습니다. 귀하가 찾고자 하는 것의 구체적인 사항을 알려주시겠습니까? <u>제가 Castro Valley에서 귀하의 기준을 충족시켜줄 수 있는 좋은 부지들을 찾아보도록 하겠습니다.</u> 귀하는 제게 이메일로 선호하는 부지 크기와 가격을 비롯한 기타 중요한 요구사항들을 답장해 주시면 됩니다.

귀하는 부동산 안내 앱에 등록하실 수도 있습니다. 매번 새로운 부동산 매물이 나올 때마다 휴대전화로 실시간 무료 문자 메시지를 받아보실 수 있습니다. 이 앱은 각 부동산 매물에 대한 상세 정보를 확인할 수 있는 기능과 앱 상에서 전달받은 매물 안내문에 대해 바로 신속하게 답장할 수 있는 기능도 제공합니다.

귀하의 답장을 고대하고 있겠습니다.

**143.** 정답 (A)

**144.** (A) 부동산 중개업자는 부동산과 관련된 거래에 관한 협상을 합니다.
(B) 몇몇 부동산 소유주들은 주택을 공개하고 이를 잠재적 구매자에게 보여줍니다.
(C) 이것은 최근 부동산 업계의 흥미로운 흐름 중 하나입니다.
(D) 제가 Castro Valley에서 귀하의 기준을 충족시켜줄 수 있는 좋은 부지들을 찾아보도록 하겠습니다. 정답 (D)

**145.** 정답 (B)

**146.** 정답 (C)

---

## Part 7

문제 147-148번은 다음 공지문을 참조하시오.

**공지**

Woodbridge News

저희는 지난 20년간 격주 화요일마다 우리 지역의 소식지인 Woodbridge News를 모든 거주민들에게 배달해온 것을 자랑스럽게 여기고 있습니다. (147/148) 그러나 안타깝게도 시장님이 지역 예산 절감 차원에서 지역 소식지를 한 달에 한 번만 배달하기로 결정하였습니다.

(147) 그로 인해 소식지는 더 이상 격주로 배송되지 않습니다. 대신 매달 20일에 월간으로 받아보시게 됩니다. 여러분의 이해에 감사 드립니다.

Woodbridge News
여러분의 지역 소식지

**147.** 공지의 목적은 무엇인가?
(A) 신문 배송 일정에 관한 변경사항을 공지하기 위해서
(B) 독자들에게 신문 내용의 변경을 알리기 위해서
(C) 신문 가격의 변경을 알리기 위해서
(D) 신문사 직원의 변경을 공지하기 위해서 정답 (A)

**148.** 이 변경사항을 결정한 사람은 누구인가?
(A) 편집장
(B) 출판사

---

(C) 시장
(D) 마을 의회  정답 (C)

문제 149-150번은 다음 광고를 참조하시오.

(149) Finalnet은 경제와 제품 시장에 관한 연구와 투자 관련 법률을 포함해 1만 가지가 넘는 웹 기반 문서들을 폭넓게 검색할 수 있는 데이터베이스를 제공합니다. 국가, 경제 분야, 주제로 분류된 이러한 자료들은 주로 World Bank Group, 투자 촉진 회사와 민간 대행사들로부터 얻습니다. (149/150) Finalnet의 비즈니스 디렉터리에는 해외 투자와 관련해서 3만 개가 넘는 기구와 사람들의 연락 정보가 들어 있습니다. (149) 또한 온라인 서비스로는, 자회사 웹사이트로 연결되는 것은 물론이고 투자 포인트와 상세 내용들이 있는 여러 사이트로 연결해 드립니다. Finalnet은 7만9천 명의 회원을 보유하고 있으며 한 달 방문자는 약 2만 명입니다. 본사의 정보 서비스는 〈Financial Times〉의 '올해의 상업 홈페이지 상' 결선에 당당히 올라갔습니다.

**149.** 이 광고에 관심을 가질 것 같은 사람은 누구인가?
(A) 회계 감사원
(B) 컴퓨터 기술자
(C) 환경 운동가
(D) 회사 중역  정답 (D)

**150.** Finalnet은 어떤 정보를 제공하는가?
(A) 공공 국제법
(B) 투자자들의 연락 정보
(C) 온라인 주식 투자 방법
(D) 비투비(B2B) 사업의 최근 경향에 대한 정보  정답 (B)

문제 151-152번은 다음 문자 메시지를 참조하시오.

NATE POTTS [오전 10:39]
귀찮게 해서 죄송하지만, 오후 3시 대신에 오후 4시에 만날 수 있을까요?

NATE POTTS [오전 10:40]
제가 비행기를 놓쳐서 다음 비행기를 타야 할 것 같습니다. 다행히도 실제 회의에는 늦지 않을 것 같아요.

MATT LEE [오전 10:42]
괜찮아요. (152) 같은 항공사를 이용하실 것인가요?

NATE POTTS [오전 10:44]
(152) 맞아요. 이름에서 알 수 있듯이, Japan Airlines는 정말 일본으로 가는 항공편을 많이 제공하네요.

MATT LEE [오전 10:45]
알겠습니다. (151) 이번에는 누구와 동반해서 오시는 건가요?

NATE POTTS [오전 10:46]
(151) 아니에요. 이번에 제 비서는 오지 않아요.

MATT LEE [오전 10:48]
그렇군요. 알겠습니다. 그럼 오후 4시에 뵙겠습니다. 하여간 저도 길이 너무 막히네요.

NATE POTTS [오전 10:51]
고마워요. 불편함을 초래해서 미안해요.

**151.** Potts 씨에 대해 암시되는 것은 무엇인가?
(A) 그는 Lee 씨의 조수이다.
(B) 그는 일본을 떠난다.

(C) 그는 일본을 방문해 본 적이 있다.
(D) 그는 비서의 수행을 받을 것이다.  정답 (C)

**152.** 오전 10시 44분에 Potts 씨가 "You got that right."라고 말한 것이 의미하는 바는 무엇인가?
(A) 그는 길이 막혀서 늦을 것이다.
(B) 그는 기계적인 문제를 처리할 수 있다.
(C) 그는 Japan Airlines사를 이용할 것이다.
(D) 그는 전에 Lee 씨를 만나본 적이 없다.  정답 (C)

문제 153-155번은 다음 편지를 참조하시오.

Fine Art Institute

1월 23일

교직원 여러분께,

(153) 유감스럽지만 제가 Oakland 대학의 교수직을 수락했음을 알려드립니다. 이것은 제가 6월 말일 자로 현재의 제자리를 사임해야 됨을 뜻합니다. 두말할 것도 없이, 제가 이곳 Fine Art Institute에서 보낸 수 년의 시간은 제 인생에서 가장 보람된 시간이었습니다. 전반적으로 아주 대단한 경험이었습니다. 그러므로 이곳을 떠나기로 결정한 것은 쉽지 않은 결정이었습니다. 하지만, 여러분 중 많은 분이 알겠지만, 저는 한동안 종신 임기를 보장할 교직 기회를 찾아왔습니다. (155) 제 경력의 다음 단계를 향해 나아가는 저의 결정을 이해해 주시기 바랍니다. Oakland 대학에서의 일자리는 제 스스로에게 세웠던 직업적 목표들 중 일부를 성취하게 해줄 것이라고 믿습니다. (154) 이곳에서 12년간 몸담으면서, 저는 여러분과 같은 많은 재능 있는 예술가들과 일할 수 있는 특권을 누렸습니다. 여러분의 노고와 헌신에 매우 감사 드리며 여러분 모두의 노력이 지속적으로 성공하기를 기원합니다.

Grace Park
Fine Art Institute
San Francisco, California

**153.** 이 편지의 목적은 무엇인가?
(A) 직무 기술
(B) 취업 제의 수락
(C) 전근 신청
(D) 사직 발표  정답 (D)

**154.** 편지에 따르면 Grace Park에 대해 무엇이 맞는가?
(A) 그녀는 Fine Art Institute의 학생들 중 하나이다.
(B) 그녀는 Fine Art Institute에서 일을 시작했다.
(C) 그녀는 Fine Art Institute에서 10년 이상을 일해왔다.
(D) 그녀는 몇 년 안에 은퇴할 계획이다.  정답 (C)

**155.** Park 씨가 Oakland 대학의 일자리에 관해 언급한 것은 무엇인가?
(A) 어느 정도의 교직 경험을 요구한다.
(B) 주로 예술 프로젝트와 관련이 있다.
(C) 그녀의 이력에 큰 도움이 될 것이다.
(D) 예술 전문가가 되기 위한 선결 요건이다.  정답 (C)

문제 156-157번은 다음 이메일을 참조하시오.

수신: Juliet Porter 〈jporter@bk.com〉
발신: Kelly Winters 〈kwinters@bk.com〉
날짜: 10월 8일, 수요일
제목: 2일 간의 광고 회의

안녕하세요, Porter 씨,

(156) 저는 결국 이틀 동안 광고 회의에 참석하기로 결정했습니다. (156/157) 10월 14일 다음 주 화요일, 회의가 시작되기 하루 전날에 떠나는 비행기를 예매해 주셨으면 합니다. 그리고 Guam에 3일 정도 추가로 머물 생각이어서 돌아오는 것은 일요일 밤이 될 것 같습니다. 저는 마지막 날에는 가능한 한 해변에서 많은 시간을 보내고 싶으니 제가 밤 비행기를 타고 Atlanta로 돌아올 수 있도록 하실 수 있는지 알아봐 주시기 바랍니다. 비행기표를 구하기에 너무 늦지 않았기를 바랍니다. 이 날짜가 가능하지 않으면 제게 전화해서 알려 주십시오.

감사합니다.

Kelly Winters

**156.** 이메일을 보낸 목적은 무엇인가?
(A) 예산의 변경사항을 제안하기 위해서
(B) 광고에 대해 문의하기 위해서
(C) 출장 준비를 하기 위해서
(D) 회의를 연기하기 위해서 　　　　　　정답 (C)

**157.** 회의는 언제 시작하는가?
(A) 월요일
(B) 화요일
(C) 수요일
(D) 목요일 　　　　　　정답 (C)

문제 158-161번은 다음 정보를 참조하시오.

### Hotel President
### 서비스 목록

President 호텔의 넓고 아름답게 장식된 객실에서 편안한 유럽풍의 분위기를 느끼실 수 있으며 편리하고 친절한 직원 서비스로 이를 돕고 있습니다.

머무시는 동안 다양한 서비스와 시설을 편안하게 즐기시기 바랍니다.

**조식** 오전 7시 30분에서 8시 30분 사이에 머무시는 객실에서 드실 수 있습니다.

**탁아서비스** 품격 높은 서비스를 이용할 수 있습니다.

**사무시설** 팩스는 페이지 당 1달러(시내). 복사는 페이지 당 10센트. (158) 정상 접수시간에만 이용 가능.

**간이침대** 무료 이용 가능.

**세탁** 월요일부터 금요일까지 당일 세탁서비스를 이용할 수 있습니다(공휴일은 제외). 매일 오전 9시 30분 전에 접수처에 맡겨주세요.

**택시** 안내 데스크 옆 현관에 있는 무료전화로 24시간 서비스를 이용할 수 있습니다.

**퇴실 시간** 체크 아웃 시간은 오전 10시입니다. 그 이후에 체크 아웃을 하시려면 사전조정이 필요합니다. 객실료 반액이 부가됩니다.

**계산** 계산은 떠나실 때 하시면 되고 현금과 신용카드 둘 다 가능합니다. (159) 지배인과의 사전 협의가 없으면 개인수표는 받지 않습니다.

**접수시간** (158) 접수시간은 오전 7시에서 오후 9시입니다.

· (160) 조간신문, 아침 커피 서비스, 헬스장 무료 이용.

**158.** 사무 서비스는 언제 이용할 수 있는가?
(A) 오전 7시 30분에서 8시 30분
(B) 오전 7시에서 오후 9시
(C) 오전 9시에서 오후 5시
(D) 오전 9시 30분에서 오후 5시 30분 　　정답 (B)

**159.** 개인수표로 계산하려는 고객은 무엇이 필요한가?
(A) 체크 아웃 3일 전 통보
(B) 사회 보장 제도 번호
(C) 지배인의 사전 승인
(D) 신분증 　　　　　　정답 (C)

**160.** 무료로 이용할 수 있는 것은 무엇인가?
(A) 주말 신문
(B) 오후 음료 서비스
(C) 헬스 클럽
(D) 탁아 서비스 　　　　　　정답 (C)

**161.** 호텔이 제공하는 서비스가 아닌 것은 무엇인가?
(A) 룸 서비스
(B) 추가 간이침대
(C) 회의시설
(D) 무료전화 　　　　　　정답 (C)

문제 162-163번은 다음 회람을 참조하시오.

### 회람

수신: 모든 직원들
발신: James Brady, 총무부장 (Ext. 5493)
날짜: 9월 11일

(162) 이번 주에 건물에 예비 전력 장치를 설치합니다. 예비 전력 장치는 정전이 일어났을 때 단기간 대체 전력을 제공하고 우리의 정보와 장비들을 보호할 것입니다. 이 장치를 컴퓨터 전원에 특수 케이블로 연결할 것입니다. (163) 정전이 발생하면 이 장치가 즉시 컴퓨터를 비상 배터리 전력으로 작동시키고 10분 동안 경고음을 보내서 정전을 알립니다. 언제든지 이 계획에 관해 조언해 주시길 바랍니다.

**162.** 이번 주에 무엇을 할 계획인가?
(A) 전기 화재 경보기가 설치된다.
(B) 컴퓨터 부품들을 추가로 구입한다.
(C) 예비 전력 장치가 설치된다.
(D) 온라인 시스템 망이 구축된다. 　　정답 (C)

**163.** 경고음은 언제 발생하는가?
(A) 발전기가 고장 났을 때
(B) 예비 전력 장치가 꺼졌을 때
(C) 컴퓨터로 연결되는 전기가 꺼졌을 때
(D) 보안 장비가 갑자기 꺼졌을 때 　　정답 (C)

문제 164-167번은 다음 공지문을 참조하시오.

### 공지

Kamon Financial Solutions

어제, 경영진과 소유주들이 회사의 장래를 논의하기 위해 회의를 열었습니다. 우리는 지난 2년 간 수익과 고객의 수가 크게 증가했습니다. 현재 많은 고객들이 우리 사무실에서 서비스를 받는 것이 불가능합니다. 그로 인해, 우리 회사를 더 성장시키기 위해서 (164) 더 큰 새 사무실로 이전하기로 결정했고, 이는 10월 2일에 개장합니다.

새 사무실로의 이전을 가능한 순조롭게 진행시키기 위해, (166) 9월 29일에 우리는 장비의 (165) 대부분을 옮기기로 결정했습니다. (167) 이날은 토요일로 우리 사무실은 주로 주말에 일을 하지 않습니다. 즉, 우리 업무에 지장을 최소화할 수 있다는 의미입니다. 경영진을 대표하여, (166) 저는 모든 직원이 토요일 새 사무실로의 이전을 돕기 위해 출근하시길 요청합니다. 여러분은 이날 시간당 50달러의 초과 수당을 받을 것입니다. 오전 11시부터 오후 3시까지 일하게 됩니다. 또한, 이전은 전날인 9월 28일, 여러분이 모든 폴더와 문서를 종이상자에 꾸려서 트럭에 쉽게 실을 수 있도록 하기 바랍니다. 여러분은 창고에서 여분의 상자를 찾을 수 있습니다.

만약 문의사항이 있으시다면, 언제든지 바로 연락하십시오. 내선 번호는 303입니다. 협조해 주셔서 감사합니다. 함께 Kamon Financial Solutions 를 시장을 주도하는 기업으로 만들어 봅시다.

Andrew Lee
최고 경영자

**164.** 이 공지의 목적은 무엇인가?
(A) 새로운 사무실로의 이전을 알리기 위해서
(B) 회사가 내놓은 신상품을 광고하기 위해서
(C) 고객들의 새로운 연락처를 제공하기 위해서
(D) 직원들에게 회의에 참석하도록 요청하기 위해서　　　정답 (A)

**165.** 두 번째 단락 두 번째 줄의 "majority"와 의미상 가장 유사한 단어는 무엇인가?
(A) 최소한
(B) 대부분
(C) 절대적인
(D) 거의　　　정답 (B)

**166.** 직원들이 9월 29일에 해달라고 요청 받은 것은 무엇인가?
(A) 영업 보고서를 작성한다.
(B) 새로운 고객에게 연락한다.
(C) 출근을 한다.
(D) 다른 주차장에 주차를 한다.　　　정답 (C)

**167.** [1], [2], [3] 그리고 [4]로 표시된 곳 중에, 아래 문장이 들어가기에 가장 적절한 곳은?
"이날은 토요일로 우리 사무실은 주로 주말에 일을 하지 않습니다. 즉, 우리 업무에 지장을 최소화할 수 있다는 의미입니다."
(A) [1]
(B) [2]
(C) [3]
(D) [4]　　　정답 (B)

**문제 168-171번은 다음 기사를 참조하시오.**

1월 10일

탄산 음료 업체에서 새롭게 선보일 새로운 탄산 음료

Chicago – 세계적인 브랜드인 Lite Soda 사는 새로 나온 다이어트 탄산음료를 곧 시장에 선보일 것이다. (168) Mountain Spring이라는 이름의 새로 나온 탄산음료는 여름 시즌이 시작되는 6월 25일에 시중에 나올 것이다. (169) Mountain Spring의 공격적인 마케팅은 5월 15일 New York, Chicago, Los Angeles, San Francisco, 그리고 Miami와 같은 주요 시장을 필두로 TV 광고와 인쇄 매체 광고를 통해 이루어질 것이다. 고속도로의 옥외광고판은 5월 말에 설치될 것이다. 이들 광고는 Ohio, Michigan 그리고 Carolina 주의 고속도로에 길게 늘어설 것이다.

(171) Lite Soda 사는 지난 5년 동안 세 가지의 새로운 탄산음료를 선보였다. (169)10칼로리를 함유한 다른 두 개의 다이어트 음료와는 달리

Mountain Spring은 칼로리가 0이고, 인공 감미료가 아닌 과일 주스로 단 맛을 냈다고 한다. (170) Lite Soda 사는 소비자들이 자연 식품을 선호하고 가공된 재료를 기피하는 시장의 흐름을 따르고 있다고 한다. 이는 최초로 출시된 이 회사의 천연 탄산 음료이다.

**168.** 새로운 탄산 음료는 언제 전국에 선보일 것인가?
(A) 5월 15일
(B) 5월 31일
(C) 6월 21일
(D) 6월 25일　　　정답 (D)

**169.** Mountain Spring의 장점은 무엇인가?
(A) 가격이 상대적으로 저렴하다.
(B) 대중에게 더 친숙하다.
(C) 천연 당분을 포함하고 있다.
(D) 열량이 10칼로리 밖에 되지 않는다.　　　정답 (C)

**170.** 새로운 탄산 음료를 개발한 이유로 언급된 것은 무엇인가?
(A) 고객의 요구
(B) 다른 업체와의 경쟁
(C) 직원 설문조사
(D) 새로운 건강 가이드라인　　　정답 (A)

**171.** [1], [2], [3] 그리고 [4]로 표시된 곳 중에, 아래 문장이 들어가기에 가장 적절한 곳은?
"Lite Soda 사는 지난 5년 동안 세 가지의 새로운 탄산음료를 선보였다."
(A) [1]
(B) [2]
(C) [3]
(D) [4]　　　정답 (C)

**문제 172-175번은 다음 온라인 채팅 토론을 참조하시오.**

Kevin Ross　　　　　　　　　　　　　　　　　　[오후 2:21]
안녕하세요, Elaine, 새로운 아파트를 찾고 있다고 들었어요. 어떻게 되어 가나요?

Elaine Trent　　　　　　　　　　　　　　　　　　[오후 2:23]
최근에 꽤 유명한 부동산 중개업자에게 연락해 두었는데, 그녀가 도심의 제 사무실 근처에 적당한 곳을 찾아보고 있어요.

Kevin Ross　　　　　　　　　　　　　　　　　　[오후 2:24]
New York 시내로 이사하려고 결정한 이유가 뭔지 물어봐도 되나요? 알다시피, New York은 주거지로서는 세계에서 가장 비싼 도시 중 한 곳이잖아요.

Elaine Trent　　　　　　　　　　　　　　　　　　[오후 2:28]
버스로 통근하면서 길에서 그렇게 많은 시간을 낭비하는 게 지긋지긋해요. 긴 통근 시간을 더 이상 감내할 수가 없어요.

Helen Smith　　　　　　　　　　　　　　　　　　[오후 2:30]
절대 동감이에요. 하지만 아파트들이 대부분 임대료가 비싸지 않아요? 그리고 생활비도 비싸고요. 감당할 수 있어요?

Elaine Trent　　　　　　　　　　　　　　　　　　[오후 2:31]
다행히 지난달에 급여가 올랐어요. (172) 큰 마케팅 프로젝트를 성공시킨 덕분에 상사가 우리 팀원 모두에게 보상을 해 준거죠.

Kevin Ross　　　　　　　　　　　　　　　　　　[오후 2:33]
그나마 다행이네요. (173) 제가 어제 신문을 읽었는데, 기사에서 Mercer Human Resource Consulting 사에서 행한 생활비 설문조사에서 New York이 전 세계에서 가장 비싼 도시로 선정되었더군요.

Helen Smith [오후 2:36]

(174) 최근에, 주택 부족으로 인해 주택 가격이 상당히 상승했어요. 마치 외곽지역으로 모든 이들이 밀려나는 것 같은 느낌이에요.

Kevin Ross [오후 2:39]

(174) 사실, 외곽 지역으로 나가는 사람들의 행렬에 합류할 수밖에 없어요. 시에서 주택난을 해소하기 위해 무엇인가 조치를 취해야 해요.

Elaine Trent [오후 2:40]

(174) 네, 저도 그렇게 생각해요. (175) 저는 New York에 어디라도 좋으니 집이나 구할 수 있었으면 해요.

Helen Smith [오후 2:42]

(175) 행운을 빌어요. 곧 당신 집을 찾을 거예요.

**172.** Trent 씨는 어떠한 회사에서 근무하는 것 같은가?

(A) 부동산 회사
(B) 디자인 회사
(C) 회계 사무소
(D) 마케팅 회사　　　　　　　　　　　정답 (D)

**173.** 기사에서 New York에 관해 언급된 것은 무엇인가?

(A) New York의 주택가격이 여전히 하락하고 있다.
(B) New York에서 거주하는 것은 비용이 많이 든다.
(C) New York은 외국인에게 점차 매력을 잃어가고 있다.
(D) New York은 고급 브랜드 상점으로 가득 찬 도시이다.　정답 (B)

**174.** 시 정부에 관해 유추할 수 있는 것은 무엇인가?

(A) 시 정부는 최근 굉장히 잘하고 있다.
(B) 시 정부는 더 많은 주거시설을 건설할 것이다.
(C) 시 정부는 주택 위기를 초래한 비판을 받아야 한다.
(D) 시 정부는 주민들의 의견에 귀를 기울이기 시작했다.　정답 (C)

**175.** 오후 2시 42분에 Smith 씨가 "I'll keep my fingers crossed."라고 말한 의도는 무엇인가?

(A) 그녀는 손가락에 문제가 있다.
(B) 그녀는 새로운 정책에 대한 Trent 씨의 의견에 동의한다.
(C) 그녀는 Trent 씨가 적당한 집을 찾을 수 있길 바라고 있다.
(D) 그녀는 환경오염 문제가 시급한 현안이라고 생각한다.　정답 (C)

**문제 176-180번은 다음 회람과 서식을 참조하시오.**

회람

모든 직원에게:

(176) 이 회람은 Ace Technology 사 직원 안내서에 나와 있는 우리 회사의 출장비 환급 정책을 상기시키고자 발송합니다.

우리 출장비 환급 정책에 의하면, 경비는 세 가지 항목으로 분류됩니다.

**카테고리 1:**
– 항공료
– 숙박

(카테고리 1의 경비는 선불로 회계부에서 사전에 처리함을 유의해 주십시오.)

**카테고리 2:**
– 현지 여행
– 식대
– 고객접대

(178) **카테고리 3:**
– 부수적인 경비

(카테고리 2와 카테고리 3 경비 모두 직원이 구매 당시 직접 지불한 뒤 항목별로 정리된 관련 영수증을 제출하면 환급됨을 유의해 주십시오.)

**여행:** 현지 여행은 환급을 받으려면 Ace Technology 사의 업무와 직접적인 관련성이 있어야 합니다. (177) 업무 목적의 철도, 개인 소유 차량, 택시, 렌터카 이용이 승인됩니다. 자가용 및 렌터카 영수증은 사용된 연료량 및 운전 거리가 포함되어 있어야 합니다. 직원들은 관련 경비를 환급 받기 위해 출장 중 사용한 모든 교통편의 영수증을 항목별로 정리하여 제시해야 합니다.

(177) **고객접대비:** 고객접대비는 명백하게 업무와 관련되어 있을 때에만 환급됩니다. 각 거래에 대해 항목별로 정리된 영수증을 제시해야 합니다.

모든 직원들은 업무와 관련된 여행 경비에 관해 필요한 정보를 언급한 출장 경비보고서를 작성해야 합니다. 직원과 직속 상사가 이 서식에 서명해야 합니다. 직원들은 작성한 출장경비 보고서와 모든 영수증을 출장을 다녀온 뒤 60일 안에 제출해야 합니다.

Ace Technology
Los Angeles, California
출장경비 보고서

이름: George Parker
일자: 8월 3일
부서: 광고부
코드번호: X6425

출발일: 7월 20일　　　　　　　　　도착일: 7월 26일

| 일자 | (178)<br>7월 22~23일 | (179)<br>7월 24~25일 | 7월 26일 |
|---|---|---|---|
| 장소 | Sydney | Auckland | Melbourne |
| 식대 및 팁 | $100 | $120 | $35 |
| 고객접대 | $0 | $0 | $0 |
| 교통편(택시, 철도 등) | $35 | $45 | $32 |
| 기타 경비 | $80 | $0 | $0 |
| | $215 | $165 | $67 |
| 총계 | | $447 | |

기타 경비 내역
(180) 7월 22일 – 팩스 발신

직원 서명: George Parker
상사 서명: Linda Wilson

**176.** 회람의 목적은 무엇인가?

(A) 일부 경비가 환급 불가능한 이유에 대해 설명한다.
(B) 직원들에게 경비 보고 요건을 전달한다.
(C) 직원 안내서의 개정을 발표한다.
(D) 환급 요청 제출 기한을 연장한다.　　　정답 (B)

**177.** 회람에서는 어떤 종류의 경비를 다루지 않는가?

(A) 팩스 수수료
(B) 고객접대비
(C) 연료비
(D) 렌터카 비용　　　　　　　　　　　정답 (A)

**178.** Parker 씨에게 카테고리 3 경비가 발생한 날은 언제인가?

(A) 7월 20일
(B) 7월 22일
(C) 7월 25일
(D) 7월 29일　　　　　　　　　　　정답 (B)

**179.** Parker 씨는 7월 25일에 어디에 있었는가?

(A) Los Angeles

(B) Auckland

(C) Sydney

(D) Melbourne          정답 (B)

**180.** Parker 씨에 대해 암시되는 것은 무엇인가?

(A) 항공 티켓을 요청했다.

(B) 호텔 예약을 직접 했다.

(C) Auckland에서 고객에게 저녁식사를 대접했다.

(D) Sydney에 있는 동안 팩스를 보냈다.          정답 (D)

**문제 181-185번은 다음 공지문과 이메일을 참조하시오.**

---

**Wallace 동물원 자원봉사 프로그램**

**자격요건:**

− 18세 이상

− (181) **고등학교 졸업자**

− (181) **과거 혹은 현재 고용인의 만족스러운 추천서**

− 매주 한 번의 근무에 전념할 수 있는 사람

− 단정하고 전문가다운 용모

− 동물원까지 믿을 수 있는 교통편

− (181) **직원연수에 참석 가능해야 함**

**근무시간:**

자원 봉사자들은 채용된 시즌에 매주 한 번 근무해야 합니다. 가을 및 겨울 자원봉사 근무 시간은 주말 오전 10시부터 오후 2시까지입니다. (184) **봄 및 여름 자원봉사자들은 평일 오전 10시부터 오후 4시까지 근무합니다.** 그러나 주말 오전 10시부터 오후 6시까지 근무해야 할 수도 있습니다. 근무일정은 동물원의 대리가 배정합니다.

우리 시 최고의 동물원에서 자원봉사를 하는 것에 관심이 있으시면, 저희 홈페이지 wz.org에 방문하여 지원해 주십시오. 질문이 있으시면 Kate Kensington 씨에게 703-221-8923 또는 katek@wz.org로 연락을 주십시오. (182) **봄 프로그램 지원서는 3월 18일 영업일이 끝나기 전에 제출되어야 합니다.** 봄 프로그램 연수는 3월 28일에 시작됩니다.

---

수신: 〈katek@wz.org〉

발신: 〈stevel@pgh.com〉

날짜: 3월 20일

제목: 자원봉사업무

첨부: 지원서, 추천서

Kensington 씨;

동물원 자원봉사 광고를 보고 연락드립니다. 저는 열흘 전에 광고를 보았으나, 질병으로 인해 지난 주 병원에 입원해 있었습니다. 그래서 지금까지 연락을 드리지 못했습니다. (183) **봄 프로그램 지원 기한이 지난 것을 압니다. 그러나 제 상황을 이해해주시고 지원할 수 있게 해주시길 바랍니다.** 빠짐없이 작성한 지원서와 현재 고용주의 추천서를 첨부하였습니다.

(184) **저는 평일에만 근무가 가능합니다.** 저는 영화관에서 일하고 있어서 토요일과 일요일에는 전일 근무해야 합니다. 저는 동물원에서 정말 일하고 싶으므로, 이 점이 문제가 되지 않길 바랍니다. 저는 (185) **능숙한** 전문가이며, 동물원에서 훌륭하게 일할 수 있다고 확신합니다.

감사합니다.

Steve Lionsgate

---

**181.** 자원봉사 직책의 자격 요건이 아닌 것은 무엇인가?

(A) 고등학교 졸업

(B) 직원연수 참가

(C) 추천서

(D) 동물원 근무 경험          정답 (D)

**182.** 봄 직책 지원서의 마감기한은 언제인가?

(A) 3월 10일

(B) 3월 18일

(C) 3월 20일

(D) 3월 28일          정답 (B)

**183.** Lionsgate 씨가 이메일에서 요청하는 것은 무엇인가?

(A) 늦은 지원에 대한 고려

(B) 동물원에서 추가 주말근무

(C) 직원 연수에 관한 정보

(D) 고등학교 졸업장 제출을 위한 더 많은 시간          정답 (A)

**184.** Lionsgate 씨는 하루에 몇 시간씩 자원봉사를 하게 될 것인가?

(A) 4시간

(B) 6시간

(C) 8시간

(D) 16시간          정답 (B)

**185.** 이메일 두 번째 단락 세 번째 줄의 "consummate"와 의미상 가장 유사한 단어는 무엇인가?

(A) 결단력이 있는

(B) 절대적인

(C) 독자적인

(D) 꼼꼼한          정답 (B)

**문제 186-190번은 다음 광고와 문서, 그리고 이메일을 참조하시오.**

---

**New Horizons**

**가족을 위한 주택이 현재 판매 중입니다!**

저는 Napa Valley 지역에 건설 중이던 고급 가족용 주택을 완공하게 되었음을 발표하게 되어 굉장히 기쁘게 생각합니다. 새로운 주택은 현대적인 가족을 염두에 두고 건설되었습니다. (187) **이 주택 단지는 숲으로 둘러 쌓여 있을 뿐만 아니라 모든 주요 대중 교통 노선 근처에 위치하여 이상적인 접근성을 지니고 있습니다.**

이 주택들은 현대적 디자인과 함께 친환경적인 건설 공법을 (186) **자랑합니다.** 주변에는 많은 학교들과 여가를 즐길 수 있는 여러 시설들이 있습니다. 이 주택들은 다양한 가족 규모와 예산에 맞춰 구매가 가능합니다.

여러분이 꿈꿔온 임대 주택에 대해 논의하고 싶으시면, 주저하지 마시고 제게 707-926-7399로 연락을 주십시오.

Susan Kang

New Horizon 주택 건설사

---

**New Horizons**

**구매 가능한 주택들**

**가족용 주택**

| 주택 번호 | 주택 코드 | 크기 | 월 임대료 | 보증금 |
|---|---|---|---|---|
| Townhouse 12번 | #MS986 | 1,200ft² | $1,200 | $600 |
| Townhouse 14번 | #MS304 | 1,500ft² | $1,500 | $750 |

| Townhouse 23번 | #MS230 | 2,000ft² | $1,800 | $900 |
| (189)<br>Townhouse 26번 | #MS129 | 2,500ft² | (189)<br>$2,000 | $1,000 |

모든 보증금들은 이사일 이전에 전액 지불되어야 합니다.

---

수신: 임대 사무소 〈rentals@newhorizons.com〉

발신: Jenna Marshall 〈j.marshall@sws.net〉

날짜: 3월 23일

제목: 아파트 임대

Kang 씨에게,

New Horizons는 마치 우리 가족 네 명을 위한 주택이란 생각이 드네요. (189) **저희는 월 임대료가 $2,000인 집을 굉장히 보고 싶어요.** 그 크기와 가격이 저희 가족에게 적합하더라고요. 홈페이지에 게재된 사진을 보니 집이 굉장히 예뻤어요! 그 집을 볼 수 있도록 일정을 잡을 수 있을까요? (188) **저는 San Francisco에 있는 한 종합병원에서 근무하지만 (190) 현재는 출산 휴가 중이라서 시간은 하루 중 언제라도 좋습니다.** 이번 주는 괜찮을까요? 그리고 집을 보러 갈 때는 제가 가져가야 할 것이 있나요? 이 가격에 좋은 임대 주택들은 바로 나가더라고요!

Jenna Marshall

---

**186.** 광고의 두 번째 단락 첫 번째 줄의 "boast"와 의미상 가장 유사한 단어는 무엇인가?

(A) 증가시키다

(B) 특징으로 하다

(C) 창조하다

(D) 보장하다 　　　　　　　　　　　　　　정답 (B)

**187.** New Horizons의 주택에 관해 언급된 것은 무엇인가?

(A) 가구가 완전히 비치되어 있다.

(B) 가까운 곳에 대중교통이 있다.

(C) 반려동물이 허용된다.

(D) 임대료 보조금을 받는다. 　　　　　　　　정답 (B)

**188.** Marshall 씨의 직업은 무엇인 것 같은가?

(A) 상품 개발자

(B) 전문 의료인

(C) 부동산 중개인

(D) 건설업자 　　　　　　　　　　　　　　정답 (B)

**189.** Marshall 씨가 가장 임대하길 원하는 곳은 어디인가?

(A) Townhouse 12

(B) Townhouse 14

(C) Townhouse 23

(D) Townhouse 26 　　　　　　　　　　　정답 (D)

**190.** Marshall 씨에게 편한 약속 시간은?

(A) 하루 중 언제든

(B) 저녁 시간에만

(C) 주말에만

(D) 오늘만 　　　　　　　　　　　　　　　정답 (A)

---

**문제 191-195번은 다음 광고와 예약 확인서, 그리고 이메일을 참조하시오.**

Speed Pass는 저희 우대 고객들에게 10월과 1월 사이의 여행에 대해 유효한 모든 기차 티켓에 대해 최고의 온라인 할인 서비스를 제공하는 것으로 보

---

답해 드리고자 합니다. (192) **Gold 레일 카드 소지자들은 모든 서비스와 노선에 대해 30%의 엄청난 할인을 이용하실 수 있으며, Silver 레일 카드를 소지하고 계신 고객들은 모든 비성수기 여행에 대해 20%를 할인 받으실 수 있습니다.** 이 놀라운 할인 가격으로 무제한으로 여행 티켓을 구매하실 수 있으며, 저희 홈페이지에는 저희 모든 노선과 서비스에 대한 정보가 들어 있습니다.

보너스로, 여러분의 레일 카드를 Platinum 서비스로 업그레이드하시면, 귀하의 첫 번째 여행이 완전히 무료일 뿐만 아니라 매달 여러분의 수신함에 곧바로 독점 할인 서비스를 받으실 수 있습니다. 일단 표의 구매가 확인되면, 표는 환불이 불가하나 10달러의 수수료를 통해 교환은 가능함에 (191) **유의하십시오.**

---

### Speed Pass 예약 확인서

고객 성명: Diane Portland

날짜: 9월 13일

**귀하의 여행 상세 정보**

| 서비스<br>번호 | 날짜 | 출발<br>시간 | 출발지 | 도착<br>시간 | 도착지 | 운행<br>시간 | 요금 |
|---|---|---|---|---|---|---|---|
| SP2581 | 10월 1일 | 10:05 | Hunter's<br>Mill | 12:31 | Pockelfields | 2시간<br>26분 | $27.00 |
| SP2582 | 10월 1일 | 19:12 | Pockelfields | 21:42 | Hunter's<br>Mill | 2시간<br>30분 | $29.00 |
| SP5665 | 11월 15일 | 10:22 | Lincoln<br>Stadium | 13:50 | Saltsburgh<br>Road | 3시간<br>28분 | $36.50 |
| (194)<br>SP5433 | 11월 17일 | 15:02 | Saltsburgh<br>Road | 18:27 | Lincoln<br>Stadium | 3시간<br>25분 | $33.00 |
| | | | | | | 할인 전 총액 | $125.50 |
| | | | | | | 할인 | 20% |
| | | | | | | 총액 | $100.40 |

---

수신: 고객 서비스부 〈cservices@sp.net〉

발신: Diane Portland 〈dp07@coolmail.net〉

날짜: 9월 14일

제목: 예약 확인

관계자께,

귀사의 웹사이트를 통해 제가 최근에 예약한 사항과 관련해 연락드립니다. (193/195) **귀사의 최근 서비스에 따르면, 제가 가입한 레일 카드는 제 여행 티켓에 30%의 할인을 받았어야 한다는 것을 의미합니다. (195) 그런데 제가 받은 할인은 실제로 20%뿐이었습니다.** 우대 고객으로서, 저는 이 차액을 제게 환불해 주실 수 있게 조정해 주시면 감사하겠습니다.

추가로, 저는 제 티켓 중 한 장을 교환하고자 합니다. (194) **저는 더 이상 15:02에 떠나는 SP5433 서비스를 이용할 수 없으며, 이를 16:02에 출발하는 것으로 바꾸고자 합니다.** 이것이 조정될 수 있으면 감사하겠습니다.

Diane Portland

---

**191.** 광고 두 번째 단락 세 번째 줄에 있는 단어 "note"와 의미가 가장 유사한 단어는 무엇인가?

(A) 등록하다

(B) 접속하다

(C) 인식하다

(D) 알아내다 　　　　　　　　　　　　　　정답 (C)

**192.** Speed Pass 고객들에게 권고되는 것은 무엇인가?

(A) 레일 카드 가입을 통해 더 저렴한 여행표를 예약할 것

(B) Speed Pass를 친구와 가족에게 추천할 것

---

(C) Speed Pass에 연락해 서비스에 대한 모든 개괄 사항을 요청할 것

(D) 추가로 2년 동안 자신의 레일 카드를 갱신할 것　　　정답 (A)

**193.** Portland 씨에 관해 유추할 수 있는 것은 무엇인가?

(A) Gold 레일 카드 소지자이다.

(B) Platinum 레일 카드로 업그레이드하기를 원한다.

(C) 자신이 구매한 모든 티켓을 취소하기를 원한다.

(D) 전에 한 번도 Speed Pass 서비스를 이용한 적이 없다.　　　정답 (A)

**194.** Portland 씨는 어느 여행을 변경하기를 원한다고 나타내는가?

(A) Hunter's Mill에서 Pockelfields로 가는 여행

(B) Pockelfields에서 Hunter's Mill로 가는 여행

(C) Lincoln Stadium에서 Saltsburgh Road로 가는 여행

(D) Saltsburgh Road에서 Lincoln Stadium으로 가는 여행　　　정답 (D)

**195.** Portland 씨의 문제점은 무엇인가?

(A) 자신의 기차 티켓에 대해 과다 청구되었다.

(B) 자신의 기차 티켓을 받지 못했다.

(C) Speed Pass 웹사이트를 이용할 수 없었다.

(D) 자신이 선택하지 않은 여행에 대해 비용이 청구되었다.　　　정답 (A)

---

문제 196-200번은 다음 공지와 교육 프로그램, 그리고 이메일을 참조하시오.

---

MK Corporation 교육 과정

BK Corporation은 다음 분기에 진행될 예정인 저희의 환상적인 교육 과정 프로그램을 소개해 드리고자 합니다. 저희는 여러분께서 각각의 과목이 제공하는 것과 그것이 어떻게 여러분 각자의 직업 계발에 도움이 될 수 있는지 뿐만 아니라 여러분의 직업 역량을 확실히 달성하는 데 대한 책임을 지실 것을 촉구합니다. (197/199) **연간 의무 교육을 아직 이수하지 않으신 분들은, 별표로 표기된 각 코스에 대한 자리를 직접 예약하셔야 할 것이며, 이 과목들은 모든 직원들에게 해마다 요구되는 요건이기 때문입니다.** (197) **또한 사내 전산망에서 여러분의 개인적 역할의 일환으로 이수해야 하는 과목들의 목록도 찾아 보실 수 있습니다.** 이 과정들에 대한 비용은 저희가 충당해 드릴 것입니다. 여러분의 업무 특성의 일부는 아니지만 여러분의 능력을 확장하는 데 도움이 될 것이라고 생각하는 어떤 과정이든지 참석하길 원하는 것이 있으면 기꺼이 그렇게 하시기를 원하지만, 개인적으로 등록비에 대한 책임을 지셔야 할 것입니다.

교육 과목에 대한 어떤 질문이라도 있거나 자리를 예약하실 분은 Brian McGowan(b.mcgowan@impulse.net) 씨에게 언제든지 이메일을 보내시기 바랍니다.

---

MK Corporation 교육 과정

| 과정 코드 | 과정 이름 | 날짜/시간 | |
|---|---|---|---|
| MK94091 | 성과 관리 능력 워크숍 | 11월 13일 | 10:00 |
| | | 11월 20일 | 10:00 |
| | | 11월 27일 | 13:00 |
| MK73112 | 효과적인 의사 소통 마스터 클래스 | 11월 10일 | 14:30 |
| | | 11월 17일 | 11:00 |
| | | 11월 24일 | 10:30 |
| (198) MK92035 | 시간 관리 워크숍 | 12월 1일 | 09:30 |
| | | 12월 8일 | 15:00 |
| | | 12월 17일 | 14:30 |
| MK74011 | 대인 관계 워크숍 | 11월 30일 | 10:00 |
| | | 12월 3일 | 14:30 |
| | | 12월 5일 | 16:00 |

---

수신: Brian McGowan〈b.mcgowan@mk.net〉

발신: Linda Wilson 〈lw@mk.net〉

날짜: 10월 10일

제목: 교육 과정

McGowan 씨께,

(198) 저는 12월 1일, 9시 30분에 MK92035 과정에 대한 자리를 예약하고자 하며, 이 코스에 참석하는 데 얼마가 드는지 궁금합니다. (200) 저는 또한 MK74011에도 관심이 있지만, 그 기간에 연차 휴가를 쓸 것입니다. 혹시 이 코스가 앞으로 언제 운영될 것인지 알고 계신가요? 마지막으로, 저는 제 성과 관리 능력에 대한 역량이 가장 최근의 것에 대한 것인지 확실하지 않습니다. (199) 저는 이전에 두 번이나 MK94091에 참석했지만, 마지막 것의 정확한 날짜에 대해 확실하지 않습니다. 이것에 대해 살펴봐 주시면 감사하겠습니다.

대단히 감사합니다.

Linda Wilson

**196.** 공지 첫 번째 단락 두 번째 줄에 있는 단어 "take"와 의미상 가장 유사한 단어는 무엇인가?

(A) 치우다

(B) 가져오다

(C) 사용하다

(D) 사로잡다　　　정답 (C)

**197.** 직원들은 무엇을 하라는 권고를 받는가?

(A) 가능한 한 빨리 4가지 교육 과정 모두에 대한 자리를 예약할 것

(B) McGowan 씨에게 과정 등록 비용을 낼 것

(C) 프로그램에 추가하고 싶은 교육 과정에 대해 제안할 것

(D) 그들의 직업적인 성장에 가장 적합한 과정을 확인해 볼 수 있는 시간을 가질 것　　　정답 (D)

**198.** "시간 관리 워크숍"에 관해 유추할 수 있는 것은 무엇인가?

(A) Wilson 씨 업무에 필요한 과목은 아니다.

(B) 올해 프로그램에 추가된 새로운 과목이다.

(C) 등록비가 가장 높다.

(D) 모든 직원들에게 의무이다.　　　정답 (A)

**199.** Wilson 씨에 관해 유추할 수 있는 것은 무엇인가?

(A) 코스들이 무엇을 수반하는지 확실히 모른다.

(B) 회사를 떠날 것이며, 의무 교육을 이수하지 않을 것이다.

(C) 1년 넘게 회사에서 일해 왔다.

(D) 자신이 직접 돈을 내야 하는 어떤 코스도 참석하기를 원하지 않는다.　　　정답 (C)

**200.** Wilson 씨는 자신의 이메일에서 무슨 문제점에 대해 설명했는가?

(A) 사내 전산망에 접속할 수 없다.

(B) 자신이 참석하실 원하는 과정 중의 하나가 진행되는 동안 휴가를 갈 것이다.

(C) 강좌 등록비를 지불할 금전적 여유가 없다.

(D) 의무 교육에 참석하고 싶어 하지 않는다.　　　정답 (B)

## Part 1

**1.** 미W
(A) The man is holding a cup.
(B) The man is speaking into a microphone.
(C) The man is wearing headphones.
(D) The man is carrying a bag on his shoulder.

(A) 남자는 컵을 손에 쥐고 있다.
(B) 남자는 마이크에 대고 말을 하고 있다.
(C) 남자는 헤드폰을 쓰고 있다.
(D) 남자는 가방을 어깨에 메고 있다. 　　　　　정답 (C)

**2.** 미M
(A) A city street is being resurfaced.
(B) A stairway is divided by a handrail.
(C) Cars are driving across a bridge.
(D) Curved metal railings border a body of water.

(A) 한 시내 도로가 재포장되고 있다.
(B) 계단 중간에 손잡이가 위치하고 있다.
(C) 차들이 다리를 가로질러 가고 있다.
(D) 구부러진 철제 난간이 물가에 위치하고 있다. 　　정답 (D)

**3.** 영W
(A) He is waxing the floor with a machine.
(B) He is using a long pole to clean a window.
(C) He is cutting the grass with a lawnmower.
(D) He is adding some detergent to a basket full of water.

(A) 그는 기계를 이용하여 바닥을 왁스칠하고 있다.
(B) 그는 긴 막대를 사용하여 유리창을 닦고 있다.
(C) 그는 잔디 깎는 기계를 사용하여 잔디를 깎고 있다.
(D) 그는 물이 가득 찬 양동이에 세제를 풀고 있다. 　정답 (B)

**4.** 호M
(A) Some people are enjoying the view of the ocean.
(B) Small tables have been placed in front of the chairs.
(C) A shirt has been hung over an empty chair.
(D) A beach umbrella has been opened to provide shade.

(A) 몇몇 사람들이 바다의 풍경을 감상하고 있다.
(B) 작은 테이블들이 의자들 앞에 놓여 있다.
(C) 셔츠 하나가 비어 있는 한 의자 위에 걸려 있다.
(D) 비치 파라솔이 펼쳐져서 그늘을 드리우고 있다. 　정답 (D)

**5.** 미W
(A) A woman is facing a group of people.
(B) Most of the participants are standing.
(C) Some lighting equipment is being installed.
(D) Some reading materials are being distributed.

(A) 한 여자가 한 무리의 사람들을 마주보고 있다.
(B) 대부분의 참석자들은 서있다.
(C) 몇몇 조명 장비가 설치되고 있다.
(D) 몇몇 읽을 자료들이 배부되고 있다. 　　　　정답 (A)

**6.** 영W
(A) Some people are standing next to a checkout counter.
(B) Groceries are being placed into plastic bags.
(C) A freezer is being stocked by a store employee.

(D) A cart is being pushed down an aisle by shoppers.

(A) 몇몇 사람들이 계산대 옆에 서있다.
(B) 식료품이 비닐봉투 안에 넣어지고 있다.
(C) 직원에 의해 냉동고에 제품이 채워지고 있다.
(D) 쇼핑하는 사람들이 카트를 밀며 통로를 다니고 있다. 　정답 (D)

## Part 2

**7.** 미M 미W
Where did you park your delivery truck?
(A) In the rear of the building.
(B) A good national park.
(C) We offer trucking services.

배송 트럭을 어디에 주차하셨나요?
(A) 건물 뒤편에요.
(B) 좋은 국립공원이에요.
(C) 저희는 트럭 운송 서비스를 제공합니다. 　　정답 (A)

**8.** 영W 미M
Who should I give this market analysis report to?
(A) Four or five pages.
(B) It's a huge market.
(C) Ms. Miyazaki, please.

이 시장 분석 보고서를 누구에게 전달해야 하나요?
(A) 네다섯 페이지요.
(B) 엄청난 규모의 시장입니다.
(C) Miyazaki 씨에게 주세요. 　　　　　　　정답 (C)

**9.** 미W 호M
What feedback did the marketing director give on our advertising campaign?
(A) Yes, it is really great.
(B) Actually, she wanted some major changes.
(C) I'll give you driving directions to the head office.

마케팅 담당 이사님이 우리의 광고 캠페인에 대해 어떤 의견을 주셨나요?
(A) 네, 그건 정말 대단해요.
(B) 사실, 그녀는 대대적인 변경을 원하고 계세요.
(C) 제가 본사까지 운전해서 가는 길을 알려 드릴게요. 　정답 (B)

**10.** 미M 영W
Should I fill the gas tank when I return this rental car?
(A) Please never be late for work.
(B) Yes, that's our policy.
(C) That's not really far.

이 임대 차량을 반납할 때 연료 탱크를 가득 채워야 하나요?
(A) 절대 늦게 출근하지 마세요.
(B) 네, 그것이 저희 방침입니다.
(C) 그리 멀지 않아요. 　　　　　　　　　정답 (B)

**11.** 미W 호M
You and Brian worked for the same accounting firm before, didn't you?
(A) He works at a small accounting firm.
(B) You can still apply for a job at the company.
(C) Yes, but we didn't know each other at that time.

당신과 Brian은 예전에 같은 회계 법인에서 일했죠, 그렇지 않나요?

(A) 그는 작은 회계 법인에서 근무해요.
(B) 당신은 여전히 그 회사에 지원할 수 있어요.
(C) 네, 하지만 저희는 그때 서로 모르던 사이였어요. 　　정답 (C)

**12.** 영W 미M
Why can't I access the computer lab?
(A) It's under maintenance now.
(B) Well, that is a good price.
(C) Yes, it's an efficient personal computer.

제가 컴퓨터실을 이용할 수 없는 이유가 뭔가요?
(A) 현재 보수 중이에요.
(B) 음, 가격이 괜찮은데요.
(C) 네, 그건 성능이 좋은 개인용 컴퓨터예요. 　　정답 (A)

**13.** 미M 미W
How would you like to pay for all of your purchases?
(A) Can I pay in cash?
(B) I bought it last Tuesday.
(C) We need to explain it to them.

구매하신 물품은 어떻게 지불하시겠습니까?
(A) 현금으로 지불할 수 있을까요?
(B) 저는 지난주 화요일에 구매했어요.
(C) 우리는 그들에게 설명해야 합니다. 　　정답 (A)

**14.** 호M 미W
Isn't the new logo supposed to be at the bottom of the page?
(A) No, the report is twenty pages long.
(B) No, it doesn't have to be.
(C) Yes, the logo was designed 10 years ago.

새로운 로고가 페이지 하단에 위치해야 하는 것 아닌가요?
(A) 아니오, 보고서는 20페이지 분량이에요.
(B) 아니오, 꼭 그럴 필요는 없어요.
(C) 네, 그 로고는 10년 전에 디자인되었어요. 　　정답 (B)

**15.** 미M 영W
Why don't you go over the sales figures after lunch?
(A) Actually, they're not for sale.
(B) I really think I should.
(C) Our monthly revenue has doubled.

점심식사 후에 매출액을 검토하는 것이 어떠세요?
(A) 사실 그것들은 비매품이에요.
(B) 정말 그래야 할 것 같아요.
(C) 우리 월 수익이 두 배로 증가했어요. 　　정답 (B)

**16.** 미W 미M
I wonder if you can cover my shift for me on Thursday.
(A) We work in three shifts.
(B) Thank you very much.
(C) Sure, if you do mine next Wednesday.

당신이 목요일에 제 교대 근무를 대신 해 줄 수 있을지 궁금해요.
(A) 우리는 3교대로 근무해요.
(B) 정말 고마워요.
(C) 물론이에요, 당신이 다음 주 수요일에 제 근무를 대신 해 준다면요.
　　정답 (C)

**17.** 미W 호M
Would you like to meet the new client in the conference room or in the boardroom?
(A) You should sign here.
(B) Either would be fine with me.
(C) Please board the flight in an hour.

새로운 고객을 회의실에서 만나실 건가요, 아니면 이사회실에서 만나실 건가요?
(A) 여기에 서명해 주세요.
(B) 저는 어느 쪽이든 좋아요.
(C) 한 시간 뒤에 비행기에 탑승하세요. 　　정답 (B)

**18.** 미M 영W
Do you want to go to see a play over the weekend?
(A) I didn't bring my wallet.
(B) Sure, but how about on Friday night?
(C) Yes, it was really disappointing.

주말에 연극 보러 갈래요?
(A) 저는 지갑을 안 가져왔어요.
(B) 그럼요, 그런데 금요일 저녁이 어때요?
(C) 네, 정말 실망스러웠어요. 　　정답 (B)

**19.** 호M 미W
What is this blouse made of?
(A) It's a hundred-percent silk.
(B) Designed by Kelvin Raymond.
(C) I really enjoyed it.

이 블라우스는 무엇으로 만들어졌나요?
(A) 100% 실크예요.
(B) Kelvin Raymond가 디자인한 겁니다.
(C) 저는 정말 즐거웠어요. 　　정답 (A)

**20.** 미M 영W
Have you been reimbursed for your business trip to London?
(A) Sorry. We're sold out.
(B) Yes, I've already received a check from the company.
(C) No, I haven't reserved my plane ticket yet.

London 출장비에 대한 환급을 받으셨나요?
(A) 죄송합니다만, 매진되었습니다.
(B) 네, 이미 회사로부터 수표를 받았어요.
(C) 아니오, 저는 아직 항공권을 예약하지 않았어요. 　　정답 (B)

**21.** 미W 미M
Ms. Parker is going to be transferred to Busan, isn't she?
(A) Yes, probably next week.
(B) It's not that far.
(C) No, I'd like to make a plane reservation.

Parker 씨가 부산으로 전근을 가게 되었죠, 그렇지 않나요?
(A) 네, 아마도 다음주일 겁니다.
(B) 그리 멀지 않아요.
(C) 아니오, 저는 항공권을 예매하려고 해요. 　　정답 (A)

**22.** 영W 호M
Has the company managed to get through the financial crisis?
(A) The company will hire a new treasurer.
(B) Yes, we're kind of strapped for funds right now.
(C) Not that I know of.

회사는 재정난을 잘 극복했나요?
(A) 회사에서는 새로운 재무 책임자를 채용할 겁니다.
(B) 네, 우리는 지금 긴축재정을 하고 있어요.
(C) 제가 알기론 아니에요.     정답 (C)

**23.** 호M 미W

Do you want to purchase a new laptop computer or use the one you currently have?
(A) Yes, about 25 percent off.
(B) Well, it depends on the price.
(C) I'm not happy with the budget.

새로운 노트북 컴퓨터를 구매하길 원하세요, 아니면 현재 갖고 있는 걸 쓰실 건가요?
(A) 네, 대략 25퍼센트 할인이에요.
(B) 음, 가격에 달려 있어요.
(C) 예산액이 만족스럽진 않아요.     정답 (B)

**24.** 미M 영W

Why can't I get this accounting program to work on my laptop computer?
(A) You should install the software update.
(B) Some interesting programs.
(C) I usually work from 9:00 to 5:00.

제 노트북 컴퓨터에서 이 회계 프로그램이 작동하지 않는 이유가 뭘까요?
(A) 소프트웨어 업데이트를 설치해야 합니다.
(B) 몇몇 흥미로운 프로그램들이요.
(C) 저는 주로 9시부터 5시까지 근무합니다.     정답 (A)

**25.** 호M 미W

Would you like to pick up your concert tickets in person or receive them by mail?
(A) It's 35 dollars for each one.
(B) Meet me at the box office.
(C) Could you send them to me by mail?

공연표를 직접 수령하시겠습니까, 아니면 우편으로 받으시겠습니까?
(A) 각 35달러예요.
(B) 저와 매표소에서 만나요.
(C) 우편으로 발송해 주시겠어요?     정답 (C)

**26.** 미M 영W

I forgot to bring my laptop computer to work today.
(A) I'm working on it now.
(B) Unfortunately, it's out of order.
(C) You can use mine if you want.

오늘 출근할 때 제 노트북 컴퓨터를 가지고 오는 걸 잊었어요.
(A) 지금 작업 중이에요.
(B) 안타깝게도, 그건 고장이 났어요.
(C) 원하시면 제 걸 사용해도 됩니다.     정답 (C)

**27.** 미W 미M

Would you prefer a desk in the corner or near the window?
(A) Either would be fine.
(B) I'd prefer a window seat.
(C) Yes, she works on the second floor.

책상이 구석에 위치하길 원하세요, 아니면 창가에 위치하길 원하세요?
(A) 어느 쪽이든 다 좋아요.
(B) 저는 창가 쪽 좌석이 좋습니다.

(C) 네, 그녀는 2층에서 근무해요.     정답 (A)

**28.** 미M 영W

You submitted an application for the vacant position of sales director, didn't you?
(A) I think it's affordably priced.
(B) Yes, in the afternoon.
(C) Sorry. No vacancies.

공석 중인 영업 이사직에 지원서를 제출하셨죠, 그렇지 않나요?
(A) 그것의 가격이 적절하게 책정되었다고 생각해요.
(B) 네, 오후에요.
(C) 죄송합니다만, 빈 방이 없습니다.     정답 (B)

**29.** 미W 호M

Would you like to join us at the fundraising charity event?
(A) Yes, I'd be glad to.
(B) Wednesday afternoons at 3:00.
(C) My sister plays in a jazz band.

자선 모금 행사에 저희와 함께 참여하시겠어요?
(A) 네, 기꺼이 그러겠습니다.
(B) 매주 수요일 오후 3시에요.
(C) 제 여동생이 재즈 밴드에서 활동하고 있어요.     정답 (A)

**30.** 미W 영W

Should we contact Mr. Ryan directly?
(A) Thanks, but I have other plans.
(B) His assistant is far easier to reach.
(C) To renew the contract as fast as possible.

Ryan 씨에게 직접 연락을 취해야 할까요?
(A) 고맙습니다만, 선약이 있어요.
(B) 그의 비서가 훨씬 더 연락하기 수월해요.
(C) 최대한 빨리 계약을 갱신하기 위해서요.     정답 (B)

**31.** 미W 호M

This photocopier is quite slow, isn't it?
(A) Yes, it's kind of an old machine.
(B) No, you should use the elevator instead.
(C) 20 copies were printed.

이 복사기는 속도가 아주 느리죠, 그렇지 않나요?
(A) 네, 기계가 좀 오래 되어서요.
(B) 아니오, 대신에 승강기를 이용하세요.
(C) 20부가 인쇄되었어요.     정답 (A)

**Part 3**

문제 32-34번은 다음 대화를 참조하시오. 미M 영W

M: Good morning. This is Nick Walker calling from the law office. I would like to speak to Mr. Watson, please.
W: I am sorry, Mr. Walker. **(33) Mr. Watson is away at an international marketing conference all week. (32) Can I take a message for you, or is this urgent?**
M: I really need to speak to him as soon as possible. Could you tell me how I might reach him?
W: **(34) I will give you the phone number of the hotel in London where he is staying for the conference.**

M: 안녕하세요. 저는 법률 사무소의 Nick Walker라고 합니다. Watson 씨와 통화하고 싶습니다.

W: 죄송합니다, Walker 씨. Watson 씨는 이번주 내내 국제 마케팅 회의에 참석차 이곳에 계시지 않습니다. 메시지를 남기시겠습니까, 아니면 긴급한 일이신가요?

M: 가능하면 빨리 그와 통화해야 합니다. 어디로 연락하면 되는지 알려주실 수 있겠습니까?

W: 그가 회의 기간 동안 머무르고 있는 London에 위치한 호텔의 연락처를 드리겠습니다.

**32.** 여자는 누구일 것 같은가?
(A) 회계사
(B) 변호사
(C) 안내 직원
(D) 호텔 직원 정답 (C)

**33.** 여자가 Watson 씨에 대해 언급한 것은 무엇인가?
(A) 그는 재판을 기다리고 있다.
(B) 그는 회의에 참석하고 있다.
(C) 그는 London에 있는 호텔을 소유하고 있다.
(D) 그는 마케팅 부장으로 근무하고 있다. 정답 (B)

**34.** 여자가 남자에게 제안하는 것은 무엇인가?
(A) 메시지를 남길 것
(B) 호텔에 연락할 것
(C) 이메일을 보낼 것
(D) 소송을 제기할 것 정답 (B)

문제 35-37번은 다음의 3자 대화를 참조하시오. ▢M ▢W ▢M

M1: (35/36) Have you all attempted to sign in with the new attendance system? (36) I can't seem to get mine registered by the system.

W: (36) Tell me about it. (35/36) There was a giant line of people trying to get their employee cards read this morning.

M2: By the time I arrived, people were just writing their names on a piece of paper.

W: (37) Ever since they announced that they will be experimenting with the attendance system, I was doubtful it would be effective.

M1: Well, you never know. It may get better and become convenient.

W: Yeah, it's possible. Or they might just return to the old system.

--------------------------------------------

M1: 다들 새로 설치된 출근 확인 시스템에 출근을 기록해 봤나요? 제 건 시스템에 등록하려고 하는데 잘 안 되는 것 같더라고요.

W: 내 말이 그 말이에요. 오늘 아침에 기기가 사원증을 인식하도록 하려는 직원들로 인해 줄이 엄청나게 길었어요.

M2: 제가 도착했을 무렵에는 사람들이 자신들의 이름을 종이에 쓰고 있던데요.

W: 저는 출근 확인 시스템을 시험한다고 했을 때부터 그 효과가 의심스러웠어요.

M1: 음, 하지만 모를 일이에요. 기능이 더 개선돼서 편리해질 수도 있어요.

W: 네, 가능하죠. 아니면 회사에서 그냥 예전 시스템을 다시 사용할지도 모를 일이고요.

**35.** 대화의 주제는 무엇인가?
(A) 광고 전략의 변화
(B) 신제품의 출시
(C) 새로 설치된 기계
(D) 보안 시스템 개발 정답 (C)

**36.** 여자가 "Tell me about it."이라고 언급한 이유는 무엇인가?
(A) 그녀는 한 남자가 방금 이야기한 내용을 듣지 못했다.
(B) 그녀는 대화에 늦게 합류했다.
(C) 그녀는 남자의 의견에 전적으로 동의하고 있다.
(D) 그녀는 이미 오전에 어떤 일이 발생했는지 알고 있다. 정답 (C)

**37.** 여자는 새로운 시스템에 대해 무엇이라고 말하는가?
(A) 수리가 되어야 한다.
(B) 제대로 작동하지 못하고 있다.
(C) 더 많은 매출을 창출했다.
(D) 더 나은 보안을 제공한다. 정답 (B)

문제 38-40번은 다음 대화를 참조하시오. ▢W ▢M

W: Hi, Tim. (38) We should discuss the details on the new ad campaign. The print layout has been approved by corporate, but we still haven't had the TV commercial tested on actual consumers in a focus group.

M: Well, I'm personally not satisfied with the commercial. The product is adequately represented, but (39) our brand isn't clearly communicated until the end. I think the brand should be clearly shown in the beginning.

W: Let's bring that up when we meet with the executives next week.

M: I'd like to get input from as many people as we can, but the campaign should be rolled out before (40) people start shopping for the holidays in November, so let's just talk with the marketing team tomorrow.

--------------------------------------------

W: 안녕하세요, Tim. 우리 새 광고 캠페인의 세부사항에 대해 의논을 해야겠어요. 회사로부터 인쇄 디자인은 승인을 받았는데 여론 조사 그룹 내의 실제 소비자들을 대상으로 TV 광고는 아직 시험해 보지 못했어요.

M: 음, 전 개인적으로 그 광고가 맘에 들지 않아요. 상품은 충분히 보여주고 있는데 우리 브랜드는 마지막까지 확실하게 전달되지 않고 있어요. 브랜드를 첫 부분에 확실하게 보여줘야 할 것 같아요.

W: 다음주에 경영진과 회의할 때 그걸 얘기해 봅시다.

M: 저는 가능한 한 많은 사람들의 조언을 얻고 싶은데, 그 광고는 11월 연휴 기간 동안 사람들이 쇼핑하기 전에 나가야 해요. 그러니 내일 마케팅 팀과 우선 이야기해 봐요.

**38.** 화자들은 무엇에 대해 논하고 있는가?
(A) 여론 조사 그룹 연구
(B) 광고 전략
(C) 인쇄 배치
(D) TV 광고 정답 (B)

**39.** 남자는 광고의 어느 부분을 변경해야 한다고 말하는가?
(A) 상품의 레이아웃
(B) 브랜드 로고의 크기
(C) 소통의 방법
(D) 클립의 길이 정답 (C)

**40.** 남자에 따르면 11월에 무슨 일이 일어날 것인가?
(A) 마케팅 팀과의 회의가 열릴 것이다.
(B) 신제품이 출시될 것이다.
(C) 쇼핑 시즌이 시작될 것이다.
(D) 경영진에 의해 결정이 이루어질 것이다. 　　　 정답 (C)

**문제 41-43번은 다음 대화를 참조하시오.** 영W 미M

W: Hello! This is Britney Wilson in the Product Development Department. **(41/42) I'm calling to let you know that I never received my paycheck for the last pay period.**

M: Ms. Wilson in the Product Development Department? Let me check. Well, we sent your paycheck by express mail to your home address last Tuesday since you were on vacation. I think you should have received it by now.

W: It hasn't arrived yet. I've already waited a week and cannot afford to wait any longer. Is there any way I can get my paycheck today? I'd like you to set this right as quickly as you can.

M: **(43) We can stop payment on the first check and issue you a new one immediately.** You can pick it up in the payroll office this afternoon. Is that okay?

------------------------------------------------

W: 안녕하세요! 저는 제품 개발 부서에서 근무하는 Britney Wilson이라고 합니다. 지난 급여 지급 기간에 급여 수표를 받지 못해서 알려드리고자 연락드렸습니다.

M: 제품 개발 부서에서 근무하는 Wilson 씨라고요? 확인 좀 해보겠습니다. 음, 당신이 휴가 중이라서 지난 화요일에 급여 수표를 빠른 우편을 통해 자택으로 발송했어요. 지금쯤이면 받으셨어야 하는데요.

W: 아직 도착하지 않았어요. 일주일이나 기다렸는데 더이상 기다릴 여력이 없어요. 오늘 급여 수표를 받을 수 있는 방법이 있을까요? 서둘러서 이 문제를 해결해 주셨으면 합니다.

M: 첫 번째 발송한 수표를 지불 중단하고 새로운 급여 수표를 바로 발급해 드리겠습니다. 오늘 오후에 급여 부서에서 수령해 가시면 됩니다. 괜찮으신가요?

**41.** 여자는 무엇 때문에 전화하는가?
(A) 환불
(B) 일정 변경
(C) 분실된 급여 수표
(D) 전기 문제 　　　 정답 (C)

**42.** 남자는 어느 부서에서 근무할 것 같은가?
(A) 급여 지급부
(B) 고객 서비스부
(C) 인사부
(D) 영업부 　　　 정답 (A)

**43.** 남자가 제안하는 것은 무엇인가?
(A) 관련 서류를 프린트한다.
(B) 즉시 돈을 지급한다.
(C) 여자에게 견본품을 배송한다.
(D) 여자에게 새로 수표를 발행한다. 　　　 정답 (D)

**문제 44-46번은 다음 대화를 참조하시오.** 미M 영W

M: Hello, Ms. Muybridge. **(44) Congratulations on your new position at Zenith Technology.** How is it going over there? We all miss you back at the office.

W: Hi, Mr. Hamilton. Everything is going pretty well so far. But things aren't as organized as they are back at Jia Electronics.

M: Oh, really? I heard Zenith Technology is one of the top companies many people want to work for.

W: **(45) But there have been a few problems. For example, I got paid late during the first two months.**

M: **(46) Oh, you don't say.** I am sorry to hear that. Did you complain about it?

W: Not yet, but I certainly will if it happens again this month.

------------------------------------------------

M: 안녕하세요, Muybridge 씨. Zenith Technology에서 새로 맡게 된 직책에 대해 축하를 드리고 싶습니다. 그곳에서 어떻게 지내고 계세요? 우리는 모두 당신이 사무실에 있던 때를 그리워하고 있어요.

W: 안녕하세요, Hamilton 씨. 지금까지는 모든 일이 아주 잘 되어가고 있어요. 하지만 Jia Electronics에서만큼 업무가 체계적이질 않아요.

M: 아, 그래요? 저는 Zenith Technology가 사람들이 가장 일하기 원하는 직장들 중 한 곳이라고 들었어요.

W: 그렇지만 몇몇 문제점들이 있었어요. 예를 들면 근무를 시작한 지 첫 두 달 동안은 급여를 늦게 받았어요.

M: 아, 설마 그런 일이 있을 줄은 몰랐어요. 그런 소식을 접하게 되어 유감이에요. 그 일에 대해 불만을 제기했나요?

W: 아직이요, 하지만 이번달에 같은 일이 재차 발생하면 분명히 그렇게 할 겁니다.

**44.** 남자가 여자에게 축하를 하는 이유는 무엇인가?
(A) 그녀는 새로운 일을 시작했다.
(B) 그녀는 승진했다.
(C) 그녀의 급여가 인상되었다.
(D) 그녀는 시험에 합격했다. 　　　 정답 (A)

**45.** 여자는 어떤 문제점에 대해 언급하는가?
(A) 새로운 상사가 경험이 부족하다.
(B) 그녀의 급여가 늦게 지급되었다.
(C) 매출이 예상보다 저조하다.
(D) 몇몇 제품들이 회수되었다. 　　　 정답 (B)

**46.** 남자가 "Oh, you don't say."라고 말한 이유는 무엇인가?
(A) 그는 무엇인가 자세하게 논의하고 싶어 한다.
(B) 그는 어떤 내용을 듣고 놀라고 있다.
(C) 그는 여자가 과장해서 말하고 있다고 생각한다.
(D) 그는 여자가 말하는 내용을 듣고 싶어하지 않는다. 　　　 정답 (B)

**문제 47-49번은 다음 대화를 참조하시오.** 미W 호M

W: Good morning. My name is April Jenkins. **(47) I ordered a leather travel bag from your online shopping mall**, but I'll be on a business trip when it's scheduled to be delivered. **(48) Could you please deliver it to my office instead? I can give you my office address now.**

M: Unfortunately, Ms. Jenkins, your order was shipped yesterday. If it arrives while you are on your trip, it will be sent back to our company, and you can call to arrange a new delivery time.

W: I understand. (49) **But will I have to pay a second shipping fee?**

M: (49) **Yes, I'm afraid there will be another shipping charge if we need to send it a second time.**

---

W: 안녕하세요. 제 이름은 April Jenkins입니다. 저는 귀사가 운영하는 온라인 쇼핑몰에서 가죽으로 제작한 여행용 가방을 주문했습니다만 배달되기로 예정된 날에 출장을 가게 되었습니다. 그래서 대신 제 사무실로 배달해 주실 수 있을까요? 지금 사무실 주소를 알려드릴 수 있습니다.

M: Jenkins 씨, 유감스럽게도 주문하신 물건은 어제 발송되었습니다. 고객님께서 출장 가 있는 동안 그 제품이 배송되면 저희 회사로 다시 반송될 겁니다. 그렇게 되면 새로운 배송 일자를 정하기 위해서 고객님께서 전화를 해주셔야 합니다.

W: 알겠습니다. 그렇지만 제가 두 번째 배송비를 지불해야 하나요?

M: 네, 죄송하지만 두 번째 발송하게 된다면 추가로 배송비가 부과될 겁니다.

**47.** 남자가 근무하는 곳은 어디일 것 같은가?
(A) 배송 회사
(B) 온라인 매장
(C) 컴퓨터 소프트웨어 회사
(D) 여행사                    정답 (B)

**48.** 여자가 남자에게 연락하는 이유는 무엇인가?
(A) 배송 비용에 대해 문의하기 위해서
(B) 주소를 변경하기 위해서
(C) 새로운 상품 소개책자를 요청하기 위해서
(D) 회사의 부실한 서비스에 대한 불만을 토로하기 위해서    정답 (B)

**49.** 여자는 이후에 무엇을 할 것 같은가?
(A) 환불을 요청한다.
(B) 소송을 제기한다.
(C) 제품을 배송한다.
(D) 추가 비용을 지불한다.        정답 (D)

**문제 50-52번은 다음의 3자 대화를 참조하시오.** 미W 미M 영W

W1: Mr. Walker, (50) **how was your interview with the personnel manager at the Ace Pharmaceutical Corporation last week?**

M: (50) **It was okay. Yesterday, I got a great job offer and accepted it.**

W2: Oh, congratulations! I'm really proud of you!

W1: I knew you could do it. Where is the Ace Pharmaceutical Corporation located?

M: It's just three blocks away from your company. (51) **All new employees are supposed to meet at the company headquarters for an orientation this Saturday at 11 A.M.** I heard it will last two hours.

W1: (52) **Then why don't we have lunch together afterward? Let's celebrate your day!**

---

W1: Walker 씨, 지난주에 있었던 Ace 제약회사의 인사부장과의 면접은 어땠어요?

M: 괜찮았어요. 어제 마침내 취업 제의를 받았고 이를 수락했어요.

W2: 아, 축하해요! 정말 자랑스럽네요!

W1: 난 당신이 해낼 줄 알았어요. Ace 제약회사는 어디에 위치하고 있나요?

M: 당신의 회사에서 세 블록 정도 떨어진 곳에 있어요. 모든 신입 직원들은

이번주 토요일 오전 11시에 회사 본사에 모여 오리엔테이션에 참석해야 해요. 제가 듣기로는 2시간 걸린다고 하더라고요.

W1: 그러면 오리엔테이션이 끝나고 우리 함께 점심식사를 하는 것은 어때요? 당신의 날을 함께 축하해요!

**50.** 화자들은 무엇에 대해 이야기하고 있는가?
(A) 새로운 채용 계획
(B) 사업 오찬
(C) 취업 시장에서의 성공
(D) 이전 제안                정답 (C)

**51.** 남자는 이번 주말에 무엇을 하도록 요청받고 있는가?
(A) 점심식사를 위한 테이블을 예약한다.
(B) 오리엔테이션에 참석한다.
(C) 취업 면접을 주최한다.
(D) 몇몇 연구원들과 만난다.        정답 (B)

**52.** 화자들은 이후에 무엇을 할 것 같은가?
(A) 함께 시간을 보낸다.
(B) 입사 지원서를 작성한다.
(C) 본사를 방문한다.
(D) 새로운 프로젝트를 시작한다.        정답 (A)

**문제 53-55번은 다음 대화를 참조하시오.** 미W 호M

W: Good afternoon. I ordered a printer last Wednesday. (53) **It was just delivered, but there is no warranty information included in the box.**

M: The manufacturer must have made an error. (54) **Can you give me your order number, please?** I'll mail you the warranty certificate by express delivery.

W: It's JIA6031123. In addition, (55) **I'd like to speak with someone in technical support about a problem I'm having with my copy machine.**

M: (55) **No problem at all.** One moment, please. (55) **I'll put you through immediately.**

---

W: 안녕하세요. 저는 지난주 수요일에 프린터를 주문했어요. 방금 배송 받았는데 상자에 품질보증서가 들어 있지 않아서요.

M: 제조사에서 실수가 있었나 보네요. 주문번호를 알려 주시겠어요? 그러면 빠른 우편을 통해 품질보증서를 보내 드리도록 하겠습니다.

W: 주문번호는 JIA6031123이에요. 그리고 제가 사용 중인 복사기에서 발생한 문제점으로 기술지원부 직원과 통화를 하고 싶습니다.

M: 문제없습니다. 잠시만 기다리세요. 제가 바로 연결해 드리겠습니다.

**53.** 여자는 어떤 문제점을 언급하고 있는가?
(A) 잘못된 물품이 배송되었다.
(B) 문서가 빠져 있다.
(C) 사무실이 일찍 문을 닫았다.
(D) 프린터가 제대로 작동하지 않는다.        정답 (B)

**54.** 남자가 여자에게 요청하는 것은 무엇인가?
(A) 기술지원
(B) 주문번호
(C) 제품 일련번호
(D) 개인 연락처                정답 (B)

**55.** 남자가 "No problem at all."이라고 말하는 이유는 무엇인가?

(A) 그는 기계를 다루는 데 아주 능숙하다.
(B) 그는 여자와 아무런 문제가 없다.
(C) 그는 품질보증서의 세부사항들에 대해 만족하고 있다.
(D) 그는 여자의 전화를 담당자에게 연결해줄 수 있다.　　　정답 (D)

**문제 56–58번은 다음 대화를 참조하시오.** 영W 호M

W: Good morning, Mr. Harrison. Did you see the e-mail from the Human Resources Department? (56) **It looks like the new team of interns won't start until the beginning of September. We'll be away at the international trade fair by then.**

M: That's not helpful at all. (57) **It would be much better to have them start in mid-August.** Do you think it might be possible for them to arrive earlier?

W: I hope so. Then, we could train them to run our company display booths and help them finish preparing our product-related materials. (58) **I'll call Sarah in Human Resources this afternoon.**

W: 안녕하세요, Harrison 씨. 인사과에서 발송한 이메일을 읽어 보셨나요? 9월 초까지는 새로운 인턴사원들로 구성된 팀이 업무를 시작하지 않을 것 같은데요. 우리는 그 때쯤이면 국제 무역 박람회에 가야 해요.

M: 그건 별로 바람직하지 않아요. 그들이 8월 중순부터 근무를 시작하는 쪽이 훨씬 나아요. 그들이 좀더 일찍 이 곳에 올 수 있을 것이라고 생각하세요?

W: 그러길 바라요. 그렇게 된다면 그들이 회사의 전시용 부스를 운영할 수 있도록 우리가 교육을 시키고 제품 관련 자료의 준비를 마무리할 수 있도록 도와줄 수 있거든요. 제가 오늘 오후에 인사과의 Sarah에게 연락을 해 봐야겠어요.

**56.** 9월 초에는 어떤 일이 발생하는가?
(A) 신제품이 출시된다.
(B) 구직자들이 지원서를 제출한다.
(C) 일부 직원들이 무역 박람회에 참여한다.
(D) 회사에서 자사 제품을 미국으로 수출한다.　　　정답 (C)

**57.** 남자가 변경하자고 제안한 것은 무엇인가?
(A) 취업 지원자들의 자격 요건
(B) 인턴직원들의 도착 날짜
(C) 신제품의 수출 가격
(D) 일부 취업 박람회의 개최지　　　정답 (B)

**58.** 여자는 오늘 오후에 무엇을 할 것인가?
(A) 동료에게 연락을 취할 것이다.
(B) 면접을 시행할 것이다.
(C) 대학 취업 박람회에 참석할 것이다.
(D) 자료를 준비할 것이다.　　　정답 (A)

**문제 59–61번은 다음 대화를 참조하시오.** 미W 미M

W: Matt, we've got a problem. (59) **We have two advertising agents joining our team next week, but we only have one desk available on our floor.**

M: Oh, I didn't think about that. That is a problem. Well, Sarah and James both work part time and usually aren't here at the same time. (60) **Maybe they could use the same desk for a while.**

W: But sometimes they are here at the same time. Won't that cause a problem?

M: It could, (61) **but I'll order a new desk through the Internet as soon as possible.** So you don't have to worry about it any longer.

W: Matt, 문제가 생겼어요. 다음주에 우리 팀에 새로운 광고 직원들이 두 명 합류하는데, 우리 층에 사용할 수 있는 책상이 하나밖에 없어요.

M: 아, 그걸 미처 생각하지 못했네요. 문제네요. Sarah와 James는 모두 시간제로 근무하니까 동시에 와 있을 일은 없어요. 아마 둘이서 잠시만 같은 책상을 사용해도 괜찮을 것 같은데요.

W: 하지만 가끔 그들이 동시에 근무를 할 때가 있어요. 문제가 되지 않을까요?

M: 그럴 수도 있겠지만 제가 인터넷을 통해 최대한 빨리 새로운 책상을 주문할 겁니다. 그러니 더이상 걱정하지 않아도 됩니다.

**59.** 무엇이 문제인가?
(A) 인력 부족 현상을 겪고 있다.
(B) 화자들의 생산성이 점차 저하되고 있다.
(C) 사무용 가구가 부족하다.
(D) 회사의 광고 비용이 너무 높다.　　　정답 (C)

**60.** 임시방편으로 논의된 것은 무엇인가?
(A) 책상을 몇 개 구입한다.
(B) 가구를 공유한다.
(C) 급여를 대폭 인상한다.
(D) 더 많은 직원들을 채용한다.　　　정답 (B)

**61.** 남자는 이후에 무엇을 할 것 같은가?
(A) 주문을 한다.
(B) 광고를 게재한다.
(C) 초과 근무를 한다.
(D) 일정을 확인한다.　　　정답 (A)

**문제 62–64번은 다음 대화와 지도를 참조하시오.** 미M 영W

M: We will arrive at the Cupertino Train Station soon. But I think (62) **it's best that we stop and put some gas in the car before we return this rental car.** (62) **The rental car company usually charges an average of three dollars per gallon, which is far more expensive than regular gas prices.**

W: You're right. (62) **We shouldn't pay more than we have to.** (63) **Is this where we should exit?**

M: No, (63) **this is the highway service area. There's a gas station at the next exit.** It's about eight miles away from here.

W: Okay. By the way, (64) **we should pick up some snacks before we take the train.**

M: 곧 Cupertino 기차역에 도착할 겁니다. 이 렌터카를 반납하기 전에 주유소에 들러서 주유를 하는 것이 좋을 것 같은데요. 렌터카 회사는 보통 휘발유 1갤런 당 평균적으로 3달러를 청구해요. 일반적인 기름값보다 훨씬 비싸죠.

W: 맞아요. 우리가 필요 이상으로 돈을 지불해야 할 필요는 없어요. 여기가 우리가 나가야 할 출구인가요?

M: 아뇨, 이번 출구는 고속도로 휴게소예요. 다음 번 출구에 주유소가 있어요. 여기서 8마일 정도 떨어져 있어요.

W: 알았어요. 그런데 우리 기차에 타기 전에 먹을 걸 좀 사야 해요.

## 도로 지도

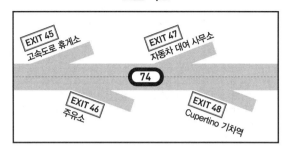

EXIT 45 고속도로 휴게소
EXIT 47 자동차 대여 사무소
74
EXIT 46 주유소
EXIT 48 Cupertino 기차역

**62.** 화자들은 무엇에 대해 걱정하고 있는가?
(A) 기차를 놓치는 것
(B) 교통체증을 겪는 것
(C) 기름값을 과하게 쓰는 것
(D) 직장에 지각하는 것 　　　　　　　　정답 (C)

**63.** 그래픽을 보시오. 화자들은 어느 출구에서 나갈 것인가?
(A) 45번 출구
(B) 46번 출구
(C) 47번 출구
(D) 48번 출구 　　　　　　　　　　　정답 (B)

**64.** 화자들은 이후에 무엇을 할 것 같은가?
(A) 먹거리를 구매한다.
(B) 좌석 배치를 확인한다.
(C) 일정을 확인한다.
(D) 온라인으로 표를 구매한다. 　　　　정답 (A)

**문제 65~67번은 다음 대화와 카탈로그를 참조하시오.** 영W 호M

W: Hi. We spoke on the phone earlier. (65) **I need a computer for work, and I'm here to pick one.**
M: Ah, you must be Jia Choi. We have several models available now, so I'm sure you'll find one that's right for you.
W: (66) **I just began working as a journalist, and frequent travel is a requirement for my job.** So I think I need something portable and light.
M: It sounds like a laptop would meet your needs. I'm sure the price is important to you, but how about the weight?
W: Well, the price isn't a huge concern for me. But (67) **I'd rather not spend more than five hundred dollars. The weight has to be under 2.5 kilograms though.**
M: I see. Here is a list of our most popular models. All of them are currently in stock.

- - - - - - - - - - - - - - - - - - - - - - - - - - - - - - -

W: 안녕하세요. 아까 통화했던 사람이에요. 제가 업무를 위해 컴퓨터가 필요해서 하나를 고르기 위해 왔습니다.
M: 아, Jia Choi 씨군요. 현재 구매 가능한 여러 모델을 보유하고 있기 때문에 꼭 알맞은 것을 찾으실 거라고 확신합니다.
W: 제가 막 기자로 일을 시작했고 제 일이 출장이 잦아요. 그래서 휴대가 용이하고 가벼운 것이 필요할 거라고 봐요.
M: 손님에게 필요한 건 노트북 컴퓨터 같은데요. 가격이 중요하다는 점은 분명하겠지만 무게에 대해서는 어떻게 생각하세요?
W: 저, 가격은 크게 걱정하는 부분이 아니에요. 하지만 5백 달러 이상 지출하고 싶지는 않아요. 그런데 무게는 2.5킬로그램 미만이어야 해요.
M: 알겠습니다. 저희 모델들 중에서 가장 인기 있는 제품들이 담긴 목록이 여기 있습니다. 이 제품들은 모두 현재 재고가 있습니다.

## 컴퓨터 부문

| 모델명 | 무게 | 가격 |
|---|---|---|
| (67) YUMI 115 | 1.8kg | $380 |
| SAMSON X5 | 2.7kg | $440 |
| HARU 4K | 1.4kg | $580 |
| GABY SUPER | 3.0kg | $590 |

**65.** 남자는 어디에서 근무할 것 같은가?
(A) 출판사
(B) 여행사
(C) 연구실
(D) 가전제품 매장 　　　　　　　　　정답 (D)

**66.** 여자가 자신의 일에 대해 언급한 것은 무엇인가?
(A) 보수가 좋다.
(B) 신체적으로 힘들다.
(C) 출장을 자주 요구한다.
(D) 기계에 대한 전문적인 지식이 필요하다. 　정답 (C)

**67.** 그래픽을 보시오. 여자는 어느 컴퓨터 모델을 선택하겠는가?
(A) YUMI 115
(B) SAMSON X5
(C) HARU 4K
(D) GABY SUPER 　　　　　　　　　정답 (A)

**문제 68~70번은 다음 대화와 목록을 참조하시오.** 미M 미W

M: Good morning. This is John Stevenson at Ruth's Restaurant. I believe you wanted to talk to me?
W: Yes, thank you for calling back. (68) **I am a reporter at _Food Magazine_,** and I'd like to write a piece about your restaurant. I think your restaurant serves absolutely superb food and is well worth a visit.
M: Oh, thank you very much. I'm glad you had a good time. That would be great for publicity.
W: (69) **I was wondering if I could visit the restaurant and maybe take some pictures and ask some questions.** When are you available?
M: Well, (70) **we usually take a break after 4 P.M., but it depends on the day.**
W: I'll send you a list of dates and times that work for me, and you can tell me which you prefer.

- - - - - - - - - - - - - - - - - - - - - - - - - - - - - - -

M: 안녕하세요. 저는 Ruth's 레스토랑의 John Stevenson입니다. 저와 통화하고 싶어하셨다고요?
W: 네, 답신 전화를 주셔서 감사드립니다. 저는 Food Magazine의 기자이고요, 귀하의 레스토랑에 관한 기사를 작성하고 싶습니다. 귀하의 레스토랑에서는 아주 훌륭한 음식을 제공하고 있어서 방문해 볼만한 가치가 있는 곳이라고 생각합니다.
M: 아, 감사합니다. 이 곳에서 좋은 시간을 보내셨다니 기쁘네요. 그러면 홍보에 아주 좋은 일이지요.
W: 제가 언제 레스토랑에 방문해서 사진을 찍고 질문을 할 수 있을지 알고 싶어요. 언제가 괜찮으세요?
M: 음, 저희는 대개 오후 4시 이후에 휴식을 취하지만 그건 날마다 달라요.
W: 제가 가능한 날짜와 시간의 목록을 보내 드릴테니 어느 때가 좋은지 알려주세요.

### 가능한 날짜와 시간

| 요일 | 시간 |
|------|------|
| 월요일 | 오전 10시 |
| 화요일 | 오후 2시 |
| (70) 수요일 | 오후 5시 |
| 목요일 | 오후 1시 |

**68.** 여자의 직업은 무엇인가?
(A) 기자
(B) 요리사
(C) 레스토랑 매니저
(D) 사진가 　　　　　　　　　　　　　　정답 (A)

**69.** 여자는 무엇을 하길 원하는가?
(A) 주문을 취소한다.
(B) 요리를 추천한다.
(C) 기사를 검토한다.
(D) 남자와 인터뷰를 한다. 　　　　　　　정답 (D)

**70.** 그래픽을 보시오. 여자는 언제 레스토랑을 방문할 것 같은가?
(A) 월요일
(B) 화요일
(C) 수요일
(D) 목요일 　　　　　　　　　　　　　　정답 (C)

## Part 4

**문제 71-73번은 다음 담화를 참조하시오.** 미M

Hi! This message is for Ms. Hayward. (71) **This is Bob Thornton from the Lakeview Terrace Hotel.** I'm calling regarding the space you reserved for the banquet on July 21. (72) **The person who took the reservation didn't check the availability of the room in advance, and it turns out that it had already been booked by someone else for the same night.** I'm very sorry for the inconvenience. I have made the Gold Hall available to you for now. It is not as big as the Platinum Hall, but it can still accommodate up to 150 guests. (73) **Could you please call me back at 927-7399 and let me know if this new arrangement is suitable for your needs?** Thank you.

--------------------------------------------

안녕하세요! 이 메시지는 Hayward 씨를 위한 메시지입니다. 저는 Lakeview Terrace Hotel의 Bob Thornton이라고 합니다. 7월 21일 연회를 위해 예약하신 공간과 관련하여 전화드립니다. 예약을 받은 직원이 그 방의 사전 예약 여부를 확인하지 않았는데, 알아보니 같은 날 저녁으로 다른 분에 의해 이미 예약된 상태였음이 확인되었습니다. 불편을 초래하여 정말 죄송합니다. 지금 Gold Hall을 예약하실 수 있도록 했습니다. 이 곳이 Platinum Hall만큼 넓진 않습니다만 150명까지 손님을 수용할 수 있는 규모입니다. 927-7399로 전화해 주셔서 새로운 예약이 원하시는 사항에 적합한지 여부에 대해서 알려주시겠습니까? 감사합니다.

**71.** 전화를 건 사람은 어디서 근무하는가?
(A) 호텔
(B) 식당
(C) 여행사

(D) 빵집 　　　　　　　　　　　　　　정답 (A)

**72.** 화자가 언급한 문제점은 무엇인가?
(A) 종업원의 수가 충분하지 않다.
(B) 방이 같은 날에 이중으로 예약되었다.
(C) 가격이 틀리게 전달되었다.
(D) 비행기 일정이 변경되었다. 　　　　　정답 (B)

**73.** 청자에게 요구된 것은 무엇인가?
(A) 이메일을 확인한다.
(B) 예약을 취소한다.
(C) 할인권을 수령한다.
(D) 전화한 사람에게 연락한다. 　　　　　정답 (D)

**문제 74-76번은 다음 광고를 참조하시오.** 미W

Have you always dreamed of traveling around the world but weren't sure where to start? (74) **Let Top Line Cruises do all the work for you! Departing from several ports on the Atlantic and Pacific coasts, Top Line can take you on almost any adventure you are able to dream up.** Visit the mysterious Mexican coast, see beautiful Antarctic ice formations, and even tour the famous cities of Europe. We offer five-star accommodations, a wide range of dining options, and fully customizable trip packages. Our new Family Voyage package line provides entertainment for children, teens, and young adults. (75) **Book more than two Family Voyages with us, and every member of your family will automatically become gold members.** (76) **Speak with a customer service representative after this talk to find out more.**

--------------------------------------------

늘 세계일주를 꿈꿨으나 어디서부터 시작해야 할지 모르신다고요? Top Line Cruises에서 여러분을 위해 모든 걸 알아서 해드리겠습니다! Top Line Cruises는 대서양 및 태평양 연안에 위치한 여러 항구에서 출발하여 여러분이 생각해낼 수 있는 거의 모든 모험을 하실 수 있도록 해드립니다. 신비로운 멕시코 해안가를 방문하고, 아름다운 남극의 빙하를 보고, 혹은 유럽의 유명한 도시들도 관광하십시오. 저희는 5성급 숙박시설과 다양한 식사 선택, 그리고 철저히 고객맞춤형 관광 상품을 제공해 드립니다. 저희의 새로운 Family Voyage 관광 상품은 아이, 청소년, 젊은 성인들을 위한 오락거리를 제공합니다. Family Voyage 상품을 두 개 이상 예약하시면 여러분의 모든 가족은 자동적으로 골드 회원이 됩니다. 이 부분에 대해 좀 더 알고 싶으시다면 광고가 끝난 후에 고객 상담원에게 말씀하세요.

**74.** 이 담화는 무엇에 관한 것인가?
(A) 가이드를 동반한 여행
(B) 아이스크림 상표
(C) 귀금속 제품
(D) 유람선 관광 상품 　　　　　　　　　정답 (D)

**75.** 두 개의 가족 상품 구매자는 어떤 혜택을 누리게 되는가?
(A) 금으로 제작된 기념품
(B) 무료 여행
(C) 자동 회원 자격
(D) 식사 특전 　　　　　　　　　　　　정답 (C)

**76.** 청자가 더 많은 정보를 원하는 경우 무엇을 해야 하는가?
(A) 발표에 참석한다.
(B) 서류를 작성한다.

(C) 점장에게 연락한다.
(D) 직원과 이야기한다. 정답 (D)

문제 77-79번은 다음 전화 메시지를 참조하시오. 미W

Hello, Mr. Stanford. **(77) This is Lisa Powell calling from Ace Style. I just checked out your e-mail regarding the sofa set you placed an order for last week. (78) I sincerely apologize for the damaged armrest. I can assure you that it was not sent out in that condition, so I think that must have happened in transit.** To rectify the situation, I will send some employees there immediately to pick it up and then have a new one shipped. **(79) There will be no additional charges for delivery.** I'll also include a couple of cotton cushions. I know they're not much, but please accept them as a token of my apology. After you check this message, please get back to me at your earliest convenience and let me know when is good for us to visit your house. Even on the weekend is fine. You can contact me at our toll-free number 1-800-857-3239 or by e-mail. Thank you. Have a nice day.

안녕하세요, Stanford 씨. 저는 Ace Style에서 전화드리는 Lisa Powell이라고 합니다. 고객님께서 지난주에 주문하신 소파 세트와 관련된 이메일을 지금 막 확인했습니다. 파손된 팔걸이 부분에 대해 진심으로 사과드립니다. 보낼 때는 분명히 그런 상태가 아니었음을 말씀드리며, 배송 중에 그러한 일이 발생한 것 같습니다. 이러한 상황을 바로잡기 위해서 파손된 제품을 수거할 직원을 그 곳으로 보내고 나서 새로운 제품을 배송하겠습니다. 배송에 따른 추가 비용은 없습니다. 그리고 면 쿠션 두 개를 함께 보내드리겠습니다. 큰 것이 아니란 건 알지만 사과의 표시로서 받아 주셨으면 합니다. 이 메시지를 확인하고 난 후 가급적 빨리 제게 연락을 주셔서 저희가 언제 방문하면 좋을지 알려주세요. 주말이라도 괜찮습니다. 저희 무료 전화번호 1-800-857-3239번으로 연락을 주시거나 이메일을 보내주시면 됩니다. 감사합니다. 좋은 하루 되세요.

**77.** 화자는 어떤 업체에서 근무할 것 같은가?
(A) 백화점
(B) 가구점
(C) 직물점
(D) 배송 회사 정답 (B)

**78.** 화자가 언급하는 문제점은 무엇인가?
(A) 배송 지연
(B) 일정 충돌
(C) 제품 파손
(D) 잘못된 연락처 기록 정답 (C)

**79.** 화자는 Stanford 씨에게 무엇을 제공하는가?
(A) 새 가구 소개책자
(B) 상품권
(C) 향후 주문에 대한 할인
(D) 무료 배송 정답 (D)

문제 80-82번은 다음 워크숍 내용을 참조하시오. 미M

Good afternoon, everyone! Welcome to the first day of the workshop. Over the next two days, **(80) you will learn how to strengthen the growth engines of your small business.**

Today, we're going to kick off with a special presenter, Sarah Baldwin, a dynamic young businesswoman. She's here to talk about her own business experience in the past. **(81) She started a small pet shop ten years ago. Now, she is the owner of the largest pet shop in the country.** I hope you listen very carefully to her advice based on her personal experience. **(82) After her presentation, we will have a 30-minute question-and-answer session.** Ladies and gentlemen, please give a warm welcome to Ms. Baldwin!

안녕하세요, 여러분! 워크숍 첫 날 과정에 오신 걸 환영합니다. 오늘부터 이틀간 여러분은 소규모 사업의 성장 동력을 어떻게 강화할 것인지에 대해 배우시게 될 겁니다. 오늘은 특별 발표로 역동적인 젊은 여성 사업가 Sarah Baldwin 씨와 함께 워크숍을 시작하도록 하겠습니다. 그녀는 과거 자신의 사업 경험에 대해 이야기를 해 드리기 위해 오셨습니다. 그녀는 10년 전에 작은 반려동물 용품점을 창업했습니다. 현재 그녀는 국내에서 가장 큰 반려동물 용품점의 소유주가 되었습니다. 그녀의 개인 경험에서 우러나오는 조언에 귀를 기울이시길 바랍니다. 그녀의 발표가 끝난 후 30분간의 질의응답 시간을 갖도록 하겠습니다. 여러분, Baldwin 씨에게 따뜻한 환영의 인사를 부탁드립니다!

**80.** 청자들은 누구일 것 같은가?
(A) 행사 기획자
(B) 재정 설계사
(C) 교육자
(D) 사업가 정답 (D)

**81.** 화자가 "Now, she is the owner of the largest pet shop in the country."라고 말한 이유는 무엇인가?
(A) 그녀의 사업 성공을 축하하기 위해서
(B) 발표자의 자질을 강조하기 위해서
(C) 그의 다음 연설의 주제를 말하기 위해서
(D) 책임감과 팀워크의 사례를 제시하기 위해서 정답 (B)

**82.** 연설이 끝난 후 청자들은 무엇을 할 것 같은가?
(A) 질문을 한다.
(B) 환영 만찬에 참석한다.
(C) 유인물의 내용을 검토한다.
(D) 몇몇 제품을 살펴본다. 정답 (A)

문제 83-85번은 다음 전화 메시지를 참조하시오. 호M

Hello, Ms. McLean. **(83) I'm calling to let you know some information regarding the employee transition plan.** Unfortunately, Mr. Shaw is leaving the company next week. As you suggested, Ms. Watt will be taking over for him. **(84) I already asked Mr. Shaw to train her on our procurement and shipping procedures a couple of days ago.** But he had a car accident this morning. **(85) So I've decided to review the procurement process with her tomorrow.** If there are any problems with that, please let me know, and I can find some workable alternatives. Thanks.

안녕하세요, McLean 씨. 직원 이동 계획에 관한 정보를 전달해 드리고자 전화 드렸습니다. 안타깝게도 Shaw 씨는 다음주에 퇴사를 할 예정입니다. 귀하가 제안하신 대로 Watt 씨가 그의 후임으로 업무를 담당하게 될 겁니다. 저는 이틀 전에 이미 Shaw 씨에게 조달 및 선적 절차에 관해 그녀에게 업무 인수인계를 해달라고 요청했습니다. 하지만 그가 오늘 오전에 자동차 사고를 당했습니다. 그래서 제가 내일 그녀와 함께 조달 절차를 검토하기로 결정했습니다. 혹시 이 부분과 관련하여 문제가 있다면 알려주십시오. 그러면 실현 가능한 대안을 마련하도록 하겠습니다. 감사합니다.

**83.** 화자가 전화한 이유는 무엇인가?
(A) 아파서 결근한다고 전하기 위해서
(B) 실수를 보고하기 위해서
(C) 좀 더 구체적인 정보를 요청하기 위해서
(D) 인사 계획을 설명하기 위해서 　　　　정답 (D)

**84.** 화자가 "But he had a car accident this morning."이라고 말할 때 의미하는 바는 무엇인가?
(A) 직원이 병가를 낼 것이다.
(B) 직원이 후임을 교육할 수 없다.
(C) 직원이 오리엔테이션에 참석할 수 없을 것이다.
(D) 직원이 최근에 많은 야근을 했다. 　　　　정답 (B)

**85.** 화자는 내일 무엇을 할 것인가?
(A) 직원과 만난다.
(B) 퇴사한다.
(C) 새로운 프로젝트를 운영한다.
(D) 제안서를 검토한다. 　　　　정답 (A)

**문제 86–88번은 다음 전화 메시지를 참조하시오.** 영W

(87) Mr. Wright, this is Rose Banks calling from Komi Pharmaceuticals. (86) I'm calling to thank you for the presentation that you gave at our sales meeting on Friday. It was a really outstanding presentation. Our employees appreciated your words about setting personal goals and staying motivated to reach those goals. (88) I'm part of the organizing committee for the Pharmaceutical National Conference in New York next month, and I would like to invite you to speak at the conference. I'm sure that your message would impress many people and contribute greatly to the event. I will e-mail you the details later. Of course, the company will pay for your airfare and hotel accommodations in addition to your speaker's fee. If you are interested, please call me back as soon as possible. Thank you.

- - - - - - - - - - - - - - - - - - - - - - - - - - - - - - - -

Wright 씨, 저는 Komi 제약사의 Rose Banks입니다. 귀하가 지난 금요일에 저희 영업 회의에서 발표해 주신 것에 감사드리고자 전화 드렸습니다. 발표는 정말 훌륭했습니다. 저희 직원들은 개인적인 목표를 설정하고 그 목표를 달성하기 위해 동기를 유지하라는 귀하의 이야기를 높이 평가했습니다. 저는 다음달에 New York에서 개최되는 전국 제약사 회의 조직위원회의 일원으로 귀하를 연설자로 초청하고 싶습니다. 귀하의 메시지는 많은 사람들을 감동시킬 것이고 이 회의에 크게 일조할 것이라고 확신합니다. 나중에 자세한 사항은 이메일을 통해 전달하겠습니다. 물론 저희 회사에서 귀하의 강연료 뿐만 아니라 항공료 및 호텔 숙박비를 지불할 것입니다. 만약에 관심이 있으시다면 최대한 서둘러 제게 전화해 주시기 바랍니다. 감사합니다.

**86.** 화자가 Wright 씨에게 감사하는 이유는 무엇인가?
(A) 그는 많은 기부금을 냈다.
(B) 그는 인상적인 발표를 했다.
(C) 그는 보건 발전에 기여를 했다.
(D) 그는 New York에서 열린 회의를 기획했다. 　　　정답 (B)

**87.** 화자가 근무하는 곳은 어디인가?
(A) 제약 회사
(B) 비즈니스 컨설팅 회사
(C) 지역 자선 단체
(D) 종합 병원 　　　　정답 (A)

**88.** 화자가 다음달에 Wright 씨에게 해달라고 요청하는 것은 무엇인가?
(A) 그녀의 출장비를 환급해 준다.
(B) 회의에서 연설을 한다.
(C) 예약을 연기한다.
(D) 그녀의 새로운 영업사원들을 훈련시킨다. 　　　정답 (B)

**문제 89–91번은 다음 안내문을 참조하시오.** 미W

Hello, everyone. This is Clay Turner, the personnel director. (89/90) There will be an emergency evacuation drill for the entire building in an hour. I know you might be a little annoyed by this inspection. But we get unexpected fire inspections at least once a year. The city fire inspector will be present to determine our emergency readiness. It is therefore crucial that all employees carefully execute the procedures. (91) Shortly after this, your department heads will show you the evacuation plan for your work area. You will know how to move quickly and safely to the nearest exit through the inspection. Thank you in advance for your cooperation.

- - - - - - - - - - - - - - - - - - - - - - - - - - - - - - - -

안녕하세요, 여러분. 저는 인사 담당 이사인 Clay Turner입니다. 한 시간 후에 전체 건물에 걸쳐 비상 대피 훈련을 실시할 것입니다. 여러분이 이 점검을 조금 번거롭게 생각하실 수도 있다는 걸 압니다. 그러나 우리는 최소 1년에 한 차례 불시 소방 점검을 받습니다. 시 소방 검사관이 참여하여 비상 상황에 대한 대비를 평가할 것입니다. 따라서 모든 직원들이 신중하게 절차를 이행해야 하는 것이 아주 중요합니다. 이 방송 직후에는 각 부서장들이 각 근무 구역에서의 대피 계획을 보여드릴 것입니다. 이 검사를 통해 여러분은 가장 가까운 출구로 안전하고 신속하게 이동하는 방법을 아시게 될 겁니다. 여러분의 협조에 미리 감사의 말씀 전합니다.

**89.** 화자는 한 시간 뒤에 어떤 일이 발생할 것이라고 말하는가?
(A) 안전 검사
(B) 교육
(C) 대피 훈련
(D) 근무 성과 평가 　　　　정답 (C)

**90.** 화자가 "I know you might be a little annoyed by this inspection."이라고 말할 때 암시하는 바는 무엇인가?
(A) 일부 장비가 제대로 작동하지 않는다.
(B) 점검이 보통 고객을 방해한다.
(C) 점검이 불시에 시행되고 있다.
(D) 직원들은 직장 내 안전에 대해 관심이 없다. 　　　정답 (C)

**91.** 화자에 따르면 직원들이 다음에 할 일은 무엇인가?
(A) 평가를 실시한다.
(B) 대피 경로를 숙지한다.
(C) 공장 견학을 간다.
(D) 업무 배정을 논의한다. 　　　　정답 (B)

Hello. I'm Michael Fox, the CEO. Today, I'd like to announce an exciting new development to all of you. We have decided to branch out into the area of cosmetics in France. The cosmetics industry in France has long achieved remarkable growth and is currently one of the dominant exporters in the world. French cosmetics are high in quality, and their brands have been growing in demand in Asia and North America. (92/93) So we, the Bella Packaging Company, have sought strategic alliances with some major cosmetics manufacturers in France for the last few months, and we finally signed a contract with a new partner, Mademoiselle, based in Paris, yesterday. (92/94) Our design team will spend the next few days working on packaging sample products for the first business meeting.

안녕하세요. 저는 최고 경영자 Michael Fox입니다. 오늘 새로운 기분 좋은 소식을 여러분 모두에게 발표하고자 합니다. 우리는 프랑스 화장품 시장으로 사업을 확장하기로 결정했습니다. 프랑스의 화장품 산업은 오랜 시간 동안 놀라운 성장을 이루어냈으며, 현재 세계에서 화장품 수출을 주도적으로 많이 하고 있는 나라들 중 하나입니다. 프랑스 화장품은 품질이 매우 뛰어나며, 그들의 화장품에 대한 아시아 및 북미 지역의 수요는 지속적으로 성장해왔습니다. 따라서 우리 Bella Packaging Company도 지난 몇 달간 프랑스의 주요 화장품 제조업체들과의 전략적 제휴 관계를 모색해왔으며, 마침내 어제 Paris에 본사를 두고 있는 새로운 협력사 Mademoiselle 사와 계약을 체결하였습니다. 우리 디자인 팀은 향후 며칠 동안 첫 번째 비즈니스 회의에 필요한 포장 견본 제품에 집중할 예정입니다.

**92.** 남자는 어떤 업종의 회사에서 일을 하는가?
(A) 화장품 회사
(B) 마케팅 회사
(C) 디자인 회사
(D) 포장 회사 　　　　　　　　　　　정답 (D)

**93.** 회사는 최근에 무엇을 했는가?
(A) 고객들에게 견본품을 발송했다.
(B) 새로운 화장품을 출시했다.
(C) 새로운 고객을 유치했다.
(D) 다른 장소로 이전했다. 　　　　　　정답 (C)

**94.** 회사가 향후 몇 주 동안 마무리해야 할 새로운 업무는 무엇인가?
(A) 견본 제품을 제작한다.
(B) 새로운 화장품을 광고한다.
(C) 새로운 제품을 개발한다.
(D) 프랑스 시장을 분석한다. 　　　　　정답 (A)

Hello. It's me, Alisa. (95) I'm calling to let you know some updates on the company outdoor party we are organizing. I already checked this week's weather forecast on the weather center's Web site. (96) According to the weather forecast, there shouldn't be any storms that day, but it is expected to rain heavily two days in a row before the day of the company outdoor party. I'm worried the ground will be too wet on that day, so it would be good to reschedule the corporate event for some time next week. I know you made arrangements

with a caterer already. (97) Please call the catering company to let someone there know about this sudden change as soon as possible.

안녕하세요. Alisa예요. 우리가 준비하는 회사 야외 파티에 대한 최근 소식을 알려드리고자 전화 드렸어요. 제가 이미 기상청의 홈페이지에서 이번주 일기 예보를 확인했어요. 일기 예보에 따르면 행사 당일엔 폭풍이 없을 것이지만 회사 야외 파티가 있기 전 이틀 동안 많은 비가 내릴 것으로 예상되고 있어요. 저는 그 날 땅이 너무 젖어 있는 상태일 것 같아 걱정이 되는데 회사 행사를 다음주 중으로 연기하는 것이 좋을 것 같아요. 당신이 출장 요리 서비스도 이미 예약한 것으로 알고 있어요. 출장 요리 회사에 전화해서 급한 일정 변화에 대해 최대한 빨리 알려주셨으면 해요.

| 월요일 | 화요일 | 수요일 | 목요일 |
|---|---|---|---|
| ☔ | ☔ | ⛅ | ☀ |

**95.** 화자는 누구일 것 같은가?
(A) 일기 예보관
(B) 출장 요리사
(C) 행사 준비자
(D) 라디오 프로그램 진행자 　　　　　정답 (C)

**96.** 그래픽을 보시오. 회사 행사가 본래 개최되기로 한 요일은 언제인가?
(A) 월요일
(B) 화요일
(C) 수요일
(D) 목요일 　　　　　　　　　　　정답 (C)

**97.** 화자가 청자에게 요청하는 것은 무엇인가?
(A) 다른 장소를 물색한다.
(B) 회사 행사를 취소한다.
(C) 주문번호를 알려준다.
(D) 서비스 제공업체에게 연락을 한다. 　　정답 (D)

Thank you for attending this meeting on such short notice. As you know, we are going to open a retail store large enough to provide our sportswear products and sports equipment to customers. (98) In today's meeting, we should look at four potential locations for the site and choose one of them. As you can see on the map, there's a large space available near the outdoor parking space. (99) But I think the location right across from the bus stop would be better because it will let us gain access to customers who frequently use public transportation. Now, (100) I'm going to distribute some handouts which contain detailed information about the four sites. After you read them, please give me your opinions and reasons for your opinions.

급한 공지에도 불구하고 회의에 참석해 주셔서 감사합니다. 아시다시피 우리는 고객들에게 스포츠 의류와 스포츠 장비를 제공할 수 있는 충분한 크기의 소매점을 개장할 예정입니다. 오늘 회의에서 우리는 상점이 입점할 수 있는 네 곳의 장소를 보고 한 곳을 결정해야 합니다. 지도를 보시면 야외 주차장 근처에 우리가 이용할 수 있는 큰 공간이 있습니다. 하지만 저는 버스

정류장 바로 맞은편 위치가 더 좋지 않을까 생각하는데, 그 이유는 그 위치가 대중교통을 자주 이용하는 고객들에게 접근성을 제공하기 때문입니다. 이제 네 곳의 부지에 대한 상세한 정보가 담긴 인쇄물을 나눠드리겠습니다. 읽어 보신 후 여러분의 견해와 그 근거를 말씀해 주십시오.

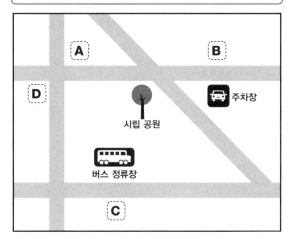

**98.** 화자가 주로 논의하는 것은 무엇인가?
(A) 시설물의 보수
(B) 사업 부지의 선정
(C) 특별 판촉 행사
(D) 스포츠 경기의 광고 　　　　　　　　정답 (B)

**99.** 그래픽을 보시오. 화자가 선호하는 위치는 어디인가?
(A) A장소
(B) B장소
(C) C장소
(D) D장소 　　　　　　　　정답 (C)

**100.** 화자는 무엇을 배부하겠다고 이야기하는가?
(A) 공사 일정표
(B) 시장 분석 보고서
(C) 인쇄물
(D) 사진 　　　　　　　　정답 (C)

## Part 5

**101.** Banks 씨는 그녀의 회사를 경영하는 법을 배우기 위해 지역 대학에서 비즈니스 인증 과정을 다녔다. 　　　　　　　　정답 (C)

**102.** Wonderful Flowers는 다양한 화환과 풍선이 달린 꽃다발을 Fremont 시에 배송하는 서비스를 제공한다. 　　　　　　　　정답 (A)

**103.** 세미나를 개최하는 동안 배포된 연간 보고서는 노동 생산성과 비용 절감 면에서 상당한 개선이 이뤄졌음을 보여줬다. 　　　　　　　　정답 (D)

**104.** 사람들에게 친절하고자 각고의 노력을 기울이는 것은 우호적인 분위기를 만들고 우리가 새로운 고객들을 유치하는 것에 도움이 될 수 있다. 　　　　　　　　정답 (A)

**105.** 고객들이 온라인으로 구매한 제품의 당일 배송을 보장받기 위해서는 추가로 3달러의 배송비를 지불해야 한다. 　　　　　　　　정답 (D)

**106.** 이렇게 빠른 성장률로 인해 그 회사가 직면하는 주요한 문제점 중의 하나가 컴퓨터 그래픽 디자이너가 부족하다는 것이다. 　　　　　　　　정답 (B)

**107.** BK Financial Group의 회장은 행사가 끝난 후 이어질 환영 만찬에서의 축하 연설을 계획했다. 　　　　　　　　정답 (A)

**108.** One International 사와 Komi 사의 합병은 향후 3주 이내에 완료될 것으로 예상된다. 　　　　　　　　정답 (C)

**109.** 공연표에 대한 엄청난 수요에 대한 조치로 Syracuse 교향악단은 정기 공연 일정에 네 번의 공연 날짜를 추가했다. 　　　　　　　　정답 (D)

**110.** 전염병이 전국에 만연하고 있지만 환자들을 위한 적절한 접종 수단이 없다. 　　　　　　　　정답 (C)

**111.** 북미 지역에서의 그의 경력 덕분에 Chan 씨는 미국인들의 작업 방식을 회사 내 다른 직원들보다 잘 이해하고 있다. 　　　　　　　　정답 (A)

**112.** 몇몇 경제 잡지들은 Hachi Technology 사가 한 중국 회사로부터 엄청난 투자 제안을 받았다고 보도했다. 　　　　　　　　정답 (C)

**113.** 선진화된 경영 기법과 기술 지식에 대한 그의 뛰어난 재능으로 Baker 씨는 자신이 우수한 최고 경영자임을 증명해 보였다. 　　　　　　　　정답 (C)

**114.** 컴퓨터 그래픽 전문가 자격증 취득과 관련된 질문은 기술 교육 부서장에게 해야 한다. 　　　　　　　　정답 (B)

**115.** 해외 부동산 구매에 관심이 있는 사람들은 그들의 행동이 국내 경제에 악영향을 미칠 수 있는 가능성이 있음을 인식해야 한다. 　　　　　　　　정답 (C)

**116.** 이사회는 만장일치로 마케팅 부장인 Beckinsale 씨를 올해의 직원으로 선정했다. 　　　　　　　　정답 (A)

**117.** 새로운 본사는 세계적인 대형 은행들과 유명한 증권사들 근처에 전략적으로 위치하고 있다. 　　　　　　　　정답 (D)

**118.** 모든 참가자들은 회의가 시작되기 전에 자신의 책상 위에 이름표를 놓아야 한다. 　　　　　　　　정답 (B)

**119.** 몇몇 사람들은 Winston 씨의 마케팅 전략이 새로 부임한 마케팅 부장의 전략과 매우 유사하다고 지적했다. 　　　　　　　　정답 (D)

**120.** Cheese Technology 사의 새로운 회계 소프트웨어는 회사들이 재무제표를 이전보다 훨씬 손쉽게 작성할 수 있도록 한다. 　　　　　　　　정답 (B)

**121.** 우리의 새로운 방침에 따라 마지막으로 사무실을 떠나는 사람이 사무실 내의 모든 등을 꺼야 할 책임이 있다. 　　　　　　　　정답 (B)

**122.** James는 새로운 업무를 하면서 회사 데이터베이스에 여기저기 분산된 정보들을 모으느라 분투했다. 　　　　　　　　정답 (C)

**123.** 정상의 자리를 유지하기 위해 우리는 고객이나 경쟁사들이 상상해본 적이 없는 새로운 상품, 서비스, 그리고 사업을 개발해내야 한다. 　　　　　　　　정답 (B)

**124.** 대부분의 서류 작업이 폐지된 덕분에 West California 은행에서 대출받기 위한 신청 과정은 그 어느 때보다 훨씬 더 빠르고 수월해질 것이다. 　　　　　　　　정답 (D)

**125.** 여러 개의 방을 예약하고 싶으시면 각 방을 다른 이름을 사용하여 예약하셔야 합니다. 그렇지 않으면 중복 예약은 호텔에 의해 취소됩니다. 　　　　　　　　정답 (A)

**126.** 석탄. 천연가스 그리고 석유와 같은 화석 연료의 사용은 지난 100년간 꾸준하게 증가해왔다. 　　　　　　　　　　　정답 (D)

**127.** 북부 해안에 혼란을 안겨준 쓰나미로 인해 대략 만 명의 사람들이 사망하거나 실종되었다. 　　　　　　　　　　　정답 (C)

**128.** 에너지 회사들은 환경오염을 감소시키고 부족한 자원을 보존할 수 있는 다양한 형태의 대체 에너지를 개발해야 할 필요가 있다. 　　　정답 (A)

**129.** 특정 상품에 대한 고객의 반응을 파악하기 위해 회사는 일 년에 두 번 설문조사를 시행한다. 　　　　　　　　　　　정답 (A)

**130.** Armitage 씨는 시장으로 선출된 이후 지역의 많은 경제 문제들에 적극적으로 관여해왔다. 　　　　　　　　　　　정답 (C)

## Part 6

문제 131-134번은 다음 이메일을 참조하시오.

Finley 씨께,

최근에 World Auction과 거래해 주셔서 감사합니다. CK 진공청소기 제품에 대한 환불 요청에 관한 서신을 받았습니다. 저희 기록을 보니 귀하는 7월 7일 저희 홈페이지를 통해 CK 진공청소기와 Speed 전자레인지를 주문하셨는데 진공청소기에 대해서만 환불을 요청하셨습니다.

해당 제품에 대한 귀하의 환불 요청을 처리했습니다. 귀하의 편의를 위해, 귀하가 다운로드하여 제품 상자에 부착하실 수 있는 반품용 배송 라벨을 동봉했습니다. 귀하가 사용하신 본래 결제수단을 통해 환불 금액을 수령하시게 될 것입니다.

환불은 처리되는 데 7일에서 15일까지 소요될 수 있음에 유의해 주시기 바랍니다. 불편함을 겪으신 점에 대해 사과드립니다. 더 궁금한 점이 있으면 주저하지 마시고 저희에게 연락을 해주십시오.

**131.** 　　　　　　　　　　　정답 (D)

**132.** (A) 귀하의 유용한 의견에 진심으로 감사드립니다.
(B) 해당 제품에 대한 귀하의 환불 요청을 처리했습니다.
(C) 귀하의 주문이 이루어졌으며 일주일 후에 귀하의 주소로 제품이 배송될 것입니다.
(D) 귀하의 요청에 대한 설명을 제공하셔서 저희가 환불이 적절한지 여부를 결정할 수 있도록 해주시기 바랍니다. 　　　정답 (B)

**133.** 　　　　　　　　　　　정답 (B)

**134.** 　　　　　　　　　　　정답 (A)

문제 135-138번은 다음 편지를 참조하시오.

Coco 난방 시스템
Pine 가 160번지
Syracuse, NY 13244

10월 1일

Stacy Nguyen
Main 가 310번지
Syracuse, NY 13244

Nguyen 씨께,

귀하의 연간 보일러 유지 보수 계약이 11월 12일자로 종료됨을 알려드리기 위해 편지 드립니다. 이달 말까지 계약을 갱신할 수 있도록 전화해 주시기 바랍니다.

겨울이 오기 전에 보일러 고장에 대비하여 보일러를 관리하는 것은 귀하와 가족의 안전하고 따뜻한 겨울나기를 위한 핵심적인 고려 사항입니다. 저희의 저렴한 유지 보수 계약은 보일러가 고장 날 경우 비싼 수리에 대해 걱정하지 않으셔도 된다는 것을 의미합니다.

오늘 전화 주셔서 저희가 긴 겨울 동안 귀하의 가정에 마음의 평화를 드릴 수 있게 해 주시기 바랍니다.

고객 관리부
Coco 난방 시스템

**135.** (A) 보일러 전문가로부터 특별 교육을 필히 받으셔야 합니다.
(B) 본인 인증을 하여 자신을 사기로부터 보호해야 할 필요가 있습니다.
(C) 새로운 보일러를 최대한 빨리 구매하셔야 합니다.
(D) 이달 말까지 계약을 갱신할 수 있도록 전화해 주시기 바랍니다. 　　　정답 (D)

**136.** 　　　　　　　　　　　정답 (D)

**137.** 　　　　　　　　　　　정답 (C)

**138.** 　　　　　　　　　　　정답 (A)

문제 139-142번은 다음 편지를 참조하시오.

Jenkins 씨께,

지난주 Joshua 증권사 면접에 와 주셔서 다시 한번 감사드립니다. 부서장들이 귀하의 이전 직장 경력 및 가능성에 모두 깊은 감명을 받았으며, 저희 Los Angeles 본사의 수석 증권거래장 직책을 제안하게 되어 기쁘게 생각합니다. 가능하다면 4월 15일에 근무를 시작해 주셨으면 합니다.

고용조건 및 혜택은 면접 때 논의한 바와 같습니다. 참고로 이 내용의 요약본을 첨부합니다. 또한 출근 첫 날에 서명하셔야 하는 고용 계약서를 동봉합니다. 귀하의 직책에 관련된 업무가 면접 때 또한 설명 드린 바와 같이 열거되어 있습니다. 명확히 해야 할 사항이 있으시면 저에게 알려 주십시오.

직책을 수락하고 싶으신지의 여부와 근무 시작일자를 확인하기 위해 저에게 전화 주시면 감사하겠습니다. 귀하로부터 답변을 듣길 기대하며 입사를 환영할 수 있길 바랍니다.

**139.** 　　　　　　　　　　　정답 (A)

**140.** (A) 우리는 급변하는 시장에서 생존하는 법에 관해 논의를 했습니다.
(B) 귀하에게 적합한 종류의 일이 무엇인지 결정하세요.
(C) 우리는 귀하의 시장 분석 보고서에 매우 감명을 받았습니다.
(D) 고용조건 및 혜택은 면접 때 논의한 바와 같습니다. 　　　정답 (D)

**141.** 　　　　　　　　　　　정답 (B)

**142.** 　　　　　　　　　　　정답 (B)

문제 143-146번은 다음 회람을 참조하시오.

회람

발신: 최고 경영자 Thomas Lee

수신: 전 직원

날짜: 6월 6일

제목: 2주간의 초과 근무

올해 세금 신고 기간이 끝날 때까지 모든 직원들은 초과 근무를 해야 함을 주지하시기 바랍니다. 올해에는 우리가 더 열심히 일해야 하는 고객들이 상당히 많습니다.

하지만 여러분의 노고는 세금 신고 기간이 끝나면 보상을 받게 될 것입니다. 세금 신고 기간 내의 휴가 신청은 저에게 직접 승인 받으셔야 합니다. 이러한 중요한 시점에는 여러분의 상사나 팀장이 휴가 신청을 승인할 수 없습니다.

바쁜 시기가 지나고 나면 회사 연회를 열 것입니다. 또한 여러분의 노고에 감사하는 뜻으로 모두에게 추가 휴가를 드릴 것입니다.

여러분의 이해와 협조에 미리 감사를 드립니다.

Thomas Lee
최고 경영자

**143.** 정답 (B)

**144.** 정답 (C)

**145.** 정답 (D)

**146.** (A) 세계적인 회계 법인으로 성장하는 것이 최우선 목표입니다.
(B) 그 도시는 낮은 세율로 인해 기업들에게 인기가 많은 곳입니다.
(C) 바쁜 시기가 지나고 나면 회사 연회를 열 것입니다.
(D) 몇몇 직원들은 회사에 의해 해외로 여행을 가는 휴가를 보상 받았습니다. 정답 (C)

## Part 7

문제 147-148번은 다음 광고를 참조하시오.

Max Interior Design

(147) **주택 소유주 각각의 취향에 맞춘 최첨단 디자인**

수십 년간의 경력이 있는 상을 받은 디자인 팀
신속한 작업완료
무료 견적
프로젝트 관리
추천인 제공 가능

(148) **Pleasant City의 Main Street에 위치한 저희의 넓은 전시실을 방문하시거나**, 온라인으로 www.maxinteriordesign.com을 방문해 주십시오.

**147.** 이 광고는 누구를 의도로 하고 있는가??
(A) 주택 소유주들
(B) 점주들
(C) 건축 설계자들
(D) 패션 디자이너들 정답 (A)

**148.** Max Interior Design에 대해 언급되는 것은 무엇인가?
(A) 곧 추가 점포를 개장한다.
(B) 경쟁사 가격과 대등하게 맞춘다.
(C) 작업 사례를 전시한다.
(D) 지역 제조업체로부터 자재를 들여온다. 정답 (C)

문제 149-150번은 다음 양식을 참조하시오.

팩스

수신: Chan Hong (510-575-4332)

발신: Andrew Kim (525-412-9267)

제목: 재발송

메시지:

(149) **고객님께서 주문하신 외장하드가 도착하지 않았음을 저희에게 알리는 편지를 주셔서 감사 드립니다.** 이로 인해 불편을 드려 죄송하며 오늘 고객님에게 다른 것을 발송하도록 조치하였습니다.

(150) **원래 주문품이 배달될 경우, 저희 웹사이트에 기재된 무료 통화번호로 전화 주시기 바랍니다.**

저희는 이 문제가 왜 발생했는지를 파악하고자 저희 배송업체에게 이 문제점에 대해 전달하였습니다. 저희 사과를 받아주시기 바라며 저희에게 주문해주신 점에 감사 드립니다.

Andrew Kim

**149.** Kim 씨가 Hong 씨에게 발송하는 것은 무엇인가?
(A) 사업계약서
(B) 주문서
(C) 새로운 소프트웨어 프로그램
(D) 저장 기기 정답 (D)

**150.** 먼저 주문한 것이 배달되면 Hong 씨는 어떻게 해야 하는가?
(A) Kim 씨에게 돌려 보낸다.
(B) 두 번째 주문을 취소한다.
(C) 회사에 도착했다고 연락한다.
(D) 쿠폰을 내려 받기 위해 새로운 홈페이지에 접속한다. 정답 (C)

문제 151-152번은 다음 문자 메시지를 참조하시오.

Lynn Jacobs [오후 3:11]
(151) **안녕하세요, Cedric, 제품 디자인이 어떻게 되어 가고 있으신지 여쭤봐도 될까요?** 우리 고객께서 이번 주말까지 우리의 진행 상황을 확인하고 싶어 하십니다.

Cedric Clark [오후 3:13]
지금 색상 작업을 하는 중입니다. 밝은 색을 사용할지 아니면 어두운 색으로 할지 모르겠어요.

Lynn Jacobs [오후 3:15]
두 가지 모두에 대한 샘플을 제게 보내 주시겠어요? 제 생각을 알려 드릴게요.

Cedric Clark [오후 3:16]
감사합니다! (152) **방금 이메일로 보내드렸습니다.**

Lynn Jacobs [오후 3:18]
(152) **확실하신가요? 제 수신함이 여전히 비어 있는데요.**

Cedric Clark [오후 3:20]
죄송해요, 실수로 예전 이메일 계정으로 보내 드렸어요. 다시 한 번 확인해 보시겠어요?

Lynn Jacobs [오후 3:21]
받았습니다. 저는 밝게 색상 처리된 버전이 더 마음에 들어요.

**151.** Clark 씨는 무슨 종류의 업체에서 근무하고 있는가?
(A) 미술 대학
(B) 자동차 제조사
(C) 회계 법인

(D) 디자인 업체 　　　　　　　　　　　　　　　　정답 (D)

**152.** 오후 3시 18분에, Jacobs 씨가 "Are you sure?"라고 썼을 때 무엇을 의미할 가능성이 가장 큰 가?
(A) Clark 씨가 선택한 색상을 묻고 있다.
(B) Clark 씨가 이메일을 보냈는지 묻고 있다.
(C) Clark 씨가 제품 디자인 프로젝트를 시작할 수 있을지 궁금해 하고 있다.
(C) Clark 씨에게 지금 온라인으로 포트폴리오를 보내 달라고 요청하고 있다. 　　　　　　　　　　　　　　　　정답 (B)

문제 153-155번은 다음 이메일을 참조하시오.

수신: Ellen Smith ⟨es@sheba.com⟩
발신: Tiffany Anderson ⟨ta@sheba.com⟩
날짜: 5월 10일
제목: 타이핑 실수

Smith 씨에게:

(153) 제가 마케팅 워크숍의 날짜에 관한 이전 이메일에서 실수한 오타를 지적하고자 합니다. (154) 날짜는 이 달 20일이며, 29일이 아닙니다. 사과 드립니다. (155) 또한 올해는 2명 더 참석을 허락한다고 했으므로, 참석을 희망하는 또 다른 사람이 있는지 사무실에 알아봐주세요. 5월 16일에 신청서를 제출해야 하기 때문에, 그 전까지 알려주세요.

감사합니다.

Tiffany Anderson
인사과

**153.** 이메일을 발송한 이유가 무엇인가?
(A) 등록을 취소하기 위해
(B) 여행 준비를 하기 위해
(C) 동료를 축하하기 위해
(D) 실수를 수정하기 위해 　　　　　　　　　　　　　　　　정답 (D)

**154.** 마케팅 워크숍은 언제 개최될 것인가?
(A) 5월 11일
(B) 5월 16일
(C) 5월 20일
(D) 5월 29일 　　　　　　　　　　　　　　　　정답 (C)

**155.** Anderson 씨가 Smith 씨에게 요청하는 것은 무엇인가?
(A) 장소를 예약한다
(B) 음식을 주문한다
(C) 정보를 제공한다
(D) 신청서를 제출한다 　　　　　　　　　　　　　　　　정답 (C)

문제 156-157번은 다음 회람을 참조하시오.

회람

발신: Brianna Palmer
수신: 전 직원
날짜: 1월 10일 화요일
제목: 공지

이번 주 목요일인 1월 12일 오후 1시부터 시작해서 약 한 시간 동안 우리 사무실의 프린터를 사용하실 수 없습니다. (156/157) 이 시간 동안 새로운 프린터가 설치되고 몇 차례 테스트가 진행될 것입니다. 그 이후엔 설치한 기술자가 이전 프린터를 가지고 가서 폐기 처분할 예정입니다.

(157) 목요일에 출력을 해야 한다면, 오후 1시 이전에 하시거나 오후 3시 이후에 하셔야 합니다. 길 건너에 있는 인쇄소를 이용하실 수도 있습니다.

불편을 초래하게 된 점 양해해주시기 바랍니다. 여러분의 이해와 협조에 미리 감사의 말씀을 드립니다.

**156.** Palmer 씨가 회람에서 언급한 것은 무엇인가?
(A) 안전검사가 실시된다.
(B) 새로운 기계가 설치된다.
(C) 새로운 방침이 시행된다.
(D) 사무실이 목요일에 문을 닫는다. 　　　　　　　　　　　　　　　　정답 (B)

**157.** 회람에서 암시하는 내용은 무엇인가?
(A) Palmer 씨는 가전제품 매장에서 근무한다.
(B) 최근에 새로운 인쇄소가 문을 열었다.
(C) 사무실에는 프린터가 한 대뿐이다.
(D) 몇몇 직원들은 대량 복사를 해야 한다. 　　　　　　　　　　　　　　　　정답 (C)

문제 158-160번은 다음 기사를 참조하시오.

새로운 레스토랑 개점 임박

존 윌슨 - 뉴 저지 데일리 텔레그래프

Jersey City - (158) 소울 푸드 카페가 이번 주 금요일 오전 8시에 아침식사를 위해 개점할 것이다. (159) 소울 푸드 카페는 이 지역 Main 가에 있는 레스토랑들에 새로 추가되는 환영할 만한 새로운 레스토랑이다.

소울 푸드 카페의 사장 Linda Hamilton 씨는 "소울 푸드는 남부 시골 스타일의 음식을 만드는 것을 전문으로 합니다. (159) 고객 여러분들을 위해 건강에 좋은 기름과 조리법을 이용한 저칼로리의 시골풍 건강식을 제공한다는 점에서 저희는 다른 레스토랑들과 차별화됩니다. 저희는 고객님들이 저지방, 저콜레스테롤로 만들어진 품격있는 음식을 드시길 원합니다. 저희의 목표는 고객님들을 다시 방문하게 해서, 저희의 음식을 지속적으로 드시도록 하여 좀더 건강하실 수 있도록 하는 것입니다."라고 말했다.

Hamilton 씨는 크레올스 홈 쿠킹의 주방장으로 일했으며, 2년 전에 본인 소유의 레스토랑을 갖고자 계획을 세웠다. 시 전역에 걸쳐 여러 지역을 둘러본 후에, 그녀는 메인 가에 위치한 카펫 상점을 사들여 레스토랑으로 수리하였다. (160) Hamilton 씨는 "제가 어린 시절 알라바마에서 갔었던 남부 레스토랑을 기억하며 그와 똑같이 보이도록 하기 위해 설계자들과 함께 작업을 했습니다."라고 말했다.

소울 푸드 카페는 내부와 외부 모두가 아름답다. 우리는 Linda와 그의 열렬한 직원들의 바람처럼 많은 주민들이 단골이 될 지 여부를 곧 알게 될 것이다. 소울 푸드 카페는 아침식사와 함께 오전 8시에 개점하여 오후 9시까지 영업한다. 일요일은 브런치와 함께 오전 10시에 개점한다.

**158.** 이 기사문의 목적은 무엇인가?
(A) 음식 조리법을 설명하기 위해서
(B) 지역 레스토랑을 평가하기 위해서
(C) 한 경영인의 사업 전략을 설명하기 위해서
(D) 새로운 레스토랑 개업을 알리기 위해서 　　　　　　　　　　　　　　　　정답 (D)

**159.** 소울 푸드 카페에 대해 언급되지 않은 것은 무엇인가?
(A) 크레올스 홈 쿠킹의 소유이다.
(B) 저칼로리의 음식을 판매한다.
(C) 도심과 가깝다.
(D) 거의 매일 아침 8시에 개점할 것이다. 　　　　　　　　　　　　　　　　정답 (A)

**160.** Hamilton 씨에 대해 암시되는 것은 무엇인가?
(A) 모든 요리를 즐긴다.

(B) 업계에 처음 뛰어들었다.

(C) 인테리어 디자인을 도왔다.

(D) 그녀는 건축 전문가이다. 　　　　　　　　정답 (C)

---

**문제 161-163번은 다음 양식을 참조하시오.**

Pegasus 전자의 휴대 전화를 구입하기로 결정해 주셔서 감사드립니다. (163) 7월 1일부터 7월 31일 사이에 구매를 하셨다면 Pegasus 전자의 액세서리가 담긴 증정품(케이스, 이어폰 세트 및 보호 화면 커버를 포함)을 받으실 수 있습니다.

(161) 하단에 요청된 세부 사항들을 입력하여 양식을 작성한 후, 구매 기록과 함께 Pegasus 전자 본사가 있는 존슨 기술 공원, 에드먼턴, 앨버타 T5A 0FH로 발송해 주십시오. 질문이 있으시다면 Pegasus 전자의 고객 서비스 부서인 customerservice@pegasus.ca로 연락해 주시길 바랍니다.

(162) 저는 Pegasus 전자의 휴대 전화 액세서리가 담긴 무료 선물을 받고 싶음을 확인합니다. ☑

이름: Brendan Baker

주소: 5 조셉 스트리트

도시/지역/우편번호: 브레이스브릿지, On P1L 5JY

전화번호: 555-9231

*이메일 주소:

구매한 휴대 전화 모델명: ☐ S350　☐ S400　☑ S450

귀하의 품목이 배송되는데 최대 2주까지 걸릴 수 있습니다. 이 할인행사는 8월 30일에 끝나는 한정된 기회입니다. 이 혜택은 Canada 외 지역이나 홈페이지에서의 구매에는 적용되지 않습니다. 또한 Pegasus 전자에 현재 고용되어 있는 직원들은 이 행사에 참여하는 것이 허락되지 않습니다.

*이메일 주소를 제공하면, 귀하는 Pegasus 전자의 출시 예정인 휴대 전화 모델들과 특별 할인 등에 관한 정보가 들어있는 월간 소식지를 받고 싶다는 의사를 표현한 것으로 간주됩니다.

**161.** Pegasus 전자에 대해 암시하는 것은 무엇인가?

(A) 에드먼턴에 본사를 두고 있다.

(B) 8월 30일자로 휴대 전화 생산을 중단할 것이다.

(C) 고객들을 위한 매장 회원제 상품을 제작했다.

(D) 최근 신규 휴대 전화 모델을 출시했다. 　　　정답 (A)

**162.** Baker 씨가 서류를 작성한 이유는 무엇인가?

(A) 제품 교환을 요구하기 위해서

(B) 서비스에 대한 견해를 전달하기 위해서

(C) 제품에 대한 환불을 요청하기 위해서

(D) 무료 제품을 수령하기 위해서 　　　　　　정답 (D)

**163.** Baker 씨에 대해 유추할 수 있는 것은 무엇인가?

(A) 그는 이전에 Pegasus 전자의 직원이었다.

(B) 그는 Pegasus 전자 홈페이지에서 휴대 전화를 주문했다.

(C) 그는 Pegasus 전자의 월간 소식지를 수령하고 싶어한다.

(D) 그는 7월에 Pegasus 전자의 휴대 전화를 구매했다. 정답 (D)

---

**문제 164-167번은 다음 회람을 참조하시오.**

회람

수신: 모든 직원

발신: Anthony Jackson

날짜: 12월 15일

---

제목: Cradle Technologies 사와의 계약

직원 여러분께,

(164/165) 사무실에서 소비되는 에너지를 절약하고자 경영진은 Cradle Technologies 사로부터 새로운 자동화 시스템을 도입하기로 결정했습니다. (167) 이 시스템은 모든 직원의 일정에 맞춰 자동으로 온도와 상단 조명을 조절합니다. 예를 들어 주중 오후 8시에는 모든 사무실 조명이 꺼지고 흐리게 표시됩니다(현관 및 비상계단 조명 제외). 마찬가지로 온도는 주중 일반적인 온도였던 섭씨 22도 대신 18도로 유지됩니다. (165) 이 새로운 시스템은 월간 공공 요금을 최소한 13% 이상 감소시키고 우리의 전기 절약 목표를 달성하는 데 도움이 될 것입니다.

(166) 이러한 변화로 인해 여러분 중 일부, 특히 근무 일정이 우리의 정규 근무 시간과 부합하지 않는 분들이 다른 분들보다 더 많은 영향을 받게 될 것임을 알고 있습니다. 건물들의 일부 구역은 야근을 할 수 있는 환경이 조성되어 있으니 만약 그러한 상황이 여러분에게 해당한다면 (166) 주저하지 마시고 시설관리부서로 연락하여 작업하시는 사무실의 변경을 요청하시기 바랍니다.

감사합니다.

Anthony Jackson

시설관리부장

**164.** 회람의 목적은 무엇인가?

(A) 직원들에게 정시 퇴근을 권장한다.

(B) 새로운 환경 보호법을 공지한다.

(C) 직원들에게 금전적 혜택을 제공한다.

(D) 직장 내 새로운 변경사항을 설명한다. 　　　정답 (D)

**165.** Cradle Technologies 사 제품의 장점으로 언급된 것은 무엇인가?

(A) 직원의 업무량을 감소시켜줄 것이다.

(B) 동종 제품들 중 최고의 품질을 지니고 있다.

(C) 어떠한 근무 환경에서도 사용이 가능하다.

(D) 회사의 에너지 비용을 감소시키는데 도움을 줄 것이다. 정답 (D)

**166.** 자주 추가 근무를 하는 직원들은 어떤 권고를 받는가?

(A) 업무 일정 변경

(B) 그들의 상사와의 면담

(C) 사무실 변경 요청

(D) 재택 근무 고려 　　　　　　　　　　　　정답 (C)

**167.** [1], [2], [3] 그리고 [4]로 표시된 곳 중에, 아래 문장이 들어가기에 가장 적절한 곳은?

"이 시스템은 모든 직원의 일정에 맞춰 자동으로 온도와 상단 조명을 조절합니다."

(A) [1]

(B) [2]

(C) [3]

(D) [4] 　　　　　　　　　　　　　　　　정답 (A)

---

**문제 168-171번은 다음 기사를 참조하시오.**

교통위원회가 산책로 건설을 승인하다

CASTRO VALLEY (7월 14일) – (168) 캐스트로 밸리 교통위원회는 도시에서 가장 붐비는 열 개의 거리에 보행자 통로를 구축하는데 300,000달러를 사용하는 사안을 표결에 부쳐 승인을 얻었다. 이 허가는 캐스트로 밸리에 살고 있는 보행자들이 보행자 통로들의 위험한 교통 상황과 긴 대기시간에 대해 불만을 토로해 시가 안전 감사를 실시한 후 바로 허가된 것이다. 감사원들은 보행자들이 제기한 문제들을 내년 안으로 다룰 것

이라고 동의했다. 이 보행자 통로들은 보행자들이 교통흐름을 방해하지 않고 길을 건널 수 있도록 할 것이며, (169) 특히 관광객들이 많이 몰리는 시기에는 강변지구의 심한 교통체증으로 인해 고생하는 운전자들에겐 희소식이라 할 수 있다.

캐스트로 밸리의 시장인 Simon Livingston 씨가 3월 12일 보행자 통로 건설을 제안했다. Livingston 씨는 11월 캐스트로 밸리 지역 주민들을 대상으로 실시한 연구 결과를 언급했다. 그 연구는 캐스트로 밸리 인구의 10퍼센트만이 도시에서 조깅 또는 산책을 즐기고 있음을 보여주었다. (168) 인근 도시에 비슷한 산책로가 건설된 경우를 바탕으로, Livingston 씨는 보행자 통로 건설이 산책이나 조깅을 하는 인구를 3배 정도 증가시킬 것이라고 믿는다.

건설을 위한 초기 단계에서 필요 시 도로의 차선을 일시적으로 차단할 수도 있다. 이런 경우 우회로가 표시될 것이다. (170) 초기 건설 단계를 거치면, 보행자 통로들은 야간에도 접근하기 쉽도록 도색이 될 것이며 조명 또한 추가될 것이다. (171) 첫 번째 통로 건설은 8월 3일에 시작될 것이며 이후 4개월 이내에 10개 모두 완성될 것이다.

**168.** 기사의 목적은 무엇인가?
(A) 관광객들을 유치할 계획을 보도하기 위해서
(B) 새로운 통근용 고속도로에 대한 세부 정보를 제공하기 위해서
(C) 보행자의 수를 증가시킬 수 있는 프로젝트를 설명하기 위해서
(D) 의회 사무소를 보수할 근로자들을 모집하기 위해서　　정답 (C)

**169.** 캐스트로 밸리에 관해 유추할 수 있는 것은 무엇인가?
(A) 강변 지구 주변은 일년 내내 많은 만성적 교통 문제들이 있다.
(B) 만 명 이상 사람들이 취미로 도심 속 산책을 한다.
(C) 주민 인구가 지난 몇 년 동안 3배로 뛰었다.
(D) 강변 지역은 관광객들에게 인기가 좋다.　　정답 (D)

**170.** 건설 과정에서 예정되어 있는 일은 무엇인가?
(A) 도로의 가로등이 교체될 것이다.
(B) 공사장 인근 일부 주차장들은 사용이 불가할 것이다.
(C) 보행자들의 눈에 잘 띌 수 있도록 보행자용 보도가 도색될 것이다.
(D) 산책이나 조깅을 할 수 있는 별도의 보도가 건설될 것이다.　　정답 (C)

**171.** [1], [2], [3] 그리고 [4]로 표시된 곳 중에, 아래 문장이 들어가기에 가장 적절한 곳은?
　"첫 번째 보도에 대한 공사는 8월 3일에 시작될 것이며, 4월 이내에 열 곳의 모든 보도가 완료될 것이다."
(A) [1]
(B) [2]
(C) [3]
(D) [4]　　정답 (D)

**문제 172-175번은 다음 온라인 채팅 토론을 참조하시오.**

Kelly Han　　[오후 1:25]
여러분, 제가 곤란한 상황을 당했어요. (173) **도움이 필요해요.**

Isabella Choi　　[오후 1:26]
무슨 일이에요? 뭔가 잘못되었어요?

Kelly Han　　[오후 1:28]
어디에요? 사무실에 있어요, 아니면 사무실로 돌아가는 길이에요?

William Smith　　[오후 1:29]
(173) 저는 여전히 점심식사 중이에요. 15분 정도 후에 사무실로 복귀할 겁니다.

Isabella Choi　　[오후 1:30]
저는 막 들어왔어요. 제 도움이 필요해요?

Kelly Han　　[오후 1:31]
(172) 제가 제 책상 위에 중요한 서류를 두고 왔어요. 사실 30분 뒤에 있을 제 발표에 그 서류가 필요해요.

Isabella Choi　　[오후 1:32]
잠시만 있어봐요. 제가 가서 확인해볼게요.

William Smith　　[오후 1:33]
(174) **당신 발표가 목요일로 예정되어 있지 않았나요?**

Kelly Han　　[오후 1:35]
맞아요, 그랬어요. 그런데 사장님이 목요일에 한국으로 출장을 가셔야 해서 일정이 앞당겨졌어요.

Isabella Choi　　[오후 1:36]
당신이 말한 서류가 VIP Sports 사 발표 파일이에요?

Kelly Han　　[오후 1:37]
맞아요. 그 파일을 제게 서둘러서 가져다 주실 수 있어요? 저는 지금 8층에 있는 회의실에 있어요.

Isabella Choi　　[오후 1:39]
(175) **좋아요. 거기로 갈게요.**

Kelly Han　　[오후 1:40]
정말 다행이에요! 고마워요. 제가 신세 한 번 지네요.

**172.** Han 씨의 문제점은 무엇인가?
(A) 그녀는 직장까지 갈 수 있는 교통수단이 없다.
(B) 그녀의 노트북 컴퓨터가 고장 났다.
(C) 그녀가 서류를 가지고 오지 않았다.
(D) 그녀는 마감시한을 맞추기 어려울 수도 있다.　　정답 (C)

**173.** 오후 1시 29분에, Smith 씨가 "I'm still at lunch."라고 썼을 때 무엇을 의미하는가?
(A) 그는 Han 씨를 도울 수 없다.
(B) 그는 오늘 발표를 하지 않는다.
(C) 그는 지금 바로 업무를 시작할 수 없다.
(D) 그는 현재 아주 맛이 있는 점심식사를 하고 있다.　　정답 (A)

**174.** Smith 씨에 대해 유추할 수 있는 것은 무엇인가?
(A) 그는 목요일에 발표를 할 것이다.
(B) 그는 현재 VIP Sports 사에서 근무하고 있다.
(C) 그는 오늘 오후에 대형 고객과 만날 것이다.
(D) 그는 발표 일정이 변경되었다는 점을 알지 못했다.　　정답 (D)

**175.** Choi 씨는 이후에 무엇을 할 것인가?
(A) 출장을 간다.
(B) 중요한 서류를 Han 씨에게 가져다 준다.
(C) 연구를 준비한다.
(D) Smith 씨에게 이메일을 보낸다.　　정답 (B)

**문제 176-180번은 다음 이메일과 주문 양식을 참조하시오.**

수신: William Jordan ⟨wj@bellamail.com⟩
발신: Samson 전자 고객 지원부 ⟨customersupport@samson.com⟩
날짜: 1월 1일
제목: 새해맞이 할인 행사

(176) 새해를 맞이하여, Samson 전자가 큰 할인행사를 개최합니다. 이전 그 어느 때보다 더 저렴한 가격으로 귀하가 선호하는 전자 제품을 구매하실 수

있습니다. 저희 지역 매장들과 홈페이지인 www.samsonelectronics.com 에서 아주 다양한 제품들에 대해 20% 할인행사 중이며 (177/180) 1월 15일 까지 온라인에서 구매하신 모든 가전제품의 배송과 설치는 무료입니다.

무료 배송과 설치 혜택을 받기 위해서는, 온라인 주문서를 작성하실 때 간단히 FREESERVE라는 코드를 입력하시면 됩니다. 아울러 아래 상품들은 놀랍게도 30% 이상 할인됩니다.

| | |
|---|---|
| (179) **Samson 고화질 TV** | **원가: $2,170** |
| | **현재: $1,519** |
| Samson 냉장고 | 원가: $1,512 |
| | 현재: $1,059 |
| Samson 디지털 캠코더 | 원가: $482 |
| | 현재: $338 |
| (179) **Samson 전자 레인지** | **원가: $182** |
| | **현재: $128** |
| Samson 전기 난방기 | 원가: $108 |
| | 현재: $76 |

저희 Samson 전자는 항상 여러분과의 거래에 감사드립니다.

---

SAMSON 전자
"우리는 여러분 삶의 방식을 바꿉니다"
Barton Springs가 721번지
Austin, TX 78704

주문서

주문번호: X4949393　　　　　　　　(180) **날짜: 1월 4일**

성명: William Jordan
주소: Hayward가 25836번지, Hayward, CA 94542
전화번호: (510) 857-7399　　　　이메일: wj@bellamail.com

주문 내역

| | |
|---|---|
| (178) **Samson 고화질 TV** | $1,519 |
| Samson 전자 레인지 | $128 |
| 판매세 | $131.76 |
| 배송료 / FREESERVE | $0 |
| (180) **설치료 / FREESERVE** | $0 |
| 총계: | $1,778.76 |
| 신용카드: **** **** **** 0603 | |

귀하의 주문이 처리되었습니다. 매우 감사합니다.
(180) **귀하의 주문은 1월 5일에 자택으로 배송될 것입니다.**

**176.** Jordan 씨에게 이메일이 발송된 이유는 무엇인가?
　(A) 채용을 광고하기 위해서
　(B) 곧 있을 새로운 상점의 개장을 알리기 위해서
　(C) 상점 영업시간의 변경을 알리기 위해서
　(D) 다양한 할인 제품들을 광고하기 위해서　　　　정답 (D)

**177.** 이메일에 따르면, 무료 배송 혜택이 언제 완료되는가?
　(A) 1월 1일
　(B) 1월 4일
　(C) 1월 5일
　(D) 1월 15일　　　　　　　　　　　　　　　　정답 (D)

**178.** 주문서에 따르면, Jordan 씨가 주문한 제품은 무엇인가?
　(A) 고화질 TV
　(B) 냉장고
　(C) 디지털 캠코더

---

　(D) 전기 난방기　　　　　　　　　　　　　　정답 (A)

**179.** Jordan 씨가 할인 제품을 주문함으로써 절약한 액수는 얼마인가?
　(A) $128
　(B) $651
　(C) $705
　(D) $1,778　　　　　　　　　　　　　　　　정답 (C)

**180.** Jordan 씨의 주문에 관해 언급된 것은 무엇인가?
　(A) 주문은 1월 15일에 배송될 것이다.
　(B) 주문은 그의 직장으로 배송될 것이다.
　(C) 그는 무료 설치 혜택을 받았다.
　(D) 그는 현금으로 계산을 했다.　　　　　　정답 (C)

**문제 181-185번은 다음 이메일과 광고를 참조하시오.**

수신: Arizona Realty 〈luxury@arizonarealty.com〉
발신: Derrick McGuire 〈derrickmac@nsumail.com〉
날짜: 6월 25일
제목: 더 많은 정보

Joseph Lowe 씨께,

귀하께서 Arizona 남부 지역에서 임대할 아파트를 여러 개 갖고 있다고 들었습니다. (182/183) **저는 3월부터 Indigo Heights 종합병원에서 근무할 예정이라 방 2개짜리 아파트가 필요합니다.** 저희는 자동차가 없으며, 제 아내는 대중 교통을 이용할 계획입니다. (181/183) **귀하께서 근처에 괜찮은 아파트를 갖고 있으셨으면 합니다.** 어떤 것들이 가능한지 제게 연락하여 알려주시기 바랍니다.

저희는 다음 주에 Arizona에 가는데, 그때 임대가 가능한 적당한 아파트를 볼 수 있었으면 합니다. 이 주소로 관련 정보를 이메일로 보내주시거나 345-555-2490으로 팩스를 보내주십시오.

Derrick McGuire

---

Arizona 부동산
Grove가 25번지
Mohave Valley, AZ 86440

임대용 아파트

Arizona 부동산은 Arizona 주 전역에 위치한 4개의 주택단지의 대개장을 공표합니다.

SANDSTONE 가든
Silicon Fields 시내에 완벽하게 위치해 있는 침실 하나와 욕실 하나가 딸린 새 아파트로 지역 수영장에서 가까운 곳에 위치해 있습니다. 월 800달러부터 있습니다.

WILLOUGHBY 빌라
Indigo Heights 시내에 위치해 있으며, 개별 발코니와 사방으로 평화로운 전망을 가진 넓은 (183) **침실 두 개에** 화장실 하나짜리 빌라입니다. 월 950달러부터 있습니다.

LENTON 아파트
번화가인 Wellington Village에 편리하게 위치해 있고, 완전히 개조한 방 3개짜리 아파트에는 케이블 TV가 설치되어 있습니다. 가격은 월 650달러부터 있습니다.

EMBER 홀
(184) **시내의 Ember Park에서 걸어서 갈 수 있는 거리에 있는 멋진 방 3개와 욕실 2개를 갖춘 이 아파트는 아주 넓습니다.** 임대료는 월 1500달러부

터 있습니다.

맘에 드는 것이 있으십니까?

(185) 더 자세한 사항은 luxury@arizonarealty.com으로 이메일 주시거나, 818-555-2837로 전화를 주시거나 저희 사무실로 방문해 주십시오.

**181.** McGuire 씨의 주된 관심사는 무엇인가?
(A) 의료 시설의 이용 가능 여부
(B) 주택의 위치
(C) 아파트의 임대료
(D) 교통비 　　　　　　　　　　　　정답 (B)

**182.** McGuire 씨가 이사하는 이유는 무엇인가?
(A) 새로운 일을 시작하려고 한다.
(B) 그는 대학원에서 공부를 할 것이다.
(C) 그는 한적한 곳에서 살길 원한다.
(D) 그는 개인병원을 개원할 것이다. 　　　정답 (A)

**183.** McGuire 씨가 관심이 있어 할 주택은 무엇일 것 같은가?
(A) Sandstone Garden
(B) Willoughby Villas
(C) Lenton Apartments
(D) Ember Hall 　　　　　　　　　　　정답 (B)

**184.** Ember Hall에 대해 암시하고 있는 것은 무엇인가?
(A) 보수되었다.
(B) 고립되어 있다.
(C) 사람으로 붐빈다.
(D) 공원 근처에 있다. 　　　　　　　　정답 (D)

**185.** Arizona 부동산에 연락할 수 있는 방법으로 언급되지 않은 것은 무엇인가?
(A) 전화
(B) 직접 방문
(C) 이메일
(D) 팩스 　　　　　　　　　　　　　정답 (D)

**문제 186-190번은 다음 광고와 정보, 그리고 이메일을 참조하시오.**

Lake Tahoe Resort

Lake Tahoe Resort 매니저로서, 저희 리조트에 대여 가능한 네 개의 새로운 객실이 있다는 점을 알려 드리게 되어 기쁘게 생각합니다. 깊은 숲 속에 위치해 있는 저희 리조트의 다른 객실들과 달리, 이 새로운 객실들은 Lake Tahoe 바로 가장자리에 지어졌습니다. 이 고급스러운 숙박시설은 유명 인테리어 디자이너인 Selena Vasquez 씨에 의해 디자인되고 가구가 비치되었으며, 대가족을 쉽게 수용할 만큼 충분히 공간이 넓습니다. (187) 저희 리조트는 공항에서 불과 차로 25분이면 도착할 수 있는 거리에 위치해 있으며, Clarkedale 시내에서 차로 15분이면 도착할 수 있는 거리에 있고, 무료 셔틀 버스가 시내와 리조트 사이를 주기적인 일정으로 운행하고 있습니다. 리조트 활동 담당 책임자인 Colin Painter 씨가 항상 손님께서 즐기실 수 있는 재미 있는 활동들을 추천해 (186) 드릴 수 있으며, (187) 수상 스키, 제트 스키, 윈드서핑, 카약, 양궁, 그리고 하이킹 탐험 활동에 관심 있는 분들을 등록해 드립니다. (188) 저희 Lake Tahoe Resort의 객실 예약을 원하시는 분은 555-0104로 Brigitte Maltin에게 연락하시기 바랍니다.

Brandon Knight
총괄 매니저
Lake Tahoe Resort

Lake Tahoe Resort

숙박 시설 B타입: 호숫가 객실

| 객실 이름 | 침실 수 | 일일 대여 요금 | 예약 선납금 |
|---|---|---|---|
| Pine Cone | 2 | $300 | $350 |
| Forest Glen | 3 | $350 | $400 |
| Green Meadow | 2 | $275 | $300 |
| (189) Sandy Shore | 3 | $325 | $350 |

예약 선납금은 예약 시에 지불되어야 합니다.

수신: Lake Tahoe Resort 〈rentals@ltr.com〉
발신: Edward Parker 〈eparker@hanamail.com〉
날짜: 6월 25일
제목: 객실 대여

관계자께,

제가 Lake Tahoe Resort에 예약한 것과 관련된 작은 문제에 대해 도움을 주실 수 있으리란 희망을 갖고 이메일 드립니다. (188) 저는 6월 20일에 귀사의 예약 담당 직원에게 전화를 걸어 일주일 동안의 휴가 기간 동안 귀사의 새로운 (189) 침실 3개짜리 호숫가 객실 중의 한 곳에 숙박 일정을 잡았습니다. 저희는 7월 3일부터 10일까지 이 객실에 머물 계획이며, 정말 많은 기대를 하고 있습니다. 귀사의 정책에 따라, 저는 예약 담당 직원과 제 객실 예약을 최종 확정하는 동안 전화 상으로 신용카드를 이용해 예약 선납금을 지불했습니다. (189/190) 그런데 제가 350달러의 비용을 승인했음에도 불구하고, 400달러가 제 계좌에서 빠져 나간 것을 막 알게 되었습니다. 저는 이것이 그저 단순한 오해였다고 생각하고 있지만, 가능한 빨리 제 계좌로 50달러를 입금해 주실 수 있으면 감사하겠습니다. 이 일이 마무리 되는 대로 제게 알려 주십시오. 감사드리며, 7월 3일에 귀하의 리조트에 도착하기를 고대하고 있겠습니다.

Edward Parker

**186.** 광고에서, 1번째 단락의 9번째 줄에 있는 표현 "on hand"와 의미가 가장 가까운 것은?
(A) 경험 많은
(B) 필수적인
(C) 시간이 나는
(D) 유용한 　　　　　　　　　　　정답 (C)

**187.** Lake Tahoe Resort에 관해 알 수 있는 내용이 아닌 것은 무엇인가?
(A) 다양한 수상 스포츠를 위한 장비가 갖춰져 있다.
(B) 편리한 지역에 위치해 있다.
(C) 시내에 지점을 운영하고 있다.
(D) 손님들을 위해 무료 교통편을 제공한다. 　정답 (C)

**188.** Parker 씨는 6월 20일에 누구와 통화했을 가능성이 큰가?
(A) Selena Vasquez
(B) Colin Painter
(C) Brigitte Maltin
(D) Brandon Knight 　　　　　　　　정답 (C)

**189.** Parker 씨는 어느 객실을 대여하기를 바랄 가능성이 큰가?
(A) Pine Cone
(B) Forest Glen
(C) Green Meadow
(D) Sandy Shore 　　　　　　　　　정답 (D)

**190.** Parker 씨는 자신의 이메일에서 무슨 문제점을 설명하는가?

    (A) 잘못된 일일 대여 요금을 전달 받았다.

    (B) 제때 예약 선납금을 지불하지 못했다.

    (C) 숙박을 할 날짜를 변경해야 한다.

    (D) 잘못된 금액을 청구 받았다.         정답 (D)

---

문제 191-195번은 다음 일정표와 이메일, 그리고 편지를 참조하시오.

<table>
<tr><td colspan="3" align="center">Austin 현대 미술관<br>예정된 전시회</td></tr>
<tr><td>날짜</td><td>전시회 제목</td><td>행사 설명</td></tr>
<tr><td>5월 7일<br>– 10월 5일</td><td>The Moon and the Sea</td><td>뛰어난 이 그림 및 사진 수집품들은 (191) 여러 카리브해 국가들을 포함한 다양한 지역에서 온 작품들로, 여러 세기에 걸쳐 인류에 영향을 미쳐 온 달과 바다의 중요성을 묘사합니다.</td></tr>
<tr><td>5월 28일<br>– 10월 5일</td><td>Furniture Is Art</td><td>우리는 가구가 도구에 불과하다고 생각하지만, 예술품이 되기도 합니다. 이 수집품들은 (191) 유럽 전역의 여러 독특한 골동품과 현대적인 가구들을 보여 줍니다.</td></tr>
<tr><td>7월 3일<br>– 12월 18일</td><td>Dance: Art by Movement</td><td>조각품과 그림, 사진, 그리고 디지털 녹화 영상들을 통해, 이 전시회는 (191) Albania에서부터 Zambia까지 모든 국가들의 공연 예술을 특징으로 합니다.</td></tr>
<tr><td>7월 24일<br>– 8월 22일</td><td>The Photography of Animals</td><td>이 전시회는 매혹적인 작품들의 모음으로서, (191) 전 세계의 다양한 야생 동물을 촬영한 사진들을 특징으로 합니다.</td></tr>
</table>

입장권에 관한 더 많은 정보가 필요하신 분은, 저희 웹사이트를 방문하시거나 cedlecon@magob.org로 이메일을 보내시기 바랍니다. (192) 모든 회원들께는 2장의 무료 입장권을 제공해 드립니다. 회원이 되시려면, 회원 자격 페이지를 방문하십시오.

---

수신: Charlie Deleon 〈Blan@Cdelion.margob.org〉

발신: Molly Hudson 〈mhudson@mason.inet〉

날짜: 5월 1일

제목: 입장권

(192) 저는 Dance: Art by Movement 전시회에 대한 무료 입장권을 갖고 있지만, 2장의 입장권을 더 구입하고자 합니다. 제 신용카드 정보가 귀사의 데이터베이스에 있으리라 확신합니다. 따라서, 제 신용카드로 비용 처리를 하시고 우편으로 입장권을 보내 주시겠습니까? (193) 저는 Furniture Is Art를 관람하기 위해 기다려 왔습니다. 이 멋진 전시회를 열어 주신 것에 대해 감사 드립니다.

Molly Hudson

---

5월 3일

Molly Hudson

사서함 N–123

NASSAU N.P.

Hudson 씨께,

---

Austin 현대 미술관의 고객이 되어 주신 것에 대해 감사드립니다. (193) 귀하께서 기다려 오신 전시회가 취소되었다는 사실을 알려 드리게 되어 유감스럽게 생각합니다. 제가 2장의 추가 입장권을 동봉해 드렸습니다. 이는 취소된 전시회를 대체하는 것입니다. 새로운 전시회는 Indigenous Cultures of the Americas라고 불리며, 순회 전시회로서 12월 18일까지 저희 미술관에서 (194) 진행될 예정입니다. 이 전시회에선 Barry Gilpin의 작품을 포함한 여러 점의 유명한 작품을 보실 수 있습니다. (195) 귀하의 JPax 신용카드로 24달러의 비용이 청구되었습니다.

Charlie Deleon

Austin 현대 미술관

첨부물

**191.** 일정표에 따르면, 모든 전시회는 무엇이 공통점인가?

    (A) 사진들을 포함한다.

    (B) 라이브 공연을 포함한다.

    (C) 카리브해 지역 출신 작가들의 작품을 특징으로 한다.

    (D) 다양한 국가에서 온 작품들을 특징으로 한다.     정답 (D)

**192.** Hudson 씨에 관해 알 수 있는 것은 무엇인가?

    (A) 환불을 요청하고 있다.

    (B) 해당 미술관의 회원 자격을 보유하고 있다.

    (C) 현대 미술가이다.

    (D) 이미 전시회들을 관람했다.     정답 (B)

**193.** 어느 전시회가 취소되었는가?

    (A) The Moon and the Sea

    (B) Furniture Is Art

    (C) Dance: Art in Movement

    (D) The Photography of Animals     정답 (B)

**194.** 편지에서, 1번째 단락 4번째 줄의 단어 "features"와 의미가 가장 가까운 어휘는 무엇인가?

    (A) 보여준다

    (B) 관리한다

    (C) 옮긴다

    (D) 덮는다     정답 (A)

**195.** Deleon 씨는 Hudson 씨를 위해 무엇을 했는가?

    (A) 다가오는 행사의 목록을 우송했다.

    (B) 전시회 날짜를 변경했다.

    (C) 예약을 확인해 주었다.

    (D) 신용카드에 비용을 청구했다.     정답 (D)

---

문제 196-200번은 다음 이메일들과 첨부 파일을 참조하시오.

수신: Mary Benson; Ramona Taylor; James Porter

발신: Tim Rolland

날짜: 6월 12일, 오후 7:54

제목: 사무실 공간

첨부: 건물들

안녕하세요, 여러분,

(198) 저는 지난 월요일에 Manke Grill에서 있었던 우리의 오찬이 대단히 즐거웠습니다. AHG Consultants의 직원으로서, 저는 Alamo 지역에서 우리의 첫 지사를 열기 위한 팀의 일부가 된 것이 흥분됩니다. 모임을 갖는 동안, 저는 우리의 첫 고객을 얻기 위해, 그리고 (196) Alamo 지역의 기업가들에게 정보 기술이 그들의 목적을 달성하는 데 얼마나 도움이 될지에 관한 조언을 제공하는 일을 시작하기 위한 우리의 노력을 느꼈습니다.

여러분께서 적합할 것 같은 타입의 사무용 공간에 관한 의견을 제게 제공해 주실 수 있다면 감사하겠습니다. 저는 우리의 기본 조건과 예산에 어울릴 만한 좋은 조건을 갖춘 것들을 찾기 위해 Syeogain.ca를 검색해 봤으며, 여러분께서 결정하실 수 있도록 최종 목록을 만들기 위해 정보를 요약했습니다. 첨부해 드린 문서를 읽어 보시고 여러분의 의견과 함께 제게 답변해 주시기 바랍니다.

Tim Rolland
AHG Consultants

---

3874 Thunderland Hilltop
보행자들이 많은 잘 개발된 시골 지역인 Alamo에 위치한 개방된 컨셉트의 사무실/소매점 공간. 건물은 놀랄 만한 외관과 함께 회사용으로 된 간판에 필요한 충분한 공간을 지니고 있습니다. 뛰어난 에너지 효율을 지닌 난방 시스템이 매년 지출 비용을 감소시켜 줄 것입니다.
월 임대료: 1,000달러

29485 Clearance Path
1층 사무실. 고급스럽게 장식되어 있음. 보안용 담장으로 둘러싸인 구내 주차장. Gasi Browse Park 인근에 위치해 있으며, 근처에 기차역이 있고, 시내에서 20분 거리임. (197) Joo Park의 보행로로 운동하는 사람들에게 매우 인기가 높습니다. Vodafone 전화 시스템이 사용 가능하도록 이미 설치되어 있습니다.
월 임대료: 950달러

4991 Commercial Park Lot
공용이 아닌 단층 건물. 유명 디자이너들이 제작한 가구가 갖춰져 있음. 거리 근처에 안전한 주차장이 있으며 세입자들에게는 할인 제공. 고속 인터넷 이용 서비스가 선택에 따라 설치될 수 있습니다. 도심의 서쪽 지역에 있는 쇼핑 구역에 위치해 있음.
월 임대료: 875달러

(200) 1432 Timothy Street
4층짜리 사무용 복합 건물. 보안 시스템과 경비 직원을 포함한 지붕이 설치된 주차 공간. (200) Alamo의 주요 상업 지구 바깥에 위치해 있음. 컬러 복사기/스캐너/프린터/팩스 기계와 같은 사무용 장비가 사용 가능하도록 준비되어 있습니다. 최신 기술 장비 및 무료 고속 무선 인터넷이 포함된 화상 회의용 스튜디오 포함.
월 임대료: 1,000달러

---

수신: Mary Benson; Tim Rolland; (199) Ramona Taylor
발신: James Porter
날짜: 6월 15일, 오후 4:39
제목: 회신: 사무실 공간

여러분께,

우리가 확인해 봤어야 하는 선택권들의 범위를 좁혀 주셔서 감사합니다, Tim. (198) 저는 지난 월요일의 팀 회의가 매우 잘 진행되었다고 생각합니다. 저도 그곳에 있었다면 기뻤겠지만, Toronto로의 제 출장은 불가피했습니다. 제 생각에 제가 이메일을 통해 의견을 전달해 드리는 마지막 사람인 것 같습니다. 여러분의 인내에 감사 드립니다.

(199/200) Ramona, 저는 넓은 공간이 있는 사무실이 마음에 들지만, 저는 우리가 시내 한복판에 위치하지 않는 것이 좋을 것 같다고 생각합니다. Alamo 지역의 대중 교통 시스템을 잘 아는 분이 계신가요? 우리가 통근을 위해 이용할 경우 알아 두면 도움이 될 겁니다.

저는 또한 우리가 Alamo에서 열리는 기술 박람회에 참석해야 한다는 Tim의 의견에 동의합니다. 저는 다음 주말에 제 주택 선택권을 알아보러 그 근처에서 약속을 잡았는데 그때 방문할 예정입니다. 또한, 저는 우리 AHG Consultants에서 근무한 적이 있었던 Alamo의 대표자와 함께 점심 식사

---

를 할 예정입니다. 전해 드릴 소식이 생길 경우 여러분께 알려 드리겠습니다.

James Porter
AHG Consultants

**196.** Rolland 씨는 누구일 가능성이 가장 큰가?
(A) 기술 컨설턴트
(B) Manke Grill의 직원
(C) 컨퍼런스 조직자
(D) 부동산 중개업체 직원 　　　　정답 (A)

**197.** 첨부 문서에 언급된 한 건물의 특징은 무엇인가?
(A) 직원들을 위한 샤워실
(B) 건물 내의 인기 레스토랑
(C) 소유주에 의해 지불되는 전기세
(D) 운동에 적합한 공원로와 가까운 위치 　　　정답 (D)

**198.** Porter 씨에 관해 알 수 있는 것은 무엇인가?
(A) Manke Grill에서의 모임을 놓쳤다.
(B) 자신의 차량을 파는 것을 고려 중이다.
(C) 공연에 참석할 계획이다.
(D) 버스로 Alamo 시를 관광할 것이다. 　　정답 (A)

**199.** Taylor 씨에 관해 알 수 있는 것은 무엇인가?
(A) 막 새로운 집으로 이사했다.
(B) 과거의 고객을 만날 것이다.
(C) 자신의 동료 직원들에게 이메일을 보냈다.
(D) 과거에 Alamo에 거주한 적이 있었다. 　　정답 (C)

**200.** Porter 씨는 어느 건물을 마음에 들어 할 가능성이 큰가?
(A) 3874 Thunderland Hilltop
(B) 29485 Clearance Path
(C) 4991 Commercial Park Lot
(D) 1432 Timothy Street 　　　정답 (D)

## Actual Test 03

### Part 1

**1.** 영W
(A) They are taking off their jackets.
(B) They are examining a piece of paper.
(C) They are searching through a backpack.
(D) They are reading a diagram on the blackboard.

(A) 그들은 상의를 벗고 있다.
(B) 그들은 서류를 검토하고 있다.
(C) 그들은 배낭을 조사하고 있다.
(D) 그들은 칠판에 있는 도표를 읽고 있다. 　　　정답 (B)

**2.** 미W
(A) Stone stairs lead down to the outdoor market.
(B) Both the road and the sidewalk are crowded.
(C) A set of escalators are located near some railroad tracks.
(D) Some people are disembarking from the train.

(A) 돌계단이 야외시장으로 이어지고 있다.
(B) 도로와 인도가 모두 붐비고 있다.
(C) 에스컬레이터가 철로 근처에 위치하고 있다.
(D) 몇몇 사람들이 열차에서 하차하고 있다. 　　　정답 (C)

**3.** 호M
(A) Some people are walking through a park.
(B) Some people are waiting at the railroad crossing.
(C) Some people are wheeling their bags on the floor.
(D) Some people are boarding a flight on the runway.

(A) 몇몇 사람들이 공원을 가로질러 가고 있다.
(B) 몇몇 사람들이 기차 건널목에서 대기하고 있다.
(C) 몇몇 사람들이 바퀴가 달린 가방들을 끌고 있다.
(D) 몇몇 사람들이 활주로에 있는 비행기에 탑승하고 있다. 　정답 (C)

**4.** 미M
(A) Fruit is being picked from a tree.
(B) The flowers are in full bloom.
(C) A piece of wood is being measured.
(D) Some flowers have been planted near the fence.

(A) 과일이 나무에서 수확되고 있다.
(B) 꽃들이 만개해 있다.
(C) 나무토막의 크기가 측정되고 있다.
(D) 몇몇 꽃들이 울타리 근처에 심어져 있다. 　　　정답 (B)

**5.** 호M
(A) She's mowing the lawn in a garden.
(B) She's fixing a sawing machine.
(C) She's walking beneath a tree.
(D) She's pushing a wheelbarrow.

(A) 그녀는 정원의 잔디를 깎고 있다.
(B) 그녀는 전기톱을 수리하고 있다.
(C) 그녀는 나무 밑을 걸어가고 있다.
(D) 그녀는 외발손수레를 밀고 있다. 　　　정답 (D)

**6.** 영W
(A) Some guitars are being displayed on a wall.
(B) A large audience is watching a concert.
(C) A cable is being connected to some equipment.
(D) Lights have been turned off in a store.

(A) 몇몇 기타들이 벽에 진열되어 있다.
(B) 많은 청중이 연주회를 관람하고 있다.
(C) 한 케이블이 장비에 연결되고 있다.
(D) 상점 내 조명들이 꺼져 있다. 　　　정답 (A)

### Part 2

**7.** 미M 영W
When is the next available flight to Tokyo?
(A) At the local airport.
(B) In about half an hour.
(C) No, it hasn't arrived yet.

Tokyo로 가는 다음 비행기는 언제 있나요?
(A) 지역 공항에서요.
(B) 대략 30분 후에요.
(C) 아니오, 아직 도착하지 않았어요. 　　　정답 (B)

**8.** 미W 미M
Where's the file cabinet?
(A) At 11 o'clock.
(B) Next to Ms. Smith's desk.
(C) We need some file folders.

서류함은 어디에 있어요?
(A) 11시에요.
(B) Smith 씨 책상 옆이요.
(C) 우리는 서류철이 몇 개 필요해요. 　　　정답 (B)

**9.** 미M 영W
Who will be attending the upcoming computer technology seminar?
(A) The performance was better than we had expected.
(B) It hasn't been decided yet.
(C) Ms. Coleman was present at the meeting.

곧 개최될 컴퓨터 기술 세미나에는 누가 참석하나요?
(A) 성능이 기대한 것보다 더 좋아요.
(B) 아직 결정된 바 없습니다.
(C) Coleman 씨는 회의에 참석 중이었어요. 　　　정답 (B)

**10.** 호M 영W
You should rewrite the sales report, shouldn't you?
(A) No, it's a little expensive.
(B) Yes, I'll do that tomorrow.
(C) The annual sale ended last week.

영업 보고서를 다시 작성하셔야 하죠, 그렇지 않나요?
(A) 아니오, 그건 조금 비싸요.
(B) 네, 내일 할 겁니다.
(C) 연례 할인 행사는 지난주에 끝났어요. 　　　정답 (B)

**11.** 영W 미M
Is the new memorandum posted on the bulletin board?
(A) No, some posts are still vacant.
(B) Yes, I've just read it.
(C) Just write him a memo and let him know.

새 회람이 게시판에 올라가 있나요?
(A) 아니오, 몇몇 자리는 여전히 공석입니다.

(B) 네, 방금 읽었어요.
(C) 그에게 메모를 써서 알려주세요. 정답 (B)

**12.** 미M 미W
Do you think it will snow tomorrow?
(A) Yes, she will.
(B) That's what the radio announcer said.
(C) I'll show you around.

내일 눈이 올까요?
(A) 네, 그녀는 그럴 겁니다.
(B) 라디오 아나운서가 그렇게 말하더군요.
(C) 제가 주변을 보여 드릴게요. 정답 (B)

**13.** 영W 호M
Did you receive the floor plans for our new manufacturing plant?
(A) That sounds like a great idea.
(B) Yes, it's very noisy in here.
(C) Well, when did you send them?

새로운 제조 공장에 대한 평면도를 받았나요?
(A) 그거 참 좋은 생각이네요.
(B) 네, 여기는 굉장히 시끄러워요.
(C) 음, 언제 보냈는데요? 정답 (C)

**14.** 영W 미M
When will the new warehouse be completed?
(A) We're temporarily out of stock now.
(B) There is one across the street.
(C) Not for another month.

새로운 창고는 언제 완공되나요?
(A) 지금 일시적으로 재고가 없어요.
(B) 길 건너편에 하나 있어요.
(C) 한 달은 더 있어야 합니다. 정답 (C)

**15.** 호M 미W
Weren't we supposed to have a meeting at 2 o'clock?
(A) About a hundred guests.
(B) Sorry. I was stuck in traffic.
(C) A full agreement on various items on the agenda.

우리가 2시에 회의하기로 하지 않았나요?
(A) 대략 100명의 손님들이요.
(B) 미안해요. 길이 너무 막혔어요.
(C) 다양한 안건에 대한 전적인 동의요. 정답 (B)

**16.** 영W 미M
Do you want to wear a jacket in case it gets cold?
(A) It was very cold yesterday.
(B) Yes, she called in sick this morning.
(C) No, I'll be in the office the whole day.

추워질 경우를 대비해서 재킷을 입으시겠어요?
(A) 어제 굉장히 추웠어요.
(B) 네, 그녀는 오늘 아침에 아파서 출근을 못한다고 전화했어요.
(C) 아니오, 오늘 하루 종일 사무실에만 있을 겁니다. 정답 (C)

**17.** 미W 영W
How did you hear about the computer graphic designer job?
(A) You can start your new job on Wednesday.
(B) The online education course was very informative.

(C) I saw a job advertisement in a local newspaper.

컴퓨터 그래픽 디자이너 직 소식은 어떻게 알았습니까?
(A) 새로운 일은 수요일부터 시작하실 수 있어요.
(B) 온라인 교육 과정이 굉장히 유익했어요.
(C) 한 지역 신문에 올라온 구인 광고를 봤습니다. 정답 (C)

**18.** 호M 미W
My car is still in the repair shop, so I can't give you a ride to work today.
(A) Thank you very much.
(B) Utilities are included in the rent.
(C) I can ask Isabella for a ride.

제 차가 여전히 정비소에서 수리 중이라서 오늘은 직장까지 태워드릴 수 없겠네요.
(A) 정말 감사합니다.
(B) 공공요금은 임대료에 포함되어 있어요.
(C) Isabella에게 태워달라고 요청할 수 있어요. 정답 (C)

**19.** 미M 영W
Excuse me, but is there a newer version of this accounting software program?
(A) It'll come next year.
(B) Some computer programmers.
(C) Yes, but he's on the phone now.

실례합니다만, 새로 나온 회계 프로그램은 없나요?
(A) 내년에 출시됩니다.
(B) 몇몇 컴퓨터 프로그래머들이요.
(C) 네, 그런데 그는 지금 통화중이에요. 정답 (A)

**20.** 미W 호M
What was the in-flight meal like when you went to Toronto last week?
(A) A reservation for four people.
(B) I slept through the flight.
(C) Consider a hotel that offers a complimentary breakfast.

지난주에 Toronto로 갈 때 기내식은 어땠어요?
(A) 네 명 예약이요.
(B) 비행하는 내내 잤어요.
(C) 무료 아침식사를 제공하는 호텔을 고려하세요. 정답 (B)

**21.** 영W 미M
Are you sure that the express train arrives at 1 o'clock?
(A) They already left for Boston.
(B) I've already checked the schedule twice.
(C) About two months of training.

급행 열차가 1시에 도착하는 게 확실한가요?
(A) 그들은 이미 Boston을 향해 출발했어요.
(B) 이미 일정표를 두 번이나 확인했어요.
(C) 대략 두 달 간의 교육 과정이에요. 정답 (B)

**22.** 호M 미W
Did you read the business magazine this afternoon?
(A) No, it's very useful information.
(B) Some leading companies.
(C) Yes, there was an article about our new product.

오늘 오후에 비즈니스 잡지를 읽었나요?

(A) 아니오, 그건 아주 유용한 정보였어요.
(B) 몇몇 업계를 선도하는 회사들이요.
(C) 네, 우리 신상품에 대한 기사가 있더군요.　　　정답 (C)

**23.** 미M 영W
Mr. Kuko revised the budget projections, didn't he?
(A) Yes, I'm sure he will.
(B) Due to the budget cuts.
(C) No, he didn't have a chance to do that yet.

Kuko 씨가 예산 예상안을 수정했죠, 그렇지 않나요?
(A) 네, 그가 할 것이라고 생각해요.
(B) 예산 삭감 때문에요.
(C) 아니오, 그는 그럴 기회가 없었어요.　　　정답 (C)

**24.** 호M 미W
Will you please update me with the production schedule?
(A) We have some state-of-the-art equipment.
(B) Sure, I definitely will.
(C) Yes, I've already updated your meeting schedule.

생산 일정에 대한 새로운 소식을 제게 전해 주시겠어요?
(A) 우리는 최신 장비를 보유하고 있어요.
(B) 물론이에요, 그렇게 할게요.
(C) 네, 이미 당신의 회의 일정을 수정했어요.　　　정답 (B)

**25.** 영W 미M
Could you help me with this new photocopier?
(A) Nice photos, I think.
(B) 20 double-sided copies, please.
(C) I'll be right back.

이 새로운 복사기 다루는 것을 도와주실 수 있나요?
(A) 좋은 사진 같아요.
(B) 양면 복사로 20부 부탁드려요.
(C) 곧 돌아올게요.　　　정답 (C)

**26.** 미W 호M
Why don't you leave right after dinner?
(A) It was really delicious.
(B) One of the nearby restaurants.
(C) That's too late. I might not catch the bus.

저녁식사 직후에 떠나는 것은 어떠세요?
(A) 그건 정말 맛있었어요.
(B) 근처에 있는 식당 중 한 곳이요.
(C) 그건 너무 늦어요. 버스를 못 탈 수 있어요.　　　정답 (C)

**27.** 미M 영W
Did you contact Mr. McDonald about repairing the cooling unit?
(A) Yes, he'll be arriving shortly.
(B) It is very hot outside today.
(C) You should call the Maintenance Department.

냉각기 수리와 관련해서 McDonald 씨에게 연락을 했나요?
(A) 네, 그는 곧 도착할 거예요.
(B) 오늘 밖이 엄청 더워요.
(C) 시설 관리 부서에 연락하셔야 해요.　　　정답 (A)

**28.** 호M 영W
Would you like to join us for lunch tomorrow?
(A) Here is your bill.

(B) Yes, I joined the company last year.
(C) I'd like to, but I have other plans.

내일 우리와 함께 점심식사를 하시겠어요?
(A) 여기 계산서입니다.
(B) 네, 저는 작년에 입사했어요.
(C) 그러고는 싶지만, 선약이 있어요.　　　정답 (C)

**29.** 미M 미W
The day after tomorrow is the last day to sign up for the accounting course the company offers.
(A) Please sign at the bottom of the page.
(B) Oh, thanks for reminding me. I almost forgot.
(C) Yes, you can use my pen.

모레가 회사에서 제공하는 회계 강좌에 등록할 수 있는 마지막 날이에요.
(A) 페이지 하단에 서명해 주세요.
(B) 아, 알려주셔서 감사해요. 깜빡하고 있었어요.
(C) 네, 제 펜을 사용하셔도 됩니다.　　　정답 (B)

**30.** 영W 미M
Are we going to discuss some marketing strategies at the staff meeting?
(A) The markets did well last year.
(B) Haven't you read the agenda?
(C) No, formal attire is required.

직원 회의에서 마케팅 전략들에 대해 논의할 예정인가요?
(A) 작년에 시장 상황이 좋았어요.
(B) 안건을 읽어보지 않았나요?
(C) 아니오, 정장을 입어야 합니다.　　　정답 (B)

**31.** 미W 호M
Do you need some help with the annual report, or can you do it yourself?
(A) I'm almost done.
(B) It should take about three days.
(C) Thanks. I think that was very helpful.

연간 보고서를 작성하는 데 도움이 필요하신가요, 아니면 혼자서 하실 수 있나요?
(A) 거의 다 마무리되었어요.
(B) 약 3일이 걸릴 겁니다.
(C) 고맙습니다. 큰 도움이 되었어요.　　　정답 (A)

## Part 3

문제 32-34번은 다음 대화를 참조하시오. 미M 미W

M: Hi, (32) **Ms. Smith.** I'm sorry I missed the staff meeting yesterday. Can you tell me what I missed?
W: No problem, Mr. Cole. (32/33) **At the meeting, I announced that we will be having extended store hours during the holiday season.**
M: That's probably a good idea with the rush of holiday shoppers. Will working extra hours be a requirement?
W: (34) **We are making it optional and will hire temporary employees to achieve our sales goal for this holiday season.**

M: 안녕하세요, Smith 씨. 어제 직원 회의에 빠져서 죄송합니다. 제가 어제

회의에서 놓친 내용이 무엇인지 알려주실 수 있나요?

W: 물론이에요, Cole 씨. 어제 회의에서 저는 연휴기간 동안 매장 영업시간을 연장할 것임을 발표했어요.

M: 연휴기간에 고객들이 많이 몰려든다는 점을 고려하면 좋은 생각이에요. 초과 근무를 하는 것은 필수사항인가요?

W: 그건 선택사항으로 할 것이고요, 이번 연휴기간 동안의 매출 목표를 달성하기 위해서 임시 직원들을 채용할 계획이에요.

**32.** 여자는 누구일 것 같은가?
(A) 고객
(B) 매장 매니저
(C) 마케팅 직원
(D) 임시 직원 　　　　　　　　　　　정답 (B)

**33.** 영업시간이 변경된 이유는 무엇인가?
(A) 매출이 급격하게 하락했다.
(B) 인력이 부족하다.
(C) 곧 연휴기간이 시작된다.
(D) 연례 할인 행사가 실시될 것이다. 　　정답 (C)

**34.** 여자는 이후에 무엇을 할 것 같은가?
(A) 새로운 직원들을 채용한다.
(B) 매장을 방문한다.
(C) 새로운 목표를 설정한다.
(D) 제품을 반품한다. 　　　　　　　　정답 (A)

**문제 35-37번은 다음의 3자 대화를 참조하시오.** 〔미W〕〔미M〕〔영W〕

W1: Mr. Powell, do you have some free time after lunch? (35) **We're preparing a new marketing campaign for Soft Touch, and we'd like your help.**

M: Oh, that's our latest skin lotion, isn't it? But I heard the marketing campaign was finalized last Friday.

W2: Yes, (36) **the commercials started airing on television last month, but since then, our sales have consistently dropped.**

M: Um... is there a problem with the commercials?

W1: Some people took issue with some of the expressions used in them. We have also received some negative feedback from customers.

W2: Please assist us in creating some new commercials. I have a few ideas on how to improve the current ones.

M: I'd be happy to help. (37) **Why don't we meet in my office at 3? I'll think about it during lunch and share my thoughts with you at our meeting.**

--------------------------------------------------

W1: Powell 씨, 점심 후에 시간 있으세요? Soft Touch를 위한 새로운 마케팅 캠페인을 준비하는 중인데요, 당신의 도움이 필요해서요.

M: 아, 그게 최신 스킨 로션 제품이 맞죠? 하지만 마케팅 캠페인은 지난주 금요일에 마무리된 것으로 알고 있는데요.

W1: 네, 지난달부터 TV 광고를 방송하기 시작했는데, 그때부터 매출이 지속적으로 하락하고 있어요.

M: 음… 광고에 어떤 문제가 있나요?

W1: 사람들이 광고에 담긴 일부 표현들을 문제 삼았어요. 또한 고객들로부터 부정적인 의견도 받았어요.

W2: 새로운 광고의 제작을 도와주셨으면 합니다. 현재의 광고를 개선시킬 수 있는 몇 가지 방안이 있어요.

M: 기꺼이 도와드릴게요. 제 사무실에서 3시에 만나는 것이 어떨까요? 점심시간 동안 제가 생각을 해보고 회의에서 의견을 나누도록 할게요.

**35.** 화자들은 누구이겠는가?
(A) TV 보도 기자
(B) 영업 사원
(C) 마케팅 전문가
(D) 레스토랑 요리사 　　　　　　　　정답 (C)

**36.** 주요 문제점은 무엇인가?
(A) 신제품의 공급이 부족하다.
(B) 광고 효과가 수익으로 이어지지 않았다.
(C) 새로운 마케팅 캠페인 비용이 너무 많이 소요된다.
(D) 일부 방송 장비가 제대로 작동하지 않는다. 　정답 (B)

**37.** 남자는 오늘 오후에 무엇을 할 것인가?
(A) 설문조사를 시행한다.
(B) 고객들과 만난다.
(C) 새로운 샴푸를 사용한다.
(D) 의견을 나눈다. 　　　　　　　　　정답 (D)

**문제 38-40번은 다음 대화를 참조하시오.** 〔미M〕〔미W〕

M: Ms. Keller, are you having any difficulties making copies? I've been trying to copy some documents, but nothing happens when I press the copy button.

W: (38) **Oh, you must be using the brand-new copier at reception.** It's quite complicated to operate, so the Human Resources supervisor sent all employees an e-mail with helpful directions on how to use it. Did you see the e-mail?

M: No, I didn't. I just got back this morning after being in New York for a weeklong trip.

W: (40) **I can show you how to work it after lunch.** (39) **You should also check your e-mail account** and read the directions for the machine.

--------------------------------------------------

M: Keller 씨, 복사하는 데 문제가 있나요? 문서를 복사하려고 했지만 복사기의 버튼을 눌러도 전혀 작동하지 않네요.

W: 아, 접수처에 있는 새 복사기를 사용하셨나 봅니다. 작동 방법이 꽤 복잡해서 인사부장이 모든 직원들에게 새로운 복사기를 사용하는 데 도움이 되는 사항들을 이메일로 보냈어요. 그 이메일을 보셨나요?

M: 아뇨, 못 봤어요. 일주일 간의 New York 출장을 마치고 오늘 아침에야 돌아왔거든요.

W: 제가 점심식사를 마치고 사용법을 알려드릴게요. 당신의 이메일 계정도 확인하고 복사기 사용법도 읽어보세요.

**38.** 여자에 따르면 최근에 구매된 것은 무엇인가?
(A) 복사기
(B) 휴대전화
(C) 카메라
(D) 노트북 컴퓨터 　　　　　　　　　정답 (A)

**39.** 여자가 남자에 요청하는 것은 무엇인가?
(A) 할인을 제공할 것
(B) 사진을 보낼 것
(C) 이메일을 확인할 것
(D) 컴퓨터의 전원을 끌 것 　　　　　　정답 (C)

**40.** 여자는 이후에 무엇을 할 것 같은가?
(A) 잉크를 구매할 것이다.
(B) 복사기를 수리할 것이다.

(C) 유사 제품을 구매할 것이다.
(D) 남자가 복사를 할 수 있도록 도움을 줄 것이다.　　　정답 (D)

**문제 41-43번은 다음 대화를 참조하시오.** 미W 미M

W: Hello. **(41) I'm calling regarding an ink cartridge I ordered for my copy machine that hasn't arrived yet.** Can you please let me know the status of this order, please?
M: Delivery usually takes three business days at the most, but sometimes there may be a delay. Can you tell me your account number, please?
W: The name of the company is the Decanix Corporation, and the account number is 510-924-7332. **(42) I ordered it on January 10.**
M: Let me see. Yes, **(43) your order was shipped out on January 15. It should be there tomorrow.**

----

W: 안녕하세요. 제가 복사기에 쓸 잉크 카트리지를 주문했는데 아직 도착하지 않아요. 주문 상태를 알려주실 수 있나요?
M: 보통은 물품 배송에 길어야 영업일 기준으로 3일이 걸리는데, 때로는 늦어지는 경우도 있습니다. 고객님 계정 번호를 좀 알려 주시겠습니까?
W: 회사 이름은 Decanix Corporation이고 계정 번호는 510-924-7332입니다. 1월 10일에 주문했어요.
M: 잠시만요. 네, 주문하신 제품이 1월 15일에 배송되었네요. 내일이면 도착할 겁니다.

**41.** 여자가 전화한 이유는 무엇인가?
(A) 환불을 요청하기 위해서
(B) 주문을 취소하기 위해서
(C) 배송 상태를 확인하기 위해서
(D) 배송 주소를 변경하기 위해서　　　정답 (C)

**42.** 여자는 언제 주문을 했는가?
(A) 1월 5일
(B) 1월 10일
(C) 1월 13일
(D) 1월 15일　　　정답 (B)

**43.** 남자는 내일 어떤 일이 발생할 것이라고 언급하는가?
(A) 복사기가 수리될 것이다.
(B) 서류가 우편으로 발송될 것이다.
(C) 배송품이 배달될 것이다.
(D) 최근에 한 주문이 취소될 것이다.　　　정답 (C)

**문제 44-46번은 다음의 3자 대화를 참조하시오.** 미W 영W 미M

W1: **(44) One of my colleagues went to see the new musical last Saturday.** She said it was really great.
W2: **(44) My sister went two weeks ago, and she said it was terrible.** Several actors missed their lines, and the light cues were all off!
M: Things usually don't go smoothly during the first few shows.
W1: You're right. Sometimes it requires time and effort to work out some problems.
W2: Should we check it out?
W1: Sounds like fun. Why don't we see it on Friday night?
M: A night out would do us some good! **(45) But today is**

Wednesday. Reservations for a Friday night show might not be possible if not made on a Monday or a Tuesday.
W1: Then **(46) I think we should reserve seats as soon as possible.**

----

W1: 제 직장동료가 지난 토요일에 새로 공연하는 뮤지컬을 봤어요. 그 뮤지컬이 너무나 좋았다고 하더라고요.
W2: 제 여동생도 2주 전에 봤는데 아주 형편없었다고 하던데요. 몇몇 배우들은 대사를 놓치고 조명은 다 꺼졌다고 하네요!
M: 초기 몇 번의 공연에서는 모든 것이 그다지 순조롭지 않지요.
W1: 맞아요. 때때로 문제점들을 해결하기 위해서는 시간과 노력이 필요해요.
W2: 그럼 우리가 가서 확인해 볼까요?
W1: 재미있겠는데요. 금요일 밤에 관람하는 것은 어떨까요?
M: 하룻밤 노는 것이 나쁠 건 없죠! 그렇지만 오늘이 수요일이에요. 금요일 저녁 공연 예약은 월요일이나 화요일에 이루어지지 않으면 쉽지가 않아요.
W1: 그러면 좌석을 최대한 빨리 예약해야 할 것 같아요.

**44.** 화자들은 무엇에 관해 이야기하는가?
(A) 극장을 보수하는 것
(B) 지역 행사에 참여하는 것
(C) 회의 일정을 정하는 것
(D) 공연을 관람하는 것　　　정답 (D)

**45.** 남자가 "But today is Wednesday."라고 말할 때 암시하는 바는 무엇인가?
(A) 이사진이 성급한 결정을 내렸다.
(B) 몇몇 동료들이 오늘이 무슨 요일인지 혼동하고 있다.
(C) 마감일이 얼마 남지 않았다.
(D) 금요일 밤 공연에 대한 표가 매진되었을 수도 있다.　　　정답 (D)

**46.** 화자들은 이후에 무엇을 할 것 같은가?
(A) 다른 영화를 관람할 것이다.
(B) 의자를 구매할 것이다.
(C) 표를 예매할 것이다.
(D) 다른 때에 다시 방문할 것이다.　　　정답 (C)

**문제 47-49번은 다음 대화를 참조하시오.** 영W 호M

W: Sorry to bother you, but my friend is an employee here, and **(47) she mentioned that your newspaper is advertising for a new photographer. (48) I have 5 years of experience in photographic journalism, so I was hoping to speak to someone about the position.**
M: **(48) Mr. Thompson is the Human Resources supervisor, and he's in charge of all recruitment matters.** However, I'm afraid he's really busy right now, so I recommend that you make an appointment to meet with him.
W: Oh, that sounds fine, but I wonder if he has a few spare minutes to answer a couple of quick questions.
M: Well, **(49) I seriously doubt he has time, but I'll call his office and check.** Can I have your name, please?

----

W: 실례합니다만, 제 친구가 귀사의 직원인데, 이 신문사에서 새로운 사진작가를 구한다고 알려줬어요. 저는 5년간 언론 매체의 사진을 담당한 경력이 있는데, 채용에 관해 이야기를 하고 싶습니다.
M: Thompson 씨가 인사부장이고 채용 문제를 담당하고 있어요. 하지만 지금은 그가 굉장히 바빠서 그와 만날 약속을 잡는 것이 좋을 것 같네요.
W: 아, 그게 좋겠네요. 하지만 두세 가지 짧은 질문에 답변해 줄 몇 분의 여

유 시간이 없으실까요?

M: 글쎄요, 그가 그럴 여유가 없는 것 같지만 그의 사무실에 전화해서 확인해 보겠습니다. 성함이 어떻게 되시죠?

**47.** 남자가 근무하는 곳은 어디인가?
(A) 취업 대행사
(B) 신문사
(C) 미술관
(D) 광고회사 　　　　　　　　　　　　　　　　정답 (B)

**48.** 여자가 Thompson 씨와 이야기해야 하는 이유는 무엇인가?
(A) 구인 중인 직책에 관해 이야기하기 위해서
(B) 서비스에 대해 항의하기 위해서
(C) 잡지 기사를 위한 인터뷰를 하기 위해서
(D) 서류를 요청하기 위해서 　　　　　　　　정답 (A)

**49.** 남자는 이후에 무엇을 할 것 같은가?
(A) 이력서를 제출한다.
(B) 약속 시간을 변경한다.
(C) 면접 일정을 정한다.
(D) 그의 동료에게 연락한다. 　　　　　　　　정답 (D)

**문제 50-52번은 다음 대화를 참조하시오.** 미M 미W

M: Hi. **(50/51) You had a dress on this mannequin yesterday. I found a few, but not in the right size. Would you happen to have one in a size 12?**
W: No, I'm sorry. We sold the last size 12 yesterday. More should come in next week though. Should I hold one for you when the shipment arrives?
M: No, that won't work. I wanted to give it to my wife to wear to a big dinner tomorrow.
W: That's sweet. There may be one in another store location. **(52) I'll call around if you don't mind waiting a couple minutes.**

--------------------------------------------------

M: 안녕하세요. 어제 이 마네킹이 입고 있던 원피스 말인데요. 그 원피스를 제가 몇 벌 찾았는데 사이즈가 안 맞아서요. 혹시 12사이즈로 한 벌 있나요?
W: 아뇨, 죄송합니다. 마지막 12사이즈를 어제 판매했거든요. 하지만 더 많은 제품이 다음주에 입고될 거예요. 입고되면 하나를 따로 보관해 둘까요?
M: 아뇨, 그러실 필요는 없어요. 내일 중요한 저녁식사가 있어서 아내에게 입으라고 갖다 주려고 했어요.
W: 참 자상하시네요. 다른 지점에 있을지도 모르겠어요. 잠시 기다리는 것이 괜찮으시다면 제가 전화를 걸어볼게요.

**50.** 화자들은 어디에 있을 것 같은가?
(A) 창고
(B) 의류 매장
(C) 식당
(D) 은행 　　　　　　　　　　　　　　　　정답 (B)

**51.** 남자가 문제점으로 언급한 것은 무엇인가?
(A) 제품이 원하는 색상이 아니다.
(B) 제품이 없어졌다.
(C) 제품의 품질이 좋지 않다.
(D) 제품의 사이즈가 맞지 않다. 　　　　　　정답 (D)

**52.** 여자는 이후에 무엇을 할 것인가?
(A) 다른 사이즈를 찾아본다.
(B) 매장의 재고를 확인한다.
(C) 남자에게 전액 환불을 해준다.
(D) 다른 지점에 전화한다. 　　　　　　　　정답 (D)

**문제 53-55번은 다음 대화를 참조하시오.** 미W 호M

W: Hi. **(53) I need to rent some storage space for about three months. I'd like to know what you have available.**
M: Our large units are now fully booked over the next year, but we do have some smaller spaces available. How much storage space do you need, ma'am?
W: Um... **(54/55) a three-by-three unit would be great as I just need to store some boxes of things from my office while the building is being renovated.**
M: **(55) No problem.** Please drop by our office at your convenience, and I'll show you the space. If you're happy with it, you can sign up for three months.

--------------------------------------------------

W: 안녕하세요. 저는 3개월 정도 보관 공간을 빌려야 합니다. 귀사에서 이용할 수 있는 것에는 무엇이 있는지 알고 싶어요.
M: 저희 대형 보관 공간은 현재 내년까지 예약이 모두 끝났지만, 그것보다 작은 보관 공간들은 이용하실 수 있습니다. 어느 정도나 되는 보관 공간을 원하십니까, 고객님?
W: 음, 가로 3미터 세로 3미터 공간이면 되겠어요. 사무실 건물이 보수되는 동안 박스 몇 개에 있는 물건들만 보관하면 되니까요.
M: 좋습니다. 시간이 편할 때 저희 사무소에 잠깐 들러 주시면 제가 보관 공간을 보여 드리겠습니다. 공간에 만족하시면 3개월 신청을 하시면 됩니다.

**53.** 여자는 무엇을 임대해야 할 필요가 있는가?
(A) 대형 상자
(B) 사무용 가구
(C) 건축 장비
(D) 보관 공간 　　　　　　　　　　　　　　정답 (D)

**54.** 여자가 자신의 사무실에 대해 언급한 것은 무엇인가?
(A) 매우 크다.
(B) 너무 오래되었다.
(C) 시내에서 멀리 떨어져 있다.
(D) 보수 공사가 진행되고 있다. 　　　　　　정답 (D)

**55.** 남자가 "No problem."이라고 말할 때 의미하는 바는 무엇인가?
(A) 그는 여자의 사무실 건물을 보수할 수 있다.
(B) 그는 여자의 구체적인 요구 조건을 충족시킬 수 있다.
(C) 그는 모든 것이 순조롭게 통제되고 있다고 생각한다.
(D) 그는 다른 곳으로 이사를 하는 것에 전혀 문제가 없다. 　정답 (B)

**문제 56-58번은 다음 대화를 참조하시오.** 영W 호M

W: Mr. Watson, I don't think I can make it to the meeting this afternoon. **(56) Could you please tell me about the details later?**
M: Well, we will deal with important research data regarding current global market trends and will analyze some of our rival companies. I think you should be there, Ms. McGowan.
W: I know. **(57) But I got an urgent phone call from the chief executive officer this morning, and he asked me to go back**

to headquarters in Scotland as soon as possible. He told me we've decided to recall thousands of our sedans in China and South Korea next week. So I don't have any choice but to take off at 1 P.M.

M: Oh, it's already 11 o'clock, Ms. McGowan. **(58) You should hurry up if you want to get to the international airport on time.**

---

W: Watson 씨, 제가 오늘 오후에 있을 회의에 참석할 수가 없을 것 같아요. 나중에 회의에서 다룬 세부사항에 대해 알려 주시겠어요?

M: 글쎄요, 현재 세계 시장의 동향과 관련된 중요한 연구 자료를 다루고 경쟁사들을 분석할 것이라서요. 회의에 참여하셔야 할 것 같아요, McGowan 씨.

W: 알아요. 하지만 오늘 오전에 최고 경영자로부터 Scotland에 있는 본사로 최대한 빨리 복귀하라는 긴급한 연락을 받았어요. 우리 회사가 다음주에 중국과 한국에서 수천 대에 달하는 자동차들을 회수하기로 결정했습니다. 그래서 오늘 오후 1시에 비행기를 타는 것 외엔 다른 방도가 없어요.

M: 아, 벌써 11시예요, McGowan 씨. 제시간에 맞춰 국제공항에 도착하려면 서두르셔야 할 것 같네요.

**56.** 여자가 남자에게 추후에 해달라고 요청하는 것은 무엇인가?
(A) 항공권을 예약한다.
(B) 새로운 시장을 분석한다.
(C) 공항까지 태워준다.
(D) 그녀가 정보를 파악할 수 있도록 돕는다.　　　정답 (D)

**57.** 여자에 따르면 본사는 어디에 위치하고 있는가?
(A) 독일
(B) 중국
(C) 한국
(D) 스코틀랜드　　　정답 (D)

**58.** 여자가 받는 조언은 무엇인가?
(A) 새로운 영업 전략을 고안한다.
(B) 서둘러 사무실을 떠난다.
(C) 회의를 취소한다.
(D) 자료를 수집한다.　　　정답 (B)

**문제 59-61번은 다음 대화를 참조하시오.** [미M] [미W]

---

M: Ms. Witherspoon, **(59) Mr. Johnson told me that you have a meeting with the budgeting committee at 2 o'clock today.**

W: Ah, yes, Mr. Redford, **(60) I need to discuss the total construction costs for the new warehouse we designed last month.**

M: Is **(61) Ms. Kellogg,** your co-designer, also going to attend the meeting?

W: I think so. **(61) I heard she came up here from San Francisco last night, and she will speak about the design features as well.**

---

M: Witherspoon 씨, Johnson 씨가 당신이 오늘 2시에 예산 위원회와 회의가 있다고 이야기하던데요.

W: 아, 네, Redford 씨, 우리가 지난달에 설계한 새로운 창고에 대한 총 건설비를 논의할 필요가 있어서요.

M: 당신의 공동 설계자인 Kellogg 씨도 그 회의에 참석할 예정인가요?

W: 그럴 겁니다. 그녀가 어젯밤에 San Francisco에서 이 곳으로 왔고 디자인의 특징들에 대해 이야기할 것이라고 들었거든요.

**59.** 대화의 주제는 무엇인가?
(A) 새로운 지점
(B) 일부 수입품
(C) 회사의 구조조정
(D) 다가올 회의　　　정답 (D)

**60.** 여자는 누구일 것 같은가?
(A) 은행원
(B) 회계부장
(C) 건축가
(D) 패션 디자이너　　　정답 (C)

**61.** 여자에 따르면 Kellogg 씨는 오늘 오후에 무엇을 할 것인가?
(A) San Francisco를 향해 출발할 것이다.
(B) 연설을 할 것이다.
(C) 새로운 계약서에 서명할 것이다.
(D) 이사회를 개최할 것이다.　　　정답 (B)

**문제 62-64번은 다음 대화와 비행기 시간표를 참조하시오.** [영W] [호M]

---

W: Hey, Mr. Longcross. We should hurry to get to the airport to pick up the client.

M: Um… **(62) I just heard that some flights have been delayed due to the inclement weather.**

W: **(62) So Ms. Travis won't be arriving at the airport as scheduled?**

M: Yes, I think it will be best if we leave for the airport in about two hours.

W: **(63) But there will be several demonstrations downtown, and they will create gridlock, which will test the patience of drivers. Why don't we leave now?**

M: Sure, we can do that. **(64) Ah, have you decided where to have dinner with Ms. Travis? I feel like taking her to an expensive and good restaurant for dinner.**

---

W: 안녕하세요, Longcross 씨. 우리는 고객을 모시러 서둘러 공항으로 가야 해요.

M: 음… 몇몇 비행기들이 악천후로 인해 도착이 지연된다는 소식을 들었어요.

W: 그러면 Travis 씨가 예정된 시간에 공항에 도착하지 못한다는 말인가요?

M: 네, 두 시간 정도 있다가 공항으로 출발하는 것이 최상이라고 생각해요.

W: 하지만 시내에 몇몇 집회들이 예정되어 있어서 운전자들의 인내심을 시험할 정도로 심한 교통체증이 있을 겁니다. 지금 떠나는 게 어때요?

M: 좋아요. 그러도록 해요. 아, Travis 씨와 어디에서 저녁 식사를 할 것인지 결정했어요? 저는 비싸면서 근사한 레스토랑으로 모시고 가서 저녁식사를 하고 싶은 생각이 드네요.

| 출발지 | 상태 | 도착 예정 시간 |
|---|---|---|
| New York | 착륙 | 오전 11:00 |
| Manchester | 정시 도착 | 오후 12:45 |
| Glasgow | 취소 | 오후 2:00 |
| Chicago | **(62) 연착** | **오후 4:30** |

**62.** 그래픽을 보시오. Travis 씨는 어느 도시에서 출발해서 오고 있는가?
(A) New York
(B) Manchester

(C) Glasgow

(D) Chicago                  정답 (D)

**63.** 여자가 제안하는 것은 무엇인가?
(A) 출장을 취소한다.
(B) 교통 정체 현상을 피하기 위해 일찍 출발한다.
(C) 다른 주차장을 이용한다.
(D) 저녁식사를 위한 테이블을 예약한다.    정답 (B)

**64.** 화자들이 Travis 씨를 만나면 무엇을 할 것 같은가?
(A) 공항으로 간다.
(B) 몇몇 안건들을 논의한다.
(C) 좌석 배치도를 확인한다.
(D) 함께 식사를 한다.            정답 (D)

문제 65-67번은 다음 대화와 회의실 일정을 참조하시오. 영W 미M

---

W: Mr. Ryan, (65) one of our important clients just called and asked for a meeting with me. I was just wondering if I could use Meeting Room 101 tomorrow.

M: Um... please hold on a second. I'm checking the meeting room calendar now. It is free at 2 P.M. Would you like me to reserve the room for you?

W: Well, I'm afraid my afternoon is fully booked tomorrow. (66) I think I'll only be free in the morning. Would it be possible to postpone the morning meeting until some other time in the afternoon?

M: (66/67) I'll contact Ms. Lane to see if she can move her meeting to 2 P.M.

---

W: Ryan 씨, 중요한 고객 중 한 분이 방금 연락해서 저와의 회의를 요청하셨어요. 그래서 내일 101호 회의실을 사용할 수 있을지 궁금해요.

M: 음… 잠시만요. 지금 회의실 일정표를 확인하고 있습니다. 오후 2시가 비어 있네요. 그 시간으로 예약을 해드릴까요?

W: 음, 내일 오후에는 이미 일정이 다 잡혀 있는데요. 오전에만 시간이 가능할 것 같아요. 혹시 오전 회의를 오후의 다른 시간으로 미루는 것이 가능할까요?

M: 제가 Lane 씨에게 연락해서 회의를 오후 2시로 미룰 수 있는지 한 번 확인해 볼게요.

### 101호 회의실

| 시간 | 일정 |
|---|---|
| (66) 오전 10:00 | 회계 회의 |
| 오후 1:00 | 마케팅 발표 |
| 오후 2:00 | |
| 오후 3:00 | 직원 회의 |

**65.** 화자들은 무엇에 관해 이야기하고 있는가?
(A) 회의 연기
(B) 연간 보고서 발표
(C) 방 예약
(D) 발표 준비             정답 (C)

**66.** 그래픽을 보시오. Lane 씨는 어느 부서에서 근무할 것 같은가?
(A) 회계부
(B) 마케팅부
(C) 인사부

(D) 시설 관리부           정답 (A)

**67.** 남자는 무엇을 하겠다고 말하는가?
(A) 발표를 취소한다.
(B) 동료에게 전화한다.
(C) 새로운 직원을 채용한다.
(D) 회의에 참석한다.        정답 (B)

문제 68-70번은 다음 대화와 목록을 참조하시오. 미M 미W

---

W: Hey, Mr. Budd, would you like to help find a studio for me in New York?

M: Sure. (68) I think you need a spacious place with high ceilings to accommodate all of your big sculptures.

W: Absolutely. (69) But I should consider the cost per month. You know, I can't free myself from budget constraints.

M: That's quite understandable. Please let me know your detailed requirements so I can recommend a good place for you in New York.

W: Um… (70) it should have extra-high ceilings more than five meters in height. Ah, and the rent should be less than $500 per month.

M: I've heard there are some decent studios looking for tenants. Would you like to search for some?

---

W: 안녕하세요, Budd 씨, 제가 New York에서 작업실을 찾을 수 있도록 도와주실 수 있나요?

M: 물론이에요. 당신의 큰 조각상들을 수용하려면 아무래도 넓으면서 높은 천장을 가진 장소가 필요할 것이란 생각이 들어요.

W: 맞아요. 하지만 월별 비용도 고려해야만 해요. 아시다시피 제가 예산 제약에서 자유롭지 못하거든요.

M: 충분히 이해합니다. 구체적인 요구 사항을 알려주시면 New York에 있는 좋은 장소를 추천해 드릴게요.

W: 음… 5미터가 넘는 높은 천장이 있어야 해요. 아, 월세가 $500 미만이어야 하고요.

M: 임차인을 찾고 있는 괜찮은 작업실들이 나와 있다고 들었어요. 그 작업실들을 보시겠어요?

| 작업실 이름 | 천장 높이 | 월세 |
|---|---|---|
| Regus | 3미터 | $200 |
| Heron | 4미터 | $300 |
| (70) Shard | 5미터 | $400 |
| Union | 6미터 | $600 |

**68.** 여자는 누구일 것 같은가?
(A) 부동산 중개업자
(B) 예술가
(C) 건축가
(D) 전시 기획자          정답 (B)

**69.** 여자에 따르면 무엇이 문제인가?
(A) 그녀는 계약을 취소하고 싶어 한다.
(B) 그녀는 충분한 자금이 없다.
(C) 그녀는 일부 작품을 완성할 수 없다.
(D) 그녀는 지역 행사에 참여할 수 없다.    정답 (B)

**70.** 그래픽을 보시오. 여자는 어느 곳과 연락을 취할 것 같은가?

(A) Regus

(B) Heron

(C) Shard

(D) Union                                                정답 (C)

## Part 4

**문제 71-73번은 다음 안내문을 참조하시오.** 호M

---

Hello, everyone. (72) **This is your senior counsel, Henry McGowan.** (71) **I know you're all excited about the new document editing software that will be installed on your laptops by Friday.** (72) **As trusted legal counsel**, it is important for us to make accurate, timely changes to reflect client feedback and to produce (72) **legal documents** on the spot and share them with our clients. The firm will offer demonstration sessions every day next week. I know all of you are very busy, and some of you might have used the application before, (73) **but you're still required to attend one session on any day of your choice next week.**

---

안녕하세요, 여러분. 저는 여러분의 수석 변호사 Henry McGowan입니다. 여러분 모두 자신의 노트북 컴퓨터에 금요일까지 설치될 새로운 문서 편집 소프트웨어에 대한 기대가 크다는 점을 알고 있습니다. 신뢰받는 변호인단 으로서 우리는 고객들의 의견을 반영하여 정확하고 빠르게 변경사항을 적 용해서 즉석에서 바로 법률 서류를 작성하고 이를 고객들과 공유하는 것이 중요합니다. 회사에서는 다음주 매일 시연회를 제공하고자 합니다. 여러분 모두가 매우 바쁘다는 점은 알고 있고 여러분 중 일부는 전에 이 응용 프로 그램을 사용해 봤을지도 모르겠지만, 그럼에도 여러분 각자 다음주 중 하루 를 선택하여 꼭 한 번은 연수에 참여하실 것을 부탁드립니다.

**71.** 이 안내문의 주제는 무엇인가?

(A) 취업 기회

(B) 새로운 소프트웨어 프로그램

(C) 기계 설치

(D) 재판 준비                                                정답 (B)

**72.** 화자의 직업은 무엇일 것 같은가?

(A) 강사

(B) 회계사

(C) 법률 전문가

(D) 컴퓨터 프로그래머                                                정답 (C)

**73.** 화자가 청자들에게 요청하는 것은 무엇인가?

(A) 소송을 제기한다.

(B) 시연에 참석한다.

(C) 새로운 노트북 컴퓨터를 구매한다.

(D) 고객에게 문서를 발송한다.                                                정답 (B)

**문제 74-76번은 다음 광고를 참조하시오.** 미W

---

Do you want something to do that isn't TV or movies? (74) **Come and join us at Patterson's! We have the state's largest supply of magazines, books, and comic books.** Our customers love to come here because we have the widest variety of titles in genres, such as fiction, history, nature, art and

photography, literature, foreign languages, and home décor. (75) **We also have a supervised fun zone so that your children can be entertained and kept safe while you shop.** Can't make it to the store? No problem! (76) **All of our titles are available for sale on our Web site. Quick delivery in under three days is guaranteed.**

---

TV나 영화 말고 다른 할 수 있는 것을 원하시나요? 그렇다면 저희 Patterson's로 오셔서 회원에 가입하세요! 저희는 우리 주에서 가장 많은 양의 잡지, 도서, 만화책을 제공합니다. 저희 고객들이 Patterson's에 오 시는 것을 좋아하는 이유는 저희가 소설, 역사, 자연, 예술과 사진, 문학, 외 국어 그리고 집안 장식과 같은 분야들의 가장 다양한 종류의 책을 보유하고 있기 때문입니다. 저희는 또한 고객분께서 쇼핑하시는 동안 아이들이 즐겁 고 안전하게 놀 수 있는 보안이 확실한 놀이 공간을 제공하고 있습니다. 매 장에 오실 수가 없나요? 문제없습니다! 모든 도서들은 저희 홈페이지를 통 해서도 구매가 가능합니다. 3일 이내의 빠른 배송을 보장해 드립니다.

**74.** Patterson's는 어떤 매장인가?

(A) 서점

(B) 가구점

(C) 의류점

(D) 스포츠 용품점                                                정답 (A)

**75.** Patterson's는 아이들과 부모들에게 무엇을 제공하는가?

(A) 무료 교통편

(B) 안전한 놀이 공간

(C) 독서 강좌

(D) 할인 쿠폰                                                정답 (B)

**76.** 화자가 홈페이지를 통한 주문에 대해 언급하는 것은 무엇인가?

(A) 배송비를 면제받는다.

(B) 일부 제품은 구매가 불가하다.

(C) 빠른 배송을 보장한다.

(D) 특별 할인이 제공된다.                                                정답 (C)

**문제 77-79번은 다음 전화 메시지를 참조하시오.** 미W

---

Hello, Mr. Miller. (77) **This is Beverley Kensington from the Big Smile Dental Clinic.** I'm calling about your regular checkup. Our records indicate that it's time for you to take care of your teeth. (78) **We upgraded our Web site last week. So you are now able to make a dental appointment online.** (79) **If you visit our Web site at www.bigsmile.com, there is a link at the bottom of the front page that says, "Make an appointment." You can't miss it.** If you have any questions about the scheduling process, please do not hesitate to call us at 776-7332. I'll see you soon, Mr. Miller. Have a good day!

---

안녕하세요, Miller 씨. 저는 Big Smile Dental Clinic의 Beverley Kensington입니다. 귀하의 정기 검진에 관해 전화 드렸습니다. 저희 기록을 보니 귀하가 치아 관리를 받으셔야 하는 시기더군요. 저희가 지난주에 홈페 이지를 개정했습니다. 그래서 이제 온라인으로 치과 예약을 하실 수 있게 되 었습니다. 저희 홈페이지 www.bigsmile.com을 방문하시면 첫 번째 페이지 의 하단 부분에 '진료 예약하기'라고 쓰인 링크가 있습니다. 찾기 어렵지 않 으실 겁니다. 만약 예약 과정에 관해 궁금한 점이 있다면 주저하지 마시고 776-7332로 전화해 주십시오. 곧 뵙겠습니다, Miller 씨. 좋은 하루 보내세요!

**77.** 화자는 어디에서 근무하는가?
(A) 치과 병원
(B) 청소 회사
(C) 자동차 판매 대리점
(D) 인터넷 서비스 업체　　　　　　　　정답 (A)

**78.** 화자가 Miller 씨에게 홈페이지를 방문할 것을 요청하는 이유는 무엇인가?
(A) 치과 서비스를 알기 위해서
(B) 길 안내를 받기 위해서
(C) 예약을 하기 위해서
(D) 유용한 정보를 읽기 위해서　　　　정답 (C)

**79.** 화자가 "You can't miss it."이라고 말할 때 암시하는 바는 무엇인가?
(A) 특별 혜택이 굉장히 매력적이다.
(B) 청자는 필히 오늘 비행기에 탑승해야 한다.
(C) 예약 변경은 허용되지 않는다.
(D) 청자가 무엇인가를 찾는 데 어려움이 전혀 없을 것이다.　　정답 (D)

문제 80-82번은 다음 연설문을 참조하시오. 영W

Good evening, ladies and gentlemen! Tonight, (80) **I'm very honored to present the entrepreneur of the year award to Brandon White.** He is the president of BK Engines, which is widely known for manufacturing durable, energy-efficient, and environment-friendly automobile engines. (81/82) **In addition, Mr. White recently announced some new company policies, such as requiring the use of renewable energy sources when manufacturing engines.** (82) **He is really amazing.** Mr. White, please come onto the stage. Ladies and gentlemen, let's give him a warm welcome! We are very happy tonight to have you, Mr. White!

------------------------------------------------

안녕하세요, 신사 숙녀 여러분! 오늘밤 저는 올해의 우수 기업인 상을 Brandon White 씨에게 수여하게 되어 매우 영광스럽게 생각합니다. 그는 BK Engines 사의 사장으로, 이 회사는 내구성이 뛰어나고, 에너지 효율성이 좋은 환경 친화적인 자동차 엔진을 제작하는 회사로 널리 알려져 있습니다. 게다가 White 씨는 최근에 엔진을 제작할 때 재생 가능한 에너지 자원을 사용하는 것과 같은 새로운 회사 방침들을 발표했습니다. 그는 정말 대단합니다. White 씨, 무대 위로 올라오세요. 신사 숙녀 여러분. 그를 따뜻하게 환영해 주십시오! 오늘밤 White 씨를 모시게 되어 매우 기쁩니다!

**80.** 연설의 주된 목적은 무엇인가?
(A) 상을 수여하기 위해서
(B) 동료들에게 이별 인사를 하기 위해서
(C) 재생 에너지를 설명하기 위해서
(D) 매출 상승을 발표하기 위해서　　정답 (A)

**81.** 화자에 따르면 Brandon White 씨가 최근에 한 것은 무엇인가?
(A) 멋진 디자인을 창작했다.
(B) 새로운 회사 방침을 만들었다.
(C) 새로운 엔진을 개발했다.
(D) 지역 자선 단체에 기부했다.　　정답 (B)

**82.** 화자가 "He is really amazing."이라고 이야기한 이유는 무엇인가?
(A) Brandon White가 인상적인 연설을 했다.
(B) Brandon White가 옷을 잘 차려 입었다.
(C) Brandon White가 수익을 사회에 환원했다.
(D) Brandon White가 큰 업적을 이루었다.　　정답 (D)

문제 83-85번은 다음 회의 내용을 참조하시오. 호W

(83) **Finally, we need to discuss the induction procedure for the new interns. They will begin arriving next Tuesday morning, and their induction is scheduled for just after lunch.** (84) **I know this is short notice, but we are going to be training twice as many interns as we had planned.** We have the office space for them, but we don't have enough materials yet. (85) **I'd like you all to postpone the rest of your work and secure employee training books and educational equipment for the additional interns by Saturday.** This will be a lot of work at first, but don't forget that more interns means more productivity later.

------------------------------------------------

마지막으로 새로운 인턴사원들을 인도하는 절차를 논의해야 합니다. 새로운 인턴사원들은 다음주 화요일 오전부터 도착하기 시작할 것이며, 그들의 인도식은 점심식사 직후로 예정되어 있습니다. 촉박한 통지임은 저도 알고 있습니다만 우리는 원래 계획했던 인원보다 두 배나 되는 인턴사원들을 훈련시켜야 합니다. 그들을 위한 사무 공간은 확보하고 있습니다만 충분한 교육자재를 보유하고 있지는 않습니다. 여러분 모두 나머지 업무를 미루고 추가 인턴사원들을 위한 직원 훈련서와 교육용 장비를 토요일까지 확보하셨으면 합니다. 이것이 처음에는 과한 업무이긴 합니다만 많은 인턴사원들이 궁극적으로 추후에 더 향상된 생산성을 의미한다는 사실을 잊지 않도록 합시다.

**83.** 화자는 주로 무엇에 관해 논의하고 있는가?
(A) 새로운 근무 일정
(B) 새로운 매출 목표
(C) 다가올 행사
(D) 생산성 향상 계획　　정답 (C)

**84.** 화자에 따르면 어떤 변경이 발생했는가?
(A) 보관할 공간이 별로 없다.
(B) 더 많은 참석자가 생겼다.
(C) 비행기들이 지연되고 있다.
(D) 도착 날짜가 변경되었다.　　정답 (B)

**85.** 화자가 청자들에게 이번주에 해야 할 일로 지시한 것은 무엇인가?
(A) 몇몇 장소들을 물색한다.
(B) 대형 화면을 설치한다.
(C) 교육 자료를 준비한다.
(D) 직원들의 사기를 진작시킨다.　　정답 (C)

문제 86-88번은 다음 전화 메시지를 참조하시오. 영W

Hello, Mr. McDonald. This is Alley Goodroad calling from AMC Properties. (86) **It was really nice meeting you on Thursday,** and I was wondering if you had any thoughts on renting the two-bedroom apartment I showed you. Um... (87) **you wanted me to find out about your own parking space, right? There are a few parking spaces available, so you can pick one of them.** Anyway, (88) **this is a very popular apartment building. You know, many people want to move into this apartment. Please let me know what you decide to do as soon as possible.** When you check this message, please get back to me. Thank you.

------------------------------------------------

안녕하세요, McDonald 씨. 저는 AMC 부동산에서 전화 드리는 Alley

60

Goodroad입니다. 지난 목요일에 만나뵙게 되어 정말 반가웠습니다. 제가 보여드린 방 두 개짜리 아파트 임대에 대해선 생각해보신 바가 있는지 궁금합니다. 음… 전용 주차 공간에 관해 제가 알아보길 원하셨죠, 그렇죠? 사용이 가능한 주차 공간이 있어서 그 중 한 자리를 선택하시면 됩니다. 어쨌든 이 아파트 건물은 인기가 아주 많습니다. 아시다시피 많은 사람들이 이 아파트로 이사하기를 원하고 있습니다. 어떻게 하실 것인지 최대한 빨리 제게 알려 주십시오. 이 메시지를 확인하시면 저에게 연락을 주십시오. 감사합니다.

**86.** 화자는 지난 목요일에 무엇을 했는가?
(A) 그녀는 일을 그만두었다.
(B) 그녀는 임대계약을 체결했다.
(C) 그녀는 고객과 만났다.
(D) 그녀는 야근을 했다. 　　　　　　　　　정답 (C)

**87.** 화자가 주차 공간에 대해 언급한 것은 무엇인가?
(A) 현재 사용이 가능하다.
(B) 도심에 위치하고 있다.
(C) 고객만 사용할 수 있다.
(D) 적은 요금으로 제공된다. 　　　　　　　정답 (A)

**88.** 화자가 "This is a very popular apartment building."이라고 언급한 이유는 무엇인가?
(A) 새로운 아파트를 홍보하기 위해서
(B) 아파트가 고품질임을 강조하기 위해서
(C) 신속한 결정을 요청하기 위해서
(D) 몇몇 장점들을 설명하기 위해서 　　　　정답 (C)

**문제 89-91번은 다음 담화를 참조하시오.** ⓂM

(89) Welcome to Scarlatti's. I am Dominique Sorrento, the executive chef. (90) We serve fresh handmade pasta, oven-baked pizzas, and many entrées using ingredients delivered from local farmers and fishermen every day. Today's special is veal cutlet served with mushroom risotto. (91) In addition, do not miss our homemade wine products that won awards at the California Chronicle's wine competition. They were even featured in Monthly Sommelier and other media outlets. Our wine cellar boasts a collection that is unmatched and famous in our region. Thank you again for coming to Scarlatti's and have a marvelous time.

Scarlatti's에 오신 것을 환영합니다. 저는 Dominique Sorrento라고 하며 수석 요리사입니다. 저희는 신선한 수제 파스타, 오븐에서 구워낸 피자, 그리고 이 지역의 농부들과 어부들로부터 매일 배송되는 재료를 이용한 많은 요리들을 제공합니다. 오늘의 특별 요리는 송아지 커틀렛과 버섯 볶음밥이 되겠습니다. 또한 저희 레스토랑에서 직접 주조한 포도주는 California Chronicle이 주최한 포도주 경연대회에서 수상했으므로 이를 맛볼 수 있는 기회를 절대 놓치지 마세요. 뿐만 아니라 Monthly Sommelier를 비롯한 언론 매체들에서도 기사로 다루었습니다. 저희 포도주 저장실은 이 지역에서 비교할 수 없을 만큼 훌륭하고 유명한 많은 포도주를 보유하고 있음을 자랑합니다. Scarlatti's을 방문해 주셔서 다시 한번 감사드리고 좋은 시간 보내시길 바랍니다.

**89.** 이 담화는 어디서 이루어지고 있는가?
(A) 포도주 양조장
(B) 레스토랑
(C) 요리 학교
(D) 슈퍼마켓 　　　　　　　　　　　　정답 (B)

**90.** 화자는 이 장소에 대해서 무엇을 강조하고 있는가?
(A) 적절한 가격
(B) 시기적절한 서비스
(C) 신선한 재료
(D) 무료 배송 　　　　　　　　　　　　정답 (C)

**91.** 레스토랑에서 직접 주조하는 포도주에 대해서 언급하고 있는 내용은 무엇인가?
(A) 모두 수입산이다.
(B) 우수한 명성을 지니고 있다.
(C) 해외로 수출이 되고 있다.
(D) 건강에 좋다. 　　　　　　　　　　　정답 (B)

**문제 92-94번은 다음 뉴스를 참조하시오.** ⒽM

(92) The major story in Business Today is the rumored purchase of HC Computer by Silver Star Technology. These companies have been star performers in growing shareholder value. (92) As the North American computer market develops at a rapid pace, numerous mergers and acquisitions are likely to take place in North America, making the computer market one of the most attractive regions in which to invest. Experts in the electronics and computing industries are eager to see the acquisition of HC Computer by Silver Star Technology (93) because Silver Star Technology will be able to produce new, revolutionary computer products after the acquisition. (94) Executives from both companies met in San Jose to negotiate the finer points of the acquisition last week. A formal announcement is expected sometime next month.

Business Today의 주요 소식은 Silver Star Technology가 HC Computer를 매입한다는 소식입니다. 이 회사들은 주가가 상승한 우량 회사들입니다. 북미 컴퓨터 시장이 빠른 속도로 발달하면서 북미 지역에서 많은 합병 및 인수가 이루어질 것으로 보이며, 이는 곧 북미 컴퓨터 시장을 가장 매력적인 투자처 중의 한 곳으로 만들고 있습니다. Silver Star Technology가 HC Computer를 인수한 후에는 새롭고 혁신적인 컴퓨터 제품을 생산할 수 있는 능력을 갖출 수 있기 때문에 전자 및 컴퓨터 업계 전문가들은 Silver Star Technology의 HC Computer 인수가 이루어지기를 강하게 원하고 있습니다. 지난주에 양쪽 회사의 중역들은 인수에 필요한 세부사항들을 협상하기 위해 San Jose에서 회동하였습니다. 공식적인 발표는 다음달 중에 이루어질 것으로 예상되고 있습니다.

**92.** 이 뉴스 보도가 주로 다루는 산업 분야는 무엇인가?
(A) 컴퓨터
(B) 자동차
(C) 제조
(D) 식품 가공 　　　　　　　　　　　　정답 (A)

**93.** 화자에 따르면 인수의 목적은 무엇인가?
(A) 생산원가의 절감
(B) 해외 시장으로의 확장
(C) 혁신적인 제품의 제작
(D) 환경 보호에 대한 도움 　　　　　　　정답 (C)

**94.** 뉴스 보도에 따르면 지난주에 무슨 일이 일어났는가?
(A) 주가가 급등하였다.
(B) 새로운 컴퓨터 제품들이 출시되었다.
(C) 협상이 진행되었다.

(D) 몇몇 회사들이 파산하였다.　　　　　　정답 (C)

문제 95-97번은 다음 전화 메시지와 설문조사지를 참조하시오. 미W

Hello, preferred customer! This is Lena Park from Oak Spa and Massage. (95) **As the owner of the company**, I want to thank you for being a vital part of our Service Excellence online poll. (96) **As a token of our appreciation, we are giving you a $30 gift card that you can use on your next visit.** You can use the gift card for any of our services and merchandise. By the way, (97) **we need some more detailed information about the category you gave five stars to. So would you mind if I asked you a few more questions?** For completing this additional survey, you will be given a 10-percent discount coupon. We are dedicated to providing the best service to every customer based on the survey results provided by our loyal customers. Thank you for your patronage at Oak Spa and Massage.

--------------------------------------------------

안녕하세요, 우수 고객님! Oak Spa and Massage의 Lena Park입니다. 회사의 사장으로서 서비스 우수성 온라인 설문조사에 참여해주신 점에 감사드리고 싶습니다. 감사의 표시로 다음 방문 시에 사용하실 수 있는 $30 상당의 상품권을 제공해 드립니다. 이 상품권은 당사의 모든 서비스 및 상품에 사용이 가능합니다. 그런데 고객님이 별 다섯 개를 주신 부문에 대해 좀 더 상세한 정보가 필요합니다. 그래서 제가 질문을 몇 개 더 드려도 괜찮으시겠습니까? 이 추가 설문을 작성해 주시면 10% 할인 쿠폰을 받으시게 됩니다. 저희는 우수 고객들을 대상으로 한 설문조사를 토대로 고객 한 분 한 분께 최고의 서비스를 제공하고자 최선을 다하고 있습니다. Oak Spa and Massage를 애용해 주셔서 감사합니다.

## 고객 의견 설문조사

| 청결 | ★★★★ |
|---|---|
| 위치 | ★★★★ |
| (97) **직원 친절도** | ★★★★★ |
| 가격 | ★★★ |

**95.** Lena Park는 누구일 것 같은가?
(A) 호텔 매니저
(B) 헬스클럽 강사
(C) 마케팅 전문가
(D) 사업가　　　　　　정답 (D)

**96.** 화자는 청자에게 무엇을 제공하겠다고 언급하는가?
(A) 상품권
(B) 할인 쿠폰
(C) 피부 관리 상품
(D) 이틀 무료 숙박　　　　　　정답 (A)

**97.** 그래픽을 보시오. 화자가 추가적인 정보를 요청하는 부문은 무엇인가?
(A) 청결
(B) 위치
(C) 직원 친절도
(D) 가격　　　　　　정답 (C)

문제 98-100번은 다음 안내와 일정표를 참조하시오. 영W

(98) **Hello, everyone, and welcome to the 25th Annual Video Game Convention,** the largest and most innovative gaming forum in the world. (98) **The Northeast Asia Video Game Developers Association is incredibly excited to feature many experts in the field who are willing to give you and your companies the insight you need to create next-generation gaming software.** I have one change to announce regarding this afternoon's schedule. At the top of your screen, you'll see that there has been a change in the lineup of today's speakers. (99) **We are sorry to announce that Brian Joo will not be speaking today because of an illness. So Mona Oh will be replacing him.** (100) **Please do not forget to submit your survey form after you complete it. All those who complete the short survey will automatically be entered in a prize-winning event for new laptop computers and popular game software.**

--------------------------------------------------

안녕하세요, 여러분. 세계에서 가장 크고 가장 혁신적인 게임 포럼인 제25회 연례 비디오 게임 컨벤션에 오신 것을 환영합니다. 동북아시아 비디오 게임 개발자 협회는 차세대 게임 소프트웨어 제작에 필요한 통찰력을 여러분 및 여러분의 회사와 기꺼이 공유하고자 하는 이 분야의 많은 전문가들을 소개하게 되어 대단히 기쁘게 생각합니다. 오늘 오후 일정과 관련하여 한 가지 변경 사항을 말씀드리고자 합니다. 화면 상단에서 오늘 발표자의 일정표에 변경이 있음을 확인하실 수 있습니다. Brian Joo 씨가 병환으로 인해 오늘 연설이 불가함을 발표하게 되어 유감으로 생각합니다. 그래서 Mona Oh 씨가 Brian Joo 씨를 대신하게 될 것입니다. 설문지를 작성한 후 이를 잊지 말고 꼭 제출해 주십시오. 짧은 설문조사를 작성하는 모든 분은 새로운 노트북 컴퓨터와 인기있는 게임 소프트웨어를 받을 수 있는 경품 행사에 자동적으로 응모가 이루어지게 됩니다.

## 연례 비디오 게임 컨벤션 연설 일정
### 6월 3일 – 6월 6일 / 서울 컨벤션 센터

| 6월 3일 오후 | 연설자 |
|---|---|
| 첫 번째 연설 | Kelly McKenzie |
| 두 번째 연설 | Sangkyu Kim |
| (99) **세 번째 연설** | **Brian Joo** |
| 네 번째 연설 | Soona Ha |

**98.** 컨벤션에 참석한 사람들은 누구일 것 같은가?
(A) 의료 전문가
(B) 전문 사진가
(C) 비디오 게임 개발자
(D) 컴퓨터 공학자　　　　　　정답 (C)

**99.** 그래픽을 보시오. 어느 연설에 변경이 발생했는가?
(A) 첫 번째 연설
(B) 두 번째 연설
(C) 세 번째 연설
(D) 네 번째 연설　　　　　　정답 (C)

**100.** 화자에 따르면 참석자들은 어떻게 경품을 받을 수 있는가?
(A) 몇몇 발표에 참석한다.
(B) 게임 잡지를 구독한다.
(C) 그들의 의견을 제공한다.
(D) 소프트웨어를 구매한다.　　　　　　정답 (C)

## Part 5

**101.** Chandler 씨는 기자 회견을 하는 동안 시장은 자유를 보장받아야 하지만 회사들은 그에 따른 책임을 존중해야 한다고 말했다. **정답 (B)**

**102.** 고객님들은 아래 수신자 요금 부담 번호로 전화하면 저희 고객 상담원과 통화하실 수 있습니다. **정답 (B)**

**103.** Sunhill 아파트는 몇몇 시립 공원들에의 근접성으로 인해 사람들 사이에서 인기가 아주 많다. **정답 (C)**

**104.** 정부는 현재 좀더 효과적인 주거 복지 정책을 시행할 수 있는 실용적인 방법을 강구하고자 열심히 노력하고 있다. **정답 (B)**

**105.** 〈World Economy〉는 미국과 캐나다 지역에서 두 번째로 광범위하게 유통이 되고 있는 잡지이다. **정답 (D)**

**106.** 몇몇 고용주들은 경쟁력 있는 임금이 높은 효율성으로 이끌지는 못한다는 잘못된 추측을 한다. **정답 (B)**

**107.** 몇몇 국내 분석가들은 중동 지역에서의 최근 유가 상승은 국가의 향후 경제 성장을 결정짓게 될 핵심 요인이라고 말했다. **정답 (B)**

**108.** 다음주에 주 정부는 단기간에 부진한 경제를 회생시키고 일자리를 창출할 수 있는 일련의 조치들을 발표할 것이다. **정답 (B)**

**109.** 몇몇 생물학자에 따르면 인간은 시각 정보를 분석할 수 있는 엄청난 능력을 보유하고 있다. **정답 (B)**

**110.** 우리 고객 서비스의 질을 향상시키기 위해서 모든 문의는 기록되어야 한다. **정답 (B)**

**111.** 최근에는 많은 사람들이 대도시에 위치한 대형 백화점에서 쇼핑하는 것에 익숙해졌다. **정답 (B)**

**112.** 직원들은 새로운 인쇄기를 가동시키기 전에 사용 설명서를 완전하게 검토하는 것이 필수라는 점을 숙지하시기 바랍니다. **정답 (C)**

**113.** 우리의 새로운 공장에서 근무하길 원하는 외국인은 관련된 취업 허가증을 신청해야만 한다. **정답 (C)**

**114.** 모든 직원들은 기밀 서류나 파일들을 컴퓨터로 고객들에게 발송할 때 보안 절차를 필히 따라야 한다. **정답 (C)**

**115.** 그 도시의 연례 여름 축제에는 수영, 파도타기, 래프팅을 비롯한 많은 즐거운 행사들을 포함하고 있다. **정답 (C)**

**116.** 수도 공급이 심각한 가뭄으로 인해 상당한 규모의 주민들에게 제공하기엔 너무 부족했다. **정답 (A)**

**117.** 과일과 야채의 높은 섭취와 포화 지방의 낮은 섭취의 조화는 대개 비만과, 당뇨, 그리고 심장 질환의 위험성을 감소시키는 데 도움을 준다. **정답 (C)**

**118.** 신문에 보도된 바에 따르면 유럽연합과의 자유 무역 협정의 시행을 승인하는 법안이 어제 통과되었다. **정답 (D)**

**119.** 누가 최고 경영자 직을 맡더라도 회사가 직면한 경영 상황이 빠르게 개선될 것이라고 기대하기엔 무리가 있다. **정답 (B)**

**120.** 60세 이상의 운전자들이 우편으로 그들의 운전면허증을 갱신할 수 없는 것은 많은 주들의 표준관행이다. **정답 (C)**

**121.** 우리 시의 관광 버스 노선들은 강북 지역과 강남 지역으로 나뉘어서 운영된다. **정답 (D)**

**122.** 이사회는 회사에서 10년 이상 근속한 일부 헌신적인 직원들에게 보상을 할 것이다. **정답 (A)**

**123.** Kamang 씨는 유럽의 많은 인상주의 화가들에 의해 영향을 받은 후 자신만의 독자적인 후기 인상주의 양식을 확립하였다. **정답 (C)**

**124.** 비행기 조종사들의 파업으로 인해 8월 15일까지 남부 휴양섬인 Cayo Costa로 가는 약 200개의 항공편이 취소될 것이다. **정답 (C)**

**125.** 우리 이사진은 본래 수요일에 New York으로 출발하기로 계획했으나 악천후로 인해 출발이 지연되었다. **정답 (D)**

**126.** 사람들이 머지 않아 쓰레기 매립지에서 살길 원하지 않는다면 시 정부는 시장에서의 비닐 봉투 사용을 금지해야만 한다. **정답 (C)**

**127.** 우리의 새로운 노트북 컴퓨터 모델이 다른 제품들에 비해 너무 비싸기 때문에 고객들은 구매를 주저하고 있다. **정답 (D)**

**128.** 마케팅 세미나 참석에 관심이 있는 사람들은 필히 마케팅 부서에 있는 Maya Cruise 씨에게 연락하셔야 합니다. **정답 (D)**

**129.** 뛰어난 예술적 기교는 오늘날 아시아 문화가 전세계에서 독특한 문화로 여겨지는 주요한 이유 중 하나이다. **정답 (A)**

**130.** Thompson 씨의 영업 실적이 9월에는 평균치에 훨씬 못 미치므로 그는 10월에 많은 잠재 고객들과 만나는 데 시간을 많이 할애하기로 결정했다. **정답 (B)**

## Part 6

**문제 131-134번은 다음 공지를 참조하시오.**

> **보수 공사 공지**
>
> New York 중앙 도서관은 8월 초부터 12월 말까지 대대적인 보수 공사를 시행할 예정입니다. 이 보수 공사는 도서관에서 책을 읽거나 공부하며 시간을 보내려고 선택한 이용객들에게 크게 확장된 좌석 공간을 제공할 것입니다.
>
> 저희는 보수 공사로 인하여 도서관 운영에 초래되는 지장을 가능한 최소화할 수 있도록 모든 노력을 다할 것입니다. 하지만 이 기간 동안 잠시 도서관 일부 구역이 폐쇄될 수 있습니다.
>
> 예정된 폐쇄 일정은 보수 공사 기간 중 도서관 게시판 및 도서관 홈페이지에 공지될 것입니다. 폐쇄로 인한 불편을 피하기 위해 일정을 확인하시기 바랍니다.
>
> 여러분의 양해와 성원에 매우 감사드립니다.

**131.** **정답 (A)**

**132.** **정답 (C)**

**133.** **정답 (C)**

**134.** (A) 도서관은 올 가을에 재개장을 할 예정입니다.
(B) 개인 소지품을 방치된 상태로 두지 마십시오.
(C) 새로 보수되는 도서관에는 2만 권이 넘는 장서들이 자리하게 될 것입니다.
(D) 폐쇄로 인한 불편을 피하기 위해 일정을 확인하시기 바랍니다.

정답 (D)

문제 135-138번은 다음 편지를 참조하시오.

Lee 씨께,

저희 편지지에 적힌 상호에서도 나타나듯이 저희는 최근에 상호를 Washington Machine에서 Washington Manufacturing으로 변경하였습니다.

경영진의 변경은 없으며, 저희는 향후에도 업계에서 지금까지 쌓아온 명성에 맞는 훌륭한 제품과 서비스를 제공할 것입니다. 이 안내문을 귀사의 회계 부서로 전달하시고 이에 맞춰 수정하도록 지시를 내려주신다면 감사하겠습니다.

저희의 소중한 고객이 되어주심에 감사드립니다. 이 문제에 대한 협조에 감사드립니다.

Cindy Walker
최고 경영자
Washington Manufacturing

**135.** 정답 (D)

**136.** 정답 (C)

**137.** 정답 (D)

**138.** (A) 저희의 소중한 고객이 되어주심에 감사드립니다.
(B) 저희는 성공적으로 새로운 혁신적인 기기를 개발했습니다.
(C) 명명에 관한 많은 관습이 오늘날에도 준수되고 있습니다.
(D) 저는 이것이야말로 가치 창출의 완벽한 모범이라고 생각합니다.

정답 (A)

문제 139-142번은 다음 이메일을 참조하시오.

발신: Yvette Chen 〈yc@klpfreight.com〉
수신: Komi Kellogg 〈kk@bellapetfactory.com〉
날짜: 3월 10일
제목: 가격 변동

Kellogg 씨께,

이 이메일은 4월 1일부로 시행되는 약간의 가격 변경에 대한 공지입니다. 가격 변동은 지난 12개월간의 운송비 증가에 따른 결과입니다.

가격 변경의 전반적인 개요는 이메일 하단에 있습니다. 향후 3년 간 추가적인 가격 변경은 발생하지 않을 것으로 예상하고 있습니다.

저희 서비스에 관한 질문이 있으시면 692-9815로 연락해 주십시오. 저희 고객 상담원들이 기꺼이 도움을 드릴 것입니다.

이번 가격 인상이 내년에도 저희 화물 서비스의 월등한 품질 기준을 유지할 수 있도록 해줄 것이란 점을 이해해 주시면 감사하겠습니다.

Yvette Chen
최고 경영자
KLP Freight Services, Inc.

**139.** 정답 (C)

**140.** 정답 (C)

**141.** (A) 저희는 해외 고객들과 소통하는 것에 큰 어려움이 있습니다.
(B) 마케팅은 고객의 요구와 고객의 만족에 관련된 것입니다.
(C) 저희 고객 상담원들이 기꺼이 도움을 드릴 것입니다.
(D) 모든 고객을 위한 더 나은 서비스는 모든 상점과 식당이 중요시하는 것입니다.

정답 (C)

**142.** 정답 (B)

문제 143-146번은 다음 이메일을 참조하시오.

안녕하세요, Hamilton 씨,

최근 저희 회사의 법무팀장 직에 지원해 주셔서 감사드립니다.

저희는 많은 지원서를 접수했으며 저희의 요구조건에 가깝게 부합하는 배경과 경력을 지닌 지원자들을 찾을 수 있었습니다.

유감스럽게도, 귀하는 이 직책에 발탁되지 못하셨습니다. 귀하가 능력을 향상시키기 위해 얼마나 열심히 노력했는지 알고 있습니다. 그래서 귀하가 자신을 그 어느 때보다 강하게 만들 것이며 훌륭한 변호사가 될 것이라고 확신합니다. 귀하의 향후 노력에 최고의 행운을 기원합니다.

관심을 가져주시고 귀하의 이력서를 송부하는 데 시간을 할애해주신 점에 많은 감사를 드립니다. 만약 질문이 있으시면 언제든 주저하지 말고 776-7323으로 전화해 주십시오.

Stacy Park
인사부장
Modern Education

**143.** 정답 (C)

**144.** 정답 (D)

**145.** (A) 고용주들이 모든 직원들에게서 찾고 싶어 하는 기술과 자질이 있습니다.
(B) 귀하의 제안서를 검토했으나 저희는 다른 업체와 계약을 하기로 결정했습니다.
(C) 귀하의 향후 노력에 최고의 행운을 기원합니다.
(D) 뛰어난 성과를 이루어낸 저희 직원들에게 항상 감사한 마음입니다.

정답 (C)

**146.** 정답 (A)

## Part 7

문제 147-148번은 다음 공지를 참조하시오.

RYAN 직물

공지

(147) 9월 1일부터 9월 8일까지, 저희 상점은 문을 닫습니다. 주립 가스 회사인 퍼시픽 가스에서 시에 필요한 새로운 가스관의 설치를 위해 저희 상점 밖에 위치한 중심 도로를 파헤치는 공사가 예정되어 있기 때문입니다. 이번에는 차도 및 인도가 모두 폐쇄될 것입니다.

(148) 회사의 임시 폐쇄 기간 동안, 저희 온라인과 전화를 통한 주문 서비스는 모두 정상적으로 운영될 것입니다. 저희 보안 홈페이지인 www.

luckysupermarket.com을 통해 혹은 무료 전화번호 1-800-741-0110으로 연락하시면 제품을 주문하실 수 있습니다. 만약 저희 제품 안내 책자를 수령하고 싶으면, 1-800-870-0603으로 전화를 주시면 됩니다.

저희 상점은 정상적으로 9월 9일에 영업을 재개합니다. 일단 상점 외부 도로 공사가 마무리되면 저희는 다시 여러분께 서비스를 제공할 수 있길 바라고 있습니다.

여러분의 인내와 양해에 감사 드립니다.

Thomas Ryan
점장

**147.** 공지의 목적은 무엇인가?
(A) 상점의 몇 가지 방침 변경을 소개하기 위해서
(B) 고객에게 임시 폐쇄를 알리기 위해서
(C) 사업 확장을 위한 새로운 사업 계획을 공표하기 위해서
(D) 주민들에게 새로운 공사 지침사항을 알리기 위해서    정답 (B)

**148.** 공지에 따르면, 9월 1일부터 9월 8일 사이에 고객이 주문할 수 있는 방법은 무엇인가?
(A) 이메일을 발송한다.
(B) 무료 전화번호로 연락한다.
(C) 상점을 직접 내방한다.
(D) 주문서를 제출한다.    정답 (B)

문제 149-151번은 다음 회람을 참조하시오.

회람

수신: 전 주방 직원
발신: Alley Goodroad
날짜: 9월 9일
제목: 새로운 지침사항

직원 여러분,

(149) 시 식품안전위원회가 사업장의 올바른 음식 취급에 대한 새로운 지침을 제시했습니다. 식품을 직접 다루든, 그렇지 않은 다음 기준을 반드시 준수해야 합니다:

1. (150) 모든 직원들은 최소 두 시간마다 손을 씻어야 합니다.
2. 4인치 이하 길이의 소매가 있는 셔츠는 허용되지 않습니다.
3. 두발은 어깨까지 내려와서는 안됩니다.(이는 묶은 머리 기준으로 적용됩니다.)
4. 손톱은 손가락 끝 부분보다 길어서는 안 됩니다.

(151) 추가적인 지침들은 다음 달에 발표되며 이는 요리를 하기 위해 생고기를 직접 만지는 직원들에게 적용될 것입니다. 필수 교육 세미나가 9월 15일(토) 오전 10시로 예정되어 있습니다.

이 문제에 관심 가져주셔서 감사합니다.

Alley Goodroad
주방 직원 관리팀장

**149.** 회람의 목적은 무엇인가?
(A) Goodroad 씨를 새로운 관리자로 공표하기 위해서
(B) 주방 직원들에게 긴급상황 시의 유용한 정보를 제공하기 위해서
(C) 일부 업무 관행의 변경에 관해 설명하기 위해서
(D) 직원들에게 향후에 있을 특별 행사에 대해 전달하기 위해서    정답 (C)

**150.** 회람에 따르면, 모든 직원들은 무엇을 해야 하는가?
(A) 요리하는 동안 앞치마를 착용한다.

(B) 교육에 등록한다.
(C) 출근 전에 샤워를 한다.
(D) 최소한 두 시간마다 손을 씻는다.    정답 (D)

**151.** 누가 추가 지침사항을 따라야 할 것 같은가?
(A) 레스토랑 종업원
(B) 요리 전문가
(C) 보건 인력
(D) 호텔 직원    정답 (B)

문제 152-153번은 다음 영수증을 참조하시오.

Target Tech Store

4893 Dresden St.
Orient, OH 40359
전화번호: 3983-7651
월요일-토요일 오전 7시-오후 10시

4월 12일 오후 3:12            4번
                          계산원: Mark Farrow

128 기가 바이트 램 (FX 전자 제조)    $210.00
드럼 머신                        $57.25
휴대전화 충전기                    $16.00
세금                           $30.52
총계                           $313.77

판매 후 수리 서비스가 포함되어 있음.
(152) Ohio 전역에 위치한 저희 지점 중 어느 곳에서든 상품을 환불하거나 교환 처리를 해야 하는 경우에 대비하여 해당 영수증을 보관하시길 바랍니다.
(153) 이 영수증 하단에 나온 코드를 입력하시면 10% 할인 쿠폰을 받으실 수 있으며 이는 저희 홈페이지인 www.targettech.com/coupon에서 상품을 구매하실 때 사용하실 수 있습니다.

**152.** Target Tech Store에 관해 언급된 것은 무엇인가?
(A) 회원 할인을 제공한다.
(B) 일요일에도 영업을 한다.
(C) 악기를 전문적으로 판매한다.
(D) Ohio 주에 다른 매장들을 운영하고 있다.    정답 (D)

**153.** 고객들이 Target Tech Store의 홈페이지를 방문할 이유는 무엇인가?
(A) 환불이나 교환을 요청하기 위해서
(B) 회원에 가입하기 위해서
(C) 고객의 의견을 제시하기 위해서
(D) 할인 쿠폰을 획득하기 위해서    정답 (D)

문제 154-155번은 다음 광고를 참조하시오.

United Health Group

다음 직책을 현재 채용 중입니다!

공인 영양사: 현재 저희는 공인 영양사 직책의 공석이 두 자리 있습니다. 지원자들은 주 위원회에서 발급한 유효한 자격증을 보유하고 있어야 합니다. 또한 공인 영양사로서 2년 이상 근무한 경력도 필요합니다. (154) 이 직책은 환자들에게 영양 지원을 제공하기 위해 의사들과 함께 일하는 것이 요구됩니다. 전일제 직책의 일정은 월요일~목요일 오전 8시~오후 4시, 토요일 오전 9시~낮 12시입니다.

행정 비서: 현재 전일제 행정 비서 직책의 공석이 한 자리 있습니다. (155)

이 직책에서는 청구서 발송 및 처리, 우편물 분류, 고객들의 전화 응대, 모든 청구서 발부 기록 정리 등의 능력이 필요합니다. (154) 또한 모든 환자들의 일정 관리를 담당합니다. 이 직책의 근무 시간은 월요일~목요일 오전 7시 30분~오후 5시입니다. (155) 지원자는 행정 비서로서 최소한 2년간 근무한 경력이 있어야 합니다.

모든 지원자들은 www.unitedhealth.com을 방문하여 인사부 링크를 선택해야 합니다. 그곳에서 이 직책들에 대한 더 많은 정보를 찾을 수 있을 것입니다. 희망하는 일자리를 클릭하여 자기소개서, 이력서, 모든 자격증의 사본, 직종 추천인의 목록을 제출해 주십시오.

**154.** United Health Group은 무엇일 것 같은가?
(A) 치과 의원
(B) 다이어트 회사
(C) 의료 센터
(D) 건강보험 제공업체     정답 (C)

**155.** 행정비서의 직무로 요구되지 않는 것은 무엇인가?
(A) 예약 일정 잡기
(B) 전화 통화하기
(C) 다른 지점으로 우편물을 보내기
(D) 지불 정보를 기록하기     정답 (C)

**문제 156-157번은 다음 문자 메시지를 참조하시오.**

Anna Gunn        [오후 2:11]
있잖아요. (157) 제 이메일에 있는 모임 초대장을 여는 방법을 모르겠어요. 실은, 직원들을 위한 온라인 비즈니스 강좌에 처음 참석하는 거라서요. 이 방법 좀 알려 주시겠어요?

Harrison Morgan        [오후 2:13]
아주 쉽습니다. 이메일을 통해 우리에게 부여된 접속 코드를 입력하시기만 하면 됩니다. 그 코드는 BK6929815입니다.

Anna Gunn        [오후 2:15]
화면에 "당신의 접속 코드는 잘못된 것입니다. 다시 시도해 주십시오."라고 나와요. 이 접속 코드에 무슨 문제라도 있는 건가요?

Harrison Morgan        [오후 2:16]
잠시만요. 제가 대신 확인해 볼게요.

Anna Gunn        [오후 2:17]
제가 받은 이메일 초대장에 문제가 있을 수도 있어요.

Harrison Morgan        [오후 2:19]
(156) 아, 죄송해요. 제가 엉뚱한 접속 코드를 알려드렸네요. 제 실수입니다. 접속 코드 BK6929825를 입력해 보세요.

Anna Gunn        [오후 2:20]
네, 작동해요! 잘 됐네요.

Harrison Morgan        [오후 2:23]
좋습니다. 제가 한 가지만 더 말씀 드릴게요. 모니터 화면의 하단에 무음 버튼이 보이시나요? (157) 헤드폰에 있는 마이크는 사용하실 필요가 없기 때문에 그것을 클릭하시면 됩니다.

**156.** 오후 2시 19분에, Morgan 씨가 "Oh, I'm sorry."라고 썼을 때 무엇을 의미할 가능성이 가장 큰가?
(A) Gunn 씨 없이 비즈니스 워크숍을 시작해야 한다.
(B) Gunn 씨에게 엉뚱한 정보를 알려 주었다.
(C) 아직 문제의 원인을 찾지 못했다.
(D) 해당 비즈니스 강좌에 등록하지 않을 것이다.     정답 (B)

**157.** Gunn 씨에 관해 무엇이 사실일 것 같은가?
(A) 최근에 새로운 헤드폰을 구입했다.
(B) 내일 비즈니스 세미나를 이끌 것이다.
(C) 온라인 강좌 중에 말을 할 필요가 없다.
(D) 이메일 초대장을 받지 못했다.     정답 (C)

**문제 158-160번은 다음 회람을 참조하시오.**

회람

수신: Best Motors 정비공들
발신: Richard Redford
날짜: 3월 8일
제목: 과정 등록

(158) Best Motors는 다양한 분야에 대한 일련의 실습 수업을 통해 정비공 팀을 교육하기 위해 National Automobile Institute (NAI)와 다시 한번 계약하였음을 발표하게 되어 기쁩니다. 모든 Best Motors 정비공들은 다음달 말까지 교육을 완료할 것입니다. 여러분이 직접 강좌에 등록해야 합니다. 등록비 지원은 과정 완료 시 제공될 것입니다.

이 강좌는 Dearborn의 Eight Mile Drive와 4th Avenue에 위치한 National Automobile Institute 캠퍼스 두 군데에서 진행될 것입니다. 각 수업은 6주간 계속될 것이며, 평일 정해진 날에 오후 4시부터 6시까지 만나게 됩니다.

여러분이 들어야 할 과정은 다음과 같습니다.

• 연료 시스템 설치: 월요일, Eight Mile Drive 캠퍼스
• 생산 허용오차: 화요일, Eight Mile Drive 캠퍼스
• 차량 안전 시스템: 목요일, 4th Avenue 캠퍼스
• 부상을 최소화하는 기법: 금요일, 4th Avenue 캠퍼스

다뤄질 내용 중 일부는 Best Motors 자동차에만 적용되는 것이며, 우리 엔지니어들이 설명을 도울 것입니다.

(160) 이 교육은 의무 참석이 아니라는 점을 알아두시기 바랍니다. 그러나 저희는 여러분이 해당 분야의 최신 정보에 능통하길 강력하게 권장합니다. (159) 여러분의 실적은 연단위로 평가되며, 이 교육은 우리 회사에서 여러분이 더 높은 직책으로 옮겨가는데 도움이 될 수 있습니다. 이 프로그램에 대해 질문이 있으시면, 여러분의 관리자와 논의해 주십시오.

감사합니다.

Richard Redford
생산 담당 이사
Best Motors

**158.** 이 회람의 목적은 무엇인가?
(A) 일부 수업의 피드백을 요청하는 것
(B) 어떤 직원들을 위한 교육을 논의하는 것
(C) 회사 교육 담당자들에게 설명을 제공하는 것
(D) 지역 자동차 정비공들을 위해 공석을 발표하는 것     정답 (B)

**159.** 직원들이 이 회람에 관심을 가질 가능성이 가장 높은 이유는 무엇인가?
(A) 제조 문제로 인해 회사가 돈을 잃고 있었다.
(B) 그들의 참여가 회사 내 직책에 영향을 줄 수 있다.
(C) 과정 완료 후 급여가 인상될 것이다.
(D) 생산 시간을 줄이는 방법을 배울 수 있다.     정답 (B)

**160.** [1], [2], [3] 그리고 [4]로 표시된 곳 중에, 아래 문장이 들어가기에 가장 적절한 곳은?
"이 교육은 의무 참석이 아니라는 점을 알아두시기 바랍니다."
(A) [1]
(B) [2]

(C) [3]

(D) [4]　　　　　　　　　　　　　　　　　　정답 (D)

---

## 문제 161-163번은 다음 이메일을 참조하시오.

수신: Michael Patterson 〈michaelw@yahomail.net〉
발신: Rebecca Ferguson 〈rf@goodtravel.com〉
날짜: 5월 9일 15:46
제목: 휴가

안녕하세요. 귀하의 여행사 담당자인 Rebecca Ferguson입니다. **(161) 고객님의 휴가 세부사항을 확인하고 싶습니다.** 고객님은 전화 상으로 저에게 7월 2일에 이탈리아로 가고 싶다고 하셨습니다. 가능하긴 하지만, 비행기 요금이 개인당 620달러입니다. **(162) 귀하의 휴가 날짜를 변경하실 수 있습니까?** 만약 귀하의 휴가를 일주일 늦춰 7월 9일 날 가시는 것이 가능하다면 요금은 개인당 450달러로 많이 낮아집니다. 이에 대해 귀하께서 원하시는 바를 제게 알려주세요.

그리고 귀하가 예약하실 호텔에 대해 몇 가지 질문이 있습니다. 성인 2명과 아동 2명을 포함하여 총 4명이 이번 휴가를 떠날 거라고 말씀하셨습니다. 큰 가족용 객실 하나와 그 보다 작은 두 개의 객실 중 어떤 것을 원하시나요? **(163) 만약 가족용 객실을 선호하신다면, 가격대에 비해 훌륭한 시설을 구비한 Paradise 호텔을 추천합니다.** 이 호텔의 객실은 욕조와 TV, 그리고 컴퓨터를 갖추고 있으며 인터넷에 접속할 수 있는 무선 와이파이를 제공합니다.

가능한 한 빨리 1-800-7767-3232로 전화하셔서 귀하의 의사를 알려주세요.

Rebecca Ferguson

---

**161.** 이 이메일의 목적은 무엇인가?

(A) Patterson 씨에게 독일에서의 할인된 휴가를 제안하기 위해서

(B) Patterson 씨에게 이번 휴가가 취소된 것을 알려주기 위해서

(C) Patterson 씨에게 여행자 보험 상품을 광고하기 위해서

(D) Patterson 씨에게 휴가 계획에 대한 몇 가지 질문을 하기 위해서

　　　　　　　　　　　　　　　　　　정답 (D)

**162.** [1], [2], [3] 그리고 [4]로 표시된 곳 중에, 아래 문장이 들어가기에 가장 적절한 곳은?

"귀하의 휴가 날짜를 변경하실 수 있으십니까?"

(A) [1]

(B) [2]

(C) [3]

(D) [4]　　　　　　　　　　　　　　　　　　정답 (B)

**163.** Ferguson 씨가 Paradise 호텔과 관련하여 언급하지 않은 것은 무엇인가?

(A) 그 호텔은 가격에 비해 훌륭한 시설을 구비하고 있다.

(B) 각 객실에는 욕조가 구비되어 있다.

(C) 이 호텔에서는 가족용 객실을 이용할 수 있다.

(D) 모든 객실은 무료 인터넷 서비스를 제공한다.　　정답 (D)

---

## 문제 164-167번은 다음 편지를 참조하시오.

Pramerica Insurance
193 레이크 스트릿
어스틴, 텍사스 49302
(800) 2020-5830

7월 3일

---

Anderson 씨께,

**(164) 저희 보험 상품에 관한 추가 정보를 요청하셨던 7월 1일의 전화통화와 관련하여 편지를 씁니다.** 동봉된 회사 상품 소개 책자를 참조하십시오.

상품 소개 책자에서 저희는 현재 제공하고 있는 여러 종류의 보험을 요약했습니다. **(166) 저는 이 기회를 빌어 사고나 응급상황의 경우 고객님과 고객님의 부군이 모두 보상을 받을 수 있는 Life Term Cover 보험을 추천해드리고 싶습니다.** 이 보험은 1년에 단돈 1200달러(또는 한 달에 100달러)의 비용이 들며 고객님이 거주하시는 지역에서 가장 인기 있는 보험 상품입니다.

저희는 적절한 보험을 선택하는 것이 간혹 스트레스를 받고, 번거로운 일이라는 것을 잘 알고 있습니다. 그것이 바로 저희가 최근에 보험 관련 세미나를 준비한 이유라고 할 수 있습니다. 세미나는 어스틴 시청에서 한 달에 한 번, 토요일에 개최되고 대략 한 시간 정도 걸립니다. **(165) 이 세미나는 어떤 보험 상품이 고객님에게 적합한지 결정하는 것을 도와주고자 고안되었습니다.** 이 세미나에서 고객님은 보험에 대한 성실한 조언가와 고객님의 개인적인 상황에 대해 논의할 수 있는 기회를 가지실 수 있습니다.

**(167) 보험 세미나에 대한 추가 정보나 약관 내용의 상세한 정보를 원하신다면, 인터넷 홈페이지 www.pramericainsurance.com을 방문해 주십시오.**

Pramerica Insurance를 선택하여 주셔서 감사합니다. 좋은 하루 보내십시오.

Linda Bush
보험 개발 부장
Pramerica Insurance

---

**164.** 이 편지의 목적은 무엇인가?

(A) 보험 상품의 약관 내용을 요약하기 위해서

(B) 고객이 요청했던 대로 추가 상품 정보를 제공하기 위해서

(C) 수신자에게 회사 직책을 제안하기 위해서

(D) 새로운 매장의 개장을 알리기 위해서　　정답 (B)

**165.** 세미나의 목적은 무엇인가?

(A) 신입직원들에게 영업기술에 대한 훈련을 시키기 위해서

(B) 웹사이트 디자인 분야에 관한 교육을 제공하기 위해서

(C) 이사회 임원들과 회사 영업 매출을 논하기 위해서

(D) 소비자가 적절한 보험을 선택하도록 도와주기 위해서　　정답 (D)

**166.** Life Term Cover 보험에 대해 언급되지 않은 내용은 무엇인가?

(A) 일 년에 1200달러 비용이 소요된다.

(B) 보험은 Anderson 씨와 그의 배우자 모두에게 유효하다.

(C) Anderson 씨의 아이들도 이 보험으로 보장받을 수 있다.

(D) 그 지역에서 가장 인기 있는 보험 상품이다.　　정답 (C)

**167.** Anderson 씨가 하도록 권유 받는 것은?

(A) 1500달러가 넘는 보험 가입하기

(B) 매주 세미나 참여하기

(C) 전문가와 온라인으로 상담하기

(D) 더 많은 정보를 위해 웹사이트 방문하기　　정답 (D)

---

## 문제 168-171번은 다음 기사를 참조하시오.

5월 10일 – 기자 회견에서 Scolan 건설의 회장 Lyle Vines는 내년 캔톤 공원 복원 계획에 회사가 150만 달러를 기부할 것이라고 밝혔다.

지난 2년간 공원 복원 계획에 대한 재정적 지원이 지속해 감소해, 자금이 크게 필요한 상태다. "Scolan 사의 후한 기부금에 굉장히 기쁩니다."라며 캔톤 공원 위원회의 Betty Judge 위원은 "캔톤 지역의 공원들

을 유지하고 개선하는 데 확실한 도움이 될 것입니다."라고 말했다.

(168) 캔톤 공원 복원 계획은 캔톤 주변의 공원과 운동장 시설들을 개선하기 위한 작업으로, 5년 전 캔톤 공원 위원회(CPC)에 의해 설립되었다. 처음 시작했을 당시에는 지역 정부에서 캔톤 공원 복원 계획을 위한 자금을 제공했으나, (169) 2년 전 캔톤 시 위원회가 캔톤 공원 복원 계획을 위한 자금을 신규 상업 지구 지원에 사용하기로 결정했다. 캔톤 공원 복원 계획은 그 이후로 자금 확보에 어려움을 겪고 있었다.

마침내 6개월 전부터 CPC는 지역 내 기업들에게 기부금을 요청하기 시작했다. "우리는 우리 공원들의 아름다움을 보여주는 책자와 편지를 여러 기업들에게 보냈습니다."라고 Judge 씨는 말했다. 책자 속 사진들은 몇 년에 걸친 공원의 경관들과 아이들이 놀고 있는 사진들을 다수 포함하고 있었다. (170) "Vines씨가 캔톤 공원 복원 계획에 기부관련 문의를 하기 전까지, 우리는 그가 이전에 이 지역 거주자였다는 것을 전혀 몰랐습니다."라고 Judge 씨는 말했다.

캔톤의 시민들과 지역장들은 캔톤 공원 복원 계획이 받을 추가 자금에 대해 반가워하고 있다. 시의원인 Carl Nesmith는 Vines 씨를 그의 기업이 한 기부에 대해 치하했다. 시의회는 공원들에 명예 명판을 배치하는 것을 논의했다. "캔톤은 지역 사회 일원 모두에게 이로운 아름다운 공원들이 여러 개 있습니다." Vines 씨가 기부를 발표하며 말했다. (171) "사실 처음 이 공원들에서 놀면서 건설에 매력을 느끼기 시작했습니다. 놀이터 속 모래사장에 작은 도시들을 만들며 보낸 시간이 아니었다면 나는 다른 직업을 선택했을 수도 있었습니다. 이번 기부로 지역 사회가 계속 공원을 즐기게 도움이 되었으면 좋겠습니다."

Michael Pyke, 현지 기자

**168.** 캔톤 공원 복원 계획은 언제 시작되었는가?
(A) 6개월 전
(B) 1년 전
(C) 2년 전
(D) 5년 전 　　　　　　　　　　　　　　　　　정답 (D)

**169.** 기사에 따르면, 캔톤 공원 복원 계획이 재정 지원을 잃었던 이유는 무엇인가?
(A) 지방 정부가 지원한 자금이 재분배되었기 때문에
(B) 유지 보수 비용이 너무 증가해서
(C) 캔톤 지역의 많은 주민들이 지역에서 이사를 가서
(D) 유지 보수 작업이 더 이상 필요하지 않았기 때문에 　　정답 (A)

**170.** 현재 캔톤 지역 주민이 아닌 사람은 누구인가?
(A) Lyle Vines
(B) Betty Judge
(C) Carl Nesmith
(D) Michael Pyke 　　　　　　　　　　　　　　정답 (A)

**171.** Vines 씨가 캔톤 지역의 공원들에 대해 무엇을 이야기했는가?
(A) 지역 사회의 일원들이 공원들을 이용하지 않는다.
(B) 공원들이 그에게 건설 분야 직업을 갖도록 이끌었다.
(C) 캔톤 지역의 회사는 공원에 지원을 제공해야 한다.
(D) 모든 공원은 기증자에 대한 정보를 제공하는 명패가 있어야 한다. 　　　　　　　　　　　　　　　　　　정답 (B)

문제 172-175번은 다음 온라인 채팅 토론을 참조하시오.

Jim Preston　　　　　　　　　　　　　　[오후 4:10]
(172) Valentina와 제가 오후 6시에 이른 저녁 식사를 위해 잠시 쉴 겁니다. 같이 가실 분 있나요?

April Armstrong　　　　　　　　　　　　[오후 4:11]
어쩌면요. (172) 어디로 가실 생각인가요?

Jim Preston　　　　　　　　　　　　　　[오후 4:12]
(172/173) Fifth Avenue에 있는 중식당에 가 볼까 합니다. Great Wall이라고 불리는 곳입니다. 그곳의 음식이 정말로 훌륭하다고 들었거든요.

Mary Barnes　　　　　　　　　　　　　[오후 4:13]
운이 없으시네요. John과 제가 지난 주에 그곳에 들렀어요. (173/174) 아쉽게도, 그곳은 이미 문을 닫았어요.

Jim Preston　　　　　　　　　　　　　　[오후 4:14]
그런 줄은 몰랐어요. (174) 안타깝네요. 인터넷에 올라와 있는 후기는 아주 좋았는데요.

Mary Barnes　　　　　　　　　　　　　[오후 4:16]
Pine Street에 있는 한식당인 Chosun Dynasty에 가 보는 것은 어때요? 한국식 바비큐를 드셔 봤나요?

Jim Preston　　　　　　　　　　　　　　[오후 4:18]
그렇게 하면 좋겠네요. 몇 달 전에 Los Angeles로 출장 갔을 때 한국식 바비큐를 먹었어요. 정말로 맛있었어요. 다른 분들도 그곳에 가실래요?

April Armstrong　　　　　　　　　　　　[오후 4:19]
네, 저도 한국 음식을 좋아합니다. 저도 끼워 주세요.

Jim Preston　　　　　　　　　　　　　　[오후 4:20]
좋습니다. 오후 6시에 로비에서 만납시다. 괜찮으신가요?

Mary Barnes　　　　　　　　　　　　　[오후 4:20]
괜찮습니다. 6시에 그곳에서 뵙겠습니다.

April Armstrong　　　　　　　　　　　　[오후 4:22]
음… (175) 하지만 저는 6시 30분이 지나서야 사무실 밖으로 갈 수 있을 거예요. Jim, 제가 다음 달에 출시될 우리 신제품에 대한 새로운 디자인을 완료해야 합니다. 하지만 오후 7시까지는 그곳으로 갈게요.

**172.** 메시지 작성자들은 무엇에 관해 이야기하고 있는가?
(A) 기업 행사를 주최할 장소
(B) 함께 갈 사람
(C) 저녁 식사를 할 장소
(D) 맛있는 음식을 제공하는 레스토랑 　　　　　　정답 (C)

**173.** 한 중식당에 관해 알 수 있는 것은 무엇인가?
(A) 새로운 곳으로 이전했다.
(B) 아주 형편 없는 평가를 받았다.
(C) 더 이상 영업하지 않는다.
(D) 오후 6시 이후에 특별 메뉴를 제공한다. 　　　　정답 (C)

**174.** 오후 4시 14분에, Preston 씨가 "That's too bad."라고 썼을 때 무엇을 의미하는가?
(A) 선약이 있다.
(B) 자신의 프로젝트에 대한 마감시한을 맞출 수 없다.
(C) 중국 음식을 한 번 먹어 보고 싶어 했다.
(D) 새로운 레스토랑이 너무 멀리 떨어져 있다고 생각한다. 　정답 (C)

**175.** Armstrong 씨는 무엇을 할 계획인가?
(A) 조금 늦게 동료들에게 합류할 것이다.
(B) 초과 근무를 할 것이다.
(C) 새로운 레스토랑으로 갈 것이다.
(D) 중국으로 출장을 떠날 것이다. 　　　　　　　정답 (A)

문제 176-180번은 다음 웹페이지와 온라인 서식을 참조하시오.

http://www.sbrg.com/about

| 홈 | SBRG에 대해 | 등록 | 연결 |

귀하의 소규모 사업체 이익을 극대화하십시오.

귀하의 소규모 사업체가 바쁘지만 여전히 이익을 내기 위해 고전하고 있습니까? (176) Small Business Resource Guide (SBRG)를 구독하시고 귀하의 소규모 사업체의 재정적 측면을 더 잘 관리하는 법을 배우십시오! (177) 저희는 20여년 이상 전국의 소규모 사업체 사장님들이 재정적 성공을 거두도록 도와드렸습니다. 여기 저희가 제공하는 것들 중 몇 가지를 소개합니다:

정보 자료 – 성공적인 소규모 사업체 사장님들이 만든 방대한 기사, 보고서, 논평에 접속하십시오. 이 자료들은 현실적이고 실제적인 조언을 제공하여 귀하의 사업체가 장기적인 수익성을 달성하도록 도움을 드릴 것입니다. (178) 저희는 매달 많은 새로운 자료를 사이트에 추가하며, 소규모 사업체 사장님들이 아셔야 할 모든 주제를 다룹니다.

다운로드 가능한 서식, 작업 계획표, 견본 – 저희는 다운로드 가능한 작업 계획표, 서식, 견본의 방대한 데이터베이스를 모두 무료로 제공합니다. 귀하의 사업체 필요에 맞게 이 자료들을 쉽게 변경하실 수 있습니다.

소규모 사업체 포럼 – 저희 온라인 포럼은 회원들이 소규모 사업체 운영의 세부사항에 대한 아이디어와 통찰력을 공유하도록 해 드립니다. 소규모 사업체 운영의 독특한 어려움을 이해하고 있는 수천 명의 회원들과 교류하세요.

온라인 및 대면 세미나 – 전문가들이 제공하는 다양한 온라인 수업에 참여하세요. 또한 저희는 주요 도시에서 자주 대면 세미나를 개최하며, 골드레벨 회원은 무료로 이 행사들에 참석하실 수 있습니다! (179) 실버레벨 회원은 이 행사에 참여하실 수 있으나, 행사 당 80달러를 지불하셔야 함에 유의해 주십시오.

지금 즉시 SBRG에 접속하세요! 일시불 비용 100달러 및 매달 30달러(실버레벨 회원) 또는 45달러(골드레벨 회원)만 내시면 됩니다.

http://www.sbrg.com/register

| 홈 | SBRG에 대해 | 등록 | 연결 |

SBRG 신규회원 정보

이름: Thomas          거리: 7891 Fields St.
성: Dekker            시: Winston
회사명: Garmon Clothing    주: North Carolina
전화번호: 800-555-8209    우편번호: 61771

이메일 주소: thomas.dekker@garmonclothing.com
회원 아이디 만들기: t.de
비밀번호 만들기: *******
비밀번호 확인: *******

지불 유형 선택: 등록비 100달러
더하기: ●실버 레벨 (월 30달러)    ●골드 레벨 (월 45달러)

(180) SBRG는 회원님들의 결과를 보장하며, 귀사의 재정이 회원가입 후 1년 안에 향상되지 않을 경우 당해 년도 회비의 절반을 배상해 드릴 것입니다.

**176.** 웹페이지 정보의 목적은 무엇인가?
(A) 웹사이트에 새로운 포럼을 발표하는 것
(B) SBRG 회원의 혜택을 설명하는 것
(C) 새로운 소규모 사업체의 창업을 홍보하는 것
(D) 소규모 사업체가 돈을 절약하는 몇 가지 방법을 서술하는 것    정답 (B)

**177.** SBRG에 대해 사실인 점은 무엇인가?
(A) 모든 회원에게 대면 행사의 비용을 청구한다.
(B) 레스토랑 소유주들을 돕는 것이 전문이다.
(C) Winston, North Carolina에 본사를 두고 있다.
(D) 20년 이상 존재했다.    정답 (D)

**178.** 웹페이지에 의하면 무엇이 매달 업데이트되는가?
(A) 정보 자료
(B) 다운로드 가능한 자료들
(C) 비즈니스 계획들
(D) 포럼 배치    정답 (A)

**179.** Dekker 씨에 대해 무엇이 암시되어 있는가?
(A) 몇 년간 SBRG의 회원이었다.
(B) 대면 세미나 참석에 관심이 있다.
(C) 최근에 사업체 위치를 변경했다.
(D) 온라인 수업을 몇 개 들었다.    정답 (B)

**180.** SBRG는 언제 환불을 제공하는가?
(A) 소규모 사업체가 자금조달을 할 수 없을 때
(B) 소규모 사업체가 이익을 내지 못할 때
(C) 세미나 비용을 이미 지불했을 때
(D) 기한 이후에 지불했을 때    정답 (B)

문제 181-185번은 다음 이메일들을 참조하시오.

수신: Andrew Kim ⟨ak@bs.com⟩
발신: 주문확인 ⟨order@acefood.com⟩
날짜: 12월 12일, 오전 11:22:19
제목: 주문 요약, 주문확인 #3232

Kim 씨께,

Ace Food Supply를 선택해 주셔서 감사합니다. (181) 이 이메일은 다음과 같이 귀하의 주문을 확인하기 위한 것입니다.

| 주문번호 | 세부내역 | 수량 |
| --- | --- | --- |
| E390 | 나파 아보카도 | 100파운드 |
| C932 | 닭가슴살 | 50파운드 |
| B820 | 야생 크랜베리 | 80파운드 |
| O400 | 고구마 | 125파운드 |

(182) 모든 주문은 수령 당일에 배송됩니다. (183) 배송품이 도착하는 정확한 시간은 저희 본사와 귀사의 거리에 따라 달라집니다.

이번 주문의 청구서는 앞으로 3영업일 안에 귀하의 레스토랑으로 보내질 것입니다.

질문이 있으시면 전화 또는 이메일로 연락 주십시오. 배송 중에는 주문을 변경하실 수 없음을 유의해 주십시오.

주문에 감사드립니다.

Ace Food Supply

수신: 주문확인 ⟨order@acefood.com⟩
발신: Andrew Kim ⟨ak@hankookmail.com⟩
날짜: 12월 13일, 오전 11:43:30
제목: 회신: 주문 요약, 주문확인 #3232

주문번호 3232 건으로 연락 드립니다. 주문 사본은 정확하지만, 가능하다면 몇 가지 변경하고 싶습니다. (184) 당초 E390을 100파운드 주문했지만, 250파운드로 주문양을 변경하고 싶습니다. 그리고 닭가슴살(품목번호

C932)은 30파운드만 필요할 것 같습니다. (185) 그런데 귀사 홈페이지에 이제는 30파운드 자루에 담긴 딸기가 없는 것을 발견했습니다. 아주 좋은 딸기였는데요. 판매가 중단된 것인가요? 그렇지 않다면 언제 다시 입고될까요?

감사합니다.

Andrew Kim
Blue Sky Restaurant

**181.** 첫 번째 이메일의 목적은 무엇인가?
(A) 대량 발주에 따른 할인을 자세하게 설명한다.
(B) 품절된 품목을 공지한다.
(C) 주문이 배송되었음을 확인한다.
(D) 최근 주문의 세부내역을 제공한다.　　　　정답 (D)

**182.** 첫 번째 이메일에서 배송에 대해 언급하고 있는 것은 무엇인가?
(A) 모든 품목에 무료로 제공된다.
(B) 주문 당일에 이루어진다.
(C) 배송된 뒤에는 반품될 수 없다.
(D) 작은 크기의 품목에 국한된다.　　　　정답 (B)

**183.** 첫 번째 이메일에서 두 번째 단락 두 번째 줄의 "proximity"와 의미상 가장 유사한 단어는 무엇인가?
(A) 가까움
(B) 방향
(C) 부족
(D) 범위　　　　정답 (A)

**184.** Kim 씨는 주문에서 어떤 품목의 수량을 늘리고 싶어하는가?
(A) 나파 아보카도
(B) 닭가슴살
(C) 야생 크랜베리
(D) 고구마　　　　정답 (A)

**185.** Kim 씨에 대해 암시되는 것은 무엇인가?
(A) 그는 주문을 취소하고 싶어한다.
(B) 그는 본래 주문에 몇 가지 품목을 추가했다.
(C) 그는 Ace Food Supply의 신규 고객이다.
(D) 그는 딸기를 주문하고 싶어한다.　　　　정답 (D)

**문제 186~190번은 다음 광고와 온라인 쇼핑 장바구니, 그리고 이메일을 참조하시오.**

Audiofile 온라인은 새로 설립된 영국 회사로, 전 세계의 음악 팬들의 사랑을 받을 것이 분명한 음악 다운로드 서비스를 제공하는 회사입니다. 저희는 가장 저렴한 가격에 전 세계 (186) **최고의** 아티스트들이 내놓는 가장 최신 음악 트랙들을 가입자 여러분께 제공해 드립니다! Audiofile 온라인에 가입하시면, 매달 다운로드 하실 수 있는 음악 트랙에 제한이 없으며, (187) **이메일로 저희 무료 월간 잡지를 받으시도록 자동으로 등록이 됩니다.** 음악 트랙에 100달러 이상을 결제하시고 무료 선물로 받으십시오! 저희 '특집 아티스트' 섹션에서는, 가입자 여러분께서 "구입하기 전에 들어보실 수 있도록" 해 드립니다. 각 특집 아티스트들의 무료 트랙 한 개를 주문하실 수 있으며, 음악이 마음에 드시면 앨범 전체를 다운로드하도록 진행하실 수 있습니다. 일반 가입자들께서는 소리가 깔끔한 128 kbit/s로 코딩된 MP3 파일을 받으실 수 있으며, (188) **Audiofile 맥스 및 Audiofile 프로 가입자 여러분께서는 각각 192 kbit/s와 320 kbit/s 트랙을 이용하실 수 있습니다.**

www.audiofile.co.uk를 방문하시면 더 자세한 정보를 얻으실 수 있습니다!

---

www.audiofileonline.co.uk/shoppingcart

Audiofile 온라인

가입자 성명: (188) **Chris Boyd**

다운로드 (특집 아티스트)

| 아티스트 | 트랙/앨범 제목 | 세부 사항 | 트랙 수 | 비트 전송률 (kbit/s) | 가격 |
|---|---|---|---|---|---|
| (189) Justin Haynes | All My Friends | 무료 트랙 | 1 | (188) 320 | $0.00 |
| One Promise | From the Heart | 무료 트랙 | 1 | 320 | $0.00 |
| Digital Dreamz | Full Evolution | 앨범 전체 | 14 | 320 | $18.06 |
| The Black Days | In Your Head | 무료 트랙 | 1 | 320 | $0.00 |
| | | | | 지불 총액: | $18.06 |

결제 진행하기

---

수신: Audiofile 온라인 고객 지원 센터 〈helpdesk@audiofile.co.uk〉
발신: Chris Boyd 〈chrisboyd79@digimail.net〉
날짜: 4월 16일
제목: 최근의 구매

안녕하세요,

최근에 귀사의 웹사이트에서 구입한 트랙에 관해 연락 드립니다. 우선, 저는 귀사의 서비스를 정말 좋아하는 팬이라는 점을 말씀 드리고자 하며, 특히 특집 아티스트 무료 트랙을 들어볼 기회를 갖는 것을 좋아합니다. 실제로, 저는 며칠 전에 몇몇 MP3 트랙을 주문했습니다. (190) **또한 Digital Dreamz의 "Full Evolution"도 구매했지만, 실제로는 그 앨범 대신에 Digital Dreamz의 "Nine Lives"를 받았습니다.** 저는 이미 이 앨범을 갖고 있기 때문에 이 상황을 바로 잡아 주실 수 있기를 바랍니다. 제가 들어본 무료 트랙들을 바탕으로 생각해 볼 때, 저는 One Promise의 앨범을 구입할 계획입니다. (189) **"All My Friends"는 들어줄 수 없을 정도지만** "In Your Head"는 제가 처음에 생각했던 것만큼 나쁘지는 않았기 때문에 이 아티스트의 앨범을 구매하는 것도 고려해 볼 수 있습니다. 좋은 서비스를 제공해 주셔서 감사 드리며, 곧 연락 주시기를 바랍니다.

Chris Boyd

**186.** 광고에서, 1번째 단락, 3번째 줄에 있는 단어 "top"과 의미가 가장 가까운 단어는 무엇인가?
(A) 가장 높은
(B) 진보한
(C) 과도한
(D) 선도하는　　　　정답 (D)

**187.** 광고에 따르면 Audiofile 온라인에 관해 사실인 것은 무엇인가?
(A) 오래 전에 설립된 회사이다.
(B) 월간 다운로드 제한을 실시하고 있다.
(C) 전자 출판물을 발간하고 있다.
(D) 여러 국가에 지사가 있다.　　　　정답 (C)

**188.** Boyd 씨에 관해 알 수 있는 것은 무엇인가?
(A) 최근에 자신이 가입한 서비스를 업그레이드했다.
(B) 네 가지 앨범 전체를 다운로드했다.
(C) Audiofile 프로 가입자이다.
(D) 무료 선물을 받았다.　　　　정답 (C)

**189.** Boyd 씨는 어느 아티스트의 음악에 가장 실망했는가?
(A) Justin Haynes
(B) One Promise

70

(C) Digital Dreamz

(D) The Black Days  정답 (A)

**190.** Boyd 씨는 자신의 이메일에서 무슨 문제점을 설명하는가?

(A) 다른 아티스트의 음악 트랙을 받았다.

(B) 음질이 좋지 않은 MP3 파일들을 받았다.

(C) 요청하지 않은 앨범을 받았다.

(D) 예상한 것보다 더 적은 파일을 받았다.  정답 (C)

---

문제 191-195번은 다음 안내 정보와, 웹페이지 양식, 그리고 이메일을 참조하시오.

---

American Elite 주식회사

(191) **9월 한 달 동안 열리는 저희 비즈니스 능력 워크숍에 관해 알려 드리게 되어 기쁩니다.** 아래에 기재된 워크숍은 한 달 내내 매주 토요일에 개최될 예정입니다. 워크숍이 열리는 도시들은 아래에 표기되어 있습니다. 장소 및 일정과 관련된 모든 상세 정보들은 저희 웹사이트에서 확인해 보실 수 있습니다.

워크숍 #091 – (CH, (192) **LA**, CI, PH, SA) – '고객과 의사 소통하는 더 나은 기술'

워크숍 #092 – (CH, NY, (192) **LA**, CI, CL) – (193) '**스마트스위트 6**를 이용해 스프레드시트 만들기'

워크숍 #093 – (CH, NY, (192) **LA**, SA, DE) – '제약 업계에서 성공하기'

워크숍 #094 – ((192) **LA**, HO, PH, SA, DE) – '웹사이트 디자인: 고객들을 유치하는 지름길'

장소 표기: Chicago (CH), New York City (NY), (192) **Los Angeles (LA)**, Houston (HO), Cincinnati (CI), Philadelphia (PH), San Antonio (SA), Cleveland (CL), Detroit (DE)

상기 행사에 관한 상세 정보 확인을 원하거나 온라인 등록 양식을 작성하려면 www.americaneliteinc.com/workshops/를 방문하시기 바랍니다.

---

www.americaneliteinc.com/workshops/registration

행사 등록 양식 – 9월 워크숍

신청자 성명:  Veronica Lamb

신청자 이메일 주소:  veronicalamb@blitzco.com

워크숍 번호:  (193) **092**

위치 코드:  CH

워크숍 날짜:  ■ (194) **9월 3일**  □ 9월 10일

  □ 9월 17일  □ 9월 24일

소속 회사:  블리츠코 주식회사

직위:  광고 이사

워크숍 등록은 선택하신 워크숍 날짜보다 최소 7일 전에 반드시 완료되어야 합니다.

**비용 지불 페이지로 가기**

---

수신: 등록 서비스 부 ⟨registration@americanelite.org⟩

발신: Veronica Lamb ⟨veronicalamb@blitzco.com ⟩

날짜: 9월 1일

제목: 워크숍 등록

안녕하세요,

제가 어제 제출한 등록 양식과 (195) **관련해** 연락 드립니다. 제가 어제 그 양식을 작성할 때 집중을 하지 못해 실수를 했습니다. 제가 날짜를 클릭할 때, 다른 것을 선택했습니다. 그 워크숍에 대한 비용이 이미 제 계좌에서 빠

---

저 나갔기 때문에 (194) **제 등록 양식의 날짜를 그 다음 토요일로 변경해 주시면 대단히 감사하겠습니다.** 제가 원하는 날짜를 뒤로 미루는 것이 불가능할 경우, 제게 등록 비용을 환불해 주시면 정확한 정보를 가지고 다시 한 번 등록하겠습니다. 곧 연락 주시기를 바랍니다.

Veronica Lamb

**191.** American Elite 주식회사는 무슨 종류의 회사일 가능성이 큰가?

(A) 광고회사

(B) 임원 채용 대행사

(C) 직무 능력 개발 회사

(D) 비즈니스 저널 출판사  정답 (C)

**192.** 목록에 표기된 모든 워크숍을 주최하는 도시는 어디인가?

(A) Chicago

(B) New York

(C) Los Angeles

(D) Detroit  정답 (C)

**193.** Lamb 씨에 관해 알 수 있는 내용은 무엇인가?

(A) 웹사이트 디자인 경력이 있다.

(B) 현재 한 제약회사에서 근무하고 있다.

(C) 자신의 의사 소통 능력을 개선하기를 원한다.

(D) 일부 소프트웨어 사용법을 배우고자 한다.  정답 (D)

**194.** Lamb 씨는 언제 워크숍에 참석하기를 원하는가?

(A) 9월 3일에

(B) 9월 10일에

(C) 9월 17일에

(D) 9월 24일에  정답 (B)

**195.** 이메일에서, 1번째 단락의 1번째 줄에 있는 단어 "concerning"과 의미가 가장 유사한 단어는 무엇인가?

(A) ~라고 가정하면

(B) ~을 포함하여

(C) ~가 있을 때까지

(D) ~와 관련해서  정답 (D)

---

문제 196-200번은 다음 광고와 웹페이지, 그리고 이메일을 참조하시오.

---

San Diego

컨벤션 센터

1201 노스 하버 가

샌디에고, 캘리포니아 92093

(858) 534-1123

"우리는 항상 귀하의 비즈니스를 생각합니다."

태평양을 바라보는 위치에 자리 잡고 있는 San Diego 컨벤션 센터는 단순한 컨벤션 센터 그 이상입니다. (196) **저희는 모든 고객님의 비즈니스 관련 요구사항을 충족시켜줄 수 있는 뛰어난 리조트 시설과 다양한 회의 서비스를 제공합니다.** (197) **저희 San Diego 컨벤션 센터는 모든 회의실에 팩스기, 컴퓨터, 프린터 및 인터넷 시설을 구비하고 있으며 또한 품격이 있는** 식당과 고급 바, 그리고 남녀 전용의 넓은 스파 및 사우나와 같은 편의시설들을 보유하고 있습니다. 게다가 태평양이 보이는 풍경은 이곳 San Diego 컨벤션 센터에서 머무는 시간을 즐겁게 해드릴 것입니다.

예약 또는 더 많은 정보를 원하시면, 저희 홈페이지 www.sdccenter.com에서 확인하시고 "예약하기"를 클릭해 주십시오.

San Diego 컨벤션 센터는 비즈니스와 사람들이 만나는 최적의 장소입니

다. 이 곳에서 귀하는 귀하의 회의를 위해 필요한 모든 것을 찾으실 수 있습니다.

---

www.sdccenter.com/reservation

| 홈 | 회의실 목록 | 숙박 | 야외 스포츠 | 연락처 |
|---|---|---|---|---|

회의실 이름  /  수용인원  /  비용

(198) 1. ORION 회의실  /  30명  /  하루 200달러
2. GALAXY 회의실  /  45명  /  하루 320달러
3. ANDROMEDA 회의실  /  70명  /  하루 480달러
4. UNIVERSE 회의실  /  100명  /  하루 630달러

---

수신: Jason Green ⟨jasongreen@pacificenergy.com⟩
발신: Belle Borden ⟨bborden@sdccenter.com⟩
날짜: 9월 11일
제목: 예약

Green 씨께,

(197) 저희는 귀하가 보내주신 10월 8일과 9일에 예약하신 2인실 그랜드 스위트의 선불금 500달러를 수령하였습니다. (199) ORION 회의실은 10월 8일 귀하의 회의를 위해 예약되었습니다. (200) 회의실 예약 완료를 위해서는 도착 1주 전에 추가 선불금인 250달러를 지불하시도록 당부 드립니다.

(198) 귀하의 발표를 위해 오리온 회의실에 필요한 전자 장비가 있으면, 저희가 미리 준비해 놓을 수 있도록 사전에 알려주시기 바랍니다.

또한, (197) 회의 시 필요한 출장 요리 서비스에 관한 문의 사항이 있으시면, 저희 주방 담당자인 Joanna Spencer 씨에게 213-767-3232, 내선 번호 7311로 전화 주시기 바랍니다.

고객님의 사업 성공을 기원합니다.

Belle Borden
예약업무 담당자
San Diego 컨벤션 센터

---

**196.** 광고가 대상으로 하는 사람은 누구일 것 같은가?
(A) 부동산 중개업자
(B) 전문 사업가
(C) 관광객
(D) 회의 기획사의 직원　　　　　　　　　정답 (B)

**197.** San Diego 컨벤션 센터에서 제공되지 않는 것은 무엇인가?
(A) 숙박
(B) 음식 서비스
(C) 사무 장비
(D) 해변 관광　　　　　　　　　정답 (D)

**198.** Green 씨에 관해 유추할 수 있는 것은 무엇인가?
(A) 그는 발표를 할 것이다.
(B) 그는 회사의 사장이다.
(C) 그는 Borden 씨와 이전에 연락한 적이 있다.
(D) 그는 Borden 씨의 일처리에 만족하고 있다.　　　　　　　　　정답 (A)

**199.** Green 씨의 회의에 대해 유추할 수 있는 것은 무엇인가?
(A) 10월 9일에 개최될 것이다.
(B) 참석자는 각자 자신이 쓸 전자 장비를 가지고 올 것이다.
(C) 30명 미만의 사람들이 참석할 것이다.
(D) 회의실은 일부 비용만이 먼저 지급되었다.　　　　　　　　　정답 (C)

**200.** Borden 씨가 그린 씨에게 요청하는 것은 무엇인가?
(A) 전액 환불 요청을 처리할 것
(B) 임대 계약서에 서명할 것
(C) 도착 전에 입금할 것
(D) 음식 서비스를 위해 스펜서 씨에게 연락할 것　　　　　　　　　정답 (C)

**1.** 미M

(A) Some customers are putting food on their plates.
(B) Some waiters are stacking dishes on a table.
(C) Some chefs are standing at a counter.
(D) Some restaurant workers are washing pans and bowls.

(A) 몇몇 손님들이 접시에 음식을 담고 있다.
(B) 몇몇 웨이터들이 테이블 위에 접시를 쌓고 있다.
(C) 몇몇 요리사들이 조리대에 서있다.
(D) 몇몇 식당 직원들이 냄비와 그릇을 닦고 있다.    정답 (C)

**2.** 미W

(A) Some people are planting flowers in a garden.
(B) Some palm trees have been cut down.
(C) Some fallen leaves are being cleared on a path.
(D) Some trees are casting large shadows in the woods.

(A) 몇몇 사람들이 정원에 꽃을 심고 있다.
(B) 몇몇 야자수들이 벌목되었다.
(C) 산책로의 낙엽이 치워지고 있다.
(D) 몇몇 나무들이 숲 속에 큰 그림자를 드리우고 있다.    정답 (D)

**3.** 영W

(A) Some waiters are serving customers.
(B) All the outdoor seats are occupied.
(C) The picnic table has been cleared of objects.
(D) The chairs are arranged in a semicircle.

(A) 몇몇 웨이터들이 손님의 시중을 들고 있다.
(B) 모든 야외 의자에 사람들이 착석하고 있다.
(C) 야외 테이블에 아무 것도 놓여 있지 않다.
(D) 의자들이 반원형으로 배치되어 있다.    정답 (D)

**4.** 미M

(A) He's removing her sunglasses.
(B) He's pressing a button in an elevator.
(C) He's standing in front of a vending machine.
(D) He's opening a file cabinet door.

(A) 그는 선글라스를 벗고 있다.
(B) 그는 승강기의 버튼을 누르고 있다.
(C) 그는 자판기 앞에 서 있다.
(D) 그는 서류함을 열고 있다.    정답 (B)

**5.** 호M

(A) The entryway is blocked off.
(B) A pathway encircles a lake.
(C) A footbridge extends over a road.
(D) A railing runs along the top of a bridge.

(A) 진입로가 막혀 있다.
(B) 호수 둘레에 오솔길이 있다.
(C) 육교가 도로 위를 지나고 있다.
(D) 난간이 다리 상단을 따라 뻗어 있다.    정답 (D)

**6.** 영W

(A) Market stalls are covered by canopies.
(B) Some shelves are being restocked with merchandise.
(C) Some customers are browsing inside a shopping mall.

(D) All of the pavilions have been erected on a grassy area.

(A) 시장 노점들이 덮개로 가려져 있다.
(B) 몇몇 선반들이 상품으로 다시 채워지고 있다.
(C) 몇몇 고객들이 쇼핑몰 안에서 구경을 하고 있다.
(D) 모든 천막들이 잔디밭에 세워져 있다.    정답 (A)

## Part 2

**7.** 미M 영W

Who's working the night shift on Thursday?
(A) I think Mr. White is.
(B) I don't have any plans tonight.
(C) Thursday would be great.

목요일에 누가 야간 근무를 하나요?
(A) White 씨인 것으로 알고 있어요.
(B) 저는 오늘밤에 약속이 없어요.
(C) 목요일이면 좋습니다.    정답 (A)

**8.** 미W 미M

Where is the art exhibition being held tomorrow?
(A) November 23 at noon.
(B) At the municipal museum, I heard.
(C) Some paintings are really impressive.

내일 미술 전시회는 어디서 개최될 예정인가요?
(A) 11월 23일 정오예요.
(B) 시립 미술관에서 열린다고 들었어요.
(C) 몇몇 그림들은 매우 인상적이에요.    정답 (B)

**9.** 영W 호M

When will the budget report be published?
(A) No later than Friday.
(B) Two weeks ago, I think.
(C) In the main office.

예산 보고서는 언제 발표되나요?
(A) 늦어도 금요일까지 될 겁니다.
(B) 2주 전인 걸로 알고 있어요.
(C) 본사에서요.    정답 (A)

**10.** 미M 영W

How do you like the new branch manager?
(A) I think he's very friendly and capable.
(B) I'd like to take them out to brunch.
(C) Sorry. We're closed.

새 지점장은 어때요?
(A) 그는 매우 친절하고 유능한 것 같아요.
(B) 저는 그들을 데리고 나가 브런치를 먹으려고 해요.
(C) 죄송합니다만, 영업이 끝났습니다.    정답 (A)

**11.** 영W 미M

Has the personnel policy changed in the past few years?
(A) Why don't you ask the personnel director?
(B) No, we need several new personal computers.
(C) Yes, I'll go to Thailand for a change.

지난 몇 년간 인사 방침에 변경이 있었나요?
(A) 인사부장에게 묻는 것이 어때요?
(B) 아니오, 우리는 몇몇 새로운 개인용 컴퓨터가 필요해요.

(C) 네, 저는 기분전환으로 태국에 갈 거예요.　　　　정답 (A)

**12.** 미W 미M

Do you think the new marketing method will increase our quarterly profits?
(A) That would save me time.
(B) I believe that it'll boost our revenues.
(C) We will increase our production to fill demand.

새로운 마케팅 방식이 우리의 분기별 수익을 증가시킬 것이라고 생각하나요?
(A) 그것이 제 시간을 절약시켜 줄 거예요.
(B) 그것이 우리의 수익을 증가시킬 것이라고 믿어요.
(C) 우리는 수요를 충족시키기 위해 생산을 늘릴 겁니다.　　　정답 (B)

**13.** 영W 미W

To whom should I direct your call?
(A) Ask someone for directions.
(B) I think it's very cold outside now.
(C) Please put me through to your marketing director.

누구에게 전화를 연결시켜 드릴까요?
(A) 누군가에게 길을 물어보세요.
(B) 지금 밖이 상당히 추운 것 같아요.
(C) 마케팅 이사에게 연결시켜 주세요.　　　정답 (C)

**14.** 미M 영W

Do you want me to help you find your seat?
(A) Yes, I'll get someone to help you.
(B) No thanks. I can manage.
(C) We'll see the show at 6:00.

좌석 찾으시는 것을 도와드릴까요?
(A) 네, 당신을 도와줄 만한 사람을 데리고 올게요.
(B) 고맙습니다만, 제가 할 수 있어요.
(C) 저희는 6시 공연을 볼 거예요.　　　정답 (B)

**15.** 호M 미M

The lunch we had yesterday was really delicious, wasn't it?
(A) No, thank you. I'm already full.
(B) Actually, it was not that good.
(C) A new restaurant on the corner.

어제 먹은 점심식사는 정말 맛있었어요, 그렇지 않나요?
(A) 고맙습니다만, 괜찮아요. 저는 이미 배가 불러요.
(B) 사실, 그다지 좋진 않았어요.
(C) 모퉁이에 있는 새로운 레스토랑이요.　　　정답 (B)

**16.** 영W 호M

Who developed the new product?
(A) Well, Mr. Hachi will.
(B) It was released last week.
(C) Let me check.

누가 신제품을 개발했나요?
(A) 음, Hachi 씨가 할 겁니다.
(B) 그건 지난주에 출시되었어요.
(C) 제가 확인해 볼게요.　　　정답 (C)

**17.** 미M 미W

Haven't you finished the new training course?
(A) I want some finalized data.

(B) Yes, two months ago.
(C) The train leaves at 9 o'clock.

새로운 연수 과정을 수료하지 않았나요?
(A) 저는 최종 자료를 원합니다.
(B) 네, 두 달 전예요.
(C) 기차는 9시에 출발합니다.　　　정답 (B)

**18.** 호M 영W

Are you giving a presentation on our new business plans on Tuesday or Wednesday?
(A) It's very interesting, isn't it?
(B) I have other plans for tonight.
(C) I'm doing that on Thursday at 1:00.

당신이 우리의 새로운 사업 계획을 발표하는 날이 화요일인가요, 아니면 수요일인가요?
(A) 굉장히 흥미롭습니다, 그렇지 않나요?
(B) 오늘밤에 선약이 있어요.
(C) 목요일 1시에 해요.　　　정답 (C)

**19.** 미W 미M

Which flight are you taking to Boston?
(A) I prefer an aisle seat.
(B) It will take about three hours.
(C) I haven't decided yet.

Boston에 갈 때 어떤 비행편을 이용하실 건가요?
(A) 복도 쪽 자리를 원합니다.
(B) 3시간 정도 걸립니다.
(C) 아직 결정하지 못했어요.　　　정답 (C)

**20.** 미M 영W

I heard Ms. Ha was promoted to floor manager.
(A) No, Ms. Kimberly was.
(B) It is on the ground floor.
(C) Yes, it's a new promotional campaign.

Ha 씨가 매장 관리자로 승진했다고 들었어요.
(A) 아니오, Kimberly 씨가 승진했어요.
(B) 그건 1층에 있어요.
(C) 네, 그건 새로운 판촉 행사예요.　　　정답 (A)

**21.** 호M 미W

I'm going to return this laptop computer to the store tomorrow.
(A) Is something wrong?
(B) Yes, I'll charge it.
(C) In the top drawer.

내일 매장에 이 노트북 컴퓨터를 반품하려고 해요.
(A) 뭐가 잘못되었나요?
(B) 네, 신용카드로 계산할게요.
(C) 상단 서랍예요.　　　정답 (A)

**22.** 미M 영W

When will Mr. Ryan be transferred to the Hong Kong branch?
(A) But it's a nice city to live in.
(B) Once the personnel manager approves it.
(C) Last Tuesday, I think.

Ryan 씨는 언제 Hong Kong 지점으로 전근을 가나요?
(A) 하지만 그 곳은 살기 좋은 도시예요.

(B) 인사부장이 승인하면요.
(C) 지난주 화요일로 알고 있어요.     정답 (B)

**23.** 호M 미W
What was the cost of the new computer monitor?
(A) Yes, I already bought it.
(B) The same price as the old one.
(C) I'm afraid you paid too much.

새로운 컴퓨터 모니터의 비용이 얼마나 들었나요?
(A) 네, 저는 이미 샀어요.
(B) 이전 것과 동일한 가격이에요.
(C) 너무 많이 지불하신 건 아닌가 싶네요.     정답 (B)

**24.** 영W 미M
Can you take this microscope to the laboratory in the basement?
(A) No, he's looking through the microscope.
(B) Yes, our labor costs are too high.
(C) I think I can do it after lunch.

이 현미경을 지하에 있는 실험실로 가져가 줄 수 있겠어요?
(A) 아니오, 그는 현미경을 통해서 보고 있어요.
(B) 네, 우리 인건비가 상당히 높습니다.
(C) 점심식사 후에 할 수 있을 것 같아요.     정답 (C)

**25.** 미W 호M
You haven't reserved a flight to Seoul for the international seminar yet, have you?
(A) Yes, the conference was held in June.
(B) No, it's a short flight.
(C) I haven't, but I'm going to call a travel agent this afternoon.

국제 세미나 참석을 위한 서울행 항공권을 아직 예매하지 못했죠, 그렇죠?
(A) 네, 회의는 6월에 열렸어요.
(B) 아니오, 비행 시간이 짧아요.
(C) 아직 못했지만, 오늘 오후에 여행사 직원에게 전화할 거예요.   정답 (C)

**26.** 미W 영W
Mr. Fonda will be returning to the office tomorrow.
(A) He's on sick leave for two days.
(B) Are you sure? I just saw him in the office.
(C) Yes, I'll return it tomorrow.

Fonda 씨는 내일 사무실로 복귀합니다.
(A) 그는 이틀간 병가 중입니다.
(B) 확실한가요? 제가 방금 사무실에서 그를 봤어요.
(C) 네, 내일 반납할 겁니다.     정답 (B)

**27.** 호M 미W
Could you please e-mail me these financial charts by tomorrow?
(A) Yes, if you insist.
(B) I can't make it to the meeting tomorrow.
(C) No, we need some shopping carts.

이 금융 차트들을 내일까지 이메일로 제게 보내 주시겠어요?
(A) 네, 원하신다면요.
(B) 저는 내일 회의에 불참합니다.
(C) 아니오, 우리는 쇼핑용 카트가 필요해요.     정답 (A)

**28.** 영W 미M
Excuse me. Do you work in the Sales Department?
(A) Yes, it's functioning well.

(B) A large firm.
(C) No, I'm here on business.

실례합니다. 영업부에서 근무하시나요?
(A) 네, 그건 잘 작동하고 있어요.
(B) 대형 회사예요.
(C) 아니오, 저는 이 곳에 업무 차 왔어요.     정답 (C)

**29.** 미M 호M
Are we going to fly to Los Angeles or take a ferry?
(A) The item your ordered has already been shipped.
(B) Yes, it's one of the biggest cities in America.
(C) I think we're going there by plane.

우리는 Los Angeles까지 비행기를 타고 가요, 아니면 여객선을 타고 가나요?
(A) 주문하신 제품은 이미 발송되었습니다.
(B) 네, 미국 내 대도시 중 하나예요.
(C) 비행기를 타고 가는 걸로 알고 있어요.     정답 (C)

**30.** 미M 영W
I wonder if this shirt comes in a bigger size.
(A) I'd like to try it on.
(B) We lowered the price this morning.
(C) I'm afraid this is the biggest size available.

이 셔츠로 더 큰 사이즈가 있는지 궁금합니다.
(A) 한 번 입어보고 싶네요.
(B) 저희는 오늘 아침에 가격을 인하했어요.
(C) 죄송합니다만 이 사이즈가 제일 큰 겁니다.     정답 (C)

**31.** 미W 호M
One of the light bulbs in the hallway has completely burned out.
(A) Oh, thank you. I hadn't noticed.
(B) We're running out of time. Hurry up!
(C) You just made a right turn.

복도에 있는 전구 하나가 완전히 나갔어요.
(A) 아, 고마워요. 몰랐어요.
(B) 우리는 시간이 없어요. 서둘러요!
(C) 당신은 지금 막 우회전을 했어요.     정답 (A)

## Part 3

문제 32-34번은 다음 대화를 참조하시오. 미W 미M

W: (32/33) I can't believe how late the bus is. I wonder what's going on.
M: (33) I asked some other people waiting, and they said they heard there was a bad accident on the highway, and it is causing a really heavy traffic jam.
W: There are always car accidents on our bus route. I think the city government should do something to raise awareness of traffic safety.
M: You can say that again. (34) Traffic accidents have recently become a serious social problem.

-------------------------------------------------

W: 버스가 이렇게 늦다니 믿을 수가 없어요. 무슨 일이 있는 건지 참 궁금하네요.
M: 기다리고 있는 다른 사람들에게 물어봤더니 고속도로에서의 교통사고로 인해 아주 극심한 교통 정체가 발생하고 있다고 알려주네요.

W: 우리가 타는 이 버스 노선에는 항상 교통사고가 많아요. 시청에서 교통
안전 의식을 향상시킬 수 있도록 무엇인가 조치를 취했으면 싶어요.

M: 동감이에요. 최근에 교통사고가 심각한 사회 문제가 되고 있어요.

**32.** 화자들은 무엇에 관해 이야기하고 있는가?
- (A) 정기 휴가
- (B) 보수 공사
- (C) 새로운 지하철 노선
- (D) 늦어지는 버스      정답 (D)

**33.** 화자들은 어디에 있을 것 같은가?
- (A) 버스
- (B) 자동차 수리점
- (C) 길가
- (D) 공사 현장      정답 (C)

**34.** 여자가 언급하는 문제점은 무엇인가?
- (A) 사람들이 종종 운전 중에 휴대폰을 사용한다.
- (B) 버스 엔진이 멈췄다.
- (C) 교통사고가 더 빈번하게 발생한다.
- (D) 에너지가 비효율적으로 사용되고 있다.      정답 (C)

**문제 35-37번은 다음 대화를 참조하시오.** 미M 미W

M: Hi. (35) **I'm looking for some light fixtures for my new café, and I have to admit I'm a little overwhelmed by your selection.**

W: Yes, we carry a wide variety of lighting, so you can find something appropriate whatever your needs. (36) **We can install them for you if you decide you'd like help.**

M: I think that would be great. How much does that service cost?

W: It's usually $75, (36/37) **but we just started a new promotion. If you buy eight or more light fixtures, then installation of all of them is absolutely free.**

------------------------------------------------

M: 안녕하세요. 저는 새로 개업하는 제 카페에 어울리는 조명기구를 찾고 있는데요. 이 가게에 있는 다양한 제품에 약간 놀랐어요.

W: 네, 저희는 아주 다양한 종류의 조명기구를 판매하고 있으니 고객님께 선 어떠한 용도가 되건 그에 적절한 제품을 찾으실 수 있을 겁니다. 그리고 원하시면 제품 설치 서비스도 제공해 드립니다.

M: 그거 좋을 것 같은데요. 그 제품 설치 서비스는 비용이 얼마나 드나요?

W: 보통 75달러인데요. 저희가 막 새로운 판촉행사를 시작했어요. 고객님 께서 조명기구를 8개 이상 구매하시면 제품 설치 서비스는 완전히 무료입 니다.

**35.** 여자는 누구일 것 같은가?
- (A) 카페 주인
- (B) 판매 직원
- (C) 기술자
- (D) 포장 디자이너      정답 (B)

**36.** 여자가 남자에게 제공하는 것은 무엇인가?
- (A) 무료 가정 배송
- (B) 무료 객실 업그레이드
- (C) 수정된 계약서
- (D) 무료 설치      정답 (D)

**37.** 남자가 판촉행사의 혜택을 받으려면 어떻게 해야 하는가?
- (A) 상당한 양의 구매를 해야 한다.
- (B) 두 명의 고객을 추천해야 한다.
- (C) 영업 회의에 참석해야 한다.
- (D) 새로운 잡지를 구독해야 한다.      정답 (A)

**문제 38-40번은 다음 대화를 참조하시오.** 미M 영W

M: Kate, (38) **I'm preparing the museum's education budget for the next quarter**, but I'm missing some figures. Do you happen to know how much we raised from private donors last year?

W: (39) **I could look it up, but I'm heading out to a fundraiser right now.** Could I send you a report tomorrow?

M: Well, (38/40) **I'd really like to finish the budget this evening.** Is there any way I could find the information myself?

W: (40) **If you log in to the donor database, you can do a search.** Set the search parameters to private donors and input the dates you need, and you'll see a list. Then, you'll just have to add up the amounts or print a summary page with the totals.

------------------------------------------------

M: Kate, 제가 다음 분기의 박물관 교육 예산을 준비 중인데요. 예산 상에 서 몇몇 수치를 분실했어요. 혹시 작년에 우리가 개인 기부자들로부터 받 은 기부금이 얼마인지 아세요?

W: 저도 찾아볼 순 있긴 한데 지금 당장 기금모금 행사에 가야 하거든요. 제가 내일 보고서를 보내드려도 될까요?

M: 글쎄요. 제가 오늘 저녁에 예산안을 마무리해야 해서요. 제가 직접 그 자료를 찾아볼 수 있는 방법이 있을까요?

W: 기부자 데이터 베이스에 접속하면 찾아볼 수 있어요. 검색 조건을 당신 에게 필요한 개인 기부자와 날짜로 맞추면 목록을 보게 될 겁니다. 그 상태 에서 액수를 그대로 더하거나 아니면 총 액수가 포함된 요약 페이지를 프 린트하면 됩니다.

**38.** 남자가 오늘 마무리해야 하는 업무는 무엇인가?
- (A) 예산안
- (B) 연간 보고서
- (C) 데이터 복구
- (D) 기부자 명단      정답 (A)

**39.** Kate가 바로 정보를 찾지 못하는 이유는 무엇인가?
- (A) 그녀는 사무실을 비운 상태이다.
- (B) 그녀는 시간이 없다.
- (C) 그녀는 더 많은 정보가 필요하다.
- (D) 그녀는 방법을 알지 못한다.      정답 (B)

**40.** 남자는 이후에 무엇을 할 것 같은가?
- (A) 자신의 상사에게 전화할 것이다.
- (B) 보고서를 제출할 것이다.
- (C) 행사에 참석할 것이다.
- (D) 데이터베이스를 찾아볼 것이다.      정답 (D)

**문제 41-43번은 다음 대화를 참조하시오.** 미W 호M

W: Hello. (41) **I've had my cellular phone for three years now. I'm looking for a new one with better features.** Could you let me know what my options are?

M: Certainly. (42) **Firstly, are you aware that you can trade** in your old device for a new one? By turning in your old phone, you'll get a 15% discount on any new model.

W: (42) Oh, that's good. Here's my current phone. Please recommend the best mobile phone I can buy today, including the best for camera, display, and battery life.

M: No problem, ma'am. This phone is the Andromeda, which is pretty new. (43) I'll be able to transfer all your contact details and any photos from that phone onto your new one.

--------------------------------------------------

W: 안녕하세요. 저는 이 휴대폰을 3년간 사용했는데요. 더 좋은 기능의 새로운 휴대폰을 찾고 있어요. 제가 선택할 수 있는 것을 알려주시겠어요?

M: 네. 우선 기존 휴대폰을 보상받아 새로운 휴대폰을 구입하실 수 있는 것을 알고 계십니까? 예전 전화기를 반납하시면 모든 신형 휴대폰 가격의 15%를 할인 받으실 수 있습니다.

W: 아, 그거 좋아요. 여기 제 전화기가 있어요. 최고의 카메라, 해상도, 그리고 배터리 수명을 지니고 있는 것으로 제가 오늘 구매할 수 있는 제일 좋은 휴대폰을 추천해 주세요.

M: 물론입니다, 고객님. 이 전화기는 Andromeda인데 아주 최근에 나온 신제품이에요. 제가 고객님의 기존 휴대폰의 모든 연락처와 사진들을 새 휴대폰으로 옮겨드릴 수도 있습니다.

**41.** 여자는 무엇에 대해 문의하는가?
    (A) 반품
    (B) 할인된 가격
    (C) 기기 갱신
    (D) 전화 수리 서비스        정답 (C)

**42.** 여자가 "Oh, that's good."이라고 말할 때 의미하는 바는 무엇인가?
    (A) 몇몇 새로운 제품들의 품질이 뛰어나다.
    (B) 교환 제의가 받아들일 만한 가치가 있다.
    (C) 다양한 할인 혜택들이 제공될 것이다.
    (D) 그녀의 현재 휴대폰에 대한 무료 수리가 가능하다.     정답 (B)

**43.** 남자가 제안한 것은 무엇인가?
    (A) 여자의 사업체를 추천한다.
    (B) 자료를 옮겨준다.
    (C) 여자의 휴대폰을 수리한다.
    (D) 일부 사진들을 출력한다.        정답 (B)

문제 44-46번은 다음의 3자 대화를 참조하시오. ⓜⓌ ⓗⓂ ⓜⓂ

W: Hi. (44) **Welcome to Cosmos Office Supplies**, I'm Catherine Miller. How may I help you?

M1: Hello. I'm here to get a refund for the pens I bought here yesterday.

W: Yes, of course. Do you have your receipt with you?

M1: Actually, I didn't keep it. Is there a problem with that?

W: Um... we can't take returns without a receipt according to our refund policy. Well, please hold on a minute. Let me ask my store manager about it. Excuse me, Mr. Goodroad?

M2: Yes, Ms. Miller?

W: (45) **This customer wants a full refund for his pens, but he lost his receipt. What should I do?**

M2: Hmm... Sir, in this case, we can't give you a full refund. (46) **All I can do is allow you to exchange your pens for some other ones.**

--------------------------------------------------

W: 안녕하세요. Cosmos 사무용품점에 오신 걸 환영합니다. 저는

---

Catherine Miller라고 합니다. 어떻게 도와드릴까요?

M1: 안녕하세요. 저는 어제 여기서 구매한 펜들을 환불하려고 왔습니다.

W: 네, 가능합니다. 영수증은 가지고 오셨는지요?

M1: 사실, 영수증을 갖고 있지 않습니다. 그게 문제가 될까요?

W: 음… 저희 환불 방침에 따르면 영수증이 없이 반품 처리를 하지 않습니다. 잠시만 기다려 보세요. 제가 점장님께 여쭤 보겠습니다. 실례합니다. Goodroad 씨?

M2: 네, Miller 씨?

W: 이 고객님께서 구매하신 펜에 대한 환불을 원하는데 영수증을 분실하셨다고 하네요. 어떻게 해야 할까요?

M2: 음… 고객님, 이런 경우에는 저희가 전액 환불을 해드릴 수가 없습니다. 저희가 해드릴 수 있는 건 고객님의 펜을 다른 제품으로 교환해 드리는 것뿐입니다.

**44.** 대화가 이루어지는 곳은 어디인가?
    (A) 은행
    (B) 가전제품 매장
    (C) 사무용 가구점
    (D) 문구점        정답 (D)

**45.** 여자가 Goodroad 씨에게 도움을 요청하는 이유는 무엇인가?
    (A) 기계가 고장 났다.
    (B) 영수증이 분실되었다.
    (C) 일부 서류가 사라졌다.
    (D) 일부 제품의 재고가 없다.     정답 (B)

**46.** 남자는 고객을 위해 무엇을 해줄 수 있다고 언급하는가?
    (A) 전액 환불을 해준다.
    (B) 제품 교환을 해준다.
    (C) 할인 쿠폰을 발송한다.
    (D) 다른 상점에 연락한다.     정답 (B)

문제 47-49번은 다음 대화를 참조하시오. ⓜⓂ ⓜⓌ

M: (47) **Did you know that the product's packaging is going to be completely changed? I received a memo about it yesterday.**

W: Yeah. (48) **It was mentioned at the supervisor's meeting on Monday.** The Advertising Department manager had several ideas for redesigning the packaging. He hopes that the changes will be implemented by the end of the year.

M: I'm quite surprised as we changed the packaging only six months ago. What were the reasons for changing it again? I think the current product packaging is excellent.

W: Well, some of the board members feel that the current packaging looks a little old fashioned. (49) **They hope that the new design will appeal to a younger age group of consumers.**

--------------------------------------------------

M: 상품 포장이 완전히 변경될 거라는 것을 알고 계셨나요? 저는 그것에 대한 회람을 어제 받았어요.

W: 네. 월요일에 있었던 관리자 회의에서 언급되었어요. 광고부 부장이 새로운 포장에 대한 몇 가지 아이디어를 갖고 있었어요. 그는 연말까지 기존의 포장이 새로운 포장으로 바뀌길 원하고 있어요.

W: 저는 굉장히 놀랐어요. 왜냐하면 불과 6개월 전에 포장을 변경했잖아요. 그것을 또 바꾸는 이유가 무엇이었나요? 제 생각에는 지금의 제품 포장도 훌륭한데 말이죠.

M: 글쎄요. 이사진 중 일부는 현재 포장이 약간 구식처럼 느껴지나 봐요. 그들은 새 디자인이 젊은 소비자 층의 호감을 사길 원하거든요.

**47.** 화자들은 무엇에 관해 이야기하는가?
(A) 제품 포장을 바꾸는 것
(B) 업무 절차를 재편하는 것
(C) 현 투자 규제를 완화하는 것
(D) 오래된 슬로건을 변경하는 것 　　　　정답 (A)

**48.** 여자는 어떻게 그 변경 사항에 대해서 알았는가?
(A) 회람
(B) 기자회견
(C) 회의
(D) 월간 사보 　　　　정답 (C)

**49.** 여자에 따르면 회사가 변화를 추구한 이유는 무엇인가?
(A) 새로운 부가가치 서비스를 시장에 선보이기 위해서
(B) 젊은 소비자들을 유치하기 위해서
(C) 회사의 이미지를 쇄신하기 위해서
(D) 차별화된 마케팅 전략을 시행하기 위해서 　　　　정답 (B)

**문제 50-52번은 다음 대화를 참조하시오.** 미M 영W

M: Hi. I'm moving out of the state, and I need to change my address. **(50) How can I sign up for mail forwarding?**
W: **(51) You can sign up online.** It's much quicker and easier than visiting the post office.
M: Great. I'm moving in three weeks. How soon should I submit the form?
W: We recommend turning in the form five to seven days in advance when possible. **(52) This will allow three full days for processing** and ensure that you don't lose any mail.

- - - - - - - - - - - - - - - - - - - - - - - - - - - - - - -

M: 안녕하세요. 제가 다른 주로 이사를 가게 되어 주소를 변경해야 할 것 같습니다. 우편물 수령지 전송 서비스에는 어떻게 등록하면 되나요?
W: 온라인으로 하실 수 있습니다. 우체국을 방문하시는 것보다 그것이 훨씬 더 빠르고 쉽습니다.
M: 좋네요. 저는 3주 후에 이사를 갑니다. 신청서를 얼마나 빨리 제출해야 하나요?
W: 저희는 가능하다면 5~7일 전에 제출하실 것을 권고해 드립니다. 신청서를 처리하는 데 3일이 소요되고 그래야 다른 우편물을 분실하지 않도록 할 수 있습니다.

**50.** 남자는 무엇이 필요한가?
(A) 포장용품 찾기
(B) 우편물 전송하기
(C) 우체국 위치 찾기
(D) 서류 작성을 도와줄 사람 찾기 　　　　정답 (B)

**51.** 여자는 남자에게 무엇을 해야 한다고 언급하는가?
(A) 우편배달부에게 연락하는 것
(B) 우체국을 방문하는 것
(C) 이사 후에 다시 연락하는 것
(D) 인터넷으로 등록하는 것 　　　　정답 (D)

**52.** 서류를 처리하는 데 소요되는 기간은 얼마나 되는가?
(A) 2일
(B) 3일
(C) 5일
(D) 7일 　　　　정답 (B)

**문제 53-55번은 다음의 3자 대화를 참조하시오.** 미M 영W 미W

M: Ms. Montague, **(53/55) could you use your security card to let me into the computer data section?**
W1: No problem, Mr. King. But what happened to yours? **(53) You lost it?**
M: **(53) Yes, a couple of days ago.** You know, since the company increased our internal security last January, no one has been allowed to enter the computer data section without a security card.
W1: Right. Have you applied for a new security card?
AM: I have. I submitted my application form yesterday. **(54) I think I should ask the head of security if it has been issued this afternoon.**
W2: Oh, Mr. King. Good to see you here. Do you know what? **(54/55) I was on my way to your office to give you your new security card.**
M: **(55) Right on time!** **(54) I really appreciate it, Ms. McDonald.**

- - - - - - - - - - - - - - - - - - - - - - - - - - - - - - -

M: Montague 씨, 당신의 보안 카드를 이용해서 저를 컴퓨터 자료 구역으로 들여보내 주실 수 있나요?
W1: 물론이에요, King 씨. 그런데 당신의 보안 카드는 어쩌고요? 분실하셨나요?
M: 네, 한 이틀 전에요. 아시다시피 회사가 지난 1월에 내부 보안을 강화한 이후 컴퓨터 자료 구역은 보안 카드 없이는 들어갈 수가 없어요.
W1: 맞아요. 새로운 보안 카드는 신청했나요?
M: 했어요. 어제 신청서를 제출했어요. 오늘 오후에 보안과장에게 보안 카드가 발급되었는지 물어보려고 해요.
W2: 아, King 씨. 여기서 보니 잘됐네요. 그거 알아요? 제가 지금 당신에게 새로운 보안 카드를 전달해 주려고 당신 사무실로 가던 길이었어요.
M: 때 맞춰 오셨네요! 정말 고마워요, McDonald 씨.

**53.** 남자는 어떤 문제점에 대해서 언급하고 있는가?
(A) 더 많은 저장 공간이 필요하다.
(B) 그의 카드가 분실되었다.
(C) 새로운 보안 시스템이 고장 났다.
(D) 그의 신청서가 아직 처리되지 않았다. 　　　　정답 (B)

**54.** McDonald 씨는 어느 부서에서 근무하겠는가?
(A) 기술 지원부
(B) 인사부
(C) 보안과
(D) 유지 보수부 　　　　정답 (C)

**55.** 남자가 "Right on time!"이라고 말할 때 의미하는 바는 무엇인가?
(A) 그가 회의에 늦지 않았다.
(B) 그는 자신의 시계가 정확하게 시간을 알려주고 있다고 생각한다.
(C) 그의 동료들은 오후 6시에 퇴근한다.
(D) 그의 카드가 필요한 시점에 맞춰 도착했다. 　　　　정답 (D)

**문제 56-58번은 다음 대화를 참조하시오.** 미W 미M

W: Oh, Richard. **(56) Some people from Marketing are planning to go to the Komi Band performance next Sunday. Do you want to go?**
M: I really love the Komi Band, Julia! **(57) I thought tickets were sold out though. How are you getting them?**
W: They were sold out, but they added a second performance.

I've got to run. (58) **Let me know by this afternoon if you want to go.** I'm going to buy them over the phone so that we can sit together, and we don't want them to sell out again! See you later.

---

W: 아, Richard. 몇몇 마케팅 부서 직원들이 다음주 일요일에 있을 Komi Band 공연에 갈 거라고 하더군요. 당신도 가고 싶으세요?

M: 저 Komi Band를 정말 좋아하거든요, Julia! 하지만 표가 다 매진된 것으로 알고 있었는데요. 어떻게 표를 구하시게요?

W: 표가 다 매진되긴 했는데, 그 밴드가 2차 공연을 추가했더라고요. 서둘러야 해요. 오늘 오후까지 제게 공연에 갈 것인지 여부를 알려주세요. 제가 전화로 표를 구매해서 같이 앉을 수 있도록 하려고 해요. 2차 공연표도 다시 매진되는 걸 원치 않아요! 그럼 나중에 봐요.

**56.** 다음 주말에 어떤 일이 발생하는가?
(A) 마케팅 회의
(B) 콘서트
(C) 기금 마련 행사
(D) 소프트웨어 시연회 　　　　　　　　정답 (B)

**57.** 남자가 우려하고 있는 것은 무엇인가?
(A) 그의 휴대폰을 수리하는 것
(B) 표를 구매하는 것
(C) 예산을 초과하는 것
(D) 발표하는 것 　　　　　　　　　　　정답 (B)

**58.** 남자가 요청받은 것은 무엇인가?
(A) 표를 예매한다.
(B) 새로운 홈페이지를 방문한다.
(C) 기술자에게 연락한다.
(D) 여자에게 참석 여부를 말한다. 　　　정답 (D)

---

문제 59~61번은 다음 대화를 참조하시오. 영W 호M

W: Hi. My name is Nina Lee, and (59) **I'm calling because I rented a pickup truck from you all last month. I had paid in full, but today I received a bill from you for $78. That can't be right.**

M: Just a moment while I pull up the record, Ms. Lee. (60) **Oh, the fee is for gasoline. It's our policy that all vehicles be returned with a full tank of gas.** If they're not, we charge a $25 filling fee plus the cost of the gas to fill up the vehicle.

W: But I know I filled up the tank. I used the station right next to your lot. Yes, I even have the return receipt noting a full gas tank.

M: Oh, well, I'm sorry about that. I am not able to change the balance on any accounts, and (61) **the branch manager is at lunch right now. Could I have her call you back so that she can clear those charges for you?**

---

W: 안녕하세요. 제 이름은 Nina Lee라고 하는데요, 제가 지난 한 달간 귀사로부터 소형 트럭을 빌려서 사용한 것과 관련하여 연락을 드려요. 저는 이용료를 전액 지불했는데 오늘 78달러에 대한 청구서를 받았어요. 그건 잘못된 것 같아요.

M: 제가 기록을 검색하는 동안에 잠시만 기다려 주십시오, Lee 씨. 아, 그 비용은 유류비입니다. 모든 차량은 기름을 가득 채워서 반납하셔야 하는 것이 저희 회사의 방침입니다. 만약 기름을 채우지 않으면 저희는 주유한 휘발유 비용에 별도로 25달러의 주유비를 부과합니다.

W: 하지만 저는 트럭의 기름을 가득 채웠거든요. 귀사의 자동차 보관장소 바로 옆에 있는 주유소를 이용했어요. 네, 저는 심지어 기름을 가득 채웠다는 내용이 적힌 반납 영수증까지 가지고 있어요.

M: 아, 죄송합니다. 제가 계정에 있는 잔액을 변경할 수 있는 권한은 없고요, 저희 지점장이 지금 점심식사 중이에요. 제가 고객님께 연락을 취하도록 하여 고객님의 요금을 지울 수 있도록 해드릴까요?

**59.** 여자가 회사에 연락을 취한 이유는 무엇인가?
(A) 차량을 예약하기 위해서
(B) 불만사항을 제기하기 위해서
(C) 청구서와 관련된 문제를 제기하기 위해서
(D) 비용에 대해 문의하기 위해서 　　　정답 (C)

**60.** 남자에 따르면 비용이 청구된 이유는 무엇인가?
(A) 차량이 늦게 반납되었다.
(B) 연료 탱크가 가득 차지 않았다.
(C) 차량에 약간의 파손이 있었다.
(D) 시간에 맞춰 비용 지불이 이루어지지 않았다. 　정답 (B)

**61.** 지점장이 여자에게 전화해야 하는 이유는 무엇인가?
(A) 예약을 확인하기 위해서
(B) 계약 조건을 마무리하기 위해서
(C) 지불을 완료하기 위해서
(D) 부과된 비용을 취소하기 위해서 　　정답 (D)

---

문제 62~64번은 다음 대화와 목록을 참조하시오. 호M 영W

M: Good morning, ma'am. How can I help you?

W: Hi. (62) **I'm looking for a good place for my company's annual banquet next month.**

M: We have several types of banquet halls here. Could you please tell me what you are looking for in a venue?

W: Um… (64) **we would like a banquet hall that can accommodate 35 employees.** (63) **I heard that your hotel has a brand-new banquet hall that can hold 50 people.** Actually, I was wondering if we could use it for our annual banquet. I think it would be the perfect place for our event.

M: That's possible, ma'am. Would you mind telling me what your budget is?

W: Not at all. (64) **We were hoping to spend 1,500 dollars on the venue.**

---

M: 안녕하십니까, 고객님. 어떻게 도와드릴까요?

W: 안녕하세요. 저는 다음달에 있을 회사 연례 연회에 적합한 장소를 물색 중이에요.

M: 저희는 여러 종류의 연회장을 보유하고 있습니다. 행사 장소를 선정함에 있어서 고객님께서 바라는 점이 있으시면 알려 주시겠어요?

W: 음… 35명의 직원들을 수용할 수 있는 장소를 원합니다. 이 호텔에 50명을 수용할 수 있는 새로운 연회장이 있다고 들었어요. 사실 저는 그 연회장을 저희 연례 연회 장소로 사용하는 것이 가능할지 궁금했어요. 그 곳이 저희 행사에 알맞은 최적의 장소란 생각이에요.

M: 가능합니다, 고객님. 혹시 예산이 어느 정도 되시는지 여쭤봐도 괜찮을까요?

W: 물론이에요. 저희는 연회 장소 비용으로 1,500달러를 예상했어요.

| 명칭 | 수용 인원 | 요금 |
|---|---|---|
| Central Hall | 30명 | $800 |
| (64) Ruby Hall | 40명 | $1,200 |
| Warren Hall | 50명 | $1,700 |
| Emerald Hall | 60명 | $2,000 |

**62.** 다음달에 어떤 일이 발생하는가?
    (A) 국제 회의
    (B) 전시회
    (C) 환영회
    (D) 회사 행사              정답 (D)

**63.** 여자에 따르면 최근에 호텔은 무엇을 했는가?
    (A) 연말 행사를 개최했다.
    (B) 새로운 연회장을 개장했다.
    (C) 숙박시설을 확장했다.
    (D) 무선 인터넷을 설치했다.    정답 (B)

**64.** 그래픽을 보시오. 행사를 위한 최적의 장소는 어디인가?
    (A) Central Hall
    (B) Ruby Hall
    (C) Warren Hall
    (D) Emerald Hall      정답 (B)

**65.** 여자가 남자에게 요청하는 것은 무엇인가?
    (A) 예약을 한다.
    (B) 문제의 원인을 파악한다.
    (C) 고객과 소통한다.
    (D) 호텔들을 비교한다.    정답 (A)

**66.** 두 호텔의 차이점은 무엇인가?
    (A) 침실의 수
    (B) 무료 서비스의 가능성
    (C) 방의 크기
    (D) 고객 서비스의 품질    정답 (B)

**67.** 그래픽을 보시오. 남자는 어떤 방을 예약하겠는가?
    (A) Castro Valley Inn – 1인실
    (B) Castro Valley Inn – 특별 1인실
    (C) Bay Hotel – 1인실
    (D) Bay Hotel – 특별 1인실    정답 (C)

---

**문제 65-67번은 다음 대화와 목록을 참조하시오.** 📻W 📻M

W: (65) **Have you booked accommodations for my New York business trip?**
M: I have a few candidates. (66/67) **The Castro Valley Inn costs less, but it doesn't provide complimentary continental breakfasts or laundry. The Bay Hotel is a bit more expensive, but it provides both.**
W: I think the Bay Hotel would be good. You know, everything is just too expensive in New York. (67) **I definitely need free breakfasts and laundry there.**
M: Right. Should I book a single room or a special single room?
W: Since I already chose the more costly hotel, (67) **I think it would be better if I chose the more affordable option for the room.**

---

W: 제가 New York으로 출장 갈 때 머무를 숙소는 예약하셨나요?
M: 고려해 볼만한 몇몇 숙소들이 있습니다. Castro Valley Inn은 가격이 상대적으로 저렴하지만 무료 아침식사와 세탁을 제공하지 않아요. Bay Hotel은 약간 더 비싸지만 그것들을 제공하고요.
W: Bay Hotel이 좋겠어요. 알겠지만 New York은 모든 것이 비싸요. 저는 무료 아침식사와 세탁이 절대적으로 필요해요.
M: 알겠습니다. 일반 1인용 객실을 예약할까요, 아니면 특별 1인용 객실을 예약할까요?
W: 이미 더 가격이 비싼 호텔을 정했으니 방은 더 저렴한 걸 선택하는 것이 나을 것 같네요.

| 호텔명 | 객실 / 가격 |
|---|---|
| Castro Valley Inn | 1인실 / $75 |
| | 특별 1인실 / $100 |
| (67) Bay Hotel | 1인실 / $125 |
| | 특별 1인실 / $200 |

---

**문제 68-70번은 다음 대화와 도표를 참조하시오.** 📻M 📻W

M: Oh, Ms. Baker. (68) **I just read the latest analysis on news in the automobile market. It said we currently have plans to acquire GD Bus.**
W: Ah, I read that last week. (68) **But I don't think it would be ideal for us to purchase GD Bus.**
M: Um... I actually agree with you there. (69) **Our company has achieved rapid growth in the field and owns the largest share of the domestic market this year at 47%.**
W: Do you know what? I read an article in *Business World* yesterday, and (70) **it said that profits at GD Bus have dropped considerably for the past two quarters.** We don't need to take a risk by purchasing GD Bus.

---

M: 아, Baker 씨. 제가 최근에 발행된 자동차 시장 뉴스에 관한 분석 보고서를 방금 읽었어요. 보고서에 보니 우리 회사가 현재 GD Bus를 인수할 계획이 있다고 나와 있어요.
W: 아, 저도 지난주에 그 보고서를 읽었어요. 하지만 저는 GD Bus를 인수하는 것이 우리 회사에게 최선의 선택은 아니란 생각이에요.
M: 음… 사실 저도 당신의 의견에 동의해요. 우리 회사는 자동차 산업 분야에서 빠른 성장을 이루어냈고 올해 국내 자동차 시장에서 가장 높은 시장 점유율인 47%를 차지하고 있어요.
W: 그거 알아요? 제가 어제 *Business World*에서 기사 하나를 읽었는데 GD Bus의 수익이 지난 두 분기 동안 상당히 하락했다고 언급하더군요. 우리가 GD Bus를 인수해서 굳이 위험을 감수해야 할 이유가 없어요.

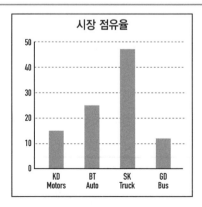

시장 점유율

**68.** 화자들은 무엇에 관해 이야기하는가?
(A) 신형 자동차 모델
(B) 인수 계획
(C) 재정 위기
(D) 새로운 마케팅 전략 　　　　　　정답 (B)

**69.** 그래픽을 보시오. 화자들은 어디에서 근무할 것 같은가?
(A) KD Motors
(B) BT Auto
(C) SK Truck
(D) GD Bus 　　　　　　정답 (C)

**70.** 여자가 GD Bus에 대해 언급한 것은 무엇인가?
(A) 재정적인 어려움을 겪고 있다.
(B) 해외 지사들을 보유하고 있다.
(C) 작년에 설립되었다.
(D) 수익이 감소해왔다. 　　　　　　정답 (D)

## Part 4

**문제 71-73번은 다음 광고를 참조하시오.** 영W

Are you interested in learning how to cook? Do you want to have a career as a chef? Are you a professional chef who works at a restaurant now? Whether you are an amateur cook or a professional chef, you always make a lot of dishes that require precise amounts of ingredients. (71) **That means you need the Perfect Balance, the best kitchen scale ever.** It always provides precise measurements and helps you feel and experience superb tastes. (72) **The Perfect Balance is so sturdy** that (73) **we promise you a five-year extended warranty.** Do you love cooking? Then place an order today!

- - - - - - - - - - - - - - - - - - - - - - - - - - - - - - - - - - -

요리를 배우는 데 관심이 있으신가요? 직업으로 요리사가 되고 싶으신가요? 현재 식당에서 근무하는 전문 요리사이신가요? 여러분이 아마추어 요리사이건 전문 요리사이건, 여러분은 항상 정확한 재료의 양을 요구하는 많은 요리들을 만듭니다. 그것은 곧 여러분에게 역대 최고의 주방 저울인 Perfect Balance가 필요하다는 것을 의미합니다. 이 저울은 언제나 정확한 계량을 제공하고 여러분이 훌륭한 맛을 느끼고 경험하실 수 있도록 도와줄 것입니다. Perfect Balance는 내구성이 매우 좋아서 여러분에게 5년의 연장된 품질 보증을 약속합니다. 요리를 사랑하세요? 그럼 오늘 주문하세요!

**71.** 어떤 제품이 광고 중인가?
(A) 믹서기
(B) 식품용 저울
(C) 커피 머신
(D) 전문가용 칼 세트 　　　　　　정답 (B)

**72.** 화자는 Perfect Balance에 대해 무엇이라고 언급하는가?
(A) 크기가 작다.
(B) 가격이 저렴하다.
(C) 내구성이 뛰어나다.
(D) 사용하기 쉽다. 　　　　　　정답 (C)

**73.** 화자에 따르면 무엇이 제공되는가?
(A) 요리책
(B) 특별 할인

(C) 연장된 품질 보증
(D) 무료 배송 　　　　　　정답 (C)

**문제 74-76번은 다음 담화를 참조하시오.** 호M

Next, (74) **I'll explain the company's policy regarding business trips.** Only business travel that is approved in advance is eligible for reimbursement. (75) **Before planning any trip, please obtain authorization from your department manager at least five days in advance.** (76) **While traveling, you must retain all receipts for transportation, accommodations, and meals.** Make sure all your receipts be ready when requesting reimbursement. Requests for reimbursement that do not include original receipts will be denied. If you have some issues over submitting the necessary documents, feel free to contact Mr. White in Accounting department. Again, you do not get reimbursed without receipts and proper consultation with the accounting departments. Thanks for your work and understanding.

- - - - - - - - - - - - - - - - - - - - - - - - - - - - - - - - - - -

다음으로, 출장과 관련된 회사의 방침에 대해 설명드리고자 합니다. 사전에 승인을 받은 출장만이 출장비 환급을 받을 수 있는 자격이 됩니다. 출장을 계획하기 전에 최소한 5일 전에 미리 부서장의 결재를 받으시기 바랍니다. 출장 기간 동안에는 필히 교통, 숙박, 그리고 식사 관련 영수증을 모두 간직하셔야 합니다. 환급 신청시에는 모든 영수증을 제출하시기 바랍니다. 영수증 원본이 포함되지 않은 환급 신청은 거부됩니다. 필요한 서류를 제출하는 데 문제가 있으시면 주저하지 말고 회계부의 White 씨에게 연락하십시오. 다시 한번 말씀드리자면, 영수증이나 회계부서와의 적절한 협의가 없으면 환급을 받으실 수 없습니다. 여러분의 수고와 이해에 감사드립니다.

**74.** 담화의 목적은 무엇인가?
(A) 몇몇 출장을 제안하기 위해서
(B) 여행사를 광고하기 위해서
(C) 방침을 소개하기 위해서
(D) 신입사원 채용을 제안하기 위해서 　　　　　　정답 (C)

**75.** 출장을 떠나기에 앞서 직원들이 꼭 해야 할 것은 무엇인가?
(A) 결재를 받는다.
(B) 항공권을 예약한다.
(C) 출장 보고서를 제출한다.
(D) 모든 비용을 환급한다. 　　　　　　정답 (A)

**76.** 화자에 따르면 직원들은 출장 기간 동안 무엇을 보관해야 하는가?
(A) 주문서
(B) 제품 견본
(C) 영수증
(D) 탑승권 　　　　　　정답 (C)

**문제 77-79번은 다음 회의 내용을 참조하시오.** 영W

Good morning, everyone. I'm glad to see all of you in the team meeting. (77) **Hmm... we've got a little time before we open the restaurant.** Let me briefly tell you a couple of things. First, you know, next month is June. (78) **We're getting close to the peak travel season. So if any of you want to put in additional hours, let me know as soon as possible.** Second, if something comes up suddenly, you can trade a work shift with another employee. (79) **But don't forget to update the work schedule.** Do I make myself clear? Okay. Let's get started working.

--------------------------------------------------

좋은 아침입니다. 여러분. 팀 회의에서 여러분 모두를 볼 수 있어서 기쁩니다. 음… 레스토랑 문을 열기까지 시간이 조금 있네요. 여러분께 간단히 두 가지만 말씀드리겠습니다. 우선, 아시다시피 다음달이 6월입니다. 우리는 점점 여행 성수기를 향해 가고 있습니다. 그러니 누구든 연장 근무를 하고 싶다면 제게 최대한 빨리 알려주세요. 두 번째로, 무슨 급한 일이 생기면 근무 일정을 다른 직원과 바꿀 수 있습니다. 하지만 근무 일정표를 수정해놓는 것을 잊지 마시길 바랍니다. 제가 하는 이야기가 잘 전달이 되었나요? 좋습니다. 그럼 일을 시작합시다.

**77.** 청자들이 근무하는 곳은 어디인가?
(A) 레스토랑
(B) 슈퍼마켓
(C) 여행사
(D) 백화점 정답 (A)

**78.** 화자가 "We're getting close to the peak travel season."이라고 말할 때 암시하는 바는 무엇인가?
(A) 가격이 인상된다.
(B) 관광객의 수가 더 많아진다.
(C) 교통 정체 현상이 더 악화된다.
(D) 사업체에 손님이 더 많아진다. 정답 (D)

**79.** 화자가 청자들에게 요청한 것은 무엇인가?
(A) 추가 근무를 한다.
(B) 청소용품을 구매한다.
(C) 근무 일정표를 갱신한다.
(D) 근무 중에 휴대전화의 전원을 끈다. 정답 (C)

**문제 80-82번은 다음 전화 메시지를 참조하시오.** 미W

Hello. It's Aurora Lane. (80) **I'm calling to see if you can meet me tomorrow morning.** (81) **We need to hire a manager for the new clothing shop as soon as possible.** Actually, the grand opening is in two weeks. Um... we have received a lot of résumés and read through them thoroughly. So when we meet tomorrow morning, we should discuss which applicants the personnel manager will interview next week. Ah, (82) **out of all the applicants, I'll e-mail you a list of the most qualified ones this afternoon.** When you check this message, please get back to me at your earliest convenience. Thank you.

--------------------------------------------------

안녕하세요. 저는 Aurora Lane이에요. 내일 오전에 저와 만나실 수 있는지 알아보고자 전화 드렸어요. 우리가 최대한 빨리 새로운 의류점의 점장을 채용해야 해서요. 사실 2주 후에 개업이에요. 음… 우리는 많은 이력서를 접수했고 모두 꼼꼼하게 살펴봤어요. 그래서 우리가 내일 아침에 만나면 인사부장이 다음주에 어떤 지원자의 면접을 봐야 하는지 논의해야 해요. 아, 지원자 중에서 제일 적격인 지원자들의 명단을 오늘 오후에 이메일로 보내 드릴게요. 이 메시지를 확인하면 가능한 빨리 제게 답변을 해주세요. 고마워요.

**80.** 메시지의 목적은 무엇인가?
(A) 일자리에 지원하기 위해서
(B) 회의 일정을 잡기 위해서
(C) 회사의 합병을 논의하기 위해서
(D) 다른 상점에서 주문을 하기 위해서 정답 (B)

**81.** 화자가 "The grand opening is in two weeks."라고 말할 때 암시하는 바는 무엇인가?
(A) 그녀는 테이블을 예약하길 원한다.
(B) 새로운 레스토랑을 다시 디자인해야 한다.
(C) 채용 결정이 빨리 이루어져야 한다.
(D) 공사는 필히 2주 안에 완공되어야 한다. 정답 (C)

**82.** 화자는 이후에 무엇을 할 것 같은가?
(A) Lane 씨의 사무실을 방문한다.
(B) 설문조사 양식을 작성한다.
(C) 일부 지원자들의 면접을 본다.
(D) 컴퓨터로 명단을 발송한다. 정답 (D)

**문제 83-85번은 다음 회의 내용을 참조하시오.** 호M

Thank you for attending this design meeting on such short notice. (83/84) **I looked over the designs for the newspaper advertisement for the Herminia Department Store.** Um... let me tell you my thoughts. (84) **They are not what the client is expecting.** As you may know, the Herminia Department Store is located in London, and it has always preferred very modern styles of advertisements. But your designs are rather traditional. I'm very sorry I didn't mention our client's preference before you started the work. I know this project is your first time to work with the Herminia Department Store. (85) **Please ask Mr. Wilson, one of your colleagues, to help you out.** He worked with the Herminia Department Store a couple of years ago.

--------------------------------------------------

급한 통보에도 불구하고 이 디자인 회의에 참석해 주셔서 감사드립니다. 저는 Herminia 백화점의 신문 광고용 디자인들을 살펴봤습니다. 음… 제 생각을 말씀드리겠습니다. 그 디자인들은 고객이 기대하던 것이 아닙니다. 여러분도 아시겠지만, Herminia 백화점은 London에 위치하고 있어서 항상 현대적인 방식의 광고들을 선호해왔습니다. 하지만 여러분의 디자인은 오히려 전통적이라고 할 수 있습니다. 여러분이 이 일을 맡기 전에 고객의 취향에 대해 말씀해 드리지 못해 무척이나 미안합니다. 저도 여러분이 Herminia 백화점과 처음 해보는 프로젝트임을 알고 있습니다. 여러분의 동료 중 한 분인 Wilson 씨에게 도움을 요청하세요. 그는 2년 전에 Herminia 백화점의 일을 해 본 경험이 있어요.

**83.** 화자는 어느 산업 분야에 종사할 것 같은가?
(A) 광고
(B) 출판
(C) 호텔 및 숙박
(D) 소매업 정답 (A)

**84.** 화자가 "They are not what the client is expecting."이라고 말한 이유는 무엇인가?
(A) 매출 하락에 놀라움을 표현하기 위해서
(B) 디자인 승인을 거절하기 위해서
(C) 고객과의 계약을 해지하기 위해서
(D) 직원들에게 최신 경향에 밝도록 요청하기 위해서 정답 (B)

**85.** 화자가 청자들에게 권고하는 것은 무엇인가?
(A) 오늘밤에 야근할 것
(B) 광고 회사에 지원할 것
(C) 마케팅 세미나에 참석할 것
(D) 동료와 협의할 것 정답 (D)

(86) **Good morning**, Oakland! This is 98.1 FM radio with your local news, weather, and up-to-date traffic information. (87) **Due to last night's big storm, there are many trees and branches on the roadways. City workers are currently hard at work trying to clear Highway 880, which has led to longer commuting times this morning.** Be sure to use extra care when passing work crews and keep an eye out for debris on the roadway. (88) **In addition, as a reminder, starting next Tuesday, 85th Avenue will be closed between Eastern Avenue and the East Oakland Sports Arena for some regular road maintenance work.** And now for our morning news with Andrea Morris.

---

좋은 아침입니다. Oakland 시민 여러분! 여기는 이 지역의 뉴스, 날씨, 그리고 최신 교통정보를 제공하는 98.1 FM 라디오입니다. 어젯밤 큰 폭풍으로 인해 많은 나무들과 가지들이 길 위에 떨어져 있습니다. 시 직원들이 현재 880번 고속도로를 치우기 위해 열심히 일하고 있는데, 이로 인해 오늘 아침 출근 시간이 평소보다 더 오래 걸렸습니다. 고속도로에서 일하는 직원들을 지나쳐 갈 때 특히 조심하시고, 도로에 놓인 나무 잔해들에 주의해 주십시오. 또한 다음주 화요일부터 Eastern Avenue와 East Oakland 스포츠 경기장 사이에 있는 85th Avenue는 정기 도로 보수 공사로 인해 폐쇄가 된다는 점 기억해 주십시오. 이제 Andrea Morris 씨가 진행하는 아침 뉴스를 들으시겠습니다.

**86.** 뉴스 보도는 언제 방송이 되고 있는가?
(A) 아침
(B) 정오
(C) 저녁
(D) 자정
정답 (A)

**87.** 화자에 따르면 교통체증을 초래하는 것은 무엇인가?
(A) 젖은 도로
(B) 떨어진 나뭇가지들
(C) 건물 공사
(D) 교량 수리
정답 (B)

**88.** 화요일에는 어떤 일이 일어나는가?
(A) 나무들이 벌목된다.
(B) 스포츠 행사가 개최된다.
(C) 폭우가 내린다.
(D) 도로가 폐쇄된다.
정답 (D)

Hi, Mr. Butler. This is Jane Stewart with the *Healthy Diet Magazine*. (89) **I'm doing some research for an upcoming article on both the health benefits and the disadvantages of reducing salt in a person's diet.** As a highly regarded expert, I would really appreciate any time you could give me in answering my questions. (90) **I've read several studies on the health sector you authored and feel you could really give an educational and interesting perspective on the issue.** (91) **Please call me back at 575-4331 at your earliest convenience to schedule either a phone or in-person interview.** I will work around your schedule. Thank you!

---

안녕하세요, Butler 씨, 저는 Healthy Diet Magazine에서 근무하는 Jane Stewart라고 합니다. 저는 현재 우리의 식단에서 소금을 줄였을 때 발생하는 건강상의 장점과 단점 모두를 다루는 기사를 작성하고자 조사 중에 있습니다. 널리 인정받는 전문가로서, 제 질문에 답변을 해 주실 시간을 할애해 주신다면 정말 감사하겠습니다. 저는 귀하가 저술하신 건강 분야에 대한 연구 내용을 읽고 나서 제가 작성하고자 하는 기사 주제에 대해 교육적이고 흥미로운 견해를 제시해주실 수 있을 분이라고 생각했습니다. 최대한 빨리 575-4331번으로 연락을 주셔서 전화 인터뷰가 되건 대면 인터뷰를 하건 그 일정을 잡을 수 있었으면 합니다. 제가 귀하의 일정에 맞추도록 하겠습니다. 감사합니다!

**89.** 화자는 어느 업종에 종사하는 것 같은가?
(A) 광고
(B) 영양
(C) 언론
(D) 정신 보건
정답 (C)

**90.** 화자에 따르면 청자가 인터뷰 대상자로 선정된 이유는 무엇인가?
(A) 그는 다른 나라의 언어를 구사할 수 있다.
(B) 그는 전통 음식에 대해 잘 알고 있다.
(C) 그는 자신의 사업체를 경영해왔다.
(D) 그는 연구 논문을 출간했다.
정답 (D)

**91.** 화자가 청자에게 요청하는 것은 무엇인가?
(A) 이메일로 의견을 발송한다.
(B) 연구시설을 방문한다.
(C) 출판 계약에 서명한다.
(D) 인터뷰를 허락한다.
정답 (D)

May I have your attention, please? I'm James Parker, the plant manager. (92/93) **This is a reminder that the Maintenance Department will be carrying out its annual maintenance checks on all manufacturing machines in the plant starting tomorrow morning and continuing tomorrow until 10:00 P.M.** Annual maintenance allows the machines in the plant to work efficiently year in and year out and ensures continued optimal performance. (94) **The plant will need to cease production on all assembly lines no later than 10 A.M. tomorrow so that the machines can cool down before they are inspected.** If you have any questions or concerns, please contact the Maintenance Department anytime you want. We appreciate your time and cooperation with us.

---

주목해 주시겠습니까? 저는 공장장인 James Parker입니다. 내일 오전부터 시작해서 내일 오후 10시까지 시설관리 부서에서 공장 내 모든 제조 기계에 대한 연례 보수 점검을 시행한다는 사실을 전달하고자 합니다. 연례 보수 점검은 공장 내 기계가 해마다 효율적으로 작동할 수 있도록 해주며, 지속적으로 최적화된 성능을 유지할 수 있도록 합니다. 공장은 보수 점검 이전에 기계가 냉각될 수 있도록 내일 오전 10시를 넘기지 말고 모든 생산 조립 라인에서의 생산 작업을 중단해야 할 것입니다. 더 궁금한 점이 있으면 언제라도 원하는 때에 시설관리 부서로 연락을 주십시오. 여러분이 내주신 시간과 협조에 감사드립니다.

**92.** 안내문이 의도하는 청자는 누구인가?
(A) 자동차 수리공
(B) 생산직 직원

(C) 시설관리 직원
(D) 안전 검사원 정답 (B)

**93.** 화자에 따르면 내일 아침에 시작되는 일은 무엇인가?
(A) 정기 감사
(B) 공장 견학
(C) 유지 보수 작업
(D) 안전 점검 정답 (C)

**94.** 청자들은 내일 오전 10시 전까지 무엇을 할 것을 요청 받는가?
(A) 다른 장비를 사용한다.
(B) 테스트 결과를 보고한다.
(C) 기계 사용을 중단한다.
(D) 양식을 작성한다. 정답 (C)

---

문제 95-97번은 다음 회의 내용과 도표를 참조하시오. 호M

Hello, everyone, and welcome to the quarterly sales meeting. (95) I called us all together to brainstorm ideas for increasing mobile tablet sales. Look at the graph. (96) You can see that tablet sales severely dropped this quarter compared to the other quarters. Therefore, we should come up with some new strategies to sell more tablets to customers. (96/97) Next year, I want to avoid the usual big drop-off, maybe by holding special sales or other events to attract customers. (96/97) Let's break up into teams and think of some good ideas for the next quarter.

---

안녕하세요, 여러분. 분기 매출 회의에 오신 걸 환영합니다. 저는 모바일 태블릿 판매 증가를 위한 아이디어를 고안해보고자 회의를 소집했습니다. 그 래프를 보십시오. 태블릿 매출이 다른 분기와 비교해 봤을 때 이번 분기에 심각하게 하락했습니다. 따라서 우리는 고객에게 보다 더 많은 태블릿을 판 매하기 위한 새로운 전략을 마련해야만 합니다. 내년에는 늘 있었던 큰 매출 하락을 피하고 싶습니다. 어쩌면 특별 할인 판매 행사, 또는 고객을 유치할 수 있는 다른 행사들을 진행해야 할 수도 있습니다. 팀별로 나누어서 다음 분기 매출을 향상시킬 수 있는 좋은 아이디어들을 고안해 봅시다.

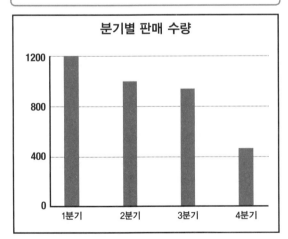

**분기별 판매 수량**

**95.** 회사가 판매하는 제품은 무엇인가?
(A) 휴대용 음악 기기
(B) 이동통신 기기
(C) 화학 제품
(D) 사무용품 정답 (B)

**96.** 그래픽을 보시오. 회의는 언제 열리는가?
(A) 1분기
(B) 2분기
(C) 3분기
(D) 4분기 정답 (D)

**97.** 화자는 이후에 무엇을 논의하고자 하는가?
(A) 매출 증가를 위한 방법
(B) 홈페이지 디자인
(C) 고객 불만사항
(D) 사업 확장 계획 정답 (A)

---

문제 98-100번은 다음 안내와 광고를 참조하시오. 미W

This is a friendly welcome to all Franklin Fresh Market shoppers! (98) **This weekend, Franklin Fresh Market is celebrating its twentieth year in business** providing you and your family a courteous and engaging environment. To show our appreciation, we'll be having a huge sale at our four locations. (99) **Here at this shop, you'll get 30 percent off all beverages, including juice and soda.** (100) Please check our Web site at Franklin. com to become a member of our Loyal Franklin Shopper Program. Then, you'll see that each location has different items on sale. (100) **Please sign up and enjoy the perks of being a loyal Franklin shopper!**

---

Franklin Fresh Market 쇼핑객 여러분 모두 따뜻하게 환영합니다! 이번 주말에 Franklin Fresh Market은 20주년을 축하하며 여러분과 가족에게 정중하고 매력적인 쇼핑 환경을 제공합니다. 감사의 뜻을 표하기 위해 4개 지점에서 엄청난 할인 판매를 시행합니다. 이 매장에선 주스와 탄산음료를 포함한 모든 음료에 30퍼센트 할인 혜택을 받으시게 됩니다. 저희 홈페이 지 Franklin.com에서 Loyal Franklin Shopper Program의 회원이 되 십시오. 그러면 각 지점마다 다른 할인 판매 제품들에 대해 아실 수 있습니 다. 회원으로 등록하셔서 Franklin 우수 회원의 특전을 누리세요!

### Franklyn Fresh Market
30% 주말 할인 행사!

| 할인 품목 | 매장 위치 |
|---|---|
| 청과물 | Fremont |
| 유제품 | San Jose |
| (99) 음료 | Cupertino |
| 제과제빵 | Oakland |

**98.** Franklin Fresh Market이 축하하는 것은 무엇인가?
(A) 창립 기념
(B) 새로운 매장 개장
(C) 국경일
(D) 수익성이 높았던 분기 정답 (A)

**99.** 그래픽을 보시오. 이 안내는 어느 매장에서 이루어지는가?
(A) Fremont
(B) San Jose
(C) Cupertino
(D) Oakland 정답 (C)

**100.** 청자들이 홈페이지에 방문해야 하는 이유는 무엇인가?
(A) 금주의 우수 직원을 위한 투표를 하기 위해서
(B) 일자리가 있는지 알아보기 위해서
(C) 회원 프로그램에 가입하기 위해서
(D) 고객 이용 후기를 작성하기 위해서 　정답 (C)

## Part 5

**101.** Keller 씨는 대개 무역 박람회에 혼자 참석하지만 Tokyo에서 개최되는 무역 박람회에는 동료 몇 명을 대동할 예정이다. 　정답 (D)

**102.** 악천후로 인해 어제 열린 지역 영화제에는 소규모의 사람들만 참석했다. 　정답 (A)

**103.** 환불 요청서는 필히 서면으로 작성되어 고객 관리 부서로 직접 전달되어야 한다. 　정답 (B)

**104.** Ryan 씨는 내일 아침 10시에 우리에게 중요한 고객과 만날 수 있는 시간적 여력이 있다. 　정답 (A)

**105.** 새로운 뮤지컬 관람표가 완전히 매진되어서 극장 측은 다음주에 추가 공연을 배정하기로 결정했다. 　정답 (D)

**106.** 지원자들 중에서 Reagan 씨가 수석 회계사 직에 가장 적격이다. 　정답 (C)

**107.** 대부분의 마케팅 부서들은 검색이 가능한 데이터베이스를 이용하여 마케팅 자료를 수집한다. 　정답 (D)

**108.** CoCo 사의 새로운 화장품을 구입하시면 멋진 선물 가방이 무료로 제공됩니다. 　정답 (C)

**109.** 그래픽 디자인 분야의 구직자들은 온라인 포트폴리오를 제작하도록 적극 권장된다. 　정답 (A)

**110.** 대부분의 금융 기관들은 고객들에게 개인 정보를 항상 안전하게 보호하기 위해 정기적으로 비밀번호를 변경하도록 권고한다. 　정답 (C)

**111.** 최근 연구에서는 10명의 사무직 근로자 중 9명이 종종 평상복을 입는 자유를 누린다는 것을 알려준다. 　정답 (B)

**112.** JH 회계법인의 회계사들은 연간 최소 40시간의 교육을 필히 이수해야 한다. 　정답 (A)

**113.** London에 있는 대부분의 분석가들은 소셜 커머스 회사들이 급속하게 성장함에 따라 온라인 마케팅 산업의 규모도 폭발적으로 증가할 것이라고 예측하고 있다. 　정답 (B)

**114.** 우리 주식들은 보통 12월과 1월 사이에 일부 주식의 가격 상승을 촉진시키는 소위 1월 효과로 인한 혜택을 본다. 　정답 (C)

**115.** 수없이 많은 열정적인 팬들은 새로운 뮤지컬 Romantic Cats의 공연 내내 열정적인 반응을 보였다. 　정답 (D)

**116.** BK 사는 직원들이 외국어를 구사할 수 있는 적절한 방법을 가르치는 특별 언어 과정을 제공한다. 　정답 (B)

**117.** Roberts 박사는 New York의 종합병원에서 은퇴했지만 여전히 자발적인 의료 봉사 활동을 하고 있다. 　정답 (D)

**118.** Nguyen 씨는 패션 산업 분야에서의 뛰어난 공로로 인하여 다음주에 수상을 하게 될 것이다. 　정답 (D)

**119.** 부서지기 쉬운 제품들은 배송 중 파손을 예방하기 위해 필히 완벽한 포장이 이루어져야 한다. 　정답 (B)

**120.** Quick Shave는 충전이 가능하여 일반 건전지가 필요없는 전기면도기이다. 　정답 (C)

**121.** Lee 씨가 Manchester의 새 지사로 전근 갔기 때문에 우리 지사는 현재 그의 후임을 선발하고 있다. 　정답 (D)

**122.** Audient Power는 세계 시장의 점유율과 수출 물량을 토대로 해외 주요 기업들이 브랜드 파워를 평가했다. 　정답 (B)

**123.** 우리 인사 담당 이사에 따르면 다음달 서울에서 개최되는 취업 박람회에서 몇몇 경력 직원들이 채용될 예정이다. 　정답 (D)

**124.** Oakland 지역 대학에서 제공하는 회계학 과정을 수료하면 졸업생들에게 학위가 발급될 것이다. 　정답 (D)

**125.** 모든 이사진은 직원들이 우리 제품에 대해 불만을 제기한 고객들에게 2일 이내에 답변을 해 주길 바라고 있다. 　정답 (B)

**126.** 판매세율은 10년 전에 3.3%로 설정되었지만 이후 정부에 의해 점진적으로 증가해왔다. 　정답 (D)

**127.** 많은 전문가들은 고객의 문제점을 지속적으로 해결하는 것이 곧 사업 성공에 있어서 가장 중요한 핵심 요인이라고 말하고 있다. 　정답 (C)

**128.** 최고 경영자가 휴가에서 복귀할 때쯤이면 영업 이사는 우리의 새로운 무선 단말기를 수입하고자 하는 몇몇 신규 고객들과 만나고 있을 것이다. 　정답 (D)

**129.** 회사가 아무리 많이 벌어도 분석 보고서에서는 우리의 현 수익 수준으로는 수입과 지출의 균형을 맞추는 것의 어려움을 강조하고 있다. 　정답 (D)

**130.** 유가가 현재 안정세에 들어서고 있음에도 불구하고 많은 사람들은 자신들의 차를 운전하기 보다는 시내에 있는 지하철과 버스를 이용하고 있다. 　정답 (B)

## Part 6

문제 131-134번은 다음 회람을 참조하시오.

수신: 전 직원
발신: David Kisling, 상점 관리자
날짜: 9월 9일
제목: 상기 사항

저는 최근에 우리 매장을 방문하신 고객들이 일부 직원들의 태도에 대해 불만을 가지고 있다는 것을 알게 되었습니다.

우리의 목표는 고객에게 언제나 최선의 서비스를 제공하는 것이며 우리가 제공하는 서비스의 질은 고객을 직접 응대하는 각 직원들에게 달려있다는 것을 기억해주시기 바랍니다.

초심으로 돌아가 미소로 고객을 응대하고 무엇이 됐든 도움이 필요한지 묻는 것에서부터 시작합시다. 아울러, 고객지원이 끝나고 그냥 자리를 떠나지 마시고, 대신에 도움이 더 필요한지 다시 한번 물어봐주시기 바랍니다.

오늘 여러분이 보인 단순한 친절이 우리 매장의 이미지를 영원히 바꿀 수 있습니다. 저는 전 직원들의 더 나아진 태도를 기대하며, 바라건대 고객들로부터 더 큰 만족도를 얻기를 또한 기대합니다.

**131.** 정답 (D)

**132.** 정답 (C)

**133.** 정답 (D)

**134.** (A) 이는 다음과 같은 이유로 우리 고객들에게 더 나은 서비스를 제공하는 데 도움을 줄 것입니다.
(B) 홍보 이벤트를 했음에도 불구하고 우리 매출은 같은 수준입니다.
(C) 오늘 여러분이 보인 단순한 친절이 우리 매장의 이미지를 영원히 바꿀 수 있습니다.
(D) 현재의 고객 만족도를 유지하기 위해 계속 수고해 주십시오. 정답 (C)

---

문제 135~138번은 다음 회람을 참조하시오.

회람

수신: 전 직원
발신: Daniel Blake, 인사부장
날짜: 9월 9일
제목: 새로운 우편물 발송 방침

우편발송 시스템을 더욱 효과적으로 운용하기 위해, Jambo Computer는 현재의 우편 정책을 변경하기로 결정했습니다.

모든 내부 우편물은 1층에 있는 우편실에서 제공하게 될 일정한 봉투를 사용하도록 바뀔 것입니다. 이 새로운 봉투들에 대한 비용은 직원들에게 청구되지 않을 것이며, 고객 발송용 우편물에 사용되는 우편 봉투들과 구별하기 위해 특별한 마크가 찍힐 것입니다.

배송 준비가 된 모든 내부 우편물은 오후까지 각 복도 끝에 있는 우편함에 넣어야 합니다.

불편부당한 우편물 발송 방침은 생산성을 감소시킵니다. 이 새로운 우편물 발송 방침은 회사뿐만 아니라 직원들을 보호할 수 있을 것임을 알아주시기 바랍니다.

**135.** 정답 (A)

**136.** 정답 (C)

**137.** 정답 (B)

**138.** (A) 최근에 우편물 소포에서 많은 물건들이 도난당했습니다.
(B) 불편부당한 우편물 발송 방침은 생산성을 감소시킵니다.
(C) 우편 발송 비용이 최근에 빠른 속도로 오르고 있습니다.
(D) 우리는 경쟁사에 사내기밀이 유출된 것으로 인해 어려움을 겪었습니다.
정답 (B)

---

문제 139~142번은 다음 편지를 참조하시오.

BK Office Machinery 사
128 South Street
Queens, New York 10111

5월 5일

---

Preston Manufacturing 사
888 Grand Avenue
Los Angeles, CA 90037

관계자 분께:

저희는 올 회계 연도가 가기 전에 새로운 사무용 복사기를 구매하고자 합니다. 저희는 귀사의 복사기를 고려하고 있으며 저희의 요구사항을 충족시킬 수 있는 제품을 보유하고 계신지 궁금합니다.

저희 회사는 소규모인지라 복사기는 대개 20명의 직원들이 사용하고 있습니다. 저희는 한 달에 대략 7천8백 장을 복사하며 일반 복사용지를 사용하는 복사기를 선호합니다. 또한 귀사의 품질 보증과 수리 서비스에 관해서도 알고 싶습니다.

저희 회계 연도가 6월 30일 부로 종료되기 때문에 귀사로부터 최대한 빨리 답변을 받을 수 있길 바랍니다.

Brandon Parker
인사부장
BK Office Machinery 사

**139.** 정답 (D)

**140.** 정답 (C)

**141.** (A) 또한 귀사의 품질 보증과 수리 서비스에 관해서도 알고 싶습니다.
(B) 스캐너와 결합된 프린터는 일종의 복사기 기능도 합니다.
(C) 귀하가 요청하신 견적을 제공해 드리게 되어 기쁘게 생각합니다.
(D) 그 회사는 마감시한이 지켜지지 못한 점에 실망스러움을 표현했습니다.
정답 (A)

**142.** 정답 (B)

---

문제 143~146번은 다음 기사를 참조하시오.

Moto Electronics는 이제 세계적인 전자회사의 선두주자로
다시 설 태세를 갖추다

Kate Thompson 작성
9월 24일 동부시간 오후 7시 48분 수정

Moto Electronics는 오늘 2천만 달러 규모의 Green Computer를 인수했다고 발표했다.

Moto Electronics의 대변인인 Andrew Kim 씨는 오늘 아침 회사가 국제 경쟁력을 높이고자 해외 사업을 강화하기 위해 Green Computer를 매입했다고 말했다. 그는 또한 Moto Electronics가 내년 말까지 세계 매출액을 두 배로 늘릴 것을 목표로 한다고 말했다.

Green Computer는 강력한 판매망과 시장 점유율을 보유하고 있다. 따라서 대부분의 업계 전문가들은 Green Computer가 Moto Electronics의 최대 약점을 상쇄할 것으로 예상되기 때문에 이번 인수로 인해 Moto Electronics가 메모리 칩과 컴퓨터 부품 부문에 있어서 선두적인 생산업체이자 판매업체가 될 것으로 강력하게 믿고 있다.

Moto Electronics는 Green Computer의 현재 인력을 그대로 유지하면서 향후 2년간 추가로 직원들을 채용할 계획이다.

**143.** 정답 (D)

**144.** 정답 (C)

**145.** (A) Green Computer는 강력한 판매망과 시장 점유율을 보유하고 있다.

(B) 이는 북미 지역에서 가장 안정적인 운영이 이루어지고 있는 대규모 회사들 중 하나로 여겨지고 있다.

(C) Moto Electronics 이사회는 내년에 외국인들을 채용하기로 큰 결정을 내렸다.

(D) 우리는 최근 개선된 생산 시설들을 사용하여 이 목표를 달성할 것이다.

정답 (A)

**146.** 정답 (C)

## Part 7

**문제 147-148번은 다음 이메일을 참조하시오.**

수신: Isabella Choi 〈ischoi@kamongcorp.com〉
발신: Office King 고객 서비스 〈infor@officeking.com〉
날짜: 9월 11일
제목: 주문 번호 1123

Choi 씨께,

(147) 요청하신 바와 같이 귀하의 주문은 취소되었습니다. 참고용으로, 귀하의 9월 9일 주문에 대한 요약 내용을 보내 드립니다.

주문 번호 1123 Apple 110 BK 프린터
상태: 취소

(148) 저희 정책에 따라, 영업일로 3일 이내에 전액 환불을 받으시게 됩니다.

추가 정보가 필요하실 경우, www.officeking.com을 방문하시거나 1-800-692-9815로 저희에게 전화 주시기 바랍니다.

귀하의 거래에 항상 감사 드립니다.

Office King

**147.** 이메일이 발송된 이유는 무엇인가?
(A) 환불 정책에 관해 문의하기 위해
(B) 고객에게 판촉 행사에 관해 알리기 위해
(C) 주문 취소를 확인해 주기 위해
(D) 실수를 바로잡기 위해

정답 (C)

**148.** Choi 씨에 관해 알 수 있는 것은 무엇인가?
(A) 이미 제품에 대한 비용을 지불했다.
(B) 다음주에 전액 환불을 받을 것이다.
(C) 3일 후에 프린터를 받을 것이다.
(D) 특별 할인을 제공 받았다.

정답 (A)

**문제 149-151번은 다음 공지를 참조하시오.**

창의적 글쓰기 수강 학생들에게 알립니다!

연례 Sandstone Short Story Writing Contest가 시작되었습니다.

(149) 현재 마감시한인 10월 30일까지 계속 참가작이 접수되고 있습니다. 모든 단편 소설 작품은 1,000자와 4,000자 사이의 길이에 해당되어야 하며, 어떤 주제도 가능합니다. 유명 작가들로 구성된 심사 위원단이(공포 소설가 Samuel J. Kingston 씨, 미스터리 소설가 Janice Bonderman 씨, 그리고 에세이 작가 Diana Jacobi 씨) 참가작들을 심사합니다.

두 가지 다른 연령 부문에 대해 수여되는 여러 상이 있습니다.
• 16세 이하
• 17세에서 19세 사이

대상인 Most Promising Writer 수상자는 1,000달러의 대학 장학금과

(151) 두 곳의 대형 출판사 방문을 위한 3일간의 모든 경비가 전액 부담되는 New York으로의 여행, 그리고 Sandstone Beacon Gazette을 통한 단편 소설 출간과 같은 혜택을 받게 됩니다.

(150) 참가 신청서는 지역 내 모든 학교의 영어 교사들을 통해 받으실 수 있습니다. 해당 양식은 우편으로 아래 주소로 제출해 주십시오.

Sandstone Short Story Writing Contest
(150) 사서함 번호 50
Sandstone, VA 65455

모든 신예 작가들께 행운을 빕니다!

**149.** 모든 참가작은 반드시 언제까지 접수되어야 하는가?
(A) 10월 3일
(B) 10월 16일
(C) 10월 19일
(D) 10월 30일

정답 (D)

**150.** 참가 신청서는 어디로 보내져야 하는가?
(A) Samuel J. Kingston 씨
(B) 지역 신문사
(C) 사서함
(D) 지역 문화 센터

정답 (C)

**151.** 대상 수상자는 무엇을 받을 것인가?
(A) 4년 전액 대학 장학금
(B) 모든 경비가 부담된 New York으로의 일주일 체류
(C) 최고의 출판업자들을 만날 수 있는 기회
(D) 유명 잡지사의 특채

정답 (C)

**문제 152-153번은 다음 문자 메시지를 참조하시오.**

| Aurora Lane | [오후 2:18] |
| 어디 계세요? B회의실에 계신가요? | |

| Holly White | [오후 2:19] |
| 네, 마지막 발표가 막 시작되었습니다. | |

| Aurora Lane | [오후 2:21] |
| 그 후에 여전히 Sally Murphy 박사님의 인공 지능 발표회에 가고 싶으신가요? (153) 이 발표는 C회의실에서 열립니다. | |

| Holly White | [오후 2:23] |
| 물론이죠, 그 발표는 놓치지 않을 겁니다. (152) 그분의 발표는 언제나 매우 흥미롭거든요. | |

| Aurora Lane | [오후 2:25] |
| (152) 전적으로 동의합니다. (152/153) 제가 당신을 위해 자리를 하나 맡아 놓을까요? | |

| Holly White | [오후 2:26] |
| 그렇게 해 주시면 좋죠. 정말 감사합니다. 그곳에서 뵙겠습니다. | |

**152.** 오후 2시 25분에, Lane 씨가 "I can't agree with you more."라고 썼을 때 무엇을 의미할 가능성이 가장 큰가?
(A) Murphy 박사의 이론을 뒷받침할 증거가 없다고 생각한다.
(B) White 씨의 의견이 자신의 것만큼 좋지 않다고 확신하고 있다.
(C) White 씨의 발표에 대단히 깊은 인상을 받았다.
(D) Murphy 박사의 연설에 대한 White 씨의 의견에 동의하고 있다.

정답 (D)

**153.** Lane 씨에 관해 무엇이 사실일 것 같은가?

(A) White 씨보다 먼저 C회의실로 갈 것이다.

(B) Murphy 박사 다음으로 발표를 할 것이다.

(C) 이미 행사를 위해 회의실을 예약해 두었다.

(D) White 씨와 함께 인공 지능에 관한 논문을 쓰고 싶어 한다.　　정답 (A)

**문제 154-155번은 다음 기사를 참조하시오.**

---

월드 이코노미 리더

비즈니스 뉴스

9월 9일, Los Angeles - Apple Republic 사의 부사장 Lance Merrier는 내년에 Chicago, Atlanta, New York, New Orleans에 새로운 매장을 열겠다는 성명서를 화요일에 발표했다.

Merrier 씨는 그가 맡은 부분에서의 실수를 인정했다. 성공적이지 못했던 사업 확장의 가장 큰 문제점은 그러한 확장을 진척시키기에 작년에 회사가 재정적으로 충분히 건실하지 못했던 점이라고 그가 고백했다. 그는 회사가 회사의 가치에 대해 잘못 판단했다고 시인했다. 강력한 마케팅 캠페인과 활력을 불어 넣은 목표로 금번에는 사업 확장이 훨씬 수월해질 것이라고 주장한다.

(155) **Los Angeles에 본사를 두고 있는 Apple Republic 사는** Christopher Lee 씨가 창립하였고 (154) **중년층을 대상으로 깔끔하고 고전적인 스타일을 유지해 왔다.** Apple Republic 사는 봄 시즌에 전 매장에서 젊은 층을 위한 새로운 의류 제품을 선보일 예정이다. Apple Republic 사는 아동복 시장에 어떻게 뛰어들 것인지 주의를 기울여 살펴볼 것이다. 초기 예상으로는 4개 매장에서 기록적인 매출을 이끌어낼 것이라고 예측되지만, 실제로는 회사의 누구도 그러한 성공을 볼 때까지는 믿지 않을 것이다.

---

**154.** Apple Republic 사에 대해 암시되는 내용은 무엇인가?

(A) 본사를 Los Angeles로 이전했다.

(B) 최근에 매장의 반을 닫았다.

(C) 아동복을 판매한다.

(D) 회사의 제품은 현재 성인용으로 제한되어 있다.　　정답 (D)

**155.** Apple Republic 본사는 어디에 위치하고 있는가?

(A) Chicago

(B) New York

(C) Los Angeles

(D) New Orleans　　정답 (C)

**문제 156-157번은 다음 회람을 참조하시오.**

---

수신: Harvey Davis 박사, 수석 레지던트

발신: Dana Kamon 박사, 소아과장

제목: (156) **간호 인력 부족**

병동 주변에서 들리는 소문을 통해 알고 계시겠지만, 인력 부족 문제가 아주 큰 방해가 되고 있습니다. (156) **우리 모두는 추가 간호사들이 필요하다는 점과 예산이 빠듯하다는 점을 알고 있습니다.** (157) **저는 직무 분담을 제안하고자 하는데,** 아마 이는 적어도 위기에 대한 임시 해결책이 될 수 있을 것이기 때문입니다.

물론, 장기적으로는, 정규직 간호사들을 고용해야 하지만, (157) **1년 넘게 직무 분담을 해 온 이곳 소아과에서, 우리는 그것이 좋은 효과가 있다고 생각합니다.** 저는 그것이 완벽한 상황임을 말씀 드리고자 하는 것은 아니지만, 직원 부족 문제에 대처하는 데 있어 그것이 효과가 있었습니다.

---

**156.** 회람에서 무엇이 논의되고 있는가?

(A) 병원 내 침대의 부족

(B) 너무 긴 시간의 교대 근무를 하는 의사들

(C) 소아과 병동 내의 환자 관리

(D) 간호 인력 문제　　정답 (D)

**157.** Kamon 박사에 의해 제안되고 있는 해결책은 무엇인가?

(A) 간호사들에 의한 직무 분담

(B) 더 많은 정규직 의사들의 고용

(C) 간호 인력의 감축

(D) 각 병동에 대한 의사들의 교대 근무　　정답 (A)

**문제 158-160번은 다음 광고를 참조하시오.**

---

Sea World

Pacific Ocean 호텔

Pacific Ocean 호텔에 오신 걸 환영합니다. 계시는 동안 매우 즐거운 시간 보내시길 기원합니다. 시내에서 맛있는 요리와 최고의 전망을 모두 갖춘 식당을 찾고 계시다면, 다른 곳 말고 저희 호텔 1층에 위치한 Sea World를 찾으세요. Albert Cardoza 주방장이 가장 신선한 요리를 저녁 내내 제공할 것이며, 여러분들을 기다리는 테이블이 있습니다.

(158) **Sea World는 화요일에서 일요일까지 오전 11시부터 오후 11시 30분까지 영업합니다.** (159) **만약 객실에서 룸서비스를 주문하고 싶으시면, 모든 객실에 룸서비스 메뉴가 준비되어 있습니다.** 식당의 정규 영업시간 동안 Sea World 메뉴에 있는 모든 음식을 주문하실 수 있습니다.

이번 주 일요일 오후 1시에서 오후 3시 사이에 방문해 주세요. 새우와 게를 마음껏 즐기실 수 있습니다. (160) **이 광고지를 식당에 가져오시기만 하면, 육즙이 많은 게다리와 커다란 새우를 무료로 무제한 드실 수 있습니다.**

---

**158.** 수요일에 식당은 몇 시에 여는가?

(A) 오전 11시

(B) 오전 11시 30분

(C) 오후 1시

(D) 오후 3시　　정답 (A)

**159.** 룸서비스에 대해 언급되지 않은 것은 무엇인가?

(A) 전체 메뉴를 포함한다.

(B) 저렴한 가격의 상품을 제공한다.

(C) 영업시간 동안 이용할 수 있다.

(D) Sea World에서 가져오는 음식이다.　　정답 (B)

**160.** Pacific Ocean 호텔이 고객들에게 제공하는 것은 무엇인가?

(A) 식당의 할인 쿠폰

(B) 무료 룸서비스

(C) 특정 고객에게 무료 해산물 음식

(D) 특별 수중 발레 공연　　정답 (C)

**문제 161-163번은 다음 회람을 참조하시오.**

---

발신: Wesley Kim, 인사부장

수신: 전 직원

날짜: 9월 15일

제목: 시설 관리 작업

동료 직원 여러분,

(163) **시설 관리 작업으로 인해 우리 지하 주차장이 10월 2일부터 5일까지**

---

이용할 수 없다는 점에 유의하시기 바랍니다. 우리는 차량들이 들어갈 충분한 공간을 제공하기 위해 지하 주차장을 확장하기로 결정했습니다. 이 주차장은 10월 6일 월요일에 다시 문을 열 예정입니다. 차를 운전해 출근하는 직원들은 (162) **시내 공영 주차장과 같은 인근의 주차장들을 이용하시기를 권해 드리며, 회사가 발생되는 모든 주차 비용을 환급해 드릴 것입니다.** 또한, (161) **통근 거리가 길 경우에 소속 부서장과 재택 근무 가능성에 관해 논의하실 수 있습니다.**

이번 시설 관리 작업이 완료되고 나면 10개의 추가 주차 공간이 생깁니다. 정규직 직원이면서 3년 넘게 재직해 오신 직원이라면, 제비 뽑기 방식을 통해 이 공간들 중의 하나를 배정 받으실 수 있습니다. 이 제비 뽑기의 대상자가 되시려면 제게 내선번호 1123으로 전화 주십시오.

여러분의 양해와 협조에 대해 미리 감사 드립니다.

Wesley Kim
인사부장
Hayward Accounting Firm

**161.** 인사부장의 말에 따르면, 직원들은 각자의 상사와 무엇에 관해 이야기할 수 있는가?
(A) 정규직 채용으로의 전환
(B) 주차 공간에 대한 제비 뽑기
(C) 재택 근무의 가능성
(D) 출장 경비에 대한 환급                              정답 (C)

**162.** 시내 공영 주차장에 관해 사실일 것 같은 내용은 무엇인가?
(A) 10월 6일에 다시 문을 열 것이다.
(B) 유료 주차장이다.
(C) Hayward Accounting Firm에서 멀리 떨어져 있다.
(D) 최근에 확장되었다.                                정답 (B)

**163.** [1], [2], [3] 그리고 [4]로 표시된 곳 중에, 아래 문장이 들어가기에 가장 적절한 곳은?
"우리는 차량들이 들어갈 충분한 공간을 제공하기 위해 지하 주차장을 확장하기로 결정했습니다."
(A) [1]
(B) [2]
(C) [3]
(D) [4]                                               정답 (A)

**문제 164-167번은 다음 이메일을 참조하시오.**

수신: Chris Bundy 〈cbundy@dahmercorp.com〉
발신: Yuliana Lim 〈ylim@trentonhotel.com〉
날짜: 8월 19일
제목: Trenton 호텔 예약 문의

Bundy 씨께,

저희 호텔 예약에 관한 이메일을 방금 받았습니다. (164) **귀하의 9월 투숙이 단골 고객들을 위한 보상 포인트 계획에 해당한다는 점은 정확합니다.**

이메일에서 귀하는 9월 1일 예정된 시간보다 일찍 입실하길 바란다고 언급하셨습니다. 알고 계시듯이 일반적인 입실 시간은 2시부터지만, 12시까지 객실을 준비할 수 있도록 노력하겠습니다. 이와 관련해서는 당일 도착에 앞서 안내 데스크에 미리 연락하시길 바랍니다. 만약 일찍 오셨는데 객실이 준비 중이면, (165) **안내 데스크 직원들에게 짐을 맡기셔도 됩니다.** 잠시 쉬거나 마을 주변을 산책하시는 동안 직원들이 짐을 안전하게 보관해드릴 것입니다.

(166) **귀하의 7월 숙박에 관한 사안 또한 정확합니다. 컴퓨터 오류로 인해**

저희는 귀하가 퇴실한 이후 보증금 100달러를 돌려드리지 못했습니다. 오늘 아침 보증금이 귀하의 신용카드로 다시 입금되는 것을 직접 확인했습니다. (167) **이러한 누락과 이로 인해 겪으셨을지도 모를 고객님의 불편함에 사과를 드립니다.** 이를 보상해드리고자, 근처 Odeon 극장에서 원하는 영화를 보실 수 있는 두 장의 영화 상품권을 준비했습니다.

추가로 질문이 있으신 경우, 555-5674로 제게 직접 문의하시기 바랍니다.

Yuliana Lim
Trenton 호텔 예약 관리자

**164.** 이메일의 목적은 무엇인가?
(A) 체크 아웃 시간이 변경되었음을 손님에게 알리기 위해서
(B) 고객에게 선금을 요청하기 위해서
(C) 특정 날짜에 방이 없음을 손님에게 알리기 위해서
(D) 손님이 특별 프로그램에 대한 자격 요건을 갖추고 있음을 확인해주기 위해서                                       정답 (D)

**165.** Trenton 호텔에 대해 언급된 것은 무엇인가?
(A) 피트니스 센터 옆에 위치하고 있다.
(B) 최근 일부 객실을 보수했다.
(C) 손님의 가방을 보관해준다.
(D) Bundy 씨에게 할인된 객실 요금에 대해 통보했다.       정답 (C)

**166.** 지난 번 Trenton 호텔에 투숙했을 당시, Bundy 씨는 어떠한 문제점을 경험했는가?
(A) 룸서비스가 초과 청구되었다.
(B) 자신의 보증금을 받지 못했다.
(C) 개인 소지품의 일부를 분실하였다.
(D) 일반 입실 시간 이후에 도착했다.                    정답 (B)

**167.** [1], [2], [3] 그리고 [4]로 표시된 곳 중에, 아래 문장이 들어가기에 가장 적절한 곳은?
"이러한 누락과 이로 인해 겪으셨을지도 모를 고객님의 불편함에 사과를 드립니다."
(A) [1]
(B) [2]
(C) [3]
(D) [4]                                               정답 (C)

**문제 168-171번은 다음 기사를 참조하시오.**

Calvert City 뉴스
도시에서 벗어날 수 있는 기회
작성자, Kelly McGowan

5월 23일 – 이곳 Calvert City를 기반으로 하는 활동과 레스토랑들에 초점을 맞추는 대신, 도시 경계에서 북쪽으로 불과 20킬로미터밖에 떨어지지 않은 아름다운 마을인 Greybridge에 관한 이야기를 하는 것으로 (169) **이번 주의 칼럼을 조금 다르게 작성하기로 결정했습니다.** Greybridge는 예스럽고 평화로운 작은 마을로, 모든 사람들에게 도시의 소음과 혼란스러움으로부터 벗어날 수 있는 기회를 제공해 줍니다. 이곳은 또한 놀랄 정도로 많은 활동과 음식을 즐길 수 있는 장소를 (168) **자랑합니다.** 다음을 보시면, Greybridge로의 즐거운 당일 여행 계획에 관한 제 제안들을 읽어 보실 수 있습니다.

(오전 8시 30분) 도착하면 곧장 Dale Bakery로 향하셔야 합니다. 기본적으로 다양한 빵과 패스트리들을 고객들에게 판매하는 제과점이지만, 또한 식사 공간으로서 제한적이면서도 맛이 뛰어난 메뉴를 자랑합니다. 이곳은 Greybridge의 터줏대감 같은 곳이며, 맛있는 아침 식사 제공 서

비스로 특히 잘 알려져 온 곳입니다. 갓 내린 커피와 함께 완전한 영국식 아침 식사를 즐겨 보시기 바랍니다.

(오전 9시 45분) 맛있는 아침 식사로 에너지를 얻은 후에는, 근처의 Glenford 강을 따라 산책해 보시기를 권해 드립니다. 강 전체 지역이 그림 같은 풍경을 지니고 있을 뿐만 아니라, 사람들의 관심을 끄는 여러 지점들이 포함되어 있습니다. 산책하는 동안, 잠시 멈춰 Balgay 예술 공원에 있는 여러 조각품과 벽화들을 확인해 보시기 바라며, 특히 어린이들의 관심을 끌 수 있는 Alton Farm Petting 동물원도 놓치지 마십시오.

(오후 1시 30분) 강을 따라 걸으면서 식욕을 북돋우셨다면, 다시 마을로 돌아가 점심 식사를 위해 Alma's Country Kitchen을 방문해 보십시오. 개장한지 오래된 곳은 아니지만, 이미 이 마을 최고의 식당들 중 한 곳으로서의 명성을 얻은 곳입니다. (170) Alma's는 오직 인근의 농장과 공급업체들을 통해 구입한 농산물만을 사용한 요리를 제공하며, 저는 특히 전문적으로 조리된 그릴에 구운 연어와 잘게 자른 샐러드를 꼽아 칭찬하고 싶습니다. 이곳의 메뉴는 www.almascountrykitchen.co.uk에서 온라인으로 보실 수 있습니다. 하지만 주말에 가실 경우에 긴 대기 시간과 맞닥뜨리실 수 있다는 점에 주의하시기 바랍니다. 또한, (171B) 바게트나 구운 감자 등과 같은 특정 음식을 포장해 가실 수 있는데, 이는 원하실 경우 근처에 있는 Meadow 공원에서 이 음식들을 즐기실 수 있다는 것을 의미합니다. 이는 날씨가 좋을 경우 아주 좋은 선택입니다.

(오후 3시) Greybridge에서의 남은 시간 동안에는, 가이드를 동반한 Greybridge 대성당 견학을 한 번 해 보십시오. 이 놀라운 건물은 15세기 후반에 지어졌으며, Greybridge Cultural Heritage Society에 의해 보존 및 유지 관리되고 있습니다. (171C) 이 대성당의 한 부속 건물은 미술관으로 개조되었으며, 지역 미술가와 조각가들이 많은 다양한 미술품들을 특징으로 하고 있습니다. 성당과 미술관 모두 월요일부터 목요일까지 입장료가 무료입니다. 그 외의 다른 날에는, 중앙 출입구에서 티켓을 구입하실 수 있습니다. www.greybridgecathedral.org를 통해 현재의 요금을 확인해 보십시오.

(171D) Greybridge에서의 당일 여행 동안 할 수 있는 활동과 관련된 여러분만의 의견이 있으신가요? 그렇다면, 여러분의 생각을 kmcgowan@calvertnews.org로 보내 주시기 바랍니다.

**168.** 첫 번째 단락, 여덟 번째 줄에 있는 단어 "boasts"와 의미가 가장 가까운 어휘는 무엇인가?
(A) 수여하다
(B) 발표하다
(C) 갖추다
(D) 제공하다 　　　　　　　　　　　　　　　정답 (D)

**169.** McGowan 씨의 칼럼에 관해 암시되는 것은 무엇인가?
(A) 자주 Greybridge에 초점을 맞춘다.
(B) 보통 인터뷰를 포함한다.
(C) 해당 출판물의 주간 특집 기사이다.
(D) 해당 출판물의 최신 칼럼이다. 　　　　　　　정답 (C)

**170.** 기사 내용에 따르면, Alma's Country Kitchen에 관해 사실인 것은 무엇인가?
(A) 아주 다양한 제과 제품을 제공한다.
(B) 매일 오후 1시 30분에 영업을 위해 문을 연다.
(C) 오직 지역에서 구한 재료만을 사용한다.
(D) 일반적으로 주말에 덜 바쁘다. 　　　　　　　정답 (C)

**171.** McGowan 씨가 권하는 사항이 아닌 것은 무엇인가?
(A) 미리 대성당 입장권을 구입하는 것
(B) 레스토랑 음식을 갖고 지역 공원으로 가는 것
(C) 그림들이 전시된 곳을 방문하는 것
(D) Greybridge에서의 활동에 대한 아이디어를 제출하는 것 　정답 (A)

---

**문제 172-175번은 다음 온라인 채팅 토론을 참조하시오.**

> **Neil Webster** 　　　　　　　　　　　　[오전 9:34]
> 안녕하세요, Lora, 주문 번호 3920의 환불 문제에 무슨 일이 생긴 건지 아시나요? 고객께서 진행 상황을 알고 싶어 하세요.
>
> **Lora McDaniel** 　　　　　　　　　　　　[오전 9:35]
> (172) 요가 매트와 아령이 포함된 주문 아니었나요? 이미 처리된 것으로 생각했는데요.
>
> **Neil Webster** 　　　　　　　　　　　　[오전 9:36]
> 그 고객께서는 아직 비용을 받지 못했다고 말씀하셨어요. (173) 그분께서 제품을 반품하고 환불을 요청하신 이후로 벌써 2주나 됐어요.
>
> **Lora McDaniel** 　　　　　　　　　　　　[오전 9:37]
> 그럼 무슨 일이지 모르겠네요. 고객 서비스부에 확인해 볼게요.
>
> **Lora McDaniel** 　　　　　　　　　　　　[오전 9:39]
> (174) Max, 주문 번호 3920에 대한 상황 좀 확인해 주시겠어요? 그 고객께서 여전히 비용을 받지 못하셨어요.
>
> **Max Francis** 　　　　　　　　　　　　[오전 9:42]
> 처리 과정에서 실수가 있었던 것 같습니다. 제가 바로 해 드릴 수는 있지만, (175) 그 고객께서 비용을 돌려 받으시기까지 여전히 일주일이 걸릴 겁니다. 그래도 괜찮은가요?
>
> **Neil Webster** 　　　　　　　　　　　　[오전 9:43]
> 어쩔 수 없을 것 같아요. (175) 하지만 처리해 주셔서 감사합니다.

**172.** 메시지 작성자들은 무슨 종류의 업체에서 근무하고 있는가?
(A) 부동산 중개업체
(B) 운동 장비 매장
(C) 회계 법인
(D) 피트니스 센터 　　　　　　　　　　　　정답 (B)

**173.** 고객은 무엇을 요청했는가?
(A) 이전의 주문품에 대한 환불
(B) 배송 주소의 변경
(C) 주문 사항의 추가
(D) 주문품 배송에 대한 정보 　　　　　　　정답 (A)

**174.** McDaniel 씨가 Francis 씨에게 연락하는 이유는 무엇인가?
(A) 제품 배송에 대한 조언을 요청하기 위해
(B) 반품된 배송 물품이 어디에 있는지 알아 보기 위해
(C) 자신의 주문품에 대한 환불을 받을 수 있는지 확인해 보기 위해
(D) 환불 문제가 아직 처리되지 않은 이유를 알아 보기 위해 　정답 (D)

**175.** 오전 9시 43분에, Webster 씨가 "I guess that can't be helped."라고 썼을 때 무엇을 의미할 가능성이 가장 높은가?
(A) Francis 씨가 즉시 문제를 처리해 주기를 원한다.
(B) 문제를 해결하는 데 불가피하게 시간이 걸린다는 사실을 받아 들이고 있다.
(C) 왜 처리 과정이 그렇게 오래 걸리는지 이해하지 못하고 있다.
(D) 고객 서비스부에 의한 추가 도움을 요청하고 있다. 　정답 (B)

---

**문제 176-180번은 다음 편지와 이메일을 참조하시오.**

> Simmons 냉난방
>
> 4월 2일
>
> Jessie Spano 씨
> Dunder Miflin 기업

스완슨 가 9923
테네시 주 92929 내시빌

Spano 씨께,

지난 며칠간 저희 기록을 살펴본 결과, (178) **귀하의 회사에 설치했던 난방
시설이 거의 1년 전에 구매되었다는 것을 알게 되었습니다.** (176) **이 메시지
는 시스템 점검을 받아보시라고 권해드리기 위한 것입니다.** 귀하의 계약서
에 언급된 바와 같이, 귀하가 구입하신 제품은 5년 동안 보증수리가 가능하
오니, 결함이 있는 부속품들을 무료로 교체하실 수 있습니다. 저희가 방문
해서 시스템을 점검해도 괜찮은 편한 일정을 이메일로 보내주시기만 하면
됩니다.

현재 기계가 잘 작동된다고 생각하실지 몰라도, 전체적인 점검을 하여 마
모되거나 고장 날 만한 것이 없는지 확인하는 일은 절대 나쁘지 않습니다.
그것은 장기적으로 볼 때 큰 돈을 절약하는 것입니다. (177) **또한, 주저하지
말고 바로 서비스를 예약하세요. 왜냐하면 겨울철에는 요구사항들이나 가
정 방문, 그리고 수리 서비스들로 매우 바쁘기 때문입니다.**

겨울철 동안 안락하고 따뜻하실 수 있도록 가능한 빨리 저희에게 연락주세
요. 606-555-0994로 전화 주시거나 customerservice@simmonshna.
com으로 이메일을 주세요.

J.K. Simmons
사장
Simmons 냉난방

---

수신: 〈customerservice@simmonshna.com〉
발신: 〈jspano@dundermif.com〉
날짜: 4월 5일
제목: 난방 시설 점검

Simmons 씨께,

현재 저희의 난방 시설 점검에 관한 편지를 받았습니다. (178) **저희가 구매
이후 한번도 시설을 점검하지 않았다는 귀하의 지적이 맞습니다.** 시설이 효
율적으로 작동되고 있는지 확인하기 위해 적절한 점검을 받아야 할 시간인
것 같습니다. 다음주 중에 누군가를 보내주실 수 있나요?

저는 또한 서비스 기사가 현재 저희 에어컨 시스템을 봐주셨으면 좋겠습니
다. (179) **현재 저희 에어컨이 낡아서 말썽이 많기 때문에** 새것을 구입하려
고 (180) **알아보고** 있습니다. 근무시간이 오전 9시부터 오후 6시까지이니,
서비스 기사를 근무시간 중 아무 때나 보내주시면 됩니다. 기사가 언제 올
것인지 이메일로 알려 주세요.

감사합니다.

Jessie Spano
관리이사
Dunder Miflin 기업

**176.** 편지의 목적은 무엇인가?
(A) 서비스를 추천하기 위해서
(B) 재시험 날짜를 보고하기 위해서
(C) 약속을 취소하기 위해서
(D) 교환 부품에 대해 문의하기 위해서              정답 (A)

**177.** Simmons 씨에 따르면, 즉시 점검 일정을 잡아야 하는 이유는 무엇인가?
(A) 겨울 날씨가 몇몇 부품을 손상시켰다.
(B) 제조 결함이 감지되었다.
(C) 가을이 끝나면 보증기간이 만료된다.
(D) 겨울철에는 점검 일정을 잡기 어렵다.        정답 (D)

---

**178.** Dunder Miflin 기업에 있는 난방 시설은 언제 점검되었는가?
(A) 1주 전
(B) 1달 전
(C) 1년 전
(D) 2년 전                                      정답 (C)

**179.** Dunder Miflin 기업의 에어컨 시스템에 대해 암시되는 내용은 무엇인가?
(A) 고장이 났다.
(B) 적절하게 작동하지 않는다.
(C) 점검을 받은 적이 없다.
(D) 최근에 설치되었다.                          정답 (B)

**180.** 이메일에서, 두 번째 단락 첫 번째 줄의 "looking into"와 가장 유사한 의미
를 지니는 어휘는 무엇인가?
(A) 예상하다
(B) 조사하다
(C) 관찰하다
(D) 연구하다                                    정답 (B)

**문제 181-185번은 다음 메모와 이메일을 참조하시오.**

메모

발신: Nancy Palosi, 부사장실 비서실장
수신: Carmina Falcone, 수석 회계사
날짜: 9월 13일
제목: Bixby 사 순방

(181/182) **다음달 El Paso에서 시작하여 San Antonio에서 끝나는
Bixby 사 시설물 순방 일정이 유감스럽게도 변경되었습니다.** Seattle에서
El Paso까지, 그리고 El Paso에서 San Antonio까지의 새로운 비행 일자
와 시간을 아래에 적어 놓았습니다. San Antonio에서 Seattle로 돌아오는
비행편은 아직 정해지진 않았지만, 제가 알게 되는 즉시 알려드리겠습니다.

비행편 E443    9월 19일 오전 10시 Seattle 출발
              9월 19일 오후 12시 50분 El Paso 도착
비행편 F559    9월 21일 오후 2시 40분 El Paso 출발
              9월 21일 오후 4시 30분 San Antonio 도착

Stern 씨께서 El Paso에에 당신보다 몇 시간 일찍 도착하시므로, 도착하
면 그에게 연락해 주시기를 원하십니다. 그리고 나서 두 분께서는 Bixby
사의 공장으로 출발하여 순방을 시작할 예정입니다. 당신 비행편의 도착시
간 때문에 (183) **회의가 오후 2시로 연기되었습니다.**

---

수신: Nancy Palosi, 〈npalosi@millerco.com〉
발신: David Thornbush 〈guestservice@grandritz.com〉
날짜: 9월 11일
제목: Falcone 씨와 Stern 씨에 대한 요청 사항

(183) **지난주 그랜드 리츠 호텔에 전화상으로 하신 Carmina Falcone 씨
와 Daniel Stern 씨의 예약 건에 대한 확인** 메일입니다. 두 개의 1인실이
귀빈층에 예약되어 있습니다. 모든 사무용 집기들이 객실 안에 있을 것입니
다. 각 객실들은 인터넷 사용이 가능한 컴퓨터, 프린터, 그리고 팩스기기를
갖추고 있습니다. 저는 Seattle에 있는 귀사에서 택배회사를 통해 보내신
소포를 받았습니다. 그것을 Falcone 씨가 도착하면 받으실 수 있도록 그녀
의 객실에 가져다 두겠습니다.

(184) **Stern 씨가 거의 오전 10시에 도착하기 때문에, 입실시간을 10시
30분으로 추가 비용 없이 정해 놓았습니다.** (183) **Stern 씨와 Falcone
씨는 도착 당일 오후 2시부터 C회의실을 단독으로 사용하실 수 있습니다.**
C회의실은 지하 1층에 위치해 있습니다. (185) **저희는 또한 두 분을 위해**

호텔 식당인 Olive에 특별 저녁 식사를 준비해 놨습니다. 식사비는 두 분의 객실 요금에 청구될 것입니다. 두 분의 숙박에 대해 문의가 있으시면, 두 분이 도착하시기 전에 미리 연락 주시면 어떠한 요청사항에 대해서도 도와드릴 것을 약속드립니다. 감사합니다.

Mina Sohn
서비스 담당 매니저
El Paso, Grand Ritz 호텔

**181.** Palosi 씨의 메모의 주된 목적은 무엇인가?
    (A) 출장의 새로운 일정을 요청하기 위해서
    (B) 누가 출장을 갈 것인지 결정하기 위해서
    (C) 출장 일정의 변경을 확인하기 위해서
    (D) 계획된 회의를 취소하기 위해서    정답 (C)

**182.** 시설물 견학은 어디에서 이루어질 것인가?
    (A) El Paso
    (B) San Antonio
    (C) Seattle과 El Paso
    (D) El Paso와 San Antonio    정답 (D)

**183.** 두 손님의 회의는 어디에서 열릴 것인가?
    (A) 호텔 회의실
    (B) San Antonio 사무실
    (C) El Paso 시설물
    (D) Falcone 씨의 사무실    정답 (A)

**184.** Stern 씨의 도착에 관해 언급된 것은 무엇인가?
    (A) 그의 비행편이 취소되었기 때문에 지연될 것이다.
    (B) 사무실에서 서류가 오기 전에 도착할 것이다.
    (C) 일반적인 호텔의 체크인 시간보다 빨리 도착할 것이다.
    (D) Falcone 씨가 도착한 후에 도착할 것이다.    정답 (C)

**185.** 예약된 객실에 대해 언급되지 않은 것은 무엇인가?
    (A) 1인실이다.
    (B) 사무집기들이 갖춰져 있다.
    (C) 같은 층에 있다.
    (D) 식당에 근접해 있다.    정답 (D)

**문제 186-190번은 다음 편지와 일정표, 그리고 이메일을 참조하시오.**

NOBLE 서점
피카딜리 대로 741번지
던디, UK
DD4 8TW

Frank Peterson 씨
미첼 대로 42번지
던디, UK
DD4 8TW

5월 23일

Peterson 씨께,

곧 있을 저희 도서 사인회 행사에 대한 귀하의 관심에 감사 드립니다. 저희 NOBLE 서점에서는, 이와 같은 즐거운 행사를 통해 고객들께서 가장 좋아하시는 작가들을 고객 여러분과 연결해 드리기 위해 열심히 노력하고 있습니다. 저희 서점의 6월과 7월 도서 사인회 행사에 대한 일정표를 동봉해 드렸습니다. 그런데 이 일정표는 변경되었습니다. 6월 22일에 있을 도서 사인회 행사가 현재 기존의 오후 3시 15분에서 5시까지 열리는 시간대에서 새로운

시간대인 오전 10시 30분에서 오후 12시까지 열리는 것으로 변경되었다는 점에 유의하시기 바랍니다. 이와 비슷하게, (186) **현재 7월 22일에 열릴 예정인 도서 사인회는 오전 10시 30분이 아닌 오후 2시 15분에 열릴 것입니다.** 동봉된 일정표에 기재되어 있는 다른 모든 세부 사항들은 (187) **정확한 정보**입니다. 저희 도서 사인회 행사에는 입장료를 내거나 등록을 하는 일은 하지 않으셔도 되므로 행사 당일에 작가가 사인을 할 수 있는 물품을 갖고 찾아오시기만 하면 됩니다. (188) **작가들은 각각 자신의 최신 소설을 홍보할 것이므로 구입하지 않은 경우에는 한 권 구입하시기 바랍니다.** 추가 문의 사항이 있으시면 ghopkins@noblebooks.com을 통해 제게 이메일을 보내시기 바랍니다.

Gerald Hopkins

---

NOBLE 서점
도서 사인회 일정 – 6월/7월

| 날짜 | 시간 | 작가 | 도서명 |
|---|---|---|---|
| 6월 5일 | 오전 10:30 – 오후 12:00 | Casey Bakke | *Forest of Echoes* |
| 6월 13일 | 오후 2:00 – 오후 3:30 | Rachel Durst | *Safe From Harm* |
| 6월 22일 | 오후 3:15 – 오후 5:00 | Karim Benzia | *A Drop In the Ocean* |
| 6월 27일 | 오후 4:15 – 오후 6:00 | Elsa Aronson | *Story of Your Life* |
| 7월 5일 | 오후 2:15 – 오후 4:00 | Viktor Fischer | *Cave of Forgotten Dreams* |
| (189) **7월 11일** | 오전 10:00 – 오전 11:30 | **Lisa Kimberly** | *Ghosts of Meliora* |
| 7월 22일 | 오전 10:30 – 오후 12:15 | Yuri Utsugi | *The Happy House* |
| 7월 25일 | 오후 5:15 – 오후 7:00 | Amanda Davis | *Blackened Feathers* |

---

수신: Gerald Hopkins ⟨ghopkins@drydenbooks.org⟩
발신: Frank Peterson ⟨fpeterson@dunhillco.com⟩
날짜: 5월 24일
제목: 여름 도서 사인회

Hopkins 씨께,

제 편지에 답변해 주시고 제게 도서 사인회 일정표도 보내 주셔서 감사 드립니다. 열성적인 독자의 한 사람으로서, 이번 여름에 도서 사인회 행사에 참여하기 위해 제가 가장 좋아하는 작가들 중의 한 분이 귀하의 서점을 방문하게 될 것이라는 사실을 알게 되어 기쁩니다. (190) **제가 귀하의 서점에 얼마나 가까운 곳에 살고 있는지를 고려하면, 예전에 귀하의 서점에서 개최하는 사인회 행사에 한 번도 참석한 것이 없다는 것이 놀랍습니다.** 제 동료직원으로부터 이 도서 사인회 행사에 관해 듣지 못했다면, 저는 전혀 알지 못했을 것입니다. 아마 서점 내에서 더 적극적으로 이 행사를 광고하는 것에 대해 고려해 보셔야 할 것 같습니다. 서점 웹사이트에 아마 도서 사인회 관련 정보가 있을 것이라고 생각하지만, 저는 온라인으로 좀처럼 책을 사지 않습니다. 저는 제가 가장 좋아하는 작가를 만나기를 진심으로 고대하고 있으며, (189) **새로 산 'Ghost of Meliora'책에 사인을 받을 수 있도록 이 책을 가져갈 것입니다.** 다시 한 번 귀하의 답변에 감사 드립니다.

Frank Peterson

**186.** 누구의 도서 사인회가 오후 시간대로 변경되었는가?
    (A) Casey Bakke
    (B) Karim Benzia
    (C) Viktor Fischer
    (D) Yuri Utsugi    정답 (D)

**187.** 편지에서 첫 번째 단락, 여섯 번째 줄에 있는 단어 "precise"와 의미가 가장 유사한 것은?
(A) 시간을 지키는
(B) 이른
(C) 계산된
(D) 정확한 　　　　　　　　　　　　　　　　　정답 (D)

**188.** Hopkins 씨는 Peterson 씨에게 무엇을 하도록 권하는가?
(A) 도서 사인회에 미리 등록할 것
(B) 하나의 행사에 대한 참석 계획을 확인할 것
(C) 최근에 출시된 출판물을 구입할 것
(D) 문서의 추가 사본을 준비할 것 　　　　　　　정답 (C)

**189.** Peterson 씨는 언제 도서 사인회에 참석할 계획인가?
(A) 6월 13일에
(B) 6월 27일에
(C) 7월 11일에
(D) 7월 25일에 　　　　　　　　　　　　　　정답 (C)

**190.** Peterson 씨의 이메일에서 그에 관해 유추할 수 있는 것은 무엇인가?
(A) 과거에 NOBLE 서점에서 열린 행사에 참석했다.
(B) 곧 있을 행사에 동료직원 한 명을 동반할 것이다.
(C) 도서 사인회에 대한 광고를 온라인으로 봤다.
(D) NOBLE 서점에서 아주 멀지 않은 곳에 산다. 　　정답 (D)

---

문제 191-195번은 다음 광고와 웹페이지를 참조하시오.

---

Sherman Tours

Sherman Tours는 Grand Canyon로 가는 특별 당일 여행을 자신 있게 선보입니다. 6명의 소수 인원으로 Grand Canyon의 South Rim으로 가는 인상 깊고 편안한 여행을 즐기실 수 있습니다. (195) 저희의 전문 가이드가 여러분을 널찍한 밴으로 Grand Canyon과 다른 주요 지역 관광 명소로 모셔다 드리고 각 명소의 역사와 전해지는 이야기도 들려 드립니다. (191) Sherman Tours의 회원만이 이 합리적인 가격의 여행상품을 이용하실 수 있는 점에 주목해 주십시오. 이 상품을 신청하시거나 Grand Canyon 여행 상품에 대한 추가적인 정보를 원하시면 저희 웹사이트 www.shermantours.com을 참조해 주십시오.

---

http://www.shermantours.com/tourinfo

| 홈 | 회사 소개 | 여행상품 정보 | 고객의 평가 글 | 예약하기 |
|---|---|---|---|---|

Sherman Tours

**(193) Grand Canyon으로 떠나는 특별한 당일 여행**

일시: 오전 10:00 – 오후 8:00
　　　일요일 – 금요일 출발 (토요일 일정 없음)

장소: Flagstaff 공항에서 Grand Canyon의 South Rim까지 (공항에서 South Rim까지 차편 제공 서비스 포함). (193) Oliviare's Italian 에서 점심식사 & Mitchell's Diner에서 저녁식사 또는 (194) 목요일에는 All about French에서 저녁식사

비용: 성인 한 명당 145달러
　　　16세 이하의 어린이 한 명당 80달러

기타: (192) 추가 200달러로 헬기를 타고 Grand Canyon을 관광할 수 있습니다. 원하시는 식단 종류는 사전에 알려주셔야 합니다. Grand Canyon과 다른 관광 명소들의 사진을 보시려면 여기를 누르세요

---

http://www.shermantours.com/testimonials

| 홈 | 회사 소개 | 여행상품 정보 | 고객의 평가 글 | 예약하기 |
|---|---|---|---|---|

"Grand Canyon으로의 멋진 여행"

Samantha Watts가 평가함
10월 10일 작성됨

이것은 Sherman Tours가 제공해준 정말 멋지고 잘 짜인 여행이었어요. 저는 특히 결코 서두를 필요 없이 아름다운 Grand Canyon의 경관을 보러 가고 자연을 감상할 수 있었던 점이 좋았어요. (195) 가이드 Joshua O'Neil 씨는 정말 유익한 정보를 알려줬고, 박식하고, 유쾌했어요. (194) All about French에서 먹었던 저녁도 정말 맛있었어요. 이 여행상품을 비교적 짧은 시간에 Grand Canyon에서 잊지 못할 경험을 하고 싶은 사람들에게 추천합니다.

**191.** Sherman Tours에 대해 맞는 것은?
(A) 회원들에게만 특정 상품을 제안하고 있다.
(B) 6명의 직원이 있다.
(C) 매달 사내 신문을 낸다.
(D) 긴 역사가 있다. 　　　　　　　　　　　　정답 (A)

**192.** 헬기 탑승에 대해 언급된 것은?
(A) 사전에 요청되어야 한다.
(B) 재구매 고객에게 주어진다.
(C) 추가 요금을 받고 제공된다.
(D) 현재 할인된 금액에 이용할 수 있다. 　　　　정답 (C)

**193.** Grand Canyon 당일 여행에 포함된 것은?
(A) 비행기 표
(B) 식사
(C) 기념품
(D) 사진촬영 서비스 　　　　　　　　　　　　정답 (B)

**194.** Watts 씨는 언제 Grand Canyon으로 여행을 갔을 것 같은가?
(A) 목요일
(B) 금요일
(C) 토요일
(D) 일요일 　　　　　　　　　　　　　　　　정답 (A)

**195.** O'Neil 씨에 대해 추론될 수 있는 것은?
(A) 그는 직업 연예인이다.
(B) 그는 Grand Canyon 여행 상품에 145달러를 냈다.
(C) 그는 Sherman Tours의 신입사원이다.
(D) 그는 Watts 씨를 Grand Canyon으로 태워다 주었다. 　정답 (D)

---

문제 196-200번은 다음 웹페이지와 양식, 그리고 이메일을 참조하시오.

---

http://www.josestexmexfiesta/employment/

| (196) 연혁 | 메뉴 | 부서 안내 | (196) 지점 찾기 | 채용 정보 |
|---|---|---|---|---|
| 회사 철학 | 행사 출장 요리 | (198) 월별 제공 서비스 | 배달 서비스 | 연락처 |

저희는 현재 여러 지점에서 근무하실 직원 및 책임자들을 채용 중입니다:

직책 #012 – 직원 (주방) (전 지점) – 반드시 열성적이어야 하며, 협업을 잘하는 분이어야 합니다. 반드시 개인 위생 관념이 뛰어나야 하며, 무거운 상자를 드는 일, 빗자루 및 대걸레를 이용한 청소를 할 수 있어야 하며, 그릴 및 토스터 기기 등을 사용할 수 있어야 합니다.

직책 #034 – 교대 근무 운영 책임자 (TH/NS/IP/IN) – 반드시 서비스 업계의 어느 분야에서든 직원들을 관리해 본 (198) **경험이 최소 12개월 이상 된 분이어야 합니다.** 반드시 제때 문서 업무를 완료할 수 있어야 합니다.

직책 #042 – 급여 업무 보조 (AH/TH/NS/LV) – 반드시 재무/회계 업무에 대해 1년의 경력이 있어야 합니다(2년 우대). 회계학 학위나 수료증 소지자 우대합니다.

직책 #024 – 레스토랑 매니저(NS/IP/WC/IN) – 반드시 레스토랑 매니저로 최소 3년의 경력이 있어야 합니다. 업무를 분배하고 하위 관리자나 직원을 격려하는데 능해야 합니다.

지점 약자: Alamo Height(AH), Terrell Hills (TH), North Star Mall (NS), Leon Valley (LV), Ingram Park Mall (IP), Wind Crest (WC), Inglewood Park (IN)

신청서를 다운로드하시려면 <u>여기를 클릭하세요.</u> 양식을 작성해서 여기로 보내주세요:
인사 관리 부서, Jose's Tex-Mex Fiesta, PO BOX 348, San Antonio, TX 78205

---

Jose's Tex - Mex Fiesta

구직 지원서 (페이지 1)

해당되는 곳에, 회사 웹사이트 구인 목록에 사용된 직책 또는 지점 코드를 입력해 주십시오. 감사합니다.

지원자 성명: Casey Grillo   생일: 1984년 7월 25일
(198) **지원 직책: 직책 #034**   이메일 주소: cgrillo@ace.com
지원 지점: NS   전화번호: 010-555-8761
자택 주소: 1007 West Heenan Street, Alamo Heights, San Antonio

(197) **다음 추가 서류를 함께 제출해 주시기 바랍니다:** 여권 또는 주민증 사본, 이력서, (200) **자기 소개서,** 추천서 최소 1부, 운전면허증 사본(배송 운전 직책에만 해당), 직무 포트폴리오(광고/마케팅/웹디자인 직책에만 해당)

---

수신: 인사부 〈recruitment@josestexmex.org〉
발신: Casey Grillo 〈cgrillo@ace.com〉
날짜: 1월 23일
제목: 최근의 채용 지원

관계자 께,

어제 제가 보내 드린 구직 지원서와 관련해 연락 드립니다. 양식을 작성하다가 제가 실수를 했다는 것을 막 알게 되었습니다. 현재 저는 Alamo Heights에 살고 있지만, North Star Mall을 자주 방문해 그곳에 있는 Jose's Tex - Mex Fiesta에서 식사를 합니다. 그곳이 제가 지원서 양식에 기재한 지점인데, 그 시점에 제대로 생각하지 못했습니다. 저와 제 가족은 2월 초에 도시 반대편으로 이사를 가기 때문에 (199) **제 지원서에 지점 "IP"로 표기했어야 했습니다.** 제 서류들을 받으시는 대로 이 부분을 수정해 주실 수 있으면 대단히 감사하겠습니다. (200) **저는 제 이력서와 전 직장의 고용주에게서 받은 추천서, 그리고 여권 사본을 지원서와 함께 보내 드렸습니다.** 제가 깜빡 잊고 보내 드리지 않은 것이 있다면 무엇이든 알려 주시기 바랍니다.

Casey Grillo

---

**196.** 웹사이트에서 이용 가능한 정보로 나타나 있지 않은 것은 무엇인가?
    (A) 업체 지점 위치 찾기 기능
    (B) 회사의 설립에 관한 상세 정보
    (C) 만족한 고객들의 의견
    (D) 특별 제공 서비스에 관한 정보           정답 (C)

**197.** 목록에 나와 있는 직책 중의 한 곳에 관심이 있는 사람은 어떻게 지원할 수 있는가?
    (A) 온라인으로 양식을 작성함으로써
    (B) 지점 한 곳을 방문함으로써
    (C) 인사부에 이메일로 보냄으로써
    (D) 문서를 우편으로 보냄으로써           정답 (D)

**198.** Grillo 씨에 관해 사실일 가능성이 가장 큰 것은 무엇인가?
    (A) 레스토랑 업계에서 뛰어난 배경을 지니고 있다.
    (B) 재무 분야에 대한 학문적 자격 요건을 갖추고 있다.
    (C) 주방 도구 및 기기를 사용해 본 경험이 있다.
    (D) 최소 1년 이상의 관리직 경력이 있다.           정답 (D)

**199.** Grillo 씨는 어느 지점에 채용되길 바라는가?
    (A) Alamo Heights
    (B) North Star Mall
    (C) Ingram Park Mall
    (D) Inglewood Park           정답 (C)

**200.** Grillo 씨는 자신의 지원서와 함께 어떤 필수 항목을 포함하는 것을 잊었는가?
    (A) 자신의 운전면허증 사본
    (B) 직무 포트폴리오
    (C) 자기 소개서
    (D) 추천서           정답 (C)

## Actual Test 05

## Part 1

**1.** 호M
(A) A person is putting on a helmet.
(B) A person is changing a tire.
(C) A person is working on a car.
(D) A person is riding a bicycle.

(A) 한 사람이 안전모를 착용하고 있다.
(B) 한 사람이 타이어를 교체하고 있다.
(C) 한 사람이 자동차를 수리하고 있다.
(D) 한 사람이 자전거를 타고 있다.　　　　　　정답 (D)

**2.** 영W
(A) A woman is signing a form.
(B) A woman is typing on a keyboard.
(C) A woman is looking at some papers.
(D) A woman is jotting something down.

(A) 여자가 서류 양식에 서명하고 있다.
(B) 여자가 자판을 치고 있다.
(C) 여자가 서류를 보고 있다.
(D) 여자가 뭔가를 쓰고 있다.　　　　　　　정답 (C)

**3.** 미W
(A) Some people are repairing a fence.
(B) Some people are talking in small groups.
(C) Some people are trimming the bushes.
(D) Some people are putting dirt into a wheelbarrow.

(A) 몇몇 사람들이 울타리를 수리하고 있다.
(B) 몇몇 사람들이 무리를 지어 이야기를 하고 있다.
(C) 몇몇 사람들이 관목을 다듬고 있다.
(D) 몇몇 사람들이 외바퀴 손수레에 흙을 담고 있다.　　정답 (D)

**4.** 호M
(A) He is getting into a car.
(B) He is lying under a car to fix it.
(C) He is bending forward to check a car.
(D) He is driving a truck into a parking garage.

(A) 그는 자동차에 탑승하고 있다.
(B) 그는 자동차를 수리하기 위해 자동차 아래에 누워 있다.
(C) 그는 자동차를 확인하기 위해 몸을 앞으로 구부리고 있다.
(D) 그는 트럭을 몰고 주차장으로 들어가고 있다.　　정답 (C)

**5.** 미M
(A) They are collaborating on some work.
(B) They are wearing protective goggles.
(C) They are hammering some nails into a wall.
(D) They are setting their helmets on a window ledge.

(A) 그들은 협동하며 작업을 하고 있다.
(B) 그들은 보안경을 착용하고 있다.
(C) 그들은 벽에 못을 박고 있다.
(D) 그들은 창틀에 안전모를 내려놓고 있다.　　정답 (A)

**6.** 영W
(A) Liquid is being poured into a mug.
(B) Some office supplies are next to a laptop computer.
(C) The phone booth is being checked.
(D) Some merchandise has been arranged on racks.

(A) 한 머그잔에 음료가 부어지고 있다.
(B) 노트북 컴퓨터 옆에 일부 사무용품들이 있다.
(C) 공중전화 부스가 점검 중이다.
(D) 일부 상품들이 옷걸이에 걸려 진열되어 있다.　　정답 (B)

## Part 2

**7.** 미W 미M
Who's in charge of the company outing in May?
(A) That would be Ms. McAdams.
(B) I was charged $100 last month.
(C) You may go back to your office now.

5월에 있을 회사 야유회의 담당자가 누구인가요?
(A) McAdams 씨일 겁니다.
(B) 저는 지난달에 100달러를 청구 받았어요.
(C) 이제 사무실로 돌아가셔도 됩니다.　　정답 (A)

**8.** 호M 영W
Where is the attendance list for the company 20th anniversary?
(A) It's our 20th new store.
(B) I think Bella has it.
(C) Next Friday at 10 A.M.

회사의 20주년 기념식에 참석하는 사람들의 명단은 어디에 있나요?
(A) 우리의 새로운 20호점이에요.
(B) Bella가 가지고 있을 거예요.
(C) 다음주 금요일 오전 10시에요.　　정답 (B)

**9.** 영W 미W
Wasn't the delivery truck repaired yesterday?
(A) No, it's being fixed now.
(B) It's a ten-minute drive.
(C) Yes, it's a little heavy.

어제 배송 트럭이 수리되지 않았나요?
(A) 아니오, 지금 수리 중이에요.
(B) 차로 10분 거리예요.
(C) 네, 좀 무겁습니다.　　정답 (A)

**10.** 미W 호M
His claims were true, weren't they?
(A) You can trust me.
(B) All but one.
(C) Yes, it's better to check.

그의 주장들이 사실이었죠, 그렇지 않나요?
(A) 당신은 나를 신뢰해도 좋아요.
(B) 하나를 빼고 전부 맞아요.
(C) 네, 확인해 보는 것이 좋겠네요.　　정답 (B)

**11.** 미M 영W
When do you expect the economic depression to end?
(A) It's much better than expected.
(B) Not until next year.
(C) I majored in economics in college.

경기 불황이 언제 끝날 것으로 예상하세요?
(A) 예상했던 것보다 훨씬 좋네요.
(B) 내년이나 되어야 할 겁니다.

(C) 저는 대학에서 경제학을 전공했어요. 정답 (B)

**12.** [호M] [미W]

Do you want me to fax the relevant documents to the client?
(A) No, I can handle it.
(B) Several tax-free retail shops.
(C) It was seven pages long.

제가 고객들에게 관련 서류를 팩스로 발송해 드릴까요?
(A) 아니오, 제가 처리할 수 있습니다.
(B) 몇몇 면세점들이요.
(C) 그건 7페이지 분량이었어요. 정답 (A)

**13.** [영W] [미M]

I think we have a staff meeting tomorrow, right?
(A) Didn't you hear that it was canceled?
(B) No, turn left at the next intersection.
(C) Yes, I've met him before.

우리 내일 직원 회의가 있죠, 그렇죠?
(A) 그게 취소되었다는 말을 못 들었나요?
(B) 아니오, 다음 사거리에서 좌회전하세요.
(C) 네, 전에 그를 만난 적이 있어요. 정답 (A)

**14.** [미W] [호M]

When can we start selling the new cellular phone model?
(A) About $400 each.
(B) Well, let me check.
(C) Please phone me at 10:00.

새로운 휴대 전화는 언제부터 판매할 수 있나요?
(A) 개당 대략 400달러예요.
(B) 음, 확인해 볼게요.
(C) 10시에 제게 전화해 주세요. 정답 (B)

**15.** [호M] [미W]

Why don't we stop for gas before we get on the highway?
(A) No, we're running out of gas.
(B) That sounds like a great idea.
(C) Because I was stuck in traffic.

고속도로를 타기 전에 주유소에 들러 주유하는 것이 어떨까요?
(A) 아니오, 기름이 떨어져 가고 있어요.
(B) 좋은 생각이에요.
(C) 제가 교통체증으로 옴짝달싹할 수가 없었어요. 정답 (B)

**16.** [영W] [호M]

How long does the annual sale last?
(A) At least two meters.
(B) Sorry. It's not for sale.
(C) Until Sunday.

연례 할인 행사는 얼마 동안 계속되나요?
(A) 최소한 2미터요.
(B) 미안합니다만 그건 판매용이 아니에요.
(C) 일요일까지요. 정답 (C)

**17.** [미W] [미M]

The new printing paper hasn't arrived yet, has it?
(A) High-quality printing paper.
(B) Ms. Wilson might know.
(C) We offer speedy delivery.

새로운 인쇄용지가 아직 도착하지 않았죠, 그렇지요?
(A) 고품질 인쇄용지예요.
(B) Wilson 씨가 알고 있을 겁니다.
(C) 저희는 빠른 배송 서비스를 제공합니다. 정답 (B)

**18.** [미M] [영W]

Would you like to discuss the new construction project today or tomorrow?
(A) Yes, it's a seven-story building.
(B) Tomorrow would be better for me.
(C) It's a new overhead projector.

새로운 건설 계획에 대한 논의를 오늘 하시겠어요, 아니면 내일 하시겠어요?
(A) 네, 그건 7층짜리 건물입니다.
(B) 저는 내일이 더 좋아요.
(C) 그건 새로운 영사기예요. 정답 (B)

**19.** [호M] [미W]

This will be your first time leading a sales presentation to the board.
(A) Yes, I hope it goes very well.
(B) You might feel nervous now.
(C) No, it's my birthday present.

이번이 이사회 앞에서 하게 되는 당신의 최초 영업 발표겠군요.
(A) 네, 잘되길 바랄 뿐입니다.
(B) 지금 긴장되시겠네요.
(C) 아니오, 그건 제 생일선물이에요. 정답 (A)

**20.** [영W] [호M]

Doesn't this mobile phone come with two free rechargeable batteries?
(A) No, I've already paid for it.
(B) Actually, I don't work here.
(C) Yes, they are provided for an additional charge.

이 휴대 전화는 두 개의 무료 충전지와 함께 나오나요?
(A) 아니오, 저는 이미 그것의 가격을 지불했어요.
(B) 사실 저는 이 곳에서 근무하지 않습니다.
(C) 네, 그것들은 추가 비용과 함께 제공됩니다. 정답 (B)

**21.** [미W] [미M]

Why were you absent from the accounting seminar yesterday?
(A) Yes, it was already sent to her.
(B) It was really informative and interesting.
(C) I thought it had been canceled.

어제 회계 세미나에 참석하지 못한 이유가 뭔가요?
(A) 네, 그건 이미 그녀에게 발송되었어요.
(B) 그건 정말 유익하고 흥미로웠어요.
(C) 저는 그게 취소된 걸로 알고 있었어요. 정답 (C)

**22.** [호M] [미W]

Why is the photocopier being moved out of the office?
(A) Some are black and white.
(B) I'm kind of busy working now.
(C) We are going to repaint the office soon.

복사기를 사무실 밖으로 꺼내는 이유가 뭔가요?
(A) 일부는 흑백이에요.
(B) 저는 지금 좀 일이 바빠요.
(C) 우리는 사무실을 다시 페인트칠할 겁니다. 정답 (C)

**23.** 영W 미M

Could you please take care of my work while I'm away?
(A) A tour of Western Canada.
(B) Yes, I'd be happy to.
(C) At the artificial intelligence conference.

제가 자리를 비운 동안에 제 업무를 봐 주시겠어요?
(A) Canada 서부 지역으로의 여행이에요.
(B) 네, 기꺼이 그렇게 할게요.
(C) 인공지능 관련 회의에서요.　　　　　정답 (B)

**24.** 미W 영W

The old museum will be restored to its original form, won't it?
(A) Admission is free for children.
(B) The exhibition is open from 10:00 A.M. to 5:00 P.M.
(C) Yes, I think it will look much better in the future.

그 오래된 박물관이 원상태로 복원된다고 하던데요, 그렇지 않나요?
(A) 아이들에게는 입장료가 무료예요.
(B) 전시회는 오전 10시에 시작하여 오후 5시에 끝나요.
(C) 네, 향후에는 더 보기가 좋을 것이라고 생각해요.　　　정답 (C)

**25.** 호M 영W

Should I send the revised contract to Ms. Ferguson?
(A) No, she has already received it.
(B) Yes, I sent them an invoice for the sale.
(C) Here's my contact number while I'm away.

수정된 계약서를 Ferguson 씨에게 보내야 하나요?
(A) 아니오, 그녀는 이미 받았어요.
(B) 네, 판매 관련 송장을 그들에게 보냈어요.
(C) 여기 제가 없는 동안 제 연락처예요.　　　정답 (A)

**26.** 미W 호M

Isn't the photocopier broken?
(A) Some broken windows.
(B) No, it's working all right.
(C) Thanks, but I can manage.

복사기가 고장 나지 않았나요?
(A) 몇몇 깨진 유리창들이요.
(B) 아니오, 잘 작동하고 있는데요.
(C) 고맙습니다만, 제가 할 수 있어요.　　　정답 (B)

**27.** 호M 미W

Did you enjoy the musical that I recommended?
(A) For about two hours.
(B) Yes, it was very impressive.
(C) No, please select the tickets you want.

제가 추천해 드린 뮤지컬이 즐거우셨어요?
(A) 대략 두 시간 동안이요.
(B) 네, 굉장히 인상적이었어요.
(C) 아니오, 원하시는 표의 종류를 선택해 주세요.　　　정답 (B)

**28.** 미M 영W

Can I borrow your wireless charger for a moment?
(A) No, I'm in charge.
(B) Yes, you can use my mobile phone.
(C) Lisa borrowed it a couple of hours ago.

무선 충전기 좀 잠시 빌려도 될까요?

(A) 아니오, 제가 책임자입니다.
(B) 네, 제 휴대전화를 쓰셔도 됩니다.
(C) Lisa가 두 시간 전에 빌려 갔어요.　　　정답 (C)

**29.** 미W 호M

Would you please fill out this loan application form?
(A) At the bank.
(B) Could I use your pen for a moment, please?
(C) Yes, I prefer to work alone.

이 대출 신청서를 작성해 주시겠어요?
(A) 은행에서요.
(B) 당신의 펜을 잠시 쓸 수 있을까요?
(C) 네, 저는 혼자서 일하는 쪽을 선호해요.　　　정답 (B)

**30.** 호M 영W

You've already spoken to our customer service manager, haven't you?
(A) No, I can speak three languages.
(B) Your order has already been shipped.
(C) Yes, she's very cooperative.

저희 고객 서비스 담당자와 이미 이야기를 나누셨지요, 그렇지 않나요?
(A) 아니오, 저는 3개 국어를 구사할 수 있어요.
(B) 주문하신 물건은 이미 배송되었어요.
(C) 네, 그녀는 굉장히 협조적이었어요.　　　정답 (C)

**31.** 미W 호M

We installed a new computer network security system last week.
(A) It looks like some kind of virus.
(B) I have it in a very safe place.
(C) But it was costly for the company.

우리는 지난주에 새로운 컴퓨터 네트워크 보안 시스템을 설치했어요.
(A) 그건 일종의 바이러스처럼 보이네요.
(B) 저는 그걸 매우 안전한 곳에 보관하고 있어요.
(C) 하지만 회사에 굉장히 많은 비용이 들었어요.　　　정답 (C)

## Part 3

문제 32-34번은 다음 대화를 참조하시오. 미M 영W

M: Hi, Ms. Clarke. (32) **Did you complete the final blueprints for DT Tower?** (33) **I need to present them to the team from the construction company at the meeting tomorrow afternoon.**

W: I'm almost finished. I had to discuss some issues with the senior engineer, so it has taken a little longer than I had expected. (34) **Can you give them the first draft of the blueprints instead?** The construction team should understand the general idea of the project.

M: Actually, I need to give them the final blueprints. To avoid delays, the construction team needs to be fully prepared. Is it possible for you to finish them by the end of today?

W: I doubt it. But if you come back first thing in the morning, they should hopefully be finished.

---------------------------------------------------------------

M: 안녕하세요, Clarke 씨. DT Tower에 대한 최종 설계도면을 완성했나요? 내일 오후에 있을 회의에서 건설회사 팀에 제출해야 해서요.

W: 거의 끝나갑니다. 수석 엔지니어와 몇 가지 문제에 대해 상의하느라 제

가 예상했던 것보다 시간이 좀 더 걸렸습니다. 대신 그들에게 초안을 보여줄 수 있는지요? 건설 팀이 이 프로젝트에 대한 전반적인 이해가 필요할 것 같아서요.

M: 사실 그들에게 최종 설계도면을 줘야 합니다. 지연을 막으려면 건설 팀이 완벽하게 준비가 되어 있어야 합니다. 오늘까지 그것들을 마칠 수 있을까요?

W: 잘 모르겠네요. 일단 아침에 출근하실 때까지 마무리하도록 해 볼게요.

**32.** 남자가 요청하는 것은 무엇인가?
(A) 사무실 가는 방법
(B) 건축 설계도면
(C) 엔지니어링 관리자
(D) 일정 변경               정답 (B)

**33.** 남자는 건설회사 팀과 언제 만날 것인가?
(A) 내일 아침
(B) 내일 오후
(C) 2주 후
(D) 오늘 오후               정답 (B)

**34.** 여자는 남자에게 무엇을 제안하는가?
(A) 기술자와 이야기할 것
(B) 발표를 준비할 것
(C) 회의를 나중에 시작할 것
(D) 이전 안을 사용할 것          정답 (D)

**문제 35-37번은 다음 대화를 참조하시오.** 미M 미W

M: Betty, I was just informed our flight will be delayed three hours. (35) **Due to the heavy rain storm, the plane cannot take off from the airport on time.**

W: Three hours? (36) **Does that mean that we will arrive in Toronto at 7 A.M.?** (37) **We won't have enough time to practice our presentation before the conference at 10 A.M.**

M: We don't need to worry about it. Most of the participants are from Vancouver like us, so the CEO just announced online that it has been rescheduled to 2 P.M. tomorrow.

--------------------------------------

M: Betty, 방금 우리 비행기가 3시간 연착될 거라고 연락 받았어요. 심한 폭풍 때문에 비행기가 공항에서 제시간에 이륙할 수가 없대요.

W: 3시간이요? 그럼 우리가 오전 7시에 Toronto에 도착할 것이란 말이에요? 오전 10시에 있을 회의 전에 우리가 발표를 연습할 시간이 충분하지 않겠는데요.

M: 그건 걱정할 필요 없어요. 대부분의 참석자가 우리처럼 Vancouver에서 오기 때문에 최고경영자가 방금 온라인으로 회의 일정이 내일 오후 2시로 재조정되었다고 발표했어요.

**35.** 남자에 따르면 비행기가 지연되는 이유는 무엇인가?
(A) 기계적인 문제
(B) 악천후
(C) 예약 초과
(D) 기내 승무원 교체           정답 (B)

**36.** 화자들이 Toronto에 도착하는 시간은 언제인가?
(A) 오전 7시
(B) 오전 10시
(C) 오후 2시
(D) 오후 3시               정답 (A)

**37.** 여자가 걱정을 하는 이유는 무엇인가?
(A) 그녀는 예약이 취소될 수도 있다.
(B) 그녀는 Toronto의 날씨를 좋아하지 않는다.
(C) 비행기에 남은 좌석이 전혀 없다.
(D) 연습할 시간이 부족하다.         정답 (D)

**문제 38-40번은 다음의 3자 대화를 참조하시오.** 미W 호M 미M

W: Hey, guys! (38) **The department supervisor just informed me that Mr. Turner will be transferring to the London office next month.**

M1: That's quite a surprise considering that he only joined the company a few months ago.

M2: You're probably right, but (38) **he's going to be in charge of the Human Resources Department there.** (39) **He worked for a European human resources firm before joining our company, so he has some experience.**

W: Oh, I was not aware of that. (40) **Anyway, he'll have a hard job over there. Our company is currently starting a new business in Europe.**

--------------------------------------

W: 안녕하세요, 여러분! 부장님이 방금 제게 Turner 씨가 다음달에 London 지사로 발령이 날 것이라고 알려줬어요.

M1: 그가 불과 몇 달 전에 회사에 들어온 점을 감안하면 매우 놀라운 일이에요.

M2: 그 말도 일리가 있긴 한데요. 그는 그곳에서 인사부장으로 근무하게 될 겁니다. 그는 우리 회사에 입사하기 전에 유럽의 인력 회사에서 근무했으니 경험이 좀 있겠지요.

W: 아, 그건 몰랐네요. 어쨌든 그는 고된 업무를 하게 될 겁니다. 현재 우리 회사가 유럽에서 새로운 사업을 시작하고 있거든요.

**38.** Turner 씨가 London으로 가는 이유는 무엇인가?
(A) 새로운 직책을 맡기 위해서
(B) 고객을 만나기 위해서
(C) 시장 조사를 하기 위해서
(D) 휴가를 즐기기 위해서          정답 (A)

**39.** 남자에 따르면 Turner 씨가 새로운 일에 적격인 이유는 무엇인가?
(A) 해박한 제품 지식
(B) 훌륭한 고객 서비스 능력
(C) 현지에서의 과거 경력
(D) 외국어 능력               정답 (C)

**40.** 여자가 Turner 씨가 바빠질 것이라는 이유로 언급한 것은 무엇인가?
(A) 곧 중요한 프로젝트가 시작된다.
(B) 신입 직원들에게 종합적인 연수가 필요하다.
(C) 그는 발표 준비를 해야 한다.
(D) 회사가 사업을 확장하고 있다.       정답 (D)

**문제 41-43번은 다음 대화를 참조하시오.** 미W 미M

W: Hi, Laurence. I received a phone call from the city council. (41/42) **They're wondering when we can show them the first draft of the blueprints for the new public library.**

M: (42) **I've been meaning to send them, but I am still considering making a few minor adjustments.** I'm not completely happy with the current position of the side entrance.

It's too close to the trash area at the rear of Garibaldi's Pizza Parlor.

W: Good point. Well, if you think you can make any improvements, go for it. (43) **I'll be meeting with them at the council building tomorrow morning**, so I'll let them know the reason for the delay. I'm sure they'll be happy to hear you're putting so much effort into getting things right.

--------------------------------

W: 안녕하세요, Laurence. 시 의회에서 전화를 받았어요. 신축 공공 도서관의 설계도 초안을 언제 볼 수 있을지 궁금해하더군요.

M: 안 그래도 설계도를 보내려고 했는데 몇 가지 수정을 해야 할 부분이 있다는 생각이 들어서요. 측면 입구의 현재 위치가 완전히 만족스럽지가 않아요. Garibaldi's Pizza Parlor 뒤에 있는 쓰레기장과 너무 가까워서요.

W: 좋은 지적이에요. 음, 설계도를 수정해야 한다고 생각한다면 그렇게 하세요. 저는 내일 오전에 시 의회 건물에서 의원들과 회의를 할 거라서 그들에게 지연 이유를 알려줄게요. 그들이 설계도면을 제대로 만들기 위한 노력을 들으면 분명 기뻐할 거예요.

**41.** 화자들은 어디에서 근무할 것 같은가?
(A) 공공 도서관
(B) 시 의회 건물
(C) 건축회사
(D) 피자 가게 　　　　　　　　　　　　정답 (C)

**42.** 남자가 "I've been meaning to send them."이라고 말할 때 의미하는 바는 무엇인가?
(A) 그는 설계도면을 보내는 것을 잊었다.
(B) 그는 고객들의 의견을 받아 보길 기다리고 있다.
(C) 그는 자신의 작업에 만족하지 않는다.
(D) 그는 여자가 피자를 가져오길 원하고 있다. 　　정답 (C)

**43.** 여자는 내일 무엇을 하고자 하는가?
(A) 배송 일정을 재조정한다.
(B) 건물을 둘러본다.
(C) 서류를 제출한다.
(D) 회의에 참석한다. 　　　　　　　　　　정답 (D)

**문제 44-46번은 다음 대화를 참조하시오.** 미M 미W

M: Good morning. (44) **I'd like to rent an apartment in the Castro Valley area.** My current lease ends on January 10, so I'm hoping to move into a new place around that time.

W: Actually, we have several properties which will be available in January. Can you give me some information about what kind of apartment you are looking for?

M: (45) **Well, my job involves a lot of overseas travel, so I'd like to have a very short distance to travel to the airport.**

W: There are several properties that are close to the international terminal. (46) **Unfortunately, our computer system is down right now, so I can't check the listings.** If you leave me your contact details, I'll check the apartment listings later on and get back to you tomorrow.

--------------------------------

M: 안녕하세요. Castro Valley 지역의 아파트를 임대하려고 합니다. 현재 살고 있는 아파트 임대 기간이 1월 10일에 끝나서 그 때쯤 새로운 곳으로 이사하려고 합니다.

W: 사실 1월에 입주 가능한 집들이 있습니다. 고객님께서 어떤 아파트를 찾고 계신지 제게 알려주시겠습니까?

M: 음, 제가 하는 일이 해외 출장 업무가 많아서 공항에서 아주 가까운 거리에 있었으면 해요.

W: 국제 공항에 가까운 집들이 있습니다. 그런데 유감스럽게도 현재 저희 컴퓨터 시스템이 고장 나서 목록을 확인할 수가 없네요. 고객님의 연락처를 남겨 주시면 나중에 아파트 목록을 확인해서 내일 다시 연락 드리겠습니다.

**44.** 남자가 전화하는 곳은 어디인가?
(A) 호텔
(B) 공항
(C) 여행사
(D) 부동산 중개업체 　　　　　　　　　정답 (D)

**45.** 남자가 중요하다고 말하는 것은 무엇인가?
(A) 공항 근처에 사는 것
(B) 차량을 위해 돈을 절약하는 것
(C) 더 나은 직장을 찾는 것
(D) 티켓 할인을 받는 것 　　　　　　　　정답 (A)

**46.** 여자가 후에 다시 전화를 걸겠다고 언급한 이유는 무엇인가?
(A) 현재 이용 가능한 정보가 없다.
(B) 목록을 만들려면 시간이 걸린다.
(C) 다른 고객들과 먼저 상담해야 한다.
(D) 남자의 여행 일정이 변경되었다. 　　　정답 (A)

**문제 47-49번은 다음 대화를 참조하시오.** 미M 미W

M: Hello. (47) **I bought a ticket for the ballet Saturday night.** I just received word that one of my colleagues will be in town this weekend, so (48) **I was wondering if it would be possible to get a ticket for him for the same night.**

W: Let me see… I'm sorry, but it looks like Saturday is sold out. We do have several seats available for the 5 P.M. Friday performance though. If you'd like, I can buy back your Saturday ticket, and then you can purchase two for Friday.

M: That might work. Thank you. (49) **I'll have to call him to see if the time is acceptable.** I'll try to call back to confirm this evening.

--------------------------------

M: 안녕하세요. 제가 토요일 저녁에 있을 발레 공연표를 한 장 구매했습니다. 그런데 제 동료가 이번 주말에 시내에 올 것이라는 이야기를 들어서, 같은 저녁 공연으로 표를 한 장 추가로 구매하는 것이 가능한지 알고 싶습니다.

W: 잠시만요… 죄송합니다만 토요일 공연표는 모두 매진이 되었어요. 하지만 금요일 오후 5시 공연은 몇 자리가 남아 있긴 합니다. 원하신다면 제가 고객님의 토요일 표를 환불해 드리고 금요일 공연표로 두 매를 구매하시는 방법도 있습니다.

M: 그 방법도 괜찮을 것 같네요. 감사합니다. 그에게 연락을 해서 시간이 괜찮은지 확인부터 해봐야겠네요. 오늘 저녁에 확인 차 다시 연락드릴게요.

**47.** 여자는 어디에서 근무할 것 같은가?
(A) 여행사
(B) 공연장
(C) 영화관
(D) 출판사 　　　　　　　　　　　　　정답 (B)

**48.** 남자는 무엇을 요청하고 있는가?
(A) 수정된 일정
(B) 추가 표
(C) 빠른 배송

(D) 더 작은 크기의 제품      정답 (B)

**49.** 남자가 여자에게 다시 전화하기 전에 무엇을 할 것 같은가?
(A) 그의 표를 환불한다.
(B) 안내책자를 요청한다.
(C) 동료와 이야기한다.
(D) 소포를 배송한다.      정답 (C)

---

**문제 50-52번은 다음 대화를 참조하시오.** 미M 미W

M: Ms. Adams, my name is Ryan Kim and I'm calling from the Union City Parks Department. We're asking local residents their opinions about Dawson Park. I see you've lived near the park for over ten years. **(50) Would you mind telling me how you feel about the park and its facilities?**

W: Well, **(51) I really enjoy visiting the park as it's the only place in the city that has tennis courts.** It's my favorite sport, so I usually use the park's courts twice a week.

M: I'm glad to hear that. Now, is there anything about the park that you think can be improved?

W: **(52) Actually, I've noticed that the children's play area is in poor condition. I think you should make some changes to that area to make it safer and more attractive.**

---

M: Adams 씨, 제 이름은 Ryan Kim이고요, Union City 공원 관리국에서 연락 드립니다. 저희는 Dawson 공원에 관한 지역 주민들의 의견을 묻고 있습니다. 귀하는 10년 넘게 공원 근처에서 살아오셨다고 알고 있습니다. 공원과 부대시설에 대해 어떻게 생각하는지 말씀해주실 수 있겠습니까?

W: 글쎄요, 테니스 코트가 있는 이 도시의 유일한 장소이기 때문에 공원에 가는 것을 즐깁니다. 제가 가장 좋아하는 스포츠라서 일주일에 두 번 공원의 코트를 이용합니다.

M: 반가운 소식이네요. 그럼 공원에 개선될 부분이 있다고 생각하시나요?

W: 사실 아이들의 놀이 구역이 열악한 상태임을 알게 되었습니다. 그 구역을 좀 더 안전하고 멋진 장소로 바꿔졌으면 하고 생각해요.

**50.** 남자가 여자에게 전화한 이유는 무엇인가?
(A) 공원으로 가는 길 안내를 받기 위해서
(B) 정보를 수집하기 위해서
(C) 스포츠 행사를 계획하기 위해서
(D) 새로운 디자인을 제공하기 위해서      정답 (B)

**51.** 여자가 Dawson 공원에 대해 좋아하는 점은 무엇인가?
(A) 아름다운 풍경을 지니고 있다.
(B) 노년층을 위한 강좌들을 제공한다.
(C) 그녀가 그곳에서 스포츠를 즐길 수 있다.
(D) 시내 중심부에 교통 접근성이 용이한 곳에 위치하고 있다.      정답 (C)

**52.** 여자가 제안하는 것은 무엇인가?
(A) 스포츠 시설을 추가한다.
(B) 다른 곳에 주차한다.
(C) 내일 그녀의 사무실을 방문한다.
(D) 특정 구역을 개선한다.      정답 (D)

---

**문제 53-55번은 다음 대화를 참조하시오.** 호M 영W

M: Hello. I would like to know how long tuxedos can be rented out for. **(53) I have to attend a company banquet next week,**

and I need one for at least two days.

W: No problem, sir. **(54) All suits and tuxedos can be rented for five days before they have to be returned.**

M: Oh, really? **(55) I'm a little confused because I'm sure I was charged a late fee last year for returning a rented suit after four days.**

W: Ah, sir, **(55) we recently changed our policy for all rented formal wear.** Items can be kept for five days now. We changed it because many of our clients rent our clothing before going abroad on business trips.

---

M: 안녕하세요. 턱시도를 며칠 동안 대여할 수 있는지 알고 싶습니다. 다음 주에 회사 연회에 참석해야 해서 최소한 이틀은 필요한데요.

W: 괜찮습니다. 모든 정장과 턱시도는 반납 전까지 5일간 대여가 가능합니다.

M: 아, 정말입니까? 좀 헷갈리는군요. 작년에는 대여했던 정장을 4일 후에 반납해서 연체료를 지불한 것으로 기억하는데요.

W: 아, 고객님, 저희가 최근에 정장 대여에 대한 방침을 변경했습니다. 이제 옷을 5일간 갖고 계실 수 있습니다. 많은 고객분들이 해외 출장 전에 저희 의류를 대여하셔서 방침을 바꾸게 되었습니다.

**53.** 남자는 다음주에 무엇을 할 예정인가?
(A) 차를 빌린다.
(B) 의류 매장을 개업한다.
(C) 연체료를 납부한다.
(D) 회사 행사에 참석한다.      정답 (D)

**54.** 현재 대여 기간은 며칠인가?
(A) 2일
(B) 3일
(C) 4일
(D) 5일      정답 (D)

**55.** 남자가 대여 기간에 대해 혼동하는 이유는 무엇인가?
(A) 연체료가 지불되지 않았다.
(B) 상품을 이용할 수 없다.
(C) 회원권이 취소되었다.
(D) 방침이 변경되었다.      정답 (D)

---

**문제 56-58번은 다음의 3자 대화를 참조하시오.** 미W 호M 영W

W1: Nick, **(56) we will have a special feature on local hotels.** Are you interested in this assignment?

M: Sure, Juliet. **(56) I think I can write a very informative article for tourists who visit our town.**

W1: Thanks, Nick. **(57) I'm going to have an interview with some general managers tomorrow afternoon. Do you want to join me?**

M: **(57) That sounds good.** Jennifer, can you come along with us to the interview and take some photographs of the hotels?

W2: No problem! I'll get ready to take some pictures.

M: Okay, Jennifer. **(58) Let's get together around 1 o'clock to discuss the details of the photo shoot.**

---

W1: Nick, 지역 호텔들에 대한 특별 기사를 작성하려고 해요. 이 일에 관심이 있어요?

M: 물론이에요, Juliet. 우리 지역을 방문하는 관광객들에게 아주 유용한 기사를 쓸 수 있다고 생각해요.

W1: 고마워요, Nick. 내일 오후에 몇몇 호텔 지배인들과 인터뷰를 하려고

해요. 함께 가실래요?

M: 아주 좋아요. Jennifer, 우리와 함께 인터뷰에 가서 호텔 사진들을 찍어 주실래요?

W2: 물론이에요! 그럼 저는 사진을 찍을 준비를 해야겠네요.

M: 그래요, Jennifer. 그러면 우리 1시쯤 만나서 사진 촬영에 관한 세부사항을 논의하도록 해요.

**56.** 화자들은 어디에서 근무할 것 같은가?
(A) 호텔
(B) 여행사
(C) 잡지사
(D) 사진 스튜디오 　　　　　　　　　　　정답 (C)

**57.** 남자가 "That sounds good."이라고 말할 때 의미하는 바는 무엇인가?
(A) 그는 더 많은 선택사항을 듣길 원한다.
(B) 그는 음질이 뛰어나다고 생각한다.
(C) 그는 여자와 함께 일할 것이다.
(D) 그는 전문 사진사를 채용하길 원한다. 　　　정답 (C)

**58.** 화자들은 점심식사 후에 무엇을 하겠는가?
(A) 다른 영화를 본다.
(B) 일정을 확인한다.
(C) 인터뷰를 한다.
(D) 회의를 한다. 　　　　　　　　　　　　정답 (D)

**문제 59–61번은 다음 대화를 참조하시오.** 미M 영W

M: Celine, (59/60) **how's the prototype of the new digital music player progressing?** I saw that your work group has logged a lot of overtime this month.

W: It's going great. (60) **The player and the earbuds are now both waterproof. They can be used while swimming laps, rafting, canoeing, and playing any water sport.**

M: That's fantastic. I swim every day, and having music would be very helpful. Do you think it can be released anytime soon?

W: (61) **We'll run a test group with a few prototypes this month.** Then, we'll have to compile the results, make changes, and have the design team get started on the packaging. It probably won't be out before the new year.

------------------------------------------------

M: Celine, 새로운 디지털 음악 재생 장치의 시험 제작 원형 작업은 잘 진행되고 있나요? 제가 보니 당신의 작업팀이 이번달에 아주 많은 야근을 기록했더군요.

W: 아주 좋아요. 이제 재생 장치와 이어폰이 모두 방수가 되어서요. 수영할 때나, 래프팅을 할 때나, 카누를 탈 때와 같이 어떤 수상 스포츠를 하는 동안에도 사용이 가능하지요.

M: 그거 아주 환상적이네요. 저도 매일같이 수영을 하는데 음악을 들을 수 있다면 도움이 될 것 같아요. 제품이 곧 출시될 수 있을 것 같아요?

W: 이번달에 시험 제작한 몇 가지 원형들에 대해 테스트 집단에게 제품 여론 조사를 할 예정이에요. 그 후에 여론 조사 결과를 규합하여 수정을 하고, 디자인 팀에게 포장 작업을 시작하도록 할 겁니다. 새해가 되면 제품을 출시할 수 있을 것 같네요.

**59.** 여자는 누구일 것 같은가?
(A) 시장 분석가
(B) 회계 담당자
(C) 제품 개발자
(D) 인사부장 　　　　　　　　　　　　　정답 (C)

**60.** 화자들은 주로 무엇에 관해 논의하고 있는가?
(A) 수영복
(B) 스포츠 센터
(C) 마케팅 설문 조사
(D) 디지털 기기 　　　　　　　　　　　정답 (D)

**61.** Celine은 이번달에 어떤 일이 발생할 것이라고 언급하는가?
(A) 스포츠 종합시설이 보수될 것이다.
(B) 사람들이 신제품을 사용해볼 것이다.
(C) 새로운 앨범이 출시될 것이다.
(D) 다양한 포장 디자인들이 제공될 것이다. 　정답 (B)

**문제 62–64번은 다음 대화와 안내판을 참조하시오.** 호M 미W

M: Lena, (62) **there are not any spots near Warren Hall. I think we should park here on the street. It's free of charge, and there's no time limit.**

W: But I don't think street parking is available now. (63) **The signs say no parking is allowed here between 5 and 8 P.M.** I think we should look for a nearby public parking garage.

M: But we have about half an hour left until the musical begins. We must hurry. You know, we haven't even bought tickets yet.

W: Um... here's the deal. (64) **I'll purchase our tickets onsite.** You should go to the box office right after you park the car in a public parking garage. Then, we won't be late for the show.

------------------------------------------------

M: Lena, Warren Hall 주변에 빈 주차 공간이 전혀 없어요. 그래서 노상 주차를 해야 해요. 주차비도 없고 시간 제한도 없네요.

W: 하지만 지금 시간은 노상 주차가 허용되지 않는 시간일 텐데요. 주차 안내판을 보면 오후 5시에서 8시까지 주차가 불가하다고 적혀 있어요. 인근에 공영 주차장을 찾아봐야 할 것 같아요.

M: 하지만 뮤지컬 공연이 시작할 때까지 30분 정도밖에 안 남았어요. 서둘러야 해요. 알겠지만 우리는 표를 예매하지 않았어요.

W: 음… 그럼 이렇게 해요. 내가 매표소에 가서 표를 구매하고 있을게요. 당신은 공영 주차장에 주차하고 바로 매표소로 오세요. 그럼 뮤지컬 공연에 늦지 않을 거예요.

### 주차 금지

| | |
|---|---|
| **월요일** | 오전 5시 – 오전 9시 |
| **(63) 화요일** | **오후 5시 – 오후 8시** |
| **토요일** | 오전 8시 – 오후 4시 |
| **일요일** | 오전 8시 – 오후 1시 |
| HAYWARD 시 | |

**62.** 남자가 노상 주차를 원하는 이유는 무엇인가?
(A) 그는 주차 허가증이 없다.
(B) 자동차의 기름을 다 소모했다.
(C) 주차비를 절약할 수 있을 것이라고 생각한다.
(D) 주차장이 극장에서 멀리 떨어져 있다. 　　정답 (C)

**63.** 그래픽을 보시오. 오늘은 무슨 요일인가?
(A) 월요일
(B) 화요일
(C) 토요일
(D) 일요일 　　　　　　　　　　　　　　정답 (B)

**64.** 여자는 이후에 무엇을 할 것 같은가?
(A) 주차 관리자와 이야기한다.
(B) 표를 구매한다.
(C) 손님들에게 지연에 대해 알린다.
(D) 운전에서 갈 수 있는 길안내를 요청한다.　　　　정답 (B)

**문제 65–67번은 다음 대화와 목록을 참조하시오.** 미W 미M

W: Excuse me. (65) **I'm here to inquire about renting a studio apartment.** I saw your advertisement in the newspaper.
M: (66) **I'm afraid there aren't any more studio apartments.** Can I interest you in a two-bedroom apartment?
W: (67) **I don't know if I can fit that into my budget of $800 a month.**
M: I'm sure we can figure something out. Why don't you look for an apartment on Harbor Road?
W: No, (67) **I'm looking for an apartment on Sunhill Boulevard.** I want to live close to where I work, and that apartment is only a 5 minute-walk from my workplace.
M: I think you're in luck! There seems to be one according to my database.

------------------------------------------------------

W: 실례합니다. 저는 원룸 아파트를 임대하는 것에 관해 문의드리고자 왔어요. 신문에 나온 광고를 봤어요.
M: 죄송합니다만 원룸 아파트는 모두 임대가 되었어요. 방 두 개짜리 아파트는 관심이 없으신가요?
W: 월 800달러인 제 예산으로 방 두 개짜리 아파트를 구할 수 있을지 모르겠네요.
M: 찾을 수 있을 겁니다. Harbor Road에 있는 아파트를 찾아보시는 건 어때요?
W: 아뇨, 저는 Sunhill Boulevard에 있는 아파트를 찾고 있는 중이에요. 저는 직장하고 근접한 곳에서 살고 싶은데 그 쪽에 있는 아파트가 직장에서 도보로 5분 거리거든요.
M: 운이 좋으세요! 제 매물 자료를 살펴보니 한 곳이 있는 것 같아요.

### EAST BAY 부동산
(방 두 개짜리 아파트)

| 호수 | 주소 | (월) 임대료 |
|------|------|------------|
| 1A | 1123 Pine Street | $400 |
| 3B | 603 Rumi Avenue | $550 |
| (67) 4B | **909 Sunhill Boulevard** | **$700** |
| 8C | 911 Harbor Road | $900 |

**65.** 여자는 무엇을 하길 원하는가?
(A) 살 곳을 찾는다.
(B) 친구의 집을 방문한다.
(C) 일자리를 구한다.
(D) 아파트를 매입한다.　　　　정답 (A)

**66.** 남자에 따르면 무엇이 문제인가?
(A) 모든 객실이 이미 예약이 되어 있다.
(B) 모든 선택사항이 여자의 예산을 초과한다.
(C) 이 지역의 대중교통이 잘 갖춰지지 않았다.
(D) 여자가 선호하는 것을 이용할 수가 없다.　　　　정답 (D)

**67.** 그래픽을 보시오. 여자는 어느 아파트를 선택할 것 같은가?
(A) 1A
(B) 3B
(C) 4B
(D) 8C　　　　정답 (C)

**문제 68–70번은 다음 대화와 도표를 참조하시오.** 영W 미M

W: Mr. Parker, (68) **have you reviewed our luxury car sales figure for this year?**
M: Yes, I have. Hmm... (69) **the sales figures for our luxury cars were high for some time, but I don't understand why we suddenly experienced such a large drop.** That is quite a shock.
W: Um... we held several aggressive sales promotions tied to a huge tax break, and we haven't had any of them since our sales peaked. I think that's why.
M: I consider the three essential conditions for our future survival to be technology, productivity, and marketing. (70) **I think we should suggest additional special promotions to the new marketing director, Ms. Witherspoon,** before it's too late.

------------------------------------------------------

W: Parker 씨, 올해 우리 회사의 고급 차량 매출 자료를 검토해 보셨어요?
M: 네, 봤어요. 음… 고급 차량 매출이 한동안 호조였는데, 갑자기 엄청나게 폭락한 이유를 이해하지 못하겠어요. 제겐 충격적인 결과예요.
W: 음… 우리 회사가 엄청난 세제 혜택과 연계한 적극적인 판촉 행사를 여러 번 했는데 매출이 정점을 찍은 이후로는 지금까지 전혀 판촉 행사를 하고 있지 않아요. 그게 이유인 것 같아요.
M: 저는 우리 회사의 향후 생존이 기술력, 생산성 그리고 마케팅, 이 세 가지 요소에 있다고 생각해요. 너무 늦기 전에 새로 부임한 마케팅 담당 이사인 Witherspoon 씨에게 새로운 특별 판촉 행사를 제안해야 할 것 같아요.

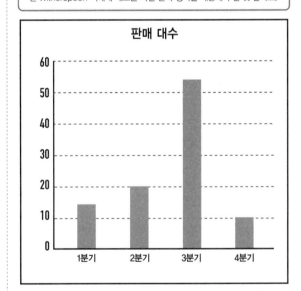

**판매 대수**

**68.** 화자들은 어디에서 근무할 것 같은가?
(A) 자동차 수리점
(B) 게임 제작업체
(C) 광고회사
(D) 자동차 제조업체　　　　정답 (D)

**69.** 그래픽을 보시오. 남자는 어떤 분기의 매출에 놀라고 있는가?

(A) 1분기

(B) 2분기

(C) 3분기

(D) 4분기 　　　　　　　　　　　정답 (D)

**70.** Witherspoon 씨는 누구일 것 같은가?

(A) 회계사

(B) 자동차 수리공

(C) 행사 기획자

(D) 마케팅 전문가 　　　　　　　　정답 (D)

## Part 4

문제 71-73번은 다음 전화 메시지를 참조하시오. 영W

Hello. This is Christine Stanwood. (71) **I'm calling because I ordered** *American Cuisine for Novices* **from your store two weeks ago but have not received it yet.** I am very disappointed because I was planning to use some recipes from the book for (72) **the party I had to host last Saturday**, but, obviously, I was not able to do so. When I processed the order on the Web site, it definitely stated that three business day delivery was guaranteed. (73) **Please give me a call at 692-4331 once you get this message to let me know how I can get my money back, including the shipping charge.**

안녕하세요. 저는 Christine Stanwood라고 합니다. 제가 2주 전에 귀사에 American Cuisine for Novices란 책을 주문했는데 아직도 받지 못해서 연락 드립니다. 제가 지난주 토요일에 열어야 했던 파티를 위해 그 책에서 다루는 일부 요리법을 사용하고자 할 계획이었는데, 그렇게 할 수 없었던 탓에 실망이 매우 큽니다. 제가 홈페이지를 통해 주문을 처리했을 때 분명히 3일 배송을 보장한다고 했습니다. 이 음성 메시지를 들으면 배송비를 포함한 책값을 환불받기 위해 어떻게 해야 하는지 692-4331로 연락해서 알려 주시길 바랍니다.

**71.** 이 메시지의 주제는 무엇인가?

(A) 파손된 제품

(B) 계약 갱신

(C) 늦은 배송

(D) 곧 있을 행사 　　　　　　　　정답 (C)

**72.** 화자는 지난주 토요일에 무엇을 했는가?

(A) 파티를 열었다.

(B) 몇몇 요리책을 읽었다.

(C) 환영 만찬에 참석했다.

(D) 한 과정에 등록했다. 　　　　　정답 (A)

**73.** 화자가 원하는 것은 무엇인가?

(A) 광고의 내용을 바로잡는다.

(B) 전액 환불을 받는다.

(C) 배송 일정을 정한다.

(D) 주문을 취소한다. 　　　　　　정답 (B)

문제 74-76번은 다음 광고를 참조하시오. 미W

Do you have a rollercoaster in your backyard? No? (74) **Then**

come to Forever Amusement Park in Victoria City this Saturday! We have the longest roller coaster in the world and provide visitors with a variety of exciting rides, such as the notorious pirate ship. (75) **Forever Amusement Park has been loved by many children and their parents for the last 30 years.** (76) **Forever Amusement Park has been recognized as a leading tourist destination and draws visitors from all over the country to our area.** We attracted almost 20 million visitors last year, making us one of the world's most popular amusement parks for 10 years in a row. One of the best ways to feel the spring spirit is to visit Forever Amusement Park.

혹시 뒷마당에 롤러코스터를 갖고 계신가요? 아니라고요? 그러면 이번 주 토요일에 Victoria City에 위치한 Forever 놀이공원으로 오세요! 저희는 전세계에서 가장 긴 롤러코스터를 보유하고 있으며 방문객들에게 그 악명높은 해적선과 같은 다양하고 신나는 놀이기구를 제공하고 있습니다. Forever 놀이공원은 지난 30년간 아이들과 부모님들의 많은 사랑을 받았습니다. Forever 놀이공원은 전국에서 방문객을 유치하는 지역 내 대표적인 관광 명소로 널리 알려져 있습니다. 작년 한 해에만 2천만 명에 육박하는 방문객들을 유치하여 10년 연속으로 세계적으로 가장 인기가 높은 놀이공원 중 한 곳이 되었습니다. 봄기운을 느끼기에 가장 좋은 방법은 바로 Forever 놀이공원을 방문하시는 겁니다.

**74.** 광고되는 업체는 무엇인가?

(A) 여행사

(B) 시립 동물원

(C) 여객선

(D) 놀이공원 　　　　　　　　　　정답 (D)

**75.** 이 업체는 얼마동안 영업을 해오고 있는가?

(A) 10년

(B) 20년

(C) 30년

(D) 40년 　　　　　　　　　　　　정답 (C)

**76.** 화자에 따르면 이 업체는 무엇으로 가장 유명한가?

(A) 가장 신나는 놀이기구 설계

(B) 지역 자선단체 기부

(C) 환경 보호

(D) 이 지역으로의 방문객 유치 　　정답 (D)

문제 77-79번은 다음 소개문을 참조하시오. 미M

Good morning, ladies and gentlemen! Today, (77) **it is a great honor and privilege to present this year's employee of the year award to Stephanie Campbell, the head researcher of vaccine development.** In addition to supervising 30 employees, Ms. Campbell has developed several vaccines to prevent deadly viruses and infections during the last ten years. (78) **Her vaccines have made the world a much safer place to live in.** (79) **I know her achievements are very important to the company.** However, it is her humanitarian spirit what sets her apart as the greatest researcher of the decade. Well, Ms. Campbell, I'd like to present you with this award. Congratulations!

좋은 아침입니다. 신사 숙녀 여러분! 오늘 백신 개발부서의 수석 연구원인 Stephanie Campbell 씨에게 올해의 우수 직원 상을 수여하게 되어 대단한 영광이자 특권이라고 생각합니다. 30명의 연구원들을 지휘하면서 Campbell 씨는 지난 10년간 치명적인 바이러스들과 감염을 예방하는 여러 개의 백신을 개발했습니다. 그녀의 백신은 세계를 좀 더 살기 안전한 곳으로 만드는 데 기여했습니다. 그녀의 업적이 우리 회사에도 굉장히 중요하다는 것을 잘 알고 있습니다. 그렇지만 그녀를 이 시대의 가장 위대한 연구자로서 격상시키는 것은 바로 그녀가 지닌 인도주의 정신에 기인합니다. 자, Campbell 씨, 이 상을 당신에게 수여합니다. 축하드립니다!

**77.** 누가 소개되고 있는가?
(A) 기조 연설자
(B) 회사 연구원
(C) 약사
(D) 시상 위원회 위원장　　　　　　　　　정답 (B)

**78.** Campbell 씨에 의해 개발된 백신에 대해 언급된 내용은 무엇인가?
(A) 가격이 저렴하다.
(B) 전세계적으로 사용되고 있다.
(C) 다음달에 출시될 예정이다.
(D) 임상 실험을 통과했다.　　　　　　　　정답 (B)

**79.** 화자가 "I know her achievements are very important to the company."라고 언급한 이유는 무엇인가?
(A) 그녀의 업적을 칭찬하기 위해서
(B) 청자들에게 인내를 종용하기 위해서
(C) 그녀의 인성을 크게 강조하기 위해서
(D) 회사의 경영 방침에 대한 불만을 제기하기 위해서　정답 (C)

**문제 80-82번은 다음 회의 내용을 참조하시오.** 호M

Okay, now let's talk about the next item. (80/81) I heard we received many customer complaints regarding our new smartphone, the IK-1123. Um... it's kind of shocking news to us, huh? (80) It was designed with all the latest technology and was supposed to be our leading mobile product. The head of Customer Service told me the majority of our customers are dissatisfied with the battery for the IK-1123, which has resulted in many angry complaints. (82) Many reported that the battery usually gets overheated and stops working after they use their phones for several hours. So here's the plan. Mr. Preston, I think it would be good if you and your staff came up with some solutions for the problem regarding the battery.

----------------------------------------

좋아요, 그러면 다음 논의 사항에 대해 이야기를 합시다. 우리가 새로 출시한 스마트폰 IK-1123에 관한 고객들의 많은 불만사항을 접하고 있다고 들었습니다. 음… 이건 좀 우리에게 충격적인 소식이네요, 그렇지요? 이 휴대폰은 모든 최첨단 기술을 동원하여 설계된 제품이고 우리 회사의 주력 이동통신 제품으로 제작한 것입니다. 고객 관리 부장이 제게 우리 고객의 대부분이 IK-1123의 배터리에 대해 만족하지 못하고 있으며, 이것이 많은 격한 불만사항들을 초래하고 있다고 이야기를 했습니다. 많은 고객들이 전화기를 몇 시간 사용한 후에는 과열되면서 작동하지 않는다고 신고를 합니다. 그러면 이렇게 합시다. Preston 씨, 당신과 직원들이 배터리 문제에 대한 해결책을 찾아내는 것이 좋을 것 같습니다.

**80.** 화자는 어디에서 근무할 것 같은가?
(A) 무선 통신업체
(B) 백화점

(C) 전자회사
(D) 시장 조사 기관　　　　　　　　　　　정답 (C)

**81.** 화자가 언급하고 있는 문제점은 무엇인가?
(A) 재고 상품 부족
(B) 고객의 높은 불만족도
(C) 가격의 갑작스러운 인상
(D) 점차 하락하는 시장 점유율　　　　　　정답 (B)

**82.** 남자가 "So here's the plan."이라고 말할 때 의미하는 바는 무엇인가?
(A) 그는 다른 의견을 듣고자 한다.
(B) 그는 회의 날짜를 변경하고자 한다.
(C) 그는 지시사항을 전달하고자 한다.
(D) 그는 다른 배터리를 개발하고자 한다.　정답 (C)

**문제 83-85번은 다음 회의 내용을 참조하시오.** 영W

(83) Thank you, everyone, for your hard work here in the studio. Now, I'd like to tell you about a new service we're going to launch in a few weeks. (83) We will install about half a dozen cameras inside the studio and provide our customers with affordable customized photographs. (84) That means that customers can create unique and personalized photo gifts such as custom photo mugs, clothing, bags, stickers, postage stamps, and calendars from their favorite photographs taken here. I think personalized photo gifts are a truly unique way to celebrate special occasions. I've just ordered the cameras, and (85) tomorrow, I'm going to interview some technicians who will work for us part time managing the equipment and running the service for us.

----------------------------------------

이 곳 스튜디오에서 열심히 일해주시는 여러분께 감사드립니다. 이제 여러분께 몇 주 후에 선보이게 될 새로운 서비스에 대해 말씀드리고자 합니다. 우리는 스튜디오 내부에 6대의 카메라를 설치하여 고객들에게 적절한 가격의 고객맞춤형 사진 서비스를 제공하고자 합니다. 다시 말해서 이 곳에서 촬영된 사진 중 고객 자신이 가장 좋아하는 사진을 이용하여 사진 머그잔, 옷, 가방, 스티커, 우표, 그리고 달력 같은 독특하고도 자신만이 지닐 수 있는 사진 제품을 만들 수 있다는 것입니다. 저는 이러한 고객 맞춤형 사진 제품들이 특별한 날을 축하할 수 있는 가장 독특한 방법이라고 생각합니다. 카메라는 제가 막 주문했고 내일은 우리를 위해 장비를 다루고 서비스를 운영하는 데 도움을 줄 수 있는 시간제 기술자의 채용을 위한 면접을 시행할 예정입니다.

**83.** 화자는 어떤 업종에 종사하는가?
(A) 카메라 판매점
(B) 사진 스튜디오
(C) 인쇄소
(D) 백화점　　　　　　　　　　　　　　　정답 (B)

**84.** 새로운 서비스를 시행하는 이유는 무엇인가?
(A) 비용을 절감하기 위해서
(B) 새로운 고객을 유치하기 위해서
(C) 특색이 있는 상품을 제공하기 위해서
(D) 언론으로부터 주목을 받기 위해서　　　정답 (C)

**85.** 화자는 내일 무엇을 할 것이라고 언급하는가?
(A) 친척을 방문한다.
(B) 지원자들을 평가한다.

(C) 인터뷰 일정을 잡는다.
(D) 사진 장비를 구매한다.　　　　　　　　정답 (B)

**문제 86-88번은 다음 전화 메시지를 참조하시오.** Ⓜ️Ⓦ

Hi. I'm Vanessa Jenkins. **(86/87) I'm calling about getting some help planning my overseas trip for this fall vacation.** Um... I don't know if you still remember my colleague, Betty. **(87) She returned from her summer vacation last year and highly recommended your travel service.** Yesterday, I went online, and I did some research about European railways. **(88) I found an unlimited Eurail pass being offered for September for 1,020€. I know the fare is high due to it being the peak travel season. But I heard I can see beautiful scenes in Europe during that time of the year.** So I thought I'd consult with you before preparing for my trip. Please call me back at 445-6928 at your earliest convenience.

------------------------------------------------

안녕하세요. 저는 Vanessa Jenkins라고 해요. 올 가을 휴가에 해외 여행을 가려고 계획 중인데 이에 대한 도움을 받고자 연락을 드렸어요. 음… 제 직장 동료인 Betty를 아직도 기억하고 계실지 모르겠어요. 그녀가 작년 여름휴가에서 복귀하고 나서 귀하의 여행사 서비스를 적극 추천하더군요. 어제 인터넷에서 유럽 철도에 대해 조사를 좀 해봤는데요. 9월에 무제한으로 사용할 수 있는 유레일 패스를 1,020유로에 판매한다는 사실을 알았어요. 저도 그 시기가 여행 성수기라서 요금이 비싸다는 건 알고 있어요. 하지만 그 시기에 유럽 전역에서 아름다운 풍경들을 볼 수 있다는 말을 들었거든요. 그래서 제가 여행을 준비하기에 앞서 상담을 해 봐야겠다고 생각했어요. 가능한 빨리 445-6928로 연락 주세요.

**86.** 화자는 무엇을 계획하고 있는가?
(A) 회사의 시상식 만찬
(B) 이직
(C) 휴가 여행
(D) 사무실 방문　　　　　　　　정답 (C)

**87.** 청자는 누구일 것 같은가?
(A) 호텔 접수처 직원
(B) 여행사 직원
(C) 열차 기관사
(D) 회의 주최자　　　　　　　　정답 (B)

**88.** 화자가 "But I heard I can see beautiful scenes in Europe during that time of the year."라고 말할 때 의미하는 바는 무엇인가?
(A) 그녀는 휴가 여행을 취소한 것을 후회한다.
(B) 그녀는 청자와 함께 여행을 가길 원한다.
(C) 그녀는 청자의 의견에 동의하지 않는다.
(D) 그녀는 요금이 구매에 소요된 비용만큼의 가치가 있을 거라고 생각한다.
　　　　　　　　정답 (D)

**문제 89-91번은 다음 안내문을 참조하시오.** Ⓜ️Ⓜ️

**(89) Attention. The Long Beach Public Library will be closing in thirty minutes.** A closing announcement is made 30 minutes and then 15 minutes before the library building closes. The library cafeteria and the bookstore will remain open for another hour. But please be aware that the photocopiers will be turned off at this time. If you checked your coat or bags when entering the library, please don't forget to retrieve them before you leave. **(89) Library patrons are asked to cooperate with the Long Beach Public Library** and the security staff in clearing the building promptly at closing time. In addition, **(91) our 34th annual book exhibit will be opening next week. (90) There are official exhibit brochures at the main entrance that can be picked up when you leave the library.** Thank you.

------------------------------------------------

주목해 주십시오. Long Beach 공공 도서관은 30분 후에 폐장합니다. 폐장 안내 방송은 도서관이 문을 닫기 전 30분 전과 15분 전에 한 번씩 나갑니다. 도서관 구내식당과 서점은 지금부터 한 시간 동안은 정상적으로 영업을 할 것입니다. 하지만 복사기는 지금 시점을 기준으로 중지된다는 점에 유의해 주십시오. 만약 도서관에 들어올 때 코트나 가방을 맡기셨다면, 잊지 말고 도서관을 나갈 때 되찾아 가십시오. 도서관을 이용하시는 분들은 폐장 시간에 맞춰 도서관 건물 밖으로 신속하게 빠져나갈 수 있도록 저희 Long Beach 공공 도서관과 경비원들에게 협조해 주시길 당부 드립니다. 그리고 다음주에는 저희 도서관의 34주년 연례 도서 전시회가 열립니다. 정문에 공식 도서 전시회 안내책자가 있사오니 나가면서 가지고 가시면 되겠습니다. 감사합니다.

**89.** 이 안내는 누구를 대상으로 하는가?
(A) 도서관 이용객
(B) 비행기 탑승객
(C) 백화점 고객
(D) 회의 참석자　　　　　　　　정답 (A)

**90.** 청자들에게 요청되는 것은 무엇인가?
(A) 신분증을 제시한다.
(B) 셔틀버스에 탑승한다.
(C) 등록처로 간다.
(D) 안내책자를 가져간다.　　　　　　　　정답 (D)

**91.** 화자에 따르면 다음주에는 어떤 일이 일어나는가?
(A) 정상 영업시간이 변경된다.
(B) 전시회가 개최된다.
(C) 또 다른 워크숍이 개최된다.
(D) 새로운 도서관이 개장한다.　　　　　　　　정답 (B)

**문제 92-94번은 다음 뉴스를 참조하시오.** Ⓔ️Ⓦ

In other news, **(92) Dicken's Food World has said that it is considering opening a manufacturing plant just east of Manchester.** The company chose Manchester for the move because of the low tax rates and the available labor force. While the local government is largely hailing the development, **(93) residents of eastern Manchester are concerned about air pollution in their neighborhoods.** A spokeswoman for Dicken's said that its plants are very clean, and that residents in the areas surrounding their other two plants have a good relationship with the company. **(94) City council member Jessica Jones asked local residents to look for the industry's annual report next month.** Dicken's usually scores well on community relations and the environment.

------------------------------------------------

다른 소식으로는, Dicken's Food World는 Manchester 동부에 제조 공장을 여는 것을 고려 중이라고 밝혔습니다. 이 회사는 낮은 세율과 채용 가능 인력으로 인해 새로운 공장을 Manchester에 유치하기로 했습니다. 주 정부는 이러한 국면을 크게 반기고 있으나 Manchester 동부 지역의 주민

들은 지역의 대기오염에 대해 우려하고 있습니다. Dicken's 사의 대변인은 자사의 공장들은 깨끗하며, 다른 두 개 공장 주변의 주민들도 회사와 좋은 관계를 유지하고 있다는 점을 언급했습니다. 시 의원 Jessica Jones 씨는 주민들에게 다음달에 나올 연례 업계 동향 보고서에 주목해 달라고 요청했습니다. Dicken's 사는 대부분 지역사회 관계와 환경 부문에서 좋은 평가를 받고 있습니다.

**92.** 뉴스 보도는 주로 무엇에 관해 다루고 있는가?
(A) 공장의 개장
(B) 다가올 선거
(C) 심각한 대기오염 문제
(D) 세율의 인하 　　　　　　　　　　　정답 (A)

**93.** 화자에 따르면 지역 주민들은 무엇을 우려하고 있는가?
(A) 시 예산 부족
(B) 공기 질 하락
(C) 학교 폐쇄
(D) 교통정체의 영향 　　　　　　　　　정답 (B)

**94.** 주민들에게 요청되는 것은 무엇인가?
(A) 설문지를 작성한다.
(B) 연간 보고서를 참조한다.
(C) 직업 훈련 과정에 참여한다.
(D) 대중교통을 이용한다. 　　　　　　　정답 (B)

---

문제 95-97번은 다음 전화 메시지와 안내를 참조하시오. [미W]

Good morning, Ms. Moore. My name is Elizabeth Shaw. (95) **I'm calling about the international sales manager position you applied for last week.** After we reviewed your résumé and letters of recommendation, we concluded that you are highly suitable for the job. (95) **The board of directors would like you to come in for a formal interview at 10 A.M. tomorrow.** Our company building is located at 603 11th Avenue. (96) **We are currently undertaking regular maintenance on all of our elevators in order to keep them in good shape and to prevent accidents. So you should take the stairs at the back of the building instead of using the elevators.** (97) **Please come to the Personnel Department.** If you need any help, please do not hesitate to call me from the lobby. I'll see you tomorrow, Ms. Moore.

- - - - - - - - - - - - - - - - - - - - - - - - - - - -

안녕하세요, Moore 씨. 저는 Elizabeth Shaw라고 합니다. 귀하가 지난주에 지원하신 해외 영업부장 직과 관련하여 연락을 드립니다. 저희는 귀하의 이력서와 추천서를 검토한 후 귀하가 영업부장 직에 매우 적합하다는 결론을 내렸습니다. 이사회에서 내일 오전 10시에 정식으로 면접을 보러 방문해 주시길 원하고 있습니다. 우리 사옥은 11번가 603번지에 위치하고 있습니다. 현재 모든 승강기의 적절한 상태를 유지하고 사고를 미연에 방지하고자 정기 점검을 시행 중에 있습니다. 그래서 승강기를 사용하는 대신에 건물 뒤편에 위치한 계단을 이용하셔야 합니다. 인사부로 오시면 됩니다. 혹시 도움이 필요하시면 주저하지 말고 로비에서 제게 연락을 주세요. 내일 뵙겠습니다. Moore 씨.

---

## Sedell International 사무 빌딩

| | 안내 |
|---|---|
| 1F | 로비 / 구내식당 / 은행 / 안내처 |
| 2F | 우편실 / 홍보부 / 회계부 / 재무부 |
| (97) 3F | 영업부(국내) / 영업부(해외) / **인사부** |
| 4F | 마케팅부 / 제품 개발부 / 연구 개발부 / 회의실 / 강당 |

**95.** 화자는 무엇에 관해 연락을 하는가?
(A) 가구 배송
(B) 면접 약속
(C) 승강기 수리 요청
(D) 정기 검진 　　　　　　　　　　　정답 (B)

**96.** 화자가 청자에게 요청하는 것은 무엇인가?
(A) 제품 목록을 보는 것
(B) 면접 일정을 잡는 것
(C) 수리 작업을 완료하는 것
(D) 계단을 이용하는 것 　　　　　　　정답 (D)

**97.** 그래픽을 보시오. 화자는 Moore 씨와 몇 층에서 만날 것 같은가?
(A) 1층
(B) 2층
(C) 3층
(D) 4층 　　　　　　　　　　　　　　정답 (C)

---

문제 98-100번은 다음 안내문과 도표를 참조하시오. [호M]

Good morning. It's great to see you all. (98) **I personally want to thank you ladies and gentlemen for participating in the survey for assembly line workers.** Everyone in the room responded in a timely fashion, and that is a testament to your dedication to our company. You are what makes our company one of the best in the business. At Turbo Machine Works, we're committed to employee satisfaction. We received a lot of suggestions on improving the factory's cafeteria, so let's take a look at those results now. Um... we'd all like a larger luncheon area, but we just can't afford an expansion right now. (99) **We can, however, address the second-most-popular suggestion. So we'll start working on that immediately.** And (100) **as a token of our thanks, everyone who filled out a survey form will receive a voucher for a free lunch.**

- - - - - - - - - - - - - - - - - - - - - - - - - - - -

안녕하십니까? 여러분 모두를 만나 뵙게 되어 반갑습니다. 개인적으로 생산조립 라인에서 근무하는 직원들을 위한 설문조사에 참여해주신 신사 숙녀 여러분께 감사를 드리고 싶습니다. 방에 있는 모든 분들이 시의 적절하게 답변을 해 주셨는데, 이는 우리 회사에 대한 헌신의 증거라고 생각합니다. 여러분이 바로 우리 회사를 업계 최고의 회사로 만들고 있습니다. Turbo Machine Works는 직원 만족을 위해 최선을 다하고 있습니다. 공장 내 구내식당을 개선해 달라는 제안을 많이 받았는데, 이제 그 설문조사 결과를 보도록 하겠습니다. 음… 우리 모두 점심식사를 위한 넓은 공간을 원하겠지만 지금은 이를 확장할 여력이 없습니다. 하지만 두 번째로 인기가 많은 제안은 시행할 수 있습니다. 그래서 즉시 이를 위한 작업을 시작할 것입니다. 그리고 감사의 표시로써 설문조사지를 작성한 분들은 무료 점심식사를 위한 교환권을 받으시게 될 것입니다.

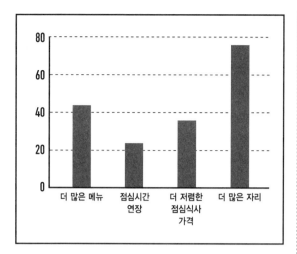

**98.** 공지는 어디에서 이루어지겠는가?
(A) 구내식당
(B) 백화점
(C) 제조 공장
(D) 요리 학교 정답 (C)

**99.** 그래픽을 보시오. 회사는 어떤 제안에 대해 조치할 것인가?
(A) 더 많은 메뉴
(B) 점심시간 연장
(C) 더 저렴한 점심식사 가격
(D) 더 많은 자리 정답 (A)

**100.** 화자에 따르면 설문지를 작성한 답변자들은 무엇을 받게 되는가?
(A) 할인 쿠폰
(B) 무료 티셔츠
(C) 무료 점심식사
(D) 상품권 정답 (C)

## Part 5

**101.** Kamon Machines 사가 구형 팩스기 모델들을 위한 교체 부품의 생산을 중단했기 때문에 우리는 그 부품들을 더 이상 구매할 수가 없다. 정답 (B)

**102.** Jones 씨는 대부분의 이전 고용주들로부터 강력한 추천을 받았다. 정답 (D)

**103.** 시 축제 참석률은 퍼레이드의 촉박한 사전 공지로 매우 낮아졌다. 정답 (B)

**104.** Tang Toys 사는 일본과 미국에서의 지속적인 매출의 확장으로 인해 2분기의 수익이 증가했다. 정답 (B)

**105.** 배송 관리자는 어제 있었던 기록적인 폭설로 인해 배송 날짜를 맞출 수 있을지 우려하고 있다. 정답 (C)

**106.** Komi Motors 사는 동유럽에 있는 제조 공장을 폐쇄함으로써 전세계적인 경제 위기를 극복했다. 정답 (B)

**107.** New York의 Fashion Academy라는 이름의 디자인 학교는 경쟁이 치열한 패션업계에 창의적이고 전문적인 디자이너들을 배출했다. 정답 (C)

**108.** 비록 눈이 많이 내리고 있었지만 많은 사람들이 도심에서의 교통 체증을 피하고자 걸어서 출근하기로 결정했다. 정답 (D)

**109.** 연간 영업 보고서에 따르면 Genelec Factory 사의 수익은 혹독한 구조조정 이후에 상당한 향상을 보였다. 정답 (B)

**110.** 20세기 초에는 부족한 교통시설 기반으로 인해 50마일 정도의 거리를 이동하는 것만으로도 매우 설레는 경험이었다. 정답 (B)

**111.** 흡연은 석유창고 내부에서 허용되지 않을 뿐만 아니라 석유화학 공장 부근에서도 허용되지 않는다. 정답 (C)

**112.** 소방훈련 중에 모든 거주민들은 예외 없이 빌딩에서 대피하라고 지시 받는다. 정답 (C)

**113.** 전략적으로 상업 지구에 위치한 관계로 그 면세점들은 해외 관광객이 이용할 수 있게 될 것이다. 정답 (D)

**114.** Jason 중공업은 회계 부장 직책에 지원하는 많은 지원서들을 받았지만 자격요건을 갖춘 사람은 거의 없다. 정답 (C)

**115.** 카지노, 환상적인 공연, 쇼핑몰, 놀라운 관광 명소에서부터 훌륭한 식사에 이르기까지 Las Vegas는 가족과 연인들 모두를 위한 세계적인 휴양지로 남아 있다. 정답 (A)

**116.** 해외 은행의 업무 처리 시간은 해당 지역 은행 시스템에 따라 달라짐을 주지하시기 바랍니다. 정답 (B)

**117.** 그 오래된 산업 단지와 이를 둘러싸고 있는 시설물은 새로운 아파트 단지로 재개발되었다. 정답 (D)

**118.** Watson 씨의 시장 분석 조사의 결과물을 필히 마케팅 발표의 마지막 슬라이드에 싣도록 하십시오. 정답 (B)

**119.** 새로운 설문조사 결과에 따르면 대부분의 사람들은 보통 예술이 선천적으로 대단한 재능을 지니거나 전문적으로 교육 받은 사람들이 하는 것이라고 생각한다. 정답 (D)

**120.** 업무 현장 내 사고 예방에 도움이 되고자 모든 직원들은 직장 내 무료 건강 및 안전 연수에 해마다 참가하는 것이 의무이다. 정답 (B)

**121.** 정기 마케팅 회의에서 Thompson 씨는 회사의 시장 점유율을 확장하는 데 도움이 되는 혁신적인 마케팅 전략을 자주 제시하곤 한다. 정답 (A)

**122.** Parker 씨는 지난주에 퇴사했기 때문에 Palo Alto에 있는 대학에서 경영학 강좌를 수강할 수 있는 시간을 가질 수 있다. 정답 (A)

**123.** 우리 직원들이 성공적으로 이달의 연수를 완료하면 그들은 회계 업무를 능숙하게 처리하게 될 것이다. 정답 (C)

**124.** 우리의 설문조사에서는 대부분의 소비자가 민트 맛의 초콜릿 칩을 매우 맛있게 여긴다는 점을 알려줬다. 정답 (B)

**125.** 새롭게 개정된 규정에 따르면 모든 회원 국가들은 필히 그들의 무역 방침과 관행에 대한 정기적인 감사를 받아야만 한다. 정답 (A)

**126.** 보험 회사는 그 사무실 건물의 화재 피해를 최대한 정확하게 평가하고자 했다. 정답 (C)

**127.** 만약 저희가 21일 내에 귀하의 가방을 찾지 못한다면, 분실된 것으로 여겨 귀하의 수하물 운송에 청구된 모든 비용을 환급해 드리도록 하겠습니다. 정답 (B)

**128.** 전국에 걸쳐 주택 시장의 매매 감소를 초래하는 일부 이유들은 명확하게 밝혀지지 않는다. 　　　　　　　　　정답 (A)

**129.** 신청자에게 사업 대출이 제공되는지 여부와 상관없이 모든 신청서는 1년간 필히 보관되어야 한다. 　　　　　　　정답 (D)

**130.** 만약 회사측이 우리의 요구에 대해 합리적인 방식으로 대응해 준다면 노조는 임금 협상을 재개할 것이다. 　　　정답 (B)

## Part 6

문제 131-134번은 다음 회람을 참조하시오.

---
회람

수신: 전 직원
발신: 홍보부장 Eric Haller
날짜: 6월 25일
제목: Warren Hall 투어

New York의 유명한 무용 연출감독인 John Baker 씨가 우리를 위해 새로운 시립 공연장인 Warren Hall에 대한 견학의 가이드를 해주시기로 했습니다.

이 가이드 투어는 다음주 토요일 Warren Hall에서 공연할 최신 뮤지컬인 Jungle Fever의 1차 리허설을 관람하는 것을 포함합니다. 이는 3000명 규모의 최신 시설인 Warren Hall을 볼 수 있는 좋은 기회가 될 것임이 분명합니다. 모든 직원들이 참여할 것을 권장합니다.

비록 비용은 무료지만, 모든 직원은 가기 전에 투어 좌석을 필히 예약해야 합니다. 투어 표가 한정되어 있고 마지막 등록일자는 6월 30일임을 알아두시기 바랍니다. 이 놀라운 투어를 등록하는 기회를 놓치지 마시기 바랍니다.

이 투어에 관해 더 많은 정보가 필요하면 홈페이지 www.warrenhall.com 을 방문하시기 바랍니다.
---

**131.** 　　　　　　　　　　　　정답 (B)

**132.** (A) 모든 직원들이 참여할 것을 권장합니다.
　　　(B) 약간의 비용이 기부 목적으로 지출되었습니다.
　　　(C) 많은 비평가들이 아름다운 무대와 의상에 대해 호평하였습니다.
　　　(D) 올해의 많은 영화들이 새로 건설된 이 극장에서 상영될 것입니다.
　　　　　　　　　　　　　　정답 (A)

**133.** 　　　　　　　　　　　　정답 (D)

**134.** 　　　　　　　　　　　　정답 (D)

문제 135-138번은 다음 편지를 참조하시오.

---
Taylor & Murphy 회계법인
110 Pine Street, San Francisco, CA 94137

관계자 분께,

Taylor & Murphy 회계법인은 당사가 필요로 하는 정보통신 기술의 운영 입찰에 대한 참여를 권고하고자 합니다. 1월부터 당사는 모든 컴퓨터 보수 관리와 데이터 관리 운영에 대한 모든 것을 외주업체에 위탁할 것입니다. 데이터 시스템 운영 정책과 기술 표준에 관한 당사의 세부적인 요구사항에 대해서는 아래의 기술 정보를 참조해 주십시오.

당사는 현재 업무의 지속성을 위해 향후 외주업체로 선정되는 회사에서 파
---

견된 직원들이 업무를 처리하길 바라고 있습니다. 그러나 당사도 그러한 상황이 언제나 가능하지 않다는 점은 이해하고 있습니다.

구리 통신망을 광대역 전송 기술을 통한 광섬유를 이용하는 통신망으로 향상시키기 위해 초기에 추가 작업이 필요할 것으로 예상하고 있습니다. 아울러 당사는 그 작업이 입찰 내용에 포함되길 원합니다. 모든 제안서와 입찰 서류는 8월 31일까지 당사 본사에 도착해야 합니다.

감사합니다.

Sally Murphy
부사장
Talyor & Murphy 회계법인

**135.** 　　　　　　　　　　　　정답 (D)

**136.** 　　　　　　　　　　　　정답 (D)

**137.** 　　　　　　　　　　　　정답 (B)

**138.** (A) 모든 제안서와 입찰 서류는 8월 31일까지 당사 본사에 도착해야 합니다.
　　　(B) 당사는 많은 입찰자들이 계약을 성사시키기 위해 서로 경쟁을 할 것으로 예상하고 있습니다.
　　　(C) 귀하는 서류 작업과 정확한 서류의 중요성에 대해 인지하셔야 합니다.
　　　(D) 당사의 노련한 직원과 기술적 인프라가 귀사의 효율성을 개선할 것입니다. 　　　　　　　　　　정답 (A)

문제 139-142번은 다음 공지를 참조하시오.

---
보수공사

Regency 아파트 단지

관리사무소는 10월부터 아파트 내부 보수공사를 준비하고 있습니다.

아파트 도처에 있는 몇몇 빈 가구들을 보수하고 난 후, 주요 보수공사가 10층부터 시작될 예정이며, 한 번에 4-6가구들이 포함될 것입니다. 보수공사가 시행되는 각 가구들은 공사가 마무리될 때까지 최소한 2주에서 3주가 소요될 것입니다.

보수공사가 시행되는 가구의 주민들은 보수공사가 시작되기 전에 지금 거주하고 계신 곳을 비워주셔야 합니다. 보수공사가 완료되고 나면 재입주를 하실 수 있습니다.

이번 보수공사를 통해 주민들의 생활이 향상되길 희망하고 있습니다. 질문이 있으면 관리사무소로 문의해 주시기 바랍니다.

여러분의 친절한 이해와 전적인 협조에 미리 감사드립니다.

Regency 아파트 단지
관리사무소
---

**139.** 　　　　　　　　　　　　정답 (D)

**140.** 　　　　　　　　　　　　정답 (C)

**141.** 　　　　　　　　　　　　정답 (C)

**142.** (A) 각 가구마다 주민들에게 이 정책을 알리는 공지가 게시될 것입니다.
　　　(B) 관리사무소는 이번주에 일시적으로 폐쇄합니다.
　　　(C) 보수공사 기간 동안 아파트 단지의 외관에 양해를 구합니다.
　　　(D) 이번 보수공사를 통해 주민들의 생활이 향상되길 희망하고 있습니다. 　　　　　　　　　　정답 (D)

3월 10일

Allie Goodroad 씨
1123 5th Avenue
Houston, TX 79038

Goodroad 씨께,

4월 1일부터 KABI 재활용 프로그램이 귀하가 거주하는 지역에서 시작될 것임을 알려 드리게 되어 기쁘게 생각합니다. 이 프로그램에 참여하고자 하는 주민들은 바퀴가 달린 녹색 용기를 지급받으실 것입니다. 이 용기를 요청하려면 1-800-575-4331로 전화해 주십시오.

도로가에 내놓는 물품의 재활용은 본래 제안대로 일주일에 한 번이 아니라 한 달에 두 번 이루어질 것입니다. 그 결과 인근 지역으로의 이동 횟수가 줄어들어 연료비와 배기가스 배출량이 감소하게 될 것입니다.

재활용 물품의 목록은 동봉된 소책자에서 찾아 보실 수 있습니다. 도시 전역의 재활용 프로그램의 일정에 관련된 더 많은 정보를 원하시면 www.kabirecycling.org를 방문해 주십시오. 여러분이 이 중요한 프로그램에 참여하시길 바랍니다.

Brandon Lee
KABI 재활용 프로그램 담당자

**143.** 정답 (A)

**144.** 정답 (D)

**145.** 정답 (C)

**146.** (A) 여러분이 이 중요한 프로그램에 참여하시길 바랍니다.
(B) 귀하의 용기는 집으로 7일 내에 도착할 것입니다.
(B) 파손된 유리를 용기에 넣지 말아 주시길 당부드립니다.
(D) 시는 이 프로젝트에 아주 큰 돈을 투자했습니다. 정답 (A)

### Part 7

문제 147-148번은 다음 영수증을 참조하시오.

현금 지급 수당 영수증

날짜 11월 23일
성명 (활자체로 기재) HANK SHREDDER

| 상세 정보 | 금액 |
|---|---|
| 제가 (147) **11월 25일부터 26일까지 New York, Manhattan에서 참석할 예정인 회계 컨퍼런스**와 관련된 모든 출장 및 식사 지출 비용을 지불하기 위함. | $1,974 |

(148) **상기 금액의 수령을 확인합니다.**
서명 Hank Shredder

**147.** Shredder 씨는 11월에 뉴욕에서 무엇을 할 것인가?
(A) 새로운 계약을 맺는다.
(B) 휴가를 떠난다.
(C) 몇몇 회계사를 고용한다.
(D) 행사에 참가한다. 정답 (D)

**148.** Shredder 씨는 무엇을 확인해 주고 있는가?
(A) 회계 소프트웨어를 구입한 것

(B) 원본 영수증을 제출한 것
(C) 호텔 비용을 지불한 것
(D) 비용을 수령한 것 정답 (D)

문제 149-150번은 다음 송장을 참조하시오.

New Line Office Supply Warehouse
25200 Carlos Bee Blvd, Hayward, CA 94542, 510-212-6313

배송 송장

날짜: 1월 10일
송장 번호: 941796
구매자: Anna Gunn
배송 주소: 540 Pine Street, Daly City, CA 94015

| | |
|---|---|
| 프리마 실버 사무용 책상/워크스테이션 | $209.95 |
| 서포트 시스템 10 책상용 의자 | $109.95 |
| 샘슨 19인치 모니터 | $149.95 |
| 샘슨 컴퓨터 (모델 번호: 안드로메다 X110) | $909.90 |
| 소계 | $1,559.75 |
| (149) **단골 구매 고객 할인** | −$100.00 |
| **세금** | $86.99 |
| (150) **총계** | $1,546.74 |

New Line Office Supply Warehouse에서 구매해 주셔서 감사합니다.

**149.** Gunn 씨에 대해 암시되는 것은 무엇인가?
(A) 주문품을 직접 찾아갈 것이다.
(B) 사무용품 회사에서 일한다.
(C) 뉴라인 오피스 서플라이 웨어하우스에서 물건을 자주 구매한다.
(D) 다음 주에 책상을 구매할 것이다. 정답 (C)

**150.** 송장 상에서 지불되어야 하는 총 금액은 얼마인가?
(A) $1,559.75
(B) $1,546.74
(C) $909.90
(D) $86.99 정답 (B)

문제 151-152번은 다음 문자 메시지를 참조하시오.

Sally Murphy [오후 4:44]
BK Building에 관한 정보를 확인해 보셨나요?

Bobby Carter [오후 4:45]
네, 봤습니다. (151) **많은 우리 건축가와 엔지니어들**이 외부에서 근무하고 있는 것을 고려하면, 우리에게 그 모든 공간이 필요할까요?

Sally Murphy [오후 4:47]
저는 정말로 그렇다고 생각해요. 회사가 이렇게 빠르게 성장하고 있는 것을 감안하면요.

Bobby Carter [오후 4:48]
하지만 그 일은 한동안 시간이 지난 후에야 가능할 거예요.

Sally Murphy [오후 4:50]
우리는 단기적인 요건과 종합적인 요건들을 모두 고려해 봐야 합니다. (152) **이 건물은 직원 규모 확대를 가능하게 할 만한 충분한 공간을 제공하고 있습니다.**

ACTUAL TEST ••• 05

Bobby Carter [오후 4:52]

(152) 알겠습니다. 우리는 하나의 회사로서 성장하기 위한 공간이 필요합니다. 우리는 나중에 옮기는 것을 원치 않을 거예요, 특히 우리가 더 많은 엔지니어들과 계약을 체결하는 일을 시작하게 되면요.

**151.** Murphy 씨와 Carter 씨는 어디에서 일하는가?
(A) 건축 회사
(B) 이사 전문 회사
(C) 부동산 중개업체
(D) 인테리어 디자인 회사  정답 (A)

**152.** 오후 4시 52분에, Carter 씨가 "Got it."이라고 썼을 때 무엇을 의미할 가능성이 가장 큰가?
(A) 회사가 현재의 사무 공간을 개선해야 한다.
(B) 새로운 공간이 너무 비쌀 것이다.
(C) 건물이 향후 성장에 대한 계획을 수용할 수 있을 것이다.
(D) 건물에 구조적인 개선 작업이 필요하다.  정답 (C)

**문제 153-155번은 다음 기사를 참조하시오.**

Bangkok, Thailand

(153) **Bangkok은 현대 여행객들을 흥분시키는 많은 매력적인 관광지들을 가진 신나고 활기찬 도시이다.** 이곳에 Thailand 문화를 경험하기 위해 왔든, 맛있는 음식들을 맛보기 위해 왔든, 혹은 쇼핑을 위해 왔든 간에, Bangkok은 모두를 위한 그 무언가를 가지고 있는 도시이다.

(153) **관광 명소들:**
Grand Palace는 도시 관광객들이 처음으로 방문하는 주요 관광명소이다. 18세기에 세워진 이 궁궐에는 귀중한 불상들이 많이 있다.

Chinatown에 있는 시장은 주말에 엄청난 관광 인파를 끌어 들인다. 이곳에서 집에 있는 가족들을 위한 훌륭한 선물이 될만한 환상적이고 저렴한 물건들을 찾을 수 있다. 흥정을 두려워하지 말되 정중히 하기 바란다. (155) **이 지역에서 활동하는 소매치기들을 경계해야 한다.**

(154) **숙박시설:**
도시 주변에는 굉장히 싼 호텔들이 많이 있다. (155) **도심지에 위치한 적절한 가격의 Royal Thai 호텔을 이용해 보는 것도 괜찮다**(1인실-10달러, 2인실-18달러). 관광 지구 중심에 있는 Bangkok 여관도 여행객들에게 인기가 높으며, TV와 뜨거운 샤워가 가능한 시설을 구비한 방을 제공한다(1인실-12달러, 2인실-20달러).

**153.** 이 기사는 어떠한 종류의 출판물에서 접할 수 있을 것 같은가?
(A) 경제 보고서
(B) 비즈니스 잡지
(C) 호텔 잡지
(D) 여행 가이드북  정답 (D)

**154.** 관광객들이 Chinatown에 있는 시장을 방문할 때 주의해야 하는 이유는 무엇인가?
(A) 도로에 교통량이 많다.
(B) 시장에 도둑들이 존재한다.
(C) 시장에 갈 때 택시가 과한 요금을 청구한다.
(D) 시장에서 많은 복제품들이 판매된다.  정답 (B)

**155.** Royal Thai 호텔에 대해 알 수 있는 것은?
(A) 중심지에 위치해 있다.
(B) 방들이 넓고 깨끗하다.
(C) 호텔에 있는 식당에서 환상적인 태국 음식을 제공한다.
(D) 호텔은 투숙객을 위한 수영장을 보유하고 있다.  정답 (A)

**문제 156-158번은 다음 광고를 참조하시오.**

Roseville 지역 센터

Roseville 시내에서 차로 10분 거리의 풍경 좋은 산과 어우러진 지역에 위치해 있는 Roseville 지역 센터(RCC)는 지역 사회에서 레저, 운동, 휴식을 위한 새로운 공간입니다. (156) **Roseville 지역 센터는 가족 단위 및 미혼 남녀들이 마사지를 받고**, 운동 및 수영을 즐기고, 심지어 일광욕실에서 낮잠을 즐길 수 있는 훌륭한 장소입니다.

다채로운 활동과 휴식을 제공하는 로즈빌 지역 센터는 가족 모임과 단기 사업 회의, 미혼 남녀들의 편안한 만남의 장소로써 최적의 장소입니다. 센터 내 관리자가 여러분의 하루를 위해 완벽한 계획을 세우도록 도와드릴 것입니다. (157) **추가 비용을 지불하시면, 개인 목욕용품을 드립니다.**

회원권 문의를 위해서는, 안내데스크 404-575-4331로 전화하시거나, members@rcc.com으로 이메일을 보내시기 바랍니다. 저희 센터 내 관리자와 연락하시려면 404-575-4331로 전화 주십시오. (158) **더 많은 정보, 사진, 오시는 길 또는 다른 회원 분들의 이용 후기를 보시려면 www.rcc. org를 방문하십시오.**

**156.** Roseville 지역 센터에 대해 언급된 것은 무엇인가?
(A) 시내 중심부에 위치해 있다.
(B) 마사지 서비스를 제공한다.
(C) 출장 연회 서비스를 제공한다.
(D) 건물 내에 커피숍이 있다.  정답 (B)

**157.** 추가 요금을 내면 이용 가능한 것은?
(A) 시내에서 오는 교통편
(B) 대형 회의실
(C) 운동 시설의 사용
(D) 목욕용품  정답 (D)

**158.** 광고에 의하면, Roseville 지역 센터로 가는 길 안내는 어떻게 받을 수 있는가?
(A) 홈페이지를 방문해서
(B) 관리자에게 전화를 걸어서
(C) 안내데스크에 연락해서
(D) 매니저에게 이메일을 보내서  정답 (A)

**문제 159-161번은 다음 편지를 참조하시오.**

Superfit 스포츠웨어
490 Over Street
London, England

11월 23일

Jeremiah Osterland
490 Rinke Strata
Vienna, Austria

Osterland 씨에게,

(159) **저희 스포츠웨어 상품을 문의하셨던 이메일 잘 받았습니다.** 우리는 역동적이고, 성장 중인 회사로 Austria 전국에 있는 귀하의 매장에 스포츠웨어를 납품할 수 있는 가능성에 기뻐하고 있습니다.

Superfit 스포츠웨어는 1992년 설립된 가족사업체입니다. 현재에는 England 전역에 30개 이상의 매장을 갖추고 있어 매년 백만 명 이상 되는 고객님들의 필요한 상품을 공급 중입니다. 우리는 신발부터 스포츠 테라피 상품에 이르기까지 다양한 상품을 제조하고 판매합니다.

(160) **귀하가 살펴보실 수 있는 카탈로그를 첨부합니다. 현재 저희가 생산하**

는 모든 상품의 목록과 설명이 포함되어 있습니다.

(161) 판매부장인 Rhodes 씨가 12월 12일 Vienna에 가서 귀하를 만나 뵐 수 있도록 하겠습니다. Rhodes 씨는 귀하와 판매 계약 조건을 협상하고 쌍방간에 이익이 되는 거래를 만들어 낼 것입니다.

귀하와 사업을 함께 할 수 있길 기대합니다.

Saul Goodman
Superfit 스포츠웨어

**159.** Goodman 씨는 어떠한 종류의 의사표현에 응답하였는가?
(A) 잡지 기사
(B) 주주의 편지
(C) 이메일 문의
(D) 전화 메시지 　　　　　　　　　　　　　　정답 (C)

**160.** Goodman 씨는 그의 편지에 무엇을 함께 보냈는가?
(A) 비행기 티켓
(B) 영업용 카탈로그
(C) 할인 쿠폰 책자
(D) 사업 계약서 목록 　　　　　　　　　　　정답 (B)

**161.** Rhodes 씨가 Vienna로 가는 이유는 무엇인가?
(A) Osterland 씨의 매장 한 곳을 살펴보기 위해서
(B) Osterland 씨와 휴가를 보내기 위해서
(C) 계약조건을 상의하기 위해서
(D) 회사의 현지 지점을 설립하기 위해서 　　정답 (C)

**문제 162-164번은 다음 이메일을 참조하시오.**

수신: 〈Bandar@bestmail.com〉
발신: 〈ClaireSaturna@ipi.org〉
날짜: 3월 20일
제목: 연례 IPI 컨퍼런스에 대한 등록

Bandar 씨께,

(162) 저희 International Petroleum Institute(IPI)에 대한 귀하의 많은 후원에 대해 감사 드리기 위해 이메일 보냅니다. 한 가지 상기시켜 드리자면, 상파울루에서 열리는 연례 IPI 컨퍼런스에 대한 등록 마감일이 10월 15일이라는 점을 명심하시기 바랍니다. 이번 컨퍼런스를 위해 (163C) 200곳이 넘는 판매업체와 제품 전시, 그리고 강연을 포함한 흥미로운 행사들이 마련되어 있으며, 모든 행사가 도심 한복판에 위치한 최신 컨벤션 시설에서 개최됩니다.

International Petroleum Institute의 프로그램들에 대한 우대 기부자로서, 저희는 귀하께 (163A) 호텔 비용에 대한 20퍼센트 할인 쿠폰과 (163D) 컨벤션 홀로 향하는 무료 셔틀 버스 서비스를 제공해 드립니다. 저희 웹사이트를 방문하여 온라인으로 등록하시기 바랍니다. (164) 또한 판매업체 부스에 대한 안내도를 포함해 그곳에서 상세한 컨퍼런스 프로그램을 찾아 보실 수 있습니다. 아니면 512-555-8760으로 저희에게 전화를 통해 연락하실 수 있습니다. (163) 귀하의 회원 번호를 준비해 주시기 바랍니다.

Claire Saturna
회원 관리 코디네이터

**162.** Bandar 씨는 누구일 가능성이 가장 큰가?
(A) 정유회사 임원
(B) 컨퍼런스 조직 책임자
(C) 기자
(D) 교사 　　　　　　　　　　　　　　　　정답 (A)

**163.** 제공되는 혜택이 아닌 것은 무엇인가?
(A) 할인된 호텔 요금
(B) 호텔 객실 업그레이드
(C) 많은 판매업체 부스
(D) 행사장으로 가는 무료 교통편 　　　　　정답 (B)

**164.** [1], [2], [3] 그리고 [4]로 표시된 곳 중에, 아래 문장이 들어가기에 가장 적절한 곳은?
"또한 판매업체 부스에 대한 안내도를 포함해 그곳에서 상세한 컨퍼런스 프로그램을 찾아 보실 수 있습니다."
(A) [1]
(B) [2]
(C) [3]
(D) [4] 　　　　　　　　　　　　　　　　정답 (D)

**문제 165-167번은 다음 기사를 참조하시오.**

Santa Fe에서 재개장하는 President 호텔
Jesse Pinkman – Santa Fe Weekly

Santa Fe – (165/166) 꼭 필요했던 수리공사가 진행되는 6개월간 문을 닫았던 President 호텔이 이번 월요일 오전 9시에 다시 문을 연다.

호텔 지배인인 Janice Ha 씨는 호텔이 그 어느 때보다 아주 훌륭하다고 말했다. 그녀는 "모든 사람들이 이 오래된 호텔을 좋아했어요."라고 운을 뗀 뒤 "하지만 이 건물 보수 작업은 저희가 현대식 성향을 반영하기 위해선 필수적이었어요. 이전에 저희는 처리할 수 없었던 수많은 관광객들의 요구를 경험했어요. 그에 따라 (166) 저희는 최신식 수영장과 체육관을 설치하고 레스토랑의 수준을 향상시키고, 손님들이 즐길 수 있는 극장을 추가했습니다. 이 곳 모든 이들이 호텔의 재개장에 들떠 있고 다시 일터로 복귀할 수 있기를 몹시 기대하고 있어요."라고 말했다.

(166) 디자이너이자 호텔의 소유주인 Chan Hong 씨는 새로운 디자인에 대한 그의 영감을 말했다. 그는 "저는 고객들에게 기억에 남는 경험을 만들어 주고 싶어요."라고 언급한 후 "저는 모든 연령대의 사람들이 이 호텔을 즐길 수 있으면 좋겠어요. 방문 목적이 사업이든 휴가든 간에 말이지요."라고 이야기했다.

Chan Hong 씨가 새 호텔이 이제껏 까다로웠던 여행 단체의 요구도 충족시킬 수 있는 시설이 구비되어 있는지 여부에 대한 질문을 받았을 때 "매우 입맛이 까다로운 손님이 와도 매우 자신 있게 응대할 수 있다"라고 대답했다.

(167) 새로운 호텔이 주는 즐거움을 최초로 직접 체험한 사람이 바로 Jim Gomez 씨로, 그는 이 곳에서 일주일에 4차례 운동을 한다. Gomez 씨는 "새 체육관은 대단해요."라고 말했다. 이어서 그는 "그곳은 휴가 때 몸매를 유지할 수 있는 모든 것들을 갖추고 있어요. 전 수영장과 레스토랑도 마음에 들어요. 다음에도 당연히 이 호텔에 체류할 겁니다."라고 이야기했다.

President 호텔은 내부와 외부를 막론하고 단연 훌륭해 보인다. 각 객실은 와이드 스크린 TV, 킹 사이즈 침대와 무선 인터넷 접속을 제공하고 있다. 만약 돈을 쓰고 싶다면, 엠퍼러 스위트 룸이 지불하는 객실료 만큼의 가치를 제공한다는 점에서 적격이라 할 수 있다. 220달러의 이 고급 방들은 단연 고상함에 딱 들어맞는다.

**165.** 이 기사문의 목적은 무엇인가?
(A) 호텔의 재개장을 홍보하기 위해서
(B) 몇몇의 다른 호텔들을 비교하기 위해서
(C) 지역사회에 무료시설 사용을 제공하기 위해서
(D) 호텔에서 일하는 직원의 공석을 광고하기 위해서 　정답 (A)

**166.** President 호텔에 대해 언급되지 않은 것은 무엇인가?

(A) 크리스마스 날에 개장할 것이다.

(B) 수영장을 가지고 있다.

(C) 6개월간 문을 닫았다.

(D) Hong 씨가 소유하고 있다.　　　　　　정답 (A)

**167.** Jim Gomez 씨에 관해 암시하고 있는 내용은 무엇인가?

(A) 그는 그의 아내와 아이들과 호텔에서 머물렀다.

(B) 그는 호텔 업계에서 일한다.

(C) 그는 운동에 열정적이다.

(D) 그는 헬스 클럽 보수 계획을 도왔다.　　　정답 (C)

문제 168-171번은 다음 다음 온라인 채팅 토론을 참조하시오.

Molly Vernon　　　　　　　　　　　　[오후 12:08]

Mike, 회사 웹사이트 좀 한 번 봐 주시겠어요? (168) **제 컴퓨터로 우리 제품들의 사진을 볼 수가 없어요.** 당신 컴퓨터에는 보이나요?

Mike Snow　　　　　　　　　　　　　[오후 12:13]

아뇨, 보이지 않는 게 분명해요. 이렇게 된지 오래됐나요?

Molly Vernon　　　　　　　　　　　　[오후 12:14]

아마 몇 시간 밖에 되지 않았을 거예요. (169) **구매한 제품에 대한 후기를 작성하고 싶어 하시는 고객 한 분으로부터 막 연락을 받았는데, 지금 보이지 않으신대요.** 오늘 이른 시간이나 어제도 불만 사항이 없었고요. 우리 IT 담당 팀에게 알려 주시겠어요?

Mike Snow　　　　　　　　　　　　　[오후 12:15]

Larry, 우리 웹사이트의 온라인 매장 코너에 있는 이미지 파일에 뭔가 문제가 발생했어요.

Larry McKee　　　　　　　　　　　　[오후 12:18]

이상하네요… (170) **그 파일들이 삭제된 것 같아요.**

Mike Snow　　　　　　　　　　　　　[오후 12:19]

(170) **우리가 백업 파일을 보관했기를 바랍니다.**

Larry McKee　　　　　　　　　　　　[오후 12:20]

만일을 위해 항상 그렇게 하죠. 지금 다시 업로드할게요.

Mike Snow　　　　　　　　　　　　　[오후 12:21]

잘됐네요. 그리고 (171) **온라인으로 간단한 해명 글을 발송해서 모든 사람들에게 고쳐졌다고 알려야 할 겁니다.**

Molly Vernon　　　　　　　　　　　　[오후 12:22]

(171) **그건 제가 처리할게요.**

**168.** Vernon 씨가 보고하고 있는 문제점은 무엇인가?

(A) 온라인 구매가 처리되지 않고 있다.

(B) 연락처가 회사의 웹사이트에 기재되어 있다.

(C) 회사의 웹사이트가 해킹된 것처럼 보인다.

(D) 제품 사진들이 온라인 매장 코너에서 보이지 않는다.　　정답 (D)

**169.** Vernon 씨는 누구로부터 문제에 대해 알게 되었는가?

(A) 회계사

(B) IT 담당 동료 직원

(C) 고객

(D) 회사의 사장　　　　　　　　　　　정답 (C)

**170.** 오후 12시 19분에, Snow 씨가 "I hope we've kept backup files."라고 썼을 때 무엇을 의미할 가능성이 가장 큰가?

(A) 회사가 많은 돈을 잃었을까 봐 걱정하고 있다.

(B) 자신의 동료직원이 파일을 다루는 절차를 설명해 주기를 원한다.

(C) 고객의 금융 거래 기록을 찾고 있다.

(D) 모든 사진들이 여전히 이용 가능하기를 바라고 있다.　정답 (D)

**171.** Vernon 씨는 곧이어 무엇을 할 것 같은가?

(A) 자신의 개인 프로필을 업데이트하는 일

(B) 보안 담당 팀에 연락하는 일

(C) IT 팀에 연락하는 일

(D) 온라인으로 메시지를 게시하는 일　　　정답 (D)

문제 172-175번은 다음 안내 정보를 참조하시오.

Sweetwater Lake State 공원
이용 가능한 활동

(172) **Sweetwater Lake State 공원에서, 여러분께서는 낚시와 카누 타기, 하이킹, 소풍, 오두막에서의 캠핑 또는 숙박, 그리고 보트 타기를 즐기실 수 있습니다.** 여러분의 다음 번 모임을 위해 저희 단체 고객용 홀을 대여하시기 바랍니다!

(174C) **공원 내에 악어들이 살고 있으므로** 방문 전에 악어 대비 안전 팁을 읽어 보시기 바랍니다.

낚시: Sweetwater Lake State 공원은 26,810에이커의 규모이며, (174C) **호수 자체에 70종이 넘는 물고기 종이 서식하고 있습니다.** 저희는 낚시용 교각과 보트 선착장을 보유하고 있습니다. 저희 국립 공원의 물가에서 낚시하는 데 낚시 허가증은 필요치 않습니다. 공원 내에서 사용하실 수 있는 낚시 장비 대여에 관해 문의하시기 바랍니다.

카누 타기: Sweetwater Lake의 구불구불한 물길을 탐험해 보십시오. 공원 내에서 카누를 대여하시거나, 보유하고 계신 카누 또는 카약을 가져오셔도 됩니다.

숙박:

● (173) **물만 제공되는 장소에서부터 모든 장비 연결이 가능한 장소에 이르기까지, 46곳의 캠프장에서 선택하십시오.**

● 방충망 처리가 된 쉼터에서 머무르실 수 있습니다.

● 역사적인 저희 오두막 중의 하나를 대여하십시오. 이 오두막은 2인실부터 6인실까지 마련되어 있으며, (174B) **몇 곳은 장애인 이용 가능 시설입니다.**

하이킹: 도보로 숲을 탐험해 보세요. (175) **Sweetwater Forest 산책로의 4분의 1마일은 장애인 이용 가능 구역입니다.** 저희 대화형 지도를 통해 더 많은 정보를 확인해 보십시오. 장애인용 산책로를 볼 수 있는 링크를 클릭하시기 바랍니다.

(174D) **자원 봉사자: 저희 자원 봉사자 페이지를 방문하셔서 도움을 제공하실 수 있는 방법을 확인해 보십시오.**

**172.** Sweetwater Lake State 공원에 관해 알 수 있는 것은 무엇인가?

(A) 고속도로에서 접근하기 어렵다.

(B) 인공 호수이며, 비교적 새로 생긴 곳이다.

(C) 다양한 활동들이 제공된다.

(D) 입장료가 매우 저렴하다.　　　　　　정답 (C)

**173.** 공원에서 캠핑하는 것에 관해 알 수 있는 것은 무엇인가?

(A) 이용 가능한 많은 선택권이 있다.

(B) 어느 캠프장에서도 전기를 이용할 수 없다.

(C) 올해는 캠핑이 허용되지 않는다.

(D) 많은 추가 캠프장들이 현재 지어지고 있다.　정답 (A)

**174.** Sweetwater Lake State 공원에 관해 암시되는 내용이 아닌 것은 무엇인가?

(A) 오직 주 내에 거주하는 주민들만을 위한 곳이다.

(B) 장애인들을 위한 선택권이 있다.
(C) 많은 종류의 야생 동물들이 있다.
(D) 현재 자원 봉사자들을 모집하고 있다.                  정답 (A)

**175.** [1], [2], [3] 그리고 [4]로 표시된 곳 중에, 아래 문장이 들어가기에 가장 적절한 곳은?

"장애인용 산책로를 볼 수 있는 링크를 클릭하시기 바랍니다."

(A) [1]
(B) [2]
(C) [3]
(D) [4]                                        정답 (D)

**문제 176~180번은 다음 이메일들을 참조하시오.**

---

수신: Eric Woodhouse, AZA 의료용품
발신: Ryan Taylor, 지배인, Ivy 호텔
날짜: 11월 29일
제목: Ivy 호텔에서의 숙박
첨부: AZAinvoice.txt

친애하는 Woodhouse 씨,

저희는 귀하와 동료들이 의료학회에 참여하기 위해 Montreal에 방문하시는 동안 저희 Ivy 호텔에 숙박하시게 된 점 매우 기쁘게 생각합니다. 저희는 여러분께서 11월 26일 저희 호텔에서 즐겁게 머무셨기를 바라고 있습니다. 저는 세금과 룸 서비스비가 포함된 최종 계산서를 이메일로 첨부 하였습니다. (178) **신용카드로** (177) **빠르게 계산하시고자 한다면** 제게 992-9599로 **전화 주십시오.**

Ivy 호텔은 신규 호텔이어서, 서비스 향상을 개선하기 위한 방법으로 고객의 소리에 항상 귀를 기울입니다. (176) **만약 귀하와 귀하의 동료들이 저희 호텔에 머무는 동안에, 호텔 숙박과 관련된 의견이 있었다면 저에게 알려주셔서 향후에는 저희가 귀하께 더 나은 서비스를 드릴 수 있도록 해주시길 바랍니다.**

저희를 방문해 주셔서 매우 기쁩니다. (180) **만약 귀하가 내년 학회 때 다시 한 번 저희 호텔을 선택해 주신다면 저희는 귀하께 20% 할인 혜택을 제공 해드리겠습니다.**

Ryan Taylor
지배인
Ivy 호텔

---

수신: Ryan Taylor, 지배인, Ivy 호텔
발신: Eric Woodhouse, AZA 의료용품
날짜: 12월 1일
제목: 답장: Ivy 호텔에서의 숙박

친애하는 Taylor 씨,

이메일 주신 점에 감사드립니다. 저와 동료들은 귀 호텔에서 머무르게 되어 정말 즐거웠습니다. 직원들은 모두 매우 유능했고, 객실이 넓어서 편히 머무를 수 있었습니다. 저희를 크게 환대해주셨지요.

저와 동료들은 영업 워크숍에 참석하기 위해 다음 달에 Montreal을 다시 방문할 예정입니다. 가능하다면 저희는 귀 호텔에 숙박하고자 4개의 객실을 예약하고 싶습니다. 지난번과 같은 객실에 머무르는 것이 가능하겠습니까? (179) **비록 오크 객실의 욕실이 약간 지저분했지만, 그 외 다른 객실들은 모두 훌륭했습니다.**

(180) **그리고 저희는 3월 1일로 예정된 다음 학회도 귀 호텔에서 개최하고자 합니다.**

---

요금을 지불하기 위해 금요일에 전화를 드리도록 하겠습니다.

Eric Woodhouse
영업 고문
AZA 의료용품

---

**176.** 첫 번째 이메일의 목적은 무엇인가?

(A) 호텔 구인 광고를 위해서
(B) 새로운 호텔의 개업을 홍보하기 위해서
(C) 호텔 숙박과 관련된 고객의 의견을 구하기 위해서
(D) 의료용품을 주문하기 위해서                  정답 (C)

**177.** 첫 번째 이메일, 첫 번째 단락 네 번째 줄 'prompt'와 가장 의미가 유사한 단어는 무엇인가?

(A) 지연된
(B) 늦은
(C) 재무상의
(D) 시간을 지키는                                정답 (D)

**178.** Taylor 씨는 Woodhouse 씨가 어떠한 수단으로 지불하길 원하는가?

(A) 현금
(B) 신용카드
(C) 수표
(D) 계좌이체                                     정답 (B)

**179.** Woodhouse 씨는 오크 객실과 관련하여 어떠한 의견을 남겼는가?

(A) 변기가 깨끗하지 않았다.
(B) 창문이 깨졌다.
(C) 욕실이 더러웠다.
(D) 객실이 환상적이었다.                         정답 (C)

**180.** Woodhouse 씨는 언제 특별 할인을 받을 수 있을 것 같은가?

(A) 11월 26일
(B) 11월 29일
(C) 12월 1일
(D) 3월 1일                                      정답 (D)

**문제 181~185번은 다음 기사와 이메일을 참조하시오.**

---

The Daily News
12월 1일

"활기를 주는 음료"

Aaron Milton 씨의 하루는 커피 콩과 달콤한 시럽, 그리고 여러 가지 독특한 맛이 더해진 크림을 중심으로 (182) **돌아간다.** 그가 최근에 개장한 매장 Daily Perk는 (183D) **여러 가지 뛰어난 매장 제조 샌드위치와 달콤한 음식들을 제공하지만,** 정말로 눈에 띄는 것은 이곳의 자체 커피 음료들이다. (181) **집에서 재배하고 볶은 커피 콩**과 맛의 조화를 위한 창의적인 솜씨가 조합되어, Aaron Milton 씨는 매장 손님들 사이에서 "미스터 커피"라는 별명으로 유명해졌다. (185) **전직 학교 교사인 Milton 씨는,** 현재 도시에서 가장 뛰어난 카페인 함유 음료들을 제조한다. 그의 혼합 음료들은 종종 계절에서 영감을 얻기 때문에(예를 들어, 가을철의 호박맛 파이나 겨울 연휴 동안의 캔디 케인 사탕이 있다) (183B) **맛의 종류가 자주 바뀐다.** 심지어 직원들조차 메뉴에 각자 원하는 개인적인 취향을 반영하도록 장려되며, 연중 구매 가능한 여러 가지 대표 제품들을 만들어 왔다.

(183C) **Milton 씨는 부모님으로부터 자금을 빌려 Daily Perk를 시작했는데,** 불과 영업 시작 1년 만에 모두 되갚을 수 있었다.

아직 그곳에 가보지 않았을 경우, Daily Perk는 Weems Lane과 Elm

---

Street가 만나는 모퉁이에 편리하게 위치해 있다. 매일 아침 6시 30분에 영업을 시작한다. 더 많은 정보는 웹사이트 www.perkup.com을 방문해 확인할 수 있다.

수신: Aaron Milton ⟨amilton@mail.com⟩
발신: Peter Vickers ⟨Pvickers@mail.com⟩
날짜: 12월 3일
제목: 기사

Aaron에게,

**(184) Daily News에서 당신에 관한 신문 기사를 읽어 보았는데, 이 기사는 제가 아직 당신의 커피 매장에 가보지 않았다는 것을 상기시켜 주었습니다.** 멋진 곳이라고 생각되었기 때문에, 곧 들를 수 있기를 바랍니다. **(185) Crown Pointe Academy에서는 당신이 그립습니다.** 여러 학생들이 여전히 당신에 관해 묻습니다. 이곳은 모든 일이 잘 되고 있습니다. 이번 여름에 과학 연구실을 개조할 예정인데, 이는 당신이 몇 년 동안 애원했던 일이라는 것을 알고 있습니다! 모든 작업이 완료되면 와 보셔야 할 것입니다.

곧 뵙겠습니다!

Peter

**181.** Milton 씨에 관해 암시되는 것은 무엇인가?
(A) 가족 사업에 합류했다.
(B) 부모님께 빚을 지고 있다.
(C) 일종의 농부이다.
(D) 직업을 바꿀 계획이다.                정답 (C)

**182.** 기사에서, 첫 번째 단락, 첫 번째 줄에 있는 단어 "revolve"와 의미가 가장 가까운 어휘는 무엇인가?
(A) 사임하다
(B) 고안하다
(C) 반복되다
(D) 연기하다                정답 (C)

**183.** Daily Perk에 관해 알 수 있는 내용이 아닌 것은 무엇인가?
(A) 오직 저녁 시간에만 문을 연다.
(B) 자주 메뉴를 바꾼다.
(C) 빠른 성공을 경험했다.
(D) 다양한 제품을 제공한다.                정답 (A)

**184.** Vickers 씨가 이메일을 보낸 이유는 무엇인가?
(A) Milton 씨에게 파티에 오도록 요청하기 위해
(B) Milton 씨에게 일자리를 부탁하기 위해
(C) 투자 기회에 대한 Milton 씨의 관심을 확인하기 위해
(D) Milton 씨에게 그의 업체에 관한 기사를 읽었음을 말하기 위해
                정답 (D)

**185.** Vickers 씨와 Milton 씨는 어디에서 함께 일했을 것 같은가?
(A) 커피 매장
(B) 학교
(C) 광고 대행사
(D) 자선 행사장                정답 (B)

**문제 186-190번은 다음 기사와 이메일들을 참조하시오.**

5월 5일
다가오는 Barrington Children's Hospital 마라톤에 대한 후원업체 결정

**(188) Pueblo Corporation**이 다가오는 Barrington Children's Hospital 마라톤 행사를 위한 가장 큰 후원업체가 될 것이라는 사실이 확인되었다. 이 업체의 후원과 관련된 상세 정보는 조만간 발표될 것이다. **(188) 이 기업은 전국에서 세 번째로 큰 제약 회사로 순위에 올라 있다.**

**(186A) Barrington Children's Hospital 마라톤 행사는 지난 15년 동안 해마다 개최되어 왔다.** 해당 기간 동안, **(186B) 1,500만 달러가 넘는 금액이 희귀 질병으로 고통 받고 있는 아이들을 돕기 위해 모금되었다.** 이 행사는 일반 마라톤(26마일)과 하프 마라톤(13마일)으로 구성되어 있다. 모든 수익금과 기부금은 Barrington Children's Hospital에 기부될 것이다. 참가자들은 각자 기금 마련과 관련된 노력을 기울이도록 장려된다.

**(186C) 이번 행사는 다음 달인 6월 16일 토요일에 열릴 것이다.** Barrington Children's Hospital 마라톤은 하프 마라톤에 10,000명이 넘는 참가자들이, 그리고 일반 마라톤에는 5,000여명의 참가자들이 찾는 전국에서 20번째로 큰 마라톤 행사이다.

수신: Jim Douglas ⟨jimdouglas@pueblo.net⟩
발신: Teresa Martinez ⟨teresamartinez@pueblo.net⟩
날짜: 5월 10일
제목: *Social Interests News*와의 인터뷰

**(187) Douglas 씨께,**

Barrington Children's Hospital 마라톤과 관련해 최근에 언론 보도가 나온 뒤로, 다수의 언론 매체들이 인터뷰를 요청해 오고 있습니다. 언론 매체들은 후원업체 결정과 관련된 **(187) 우리 홍보부의 의견**을 들어 보고 싶어 합니다. 이 매체들 중에서, 가장 명성이 높은 매체인 *Social Interest News*를 골랐습니다. *Social Interest News*의 기자 한 분이 인터뷰 일정을 잡기 위해 곧 연락 드릴 것입니다. **(190) 일정을 고려해 보면, 5월 12일, 14일, 15일, 그리고 20일에 시간이 있으실 것 같습니다.** 이 중에서 하루 시간이 괜찮으시길 바랍니다.

Teresa Martinez
**(187) 비서**
Pueblo Corporation

수신: Jim Douglas ⟨jimdouglas@pueblo.net⟩
발신: Matthew Stokes ⟨mstokes12@socialinterestnews.com⟩
날짜: 5월 10일
제목: Pueblo Corporation의 인터뷰 요청

Douglas 씨께,

제 이름은 Matthew이며, 저는 *Social Interest News*의 기자입니다. 제가 이미 귀하의 비서이신 Teresa Martinez 씨께 인터뷰와 관련해 연락 드렸습니다. 저는 다가오는 Barrington Children's Hospital 마라톤 행사의 후원업체가 되기 위한 귀사의 결정에 관해 들었습니다. 저희 신문사는 저희가 일반 대중에게 주요 후원업체를 소개할 수 있는 아주 좋은 기회가 될 것이라는 생각이 들었습니다. 저희는 이번 인터뷰가 귀사의 대외 홍보에도 **(189) 이득이 될 수 있다**는 점에 의심의 여지가 없습니다. **(190) 귀하께서는 13일과 14일, 또는 16일 중의 하루에 시간이 되시는지요?** 그렇지 않으실 경우, 다른 날로 일정을 잡을 수 있습니다.

Matthew Stokes
*Social Interest News*

**186.** Barrington Children's Hospital 마라톤에 관해 알 수 있는 내용이 아닌 것은 무엇인가?
(A) 15년 동안 매년 개최되어 왔다.
(B) 병을 앓고 있는 아이들을 위한 모금 행사이다.
(C) 오직 26마일 길이의 마라톤으로만 구성된다.

114

(D) 올해는 6월 중순에 개최될 것이다.　　　　　　정답 (C)

**187.** Douglas 씨는 누구일 가능성이 가장 큰가?
(A) Pueblo의 홍보부장
(B) Pueblo Corporation의 비서
(C) Social Interest News의 편집장
(D) Barrington Children's Hospital의 직원　　정답 (A)

**188.** Pueblo Corporation에 관해 알 수 있는 것은 무엇인가?
(A) 직원들이 마라톤에 참가한다.
(B) 항상 해당 마라톤 행사의 후원업체였다.
(C) 전국에서 가장 큰 제약 회사이다.
(D) 의약품 제조를 전문으로 한다.　　　　　정답 (D)

**189.** 두 번째 이메일에서, 첫 번째 단락의 다섯 번째 줄에 있는 단어 "beneficial"과 의미가 가장 가까운 것은 무엇인가?
(A) 도움이 되는
(B) 호의적인
(C) 수익성이 좋은
(D) 널리 알려진　　　　　　　　　　　　정답 (A)

**190.** 인터뷰는 언제 진행될 가능성이 가장 큰가?
(A) 5월 13일
(B) 5월 14일
(C) 5월 16일
(D) 6월 16일　　　　　　　　　　　　　정답 (B)

**문제 191-195번은 다음 웹페이지들과 이메일을 참조하시오.**

---
http://www.allhousinglondon.uk

시내에 아파트를 구하는 초빙 교수

게시 제목: 6개월 기간의 전대
날짜: 9월 12일

(191/195) **저는 Coleridge College에서의 강의를 위해 1월부터 6월까지 London에 있을 예정입니다.** 저는 내년을 위해 6개월 기간의 임대(또는 전대) 계약을 찾고 있습니다.

저는 고급스러운 것을 찾고 있는 것이 아닙니다. 저는 가스 레인지와 냉장고 같은 기본적인 편의 시설이 있는 깨끗하고 괜찮은 (192B) **침실 하나 또는 두 개짜리 아파트를** 구입하는 데 관심이 있습니다. 그 외의 것들은 추가적인 보너스와 같을 것입니다. 테라스나 개방된 발코니가 있으면 이상적일 텐데, 친구들이나 동료들과 즐거운 시간을 보내고 싶기 때문입니다. 하지만 저는 대학교 근처에서 거주할 계획인데, 미국에서 제 차를 가져가지 않을 것이기 때문입니다. 제 예산은 수도와 가스, 전기를 포함한 비용으로 미화 1,600달러입니다. (192D) **저는 비흡연자입니다.**

---
http://www.allhousinglondon.uk

London의 아파트 임대

게시 제목: 부동산 및 주택
날짜: 9월 13일

건물이 완전히 개조중인 이 훌륭한 (192B) **침실 하나짜리 아파트를** 즐겨 보세요. 이 깨끗하고 단순하면서도 현대적인 아파트는 (195) **12월 15일에 입주 준비가 될 것입니다.** 이곳은 멋진 발코니와 구석구석 새롭게 깔린 바닥재, 그리고 모두 새로운 가전 기기들을 특징으로 합니다. 이 아파트는 London 시내 바로 외곽에 위치해 있지만 주요 대중 교통 거점들과 가까

---
운 곳에 있습니다. 이곳은 Coleridge College의 학생과 직원들뿐만 아니라 우체국과 기타 정부 관청 근무 직원들에게도 이상적인 선택권입니다. 주요 지역 공원에서 불과 1킬로미터도 떨어지지 않은 곳에 있습니다. 1,000파운드 비용이면 상수도와 하수 처리, 쓰레기 수거, 그리고 일반적인 건물 관리비를 지불하실 수 있습니다. 전기와 천연 가스는 세입자에게 지불 책임이 있습니다. (192D) **오직 비흡연자만 가능합니다.** 한 달의 방세와 동일한 금액으로 한 번만 지불하면 되는 보증금은 임대 계약을 맺는 즉시 지불되어야 합니다.

---
수신: Martha Turner ⟨turnerproperties@hmail.net⟩
발신: Reed McMahon 박사 ⟨reed.mc@talkmail.com⟩
날짜: 9월 14일
제목: 아파트

Turner 씨께,

시내 바로 외곽에 위치한 새롭게 개조된 침실 하나짜리 아파트에 대한 귀하의 게시물과 관련해 연락 드립니다. 이 아파트는 제게 매우 매력적인 곳으로 보이며, (192A) **제 예산에도 분명 적합합니다.** 안타깝게도, (193/194) **제가 직접 아파트를 보러 갈 수 없기 때문에,** (193) **집을 찍은 몇몇 사진이라도 가지고 계셨으면 합니다.** 분명히 아직 개조 공사 중이겠지만, 틀림 없이 그 이후의 모습을 상상할 수 있습니다. 이 이메일 주소를 이용해 제게 답변하시거나 원하실 경우에 언제든지 제게 전화 주시기 바랍니다.

감사합니다.

Reed McMahon 박사
512.578.6090

---
**191.** McMahon 박사가 이사하는 이유는 무엇인가?
(A) 학생들을 가르치기 위해
(B) 집으로 돌아가기 위해
(C) 파트 타임으로 공부하기 위해
(D) 코치로 일하기 위해　　　　　　　　　정답 (A)

**192.** 집의 어떤 면이 McMahon 박사의 선호 사항과 일치하지 않는가?
(A) 월 비용
(B) 크기
(C) 위치
(D) 흡연 규정　　　　　　　　　　　　　정답 (C)

**193.** McMahon 박사는 무슨 추가 정보를 요청하는가?
(A) 아파트에 입주 가능한 시점
(B) 미국 달러의 파운드 환전
(C) 수리와 관련해 전화해야 하는 사람
(D) 아파트 사진들　　　　　　　　　　　정답 (D)

**194.** McMahon 박사가 이메일을 발송한 이유는 무엇인가?
(A) 아파트의 실내 배치를 알아 보기 위해
(B) 주택 관련 광고의 상세 정보를 변경하기 위해
(C) 교통편 선택권에 관해 문의하기 위해
(D) 지역 기업들에 관해 문의하기 위해　　정답 (A)

**195.** McMahon 박사는 언제 이사할 가능성이 가장 큰가?
(A) 2월
(B) 12월
(C) 1월
(D) 9월　　　　　　　　　　　　　　　　정답 (B)

문제 196-200번은 다음 양식과 이메일, 그리고 웹페이지를 참조하시오.

---

### AMERICAN AIR
### 연착 수하물 양식

American Air 고객 여러분,

여러분의 수하물에 대한 연착 소식을 알려 드리게 되어 사과 드립니다. 여러분의 물품들을 파악해 가능한 한 빨리 돌려 드리는 데 도움이 될 수 있도록 아래에 상세 정보를 기재해 주시기 바랍니다. (196) **저희 American Air 직원이 여러분의 수하물을 찾는 대로 전화로 연락 드릴 것입니다.** 대부분의 가방들이 추적되어 이틀 이내에 소유주에게 전달이 됩니다. 만약 수하물이 발견되지 않을 경우, 분실된 상태가 21일간 지속될 때까진 수하물은 "분실 상태"가 아니라 "지연 상태"로 분류가 됩니다.

날짜: 11월 16일
(196) **성명: Raymond Walker**
지역 주소: Forest 호텔, Downtown, 984-2 Auckland, New Zealand
전화번호: +62 185 0253
항공편 번호: K53GC6

연착 수하물 정보

| | 수량 | 설명 |
|---|---|---|
| 여행 가방 | 1 | 바퀴가 2개 달린 붉은색 소형 여행 가방, 이름표에 "Raymond Walker"라고 기재됨 |
| 배낭 | | |
| 핸드백 | | |
| (197) 상자 | 1 | "Raymond Walker, Samion Foods"라고 쓰여 있는 소형 플라스틱 상자 |
| 기타 | | |

---

수신: Raymond Walker 〈rwalker@samionfood.com〉
발신: Harry Hernandez 〈hhomez@samionfood.com〉
날짜: 11월 16일, 오후 5:23
제목: 회신: 식품 샘플

Walker 씨께,

(197) 당신의 수하물이 언제 발견되어 되돌려 받으실지 장담할 수 없기 때문에 야간 배송으로 소스 샘플들을 보내 드렸습니다. 따라서, 이 물품을 내일 회의에 가져 가시면 됩니다. (198/199/200) 라벨이 붙은 두 개의 소형 소스 병들뿐만 아니라 따로 포장된 다섯 가지 맛이 있습니다. TWS Shipping을 통해 당신의 숙소로 이 물품들을 보냈습니다. 이 배송 물품이 오전 9시 30분까지 도착할 것이므로 11시에 발표하실 때 샘플들을 보여주실 수 있을 겁니다.

Harry Hernandez
Samion Foods

---

https://www.twsshipping.co.au/overnight

### TWS SHIPPING

귀하의 배송 정보
배송 출발지:
Samion Foods, 27 Earot Street, Archeis 1, 1UE, AU
배송 도착지:
Forest 호텔, Downtown, 984-2 Auckland, New Zealand
중량: 0.68kg

☐ 동봉물    ■ 상자    ☐ 지정 패키지

---

야간 배송 선택권
TWS 이른 오전: (200) **내일 오전 9시 30분까지 배송 [62달러 지금 배송]**
TWS 오전: 내일 오전 11시 30분까지 배송 [49달러 지금 배송]
TWS 오후: 내일 오후 3시까지 배송 [3달러 지금 배송]
TWS 저녁: 내일 오후 8시 30분까지 배송 [35달러 지금 배송]

**196.** American Air에 관해 알 수 있는 것은 무엇인가?
(A) 모든 수하물에 이름표를 포함하도록 고객들에게 요청한다.
(B) 분실된 수하물이 3일 안에 되돌려 보내진다는 점을 보장한다.
(C) Walker 씨의 수하물을 찾을 경우 통보해 줄 것이다.
(D) Walker 씨에게 분실 수하물에 대한 비용을 환급해 줄 것이다.
정답 (C)

**197.** Walker 씨는 샘플을 어디에 넣었을 가능성이 가장 큰가?
(A) 상자
(B) 냉장고
(C) 서류 가방
(D) 배낭
정답 (A)

**198.** Hernandez 씨에 관해 유추되는 것은 무엇인가?
(A) New Zealand에서 고객들과 만난다.
(B) Samion Foods를 위해 자주 출장을 간다.
(C) American Air의 고객 서비스 직원이다.
(D) 고객이 일부 제품을 검토해 보기를 원하고 있다.
정답 (D)

**199.** 이메일에 따르면, Walker 씨는 내일 오전 11시에 무엇을 할 것인가?
(A) 배송 물품을 받는다.
(B) 발표를 한다.
(C) 호텔에서 체크 아웃한다.
(D) 돌아가는 항공편을 확인한다.
정답 (B)

**200.** Hernandez 씨는 배송에 대해 얼마를 청구 받았는가?
(A) 35달러
(B) 31달러
(C) 49달러
(D) 62달러
정답 (D)

### 점수 환산표

자신의 정답 개수를 기준으로 본인의 점수를 개략적으로 환산해 볼 수 있는 자료입니다.
정확한 계산법이 아닌 추정치임을 참고하시기 바랍니다.

| Listening Comprehension | | Reading Comprehension | |
|---|---|---|---|
| 정답 개수 | 환산점수 | 정답 개수 | 환산점수 |
| 96-100 | 470-495 | 96-100 | 470-495 |
| 91-95 | 440-470 | 91-95 | 450-470 |
| 86-90 | 410-440 | 86-90 | 420-450 |
| 81-85 | 370-410 | 81-85 | 380-420 |
| 76-80 | 340-370 | 76-80 | 350-380 |
| 71-75 | 310-340 | 71-75 | 330-350 |
| 66-70 | 280-310 | 66-70 | 300-330 |
| 61-65 | 250-280 | 61-65 | 270-300 |
| 56-60 | 230-250 | 56-60 | 240-270 |
| 51-55 | 200-230 | 51-55 | 210-240 |
| 46-50 | 170-200 | 46-50 | 190-210 |
| 41-45 | 150-170 | 41-45 | 170-190 |
| 36-40 | 120-150 | 36-40 | 140-170 |
| 31-35 | 90-120 | 31-35 | 110-140 |
| 26-30 | 70-90 | 26-30 | 90-110 |
| 21-25 | 40-70 | 21-25 | 70-90 |
| 16-20 | 30-40 | 16-20 | 50-70 |
| 11-15 | 10-30 | 11-15 | 30-50 |
| 6-10 | 5-10 | 6-10 | 10-30 |
| 1-5 | 5 | 1-5 | 0 |
| 0 | 5 | 0 | 0 |

# Actual Test 01

## LISTENING (Part I ~ IV)

| NO. | ANSWER | NO. | ANSWER | NO. | ANSWER | NO. | ANSWER | NO. | ANSWER |
|-----|--------|-----|--------|-----|--------|-----|--------|-----|--------|
|  | A B C D |  | A B C D |  | A B C D |  | A B C D |  | A B C D |
| 1 | a b c d | 21 | a b c d | 41 | a b c d | 61 | a b c d | 81 | a b c d |
| 2 | a b c d | 22 | a b c d | 42 | a b c d | 62 | a b c d | 82 | a b c d |
| 3 | a b c d | 23 | a b c d | 43 | a b c d | 63 | a b c d | 83 | a b c d |
| 4 | a b c d | 24 | a b c d | 44 | a b c d | 64 | a b c d | 84 | a b c d |
| 5 | a b c d | 25 | a b c d | 45 | a b c d | 65 | a b c d | 85 | a b c d |
| 6 | a b c d | 26 | a b c d | 46 | a b c d | 66 | a b c d | 86 | a b c d |
| 7 | a b c d | 27 | a b c d | 47 | a b c d | 67 | a b c d | 87 | a b c d |
| 8 | a b c d | 28 | a b c d | 48 | a b c d | 68 | a b c d | 88 | a b c d |
| 9 | a b c d | 29 | a b c d | 49 | a b c d | 69 | a b c d | 89 | a b c d |
| 10 | a b c d | 30 | a b c d | 50 | a b c d | 70 | a b c d | 90 | a b c d |
| 11 | a b c d | 31 | a b c d | 51 | a b c d | 71 | a b c d | 91 | a b c d |
| 12 | a b c d | 32 | a b c d | 52 | a b c d | 72 | a b c d | 92 | a b c d |
| 13 | a b c d | 33 | a b c d | 53 | a b c d | 73 | a b c d | 93 | a b c d |
| 14 | a b c d | 34 | a b c d | 54 | a b c d | 74 | a b c d | 94 | a b c d |
| 15 | a b c d | 35 | a b c d | 55 | a b c d | 75 | a b c d | 95 | a b c d |
| 16 | a b c d | 36 | a b c d | 56 | a b c d | 76 | a b c d | 96 | a b c d |
| 17 | a b c d | 37 | a b c d | 57 | a b c d | 77 | a b c d | 97 | a b c d |
| 18 | a b c d | 38 | a b c d | 58 | a b c d | 78 | a b c d | 98 | a b c d |
| 19 | a b c d | 39 | a b c d | 59 | a b c d | 79 | a b c d | 99 | a b c d |
| 20 | a b c d | 40 | a b c d | 60 | a b c d | 80 | a b c d | 100 | a b c d |

## READING (Part V ~ VII)

| NO. | ANSWER | NO. | ANSWER | NO. | ANSWER | NO. | ANSWER | NO. | ANSWER |
|-----|--------|-----|--------|-----|--------|-----|--------|-----|--------|
|  | A B C D |  | A B C D |  | A B C D |  | A B C D |  | A B C D |
| 101 | a b c d | 121 | a b c d | 141 | a b c d | 161 | a b c d | 181 | a b c d |
| 102 | a b c d | 122 | a b c d | 142 | a b c d | 162 | a b c d | 182 | a b c d |
| 103 | a b c d | 123 | a b c d | 143 | a b c d | 163 | a b c d | 183 | a b c d |
| 104 | a b c d | 124 | a b c d | 144 | a b c d | 164 | a b c d | 184 | a b c d |
| 105 | a b c d | 125 | a b c d | 145 | a b c d | 165 | a b c d | 185 | a b c d |
| 106 | a b c d | 126 | a b c d | 146 | a b c d | 166 | a b c d | 186 | a b c d |
| 107 | a b c d | 127 | a b c d | 147 | a b c d | 167 | a b c d | 187 | a b c d |
| 108 | a b c d | 128 | a b c d | 148 | a b c d | 168 | a b c d | 188 | a b c d |
| 109 | a b c d | 129 | a b c d | 149 | a b c d | 169 | a b c d | 189 | a b c d |
| 110 | a b c d | 130 | a b c d | 150 | a b c d | 170 | a b c d | 190 | a b c d |
| 111 | a b c d | 131 | a b c d | 151 | a b c d | 171 | a b c d | 191 | a b c d |
| 112 | a b c d | 132 | a b c d | 152 | a b c d | 172 | a b c d | 192 | a b c d |
| 113 | a b c d | 133 | a b c d | 153 | a b c d | 173 | a b c d | 193 | a b c d |
| 114 | a b c d | 134 | a b c d | 154 | a b c d | 174 | a b c d | 194 | a b c d |
| 115 | a b c d | 135 | a b c d | 155 | a b c d | 175 | a b c d | 195 | a b c d |
| 116 | a b c d | 136 | a b c d | 156 | a b c d | 176 | a b c d | 196 | a b c d |
| 117 | a b c d | 137 | a b c d | 157 | a b c d | 177 | a b c d | 197 | a b c d |
| 118 | a b c d | 138 | a b c d | 158 | a b c d | 178 | a b c d | 198 | a b c d |
| 119 | a b c d | 139 | a b c d | 159 | a b c d | 179 | a b c d | 199 | a b c d |
| 120 | a b c d | 140 | a b c d | 160 | a b c d | 180 | a b c d | 200 | a b c d |

# Actual Test 02

## LISTENING (Part I ~ IV)

| NO. | ANSWER | NO. | ANSWER | NO. | ANSWER | NO. | ANSWER | NO. | ANSWER |
|---|---|---|---|---|---|---|---|---|---|
| | A B C D | | A B C D | | A B C D | | A B C D | | A B C D |
| 1 | a b c d | 21 | a b c | 41 | a b c d | 61 | a b c d | 81 | a b c d |
| 2 | a b c d | 22 | a b c | 42 | a b c d | 62 | a b c d | 82 | a b c d |
| 3 | a b c d | 23 | a b c | 43 | a b c d | 63 | a b c d | 83 | a b c d |
| 4 | a b c | 24 | a b c | 44 | a b c d | 64 | a b c d | 84 | a b c d |
| 5 | a b c | 25 | a b c | 45 | a b c d | 65 | a b c d | 85 | a b c d |
| 6 | a b c | 26 | a b c | 46 | a b c d | 66 | a b c d | 86 | a b c d |
| 7 | a b c | 27 | a b c | 47 | a b c d | 67 | a b c d | 87 | a b c d |
| 8 | a b c | 28 | a b c | 48 | a b c d | 68 | a b c d | 88 | a b c d |
| 9 | a b c | 29 | a b c | 49 | a b c d | 69 | a b c d | 89 | a b c d |
| 10 | a b c | 30 | a b c | 50 | a b c d | 70 | a b c d | 90 | a b c d |
| 11 | a b c | 31 | a b c | 51 | a b c d | 71 | a b c d | 91 | a b c d |
| 12 | a b c | 32 | a b c | 52 | a b c d | 72 | a b c d | 92 | a b c d |
| 13 | a b c | 33 | a b c | 53 | a b c d | 73 | a b c d | 93 | a b c d |
| 14 | a b c | 34 | a b c | 54 | a b c d | 74 | a b c d | 94 | a b c d |
| 15 | a b c | 35 | a b c | 55 | a b c d | 75 | a b c d | 95 | a b c d |
| 16 | a b c | 36 | a b c | 56 | a b c d | 76 | a b c d | 96 | a b c d |
| 17 | a b c | 37 | a b c | 57 | a b c d | 77 | a b c d | 97 | a b c d |
| 18 | a b c | 38 | a b c | 58 | a b c d | 78 | a b c d | 98 | a b c d |
| 19 | a b c | 39 | a b c | 59 | a b c d | 79 | a b c d | 99 | a b c d |
| 20 | a b c | 40 | a b c | 60 | a b c d | 80 | a b c d | 100 | a b c d |

## READING (Part V ~ VII)

| NO. | ANSWER | NO. | ANSWER | NO. | ANSWER | NO. | ANSWER | NO. | ANSWER |
|---|---|---|---|---|---|---|---|---|---|
| | A B C D | | A B C D | | A B C D | | A B C D | | A B C D |
| 101 | a b c d | 121 | a b c d | 141 | a b c d | 161 | a b c d | 181 | a b c d |
| 102 | a b c d | 122 | a b c d | 142 | a b c d | 162 | a b c d | 182 | a b c d |
| 103 | a b c d | 123 | a b c d | 143 | a b c d | 163 | a b c d | 183 | a b c d |
| 104 | a b c d | 124 | a b c d | 144 | a b c d | 164 | a b c d | 184 | a b c d |
| 105 | a b c d | 125 | a b c d | 145 | a b c d | 165 | a b c d | 185 | a b c d |
| 106 | a b c d | 126 | a b c d | 146 | a b c d | 166 | a b c d | 186 | a b c d |
| 107 | a b c d | 127 | a b c d | 147 | a b c d | 167 | a b c d | 187 | a b c d |
| 108 | a b c d | 128 | a b c d | 148 | a b c d | 168 | a b c d | 188 | a b c d |
| 109 | a b c d | 129 | a b c d | 149 | a b c d | 169 | a b c d | 189 | a b c d |
| 110 | a b c d | 130 | a b c d | 150 | a b c d | 170 | a b c d | 190 | a b c d |
| 111 | a b c d | 131 | a b c d | 151 | a b c d | 171 | a b c d | 191 | a b c d |
| 112 | a b c d | 132 | a b c d | 152 | a b c d | 172 | a b c d | 192 | a b c d |
| 113 | a b c d | 133 | a b c d | 153 | a b c d | 173 | a b c d | 193 | a b c d |
| 114 | a b c d | 134 | a b c d | 154 | a b c d | 174 | a b c d | 194 | a b c d |
| 115 | a b c d | 135 | a b c d | 155 | a b c d | 175 | a b c d | 195 | a b c d |
| 116 | a b c d | 136 | a b c d | 156 | a b c d | 176 | a b c d | 196 | a b c d |
| 117 | a b c d | 137 | a b c d | 157 | a b c d | 177 | a b c d | 197 | a b c d |
| 118 | a b c d | 138 | a b c d | 158 | a b c d | 178 | a b c d | 198 | a b c d |
| 119 | a b c d | 139 | a b c d | 159 | a b c d | 179 | a b c d | 199 | a b c d |
| 120 | a b c d | 140 | a b c d | 160 | a b c d | 180 | a b c d | 200 | a b c d |

# Actual Test 03

## LISTENING (Part I ~ IV)

| NO. | ANSWER A B C D | NO. | ANSWER A B C D | NO. | ANSWER A B C D | NO. | ANSWER A B C D | NO. | ANSWER A B C D |
|---|---|---|---|---|---|---|---|---|---|
| 1 | ⓐ ⓑ ⓒ ⓓ | 21 | ⓐ ⓑ ⓒ ⓓ | 41 | ⓐ ⓑ ⓒ ⓓ | 61 | ⓐ ⓑ ⓒ ⓓ | 81 | ⓐ ⓑ ⓒ ⓓ |
| 2 | ⓐ ⓑ ⓒ ⓓ | 22 | ⓐ ⓑ ⓒ ⓓ | 42 | ⓐ ⓑ ⓒ ⓓ | 62 | ⓐ ⓑ ⓒ ⓓ | 82 | ⓐ ⓑ ⓒ ⓓ |
| 3 | ⓐ ⓑ ⓒ ⓓ | 23 | ⓐ ⓑ ⓒ ⓓ | 43 | ⓐ ⓑ ⓒ ⓓ | 63 | ⓐ ⓑ ⓒ ⓓ | 83 | ⓐ ⓑ ⓒ ⓓ |
| 4 | ⓐ ⓑ ⓒ ⓓ | 24 | ⓐ ⓑ ⓒ ⓓ | 44 | ⓐ ⓑ ⓒ ⓓ | 64 | ⓐ ⓑ ⓒ ⓓ | 84 | ⓐ ⓑ ⓒ ⓓ |
| 5 | ⓐ ⓑ ⓒ ⓓ | 25 | ⓐ ⓑ ⓒ | 45 | ⓐ ⓑ ⓒ ⓓ | 65 | ⓐ ⓑ ⓒ ⓓ | 85 | ⓐ ⓑ ⓒ ⓓ |
| 6 | ⓐ ⓑ ⓒ ⓓ | 26 | ⓐ ⓑ ⓒ | 46 | ⓐ ⓑ ⓒ ⓓ | 66 | ⓐ ⓑ ⓒ ⓓ | 86 | ⓐ ⓑ ⓒ ⓓ |
| 7 | ⓐ ⓑ ⓒ | 27 | ⓐ ⓑ ⓒ | 47 | ⓐ ⓑ ⓒ ⓓ | 67 | ⓐ ⓑ ⓒ ⓓ | 87 | ⓐ ⓑ ⓒ ⓓ |
| 8 | ⓐ ⓑ ⓒ | 28 | ⓐ ⓑ ⓒ | 48 | ⓐ ⓑ ⓒ ⓓ | 68 | ⓐ ⓑ ⓒ ⓓ | 88 | ⓐ ⓑ ⓒ ⓓ |
| 9 | ⓐ ⓑ ⓒ | 29 | ⓐ ⓑ ⓒ | 49 | ⓐ ⓑ ⓒ ⓓ | 69 | ⓐ ⓑ ⓒ ⓓ | 89 | ⓐ ⓑ ⓒ ⓓ |
| 10 | ⓐ ⓑ ⓒ | 30 | ⓐ ⓑ ⓒ ⓓ | 50 | ⓐ ⓑ ⓒ ⓓ | 70 | ⓐ ⓑ ⓒ ⓓ | 90 | ⓐ ⓑ ⓒ ⓓ |
| 11 | ⓐ ⓑ ⓒ | 31 | ⓐ ⓑ ⓒ ⓓ | 51 | ⓐ ⓑ ⓒ ⓓ | 71 | ⓐ ⓑ ⓒ ⓓ | 91 | ⓐ ⓑ ⓒ ⓓ |
| 12 | ⓐ ⓑ ⓒ | 32 | ⓐ ⓑ ⓒ ⓓ | 52 | ⓐ ⓑ ⓒ ⓓ | 72 | ⓐ ⓑ ⓒ ⓓ | 92 | ⓐ ⓑ ⓒ ⓓ |
| 13 | ⓐ ⓑ ⓒ | 33 | ⓐ ⓑ ⓒ ⓓ | 53 | ⓐ ⓑ ⓒ ⓓ | 73 | ⓐ ⓑ ⓒ ⓓ | 93 | ⓐ ⓑ ⓒ ⓓ |
| 14 | ⓐ ⓑ ⓒ | 34 | ⓐ ⓑ ⓒ ⓓ | 54 | ⓐ ⓑ ⓒ ⓓ | 74 | ⓐ ⓑ ⓒ ⓓ | 94 | ⓐ ⓑ ⓒ ⓓ |
| 15 | ⓐ ⓑ ⓒ | 35 | ⓐ ⓑ ⓒ ⓓ | 55 | ⓐ ⓑ ⓒ ⓓ | 75 | ⓐ ⓑ ⓒ ⓓ | 95 | ⓐ ⓑ ⓒ ⓓ |
| 16 | ⓐ ⓑ ⓒ | 36 | ⓐ ⓑ ⓒ ⓓ | 56 | ⓐ ⓑ ⓒ ⓓ | 76 | ⓐ ⓑ ⓒ ⓓ | 96 | ⓐ ⓑ ⓒ ⓓ |
| 17 | ⓐ ⓑ ⓒ | 37 | ⓐ ⓑ ⓒ ⓓ | 57 | ⓐ ⓑ ⓒ ⓓ | 77 | ⓐ ⓑ ⓒ ⓓ | 97 | ⓐ ⓑ ⓒ ⓓ |
| 18 | ⓐ ⓑ ⓒ | 38 | ⓐ ⓑ ⓒ ⓓ | 58 | ⓐ ⓑ ⓒ ⓓ | 78 | ⓐ ⓑ ⓒ ⓓ | 98 | ⓐ ⓑ ⓒ ⓓ |
| 19 | ⓐ ⓑ ⓒ | 39 | ⓐ ⓑ ⓒ ⓓ | 59 | ⓐ ⓑ ⓒ ⓓ | 79 | ⓐ ⓑ ⓒ ⓓ | 99 | ⓐ ⓑ ⓒ ⓓ |
| 20 | ⓐ ⓑ ⓒ | 40 | ⓐ ⓑ ⓒ ⓓ | 60 | ⓐ ⓑ ⓒ ⓓ | 80 | ⓐ ⓑ ⓒ ⓓ | 100 | ⓐ ⓑ ⓒ ⓓ |

## READING (Part V ~ VII)

| NO. | ANSWER A B C D | NO. | ANSWER A B C D | NO. | ANSWER A B C D | NO. | ANSWER A B C D | NO. | ANSWER A B C D |
|---|---|---|---|---|---|---|---|---|---|
| 101 | ⓐ ⓑ ⓒ ⓓ | 121 | ⓐ ⓑ ⓒ ⓓ | 141 | ⓐ ⓑ ⓒ ⓓ | 161 | ⓐ ⓑ ⓒ ⓓ | 181 | ⓐ ⓑ ⓒ ⓓ |
| 102 | ⓐ ⓑ ⓒ ⓓ | 122 | ⓐ ⓑ ⓒ ⓓ | 142 | ⓐ ⓑ ⓒ ⓓ | 162 | ⓐ ⓑ ⓒ ⓓ | 182 | ⓐ ⓑ ⓒ ⓓ |
| 103 | ⓐ ⓑ ⓒ ⓓ | 123 | ⓐ ⓑ ⓒ ⓓ | 143 | ⓐ ⓑ ⓒ ⓓ | 163 | ⓐ ⓑ ⓒ ⓓ | 183 | ⓐ ⓑ ⓒ ⓓ |
| 104 | ⓐ ⓑ ⓒ ⓓ | 124 | ⓐ ⓑ ⓒ ⓓ | 144 | ⓐ ⓑ ⓒ ⓓ | 164 | ⓐ ⓑ ⓒ ⓓ | 184 | ⓐ ⓑ ⓒ ⓓ |
| 105 | ⓐ ⓑ ⓒ ⓓ | 125 | ⓐ ⓑ ⓒ ⓓ | 145 | ⓐ ⓑ ⓒ ⓓ | 165 | ⓐ ⓑ ⓒ ⓓ | 185 | ⓐ ⓑ ⓒ ⓓ |
| 106 | ⓐ ⓑ ⓒ ⓓ | 126 | ⓐ ⓑ ⓒ ⓓ | 146 | ⓐ ⓑ ⓒ ⓓ | 166 | ⓐ ⓑ ⓒ ⓓ | 186 | ⓐ ⓑ ⓒ ⓓ |
| 107 | ⓐ ⓑ ⓒ ⓓ | 127 | ⓐ ⓑ ⓒ ⓓ | 147 | ⓐ ⓑ ⓒ ⓓ | 167 | ⓐ ⓑ ⓒ ⓓ | 187 | ⓐ ⓑ ⓒ ⓓ |
| 108 | ⓐ ⓑ ⓒ ⓓ | 128 | ⓐ ⓑ ⓒ ⓓ | 148 | ⓐ ⓑ ⓒ ⓓ | 168 | ⓐ ⓑ ⓒ ⓓ | 188 | ⓐ ⓑ ⓒ ⓓ |
| 109 | ⓐ ⓑ ⓒ ⓓ | 129 | ⓐ ⓑ ⓒ ⓓ | 149 | ⓐ ⓑ ⓒ ⓓ | 169 | ⓐ ⓑ ⓒ ⓓ | 189 | ⓐ ⓑ ⓒ ⓓ |
| 110 | ⓐ ⓑ ⓒ ⓓ | 130 | ⓐ ⓑ ⓒ ⓓ | 150 | ⓐ ⓑ ⓒ ⓓ | 170 | ⓐ ⓑ ⓒ ⓓ | 190 | ⓐ ⓑ ⓒ ⓓ |
| 111 | ⓐ ⓑ ⓒ ⓓ | 131 | ⓐ ⓑ ⓒ ⓓ | 151 | ⓐ ⓑ ⓒ ⓓ | 171 | ⓐ ⓑ ⓒ ⓓ | 191 | ⓐ ⓑ ⓒ ⓓ |
| 112 | ⓐ ⓑ ⓒ ⓓ | 132 | ⓐ ⓑ ⓒ ⓓ | 152 | ⓐ ⓑ ⓒ ⓓ | 172 | ⓐ ⓑ ⓒ ⓓ | 192 | ⓐ ⓑ ⓒ ⓓ |
| 113 | ⓐ ⓑ ⓒ ⓓ | 133 | ⓐ ⓑ ⓒ ⓓ | 153 | ⓐ ⓑ ⓒ ⓓ | 173 | ⓐ ⓑ ⓒ ⓓ | 193 | ⓐ ⓑ ⓒ ⓓ |
| 114 | ⓐ ⓑ ⓒ ⓓ | 134 | ⓐ ⓑ ⓒ ⓓ | 154 | ⓐ ⓑ ⓒ ⓓ | 174 | ⓐ ⓑ ⓒ ⓓ | 194 | ⓐ ⓑ ⓒ ⓓ |
| 115 | ⓐ ⓑ ⓒ ⓓ | 135 | ⓐ ⓑ ⓒ ⓓ | 155 | ⓐ ⓑ ⓒ ⓓ | 175 | ⓐ ⓑ ⓒ ⓓ | 195 | ⓐ ⓑ ⓒ ⓓ |
| 116 | ⓐ ⓑ ⓒ ⓓ | 136 | ⓐ ⓑ ⓒ ⓓ | 156 | ⓐ ⓑ ⓒ ⓓ | 176 | ⓐ ⓑ ⓒ ⓓ | 196 | ⓐ ⓑ ⓒ ⓓ |
| 117 | ⓐ ⓑ ⓒ ⓓ | 137 | ⓐ ⓑ ⓒ ⓓ | 157 | ⓐ ⓑ ⓒ ⓓ | 177 | ⓐ ⓑ ⓒ ⓓ | 197 | ⓐ ⓑ ⓒ ⓓ |
| 118 | ⓐ ⓑ ⓒ ⓓ | 138 | ⓐ ⓑ ⓒ ⓓ | 158 | ⓐ ⓑ ⓒ ⓓ | 178 | ⓐ ⓑ ⓒ ⓓ | 198 | ⓐ ⓑ ⓒ ⓓ |
| 119 | ⓐ ⓑ ⓒ ⓓ | 139 | ⓐ ⓑ ⓒ ⓓ | 159 | ⓐ ⓑ ⓒ ⓓ | 179 | ⓐ ⓑ ⓒ ⓓ | 199 | ⓐ ⓑ ⓒ ⓓ |
| 120 | ⓐ ⓑ ⓒ ⓓ | 140 | ⓐ ⓑ ⓒ ⓓ | 160 | ⓐ ⓑ ⓒ ⓓ | 180 | ⓐ ⓑ ⓒ ⓓ | 200 | ⓐ ⓑ ⓒ ⓓ |

# Actual Test 04

## LISTENING (Part I ~ IV)

## READING (Part V ~ VII)

# Actual Test 05

## LISTENING (Part I ~ IV)

| NO. | ANSWER A B C D | NO. | ANSWER A B C D | NO. | ANSWER A B C D | NO. | ANSWER A B C D | NO. | ANSWER A B C D |
|---|---|---|---|---|---|---|---|---|---|
| 1 | ⓐ ⓑ ⓒ | 21 | ⓐ ⓑ ⓒ ⓓ | 41 | ⓐ ⓑ ⓒ ⓓ | 61 | ⓐ ⓑ ⓒ ⓓ | 81 | ⓐ ⓑ ⓒ ⓓ |
| 2 | ⓐ ⓑ ⓒ | 22 | ⓐ ⓑ ⓒ ⓓ | 42 | ⓐ ⓑ ⓒ ⓓ | 62 | ⓐ ⓑ ⓒ ⓓ | 82 | ⓐ ⓑ ⓒ ⓓ |
| 3 | ⓐ ⓑ ⓒ | 23 | ⓐ ⓑ ⓒ ⓓ | 43 | ⓐ ⓑ ⓒ ⓓ | 63 | ⓐ ⓑ ⓒ ⓓ | 83 | ⓐ ⓑ ⓒ ⓓ |
| 4 | ⓐ ⓑ ⓒ | 24 | ⓐ ⓑ ⓒ ⓓ | 44 | ⓐ ⓑ ⓒ ⓓ | 64 | ⓐ ⓑ ⓒ ⓓ | 84 | ⓐ ⓑ ⓒ ⓓ |
| 5 | ⓐ ⓑ ⓒ | 25 | ⓐ ⓑ ⓒ ⓓ | 45 | ⓐ ⓑ ⓒ ⓓ | 65 | ⓐ ⓑ ⓒ ⓓ | 85 | ⓐ ⓑ ⓒ ⓓ |
| 6 | ⓐ ⓑ ⓒ | 26 | ⓐ ⓑ ⓒ ⓓ | 46 | ⓐ ⓑ ⓒ ⓓ | 66 | ⓐ ⓑ ⓒ ⓓ | 86 | ⓐ ⓑ ⓒ ⓓ |
| 7 | ⓐ ⓑ ⓒ | 27 | ⓐ ⓑ ⓒ ⓓ | 47 | ⓐ ⓑ ⓒ ⓓ | 67 | ⓐ ⓑ ⓒ ⓓ | 87 | ⓐ ⓑ ⓒ ⓓ |
| 8 | ⓐ ⓑ ⓒ | 28 | ⓐ ⓑ ⓒ ⓓ | 48 | ⓐ ⓑ ⓒ ⓓ | 68 | ⓐ ⓑ ⓒ ⓓ | 88 | ⓐ ⓑ ⓒ ⓓ |
| 9 | ⓐ ⓑ ⓒ | 29 | ⓐ ⓑ ⓒ ⓓ | 49 | ⓐ ⓑ ⓒ ⓓ | 69 | ⓐ ⓑ ⓒ ⓓ | 89 | ⓐ ⓑ ⓒ ⓓ |
| 10 | ⓐ ⓑ ⓒ | 30 | ⓐ ⓑ ⓒ ⓓ | 50 | ⓐ ⓑ ⓒ ⓓ | 70 | ⓐ ⓑ ⓒ ⓓ | 90 | ⓐ ⓑ ⓒ ⓓ |
| 11 | ⓐ ⓑ ⓒ | 31 | ⓐ ⓑ ⓒ ⓓ | 51 | ⓐ ⓑ ⓒ ⓓ | 71 | ⓐ ⓑ ⓒ ⓓ | 91 | ⓐ ⓑ ⓒ ⓓ |
| 12 | ⓐ ⓑ ⓒ | 32 | ⓐ ⓑ ⓒ ⓓ | 52 | ⓐ ⓑ ⓒ ⓓ | 72 | ⓐ ⓑ ⓒ ⓓ | 92 | ⓐ ⓑ ⓒ ⓓ |
| 13 | ⓐ ⓑ ⓒ | 33 | ⓐ ⓑ ⓒ ⓓ | 53 | ⓐ ⓑ ⓒ ⓓ | 73 | ⓐ ⓑ ⓒ ⓓ | 93 | ⓐ ⓑ ⓒ ⓓ |
| 14 | ⓐ ⓑ ⓒ | 34 | ⓐ ⓑ ⓒ ⓓ | 54 | ⓐ ⓑ ⓒ ⓓ | 74 | ⓐ ⓑ ⓒ ⓓ | 94 | ⓐ ⓑ ⓒ ⓓ |
| 15 | ⓐ ⓑ ⓒ | 35 | ⓐ ⓑ ⓒ ⓓ | 55 | ⓐ ⓑ ⓒ ⓓ | 75 | ⓐ ⓑ ⓒ ⓓ | 95 | ⓐ ⓑ ⓒ ⓓ |
| 16 | ⓐ ⓑ ⓒ | 36 | ⓐ ⓑ ⓒ ⓓ | 56 | ⓐ ⓑ ⓒ ⓓ | 76 | ⓐ ⓑ ⓒ ⓓ | 96 | ⓐ ⓑ ⓒ ⓓ |
| 17 | ⓐ ⓑ ⓒ | 37 | ⓐ ⓑ ⓒ ⓓ | 57 | ⓐ ⓑ ⓒ ⓓ | 77 | ⓐ ⓑ ⓒ ⓓ | 97 | ⓐ ⓑ ⓒ ⓓ |
| 18 | ⓐ ⓑ ⓒ | 38 | ⓐ ⓑ ⓒ ⓓ | 58 | ⓐ ⓑ ⓒ ⓓ | 78 | ⓐ ⓑ ⓒ ⓓ | 98 | ⓐ ⓑ ⓒ ⓓ |
| 19 | ⓐ ⓑ ⓒ | 39 | ⓐ ⓑ ⓒ ⓓ | 59 | ⓐ ⓑ ⓒ ⓓ | 79 | ⓐ ⓑ ⓒ ⓓ | 99 | ⓐ ⓑ ⓒ ⓓ |
| 20 | ⓐ ⓑ ⓒ | 40 | ⓐ ⓑ ⓒ ⓓ | 60 | ⓐ ⓑ ⓒ ⓓ | 80 | ⓐ ⓑ ⓒ ⓓ | 100 | ⓐ ⓑ ⓒ ⓓ |

## READING (Part V ~ VII)

| NO. | ANSWER A B C D | NO. | ANSWER A B C D | NO. | ANSWER A B C D | NO. | ANSWER A B C D | NO. | ANSWER A B C D |
|---|---|---|---|---|---|---|---|---|---|
| 101 | ⓐ ⓑ ⓒ ⓓ | 121 | ⓐ ⓑ ⓒ ⓓ | 141 | ⓐ ⓑ ⓒ ⓓ | 161 | ⓐ ⓑ ⓒ ⓓ | 181 | ⓐ ⓑ ⓒ ⓓ |
| 102 | ⓐ ⓑ ⓒ ⓓ | 122 | ⓐ ⓑ ⓒ ⓓ | 142 | ⓐ ⓑ ⓒ ⓓ | 162 | ⓐ ⓑ ⓒ ⓓ | 182 | ⓐ ⓑ ⓒ ⓓ |
| 103 | ⓐ ⓑ ⓒ ⓓ | 123 | ⓐ ⓑ ⓒ ⓓ | 143 | ⓐ ⓑ ⓒ ⓓ | 163 | ⓐ ⓑ ⓒ ⓓ | 183 | ⓐ ⓑ ⓒ ⓓ |
| 104 | ⓐ ⓑ ⓒ ⓓ | 124 | ⓐ ⓑ ⓒ ⓓ | 144 | ⓐ ⓑ ⓒ ⓓ | 164 | ⓐ ⓑ ⓒ ⓓ | 184 | ⓐ ⓑ ⓒ ⓓ |
| 105 | ⓐ ⓑ ⓒ ⓓ | 125 | ⓐ ⓑ ⓒ ⓓ | 145 | ⓐ ⓑ ⓒ ⓓ | 165 | ⓐ ⓑ ⓒ ⓓ | 185 | ⓐ ⓑ ⓒ ⓓ |
| 106 | ⓐ ⓑ ⓒ ⓓ | 126 | ⓐ ⓑ ⓒ ⓓ | 146 | ⓐ ⓑ ⓒ ⓓ | 166 | ⓐ ⓑ ⓒ ⓓ | 186 | ⓐ ⓑ ⓒ ⓓ |
| 107 | ⓐ ⓑ ⓒ ⓓ | 127 | ⓐ ⓑ ⓒ ⓓ | 147 | ⓐ ⓑ ⓒ ⓓ | 167 | ⓐ ⓑ ⓒ ⓓ | 187 | ⓐ ⓑ ⓒ ⓓ |
| 108 | ⓐ ⓑ ⓒ ⓓ | 128 | ⓐ ⓑ ⓒ ⓓ | 148 | ⓐ ⓑ ⓒ ⓓ | 168 | ⓐ ⓑ ⓒ ⓓ | 188 | ⓐ ⓑ ⓒ ⓓ |
| 109 | ⓐ ⓑ ⓒ ⓓ | 129 | ⓐ ⓑ ⓒ ⓓ | 149 | ⓐ ⓑ ⓒ ⓓ | 169 | ⓐ ⓑ ⓒ ⓓ | 189 | ⓐ ⓑ ⓒ ⓓ |
| 110 | ⓐ ⓑ ⓒ ⓓ | 130 | ⓐ ⓑ ⓒ ⓓ | 150 | ⓐ ⓑ ⓒ ⓓ | 170 | ⓐ ⓑ ⓒ ⓓ | 190 | ⓐ ⓑ ⓒ ⓓ |
| 111 | ⓐ ⓑ ⓒ ⓓ | 131 | ⓐ ⓑ ⓒ ⓓ | 151 | ⓐ ⓑ ⓒ ⓓ | 171 | ⓐ ⓑ ⓒ ⓓ | 191 | ⓐ ⓑ ⓒ ⓓ |
| 112 | ⓐ ⓑ ⓒ ⓓ | 132 | ⓐ ⓑ ⓒ ⓓ | 152 | ⓐ ⓑ ⓒ ⓓ | 172 | ⓐ ⓑ ⓒ ⓓ | 192 | ⓐ ⓑ ⓒ ⓓ |
| 113 | ⓐ ⓑ ⓒ ⓓ | 133 | ⓐ ⓑ ⓒ ⓓ | 153 | ⓐ ⓑ ⓒ ⓓ | 173 | ⓐ ⓑ ⓒ ⓓ | 193 | ⓐ ⓑ ⓒ ⓓ |
| 114 | ⓐ ⓑ ⓒ ⓓ | 134 | ⓐ ⓑ ⓒ ⓓ | 154 | ⓐ ⓑ ⓒ ⓓ | 174 | ⓐ ⓑ ⓒ ⓓ | 194 | ⓐ ⓑ ⓒ ⓓ |
| 115 | ⓐ ⓑ ⓒ ⓓ | 135 | ⓐ ⓑ ⓒ ⓓ | 155 | ⓐ ⓑ ⓒ ⓓ | 175 | ⓐ ⓑ ⓒ ⓓ | 195 | ⓐ ⓑ ⓒ ⓓ |
| 116 | ⓐ ⓑ ⓒ ⓓ | 136 | ⓐ ⓑ ⓒ ⓓ | 156 | ⓐ ⓑ ⓒ ⓓ | 176 | ⓐ ⓑ ⓒ ⓓ | 196 | ⓐ ⓑ ⓒ ⓓ |
| 117 | ⓐ ⓑ ⓒ ⓓ | 137 | ⓐ ⓑ ⓒ ⓓ | 157 | ⓐ ⓑ ⓒ ⓓ | 177 | ⓐ ⓑ ⓒ ⓓ | 197 | ⓐ ⓑ ⓒ ⓓ |
| 118 | ⓐ ⓑ ⓒ ⓓ | 138 | ⓐ ⓑ ⓒ ⓓ | 158 | ⓐ ⓑ ⓒ ⓓ | 178 | ⓐ ⓑ ⓒ ⓓ | 198 | ⓐ ⓑ ⓒ ⓓ |
| 119 | ⓐ ⓑ ⓒ ⓓ | 139 | ⓐ ⓑ ⓒ ⓓ | 159 | ⓐ ⓑ ⓒ ⓓ | 179 | ⓐ ⓑ ⓒ ⓓ | 199 | ⓐ ⓑ ⓒ ⓓ |
| 120 | ⓐ ⓑ ⓒ ⓓ | 140 | ⓐ ⓑ ⓒ ⓓ | 160 | ⓐ ⓑ ⓒ ⓓ | 180 | ⓐ ⓑ ⓒ ⓓ | 200 | ⓐ ⓑ ⓒ ⓓ |

# 파트 5, 6 문제 중
# 이 책에서 비껴나가는 문제는 없다!

시험에 나오는 것만 공부한다!

시나공 토익

# 850
# 실전
# 모의고사

김병기 지음

문제집

Actual Test 06~10

**시나공 토익**

# 850 실전 모의고사

**초판 1쇄 발행** · 2020년 7월 10일
**초판 2쇄 발행** · 2021년 2월 10일

**지은이** · 김병기
**발행인** · 이종원
**발행처** · ㈜도서출판 길벗
**출판사 등록일** · 1990년 12월 24일
**주소** · 서울시 마포구 월드컵로 10길 56(서교동)
**대표전화** · 02) 332-0931 | **팩스** · 02) 322-6766
**홈페이지** · www.gilbut.co.kr | **이메일** · eztok@gilbut.co.kr

**기획 및 책임편집** · 고경환 (kkh@gilbut.co.kr) | **디자인** · 황애라 | **제작** · 이준호, 손일순, 이진혁
**영업마케팅** · 김학흥, 장봉석 | **웹마케팅** · 이수미, 최소영 | **영업관리** · 심선숙 | **독자지원** · 송혜란, 윤정아

**CTP 출력 및 인쇄** · 예림인쇄 | **제본** · 예림바인딩

ISBN 979-11-6521-213-1 03740
(이지톡 도서번호 300993)

정가 19,500원

· · · · · · · · · · · · · · · · · · · · · · · · · · · · · · · · · · · · · · · · · · · · · · · · · · · · · · ·

**독자의 1초까지 아껴주는 정성 길벗출판사**

**(주)도서출판 길벗** | IT실용, IT/일반 수험서, 경제경영, 취미실용, 인문교양(더퀘스트) www.gilbut.co.kr
**길벗이지톡** | 어학단행본, 어학수험서 www.eztok.co.kr
**길벗스쿨** | 국어학습, 수학학습, 어린이교양, 주니어 어학학습, 교과서 www.gilbutschool.co.kr

## 목차

＊자세한 해설을 확인하고 싶으시면 홈페이지에서 해설집을 다운로드하세요.(www.gilbut.co.kr)

# Actual Test

MP3 해설집

**120 min**

시작 시간 ___시 ___분

종료 시간 ___시 ___분

중간에 멈추지 말고 처음부터 끝까지 풀어보세요.
문제를 풀 때에는 실전처럼 답안지에 마킹하세요.

---

목표 개수 _____ / 200  실제 개수 _____ / 200

예상 점수는 번역 및 정답에 있는 점수 환산표를 참조하세요.

# LISTENING TEST

In the Listening test, you will be asked to demonstrate how well you understand spoken English. The entire Listening test will last approximately 45 minutes. There are four parts, and directions are given for each part. You must mark your answers on the separate answer sheet. Do not write your answers in your test book.

## PART 1

**Directions:** For each question in this part, you will hear four statements about a picture in your test book. When you hear the statements, you must select the one statement that best describes what you see in the picture. Then find the number of the question on your answer sheet and mark your answer. The statements will not be printed in your test book and will be spoken only one time.

Statement (B), "They are sitting at a table," is the best description of the picture. So you should select answer (B) and mark it on your answer sheet.

**1.**

**2.**

▶ ▶ ▶ GO ON TO THE NEXT PAGE

**3.**

**4.**

**5.**

**6.**

▶ ▶ ▶GO ON TO THE NEXT PAGE

## PART 2

**Directions:** You will hear a question or statement and three responses spoken in English. They will not be printed in your test book and will be spoken only one time. Select the best response to the question or statement and mark the letter (A), (B), or (C) on your answer sheet.

7. Mark your answer on your answer sheet.

8. Mark your answer on your answer sheet.

9. Mark your answer on your answer sheet.

10. Mark your answer on your answer sheet.

11. Mark your answer on your answer sheet.

12. Mark your answer on your answer sheet.

13. Mark your answer on your answer sheet.

14. Mark your answer on your answer sheet.

15. Mark your answer on your answer sheet.

16. Mark your answer on your answer sheet.

17. Mark your answer on your answer sheet.

18. Mark your answer on your answer sheet.

19. Mark your answer on your answer sheet.

20. Mark your answer on your answer sheet.

21. Mark your answer on your answer sheet.

22. Mark your answer on your answer sheet.

23. Mark your answer on your answer sheet.

24. Mark your answer on your answer sheet.

25. Mark your answer on your answer sheet.

26. Mark your answer on your answer sheet.

27. Mark your answer on your answer sheet.

28. Mark your answer on your answer sheet.

29. Mark your answer on your answer sheet.

30. Mark your answer on your answer sheet.

31. Mark your answer on your answer sheet.

# PART 3

**Directions:** You will hear some conversations between two or three people. You will be asked to answer three questions about what the speakers say in each conversation. Select the best response to each question and mark the letter (A), (B), (C), or (D) on your answer sheet. The conversations will not be printed in your test book and will be spoken only one time.

**32.** Why is the man calling?
(A) To apply for a job
(B) To advertise a special offer
(C) To get a tire changed
(D) To report an accident

**33.** Who most likely is the woman?
(A) A tour guide
(B) A radio reporter
(C) An auto dealer
(D) A customer service representative

**34.** What is the man concerned about?
(A) The cost of a service
(B) The changes in his schedule
(C) The size of his new office
(D) The availability of a technician

**35.** Where does the man work?
(A) At an investment firm
(B) At a landscaping company
(C) At a real estate agency
(D) At a government office

**36.** What is the woman concerned about?
(A) A location
(B) A price
(C) A loan rate
(D) A size

**37.** What will the speakers probably do in the afternoon?
(A) Visit a house
(B) Apply for a loan
(C) Start renovation works
(D) Sign a rental agreement

**38.** What are the speakers discussing?
(A) A missing document
(B) An internship program
(C) A technical problem
(D) A conference agenda

**39.** What does Mr. Murphy need to do before his meeting?
(A) Complete a report
(B) Train some interns
(C) Repair a server
(D) Prepare for a presentation

**40.** What does the woman offer to do?
(A) Send a repairperson
(B) Provide some data
(C) Deliver some samples
(D) Show him the location of a server

**41.** What does the man say he will do?
(A) Book a sightseeing tour
(B) Sell a property
(C) Move into a new apartment
(D) Perform a safety inspection

**42.** Who will be visiting the apartments?
(A) Real estate agents
(B) Safety inspectors
(C) Interior designers
(D) City developers

**43.** What does the woman suggest doing?
(A) Calling a neighbor
(B) Advertising some merchandise
(C) Speaking with a building owner
(D) Visiting her unit at a certain time

▶▶▶GO ON TO THE NEXT PAGE

44. What is the purpose of the man's visit?

(A) To paint a new office
(B) To sign a contract
(C) To do some repair work
(D) To perform a safety inspection

45. What did the woman do for the man?

(A) She interviewed job applicants.
(B) She moved some office furniture.
(C) She ordered some office supplies.
(D) She set up a meeting with a client.

46. What will the man do in about half an hour?

(A) Complete a repair
(B) Clean a new office
(C) Provide a cost estimate
(D) Discuss the terms of a contract

47. What type of business do the speakers own?

(A) An accounting firm
(B) A restaurant
(C) A consulting agency
(D) A food processing company

48. Why does the woman say, "We don't have enough management experience for that"?

(A) To object to hiring more employees
(B) To explain a decrease in profits
(C) To recommend taking a management course
(D) To express concern about a proposal

49. What does the man suggest doing?

(A) Creating new items for a menu
(B) Hiring a professional
(C) Requesting customer feedback
(D) Advising a new business

50. Why will some city council members go to Montreal?

(A) To review the budget plans for the next year
(B) To discuss the design of a new structure
(C) To do some sightseeing at several historic sites
(D) To attend the opening ceremony of a museum

51. Why was the man unable to make a reservation?

(A) The date of a meeting was not decided.
(B) He didn't know how many people would visit.
(C) The board didn't want to have lunch outside.
(D) Some restaurants were closed for renovations.

52. Why does the man recommend Hurricane?

(A) It offers special discounts.
(B) It is close to the company.
(C) It has a quiet atmosphere.
(D) It provides great Canadian dishes.

53. What are the speakers discussing?

(A) A new restaurant
(B) A city tour
(C) A radio show
(D) An advertising campaign

54. What is the man concerned about?

(A) Reserving a large table
(B) Completing an assignment on time
(C) Keeping costs within budget
(D) Finding the best route

55. What does the woman say she will do?

(A) Consult with a relative
(B) Write down some ideas
(C) Create an itinerary
(D) Change a schedule

**56.** Where most likely are the speakers?

(A) At a hotel
(B) At a bus terminal
(C) At an airport
(D) At a convention center

**57.** What does the woman say she will do?

(A) Go on a city tour
(B) Attend a meeting
(C) Write a contract
(D) Contact a client

**58.** Why does the man say, "There are several seats left on Air Atlas at 8:30 P.M."

(A) To provide a different option
(B) To cancel a flight ticket
(C) To urge the woman to hurry
(D) To decline an offer

**59.** What are the speakers mainly discussing?

(A) A package tour
(B) A major sale
(C) A damaged computer
(D) A new software demonstration

**60.** What does the man imply when he says, "I already did that a couple of hours ago"?

(A) He purchased a warranty.
(B) He completed his work earlier than expected.
(C) The woman's laptop computer has already been repaired.
(D) What the woman suggested didn't work.

**61.** What does the woman suggest the man do?

(A) Reschedule his business trip
(B) Visit her workplace
(C) Stay in a waiting area
(D) Speak to the store manager

## STAR BAY HOTEL

| BUILDING 1 | ROOM 1~100 |
| --- | --- |
| BUILDING 2 | ROOM 101~200 |
| BUILDING 3 | ROOM 201~300 |
| BUILDING 4 | ROOM 301~400 |

**62.** Who most likely are the speakers?

(A) Caterers
(B) Plumbers
(C) Front desk receptionists
(D) Housekeeping staff members

**63.** Look at the graphic. Where is the man currently working?

(A) In Building 1
(B) In Building 2
(C) In Building 3
(D) In Building 4

**64.** What are the speakers probably going to do next?

(A) Clean a bathroom
(B) Fold some towels
(C) Order some bedsheets
(D) Wash some dirty dishes

▶ ▶ ▶ GO ON TO THE NEXT PAGE

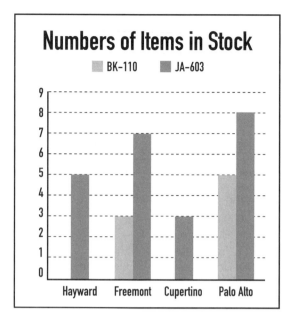

**Numbers of Items in Stock**

BK-110    JA-603

| Shop | Print Quality | Price per Page |
|---|---|---|
| Office King | Black & White | 4 cents |
| Kelly Print | Black & White | 5 cents |
| Copy Factory | Color | 7 cents |
| Komi Print Solutions | Color | 9 cents |

**65.** What does the woman want to know?

(A) The name of a new product
(B) The availability of an item
(C) The status of an order
(D) The location of a new store

**66.** According to the man, what is the problem?

(A) A shipment was sent to the wrong place by mistake.
(B) A certain product is not in the store's inventory.
(C) The release of a new product has been delayed.
(D) Tomorrow is expected to be a day with heavy rainfall.

**67.** Look at the graphic. Which location will the woman probably visit?

(A) Hayward
(B) Freemont
(C) Cupertino
(D) Palo Alto

**68.** What problem does the woman mention?

(A) Some employees were late for a meeting.
(B) Some office equipment is malfunctioning.
(C) Certain products cannot be exchanged.
(D) A special store promotion has ended.

**69.** What does the man say he did?

(A) Conducted an interview
(B) Copied some documents
(C) Set a sales record
(D) Contacted a repairperson

**70.** Look at the graphic. Which shop will the woman most likely choose?

(A) Office King
(B) Kelly Print
(C) Copy Factory
(D) Komi Print Solutions

**Directions:** You will hear some short talks given by a single speaker. You will be asked to answer three questions about what the speaker says in each short talk. Select the best response to each question and mark the letter (A), (B), (C), or (D) on your answer sheet. The talks will not be printed in your test book and will be spoken only one time.

71. Who is the message intended for?

    (A) Engineers
    (B) Visitors
    (C) Shoppers
    (D) Curators

72. What kind of procedures does the speaker provide?

    (A) Finding a particular building
    (B) Registering for membership
    (C) Using equipment on a tour
    (D) Buying items at a store

73. What should the listeners do if they need immediate assistance?

    (A) Use a device
    (B) Visit the admissions desk
    (C) Call another number
    (D) Speak with a supervisor

74. What is the radio show mainly about?
    (A) Finance
    (B) Health
    (C) Tourism
    (D) Technology

75. What type of business does Spencer Macintyre own?

    (A) A securities firm
    (B) A publishing company
    (C) An investment company
    (D) A software company

76. Why does the speaker say, "It is currently available at online and offline bookstores"?

    (A) To clarify a misunderstanding
    (B) To indicate that a book is not successful
    (C) To encourage the listeners to make a purchase
    (D) To express dissatisfaction with a decision

77. What is being announced?

    (A) A merger
    (B) An opening ceremony
    (C) An interest rate change
    (D) A new business travel policy

78. What will business travelers receive?

    (A) A list of cheap hotels
    (B) A company credit card
    (C) New traveler's checks
    (D) Full reimbursement

79. According to the speaker, what can be accessed on a Web site?

    (A) Fight schedules
    (B) Company policies
    (C) Bank locations
    (D) Approved hotel names

80. What will the speaker make a presentation about?

    (A) Sales strategies
    (B) Accounting procedures
    (C) Cost-reduction suggestions
    (D) Company health plans

81. According to the speaker, what changed?

    (A) A company logo
    (B) A presentation date
    (C) A production deadline
    (D) A conference venue

82. Why does the speaker say, "You know Stacy from Accounting, right?"

    (A) To confirm an appointment
    (B) To suggest a staffing change
    (C) To ask the listener to contact a colleague
    (D) To express concerns about an expense

▶ ▶ ▶GO ON TO THE NEXT PAGE

83. Who most likely is the speaker?

(A) A news reporter
(B) A radio host
(C) A professional chef
(D) A television actor

84. According to the speaker, what will Raymond Wilson talk about?

(A) His successful diet
(B) His research conclusions
(C) His academic career
(D) His theories on health

85. What does the speaker say Raymond Wilson will do next?

(A) Take a short break
(B) Play some music
(C) Go to a commercial break
(D) Answer the audience's questions

86. For whom is this message intended?

(A) A flight attendant
(B) A hotel concierge
(C) A delivery driver
(D) A passenger

87. What is the main purpose of the recorded message?

(A) To confirm a flight reservation
(B) To postpone an appointment
(C) To give notice of a shipment
(D) To return a defective item

88. What does the speaker suggest the listener do?

(A) Meet in person
(B) Visit an office
(C) Bring an original receipt
(D) Return a phone call

89. Where did William Carnegie work previously?

(A) At a film studio
(B) At a real estate agency
(C) At an accounting firm
(D) At a local college

90. What did William Carnegie do in college?

(A) He won a prestigious award.
(B) He was involved in acting.
(C) He founded his own company.
(D) He studied corporate finance.

91. According to the speaker, what will William Carnegie be responsible for?

(A) Directing some movies
(B) Running a theater company
(C) Teaching college students
(D) Managing funds

92. Where does the speaker most likely work?

(A) On a local farm
(B) At a sandwich shop
(C) At a restaurant
(D) At a trucking company

93. What problem does the speaker mention?

(A) A delivery truck broke down.
(B) Some machines are not working properly.
(C) Some employees called in sick.
(D) An order has not been delivered yet.

94. Why does the speaker say, "We open in just two hours"?

(A) To express dissatisfaction with a decision
(B) To remind employees of a deadline
(C) To explain the seriousness of a situation
(D) To ask a customer to return later

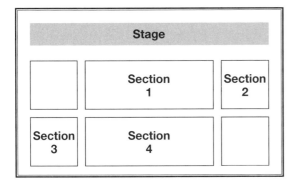

| | Stage | |
|---|---|---|
| | Section 1 | Section 2 |
| Section 3 | Section 4 | |

## Schedule for Training Sessions

Instructor: Mr. Chan Hong / Mechanical Engineer

| Training 1 | Monday | 10 A.M. - 11 A.M. |
|---|---|---|
| Training 2 | Tuesday | 2 P.M. - 3 P.M. |
| Training 3 | Wednesday | 2 P.M. - 3 P.M. |
| Training 4 | Thursday | 10 A.M. - 11 P.M. |

95. What is the speaker calling about?

(A) Making an appointment
(B) Extending an invitation
(C) Repairing some equipment
(D) Giving driving directions

96. Look at the graphic. Which section does the speaker have tickets for?

(A) Section 1
(B) Section 2
(C) Section 3
(D) Section 4

97. According to the speaker, who is Susan Kang?

(A) An actress
(B) An event planner
(C) A colleague
(D) A dancer

98. Who most likely is the speaker?

(A) A company spokesman
(B) A personnel manager
(C) A professional technician
(D) A plant manager

99. What are the listeners asked to do?

(A) Read an instruction manual
(B) Attend an information session
(C) Stop using a new machine
(D) Look at a new work schedule

100. Look at the graphic. When will the last session be?

(A) Monday
(B) Tuesday
(C) Wednesday
(D) Thursday

This is the end of the Listening test. Turn to Part 5 in your test book.

# READING TEST

In the Reading test, you will read a variety of texts and answer several different types of reading comprehension questions. The entire Reading test will last 75 minutes. There are three parts, and directions are given for each part. You are encouraged to answer as many questions as possible within the time allowed.

You must mark your answers on the separate answer sheet. Do not write your answers in your test book.

## PART 5

**Directions**: A word or phrase is missing in each of the sentences below. Four answer choices are given below each sentence. Select the best answer to complete the sentence. Then mark the letter (A), (B), (C), or (D) on your answer sheet.

**101.** Eugene Peters will meet with the chief executive officer ------- 3 P.M. this afternoon.

(A) on
(B) in
(C) at
(D) within

**102.** Sales of the new cold medicine will be ------- by the Food and Drug Administration until more tests are completed.

(A) expired
(B) delivered
(C) involved
(D) suspended

**103.** Delta Computer, which has the potential to become one of the fastest ------- companies in the computer industry, has struggled to attract foreign investment.

(A) demanding
(B) engaging
(C) distinguishing
(D) emerging

**104.** The merger of Mando Technology and Komi International is expected to be complete ------- the next two weeks.

(A) along
(B) until
(C) within
(D) about

**105.** ------- to *World Business* can be renewed online or with the automated telephone renewal service.

(A) Subscriptions
(B) Subscribers
(C) Subscribes
(D) Subscribed

**106.** If you have tires that are too ------- on a small vehicle, you may not feel comfortable while driving.

(A) width
(B) wide
(C) widen
(D) widely

**107.** Our goal is to provide every customer with full service and complete satisfaction, and we look forward to ------- you for many years to come.

(A) serve
(B) server
(C) serving
(D) served

**108.** For over a decade, jazz ------- both young and old have made 105.8 FM the place to be on the radio.

(A) enthusiasm
(B) enthusiasts
(C) enthusiastic
(D) enthusiastically

**109.** Mr. Kensington established ------- as one of the most competent biochemists in the world as he published six papers in *Bio World* last year alone.

(A) he
(B) his
(C) him
(D) himself

**110.** One of the greatest ------- of the social network system is that it offers instant access to the databases of plenty of libraries and educational institutions all over the world.

(A) profits
(B) flaws
(C) favors
(D) advantages

**111.** The revised regulations require that all customers ------- at least two forms of identification when opening a new checking account at a bank.

(A) supply
(B) supplies
(C) are supplied
(D) will supply

**112.** According to a newspaper report today, it is expected that the euro will fall to $1.28 ------- the next three weeks.

(A) into
(B) up to
(C) around
(D) over

**113.** Our Monday meetings are always held in the seminar room ------- otherwise indicated in the weekly schedule.

(A) before
(B) because
(C) despite
(D) unless

**114.** When ------- a customer service representative to ask questions, it would be better to have a list of them ready.

(A) call
(B) to call
(C) called
(D) calling

**115.** Customers are required to present a valid form of ------- to a teller when transferring a large sum of money from a bank.

(A) currency
(B) demonstration
(C) withdrawal
(D) identification

**116.** Several leading oil companies have been trying to gain access to the rights ------- crude oil in the oil fields in South America.

(A) produce
(B) production
(C) being produced
(D) to produce

**117.** ------- the state of the economy these days, most consumers cannot afford to buy expensive new products.

(A) If
(B) Given
(C) Considered
(D) Provided

**118.** Some stock brokerage companies have been reducing fees for trading stocks in order to ------- new customers.

(A) provide
(B) attract
(C) discover
(D) lose

**119.** Some stock analysts strongly suggested to ------- that they pull out of the project to develop the copper mine in Venezuela.

(A) invest
(B) investing
(C) investment
(D) investors

**120.** Transcent Telecom, which announced its plan to ------- with Ciao, Inc., the largest domestic software development company, will increase its influence in the telecommunication industry.

(A) acquire
(B) sell
(C) merge
(D) deal

▶ ▶ ▶ GO ON TO THE NEXT PAGE

121. The federal government has so far not tried to raise the retirement age ------- questions regarding the long-term adequacy of the national pension plan.

(A) nevertheless
(B) however
(C) although
(D) in spite of

122. Some economists expect that fuel -------, which have been stable for the past ten years, will likely soar next year.

(A) price
(B) priced
(C) prices
(D) pricing

123. Mr. Wilson ------- from jet lag since he came to London the day before the meeting with some important clients.

(A) suffer
(B) is suffered
(C) had suffered
(D) was suffering

124. The shutdown of the power plant was very ------- as the mechanical problems were repaired more quickly than expected.

(A) sure
(B) ready
(C) prompt
(D) brief

125. Drug prices have been rising at ------- an unprecedented rate that people are worried that the drugs they need will be beyond their ability to purchase.

(A) so
(B) too
(C) very
(D) such

126. Employees who wish to attend the upcoming seminar are required to register online by October 8, and then details ------- it will be e-mailed to them.

(A) pertaining to
(B) after
(C) related
(D) as soon as

127. ------- trivial the mistranslation of a passage in a contract may appear to be, it could lead to a lawsuit and the loss of money between the two companies.

(A) However
(B) Nevertheless
(C) Despite
(D) Although

128. It is very hard to determine ------- proposal will be more effective when implementing a new financial policy.

(A) whenever
(B) how
(C) whichever
(D) whose

129. ------- you require more information, please visit the Oxford Film Festival Web site at www.off.org and click on "Upcoming Events."

(A) Had
(B) Should
(C) Were
(D) Did

130. The financial manager rejected the new budget proposal to remodel the boardroom and chose ------- to make the spare room into a new employee lounge.

(A) so as
(B) exchangeably
(C) instead
(D) somewhere else

# PART 6

**Directions:** Read the texts that follow. A word, phrase, or sentence is missing in parts of each text. Four answer choices for each question are given below the text. Select the best answer to complete the text. Then mark the letter (A), (B), (C), or (D) on your answer sheet.

**Questions 131-134** refer to the following letter.

Dear Ms. Kim,

I am writing to let you know that the bicycle you inquired about is currently out of stock and can only be purchased with a special order. You can get your order ------- a week from today
**131.**
if you pay for express delivery service in advance.

Please reply to this letter or call me directly at 692-9815 at your earliest convenience and let me know ------- you still want to purchase the bicycle. If so, I will contact the manufacturer as
**132.**
quickly as possible. -------.
**133.**

I look forward to ------- from you.
**134.**

Yours truly,

Brandon Lee

131. (A) by
(B) over
(C) within
(D) between

132. (A) whether
(B) what
(C) even though
(D) since

133. (A) Some highly customized bicycles are specifically designed for touring.
(B) Then, you will be notified by e-mail when you can receive your dream bicycle.
(C) In this situation, bicyclists are usually concerned about the risk of accidents.
(D) The city will build new bicycle lanes to help its residents exercise.

134. (A) hear
(B) hearing
(C) being heard
(D) heard

▶ ▶ ▶ GO ON TO THE NEXT PAGE

To: Ethan McGowan <em@mimielectronics.com>
From: Wesley Park <wp@zenithtech.com>
Subject: Alternative Product Redress
Date: July 3

Dear Mr. McGowan,

We received the e-mail you sent yesterday to place an order for product Belden 192.

Unfortunately, the Belden 192 is no longer being manufactured, and we currently do not have

any belden 192 models available at any of ------- stores.
                                            **135.**

------- we would like to suggest our new model, the Belden 201, which basically has the
**136.**
same functions as the Belden 192, except for its sound quality, which is more advanced.

-------. Once you do that, we will change your order request and arrange a shipment of the
**137.**
Belden 201 right away. We will be awaiting your ------- of our offer.
                                                 **138.**

Sincerely yours,

Wesley Park

**135.** (A) your
(B) its
(C) their
(D) our

**136.** (A) Unfortunately
(B) Therefore
(C) In addition
(D) To make things worse

**137.** (A) Let us give you the details on the quality of sound that this model can produce.
(B) If this model sounds acceptable to you, please let us know.
(C) Please report any technical defects in the Belden 192 you purchased.
(D) It is an honor to produce the best audio system in collaboration with you.

**138.** (A) approval
(B) dedication
(C) favor
(D) advice

Mr. Thomas Lee
Komi Electronics
909 Sunhill Street
San Diego, CA 92110

Dear Mr. Lee,

We are pleased to ------- your order of November 23.
**139.**

------- because of an unexpected shortage of computer chips, the digital computer graphic
**140.**
card is out of stock, and we are unable to fill your order at this time.

We can provide a substitute product, called the ultimate computer graphic card, for you. It is

a minor upgraded version of the graphic card you are looking for, and there is no big

difference between them. Please let me know how you feel about ------- proposal.
**141.**

-------.
**142.**

Sincerely yours,

Kelly Ha
Head of Sales
Choff Electronics Outlet

---

**139.** (A) acknowledge
(B) place
(C) fulfill
(D) terminate

**140.** (A) Although
(B) However
(C) Thus
(D) In addition

**141.** (A) our
(B) its
(C) which
(D) one

**142.** (A) We will return your payment for this order.
(B) Thank you for giving us this opportunity to serve you.
(C) We look forward to serving you soon again.
(D) I am confident you will find it was worth waiting for.

SARA DESIGN FACTORY
Notice Number: 7399

**NOTICE OF POLICY CHANGES**

The Accounting Department has just finished ------- its new payroll software package, and
                                            **143.**
there are some changes we all need to be aware of.

From now on, all time sheets for the preceding calendar month need to be submitted by the

3rd of the month. -------. The use of regular vacation and personal leave is ------- to the
                  **144.**                                                    **145.**
personnel director's approval. Ideally, regular vacation and personal leave requests should be

made with at least ten days' notice.

Expense reports are also due on the 3rd of the month. Purchase orders may be submitted at

any time, but they ------- on Fridays.
                    **146.**

If you have any urgent requests or questions about the new time sheet system, please feel

free to talk to Ms. Ryan in the accounting office in person. Thank you for your cooperation in

advance.

John Wilson
Chief Executive Officer

---

**143.** (A) install
(B) installation
(C) installed
(D) installing

**144.** (A) Paychecks will now be issued on the
10th of each month.
(B) All employees are allowed to adjust
their work hours.
(C) We need to understand why we've
done our accounting the way we
have.
(D) Some experts are appropriately
handling our accounting troubles.

**145.** (A) subject
(B) ready
(C) entitled
(D) responsible

**146.** (A) process
(B) were processed
(C) are processing
(D) will be processed

## PART 7

**Directions:** In this part you will read a selection of texts, such as magazine and newspaper articles, e-mails, and instant messages. Each text or set of texts is followed by several questions. Select the best answer for each question and mark the letter (A), (B), (C), or (D) on your answer sheet.

**Questions 147-148** refer to the following message.

For the attention of: Peter Jones
Date: Friday, April 20, 2:35 P.M.
Caller: Adam Johnson
Business: The Woolshed Clothing Store
Phone number: 925-7399

Message:
Mr. Johnson from the Woolshed Clothing Store called to inquire about the location of his order. He claims that he ordered 500 sweaters from our company last Monday, but they have not yet been delivered to his store. He would like you to e-mail the order tracking number to him so that he can contact the delivery company. His e-mail address is A.Johnson@woolshed.net.

Message taken by: Barbara Lewis

**147.** Why did Mr. Johnson telephone Mr. Jones?

(A) To schedule a meeting
(B) To pay an invoice
(C) To make an inquiry about an order
(D) To check whether some sweaters are available

**148.** What did Mr. Johnson ask Mr. Jones to do?

(A) Send him some information by e-mail
(B) Fax him a copy of a contract
(C) Phone him at his home
(D) Send him a catalogue by post

# Get away from it all on one of our luxury cruises!

Caribbean Cruises Ltd. offers luxury family-oriented cruises at affordable prices for large families.

Our cruise packages include:
- A visit to 3 different Caribbean islands
- 7 days aboard our luxury cruise ship *The Princess*
- Free rental of scuba and snorkeling equipment
- Three hot meals served daily at our exclusive 4-star restaurant

Don't delay. Book your vacation today!

To make a reservation, please call 1-800-2992. Our sales staff is available to take your call from 9 A.M. to 5 P.M. from Monday to Saturday.

Earn a 10% special discount with our "Refer a Friend" program. You will receive a discount if your friend mentions your name when making a reservation!

**149.** What is NOT included in the cruise package?

(A) Seven days aboard a ship
(B) A free pass to the ship's movie theater
(C) Free use of diving equipment
(D) Free meals in the restaurant

**150.** What special offer does the advertisement mention?

(A) A $100 discount for booking online
(B) Free hotel pickup if a reservation is made before October 1
(C) A discount if a friend also makes a reservation
(D) A free souvenir T-shirt for every child on board the ship

**151.** On what day does the booking staff NOT take calls?

(A) Monday
(B) Tuesday
(C) Wednesday
(D) Sunday

**Questions 152-153** refer to the following text message chain.

**Debra Morgan** [2:28 P.M.]
Did you get the laundry delivered to the Memorial house?

**Arthur Mitchell** [2:30 P.M.]
I'm on my way now. Traffic is bad on this side of town.

**Debra Morgan** [2:31 P.M.]
The client called. He needs the delivery by 3 P.M.

**Arthur Mitchell** [2:32 P.M.]
I am sure that it will be there on time. Don't worry.

**Debra Morgan** [2:33 P.M.]
Can you take a different route?

**Arthur Mitchell** [2:33 P.M.]
No idea. I will check for the best route on my phone. I think there was a car accident.

**Debra Morgan** [2:34 P.M.]
Okay. Get there safely and quickly. And send a text message after you're done with the delivery.

**152.** What type of business does Mr. Mitchell work at?

(A) A shipping company
(B) A moving company
(C) A laundry service
(D) A law firm

**153.** At. 2:31 P.M. what does Ms. Morgan most likely mean when she writes, "He needs the delivery by 3 P.M."?

(A) She has plans for her golf game today.
(B) There are more deliveries to be done.
(D) She is angry about the car accident.
(D) The client needs the job done on time.

# Southshore Business News

Gaby Motor Co. expects record sales and profits for the second straight year. Spurred by a sales growth in North America and South Korea, along with the sales recovery in Europe, Gaby Motor Co. is the fastest growing automobile manufacturer in the world. In this fiscal year, which started April 1, Gaby expects minimum support from the weak dollar, but is confident in increasing sales volume, especially in its line of sports utility vehicles.

**154.** What does the article discuss?

(A) The expansion of the sports utility vehicle market

(B) The financial status of Gaby Motor Co.

(C) The advertising strategy of Gaby Motor Co.

(D) The sales predictions of Gaby Motor Co.

**155.** Which is NOT a factor that contributed to the increase in sales at Gaby Motor Co.?

(A) The revival of European markets

(B) The depreciation of the dollar

(C) Growing customer demand in South Korea

(D) Improved sales performance in North America

**Questions 156-157** refer to the advertisement.

# Summer Promotion

Starling Leisure Center
47 Bell Street
Miami, Florida
Phone: 404-466-0278

Take advantage of our discounted prices this summer.
Swimming and mini-golf: 50% off in July!
Enjoy lunch in our cafeteria, served from 1 PM.

Opening Hours
Monday to Friday: 09:30 AM – 6:00 PM
Saturday and Sunday 10.00 AM – 09:00 PM
Closed on public holidays.

**156.** What is the announcement for?

(A) A summer promotion at a leisure center
(B) Changes in a lunch menu
(C) The reopening of a store
(D) The dates of some public holidays

**157.** What is indicated about the Starling Leisure Center?

(A) It is famous throughout Florida.
(B) It opens later than usual on weekends.
(C) Lunch is served all day.
(D) Its prices have recently increased.

# New College Dormitory Complex
# For Hayward State University

### by Alicia Adams, Beat Reporter

June 27 - The new plans were finalized and the appropriate personnel put into place. Construction has started for the new college dormitory complex. A ceremony took place last Thursday at the intersection of Brompton Avenue and Route 20, where Hayward State University is building its new dormitory complex, Pioneers Lofts. Delilah Sorcarro, the president of Hayward State University, turned over the first shovelful of dirt at the site, located three miles north of the main campus. —[1]—.

Pioneers Lofts is a joint venture between the college, a public institution, and the Weingarten Group, a local property-development firm. It will consist of three large mixed-use buildings. —[2]—. The Weingarten Group will develop the site and manage the retail operations. "Until recently, most of our students have been commuters," Ms. Sorcarro said. "Now we are seeing a sharp increase in the number of applicants who request campus housing. —[3]—. The high-rise dormitory we built last spring has helped to some extent. But when this project is completed, we will be in a much better position to serve our students."

Daniel Ho, the Weingarten Group's city planner, told the university board that several retailers have already expressed interest in leasing space in the complex, including a number of clothing stores and health food outlets, and he has invited a large supermarket chain in the area to open a store. —[4]—. The complex and the campus will be connected by a scenic footpath.

---

**158.** Who is Ms. Sorcarro?

(A) A resident
(B) A property developer
(C) A college administrator
(D) A store owner

**159.** What business did the Weingarten Group invite to the new establishment?

(A) A construction firm
(B) A travel agency
(C) A private education institute
(D) A grocery store

**160.** In which of the positions marked [1], [2], [3], and [4] does the following sentence best belong?

"Each will have retail space at ground level and just above that, student apartments."

(A) [1]
(B) [2]
(C) [3]
(D) [4]

HARTVILLE (September 3) - The Hartville Transit Board would like to update residents on the current status of various infrastructure improvements that are taking place throughout the city, and their impact on commuting and foot traffic. "Please take note of the effect that many of these projects will have on the main commuter routes," says Gary Rondell, the chairman of the transit board.

Two lanes of the Dayton Valley Bridge have been closed for urgent repaving since August 29. Due to this closure, it is common for motorists to face delays of up to one hour during morning and evening rush hour. Additionally, the underground tunnel that crosses under 14th Avenue downtown is inaccessible due to construction work that will continue until mid-September. The Carson Avenue Bridge, just 100 meters further down 14th Avenue, serves as an alternative, safe pedestrian-crossing point until the tunnel construction is finished.

University lecturer Harold Blackley reported delays of at least 45 minutes during his daily commute between New Haven and Angler University in downtown Hartville. "Traffic on Wells Boulevard is often at a complete standstill," Mr. Blackley said. "These days, if I want to make it on time for my first class, I have no choice but to leave one hour earlier than I normally would." Chet Landry, a motorbike courier, has also encountered many problems. "At my job, things have to run smoothly so that my packages are delivered on time. Clients depend on me to deliver packages promptly, but that is increasingly difficult with all the street maintenance that is going on."

Mr. Rondell warns drivers to take increased care when traveling through busy road maintenance areas. "Motorists should try to remain patient and stay vigilant regarding the environment. There are many obstacles and a large number of road crew workers on the streets, and we don't want any unnecessary accidents to occur."

**161.** What is the purpose of the article?
(A) To encourage residents to make use of public transportation
(B) To outline a proposal for a citywide urban development project
(C) To describe the construction of a new commuter route to New Haven
(D) To inform local residents of the effects of ongoing maintenance

**162.** According to the article, where can pedestrians walk while the underground tunnel is closed?
(A) On the Dayton Valley Bridge
(B) On 14th Avenue
(C) On the Carson Avenue Bridge
(D) On Wells Boulevard

**163.** In paragraph 3, line 11, the word "run" is closest in meaning to
(A) send
(B) operate
(C) drive
(D) improve

**164.** What does the chairman of the transit board advise people to do?
(A) Leave for work earlier than usual
(B) Try to carpool with other people
(C) Exercise caution when driving
(D) Avoid using cars whenever possible

**Questions 165-168** refer to the following online chat discussion.

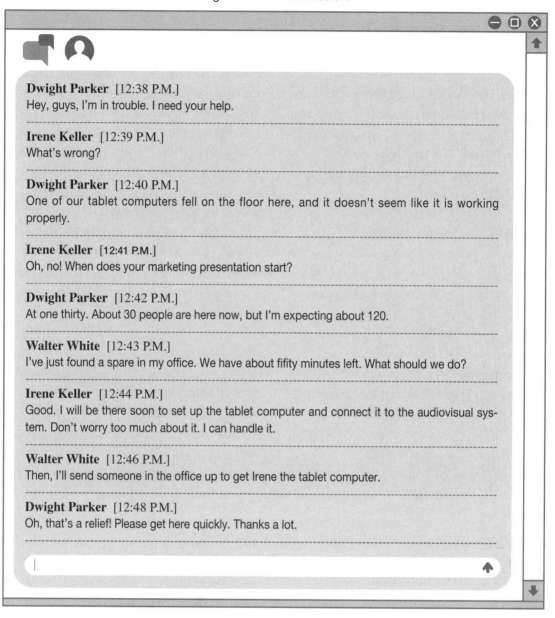

**Dwight Parker** [12:38 P.M.]
Hey, guys, I'm in trouble. I need your help.

**Irene Keller** [12:39 P.M.]
What's wrong?

**Dwight Parker** [12:40 P.M.]
One of our tablet computers fell on the floor here, and it doesn't seem like it is working properly.

**Irene Keller** [12:41 P.M.]
Oh, no! When does your marketing presentation start?

**Dwight Parker** [12:42 P.M.]
At one thirty. About 30 people are here now, but I'm expecting about 120.

**Walter White** [12:43 P.M.]
I've just found a spare in my office. We have about fifity minutes left. What should we do?

**Irene Keller** [12:44 P.M.]
Good. I will be there soon to set up the tablet computer and connect it to the audiovisual system. Don't worry too much about it. I can handle it.

**Walter White** [12:46 P.M.]
Then, I'll send someone in the office up to get Irene the tablet computer.

**Dwight Parker** [12:48 P.M.]
Oh, that's a relief! Please get here quickly. Thanks a lot.

**165.** Where most likely is Mr. Parker?

(A) In a conference room
(B) In an electronics store
(C) At a movie theater
(D) In his office

**166.** At 12:41 P.M., why does Ms. Keller say, "Oh, no"?

(A) An event has been canceled.
(B) Some people have not arrived.
(C) An employee called in sick this morning.
(D) A piece of equipment is damaged.

**167.** What is implied about Ms. Keller?

(A) She is a marketing manager.
(B) She is Mr. Parker's supervisor.
(C) She is good at handling machines.
(D) She is one of Mr. Parker's biggest clients.

**168.** What will Mr. White most likely do next?

(A) Give a marketing presentation
(B) Buy a new tablet computer
(C) Have someone bring a machine up
(D) Install a machine with Mr. Parker

# Special Announcement

To: The Editor, Bradford University's Student Magazine
From: Kelly Francis, Keepsafe Insurance

These days, it can often be difficult for young people to find affordable travel insurance to cover them for vacations or trips abroad. That is why we at Keepsafe Insurance are launching our new Backpacker Insurance package, which is aimed specifically at people aged eighteen to twenty-five.

When traveling, there are a number of dangers and risks that travelers need to be protected from. Our Backpacker Insurance package will allow you to claim compensation in the event of theft or loss of luggage. It will also allow you to claim a refund if your flight is canceled. The policy covers you in the event of a medical emergency as Keepsafe Insurance will pay all hospital bills up to $10,000.

To find out more information about our Backpacker Insurance package, you are invited to attend my twenty-minute presentation in the student auditorium at 4 P.M. on Thursday, March 18. If this is not convenient for you, you can e-mail me with any questions at kellyfrancis@keepsafe.com or phone the office at 1-800-3020-5939 and ask for Kelly.

**169.** What age group is the Backpacker Insurance package designed for?

(A) 30- to 40-year-olds
(B) 10- to 15-year-olds
(C) 18- to 25-year-olds
(D) 60- to 75-year-olds

**170.** What is NOT stated as being covered by the insurance package?

(A) The cancellation of a flight
(B) Medical expenses
(C) The theft of luggage
(D) Legal bills

**171.** Which of the following is NOT mentioned as a way to learn more about the Backpacker Insurance package?

(A) Telephoning Ms. Francis at the office
(B) Sending an e-mail to Ms. Francis
(C) Sending a letter to Ms. Francis at her private address
(D) Attending a presentation given by Ms. Francis

Nagasaki (June 14) - Artist Akemi Kitagawa, who specializes in landscape watercolors, has been traveling the more rural parts of her country for the past 5 years and painting the entire time. —[1]—. She takes photos of her pieces and posts them almost daily on her blog, which can be viewed at www.travelandpaint.com.

—[2]—. She describes individuals she meets as well as different cultures and dialects she encounters, and she shares her thoughts while on long, lonely stretches of road.

Ms. Kitagawa's site has drawn a large following as her blog statistics report an average of 3.2 thousand hits each day. For those blog readers who agree to take a brief survey, the top demographic for these readers is female college graduates in their mid-twenties and early thirties. —[3]—. One anonymous reader commented on the blog, "I visit here every day because Akemi is living the life I feel I missed out on – one of adventure and self-discovery."

When asked what inspired her to start her blog, Ms. Kitagawa explained, "Honestly, it first started out simply as a digital journal – a way to record my thoughts while on this journey. Only after my readership kept increasing did I realize that others would be interested in what I had to say. I'm happy to share my thoughts, however personal or simple, with the world." —[4]—.

**172.** What is the subject of the article?

(A) A painter's personal experiences
(B) New trends in photography
(C) Different cultures in Japan
(D) Traveling rural roads in Japan

**173.** In the article, the word 'drawn' in paragraph 3, line 1 is closest in meaning to

(A) described
(B) illustrated
(C) attracted
(D) labeled

**174.** What is NOT featured on Akemi Kitagawa's blog?

(A) Descriptions of her surroundings
(B) The cost of her artwork
(C) Her personal feelings
(D) Tales of her adventures

**175.** In which of the positions marked [1], [2], [3], and [4] does the following sentence best belong?

"Also on her blog are diary-like entries recording her adventures on her travels."

(A) [1]
(B) [2]
(C) [3]
(D) [4]

# ARTHOUSE.COM
## the leading online art supply retailer

Art House has everything modern artists need to create their next great masterpiece. For the next five days only, we are offering deep discounts on...

- 12 pack assorted clipart stencils $7
- Brandt easel-carrying case $27
- Art House brand 24 color charcoal set $9

In addition, with purchases of $75 or more, customers will receive a 4 pack of dry erase markers.

If you need any assistance with your purchases, let one of our online customer service representatives assist you. Just click the customer service tab at the top left of our main page.

# Art Today
## Your place for the latest on everything for art

**An art guide: Featured store of the month**

Art House is a great place to find good deals and is different from well-known art supply stores that often have higher prices and lower-quality products. Art House actually produces some of its own products and sells them along with other popular brands. It has a growing selection of items on its site, ranging from brushes to plaster and pencils. The quality of its products is not as high as some of the more popular brands, but for artists that need more affordable supplies, this is the place to go.

Art House also offers discounts on shipping with purchases over $80. However, since it does most of its shipping itself, it takes a lot longer for customers to get its items. But the lower prices are worth the wait. Visit its Web site at www.arthouse.com for hundreds of great deals.

176. What special offer is being advertised?

(A) Canvases for half price
(B) A gift with the purchase of $75
(C) Free shipping on all purchases
(D) A discount on all coloring supplies

177. What is suggested about Art House?

(A) It is attractive to artists who need to save.
(B) It does not advertise in newspapers and magazines.
(C) It has more than one store location.
(D) It allows only a certain number of purchases each day.

178. Which of the advertised products is produced by Art House?

(A) The stencils
(B) The easel case
(C) The charcoal set
(D) The markers

179. What does the reviewer consider a disadvantage of Art House?

(A) The low quality of its customer service
(B) The high cost of many of its products
(C) The time it takes to receive its products
(D) The smaller selection of brushes

180. In the review, the word "deals" in paragraph 1, line 1 is closest in meaning to

(A) quantities
(B) bargains
(C) contracts
(D) compromises

**Questions 181-185** refer to the following e-mails.

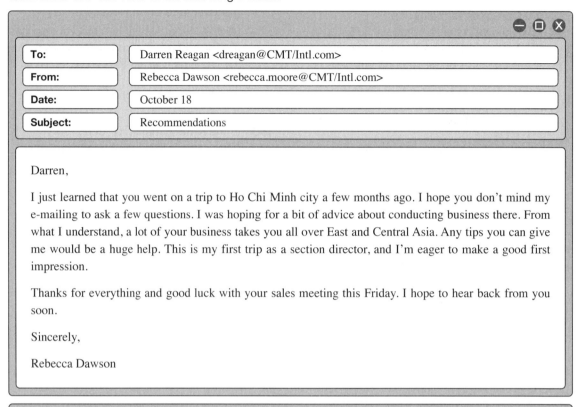

To: Darren Reagan <dreagan@CMT/Intl.com>
From: Rebecca Dawson <rebecca.moore@CMT/Intl.com>
Date: October 18
Subject: Recommendations

Darren,

I just learned that you went on a trip to Ho Chi Minh city a few months ago. I hope you don't mind my e-mailing to ask a few questions. I was hoping for a bit of advice about conducting business there. From what I understand, a lot of your business takes you all over East and Central Asia. Any tips you can give me would be a huge help. This is my first trip as a section director, and I'm eager to make a good first impression.

Thanks for everything and good luck with your sales meeting this Friday. I hope to hear back from you soon.

Sincerely,

Rebecca Dawson

To: Rebecca Dawson <rebecca.moore@CMT/Intl.com>
From: Darren Reagan <dreagan@CMT/Intl.com>
Date: October 19
Subject: Re: Recommendations

Rebecca,

I'd be happy to help you in any way that I can. Well, I can gather that you will most likely do a bit of research about Ho Chi Minh before you depart. I would suggest seeing a few cultural sites or something of historical significance right when you arrive. This will give you a few topics of conversation with the business contacts you will be meeting there.

In addition, remember that the traffic laws there are very different from back at home, and people don't pay as much attention to pedestrians as in other places I've been to. Be sure to leave plenty of time in advance to get to meetings and appointments. The traffic is out of control and a bit unnerving to maneuver around.

If you have any other questions, let me know. I'm trying to deliver a great presentation this Friday. But I'm not counting on anything yet. I still have some more things to prepare for it. I hope to wrap them up by the end of the day.

Have a safe trip and enjoy yourself. Vietnam is a beautiful country.

Darren

**181.** What is the main purpose of Ms. Dawson's e-mail?

(A) To ask about an upcoming sales meeting

(B) To inquire about tourist attractions in Ho Chi Minh city

(C) To ask a colleague about a business meeting

(D) To request advice for a business trip to Ho Chi Minh city

**182.** What is suggested about Ms. Dawson?

(A) She will move to another country in Asia next month.

(B) She just started a new position.

(C) She has visited Vietnam several times.

(D) She has just been introduced to Mr. Reagan.

**183.** Why does Mr. Reagan mention his business dealings in his e-mail?

(A) To address a comment made by Ms. Dawson

(B) To celebrate the closing of a deal

(C) To invite Ms. Dawson to be a part of the meeting

(D) To emphasize the importance of advance research

**184.** What is NOT one of Mr. Reagan's suggestions?

(A) Visit some cultural and historical sites

(B) Be on time for business meetings

(C) Have a good time

(D) Be difficult with clients to earn their respect

**185.** In the second e-mail, the phrase "counting on" in paragraph 3, line 2, is closest in meaning to

(A) being certain of

(B) coming up with

(C) measuring up to

(D) keeping records of

▶ ▶ ▶ GO ON TO THE NEXT PAGE

# CINEPLUS THEATERS
## Weston Park, Fairfield

Attention All Movie Fans! Construction of our brand new IMAX screen is complete and we want to celebrate its launch with you. The IMAX screen, Screen 8, opened on June 2nd, just in time for the premiere of the latest *Star Voyager* blockbuster movie. To commemorate this expansion, we will be marking down all tickets at our box office by 15 percent until the end of June. Additionally, Cineplus Theaters members qualify for bigger discounts by booking on our Web site during this month! Book tickets online for a Friday showing and receive a 20 percent discount! Book tickets for any Saturday showing and get a 25 percent discount! Come on Sunday and get a 30 percent discount! Finally, we're giving away vouchers for snacks and beverages to customers who select Premium seats!

http://www.cineplus.co.uk/theaters/location1089/

Cineplus Theaters – Search by Location  You are signed in as: Josh Furman (Member)

Selected Location:  Weston Park, Fairfield  ▼

Selected Date:  Saturday, June 19th  ▼

Number of Tickets:  2  ▼

The following movies are playing at the selected location on the selected date. Please click on a show time and you will be taken to our seat selection and payment screen. Thank you.

| Movie | Director | Starring | Run Time (Minutes) | Show Times |
|---|---|---|---|---|
| Into the Abyss | Cathy Bridges | Tom Hoffman, Alice Cruz | 98 | 10:30/16:30/21:30 |
| Love Recipe | Leo Cresswell | Julia Holt, Sally Nash | 134 | 09:30/12:45/20:30 |
| Star Voyager | Joe Wilcox | Edward Brooks, Lisa Wincot | 117 | 11:30/15:00/21:30 |
| The Dependables | Oliver Phelps | Bernie Jones, Tre Sawyer | 99 | 14:00/17:00/21:30 |
| Secret Identity | Elisa Finch | Tim Sherman, Rita Stone | 108 | 09:30/15:00/20:30 |
| Above Suspicion | Joe Wilcox | Clarke Grey, Tom Hoffman | 122 | 11:30/15:45/21:30 |
| On the Battlefield | Sarah Mulder | Sally Nash, Dave Mathis | 113 | 09:30/14:30/21:00 |

**ANNIE WOODS** [1:47 P.M.]

Hey, Josh. Thanks for buying those cinema tickets for us online. I totally loved the movie.

------------------------------------------------------------

**JOSH FURMAN** [1:48 P.M.]

No problem, Annie. And, ...me too! What a fantastic film. It's just a shame it didn't start until 9:30 p.m. And, it was pretty long.

------------------------------------------------------------

**ANNIE WOODS** [1:50 P.M.]

Yes, I got home pretty late, but it was worth it. It had a much more serious tone than Joe Wilcox's other films. I was kind of surprised. Although it had some funny moments, too.

------------------------------------------------------------

**JOSH FURMAN** [1:52 P.M.]

Right! It was pretty intense for the most part! Right up until the end, I had no idea that Tom Hoffman's character was the Russian spy!

------------------------------------------------------------

**ANNIE WOODS** [1:53 P.M.]

Same here! You just couldn't see it coming, could you? Let's go back next weekend. I'll let you choose a film again!

**186.** What is the main purpose of the advertisement?

(A) To announce a cinema expansion plan
(B) To promote the launch of a new movie
(C) To inform customers about special offers
(D) To introduce a new cinema membership plan

**187.** What is NOT true about the movies shown on the Web page schedule?

(A) One of them starts at 10:30 p.m.
(B) Most of them are under two hours long.
(C) All of them are shown three times per day.
(D) Two of them star Sally Nash.

**188.** What can be inferred about Mr. Furman?

(A) He was given a voucher for complimentary snacks.
(B) He purchased tickets for a film premiere.
(C) He received a 25 percent discount on movie tickets.
(D) He is an employee at Cineplus Weston Park.

**189.** Which movie did Ms. Woods and Mr. Furman most likely watch together?

(A) Into The Abyss
(B) Star Voyager
(C) Secret Identity
(D) Above Suspicion

**190.** What is suggested about Ms. Woods?

(A) She would like to watch the same movie again.
(B) She typically prefers comedic movies.
(C) She has a membership with Cineplus Theaters.
(D) She was surprised by the ending of the movie.

▶ ▶ ▶GO ON TO THE NEXT PAGE

# Memorandum

To: Borelli Tires Inc. Department Managers
From: Charles Mulgrew, Chief Executive Officer
Date: November 30
Re: December Management Meeting

Managers:

It is imperative that you all attend next week's meeting, as both our chief operations officer (Diana Hayworth) and the chairman of our company (David Ashcroft) will be leading discussions on some important topics. I will also be giving a presentation during the meeting. Please come prepared with ideas and suggestions so that you can contribute productively during the meeting. If, for whatever reason, you are unable to join the meeting, please inform my secretary, Ms. Naylor, at least one day beforehand. The location of the meeting depends on the progress of the renovation work in Meeting Room A. If the work is done and the room is ready, the meeting will be held there from 9:30 a.m. onwards. However, if it is not ready by December 6, we will use Meeting Room B instead. That room will be in use for employee training during the morning, so the meeting will begin after lunch. As with previous meetings, this one should last no longer than three hours. I'll update you on the meeting location one or two days in advance.

# BORELLI TIRES INC.

Management Meeting Agenda
December 6, Meeting Room B
Minutes Taken By: Veronica Naylor, Secretary

| Item | Topic | Presenter/Discussion Leader |
|------|-------|------------------------------|
| 1 | Sales Targets and Projections for Next Quarter | Bob Tunstall |
| 2 | Staff Performance-Based Rewards Programs | Khezar Hayat |
| 3 | Expansion into European and Asian Markets | Diana Hayworth |
| 4 | Evaluation of Recent Market Trends | Charles Mulgrew |
| 5 | Strategies for Enhancing the Company's Image | David Ashcroft |
| 6 | Demand for New Workers at Production Plants | Sandra Davis |

Meeting attendees may contact Ms. Naylor the day after the meeting if they wish to obtain a copy of the minutes or any supplementary materials.

To: Veronica Naylor <vnaylor@borellitires.org>

From: Bernadette Kidman <bkidman@borellitires.org>

Date: December 7

Subject: Yesterday's Meeting

Hi Veronica,

I'd very much appreciate it if you could send me the minutes from yesterday's management meeting. As you know, I had to step out of the room to take an urgent client phone call for around 30 minutes, so I missed the entirety of Item 2 on our meeting agenda. Also, I was particularly interested in what our chairman, Mr. Ashcroft, had to say, so I'd like to read over his comments again. In addition to the minutes, can you send me some extra copies of the handouts that accompanied our CEO's presentation? I'm planning to distribute them among the employees in my department. Thanks in advance for your assistance.

Have a nice day,

Bernadette Kidman

**191.** What are Borrelli Tires Inc.'s department managers requested to do?

(A) Forward topic suggestions to Mr. Mulgrew
(B) Obtain a meeting agenda from Ms. Naylor
(C) Give advance notification of non-attendance
(D) Organize an employee training session

**192.** What is most likely true about the management meeting in December?

(A) It lasted for more than three hours.
(B) It was held in a newly-renovated room.
(C) It took place in the afternoon.
(D) It was rescheduled for a different day.

**193.** Who most likely spoke about employee incentives?

(A) Sandra Davis
(B) Diana Hayworth
(C) Bob Tunstall
(D) Khezar Hayat

**194.** For which agenda item does Ms. Kidman request additional handouts?

(A) Item 2
(B) Item 3
(C) Item 4
(D) Item 5

**195.** In the e-mail, the word "missed" in paragraph 1, line 3, is closest in meaning to

(A) failed
(B) desired
(C) skipped
(D) misplaced

# For the Attention of Pebble Country Club Members!

As you all know, we work hard to provide you with the highest quality of services and amenities. Accordingly, we are delighted to announce that we will be introducing some new sports classes for the enjoyment of our members, starting in September. Full details of these classes can be found on our Web site. Throughout September, we will celebrate the start of these classes by giving our members an opportunity to take one free trial class per sport completely free! If you enjoy your trial classes, you can then sign up for more sessions with our experienced instructors! Additionally, individuals who have been members of our club for at least one year will receive a 15 percent savings on all classes attended in September, while those who have been members for at least two years will receive a 25 percent discount.

http://www.pebblecountryclub.ca/member/accountsummary/028178/4

# Pebble Country Club

**Member's Name:** Aurora Lanes
**Member's Account Number:** 028178
**Member's Account Summary:** September 1 – September 30

## Section 4: Additional Sports Instruction Fees

| Sports Class | Archery | Tennis | Squash | Golf |
|---|---|---|---|---|
| **Instructor** | Joshua Paek | Matthew Clarke | Kate Hutchson | Franz Schultz |
| **Class Rate** | Free Trial | Standard Rate | Free Trial | Free Trial |
| **No. of Lessons** | 1 | 4 | 1 | 1 |
| **Total Price** | $0.00 | $140.00 | $0.00 | $0.00 |
| **Total Fees** | $140.00 | | | |
| **Membership Discount Applied (15%)** | - $21.00 | | | |

Please pay the appropriate amount to Member's Services by October 10th.
Thank you. **Click Here** to make a payment.

To:     Pebble Country Club <inquires@pebblecc.com>

From:     Aurora Lanes <al@briggsinc.org>

Date:     October 3

Subject:     Sports Fees for September

Dear sir/madam,

I was just looking at my member's account summary when I noticed an error. I enjoyed having a chance to take free trial classes in September, and I even took extra classes at the discounted rate. However, my account summary shows that I took tennis classes with Matthew Clarke, but I actually took badminton classes with James LeBlanc. I know that the fee is the same for both classes, so that isn't my main concern. I'm worried that there may be an issue when I try to sign up for more classes with Mr. LeBlanc this month. Please amend my online account summary before I continue with my payment. Also, can you sign me up for four more classes with Mr. Paek this month? While I found Mr. Schultz and Ms. Hutchson to be excellent instructors, I don't think those sports are suitable for me.

Best wishes,

Aurora Lanes

**196.** In the notice, the word "introducing" in paragraph 1, line 2, is closest in meaning to

(A) meeting
(B) participating
(C) concluding
(D) launching

**197.** What are Pebble Country Club members encouraged to do?

(A) Offer suggestions for new sports classes
(B) Renew their club memberships in September
(C) Take advantage of a limited-time offer
(D) Update their personal details on the Web site

**198.** What is most likely true about Ms. Lanes?

(A) She has provided sports instruction to country club members.
(B) She has been a member of the club for less than two years.
(C) She is required to pay $140.00 in fees for sports classes.
(D) She should pay her outstanding fees within 30 days.

**199.** Which sports class does Ms. Lanes plan to join again in the future?

(A) Tennis
(B) Squash
(C) Archery
(D) Golf

**200.** What problem does Ms. Lanes mention in her e-mail?

(A) She was unable to sign up for a badminton class.
(B) She did not receive an advertised member's discount.
(C) She was billed for a class that she did not take.
(D) She was disappointed with one of the sports instructors.

STOP! This is the end of the test. If you finish before time is called, you may go back to Parts 5, 6, and 7 and check your work.

# Actual Test

MP3

해설집

시작 시간 ___시 ___분

종료 시간 ___시 ___분

중간에 멈추지 말고 처음부터 끝까지 풀어보세요.
문제를 풀 때에는 실전처럼 답안지에 마킹하세요.

목표 개수 _____ / 200    실제 개수 _____ / 200

예상 점수는 번역 및 정답에 있는 점수 환산표를 참조하세요.

# LISTENING TEST

In the Listening test, you will be asked to demonstrate how well you understand spoken English. The entire Listening test will last approximately 45 minutes. There are four parts, and directions are given for each part. You must mark your answers on the separate answer sheet. Do not write your answers in your test book.

## PART 1

**Directions:** For each question in this part, you will hear four statements about a picture in your test book. When you hear the statements, you must select the one statement that best describes what you see in the picture. Then find the number of the question on your answer sheet and mark your answer. The statements will not be printed in your test book and will be spoken only one time.

Statement (B), "They are sitting at a table," is the best description of the picture. So you should select answer (B) and mark it on your answer sheet.

**1.**

**2.**

▶ ▶ ▶ GO ON TO THE NEXT PAGE

**3.**

**4.**

**5.**

**6.**

## PART 2

**Directions:** You will hear a question or statement and three responses spoken in English. They will not be printed in your test book and will be spoken only one time. Select the best response to the question or statement and mark the letter (A), (B), or (C) on your answer sheet.

7. Mark your answer on your answer sheet.

8. Mark your answer on your answer sheet.

9. Mark your answer on your answer sheet.

10. Mark your answer on your answer sheet.

11. Mark your answer on your answer sheet.

12. Mark your answer on your answer sheet.

13. Mark your answer on your answer sheet.

14. Mark your answer on your answer sheet.

15. Mark your answer on your answer sheet.

16. Mark your answer on your answer sheet.

17. Mark your answer on your answer sheet.

18. Mark your answer on your answer sheet.

19. Mark your answer on your answer sheet.

20. Mark your answer on your answer sheet.

21. Mark your answer on your answer sheet.

22. Mark your answer on your answer sheet.

23. Mark your answer on your answer sheet.

24. Mark your answer on your answer sheet.

25. Mark your answer on your answer sheet.

26. Mark your answer on your answer sheet.

27. Mark your answer on your answer sheet.

28. Mark your answer on your answer sheet.

29. Mark your answer on your answer sheet.

30. Mark your answer on your answer sheet.

31. Mark your answer on your answer sheet.

## PART 3

**Directions:** You will hear some conversations between two or three people. You will be asked to answer three questions about what the speakers say in each conversation. Select the best response to each question and mark the letter (A), (B), (C), or (D) on your answer sheet. The conversations will not be printed in your test book and will be spoken only one time.

**32.** Where does this conversation most likely take place?

(A) At an airport
(B) At a post office
(C) At a bus terminal
(D) At a department store

**33.** Why is the woman concerned?

(A) She doesn't have enough money.
(B) The price of a new product is too high.
(C) It will take too long to deliver a package.
(D) All of the tickets are already sold out.

**34.** What does the man suggest doing?

(A) Paying with cash
(B) Ordering additional items
(C) Using an alternate service
(D) Booking a flight ticket

**35.** Who is the woman?

(A) A taxi driver
(B) A journalist
(C) A supermarket cashier
(D) A restaurateur

**36.** How did the men hear about the business?

(A) From a television program
(B) From a newspaper advertisement
(C) From a travel guide
(D) From a magazine article

**37.** What does the woman say will happen next year?

(A) Another location will open.
(B) Some employees will be hired.
(C) A new menu will be offered.
(D) A special promotion will begin.

**38.** Why does the man want to leave the office space?

(A) He needs a smaller space.
(B) He needs to relocate his business.
(C) His monthly rent is too expensive.
(D) His office has deteriorated.

**39.** What is the woman asked to do?

(A) Take a regular examination
(B) Make some repairs
(C) Cancel a current agreement
(D) Lower the man's monthly rent

**40.** What does the man offer to do?

(A) Sign a new lease
(B) Search for a new tenant
(C) Purchase some replacement parts
(D) Pay for the man's moving expenses

**41.** What is the conversation mainly about?

(A) The new sales agenda
(B) The distribution of new devices
(C) The change in sales team members
(D) The efficiency of the tablets

**42.** Why does the woman say, "It's about time"?

(A) She is unsatisfied.
(B) She has been waiting.
(C) She wants more time.
(D) She feels skeptical

**43.** What do the man imply about the management?

(A) They think sales will improve.
(B) They dislike investing.
(C) They are preoccupied.
(D) They plan to hire more people.

44. What position are the candidates applying for?

   (A) Personnel manager
   (B) Security guard
   (C) Sales representative
   (D) Accountant

45. According to the woman, how many applicants will be interviewed?

   (A) One
   (B) Two
   (C) Three
   (D) Four

46. What does the man say he will do on Wednesday?

   (A) Call a hotel
   (B) Attend a conference
   (C) Talk to some applicants
   (D) Go on vacation

47. Which department does the man work in?

   (A) Accounting
   (B) Personnel
   (C) Marketing
   (D) Maintenance

48. What does the man mean when he says, "I don't have anything scheduled on Friday"?

   (A) He will take some time off.
   (B) He can make a presentation.
   (C) He wants to cancel a meeting.
   (D) He didn't receive an invitation.

49. What will the woman do in thirty minutes?

   (A) Complete a survey form
   (B) Provide some information
   (C) Talk to a department manager
   (D) Send some marketing data

50. Why was the woman absent from the conference?

   (A) She thought it had been canceled.
   (B) She didn't take a train on time.
   (C) She came down with a severe cold.
   (D) She went to the wrong location.

51. What does the woman want to know?

   (A) A registration period
   (B) A schedule change
   (C) The number of participants
   (D) The location of a printshop

52. What does the woman plan to do next?

   (A) Finalize her report
   (B) Print some documents
   (C) Reserve a conference room
   (D) Organize a corporate event

53. Who most likely is Mr. Winston?

   (A) An advertising expert
   (B) A personnel manager
   (C) A bank teller
   (D) A new employee

54. What does the man say he needs to do?

   (A) Get an employee badge
   (B) Show some samples
   (C) Finish some paperwork
   (D) Attend an orientation session

55. What does the woman imply when she says, "I'm about to start a meeting"?

   (A) She needs to read some reports.
   (B) She cannot reschedule a meeting.
   (C) She doesn't have time to fix a problem.
   (D) She is not available to help.

56. What kind of business does the woman work for?

(A) An advertising company
(B) A department store
(C) A real estate agency
(D) A magazine

57. What does the woman say about the special deal?

(A) It is only for fashion professionals.
(B) It will expire soon.
(C) It will help develop a huge readership.
(D) It includes a new Web site design.

58. What does the man ask the woman to do?

(A) Pay in advance
(B) Create a new marketing strategy
(C) Reserve some spots for him
(D) Subscribe to a new magazine

59. According to the man, what will happen in March?

(A) A new branch manager will be appointed.
(B) An anniversary celebration will be held.
(C) Some special promotions will take place.
(D) Some upgrades will begin.

60. What will be offered to regular members?

(A) A free locker
(B) A discount
(C) A medical checkup
(D) A free beverage

61. What does the woman say she will do in the afternoon?

(A) Have a late lunch
(B) Teach new regular members
(C) Send a notice electronically
(D) Call another colleague

| Name | Department | Comment |
|---|---|---|
| Andrew Kim | Maintenance | Ergonomic chairs |
| Yejin Hwang | Accounting | A decent corporate cafeteria |
| David Kiesling | Technical Support | More time off |
| Sally Murphy | Marketing | A longer lunch break |

62. In which department do the speakers probably work?

(A) Accounting
(B) Maintenance
(C) Human Resources
(D) Technical Support

63. Look at the graphic. Whose opinion are the speakers talking about?

(A) Andrew Kim's
(B) Yejin Hwang's
(C) David Kiesling's
(D) Sally Murphy's

64. What will the speakers probably do next?

(A) Print more survey forms
(B) Discuss the budget for a new cafeteria
(C) Review other suggestions
(D) Make some changes to a work schedule

▶ ▶ ▶ GO ON TO THE NEXT PAGE

## SUNSHADE SAMPLE DESIGN

25200 Carlos Bee Blvd #310
510-575-4331
www.charilesinteriors.com

· **Designer:** Charlie McDonell
· **Date:** June 3

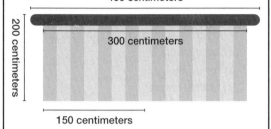

400 centimeters

200 centimeters

300 centimeters

150 centimeters

## MEETING ROOM SCHEDULE

September 9 / TUESDAY

※ Schedule Manager: Jennifer Lee / EXT 1123

| Meeting Room 401 | | |
|---|---|---|
| 8:00 A.M. | Monthly meeting (Accounting) | Chris Froom |
| 9:00 A.M. | Sales Presentation | William Parker |
| 10:00 A.M. | | |
| 11:00 A.M. | Training Session | Jia Choi |
| 2:00 P.M. | Marketing Meeting | Thomas Baker |

**65.** Where does the man work?

(A) At an interior company
(B) At a home improvement store
(C) At a clothing store
(D) At an accounting firm

**66.** Look at the graphic. Which measurement does the man want to change?

(A) 400 centimeters
(B) 300 centimeters
(C) 200 centimeters
(D) 150 centimeters

**67.** What will the woman probably do next?

(A) Calculate a new tax rate
(B) Begin interior repairs
(C) Install new office equipment
(D) Determine a new cost

**68.** Where most likely do the speakers work?

(A) At an accounting firm
(B) At a business consulting firm
(C) At a financial institution
(D) At an apartment management office

**69.** Look at the graphic. Who should the woman contact?

(A) Chris Froom
(B) William Parker
(C) Jia Choi
(D) Thomas Baker

**70.** What does the woman say she will do?

(A) Cancel a meeting
(B) Contact a colleague
(C) Prepare for a company event
(D) Tell a client about a change in a schedule

# PART 4

**Directions:** You will hear some short talks given by a single speaker. You will be asked to answer three questions about what the speaker says in each short talk. Select the best response to each question and mark the letter (A), (B), (C), or (D) on your answer sheet. The talks will not be printed in your test book and will be spoken only one time.

**71.** What is the message mainly about?

(A) A new library policy
(B) An upgraded computer room
(C) A special reading program
(D) A temporary location

**72.** According to the speaker, what can be accessed on a Web site?

(A) A new location
(B) A moving schedule
(C) Specific directions
(D) Discount coupons

**73.** What should the listeners do to borrow a laptop computer?

(A) Complete a form
(B) Show a membership card
(C) Pay a security deposit
(D) Join a free rental service

**74.** Who are the listeners?

(A) Sales representatives
(B) Marketing experts
(C) Foreign investors
(D) Stockholders

**75.** Why have the sales of Yellow Farm Cheese decreased?

(A) Its customer service is very poor.
(B) Its commercial was not effective.
(C) Most of its products are very expensive.
(D) A series of new products failed.

**76.** According to the speaker, what will happen on March 10?

(A) A new brand will be launched.
(B) Special promotional events will start.
(C) More marketing experts will be hired.
(D) New TV advertisements will be aired.

**77.** What is the speaker mainly discussing?

(A) A high-quality product
(B) A pay raise
(C) A new sales strategy
(D) An annual sale

**78.** Why does the speaker say, "You won't see prices this low again for another year"?

(A) He is considering ending a store's discount programs.
(B) He wants to emphasize the benefits of medical insurance.
(C) He is encouraging the listeners to buy shoes at discount prices.
(D) He feels regret over missing a good chance to get good deals.

**79.** According to the speaker, who is available to answer questions?

(A) Cashiers
(B) Store managers
(C) Store clerks
(D) Customer service representatives

**80.** What is the purpose of the message?

(A) To inquire about a business
(B) To make a reservation
(C) To advertise some services
(D) To find some information

**81.** Where does the listener probably work?

(A) At a restaurant
(B) At a shopping mall
(C) At an interior design company
(D) At a cleaning company

**82.** What does the speaker say about her business?

(A) It was recently established.
(B) It offers special discounts.
(C) It will be relocated.
(D) It has locations across the country.

83. What is the news report mainly about?

    (A) A city budget
    (B) A new exhibit
    (C) A transportation problem
    (D) A small price increase

84. Who is Katherine Carter?

    (A) A news presenter
    (B) A truck driver
    (C) An artist
    (D) A local government official

85. According to the speaker, what may occur at the end of the month?

    (A) Some construction plans may be canceled.
    (B) Museum admission fees may be increased.
    (C) Some community groups may be supported.
    (D) The number of bike lanes may be decreased.

86. What did the speaker recently do?

    (A) She authored a book.
    (B) She started his own company.
    (C) She changed jobs.
    (D) She reviewed many résumés.

87. What does the speaker imply when she says, "Don't waste time filling out a bunch of applications"?

    (A) She is currently unemployed.
    (B) She is ready to start her new job.
    (C) She provides reliable advice.
    (D) She does not have experience with small businesses.

88. According to the speaker, what can the listeners receive by visiting a Web site?

    (A) An autographed book
    (B) A promotional item
    (C) A free membership
    (D) A free consultation

89. What is the subject of the workshop?

    (A) Enhancing team communication
    (B) Making a commercial Web site
    (C) Developing public-speaking skills
    (D) Learning new market trends

90. Why does the speaker say, "Many people have that problem"?

    (A) To criticize a lack of effort
    (B) To suggest a solution
    (C) To complain about a company
    (D) To reassure the attendees

91. What does the speaker ask the listeners to do?

    (A) Review some data
    (B) Fill out a survey
    (C) Sign up for a course
    (D) Look for a partner

92. Where does the speaker probably work?

    (A) At a department store
    (B) At a train station
    (C) In an inspection office
    (D) At a factory

93. What change will workers experience?

    (A) New schedules
    (B) Renovations to the building
    (C) Working on different production lines
    (D) Revised benefits packages

94. According to the speaker, what should the listeners go over?

    (A) An instruction manual
    (B) A schedule of inspections
    (C) A training handbook
    (D) A description of benefits

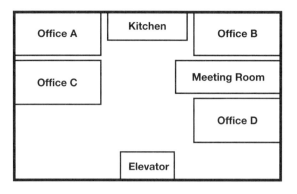

95. What type of document does the speaker request?

(A) An expense report
(B) A performance evaluation
(C) A quarterly sales report
(D) A financial statement

96. Why does the speaker reschedule a deadline?

(A) He has no time to review a document.
(B) He cannot proceed with a project.
(C) He will go on a business trip next week.
(D) He needs more time to get his work done.

97. Look at the graphic. Which office belongs to the speaker?

(A) Office A
(B) Office B
(C) Office C
(D) Office D

## MONA PET FURNITURE
### SUMMER WORKSHOP SCHEDULE
July 17 / Venice Resort California

| Presenter | Venue | Time |
|-----------|-------|------|
| Cindy Nelson | Diamond Room | 10:00 – 11:00 |
| Gina Davidson | Crystal Room | 11:00 – 12:00 |
| Oliver Tylor | Ocean Room | 1:00 – 2:30 |
| Andrew Kim | Island Room | 3:00 – 4:30 |

98. What does the speaker say about the resort?

(A) It provides healthy meals for free.
(B) It is well known for its golf courses.
(C) It has magnificent views.
(D) It is regarded as one of the top resorts.

99. What does the speaker remind the listeners about?

(A) A company outing
(B) A reception
(C) A client meeting
(D) An anniversary ceremony

100. Look at the graphic. When will John Scofield begin his presentation?

(A) At 10:00 A.M.
(B) At 11:00 A.M.
(C) At 1:00 P.M.
(D) At 3:00 P.M.

This is the end of the Listening test. Turn to Part 5 in your test book.

▶ ▶ ▶ GO ON TO THE NEXT PAGE

# READING TEST

In the Reading test, you will read a variety of texts and answer several different types of reading comprehension questions. The entire Reading test will last 75 minutes. There are three parts, and directions are given for each part. You are encouraged to answer as many questions as possible within the time allowed.

You must mark your answers on the separate answer sheet. Do not write your answers in your test book.

## PART 5

**Directions**: A word or phrase is missing in each of the sentences below. Four answer choices are given below each sentence. Select the best answer to complete the sentence. Then mark the letter (A), (B), (C), or (D) on your answer sheet.

101. All the participants in the trade seminar are required to bring ------- laptop computers and employee badges.
    (A) they
    (B) their
    (C) them
    (D) theirs

102. Every employee in our office must be able to work independently in an ------- busy environment.
    (A) accidentally
    (B) accessibly
    (C) extremely
    (D) energetically

103. Her cultural background is different than -------, so she can view the matter from an entirely unique perspective.
    (A) I
    (B) my
    (C) me
    (D) mine

104. Both the exteriors and the interiors of our cars have been ------- redesigned to appeal to domestic and foreign customers.
    (A) complete
    (B) completing
    (C) completely
    (D) completion

105. A discount coupon is a kind of ticket or document that can be ------- for a financial discount or rebate when purchasing a product.
    (A) refunded
    (B) exchanged
    (C) purchased
    (D) subtracted

106. The library contains a wide range of fiction and nonfiction books and is open to the public ------- regular business hours.
    (A) for
    (B) total
    (C) down
    (D) during

107. SK Penny, Inc. currently awards long-serving employees with up to 14 days of vacation ------- two years.
    (A) all
    (B) much
    (C) every
    (D) some

108. ------- receiving his law degree from a local law school, Mr. Kennedy began his career in law enforcement.
    (A) Unlike
    (B) About
    (C) Upon
    (D) For

**109.** The new desktop computers are equipped ------- the latest word-processing software and high-resolution monitors.

(A) by
(B) with
(C) through
(D) for

**110.** ------- the personnel head's absence, the staff meeting on the welfare of the employees will be held as planned.

(A) Due to
(B) Ahead of
(C) Regardless of
(D) Nonetheless

**111.** If you are interested in any of our new items, please contact us via e-mail, telephone, or fax so that we can send you ------- information.

(A) further
(B) few
(C) little
(D) detail

**112.** In an effort ------- prices, our company streamlined the production process and minimized package volume and weight.

(A) reduced
(B) reduces
(C) would reduce
(D) to reduce

**113.** The recently purchased fax machine on the third floor works ------- more quietly than the old one on the second floor.

(A) very
(B) quite
(C) even
(D) so

**114.** The sales contract ------- indicates that some photo files may be used for commercial purposes.

(A) recently
(B) courteously
(C) straightforwardly
(D) elegantly

**115.** Providing a toll-free number for its ------- customers, the company will get more orders and calls for information on its products.

(A) potential
(B) confidential
(C) artificial
(D) progressive

**116.** Financial institutions need ------- storage space to upload all of the information about their monetary transactions.

(A) security
(B) securely
(C) secure
(D) securing

**117.** Many single people are not ------- for some tax benefits that married couples can enjoy.

(A) responsible
(B) eligible
(C) easy
(D) possible

**118.** The Cal State Union Bank closes at 5:00 P.M., ------- you can withdraw money from your account all day.

(A) or
(B) but
(C) even
(D) which

**119.** Our sales manager ------- next quarter's sales to increase twofold.

(A) project
(B) projecting
(C) are projected
(D) projects

**120.** The Yellow Chip Travel Agency will ------- package tours to New York with free hotel accommodations next year.

(A) inform
(B) remind
(C) offer
(D) notify

121. If ------- by the board of directors, the relocation of General Steel to Detroit will probably occur in October.

(A) approve
(B) approval
(C) approved
(D) approving

122. Neither the quality of products ------- workplace safety should be compromised in the name of profits.

(A) and
(B) or
(C) nor
(D) but also

123. ------- concerns about the possibility of complaints by the residents, the city government will grant a new development contract to the housing developer.

(A) But
(B) Despite of
(C) Even though
(D) In spite of

124. A lot of people who showed up at the art auction in Chicago ------- great interest in purchasing works from the famous art collection.

(A) express
(B) expressed
(C) expression
(D) expressing

125. Due to a massive gas -------, the gas pipelines running along the bottom of the Straits of Mackenzie were shut down yesterday.

(A) leak
(B) leaks
(C) leaked
(D) to leak

126. Located in the center of Toronto, the Royal Ontario Museum makes the history of Ontario ------- to every resident and visitor.

(A) access
(B) accessing
(C) accessible
(D) accessibly

127. Last week, some scuba divers went underwater without any protective gear, ------- could be very dangerous and even fatal.

(A) that
(B) who
(C) when
(D) which

128. Economists and financial market analysts need to pinpoint the exact cause of the global financial crisis ------- find some working solutions.

(A) In order that
(B) rather than
(C) so as to
(D) provided that

129. Astronomical studies in the past few decades have shown that the gravity of the moon is about 20 percent of ------- of the Earth.

(A) it
(B) one
(C) that
(D) those

130. This type of heater is a good choice for the quick heating of enclosed spaces; however, it should not be left -------.

(A) unused
(B) unorganized
(C) unattended
(D) unexpected

# PART 6

**Directions:** Read the texts that follow. A word, phrase, or sentence is missing in parts of each text. Four answer choices for each question are given below the text. Select the best answer to complete the text. Then mark the letter (A), (B), (C), or (D) on your answer sheet.

**Questions 131-134** refer to the following letter.

## JOB TRANSFER REQUEST LETTER

Dear Head of Human Resources,

I would like to respectfully inquire about the possibility of a transfer to the Columbus, Ohio location. My spouse has received a job offer there, ------- will begin next month.
                                                                    **131.**

I ------- working here for the past six years, first as an assistant manager, and now in my
   **132.**

current position as department head. I feel that I have been an asset in Accounting and

would like to continue my association with the company.

I am ------- to stay on for several weeks to help train someone to fill the position I will leave.
       **133.**

I know several employees who would make good candidates for the position and would be

happy to share my thoughts with you.

My experience at Syracuse's has been very rewarding, and I would appreciate the

opportunity to continue my career with the company. -------.
                                                    **134.**

Sincerely,
Michael Moore

---

**131.** (A) that
(B) which
(C) who
(D) since

**132.** (A) enjoying
(B) am enjoying
(C) have enjoyed
(D) will have enjoyed

**133.** (A) ready
(B) possible
(C) considerate
(D) able

**134.** (A) I look forward to having the opportunity to work with you soon.
(B) Your thoughtful consideration of my request will be greatly appreciated.
(C) We decided to cut the budget to maximize cost efficiency in hiring new employees.
(D) I would like to inform you that I am resigning from my position as head of Accounting.

▶ ▶ ▶ GO ON TO THE NEXT PAGE

**BK Computer World**
1123 Orchard Ave
Fremont, CA 94513

Dear Mr. Pinkman:

Thank you for your letter describing the problem you had with your laptop computer. We

believe, as you do, that electronic equipment should be built to last. ------- laptop computers
**135.**

are highly reliable, occasionally, units fail for a number of reasons.

Although we cannot provide you with a replacement since it is now past the 30-day return

period, we can provide you with information to get your unit -------. You need to call BK
**136.**

technical support at (510) 603-0110. Someone there will provide you with instructions on how

to package and return your unit for repairs.

-------, you may purchase a new unit from us. We have several of the Andromeda units in
**137.**

stock and have recently dropped the price to $299. We also have plenty of the new G909

and G911 units in stock.

Whatever route you choose, feel free to visit us for a product demonstration anytime. -------.
**138.**

Sincerely,

Stacy McKintire
Customer Service Head
BK Computer World

**135.** (A) Despite
(B) Once
(C) While
(D) As if

**136.** (A) repair
(B) to repair
(C) repairing
(D) repaired

**137.** (A) Additionally
(B) Consequently
(C) Apparently
(D) Alternatively

**138.** (A) We apologize for our carelessness.
(B) We're glad to serve you and hope to continue to do so in the future.
(C) We hope that you will strongly consider joining us.
(D) On behalf of us all, I would like to express our sincere thanks.

Aifa Apartment Communities
The Office of Resident Services
Palm Tree Avenue, Miami, FL 32003

Dear Ms. Jordan,

I am writing to notify you of the current status of your apartment renter's insurance. As of

March 31, your insurance has expired. You must ------- a new renter's insurance application
**139.**
form before May 1. Failure to supply complete coverage of your rented property will ------- in
**140.**
the termination of your lease for apartment #310 at Aifa Apartment Communities.


-------. It will protect you and your family from fire, water, and wind damage and will also
**141.**
reimburse you for any losses ------- in case of theft. It can't stop something from happening.
**142.**
However, if something unexpected does happen and it is covered by your policy, you won't

have to pay the full cost of a loss. Please bring proof of insurance to the office of Resident

Services before the May 1 deadline.

Sincerely,

Charles Parker
Manager
The Office of Resident Services

---

**139.** (A) agree
(B) understand
(C) renew
(D) complete

**140.** (A) give
(B) cause
(C) result
(D) cancel

**141.** (A) The primary purpose of renter's
insurance is peace of mind.
(B) It will protect your assets from
financial risk if something goes wrong.
(C) You may have to pay for expensive
surgeries and treatments if you have
no insurance.
(D) We currently provide top security to
meet the needs of our residents.

**142.** (A) be incurred
(B) incurring
(C) incurs
(D) incurred

**The City of Spokane**
**Public Notice**

ORDINANCE NO. 1123

Next month, the city of Spokane will host a big parade for the fire department. -------. These
**143.**

brave men have been sorely neglected, and we would like ------- them to the forefront of our
**144.**

memories and remind ourselves that we are protected by these men every day.

Their sacrifices were not in vain because the local firefighting community will always be -------
**145.**

to saving the lives of those caught in house and forest fires.

Residents are invited to pay their -------. If you are unable to attend the event, please send
**146.**

flowers to let our heroes' loved ones know that they are still in your thoughts.

143. (A) For some people, saving lives is just a
     part of their job description.
     (B) There will be different events related
     to fire safety in other regions.
     (C) We must improve the treatment
     of firefighters and their working
     conditions.
     (D) The parade will honor fallen heroes
     who tragically lost their lives while
     saving others.

144. (A) bring
     (B) to bring
     (C) brought
     (D) being brought

145. (A) dedicated
     (B) dedicating
     (C) dedication
     (D) dedicate

146. (A) expectations
     (B) earnings
     (C) proceeds
     (D) respects

## PART 7

**Directions:** In this part you will read a selection of texts, such as magazine and newspaper articles, e-mails, and instant messages. Each text or set of texts is followed by several questions. Select the best answer for each question and mark the letter (A), (B), (C), or (D) on your answer sheet.

**Questions 147-148** refer to the following letter.

May 10

Bob Miller
Jamestown High School Choir
8923 Charleston Blvd
Jamestown, Delaware 67830

Dear Mr. Miller,

I am happy to inform you that your choir has been selected to perform at the Jamestown Parade next month. The parade begins at 11:00 A.M. on June 15. Please have everyone in your group assemble at the Fulton Center parking lot no later than 10:00 A.M. We will need to put all of the groups participating in the parade in order, so it is crucial that all performers be on hand no later than one hour before the start of the parade. The parade starts at the Jamestown Botanical Gardens and runs the entire length of Moore Street. There will be shuttle buses to return all performers back to the Fulton Center parking lot. They will be located behind Jamestown City Hall.

Thank you,

Bonnie Cutler
Event Coordinator

**147.** Who most likely is Mr. Miller?

(A) A parade organizer
(B) A local music critic
(C) A professional singer
(D) The head of a school choir

**148.** Where will the parade begin?

(A) At a high school
(B) At a parking lot
(C) At Jamestown City Hall
(D) At some botanical gardens

# Wilson Windows

85 Kent Street
Tilford, MA 28191
800-555-1988
www.wilsonwindows.com

## *Hot New Product!*

Since you are one of our best customers, we would like to let you know about a revolutionary product we are now carrying. It is called Security Film, and with it, any window can be transformed into an unbreakable security window. This product will allow businesses to increase their security at surprisingly low prices. In fact, your business can now convert your existing windows with Security Film for 10% of the cost of new high-security windows. So come in and see how good Security Film is.

We are now running a special offer. Until March 10, if you purchase 1,000 feet of Security Film, we will take half off the price of installation. We look forward to seeing you soon!

---

**149.** What is indicated about Security Film?

(A) It has been approved by security companies.
(B) It can only be applied to high-security windows.
(C) It prevents windows from chipping.
(D) It is available at Wilson Windows.

**150.** What can a customer get through the special offer?

(A) A discount on installation
(B) Installation before March 10
(C) Additional Security Film to install
(D) A better price for Security Film

**Questions 151-152** refer to the following text message chain.

**Richard Crane** [11:02 A.M.]

I have a problem, Lisa. I bought two tickets for the Royal King's Orchestra performance next Friday night, but something just came up, so I can't attend the concert. It's such a shame I can't go.

---

**Lisa Livingstone** [11:03 A.M.]

That's too bad. You are really out of luck. What are you going to do with those tickets?

---

**Richard Crane** [11:05 A.M.]

I remember you said you have a friend who will be visiting from out of town next week. Would you like the tickets so that you can go together with your friend?

---

**Lisa Livingstone** [11:08 A.M.]

You're sweet, Richard! That's a nice thought, and I do love the Royal King's Orchestra. But we already have plans for Friday night. You know, Scott is also a huge fan of the Royal King's Orchestra.

---

**Richard Crane** [11:09 A.M.]

I know. I already checked with him. He told me he's going to bury himself under a mountain of paperwork next week. Actually, I paid for the most expensive tickets, and they are nonrefundable. It seems there's nothing I can do.

---

**Lisa Livingstone** [11:11 A.M.]

Why don't you post a notice about your tickets on the company intranet? I'm sure there will be somebody who wants to buy them.

---

**Richard Crane** [11:12 A.M.]

That sounds like a great idea. I think I'll do that right away. As you said, someone's sure to snap them up.

---

**Lisa Livingstone** [11:14 A.M.]

That's what I'm saying, Richard. Go for it, man! I'll also ask some of my colleagues if they want to go to the concert.

**151.** What problem does Mr. Crane have?

(A) He has to do too much paperwork.
(B) He can't afford to buy a ticket.
(C) He can't take time off from his job.
(D) He will miss a music performance.

**152.** At 11:08 A.M., what does Ms. Livingstone mean when she writes, "You're sweet, Richard"?

(A) Mr. Crane loves sweets.
(B) Mr. Crane is flattering her.
(C) Mr. Crane is very kind.
(D) Mr. Crane is a little indecisive.

▶ ▶ ▶GO ON TO THE NEXT PAGE

# Mario's Pizza Place

**728 North Capital Street, Baltimore**
**301-555-8291**

Mario's Pizza Place, a Baltimore landmark, has been in business for over 50 years. Our traditional New York-style pizza has won countless awards. So drop in for a slice. You'll love it!

**We also offer the following:**
- Hoagies, meatball sandwiches, and steak and cheese sandwiches all served on bread we bake daily
- Calzones that are served to order
- A salad bar with 40 items to choose from
- Ten different desserts, all made in house

**Hours:** Monday through Saturday from 10:30 A.M. to 8:00 P.M.
**Summer (May through September):** We stay open an hour later than usual.

Wednesday is Family Night. Families get half off a large cheese pizza. Additional toppings may be added for $1.50 each.

**153.** What is mentioned about Mario's Pizza Place?

(A) It opened one decade ago.
(B) Its pizzas are available in supermarkets.
(C) It is a national franchise that is expanding.
(D) It makes its desserts at the restaurant.

**154.** According to the advertisement, what happens in May?

(A) The restaurant has summer specials.
(B) The restaurant opens on Sundays.
(C) The restaurant offers a special menu.
(D) The restaurant closes at 9:00 P.M.

**154.** What is indicated about Family Night?

(A) It is the busiest night at the restaurant.
(B) It takes place on a weekday night.
(C) It is only held during the summer months.
(D) It is a new promotional offer.

**Questions 156-158** refer to the following memo.

To: All staff
From: Eugene Claire
Date: June 18
Subject: Busy season hiring

Hello,

As you know, we get most of our work during the summer. For this reason, it is important that we have enough employees at this time of the year. Right now, we don't have enough workers to complete all of the projects we have scheduled for the summer. Before I put an advertisement out in the local newspapers, I would like to know if any of you know people you could recommend. Of course, I would rather hire individuals who come with solid recommendations from current employees. That way, I know I am hiring someone who will not only be able to do the work but will also fit in with all of us.

To make the deal good for both you and the company, I will provide a $150 bonus to anyone who refers a person that takes a job at the company. Please get in touch with me within the next week if you know the right person. If we can't meet our hiring needs by then, I will contact the local newspapers.

Sincerely,

Eugene Claire
Personnel director
Enton Travel

---

**156.** What is the purpose of the memo?

(A) To report an increase in employee salaries
(B) To announce this season's construction projects
(C) To ask employees to refer people for employment
(D) To remind employees that bonuses will be based on efficiency

**157.** Who is Mr. Claire?

(A) A company client
(B) A company executive
(C) A temporary employee
(D) A public accountant

**158.** According to the memo, what might Mr. Claire do soon after June 25?

(A) Get in touch with some local newspapers
(B) Review some projects completed by new staff members
(C) Provide training to improve employee efficiency
(D) Announce a need for seasonal employees to workers

# Smith Lawn and Garden

**Providing Australia with quality outdoor products for over three decades**

__Click here__ to make a purchase as a guest of Smith Lawn and Garden.

__Click here__ to register for a Smith Lawn and Garden online shopper account.

**The benefits of being a registered user at Smith Lawn and Garden:**

Regular updates on new products and sales through e-mail

Access to members-only discounts on new and discontinued items

Fast, two-step purchases through our Web site

Free shipping within Australia (international packages are subject to international delivery rates)

It's safe and easy to register. You can also choose to save your billing details. We encrypt everything, so it is safe, and you won't need to reenter it for every purchase. So sign up on our site today. You can even get assistance from our online help desk when registering. It only takes a minute!

**159.** What is the purpose of the Web page?

(A) To describe the advantages of an online shopping account

(B) To tell a customer that an item has been discontinued

(C) To promote a new line of lawn and garden supplies

(D) To inform a customer of a new online service

**160.** What is NOT indicated as an advantage of registration?

(A) Information about new items in stock

(B) Online assistance during purchases

(C) Discounted merchandise

(D) Stored billing information

**161.** What is suggested about Smith Lawn and Garden?

(A) It recently built a new warehouse.

(B) It has been open for 20 years.

(C) It runs an overseas office in the U.S.

(D) It does not charge for domestic shipping.

## Hollywood Post

# Celebrities and Entertainment

**By Alliso Bank**

*City Life*, an upcoming television drama on Channel 4, stars Wendy Smith in the leading role of Margie Banks, the director of publishing at a popular New York newspaper. Directed by Steven Wentworth and shot entirely in New York City, the show provides an entertaining look at the life of a single woman in New York City. The first show airs on Wednesday, September 4, at 9:00 P.M. following The Greg Henderson Comedy Hour.

**162.** Who is the main character in *City Life*?

(A) Wendy Smith
(B) Margie Banks
(C) Steven Wentworth
(D) Greg Henderson

**163.** According to the article, what will happen on September 4?

(A) A news broadcast will be produced.
(B) A newspaper will introduce a director.
(C) A television series will begin.
(D) A television drama will receive an award.

▶ ▶ ▶ GO ON TO THE NEXT PAGE

# Singapore Business Expo

May 8

Jaheed Gupta
9201 Hearth Place
San Diego, CA 90182

Dear Mr. Gupta,

I am contacting you regarding your participation at this year's Singapore Business Expo, which will take place from August 5-8. We have you scheduled to deliver your talk on the afternoon of the 7th. —[1]—.

I would like to let you know that my assistant has booked a room for you at the Plaza Hotel, where the event will be taking place. We have reserved the Grand Ballroom there for all of the expo's events. —[2]—. Obviously, you will have no problems getting to and from the event each day.

I am certain you will find the hotel a comfortable and luxurious place. What's more, the city is beautiful with attractions such as City Harbor, Freedom Tower, and the Xialou Shopping District. We will spend some time sightseeing in the afternoons. Since the hotel is in the downtown area, we can see a lot of great things in just a short time.

—[3]—. Please submit it to me at least three weeks before the event. The reason for this is that our legal and public affairs teams need to approve the information you will be providing.

It will be great to see you again. We have run into each other at several conferences, none of which I have organized, however. —[4]—.

Regards,

Zao Li
Vice President, Singapore Business Association

**164.** The word "deliver" in paragraph 1, line 2, is closest in meaning to

(A) bring
(B) grant
(C) present
(D) donate

**165.** What is NOT mentioned in the letter?

(A) Transportation details
(B) The location of the hotel
(C) The venue of the event
(D) The dates of the event

**166.** How does Mr. Li know Mr. Gupta?

(A) Through his many awards
(B) Through his published works
(C) Through his application for the expo
(D) Through his attendance at previous events

**167.** In which of the positions marked [1], [2], [3], and [4] does the following sentence best belong?

"I would like to remind you that we need a copy of the talk you plan to give at the expo."

(A) [1]
(B) [2]
(C) [3]
(D) [4]

▶ ▶ ▶GO ON TO THE NEXT PAGE

(April 2) Winston County has a reason to be happy. Two weeks ago, county officials voted to increase its road repair budget to take care of the county's pothole problem.

The winter was extreme this year, and due to the increased use of snowplows and anti-ice chemicals, the county's road surfaces were left with extensive problems. —[1]—. For this reason, the county has received numerous complaints about automobile damage caused by potholes.

—[2]—. The county usually spends 2 million dollars per year on road repairs. However, it was estimated that it will cost over 4 million dollars to repair the potholes caused by this winter alone.

Obviously, this budget increase is necessary. —[3]—. Most county residents rely on their automobiles to get around, and people that do not drive use the county's public bus system, which also needs the roads to be in good condition. —[4]—. The county's economy relies heavily on automobiles, so the measure will allow business to go on as usual.

**168.** What problem is Winston County experiencing?

(A) Errors in the budget planning
(B) Road repair failures
(C) Roadway damage
(D) Increased traffic

**169.** The word "extensive" in paragraph 2, line 4, is closest in meaning to

(A) sufficient
(B) longing
(C) periodical
(D) considerable

**170.** What is NOT mentioned about the county's road repair budget?

(A) It had been insufficient.
(B) It needed to be reexamined.
(C) It increased two weeks ago.
(D) It was based on increased traffic.

**171.** In which of the positions marked [1], [2], [3], and [4] does the following sentence best belong?

"In order to take care of the problem, officials asked for a budget increase for road repairs."

(A) [1]
(B) [2]
(C) [3]
(D) [4]

**Questions 172-175** refer to the following online chat discussion.

**Agatha Franklin** [2:10 P.M.]
Mr. Campbell, the air conditioner in my second-floor office doesn't seem to be working. When I turn it on with the remote control, the lights come on but no cold air comes out.

-------------------------------------------------------------------------------

**Michael Campbell** [2:13 P.M.]
I'm sorry, Ms. Franklin. But all our maintenance staff are occupied right now. I'm afraid I might not be able to get the air conditioner fixed for some time.

-------------------------------------------------------------------------------

**Agatha Franklin** [2:14 P.M.]
You know, I can't focus on my work even if I try due to the dry heat. Unfortunately, all I can do is just sit back and drink as much water as possible.

-------------------------------------------------------------------------------

**Rene Girard** [2:15 P.M.]
Yeah, it's too hot in here. Mr. Campbell, why don't we move to another office on the third floor and get back to work?

-------------------------------------------------------------------------------

**Agatha Franklin** [2:16 P.M.]
I think working in hot conditions can result in a number of adverse health effects.

-------------------------------------------------------------------------------

**Michael Campbell** [2:16 P.M.]
Okay. I'll call the personnel head to fix this problem.

-------------------------------------------------------------------------------

**Michael Campbell** [2:18 P.M.]
All right. The head has allowed you guys to use the third-floor office.

-------------------------------------------------------------------------------

**Rene Girard** [2:18 P.M.]
Thanks a lot. Now I can do some work.

-------------------------------------------------------------------------------

**Agatha Franklin** [2:19 P.M.]
Great, that's a load off my mind. Thanks.

-------------------------------------------------------------------------------

**Michael Campbell** [2:20 P.M.]
Not at all. I'm glad I could be of some help.

-------------------------------------------------------------------------------

**Agatha Franklin** [2:21 P.M.]
Could you do me a favor? Please arrange for someone to move my desktop computer, monitors, fax machine and other stuff into the third-floor office?

-------------------------------------------------------------------------------

**Rene Girard** [2:21 P.M.]
There are too many things for us to carry all of them at once.

-------------------------------------------------------------------------------

**Michael Campbell** [2:22 P.M.]
No problem. I'll send someone up in five minutes. If there is anything else you need, please feel free to talk to me through text.

-------------------------------------------------------------------------------

**Agatha Franklin** [2:23 P.M.]
Okay. Thanks again for everything.

**172.** What is Ms. Franklin's problem?

(A) She has much baggage to carry.
(B) She has a lot of paperwork to do.
(C) She can't work comfortably.
(D) She hasn't been paid proper salary.

**173.** What does Mr. Girard wants to do?

(A) Remodel his office
(B) Share some information
(C) Move to another place
(D) Call someone to help

**174.** What is suggested about Ms. Franklin and Mr. Girard?

(A) They want to purchase a new machine.
(B) They work in the same office.
(C) They have known each other since college.
(D) They have recently been hired.

**175.** At 2:19 P.M., what does Ms. Franklin mean when she writes, "Great, that's a load off my mind"?

(A) She is worried too much about her new job assignment.
(B) She has removed some items from her luggage to lighten weight.
(C) Mr. Girard has found a suitable person to take over her work.
(D) Mr. Campbell has taken a proper measure to relieve her discomfort.

# Vitamin House

# Invoice

**Customer Name:** Betty Farmer

**Order Date:** August 10

**Delivery Address:** 1800 Benson Road, Saint Petersburg, FLA 39422

**Estimated Delivery Date:** August 12–14

**Home Telephone:** (800) 555-1000

**Order Number:** 829201

**Order Taken By:** Frank Miller

**Work Telephone:** (800) 800-9000

| Quantity | Item | Description | Price |
|:---:|:---:|:---|---:|
| 1 | Vitamin 181 | 200-count bottle of chewable vitamin C | $6.00 |
| 1 | Fiber 561 | 5lb container of orange-flavored fiber mix | $11.00 |
| 1 | Herbal 891 | 100-count bottle of gingko biloba capsules | $12.00 |
| 2 | Herbal 913 | 200-count bottle of saw palmetto capsules | $32.00 |
| | | | **Shipping: $5.00** |
| | | | **Total: $66.00** |

**Payment method:** Billed to customer's credit card account ending in 7813

Please contact customerservice@vitaminhouse.com if you have any questions regarding your order.

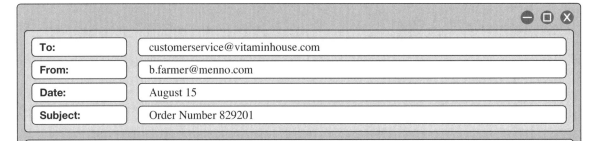

| To: | customerservice@vitaminhouse.com |
|---|---|
| From: | b.farmer@menno.com |
| Date: | August 15 |
| Subject: | Order Number 829201 |

Hello,

I recently placed an order by phone for several products from your company. I was helped by Frank Miller. I received the order by mail yesterday, and it contained all of the items I had ordered. However, I noticed a problem with the invoice. It stated that I had ordered an additional bottle of the saw palmetto capsules when I hadn't. My credit card was also billed for this additional bottle.

I hope you will be able to quickly resolve this issue. I did not order the additional bottle, nor did I receive an additional bottle, yet I was charged for one. Please credit my account for the amount I was charged for the additional bottle.

Please confirm that the issue has been resolved by contacting me at this e-mail address.

Thank you,

Betty Farmer

**176.** Who most likely is Mr. Miller?

(A) A Vitamin House employee
(B) One of Ms. Farmer's employees
(C) A nutritionist at a local hospital
(D) An employee for a shipping company

**177.** When did Ms. Farmer receive her order?

(A) On August 10
(B) On August 12
(C) On August 14
(D) On August 15

**178.** Why did Ms. Farmer send the e-mail?

(A) Her credit card expired.
(B) There was a billing error.
(C) She received the wrong product.
(D) A product's use-by date had passed.

**179.** How much money should Ms. Farmer expect to be added to her credit card?

(A) $6
(B) $11
(C) $12
(D) $16

**180.** How should Vitamin House customer service respond to Ms. Farmer?

(A) By e-mailing her
(B) By calling her on her home phone
(C) By calling her on her work phone
(D) By sending a letter through the mail

**Questions 181-185** refer to the following article and e-mail.

March 23 – Tom Stanford, the owner of the Prime Hotel, believes in utilizing as many products and services from local sources as possible. Most meats and vegetables served at the hotel's restaurant come from Virginia farms. He even showcases the talents of local performers on the hotel's theater stage. And for the entire month of August, the hotel will feature the music of Edgar Stevenson, a Virginia resident and Grand Award winner.

"I always buy local when I can. Why not have local talents perform at our luxurious hotel as well?" Mr. Stanford said, inviting guests to check out why Mr. Stevenson is so well known. "Unless people follow the local music scene, they won't know most of the artists that perform at our hotel. But the performances are always amazing."

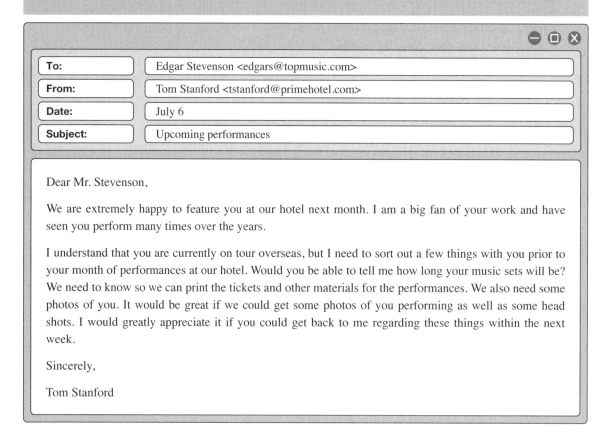

| To: | Edgar Stevenson <edgars@topmusic.com> |
| --- | --- |
| From: | Tom Stanford <tstanford@primehotel.com> |
| Date: | July 6 |
| Subject: | Upcoming performances |

Dear Mr. Stevenson,

We are extremely happy to feature you at our hotel next month. I am a big fan of your work and have seen you perform many times over the years.

I understand that you are currently on tour overseas, but I need to sort out a few things with you prior to your month of performances at our hotel. Would you be able to tell me how long your music sets will be? We need to know so we can print the tickets and other materials for the performances. We also need some photos of you. It would be great if we could get some photos of you performing as well as some head shots. I would greatly appreciate it if you could get back to me regarding these things within the next week.

Sincerely,

Tom Stanford

**181.** What does the article discuss?

(A) Some remodeling at a local business

(B) The purchase of a local hotel

(C) Some upcoming performances

(D) A new restaurant in the area

**182.** What is mentioned about Mr. Stanford?

(A) He prefers to use local sources for hotel supplies.

(B) He used to be a member of a local music band.

(C) He is well known to musicians in the area.

(D) He has some other businesses in Virginia.

**183.** What does Mr. Stanford invite guests to do at the hotel?

(A) Request music at their table during dinner

(B) Get involved in the local music scene

(C) Spend the night at his hotel

(D) See a musical performance

**184.** What is implied about Mr. Stevenson?

(A) He received an award for his work last year.

(B) He no longer has a home in Virginia.

(C) He is currently outside of Virginia.

(D) He may not perform next month.

**185.** According to the e-mail, what does Mr. Stanford need from Mr. Stevenson?

(A) Some images of Mr. Stevenson

(B) The venue for the Mr. Stevenson's performance

(C) Mr. Stevenson's bank account number

(D) A list of songs Mr. Stevenson will be playing

Questions 186-190 refer to the following Web pages and e-mail.

http://www.fellasshoeorthotics.com

**Fellas Custom Shoe Orthotics**

# Frequently Asked Questions

### What types of products does Fellas Custom Shoe Orthotics produce?

Fellas Custom Shoe Orthotics manufactures shoe orthotics for men's, women's, and children's shoes. Most of our shoe orthotics are created for normal daily use. They typically use a proprietary thermoplastic or fiberglass composite that can be heat molded to match the customer's foot. However, we also offer specialized shoe orthotics. For example, our heat moldable carbon fiber shoe orthotics were developed specifically for use in athletics shoes. These shoe orthotics are light, durable, and extremely rigid.

### Who uses our products?

We provide our shoe orthotics for many companies in both the United States and Asia. All of our products can be heat molded with a simple, foolproof process, allowing for a custom fit each and every time.

### How can I request Fellas Custom Shoe Orthotics to become a supplier for my company?

Please contact one of our representatives to schedule a meeting. Our representatives can provide you with free product samples and contract requirements.

http:// www.fellasshoes.com/personneldepartment/personnelroaster

# The List of Sales Representatives

**Asia:** Daisuke Tanaka / <d.tanaka@ fellashoeorthotics.co.jp>

**Australia:** Devora Morgan / <dmorgan@ fellashoeorthotics.co.au>

**Western Europe:** François Jalabert / <f.jalabert@ fellashoeorthotics.co.fr>

**Eastern Europe:** Anatoly Konenko / <akonenko@ fellashoeorthotics.co.ru>

**North America:** Stanley Parker / <s.parker@ fellashoeorthotics.com>>

**Central America:** Julian Sanchez / <js@ fellashoeorthotics.com>

**South America:** Maria Jimenez / < m.jimenez@ fellashoeorthotics.co.ar>

| To: | Stanley Parker <s.parker@fellashoeorthotics.com> |
| From: | Jaime Foster < jaimefoster@vista.co.ar> |
| Date: | June 12 |
| Subject: | Interested in your products |

Dear Mr. Parker,

My company is a South America-based orthotics distributor. We provide orthotics for the medical industry, with goods such as shoe orthotics, artificial limbs, and orthopedic back and neck braces. Last month, I attended the US National Orthotics trade show in Las Vegas, and I visited your company's booth several times. I was quite impressed by the quality and pricing of your athletic shoe orthotics and intend to place a large order for them. Your company's products are far superior to the rubber products that we are getting from our current supplier. We have been looking for a lighter product for some time, and some of your products definitely fit the bill.

I would like to speak to one of your company's representatives about sampling your products and possibly entering into a contract. Please let me know whom I can meet with in this region so I can start doing business with your company.

Sincerely,

Jaime Foster
Vista Orthopedic Medical Suppliers

---

**186.** What is stated about Fellas Custom Shoe Orthotics?

(A) It only manufactures athletic footwear.
(B) It sells its products solely to hospitals.
(C) It usually works with domestic companies.
(D) It does business in many countries.

**187.** What is most likely true about Mr. Parker?

(A) He is able to send samples of shoe orthotics.
(B) He works in both North and South America.
(C) He met with Mr. Foster on several occasions.
(D) His office is based on the West Coast of the United States.

**188.** What type of materials will Mr. Foster most likely want to be used in products that he purchases?

(A) Rubber
(B) Thermoplastic
(C) Fiberglass composite
(D) Carbon fiber

**189.** In the e-mail, the word "intend" in paragraph 1, line 5, is closest in meaning to

(A) plan
(B) seem
(C) request
(D) ask

**190.** Who will Mr. Foster most likely contact to receive the sample products?

(A) Debora Morgan
(B) François Jalabert
(C) Julian Sanchez
(D) Maria Jimenez

# Pearl Fabrics
769 Creek Road
Clayton, NC 27520

October 18

Nancy Granger
57 Central Avenue
New York, NY 10002

Dear Ms. Granger,

I am sorry to inform you that the following item you requested has been discontinued.

PRODUCT #00013834 (Jenny's) Cotton, Pink 101, no pattern (12ft long), $19.99

The manufacturer of that product, Jenny's, discontinued the product just a week ago. We still have some of it in stock, but other than that, I'm afraid we cannot get more of it. Therefore, I suggest that you look into the following:

PRODUCT #00081230 (Fabricland) Cotton, Rose Pink, no pattern (6ft long), $10.99 or
PRODUCT #00109314 (Fabricland) Cotton, Pink Salmon, no pattern (6ft long), $13.99 or
PRODUCT #00056918 (Inkcloth) Cotton, Light Pink, no pattern (12ft long) $11.99

We have sorted the ones that have a similar texture and color of the fabric you desire. The differences in the products are the prices, the lengths, and the colors. The screen monitor may not display the subtle differences in the colors. We can send you samples of all three for a more in-depth examination. I hope this helps.

Thank you always.

Kara Strong
Customer Service Specialist
Pearl Fabrics

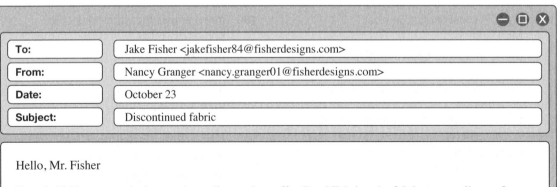

| To: | Jake Fisher <jakefisher84@fisherdesigns.com> |
| From: | Nancy Granger <nancy.granger01@fisherdesigns.com> |
| Date: | October 23 |
| Subject: | Discontinued fabric |

Hello, Mr. Fisher

I'm afraid I have some bad news. According to the staff at Pearl Fabrics, the fabric we usually use for our Spring Flash curtains, Pink 101, has been discontinued. I ordered all of the fabric it had remaining in stock, but unless Jenny's decides to bring back the fabric, I don't think we have any choice but to choose a different kind of fabric. The company sent me some samples of products it recommend as a substitute. All of them are cotton, but they differ slightly in color and texture. In addition, all of the fabrics from Fabricland are heavier than Pink 101.

The one that has the most similar color and texture is Pink Salmon. However, I don't want to recommend it. The second-most similar product is from Inkcloth. The color looks pretty similar, but it's lighter than the original product. I'm not sure if we can make sturdy curtains with this kind of material. If we use the fabric from Fabricland, we will have to increase the prices of the curtains. If we use the fabric from Inkcloth, we'll have to sacrifice the quality of our products. I'll bring all the samples to tomorrow's meeting so you can have a better look. See you tomorrow.

Nancy Granger

---

## TRANSACTION RECEIPT

Pearl Fabrics
769 Creek Road
Clayton, NC 27520
(919) 319-4928

02/16 11:55
**Name**: Nancy Granger
**Requested Package Number**: #000000AA19317
**Receiver**: Fisher Designs
**Contents**: PRODUCT #00109314 (Fabricland) Cotton, Pink Salmon, no pattern (6ft long), $13.99
**Quantity:** 20

**Tax (6%)**: $16.79
**Total**: $296.59

Thank you for shopping with us.

---

**191.** In the letter, the word "subtle" in paragraph 3, line 3, is closest in meaning to

(A) rational
(B) minor
(C) decisive
(D) influential

**192.** What is the purpose of the letter?

(A) To explain why a delivery was late
(B) To recommend a different fabric shop
(C) To offer a special promotion that features free delivery
(D) To notify a buyer about a product

**193.** What will most likely happen to Fisher Designs?

(A) It will increase the price of its Spring Flash curtains.
(B) It will stop producing Spring Flash curtains.
(C) it will find another source of fabric.
(D) It will provide its own fabric.

**194.** Which fabric is the lightest?

(A) Pink 101
(B) Rose Pink
(C) Pink Salmon
(D) Light Pink

**195.** What most likely is the problem with Pink Salmon?

(A) It is too expensive.
(B) It is too light.
(C) It has a reputation for poor quality.
(D) It is made with microfibers.

# Books World

| HOME | RECENT | CATEGORY | ORDER |
|------|--------|----------|-------|

### Bestselling books by category: culinary arts

1. *Behind the Kitchen* by Anthony Barry
   Dreaming of opening a restaurant? Learn to make good money in the food industry with Mr. Barry's insights and advice.

2. *Happy Table* by Karen Wilson
   The food on your table determines your and your family's health and happiness. Directions on choosing the right ingredients and using the right cooking methods.

3. *Understanding the Food Industry* by Rodney Sanford
   You have to understand the industry in order to become successful in it. See how to avoid mistakes that people new to the food industry often make. If you are interested in owning a restaurant, this is a must-read for you.

4. *Food, Language, and Culture* by Rodney Sanford
   What determines the food, language, and culture of a nation? And how do they, in turn, affect the nation and its people? Find out in Mr. Sanford's book that has been translated into more than 10 languages.

# Bloomfield Public Library
## Events in the Fourth Week of June

June 20, Monday – Successful author and restaurant owner Rodney Sanford visits our library to discuss methods regarding operating a restaurant that are demonstrated in his latest book. Mr. Sanford will sign his book for participants after the event.

June 22, Wednesday – A fun, interactive event full of music for preschoolers and toddlers with their guardians. Songs about the different seasons and weather will be played along with various instruments. No registration required to join this exciting musical class.

| To: | <customerservice@bloomfieldpl.org> |
| From: | Melvin Charles <mcharles@opmail.com> |
| Date: | June 27 |
| Subject: | Bloomfield Public Library |

To Whom It May Concern,

I recently attended an event held at the Bloomfield Public Library. I was greatly impressed by Mr. Sanford's knowledge and ideas. What he taught me during the discussion session will be a great asset when it comes to executing my own business plan.

In addition, I would like to be notified by text message when the book *Behind the Kitchen* becomes available. It was already checked out when I tried to borrow it. My mobile number is (210) 555-3918. Thank you.

Melvin Charles

**196.** In the Web page, the word "good" in paragraph 1, line 2, is closest in meaning to

(A) pleasant
(B) substantial
(C) generous
(D) real

**197.** What is indicated about the Bloomfield Public Library?

(A) It hosts events for children.
(B) It requires a membership card for event registration.
(C) It is currently hiring new employees.
(D) Its operating hours vary seasonall

**198.** What book was signed at the Bloomfield Public Library by its author recently?

(A) *Behind the Kitchen*
(B) *Happy Table*
(C) *Understanding the Food Industry*
(D) *Food, Language, and Culture*

**199.** What is probably true about Mr. Charles?

(A) He frequently visits the Bloomfield Public Library.
(B) He works at the Bloomfield Public Library.
(C) He would like to buy one of Mr. Sanford's books.
(D) He is interested in opening a restaurant.

**200.** What does Mr. Charles request the Bloomfield Public Library do?

(A) Inform him of the release date of a book
(B) Notify him of when there will be another event with Mr. Sanford
(C) Let him know when a book is returned to the library
(D) Send a new book to his address

STOP! This is the end of the test. If you finish before time is called,
you may go back to Parts 5, 6, and 7 and check your work.

# Actual Test

MP3

해설집

시작 시간 ___시 ___분

종료 시간 ___시 ___분

중간에 멈추지 말고 처음부터 끝까지 풀어보세요.
문제를 풀 때에는 실전처럼 답안지에 마킹하세요.

목표 개수 _____ / 200    실제 개수 _____ / 200

예상 점수는 번역 및 정답에 있는 점수 환산표를 참조하세요.

# LISTENING TEST

In the Listening test, you will be asked to demonstrate how well you understand spoken English. The entire Listening test will last approximately 45 minutes. There are four parts, and directions are given for each part. You must mark your answers on the separate answer sheet. Do not write your answers in your test book.

## PART 1

**Directions:** For each question in this part, you will hear four statements about a picture in your test book. When you hear the statements, you must select the one statement that best describes what you see in the picture. Then find the number of the question on your answer sheet and mark your answer. The statements will not be printed in your test book and will be spoken only one time.

Statement (B), "They are sitting at a table," is the best description of the picture. So you should select answer (B) and mark it on your answer sheet.

**1.**

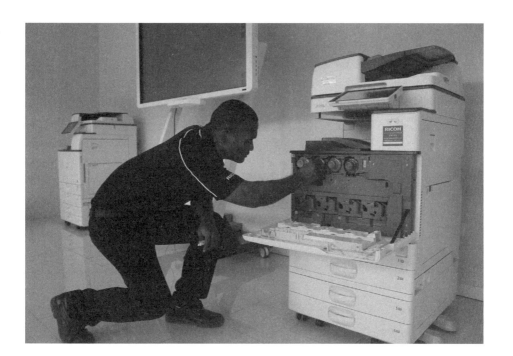

**2.**

▶ ▶ ▶GO ON TO THE NEXT PAGE

**3.**

**4.**

**5.**

**6.**

# PART 2

**Directions:** You will hear a question or statement and three responses spoken in English. They will not be printed in your test book and will be spoken only one time. Select the best response to the question or statement and mark the letter (A), (B), or (C) on your answer sheet.

**7.** Mark your answer on your answer sheet.

**8.** Mark your answer on your answer sheet.

**9.** Mark your answer on your answer sheet.

**10.** Mark your answer on your answer sheet.

**11.** Mark your answer on your answer sheet.

**12.** Mark your answer on your answer sheet.

**13.** Mark your answer on your answer sheet.

**14.** Mark your answer on your answer sheet.

**15.** Mark your answer on your answer sheet.

**16.** Mark your answer on your answer sheet.

**17.** Mark your answer on your answer sheet.

**18.** Mark your answer on your answer sheet.

**19.** Mark your answer on your answer sheet.

**20.** Mark your answer on your answer sheet.

**21.** Mark your answer on your answer sheet.

**22.** Mark your answer on your answer sheet.

**23.** Mark your answer on your answer sheet.

**24.** Mark your answer on your answer sheet.

**25.** Mark your answer on your answer sheet.

**26.** Mark your answer on your answer sheet.

**27.** Mark your answer on your answer sheet.

**28.** Mark your answer on your answer sheet.

**29.** Mark your answer on your answer sheet.

**30.** Mark your answer on your answer sheet.

**31.** Mark your answer on your answer sheet.

## PART 3

**Directions:** You will hear some conversations between two or three people. You will be asked to answer three questions about what the speakers say in each conversation. Select the best response to each question and mark the letter (A), (B), (C), or (D) on your answer sheet. The conversations will not be printed in your test book and will be spoken only one time.

**32.** What are the speakers doing?

(A) Purchasing some plants
(B) Working on a fence
(C) Repairing a vehicle
(D) Painting a truck

**33.** What do the speakers need?

(A) Wooden planks
(B) Spare parts
(C) Paint
(D) Brushes

**34.** When will the task probably be completed?

(A) This morning
(B) This afternoon
(C) Tomorrow morning
(D) The day after tomorrow

**35.** According to the man, what is the problem?

(A) He has a scheduling conflict.
(B) He missed his flight.
(C) He is suffering from a toothache.
(D) He can't start a meeting on time.

**36.** What does the man want to do?

(A) Locate a dentist
(B) Make a presentation
(C) Delay a meeting
(D) Reserve a plane ticket

**37.** What does the woman say she will do?

(A) Arrive early tomorrow
(B) Send Kate to the meeting room
(C) Prepare for a company event
(D) Inform the staff about a change in a schedule

**38.** What does the woman mean when she says, "Can you see all these cars at the intersection?"

(A) She is concerned about her presentation.
(B) She feels proud of working at a car manufacturer.
(C) She wants to introduce new cars to customers.
(D) She is surprised by heavy traffic.

**39.** Why will the speakers meet with Mr. Edward?

(A) To give a sales presentation
(B) To provide a job offer
(C) To discuss the design of a new car
(D) To sign a contract

**40.** What does the woman suggest?

(A) Canceling a meeting
(B) Inspecting a company vehicle
(C) Rescheduling her presentation
(D) Using public transportation

**41.** What are the speakers discussing?

(A) A defective product
(B) A new prescription
(C) A surgical operation
(D) A medical appointment

**42.** What does the woman say she will do immediately?

(A) Call a doctor
(B) Accept a returned product
(C) Cancel an order
(D) Schedule a new appointment

**43.** What does the man agree to do?

(A) Call a taxi
(B) Postpone an appointment
(C) Visit a clinic
(D) Issue a prescription

44. Who most likely are the men?

(A) Recording engineers
(B) Photographers
(C) Event planners
(D) Musicians

45. What do the men ask the woman to do?

(A) Take some commercial videos
(B) Offer new tour packages
(C) Record some songs for an album
(D) Create images for merchandise

46. What does the woman request from the men?

(A) A completed questionnaire
(B) An employment contract
(C) A new musical instrument
(D) A promotional item

47. Who most likely is the woman?

(A) A financial analyst
(B) An investor
(C) A project accountant
(D) A Human Resources manager

48. What is the man asking about?

(A) His salary
(B) His starting date
(C) His vacation time
(D) His training opportunities

49. What will the woman do before the man starts working?

(A) Conduct a background check
(B) Negotiate the man's salary
(C) Lead an employee orientation
(D) Conduct a job interview

50. What problem are the speakers addressing?

(A) A reduced budget
(B) Negative feedback
(C) The loss of market share
(D) Poor packaging

51. What does the women say about the company's products?

(A) Their logos were redesigned.
(B) Their sales have been declining.
(C) The quality of their packaging has improved.
(D) Their promotional events were not successful.

52. What will the man probably do next?

(A) Cancel an event
(B) Contact an advertising agency
(C) Try to gain more funding
(D) Speak to a shop manager

53. What is the problem with the product?

(A) It is expensive.
(B) It has failed to attract customers.
(C) It has a scent that is too strong.
(D) It hasn't passed a quality test.

54. What does the woman tell the man to do?

(A) Cancel a quality control test
(B) Review customer feedback
(C) Give her some advice
(D) Manage a project

55. What does the man offer to do?

(A) Develop a new product
(B) Buy some cosmetics
(C) Make revisions to the product
(D) Share some information

**56.** What are the speakers discussing?

(A) A method for tracking orders
(B) A proposal for extending hours of operation
(C) An introduction for a new inventory system
(D) A new policy for obtaining materials

**57.** According to the woman, why was a decision made?

(A) To reduce expenses
(B) To save time
(C) To increase productivity
(D) To comply with a new law

**58.** What does the woman suggest?

(A) Purchasing more office supplies
(B) Changing a shipping policy
(C) Making a process easier
(D) Posting a job opening online

**59.** Where do the speakers probably work?

(A) At an accounting firm
(B) At an advertising company
(C) At a game manufacturer
(D) At a department store

**60.** What does the woman mean when she says, "Motion Sportwear was my second account here"?

(A) She has several bank accounts.
(B) She has knowledge of the man's job.
(C) She doesn't work with the client any longer.
(D) She fully understands why the man is angry.

**61.** What does the woman suggest the man do?

(A) Find another job
(B) Revise a graphic design
(C) Attract a new client
(D) Get some help from his manager

## Common Access Card Error Codes

| 001 | Database access restricted |
| --- | --- |
| 002 | Access card damaged |
| 003 | Printer malfunction |
| 004 | Vehicle not registered |

**62.** Who most likely is the man?

(A) A lab technician
(B) A receptionist
(C) A security expert
(D) A software developer

**63.** Look at the graphic. Why did the woman's card fail to work in the morning?

(A) Her card is damaged.
(B) The database system has a problem.
(C) Some security devices malfunctioned.
(D) Her car has not been registered yet.

**64.** What does the woman say she will do?

(A) Visit the security office
(B) Publish her research papers
(C) Come to work early tomorrow
(D) Issue a new access card

▶ ▶ ▶GO ON TO THE NEXT PAGE

## OAKLAND CAR RENTAL CHART

| Small Pickup Truck<br>12 feet long | Cargo Van<br>15 feet long |
|---|---|
| Standard Mover<br>18 feet long | Large Moving Truck<br>22 feet long |

65. Why does the man need to rent a vehicle?

    (A) To go on vacation
    (B) To move his office
    (C) To transport some furniture from his home
    (D) To assist with the opening of a new store

66. Look at the graphic. Which vehicle does the man want?

    (A) A small pickup truck
    (B) A cargo van
    (C) A standard mover
    (D) A large moving truck

67. What does the woman request from the man?

    (A) His driver's license
    (B) A copy of a rental contract
    (C) A security deposit
    (D) The date of a rental

---

## London 46 Theater Presents

### *Live Once, Buried Twice*

**BOX OFFICE REGULAR HOURS**
11:00 A.M. – 7:00 P.M.
DOORS OPEN 6:30 P.M.
SHOW BEGINS 8:00 P.M.
SHOW ENDS 10:30 P.M.
NO ENTRANCE AFTER 8:20 P.M.

68. Look at the graphic. When do the speakers plan to arrive at the theater?

    (A) 6:30 P.M.
    (B) 8:00 P.M.
    (C) 8:30 P.M.
    (D) 10:30 P.M.

69. What does the man mention about the theater?

    (A) It hosts various performances.
    (B) It doesn't have assigned seating.
    (C) It has a long history and wonderful traditions.
    (D) It sells a limited number of tickets at discounted prices.

70. What will the speakers probably do before the play?

    (A) Reserve tickets
    (B) Have a meal
    (C) Buy some souvenirs
    (D) Confirm a schedule

## PART 4

**Directions:** You will hear some short talks given by a single speaker. You will be asked to answer three questions about what the speaker says in each short talk. Select the best response to each question and mark the letter (A), (B), (C), or (D) on your answer sheet. The talks will not be printed in your test book and will be spoken only one time.

**71.** What is the speaker talking about?

(A) A meeting agenda
(B) A work schedule
(C) A job application
(D) A new Web site

**72.** Who is the speaker?

(A) A human resources manager
(B) A senior researcher
(C) A financial analyst
(D) A computer programmer

**73.** What does the speaker suggest the listener do?

(A) Attend a staff meeting
(B) Complete an application form online
(C) Provide a reference letter
(D) Make a telephone call

**74.** Which department does the speaker work in?

(A) Marketing
(B) Public Relations
(C) Security
(D) Personnel

**75.** According to the speaker, what will be given to the employees next week?

(A) New passwords
(B) Access cards
(C) Parking spaces
(D) Office keys

**76.** What will the speaker do next?

(A) Offer technical training
(B) Hand out samples
(C) Install some new software
(D) Complete a project

**77.** According to the speaker, why is the event being held?

(A) To thank volunteers
(B) To raise funds
(C) To publicize adoption efforts
(D) To celebrate an anniversary

**78.** What kind of organization does the speaker probably work at?

(A) A research and consulting agency
(B) A consumer rights group
(C) A media organization
(D) An animal welfare group

**79.** What does the speaker mention about the adoption campaign?

(A) It was very successful.
(B) It required a lot of volunteers.
(C) It was mentioned in the press.
(D) It was not effective.

**80.** Where does the speaker most likely work?

(A) At a catering service
(B) At a lumber supply store
(C) At a printing firm
(D) At an event planning company

**81.** Why is the man calling?

(A) To cancel an event
(B) To reserve a venue
(C) To make catering requests
(D) To confirm a location

**82.** What will the speaker do tomorrow?

(A) Visit a catering company
(B) Summarize feedback
(C) Take customers' orders
(D) Attend a cooking demonstration

▶ ▶ ▶GO ON TO THE NEXT PAGE

**83.** What problem does the speaker mention?

(A) A billing issue
(B) A decline in sales
(C) Customer complaints
(D) Possible massive layoffs

**84.** What does the woman mean when she says, "I need everyone on deck with our restructuring plans to improve our sales"?

(A) She is disappointed with some errors in work.
(B) She is uncertain about following a recommendation.
(C) She wants the listeners to be involved.
(D) She needs more creative ideas to increase sales.

**85.** According to the speaker, who is Ms. Jenkins?

(A) A market researcher
(B) A board member
(C) An electric engineer
(D) A sales professional

**86.** What will the listeners do at 4 P.M.?

(A) Have some ice cream
(B) Board a trolley
(C) Attend a concert
(D) Visit a cultural museum

**87.** Why does the speaker say, "Sandy's Donut Shop's ice cream is delicious"?

(A) To compare two ice cream brands
(B) To encourage the listeners to try delicious donuts
(C) To recommend that the listeners visit there
(D) To explain why a shop is widely known

**88.** What will the speaker probably do next?

(A) Watch a show
(B) Make a reservation
(C) Buy some souvenirs
(D) Distribute some tickets

**89.** What problem does the speaker mention?

(A) A construction delay
(B) Traffic problems
(C) A mechanical breakdown
(D) Inclement weather

**90.** Who most likely is the speaker?

(A) A computer repairperson
(B) A construction supervisor
(C) A news reporter
(D) A government official

**91.** What is the speaker going to do later?

(A) Perform a safety inspection
(B) Train new employees
(C) Announce a new update
(D) Discuss upcoming events

**92.** Where is this announcement heard?

(A) On an airplane
(B) On a cruise ship
(C) At a harbor office
(D) At a press conference

**93.** According to the speaker, what has caused the delay?

(A) Mechanical problems
(B) Heavy vessel traffic
(C) Weather conditions
(D) System software malfunctions

**94.** What will the listeners most likely do next?

(A) Take a boat trip
(B) Get refunds on their tickets
(C) Learn safety procedures
(D) Wait for another announcement

## Order Form

| Item | Quantity |
|------|----------|
| T-shirts | 100 |
| Postcards | 150 |
| Coffee cups | 500 |
| Candy bars | 700 |

| Time 10:00-12:00 | Reserved By |
|------------------|-------------|
| Presidential Library | Mr. Baker |
| Convention Room | Ms. Lawrence |
| Conference Room A | Ms. Wallace |
| Conference Room B | Open |

**95.** Look at the graphic. Which quantity of the order form may be changed?

(A) 100
(B) 150
(C) 500
(D) 700

**96.** What will the speaker do next week?

(A) He will release a new beverage.
(B) He will be out of the office.
(C) He will begin work on a new job.
(D) He will use some special equipment.

**97.** What does the speaker say Ms. Kensington will do?

(A) She will ask for a full refund.
(B) She will train some new employees.
(C) She will send new coffee cups.
(D) She will be taking care of the man's work.

**98.** Why did the speaker reserve a room?

(A) To meet with some clients
(B) To give a lecture
(C) To hold a seminar
(D) To rehearse a presentation

**99.** Look at the graphic. Which room does the speaker want to use?

(A) The Presidential Library
(B) The Convention Room
(C) Conference Room A
(D) Conference Room B

**100.** What does the speaker say he wants to do?

(A) Get a complimentary beverage
(B) Print some handouts
(C) Reschedule his reservation
(D) Set up some video equipment

This is the end of the Listening test. Turn to Part 5 in your test book.

▶ ▶ ▶ GO ON TO THE NEXT PAGE

# READING TEST

In the Reading test, you will read a variety of texts and answer several different types of reading comprehension questions. The entire Reading test will last 75 minutes. There are three parts, and directions are given for each part. You are encouraged to answer as many questions as possible within the time allowed.

You must mark your answers on the separate answer sheet. Do not write your answers in your test book.

## PART 5

**Directions**: A word or phrase is missing in each of the sentences below. Four answer choices are given below each sentence. Select the best answer to complete the sentence. Then mark the letter (A), (B), (C), or (D) on your answer sheet.

**101.** European financial institutions will pull ------- funds out of China due to monetary difficulties occurring in America.

(A) they
(B) them
(C) their
(D) theirs

**102.** All of the department heads are expected to perform well on both familiar ------- new tasks.

(A) and
(B) but
(C) or
(D) nor

**103.** The municipal gallery is ------- closed for refurbishment and is due to reopen in September of next year.

(A) currently
(B) quickly
(C) instantly
(D) lately

**104.** Thousands of researchers from almost 100 countries will be in ------- at the international academic conference on climate change in Stockholm next month.

(A) attention
(B) attendee
(C) attendance
(D) attendant

**105.** In recent years, increased college student enrollment at the city's universities has led to greater demand for ------- properties.

(A) rent
(B) rents
(C) rental
(D) renting

**106.** For a ------- time only, customers can purchase our new powerful laptop computers with 0% financing and no money down.

(A) limit
(B) limits
(C) limiting
(D) limited

**107.** The number of American overseas travelers fell ------- as it dropped by 12% from the previous year due to the economic recession.

(A) sharp
(B) sharpen
(C) sharply
(D) sharpness

**108.** According to the forest service, ------- who does not follow the rules will be fined or barred from visiting the mountain again.

(A) they
(B) those
(C) anyone
(D) people

**109.** This method sometimes helps clarify topics that we may misunderstand or not ------- understand.

(A) partially
(B) fully
(C) hardly
(D) incidentally

**110.** Due to unexpected audio teleconference system failures, the ------- was postponed until next Wednesday.

(A) present
(B) presenter
(C) presentation
(D) presented

**111.** Our security teams are on duty 24 hours a day to give ------- attention to any situations that may arise.

(A) prompt
(B) promptness
(C) prompting
(D) promptly

**112.** One of the oldest manufacturing plants in Alabama finally ------- operations following a month-long suspension.

(A) stopped
(B) renovated
(C) completed
(D) resumed

**113.** Highly advanced medical technology can help surgeons conduct delicate surgeries more -------.

(A) urgently
(B) promptly
(C) precisely
(D) seriously

**114.** Last month, Mandoo Tech debuted a new computer half the size of the computers most people use, making it the ------- computer on the market.

(A) better
(B) smallest
(C) worst
(D) widest

**115.** The newly improved container trucks are almost as ------- as the conventional ones, but they are stronger and easier to control.

(A) heavy
(B) heavier
(C) heaviest
(D) heavily

**116.** To retain their freshness, these onions and tomatoes should be put into the refrigerator and stored ------- 36 degrees Fahrenheit.

(A) more
(B) less
(C) low
(D) below

**117.** Once the pharmaceutical patents -------, other companies can produce identical versions of the original drugs four times cheaper than the current rates.

(A) expire
(B) expires
(C) is expired
(D) will be expired

**118.** The individual ------- responsibility is to process all sales paperwork is Andrew Kim, the assistant director.

(A) what
(B) whether
(C) whose
(D) this

**119.** ------- studying the personal and social economic activities which affect the national economy, economists regularly attempt to predict future global economic trends.

(A) In addition to
(B) Furthermore
(C) In place of
(D) as a result of

▶▶▶GO ON TO THE NEXT PAGE

120. The shoe store located on 11th Street provides a wide ------- of brands for customers to choose from.

(A) type
(B) preference
(C) difference
(D) selection

121. An industrial expert said Zayo Auto's ------- of SS Motors will narrow the gap in automobile technology between the two companies from six years to three years.

(A) acquisition
(B) competition
(C) advances
(D) development

122. According to a news report, our company's brand value ranked 13th ------- 120 multinational corporations around the world.

(A) of
(B) among
(C) from
(D) throughout

123. This museum is one of the oldest institutions in the United States dedicated to ------- the nation's railroad history.

(A) preserve
(B) preservation
(C) preserving
(D) preserved

124. If the company ------- these new energy drinks in China, they probably wouldn't have been popular.

(A) sells
(B) sold
(C) had sold
(D) should sell

125. Many factors, including a lack of oxygen, extreme weather, and frostbite, make it ------- to climb some high mountains.

(A) difficulty
(B) difficulties
(C) difficult
(D) difference

126. Any customer who makes a ------- payment must pay the remaining balance plus a $5 late charge the next month.

(A) partial
(B) immediate
(C) total
(D) reliable

127. ------- some people are very different from us, we should still respect their cultures and local customs.

(A) Even though
(B) Nevertheless
(C) Despite
(D) Even

128. Customers who take their computers to the service center for repairs will be ------- contacted, typically within one hour, after the repairs are completed.

(A) randomly
(B) promptly
(C) periodically
(D) recently

129. Due to the poor economy, most of the employees will put off taking their summer vacation until the domestic economy -------.

(A) improve
(B) had improved
(C) will improve
(D) has improved

130. It appears that many office workers overuse caffeine like coffee ------- they get tired or stressed from work and their daily routines.

(A) so that
(B) even if
(C) whenever
(D) whichever

## PART 6

**Directions:** Read the texts that follow. A word, phrase, or sentence is missing in parts of each text. Four answer choices for each question are given below the text. Select the best answer to complete the text. Then mark the letter (A), (B), (C), or (D) on your answer sheet.

**Questions 131-134** refer to the following advertisement.

### The East Seafood Restaurant

The East Seafood Restaurant is a great choice for people who want a quick meal and for families with kids. We guarantee you'll get your king crabs in 15 minutes, ------- your meal is
**131.**
on us! Our meals include hand-cut French-fries, a healthy salad bar selection, and a variety of soft drinks.

Apply today to become a member of our restaurant. Every time you visit, a stamp will be put on your membership card. ------- 10 visits, you will receive a free lobster meal. Members will
**132.**
receive a 20% discount on Blue Ocean merchandise like T-shirts and caps with the East Seafood Restaurant logo. -------.
**133.**

The East Seafood Restaurant ------- an annual membership fee of $40. Please note that the
**134.**
membership card cannot be used to pay for meals; it is not a credit card.

---

**131.** (A) for
(B) either
(C) or
(D) and

**132.** (A) Before
(B) While
(C) Since
(D) After

**133.** (A) Members will also get priority seating when the restaurant is crowded.
(B) Our restaurant is conveniently accessible by bus and subway.
(C) The number of our restaurant members has increased considerably.
(D) Super seafoods such as salmon and tuna are known to promote heart health.

**134.** (A) charges
(B) joins
(C) costs
(D) transfers

---

**MEMORANDUM**

From: North America Corporation HR & Payroll Services
To: All employees
Date: January 8
Subject: Change in the delivery of your pay statement

Over the past few months, electronic pay statements have replaced paper pay statements for

many employees ------- pay is directly deposited into an account. Your final paper pay
          **135.**

statement ------- and delivered to you on January 15. If you want to continue to receive a
      **136.**

paper pay statement, you can follow the instructions that will be sent to you in mid-January.

Electronic delivery of your pay statement is part of our goal to encourage the use of HR and

payroll self-service.

By using HR and payroll self-service, you will have easy ------- to current and past pay
          **137.**

information in seconds. In addition, some of the company's costs associated with producing

and delivering pay statements will be reduced. -------. We believe finding ways to improve
          **138.**

employee convenience is one of the top priorities of the Human Resources Department.

Thank you.

---

135. (A) who
(B) which
(C) while
(D) whose

136. (A) prints
(B) were printed
(C) has printed
(D) will be printed

137. (A) search
(B) access
(C) insight
(D) control

138. (A) Our employees have played a vital role in the company's success.
(B) Management is willing to increase the bonuses of all employees as requested.
(C) This policy change will ultimately contribute to the convenience of our employees.
(D) The objective of technology in the workplace is to facilitate everyday work for employees.

---

EFFECTIVE MONDAY, JULY 1

**RELOCATION NOTICE**

As of July 1, the Cheese Pastry Factory will no longer be in its current location. We have

closed our head office in Hayward and have begun the process of relocating to our new

offices in Oakland.


Any ------- about concerns or problems with products or services must now be sent to the
     **139.**
following address: Cheese Pastry Factory, 110 Telegraph Lane, Oakland, California 94577.


However, our online store, www.cpf.com, and our employee e-mail addresses will remain

-------. Unfortunately, we have not yet received our new telephone and fax numbers from
  **140.**
Oakland Telephone Services. -------.
           **141.**


------- the Cheese Pastry Factory, we would like to thank you for your patience and hope you
  **142.**
continue to shop with the largest pastry supplier in the Northern California area.

---

**139.** (A) response
    (B) complaint
    (C) questionnaire
    (D) correspondence

**140.** (A) unchange
    (B) unchangingly
    (C) unchanging
    (D) unchanged

**141.** (A) Our company is well known for producing various types of breads and pastries.
    (B) Personal information like your home address or phone number should be kept private.
    (C) We hope to have these numbers listed on our Web site in the next 48 hours.
    (D) Other social networking services will become crucial communication channels with customers.

**142.** (A) On behalf of
    (B) Regardless of
    (C) Instead of
    (D) In place of

▶ ▶ ▶GO ON TO THE NEXT PAGE

**Questions 143-146** refer to the following letter.

---

**OLIVER TOYS**

Ms. Rita White
909 Star Avenue
Bakersfield, CA 90232

Dear Ms. White,

Thank you for your letter dated October 26. I am writing to ------- receipt of your request for a
**143.**
replacement item. We are always happy to replace items that fail to meet the expectations of
our customers provided that the items are in perfect condition.

In order to return the item to us, please send it in its original packaging ------- the invoice that
**144.**
you received with the delivery. In addition, please print a return label from the customer
services section of our Web site and attach it to the returned item.

Please remember that our return policy requires that items be sent back in good condition
and within 30 days of purchase. -------. However, you may rest assured that we will do
**145.**
everything that we can to deal with your return in a timely -------.
**146.**

Yours sincerely,
Brian McGrigger
Head of Customer Services Division

---

143. (A) deliver
(B) acknowledge
(C) purchase
(D) return

144. (A) aside from
(B) on top of
(C) together with
(D) regardless of

145. (A) Thank you for your many years of patronage.
(B) Many of the complaints are due to the poor quality of products or services.
(C) We are very sorry that you are not pleased with your purchase.
(D) We rely on market surveys to know which products are satisfying customers.

146. (A) fashion
(B) matter
(C) decision
(D) treatment

## PART 7

**Directions:** In this part you will read a selection of texts, such as magazine and newspaper articles, e-mails, and instant messages. Each text or set of texts is followed by several questions. Select the best answer for each question and mark the letter (A), (B), (C), or (D) on your answer sheet.

**Questions 147-148** refer to the following text message.

---

From: Harry Robinson, (212)545-6313
Received: Wednesday, June 3, 5:30 P.M.

Hello, Ms. Johansson.

I ran the battery down trying to get my car started. So I had to call a tow truck to get it out and to tow it to an auto repair shop on 11th Street. Now, I'm waiting to have my car's battery replaced here.

I wonder if you could take my dinner shift today. Please let me know as soon as possible if you can fill in for me tonight. Of course, if you can do that, I'll do one of your shifts next week. Thanks.

---

**147.** Why did Mr. Robinson send the text message?

(A) To have his car repaired
(B) To request a ride to work
(C) To take a leave of absence
(D) To ask a person to cover his night shift

**148.** What is Ms. Johansson asked to do quickly?

(A) Pick up Mr. Robinson
(B) Send a reply
(C) Make dinner for customers
(D) Recharge a battery

▶ ▶ ▶GO ON TO THE NEXT PAGE

May 10

Ms. Catherine Townsend
8290 Sears Street
Nassau, Bahamas

Dear Ms. Townsend,

I would like to thank you for completing our online survey. To show our thanks, we have sent a voucher to your home address. You will be able to redeem the voucher on your next visit to our spa for 20 percent off your entire visit. The voucher has no expiration date, and you can use it toward spa services for yourself and one other guest.

I would also like to let you know about the Wilson Spa Rewards Club. Members of the club are entitled to 15 percent off all services at our spa. What's more, Wilson Spa Rewards Club members can also use the card for discounts at the Wimbledon Resort, the Belington Inn, the Kudhara Yoga Center, and the Cool Island Café.

Thanks again. We look forward to providing you with our usual high level of service on your next visit.

Sincerely,

Amy Banks
Owner, Wilson Spa

---

**149.** What does the letter suggest about the Wilson Spa?

(A) It is looking to hire additional staffers.
(B) It asks customers for feedback.
(C) It does offline surveys for businesses.
(D) It recently opened an additional location.

**150.** According to the letter, what can Ms. Townsend do during her next visit?

(A) Complete a job application
(B) Purchase a discount card
(C) Extend her contract
(D) Get a discount

**Questions 151-152** refer to the following text message chain.

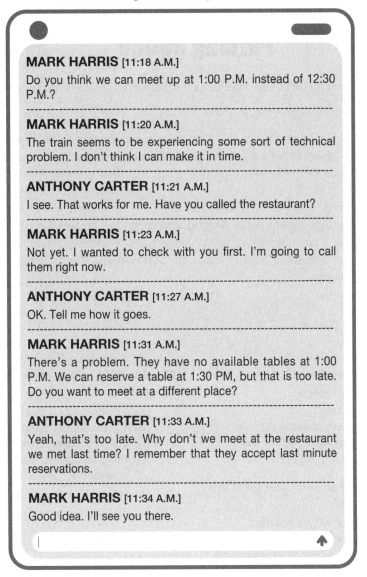

**MARK HARRIS** [11:18 A.M.]

Do you think we can meet up at 1:00 P.M. instead of 12:30 P.M.?

----

**MARK HARRIS** [11:20 A.M.]

The train seems to be experiencing some sort of technical problem. I don't think I can make it in time.

----

**ANTHONY CARTER** [11:21 A.M.]

I see. That works for me. Have you called the restaurant?

----

**MARK HARRIS** [11:23 A.M.]

Not yet. I wanted to check with you first. I'm going to call them right now.

----

**ANTHONY CARTER** [11:27 A.M.]

OK. Tell me how it goes.

----

**MARK HARRIS** [11:31 A.M.]

There's a problem. They have no available tables at 1:00 P.M. We can reserve a table at 1:30 PM, but that is too late. Do you want to meet at a different place?

----

**ANTHONY CARTER** [11:33 A.M.]

Yeah, that's too late. Why don't we meet at the restaurant we met last time? I remember that they accept last minute reservations.

----

**MARK HARRIS** [11:34 A.M.]

Good idea. I'll see you there.

**151.** What is suggested about Mr. Carter?

(A) He will be late due to the poor weather.
(B) He has met Mr. Harris before.
(C) He is trying to reserve a table at a restaurant.
(D) He usually drives to work.

**152.** At 11:31 A.M., what does Mr. Harris mean by "There's a problem"?

(A) He was stuck in traffic.
(B) He needs to get his car repaired.
(C) He has already eaten his lunch.
(D) He failed to reserve a table at the preferred time.

▶ ▶ ▶ GO ON TO THE NEXT PAGE

# Parking Notice

Now that the parking lot has been resurfaced and repainted, there is finally enough space for everyone.

Please respect the No Parking signs near the fire exits and loading dock. Spaces near the front entrance are reserved for visitors and handicapped individuals. Employee vehicles parked in these areas will be towed.

Due to the numerous requests by employees, company management has established a women-only parking lot. Even the car parking attendants will be female to create a safe and comfortable environment for our female employees. Company management hopes that this effort, the first of its kind in our state and perhaps the country, will spread throughout the country.

**153.** Where is parking prohibited?

(A) Near the front entrance
(B) At the loading dock
(C) In the women-only parking lot
(D) In the parking lot reserved for the disabled

**154.** What will happen if an employee parks in the area for visitors?

(A) The person's car will be ticketed.
(B) The person's car will be towed away.
(C) The person's parking privileges will be suspended for a week.
(D) The person's parking privileges will be revoked.

**155.** What is a feature of the women-only parking lot?

(A) It is located on the first floor.
(B) It is the safest parking lot in the state.
(C) It will be open to the public.
(D) It will be operated by female attendants.

# Southwest Air Cargo

Southwest Air Cargo is the pioneer airfreight forwarder in transporting documents, packages and freight shipments worldwide.

Southwest Air Cargo connects markets, within just 1 to 2 business days that comprise 70 percent of the world's economic activity. We even offer pickup in less than 90 minutes of your call, 24 hours a day. That means no advance scheduling or cutoff times for those really urgent shipments. And you can rest assured that your freight gets to its destination safely and securely because there's no extra handling or freight transfers, virtually eliminating the possibility for en route damage.

For more information or to arrange for your emergency shipment, call (800) 762-3787.

**156.** What is being advertised?

(A) A shipping service
(B) A new postal system
(C) A travel agency
(D) A commercial airliner

**157.** What is stated about Southwest Air Cargo?

(A) Delivery time is much shorter.
(B) Reservation is not necessary.
(C) Transporting expenses are less expensive.
(D) Thorough maintenance checks are regularly performed.

# Wonder Fresh Organic Grocery

May 2

Dear VIP Member,

We would like to update you on the latest developments at Wonder Fresh Organic Grocery. As you probably know, we purchased the building next door. We are currently expanding the grocery store into that space, which will add an additional 6,000 square meters to the store. Furthermore, we are also renovating our existing store.

We would also like to let you know that our bakery will increase in size due to the expansion. It will offer many more types of breads, pastries, and other baked goods. We expect the grocery store to be completely renovated and expanded by Saturday, June 7. And to celebrate all of these great developments, we will have a grand reopening celebration on the following Saturday.

We will be offering many great specials as well as free items for VIP members. What's more, you will get a voucher for a complimentary lunch at our new food court. You will also notice that we have included a $15 prepaid card with this letter. We included it as a gift to show you our appreciation for your continued business at our store. You will be able to use it toward the purchase of any items during the entire month of June.

Thank you.

Wonder Fresh Organic Grocery

---

**158.** What is the purpose of the letter?

(A) To inform a customer that a membership will soon expire
(B) To announce some construction work at a grocery store
(C) To advertise a new line of organic food products
(D) To relay information about available retail space

**159.** When will Wonder Fresh Organic Grocery host a special event?

(A) On May 2
(B) On May 9
(C) On June 7
(D) On June 14

**160.** What is NOT mentioned in the letter?

(A) The store will become larger.
(B) There will be a new food court.
(C) Vouchers will be offered.
(D) New products will drive up sales records.

**160.** What was enclosed with the letter?

(A) A thank-you note
(B) A new membership card
(C) A discount coupon
(D) A prepaid card

# The Cheese Online Shopping Mall
## Shipping Terms and Conditions

- If you purchase items from our online shopping mall, they are usually delivered within two business days of the placement of your order.

- If products you want to order are temporarily out of stock, they may take up to a week to be delivered to you. We hope you understand it normally takes about two or three days to store goods in our warehouse.

- If an item you ordered is out of stock and must be backordered, we will contact you immediately upon receipt of your request.

- We offer gift wrapping for a small fee. If you want to select this option, simply mark the appropriate box on the online order form. Free gift shipping is provided when your order is over $100.

- We offer free delivery service on all orders of three items or more or if you spend a minimum of $150 and you are within the Los Angeles metropolitan area. You will find delivery rates and other fees on our Web site at www.speedshopping.net.

**ACTUAL TEST··· 08**

162. What is the stated purpose of the information?

(A) To promote new products
(B) To explain a company policy
(C) To note an address change
(D) To announce an increase in shipping costs

163. What will be offered if a customer makes a purchase of $150?

(A) Free gift wrapping
(B) Giveaways
(C) Free shipping
(D) Discount coupons

# MEMORANDUM

From: Brandon McGraw
To: All employees
Date: October 14
Subject: Thermotex lab freezer

Dear employees,

It has caught my attention that some of you are unaware of the presence and usage of our recently purchased Thermotex lab freezer. —[1]—. It is currently situated next to the BioWare freezer on the 3rd floor biological lab. This lab freezer is set at -70 degrees Celsius, providing an ideal storage place for biological samples and certain bacterial strains. It is equipped with an advanced temperature control system with alarms connected to the 1st floor security department. If the temperature increases by 5 degrees, the alarm will activate and contact security. —[2]—.

In an effort to keep the freezer in prime condition, we ask you observe the following instructions. Even though the freezer is explosive-proof, please avoid storing flammable and volatile chemicals or placing such chemicals near the freezer. —[3]—. Also, when opening the freezer for a prolonged time (more than 5 minutes), contact the security department so they are aware if the alarm goes off. Please clean and check the freezer at least every 6 months and contact the maintenance team immediately if there are any problems. —[4]—. After lunch, I will send the instruction manual electronically to all of you.

Sincerely,

Brandon McGraw
Research Laboratory Manager

**164.** What is the purpose of the memo?

(A) To inform employees of a new purchase plan

(B) To alert about security in the company

(C) To address some problems in research

(D) To provide information about a new machine

**165.** According to the memo, what is a notable feature of the Thermotex lab freezer?

(A) It can only store certain biological samples.

(B) Its temperature can rise above 5 degrees and have no consequences.

(C) It is sensitive to explosive and flammable chemicals.

(D) It has a control system that maintains steady temperature.

**166.** What will Mr. McGraw probably do this afternoon?

(A) Make a presentation to researchers

(B) Send some technician to repair a machine

(C) Store some biological samples in the freezer

(D) E-mail a guidebook to employees

**167.** In which of the positions marked [1], [2], [3], and [4] does the following sentence best belong?

"This will allow the constant maintenance of freezing temperature and ensure the integrity of the stored organic samples."

(A) [1]

(B) [2]

(C) [3]

(D) [4]

# *Thompson Air Conditioning*
# *Get the best for less!*

How long has it been since you replaced your home's air conditioner? If it has been over ten years, you may want to consider getting a new air conditioner unit to prepare your home for this summer.

—[1]—. This results in longer running times and higher utility bills. You'll also notice that your home is less comfortable because the air conditioner does not remove the humidity that's in the hot summer air.

If you think that it's time to replace your home's air conditioner, give Thompson Air Conditioning a call. —[2]—. We have over twenty different air conditioner models available, all of which have a National Energy Saver rating of five. What's more, our air conditioners cost ten percent less than comparable units from our competitors.

We now have a special offer for the entire month of April. —[3]—. Purchase one of our air conditioners and get half off installation. That's right! You can get 50 percent off installation, but the purchase has to be made before the end of the month.

Lastly, at the time of installation, we will inspect your home's ductwork free of charge. —[4]—. This means that we can locate any areas in your home's central heating and air system that may need cleaning or repairing.

Thank you!

**168.** For whom is the advertisement most likely intended?

(A) Repairmen
(B) Homeowners
(C) Building managers
(D) Air conditioner distributors

**169.** What advantage of Thompson Air Conditioning is discussed?

(A) Its air conditioners are cheap to repair.
(B) Its air conditioners come in two different models.
(C) Its air conditioners are cheaper to run than those of other companies.
(D) Its air conditioners are more affordable than those of their competitors.

**170.** How can a customer receive a discount?

(A) By using a discount code
(B) By purchasing other products
(C) By showing a copy of the advertisement
(D) By purchasing an air conditioner before May

**171.** In which of the positions marked [1], [2], [3], and [4] does the following sentence best belong?

"When an air conditioner gets older, it becomes less efficient."

(A) [1]
(B) [2]
(C) [3]
(D) [4]

▶ ▶ ▶ GO ON TO THE NEXT PAGE

**Questions 172-175** refer to the following online chat discussion.

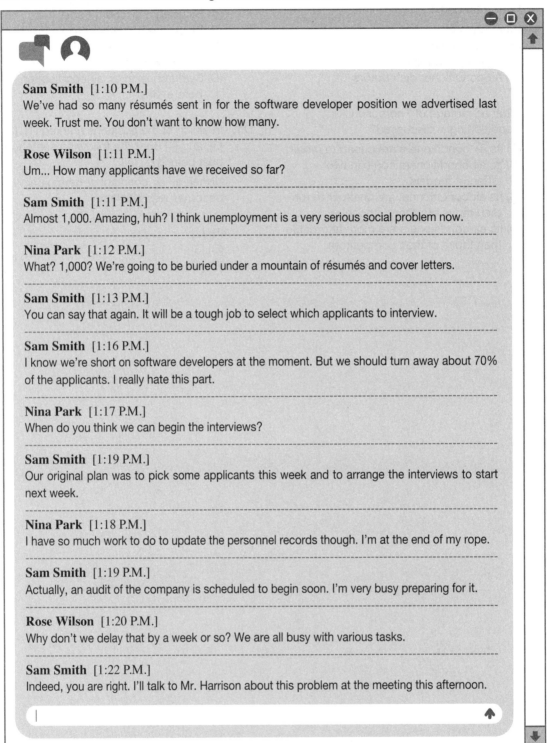

**Sam Smith** [1:10 P.M.]
We've had so many résumés sent in for the software developer position we advertised last week. Trust me. You don't want to know how many.

**Rose Wilson** [1:11 P.M.]
Um... How many applicants have we received so far?

**Sam Smith** [1:11 P.M.]
Almost 1,000. Amazing, huh? I think unemployment is a very serious social problem now.

**Nina Park** [1:12 P.M.]
What? 1,000? We're going to be buried under a mountain of résumés and cover letters.

**Sam Smith** [1:13 P.M.]
You can say that again. It will be a tough job to select which applicants to interview.

**Sam Smith** [1:16 P.M.]
I know we're short on software developers at the moment. But we should turn away about 70% of the applicants. I really hate this part.

**Nina Park** [1:17 P.M.]
When do you think we can begin the interviews?

**Sam Smith** [1:19 P.M.]
Our original plan was to pick some applicants this week and to arrange the interviews to start next week.

**Nina Park** [1:18 P.M.]
I have so much work to do to update the personnel records though. I'm at the end of my rope.

**Sam Smith** [1:19 P.M.]
Actually, an audit of the company is scheduled to begin soon. I'm very busy preparing for it.

**Rose Wilson** [1:20 P.M.]
Why don't we delay that by a week or so? We are all busy with various tasks.

**Sam Smith** [1:22 P.M.]
Indeed, you are right. I'll talk to Mr. Harrison about this problem at the meeting this afternoon.

**172.** What department do the speakers probably work in?

(A) Maintenance
(B) Accounting
(C) Personnel
(D) Software Development

**173.** What is indicated about the company?

(A) It doesn't have enough workers.
(B) It will advertise a job vacancy.
(C) It will move to a new location.
(D) It needs financial stability.

**174.** What does Ms. Wilson suggest doing?

(A) Selecting successful candidates
(B) Operating software development centers
(C) Postponing some scheduled events
(D) Discussing a new hiring plan with Mr. Harrison

**175.** At 1:13 P.M., what does Mr. Smith mean when he writes, "You can say that again"?

(A) He needs to cooperate with his colleagues.
(B) He has recognized some problems in a new plan.
(C) He accepts his colleague's opinion.
(D) He wants to give another employee a chance to speak.

# CompuMax Computing Workshops

Are you a novice when it comes to computers? Do you need to improve your computing skills for a new job? Do you have to learn about new file management software or discover how to use the latest software and programs? CompuMax Computing Workshops offers something for everyone, from students to executives. We deliver comprehensive workshops that can benefit you in many ways. Check out our website at www.compumax.com. Some of our most popular workshops are listed below.

### 1. Databases and Spreadsheets

Learn how to build databases and spreadsheets as well as organize, track, and chart data.
- Saturday, March 26     09:00 a.m.-11:00 a.m.     Cost: $45

### 2. Computing Basics

Learn how to get the most out of your computer and how to protect it from viruses.
- Saturday, May 22     09:00 a.m.-11:00 a.m.     Cost: $20

### 3. Document Creation

Learn how to make professional documents such as newsletters and how to effectively format and print your documents.
- Saturday, July 7     08:30 a.m.-10:30 a.m.     Cost: $35

### 4. Graphics and Presentations

Learn how to make effective slide shows, how to design graphics and logos, how to edit digital photos, and how to present them online.
- Saturday, September 9     08:30 a.m.-10:30 a.m.     Cost: $50

# Workshop Application Form

| | |
|---|---|
| **Name:** | Bob Forrest |
| **Address:** | 4319 San Pedro Blvd, Los Angeles CA 92001 |
| **Phone No:** | (213) 5678-8376 |
| **E-mail:** | bforrest@quikmail.com |
| **Workshop No:** | 4 |
| **Date:** | September 9 |
| **Comments:** | Please let me know the location of the workshop. I didn't see it mentioned in the announcement. |

**176.** What is the purpose of the announcement?

(A) To confirm registration in a class
(B) To promote a series of workshops
(C) To announce a discount on computer software
(D) To reschedule some presentations

**177.** In the announcement, the word "deliver" in paragraph 1, line 4 is closest in meaning to

(A) transmit
(B) order
(C) provide
(D) send

**178.** What is NOT a subject of the workshops?

(A) Document creation
(B) The organization of data
(C) Fundamental computing skills
(D) Video and audio software

**179.** What is the fee for the workshop Bob Forrest plans to attend?

(A) $20
(B) $35
(C) $45
(D) $50

**180.** What does Mr. Forrest want to know?

(A) What the workshop fee covers
(B) Whether group discounts are available
(C) Where the classes will be held
(D) Who will be instructing the class

# THE INSTITUTE OF FINE ARTS

## Rose Douglass
## Director

The Institute of Fine Arts
1001 North Michigan Avenue
Chicago, IL 60603
Web: www.ifa.edu
Phone: (312) 444-3800
E-mail: rdouglass@ifa.edu

| To: | Rose Douglass <rdouglass@ifa.edu> |
| From: | Kelly Preston <kpreston@coolmail.com> |
| Date: | June 3 |
| Subject: | My Information |

Dear Ms. Douglass,

It was an honor to meet and talk about the modern arts with you at the Anderson Museum's 50th anniversary celebration in Boston last week.

I really appreciate your mentioning that the Institute of Fine Arts, where you work, is looking for a curator. I firmly believe that I am the perfect candidate for your galley curator's job. I am currently the lead archivist in Atlanta at the Georgia Museum of Arts. At my current job, I assess, collect, organize, and preserve pieces of art that have long-term value in the artistic world.

Ever since I was in college, I have been in awe of all that museums stand for. The mystery and the aura are such an amazing combination that makes me want to work in this arena all the more. My love for museums and artworks is the only driving force that would make me want to apply for the position of curator at the Institute of Fine Arts. You told me at the celebration party that you are looking for someone with expertise in identifying works of art and their placement in world history, and I can assure you that I possess that acumen. That's why I am confident that I am the perfect choice for this position.

I am very excited at the prospect of working with you at this position and would like to meet you in person so we can discuss how I may add to your organization. I will call your office to ask for an interview date, and I am available at (404) 814-4000 if you need to contact me.

Thank you for your time and consideration. I look forward to having an opportunity to discuss my qualifications for the position of curator further.

Sincerely,

Kelly Preston

**181.** Why was the e-mail written?

(A) To suggest hiring new employees
(B) To obtain help organizing a celebration party
(C) To apply for a job
(D) To request an interview for a newspaper article

**182.** What is mentioned about Ms. Douglass?

(A) She has never met Ms. Preston before.
(B) She currently works for a museum in Atlanta.
(C) She attended an event in Boston.
(D) She possesses excellence in planning and organizing exhibitions.

**183.** What does Ms. Preston express interest in?

(A) Hosting her first art exhibition
(B) Working for the Institute of Fine Arts
(C) Interning at the Georgia Museum of Arts
(D) Buying some paintings from the Anderson Museum

**184.** Why is Ms. Preston so sure that she is the perfect choice for Ms. Douglass?

(A) She has an insight into the true quality of art.
(B) She has organized many rotating exhibitions.
(C) She has collected modern artworks and studied Impressionism.
(D) She can return faded paintings to their previous states.

**185.** What city does Ms. Preston want to meet Ms. Douglass in?

(A) Boston
(B) Atlanta
(C) Chicago
(D) Philadelphia

# How to Transfer Data between Memory Cards

On this page, step-by-step instructions will be provided on how to transfer data from one memory card to another.

**WHAT YOU WILL NEED:**
- Two compatible memory cards (must be of the same class)
- A computer that can recognize the cards (through a commercially available card reader/ writer or a built-in card slot)

**IMPORTANT:**
- Do not alter, move, or erase files in the folder.
- Do not overwrite data by recopying the folder to the original memory card.

**WHAT TO DO:**
- Insert the card with the data into the card slot or the card reader/writer.
- Locate the memory card on your computer device and access the card.
- Select the data and copy it to your desktop.
- Eject the memory card.
- nsert the memory card you want to transfer the data to.
- Locate the memory card on your computer device and access the card.
- Select the copied folder from your desktop and move it to the second memory card.

http://www.ponetocards.com/contact_us

**Name**:   Eugene Daniels

**E-mail**:  eugene.daniels@email.com

**Subject**: My memory card won't register

**Message (explain in as much detail as possible to receive an accurate answer):**

As I wrote in the subject line, my memory card won't register with my camera. I don't understand why since I followed everything in the instruction manual. I went ahead and purchased a 32GB memory card since the original memory card I have is 8GB, which is too small for all my pictures and music. The new 32GB memory card says that the model is "Poneto: Kamang memory card 32GB," and my original memory card is "Poneto: Haru memory card 8GB." I copied and pasted everything without any alteration, but my camera keeps saying, "The card is corrupt: Error 403." What should I do?

**To:** Eugene Daniels <eugene.daniels@email.com>

**From:** Poneto Support <noreply@poneto.net>

**Date:** June 8

**Subject:** Re: My memory card won't register

• Please note that this is an auto-generated message from Poneto Support based on your recently submitted message. Please do not reply to this message as it will not be seen by the Poneto Support Staff.

Hello, Mr. Daniels,

Thank you for your recent submission to Poneto Support. We have created a case file for your report and evaluated the issue in order to provide the best response.

Unfortunately, it seems that you are using the wrong line of cards. Kamang and Haru are two different lines that support different systems. It seems like your camera only supports the Haru line. My suggestion is that you return the Kamang memory card and buy a Haru card. If you encounter any further problems, please feel free to contact us again. Thank you.

Poneto Support Team

---

**186.** In the instructions, the word "compatible" in paragraph 2, line 2, is closest in meaning to

(A) competitive
(B) similar
(C) complicated
(D) exchangeable

**187.** Why did Mr. Daniels submit his message to the Poneto Web site?

(A) To submit some reviews of the company's products
(B) To get more information about the new products
(C) To complain about Poneto's poor customer service
(D) To ask for a solution to a product malfunction

**188.** What should Mr. Daniels do if he wants to use his camera with a memory card?

(A) He should follow the instructions correctly.
(B) He should use only Haru memory cards.
(C) He should have his item repaired by Poneto.
(D) He should secure enough space on his Kamang memory card.

**189.** What is mentioned in the e-mail?

(A) Poneto will reimburse Mr. Daniels for the faulty camera.
(B) The Poneto support staff cannot be reached by e-mail.
(C) Mr. Daniels has lost all his data.
(D) Mr. Daniels' camera is an old model.

**190.** What is NOT true about Poneto memory cards?

(A) It is impossible to transfer data between memory cards.
(B) There are more than one line of products.
(C) They usually come in various sizes.
(D) Data can be altered by the user through a computer.

▶▶▶GO ON TO THE NEXT PAGE

# SUNHILL SUMMER RENTALS

This SUNHILL APARTMENT is offered and managed by South Beach Vacations LLC with amenities and furnishings consistent with the high standards required of a 5 star quality resort accommodation.

NO OTHER APARTMENTS in South Beach offer this harmony of Extra Private Ocean View Features, Beauty & Ambiance, 5 Star Quality Amenities & Service, Private Patio, Prestigious, Tranquil & Convenient Art Deco District Location. It is located right in the heart of the historic South Beach Art Deco District. If you need more information or want to make a reservation, please e-mail Ms. Everton at meverton@shsl.com.

**SUNHILL APARTMENT**

1000 Beach Drive
Miami, Florida 23711

| To: | Maria Casares <mcasares@bkmail.com> |
|---|---|
| From: | Marsha Everton <meverton@shsl.com.> |
| Date: | May 23 |
| Subject: | Reservation |

Dear Ms. Casares,

Thank you for choosing Sunhill Summer Rentals again. We are sending this e-mail to confirm that we have received your Internet request for Sunhill Apartment at 1000 Beach Drive in Miami. One of our representatives has reviewed your reservation and has verified that #403 will be available for you on the dates you requested. You will be staying in #403 from the date of June 8 to June 14. Your transaction number is 72877771.

The credit card you submitted (ending 8891) has been charged $872.40. Please be aware that your booking is final and that this charge cannot be refunded if you choose to cancel your stay.

One of our representatives will be in touch with you before the end of the month to provide you with our new guidelines for staying at one of our properties.

If you have any questions or concerns, please feel free to call us at 800-555-1000. You will be asked your transaction number at the time of your call, so please have it ready. We appreciate your business and wish you a great stay.

Sincerely,

Marsha Everton
Guest Services Manager
Sunhill Summer Rentals

| To: | Marsha Everton <meverton@shsl.com> |
|---|---|
| From: | Maria Casares <mcasares@bkmail.com> |
| Date: | June 5 |
| Subject: | Re: Reservation |

Dear Ms. Everton,

I am contacting you about my reservation (#72877771) with Sunhill Summer Rentals for the dates of June 8 to June 14. Your e-mail indicated that I would be contacted with important details for my stay. You also wrote that this would happen by the end of last month. However, I have had no more contact from your company.

I would very much appreciate receiving this information prior to my departure, so please provide me with it as soon as possible. I repeatedly tried to reach your company at the phone number you provided in your e-mail, but the call goes straight to voicemail every time.

Please contact me as soon as you can.

Thank you.

Sincerely,
Maria Casares
(800) 692-9815

**191.** What is the purpose of the first e-mail?

(A) To request more information
(B) To seek payment for some services
(C) To indicate a problem with a reservation
(D) To verify that a reservation has been made

**192.** What is implied about Ms. Casares?

(A) She works at South Beach Vacations LLC.
(B) She rented Sunhill Apartment last year.
(C) She previously spoke to Ms. Everton on the phone.
(D) She comes to Miami for her vacation every summer.

**193.** What is Ms. Casares asked to provide when contacting Sunhill Summer Rentals?

(A) Her bank account number
(B) Her transaction number
(C) Her legal identification
(D) Her original receipt

**194.** What does Ms. Casares request from Ms. Everton?

(A) Revised residential policies
(B) An apartment room number
(C) Payment options
(D) Directions to a property

**195.** In the second e-mail, the word "reach" in paragraph 2, line 2, is closest in meaning to

(A) arrive
(B) contact
(C) overtake
(D) stretch

# *The Verdi Opera House*

## For immediate release

Philadelphia, Pennsylvania, March 10 – The Verdi Opera House, the region's oldest opera house, has announced the dates of its spring performances. The five shows will include a performance by the Philadelphia Opera Company, which debuted at the Verdi Opera House 20 years ago.

**The performance schedule is as follows:**

| DATE | Opera Title | Opera Company |
|------|-------------|---------------|
| March 29 | The Medium | The Wilson Opera Company |
| April 9 | The Spring Marriage | The Philadelphia Opera Company |
| April 18 | Gloriana | Opera La Fezzata |
| May 2 | Carmen | The California Opera Company |
| May 12 | La Giaconda | Opera Cornuti |

Tickets will be available from $140. To purchase tickets, visit our online store at verdioperahouse. com/tickets. Those with a Verdi Opera House VIP Membership can get 20 percent off of tickets for themselves and half off for their guests. Just use your member ID number at the time of purchasing.

For more information on the performances, please contact our information desk at 800-555-8921.

# *The Verdi Opera House*

## For immediate release

Philadelphia, Pennsylvania, March 19 – Recent storms in the area have caused considerable damage to our building. Since the resultant repair work will take a couple of months to complete, we have to change our spring schedule considerably. Now, we do plan to reschedule all the spring events for the summer. With the exception of the performance by Opera Cornuti, there will be no performances at our venue this spring. If you already have a ticket for a postponed event, we encourage you to hold onto it. You will be able to exchange it for a ticket at a later date. To find out more about the rescheduling of the performances, visit our Web site at www.verdioperahouse.com /news. To request a full refund for tickets, call 800-222-7391.

# OPERA PERFORMANCE TICKET

## *The Verdi Opera House*

**NAME: Ms. Hannah Palmer / Verdi Opera House VIP Membership**

# La Giaconda

**BALCONY STALLS / B46-5**

0  36000  29145  2

---

**196.** Who performed at the Verdi Opera House over 20 years ago?

(A) The Wilson Opera Company
(B) The Philadelphia Opera Company
(C) Opera La Fezzata
(D) Opera Cornuti

**197.** Why does The Verdi Opera House want to delay all the events until this summer?

(A) It needs more time to prepare for new performances.
(B) It has experienced severe financial difficulty.
(C) The performing art facility has been damaged.
(D) Fewer people are interested in its spring events.

**198.** What is suggested about Ms. Palmer?

(A) She owns the Verdi Opera House.
(B) She received a 20% discount.
(C) She will demand a full refund for her ticket.
(D) She will watch a performance with her friends.

**199.** When will Ms. Palmer watch her performance?

(A) April 18
(B) April 27
(C) May 2
(D) May 12

**200.** According to the second press release, what can people do if they have already bought a ticket?

(A) Trade it in for two tickets
(B) Use it for any scheduled opera
(C) Return it for a partial refund
(D) Exchange it for another ticket later

STOP! This is the end of the test. If you finish before time is called, you may go back to Parts 5, 6, and 7 and check your work.

# Actual Test

MP3 해설집

적정 풀이 시간 120분

120 min

시작 시간 ___시 ___분

종료 시간 ___시 ___분

중간에 멈추지 말고 처음부터 끝까지 풀어보세요.
문제를 풀 때에는 실전처럼 답안지에 마킹하세요.

목표 개수 _____ / 200   실제 개수 _____ / 200

예상 점수는 번역 및 정답에 있는 점수 환산표를 참조하세요.

# LISTENING TEST

In the Listening test, you will be asked to demonstrate how well you understand spoken English. The entire Listening test will last approximately 45 minutes. There are four parts, and directions are given for each part. You must mark your answers on the separate answer sheet. Do not write your answers in your test book.

## PART 1

**Directions:** For each question in this part, you will hear four statements about a picture in your test book. When you hear the statements, you must select the one statement that best describes what you see in the picture. Then find the number of the question on your answer sheet and mark your answer. The statements will not be printed in your test book and will be spoken only one time.

Statement (B), "They are sitting at a table," is the best description of the picture. So you should select answer (B) and mark it on your answer sheet.

**1.**

**2.**

▶ ▶ ▶GO ON TO THE NEXT PAGE

**3.**

**4.**

**5.**

**6.**

▶ ▶ ▶GO ON TO THE NEXT PAGE

## PART 2

**Directions:** You will hear a question or statement and three responses spoken in English. They will not be printed in your test book and will be spoken only one time. Select the best response to the question or statement and mark the letter (A), (B), or (C) on your answer sheet.

7. Mark your answer on your answer sheet.

8. Mark your answer on your answer sheet.

9. Mark your answer on your answer sheet.

10. Mark your answer on your answer sheet.

11. Mark your answer on your answer sheet.

12. Mark your answer on your answer sheet.

13. Mark your answer on your answer sheet.

14. Mark your answer on your answer sheet.

15. Mark your answer on your answer sheet.

16. Mark your answer on your answer sheet.

17. Mark your answer on your answer sheet.

18. Mark your answer on your answer sheet.

19. Mark your answer on your answer sheet.

20. Mark your answer on your answer sheet.

21. Mark your answer on your answer sheet.

22. Mark your answer on your answer sheet.

23. Mark your answer on your answer sheet.

24. Mark your answer on your answer sheet.

25. Mark your answer on your answer sheet.

26. Mark your answer on your answer sheet.

27. Mark your answer on your answer sheet.

28. Mark your answer on your answer sheet.

29. Mark your answer on your answer sheet.

30. Mark your answer on your answer sheet.

31. Mark your answer on your answer sheet.

## PART 3

**Directions:** You will hear some conversations between two or three people. You will be asked to answer three questions about what the speakers say in each conversation. Select the best response to each question and mark the letter (A), (B), (C), or (D) on your answer sheet. The conversations will not be printed in your test book and will be spoken only one time.

32. Where does the conversation take place?
   (A) At a bookstore
   (B) At a printing company
   (C) At a bank
   (D) At a library

33. What does the man need to do if he wants to become a member?
   (A) Speak to a store manager
   (B) Fill out an application form
   (C) Find another cashier
   (D) Order a copy of a book

34. What can the man receive by becoming a member?
   (A) A coupon
   (B) A free subscription
   (C) Price reductions
   (D) A gift certificate

35. What is the woman asked to do?
   (A) Attend a company outing
   (B) Receive a package
   (C) Draw up a new contract
   (D) Send some documents

36. What kind of information does the woman ask for?
   (A) A specific time
   (B) An order number
   (C) An estimated cost
   (D) A shipping destination

37. What will the man do next?
   (A) Resume negotiations
   (B) Make a delivery
   (C) Set up a meeting
   (D) Make a phone call

38. What is the conversation mainly about?
   (A) Attracting more clients
   (B) Planning a training event
   (C) Creating new commercials
   (D) Improving management

39. What problem does the company have?
   (A) The possibility of bankruptcy
   (B) The loss of market share
   (C) The high cost of advertising
   (D) A worsening financial situation

40. What does the man suggest?
   (A) Attending an advertising seminar
   (B) Using a different marketing strategy
   (C) Asking for financial support
   (D) Organizing a charity event

41. Who most likely is the woman?
   (A) A parking manager
   (B) A marketing expert
   (C) A legal adviser
   (D) A truck driver

42. According to the man, how long will the project last?
   (A) One month
   (B) Two months
   (C) Six months
   (D) A year

43. What does the woman say about the parking permit?
   (A) It usually takes about a week to get issued.
   (B) A monthly parking permit is available for anyone to buy.
   (C) Only building residents are eligible for one.
   (D) A driver's license must be presented to get one.

44. What is the conversation about?
    (A) A home renovation
    (B) A construction schedule
    (C) A business loan
    (D) A regular bargain sale

45. Why was the man unable to finish the work today?
    (A) Some workers were unavailable.
    (B) A piece of furniture did not arrive.
    (C) His funds for the renovations were low.
    (D) A supplier delivered the wrong materials.

46. What does the woman ask the man to do by Friday?
    (A) Complete some paperwork
    (B) Check a procedure
    (C) Order some kitchen appliances
    (D) Submit an estimate

47. Which industry do the speakers most likely work in?
    (A) Fashion
    (B) Tourism
    (C) Architecture
    (D) Publishing

48. What does the man imply when he says, "My meeting was delayed"?
    (A) He can go on vacation next week.
    (B) He is concerned about his project.
    (C) He has some time to discuss an issue.
    (D) He is irritated by a change in his work schedule.

49. What will the man most likely do next?
    (A) Contact some colleagues
    (B) Collect some questionnaires
    (C) Change a design
    (D) Send some information to a vendor

50. What does the customer want to change about his order?
    (A) The quantity
    (B) The color
    (C) The shipping address
    (D) The shipping method

51. What problem does one of the women mention?
    (A) An invoice is missing.
    (B) An item has been discontinued.
    (C) An order has already been shipped.
    (D) An item is temporarily out of stock.

52. What will the man most likely do next?
    (A) Suggest other colors to his client
    (B) Offer his client a full refund
    (C) Put a complaint in writing
    (D) Revise an estimate

53. What is the woman's problem?
    (A) Her car is not running.
    (B) Her paperwork is incomplete.
    (C) Her flight has been canceled.
    (D) Her office is hot.

54. Who is most likely the man?
    (A) A plumber
    (B) An airport employee
    (C) A facility manager
    (D) An auto mechanic

55. What is the woman going to do this afternoon?
    (A) Reschedule a meeting
    (B) Complete a report
    (C) Meet with some clients
    (D) Order some cooling equipment

56. Why does the woman say, "I'm very pleased with it"?

(A) Her new computer is very powerful.
(B) Her order arrived faster than expected.
(C) A recently installed program is very useful.
(D) Her company reported an increase in sales.

57. What does the woman say about the new software program?

(A) It is good for drawing.
(B) It is reasonably priced.
(C) It has a simple manual.
(D) It allows orders to be entered by servers.

58. What will happen next week?

(A) A new employee will begin working.
(B) A software program will be installed.
(C) A special performance will be given.
(D) An employee will be transferred.

59. Where does the conversation probably take place?

(A) At a bank
(B) At a shipping company
(C) At a restaurant
(D) At a furniture store

60. On which day does Ms. Wallace request that the delivery be made?

(A) Thursday
(B) Friday
(C) Saturday
(D) Sunday

61. What should Ms. Wallace do if she wants her old furniture removed?

(A) Pay a fee
(B) Hire more workers
(C) Rent a delivery truck
(D) Donate to a local charity

## Monthly Bill

**Customer Account: Vanessa Finley**

| Charges | |
|---|---|
| Monthly Service: | $28.00 |
| Late Fee: | $4.00 |
| Taxes: | $2.50 |
| **Total Amount:** | **$34.00** |

62. What kind of business does the man most likely work for?

(A) A computer manufacturer
(B) A construction company
(C) A mobile phone company
(D) A real estate agency

63. Look at the graphic. What amount will be taken off the woman's bill?

(A) $2.50
(B) $4.00
(C) $28.00
(D) $34.00

64. Why does the man ask the woman to wait?

(A) To confirm her appointment
(B) To transfer her call to a supervisor
(C) To introduce some new mobile phones
(D) To give her information about benefits

▶ ▶ ▶ GO ON TO THE NEXT PAGE

## Lucky 7 Supermarket

### Special Summer Promotion

| Total Purchase | Additional Discount |
|---|---|
| $10 - $49 | 7% |
| $50 - $99 | 15% |
| $100 - $199 | 20% |
| $200 or more | 25% |

## DALY CITY STATION TRAIN SCHEDULE

| Destination | Departure Time | Current Status |
|---|---|---|
| Fairfield | 2:10 P.M. | Departing |
| Napa Valley | 2:20 P.M. | On Time |
| Richmond | 2:30 P.M. | On Time |

65. What is the woman trying to do?

(A) Cancel a transaction
(B) Return a phone call
(C) Complain about a product
(D) Purchase some merchandise

66. What does the man say about the problem?

(A) An order cannot be processed.
(B) An item is currently unavailable.
(C) A delivery will arrive later than usual.
(D) A Web site is not working properly.

67. Look at the graphic. What discount will the woman receive?

(A) 7%
(B) 15%
(C) 20%
(D) 25%

68. What was the man unable to do?

(A) Locate the train station
(B) Print his ticket
(C) Change his reservation
(D) Show his identification card

69. Look at the graphic. What is the man's destination?

(A) Daly City
(B) Fairfield
(C) Napa Valley
(D) Richmond

70. According to the woman, what is available free of charge?

(A) Seating upgrades
(B) Refreshments
(C) Baggage handling
(D) Wireless Internet

## PART 4

**Directions:** You will hear some short talks given by a single speaker. You will be asked to answer three questions about what the speaker says in each short talk. Select the best response to each question and mark the letter (A), (B), (C), or (D) on your answer sheet. The talks will not be printed in your test book and will be spoken only one time.

71. What is the main purpose of the talk?

    (A) To demonstrate new products
    (B) To say farewell to a colleague
    (C) To honor an employee
    (D) To announce a retirement

72. Who most likely is the audience?

    (A) Store managers
    (B) Foreign investors
    (C) Employees
    (D) Medical doctors

73. How long has Mr. Clinton been with the company?

    (A) Two years
    (B) Ten years
    (C) Twelve years
    (D) Twenty years

74. Where most likely do the listeners work?

    (A) At a research laboratory
    (B) At an automobile manufacturer
    (C) At a an architectural firm.
    (D) At a clothing company

75. What does the speaker imply when she says, "Please keep in mind that many architects like us want to attend this course"?

    (A) She needs to make the seminar room larger.
    (B) She wants to order more office supplies.
    (C) The listeners should register as soon as possible.
    (D) The listeners should feel proud of themselves.

76. What does the speaker remind the listeners to do?

    (A) Give some updates on their progress
    (B) Learn enough to draw some designs
    (C) Suggest some ideas to save money
    (D) Search for a construction site

77. What is the purpose of the event?

    (A) To raise funds for a new construction project
    (B) To present awards to entrepreneurs
    (C) To promote new housing facilities
    (D) To congratulate a person on the completion of a project

78. What will the mayor speak about?

    (A) Business conditions
    (B) Upcoming public elections
    (C) Direct investments
    (D) New real estate trends

79. According to the speaker, what will take place in the afternoon?

    (A) A public hearing
    (B) A sales presentation
    (C) A business luncheon
    (D) A new residence tour

80. According to the speaker, what will happen this weekend?

    (A) A construction project will begin.
    (B) A hotel will celebrate its founding.
    (C) A retailer will start a seasonal sale.
    (D) A spa will open for business.

81. How can the listeners receive a discount?

    (A) By visiting a Web site
    (B) By sending an e-mail
    (C) By attending an event
    (D) By making an appointment

82. What does the speaker mean when he says, "You're in luck"?

    (A) He thinks the town has many excellent amenities.
    (B) He will provide some pleasing news to the listeners.
    (C) He will announce the results of a radio competition.
    (D) He believes that the listeners will receive a free gift.

83. According to the speaker, what is the business known for?

(A) Fast deliveries
(B) Consumer amenities
(C) Large selections
(D) Reasonable prices

84. What does the speaker imply when she says, "Can you believe it"?

(A) She can't believe the contents of the advertisement.
(B) She is impressed with a store's services.
(C) She thinks the bargain is incredible.
(D) She is surprised by the quality of a company's goods.

85. What will the store begin selling next month?

(A) Catering services
(B) Home appliances
(C) Home furniture
(D) Specialist products

86. Where most likely does the speaker work?

(A) At a hotel
(B) At a marketing firm
(C) At a radio station
(D) At a theater

87. What does the speaker say will happen in three days?

(A) A theatrical performance will end.
(B) A party will be held.
(C) A film will be released.
(D) A play will have its first showing.

88. What does the speaker ask for help with?

(A) Promoting a play
(B) Distributing posters
(C) Arranging a store opening
(D) Preparing for a party

89. Who most likely is the speaker?

(A) A customer
(B) An intern
(C) A customer service representative
(D) An advertising expert

90. What is the purpose of the message?

(A) To request an interview
(B) To confirm an appointment
(C) To promote a special offer
(D) To double-check a quantity

91. What will the listener most likely do next?

(A) Talk to an intern
(B) Send an e-mail
(C) Look at available products
(D) Print a flyer

92. What change is being announced?

(A) Employees are able to use a parking garage.
(B) There is a new parking manager.
(C) Street parking is no longer allowed.
(D) A garage is temporarily closed.

93. What is Mr. Bobby Singh's occupation?

(A) Construction worker
(B) Project manager
(C) Architect
(D) Human Resources professional

94. Why is the event happening?

(A) To give a place a new paint job
(B) To allow for more customer parking
(C) To demolish a garage
(D) To prevent employees from being late

## CENTURY 74 CINEMA TICKET

**Movie:** We Were Brave Soldiers
**Date:** Saturday, January 10
**Time:** 10:40 A.M.

**Mr. Brandon White**

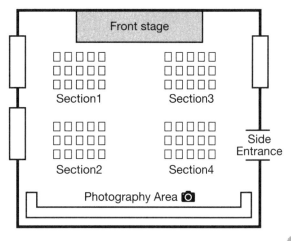

**95.** Why is the woman calling?

(A) To answer some questions
(B) To confirm an order
(C) To ask about an employee benefit
(D) To request some information

**96.** What does the speaker say about Century 74 Cinema?

(A) It is only open on weekdays.
(B) It is conveniently located.
(C) It offers discounted tickets.
(D) It will be closed soon.

**97.** Look at the graphic. How much did Mr. White's ticket most likely cost?

(A) $6
(B) $7
(C) $8
(D) $14

**98.** Who probably is the speaker?

(A) An art critic
(B) A performer
(C) A program producer
(D) A professional photographer

**99.** Look at the graphic. Which seating area will the listeners most likely sit in?

(A) Seating Area 1
(B) Seating Area 2
(C) Seating Area 3
(D) Seating Area 4

**100.** What should the listeners who want to take photographs with performers do?

(A) Move to the studio setting
(B) Bring their own cameras
(C) Go to the photo shoot zone
(D) Donate to local charities

This is the end of the Listening test. Turn to Part 5 in your test book.

▶ ▶ ▶GO ON TO THE NEXT PAGE

# READING TEST

In the Reading test, you will read a variety of texts and answer several different types of reading comprehension questions. The entire Reading test will last 75 minutes. There are three parts, and directions are given for each part. You are encouraged to answer as many questions as possible within the time allowed.

You must mark your answers on the separate answer sheet. Do not write your answers in your test book.

## PART 5

**Directions**: A word or phrase is missing in each of the sentences below. Four answer choices are given below each sentence. Select the best answer to complete the sentence. Then mark the letter (A), (B), (C), or (D) on your answer sheet.

101. Every year, many tourists ------- all over the world go to Arizona to see popular tourist attractions.
    (A) from
    (B) who
    (C) along
    (D) where

102. Best Business Consulting always sends their pamphlets highlighting the reasons behind the success of their projects to attract ------- clients from abroad.
    (A) prospect
    (B) prospective
    (C) prospectively
    (D) prospecting

103. Several local businesses in Syracuse, including mine, usually donate a ------- of our sales to the municipal orphanage.
    (A) variety
    (B) percentage
    (C) charge
    (D) value

104. Cashiers usually spend most of their time on their feet, which can be very -------.
    (A) tire
    (B) tires
    (C) tired
    (D) tiring

105. The mayor said that the city has severe traffic congestion problems, so it will vigorously invest in trains, buses, and the aging subway system ------- the next 10 years.
    (A) approximately
    (B) nearly
    (C) over
    (D) above

106. The city council appointed some aviation experts to the airport technical committee, which will ------- the airport controlling system.
    (A) supply
    (B) oversee
    (C) transport
    (D) instruct

107. All of the sales ------- need to pay more attention to keeping their promises with their foreign clients.
    (A) represent
    (B) representatives
    (C) representing
    (D) representation

108. Please note that ------- employees are not permitted to enter the restricted area at any time.
    (A) dedicated
    (B) experienced
    (C) unauthorized
    (D) approved

**109.** Although the economy has been prosperous in the past three years, the income growth rate has been ------- declining.

(A) consist
(B) consistency
(C) consistent
(D) consistently

**110.** All of your medical records will be kept ------- and will not be provided to any related or unrelated third parties.

(A) security
(B) secure
(C) secured
(D) securely

**111.** The company decided ------- 10% of its workforce as a part of a restructuring effort due to slow demand for new yachts.

(A) downsize
(B) to downsize
(C) downsizing
(D) downsized

**112.** This city has 10 municipal parks spread ------- its downtown area, meaning that most residents live near areas with lots of trees and can breathe clean air.

(A) between
(B) with
(C) throughout
(D) nearby

**113.** ------- receiving her diploma in business administration, she returned to South Africa, where she joined the family business in the gem trade.

(A) For
(B) From
(C) Upon
(D) Besides

**114.** If the photocopier does not work at all, please check to see that it is plugged in ------- and that the power switch is turned to "On."

(A) correct
(B) correction
(C) correcting
(D) correctly

**115.** Whenever purchasing boxed lunches from convenience stores, customers are advised always to check details such as the production dates, manufacturers, and ------- dates.

(A) expire
(B) expires
(C) expired
(D) expiration

**116.** Under the revised law, every guest should pay a special state sales tax ------- all alcoholic beverages.

(A) on
(B) with
(C) by
(D) at

**117.** ------- the order is delivered by October, the company will have to cancel it and search for another supplier.

(A) When
(B) Ever since
(C) Unless
(D) However

**118.** The survey results showed that auto insurance rates in New York are ------- higher than those in other cities in the United States.

(A) very
(B) more
(C) so that
(D) considerably

**119.** As -------, our company is sending you its latest brochure along with a price list by courier service.

(A) request
(B) requests
(C) requested
(D) requesting

**120.** Unlike ------- companies, ours is equipped with the most modern machinery, so you're assured of outstanding quality each time we deliver your order.

(A) few
(B) more
(C) many
(D) much

▶ ▶ ▶GO ON TO THE NEXT PAGE

121. ------- for Southeast Asian countries to create economic growth, it is necessary to establish sound economic development plans and domestic environments friendly to foreign direct investment and trade.

(A) In order
(B) But
(C) So that
(D) In addition

122. People in the northeast region, which suffered from record floods last week, moved quickly to recover from the damage as the rainfall -------.

(A) recurred
(B) continued
(C) threatened
(D) subsided

123. The head architect ------- the new office building design by the time the client visits us to meet with the board members next month.

(A) complete
(B) has completed
(C) will be completed
(D) will have completed

124. ------- the probationary period is complete, some of the interns will be employed fulltime, and the company will provide them with competitive salaries and extra benefits.

(A) While
(B) Once
(C) So that
(D) As though

125. KS Electronics, one of the world's largest multinational companies, now has more than 15,000 employees ------- represent over 20 nationalities.

(A) whichever
(B) who
(C) whom
(D) whoever

126. Ryan Films has a vacancy for an ------- accountant to manage the full accounting functions of the top movie production company in the country.

(A) experienced
(B) absolute
(C) optimal
(D) advantageous

127. Some people believe that nuclear power plants provide safe, consistent, and ------- sources of clean energy.

(A) extensive
(B) unreliable
(C) expressive
(D) affordable

128. Auctions are proving to be ------- exciting and effective for both buyers and sellers.

(A) financially
(B) carefully
(C) extraneously
(D) simultaneously

129. Researchers who do not wear safety glasses to protect their eyes are not ------- to enter the chemistry laboratory.

(A) expected
(B) permitted
(C) attached
(D) intervened

130. You should inform the hospital receptionist of your expected absence ------- an alternate date for your medical appointment can be discussed.

(A) owing to
(B) so that
(C) therefore
(D) once

## PART 6

**Directions:** Read the texts that follow. A word, phrase, or sentence is missing in parts of each text. Four answer choices for each question are given below the text. Select the best answer to complete the text. Then mark the letter (A), (B), (C), or (D) on your answer sheet.

**Questions 131-134** refer to the following memorandum.

### MEMORANDUM

To: All Employees
From: Joseph C. Smith, Senior Vice President

Randy Jones has informed me ------- his decision to step down as the president of Red Jet
**131.**
Airlines, effective immediately, to pursue other opportunities. Randy was ------- in shaping
**132.**
the growth and direction of one of the nation's leading regional air carriers. -------. We wish
**133.**
him well.

Effective today, Fred Martin will assume the duties of president of Red Jet Airlines. Fred

brings ------- experience in airline planning, operations, finance, and leadership to this
**134.**
position. He served as head of customer service, senior director of strategy and business

development, and director of operational planning in the past. He brings passion and

professionalism to our airline, and I know he will lead our company to new levels of

excellence with your support. Thank you for your effort to keep our airline flying strong.

**131.** (A) with
(B) of
(C) toward
(D) against

**132.** (A) instrument
(B) instrumenting
(C) instrumental
(D) instrumented

**133.** (A) Then, he became the youngest chief executive officer at the age of 38.
(B) Let's wait and see how the new chief executive officer leads our company.
(C) The former chief executive officer has used innovative ideas to make outstanding airplanes.
(D) His significant contributions and strong leadership over many years are appreciated.

**134.** (A) extend
(B) extensive
(C) extended
(D) extension

---

To: Sheldon King <kingsh@hoi.com>
From: Linda Hamilton <lh@cosmopolitangazette.com>
Date: August 1
Subject: About a new Web site

Dear Ms. King,

As you are a valued subscriber to the *Cosmopolitan Gazette*, we want to let you know -------
**135.**
about the upcoming launch of our exciting new Web site, cosmopolitangazette.com.

Starting on Monday, August 12, you'll be able to enjoy our latest news coverage on the Web

site. ------- the printed version of the newspaper will continue to offer exclusive print-only
**136.**
content, the Web site will also have content of its own, such as interactive crosswords and

forums that harness the power of the Internet. We have no doubt that ------- will mean that
**137.**
readers will enjoy both the newspaper and the Web site in equal measure.

While the main part of the Web site will be open to the public, subscribers such as yourself

will have access to a special subscriber's area, where you will find premium content reserved

only for our subscribers. -------.
**138.**

Sincerely yours,

Linda Hamilton

---

135. (A) direct
 (B) directed
 (C) director
 (D) directly

136. (A) While
 (B) Unless
 (C) Since
 (D) Once

137. (A) them
 (B) this
 (C) those
 (D) their

138. (A) Here are ten of the most common Web
 site errors and issues to look out for.
 (B) We appreciate your continued
 patronage of the Cosmopolitan
 Gazette.
 (C) We would like to apologize in advance
 for all the problems that the sudden
 changes may cause.
 (D) Tell your subscribers how grateful you
 are for their support with a thoughtful,
 timely thank-you e-mail.

---

Dear Mr. Kane,

Passion. Dedication. Industry know-how.

These are the attributes that drive me, and these are the attributes that I bring to my work.

I am passionate about the job that I do. ------- opening a new market territory, I always start
**139.**
from the ground up. No one ever gave me a $30 million brand and told me to grow it into a

$40 million brand. Instead, they gave me a new brand or a new territory and watched as I

drove it to success.

I'm dedicated to ------- my best. I'm a "roll up your sleeves" kind of worker who makes
**140.**
work a priority and who believes wholeheartedly in customer service. -------. With more
**141.**
than 15 years in the field, I am well-known and respected by manufacturers, retailers, and

other representatives of all sizes, from big-box retailers to mom-and-pop stores.

I'd like the ------- to share more of my passion, dedication, and know-how in person. I look
**142.**
forward to following up with you soon.

Regards,

Mina Weston

---

**139.** (A) With
(B) Aside from
(C) When
(D) Even so

**140.** (A) perform
(B) performing
(C) performed
(D) performer

**141.** (A) I know how to deal with difficult
situations.
(B) I have deep industry expertise and
knowledge.
(C) I have been with this company for a
long time.
(D) I can give you good advice based on
my experience.

**142.** (A) plan
(B) right
(C) opportunity
(D) authority

▶ ▶ ▶ GO ON TO THE NEXT PAGE

ACTUAL TEST··· **09**

Dear Ms. Murphy:

Thank you for attending the Manchester Air Quality Workshop. We hope that you found the

workshop ------- and worthwhile. Our primary goal was to increase your understanding of air
**143.**

quality and other environmental issues and to introduce and provide resources ------- will
**144.**

support your classroom instruction.

There were many topics covered during the workshop, and the presenters did outstanding

jobs of sharing their expertise with you. If you would like to contact any of the presenters with

questions, please see the attachment for their contact information.

-------. Thank you for your comments and suggestions on the evaluations, and I assure you
**145.**

that each will ------- consideration so that future workshops will be even more of a success.
**146.**

Again, thank you for being a part of our Air Quality Workshop. Please recommend this

training course to others in the future. I wish you the best.


Sincerely,

Isabella Choi
President
The Manchester Air Quality Association


**143.** (A) inform
(B) informative
(C) informed
(D) information

**144.** (A) they
(B) it
(C) who
(D) that

**145.** (A) We have also experienced problems emerging from environmental pollution.
(B) A new workshop on the environment will be held on November 11-13.
(C) Your enthusiasm helped make our time together both productive and fun.
(D) The study indicates vehicle emissions are a leading contributor to poor air quality.

**146.** (A) be given
(B) give
(C) to give
(D) giving

**Directions:** In this part you will read a selection of texts, such as magazine and newspaper articles, e-mails, and instant messages. Each text or set of texts is followed by several questions. Select the best answer for each question and mark the letter (A), (B), (C), or (D) on your answer sheet.

**Questions 147-148** refer to the following letter.

# Fairway Car Insurance

899 Potomac Avenue
Nelsonville, MD 77181

February 28

Theodore Houston
Re: Customer Account #091182

Dear Mr. Houston,

Thank you for updating your account information with your new address. You also selected to have all correspondence sent in the form of paper documents be delivered to your new mailing address at 899 Filmore Street, Milton, MD 77172.

Please note that you made the account changes on the last day of the month, and your monthly bill had already been sent to your previous address. We have put in an order for another statement for this month to the Billing Department, and you should receive the statement at your new address within the next two days. Should you wish to access the bill for this past month during that time, you can access your online customer account at fairway.com. You only need to type in your customer account number and password to access this feature of your policy.

Thank you, Mr. Houston.

Sincerely,
Amy Raymond
Customer Service Associate

**147.** What is the letter about?

(A) A question about insurance
(B) The purchase of a new policy
(C) A change in a mailing address
(D) A new feature added to all policies

**148.** What does Ms. Raymond indicate to Mr. Houston?

(A) His February bill will arrive soon.
(B) He must get all of his policy information online.
(C) He sent a bill to the wrong department.
(D) He needs to fill out a form to get a new statement.

Questions 149-150 refer to the following notice.

# ASIAN AIRWAYS

### 250 Hungda Road Wai Kee Industrial B/D 1F – 7F
### Kwun Tong District, Hong Kong

Airline flights may be overbooked, and there is a slight chance that a seat will not be available on a flight on which a person has a confirmed reservation. If the flight is overbooked, no one will be denied a seat until airline personnel first ask for volunteers willing to give up their reservations in exchange for a payment of the airline's choosing. If there are not enough volunteers, the airline will deny boarding to other people in accordance with its particular boarding priority.

Under the compensation system, a passenger who is denied boarding on an overbooked flight is entitled to choose between reimbursement without penalty of the cost of the ticket for the journey not made, rerouting to his final destination at the earliest opportunity, and rerouting at a later date at the passenger's convenience. The passenger is also entitled to immediate payment by the air carrier of minimum financial compensation. In any event, this compensation may not exceed the price of the ticket to the final destination.

**149.** Who will probably be denied boarding in case of overbooking?

(A) A person who reserved a ticket late

(B) A person who has not checked in any baggage

(C) A person who has not confirmed the reservation

(D) A person who has low priority boarding

**150.** What is NOT a type of compensation for people who cannot board?

(A) Extra air miles

(B) Rescheduling at a later date

(C) A refund of the fare paid without a penalty

(D) An additional payment for waiting

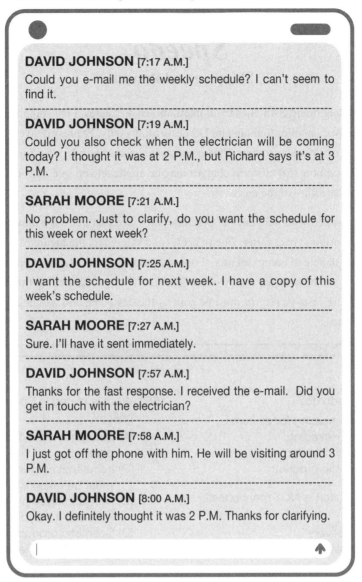

**DAVID JOHNSON** [7:17 A.M.]

Could you e-mail me the weekly schedule? I can't seem to find it.

---

**DAVID JOHNSON** [7:19 A.M.]

Could you also check when the electrician will be coming today? I thought it was at 2 P.M., but Richard says it's at 3 P.M.

---

**SARAH MOORE** [7:21 A.M.]

No problem. Just to clarify, do you want the schedule for this week or next week?

---

**DAVID JOHNSON** [7:25 A.M.]

I want the schedule for next week. I have a copy of this week's schedule.

---

**SARAH MOORE** [7:27 A.M.]

Sure. I'll have it sent immediately.

---

**DAVID JOHNSON** [7:57 A.M.]

Thanks for the fast response. I received the e-mail. Did you get in touch with the electrician?

---

**SARAH MOORE** [7:58 A.M.]

I just got off the phone with him. He will be visiting around 3 P.M.

---

**DAVID JOHNSON** [8:00 A.M.]

Okay. I definitely thought it was 2 P.M. Thanks for clarifying.

151. What is indicated about Mr. Johnson?

(A) He is expecting a client today.
(B) He is a skilled electrician.
(C) He has a copy of the current work schedule.
(D) He will be visiting Ms. Moore's office at 3:00 P.M.

152. At 8:00 A.M., what does Mr. Johnson mean when he writes, "Thanks for clarifying"?

(A) Ms. Moore sent the correct files to Mr. Johnson.
(B) Ms. Moore told the electrician about the changed appointment time.
(C) Ms. Moore clearly answered Mr. Johnson's question.
(D) Ms. Moore helped Mr. Johnson do his paperwork more accurately.

# *Speedo*
## Shipping and Returns

We ship our leading brand cosmetics to all international addresses. Free shipping, overnight, and two-day delivery applies to mainland US destinations only. Express delivery (5–7 days) is available for international customers. Please contact Customer Services for further information. Please note that customs charges may be applicable on international orders and are the sole responsibility of the customer.

Items may be returned within 30 days of purchase, provided that items are unused and returned in their original packaging. Due to health and safety and the nature of cosmetics products, we are unable to accept returns of opened products unless faulty. Purchases made by phone or on-line can be returned to any of our stores, or by mailing them to the returns address provided. Shipping costs on returns must be paid by the customer, and will be refunded in the case of faulty items.

**153.** What does Speedo do?

(A) It offers free shipping for all items.
(B) It produces packaging.
(C) It offers healthcare items.
(D) It sells cosmetic products.

**154.** What delivery option is NOT mentioned?

(A) Free delivery
(B) Same-day delivery
(C) Overnight delivery
(D) Two-day delivery

**155.** What is stated in Speedo's returns policy?

(A) Returned items can be mailed free of charge.
(B) Items that customers wish to return must be taken to a store.
(C) Non-damaged products may only be returned if they are unopened.
(D) Cosmetic products cannot be returned for reasons of health and safety.

Questions 156-157 refer to the following message.

**FOR:** Mr. Gilbert Porter
**DATE/TIME:** Tuesday, November 23 / 3:30 P.M.
**CALLER:** Ms. Jane Keller
**OF:** Anderson Accounting Corporation
**PHONE:** (510) 882-3845

**MESSAGE:**
Ms. Keller called to postpone the tomorrow meeting with you until next Wednesday at 11:00 A.M. She needs to know whether it will inconvenience you if she puts off the meeting. You should call Ms. Keller before she leaves the office and let her know if this is okay with you. She also wants me to remind you to fax the financial statements for the last five years before you visit her office.

**TAKEN BY:** Lee Thompson

ACTUAL TEST... 09

156. Why did Ms. Keller call Mr. Porter?
    (A) To cancel a meeting tomorrow
    (B) To confirm her recent order
    (C) To arrange a new time for a meeting
    (D) To ask for some paperwork

157. What is Mr. Porter asked to do?
    (A) Arrive on time
    (B) Organize a company event
    (C) Check some documents
    (D) Send his financial information

# FRANCONIA DAILY NEWS

Saturday, May 16 – Franconia Mayor Cynthia Barber announced yesterday that the city will fund a project to widen Main Street from 8th Avenue to Garner Street. Not only will a widened Main Street improve the traffic problem that has existed in the area for the last decade, but it will also bring in more customers to the businesses on Main Street. —[1]—.

The project was met with opposition for several years. —[2]—. However, the growing issues warranted a change with people and the city council concluded that the majority of residents supported the project.

Mayor Barber stated that the work would commence before the start of next month. —[3]—. The project is expected to shut down Main Street, as well as portions of 8th Street, 9th Street, Garner Street, and Brown Avenue, for extended periods of time. —[4]—.

**158.** Why is the roadwork necessary?

(A) Franconia has traffic problems.
(B) Businesses near Main Street are losing money.
(C) A road is often flooded due to rain in the summer.
(D) There are frequent accidents caused by unsafe road conditions.

**159.** What will probably be under construction for most of next year?

(A) Main Street
(B) 8th Street
(C) Garner Street
(D) Brown Avenue

**160.** The word "warranted" in paragraph 2, line 3, is closest in meaning to

(A) opposed
(B) clarified
(C) justified
(D) exaggerated

**161.** In which of the positions marked [1], [2], [3], and [4] does the following sentence best belong?

"The tentative date for the completion of the project is December of next year."

(A) [1]
(B) [2]
(C) [3]
(D) [4]

Securecar.com would like to announce the new Safe2U real-time security alert system for your vehicle. With Safe2U, you will know the security status of your vehicle 24 hours a day, 7 days a week, and 365 days a year. —[1]—.

Safe2U is available for all models. For owners with vehicles featuring mobile data communication systems, signing up for Safe2U is as easy as getting online and registering. —[2]—. For those with older models, you will need to bring your vehicle in to any one of our service centers located all over the country to have the Safe2U hardware module installed.

The Safe2U system uses an app that alerts you if anything happens to your vehicle. Is someone trying to unlock the doors? Did someone break a window? —[3]—. Is someone trying to break the steering wheel lock? If so, you will be notified the moment it happens by the Safe2U system.

You will also be happy to know that the Safe2U system can also be used to track your vehicle, if by chance it is stolen. We can also unlock your car for you if you lock your keys in the car!

Sound expensive? It isn't! —[4]—.

**162.** For whom is the information intended?

(A) Home buyers
(B) Car dealers
(C) Security professionals
(D) Automobile owners

**163.** What is mentioned about securecar.com?

(A) It has locations all over the country.
(B) It produces some automobile safety gear.
(C) It has recently been merged with one of its competitors.
(D) It provides a new service only to existing customers.

**164.** In which of the positions marked [1], [2], [3], and [4] does the following sentence best belong?

"A subscription to the service can be as low as $9 per month."

(A) [1]
(B) [2]
(C) [3]
(D) [4]

# Attention,
# All Tenants of the Merrifield Professional Center

June 21

At the beginning of next month, the Merrifield Professional Center will begin a recycling program. The program, which involves recycling paper, cans, and plastic containers, aims to preserve the environment and to reduce costs for tenants. The plan is to set up recycling bins in each office in the building. Tenants are encouraged to separate materials and to place them in the appropriate bins. Each week, the A1 Recycling Company will come and pick up the recycled materials. A1 will then sell the materials to a recycling center and pay us a portion of the profits. Our building's portion of the profits will be provided to tenants in the form of a reduction in the monthly maintenance fee.

The recycling bins will indicate the types of materials that may be placed in them. However, if you are unsure about whether an item can be recycled or not, please contact A1 representative Alfred Morris at 555-1212, ext. 728.

If you have any questions about the program, please contact Cynthia Moore at 555-1000, ext. 378.

Sincerely,

Building Management
Merrifield Professional Center

**164.** What is the purpose of the notice?

(A) To promote a product
(B) To announce a new program
(C) To indicate the date of a meeting
(D) To ask for donations of canned goods

**165.** How does building management plan to decrease the monthly maintenance fee?

(A) By reducing staffing costs
(B) By charging more for parking
(C) By selling its recyclable materials
(D) By using new energy-efficient lights

**167.** What is indicated in the notice as a reason to contact Mr. Morris?

(A) To find out which items can be put in the new bins
(B) To ask for details about increased rents
(D) To request materials for a new project
(C) To report security concerns

▶ ▶ ▶ GO ON TO THE NEXT PAGE

**Questions 168–171** refer to the following e-mail.

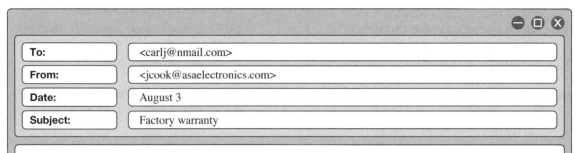

To: <carlj@nmail.com>

From: <jcook@asaelectronics.com>

Date: August 3

Subject: Factory warranty

Dear Mr. Jahini,

Thank you for contacting us regarding your recent purchase from ASA Electronics. Every product we sell is covered by a factory warranty. Here are the warranty details:

- The basic factory warranty covers the product for 24 months.
- If a product has a problem while it is still under warranty, the machine will either be replaced or repaired for free.
- Warranties can be extended for $25 per month for six months once the factory warranty has expired.
- Repairs under warranty must be handled by ASA Electronics. Any repairs not made by ASA Electronics will automatically void the warranty of the product.
- Every item must be preapproved for warranty before it is returned to ASA Electronics. Please contact the Customer Service Department with a brief explanation of the warranty issue. You will hear back from us within the same business day.

Should you need any more information regarding warranties or if I can help you with anything else, please feel free to contact me.

Sincerely,

John Cook
Product Support
ASA Electronics
TEL: 800-555-6817
FAX: 800-555-6889

**168.** What is the purpose of the e-mail?

(A) To detail the charges for a repaired item
(B) To give a customer information about warranties
(C) To inform a customer on how to return a warrantied item
(D) To provide billing details for a recent product purchase

**169.** What is indicated about the products offered by ASA Electronics?

(A) They are sold with a two-year warranty.
(B) They can be covered by a warranty for $50 a year.
(C) They can be returned if the customer is not satisfied.
(D) They are eligible for free repairs for the lifetime of the products.

**170.** What is NOT stated in the e-mail?

(A) All products offered by ASA Electronics have a warranty.
(B) ASA Electronics produces all of the products it sells.
(C) Warranties may be extended by paying an additional fee.
(D) Warrantied products must be repaired by ASA Electronics.

**171.** What should a customer do if a product needs to be repaired?

(A) Take it to a local electronics repair shop
(B) Contact the Customer Service Department
(C) Send the product back in its original packaging
(D) Send in a warranty claim along with a copy of the receipt

▶ ▶ ▶GO ON TO THE NEXT PAGE

**Questions 172-175** refer to the following online chat discussion.

**David Faraday** [2:10 P.M.]
Charlotte, how are you getting on with the design for the new camera? I heard your team has been putting in some long hours over the last few months.

**Charlotte McGowan** [2:13 P.M.]
We certainly have. We've come up with a design for a camera that can be mounted safely on the handlebars of a bicycle.

**Rita Hamilton** [2:14 P.M.]
Awesome! I'm a cyclist myself and I'd certainly like something like that.

**Charlotte McGowan** [2:15 P.M.]
It will allow customers to take pictures while they're cycling, even at high speeds. I think we will outsmart our competitors with this innovative product.

**David Faraday** [2:17 P.M.]
I know it will sweep through the market, winning the hearts of tens of millions of Americans.

**Charlotte McGowan** [2:18 P.M.]
I hope so. You know, it is usually hard about designing this kind of product. It's hard in part because it requires a combination of two things.

**David Faraday** [2:21 P.M.]
You finally made it. When do you expect it to be ready for launch?

**Charlotte McGowan** [2:25 P.M.]
The first step is to run some focus groups. We've invited some consumers in to try a prototype next week. We'll make any necessary adjustments to the design based on their feedback. I hope we can then move onto full production by the final quarter.

**David Faraday** [2:27 P.M.]
We will see the greatest revenue growth among major players in the market. Me and our sales representatives will make this happen.

**Charlotte McGowan** [2:31 P.M.]
Good to hear that. I believe we will definitely get a special bonus for our excellent performance at the end of the year.

**172.** What is implied about Ms. McGowan's new design project?

(A) It has created several stylish designs.
(B) It has been delayed due to lack of funds.
(C) It has been completed ahead of schedule.
(D) It has been a demanding work.

**173.** What type of work does Mr. Faraday probably do?

(A) He provides services in product design.
(B) He produces commercial films for his clients.
(C) He develops different types of bicycles.
(D) He sells products through sales channels.

**174.** What will happen next week?

(A) Some designers will be hired.
(B) A new product will be tested.
(C) The company will have seasonal clearance sales.
(D) An advertisement will be launched.

**175.** At 2:21 P.M., what does Mr. Faraday mean when he writes, "You finally made it"?

(A) Ms. McGowan organized a popular design exhibition.
(B) Ms. McGowan made a new innovative camera.
(C) Ms. McGowan finalized an important contract.
(D) Ms. McGowan completed her project successfully.

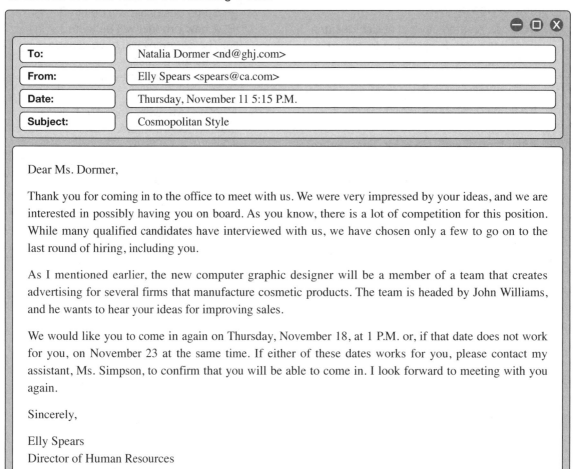

Dear Ms. Dormer,

Thank you for coming in to the office to meet with us. We were very impressed by your ideas, and we are interested in possibly having you on board. As you know, there is a lot of competition for this position. While many qualified candidates have interviewed with us, we have chosen only a few to go on to the last round of hiring, including you.

As I mentioned earlier, the new computer graphic designer will be a member of a team that creates advertising for several firms that manufacture cosmetic products. The team is headed by John Williams, and he wants to hear your ideas for improving sales.

We would like you to come in again on Thursday, November 18, at 1 P.M. or, if that date does not work for you, on November 23 at the same time. If either of these dates works for you, please contact my assistant, Ms. Simpson, to confirm that you will be able to come in. I look forward to meeting with you again.

Sincerely,

Elly Spears
Director of Human Resources

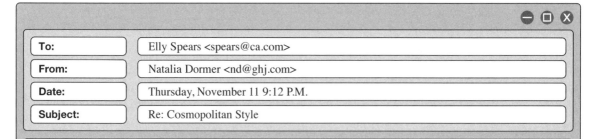

Dear Ms. Spears,

Thank you for contacting me regarding the computer graphic designer position. I am still interested in the position, and I would greatly appreciate the opportunity to speak to you about my experience in advertising and my ideas for the direction of the advertising at your firm. Unfortunately, I am already committed to giving a presentation at an advertising conference in Seattle on November 18, but I am certainly available on the later date.

Furthermore, regarding your request for a letter of reference, I have asked my supervisor, Brian Stone, to provide a letter of reference for me. He will be in touch with you soon. I can bring samples of my work with me to the next interview.

Thank you.

Sincerely,

Natalia Dormer

**176.** What is the purpose of the first e-mail?

(A) To ask for some documents
(B) To schedule a job interview
(C) To ask for advertising ideas
(D) To assign a work project

**177.** What type of business does Ms. Spears most likely work for?

(A) A magazine publisher
(B) A computer graphic software developer
(C) A staffing company
(D) An advertising agency

**178.** According to the first e-mail, what does Mr. Williams do?

(A) He handles contracts with retailers.
(B) He serves as a spokesperson for his company.
(C) He manages a team that markets beauty products.
(D) He directs a group of engineers who develop software programs.

**179.** When will Ms. Dormer meet with Ms. Spears?

(A) On November 11
(B) On November 18
(C) On November 23
(D) On November 25

**180.** Who is NOT an employee at Cosmopolitan Style?

(A) Ms. Spears
(B) Mr. Williams
(C) Ms. Simpson
(D) Ms. Dormer

# Island Creek Books
160 Elm Drive, Sacramento, CA

## *Book Signing on Sunday, June 4!*
## *Meet authors Jerry Miller, Sharon Woodman, Maria Jimenez,*
## *and Cindy Sanders*

On Sunday, June 4, Island Creek Books will host four bestselling authors. The authors' most recent books will be available for purchase and can be autographed by the authors themselves. In addition to signing books, each author will hold a panel discussion along with a Q&A session with the public. The Island Creek Café will be providing refreshments, including coffee, pastries, and sandwiches.

This will be the fourth such event that we have held at the bookstore, and as always, it is free and open to the public. Please join us for a delightful day with the authors.

### Guest Lineup

| | |
|---|---|
| **Mr. Miller** | 11:00 A.M |
| **Ms. Woodman** | 12:30 P.M. |
| **Ms. Jimenez** | 2:00 P.M. |
| **Ms. Sanders** | 3:30 P.M. |

| | |
|---|---|
| **To:** | <woodman@1writer.net> |
| **From:** | <bjackson@islandcreekbooks.com> |
| **Date:** | June 1 |
| **Subject:** | Sunday's schedule |

Dear Ms. Woodman,

Thank you for sending me the message. After I received it, I contacted Mr. Miller with regard to exchanging time slots with him. He indicated that he would be happy to exchange time slots with you.

We understand you need to move your time slot up earlier in the day to travel to Los Angeles to receive the National Writer's Guild Novel of the Year Award. We know you will be pressed for time by attending our event and traveling to Los Angeles for the awards ceremony, and we sincerely thank you for honoring your commitment to our book signing.

Regards,

Brenda Jackson

**181.** According to the advertisement, what will happen in Sacramento on June 4?

(A) A store will hold a clearance event.
(B) A bookstore will have a grand opening event.
(C) Some authors will sign their books for the public.
(D) A group of authors will release their new books to the public.

**182.** What is NOT suggested about the event?

(A) It will offer refreshments to attendees.
(B) It will be free to attend.
(C) It will give awards to the authors.
(D) It has been held before.

**183.** When will Mr. Miller most likely make a presentation?

(A) At 11:00 A.M.
(B) At 12:30 P.M.
(C) At 2:00 P.M.
(D) At 3:30 P.M.

**184.** Why did Ms. Jackson send the e-mail?

(A) To discuss some payment details
(B) To inform an author about an award
(C) To reply to a request
(D) To plan a meeting

**185.** What will probably happen in Los Angeles?

(A) An author will be recognized for her work.
(B) An author will give a presentation.
(C) An author will build her own house.
(D) An author will retire.

**Questions 186-190** refer to the following e-mails and receipt.

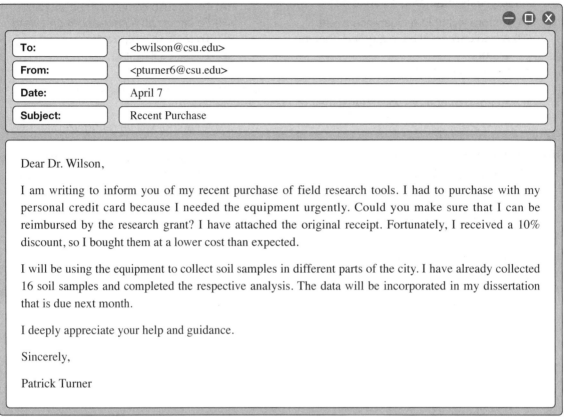

To: <bwilson@csu.edu>

From: <pturner6@csu.edu>

Date: April 7

Subject: Recent Purchase

Dear Dr. Wilson,

I am writing to inform you of my recent purchase of field research tools. I had to purchase with my personal credit card because I needed the equipment urgently. Could you make sure that I can be reimbursed by the research grant? I have attached the original receipt. Fortunately, I received a 10% discount, so I bought them at a lower cost than expected.

I will be using the equipment to collect soil samples in different parts of the city. I have already collected 16 soil samples and completed the respective analysis. The data will be incorporated in my dissertation that is due next month.

I deeply appreciate your help and guidance.

Sincerely,

Patrick Turner

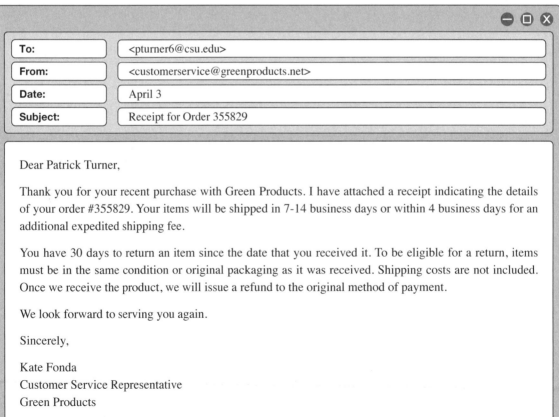

To: <pturner6@csu.edu>

From: <customerservice@greenproducts.net>

Date: April 3

Subject: Receipt for Order 355829

Dear Patrick Turner,

Thank you for your recent purchase with Green Products. I have attached a receipt indicating the details of your order #355829. Your items will be shipped in 7-14 business days or within 4 business days for an additional expedited shipping fee.

You have 30 days to return an item since the date that you received it. To be eligible for a return, items must be in the same condition or original packaging as it was received. Shipping costs are not included. Once we receive the product, we will issue a refund to the original method of payment.

We look forward to serving you again.

Sincerely,

Kate Fonda
Customer Service Representative
Green Products

## Equipment Receipt

# Green Products

**Order #:** 355829

**Details**

| | |
|---|---|
| Rapid Soil Test Kit<br>Item No. 1000459 | $34.00 USD |
| Small Containers(20 pieces)<br>Item No. 1003294 | $10.00 USD |
| Shovel<br>Item No. 120024 | $8.00 USD |
| Moisture Meter<br>Item No. 19001 | $22.00 USD |
| Expedited Shipping | $8.50 USD |
| Regular Customer Discount 10% | $8.25 USD |
| **Total** | **$74.25 USD** |

Thank you for shopping at Green Products.

**186.** What does Mr. Turner ask Dr. Wilson to do?

(A) Return the field equipment to the buyer
(B) Purchase field equipment for his dissertation
(C) Analyze collected soil samples
(D) Enable him to be compensated by a grant

**187.** What does Mr. Turner want to collect?

(A) Air moisture
(B) Soil samples
(C) Test information
(D) Product receipts

**188.** What is suggested about Mr. Turner?

(A) He has a spacious ranch in the countryside.
(B) He has known Dr. Wilson since college.
(C) He has bought items before at Green Products.
(D) He has an outstanding reputation in agricultural education.

**189.** What are the conditions for returning an item?

(A) Visit a store in person
(B) Send a copy of the original receipt
(C) Notify an item to be returned in advance
(D) Return an item within a certain time period

**190.** What most likely is true about Mr. Turner's order?

(A) He can't get reimbursed for his expenses.
(B) He has been overcharged for his order.
(C) His order will arrive within four business days.
(D) Some items Mr. Turner wanted were out of stock.

# Predictive Analytics Business Conference

2233 Bainbridge St.
Philadelphia PA 19119

February 3

Dear Mr. Mason,

It is with great pleasure that I extend this invitation to attend and present your case for the Predictive Analytics Business Conference. The conference will be held in Philadelphia, Pennsylvania, March 10-18. You are scheduled to present the following item(s):

Revenue Modeling & Predictive Maintenance
Wednesday, March 11, 10:00-11:45 A.M.
Conference Room 481 of Madison Hills Hotel
Presenter: Mr. Frances Mason of Triotex Enterprise

The conference room is equipped with chairs, tables, public address system, screen, an overhead projector, and computers. Extra chairs and tables are available for larger groups. You are responsible for any other additional audio-visual equipment. In the event that you need to make arrangements to rent additional audio-visual equipment or have any further questions concerning the matter, please contact Richard Lee, our media engineer at the following: 783-324-9325.

Thank you for your participation. If we can be of any further assistance to you, please contact Kylie Turner at kturner@pab.org or 783-109-9546.

Sincerely,
Anna Rodriguez
Predictive Analytics Business Conference

---

| To: | Carl Hawkins <carlhawkins130@triotex.com> |
| --- | --- |
| From: | Frances Mason <francesmason.14@bkmail.com> |
| Date: | February 6 |
| Subject: | Change session? |

Good morning, Mr. Hawkins.

I was recently asked to present at the Predictive Analytics Business Conference. I'm so honored to be presenting, since it's one of the most prestigious conferences in the North America when it comes to predictive analytics. There's a small problem though; I am supposed to present at the company's weekly analytics meeting on the same week of the conference. I was able to take the whole week off to attend the conference, but I have completely forgotten about the company meeting. I'm really sorry to ask, but do you mind if I give my lecture on 18th? I think it's a really good opportunity to attend this conference, for myself and Triotex.

Frances Mason

# Predictive Analytics Business Conference
## OFFICIAL NOTICE

We are sorry to inform you that the class "Revenue Modeling & Predictive Maintenance" has been moved to March 18, Wednesday due to the instructor's condition. Instead, we will be offering a class named "What exactly is Predictive Analytics?" presented by Mr. Carl Hawkins. It will explain what Predictive Analytics is in detail and prepare the audience for the next week's course. Thank you for your cooperation.

**191.** In the letter, the word "extend" in paragraph 1, line 1, is closest in meaning to

(A) develop
(B) expand
(C) offer
(D) lengthen

**192.** What is indicated about the Predictive Analytics Business Conference?

(A) The conference will last only one day.
(B) Attendees are offered free parking during the conference.
(C) Presenters are asked to bring their own extra audio visual equipment.
(D) Speakers are required to fill out an application for presentation gear.

**193.** According to the e-mail, what is Mr. Mason's problem?

(A) He has a scheduling conflict.
(B) He has failed to prepare for his next presentation.
(C) He lacks proper equipment for his speech.
(D) His request to take a vacation has been rejected.

**194.** What is implied about Mr. Hawkins?

(A) He will postpone his presentation.
(B) He will preside over a company meeting.
(C) He was pleased with the quality of Mr. Mason's work.
(D) He was supposed to make a presentation on March 18th.

**195.** What will most likely happen on March 11?

(A) Mr. Mason will make a speech.
(B) The conference will conclude.
(C) Mr. Hawkins' lecture will take place.
(D) New equipment will be installed in the conference room.

March 2

Ms. Emma Petrie
3007 Mallory Terrace
Ottawa, ON K1A 1L1

Ms. Petrie:

I am delighted to inform you that you have been selected to fill the role of Sales Team Manager at Futurecom Plasticware Inc. On April 1st, you will assume responsibility for a team of twenty-five experienced sales representatives at our Mulberry location. You and your team will sell our range of cell phone cases and accessories to both existing and potential clients.

Prior to your first official work day, you must attend an employee orientation. The orientation will most probably be held at the Mulberry branch office on March 28th. However, there is a slight chance that we will hold it one day earlier. If we do decide to move it forward by one day, we will use the Hexford branch office instead, as the Mulberry branch office will be unavailable on that day. You will be informed of the finalized details within the next few days, and an orientation schedule will be sent out to you promptly.

Kind regards,

Pamela Kane
Human Resources Manager
Futurecom Plasticware Inc.

---

## Futurecom Plasticware Inc.
# Employee Orientation Schedule
### Room 301, Hexford Branch Office

| Time | Training Session | Speaker/Instructor |
|------|------------------|--------------------|
| 9:15-9:45 | Welcome Address & Orientation Outline | Mr. Aaron Myles |
| 9:45-10:45 | Futurecom Plasticware Inc.: Philosophy & History | Ms. Tracey Dugan |
| 10:45-12:15 | Innovative Product Design & Unique Selling Points | Mr. Greg Parker |
| 1:30-2:45 | Communicating with Existing and Potential Buyers | Ms. Jane Lewis |
| 2:45-4:15 | Strategies for Maximizing Your Time & Efficiency | Ms. Emily Hong |
| 4:15-5:30 | Upcoming Projects, Developments & Goals | Mr. Luke Thewlis |

Orientation participants may contact the administration manager, Ms. Kim Christie, at k_christie@futurecom.net or 555-2134 if they have any questions.

**To:** Kim Christie <k_christie@futurecom.net>

**From:** Emma Petrie <e_petrie@futurecom.net>

**Date:** April 1

**Subject:** Recent Orientation

Dear Ms. Christie,

I am the new Sales Team Manager at the Mulberry branch office, and I recently attended the staff orientation. I hope you don't mind assisting me with a couple of things. First, my dental appointment caused me to miss the start of Mr. Myles's talk, so I was wondering if there were any handouts distributed at the beginning. If so, would I still be able to receive a copy? Also, I have a slightly embarrassing problem. The manager who spoke about the company's founding suggested that we get together for lunch this week. The problem is that I cannot recall the manager's name, and I haven't heard of the schedule yet. Can you please let me know the manager's name and extension number? Thank you very much.

Sincerely,

Emma Petrie

---

**196.** In the letter, the word "assume" in paragraph 1, line 2, is closest in meaning to

(A) inquire
(B) undertake
(C) suppose
(D) raise

**197.** What is most likely true about the employee orientation?

(A) It took place in two locations.
(B) It included a 90-minute lunch break.
(C) It was held on March 27th.
(D) It was attended by twenty-five people.

**198.** What is NOT a topic that was covered at the employee orientation?

(A) Design features of products
(B) Interaction with customers
(C) Advertising strategies
(D) Future objectives

**199.** According to the e-mail, what was the problem of Ms. Petrie?

(A) She didn't practice her presentation.
(B) She was not familiar with Ms. Christie.
(C) She started work later than scheduled.
(D) She missed the beginning of Mr. Myles' speech.

**200.** Which orientation instructor most likely invited Ms. Petrie to lunch?

(A) Tracey Dugan
(B) Greg Parker
(C) Jane Lewis
(D) Emily Hong

STOP! This is the end of the test. If you finish before time is called,
you may go back to Parts 5, 6, and 7 and check your work.

# Actual Test 10

MP3         해설집

적정 풀이 시간 120분

**120 min**

시작 시간 ___시 ___분

종료 시간 ___시 ___분

중간에 멈추지 말고 처음부터 끝까지 풀어보세요.
문제를 풀 때에는 실전처럼 답안지에 마킹하세요.

목표 개수 _____ / 200    실제 개수 _____ / 200

예상 점수는 번역 및 정답에 있는 점수 환산표를 참조하세요.

# LISTENING TEST

In the Listening test, you will be asked to demonstrate how well you understand spoken English. The entire Listening test will last approximately 45 minutes. There are four parts, and directions are given for each part. You must mark your answers on the separate answer sheet. Do not write your answers in your test book.

## PART 1

**Directions:** For each question in this part, you will hear four statements about a picture in your test book. When you hear the statements, you must select the one statement that best describes what you see in the picture. Then find the number of the question on your answer sheet and mark your answer. The statements will not be printed in your test book and will be spoken only one time.

Statement (B), "They are sitting at a table," is the best description of the picture. So you should select answer (B) and mark it on your answer sheet.

**1.**

**2.**

**3.**

**4.**

**5.**

**6.**

▶ ▶ ▶GO ON TO THE NEXT PAGE

# PART 2

**Directions:** You will hear a question or statement and three responses spoken in English. They will not be printed in your test book and will be spoken only one time. Select the best response to the question or statement and mark the letter (A), (B), or (C) on your answer sheet.

7. Mark your answer on your answer sheet.

8. Mark your answer on your answer sheet.

9. Mark your answer on your answer sheet.

10. Mark your answer on your answer sheet.

11. Mark your answer on your answer sheet.

12. Mark your answer on your answer sheet.

13. Mark your answer on your answer sheet.

14. Mark your answer on your answer sheet.

15. Mark your answer on your answer sheet.

16. Mark your answer on your answer sheet.

17. Mark your answer on your answer sheet.

18. Mark your answer on your answer sheet.

19. Mark your answer on your answer sheet.

20. Mark your answer on your answer sheet.

21. Mark your answer on your answer sheet.

22. Mark your answer on your answer sheet.

23. Mark your answer on your answer sheet.

24. Mark your answer on your answer sheet.

25. Mark your answer on your answer sheet.

26. Mark your answer on your answer sheet.

27. Mark your answer on your answer sheet.

28. Mark your answer on your answer sheet.

29. Mark your answer on your answer sheet.

30. Mark your answer on your answer sheet.

31. Mark your answer on your answer sheet.

## PART 3

**Directions:** You will hear some conversations between two or three people. You will be asked to answer three questions about what the speakers say in each conversation. Select the best response to each question and mark the letter (A), (B), (C), or (D) on your answer sheet. The conversations will not be printed in your test book and will be spoken only one time.

**32.** What are the speakers mainly discussing?

(A) Office supplies
(B) Delayed orders
(C) Missing documents
(D) An inventory check

**33.** What will the woman most likely do this afternoon?

(A) Order some supplies
(B) Call a vendor
(C) Complete a form
(D) Send an e-mail

**34.** According to the man, what will probably happen next Monday?

(A) An order will be placed.
(B) Some office supplies will arrive.
(C) Free lunch will be served.
(D) Production will resume.

**35.** What does the man want to know about the apartment?

(A) Its monthly rent
(B) Its location
(C) Its availability
(D) Its nearness to public transportation

**36.** What does the woman say about the apartment?

(A) It is near his workplace.
(B) It is currently occupied.
(C) It is convenient for transportation.
(D) It is luxuriously furnished.

**37.** What time will the speakers probably meet?

(A) At 1 P.M.
(B) At 2 P.M.
(C) At 3 P.M.
(D) At 4 P.M.

**38.** Why is the woman calling the man?

(A) To ask about a missing item
(B) To discuss a recent purchase
(C) To report an equipment problem
(D) To reschedule a meeting

**39.** What does the man offer the woman?

(A) A discount on repairs
(B) A different suite
(C) A temporary pass
(D) Free delivery

**40.** What does the woman ask the man to do?

(A) Have her luggage moved
(B) Discuss some prices
(C) Repair some equipment
(D) Recommend a place for dinner

**41.** What does the woman want to know about?

(A) Computer training
(B) Flexible work hours
(C) A courtesy shuttle bus service
(D) Exercise classes

**42.** What does the woman say she is concerned about?

(A) Space requirements
(B) Health insurance programs
(C) Time limitations
(D) Instructor qualifications

**43.** What does David offer the woman?

(A) Some pamphlets
(B) Some refreshments
(C) His mobile phone number
(D) A free locker

**44.** What is the man preparing for?

(A) A conference
(B) An intern orientation
(C) A job interview
(D) A conference call

**45.** What should the interns do before lunch?

(A) Arrange some materials
(B) Greet some special guests
(C) Attend an orientation event
(D) Order some lunch

**46.** What will Mr. Grant do after the meeting begins?

(A) Get some rest
(B) Buy some folders
(C) Prepare for another event
(D) Confirm a food order

---

**47.** Who most likely is the woman?

(A) A personnel director
(B) A secretary
(C) A coffee shop owner
(D) An interviewee

**48.** Why is Sally Murphy currently out of the office?

(A) She is working outside.
(B) She is attending a meeting.
(C) She is having a late lunch.
(D) She is interviewing some applicants.

**49.** What does Mr. Moore offer to do for the woman?

(A) Send a repairperson
(B) Contact her later
(C) Make a presentation
(D) Provide some refreshments

---

**50.** Where do the speakers mostly like work?

(A) At a fitness center
(B) At a sporting goods store
(C) At a manufacturing plant
(D) At a community college

**51.** What does the man imply when he says, "That is going to be pretty hard"?

(A) He is asking for a volunteer.
(B) He wants to know the name of a staff member.
(C) He thinks that a task is almost impossible.
(D) He is interested in an applicant's qualifications.

**52.** What does the woman offer to do?

(A) Check the inventory
(B) Clean up a workspace
(C) Respond to an inquiry
(D) Change a schedule

---

**53.** What kind of business does the woman work for?

(A) A dry cleaner's
(B) A bookstore
(C) A painting company
(D) A medical clinic

**54.** What does the woman ask the man for?

(A) A specific file
(B) The cost of a file folder
(C) A tracking number
(D) The name of a patient

**55.** Why did the man pull all of the hard copy files?

(A) There are a large number of appointments today.
(B) The computer lab will be inaccessible.
(C) Some employees will back up the data.
(D) Some renovation work will be happening soon.

---

56. What are the speakers mainly taking about?

(A) A damaged office
(B) A new restaurant
(C) A building renovation plan
(D) A plumbing issue

57. What does the man want the woman to do?

(A) Replace an old kitchen sink
(B) Provide a full refund
(C) Move into a new office
(D) Inspect a ceiling

58. What does the man mean when he says, "That's all"?

(A) He selected the office he wanted.
(B) He already gave everything he had.
(C) He does not want anything else.
(D) He repaired the damaged machines himself.

59. What is the topic of the conversation?

(A) Analyzing market data
(B) Making a presentation
(C) Scheduling a meeting
(D) Submitting a budget on time

60. What does the woman mention?

(A) She will work late tonight.
(B) Her report is not complete yet.
(C) She will take a training course on Friday.
(D) Her report is about marketing activities.

61. Who most likely is Frank Marshall?

(A) Rachel's former employer
(B) Matt's subordinate
(C) Rachel's department head
(D) Matt's immediate supervisor

## Farm Bistro
### Lunch Menu Today!

| Beverage | |
| --- | --- |
| Soda | $1.00 |
| Coffee | $1.50 |
| Lemonade | $2.00 |
| Green Tea | $2.50 |

| Main Dish | |
| --- | --- |
| Apple Salad | $5.00 |
| Potato Salad | $6.00 |
| Tuna Sandwich | $8.0 |

62. Why did the woman's colleague recommend the Farm Bistro?

(A) It has a good reputation.
(B) It is conveniently located.
(C) It has great vegetarian dishes.
(D) It offers cheap prices at certain times of the day.

63. What does the man say about the watermelon salad?

(A) It is offered only in summer.
(B) It is a new item on the menu.
(C) It is one of the chef's specialties.
(D) It is served only as an appetizer.

64. Look at the graphic. How much does the woman's dish cost?

(A) $5.00
(B) $6.00
(C) $7.00
(D) $8.00

▶ ▶ ▶ GO ON TO THE NEXT PAGE

| Internet Service Plan | Service Fee |
|---|---|
| Quarter Plan | $21.00 |
| Six-Month Plan | $30.00 |
| One-Year Plan | $38.00 |
| Two-Year Plan | $65.00 |

**65.** When will an additional fee be charged?

(A) When a customer moves to a new area
(B) When a contract is canceled early
(C) When a monthly payment is overdue
(D) When a new option is added to the original plan

**66.** According to the man, what will happen in six months?

(A) He will go on a business trip.
(B) A contract will be renewed.
(C) He will move overseas.
(D) A new Internet system will be developed.

**67.** Look at the graphic. How much will the man probably pay for his service?

(A) $21
(B) $30
(C) $38
(D) $65

## Renovation Schedule

| Week 1 | Electric wiring |
|---|---|
| Week 2 | Install flooring |
| Week 3 | Paint inside |
| Week 4 | Paint outside |

**68.** What most likely is the man's occupation?

(A) Construction manager
(B) Warehouse worker
(C) Hardware store owner
(D) Architect

**69.** Look at the graphic. Which part of the renovation process will begin next week?

(A) Week 1
(B) Week 2
(C) Week 3
(D) Week 4

**70.** What is the man asked to do?

(A) Send a list of costs
(B) Design a new Web site
(C) Write an invitation
(D) Work in the woman's place next week

## PART 4

**Directions:** You will hear some short talks given by a single speaker. You will be asked to answer three questions about what the speaker says in each short talk. Select the best response to each question and mark the letter (A), (B), (C), or (D) on your answer sheet. The talks will not be printed in your test book and will be spoken only one time.

**71.** Why is the woman calling?

(A) To provide some information
(B) To terminate a contract
(C) To confirm a reservation
(D) To advertise a new wireless network

**72.** According to the speaker, how long will the work take?

(A) One day
(B) Two days
(C) Three days
(D) A week

**73.** What is the problem with the wireless network?

(A) It will be shut down soon.
(B) It has low speed.
(C) It needs some complicated equipment.
(D) It is still expensive to use.

**74.** What is the talk mainly about?

(A) A travel budget
(B) Internet access
(C) A company's new policy
(D) Business relocation

**75.** According to the speaker, what does the company want to know?

(A) The status of an order
(B) A new business travel policy
(C) Detailed spending information
(D) Accounting standards

**76.** What does the speaker ask the listeners to do?

(A) Upgrade the accuracy of their data
(B) Put related information into the system
(C) Arrive early for a corporate event
(D) Save receipts from their vacations

**77.** What is the speaker mainly discussing?

(A) A new parking supervisor
(B) An efficient payroll system
(C) An improved parking facility
(D) A lot of paperwork

**78.** What does the speaker imply when he says, "But here's the thing"?

(A) He will introduce a point to consider.
(B) He will indicate a controversial issue.
(C) He will complain about the company's poor service.
(D) He will show something that people want to get.

**79.** What are the listeners asked to do by later in the week?

(A) Pick up their new permits
(B) Make new bank accounts
(C) Fill out some documents
(D) Get ready to submit their insurance cards

**80.** What type of business does the speaker work for?

(A) An electronics company
(B) An Internet service provider
(C) A carpet manufacturer
(D) A trucking company

**81.** What does the speaker imply when she says "They are blocking the road from our factory"?

(A) She cannot operate her factory.
(B) She will take a detour.
(C) She needs to repair a truck.
(D) She cannot deliver an order on time.

**82.** What does the speaker suggest the listener do?

(A) Cancel an order
(B) Call her on her mobile phone
(C) Pay a late delivery fee
(D) Compare the prices of two products

▶ ▶ ▶GO ON TO THE NEXT PAGE

83. Why is the speaker calling?

(A) To update her address book
(B) To confirm an appointment
(C) To sign up for insurance
(D) To change an order

84. What should Mr. Foster do on June 3?

(A) Eat a healthy lunch
(B) Confirm his appointment
(C) Update his insurance information
(D) Fill out some papers

85. What does the speaker ask the listener to do?

(A) Exercise regularly
(B) Check his previous medical history
(C) Provide a fax number
(D) Send his insurance information

86. What type of business does the speaker work for?

(A) A hospital
(B) A real estate agency
(C) A fitness club
(D) A cable TV company

87. According to the speaker, what is the business known for?

(A) Innovative products
(B) Qualified doctors
(C) Reasonable prices
(D) Varied equipment

88. What does the speaker mean when she says, "You won't be disappointed at all"?

(A) Some new products are high in quality.
(B) People are satisfied with high returns.
(C) Customers will have healthy lives.
(D) Some problems won't happen again.

89. What is the purpose of the talk?

(A) To announce a recruiting initiative
(B) To remind department heads of a scheduled meeting
(C) To introduce a new board member
(D) To provide a summary of a new business expansion plan

90. What kind of experience does Daniel Stevens have?

(A) Marketing
(B) Public relations
(C) Foreign sales
(D) Human resources

91. According to the speaker, what will the company do the following year?

(A) Hire more employees
(B) Construct a new plant
(C) Develop some overseas markets
(D) Start an aggressive advertising campaign

92. What is the speaker talking about?

(A) A new safety system
(B) A management training program
(C) Revised delivery routes
(D) Adopting new technology

93. Where does the speaker probably work?

(A) At a moving company
(B) At a software development firm
(C) At a courier service
(D) At a computer factory

94. What should the listeners do before Sunday?

(A) Read an instruction manual
(B) Buy some books
(C) Install some software
(D) Return some equipment

## Richmond Island Ferry Timetable

| Departure Time | Arrival Time |
|----------------|--------------|
| 8:30 A.M. | 9:00 A.M. |
| 10:00 A.M. | 10:30 A.M. |
| 7:00 P.M. | 7:30 P.M. |
| 9:30 P.M. | 10:00 P.M. |

## Sale of the Week Program

| Type of Furniture | Date |
|-------------------|------|
| Wood Furniture | February 21 |
| Glass Furniture | February 22 |
| Marble Furniture | February 23 |
| Metal Furniture | February 24 |

**95.** What has caused the suspension of operations?

(A) Technical problems
(B) A lack of crew members
(C) Inclement weather
(D) A problem with the boarding procedures

**96.** Look at the graphic. What time will the ferry probably leave?

(A) 8:30 A.M.
(B) 10:00 A.M.
(C) 7:00 P.M.
(D) 9:30 P.M.

**97.** What does the speaker recommend the listeners do?

(A) Wear thick clothes
(B) Take a vacation
(C) Go to work later
(D) Keep a sales receipt

**98.** What is being advertised?

(A) Commercial properties
(B) The relocation of a store
(C) An anniversary discount promotion
(D) Special pricing for members

**99.** What are the listeners asked to do?

(A) Call the store to check the sale schedule
(B) Visit only on specific days to receive coupons
(C) Bring their identification cards with them
(D) Present a brochure for an extra discount

**100.** Look at the graphic. When will marble furniture be on sale?

(A) February 21
(B) February 22
(C) February 23
(D) February 24

This is the end of the Listening test. Turn to Part 5 in your test book.

▶ ▶ ▶ GO ON TO THE NEXT PAGE

# READING TEST

In the Reading test, you will read a variety of texts and answer several different types of reading comprehension questions. The entire Reading test will last 75 minutes. There are three parts, and directions are given for each part. You are encouraged to answer as many questions as possible within the time allowed.

You must mark your answers on the separate answer sheet. Do not write your answers in your test book.

## PART 5

**Directions**: A word or phrase is missing in each of the sentences below. Four answer choices are given below each sentence. Select the best answer to complete the sentence. Then mark the letter (A), (B), (C), or (D) on your answer sheet.

**101.** The winner of this year's award will get a tour ------- the manufacturing plant in Alabama and wonderful prizes.

(A) for
(B) with
(C) before
(D) of

**102.** A ------- of the proceeds will be donated to local charity organizations to help homeless and hungry New Yorkers.

(A) level
(B) fund
(C) section
(D) portion

**103.** Ruby & Kabi Furniture has provided various kinds of do-it-yourself unassembled furniture for customers ------- the past five years.

(A) from
(B) with
(C) of
(D) for

**104.** Several excellent and unique restaurants are located ------- walking distance of the new branch office in London.

(A) within
(B) from
(C) by
(D) through

**105.** The amount of the yearly bonus ------- every year depending on the profitability of the company.

(A) vary
(B) varies
(C) variety
(D) various

**106.** Almost all of our department heads attended yesterday's meeting, ------- the inclement weather that included wind storms and hail.

(A) furthermore
(B) whereas
(C) however
(D) notwithstanding

**107.** Some customers were ------- with the overall quality of the new products manufactured by the Ryan Corporation.

(A) disappointing
(B) disappointed
(C) disappoint
(D) disappointment

**108.** The central bank's monetary policy committee voted ------- to leave the standard interest rate unchanged.

(A) singly
(B) unanimously
(C) immediately
(D) separately

**109.** ------- the company's brand image is one of the most effective ways to increase its sales in the European market.

(A) Photocopying
(B) Enhancing
(C) Representing
(D) Simplifying

**110.** Due to numerous requests, the ------- deadline for the submission of the revised market analysis report is January 10.

(A) extend
(B) extension
(C) extensive
(D) extended

**111.** The new laundry detergent products have been ------- tested by our researchers, so they are perfectly safe for customers to use.

(A) hardly
(B) thoroughly
(C) exceptionally
(D) previously

**112.** The government ------- believes tax cuts will help revive the economy and get it to emerge from the current economic recession.

(A) exactly
(B) firmly
(C) effectively
(D) respectively

**113.** Most of the assembly line workers finally ------- the plant relocation plan after the company promised them job security and medical benefits.

(A) agreed
(B) made
(C) endorsed
(D) appealed

**114.** These savings points are ------- for discounted meals and merchandise from the Maxie Department Store.

(A) calculative
(B) redeemable
(C) dependable
(D) transferable

**115.** This gas field was ------- our company discovered natural gas with commercial value for the first time.

(A) which
(B) what
(C) when
(D) where

**116.** The investment by Komi International is the ------- largest foreign direct investment in the nation's financial industry.

(A) quite
(B) much
(C) every
(D) single

**117.** In appreciation of your -------, we would like to offer you a 20% discount coupon you can use for any online or in-store purchase.

(A) eligibility
(B) efforts
(C) refund
(D) patronage

**118.** Please be ------- and refrain from activities in the theater that may cause any inconvenience to other members of the audience and the actors on stage.

(A) consideration
(B) considerable
(C) considered
(D) considerate

**119.** ------- our new car models were released last quarter, they have been astonishingly popular.

(A) During
(B) Since
(C) When
(D) As though

**120.** ------- is a questionnaire designed to provide the information needed for a thorough evaluation of your particular spinal problem.

(A) Attach
(B) Attached
(C) Attaching
(D) Attachment

▶ ▶ ▶ GO ON TO THE NEXT PAGE

121. Some renowned meteorologists said that deforestation is responsible for ------- 25% of the global climate change problem.
(A) near
(B) approximately
(C) mostly
(D) highly

122. According to a recent report published by an international health organization, there are a number of regional and national ------- of the cold virus.
(A) variety
(B) variation
(C) variations
(D) variability

123. Employees at KBG Electronics will receive a significant bonus ------- the company's net profits exceed the expectations of the president and the board.
(A) provided that
(B) while
(C) in that
(D) unless

124. This new approach will ------- reduce the size and complexity of the library and decrease the number of librarians required to maintain books and reference material.
(A) significance
(B) significant
(C) more significant
(D) significantly

125. All damage to building materials must be reported ------- to the construction manager within 24 hours of the damage occurring.
(A) soon
(B) directly
(C) especially
(D) recently

126. There are some employees who prefer to work independently and others who do better when ------- with their colleagues.
(A) work
(B) to work
(C) working
(D) worked

127. What matters the most is ------- soon our company will be able to make inroads into the Korean market.
(A) when
(B) how
(C) where
(D) which

128. Mr. Winters ------- a managerial position but declined it since he was looking for something more lucrative.
(A) offers
(B) offered
(C) was offered
(D) will be offered

129. GE Technology claims its new computer software is compatible with most computer operating systems, but some of its customers suggest -------.
(A) instead
(B) comparably
(C) otherwise
(D) on the other hand

130. All the participants in the upcoming international business conference may stay at the Top Hotel or the Presidential Hotel, ------- they find more pleasant and convenient.
(A) everyone
(B) that
(C) whoever
(D) whichever

# PART 6

**Directions:** Read the texts that follow. A word, phrase, or sentence is missing in parts of each text. Four answer choices for each question are given below the text. Select the best answer to complete the text. Then mark the letter (A), (B), (C), or (D) on your answer sheet.

**Questions 131-134** refer to the following letter.

Dear Ms. Hwang,

Please accept this letter as formal notification that I am stepping down from my current position. -------. However, if at all possible, I would appreciate you releasing me from
**131.**
my employment with the company as soon as possible. If I could provide any assistance in

training my replacement or otherwise facilitating the -------, I would be happy to do so.
**132.**

Thank you for the opportunities for professional and personal development that you have

provided me ------- the last seven years. I have enjoyed working for the company and
**133.**
appreciate the support ------- me during my tenure here. I look forward to hearing from you
**134.**
regarding the end date of my employment.

Sincerely,

James Taylor
Head of International Sales

131. (A) I understand that two weeks' notice is standard.
   (B) Some employees were severely criticized and eventually fired.
   (C) You will have deeper knowledge and the ability to think logically.
   (D) I have argued that trade is good for peace and prosperity.

132. (A) career
   (B) turnover
   (C) transition
   (D) change

133. (A) within
   (B) during
   (C) except
   (D) across

134. (A) provide
   (B) provision
   (C) providing
   (D) provided

Dear Ms. Winston:

I received a collection notice from Union City Telecom on February 1. The letter states that I owe a past due balance from the November 16 to December 15 billing period. The letter also states that my mobile phone service will be disconnected ------- I act immediately;
**135.**
however, I am informing you for the second time that I paid that bill on January 10.

On January 18, I received a call from one of your representatives about this matter, and I told him that I had sent a check to your office for the due amount of $46.92 ten days ago. Unfortunately, I failed to get his name. I am ------- that you have not taken care of this
**136.**
matter. I am also ------- a copy of the check herewith.
**137.**


-------.
**138.**


Sincerely yours,

John Kensington
(510) 692-3355
Encl: copy of check

135. (A) if
(B) whether
(C) unless
(D) as if

136. (A) irritate
(B) irritation
(C) irritating
(D) irritated

137. (A) issuing
(B) enclosing
(C) endorsing
(D) writing

138. (A) The judgment is expected to result in other lawsuits.
(B) The company decided to cut monthly rates starting next month.
(C) The city is well covered by major mobile phone service providers.
(D) I hope that this settles the matter once and for all.

**Questions 139-142** refer to the following e-mail.

To: Elizabeth Giles <eg@eventspace.com>
From: Robert Shaw <rshaw@alphabusiness.com>
Date: October 26
Subject: About one-day computer class

Dear Ms. Giles,

Our company will be hosting a one-day computer class on Saturday, November 10. -------,
**139.**
the main office over-registered us, so we now have to look for a larger space.

We need a large conference room with at least 16 power outlets and several long tables

------- we can set up computer equipment. We also need a lunch buffet for ------- 50
**140.**                                                                    **141.**
people.

We have received many recommendations from other businesses that have used your

facilities for similar classes and found both the rooms and the staff to be first rate. -------.
**142.**

Thank you.

Robert Shaw
Head of Personnel
(610) 837-2454 / EXT 119

139. (A) Similarly
(B) Reasonably
(C) Additionally
(D) Unfortunately

140. (A) which
(B) whose
(C) whom
(D) where

141. (A) roughly
(B) incrementally
(C) considerably
(D) straightforwardly

142. (A) Please inform us if you identify any
maintenance needs.
(B) We are thankful for the public
investment in schooling.
(C) Please call me at your convenience to
discuss availability and prices.
(D) It is no secret that computers are
becoming faster and faster.

▶ ▶ ▶GO ON TO THE NEXT PAGE

http:www.westerndairyguild.org

Every year, the Western Dairy Guild (WDG) hosts a major trade fair for dairy products and conducts educational forums on dairy technology and science ------- the dairy farming
**143.**
industry. Nowadays, the dairy farming industry in the United States is growing fast because most dairy farms are using the latest technology. Dairy and food products from the western United States are recognized for their quality both domestically and internationally.

Most world-renowned chefs have long used dairy products produced from this region. State Milk Quality Contest, which is one of the ------- dairy product events in the United States, will
**144.**
be held by the WDG next month. -------. Paul Edwards was last year's -------. His cow milk
**145.** **146.**
received the best score, which was 97.4 out of 100.

**143.** (A) to advance
(B) is advancing
(C) has been advanced
(D) will advance

**144.** (A) prestigious
(B) more prestigious
(C) most prestigious
(D) most prestigiously

**145.** (A) You can book your stay directly on the hotel's own Web site.
(B) Milk producers from all around the globe go there to compete.
(C) Automation technology is changing the way farms produce dairy products.
(D) A large number of events will be held to capture the attention of visitors.

**146.** (A) judge
(B) expert
(C) organizer
(D) winner

## PART 7

**Directions:** In this part you will read a selection of texts, such as magazine and newspaper articles, e-mails, and instant messages. Each text or set of texts is followed by several questions. Select the best answer for each question and mark the letter (A), (B), (C), or (D) on your answer sheet.

**Questions 147-148** refer to the following notice.

# NOTICE

This notice is to inform all Good Times Café customers that the premises will be closed for renovations from June 2 to 14. To provide a more pleasurable atmosphere for our patrons, we will be redecorating all the floors and will also be adding a mini-library on the first floor so that you can enjoy an assortment of magazines and novels with your coffee.

To celebrate the new and improved Good Times Café, we will be giving away a Good Times coffee mug to every customer on June 15. In addition, we will be offering discounts on all beverages on our reopening day!

We are open seven days a week for your convenience: from 10 A.M. to 11 P.M. on weekdays and from 10 A.M. to midnight on weekends.

As always, we appreciate your patronage, and we are looking forward to serving you soon.

**147.** What is stated about the store?

(A) It will be adding an additional floor.
(B) It will have a reading area.
(C) It will change its hours of operation.
(D) It will have a new menu.

**148.** What will customers get free of charge on June 15?

(A) A mug
(B) A magazine
(C) Desserts
(D) Coffee

# Moab Forrest Cabins

Moab Forrest National Park Service is pleased to announce a project to build 25 beautiful log cabins in Moab Forrest National Park. Work is expected to begin in approximately two weeks. If all goes according to plan, we hope to have the site prepared and the main structural foundations in place within a month. That may seem like quite a huge task, but we are desperate to have everything finished before the summer season begins. The new cabins should be completed by June this year.

There will be two types of cabins available: standard cabins that have two floors and sleep up to 5 people and group cabins that have three floors and sleep up to 10 people. Both kinds of cabins will be fully air conditioned and will have modern bathrooms, including hot tubs. The kitchens in both cabin types will be equipped with a full range of appliances, including a refrigerator, microwave, washing machine, and gas range.

The Moab Forrest cabins will be conveniently located beside beautiful Pleasant Lake. This will make them perfect for anyone who wishes to escape the city heat and enjoy some fishing, swimming, and water sports in the national park. Contact an agent from the Moab Forrest National Park Service today to make an advance booking for one of the cabins.

Most cabins will be available to rent starting June 4. Contact us at 555-6892 for further details.

**149.** What is stated about the cabins?

(A) Construction began two weeks ago.
(B) Kitchen appliances are included.
(C) The bedrooms are very spacious.
(D) They cannot accommodate large groups.

**150.** What information is NOT included in the advertisement?

(A) The date the first cabins open
(B) The cabin styles available
(C) The cost of a cabin rental
(D) The location of the cabins

**Questions 151-152** refer to the following text message chain.

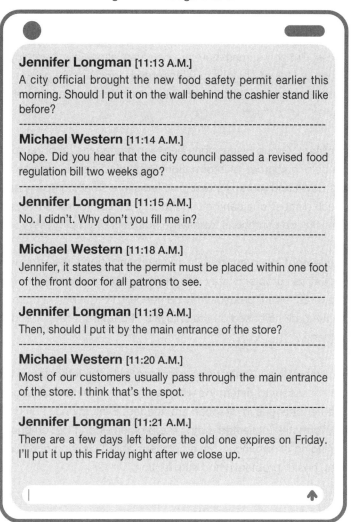

**Jennifer Longman** [11:13 A.M.]
A city official brought the new food safety permit earlier this morning. Should I put it on the wall behind the cashier stand like before?
--------------------------------------------------------
**Michael Western** [11:14 A.M.]
Nope. Did you hear that the city council passed a revised food regulation bill two weeks ago?
--------------------------------------------------------
**Jennifer Longman** [11:15 A.M.]
No. I didn't. Why don't you fill me in?
--------------------------------------------------------
**Michael Western** [11:18 A.M.]
Jennifer, it states that the permit must be placed within one foot of the front door for all patrons to see.
--------------------------------------------------------
**Jennifer Longman** [11:19 A.M.]
Then, should I put it by the main entrance of the store?
--------------------------------------------------------
**Michael Western** [11:20 A.M.]
Most of our customers usually pass through the main entrance of the store. I think that's the spot.
--------------------------------------------------------
**Jennifer Longman** [11:21 A.M.]
There are a few days left before the old one expires on Friday. I'll put it up this Friday night after we close up.

**151.** What does Mr. Western ask Ms. Longman to do?

(A) Put up a sign for sale
(B) Place a package near a cashier stand
(C) Prepare some dishes for an event
(D) Post a document on a new location

**152.** At 11:15 A.M., what does Ms. Longman mean when she writes, "Why don't you fill me in?"

(A) She wants to have lunch with Mr. Western.
(B) She has some time to help Mr. Western.
(C) She is impressed by Mr. Western's comments.
(D) She needs to get some information from Mr. Western.

▶ ▶ ▶GO ON TO THE NEXT PAGE

**Questions 153-154** refer to the following information.

Low morale, health problems, complaints, and employee turnover often provide the first signs of job stress. But sometimes there are no clues, especially if employees are fearful of losing their jobs. A lack of obvious or widespread signs is not a good reason to dismiss concerns about job stress or to minimize the importance of a prevention program.

**Identify the problem.** Group discussions between managers, labor representatives, and employees can be rich sources of information. Such discussions may be all that is needed to track down and remedy stress problems in a small company. In a larger organization, such discussions can be used to help design formal surveys for gathering input about stressful job conditions from large numbers of employees.

**Design and implement interventions.** In small organizations, the informal discussions that help identify stress problems may also produce fruitful ideas for prevention. In large organizations, a more formal process may be needed. Frequently, a team is asked to develop recommendations based on the analysis of data from Step 1 and consultation with outside experts.

**Evaluate the interventions.** Evaluations are essential to the intervention process. Evaluations are necessary to determine whether interventions are producing the desired effects and whether changes in direction are needed. Evaluations should focus on the same types of information collected during the problem-identification phase of the intervention, including information from employees about working conditions, levels of perceived stress, health problems, and satisfaction.

---

**153.** What is the main topic of the information?

(A) What job stress is
(B) The relationship between job stress and health
(C) Steps for preventing job stress
(D) The effects of job stress on productivity

**154.** For what purpose can informal discussions be used in small companies?

(A) Remedying some dangerous mental illnesses
(B) Uniting labor and management
(C) Identifying stressful job conditions
(D) Finding solutions to prevent stress problems

**155.** According to the information, what is determined by evaluations?

(A) The true effects of interventions
(B) How to get the best productivity
(C) The health conditions of employees
(D) Future possibilities of job stress

# NOTICE

We have always made a commitment to conservation and preservation by operating in an environmentally sensitive manner. Installing energy- and water-efficient equipment in all our rooms, reducing the amount of waste produced and recycling the waste that is produced, and integrating conservation techniques into every employee's job description – these are the measures that distinguish us, an environmentally responsible organization, from conventional lodging operations. We suggest the following to our guests to help conserve water:

- Turn off the faucet while brushing your teeth, washing your face, and shaving.
- Rinse your razor in the sink with the bottom of the sink filled with a few inches of water.
- In the shower, turn the water on to get wet. Turn it off to lather up. Then, turn it back on to rinse off. Repeat when washing your hair.
- Limit yourself to five-minute showers and fill the tub with only ten inches of water for baths.
- Avoid flushing the toilet needlessly. Throw tissues and other waste in the garbage.

**ACTUAL TEST··· 10**

**156.** What is the notice about?

(A) Tips to help conserve water
(B) Newly adopted conservation techniques
(C) Methods to prevent water pollution
(D) Policies to protect the environment

**157.** Where would this notice most likely be seen?

(A) In a tourism magazine
(B) In an apartment lobby
(C) In a hotel room
(D) In a train car

# Daily Fresh Introduces a New Collection of Soaps

Los Angeles – Daily Fresh, a subsidiary company of KB Industries, Inc., has announced it will enter the liquid hand soap market. —[1]—. The new product, named Flow 'n' Fresh, will go on sale in stores across California on March 15. The rest of the states can expect to see Flow 'n' Fresh in stores starting on May 21.

—[2]—. A television and Internet advertisement campaign will begin in California on February 25. Advertisements in print media are scheduled to start on May 1.

Daily Fresh is California's oldest soap manufacturer. Daily Fresh's release of the liquid soap comes after sales of its traditional solid soap products have fallen. —[3]—. As a result,

Fresh Day, the company's oldest and top-selling soap, has seen a thirty-percent decrease in sales over the last two years. The company's move into the liquid soap market has been made in the hope that Daily Fresh can reestablish itself as a leading soap company.

Over the next 12 months Daily Fresh will release four varieties of liquid soap: melon, strawberry, olive, and honey. —[4]—. During the following 12 months, three more scents – lemon, lavender, and rose petal – will hit the market.

Early market tests conducted in Las Vegas, San Diego, and Rochester have indicated Flow 'n' Fresh will be well received by consumers across the country.

**158.** When will Flow 'n' Fresh be available nationwide?

(A) On February 25
(B) On March 15
(C) On May 1
(D) On May 21

**159.** Why has Daily Fresh entered the liquid soap market?

(A) To increase the company's profile in California
(B) To increase sales of current products
(C) To return to market leader status
(D) To open new stores in various countries

**160.** What recently happened to Daily Fresh?

(A) It expanded its market share.
(B) It grew bigger than ever.
(C) It developed new fresh and organic products.
(D) It saw a sharp turn downward in sales.

**161.** In which of the positions marked [1], [2], [3], and [4] does the following sentence best belong?

"The release of Flow 'n' Fresh will be accompanied by an advertising campaign targeting television, print media, and the Internet."

(A) [1]
(B) [2]
(C) [3]
(D) [4]

# MEMORANDUM

To: All employees
From: Jill Larson, Personnel Director

Employees will be granted sick leave when it is requested for a qualifying reason. All regular employees working 20 hours or more per week are eligible for paid sick leave and begin to accrue hours from the date they are hired. For extended leave (more than 6 days), medical certification is required. If it is not provided, the time off will be reclassified as vacation, compensatory time, or leave without pay. Employees are obligated to complete and submit a leave of absence form 2 weeks before the leave if the situation permits.

Full-time employees eligible for sick leave allowances may use accrued sick leave for purposes of routine physician appointments if the time has been approved in advance by the employee's supervisor. Sick leave is not paid until the employee completes three months of service.

Thank you for your understanding and full cooperation in advance.

Jill Larson
Personnel Director

**162.** What is the memo mainly about?

(A) Guidelines for taking sick leave
(B) The amounts of sick leave employees have
(C) Extensions of sick leave periods
(D) Requirements for receiving sick leave

**163.** What is required for employees who want to use accrued sick leave for regular physical checkups?

(A) A doctor's signature
(B) A supervisor's approval
(C) A leave of absence form
(D) A medical insurance form

# Sky Cycles: Our Passion, Our Cycles!

Commuters, are you tired of the endless traffic hold-ups, or the overcrowded, overpriced trains? Do you remember the happy days when you went everywhere by bicycle? Why not do it again? —[1]—.

Now is the perfect time to return to the bicycle. Throughout June, we have reductions of up to 25% on all bicycles in our stores. —[2]—. Plus, we have up to 30% off accessories, and up to 35% off cycling attire. Plus, safety equipment such as helmets and reflectors are up to 50% off! —[3]—.

And don't forget, Sky Cycles partners with the local government to offer you a range of competitive financing supports on your purchases.

—[4]—. We have bicycles of all kinds, from mountain bikes and road bikes, to commuter bikes that are ideal for those desiring a comfortable ride to and from work each day.

**164.** What advantage of cycling is implied in the advertisement?

(A) It is beneficial for commuters' health.
(B) It is better than driving during the summer months.
(C) It is cheaper than other forms of transportation.
(D) It helps people feel more relaxed.

**165.** What discount is offered on clothing?

(A) 25%
(B) 30%
(C) 35%
(D) 50%

**166.** What is mentioned about Sky Cycles?

(A) It recently opened for business.
(B) It works with government.
(C) It specializes in commuter bicycles.
(D) It prioritizes environmental protection.

**167.** In which of the positions marked [1], [2], [3], and [4] does the following sentence best belong?

"Sky Cycles was founded ten years ago with the aim of making lives better through cycling."

(A) [1]
(B) [2]
(C) [3]
(D) [4]

Dear Mr. Carmichael,

Thank you for all your help with everything we've gone through regarding my property during the past year and a half. There's no way I could have made it through the sale of my home without your help, knowledge, hard work, and support.

Robin Jenkins, one of your staff members, was patient and helpful when I was looking for a house to buy several years ago. We must have looked at homes for three or four months before finding the right one. Once I decided on a house, he got to work for me and made sure we closed the deal in a professional manner. Then, once I left Boston for Sacramento due to my new job, I immediately chose your company again to sell my house. Unfortunately, I ran into quite a few snags along the way to selling the property. My tenant, Ailey Taylor, didn't pay her rent for two months. I demanded that she move out according to the lease, but she refused to leave. That roadblock wasn't a problem for you, however. Your staff made the large problem I had only minor, and you took it in stride and handled the work with ease. I felt I could relax because my house was in good hands.

Whenever I have the opportunity to share the story of how I bought and sold my first home with someone, I'm sure to include how I couldn't have gotten through the process without Imperial Realty. You might think it's bizarre to give so much credit to a realtor, but it's all true.

Please let me know if I can ever do anything else for you.

Sincerely,

David Ferguson

**168.** What is the purpose of the letter?

(A) To introduce a property
(B) To ask for legal advice
(C) To give thanks for good service
(D) To notify a realtor of an upcoming move

**169.** Why did Mr. Ferguson sell his house again?

(A) He needed some quick cash.
(B) He wanted to move to a bigger house.
(C) He had to go to another city to work.
(D) He fell behind in his mortgage payments.

**170.** Who most likely is Mr. Carmichael?

(A) A lawyer
(B) A real estate agent
(C) An architect
(D) A landlord

**171.** What did Mr. Ferguson request that Ms. Taylor do?

(A) Sell the house to avoid higher taxes
(B) Modify some terms on the contact
(C) Vacate the house immediately
(D) Settle the problem without going to court

**Questions 172-175** refer to the following online chat discussion.

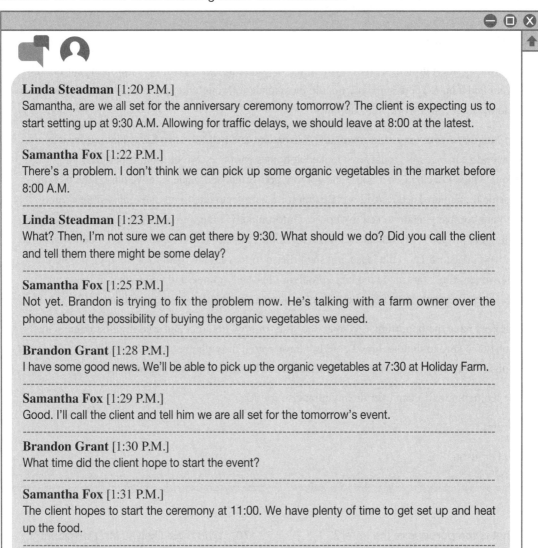

**Linda Steadman** [1:20 P.M.]
Samantha, are we all set for the anniversary ceremony tomorrow? The client is expecting us to start setting up at 9:30 A.M. Allowing for traffic delays, we should leave at 8:00 at the latest.

--------------------------------------------------------

**Samantha Fox** [1:22 P.M.]
There's a problem. I don't think we can pick up some organic vegetables in the market before 8:00 A.M.

--------------------------------------------------------

**Linda Steadman** [1:23 P.M.]
What? Then, I'm not sure we can get there by 9:30. What should we do? Did you call the client and tell them there might be some delay?

--------------------------------------------------------

**Samantha Fox** [1:25 P.M.]
Not yet. Brandon is trying to fix the problem now. He's talking with a farm owner over the phone about the possibility of buying the organic vegetables we need.

--------------------------------------------------------

**Brandon Grant** [1:28 P.M.]
I have some good news. We'll be able to pick up the organic vegetables at 7:30 at Holiday Farm.

--------------------------------------------------------

**Samantha Fox** [1:29 P.M.]
Good. I'll call the client and tell him we are all set for the tomorrow's event.

--------------------------------------------------------

**Brandon Grant** [1:30 P.M.]
What time did the client hope to start the event?

--------------------------------------------------------

**Samantha Fox** [1:31 P.M.]
The client hopes to start the ceremony at 11:00. We have plenty of time to get set up and heat up the food.

--------------------------------------------------------

**Linda Steadman** [1:33 P.M.]
You know, we'll need quite a bit of space for all the dishes the client asked for.

--------------------------------------------------------

**Brandon Grant** [1:33 P.M.]
The event venue is kind of a large ballroom. It's pretty huge. We don't have to worry about it.

--------------------------------------------------------

**Linda Steadman** [1:34 P.M.]
Okay. It seems like we have everything under control. I'm confident things will run smoothly tomorrow. Now, I think we can all relax.

**172.** Where do the writers most likely work?

    (A) At a catering company
    (B) At a healthcare center
    (C) At a local farm
    (D) At a restaurant

**173.** When will the writers arrive at the event venue?

    (A) At 7:30 A.M.
    (B) At 8 A.M.
    (C) At 9:30 A.M.
    (D) At 11 A.M.

**174.** What will Ms. Fox probably do next?

    (A) Order some organic foods
    (B) Contact the client
    (C) Prepare for her presentation
    (D) E-mail a local farm

**175.** At 1:34 P.M., what does Ms. Steadman mean when she writes, "Now, I think we can all relax"?

    (A) She feels tired after the ceremony.
    (B) She thinks they are well prepared for the event.
    (C) She hopes the client will be pleased.
    (D) She suggests having a coffee break.

# BELLE BOOKS
# Book talks for Business February!

| Sunday Evenings, 7:00 P.M. | Event Coordinator | Author | Most recent book |
|---|---|---|---|
| February 2 | Charles Winters | Margaret Michaels | Risk to Gain |
| February 9 | Deborah Stokes | Ashley Dedham | Modern Investment Strategies |
| February 16 | Thomas Racine | Stanley Mills | The Psychology of Business Gurus |
| February 23* | Amy Kane | | |

*On February 23, there will be a homecoming ceremony at nearby Mason College. Parking will likely be limited at that time, so please plan ahead.

| To: | Thomas Racine <tracine@loneowl.com> |
|---|---|
| From: | Charles Winters <cw@bellebooks.com> |
| Date: | January 10 |
| Subject: | Book talk dates |

Hello, Thomas,

I just learned about a great opportunity to host a book talk with Robin Baker, the author of several internationally acclaimed books on business. He will be in town from February 13 to 16 and is currently available on Sunday the 16th. The current schedule for next month's book talks has Stanley Mills set to talk on that evening. However, I know Mr. Mills personally. And I know that he lives locally and would likely not object to being rescheduled to the final book talk of next month. That would work out well for us since we do not currently have anyone scheduled for that date.

Would you be so kind as to contact Mr. Mills and see if he wouldn't mind us rescheduling his book talk to the later date? Then, contact Mr. Baker and let him know that we would love to have him on the 16th. Lastly, please inform Amy Kane that Mr. Mills will be appearing on the date she is responsible for coordinating.

Thank you.

Sincerely,

Charles Winters

**176.** What is suggested about Belle Books?

(A) It only sells books about investments.
(B) It has special prices for business books.
(C) It will host a regular event next month.
(D) It is located on the campus of a local college.

**177.** Why was the e-mail sent?

(A) To request more information about an author
(B) To ask an employee to host a book talk
(C) To get help changing some plans
(D) To ask about publishing expenses

**178.** What is indicated about Mr. Baker?

(A) He has already been to Belle Books.
(B) He will have to reschedule his visit.
(C) He is known in other countries.
(D) He is asking for a raise.

**179.** Which book does Mr. Winters hope to feature on February 23?

(A) Risk to Gain
(B) Modern Investment Strategies
(C) The Psychology of Business Gurus
(D) Buy and Sell Houses Now

**180.** In the e-mail, the word "appearing" in paragraph 2, line 3, is closest in meaning to

(A) sitting down
(B) taking part
(C) turning up
(D) going away

▶ ▶ ▶GO ON TO THE NEXT PAGE

# BUSINESS TRAVEL EXPENSE REPORT

**Employee:** Sophia Jones *Sophia Jones*
**For period ending:** August 15

## REIMBURSABLE EXPENSES INCURRED

| ITEM | AMOUNT |
|---|---|
| Hotel/Lodging | $798.67 |
| Meals | $224.58 |
| Airfare | $985.74 |
| 2-Day Auto Rental | $176.00 |
| Parking | $18.00 |
| Cab Fare (Includes Tips) | $42.00 |
| Tax | $84.03 |
| **TOTAL** | **$2,329.02** |

All of the original receipts are attached on the back of the report.

| To: | Sophia Jones <sjones@bellecorporation.com> |
|---|---|
| From: | Charlotte Miller <cmiller@bellecorporation.com> |
| Date: | August 20 |
| Subject: | Reimbursement |

Dear Ms. Jones,

I received your business travel expense report yesterday and closely examined your report and original receipts that you presented. But there is a problem that we need to deal with.

Unfortunately, the expense for your three nights of lodging exceeds the company's business travel expense guidelines. Considering that standard reimbursement allowance is $200 per night, your lodging expense, $798.67, is $198.67 over the maximum, and it must be paid by you.

However, the company fully acknowledges that hotel charges in Boston were suddenly inflated due to the international business convention and that the board's late decision to attend the convention limited your options to costly hotels. Therefore, I'd like you to fill in a RBSAE (Reimbursement Beyond Standard Allowable Expenses) form if you want to be fully reimbursed for the cost of your lodging. You can download it from our Web site at www.bellecorporation.com/forms.

Please submit it by Thursday, August 29, and the total amount on your report will be added to your next paycheck.

Thank you for your cooperation.

Regards,

Charlotte Miller
Accounting Manager

**181.** Why was the report sent?

(A) To authorize reimbursement
(B) To request repayment for travel costs
(C) To ask for a travel budget
(D) To provide basic information about a work procedure

**182.** Which expenditure went over the maximum limit?

(A) Accommodations
(B) Meals
(C) Parking
(D) Transportation

**183.** How long did Ms. Jones stay at the hotel?

(A) Two nights
(B) Three nights
(C) Four nights
(D) Five nights

**184.** What should Ms. Jones do to get fully reimbursed?

(A) Submit proof of employment
(B) Download some files for a conference
(C) Attach the original travel receipts to a report
(D) Complete a document for additional repayment

**185.** What can be inferred about Ms. Jones' business trip?

(A) She didn't rent a car.
(B) She stayed at an inexpensive hotel.
(C) The convention was held in Boston.
(D) Some of her receipts were lost.

# Shakespeare Fans:
# The Royal Theater Group is coming to San Francisco!

*RTG will perform William Shakespeare's classic play*
*The Merchant of Venice.*

**Venue:** San Francisco Downtown Theater
**Dates:** Sunday, October 12, 7 P.M.
Saturday, October 18, 7 P.M.
Friday, October 24, 7 P.M.
Sunday, October 26, 7 P.M.
**Ticket Prices:** $75 adults / $25 children under sixteen

Advance bookings can be made by visiting our Web site at www.sfdtheater.com and clicking on the ticket reservations link. To pay, either send a personal check to San Francisco Downtown Theater or choose to make a reservation payment online by credit card on our Web site.

Tickets can also be bought directly at the box office 2 hours prior to show time, but we can't guarantee that there will be any left at that time. Tickets bought at the box office must be paid for with cash. Thank you.

For more details, please call 510-575-4331 or e-mail our customer service department at cs@sfdtheater.com.

## SAN FRANCISCO DOWNTOWN THEATER

2301 Orchard Ave.
San Francisco, CA 94105

October 3

Dear Ms. West,

I am very excited to introduce the upcoming theater performance by the Royal Theater Group. *The Merchant of Venice* will be staged on October 12 and October 18 at the San Francisco Downtown Theater.

Details of the performance are as follows:

Date and time: October 12 7 P.M.
October 18 7 P.M.
October 24 7 P.M.
October 26 7 P.M.
Venue: San Francisco Downtown Theater
Ticket Prices: $75 adults / $25 children under sixteen
Remarks: Children below the age of 5 will not be admitted.

*The Merchant of Venice* has always been the beloved play by William Shakespeare, but it is very hard to get a chance to see it performed on stage. You are cordially invited to The Merchant of Venice and are welcome to order tickets for the show. As always, our VIP guests will be offered free parking and complimentary dinner.

Please honor us with your presence. I'm sure it will be a wonderful evening. Thank you, in advance, for your consideration of this request.

Truly yours,

William Baker
Chief Executive Officer
San Francisco Downtown Theater

---

**SAN FRANCISCO DOWNTOWN THEATER**

# PARKING TICKET FOR VIP

### Saturday, October 18

**IN:** 6:18 P.M.
**OUT:** 9:40 P.M.
**PARKING FEE:** $0

---

**186.** What is NOT mentioned as a payment option?

(A) Credit cards
(B) Money orders
(C) Personal checks
(D) Cash

**187.** In the flyer, the word "guarantee" in paragraph 3, line 1 is closest in meaning to

(A) endorse
(B) retain
(C) secure
(D) reserve

**188.** What is suggested about Ms. West?

(A) She has seen other plays in the theater.
(B) She has already paid for her tickets by credit card.
(C) She will pick up her tickets on the night of the event.
(D) She will go to the performance by herself.

**189.** According to the letter, what is stated about *The Merchant of Venice*?

(A) It has not been popular among fans.
(B) It has been received favorably by many critics.
(C) It has not been frequently performed.
(D) It has been reproduced in modern form.

**190.** When did Ms. West probably watch the performance?

(A) October 12
(B) October 18
(C) October 24
(D) October 26

⊖ ▢ ⊗

| To: | Kris Livingstone <klivingstone@rantzen.com> |
|---|---|
| From: | Brenda Fabian <bfian@rantzen.com> |
| Date: | August 29 |
| Subject: | London Trip |
| Attachment: | Train Schedule |

As you requested, I am sending you a schedule file including details of all the trains leaving Glasgow for London on September 5. As you can see, you have the option to take an express train which arrives in London around half an hour faster than any of the regular trains do. When you've decided, just let me know, and I'll take care of the reservations.

Did you say that you also want me to book tickets for Ms. Debbie Gibson? Does she require the same tickets as you?

Sincerely,

Brenda Fabian
Personnel Department

# TRAIN SCHEDULE

## September 5

| Train Number | 78 (Express) | 23 (Regular) | 77 (Express) | 24 (Regular) |
|---|---|---|---|---|
| Depart: Glasgow | 7:24 A.M. | 7:30 A.M. | 7:54 A.M. | 8:01 A.M. |
| Arrive: London | 1:13 P.M. | 1:55 P.M. | 1:43 P.M. | 2:26 P.M. |

## September 7

| Train Number | 81 (Express) | 33 (Regular) | 82 (Express) | 32 (Regular) |
|---|---|---|---|---|
| Depart: London | 1:35 P.M. | 1:55 P.M. | 2:10 P.M. | 2:45 P.M. |
| Arrive: Glasgow | 7:27 P.M. | 8:00 P.M. | 7:58 P.M. | 8:52 P.M. |

To: Brenda Fabian <bfabian@rantzen.com>

From: Kris Livingstone <klivingstone@rantzen.com>

Date: August 30

Subject: Re: London Trip

Hi, Brenda.

I really appreciate the time you have taken to organize this trip. I need to arrive in London before 1:30 P.M. so that I can meet up with our branch manager from the Manchester branch and go over our presentation one final time. For my return train, could you please book the earliest one that you mentioned?

Ms. Gibson plans to leave for London the day after me, September 6. However, we will return together at the same time on September 7. Could you please just book a ticket back to Glasgow for Ms. Gibson?

In addition, could you give the Manchester office a quick call and find out what hotel they will be staying at? We need to deliver the presentation on sales techniques together, so I'd like to book the same hotel as them so that we can work closely together.

Thanks again.

Kris Livingstone

191. What is Mr. Livingstone asked to do?

(A) Contact Ms. Gibson
(B) Reserve a ticket
(C) Fill out paperwork
(D) Provide further information

192. What is the number of the train Mr. Livingstone probably wants to take to London?

(A) 78
(B) 23
(C) 77
(D) 24

193. At what time does Mr. Livingstone most likely want to take the train from London to Glasgow?

(A) 1:35 P.M.
(B) 1:55 P.M.
(C) 2:10 P.M.
(D) 2:45 P.M.

194. What does Mr. Livingstone ask Ms. Fabian to do?

(A) Contact Ms. Gibson for approval
(B) Accompany him to a convention
(C) Cancel a hotel reservation
(D) Contact the Manchester office

195. What is indicated about Mr. Livingstone?

(A) He will return to Glasgow on September 6.
(B) He will travel with Ms. Gibson to London.
(C) He has already reserved a hotel room.
(D) He will work with his Manchester colleagues.

# Regular Workshop for Newly Hired Employees

Our company will hold regular workshops next month for new employees who have been with the company for fewer than six months. Attendance is mandatory.

**Date:** January 15-17 6:00 P.M. - 9:00 P.M. (after business hours)
**Place:** King Hotel in New York City - Conference Room on 2nd Floor

These workshops are designed to provide the most updated training to new employees at our company. During the workshops, each employee will get a chance to become acquainted with our executive personnel as well as employees in other departments. New employees will also be exposed to our new line of products and will be informed of the company's new sales strategies and goals for this year.

Any new employee who cannot attend for medical or personal reasons must inform Ms. Juliet Hwang, the head of Human Resources, of his or her expected absence and get permission from her.

Thank you. I really look forward to seeing all of you there.

George Winston
Chief Executive Officer
Yellow Chip, Inc.

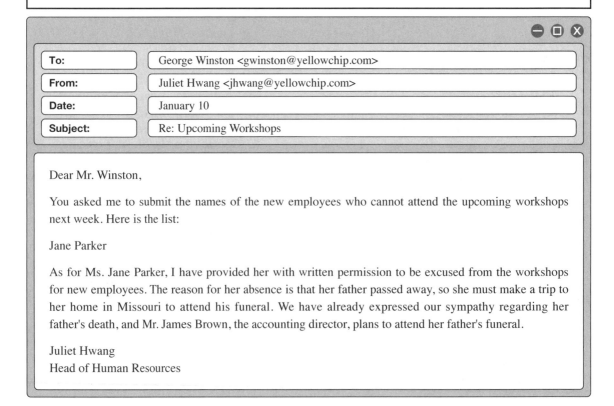

| To: | George Winston <gwinston@yellowchip.com> |
| --- | --- |
| From: | Juliet Hwang <jhwang@yellowchip.com> |
| Date: | January 10 |
| Subject: | Re: Upcoming Workshops |

Dear Mr. Winston,

You asked me to submit the names of the new employees who cannot attend the upcoming workshops next week. Here is the list:

Jane Parker

As for Ms. Jane Parker, I have provided her with written permission to be excused from the workshops for new employees. The reason for her absence is that her father passed away, so she must make a trip to her home in Missouri to attend his funeral. We have already expressed our sympathy regarding her father's death, and Mr. James Brown, the accounting director, plans to attend her father's funeral.

Juliet Hwang
Head of Human Resources

# OBITUARY

## IN LOVING MEMORY OF ROBERT PARKER

Mr. Robert Parker, an aged resident of Joplin, died early Saturday morning of general debility, and his death has caused widespread sorrow in the community.

The funeral will be held from the home of Mr. Robert Parker with her daughter, Jane Parker, on the morning of January 17, with the services in St. John's church and interment in St. John's cemetery.

**196.** What is stated about the regular workshops for new employees?

(A) The company guarantees they will have adequate accommodations.

(B) Every employee is required to attend.

(C) No new employees can skip them without an appropriate reason.

(D) They offer a wide selection of professional development programs.

**197.** What can be implied about Yellow Chip?

(A) It is located in New York City.

(B) It offers professional funeral services.

(C) It holds regular workshops twice a year.

(D) It hasn't hired new employees for several years.

**198.** Why did Ms. Hwang send an e-mail?

(A) To schedule a time to visit Missouri

(B) To contradict claims made at a workshop

(C) To offer her condolences to Ms. Parker's family

(D) To provide the name of an absentee

**199.** What can be inferred about Ms. Jane Parker?

(A) She will go on a business trip to Missouri.

(B) She will give a presentation at a corporate event.

(C) She has been with the company for less than half a year.

(D) She has attended many workshops in recent years.

**200.** What will probably happen on January 17?

(A) A new product will be released.

(B) A corporate event will begin.

(C) An executive won't attend a workshop.

(D) Some employees will visit another country.

STOP! This is the end of the test. If you finish before time is called, you may go back to Parts 5, 6, and 7 and check your work.

# 자세한 해설로 유명한
# 실전 모의고사 분야 최고의 베스트셀러!

**8회분 15,000원!**
〈본책 6회 + PDF 2회〉
**시즌 2**

## 실전 모의고사 8회에 15,000원!
## 타의 추종을 불허하는 압도적인 가성비!

❶ 강의보다도 더 쉽고 자세한 해설집!

❷ 틈틈이 공부하는 휴대용 단어 암기장!

❸ MP3 3종 세트(실전용 | 영국·호주발음 훈련용 | 고사장용)!

| 권장하는 점수대 | 400 | 500 | 600 | 700 | 800 | 900 |
|---|---|---|---|---|---|---|

| 이 책의 난이도 | 쉬움 | 비슷함 | 어려움 |
|---|---|---|---|

시험에 나오는 것만 공부한다!

# 시나공 토익

# 850 실전 모의고사

김병기 지음

## 번역 및 정답

Actual Test 06~10

## 시나공 토익
# 850 실전 모의고사

**초판 1쇄 발행** · 2020년 7월 10일
**초판 2쇄 발행** · 2021년 2월 10일

**지은이** · 김병기
**발행인** · 이종원
**발행처** · ㈜도서출판 길벗
**출판사 등록일** · 1990년 12월 24일
**주소** · 서울시 마포구 월드컵로 10길 56(서교동)
**대표전화** · 02) 332-0931 | **팩스** · 02) 322-6766
**홈페이지** · www.gilbut.co.kr | **이메일** · eztok@gilbut.co.kr

**기획 및 책임편집** · 고경환 (kkh@gilbut.co.kr) | **디자인** · 황애라 | **제작** · 이준호, 손일순, 이진혁
**영업마케팅** · 김학흥, 장봉석 | **웹마케팅** · 이수미, 최소영 | **영업관리** · 심선숙 | **독자지원** · 송혜란, 윤정아

**CTP 출력 및 인쇄** · 예림인쇄 | **제본** · 예림바인딩

ISBN 979-11-6521-213-1 03740
(이지톡 도서번호 300993)

정가 19,500원

# 목차

*자세한 해설을 확인하고 싶으시면 홈페이지에서 해설집을 다운로드하세요.(www.gilbut.co.kr)

# Actual Test 정답표

**Listening Comprehension**　　　　　　　　**Reading Comprehension**

## 06

| | | | | | | | | | |
|---|---|---|---|---|---|---|---|---|---|
| 1. (B) | 2. (D) | 3. (B) | 4. (C) | 5. (C) | 101. (C) | 102. (D) | 103. (D) | 104. (C) | 105. (A) |
| 6. (A) | 7. (B) | 8. (C) | 9. (A) | 10. (A) | 106. (B) | 107. (C) | 108. (B) | 109. (D) | 110. (D) |
| 11. (C) | 12. (B) | 13. (C) | 14. (B) | 15. (C) | 111. (A) | 112. (D) | 113. (D) | 114. (D) | 115. (D) |
| 16. (B) | 17. (A) | 18. (A) | 19. (B) | 20. (C) | 116. (D) | 117. (B) | 118. (B) | 119. (D) | 120. (C) |
| 21. (B) | 22. (C) | 23. (C) | 24. (A) | 25. (C) | 121. (D) | 122. (C) | 123. (D) | 124. (D) | 125. (C) |
| 26. (B) | 27. (B) | 28. (B) | 29. (B) | 30. (C) | 126. (A) | 127. (A) | 128. (D) | 129. (B) | 130. (C) |
| 31. (A) | 32. (C) | 33. (D) | 34. (A) | 35. (C) | 131. (C) | 132. (A) | 133. (B) | 134. (B) | 135. (D) |
| 36. (B) | 37. (A) | 38. (C) | 39. (A) | 40. (B) | 136. (B) | 137. (B) | 138. (A) | 139. (A) | 140. (B) |
| 41. (B) | 42. (A) | 43. (D) | 44. (C) | 45. (B) | 141. (A) | 142. (C) | 143. (D) | 144. (A) | 145. (A) |
| 46. (C) | 47. (B) | 48. (D) | 49. (B) | 50. (B) | 146. (D) | 147. (C) | 148. (A) | 149. (B) | 150. (C) |
| 51. (B) | 52. (B) | 53. (D) | 54. (C) | 55. (A) | 151. (D) | 152. (C) | 153. (D) | 154. (C) | 155. (B) |
| 56. (C) | 57. (B) | 58. (A) | 59. (C) | 60. (D) | 156. (A) | 157. (B) | 158. (C) | 159. (D) | 160. (B) |
| 61. (C) | 62. (D) | 63. (C) | 64. (A) | 65. (B) | 161. (D) | 162. (C) | 163. (B) | 164. (C) | 165. (A) |
| 66. (B) | 67. (D) | 68. (B) | 69. (D) | 70. (C) | 166. (D) | 167. (C) | 168. (C) | 169. (C) | 170. (D) |
| 71. (B) | 72. (C) | 73. (B) | 74. (A) | 75. (C) | 171. (C) | 172. (A) | 173. (C) | 174. (B) | 175. (B) |
| 76. (C) | 77. (D) | 78. (B) | 79. (D) | 80. (C) | 176. (B) | 177. (A) | 178. (C) | 179. (C) | 180. (B) |
| 81. (B) | 82. (C) | 83. (B) | 84. (B) | 85. (D) | 181. (D) | 182. (B) | 183. (A) | 184. (D) | 185. (A) |
| 86. (D) | 87. (C) | 88. (D) | 89. (C) | 90. (B) | 186. (C) | 187. (A) | 188. (D) | 189. (D) | 190. (D) |
| 91. (D) | 92. (B) | 93. (D) | 94. (C) | 95. (B) | 191. (C) | 192. (C) | 193. (D) | 194. (C) | 195. (B) |
| 96. (A) | 97. (D) | 98. (D) | 99. (B) | 100. (C) | 196. (D) | 197. (C) | 198. (B) | 199. (C) | 200. (C) |

## 07

| | | | | | | | | | |
|---|---|---|---|---|---|---|---|---|---|
| 1. (B) | 2. (B) | 3. (D) | 4. (D) | 5. (C) | 101. (B) | 102. (C) | 103. (D) | 104. (C) | 105. (B) |
| 6. (B) | 7. (B) | 8. (B) | 9. (A) | 10. (C) | 106. (D) | 107. (C) | 108. (C) | 109. (B) | 110. (C) |
| 11. (B) | 12. (B) | 13. (B) | 14. (C) | 15. (C) | 111. (A) | 112. (D) | 113. (C) | 114. (C) | 115. (A) |
| 16. (B) | 17. (A) | 18. (A) | 19. (B) | 20. (A) | 116. (C) | 117. (B) | 118. (B) | 119. (D) | 120. (C) |
| 21. (B) | 22. (B) | 23. (A) | 24. (B) | 25. (C) | 121. (C) | 122. (C) | 123. (D) | 124. (B) | 125. (A) |
| 26. (A) | 27. (A) | 28. (B) | 29. (A) | 30. (B) | 126. (C) | 127. (C) | 128. (C) | 129. (C) | 130. (C) |
| 31. (B) | 32. (B) | 33. (C) | 34. (C) | 35. (D) | 131. (B) | 132. (C) | 133. (D) | 134. (B) | 135. (C) |
| 36. (D) | 37. (A) | 38. (B) | 39. (C) | 40. (B) | 136. (D) | 137. (A) | 138. (B) | 139. (D) | 140. (C) |
| 41. (B) | 42. (B) | 43. (A) | 44. (D) | 45. (B) | 141. (A) | 142. (D) | 143. (D) | 144. (B) | 145. (A) |
| 46. (C) | 47. (C) | 48. (B) | 49. (B) | 50. (B) | 146. (D) | 147. (D) | 148. (D) | 149. (D) | 150. (A) |
| 51. (C) | 52. (B) | 53. (D) | 54. (D) | 55. (D) | 151. (D) | 152. (C) | 153. (D) | 154. (D) | 155. (B) |
| 56. (D) | 57. (B) | 58. (C) | 59. (D) | 60. (B) | 156. (C) | 157. (B) | 158. (A) | 159. (A) | 160. (B) |
| 61. (C) | 62. (C) | 63. (D) | 64. (C) | 65. (D) | 161. (D) | 162. (B) | 163. (C) | 164. (C) | 165. (A) |
| 66. (C) | 67. (D) | 68. (C) | 69. (D) | 70. (B) | 166. (D) | 167. (C) | 168. (C) | 169. (D) | 170. (D) |
| 71. (D) | 72. (C) | 73. (B) | 74. (D) | 75. (B) | 171. (B) | 172. (C) | 173. (C) | 174. (B) | 175. (D) |
| 76. (D) | 77. (D) | 78. (C) | 79. (C) | 80. (C) | 176. (A) | 177. (C) | 178. (B) | 179. (D) | 180. (A) |
| 81. (A) | 82. (D) | 83. (A) | 84. (D) | 85. (B) | 181. (C) | 182. (A) | 183. (D) | 184. (C) | 185. (A) |
| 86. (A) | 87. (C) | 88. (D) | 89. (C) | 90. (D) | 186. (D) | 187. (A) | 188. (D) | 189. (A) | 190. (D) |
| 91. (D) | 92. (D) | 93. (C) | 94. (B) | 95. (A) | 191. (B) | 192. (D) | 193. (A) | 194. (D) | 195. (A) |
| 96. (A) | 97. (C) | 98. (D) | 99. (B) | 100. (B) | 196. (B) | 197. (A) | 198. (C) | 199. (D) | 200. (C) |

# Actual Test 정답표

**Listening Comprehension**     **Reading Comprehension**

## 08

| | | | | | | | | | |
|---|---|---|---|---|---|---|---|---|---|
| 1. (B) | 2. (C) | 3. (B) | 4. (A) | 5. (D) | 101. (C) | 102. (A) | 103. (A) | 104. (C) | 105. (C) |
| 6. (C) | 7. (C) | 8. (C) | 9. (C) | 10. (B) | 106. (D) | 107. (C) | 108. (C) | 109. (B) | 110. (C) |
| 11. (A) | 12. (B) | 13. (C) | 14. (C) | 15. (B) | 111. (A) | 112. (D) | 113. (C) | 114. (B) | 115. (A) |
| 16. (B) | 17. (B) | 18. (B) | 19. (C) | 20. (A) | 116. (D) | 117. (A) | 118. (C) | 119. (A) | 120. (D) |
| 21. (B) | 22. (B) | 23. (B) | 24. (B) | 25. (C) | 121. (A) | 122. (B) | 123. (C) | 124. (C) | 125. (C) |
| 26. (C) | 27. (C) | 28. (B) | 29. (A) | 30. (B) | 126. (A) | 127. (A) | 128. (B) | 129. (D) | 130. (C) |
| 31. (C) | 32. (B) | 33. (D) | 34. (B) | 35. (D) | 131. (C) | 132. (D) | 133. (A) | 134. (A) | 135. (D) |
| 36. (C) | 37. (B) | 38. (D) | 39. (D) | 40. (D) | 136. (D) | 137. (B) | 138. (C) | 139. (D) | 140. (D) |
| 41. (D) | 42. (D) | 43. (C) | 44. (D) | 45. (D) | 141. (C) | 142. (A) | 143. (B) | 144. (C) | 145. (C) |
| 46. (A) | 47. (D) | 48. (B) | 49. (A) | 50. (A) | 146. (A) | 147. (D) | 148. (B) | 149. (B) | 150. (D) |
| 51. (A) | 52. (C) | 53. (C) | 54. (C) | 55. (D) | 151. (B) | 152. (D) | 153. (B) | 154. (B) | 155. (D) |
| 56. (D) | 57. (A) | 58. (C) | 59. (B) | 60. (D) | 156. (D) | 157. (A) | 158. (B) | 159. (B) | 160. (D) |
| 61. (D) | 62. (C) | 63. (D) | 64. (A) | 65. (B) | 161. (D) | 162. (B) | 163. (C) | 164. (B) | 165. (D) |
| 66. (B) | 67. (D) | 68. (A) | 69. (B) | 70. (B) | 166. (D) | 167. (B) | 168. (B) | 169. (B) | 170. (D) |
| 71. (C) | 72. (A) | 73. (D) | 74. (C) | 75. (B) | 171. (A) | 172. (C) | 173. (A) | 174. (C) | 175. (C) |
| 76. (A) | 77. (A) | 78. (D) | 79. (A) | 80. (B) | 176. (B) | 177. (C) | 178. (D) | 179. (D) | 180. (C) |
| 81. (C) | 82. (A) | 83. (B) | 84. (C) | 85. (D) | 181. (C) | 182. (C) | 183. (B) | 184. (A) | 185. (D) |
| 86. (C) | 87. (C) | 88. (D) | 89. (B) | 90. (C) | 186. (C) | 187. (D) | 188. (B) | 189. (B) | 190. (A) |
| 91. (C) | 92. (C) | 93. (C) | 94. (D) | 95. (C) | 191. (C) | 192. (B) | 193. (B) | 194. (A) | 195. (B) |
| 96. (B) | 97. (D) | 98. (A) | 99. (B) | 100. (D) | 196. (B) | 197. (C) | 198. (B) | 199. (D) | 200. (D) |

## 09

| | | | | | | | | | |
|---|---|---|---|---|---|---|---|---|---|
| 1. (D) | 2. (D) | 3. (A) | 4. (C) | 5. (C) | 101. (A) | 102. (B) | 103. (B) | 104. (D) | 105. (C) |
| 6. (C) | 7. (B) | 8. (A) | 9. (B) | 10. (C) | 106. (B) | 107. (B) | 108. (C) | 109. (D) | 110. (B) |
| 11. (C) | 12. (C) | 13. (A) | 14. (B) | 15. (B) | 111. (B) | 112. (C) | 113. (C) | 114. (D) | 115. (D) |
| 16. (C) | 17. (C) | 18. (C) | 19. (B) | 20. (C) | 116. (A) | 117. (C) | 118. (D) | 119. (C) | 120. (C) |
| 21. (A) | 22. (B) | 23. (C) | 24. (C) | 25. (C) | 121. (A) | 122. (D) | 123. (D) | 124. (B) | 125. (B) |
| 26. (C) | 27. (D) | 28. (D) | 29. (A) | 30. (B) | 126. (A) | 127. (D) | 128. (D) | 129. (B) | 130. (B) |
| 31. (B) | 32. (A) | 33. (B) | 34. (C) | 35. (B) | 131. (B) | 132. (C) | 133. (D) | 134. (B) | 135. (D) |
| 36. (A) | 37. (D) | 38. (A) | 39. (D) | 40. (D) | 136. (A) | 137. (B) | 138. (B) | 139. (C) | 140. (B) |
| 41. (A) | 42. (B) | 43. (B) | 44. (A) | 45. (B) | 141. (B) | 142. (C) | 143. (B) | 144. (D) | 145. (C) |
| 46. (D) | 47. (A) | 48. (C) | 49. (C) | 50. (B) | 146. (A) | 147. (C) | 148. (A) | 149. (D) | 150. (A) |
| 51. (D) | 52. (A) | 53. (D) | 54. (C) | 55. (C) | 151. (C) | 152. (C) | 153. (D) | 154. (B) | 155. (C) |
| 56. (C) | 57. (C) | 58. (A) | 59. (D) | 60. (C) | 156. (C) | 157. (D) | 158. (A) | 159. (A) | 160. (C) |
| 61. (A) | 62. (C) | 63. (B) | 64. (D) | 65. (D) | 161. (D) | 162. (D) | 163. (A) | 164. (D) | 165. (B) |
| 66. (C) | 67. (C) | 68. (B) | 69. (D) | 70. (C) | 166. (C) | 167. (A) | 168. (B) | 169. (A) | 170. (B) |
| 71. (C) | 72. (C) | 73. (C) | 74. (C) | 75. (C) | 171. (B) | 172. (D) | 173. (D) | 174. (B) | 175. (D) |
| 76. (A) | 77. (C) | 78. (A) | 79. (D) | 80. (D) | 176. (B) | 177. (D) | 178. (C) | 179. (C) | 180. (D) |
| 81. (A) | 82. (B) | 83. (C) | 84. (C) | 85. (B) | 181. (C) | 182. (C) | 183. (B) | 184. (C) | 185. (A) |
| 86. (D) | 87. (D) | 88. (D) | 89. (C) | 90. (D) | 186. (D) | 187. (B) | 188. (C) | 189. (D) | 190. (C) |
| 91. (B) | 92. (C) | 93. (B) | 94. (A) | 95. (A) | 191. (C) | 192. (C) | 193. (A) | 194. (D) | 195. (C) |
| 96. (C) | 97. (C) | 98. (C) | 99. (D) | 100. (C) | 196. (B) | 197. (C) | 198. (C) | 199. (D) | 200. (A) |

# Actual Test 정답표

**10**

| | | | | | | | | | |
|---|---|---|---|---|---|---|---|---|---|
| **1.** (A) | **2.** (B) | **3.** (C) | **4.** (D) | **5.** (B) | **101.** (D) | **102.** (D) | **103.** (D) | **104.** (A) | **105.** (B) |
| **6.** (D) | **7.** (B) | **8.** (B) | **9.** (A) | **10.** (C) | **106.** (D) | **107.** (B) | **108.** (B) | **109.** (B) | **110.** (D) |
| **11.** (A) | **12.** (B) | **13.** (C) | **14.** (B) | **15.** (A) | **111.** (B) | **112.** (B) | **113.** (C) | **114.** (B) | **115.** (D) |
| **16.** (C) | **17.** (C) | **18.** (B) | **19.** (C) | **20.** (A) | **116.** (D) | **117.** (D) | **118.** (D) | **119.** (B) | **120.** (B) |
| **21.** (A) | **22.** (C) | **23.** (B) | **24.** (C) | **25.** (A) | **121.** (B) | **122.** (C) | **123.** (A) | **124.** (D) | **125.** (B) |
| **26.** (C) | **27.** (B) | **28.** (C) | **29.** (B) | **30.** (B) | **126.** (C) | **127.** (B) | **128.** (C) | **129.** (C) | **130.** (D) |
| **31.** (B) | **32.** (A) | **33.** (D) | **34.** (B) | **35.** (C) | **131.** (A) | **132.** (C) | **133.** (B) | **134.** (D) | **135.** (C) |
| **36.** (C) | **37.** (A) | **38.** (C) | **39.** (B) | **40.** (A) | **136.** (D) | **137.** (B) | **138.** (D) | **139.** (D) | **140.** (D) |
| **41.** (D) | **42.** (C) | **43.** (A) | **44.** (A) | **45.** (A) | **141.** (A) | **142.** (C) | **143.** (A) | **144.** (C) | **145.** (B) |
| **46.** (D) | **47.** (D) | **48.** (B) | **49.** (B) | **50.** (A) | **146.** (D) | **147.** (B) | **148.** (A) | **149.** (B) | **150.** (C) |
| **51.** (C) | **52.** (D) | **53.** (D) | **54.** (A) | **55.** (D) | **151.** (D) | **152.** (D) | **153.** (C) | **154.** (D) | **155.** (A) |
| **56.** (D) | **57.** (D) | **58.** (C) | **59.** (D) | **60.** (B) | **156.** (A) | **157.** (C) | **158.** (D) | **159.** (C) | **160.** (D) |
| **61.** (D) | **62.** (C) | **63.** (A) | **64.** (D) | **65.** (B) | **161.** (B) | **162.** (A) | **163.** (B) | **164.** (C) | **165.** (C) |
| **66.** (C) | **67.** (B) | **68.** (A) | **69.** (C) | **70.** (A) | **166.** (B) | **167.** (D) | **168.** (C) | **169.** (C) | **170.** (B) |
| **71.** (A) | **72.** (B) | **73.** (B) | **74.** (C) | **75.** (C) | **171.** (C) | **172.** (A) | **173.** (C) | **174.** (B) | **175.** (B) |
| **76.** (B) | **77.** (C) | **78.** (A) | **79.** (C) | **80.** (C) | **176.** (C) | **177.** (C) | **178.** (C) | **179.** (C) | **180.** (B) |
| **81.** (D) | **82.** (B) | **83.** (B) | **84.** (A) | **85.** (D) | **181.** (B) | **182.** (A) | **183.** (B) | **184.** (D) | **185.** (C) |
| **86.** (C) | **87.** (D) | **88.** (C) | **89.** (C) | **90.** (C) | **186.** (B) | **187.** (C) | **188.** (A) | **189.** (C) | **190.** (B) |
| **91.** (C) | **92.** (D) | **93.** (C) | **94.** (A) | **95.** (C) | **191.** (D) | **192.** (A) | **193.** (A) | **194.** (D) | **195.** (D) |
| **96.** (D) | **97.** (A) | **98.** (C) | **99.** (D) | **100.** (B) | **196.** (C) | **197.** (A) | **198.** (D) | **199.** (C) | **200.** (C) |

# Actual Test

## 번역 및 정답

**1.** 미W

(A) She is sipping a cup of coffee.
(B) She is talking on a cellular phone while walking.
(C) She is standing near the entrance of a building.
(D) She is looking through her bag.

(A) 그녀는 커피를 마시고 있다.
(B) 그녀는 걸으면서 휴대전화로 통화하고 있다.
(C) 그녀는 건물 입구 근처에 서 있다.
(D) 그녀는 가방 안을 살펴보고 있다. 　　　정답 (B)

**2.** 영W

(A) A woman is grasping a handrail.
(B) A microphone is being set up on a stage.
(C) Tourists are taking a group picture.
(D) Some filming equipment is being adjusted.

(A) 여자가 손잡이를 잡고 있다.
(B) 마이크가 무대 위에 설치되고 있다.
(C) 관광객들이 단체 사진을 찍고 있다.
(D) 촬영 장비가 조정되고 있다. 　　　정답 (D)

**3.** 미M

(A) The woman is bending down to tie her shoe.
(B) The woman is kneeling down to do some exercise.
(C) The woman is grasping onto an escalator handrail.
(D) The woman is assembling some equipment in a shop.

(A) 여자는 신발 끈을 묶기 위해 몸을 수그리고 있다.
(B) 여자는 무릎을 꿇은 상태에서 운동을 하고 있다.
(C) 여자는 에스컬레이터의 손잡이를 쥐고 있다.
(D) 여자는 가게에서 장비를 조립하고 있다. 　　　정답 (B)

**4.** 호M

(A) The path winds through the trees.
(B) A boat is being paddled down a river.
(C) Some branches are hanging over the water.
(D) A row of fishing boats is docked at a pier.

(A) 나무들 사이로 휘어진 오솔길이 있다.
(B) 배 한 척이 강을 따라 움직이고 있다.
(C) 몇몇 나뭇가지들이 물 위로 드리워져 있다.
(D) 낚싯배들이 일렬로 부두에 정박해 있다. 　　　정답 (C)

**5.** 미W

(A) Some people are enjoying the view of the ocean.
(B) A pile of leaves has been left near a walkway.
(C) Some tables and chairs have been placed along a canal.
(D) An awning has been stretched across a building entrance.

(A) 몇몇 사람들이 바다 풍경을 감상하고 있다.
(B) 낙엽 더미가 보도 근처에 남아 있다.
(C) 몇몇 테이블과 의자들이 수로를 따라 위치해 있다.
(D) 건물 입구에 걸쳐 차양이 설치되어 있다. 　　　정답 (C)

**6.** 미M

(A) The woman is sawing a wooden plank.
(B) The woman is carrying building materials.
(C) The woman is operating a sewing machine.

(D) The woman is walking through a garden.

(A) 여자가 나무 판자를 톱으로 자르고 있다.
(B) 여자가 건축 자재를 운반하고 있다.
(C) 여자가 재봉틀을 작동하고 있다.
(D) 여자가 정원을 걷고 있다. 　　　정답 (A)

### Part 2

**7.** 미M 영W

When is Mr. Watson coming back to the office?
(A) By subway.
(B) I have no idea.
(C) Yes, I think so.

Watson 씨는 언제 사무실에 복귀하나요?
(A) 지하철을 이용해서요.
(B) 잘 모르겠어요.
(C) 네, 그렇게 생각해요. 　　　정답 (B)

**8.** 미W 미M

Why were you so late for the regular meeting today?
(A) Sure, I can meet the deadline.
(B) I drive to work every day.
(C) Because of a minor car accident.

오늘 정기 회의에 늦은 이유가 뭔가요?
(A) 물론이에요, 마감시한을 맞출 수 있어요.
(B) 저는 매일 차를 몰고 출근해요.
(C) 작은 교통사고 때문에요. 　　　정답 (C)

**9.** 미M 영W

Do you know Cheese Electronics offers an extended warranty?
(A) Yes, but there is an additional fee for that.
(B) Yes, she's extremely knowledgeable.
(C) May I have extension 110, please?

Cheese Electronics 사에서 연장된 품질 보증을 제공해 준다는 사실을 알고 있어요?
(A) 네, 그렇지만 그에 따른 추가 비용이 있어요.
(B) 네, 그녀는 굉장히 박식해요.
(C) 내선번호 110번으로 연결해 주시겠어요? 　　　정답 (A)

**10.** 미W 미M

When is the market analysis report due?
(A) Not until November 23.
(B) We only have 7% of the domestic market share.
(C) Yes, I reported it to the police.

시장 분석 보고서의 마감시한은 언제인가요?
(A) 11월 23일이에요.
(B) 우리의 국내 시장 점유율은 7%에 불과해요.
(C) 네, 경찰에 신고했습니다. 　　　정답 (A)

**11.** 미M 영W

How long have you been with the company?
(A) It was founded 35 years ago.
(B) All right. It'll take about ten minutes.
(C) Since I graduated from college.

그 회사에서 얼마 동안 근무하셨습니까?
(A) 35년 전에 설립되었습니다.

(B) 좋습니다. 10분 정도 걸릴 겁니다.
(C) 대학을 졸업한 이후부터요.　　　　　　　정답 (C)

**12.** 호M 영W

Where is the best place to buy fresh produce downtown?
(A) We need to buy carrots, lettuce, and potatoes.
(B) Why don't you go to the market on Main Street?
(C) I'll be out of town tomorrow.

시내에서 신선한 농산물을 구매할 수 있는 가장 좋은 장소가 어디인가요?
(A) 우리는 당근, 상추, 그리고 감자를 사야 해요.
(B) Main Street에 있는 시장으로 가는 건 어때요?
(C) 저는 내일 출장을 갑니다.　　　　　　　정답 (B)

**13.** 미W 미M

Why has the opening of our new branch office been postponed?
(A) It usually opens at 9:00.
(B) To the Paris branch office.
(C) The building is still under maintenance.

우리의 새로운 지사의 개장이 연기된 이유는 무엇인가요?
(A) 대개 9시에 열어요.
(B) Paris 지사로요.
(C) 건물이 여전히 보수 공사 중이에요.　　　　정답 (C)

**14.** 미M 영W

I have an appointment with the eye doctor later this afternoon.
(A) The pharmaceutical section.
(B) Then I'll do the paperwork for you.
(C) Thank you for your time and consideration.

저는 오늘 늦은 오후에 안과 의사와 진료 예약이 있어요.
(A) 약품 코너요.
(B) 그러면 제가 서류 작업을 해 드릴게요.
(C) 시간 내주고 배려해 주셔서 감사합니다.　　정답 (B)

**15.** 미W 호M

Will you be attending the seminar on new computer technology?
(A) The computer has already been repaired.
(B) I think Dr. Johnson is an excellent speaker.
(C) Has it been canceled?

새로운 컴퓨터 기술에 관한 세미나에 참석하실 건가요?
(A) 컴퓨터는 이미 수리가 되었어요.
(B) Johnson 박사님이 훌륭한 연설자라고 생각해요.
(C) 그게 취소되었나요?　　　　　　　　　정답 (C)

**16.** 영W 미M

Would you like to call Ms. Mako now, or do you want me to talk to her later?
(A) Yes, it's very cold outside now.
(B) I think I can handle it myself.
(C) She called in sick this morning.

지금 Mako 씨에게 전화하실 건가요, 아니면 나중에 제가 그녀에게 이야기하길 원하시나요?
(A) 네, 지금 밖은 굉장히 추워요.
(B) 제가 처리할 수 있을 것 같아요.
(C) 그녀는 오전에 아파서 결근한다고 전화했어요.　정답 (B)

**17.** 호M 미W

How often do you visit the manufacturing plant?

(A) Whenever it is necessary.
(B) Three years in a row.
(C) It will open next Monday.

제조 공장에는 얼마나 자주 방문하시나요?
(A) 필요할 때마다요.
(B) 3년 연속으로요.
(C) 다음주 월요일에 개장할 겁니다.　　　　정답 (A)

**18.** 미M 영W

Would you like to see this laptop computer in another color?
(A) Sure, which colors do you have?
(B) No, I'd like to pay with my credit card.
(C) No, thank you. I'm already full.

다른 색상의 노트북 컴퓨터를 보시겠습니까?
(A) 물론이에요, 어떠한 색상을 보유하고 계세요?
(B) 아니오, 신용카드로 계산하겠습니다.
(C) 감사합니다만 사양할게요, 이미 배가 불러요.　정답 (A)

**19.** 호M 미M

We will expand the assembly plant to meet seasonal peak demand.
(A) The building wasn't ready.
(B) We should hire extra staff, too.
(C) Some stores are currently disappearing.

우리는 계절에 따른 수요의 증가를 충족시키고자 조립 공장의 규모를 확장할 겁니다.
(A) 건물이 준비되지 않았어요.
(B) 추가 인력도 채용해야 해요.
(C) 몇몇 상점들이 현재 사라져가고 있어요.　　정답 (B)

**20.** 영W 미M

What's the fax number for Andrew Accounting Services?
(A) 25,200 Carlos Bee Blvd.
(B) About the preparation of financial statements.
(C) I have to look it up.

Andrew Accounting Services의 팩스 번호는 어떻게 되나요?
(A) Carlos Bee 가 25200번지예요.
(B) 재무제표 준비에 관해서요.
(C) 찾아봐야 해요.　　　　　　　　　　정답 (C)

**21.** 미W 호M

This is a cheap watch, but it runs great and keeps good time.
(A) He is very punctual.
(B) How much did you pay for it?
(C) I think the interview went really well.

이 시계가 싸긴 하지만 시계도 잘 가고 시간도 정확하게 잘 맞아요.
(A) 그는 시간 약속을 잘 지켜요.
(B) 얼마를 지불하셨어요?
(C) 면접은 아주 순조로웠던 것 같아요.　　　정답 (B)

**22.** 영W 호M

Where can I find more information about recently launched products?
(A) Yes, it was just released.
(B) This is a perfect place for a business lunch.
(C) You should visit the manufacturer's Web site.

최근 출시된 제품들에 대한 추가 정보는 어디서 찾을 수 있을까요?
(A) 네, 그건 막 출시되었어요.
(B) 이곳이 사업상 점심식사를 하기에 아주 좋은 장소예요.
(C) 제조업체의 홈페이지를 참조하세요.     정답 (C)

**23.** 영W 미M

Haven't the new tires for Ms. Tyler's van arrived yet?
(A) Sorry. I'm very tired tonight.
(B) Yes, she is a good delivery truck driver.
(C) Do you mean the ones for the van parked in the rear of the garage?

Tyler 씨 승합차에 필요한 새로운 타이어들은 아직 도착하지 않은 건가요?
(A) 미안해요. 제가 오늘밤에 굉장히 피곤하네요.
(B) 네, 그녀는 좋은 배송 트럭 기사예요.
(C) 자동차 수리점 뒤쪽에 주차한 승합차에 사용할 타이어들을 말씀하시는 건가요?     정답 (C)

**24.** 호M 미W

Would you like a copy of our itinerary?
(A) That would be great. Thanks.
(B) We had a good time in San Francisco.
(C) Please make mine black.

여행 일정표를 한 부 원하십니까?
(A) 그러면 좋죠, 고맙습니다.
(B) 우리는 San Francisco에서 좋은 시간을 보냈어요.
(C) 제 건 블랙 커피로 해주세요.     정답 (A)

**25.** 미M 영W

The General Affairs Department is on the seventh floor.
(A) No, I think it's on the seventh floor.
(B) The department store is two blocks away from here.
(C) Isn't the Personnel Department there, too?

총무부는 7층에 위치하고 있습니다.
(A) 아니오, 7층에 있는 걸로 알고 있어요.
(B) 백화점은 이 곳에서 두 블록 떨어진 곳에 있어요.
(C) 그 곳에 인사부도 있지 않나요?     정답 (C)

**26.** 미W 미M

Will you accept a personal check?
(A) I'll check out of the hotel at 10:00 A.M.
(B) Sorry. Cash or charge only.
(C) It's already in the mail.

개인 수표도 받으시나요?
(A) 저는 오전 10시에 호텔에서 퇴실할 겁니다.
(B) 죄송합니다만, 현금이나 신용카드만 가능합니다.
(C) 그건 이미 우편물 속에 있어요.     정답 (B)

**27.** 호M 영W

Would you be able to lead the safety education session for our employees?
(A) It'll last about an hour.
(B) It depends on when it is.
(C) Unfortunately, it's out of stock.

우리 직원들을 대상으로 하는 안전 교육을 진행해 주실 수 있나요?
(A) 그건 한 시간 정도 걸릴 겁니다.
(B) 언제 하는지에 달려 있어요.
(C) 안타깝게도 재고가 없네요.     정답 (B)

**28.** 미M 미W

We're scheduled to go on a business trip on Monday, aren't we?
(A) Yes, I'm glad they can do it.
(B) Yes, we're going to meet with some foreign buyers there.
(C) No, you should bring me your original receipts.

우리는 월요일에 출장을 가기로 되어 있어요, 그렇지 않아요?
(A) 네, 그들이 할 수 있어서 기뻐요.
(B) 네, 우리는 그 곳에서 해외 구매자들과 만날 겁니다.
(C) 아니오, 영수증 원본들을 제게 가져다 주셔야 합니다.     정답 (B)

**29.** 영W 미M

Do you want me to schedule the job interview for the morning or the afternoon?
(A) Yes, if you don't mind.
(B) Either would be fine.
(C) Mr. Stanford quit his job in the morning.

취업 면접 시간을 오전에 잡길 원하세요, 아니면 오후에 잡길 원하세요?
(A) 네, 당신만 좋다면요.
(B) 어느 쪽이든 좋습니다.
(C) Stanford 씨는 오전에 퇴사했습니다.     정답 (B)

**30.** 미M 미W

Why do you want to send the documents by express mail?
(A) You can track the ordered item.
(B) Because I just checked your e-mail.
(C) They must be delivered by Thursday.

그 서류들을 속달 우편으로 보내고 싶어 하는 이유가 뭐예요?
(A) 주문한 물건의 배송 경로를 추적할 수 있어요.
(B) 제가 방금 당신의 이메일을 확인했거든요.
(C) 그 서류들이 목요일까지 전달되어야 합니다.     정답 (C)

**31.** 영W 호M

The post office closes at 5:00 P.M., doesn't it?
(A) As far as I know, yes.
(B) Yes, much better. Thank you.
(C) It's very close to our office.

우체국은 오후 5시에 문을 닫죠, 그렇지 않나요?
(A) 제가 알기론 그렇습니다.
(B) 네, 훨씬 낫습니다. 감사합니다.
(C) 우리 사무실과 굉장히 가깝습니다.     정답 (A)

## Part 3

문제 32-34번은 다음 대화를 참조하시오. 호M 미W

M: Hello. My name is William Terry, and I'm a member of the Specialized Automobile Service. I'm on my way to Oakland now, but, **(32) unfortunately, one of the front tires is flat now after I dropped by a place to get some dinner. Can someone help me to change my tire?**

W: Sure, Mr. Terry. **(33) I'll contact the auto maintenance technician closest to your location, and he'll go to you as soon as possible.** He will check your tire and take the necessary steps to change it.

M: Oh, great. I'm on Freeway 5 near exit 74B. **(34) How much do you charge to change a tire? I wonder I have enough money to pay for the service.**

10

W: Your annual membership fee for the Specialized Automobile Service will cover it this time.

---

M: 안녕하세요. 저는 William Terry라고 하는데요, Specialized Automobile Service의 회원이에요. 제가 지금 Oakland로 가는 길이고, 저녁식사를 하느라 잠시 식당에 들렀는데 공교롭게도 지금 자동차 앞바퀴 하나가 펑크가 났어요. 누군가 타이어 교체를 도와주실 수 있을까요?
W: 물론이에요, Terry 씨. 제가 고객님이 계신 위치에서 가장 가까운 곳에 있는 자동차 수리 기술자와 연락을 취해서, 그가 최대한 빨리 고객님께 갈 겁니다. 저희 기술자가 자동차 타이어를 점검하고 교체하는 데 필요한 조치들을 취할 겁니다.
M: 아, 좋아요. 저는 지금 5번 고속도로의 74B 출구 근처에 있어요. 타이어 교체 비용은 얼마나 될까요? 제가 서비스에 지불할 돈이 충분한지 모르겠네요.
W: Specialized Automobile Service에 지불하신 고객님의 연회비가 이번에 받는 서비스의 비용을 부담할 겁니다.

**32.** 남자가 전화하는 이유는 무엇인가?
(A) 일자리 지원을 하기 위해서
(B) 특별 할인 행사를 홍보하기 위해서
(C) 타이어를 교체하기 위해서
(D) 사고를 보고하기 위해서　　　　정답 (C)

**33.** 여자는 누구일 것 같은가?
(A) 관광 가이드
(B) 라디오 기자
(C) 자동차 판매상
(D) 고객 서비스 직원　　　　정답 (D)

**34.** 남자가 우려하는 것은 무엇인가?
(A) 서비스 비용
(B) 그의 일정 변경
(C) 새로운 사무실의 크기
(D) 기술자의 가용 상태　　　　정답 (A)

**문제 35-37번은 다음 대화를 참조하시오.** ⓜM ⓜW

M: Good morning, Ms. Anderson? (35) This is Oliver Stone, the realtor with Century Realty. I'd like to tell you a new single house on Orchard Avenue is put up for sale. I was wondering if you were interested in it.
W: Oh, that's a good neighborhood. Could you please tell me more about the house?
M: Well, it's a two-story home with a front lawn and a back porch. (36) It's selling for 300,000 dollars.
AW: Um…I really like the house, (36) but it's just a bit out of my price range. Is there any room to negotiate the price down?
M: I think it's possible. (37) But why don't you look at the property first? When will you be available? I'm free this afternoon around 2 o'clock.
W: (37) I think I can meet you there at 2. Please text me the address.

---

M: 안녕하세요, Anderson 씨? 저는 Century Realty에서 근무하는 Oliver Stone이에요. Orchard 대로에 위치한 새로운 단독주택이 매물로 나와서 말씀드리려고요. 혹시 관심이 있으실까 싶어서요.
W: 오, 좋은 동네에 있네요. 그 집에 대해서 더 알려주실 수 있나요?
M: 음, 전면에는 잔디밭이 있고 후면에 베란다가 있는 2층 주택이에요. 가

---

격은 30만 달러이고요.
W: 음… 그 집이 정말 좋은데요. 제 예산을 살짝 벗어나네요. 가격을 인하시킬 수 있는 협상의 여지가 있을까요?
M: 가능할 거라고 봅니다. 하지만 일단 주택부터 먼저 보시는 것이 어떨까요? 언제 시간이 되세요? 저는 오늘 오후 2시쯤에 시간이 납니다.
W: 그 곳에서 2시에 뵐 수 있을 것 같네요. 제게 문자로 그 곳의 주소를 알려주세요.

**35.** 남자는 어디에서 근무하는가?
(A) 투자 회사
(B) 조경 회사
(C) 부동산 중개업체
(D) 관공서　　　　정답 (C)

**36.** 여자는 무엇에 관해 우려하고 있는가?
(A) 위치
(B) 가격
(C) 대출 금리
(D) 규모　　　　정답 (B)

**37.** 화자들은 오후에 무엇을 할 것 같은가?
(A) 주택을 방문한다.
(B) 대출을 신청한다.
(C) 보수공사를 시작한다.
(D) 임대 계약서에 서명한다.　　　　정답 (A)

**문제 38-40번은 다음의 3자 대화를 참조하시오.** ⓜM ⓗM ⓔW

M1: Hey, Mr. Budd, (38) have you been able to access the server today? I can't get to any of the folders. I just receive an error message.
M2: Yes, Mr. Murphy. (38) I've been experiencing the same thing. I called the IT Department, and the department head said the server will be down until tomorrow.
M1: That's the problem. (39) I need to finish this sales report for a meeting with a client at 3 o'clock. I need last year's revenue numbers to do that.
W: Oh, Mr. Murphy, I think I can help you with that. (40) I've got those numbers printed if you want them. It's not ideal, but you could recruit a couple of interns to enter the numbers on a spreadsheet program.

---

M1: 안녕하세요, Budd 씨, 오늘 서버에 접속이 가능했어요? 저는 어떤 폴더도 접근이 안되던데요. 오류 메시지만 뜨더라고요.
M2: 네, Murphy 씨. 저도 내내 똑같은 경험을 했어요. IT 부서에 연락을 했더니 그 곳 부장님이 서버가 내일까지 열리지 않는다고 하네요.
M1: 그거 문제네요. 오늘 오후 3시에 고객과 회의가 있어서 이 영업 보고서를 마무리 지어야 하는데 말이죠. 보고서를 작성하려면 작년 수익 수치가 필요하거든요.
W: 아, Murphy 씨, 그 부분은 제가 도와드릴 수 있어요. 원한다면 그 수치들은 제가 프린트한 게 있어요. 이상적인 방법은 아니지만 스프레드시트 프로그램에 그 수치를 입력할 인턴을 두어 명 정도 찾을 수 있을 거예요.

**38.** 화자들은 무엇을 논의하고 있는가?
(A) 잃어버린 서류
(B) 인턴 프로그램
(C) 기술적인 문제
(D) 회의 안건　　　　정답 (C)

**39.** Murphy 씨는 회의 전에 무엇을 해야 하는가?
(A) 보고서를 작성해야 한다.
(B) 인턴들을 훈련시켜야 한다.
(C) 서버를 수리해야 한다.
(D) 발표를 준비해야 한다. 정답 (A)

**40.** 여자가 제안하는 것은 무엇인가?
(A) 기술자를 보낸다.
(B) 자료를 제공한다.
(C) 견본품을 배송한다.
(D) 서버가 위치한 곳으로 안내한다. 정답 (B)

---

문제 41-43번은 다음 대화를 참조하시오. 호M 미W

M: Hi, Ms. Campbell. (41) **This is Steve Jones. I own the apartment complex you're living in. I'm calling to let you know that I've put your building up for sale.**
W: Oh? I was planning on staying here until next May. When will I have to leave?
M: I expect the process could take a full month, but I'll keep you updated. During the next few weeks though, (42) **some realtors will be looking at the individual units.**
W: I see. (43) **Could I ask that they visit my unit on the weekend?** I'm not really comfortable with them being in my apartment while I'm not there.

---

M: 안녕하세요, Campbell 씨. 저는 Steve Jones라고 합니다. 저는 당신이 임대하고 있는 아파트 단지의 소유주예요. 제가 아파트를 매물로 내놓았다는 사실을 알려드리고자 연락을 드렸습니다.
W: 그래요? 저는 이 아파트에 5월까지 머무르려고 계획했는데요. 제가 언제 비워드려야 하나요?
M: 아파트를 매각하는 과정이 한 달은 족히 걸릴 것으로 예상하고 있지만, 상황이 어떻게 되어 가는지 계속 알려드리도록 할게요. 그렇지만 향후 몇 주간은 몇몇 부동산 중개업자들이 각 집을 보러 가게 될 겁니다.
W: 알겠습니다. 그런데 부동산 중개업자들이 주말에 제 집을 보러 와 달라고 당부 드려도 될까요? 제가 집에 없는 동안에 살펴보는 것은 정말 불편하거든요.

**41.** 남자는 무엇을 할 것이라고 말하는가?
(A) 관광 여행을 예약한다.
(B) 부동산을 매각한다.
(C) 새로운 아파트로 이사한다.
(D) 안전 검사를 실시한다. 정답 (B)

**42.** 아파트에 누가 방문할 것인가?
(A) 부동산 중개업자
(B) 안전 검사관
(C) 인테리어 디자이너
(D) 도시 개발업자 정답 (A)

**43.** 여자가 제안하는 것은 무엇인가?
(A) 이웃에게 전화한다.
(B) 몇몇 제품의 광고를 한다.
(C) 건물주와 이야기한다.
(D) 그녀의 아파트를 특정 시간에 방문한다. 정답 (D)

---

문제 44-46번은 다음 대화를 참조하시오. 호M 영W

M: Excuse me. I'm Allen Smith from Best Maintenance Center. (44) **I'm here to fix a leak in the ceiling in this office.**
W: Thank you for coming, Mr. Smith. There's some dripping water coming directly from the ceiling. (45) **I've already moved some of the desks and chairs in that area so that you can have some space to work.** I wonder how much it will cost to get it repaired.
M: Well, I can't get into that right now. I don't know what's causing the water leak yet. I'll have to check the ceiling and find out the cause of the leak first. (46) **Please give me about 30 minutes. Then, I'll be able to give you an estimate.**

---

M: 실례합니다. 저는 Best Maintenance Center에서 근무하는 Allen Smith라고 합니다. 이 사무실 천장의 누수를 수리하러 왔습니다.
W: 방문해 주셔서 감사합니다, Smith 씨. 천장에서 물이 바로 뚝뚝 떨어지더군요. 작업하실 수 있는 공간을 확보하기 위해서 물이 떨어지는 쪽에 있는 몇몇 책상과 의자들은 이미 치웠어요. 누수 수리 비용은 얼마나 될지 궁금합니다.
M: 글쎄요, 지금 당장은 뭐라고 말씀드리기 어렵습니다. 누수를 일으키는 원인을 아직 알 수가 없어서요. 우선 천장을 살펴보고 누수 원인을 찾아야 합니다. 제게 30분 정도 시간을 주십시오. 그 때는 견적을 내드리는 것이 가능할 겁니다.

**44.** 남자의 방문 목적은 무엇인가?
(A) 새로운 사무실을 페인트칠하기 위해서
(B) 계약서에 서명하기 위해서
(C) 수리를 하기 위해서
(D) 안전검사를 실시하기 위해서 정답 (C)

**45.** 여자는 남자를 위해 무엇을 했는가?
(A) 입사 지원자들의 면접을 실시했다.
(B) 일부 사무 가구를 옮겼다.
(C) 사무용품을 주문했다.
(D) 고객과의 회의 일정을 잡았다. 정답 (B)

**46.** 남자는 대략 30분 후에 무엇을 할 것인가?
(A) 수리 작업을 마무리한다.
(B) 새로운 사무실을 청소한다.
(C) 가격 견적을 제공한다.
(D) 계약 조건을 말한다. 정답 (C)

---

문제 47-49번은 다음 대화를 참조하시오. 미M 미W

M: Oh, Ms. Wilson. (47) **The restaurant has been so successful since we opened it last June.** I'm very glad to see it prospering.
W: Yes, our net profits have risen sharply every month. People are even coming to our restaurant from the other side of the city to have meals.
M: Precisely! (48) **I think it's time to open a second location. What do you say?**
W: Um... (48) **we don't have enough management experience for that.**
M: Right. (49) **That's why we should hire a business consulting expert to lead us.** That person will be able to advise us on how we can manage two restaurants.

---

M: 아, Wilson 씨. 우리 식당이 지난 6월에 개업한 이후 무척이나 잘 되고 있어요. 이렇게 영업이 잘 되는 걸 보니 굉장히 기쁘네요.

W: 네, 우리 순이익도 매달 급증하고 있어요. 사람들이 심지어는 도시 반대편에서도 우리 식당에서 식사를 하려고 방문하고 있어요.

M: 그렇죠! 저는 2호점을 개장해야 할 시점이라고 생각해요. 어떻게 생각하세요?

W: 음… 우리는 그렇게 운영해본 경험이 없어요.

M: 맞아요. 그래서 우리를 잘 이끌어 줄 비즈니스 컨설팅 전문가를 고용해야 해요. 그 사람은 우리가 어떻게 두 개의 식당을 운영해야 할지 조언해 줄 수 있을 겁니다.

**47.** 화자들은 어떤 종류의 사업체를 소유하고 있는가?
(A) 회계사무소
(B) 식당
(C) 컨설팅 회사
(D) 식품가공 회사 　　　　　　　　　　　　정답 (B)

**48.** 여자가 "We don't have enough management experience for that."이라고 말한 이유는 무엇인가?
(A) 더 많은 직원들을 채용하는 것에 반대하기 위해서
(B) 수익 하락에 대해 설명하기 위해서
(C) 경영 과정 수강을 권고하기 위해서
(D) 제안에 대해 우려를 표하기 위해서 　　　　정답 (D)

**49.** 남자가 제안하는 것은 무엇인가?
(A) 새로운 메뉴를 만든다.
(B) 전문가를 고용한다.
(C) 고객 의견을 요청한다.
(D) 새로운 사업에 대해 조언한다. 　　　　　정답 (B)

---

문제 50-52번은 다음 대화를 참조하시오. 영W 호M

W: Ms. Davis just e-mailed me. (50) **It looks like we will have four city council members from Toronto coming here on Friday to go over the plans for the new city government building.**

M: Good. (51) **I was waiting to get the final number of how many people would be coming for the luncheon meeting with the board. Now I can make the reservation.**

W: We should make the reservation for noon. I know that they need to catch the 4:30 airplane leaving for Toronto.

M: Then (52) **we have to pick a nearby restaurant.** I think Hurricane in downtown Montreal is becoming really popular and should be a fantastic spot for a relaxed lunch on its outdoor terrace. What do you say to that?

- - - - - - - - - - - - - - - - - - - - - - - - - - - - - - - - - -

W: Davis 씨가 방금 제게 이메일을 보냈어요. 금요일에 시 의원 네 분이 새로운 시청 건물의 설계를 검토하기 위해서 Toronto에서 여기로 올 것 같아요.

M: 잘됐네요. 최종적으로 몇 명이 이사회와의 오찬 회의에 참석할 것인지 기다리고 있던 참이에요. 이제야 예약을 할 수 있겠군요.

W: 정오로 예약을 해야 해요. 시 의원들이 4시 30분 Toronto 행 비행기를 타야 하는 것으로 알고 있거든요.

M: 그러면 근처에 있는 레스토랑을 선택할 수밖에 없네요. 저는 요즘 Hurricane이 Montreal 시내에서 가장 인기가 좋고, 멋진 야외 테라스에서 편안한 점심식사를 할 수 있는 최적의 장소일 것이란 생각이 들어요. 어떻게 생각하세요?

**50.** 시 의원들이 Montreal을 방문하는 이유는 무엇인가?
(A) 내년 예산안을 검토하기 위해서
(B) 새로운 건물의 설계에 관해 논의하기 위해서
(C) 유적지를 관광하기 위해서
(D) 박물관 개관식에 참석하기 위해서 　　　　정답 (B)

**51.** 남자가 예약을 할 수 없었던 이유는 무엇인가?
(A) 회의 일정이 정해지지 않았다.
(B) 그는 몇 명이 방문할 지 알 수 없었다.
(C) 이사회는 밖에서 점심식사를 하길 원하지 않았다.
(D) 몇몇 식당들이 보수 공사로 문을 닫았다. 　　정답 (B)

**52.** 남자가 Hurricane을 추천하는 이유는 무엇인가?
(A) 특별 할인을 제공한다.
(B) 회사와 가까운 거리에 있다.
(C) 조용한 분위기를 지니고 있다.
(D) 훌륭한 캐나다 음식을 제공한다. 　　　　정답 (B)

---

문제 53-55번은 다음의 3자 대화를 참조하시오. 영W 호M 미M

W: (53) **Last night, I was talking to my cousin, who works in advertising. She said she thinks we'd benefit from advertising our new restaurant on the subway.**

M1: That's not a bad idea at all. Thousands of people would see the ads every day, and we could target subway trains that pass nearby the restaurant.

M2: (54) **How much do you think it would cost though? We don't have a large advertising budget, and we can't overspend.**

M1: I don't know for sure, but it would likely be expensive.

W: Another idea my cousin had was to use radio ads. I guess they'd be more affordable. (55) **I'll talk with her again tonight and ask for more information.**

- - - - - - - - - - - - - - - - - - - - - - - - - - - - - - - - - -

W: 어젯밤에 광고업계에서 일하는 제 사촌과 이야기를 했어요. 우리의 새 레스토랑을 지하철에 광고하면 좋을 것 같다고 말하더군요.

M1: 나쁜 생각이 아닌데요. 매일 수천 명의 사람들이 광고를 볼테고, 레스토랑 근처를 지나가는 지하철을 목표로 삼을 수 있을 거예요.

M2: 하지만 비용이 얼마나 들 것 같아요? 광고 예산이 많지 않고 초과 지출할 수는 없으니까요.

M1: 확실히는 모르겠지만 비쌀 것 같아요.

W: 제 사촌이 말한 다른 아이디어는 라디오 광고를 이용하는 것이었어요. 그게 더 저렴할 것 같아요. 오늘밤에 제 사촌과 다시 이야기해보고 더 많은 정보를 요청할게요.

**53.** 화자들은 무엇에 대해 논의하고 있는가?
(A) 새로운 식당
(B) 시내 관광
(C) 라디오 프로그램
(D) 광고 캠페인 　　　　　　　　　　　　정답 (D)

**54.** 남자는 무엇에 관해 우려하고 있는가?
(A) 큰 테이블을 예약하는 것
(B) 제시간에 업무를 완료하는 것
(C) 예산 내로 비용을 유지하는 것
(D) 최적의 노선을 찾는 것 　　　　　　　　정답 (C)

**55.** 여자는 무엇을 하겠다고 언급하는가?
(A) 친척과 상의한다.
(B) 아이디어들을 적는다.
(C) 여행 일정표를 작성한다.
(D) 일정을 변경한다. 　　　　　　　정답 (A)

---

문제 56-58번은 다음 대화를 참조하시오. 〔미W〕〔미M〕

W: Excuse me. My name is Cindy Hwang, and **(56) I'd like to make a booking for the flight leaving from Los Angeles to New York at 6:00 P.M.**

M: Please hold on, ma'am. Let me check the flight reservation data. Um… **(58) I'm afraid no tickets for the flight are currently available.**

W: Oh, no! **(57) I must go to New York tonight to attend an important meeting at 11 o'clock tomorrow.** What should I do now?

M: Um… let me check the reservation systems of other airlines. **(58) There are several seats left on Air Atlas at 8:30 P.M.** Would that work for you?

W: Certainly. Please reserve a seat for me on that flight. I really appreciate your assistance in finding me a seat.

---

W: 실례합니다. 제 이름은 Cindy Hwang이고요, 저는 오후 6시에 Los Angeles에서 출발하여 New York으로 가는 항공권을 예약하고 싶습니다.

M: 잠시만 기다려 주세요, 고객님. 항공권 예약 자료를 확인해 보도록 하겠습니다. 음… 죄송합니다만 그 비행편의 좌석은 현재 예약이 불가합니다.

W: 안 되는데요! 저는 내일 오전 11시에 있을 중요한 회의에 참석해야 해서 오늘밤에 꼭 New York에 가야만 합니다. 어떻게 해야 할까요?

M: 음… 제가 타 항공사의 예약 현황 시스템을 살펴보도록 하겠습니다. 오후 8시 30분에 출발하는 Air Atlas에 몇몇 좌석들이 남아 있습니다. 그거면 괜찮으실까요?

W: 물론입니다. 그 비행기에 좌석을 예약해 주세요. 좌석을 찾는 데 도움을 주셔서 정말 감사합니다.

**56.** 화자들은 어디에 있을 것 같은가?
(A) 호텔
(B) 버스 터미널
(C) 공항
(D) 컨벤션 센터 　　　　　　　정답 (C)

**57.** 여자는 무엇을 할 것이라고 언급하는가?
(A) 시내 관광을 한다.
(B) 회의에 참석한다.
(C) 계약서를 작성한다.
(D) 고객에게 연락한다. 　　　　　　　정답 (B)

**58.** 남자가 "There are several seats left on Air Atlas at 8:30 P.M."이라고 말한 이유는 무엇인가?
(A) 다른 선택사항을 제공하기 위해서
(B) 항공권을 취소하기 위해서
(C) 여자에게 서두르도록 재촉하기 위해서
(D) 제안을 거절하기 위해서 　　　　　　　정답 (A)

---

문제 59-61번은 다음의 대화를 참조하시오. 〔영W〕〔미M〕

W: Welcome to Andrew's Electronics. How may I help you today, sir?

M: Oh, hi! **(59) I'm here to have my laptop computer repaired.** It stopped working after I spilled some coffee on it.

W: Oh I see. **(60) Did you do the things like turning your laptop computer upside down and putting it over something absorbent such as a towel or a dry cloth?**

M: **(60) I already did that a couple of hours ago.** But it's still not working. **(60) Could you repair it by Wednesday?** I'm going on a business trip to Berlin on Thursday.

W: Okay. I'll examine it and talk to you in 10 minute. **(61) Why don't you sit in the waiting room over there while I'm doing my job?** I will call your name when it's done.

M: Thank you.

---

W: Andrew's 전자 매장에 오신 걸 환영합니다. 오늘은 무엇을 도와드릴까요, 고객님?

M: 아, 안녕하세요! 제 노트북 컴퓨터를 수리하러 왔습니다. 제가 노트북 컴퓨터에 커피를 쏟은 이후부터 작동을 멈췄어요.

W: 아, 알겠습니다. 노트북 컴퓨터를 뒤집어서 수건이나 마른 천과 같이 물기를 흡수할 수 있는 것에 올려두는 것도 해보셨나요?

M: 이미 두어 시간 전에 그렇게 했어요. 그런데 아직도 작동을 안 합니다. 제 노트북 컴퓨터를 수요일까지 수리해주실 수 있나요? 제가 목요일에 Berlin으로 출장을 가야 하거든요.

W: 네, 제가 자세히 살펴보고 10분 뒤에 말씀드릴게요. 제가 살펴보는 동안에 저쪽 대기실에 앉아 계시는 게 어떤가요? 끝나면 성함을 불러드리겠습니다.

M: 감사합니다.

**59.** 화자들은 주로 무엇에 대해 논의하는가?
(A) 패키지 여행
(B) 대규모 할인 행사
(C) 파손된 컴퓨터
(D) 새로운 소프트웨어 시연회 　　　　　　　정답 (C)

**60.** 남자가 "I already did that a couple of hours ago."라고 말할 때 의미하는 바는 무엇인가?
(A) 그는 품질 보증서를 구매했다.
(B) 그는 예상보다 일찍 자신의 업무를 마쳤다.
(C) 여자의 컴퓨터는 이미 수리된 상태이다.
(D) 여자가 제안한 것은 효과가 없었다. 　　　　　　　정답 (D)

**61.** 여자가 남자에게 제안한 것은 무엇인가?
(A) 출장 일정을 재조정한다.
(B) 그녀의 직장을 방문한다.
(C) 대기실에 머무른다.
(D) 점장에게 이야기한다. 　　　　　　　정답 (C)

---

문제 62-64번은 다음 대화와 안내판을 참조하시오. 〔미M〕〔영W〕

M: Hi, Ms. Walter. I'm just giving you a quick call to see how you're doing. **(62) Have you finished cleaning room 337 yet?**

W: I'm afraid not, Mr. Robertson. The guests that stayed in this room must have ordered a lot of food from the kitchen. There are dirty plates and trash all over the place, and the bed linens are all stained. It might take me a while.

M: Well, before you tidy up, (63) I'd like you to come over to room 250. There's a bit of an emergency. (64) The toilet is blocked, so the bathroom is flooded.

W: Oh, dear! (63/64) I'll go right over there to help you. (64) I'll bring plenty of towels with me.

--------------------------------

M: 안녕하세요, Walter 씨. 어떻게 일은 잘 되고 있는지 알아보려고 급한 전화 드렸어요. 337호실 청소는 다 끝났나요?

W: 안타깝게도 그렇질 못하네요, Robertson 씨. 이 방에 묵었던 손님들이 우리 주방에서 아주 많은 음식을 시켜 드신 모양입니다. 객실 곳곳에 지저분한 접시들과 쓰레기들 천지이고, 침구에도 얼룩들이 묻어 있어요. 이걸 다 청소하려면 시간이 꽤나 걸릴 것 같아요.

M: 음, 그 객실을 청소하기 전에 250호실로 와 주셨으면 해요. 여긴 좀 비상 상황이에요. 변기가 막혀서 욕실이 아주 물바다예요.

W: 이런, 세상에! 제가 바로 도와드리러 갈게요. 수건을 많이 가지고 갈게요.

---

## STAR BAY 호텔

| 건물 1 | 1~100호실 |
| --- | --- |
| 건물 2 | 101~200호실 |
| 건물 3 | 201~300호실 |
| 건물 4 | 301~400호실 |

**62.** 화자들은 누구일 것 같은가?
(A) 출장 요리사
(B) 배관공
(C) 접수처 직원
(D) 객실 청소 직원 　　　　정답 (D)

**63.** 그래픽을 보시오. 남자는 현재 어디에서 일하고 있는가?
(A) 건물 1
(B) 건물 2
(C) 건물 3
(D) 건물 4 　　　　정답 (C)

**64.** 화자들은 이후에 무엇을 할 것 같은가?
(A) 욕실을 청소한다.
(B) 수건을 접는다.
(C) 침대 시트를 주문한다.
(D) 지저분한 접시들을 설거지한다. 　　　　정답 (A)

**문제 65-67번은 다음 대화와 도표를 참조하시오.** ⓜⓜ ⓜⓦ

M: Good afternoon, ma'am. How may I help you?

W: Oh, hi! (65) I'm looking for the new laptop computer model BK-110. Could you please tell me where I can find it?

M: (66) I regret to say that it is currently out of stock, ma'am. The BK-110 has been one of the best-selling products for the past couple of months.

W: Yeah, I can tell. I know the BK-110 has been on everyone's tongue and is really popular in many countries. (65) Can I buy it at any of your nearby stores?

M: Please hold on. Let me take a look at the database of

---

all the branches in this area. Well, (67) the computer says it is stocked at the stores in Freemont and Palo Alto. I recommend the one with more stocks. As you can see it on the screen here, there's not much left to buy. It could be out of stock soon.

W: Um… I see. I should drive there right now. Thanks.

--------------------------------

M: 안녕하세요, 고객님. 어떻게 도와드릴까요?

W: 아, 안녕하세요! 저는 새로운 노트북 컴퓨터인 BK-110을 찾고 있어요. 어디서 찾을 수 있는지 알려주시겠어요?

M: 죄송하게도 지금 재고가 없는 상태입니다, 고객님. BK-110은 지난 두 달간 제일 많이 팔린 제품들 중 하나입니다.

W: 네, 맞아요. 저도 BK-110이 사람들에게 회자되고 많은 나라에서 엄청난 인기를 구가하고 있는 제품인 것은 알고 있어요. 인근의 다른 상점들 중에서 제가 이 노트북 컴퓨터를 구매할 수 있는 곳이 있나요?

M: 잠시만 기다려 주세요. 제가 이 지역의 모든 지점들의 재고 현황 자료를 살펴보겠습니다. 음, Freemont와 Palo Alto 상점에 재고가 있는 것으로 나옵니다. 저는 재고를 더 많이 가지고 있는 매장에 가시는 것을 추천 드립니다. 여기 화면에서 보시듯이 재고가 얼마 남지 않았습니다. 금방 품절이 될지도 모릅니다.

W: 음… 알겠습니다. 바로 운전해서 가야겠네요. 감사합니다.

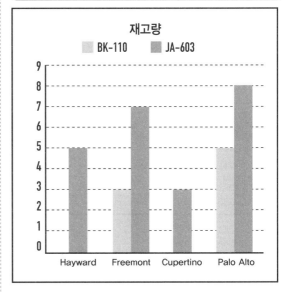

**65.** 여자가 알고 싶어 하는 것은 무엇인가?
(A) 신제품의 이름
(B) 제품의 구매 가능성
(C) 주문 현황
(D) 새로운 상점의 위치 　　　　정답 (B)

**66.** 남자에 따르면 무엇이 문제인가?
(A) 배송이 실수로 잘못된 주소로 되었다.
(B) 특정 제품의 재고가 없다.
(C) 신제품의 출시가 지연되었다.
(D) 내일 폭우가 내릴 것으로 예상되고 있다. 　　　　정답 (B)

**67.** 그래픽을 보시오. 여자는 어느 지점을 방문할 것 같은가?
(A) Hayward
(B) Freemont
(C) Cupertino
(D) Palo Alto 　　　　정답 (D)

W: Mr. White, I have to copy the yearly sales report and provide them to the new sales representatives tomorrow. (68) **But the copier suddenly stopped working a couple of hours ago.**
M: (69) **I've already called a technician,** and he'll get here to repair it tomorrow morning. There are some print shops around the office. I think you should visit one of them to make the copies.
W: It's really good to have some options. But, you know, I've never visited any of the nearby print shops. (70) **Could you please recommend a shop for me?**
M: Um… (70) **most of the diagrams in the report are color coded, so you need color copies. But you should also try to save as much money as you can.**

--------

W: White 씨, 제가 연간 영업 보고서를 복사해서 내일 신입 영업 직원들에게 제공해야 합니다. 그런데 복사기가 두 시간 전에 갑자기 작동이 중단되었어요.
M: 제가 이미 기술자에게 연락은 했는데요, 내일 오전에나 방문해서 복사기를 수리할 수 있다고 하네요. 사무실 주변에 인쇄소들이 여럿 있어요. 그 중 한 곳을 방문해서 복사하셔야 할 것 같습니다.
W: 선택사항이 있으니 정말 다행이긴 합니다. 그런데 저는 인근에 있는 인쇄소를 한 곳도 이용해본 적이 없어요. 제게 상점을 하나 추천해주실 수 있나요?
M: 음… 그 영업 보고서에 있는 대부분의 도표들은 컬러로 되어 있으니 컬러 복사를 하셔야 할 거예요. 하지만 한편으로는 복사 비용을 최대한 절감하도록 하셔야 할 겁니다.

| 상점 | 복사 방식 | 페이지 당 가격 |
|---|---|---|
| Office King | 흑백 | 4센트 |
| Kelly Print | 흑백 | 5센트 |
| Copy Factory | 컬러 | 7센트 |
| Komi Print Solutions | 컬러 | 9센트 |

**68.** 여자는 어떤 문제점을 언급하는가?
(A) 몇몇 직원들이 회의에 늦었다.
(B) 일부 사무 기기가 고장 났다.
(C) 특정 제품들은 교환이 되지 않는다.
(D) 특별 판촉 행사가 종료되었다. 정답 (B)

**69.** 남자는 자신이 무엇을 했다고 언급하는가?
(A) 면접을 실시했다.
(B) 몇몇 서류를 복사했다.
(C) 판매 기록을 수립했다.
(D) 수리 기술자에게 연락을 취했다. 정답 (D)

**70.** 그래픽을 보시오. 여자는 어느 상점을 선택하겠는가?
(A) Office King
(B) Kelly Print
(C) Copy Factory
(D) Komi Print Solutions 정답 (C)

(71) Good morning and thank you for visiting the National History Museum. This audio tour device is designed to give you a better understanding of the exhibits in the museum. (72) **To hear an audio explanation for an exhibit, simply hold this device over the electronic scanner near the exhibit and press the "Information" button on your device.** (73) **If you need immediate help with this audio tour device, simply return to the admissions desk and speak to one of our employees.** We hope that you enjoy your visit to the museum today, and don't forget to sign the visitor's book and to visit the gift shop before you leave.

--------

안녕하세요. 국립 역사박물관을 방문해 주셔서 감사합니다. 이 오디오 안내 기기는 박물관 전시품들에 대한 더 나은 이해를 제공하고자 고안되었습니다. 전시품에 대한 오디오 설명을 들으려면 이 기기를 전시품 옆의 전자 스캐너 위에 들고 기기의 "안내" 버튼을 누르시면 됩니다. 이 오디오 안내기기에 대한 즉각적인 도움이 필요하면 입구 데스크로 와서 저희 직원에게 말씀하시면 됩니다. 오늘 즐거운 박물관 관람이 되시길 바라며, 방명록에 서명하는 것을 잊지 마시고 가기 전에 기념품점에 들러주시길 바랍니다.

**71.** 누구를 위한 메시지인가?
(A) 기술자
(B) 방문객
(C) 쇼핑객
(D) 전시 책임자 정답 (B)

**72.** 화자가 제공하는 방법은 무엇인가?
(A) 특정 건물을 찾는 방법
(B) 회원 가입 방법
(C) 관람 장비 이용 방법
(D) 상점에서의 물건 구매 방법 정답 (C)

**73.** 청자들은 즉각적인 도움이 필요하면 무엇을 해야 하는가?
(A) 기기를 사용한다.
(B) 입구 데스크를 방문한다.
(C) 다른 번호로 연락한다.
(D) 관리자와 이야기한다. 정답 (B)

(74) Hello! Welcome to Afternoon Finance, the best radio program where we discuss the latest financial news and provide the latest updates that can affect your money, investment, and savings. This afternoon, we have a special guest who is sitting here right next to me, Spencer Macintyre. (75) **He is one of the most popular financial experts and manages his own investment firm in London.** His seminars are always crowded. (76) **He recently published his second book, *Invest or What?*** It is currently available at online and offline bookstores. Hello, Mr. Macintyre! Thank you for joining us today.

--------

안녕하세요! Afternoon Finance를 청취해 주시는 여러분, 환영합니다. 우리 프로그램은 최신 금융 소식 외에도 여러분의 자금, 투자, 저축에 영향을 미치는 최근의 소식들도 함께 다루고 있습니다. 오늘 오후에는 제 바

로 옆에 특별 손님인 Spencer Macintyre 씨를 모셨습니다. 그는 가장 유명한 재정 전문가들 중 한 분이시고 London에서 투자 회사를 직접 경영하고 있습니다. 그의 세미나는 항상 사람들로 북새통을 이룹니다. 그는 최근에 두 번째 저서인 〈Invest or What?〉을 출간했습니다. 현재 온라인과 오프라인 서점에서 모두 구매가 가능합니다. 안녕하세요, Macintyre 씨! 오늘 저희와 함께 해 주셔서 감사합니다.

**74.** 라디오 방송의 주제는 무엇인가?
(A) 재정
(B) 건강
(C) 여행
(D) 기술 정답 (A)

**75.** Spencer Macintyre는 어떤 회사를 소유하고 있는가?
(A) 증권 회사
(B) 출판사
(C) 투자 회사
(D) 소프트웨어 회사 정답 (C)

**76.** 화자가 "It is currently available at online and offline bookstores."라고 언급한 이유는 무엇인가?
(A) 오해를 바로잡기 위해서
(B) 책이 그다지 성공적이지 않음을 알리기 위해서
(C) 청자들에게 구매를 권장하기 위해서
(D) 결정에 대한 불만족을 표출하기 위해서 정답 (C)

**문제 77–79번은 다음 안내문을 참조하시오.** ⓜM

(77) The most pressing matter on the agenda for today's meeting is the company's new travel policy. There have been a couple of major changes that will affect all employees who must travel on business. The first change regards currency exchange. The company will no longer be issuing traveler's checks for international business trips. The exchange rates for traveler's checks are not as favorable as those of automatic banking machines. (78) So the company will issue company credit cards to business travelers. Another major change is regarding hotels. From now on, people traveling on business will only be allowed to stay at company-approved hotels. (79) The hotels that the company has approved can be found on our Web site and are searchable by city.

-------------------------------------

오늘 회의의 안건으로 가장 긴급한 현안은 회사의 새로운 출장 방침이 되겠습니다. 출장을 가는 모든 직원들에게 영향을 미치는 두 가지 큰 변경 사항이 있습니다. 첫 번째 변경 사항은 환전과 관련된 것입니다. 회사는 해외 출장에 더 이상 여행자 수표를 발급하지 않습니다. 여행자 수표에 대한 환율이 은행 자동 입출금기만큼 좋지 않습니다. 따라서 회사는 출장자들에게 법인 신용 카드를 발급해줄 겁니다. 또 다른 변경 사항은 호텔 관련입니다. 지금부터 출장을 가는 직원들에게는 오직 회사에 의해 승인된 호텔에서만 숙박하는 것이 허용됩니다. 회사가 승인한 호텔들은 회사 홈페이지에서 도시별로 검색하여 알 수 있습니다.

**77.** 무엇이 발표되고 있는가?
(A) 합병
(B) 개업식
(C) 금리 변동
(D) 새로운 출장 정책 정답 (D)

**78.** 출장 가는 사람들은 무엇을 받게 되는가?
(A) 저렴한 호텔 목록
(B) 법인 신용 카드
(C) 새로운 여행자 수표
(D) 전액 환급 정답 (B)

**79.** 화자에 따르면 홈페이지에서 이용할 수 있는 것은 무엇인가?
(A) 비행기 일정
(B) 회사 정책
(C) 은행 위치
(D) 승인된 호텔 이름 정답 (D)

**문제 80–82번은 다음 전화 메시지를 참조하시오.** ⓜM

Good morning, Kenneth. It's David. (80) Did you hear that the vice president asked for our suggestions on reducing production costs? (80/81) We were supposed to present our cost-cutting proposal in two weeks. (81) But he wants us to present it next Tuesday instead. So we're in trouble now. I think I can manage to make the presentation slides, (82) but the problem is that we're short on the financial data we need to give the presentation. You know Stacy from Accounting, right? I am not sure how you feel but I think you should talk to her and ask for help on the financial data we need. (82) Please let me know what you know. Thanks. I owe you one.

-------------------------------------

좋은 아침이에요, Kenneth. David입니다. 부사장님이 우리에게 생산 원가 절감을 위한 제안을 요청하셨다는 소식 들었어요? 우리가 원래 비용 절감안에 관한 발표를 2주 뒤에 하기로 되어 있었어요. 그런데 부사장님이 대신 다음주 화요일에 발표하길 원한다고 하시네요. 그래서 참 곤란하게 되었어요. 제 생각에 발표에 쓸 슬라이드 제작 작업은 어떻게 해나갈 수 있을 것 같긴 한데, 문제는 발표를 위해 필요한 재정 관련 자료가 부족해요. 당신이 회계부서의 Stacy를 알잖아요, 그렇죠? 어떻게 생각하실지 모르겠지만 저는 당신이 Stacy와 얘기해서 우리가 필요한 재정 자료에 대해 도움을 받아야 할 것 같아요. 뭔가 아는 것이 생기면 제게도 좀 알려주세요. 고마워요. 제가 신세 한 번 집니다.

**80.** 화자가 발표할 주제는 무엇인가?
(A) 영업 전략
(B) 회계 절차
(C) 비용 절감안
(D) 직장 의료 보험 정답 (C)

**81.** 화자에 따르면 무엇이 변경되었는가?
(A) 회사 로고
(B) 발표 날짜
(C) 생산 마감일
(D) 회의 장소 정답 (B)

**82.** 화자가 "You know Stacy from Accounting, right?"라고 말하는 이유는 무엇인가?
(A) 약속을 확인하기 위해
(B) 직원 변경을 제안하기 위해
(C) 청자가 동료에게 연락할 것을 요청하기 위해
(D) 비용에 대한 우려를 표기 위해 정답 (C)

(83) **Thanks for tuning into Your Life, Your Now, the only lifestyle coaching show on the air.** Today, we're going to discuss eating habits and how they can affect your health. This subject is always popular right after the holidays. We've all heard so much advice about what to eat, when to eat, and even where to eat. (84) **A special guest, Raymond Wilson, will talk about his findings from several research studies conducted over the past year.** Surprising evidence shows that eating slowly and not eating on the go can lead to better diet decisions. (85) **Want to ask him something? Get on the line now so that you can ask him a question.** Mr. Wilson will answer your questions himself soon!

생활방식에 대해 조언해주는 유일한 방송 프로그램인 Your Life, Your Now를 청취해 주셔서 감사합니다. 오늘은 식습관과 이러한 식습관이 여러분의 건강에 어떠한 영향을 미치는지 이야기해 보고자 합니다. 이 주제는 연휴가 끝난 직후에 늘 등장합니다. 우리는 지금까지 무엇을 먹어야 하는지, 언제 먹어야 하는지, 그리고 심지어는 어디서 먹어야 하는지에 관련해 엄청나게 많은 조언을 들어왔습니다. 특별 초청 손님인 Raymond Wilson 씨가 작년에 행해진 몇몇 연구들을 통한 결과에 대하여 이야기해주실 겁니다. 식사를 천천히 하고 이동중에 음식 섭취를 금하는 것이 좀 더 바람직한 체중 감량을 유도한다는 점을 보여주는 놀라운 증거도 있습니다. 그에게 질문하고 싶은가요? 지금 전화해서 질문하십시오. Wilson 씨가 곧 여러분의 질문에 직접 답변을 해주실 겁니다!

**83.** 화자는 누구일 것 같은가?
(A) 뉴스 보도 기자
(B) 라디오 진행자
(C) 전문 요리사
(D) 텔레비전 배우　　　　　　　　정답 (B)

**84.** 화자에 따르면 Raymond Wilson 씨는 무엇에 관해 이야기를 할 것인가?
(A) 그의 성공적인 체중 감량
(B) 그의 연구 결과
(C) 그의 학력
(D) 그의 건강 이론　　　　　　　　정답 (B)

**85.** 화자는 Raymond Wilson 씨가 이후에 무엇을 할 것이라고 언급하는가?
(A) 짧은 휴식을 취한다.
(B) 음악을 연주한다.
(C) 광고를 틀어준다.
(D) 청취자 질문에 답변을 한다.　　정답 (D)

Hi, Ms. Hopkins. This is Jim Carter calling from Red Jet Airlines customer service. (86/87) **I'm pleased to inform you that we've located your luggage from Flight 575.** Unfortunately, your luggage has been slightly damaged, but you will be glad to know that the contents are all right. (87) **We'll be shipping it to the Riverside Hotel tonight.** We've been told that you're staying there while you're in New York. It should arrive at the hotel tomorrow morning. If you have any questions, please feel free to contact me at 1-800-767-3232. We regret any inconvenience this may be causing you and fully understand if you want the company to reimburse for your damaged luggage.

(88) **Would you please call me back as soon as possible when you return to the hotel and check my message, Ms. Hopkins?** I'll be waiting your call. Thank you.

안녕하세요, Hopkins 씨. 저는 Red Jet Airlines 고객 서비스 부서에서 연락드리는 Jim Carter라고 합니다. 575편 비행기에서 귀하의 짐을 발견했다고 알려드리게 되어 기쁘게 생각합니다. 안타깝게도 귀하의 짐이 약간 파손된 상태지만, 다행스럽게도 가방 안에 있는 내용물은 모두 이상이 없습니다. 저희가 오늘밤에 짐을 Riverside Hotel로 배송해 드리고자 합니다. 귀하가 New York에 체류하는 동안 그 곳에 머무신다고 들었습니다. 짐은 내일 아침에 호텔에 도착할 겁니다. 질문이 있으시면 1-800-767-3232로 언제라도 연락을 주십시오. 이 일로 겪으신 불편함에 대해서 죄송하게 생각하며, 파손된 짐에 대해 보상을 요구하셔도 충분히 이해합니다. Hopkins 씨, 호텔로 돌아와서 제 메시지를 확인하면 바로 연락을 주시겠습니까? 연락 기다리고 있겠습니다. 감사합니다.

**86.** 이 메시지는 누구를 대상으로 하는가?
(A) 비행기 승무원
(B) 호텔 직원
(C) 배송 기사
(D) 탑승객　　　　　　　　　　　　정답 (D)

**87.** 녹음 메시지를 남긴 목적은 무엇인가?
(A) 비행기 예약을 확인하기 위해서
(B) 약속을 연기하기 위해서
(C) 물건 배송을 통보하기 위해서
(D) 불량품을 반품하기 위해서　　　정답 (C)

**88.** 화자가 청자에게 제안하는 것은 무엇인가?
(A) 직접 만난다.
(B) 사무실을 방문한다.
(C) 영수증 원본을 가지고 온다.
(D) 답신 전화를 한다.　　　　　　　정답 (D)

Before our meeting starts, I'd like to introduce our new accountant, William Carnegie. Mr. Carnegie not only is an able accountant, but he also has years of money management experience that will be a great asset to our theater. For the past few years, (89) **he has worked as the manager in charge of corporate accounting at Andrew & Wesley Accounting Services here in Los Angeles.** He also, luckily for us, has experience working at theaters both on the stage and behind the scenes. He was on the board of directors of the Broadway Theater, where he served as the board president. (90) **He even appeared on stage in a few shows during his college years.** (91) **I'm sure he will help us in all of our financial matters for the new theater season in October.**

회의를 시작하기에 앞서 새로운 회계사인 William Carnegie 씨를 소개하고자 합니다. Carnegie 씨는 능력 있는 회계사일 뿐만 아니라 우리 극장에 큰 자산이 될 수년간의 자산 운용 경험을 지니고 있습니다. 지난 몇 년 동안 그는 이 곳 Los Angeles에 있는 기업 회계를 담당하는 Andrew & Wesley 회계법인에서 책임자로 일했습니다. 또한 우리로서는 행운입니다만, 그는 극장에서 무대에 오른 경험과 무대 뒤에서 일을 해본 경험을 모두 갖추고 있습니다. 그는 Broadway Theater의 이사회에서 이사회 의장으로 활동했습니다. 대학 시절에는 몇몇 연극 무대에 서기까지 했습니다. 저는 그가 새로운 연극 시즌인 10월에 우리의 재정 문제를 해결하는 데 도움을 줄 것으로 확신합니다.

**89.** William Carnegie 씨는 전에 어디서 일했는가?
(A) 영화사
(B) 부동산 중개업체
(C) 회계 법인
(D) 지역 대학 　　　　　　　　　　　　　　　　정답 (C)

**90.** William Carnegie 씨는 대학에서 무엇을 했는가?
(A) 그는 저명한 상을 수상했다.
(B) 그는 연기를 했다.
(C) 그는 창업을 했다.
(D) 그는 기업 금융을 공부했다. 　　　　　　　　정답 (B)

**91.** 화자에 따르면 William Carnegie 씨는 무엇을 담당하게 되는가?
(A) 영화 감독
(B) 극단 경영
(C) 대학생 교육
(D) 자금 관리 　　　　　　　　　　　　　　　　정답 (D)

**문제 92-94번은 다음 전화 메시지를 참조하시오.** 영W

Hi, Mr. Hernandez. It's Diana. I know it's your day off, but we are experiencing a major problem at the shop. We're preparing for the busy lunch hour right now, and (93) **I'm getting worried because the baker hasn't delivered our bread yet.** (92) **How can we make sandwiches without bread?** He always drops off our order first thing in the morning. I tried calling the bakery and sent an e-mail, but I haven't heard back from anyone. We may need to go to a grocery store to buy some bread. I really hope you can help us out. (94) **We need your help. We open in just two hours! Please call me back and let me know what to do.**

--------

안녕하세요, Hernandez 씨. Diana예요. 오늘 쉬는 날인 걸 알지만 가게에 지금 큰 문제가 발생했어요. 지금 바쁜 점심시간을 준비하고 있는데 제 빵업자가 아직 빵을 배송하지 않아서 걱정이에요. 빵 없이 샌드위치를 어떻게 만들겠어요? 그는 항상 아침 일찍 우리 가게가 주문한 제품을 우선적으로 배송해 주었거든요. 제가 제빵업체에게 연락을 취하려고 애쓰고 이메일도 보냈지만 아직까지 아무에게도 답변을 듣지 못했어요. 어쩌면 식료품점에 가서 빵을 사와야 할지도 모르겠어요. 당신이 우리를 도와주셨으면 해요. 당신의 도움이 필요해요. 우리는 딱 두 시간 뒤에 문을 열어야 해요! 제게 연락 주셔서 어떻게 해야 할지 알려주세요.

**92.** 화자는 어디에서 근무할 것 같은가?
(A) 지역 농장
(B) 샌드위치 가게
(C) 레스토랑
(D) 운송 회사 　　　　　　　　　　　　　　　　정답 (B)

**93.** 화자는 어떤 문제에 대해 언급하는가?
(A) 배송 트럭이 고장이 났다.
(B) 몇몇 기계들이 제대로 작동하지 않는다.
(C) 몇몇 직원들이 아파서 결근한다고 연락했다.
(D) 주문한 물건이 아직까지 배송되지 않았다. 　　정답 (D)

**94.** 화자가 "We open in just two hours!"라고 말한 이유는 무엇인가?
(A) 결정에 대한 불만을 표현하기 위해서
(B) 직원들에게 마감시한을 상기시키기 위해서
(C) 상황의 심각성을 표현하기 위해서
(D) 고객에게 나중에 다시 오라고 요청하기 위해서 　정답 (C)

**문제 95-97번은 다음 전화 메시지와 좌석 배치도를 참조하시오.** 미W

Hey, Harry! It's Dorothy. (95) **I'm calling to see if you're available on Wednesday night.** A co-worker has season tickets to the Classical Season Spectacular, but she can't go. So (95) **I have two tickets to see the ballet being performed at the Star Arts Theater. I thought you might like to go with me.** I just looked at the theater's seating chart, and the seats are really good. (96) **They're in the center section on the main floor and are pretty close to the stage.** Anyway, I know you like ballet and dance, so I thought you might be interested in going. (97) **Susan Kang is the guest prima ballerina that night.** I've never seen her perform, but I heard from some friends on the Internet that she is really amazing. It would be great to see her there. Let me know your availability.

--------

안녕하세요, Harry! 저 Dorothy예요. 수요일 밤에 시간이 나는지 알아보려고 연락드려요. 직장 동료 한 사람이 Classical Season Spectacular의 시즌권이 있는데 못 가게 됐어요. 그래서 제게 Star Arts Theater에서 열리는 발레 관람표 두 장이 생겼어요. 저는 당신이 같이 가고 싶어할 지도 모르겠다고 생각했어요. 제가 극장의 좌석 배치도를 살펴봤는데 좌석의 위치도 정말 좋아요. 1층 중앙이고 무대하고 상당히 가까운 곳이에요. 어쨌든 당신이 발레와 무용을 좋아하는 걸로 알고 있어서 관람하러 가는 것에 관심이 있을지도 모르겠다고 생각했어요. 그날 밤에 Susan Kang이 초청 주연 발레리나로 출연해요. 그녀가 공연하는 것을 관람한 적이 없지만 인터넷에서 몇몇 친구들이 그녀가 정말 대단한 발레리나라고 하는 걸 들었어요. 그녀를 보면 정말 좋을 것 같네요. 같이 갈 수 있는지 여부를 알려주세요.

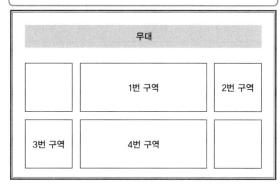

**95.** 화자는 무엇에 관해 전화하는가?
(A) 예약
(B) 초대
(C) 장비 수리
(D) 운전 길 안내 　　　　　　　　　　　　　　　정답 (B)

**96.** 그래픽을 보시오. 화자는 어느 관람 구역의 관람표를 보유하고 있는가?
(A) 1번 구역
(B) 2번 구역
(C) 3번 구역
(D) 4번 구역 　　　　　　　　　　　　　　　　　정답 (A)

**97.** 화자에 따르면 Susan Kang은 누구인가?
(A) 여배우
(B) 행사 기획자
(C) 직장 동료
(D) 무용가 　　　　　　　　　　　　정답 (D)

**문제 98-100번은 다음 안내문과 일정표를 참조하시오.** 영M

Attention, everyone. I have an announcement to make before we begin today. **(98) As you all know, there have been some recent accidents with the new machines.** While we did hand out instruction manuals to all employees in the factory, the manual can be quite hard to navigate through, which is why I'm guessing there have been some accidents. **(98) So I decided to hold some mandatory training sessions. (99) All employees are required to attend these sessions.** The schedule has already been posted on our Web site. **(100) However, please be aware that all morning sessions have been canceled due to the instructor's personal reasons.**

- - - - - - - - - - - - - - - - - - - - - - - - - - - - - - - - - - - - -

주목해 주십시오, 여러분. 오늘 시작 전에 공지해야 할 내용이 있습니다. 모두 아시다시피, 최근 새로 도입한 기계와 관련된 사고들이 있었습니다. 공장의 모든 직원에게 취급 설명서를 배포하긴 했지만, 그 설명서가 너무 이해하기 어려워서 사고들이 발생하는 것이 아닌가 생각하고 있습니다. 따라서 의무 교육을 개최하기로 결정했습니다. 모든 직원은 필히 이 교육을 참여해야만 합니다. 교육 일정은 이미 회사 홈페이지에 게재되어 있습니다. 그러나 모든 오전 교육은 강사의 일신상의 사유로 취소되었음을 유의하시기 바랍니다.

### 교육 일정표
#### 강사: Chan Hong 씨 / 기계 공학자

| 교육 1 | 월요일 | 오전 10시 – 오전 11시 |
|---|---|---|
| 교육 2 | 화요일 | 오후 2시 – 오후 3시 |
| 교육 3 | 수요일 | 오후 2시 – 오후 3시 |
| 교육 4 | 목요일 | 오전 10시 – 오전 11시 |

**98.** 화자는 누구이겠는가?
(A) 회사 대변인
(B) 인사부장
(C) 전문 기술자
(D) 공장장 　　　　　　　　　　　　정답 (D)

**99.** 청자들에게 요청되는 것은 무엇인가?
(A) 취급 설명서를 읽는다.
(B) 설명회에 참석한다.
(C) 새로운 기계의 사용을 중단한다.
(D) 새로운 근무 일정표를 살펴본다. 　　정답 (B)

**100.** 그래픽을 보시오. 마지막 교육은 언제인가?
(A) 월요일
(B) 화요일
(C) 수요일
(D) 목요일 　　　　　　　　　　　　정답 (C)

## Part 5

**101.** Eugene Peters는 오늘 오후 3시에 최고 경영자와 만날 것이다. 　정답 (C)

**102.** 새로운 감기약의 판매는 더 많은 시험이 완료될 때까지 식품의약국에 의해 유보되었다. 　　　　　　　　　　정답 (D)

**103.** 컴퓨터 산업 분야에서 가장 빠르게 성장할 잠재력을 지닌 회사 중 하나인 Delta Computer 사는 해외 투자를 유치하기 위해 분투해왔다. 　　　　　　　　　　　　　　정답 (D)

**104.** Mando Technology 사와 Komi International 사의 합병은 향후 2주 이내에 완료될 것으로 예상된다. 　　정답 (C)

**105.** World Business 구독은 온라인이나 자동 전화 갱신 서비스를 통해 갱신이 가능하다. 　　　　　　　　　정답 (A)

**106.** 만약 타이어가 소형 차량에 장착하기에 너무 넓은 타이어라면 운전할 때 안락함을 느끼지 못할 수도 있다. 　정답 (B)

**107.** 저희의 목표는 모든 고객에게 완전한 서비스 및 만족을 제공하는 것이며 앞으로도 오랫동안 귀하에게 서비스를 제공할 수 있길 기대합니다. 　　　　　　　　　　　정답 (C)

**108.** 10년이 넘도록 재즈 애호가들은 연령과 무관하게 라디오에서 FM 105.8 방송을 즐겨 들어왔다. 　　　　정답 (B)

**109.** Kensington 씨는 작년 한 해에만 Bio World에 여섯 편의 논문을 게재하며 세계적으로 유능한 생화학자들 중 한 사람이라는 명성을 쌓았다. 　　　　　　　　　정답 (D)

**110.** 소셜 네트워크 시스템의 가장 큰 장점 중 한 가지는 바로 전세계에 있는 많은 도서관과 교육 기관들이 보유한 자료에 대한 즉각적인 접근을 제공한다는 것이다. 　　　　　　　정답 (D)

**111.** 새로 개정된 규정은 모든 고객이 은행에서 새로운 당좌예금 계좌를 개설할 때 최소한 두 종류의 신분증을 제시하도록 요구하고 있다. 　정답 (A)

**112.** 오늘 신문 보도에 따르면 유로화는 향후 3주간 1.28달러로 가치가 하락할 것으로 예상된다. 　　　　정답 (D)

**113.** 주간 일정에서 공지되지 않는다면 우리의 월요일 정기회의는 항상 세미나실에서 개최된다. 　　　　　정답 (D)

**114.** 고객 상담원에게 문의하고자 전화할 때는 질문 목록을 준비해 놓는 것이 바람직하다. 　　　　　　　정답 (D)

**115.** 고객들은 은행으로부터 큰 금액을 송금할 때 은행원에게 유효한 형태의 신분증을 제시할 것을 요청받는다. 　정답 (D)

**116.** 몇몇 주요 정유회사들은 남미의 유전에서 원유를 생산할 수 있는 권리를 획득하고자 노력하고 있다. 　정답 (D)

**117.** 요즘 경제 사정을 고려하면 대부분의 소비자들은 비싼 신제품을 구매할 여력이 없다. 　　　　　　　정답 (B)

**118.** 몇몇 증권 회사들은 새로운 고객들을 유치하기 위해 주식 거래 수수료를 인하하고 있다. 　　　　　정답 (B)

**119.** 몇몇 주식 분석가들은 투자자들에게 Venezuela의 구리 광산을 개발하는 프로젝트에서 손을 뗄 것을 강력하게 제안했다. 　정답 (D)

**120.** 국내에서 가장 큰 소프트웨어 개발 회사인 Ciao 사와의 합병 계획을 발표한 Transcent Telecom 사는 이동통신 산업 분야에서 영향력을 증대시켜 나갈 것이다. 　정답 (C)

**121.** 국가 연금 제도가 장기적으로 운용이 적절한지 여부와 관련된 의문에도 불구하고 연방 정부는 지금까지 퇴직 연령을 높이고자 시도하지 않았다. 　정답 (D)

**122.** 일부 경제학자들은 지난 10년간 안정세였던 연료비가 내년에 급등할 것으로 예상하고 있다. 　정답 (C)

**123.** Wilson 씨는 몇몇 중요한 고객들과의 회의가 있기 바로 전날에 London에 도착했기 때문에 시차증으로 고생하고 있었다. 　정답 (D)

**124.** 기계적인 문제점들이 예상보다 빠르게 수리가 되어서 발전소가 폐쇄된 기간은 매우 짧았다. 　정답 (D)

**125.** 약값이 전례 없이 빠른 속도로 상승하고 있어서 사람들은 필요한 약품들의 가격이 자신들이 구매할 수 있는 능력을 넘어설까 우려하고 있다. 　정답 (D)

**126.** 곧 있을 세미나에 참석하길 원하는 직원들은 10월 8일까지 온라인으로 등록해야 하며, 그 후엔 세미나에 대한 세부사항이 등록자들에게 이메일로 발송될 것이다. 　정답 (A)

**127.** 계약서 내의 한 구절에 대한 오역이 아무리 미미하게 보인다 하더라도 이는 두 회사 사이에 법적 소송 및 비용의 손실로 이어질 수 있다. 　정답 (A)

**128.** 새로운 금융 정책을 시행함에 있어서 누구의 제안이 더 효과적일지 결정을 내리기가 매우 어렵다. 　정답 (D)

**129.** 더 많은 정보를 요청하시려면 Oxford 영화제 홈페이지인 www.off.org에 접속하셔서 "다가올 행사"를 클릭해 주십시오. 　정답 (B)

**130.** 재무부장은 중역 회의실을 보수하기 위한 새로운 예산안을 거부하고 대신에 여분의 공간을 새 직원용 휴게실로 변경할 것을 선택했다. 　정답 (C)

## Part 6

**문제 131~134번은 다음 편지를 참조하시오.**

Kim 씨께,

귀하가 문의하신 자전거는 현재 재고가 없는 상태이며 특별 주문을 통해서만 구매가 가능함을 알려드리고자 편지를 씁니다. 만약 사전에 빠른 배송 요금을 지불하신다면 오늘로부터 일주일 이내에 주문품을 수령하실 수 있습니다.

이 편지에 대해 빠른 시일 내에 답장을 주시거나 제게 직접 692-9815로 전화해 주셔서 여전히 이 자전거를 구매하길 원하시는지 여부를 알려주시기 바랍니다. 만약에 그렇다면 자전거 제조업체에 최대한 빨리 연락하겠습니다. 그러면 이메일을 통해 귀하가 원하시는 자전거를 수령할 수 있는 날짜에 대해 연락을 받으시게 될 것입니다.

귀하의 답장을 기대합니다.

Brandon Lee

**131.** 　정답 (C)

**132.** 　정답 (A)

**133.** (A) 일부 상당한 수준의 고객 맞춤형 자전거들은 특별히 활주 대회를 위해 설계되었습니다.
(B) 그러면 이메일을 통해 귀하가 원하시는 자전거를 수령할 수 있는 날짜에 대해 연락을 받으시게 될 것입니다.
(C) 이러한 상황에서는 자전거를 타는 사람들이 대개 사고의 위험성에 대해 우려합니다.
(D) 시에서는 시민들의 운동에 도움을 주기 위해 새로운 자전거 도로를 건설할 것입니다. 　정답 (B)

**134.** 　정답 (B)

**문제 135~138번은 다음 이메일을 참조하시오.**

수신: Ethan McGowan 〈em@mimielectronics.com〉
발신: Wesley Park 〈wp@zenithtech.com〉
제목: 대체상품 보상
날짜: 7월 3일

McGowan 씨께,

어제 귀하께서 보내신 제품 Belden 192의 주문 신청 이메일을 받았습니다. 안타깝게도 Belden 192는 더 이상 제작되지 않고 있어서 현재 저희 지점 어디에서도 Belden 192 모델은 찾아볼 수 없습니다.

따라서 더 나아진 음질을 제외하고는 기본적으로 Belden 192와 똑같은 기능을 가진 새로운 모델 Belden 201을 추천해 드리고 싶습니다.

이 모델이 귀하의 기준에 맞는 것 같다면 알려주시기 바랍니다. 그렇게 하시면 귀하의 주문 신청을 변경하고 Belden 201의 배송을 즉시 진행할 것입니다. 저희의 제안에 대한 동의를 기다리고 있겠습니다.

Wesley Park

**135.** 　정답 (D)

**136.** 　정답 (B)

**137.** (A) 이 모델이 만들어내는 음질에 관한 상세한 설명을 드리겠습니다.
(B) 이 모델이 귀하의 기준에 맞는 것 같다면 알려주시기 바랍니다.
(C) 구매하신 Belden 192의 기술적인 결함이 있으면 알려주시기 바랍니다.
(D) 귀사와 협력하여 최고의 오디오 시스템을 만들게 되어 영광으로 생각합니다. 　정답 (B)

**138.** 　정답 (A)

**문제 139~142번은 다음 편지를 참조하시오.**

Thomas Lee 씨
Komi 전자
909 Sunhill Street
San Diego, CA 92110

Lee 씨께,

귀하의 11월 23일자 주문을 받게 되어 기쁘게 생각합니다.

하지만 예상하지 못한 컴퓨터 칩의 공급 부족으로 인해 디지털 컴퓨터 그래픽카드는 재고가 없으므로 현재 귀하의 주문품을 준비할 수가 없습니다.

얼티미트 컴퓨터 그래픽카드라는 대체 상품으로는 보내드릴 수 있습니다. 귀하가 찾는 그래픽카드 제품에서 약간 업그레이드된 제품이며 두 제품 사이에 큰 차이점은 없습니다. 저희의 제안에 대해 어떻게 생각하시는지 알려주시기 바랍니다.

곧 다시 귀하에게 서비스를 제공할 수 있길 고대합니다.

Kelly Ha
영업부장
Choff 전자매장

**139.**                                                        정답 (A)

**140.**                                                        정답 (B)

**141.**                                                        정답 (A)

**142.** (A) 이 주문에 대해 지불하신 금액을 환불해드릴 것입니다.
   (B) 귀하에게 서비스를 제공할 수 있는 기회를 주신 점에 감사드립니다.
   (C) 곧 다시 귀하에게 서비스를 제공할 수 있길 고대합니다.
   (D) 이것을 기다릴만한 가치가 있음을 아시게 될 것이라고 확신합니다.
                                                                정답 (C)

문제 143-146번은 다음 공지를 참조하시오.

SARA DESIGN FACTORY
공지 번호: 7399

정책 변경에 따른 공지

회계부에서 새로운 급여 정산용 소프트웨어 패키지 설치 작업을 완료하여 이에 따라 우리가 알아두어야 할 몇 가지 변경사항들이 있습니다.

향후 모든 전월 출퇴근 기록부는 익월 3일까지 제출하셔야 합니다. 급여는 이제 매달 10일에 지급될 것입니다. 정규 휴가 및 개인 휴가를 사용하려면 인사 담당자의 결재가 필요합니다. 이상적으로는 정규 휴가 및 개인 휴가 신청은 최소한 10일 전에 이루어져야 합니다.

비용 보고서 또한 매달 3일이 마감기한입니다. 구입 요청서는 언제라도 제출이 가능하지만 매주 금요일에 처리될 것입니다.

새로운 출퇴근 관리 시스템에 대한 긴급한 요청이나 질문이 있으면 주저하지 말고 회계부의 Ryan 씨에게 직접 말씀하시기 바랍니다. 여러분의 협조에 미리 감사의 말씀 드립니다.

John Wilson
최고 경영자

**143.**                                                        정답 (D)

**144.** (A) 급여는 이제 매달 10일에 지급될 것입니다.
   (B) 모든 직원이 자신들의 근무 시간을 조정하는 것이 가능합니다.
   (C) 우리는 왜 지금까지 기존의 방식으로 회계를 해왔는지 이해해야 할 필요가 있습니다.
   (D) 몇몇 전문가들이 우리가 겪고 있는 회계의 문제점들을 적절하게 다루고 있습니다.
                                                                정답 (A)

**145.**                                                        정답 (A)

**146.**                                                        정답 (D)

## Part 7

문제 147-148번은 다음 메시지를 참조하시오.

Peter Jones 앞
날짜: 4월 20일 금요일 오후 2:35
발신자: Adam Johnson
사업체: Woolshed 의류점
연락처: 925-7399

메시지:
(147) Woolshed 의류점의 Johnson 씨가 주문품의 위치에 관해 문의하기 위해 전화했습니다. 그는 지난 주 월요일 우리 회사에 500벌의 스웨터를 주문했는데 아직 그의 가게로 배송되지 않았습니다. (148) 그는 주문 송장번호를 그에게 이메일로 보내주길 원했으며 그 번호로 배송 회사에 연락을 취하겠다고 했습니다. 그의 이메일 주소는 A.Johnson@woolshed.net입니다.

메시지 수신자: Barbara Lewis

**147.** Johnson 씨가 Jones 씨에게 전화를 한 이유는 무엇인가?
   (A) 회의 일정을 잡기 위해서
   (B) 청구서 지불을 위해서
   (C) 주문품에 대해 문의하기 위해서
   (D) 스웨터가 주문 가능한지 확인하기 위해서         정답 (C)

**148.** Johnson 씨가 Jones 씨에게 요청한 것은 무엇인가?
   (A) 그에게 관련 정보를 이메일로 보낼 것
   (B) 그에게 계약서 사본을 팩스로 보낼 것
   (C) 그의 집으로 전화를 해줄 것
   (D) 그에게 우편을 통해 카탈로그를 보낼 것          정답 (A)

문제 149-151번은 다음 광고를 참조하시오.

럭셔리 크루즈로 모든 것을 떨쳐버리세요!

Caribbean 크루즈사는 대가족에게 적절한 가격으로 럭셔리 가족 맞춤형 크루즈 상품을 제공합니다.

당사의 크루즈 상품은 아래와 같은 내용들을 포함하고 있습니다:

• 세 곳의 캐리비안 섬 방문
• (149) 7일간의 럭셔리 크루즈 '프린세스 호' 탑승
• (149) 스쿠버와 스노클 장비 무료 대여
• (149) 타의 추종을 불허하는 우리 4성급 레스토랑에서 매일 따뜻한 세 끼 식사 제공

늦지 마세요! 오늘 당신의 휴가를 예약하세요!

예약하시려면 1-800-2992로 전화하세요. (151) 저희 직원이 월요일부터 토요일, 오전 9시~오후 5시까지 전화 상담이 가능합니다.

(150) "친구 추천" 프로그램으로 10% 특별 할인을 받으세요. 친구가 예약 시에 귀하의 이름을 말하면 고객님은 할인 혜택을 받을 수 있습니다.

**149.** 크루즈 상품에 포함되지 않는 것은 무엇인가?
   (A) 7일간의 승선
   (B) 선내 극장의 무료티켓
   (C) 다이빙 장비의 무료 이용권
   (D) 레스토랑 무료 식사권                           정답 (B)

**150.** 광고에서 언급하고 있는 특별 혜택은 무엇인가?
   (A) 인터넷 예약을 통한 100달러 할인

(B) 10월 1일 이전 예약에 한해 제공받는 무료 호텔 픽업 서비스

(C) 친구가 예약을 하게 되면 받는 할인

(D) 승선하는 모든 아동들에게 무료 기념 티셔츠 제공　　　정답 (C)

**151.** 예약 담당 직원이 전화를 받지 않는 날은 언제인가?

(A) 월요일

(B) 화요일

(C) 수요일

(D) 일요일　　　정답 (D)

**문제 152-153번은 다음 문자 메시지 대화를 참조하시오.**

> Debra Morgan　　　　　　　　　　　　[오후 2:20]
>
> (152) 세탁한 옷을 메모리얼 하우스로 배달했나요?
>
> Arthur Mitchell　　　　　　　　　　　　[오후 2:30]
>
> 가고 있는 길이에요. 이 쪽 동네의 교통 정체 현상이 심하네요.
>
> Debra Morgan　　　　　　　　　　　　[오후 2:31]
>
> (153) 고객이 연락을 했어요. 그는 세탁한 옷이 오후 3시까지 필요하다고 하네요.
>
> Arthur Mitchell　　　　　　　　　　　　[오후 2:32]
>
> (153) 그 시간에 맞춰서 확실하게 배송할게요. 염려 마세요.
>
> Debra Morgan　　　　　　　　　　　　[오후 2:33]
>
> 다른 길로 가는 것이 어때요?
>
> Arthur Mitchell　　　　　　　　　　　　[오후 2:33]
>
> 모르겠어요. 최상의 길이 무엇인지 휴대전화를 통해 검색해볼게요. 차 사고가 발생한 것이 아닐까 싶어요.
>
> Debra Morgan　　　　　　　　　　　　[오후 2:34]
>
> 좋아요. 그 곳까지 안전하고 신속하게 가도록 하세요. 배송이 끝난 후 문자 메시지를 보내 주세요.

**152.** Mitchell 씨는 어느 회사에서 근무하고 있는가?

(A) 배송 회사

(B) 이삿짐 회사

(C) 세탁 서비스 제공 회사

(D) 법률 회사　　　정답 (C)

**153.** 오후 2시 31분에 Morgan 씨가 "He needs the delivery by 3 P.M."이라고 쓴 것이 의미하는 바는 무엇인가?

(A) 그녀는 오늘 골프를 할 계획이다.

(B) 처리해야 할 더 많은 배송이 있다.

(D) 자동차 사고로 인해 화가 났다.

(D) 그 고객은 시간에 맞춰 배달이 이뤄지길 바라고 있다.　　　정답 (D)

**문제 154-155번은 다음 기사를 참조하시오.**

> **Southshore Business News**
>
> (154) **Gaby Motor 사는 2년 연속으로 기록적인 영업과 이윤을 기대하고 있다.** 유럽에서의 판매 회복과 함께 북미 지역과 한국의 판매 증가에 힘입어 Gaby Motor 사는 세계에서 가장 빠른 성장을 보이는 자동차 제조업체가 되었다. 4월 1일로 시작된 이번 회계연도에서 (155) **Gaby Motor 사는 달러 약세에서 비롯되는 혜택은 기대하지 않고 있는** 반면, SUV 차량의 판매량 증가를 확신하고 있다.

**154.** 뉴스가 보도하고 있는 내용은 무엇인가?

(A) SUV 차량 시장의 확대

(B) Gaby Motor 사의 재정 상태

(C) Gaby Motor 사의 광고 전략

(D) Gaby Motor 사의 판매 예상　　　정답 (D)

**155.** Gaby Motor 사의 판매량 증가에 기여하는 요소가 아닌 것은 무엇인가?

(A) 유럽 시장의 부활

(B) 달러화 가치의 하락

(C) 한국에서의 소비자 수요 증가

(D) 북미 지역에서의 판매 증가　　　정답 (B)

**문제 156-157번은 다음 광고를 참조하시오.**

> (156) **하계 판촉 행사**
>
> (156) **Starling 레저 센터**
>
> 47 벨 가
>
> 마이애미, 플로리다
>
> 전화: 404-466-0278
>
> 올 여름 저희가 제공하는 할인 특가를 활용하세요.
>
> 수영과 미니 골프: 7월에는 50% 할인
>
> 1시부터 제공되는 점심을 카페테리아에서 즐기세요!
>
> (157) **영업시간**
>
> **월요일~금요일: 오전 9:30 - 오후 6:00**
>
> **토요일과 일요일: 오전 10:00 - 오후 9:00**
>
> 공휴일은 휴무

**156.** 이 공지의 목적은 무엇인가?

(A) 레저 센터의 여름 판촉 행사

(B) 점심메뉴의 변경사항

(C) 가게의 재개장

(D) 몇몇 공휴일 날짜　　　정답 (A)

**157.** Starling 레저 센터에 대해 암시되는 것은 무엇인가?

(A) 플로리다 전역에서 유명하다.

(B) 주말에는 평소보다 늦게 연다.

(C) 점심은 온종일 제공된다.

(D) 가격이 최근에 올랐다.　　　정답 (B)

**문제 158-160번은 다음 기사를 참조하시오.**

> Hayward 주립 대학교의 새로운 기숙사
>
> Alicia Adams, Beat Reporter
>
> 6월 27일 — 새로운 계획이 확정되었고 적절한 인원이 배치되었다. 새로운 기숙사 복합 시설의 공사가 시작되었다. 기공식은 지난 목요일 브롬톤 가 20번 도로 교차로에서 열렸으며 이 곳은 주립 대학교에서 새로운 기숙사 단지인 Pioneers Lofts를 건설하게 될 지역이다. (158) **대학 총장인 Delilah Sorcarro 씨는** 본교에서 북쪽으로 3마일 떨어진 이 곳에서 공사의 첫 삽을 떴다.
>
> Pioneers Lofts는 대학 (공공 기관)과 Weingarten 그룹 (지역 부동산 개발 회사) 간의 합작 투자이다. (160) **기숙사 복합 시설은 3개의 대형 복합 건물로 구성된다.** 각 건물의 1층에는 소매업을 할 수 있는 공간을 보유하게 되며 바로 그 위에는 기숙사가 위치하게 될 것이다. Weingarten은 부지를 개발하고 소매업 운영을 관리한다. "최근까지 대부분의 학생들은 통학했습니다."라고 대학 총장인 Sorcarro 씨는 말했으며 이어서 "현

재 캠퍼스 내 기숙사 거주를 신청하는 지원자의 수가 급격히 증가하고 있습니다. 지난 봄에 우리가 지은 고층 기숙사는 어느 정도 도움이 되었습니다. 그러나 이 공사가 완료되면 우리는 학생들에게 봉사할 수 있는 훨씬 좋은 입장에 있게 될 것입니다."라고 언급했다.

Weingarten 그룹의 도시 계획가인 Daniel Ho는 대학 위원회에 몇몇 소매상은 이미 많은 의류 매장과 건강 식품 매장을 포함하여 이미 단지를 임대하는 것에 관심을 표명하고 있으며 (159) **매장을 열기위해 이 지역에 대형 슈퍼마켓 체인을 유치했다**고 말했다. 복합 단지와 캠퍼스는 경치가 좋은 인도로 연결된다.

**158.** Sorcarro 씨는 누구인가?
(A) 거주민
(B) 부동사 개발업자
(C) 대학 관리자
(D) 점주 　　　　　　　　　　　　정답 (C)

**159.** Weingarten 그룹이 새로운 시설에 유치한 업종은 무엇인가?
(A) 건설사
(B) 여행사
(C) 사교육 기관
(D) 식료품점 　　　　　　　　　　정답 (D)

**160.** [1], [2], [3] 그리고 [4]로 표시된 곳 중에, 아래 문장이 들어가기에 가장 적절한 곳은?
"각 건물의 1층에는 소매업을 할 수 있는 공간을 보유하게 되며 바로 그 위에는 기숙사가 위치하게 될 것이다."
(A) [1]
(B) [2]
(C) [3]
(D) [4] 　　　　　　　　　　　　　정답 (B)

**문제 161-164번은 다음 기사를 참조하시오.**

Hartville (9월 3일) – (161) **Hartville 교통위원회가 현재 도시 전역에 일어나고 있는 각종 인프라 개선 현황과, 이것이 통근과 왕래에 미치는 영향에 관한 최신 소식을 전한다.** "여러 프로젝트들이 주요 통근 노선에 끼치는 영향에 주목하시길 바랍니다."라고 교통위원회의 회장인 개리 론델 씨가 말했다.

8월 29일부터 데이튼 밸리 다리의 두 차선이 긴급 재포장 공사를 위해 폐쇄되었다. 이 폐쇄 탓에, 운전자들은 아침과 저녁 출퇴근 시간에 최대 1시간 지연될 수 있다. (162) **또한 9월 중순까지 진행되는 건설 공사로 인해 시내 14번가 밑으로 가로질러 가는 지하 터널 접근이 불가하다. 대신 14번가를 따라 100미터를 내려가면 있는 카슨 애비뉴 다리가 터널 공사가 완성되기 전까지 보행자들을 위해 안전한 우회 횡단보도로 이용된다.**

대학 강사인 Harold Blackley 씨는 New Haven에서 시내 Hartville에 있는 Angler 대학까지의 통근거리가 최소 45분 이상 지연되었다고 보고했다. "웰스 가는 자꾸 교통이 완전히 정지 상태가 되곤 합니다. 요즘 첫 수업 시간에 늦지 않으려면 원래 출근하던 것보다 한 시간 일찍 나가는 수밖에 없어요."라고 Blackley 씨는 말했다. 오토바이 택배원인 Chet Landry 씨 또한 많은 문제에 직면해 있다. "직업 특성상 소포가 제시간에 배달되려면 모든 게 원활히 (163) **진행되어야** 합니다. 고객들은 제가 제 시간에 소포를 배달할 것이라고 믿고 있는데, 이렇게 많은 도로 보수로 제 시간에 배달하는 것이 점점 어려워지고 있습니다."

(164) **Rondell 씨는 바쁜 도로 보수 지역들을 지나갈 때 운전자들에게 더 많이 주의할 것을 경고하고 있다.** "운전자들은 인내심을 갖고 주변 환경을 확인해야 합니다. 도로에 장애물도 많고 도로 작업인부도 많

이 있기에, 불필요한 사고가 발생하는 것을 원하지 않습니다."

**161.** 이 기사의 목적은 무엇인가?
(A) 지역 주민들에게 대중 교통 사용을 장려하기 위해서
(B) 도시 전역에 걸친 도시 개발 프로젝트에 관한 제안서를 설명하기 위해서
(C) 뉴 헤이븐으로 이어지는 새로운 통근 경로 건설을 설명하기 위해서
(D) 진행중인 보수공사의 영향을 지역 주민들에게 알려주기 위해서
　　　　　　　　　　　　　　　정답 (D)

**162.** 기사에 따르면, 지하 터널이 폐쇄되는 동안 보행자들은 어디로 가야 하는가?
(A) 데이튼 밸리 다리
(B) 14번가
(C) 카슨 애비뉴 다리
(D) 웰스가 　　　　　　　　　　　정답 (C)

**163.** 세 번째 단락 열한 번째 줄의 단어 "run"과 가장 유사한 의미의 단어는 무엇인가?
(A) 보내다
(B) 운영하다
(C) 운전하다
(D) 개선되다 　　　　　　　　　　정답 (B)

**164.** 교통위원회의 회장은 사람들에게 어떠한 조언을 했는가?
(A) 평소보다 일찍 출근할 것.
(B) 다른 사람들과 카풀 제도를 시행할 것.
(C) 운전시 주의할 것.
(D) 가능하면 자동차 사용을 피할 것. 　　정답 (C)

**문제 165-168번은 다음 온라인 채팅 토론을 참조하시오.**

Dwight Parker 　　　　　　　　　　[오후 12:38]
여러분, 제가 좀 곤란한 상황인데 도움을 주실 수 있나요?

Irene Keller 　　　　　　　　　　　[오후 12:39]
뭐가 잘못되었나요?

Dwight Parker 　　　　　　　　　　[오후 12:40]
(165/166) **우리 태블릿 컴퓨터 하나가 이 곳 바닥에 떨어졌어요. 그런데 제대로 작동하는 것처럼 보이질 않네요**

Irene Keller 　　　　　　　　　　　[오후 12:41]
(166) **오, 어떡하죠! 마케팅 발표는 언제 시작하나요?**

Dwight Parker 　　　　　　　　　　[오후 12:42]
오후 1시 30분에요. 지금 대략 30분이 오셨는데, 궁극적으로 약 120분 정도가 오실 겁니다.

Walter White 　　　　　　　　　　[오후 12:43]
제가 사무실에서 여분의 태블릿 컴퓨터를 찾았어요. 한 50분 정도 시간이 남았지요. 어떻게 할까요?

Irene Keller 　　　　　　　　　　　[오후 12:44]
좋아요. (167) **제가 곧 거기에 가서 태블릿 컴퓨터를 설치하고 이를 시청각 자료와 연결시켜줄 겁니다.** 너무 걱정하지 마세요. 제가 알아서 처리할게요.

Walter White 　　　　　　　　　　[오후 12:46]
그럼, (168) **제가 사무실에 있는 사람을 시켜 Irene에게 태블릿 컴퓨터를 가져다 주도록 할게요.**

Dwight Parker 　　　　　　　　　　[오후 12:48]
정말 안심이 되네요. 얼른 서둘러서 와주세요. 정말 고마워요.

**165.** Parker 씨는 어느 곳에 있을 것 같은가?

    (A) 회의실

    (B) 전자제품 매장

    (C) 영화관

    (D) 그의 사무실                      정답 (A)

**166.** 오후 12시 41분에 Keller 씨가 "Oh, no."라고 말한 이유는 무엇인가?

    (A) 행사가 취소되었다.

    (B) 몇몇 사람들이 도착하지 않았다.

    (C) 한 직원이 아파서 결근한다고 연락을 했다.

    (D) 장비의 파손이 발생했다.            정답 (D)

**167.** Keller 씨에 대해 유추할 수 있는 것은 무엇인가?

    (A) 그녀는 마케팅 담당자이다.

    (B) 그녀는 Parker 씨의 상사이다.

    (C) 그녀는 기계를 다루는 것에 능하다.

    (D) 그녀는 파커 씨의 가장 큰 고객 중 하나이다.    정답 (C)

**168.** White 씨는 이후에 무엇을 할 것 같은가?

    (A) 마케팅 발표를 할 것이다.

    (B) 새로운 태블릿 컴퓨터를 구매할 것이다.

    (C) 누군가에게 장비를 가지고 올라가게 할 것이다.

    (D) Parker 씨와 함께 기계를 설치할 것이다.       정답 (C)

**문제 169-171번은 다음 광고를 참조하시오.**

---

**특별 공지**

수신: Bradford 대학교 내 학생잡지사, 편집장

발신: Keepsafe 보험사, Kelly Francis

오늘날, 젊은이들이 방학이나 해외여행에 대해 보상받을 수 있는 적절한 여행보험을 찾는 것은 어렵습니다. (169) **이것이 우리 Keepsafe 보험사가 특별히 18살~25살의 젊은이들만을 대상으로 한, 백패커 보험 상품을 출시하는 이유입니다.**

여행시에, 여행자가 보호받아야 마땅한 많은 어려움과 위험이 있습니다. (170) **백패커 보험 상품은 수하물 분실이나 강도의 경우에도 당신의 보상 요구를 받아들일 것입니다.** 또한 항공편이 취소되는 경우에도 환불을 요청하실 수 있습니다. 킵세이프 보험사는 만 달러까지 의료비를 지원하기 때문에 의료사고의 경우에도 보장받으실 수 있습니다.

(171) **백패커 보험 상품의 더 많은 정보를 위해, 3월 18일 목요일 오후 4시 학생 대강당에서 개최되는 20분짜리 설명회에 참석하세요.** 참석이 어려우시다면, 이메일 kellyfrancis@keepsafe.com을 통해 문의하거나 1-800-3020-5939번으로 사무실로 전화하셔서 켈리를 찾아주세요.

---

**169.** 백패커 보험상품이 대상으로 하는 고객의 연령대는 무엇인가?

    (A) 30~40살

    (B) 10~15살

    (C) 18~25살

    (D) 60~75살                    정답 (C)

**170.** 이 보험 상품으로 보상받지 못하는 것은 무엇인가?

    (A) 비행편의 취소

    (B) 의료 비용

    (C) 수하물 도난

    (D) 법정 비용                    정답 (D)

**171.** 다음 중 백패커 보험상품에 대한 정보를 얻을 수 있는 방법으로 언급되지 않은 것은 무엇인가?

    (A) 사무실에 있는 Francis 씨에게 전화할 것

    (B) Francis 씨에게 이메일을 전송할 것

    (C) Francis 씨의 개인 주소로 편지를 발송할 것

    (D) Francis 씨가 주최하는 세미나에 참석할 것     정답 (C)

**문제 172-175번은 다음 기사를 참조하시오.**

---

Nagasaki (6월 14일) – (172) **풍경 수채화를 전문으로 하는 화가 아케미 기타가와는 지난 5년 동안 국내의 많은 시골 지역을 여행하면서 그림을 그려왔다.** 그녀는 자신의 작품을 사진으로 촬영해 거의 매일 자신의 블로그에 올리고 있는데, www.travelandpaint.com에서 볼 수 있다.

(174/175) 그녀의 블로그에는 또한 여행 중에 있었던 모험들을 기록한 일기와도 같은 작품들도 있다. (174) 그녀는 자신이 만나는 사람들, 다양한 문화 또는 마주치는 방언들을 서술하기도 하며, 길 위에서의 외로운 발걸음을 재촉하면서 느끼는 자신만의 생각들도 공유해 나간다.

기타가와 씨의 사이트는 엄청난 팔로잉을 (173) **보유하고** 있는데, 그녀의 블로그 통계치가 하루 평균 3천 2백의 조회 수를 보여주고 있다. 짧은 설문조사에 동의한 블로그 독자들을 보면, 이들의 최대 인구집단은 20대 중반이나 30대 초반의 여성 대졸자이다. 어느 익명의 독자가 블로그에 남긴 말이 있다. "내가 매일 여기 들리는 이유는, 아케미가 내가 잃어버렸다고 생각한 일종의 모험과 자기 발견의 삶을 살고 있기 때문입니다."

무엇이 자신의 블로그를 시작하게 영향을 주었냐는 질문을 받았을 때, 기타가와 씨는 "솔직히 말해, 처음에는 단순히 하나의 디지털 일기로 시작됐어요. 여행을 하는 동안 내 생각들을 기록하는 하나의 방법일 뿐이었죠. 제 독자들이 계속 늘어나기 시작한 후에야 저는 다른 사람들이 내가 말하는 것에 관심을 가질 수도 있다는 점을 깨달았습니다. 내 생각을 세상과 공유하는 것이 행복합니다. 그것이 아무리 개인적인 것이고 단순한 것이든 말이죠."라고 설명했다.

---

**172.** 기사의 주제는 무엇인가?

    (A) 어느 화가의 개인적 경험

    (B) 사진의 새로운 트렌드

    (C) 일본의 다양한 문화들

    (D) 일본의 시골길 여행               정답 (A)

**173.** 기사에서, 셋째 단락 첫 줄의 'drawn'과 의미가 가장 가까운 어휘는 무엇인가?

    (A) 서술했다

    (B) 그려냈다

    (C) 끌어들였다

    (D) 부착했다                    정답 (C)

**174.** 아케미 기타가와 씨의 블로그에 담겨있지 않은 것은 무엇인가?

    (A) 자신의 주변에 대한 서술

    (B) 그녀의 작품 가격

    (C) 그녀 개인의 감정

    (D) 자신의 모험에 대한 이야기           정답 (B)

**175.** [1], [2], [3] 그리고 [4]로 표시된 곳 중에, 아래 문장이 들어가기에 가장 적절한 곳은?

    "그녀의 블로그에는 또한 여행 중에 있었던 모험들을 기록한 일기와도 같은 작품들도 있다."

    (A) [1]

    (B) [2]

    (C) [3]

    (D) [4]                      정답 (B)

문제 176-180번은 다음 광고와 평론을 참조하시오.

---

ARTHOUSE.COM
선두적인 온라인 미술용품 소매업체

Art House는 현대 미술가가 다음 명작을 창조하는 데 필요로 하는 모든 것을 갖추고 있습니다. 다음 5일 동안만, 다음의 목록에 대해 엄청난 할인을 해 드립니다.

- 여러 가지 종류의 클립아트 스텐실 12통 7달러
- 브란트 이젤 가방 27달러
- (178) Art House 상표의 24색 목탄 세트 9달러

또한, (176) 75달러 이상 구매 시, 화이트보드 마커 4개 세트를 드립니다.

구매 물품에 대해 도움이 필요하시면, 저희 온라인 고객 서비스 직원이 도와 드리겠습니다. 홈페이지 메인 화면 왼쪽 상단에 있는 고객 서비스 탭을 클릭하세요.

---

아트 투데이
미술에 필요한 모든 최신품들이 있는 곳

미술 가이드: 이달의 우수 상점

Art House는 저렴한 (180) 가격으로 물건을 살 수 있는 곳이며, 품질이 낮은 제품을 비싼 가격에 판매하는 유명한 미술용품점과는 다릅니다. Art House는 실제로 Art House만의 제품을 생산하고 있으며, 다른 인기 있는 브랜드와 함께 판매합니다. 붓에서 회반죽과 연필에 이르기까지 점점 더 다양한 제품을 사이트에서 취급합니다. (177) 그것의 품질이 더 유명한 브랜드의 제품만큼 좋진 않지만, 적절한 가격의 미술용품을 필요로 하는 미술가에게는 좋은 곳입니다.

또한, Art House는 80달러 이상 구매시 배송비 할인을 해줍니다. (179) 하지만 Art House가 대부분 직접 배송을 하기 때문에, 고객에게 배송 완료되기까지 시간이 훨씬 더 오래 걸릴 것입니다. 저렴한 가격은 기다릴 만한 가치가 있습니다. 홈페이지인 www.arthouse.com을 방문하여 수백 가지의 좋은 제품들을 확인하세요.

---

**176.** 어떠한 특별 할인이 광고되고 있는가?
(A) 반값의 캔버스
(B) $75 구매시 사은품
(C) 모든 구매의 무료 배송
(D) 모든 채색용품의 할인 　　　　　정답 (B)

**177.** Art House에 대해 유추할 수 있는 것은 무엇인가?
(A) 절약해야 하는 미술가들에게 매력적이다.
(B) 신문이나 잡지에는 광고되지 않는다.
(C) 한 곳 이상의 상점이 있다.
(D) 매일 특정한 구매 횟수가 정해져 있다. 　　　정답 (A)

**178.** 광고된 제품 중 어떠한 제품이 Art House가 제작한 것인가?
(A) 스텐실
(B) 이젤 가방
(C) 목탄 세트
(D) 마커 　　　　　정답 (C)

**179.** 평론가가 Art House의 단점으로 언급한 것은 무엇인가?
(A) 고객 서비스의 낮은 질
(B) 많은 제품의 비싼 가격
(C) 제품을 수령하기까지의 소요 시간
(D) 덜 다양한 붓의 종류 　　　　정답 (C)

---

**180.** 논평에서, 첫 번째 단락 첫 번째 줄의 "deals"와 의미상 가장 유사한 단어는 무엇인가?
(A) 다량
(B) 염가 판매
(C) 계약
(D) 타협 　　　　　정답 (B)

---

문제 181-185번은 다음 이메일들을 참조하시오.

---

수신: Darren Reagan 〈dreagan@CMT/Intl.com〉
발신: Rebecca Dawson 〈rebecca.moore@CMT/Intl.com〉
날짜: 10월 18일
제목: 추천

Darren,

(181) 당신이 몇 달 전 Ho Chi Minh 출장을 다녀왔다는 사실을 이제 막 알게 되었습니다. 제가 몇 가지를 여쭤보기 위해 이메일을 보내는 것을 이해해 주시기를 바랍니다. 저는 그 곳에서 사업을 펼치는 것에 대해 약간의 조언을 듣고자 합니다. 제가 이해한 바로는, 당신이 동아시아에서 중앙아시아까지 사업차 곳곳을 다니신다고 들었습니다. 그래서 당신이 해 주실 수 있는 조언이 저에게 큰 도움이 될 수 있을 것입니다. (182) 이번이 제가 지역 담당 이사로써 처음으로 출장가는 것이며 좋은 첫 인상을 만들 수 있기를 바랍니다.

감사드리며, (183) 이번 주 금요일에 있을 영업회의에서 좋은 성과를 거두시길 바랍니다. 곧 답장 받기를 희망합니다.

Rebecca Dawson

---

수신: Rebecca Dawson 〈rebecca.moore@CMT/Intl.com〉
발신: Darren Reagan 〈dreagan@CMT/Intl.com〉
날짜: 10월 19일
제목: 답장: 추천

Rebecca,

제가 어떤 방법으로든 도와드릴 수 있다면 기꺼이 도와드리겠습니다. 출발 전에 Ho Chi Minh에 대해 어느 정도 조사를 해 보시리라 생각합니다. (184) 도착하시면 몇몇 문화 유적이나 역사적으로 중요한 장소 등을 방문해 보시길 권해 드립니다. 현지에서 만날 사업 관계자들과 대화할 때 대화의 화제로 사용하실 수 있을 것입니다.

또한, 현지의 교통법이 우리나라와 많이 다르다는 것을 기억하십시오. 사람들이 제가 겪은 여러 곳만큼 보행자들에게 주의를 기울이지 않습니다. (184) 회의나 약속에 가실 때 충분한 시간을 가지고 출발하십시오. 교통 체증이 상당히 심각하며 이동하는 것이 뜻대로 잘 되지 않습니다.

다른 질문이 있으면 알려 주십시오. (183) 이번 금요일에 큰 프리젠테이션을 할 예정입니다. 하지만 아직은 아무것도 (185) 확인하지는 않습니다. 아직 준비할 것들이 좀 남아 있습니다. 오늘 퇴근 전에 마무리할 예정입니다.

(184) 안전한 여행 하시고 즐거운 시간 보내십시오. Vietnam은 아름다운 나라입니다.

Darren

---

**181.** Dawson 씨가 이메일을 발송한 주된 목적은 무엇인가?
(A) 다가오는 영업 회의에 대해 물어보기 위해서
(B) Ho Chi Minh의 관광 명소에 대해 물어보기 위해서
(C) 사업 회의에 대해 동료에게 물어보기 위해서
(D) Ho Chi Minh으로 출장 가는 것에 대한 조언을 구하기 위해서
　　　　　정답 (D)

**182.** Dawson 씨에 대해 암시되는 것은 무엇인가?
(A) 그녀는 다음 달에 아시아의 다른 도시로 이사할 것이다.
(B) 그녀는 막 새로운 직책을 맡았다.
(C) 그녀는 베트남을 여러 번 방문한 적이 있다.
(D) 그녀는 최근 레이건 씨와 알게 되었다.　　　　정답 (B)

**183.** Reagan 씨가 이메일에서 그의 사업 거래에 대해 언급한 이유는 무엇인가?
(A) Dawson 씨가 한 언급에 대답하기 위해서
(B) 거래의 성사를 축하하기 위해서
(C) Dawson 씨를 회의의 일원으로 초대하기 위해서
(D) 사전 조사의 중요성을 강조하기 위해서　　　　정답 (A)

**184.** Reagan 씨의 제안 사항이 아닌 것은 무엇인가?
(A) 문화 및 역사 유적지에 방문할 것
(B) 사업 회의에 정시에 도착할 것
(C) 좋은 시간을 보낼 것
(D) 존경을 받기 위해 고객에게 까다롭게 굴 것　　　　정답 (D)

**185.** 두 번째 이메일에서, 세 번째 단락 두 번째 줄의 "counting on"과 의미상 가장 유사한 표현은 무엇인가?
(A) 확신하는
(B) 고안하는
(C) 달하는
(D) 기록하는　　　　정답 (A)

문제 186~190번은 다음 광고, 온라인 일정, 그리고 문자 메시지를 참조하시오.

---

Cineplus 극장
Weston Park, Fairfield

(186) 모든 영화 팬들은 주목해 주십시오! 완전히 새로운 저희 IMAX 스크린 공사가 완료되어 여러분과 함께 개관을 기념하고자 합니다. IMAX 스크린인 스크린 8이 최신 블록버스터 영화 Star Voyager 시사회에 맞춰 6월 2일에 문을 열었습니다. (186) 이 규모 확장을 기념하기 위해, 저희는 6월 말까지 매표소에서 모든 입장권을 15퍼센트 할인해드릴 것입니다. 추가로, Cineplus 극장 회원들께서는 이번 달 동안에 저희 웹사이트에서 예약하시면 더 큰 할인을 받습니다! 금요일 상영작을 온라인으로 예약하시고 20퍼센트의 할인을 받으세요! (188) 토요일 상영작 표를 예약하시고 25퍼센트의 할인을 받으십시오! 일요일에 오시면 30퍼센트의 할인을 받으실 수 있습니다! 마지막으로, 저희는 프리미엄 좌석을 선택한 고객들께 스낵과 음료 쿠폰을 나눠 드릴 것입니다!

---

http://www.cineplus.co.uk/theaters/location1089/

Cineplus 극장 - 위치 검색

귀하는 등록되어 있습니다: Josh Furman(회원)

선택된 장소: Weston Park, Fairfield ▼

선택된 날짜: (188) 토요일, 6월 19일 ▼

표 수량: 2 ▼

아래의 영화는 선택된 날짜에 선택된 장소에서 상영 중입니다. 상영 시작 시간을 클릭하시면 좌석 선택 화면 및 지불 화면으로 넘어가게 될 것입니다. 감사합니다.

| 영화 | 감독 | 주연 | 상영 시간 (분) | 상영 시작 시간 |
|------|------|------|--------|----------------|

| Into the Abyss | Cathy Bridges | Tom Hoffman, Alice Cruz | 98 | (187) **10:30**/16:30/21:30 |
| Love Recipe | Leo Cresswell | Julia Holt, Sally Nash | 134 | 09:30/12:45/20:30 |
| Star Voyager | Joe Wilcox | Edward Brooks, Lisa Wincot | 117 | 11:30/15:00/21:30 |
| The Dependables | Oliver Phelps | Bernie Jones, Tre Sawyer | 99 | 14:00/17:00/21:30 |
| Secret Identity | Elisa Finch | Tim Sherman, Rita Stone | 108 | 09:30/15:00/20:30 |
| (189) **Above Suspicion** | **Joe Wilcox** | Clarke Grey, **Tom Hoffman** | 122 | 11:30/15:45/21:30 |
| On the Battlefield | Sarah Mulder | Sally Nash, Dave Mathis | 113 | 09:30/14:30/21:00 |

---

ANNIE WOODS　　　　[오후 1:47]
안녕, 조쉬. 우리를 위해 온라인에서 영화 표를 사줘서 고마워요. 그 영화 정말 재미있었어요.

JOSH FURMAN　　　　[오후 1:48]
고맙기는요, 애니. 그리고… 나도 그랬어요! 엄청난 영화였어요! 오후 9시 30분까지 시작하지 않은 게 유감스러웠어요. 그리고, 영화가 꽤 길었어요.

ANNIE WOODS　　　　[오후 1:50]
네, 집에 꽤 늦게 가긴 했지만 그럴 만한 가치가 있었어요. (189) **조 윌콕스의 다른 영화들보다 꽤 많이 진지한 분위기였어요.** 난 좀 놀랐어요. 그럼에도 몇몇 웃긴 순간도 있었어요.

JOSH FURMAN　　　　[오후 1:52]
맞아요! 대체적으로 무척 강렬했어요! (190) **끝나기 바로 직전까지,** (189) **Tom Hoffman의 배역이 러시아 첩자였다는 것을 전혀 생각하지 못했어요!**

ANNIE WOODS　　　　[오후 1:53]
저도요! 그렇게 될 줄 몰랐어요, 그렇죠? 다음 주말에 또 가요. 당신이 또 영화를 고르게 해줄게요!

---

**186.** 광고의 주된 목적은 무엇인가?
(A) 영화관 확장 계획을 발표하는 것
(B) 새로운 영화 개봉을 홍보하는 것
(C) 특별 제공 서비스에 관해 고객에게 알리는 것
(D) 새로운 영화 회원제를 소개하는 것　　　　정답 (C)

**187.** 웹페이지 일정표에 보이는 영화들에 관해 사실이 아닌 것은?
(A) 영화들 중 하나가 오후 10시 30분에 시작한다.
(B) 대부분의 영화가 2시간 이하의 길이이다.
(C) 모든 영화가 하루에 3번 상영된다.
(D) 영화들 중의 두 개에 Sally Nash가 주연이다.　　　　정답 (A)

**188.** FURMAN 씨에 관해 유추할 수 있는 것은 무엇인가?
(A) 무료 스낵 쿠폰을 받았다.
(B) 영화 시사회 표를 구매했다.
(C) 영화 표에 대해 25퍼센트의 할인을 받았다.
(D) Cineplus Weston Park 지점의 직원이다.　　　　정답 (C)

**189.** WOODS 씨와 FURMAN 씨는 어떤 영화를 함께 보았을 가능성이 큰가?
(A) Into The Abyss
(B) Star Voyager
(C) Secret Identity
(D) Above Suspicion　　　　정답 (D)

**190.** WOODS 씨에 관해 알 수 있는 것은 무엇인가?
  (A) 똑같은 영화를 다시 보고 싶어 한다.
  (B) 보통 코미디 영화를 선호한다.
  (C) Cineplus 극장의 회원이다.
  (D) 영화의 결말에 놀랐다.      정답 (D)

**문제 191-195번은 다음 회람과 회의 안건, 그리고 이메일을 참조하시오.**

---

**회람**

수신: Borelli 타이어 사의 부서장들
발신: (194) **Charles Mulgrew, 대표이사**
제목: 12월 경영진 회의
날짜: 11월 30일

부서장 여러분께:

우리 회사의 최고 운영책임자(Diana Hayworth)와 회장님(David Ashcroft)께서 몇몇 중요한 주제에 관한 논의를 진행하실 예정이므로 여러분 모두 반드시 다음 주에 있을 회의에 참석하셔야 합니다. 저 또한 회의 중에 발표를 할 예정입니다. 회의 중에 생산적으로 참여하실 수 있도록 아이디어와 제안 사항들을 준비해 오시기 바랍니다. (191) **이유가 무엇이든, 회의에 참석할 수 없는 분은 제 비서인 네일러 씨에게 최소 하루 전에 알려 주시기 바랍니다.** 회의 장소는 A회의실의 보수 작업 경과에 따라 달라질 수 있습니다. 작업이 완료되어 회의실이 준비되면, 회의는 오전 9시 30분부터 계속 그곳에서 열릴 것입니다. (192) **하지만 12월 6일까지 준비가 되지 않는다면, B회의실을 대신 사용할 것입니다. 이 회의실은 오전에는 직원 교육을 위해 사용될 것이므로 회의는 점심 시간 이후에 시작될 것입니다.** 과거의 회의에서와 마찬가지로 이번 회의도 3시간이 넘지 않을 것입니다. 제가 하루 또는 이틀 전에 미리 회의 장소에 대해 여러분께 알려 드리겠습니다.

---

Borelli 타이어 사

경영 회의 안건
(192) **12월 6일, B회의실**
회의록 작성자: 비서 Veronica Naylor

| 항목 | 주제 | 발표자/논의 진행자 |
|------|------|-------------------|
| 1 | 다음 분기 영업 대상 및 예상 | Bob Tunstall |
| 2 | (193) **직원 성과 기반 보상 프로그램** | **Khezar Hayat** |
| 3 | 유럽 및 아시아 시장으로의 사업 확장 | Diana Hayworth |
| (194) 4 | 최근의 시장 경향에 대한 평가 | **Charles Mulgrew** |
| 5 | 기업 이미지 강화를 위한 전략 | David Ashcroft |
| 6 | 생산 공장 내 신규 직원 채용 요청 | Sandra Davis |

회의 참석자들은 회의록 사본이나 보조 자료를 얻고자 하시는 경우 회의 다음 날 네일러 씨에게 연락하시면 됩니다.

---

수신: Veronica Naylor 〈vnaylor@borellitires.org〉
발신: Bernadette Kidman 〈bkidman@borellitires.org〉
날짜: 12월 7일
제목: 어제 회의

안녕하세요, Veronica,

어제 있었던 경영진 회의의 회의록을 제게 보내주시면 매우 감사하겠습니다. 아시다시피, 약 30분 동안 긴급한 고객 전화를 받기 위해 회의실 밖

---

으로 나와야 했기 때문에 회의 안건의 2번 항목 전체를 (195) **놓쳤습니다.** 또한, Ashcroft 회장님께서 말씀하시려고 했던 것에 특히 관심이 있어서 그 내용을 다시 한 번 읽어 보고 싶습니다. 회의록 외에도, (194) **대표이사님의 발표에 동반된 유인물 추가 사본도 보내 주시겠습니까?** 제 부서에 근무하는 직원들에게 그것을 나눠줄 계획입니다. 도움 주시는 것에 대해 미리 감사 드립니다.

좋은 하루 되세요,

Bernadette Kidman

**191.** Borelli 타이어 사의 부서장들은 무엇을 하도록 요청 받는가?
  (A) Mulgrew 씨에게 주제에 대한 제안사항을 보내는 것
  (B) Naylor 씨에게서 회의 안건을 받는 것
  (C) 불참하는 것에 대해 사전에 알려주는 것
  (D) 직원 연수를 준비하는 것      정답 (C)

**192.** 12월 경영진 회의에 관해 사실일 가능성이 큰 것은 무엇인가?
  (A) 3시간 넘게 지속됐다.
  (B) 새로 보수된 회의실에서 열렸다.
  (C) 오후에 열렸다.
  (D) 다른 날로 일정이 재조정됐다.      정답 (C)

**193.** 직원 장려 정책에 관해 누가 이야기했을 가능성이 큰가?
  (A) Sandra Davis
  (B) Diana Hayworth
  (C) Bob Tunstall
  (D) Khezar Hayat      정답 (D)

**194.** Kidman 씨는 어느 안건 항목에 대한 추가 유인물을 요청하는가?
  (A) 항목 2
  (B) 항목 3
  (C) 항목 4
  (D) 항목 5      정답 (C)

**195.** 이메일에서 첫 번째 단락, 세 번째 줄에 있는 단어 "missed"와 의미가 가장 유사한 단어는 무엇인가?
  (A) 실패했다
  (B) 희망했다
  (C) 건너뛰었다
  (D) 잘못 놓아 두었다      정답 (C)

**문제 196-200번은 다음 공지와 온라인 계정 내역, 그리고 이메일을 참조하시오.**

---

Pebble 컨트리 클럽 회원 여러분께 알립니다!

여러분 모두 아시다시피, 저희는 여러분께 최상의 서비스와 편의 시설을 제공해 드리기 위해 열심히 노력하고 있습니다. 그에 따라, 9월부터 회원 여러분께서 즐기실 수 있도록 새로운 스포츠 강좌를 (196) **도입한다는 점을 알려 드리게 되어 기쁘게 생각합니다.** 이 강좌들에 대한 모든 상세 정보는 저희 웹사이트에서 찾아보실 수 있습니다. 9월 한 달 동안, (197) **회원 여러분께 각 운동 종목마다 전액 무료로 한 개의 무료 시범 강좌를 들으실 수 있는 기회를 제공해 드림으로써 이 강좌들의 시작을 기념할 것입니다!** 신청하신 시범 강좌가 마음에 드실 경우, 그 후에 경험 많은 저희 강사들과 함께 하는 더 많은 수업에 등록하실 수 있습니다! 추가로, 최소 1년 동안 저희 클럽의 회원으로 가입되어 있으신 분들께서는 9월에 참석하시는 모든 강좌에 대해 15퍼센트 할인을 받으실 수 있으며, (198) **최소 2년 동안 회원이신 분들은 25퍼센트의 할인을 받으실 수 있습니다.**

http://www.pebblecountryclub.ca/member/accountsummary/028178/4

Pebble 컨트리 클럽

회원 성명: Aurora Lanes
회원 계정 번호: 028178
회원 계정 내역: 9월 1일 – 9월 30일

4구역: 추가 운동 수강료

| 스포츠 강좌명 | (199) 양궁 | 테니스 | 스쿼시 | 골프 |
|---|---|---|---|---|
| 강사 | Joshua Paek | Matthew Clarke | Kate Hutchson | Franz Schultz |
| 수강료 | 무료 시범 수강 | 일반 요금 | 무료 시범 수강 | 무료 시범 수강 |
| 강의 수 | 1회 | 4회 | 1회 | 1회 |
| 총액 | $0 | $140 | $0 | $0 |
| 총 수강료 | $140 | | | |
| (198) 회원 할인가 적용 | −$21 | | | |

해당 금액을 10월 10일까지 회원 서비스부에 납부해 주시기 바랍니다.
감사합니다. 비용 납부를 원하시면 여기를 클릭하십시오.

---

수신: Pebble 컨트리 클럽 〈inquires@pebblecc.com〉
발신: Aurora Lanes 〈al@briggsinc.org〉
날짜: 10월 3일
제목: 9월 스포츠 요금

관계자께,

제 회원 계정 내역을 읽어 보다가 오류가 있다는 것을 알았습니다. 9월에 있었던 무료 시범 강좌를 수강할 기회가 있어서 좋았으며, 심지어 할인된 요금으로 추가 강좌도 들었습니다. (200) **그런데 제 계정 내역을 보니 제가 Matthew Clarke 씨와 함께 하는 테니스 강좌를 수강했다고 나타나 있는데, 저는 실제로 James LeBlanc 씨와 함께 하는 배드민턴 강좌를 들었습니다.** 두 강좌에 대한 수강료가 같다는 것을 알고 있기 때문에 이 부분에 대해서는 크게 걱정하지 않습니다. (200) **저는 이번 달에 LeBlanc 씨와 함께 하는 추가 강좌에 등록하려 할 때 문제가 있을까 걱정됩니다.** 제가 요금 납부를 계속 진행하기 전에 제 온라인 계정 내역을 수정해 주시기 바랍니다. 또한, (199) **이번 달에 Paek 씨와 함께 하는 4개의 추가 강좌에 대해 저를 등록해 주시겠습니까?** 비록 Schultz 씨와 Hutchson 씨가 훌륭한 강사들이라는 것을 알게 되었지만, 저는 그 운동 종목이 제게 맞지 않다고 생각합니다.

Aurora Lanes

**196.** 공지에서, 1번째 단락 2번째 줄에 있는 단어 "introducing"과 의미가 가장 가까운 것은?
(A) 만나는
(B) 참가하는
(C) 결정짓는
(D) 시작하는  정답 (D)

**197.** Pebble 컨트리 클럽 회원들은 무엇을 하도록 권고 받는가?
(A) 새로운 스포츠 강좌에 대한 제안사항을 말할 것
(B) 9월에 각자의 회원 자격을 갱신할 것
(C) 기간이 한정되어 있는 제공 서비스를 이용할 것
(D) 웹사이트에서 각자의 개인 상세 정보를 업데이트할 것  정답 (C)

**198.** Lanes 씨에 관해 사실일 가능성이 큰 것은 무엇인가?
(A) 컨트리 클럽 회원들에게 스포츠를 가르쳐 왔다.
(B) 2년이 채 되지 않는 기간 동안 클럽의 회원 자격을 유지해 왔다.
(C) 스포츠 강좌에 대한 요금으로 140달러를 지불해야 한다.
(D) 30일 이내에 미납 요금을 지불해야 한다.  정답 (B)

**199.** Lanes 씨는 앞으로 어느 스포츠 강좌를 다시 들을 계획인가?
(A) 테니스
(B) 스쿼시
(C) 양궁
(D) 골프  정답 (C)

**200.** Lanes 씨는 자신의 이메일에서 무슨 문제점을 언급하는가?
(A) 배드민턴 강좌에 등록할 수 없었다.
(B) 광고에 나온 회원 할인 서비스를 받지 못했다.
(C) 수강하지 않은 강좌에 대한 요금이 청구되었다.
(D) 스포츠 강사들 중의 한 명에게 실망했다.  정답 (C)

**1.** 미W
(A) The woman is wearing an apron.
(B) The woman is mopping the floor.
(C) The woman is refinishing the floor.
(D) The woman is bending over a kitchen sink.

(A) 여자는 앞치마를 착용하고 있다.
(B) 여자는 바닥을 대걸레로 닦고 있다.
(C) 여자는 바닥 표면을 재작업하고 있다.
(D) 여자는 부엌 싱크대 위로 몸을 숙이고 있다.   정답 (B)

**2.** 영W
(A) Some people are sunbathing on the deck.
(B) Some people are paddling a boat on the water.
(C) A boat is being pulled onto the shore.
(D) Some boats are competing against one another.

(A) 몇몇 사람들이 갑판 위에서 일광욕을 하고 있다.
(B) 몇몇 사람들이 물 위에 있는 배에서 노를 젓고 있다.
(C) 배 한 척이 해변으로 끌려오고 있다.
(D) 몇몇 배들이 서로 경쟁하고 있다.   정답 (B)

**3.** 호M
(A) The man is performing before a large audience.
(B) The man is adjusting a microphone stand.
(C) Most of the seats are occupied.
(D) The clock has been mounted on a wall.

(A) 남자는 많은 청중들 앞에서 연주하고 있다.
(B) 남자는 마이크 거치대의 높이를 조정하고 있다.
(C) 대부분의 의자에는 사람들이 착석해 있다.
(D) 시계가 벽에 부착되어 있다.   정답 (D)

**4.** 미M
(A) She's packing a camera into a case.
(B) She's dusting a camera lens off.
(C) She's checking information on a monitor.
(D) She's adjusting some photographic equipment.

(A) 그녀는 케이스에 카메라를 넣고 있다.
(B) 그녀는 카메라 렌즈의 먼지를 털어내고 있다.
(C) 그녀는 모니터를 통해 정보를 확인하고 있다.
(D) 그녀는 사진 촬영 장비를 조정하고 있다.   정답 (D)

**5.** 영W
(A) Several people are gathered around the table.
(B) Some lampposts are lined up along the motorway.
(C) Cement steps lead down to the waterfront pathway.
(D) There is a handrail on both sides of the circular staircase.

(A) 몇몇 사람들이 테이블 주변에 모여 있다.
(B) 몇몇 가로등이 고속도로를 따라 줄지어 늘어서 있다.
(C) 시멘트로 만든 계단이 물가에 있는 길로 연결되어 있다.
(D) 나선형 계단의 양쪽에 손잡이가 있다.   정답 (C)

**6.** 호M
(A) Some containers are filled with vegetables.
(B) Some kitchen appliances are on a counter.
(C) Some windows are being cleaned.
(D) Some dishes are piled up on the table.

(A) 몇몇 용기들이 야채들로 채워져 있다.
(B) 몇몇 주방용품들이 조리대 위에 있다.
(C) 몇몇 창문들이 청소되고 있다.
(D) 몇몇 접시들이 테이블 위에 쌓여 있다.   정답 (B)

**7.** 미W 호M
When does the convenience store open?
(A) Last week.
(B) At 6:00 o'clock, I heard.
(C) Some job openings.

편의점은 언제 문을 여나요?
(A) 지난주에요.
(B) 6시라고 들었어요.
(C) 몇몇 일자리들이요.   정답 (B)

**8.** 호M 미W
Which necktie will you buy to go with your business suit?
(A) I bought it last month.
(B) The brown one.
(C) For my business trip to Shanghai.

당신의 정장에 어울리는 어떤 넥타이를 사시겠어요?
(A) 지난달에 샀어요.
(B) 갈색이요.
(C) Shanghai로 가는 출장을 위해서요.   정답 (B)

**9.** 영W 호M
Why is Ms. Witherspoon rewriting the sales report?
(A) Because there were some numerical errors.
(B) Twenty-one pages long.
(C) To New York and Syracuse.

Witherspoon 씨가 판매 보고서를 다시 작성하는 이유가 뭔가요?
(A) 숫자상의 오류들이 있어서요.
(B) 21페이지 분량이에요.
(C) New York과 Syracuse로요.   정답 (A)

**10.** 미W 호M
How long does it take to drive to the trade center?
(A) The shipment of export goods to China.
(B) About 10 miles or so.
(C) I usually take the subway to get there.

무역 센터까지 운전해서 가는 데 시간이 얼마나 걸리나요?
(A) 중국으로 수출하는 제품들의 배송이요.
(B) 약 10마일 정도요.
(C) 저는 그 곳에 갈 때 주로 지하철을 이용합니다.   정답 (C)

**11.** 영W 미M
Where can I find a good printing shop around here?
(A) Much better than I thought.
(B) Ms. Thompson might know.
(C) Yes, we distributed 100 hard copies.

이 주변에 좋은 인쇄소가 어디에 있을까요?
(A) 내가 생각했던 것보다 훨씬 더 좋아요.
(B) Thompson 씨가 알지도 몰라요.

(C) 네, 우리가 100부를 배포했어요.                                정답 (B)

**12.** 호M 미W

Would you like some dessert after your dinner?
(A) Yes, the street looks deserted.
(B) No, thanks. Just bring the check, please.
(C) The food was exceptional.

저녁식사 후에 후식을 드시겠어요?
(A) 네, 거리는 한적해 보여요.
(B) 감사합니다만 사양할게요. 계산서를 가져다 주세요.
(C) 음식은 아주 훌륭했어요.                                정답 (B)

**13.** 미W 호M

Could you forward me the research files electronically?
(A) Just go forward.
(B) Sure, I'll do that after lunch.
(C) No, through the Internet.

연구 파일들을 이메일로 보내 주시겠어요?
(A) 그냥 앞으로 가세요.
(B) 그러죠. 점심식사 후에 그렇게 할게요.
(C) 아니오, 인터넷을 통해서요.                                정답 (B)

**14.** 영W 미M

How can I get to the Redstone Hotel in Seoul?
(A) Yes, I'm getting tired.
(B) We have a long way to go.
(C) I'll drive you there.

서울에 있는 Redstone Hotel까지 어떻게 가면 되나요?
(A) 네, 점점 피곤해지네요.
(B) 우리는 갈 길이 멀어요.
(C) 제가 그 곳까지 차로 모셔다 드릴게요.                                정답 (C)

**15.** 미W 호M

Which flight are you taking to New York?
(A) On the morning of November 23.
(B) Please arrive at the airport an hour earlier.
(C) Actually, I haven't reserved a ticket yet.

어떤 항공편을 이용하여 New York에 가시나요?
(A) 11월 23일 오전에요.
(B) 한 시간 일찍 공항에 도착하세요.
(C) 사실, 아직 항공권을 예약하지 못했어요.                                정답 (C)

**16.** 미W 영W

Who will lock the computer lab tonight?
(A) James will get off work at 5:00.
(B) I think Ms. Austin will be the last to leave.
(C) There will be a new software demonstration tonight.

오늘밤에 컴퓨터실의 문을 잠글 사람이 누구인가요?
(A) James는 5시에 퇴근할 거예요.
(B) Austin 씨가 마지막으로 퇴근하는 걸로 알고 있어요.
(C) 오늘밤에 새로운 소프트웨어 시연회가 있어요.                                정답 (B)

**17.** 호M 미W

Who's in charge of handing out our new brochures today?
(A) I wish I knew.
(B) The first printing had only 100 copies.
(C) We need to recharge the battery.

오늘 새로운 소개책자를 배부하는 일은 누가 담당하나요?
(A) 저도 알았으면 좋겠네요.
(B) 초판은 단지 100부였어요.
(C) 우리는 배터리를 재충전해야 해요.                                정답 (A)

**18.** 미W 미M

Are we still planning to meet at 2:00?
(A) Yes, that's the plan.
(B) We haven't met before.
(C) There will be about twenty people.

우리는 여전히 2시에 만날 계획이죠?
(A) 네, 그럴 계획이에요.
(B) 우리는 전에 만난 적이 없어요.
(C) 20명 정도가 있을 겁니다.                                정답 (A)

**19.** 영W 호M

What's the bus fare to Spokane?
(A) At the express bus terminal.
(B) I think it's $7.25.
(C) The job fair was held in Spokane.

Spokane까지 가는 버스요금은 얼마인가요?
(A) 고속버스 터미널에서요.
(B) 7달러 25센트인 것으로 알고 있어요.
(C) 취업 박람회가 Spokane에서 개최되었어요.                                정답 (B)

**20.** 영W 미W

Would you like to meet with the foreign client, or should I ask someone else to do it?
(A) I think Andrew will do it.
(B) No, they're off duty today.
(C) We talked about many issues.

해외 고객과 만나시겠어요, 아니면 다른 사람에게 만나보라고 할까요?
(A) Andrew가 만나는 것으로 알고 있는데요.
(B) 아니오, 그들은 오늘 비번이에요.
(C) 우리는 많은 안건에 대해 이야기했어요.                                정답 (A)

**21.** 영W 호M

Why are they expanding their manufacturing plant in China?
(A) Yes, the prices are very competitive.
(B) To meet the high demand for their products.
(C) One of my clients wants the floor plans.

그들은 왜 중국의 제조 공장을 확장하는 거죠?
(A) 네, 가격이 매우 경쟁력이 있어요.
(B) 그들의 제품에 대한 높은 수요를 충족시키기 위해서요.
(C) 우리 고객 중 한 분이 평면도를 보고 싶어 해요.                                정답 (B)

**22.** 미M 미W

Should we start the seminar now or wait for Mr. Stanley for a little while?
(A) I think I have to miss it.
(B) We have a lot to do, so don't waste our time.
(C) To be honest, I didn't like it at all.

세미나를 지금 시작할까요, 아니면 Stanley 씨를 좀 기다려 볼까요?
(A) 저는 불참할 것 같아요.
(B) 우리가 다룰 것이 많으니 시간을 낭비하지 맙시다.
(C) 솔직히 말하자면, 저는 그게 전혀 좋지 않았어요.                                정답 (B)

**23.** 미W 호M

Have you taken care of all the paperwork for your small business loan?

(A) I've already submitted all the required documents.

(B) The loan application will take a while to be approved.

(C) Bank interest rates are higher than I anticipated.

소규모 사업 대출을 위한 서류 작업은 다 처리하셨나요?

(A) 모든 요청 서류들을 다 제출했어요.

(B) 대출 신청이 승인되는 데 한동안 시간이 걸려요.

(C) 은행 금리가 예상했던 것보다 높네요. 　　　정답 (A)

**24.** 미M 영W

I really enjoyed the Impressionist art exhibition yesterday.

(A) Her exhibition was really impressive.

(B) I wish I could have gone there with you.

(C) The gallery is located on Pine Street.

어제 인상주의 미술 전시회를 정말 즐겁게 보고 왔습니다.

(A) 그녀의 전시회는 정말 인상적이었어요.

(B) 저도 같이 갔으면 좋았을 텐데요.

(C) 미술관은 Pine Street에 위치하고 있어요. 　정답 (B)

**25.** 미W 호M

Uh-oh, my laptop computer just crashed.

(A) I need some time to think.

(B) Sure, I'll do it immediately.

(C) Why don't you try restarting it?

아, 이런, 제 노트북 컴퓨터가 방금 멈춰 버렸어요.

(A) 생각할 시간이 좀 필요해요.

(B) 물론이에요, 바로 하겠습니다.

(C) 재부팅을 해보는 게 어때요? 　　　　　정답 (C)

**26.** 영W 미M

Do you know why the government wants to expand the local airport?

(A) To accommodate future air traffic growth.

(B) Yes, we're trying to expand our business.

(C) It'll take nearly three years to complete.

정부에서 지역 공항을 확장하고자 하는 이유가 뭐가요?

(A) 향후 증가할 항공 교통량을 수용하기 위해서죠.

(B) 네, 우리는 사업을 확장하고자 노력하고 있어요.

(C) 완공하는 데 거의 3년이 소요될 겁니다. 　정답 (A)

**27.** 미W 호M

How do you turn this fax machine on?

(A) Push the red button on the far-right side.

(B) At a tax-free retail shop.

(C) Please turn it off when you leave the office.

이 팩스기는 어떻게 켜나요?

(A) 맨 오른쪽에 있는 빨간색 버튼을 누르세요.

(B) 한 면세점에서요.

(C) 퇴근할 때는 꼭 꺼주세요. 　　　　　정답 (A)

**28.** 미M 미W

Do you want to open a personal or corporate account?

(A) Shops are open in the morning until noon.

(B) I'm considering both of them.

(C) Our accountants are busy working today.

개인 계좌를 열길 원하시나요, 아니면 기업용 계좌를 열길 원하시나요?

(A) 가게들은 오전에서 정오까지 열어요.

(B) 둘 다 여는 것을 고려하고 있습니다.

(C) 우리 회계사들이 오늘 일하느라 바쁩니다. 　정답 (B)

**29.** 영W 미M

I haven't signed up to attend the basic computer skills course yet.

(A) Well, registration is already closed.

(B) We need some tablet and desktop computers.

(C) This is a free utility on the Internet.

아직까지 기초 컴퓨터 기술 강좌 참석을 위한 등록을 하지 못했어요.

(A) 음, 등록은 이미 종료되었어요.

(B) 우리는 태블릿 및 데스크톱 컴퓨터들이 필요해요.

(C) 이건 인터넷에 있는 무료 소프트웨어예요. 　정답 (A)

**30.** 미W 호M

Why haven't you restocked the shelves yet?

(A) Five dollars per share.

(B) There have been so many customers today.

(C) We accept cash, checks, and charge cards.

선반에 상품들을 다시 채워 넣지 않은 이유가 뭔가요?

(A) 한 주당 5달러예요.

(B) 오늘 손님들이 너무 많았어요.

(C) 저희는 현금, 수표, 그리고 신용카드를 모두 받습니다. 　정답 (B)

**31.** 영W 미M

None of the clients visited our office yesterday, right?

(A) About an hour-long meeting.

(B) I was out of the office.

(C) No, I haven't received any packages yet.

어제 우리 사무실을 방문한 고객은 전혀 없었지요, 그렇죠?

(A) 약 한 시간에 달하는 회의예요.

(B) 저는 사무실에 없었어요.

(C) 아니오, 아직까지 어떤 소포도 받지 못했어요. 　정답 (B)

## Part 3

문제 32-34번은 다음 대화를 참조하시오. 미W 미M

W: (32) **I need to ship this package quickly to my brother in South Korea.** How much will it cost to ship it there?

M: (33) **Standard deliveries to Korea are $18 per pound. It will take about 14 days to arrive. If you pay $30 per pound, you can have it arrive in one week.**

W: Is there any faster way to ship it, such as overnight express or something? (33) **My brother really needs this package in four days, and I want to have it delivered to him as soon as possible.**

M: (34) **We do have World Express Shipping. But the price is very high at $42 per pound.** If you send it today, your brother will receive it in two business days.

--------------------------------------------------

W: 한국에 있는 제 남동생에게 이 소포를 빨리 배송해야 하는데요. 그 곳까지 배송하는 데 비용이 얼마나 들까요?

M: 한국까지의 일반 배송은 파운드당 18달러입니다. 도착하는 데 14일 정도 걸리고요. 만약 파운드당 30달러를 지불하시면 소포가 일주일 후에 도

착할 겁니다.

W: 익일 배송같이 더 빠르게 배송할 수 있는 방법이 있나요? 제 동생이 4일 후에 이 소포가 정말 필요해서 저는 최대한 빨리 이 소포가 제 동생에게 배달되었으면 합니다.

M: World Express Shipping도 있습니다. 그렇지만 가격이 굉장히 비싸서 파운드당 42달러입니다. 만약에 손님이 오늘 소포를 보내시면 동생은 2일 후에 받으시게 됩니다.

**32.** 대화는 어디에서 이루어지는 것 같은가?
(A) 공항
(B) 우체국
(C) 버스 터미널
(D) 백화점 　　　　　　　　　　　정답 (B)

**33.** 여자가 걱정하는 이유는 무엇인가?
(A) 그녀가 가지고 있는 돈이 충분하지 않다.
(B) 신제품의 가격이 너무 비싸다.
(C) 소포를 배달하는 데 너무 오래 걸린다.
(D) 모든 표가 이미 매진되었다. 　　　　정답 (C)

**34.** 남자가 여자에게 제안하는 것은 무엇인가?
(A) 현금으로 결제한다.
(B) 추가로 제품을 주문한다.
(C) 다른 서비스를 이용한다.
(D) 항공권을 예약한다. 　　　　　　　정답 (C)

**문제 35-37번은 다음의 3자 대화를 참조하시오.** 영W 미M 호M

W: Excuse me. (35) **I'm the owner of Vibendum. How was your meal?**
M1: Oh, superb. I can't complain. It was well worth the drive.
W: Thank you for the compliment. Where are you visiting us from?
M2: We live in Manchester. It's a three-hour drive from here.
W: Wow, that's quite a drive. (36) **How did you learn about this restaurant?**
M2: Um… (36) **we read a review in our local food magazine last week,** which said Vibendum provides exceptional food, great service, and nice ambience. We've wanted to come here ever since.
M1: Your food today certainly lived up to your reputation. I hope you open another restaurant closer to Manchester.
W: Oh, (37) **I'm opening a new restaurant there early next year.** When it opens, I'll invite both of you. Please come by and enjoy our delicious food surrounded by beautiful oak trees in a country setting.

----------------------------------------

W: 실례합니다. 저는 Vibendum 주인입니다. 식사는 어떠신가요?
M1: 아, 훌륭합니다. 전혀 불만이 없습니다. 운전해서 올 만한 가치가 있습니다.
W: 칭찬에 감사드립니다. 어디에서 오셨습니까?
M2: 우리는 Manchester에서 삽니다. 운전해서 3시간 거리에 있어요.
W: 와, 정말 먼 거리를 운전해 오셨네요. 저희 식당은 어떻게 알게 되셨나요?
M2: 음… 지난 주에 지역 음식 잡지에 나온 평가를 읽었는데, Vibendum이 훌륭한 음식, 뛰어난 서비스, 그리고 좋은 분위기를 지닌 곳이라고 하더군요. 저희는 그 이후로 이 곳을 방문하고 싶었어요.
M1: 오늘 음식은 확실히 이 곳의 명성에 부족함이 없었습니다. Manchester

근처에도 식당 하나를 더 개업하시길 바랍니다.

W: 아, 내년 초에 그 곳에도 새로운 식당을 개업하려고 합니다. 개업하면 제가 두 분을 초대하겠습니다. 방문하셔서 전원에 있는 아름다운 떡갈나무들 밑에서 맛있는 음식을 즐기시길 바랄게요.

**35.** 여자는 누구인가?
(A) 택시 기사
(B) 기자
(C) 슈퍼마켓 계산원
(D) 레스토랑 주인 　　　　　　　　　정답 (D)

**36.** 남자들은 이 업체에 대해 어떻게 알게 되었는가?
(A) 텔레비전 프로그램을 통해서
(B) 신문 광고를 통해서
(C) 여행 가이드를 통해서
(D) 잡지 기사를 통해서 　　　　　　　정답 (D)

**37.** 여자는 내년에 어떤 일이 일어날 것이라고 언급하는가?
(A) 또 다른 지점이 개장할 것이다.
(B) 몇몇 직원들이 채용될 것이다.
(C) 새로운 메뉴가 제공될 것이다.
(D) 특별한 판촉 행사가 시작될 것이다. 　정답 (A)

**문제 38-40번은 다음 대화를 참조하시오.** 미M 미W

M: Hi. This is Brian Stockton. I rent the office space in 110B. (38) **I bought a new office space for my dental practice downtown, so I need to move out of here soon.** (39) **How soon can I cancel my lease?**
W: Congratulations, Mr. Stockton. That is very good news for you. All of our leases require 60 days' notice before you can get out of them, so you'll be responsible for the lease for 60 days from today.
M: That will be difficult for me to manage along with the moving expenses. I know a few people looking for locations to rent. (40) **If I refer a new tenant to you, would you be able to cancel the lease earlier?**

----------------------------------------

M: 안녕하세요. 저는 Brian Stockton이라고 합니다. 제가 110B 사무실을 임대하고 있는데요. 제가 시내에서 치과 개업에 적합한 새로운 사무실을 매입해서 이곳에서 곧 나가야 합니다. 제가 임대 계약을 최대한 빠르게 해지할 수 있는 시점이 언제일까요?
W: 축하드려요, Stockton 씨. 좋은 소식이네요. 저희의 모든 임대 계약은 이사를 가기 60일 전에 통보해줄 것을 요청하고 있어서 오늘부터 60일 동안의 임대 비용에 대해 책임지셔야 합니다.
M: 이사 비용까지 고려한다면 그건 좀 어렵겠군요. 제가 임대 장소를 찾고 있는 몇몇 사람들을 알고 있습니다. 제가 새로운 입주자를 알아보면 임대 계약을 좀 더 빠르게 해지하는 것이 가능할까요?

**38.** 남자가 사무실에서 나가길 원하는 이유는 무엇인가?
(A) 그는 더 작은 규모의 사무실을 원한다.
(B) 그는 사업체를 이전하길 원한다.
(C) 그의 월 임대료가 너무 비싸다.
(D) 그의 사무실이 노후되었다. 　　　　정답 (B)

**39.** 여자에게 요구되는 것은 무엇인가?
(A) 정기 검진을 받는다.
(B) 수리를 한다.

(C) 현재 계약을 해지한다.
(D) 남자의 월세를 인하한다.　　　　　　　정답 (C)

**40.** 남자가 하겠다고 제안하는 것은?
(A) 새로운 임대 계약서에 서명한다.
(B) 새로운 입주자를 찾는다.
(C) 일부 교체용 부품을 구매한다.
(D) 남자의 이사 비용을 지불한다.　　　　정답 (B)

---

**문제 41-43번은 다음의 3자 대화를 참조하시오.** 미W 영W 미M

> W1: **(41/42) I just spoke with Mr. Jones in IT, and he told me that the entire sales team is being issued new tablets.**
> W2: It's about time. They will help us work more efficiently.
> M: You're right. We can check and show our clients up-to-date data right in front of them.
> W1: I wonder what took them so long. We had been requesting the tablets for some time.
> W2: Maybe it's a response to the disappointing numbers last quarter.
> W1: Yeah. You might be right about that.
> M: **(43) Management probably expects a strong return on this investment in the tablets.**
>
> ---
>
> W1: 방금 막 IT의 Jones 씨와 이야기를 나눴는데, 전체 판매팀에게 새로운 태블릿PC가 지급될 예정이라네요.
> W2: 진작 그랬어야죠. 업무를 더 효율적으로 처리하는 데 도움이 되겠네요.
> M: 당신 말이 맞아요. 고객들의 최신자료를 그들 바로 앞에서 확인하고 보여줄 수 있겠어요.
> W1: 왜 그렇게 오래 걸렸는지 궁금하네요. 우리는 한참 동안 태블릿PC를 요청했어요.
> W2: 아마도 지난 분기의 저조한 수치에 대한 반응인 것 같아요.
> W1: 예, 당신 말이 맞을 거예요.
> M: 경영진은 태블릿PC 투자함으로써 큰 수익을 기대하고 있을 거예요.

**41.** 대화는 주로 무엇에 관한 것인가?
(A) 새로운 판매 안건
(B) 새로운 기기배급
(C) 영업팀 구성원의 변화
(D) 태블릿PC의 효율성　　　　　　　　정답 (B)

**42.** 여자는 왜 "It's about time"이라고 말하고 있는가?
(A) 그녀는 만족스럽지 않다.
(B) 그녀는 기대하고 있었다.
(C) 그녀는 시간이 더 필요하다.
(D) 그녀는 정해진 시간을 맞추길 원한다.　　정답 (B)

**43.** 남자가 경영진에 관해 암시하는 것은 무엇인가?
(A) 그들은 판매실적이 향상될 것을 예상한다.
(B) 그들은 투자를 싫어한다.
(C) 그들은 투자를 더 할 것이다.
(D) 그들은 더 많은 사람을 고용할 계획이다　정답 (A)

---

**문제 44-46번은 다음 대화를 참조하시오.** 호M 영W

> M: Hello, Ms. Watson. **(44) Have we managed to find a suitable candidate for the senior accountant position?**

---

> W: **(45) We have received four applications, but only two of them seem qualified for the position. I plan to call them this afternoon to arrange interviews.** Would you be able to interview them on Monday afternoon?
> M: I'm afraid not. I'll be in London for a two-day conference. **(46) I could meet them on Wednesday though.**
> W: Great. I'll schedule the interviews for Wednesday afternoon.
>
> ---
>
> M: 안녕하세요, Watson 씨. 수석 회계사 직에 적합한 후보자를 찾을 수 있었나요?
> W: 네 명의 지원서를 받았지만 그 직책에 자격이 있는 사람은 두 명뿐인 것 같아요. 오늘 오후에 그들에게 전화해서 면접 일정을 잡을 계획입니다. 월요일 오후에 그들을 면접하시겠어요?
> M: 안되겠는데요. 이틀간 열리는 회의 참차로 London에 가 있을 겁니다. 하지만 수요일에는 그들을 만나볼 수 있겠네요.
> W: 좋습니다. 수요일 오후로 면접 일정을 잡겠습니다.

**44.** 지원자들이 지원한 직책은 무엇인가?
(A) 인사부장
(B) 경비원
(C) 영업사원
(D) 회계사　　　　　　　　　　　　　　정답 (D)

**45.** 여자에 따르면 몇 명의 지원자들이 면접을 보게 되는가?
(A) 한 명
(B) 두 명
(C) 세 명
(D) 네 명　　　　　　　　　　　　　　정답 (B)

**46.** 남자는 수요일에 무엇을 할 것이라고 언급하는가?
(A) 호텔에 전화한다.
(B) 회의에 참석한다.
(C) 몇몇 지원자들과 이야기한다.
(D) 휴가를 떠난다.　　　　　　　　　　정답 (C)

---

**문제 47-49번은 다음 대화를 참조하시오.** 영W 호M

> W: Hi, Mr. Baker. **(48) I have a meeting with the chief financial officer on Friday to discuss the budget for next year. (47) Since you're the head of Marketing, (48) I would like you to present the marketing expenses from last year.**
> M: Um… let me check my calendar. **(48) I don't have anything scheduled on Friday.**
> W: Sounds good. Your data will be of a big help to gauge the precise size of the budget. I think we should be more careful in setting a budget due to the current recession. **(49) I'll send you the other agenda items discussed at the meeting by e-mail in half an hour.**
>
> ---
>
> W: 안녕하세요, Baker 씨. 제가 금요일에 내년 예산을 논의하기 위해 최고 재무 책임자와 회의를 할 예정이에요. 당신이 마케팅 부장이니까 그 회의에서 작년 마케팅 비용에 관해 발표해 주셨으면 합니다.
> M: 음… 제 일정을 한 번 볼게요. 금요일에 특별한 일정이 없네요.
> W: 잘됐네요. 당신의 자료는 정확한 규모의 예산을 가늠하는 데 큰 도움이 될 겁니다. 현재 불경기로 인해 예산을 책정하는 데 더욱 신중해야 할 필요가 있다고 생각해요. 30분 후에 그 회의에서 논의될 다른 안건들을 이메일로 보내 드릴게요.

**47.** 남자는 어느 부서에서 근무하는가?
(A) 회계부
(B) 인사부
(C) 마케팅부
(D) 시설 관리부　　　　　　　　　　　　정답 (C)

**48.** 남자가 "I don't have anything scheduled on Friday."라고 말할 때 의미하는 바는 무엇인가?
(A) 그는 휴가를 떠날 것이다.
(B) 그는 발표를 할 수 있다.
(C) 그는 회의를 취소하길 원한다.
(D) 그는 초대장을 받지 못했다.　　　　　정답 (B)

**49.** 여자는 30분 후에 무엇을 할 것인가?
(A) 설문지를 작성한다.
(B) 정보를 제공한다.
(C) 부서장과 이야기한다.
(D) 마케팅 자료를 발송한다.　　　　　정답 (B)

**문제 50~52번은 다음 대화를 참조하시오.** 미M 영W

M: Good morning, Ms. McGowan. I didn't see you at the seminar on international politics and trade yesterday. What happened to you?
W: Well, Mr. Powell, (50) **I missed the courtesy shuttle bus from the hotel yesterday morning, and I failed to catch the commuter train on time.** When I arrived here, the seminar was already finished. (51) **Were there many people there yesterday?**
M: I think it was very well attended. I would say about 40 people were there yesterday, and I guess that more than 70 people will attend your seminar.
W: (52) **Oh, then I definitely need to print some more handouts.** I should look for a copy shop around here.

--------------------------------------------------

M: 안녕하세요, McGowan 씨. 어제 국제 정치와 무역 세미나에서 못 뵀었네요. 무슨 일이 있었나요?
W: 음, Powell 씨, 어제 아침에 호텔에서 출발하는 셔틀버스를 놓쳐서 제 시간에 맞춰 통근 열차를 탈 수가 없었어요. 제가 도착했을 때 이미 세미나는 끝이 난 상태였어요. 어제 세미나에 사람들이 많이 참석했나요?
M: 아주 많이 온 것 같아요. 어제 한 40명 정도 참석했고, 당신의 세미나에는 70명 넘게 참석할 것으로 생각해요.
W: 아, 그럼 유인물을 더 프린트해야 할 것 같아요. 이 주변에 인쇄소가 있는지 찾아봐야겠어요.

**50.** 여자가 회의에 결석한 이유는 무엇인가?
(A) 그녀는 회의가 취소된 것으로 생각했다.
(B) 그녀는 제시간에 열차를 타지 못했다.
(C) 그녀는 독감에 걸렸다.
(D) 그녀는 엉뚱한 장소로 갔다.　　　　정답 (B)

**51.** 여자는 무엇을 알고 싶어 하는가?
(A) 등록 기간
(B) 일정 변경
(C) 참석자 수
(D) 인쇄소의 위치　　　　　　　　　정답 (C)

**52.** 여자는 이후에 무엇을 할 것인가?
(A) 보고서 작성을 마무리한다.
(B) 문서를 프린트한다.
(C) 회의실을 예약한다.
(D) 회사 행사를 주관한다.　　　　　정답 (B)

**문제 53~55번은 다음의 대화를 참조하시오.** 미M 미W

M: Excuse me. I'm here to meet Ms. Bush, the head of the Personnel Department.
W: Oh, (53) **you must be Charles Winston, our new accountant.** I'm Kelly Bush. Nice to meet you.
M: Nice to meet you, too. (53) **I'm thrilled to be joining Jin Enterprise North America.** I think it's going to make some big changes in my life.
W: That's good to hear. We're very glad to have you. Here's your employee badge.
M: Ah, Ms. Bush, (54) **I have to go to Room 401 to attend the new employee orientation.** (55) Um… could you show me to Room 401?
W: (55) **I'm about to start a meeting.** But Ms. Taylor is available to help you. Her desk is just around the corner.

--------------------------------------------------

M: 실례합니다. 저는 인사부장님인 Bush 씨를 만나러 왔습니다.
W: 아, 새로 입사한 회계사 Charles Winston 씨죠? 제가 Kelly Bush입니다. 만나서 반갑습니다.
M: 저도 반갑습니다. Jin Enterprise North America에 입사하게 되어 기쁩니다. 이 곳에서의 근무가 제 인생에 큰 변화를 가지고 올 것이라고 생각합니다.
W: 듣던 중 반가운 말이네요. 저희도 Winston 씨를 맞이하게 되어 기쁩니다. 여기 당신의 사원증이 있습니다.
M: 아, Bush 씨, 제가 신입 사원 오리엔테이션에 참석하기 위해 401호로 가야 합니다. 음… 401호까지 안내해주실 수 있을까요?
W: 제가 곧 회의를 시작해야 합니다. 하지만 Taylor 씨가 당신을 도와줄 겁니다. 모퉁이를 돌자 마자 바로 그녀의 책상이 있어요.

**53.** Winston 씨는 누구일 것 같은가?
(A) 광고 전문가
(B) 인사부장
(C) 은행 창구 직원
(D) 신입 직원　　　　　　　　　　정답 (D)

**54.** 남자는 무엇을 해야 한다고 언급하는가?
(A) 사원증을 받는다.
(B) 견본품을 보여준다.
(C) 서류 작업을 마무리한다.
(D) 오리엔테이션에 참석한다.　　　정답 (D)

**55.** 여자가 "I'm about to start a meeting."이라고 말할 때 암시하는 것은 무엇인가?
(A) 그녀는 몇몇 보고서를 읽어야 할 필요가 있다.
(B) 그녀는 회의 일정을 재조정할 수가 없다.
(C) 그녀는 문제를 해결할 시간적 여력이 없다.
(D) 그녀는 도움을 줄 수가 없다.　　　정답 (D)

W: Hello. Fashion Style. How can I help you?

M: Oh, hi. This is William Baker. (56) **I'm calling from Rebecca Apparel about the price of an advertising spot in your magazine.** I've heard of your reputation in the industry.

W: Thanks for the compliment, Mr. Baker. (57) **For the last two weeks, we have been offering a special promotion where ads cost 40% off the regular price. But it will end tomorrow.** We have three open advertising spots available on our magazine and its Web site.

M: Ad spots are filling up quickly. Well, my company is releasing a new line of clothing dedicated to young professionals next month, and we would like to have some new ads run for two months. (58) **Could you set two advertising spots aside for us?**

--------------------------------------------------

W: 안녕하세요. Fashion Style입니다. 어떻게 도와드릴까요?

M: 아, 안녕하세요. 저는 William Baker입니다. Rebecca Apparel에서 귀 잡지사의 광고 가격에 대해 문의하고자 연락 드립니다. 이 분야에서 명성이 자자하다고 들었습니다.

W: 칭찬 감사합니다, Baker 씨. 지난 2주간 저희가 정규 광고가의 40%를 할인해 드리는 특별 판촉행사를 진행해 왔습니다. 그런데 판촉 행사는 내일 종료합니다. 저희 잡지와 홈페이지에서 이용할 수 있는 광고란은 3개가 있네요.

M: 광고란이 빠르게 차는군요. 음, 저희 회사에서 다음달에 젊은 전문직 종사자들을 대상으로 하는 새로운 의류 상품을 출시할 예정이라서 두 달간 귀사에 광고를 게재하고 싶습니다. 광고란 2개를 확보해 주실 수 있나요?

**56.** 여자는 어떤 업종의 회사에서 근무하는가?
(A) 광고회사
(B) 백화점
(C) 부동산 중개업체
(D) 잡지사　　　　　　　　　　　　　　　　정답 (D)

**57.** 여자는 특별 행사에 대해서 무엇이라고 이야기하는가?
(A) 패션 전문가들에게만 해당된다.
(B) 곧 종료된다.
(C) 구독자 수를 엄청나게 증가시키는 데 도움을 줄 것이다.
(D) 새로운 홈페이지 디자인이 포함되어 있다.　　정답 (B)

**58.** 남자는 여자에게 무엇을 요청하는가?
(A) 선불로 지불한다.
(B) 새로운 마케팅 전략을 고안한다.
(C) 일부 공란을 확보한다.
(D) 새로운 잡지를 구독한다.　　　　　　　　정답 (C)

M: Hi, Kelly. I received a call from the regional manager for all Fat-Free Fitness World locations in California. (59) **He told me that we'll be closed for two months due to the scheduled renovations starting in March.**

W: Then we should notify our regular members of the upcoming temporary closure and ask them to use another location nearby during that time.

M: Right. And (60) **the regional manager also told me that members will get 60 percent off their monthly membership fee** while they have to work out at a different location.

W: I think that's a good offer. (61) **I'll send an e-mail to all our members after lunch.**

--------------------------------------------------

M: 안녕하세요, Kelly. 제가 California에 소재한 모든 Fat-Free Fitness World 지점들을 관리하는 지역 총괄 담당자에게 전화를 받았어요. 그가 3월로 예정된 보수공사로 인해 우리 지점이 두 달간 문을 닫아야 한다고 말하더군요.

W: 그러면 우리 정기 회원들에게 곧 있을 임시 폐쇄에 대해 알려주고 그 기간 동안 인근 다른 지점을 이용하도록 요청해야겠네요.

M: 네. 그리고 지역 총괄 담당자가 또한 회원들은 다른 지점에서 운동을 하는 동안 월 회비의 60% 할인 혜택을 받게 될 것이라고 말했어요.

W: 좋은 제안이라는 생각이에요. 점심식사 후에 제가 회원들에게 이메일을 보내도록 할게요.

**59.** 남자에 따르면 3월에 발생하는 일은 무엇인가?
(A) 새로운 지점장이 임명될 것이다.
(B) 기념식이 개최될 것이다.
(C) 특별 판촉행사가 시행될 것이다.
(D) 보수공사가 시작될 것이다.　　　　　　정답 (D)

**60.** 정기 회원들에게 제공되는 것은?
(A) 무료 라커
(B) 할인
(C) 건강 검진
(D) 무료 음료　　　　　　　　　　　　　　정답 (B)

**61.** 여자는 오후에 무엇을 할 것이라고 언급하는가?
(A) 늦은 점심식사를 한다.
(B) 새로운 정기 회원을 가르친다.
(C) 이메일로 공지를 발송한다.
(D) 다른 동료에게 전화한다.　　　　　　　정답 (C)

M: Did our employees submit their ideas during the staff meeting on Tuesday?

W: Yes, (62) **each of them completed a form and put it in the collection box near the Personnel Department.** I just finished reading one of them.

M: Could you tell me what the employee wrote on the form?

W: No problem. (63) **She wants a longer lunch break.** She wrote, "There is scarcely any time for lunch," and, mm... she always has to rush back to the office after having lunch in the shopping mall across the street.

M: Yeah, that's a good point. It can make mealtime more stressful and frustrating for every employee. (62) **As members of the Personnel Department,** we should really consider all their suggestions to make working here more convenient.

W: Absolutely. (64) **After we read all their suggestions, we should discuss which actions we will be able to take.**

--------------------------------------------------

M: 우리 직원들이 화요일 직원 회의 시간에 의견들을 제출했나요?

W: 네, 각자 양식을 작성하고 인사부 옆에 있는 수거함에 넣었어요. 안 그래도 지금 막 한 의견을 읽었어요.

M: 그 직원이 양식에 뭐라고 썼는지 알려줄 수 있어요?

W: 물론이에요. 그녀는 점심시간이 연장되길 원한데요. 그녀는 이렇게 썼는데요, "점심식사를 할 만한 시간이 되질 않아요." 그리고 음... 길 건너에 있는 쇼핑몰에서 점심식사를 마치고 늘 급하게 사무실로 복귀해야 한다

고 하네요.

M: 네, 좋은 지적이에요. 점심식사 시간이 부족하면 직원들에게 식사 시간 자체가 스트레스를 받고 불만스러운 시간이 될 겁니다. 우리가 인사부 직원으로서 직원들의 편의 향상을 위해서 정말 그들의 모든 의견을 다 고려해 봐야겠어요.

W: 맞습니다. 그들의 의견을 다 읽은 후에 어떤 개선 조치를 취할 수 있을지 논의해야겠어요.

| 이름 | 부서 | 의견 |
|---|---|---|
| Andrew Kim | 시설관리부 | 인체 공학적 의자 |
| Yejin Hwang | 회계부 | 적절한 회사 구내식당 |
| David Kiesling | 기술지원부 | 더 많은 휴가 |
| (63) Sally Murphy | 마케팅부 | 점심식사 시간 연장 |

**62.** 화자들은 어느 부서에서 일하겠는가?
(A) 회계부
(B) 시설관리부
(C) 인사부
(D) 기술지원부 　　　　　　　　　정답 (C)

**63.** 그래픽을 보시오. 화자들은 누구의 의견에 대해 이야기하는가?
(A) Andrew Kim의 의견
(B) Yejin Hwang의 의견
(C) David Kiesling의 의견
(D) Sally Murphy의 의견 　　　　　정답 (D)

**64.** 화자들은 이후에 무엇을 할 것인가?
(A) 더 많은 설문지를 프린트한다.
(B) 새로운 구내식당을 위한 예산을 논의한다.
(C) 다른 제안 내용들을 검토한다.
(D) 근무 일정을 약간 변경한다. 　　　정답 (C)

---

문제 65-67번은 다음 대화와 디자인을 참조하시오. 〔미W〕〔호M〕

W: Welcome to Charlie's Interiors. What can I do for you?

M: Hi. (65) **Last week, we talked on the phone about installing five sunshades on the windows in the accounting office I work at.**

W: Oh, yes, Mr. Porter. Did your boss see our sunshade sample? Did he like it?

M: Yes, he wants to order your sunshades, (66) **but he wants them to hang down a little longer than what you designed in the sample. Could you redesign them to be 270 centimeters long instead?**

W: Sure, no problem. I'll revise them and send it to you this afternoon. (67) **I think this will change the estimated cost slightly. Could you give me a minute to figure out the new one?**

- - - - - - - - - - - - - - - - - - - - - - - - - - - - - - - - - - - - - - - -

W: Charlie's Interiors에 오신 걸 환영합니다. 어떻게 도와드릴까요?

M: 안녕하세요. 지난주에 제가 근무하는 회계사무소 창문에 설치할 5개의 차양막에 대해 전화 통화를 한 바 있어요.

W: 아, 네, Porter 씨. 사장님께서 저희 차양막 견본품을 보셨나요? 좋아하시던가요?

M: 네, 귀사의 차양막을 주문하길 원하시는데, 본래 디자인하신 견본품보다 길이를 연장해서 차양막이 좀 아래까지 늘어지기를 바라시더라고요. 본래 길이 대신 270센티미터로 다시 디자인해주실 수 있을까요?

W: 물론이에요. 문제없습니다. 수정해서 오후에 보내 드리도록 하겠습니

---

다. 이 변경으로 인해 견적 비용이 약간 달라질 수 있어요. 새로운 견적가가 얼마나 되는지 계산을 하도록 잠시 시간을 주시겠어요?

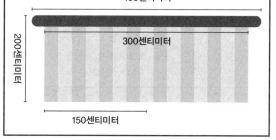

**차양막 견본품 디자인**

25200 Carlos Bee Blvd #310
510-575-4331
www.charilesinteriors.com

- 디자이너: Charlie McDonell
- 일시: 6월 3일

**65.** 남자는 어디에서 근무하는가?
(A) 인테리어 회사
(B) 주택 개조용품점
(C) 의류 매장
(D) 회계사무소 　　　　　　　　　정답 (D)

**66.** 그래픽을 보시오. 남자는 어떠한 치수를 변경하길 원하는가?
(A) 400센티미터
(B) 300센티미터
(C) 200센티미터
(D) 150센티미터 　　　　　　　　정답 (C)

**67.** 여자는 이후에 무엇을 할 것 같은가?
(A) 새로운 세율을 계산한다.
(B) 인테리어 공사를 시작한다.
(C) 새로운 사무기기를 설치한다.
(D) 새로운 비용을 산정한다. 　　　정답 (D)

---

문제 68-70번은 다음 대화와 회의실 일정표를 참조하시오. 〔영W〕〔미M〕

W: Mr. Simpson, one of your clients from the Tellink Corporation just called. (68) **She needs some urgent advice on her business loan application.** She asked if you were available tomorrow.

M: Ah, you must be talking about Ms. Hudson. I read her e-mail. She's one of the most important clients at our company. It would be great if I could use Meeting Room 401.

W: I checked the schedule, and it looks like the room is free at 10:00 A.M. Should I go ahead and reserve the room?

M: Um… It looks like my morning is fully booked tomorrow. (69) **I am available only in the afternoon.** Do you think it'd be possible to move a meeting so that I can use the room in the afternoon?

W: (69/70) **I will try to contact to see if I can move the event to 10:00 A.M.**

W: Simpson 씨, Tellink의 당신 고객 한 분이 방금 연락을 하셨어요. 그녀의 사업자 대출 신청건과 관련하여 급히 조언을 구할 것이 있다고 하시던데요. 당신이 내일 시간이 있는지 물어보셨어요.

M: 아, Hudson 씨 말씀이시군요. 저도 그 분이 보낸 이메일을 읽어봤어요. 그 분이 우리 회사에서 아주 중요한 고객들 중 한 분이에요. 제가 내일 401호 회의실을 사용할 수 있으면 좋겠는데요.

W: 제가 일정을 살펴봤는데 그 회의실은 오전 10시에 비어 있어요. 그러면 제가 그 회의실을 예약해 놓을까요?

M: 음… 내일 오전은 이미 일정이 가득 차 있어요. 오후만 가능한데요. 혹시 제가 오후에 그 방을 사용할 수 있도록 다른 회의 일정을 조정해주실 수 있나요?

W: 제가 연락을 해서 행사 시간을 오전 10시로 옮기는 것이 가능한지 여부를 확인해 볼게요.

## 회의실 일정

9월 9일 / 화요일

※ 일정 관리자: Jennifer Lee / 내선번호 1123

| 401호 회의실 | | |
|---|---|---|
| 오전 8:00 | 월간 회의(회계부) | Chris Froom |
| 오전 9:00 | 영업 발표 | William Parker |
| 오전 10:00 | | |
| 오전 11:00 | 교육 | Jia Choi |
| (70) 오전 2:00 | 마케팅 회의 | Thomas Baker |

**68.** 화자들은 어디에서 근무할 것 같은가?
(A) 회계사무소
(B) 비즈니스 컨설팅 회사
(C) 금융기관
(D) 아파트 관리사무소　　　　　정답 (C)

**69.** 그래픽을 보시오. 여자는 누구에게 연락해야 하는가?
(A) Chris Froom
(B) William Parker
(C) Jia Choi
(D) Thomas Baker　　　　　정답 (D)

**70.** 여자는 무엇을 할 것이라고 언급하는가?
(A) 회의를 취소한다.
(B) 동료에게 연락한다.
(C) 회사 행사를 준비한다.
(D) 고객에게 일정 변경에 관해 이야기한다.　　정답 (B)

## Part 4

**문제 71-73번은 다음 녹음 메시지를 참조하시오.** 〔M〕

Thank you for calling the Warren Public Library. The Warren Public Library will be closed at the end of August for six months for upgrades and remodeling. (71) **For your convenience, we are going to open a temporary library located at 911 Harder Street next Monday.** Please be advised that we will not provide computer rooms for library patrons due to the limited amount of space there. However, (73) **you can borrow library laptop computers as usual if you present your library card to any of our librarians.** (72) If you need to get step-by-step driving

or walking directions to the temporary library, please visit our Web site at www.warrenpl.org. Thank you.

Warren 공공 도서관에 전화해 주셔서 감사합니다. Warren 공공 도서관은 8월 말에 시설 개선 및 내부 개조 공사로 인해 6개월간 폐관합니다. 여러분의 편의를 위해 다음주 월요일에 Harder 가 911번지에 위치한 임시 도서관을 개장할 예정입니다. 공간이 협소한 관계로 도서관 이용자들에게 컴퓨터실을 일체 제공하지 못하게 된 점 주지해 주시기 바랍니다. 하지만 평소와 마찬가지로 도서관 카드를 사서에게 제시하면 도서관의 노트북 컴퓨터를 대여하여 사용하시는 것이 가능합니다. 임시 도서관까지 운전이나 도보를 통해 오는 상세한 길 안내를 원하시면 저희 홈페이지 www.warrenpl.org를 방문해 주시기 바랍니다. 감사합니다.

**71.** 메시지는 무엇에 관한 내용인가?
(A) 새로운 도서관 방침
(B) 개선된 컴퓨터실
(C) 특별 독서 프로그램
(D) 임시 장소　　　　　정답 (D)

**72.** 화자에 따르면 홈페이지를 통해 접할 수 있는 것은 무엇인가?
(A) 새로운 위치
(B) 이사 일정
(C) 상세한 길안내
(D) 할인 쿠폰　　　　　정답 (C)

**73.** 청자가 노트북 컴퓨터를 빌리려면 해야 하는 것은 무엇인가?
(A) 서류를 작성한다.
(B) 회원카드를 제시한다.
(C) 보증금을 지불한다.
(D) 무료 대여 서비스에 가입한다.　　정답 (B)

**문제 74-76번은 다음 안내문을 참조하시오.** 〔W〕

Good morning. (74) **It's my pleasure to speak to all of our company shareholders in person.** As the sales director, I realize that over the past few months, sales of our cheeses have dropped considerably. To address this problem, we conducted a customer survey and discovered that (75) **the new television advertising campaign for Yellow Farm Cheese is the main reason for the decrease in sales.** Customers stated that the current advertisement has a negative impact on their consuming desire. So we are filming new TV commercials now. We have invested a lot of funds in advertising to compete with our rivals. (76) **We aim to introduce our new TV commercials on March 10.** I'm sure we will have noticed a significant rise in sales by the next shareholders' meeting.

안녕하세요. 회사의 모든 주주님께 직접 이야기할 수 있게 되어 기쁩니다. 영업 이사로서 저는 지난 몇 달간 저희 치즈 판매량이 상당히 하락했음을 알게 되었습니다. 이 문제를 다루기 위해 고객 설문조사를 실시했으며, 그 결과 Yellow Farm Cheese의 새로운 TV 광고가 판매 하락의 주된 원인임을 발견했습니다. 고객들은 새로운 광고가 소비 욕구에 부정적인 영향을 미친다고 이야기했습니다. 그래서 현재 새로운 TV 광고들을 촬영 중에 있습니다. 경쟁사들과 경쟁을 하기 위해 광고에 많은 자금도 투입했습니다. 3월 10일에 새로운 TV 광고를 선보이는 것이 목표입니다. 다음 주주총회 때는 상당한 매출 향상을 보게 될 것이라고 확신합니다.

**74.** 청자는 누구인가?
(A) 영업 직원들
(B) 마케팅 전문가들
(C) 해외 투자자들
(D) 주주들 　　　　　　　　　　　정답 (D)

**75.** Yellow Farm Cheese의 매출이 하락한 이유는 무엇인가?
(A) 고객 서비스가 매우 부실하다.
(B) 광고가 효과적이지 못했다.
(C) 대부분의 제품이 매우 비싸다.
(D) 신제품들이 실패했다. 　　　　　　정답 (B)

**76.** 화자에 따르면 3월 10일에는 어떤 일이 발생하는가?
(A) 새로운 브랜드가 출시된다.
(B) 특별 판촉 행사가 시작된다.
(C) 더 많은 마케팅 전문 인력이 채용된다.
(D) 새로운 TV 광고들이 방송된다. 　　정답 (D)

**문제 77-79번은 다음 안내문을 참조하시오.** 미M

Attention, Wonderful Shoes customers! (77) **This weekend, we will be starting our yearly sale with fantastic bargains for all of our customers.** Adults shoes will be discounted up to 35%, and children's shoes will be discounted 50% off our already low prices. (78) **We hope you will take advantage of these great prices. The sale prices will only be available on Saturday and Sunday. You won't see prices this low again for another year.** (79) **If you have any questions about our amazing discounts, please ask our sales associates in the store.** Have a great day and thank you for shopping at Wonderful Shoes in San Diego.

------------------------------------------------

주목해 주십시오, Wonderful Shoes 고객님! 이번 주말에 고객님들을 대상으로 엄청난 혜택의 연례 할인 행사를 시행합니다. 이미 저렴한 가격임에도 성인용 신발은 최대 35%, 그리고 아동용 신발은 50% 할인됩니다. 여러분께서 이 엄청난 할인으로 가격 혜택을 누리시길 바랍니다. 이 판매가는 오직 토요일과 일요일 주말에만 제공됩니다. 앞으로 1년 동안은 이만큼 저렴한 가격은 보시지 못할 겁니다. 만약 저희의 놀라운 할인 혜택에 관해 질문이 있으시면 매장에 있는 판매 직원들에게 문의해 주십시오. 좋은 하루 보내시고 San Diego의 Wonderful Shoes에서 쇼핑해 주셔서 감사합니다.

**77.** 화자가 주로 논의하는 것은 무엇인가?
(A) 고품질 제품
(B) 급여 인상
(C) 새로운 판매 전략
(D) 연례 할인 　　　　　　　　　　정답 (D)

**78.** 화자가 "You won't see prices this low again for another year."라고 말하는 이유는 무엇인가?
(A) 매장의 할인 프로그램을 종료하는 것을 고려하고 있다.
(B) 의료 보험 혜택을 강조하고자 한다.
(C) 청자들이 할인 가격에 신발을 사길 권장하고 있다.
(D) 좋은 가격에 구매할 수 있는 좋은 기회를 놓치는 것을 유감스럽게 생각한다. 　　　　　　　정답 (C)

**79.** 화자에 따르면 질문에 답할 수 있는 사람은 누구인가?
(A) 계산원

(B) 점장
(C) 점원
(D) 고객 상담원 　　　　　　　　　정답 (C)

**문제 80-82번은 다음 전화 메시지를 참조하시오.** 미W

Good afternoon. My name is Tiffany Houston. I'm the head manager of Sunny Cleaning Services, which specializes in the cleaning and maintenance of commercial spaces. (80/81) **I am calling in case you are interested in using our cleaning services for your new restaurant.** We have extensive experience cleaning all sorts of businesses, including hotels, hospitals, and shopping centers, and our services range from carpet cleaning to landscaping. (82) **We have twelve branches throughout the country,** so we provide quality services to customers everywhere. For more information, please give us a call at 903-924-7321. Thank you.

------------------------------------------------

안녕하세요. 제 이름은 Tiffany Houston입니다. 상업 공간의 청결과 유지 관리 업무를 전문으로 하는 Sunny Cleaning Services의 책임자입니다. 귀하의 새로운 식당이 저희 서비스를 이용하는 데 관심이 있으실 것으로 생각해 연락 드립니다. 저희는 호텔이나 병원, 쇼핑센터 등을 포함하는 모든 업체 청소에 풍부한 경험이 있으며 저희 서비스는 카펫 청소에서부터 조경까지 범위가 다양합니다. 저희는 전국에 12개의 지점을 보유하고 있어서 어느 곳에서나 고품질의 서비스를 제공할 수 있습니다. 더 많은 관련 정보를 원하시면 903-924-7321로 연락 주십시오. 감사합니다.

**80.** 메시지의 목적은 무엇인가?
(A) 업체에 대해 문의하기 위해서
(B) 예약하기 위해서
(C) 서비스를 홍보하기 위해서
(D) 정보를 찾기 위해서 　　　　　　정답 (C)

**81.** 청자는 어디에서 근무할 것 같은가?
(A) 식당
(B) 쇼핑몰
(C) 인테리어 디자인 업체
(D) 청소 회사 　　　　　　　　　　정답 (A)

**82.** 화자가 자신의 업체에 대해 언급한 것은 무엇인가?
(A) 최근에 설립된 회사이다.
(B) 특별 할인가를 제공한다.
(C) 다른 곳으로 이전한다.
(D) 전국적으로 여러 지점을 보유하고 있다. 　정답 (D)

**문제 83-85번은 다음 뉴스를 참조하시오.** 미W

Good afternoon and welcome to the Channel 7 lunchtime news. I'm Nancy Stevens. (83) **Our top story this lunchtime is this morning's announcement about the city budget for the coming year.** As expected, less money will be available for city museums and community groups. However, extra funding will be allocated to transportation in an attempt to solve the city's traffic problems. (84) **Mayor Katherine Carter** said the budget was tough but fair. She told members of the city council that spending cuts were necessary in view of the current financial situation. Community groups are planning some protests against the cuts, and (85) **museums said they will consider raising admission prices at the end of this month.**

---

안녕하십니까, Channel 7 점심 뉴스에 오신 것을 환영합니다. 저는 Nancy Stevens입니다. 오늘 점심 뉴스의 첫 번째 소식은 오늘 아침에 있었던 내년 시 예산 발표입니다. 예상과 같이 시립 박물관과 지역 단체에 대한 예산이 삭감되어 할당될 것이란 소식입니다. 그러나 이로 인한 여분의 예산은 시의 교통 문제를 해결하기 위한 추가 기금으로 교통 부문에 할당될 것이라고 합니다. Katherine Carter 시장이 이 예산안을 결정짓는 것이 어렵긴 했으나 공정했다고 말했습니다. 시장은 현재의 재정 상황을 감안할 때 지출 삭감이 필요했음을 시 의회에 설명했습니다. 지역 단체들은 이번 예산 삭감에 대한 항의를 계획 중이며, 박물관들은 이달 말에 입장료 인상을 고려 중이라고 밝혔습니다.

**83.** 뉴스 보도의 주제는 무엇인가?
(A) 시 예산
(B) 새로운 전시회
(C) 교통 문제
(D) 소폭의 물가 인상 　　　　　　　정답 (A)

**84.** Katherine Carter는 누구인가?
(A) 뉴스 앵커
(B) 트럭 기사
(C) 예술가
(D) 지방 정부 공무원 　　　　　　　정답 (D)

**85.** 화자에 따르면 이달 말에 어떤 일이 일어날 수 있다고 하는가?
(A) 일부 공사 계획이 취소될 수 있다.
(B) 박물관 입장료가 인상될 수 있다.
(C) 일부 지역 단체들이 지원을 받을 수 있다.
(D) 자전거 도로의 수가 감소할 수 있다. 　　정답 (B)

**문제 86-88번은 다음 발표문을 참조하시오.** 영W

---

Are you considering a change in careers? Deciding on a change of career or job is never easy. Trust me. I know. I spent so many hours writing my résumé and filling out applications, but I didn't hear from any employers. Maybe for many of us, submitting a job application and getting no response is quite common, huh? (86/87) **My new book, *Pursuit of Your Dream Job*, will help you not to make mistakes in the job-hunting process.** (87) **It also explains how to find the right employer and to prepare for job interviews. Don't waste time filling out a bunch of applications. Plus, I worked as the personnel director for several multinational companies.** As a personnel director, I took a lot of job applications everyday. So I'm pretty sure I know how to make your résumé look more professional and convincing.  After my presentation, (88) **please visit my Web site and sign up for a free 30-minute consultation.**

---

이직을 고려 중이신가요? 이직은 결코 쉽지가 않습니다. 제 말을 믿으세요. 저도 압니다. 저도 이력서를 쓰고 지원서를 작성하는 데 엄청나게 많은 시간을 할애했지만, 고용주로부터 소식을 듣지 못했습니다. 아마도 우리 중에 많은 이들에게 이력서를 제출했지만 회사로부터 소식을 듣지 못한 일은 비일비재할 겁니다. 그렇죠? 제 신간 Pursuit of Your Dream Job이 구직 과정에서 실수를 하지 않도록 도움을 줄 겁니다. 또한 여러분에게 딱 맞는 고용주를 찾는 방법과 면접을 어떻게 준비해야 하는지에 대해 설명해 줍니다. 많은 지원서를 작성하느라 시간을 낭비하지 마세요. 그리고 저

---

는 몇몇 다국적 기업에서 인사 담당자로도 근무했습니다. 인사 담당자로서 매일 많은 지원서를 받았습니다. 그래서 제가 여러분의 이력서를 더 전문적이고 설득력 있어 보이게 만들 수 있다고 확신합니다. 제 발표가 끝난 후엔 제 홈페이지를 방문하셔서 30분간의 무료 상담에 등록하세요.

**86.** 화자는 최근에 무엇을 했는가?
(A) 책을 저술했다.
(B) 창업을 했다.
(C) 이직했다.
(D) 많은 이력서를 검토했다. 　　　　정답 (A)

**87.** 그녀가 "Don't waste time filling out a bunch of applications."라고 말할 때 암시하는 바는 무엇인가?
(A) 그녀는 지금 무직인 상태이다.
(B) 그녀는 새로운 일을 시작할 준비가 되어 있다.
(C) 그녀는 믿을 만한 조언을 제시한다.
(D) 그녀는 중소 기업에서의 경험이 없다. 　정답 (C)

**88.** 화자에 따르면 청자들이 홈페이지에 방문하면 무엇을 받을 수 있는가?
(A) 사인이 된 책
(B) 홍보용 상품
(C) 무료 회원
(D) 무료 상담 　　　　　　　　　정답 (D)

**문제 89-91번은 다음 워크숍 내용을 참조하시오.** 호M

---

Greetings, everyone. As you know, (89) **we're here to learn more to enhance our public-speaking skills, which are vital skills for corporate leaders and management.** (90) **Do you prepare for days for important work presentations but still fail to make the impression you want to?** Well, many people have that problem. In fact, the majority of people rank public speaking as their greatest fear. But have no fear: Good public speaking is not just a talent. It's a skill within us all and can be harnessed in a way that communicates the best you and your company have to offer. Today, I'll teach you the simplest ways to project a confident demeanor whenever you speak in front of other people. (91) **I'd like everyone to find a partner now.** We're going to start with a quick exercise.

---

안녕하세요, 여러분. 아시다시피, 우리는 대중 연설 기술을 향상하기 위해 더 많은 것을 배우고자 여기에 있습니다. 대중 연설 기술은 기업 리더와 경영진에게 중요한 기술입니다. 중요한 업무 발표를 위해 며칠 동안 준비를 하지만 여전히 원하는 인상을 주지 못하십니까? 음, 많은 사람들이 그 문제를 안고 있습니다. 사실 대다수의 사람들이 대중 연설을 가장 큰 두려움으로 생각합니다. 그러나 두려움을 없애야 합니다. 좋은 대중 연설은 단순히 재능이 아닙니다. 그것은 우리 모두에게 내재된 기술이며 여러분과 여러분의 회사가 제공해야 할 최선의 것을 전달하는 방식으로 활용될 수 있습니다. 오늘은 다른 사람들 앞에서 연설을 할 때마다 자신감 있는 태도를 보여줄 수 있는 가장 간단한 방법을 가르쳐 드리겠습니다. 지금 모든 분이 같이 연습할 파트너를 찾으셨으면 합니다. 빠른 연습과 함께 이 워크숍을 시작하도록 하겠습니다.

**89.** 워크숍의 주제는 무엇인가?
(A) 팀 소통의 강화
(B) 상업적 홈페이지의 제작
(C) 대중 연설 기술의 발전
(D) 새로운 시장 경향의 학습 　　　　정답 (C)

**90.** 화자가 "Many people have that problem."이라고 이야기한 이유는 무엇인가?

(A) 노력 부족을 질타하기 위해서
(B) 해결책을 제시하기 위해서
(C) 회사에 대한 불만을 토로하기 위해서
(D) 참석자들을 안심시키기 위해서 　　　　　정답 (D)

**91.** 화자가 청자들에게 요청하는 것은 무엇인가?

(A) 자료를 검토한다.
(B) 설문지를 작성한다.
(C) 과정에 등록한다.
(D) 같이 할 사람을 찾는다. 　　　　　　　정답 (D)

**문제 92-94번은 다음 담화를 참조하시오.** 호M

Good afternoon. Next month, an inspector from the city will visit to assess the safety of this workplace after the recent renovations. Each workstation will be inspected separately, and the equipment cannot be in use while being inspected. (92/93) **While your station is being looked at, you will be moved temporarily to a support role on another production line.** Your foremen will give you more details and any necessary training in the coming weeks. (92/93) **Care will be taken to ensure that you will be moved to a production line for which you have the necessary skills.** (94) **Your foremen will also give you an inspection schedule at your station meetings this afternoon. Make sure you review it carefully** and ask them any questions you may have.

--------------------------------

안녕하세요. 다음달에 시에서 검사관이 방문하여 최근 보수공사가 끝난 우리 작업장의 안전도에 대한 평가를 할 것입니다. 각각의 작업대는 별도로 검사를 받을 것이며, 검사를 받는 동안에는 장비를 사용할 수 없습니다. 여러분의 작업대가 검사를 받는 동안 여러분은 임시로 다른 생산 라인을 지원하는 자리로 옮겨가게 될 것입니다. 생산 현장 책임자들이 향후 몇 주간 세부 사항과 필요한 훈련을 제공할 것입니다. 여러분이 지니고 있는 필요한 기술에 적합한 생산 라인으로 옮겨갈 수 있도록 세심한 배려가 이루어질 것입니다. 생산 현장 책임자들이 오늘 오후에 있을 작업장 회의에서 각 작업대의 검사 일정을 알려줄 것입니다. 그 일정을 필히 주의깊게 검토하고 궁금한 점이 있으면 현장 책임자들에게 질문하도록 하십시오.

**92.** 화자는 어디에서 근무할 것 같은가?

(A) 백화점
(B) 기차역
(C) 검사국
(D) 공장 　　　　　　　　　　　　　　정답 (D)

**93.** 직원들은 어떤 변화를 겪게 되는가?

(A) 새로운 근무 일정
(B) 건물 보수 공사
(C) 다른 생산 라인 근무
(D) 개정된 복리후생 제도 　　　　　　　정답 (C)

**94.** 화자에 따르면 청자들은 무엇을 검토해야 하는가?

(A) 취급 설명서
(B) 검사 일정
(C) 교육 안내책자
(D) 복리후생 제도에 대한 설명 　　　　　정답 (B)

**문제 95-97번은 다음 전화 메시지와 평면도를 참조하시오.** 미M

Hello, Marsha. It's Michael. I'm sorry to bother you. (95) **When we spoke earlier this morning, I requested the travel expense report released by the Sales Department last week,** but (96) **I just remembered that I'm taking a few days off. I won't have a chance to review the report until I return.** Please just put the report on top of the stack of papers on my desk by the time I return on Thursday. In addition, my new office is the corner on the third floor. (97) **To get here, exit the elevator and start heading toward the kitchen. My office is on the left directly across from the meeting room.**

--------------------------------

안녕하세요, Marsha. Michael이에요. 번거롭게 해서 미안해요. 우리가 앞서 오늘 아침에 이야기했을 때 제가 지난주에 영업부가 작성한 출장 경비 보고서를 요청했는데요, 제가 곧 휴가라는 점이 막 기억이 났어요. 제가 복귀를 해야 보고서를 검토할 시간이 있을 겁니다. 그 보고서는 제가 목요일에 복귀할 때까지 제 책상 위에 있는 서류 위에 그냥 놔두세요. 그리고 제 새로운 사무실은 3층 모퉁이에 위치하고 있어요. 이 곳에 오시려면 엘리베이터를 나와서 탕비실 쪽으로 향하셔야 합니다. 제 사무실은 회의실 바로 맞은편으로 좌측에 있습니다.

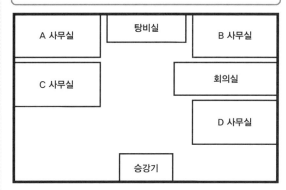

**95.** 화자는 어떤 종류의 서류를 요청하는가?

(A) 비용 보고서
(B) 실적 평가서
(C) 분기별 매출 보고서
(D) 재무제표 　　　　　　　　　　　　정답 (A)

**96.** 화자가 마감시한을 재조정한 이유는 무엇인가?

(A) 그는 서류를 검토할 시간이 없다.
(B) 그는 프로젝트를 진행할 수 없다.
(C) 그는 다음주에 출장을 간다.
(D) 그는 일을 마무리하려면 더 많은 시간이 필요하다. 　정답 (A)

**97.** 그래픽을 보시오. 화자에게 속한 사무실은 어느 것인가?

(A) A 사무실
(B) B 사무실
(C) C 사무실
(D) D 사무실 　　　　　　　　　　　정답 (C)

**문제 98-100번은 다음 담화와 일정표를 참조하시오.** 미W

Hello, everyone. Welcome to the 15th regular workshop here at the Genesis Valley Resort. On behalf of the company, I'd like to express my deep gratitude for the time we will share here. (98)

This resort is one of the best vacation resorts in California. You are more than welcome to make use of all the facilities here over the course of the weekend. You will find details of the workshops on the board in the lobby. (100) Unfortunately, Gina Davidson is unable to make her speech due to unexpected personal reasons. She will be replaced by John Scofield. (99) Please let me remind you that a reception will take place at 7 P.M. in Green Hall. Thank you. Enjoy the workshop.

--------------------------------

안녕하세요, 여러분. Genesis Valley Resort에서 개최되는 제 15회 정기 워크숍에 오신 걸 환영합니다. 회사를 대표하여 우리가 함께 할 수 있는 시간을 내주신 점에 깊은 감사의 말씀을 전해드리고 싶습니다. 이 리조트는 California 주에서 최고 휴양지 중 한 곳이라고 할 수 있습니다. 여러분은 주말 동안 이 곳의 모든 시설을 얼마든지 사용하실 수 있습니다. 로비에 있는 게시판에서 워크숍에 대한 세부사항을 확인하실 수 있습니다. 안타깝게도 Gina Davidson 씨가 예기치 못한 개인 사정으로 인해 연설을 할 수 없게 되었습니다. 그녀 대신에 John Scofield 씨가 연설을 하게 될 것입니다. 그리고 저녁 7시에 Green Hall에서 환영 만찬이 예정되어 있다는 점을 상기시켜 드립니다. 감사합니다. 즐거운 워크숍이 되시길 바랍니다.

--------------------------------

## Mona 반려동물 가구

### 여름 워크숍 일정
### 7월 17일 / Venice Resort California

| 발표자 | 장소 | 시간 |
|---|---|---|
| Cindy Nelson | Diamond Room | 10:00 - 11:00 |
| (97) Gina Davidson | Crystal Room | 11:00 - 12:00 |
| Oliver Tylor | Ocean Room | 1:00 - 2:30 |
| Andrew Kim | Island Room | 3:00 - 4:30 |

**98.** 화자가 리조트에 관해 언급하는 것은 무엇인가?
(A) 건강식을 무료로 제공한다.
(B) 골프 코스로 유명하다.
(C) 멋진 풍경을 제공한다.
(D) 최고의 휴양지들 중 한 곳으로 여겨진다.  정답 (D)

**99.** 화자가 청자들에게 상기시키는 것은 무엇인가?
(A) 회사 야유회
(B) 환영 만찬
(C) 고객 회의
(D) 기념식  정답 (B)

**100.** 그래픽을 보시오. John Scofield 씨는 언제 발표를 시작하는가?
(A) 오전 10시
(B) 오전 11시
(C) 오후 1시
(D) 오후 3시  정답 (B)

**101.** 무역 세미나의 모든 참석자들은 노트북 컴퓨터와 사원증을 구비하도록 요청 받는다.  정답 (B)

**102.** 우리 사무실의 모든 직원은 매우 바쁜 상황에서 독자적으로 일하는 것이 가능해야만 한다.  정답 (C)

**103.** 그녀의 문화적 배경이 나와는 다르기 때문에 그녀는 그 문제를 전적으로 독특한 관점에서 바라볼 수 있다.  정답 (D)

**104.** 우리 자동차들의 외장과 내장은 국내외 고객들의 마음을 끌기 위해 완전히 새롭게 재설계되었다.  정답 (C)

**105.** 할인 쿠폰은 제품을 구매할 때 금전적 할인이나 환급을 받을 수 있는 일종의 표나 문서와 같은 것이다.  정답 (B)

**106.** 그 도서관에는 매우 다양한 소설과 비소설 도서들이 구비되어 있으며 정규 운영시간 동안 대중이 이용할 수 있다.  정답 (D)

**107.** SK Penny 사는 현재 장기 근속 직원들에게 2년마다 최대 14일간의 휴가를 제공하고 있다.  정답 (C)

**108.** 지역의 법과 대학원에서 학위를 취득하자마자, Kennedy 씨는 법 집행기관에서 근무하기 시작했다.  정답 (C)

**109.** 새로운 데스크톱 컴퓨터들은 최신 문서 작성 소프트웨어와 고해상도의 모니터들이 장착되어 있다.  정답 (B)

**110.** 인사부장의 결근과 무관하게 직원들의 복리후생을 논의하기 위한 직원 회의는 예정대로 진행될 것이다.  정답 (C)

**111.** 저희 신제품에 관심 있으시면 이메일, 전화, 혹은 팩스기를 통해 저희에게 연락하시면 추가 정보를 보내 드리도록 하겠습니다.  정답 (A)

**112.** 가격을 낮추고자 우리 회사는 생산 과정을 간소화하고 포장의 부피와 무게를 최소화했다.  정답 (D)

**113.** 최근에 구입한 3층의 팩스기는 2층에 있는 오래된 팩스기보다 훨씬 더 조용하게 작동한다.  정답 (C)

**114.** 그 매매 계약서에는 일부 사진 파일들이 상업적인 목적으로 사용이 가능하다는 점이 분명하게 명시되어 있다.  정답 (C)

**115.** 수신자 요금 부담 전화번호를 잠재 고객들에게 제공함으로써 회사는 더 많은 주문을 받고 제품과 관련된 정보를 얻기 위한 전화를 더 많이 받을 것이다.  정답 (A)

**116.** 금융 기관들은 금융 거래에 관한 모든 정보를 업로드할 수 있는 안전한 저장 공간이 필요하다.  정답 (C)

**117.** 많은 독신자들은 기혼자들이 누릴 수 있는 일부 세금 혜택에 대한 수령 자격이 되지 않는다.  정답 (B)

**118.** Cal State Union 은행은 오후 5시에 영업을 종료하지만 계좌에서 출금하는 업무는 하루 종일 가능하다.  정답 (B)

**119.** 우리 영업부장은 다음 분기 매출액이 두 배로 증가할 것으로 예상하고 있다.  정답 (D)

**120.** Yellow Chip 여행사는 내년에 무료 호텔 숙박이 포함된 New York 패키지 여행 상품을 제공할 것이다. 　　　정답 (C)

**121.** 만약 이사회에 의해 승인이 된다면 General Steel 사의 Detroit 이전은 아마도 10월에 이루어질 것이다. 　　　정답 (C)

**122.** 제품의 품질과 작업장의 안전이 수익을 얻겠다는 명목으로 타협되어서는 안 된다. 　　　정답 (C)

**123.** 주민들에게서 불만이 제기될 가능성에 대한 우려에도 불구하고 시 정부는 주택 개발업체와 새로운 개발 계약을 체결할 것이다. 　　　정답 (D)

**124.** Chicago에서 미술품 경매에 참석한 많은 사람들이 유명한 미술품을 구매하는 것에 큰 관심을 보였다. 　　　정답 (B)

**125.** 대규모 가스 누출로 인해 Mackenzie 해협의 해저를 지나는 가스 파이프라인은 어제 폐쇄되었다. 　　　정답 (A)

**126.** Toronto 중심에 위치하고 있는 Royal Ontario 박물관은 모든 거주민과 방문객들이 Ontario 주의 역사를 쉽게 접할 수 있도록 한다. 　　　정답 (C)

**127.** 지난주에 몇몇 스쿠버 다이버들이 보호 장비도 없이 입수를 했는데, 이는 굉장히 위험하고 치명적일 수 있다. 　　　정답 (D)

**128.** 경제학자들과 금융 시장 분석가들은 적절한 해결책을 찾을 수 있도록 세계 금융 위기의 정확한 원인을 설명해야 할 필요가 있다. 　　　정답 (C)

**129.** 지난 수십년간 천문학 연구는 달의 중력이 지구 중력의 대략 20%임을 보여주고 있다. 　　　정답 (C)

**130.** 이런 종류의 난방기는 폐쇄된 공간에서 빠른 난방을 위한 좋은 선택이지만 이 제품은 지켜보는 사람이 없이 방치되면 안된다. 　　　정답 (C)

## Part 6

**문제 131-134번은 다음 편지를 참조하시오.**

> 전근 요청서
>
> 인사부장님께,
>
> 저는 정중히 Ohio 주 Columbus 지사로의 전근 가능성에 대해 문의하고자 합니다. 제 배우자가 다음 달부터 그 곳에서 근무하는 취업 제의를 받았습니다.
>
> 저는 지난 6년 동안 이곳에서 처음에는 대리로 근무하기 시작하여, 현재에는 부장으로 승진하며 즐겁게 근무해왔습니다. 저는 제가 회계 부서에서 중요한 직원이었음을 느끼고 있으며 이후에도 회사와의 유대 관계를 지속적으로 유지하고 싶습니다.
>
> 저는 이 곳에 몇 주간 머무르며 제가 떠나게 될 직책의 후임자에게 업무 인수인계를 하도록 도움을 주는 것이 가능합니다. 제 직책에 적합한 후보자가 되는 몇몇 직원들을 알고 있으며 그 부분에 대해 기꺼이 인사부장님께 제 의견을 공유해드릴 것입니다.
>
> Syracuse에서 쌓은 제 경험은 무척이나 보람이 있었으며, 이후에도 회사에서 제 경력을 지속적으로 이어갈 수 있도록 배려해 주신다면 감사하겠습니다. 제 전근 요청에 대해 인사부장님께서 사려 깊은 배려를 해주신다면 정말 감사하겠습니다.
>
> Michael Moore

**131.** 　　　정답 (B)

**132.** 　　　정답 (C)

**133.** 　　　정답 (D)

**134.** (A) 귀하와 곧 함께 일할 수 있는 기회를 고대하고 있습니다.
(B) 제 전근 요청에 대해 인사부장님께서 사려 깊은 배려를 해주신다면 정말 감사하겠습니다.
(C) 저희는 신입 사원들을 채용하는 데 있어서 비용의 효율성을 극대화시키고자 예산을 삭감하기로 결정했습니다.
(D) 회계부장 직에서 사임하고자 함을 알려드리고 싶습니다. 　　　정답 (B)

**문제 135-138번은 다음 편지를 참조하시오.**

> BK Computer World
> 1123 Orchard Ave
> Fremont, CA 94513
>
> Pinkman 씨께,
>
> 귀하의 노트북 컴퓨터에 관해 겪고 계신 문제점을 설명하는 편지를 보내주신 점에 감사드립니다. 귀하도 그러시겠지만 저희도 전자 기기는 내구성이 좋도록 만들어져야 한다고 생각합니다. 노트북 컴퓨터는 상당히 신뢰할 수 있는 전자 기기이지만 종종 여러 가지 이유로 제 기능을 발휘하지 못하는 경우도 발생합니다.
>
> 30일의 반품 기한이 지나서 노트북 컴퓨터를 교환해 드리지는 못합니다만, 귀하의 노트북 컴퓨터를 수리하실 수 있도록 관련 정보를 제공해드릴 수 있습니다. (510) 603-0110으로 BK 기술 지원부에 전화하셔야 합니다. 그쪽 직원이 수리를 받으실 수 있도록 귀하의 노트북 컴퓨터를 어떻게 포장해서 발송해야 하는지 알려드릴 것입니다.
>
> 다른 대안으로는, 새로운 노트북 컴퓨터를 저희에게서 구매하시는 방법도 있습니다. 현재 몇몇 Andromeda 제품을 보유하고 있으며 최근에 가격을 299달러로 인하했습니다. 또한 신제품인 G909와 G911에 대한 재고 또한 많습니다.
>
> 어떠한 방법을 선택하시건 제품 시연을 원하시면 언제든 저희를 방문해 주십시오. 고객님께 서비스를 제공하게 되어 기쁘게 생각하며 향후에도 지속적으로 서비스를 제공할 수 있길 바랍니다.
>
> Stacy McKintire
> 고객 서비스 부장
> BK Computer World

**135.** 　　　정답 (C)

**136.** 　　　정답 (D)

**137.** 　　　정답 (D)

**138.** (A) 저희의 부주의함에 대해 사과드립니다.
(B) 고객님께 서비스를 제공하게 되어 기쁘게 생각하며 향후에도 지속적으로 서비스를 제공할 수 있길 바랍니다.
(C) 귀하가 저희와 함께 할 것을 강력하게 고려해 주시길 바라고 있습니다.
(D) 저희 모두를 대표하여 제가 진심으로 감사함을 전하고 싶습니다. 　　　정답 (B)

Aifa 아파트 단지
주민 서비스 사무실
Palm Tree Avenue, Miami, FL 32003

Jordan 씨께,

귀하의 아파트 세입자 보험의 현재 상황을 전달해 드리기 위해 편지를 씁니다. 3월 31일자로 귀하의 보험이 만료되었습니다. 새 세입자 보험 신청서를 5월 1일 전에 작성하셔야 합니다. 임차한 부동산에 대해 완전한 보험 보장을 하지 못할 경우 Aifa 아파트 단지 310호의 임대차 계약이 종료될 것입니다.

세입자 보험의 주된 목적은 바로 세입자의 안심에 있습니다. 이 보험은 귀하와 귀하의 가족을 화재, 수해, 풍해로부터 보호해 드릴 것이며, 또한 절도 발생 시 초래된 손실을 배상해 드릴 것입니다. 보험이 이러한 일이 발생하는 것 자체를 막을 순 없습니다. 하지만 예상치 못한 일이 발생했을 경우 보험으로 처리가 가능하다면, 귀하가 모든 피해액을 부담하지 않으셔도 될 것입니다. 보험 가입 증빙 서류를 5월 1일 마감기한 전에 주민 서비스 사무실로 가져와 주시기 바랍니다.

Charles Parker
관리소장
주민 서비스 사무소

**139.** 정답 (D)

**140.** 정답 (C)

**141.** (A) 세입자 보험의 주된 목적은 바로 세입자의 안심에 있습니다.
(B) 이는 뭔가 잘못되는 경우 귀하의 자산을 재정적인 위험으로부터 보호해 줄 것입니다.
(C) 보험이 없다면 귀하는 값비싼 수술비와 치료비를 지불해야만 합니다.
(D) 저희는 현재 주민들의 필요사항을 충족시키고자 최고 수준의 보안을 제공합니다. 정답 (A)

**142.** 정답 (D)

문제 143~146번은 다음 공지를 참조하시오.

Spokane 시
공시

조례 공시 번호 1123

다음달 Spokane 시는 소방서를 위한 대규모의 가두 행진을 주최할 것입니다. 이 행진은 타인을 구하기 위해 비극적으로 목숨을 잃은 영웅들을 기릴 것입니다. 이 용감한 분들은 매우 등한시되어 왔으므로 그들을 우리 기억의 중심으로 가져와서 우리가 매일 그들에게 보호받고 있음을 상기하고자 합니다.

그들의 희생은 헛되지 않았습니다. 지역 소방 공동체가 주택 화재 및 산불로 갇힌 사람들의 생명을 구하기 위해 항상 헌신할 것이기 때문입니다.

주민 여러분은 경의를 표해 주시기 바랍니다. 만약 행사에 참여가 불가하다면 헌화를 통해 우리 영웅들의 가족에게 우리가 여전히 그 분들을 기억하고 있음을 알려주시기 바랍니다.

**143.** (A) 몇몇 사람들에게는 생명을 구한다는 것이 단순히 직무의 일부일 수도 있습니다.
(B) 다른 지역에서도 소방 안전과 관련된 다양한 행사들이 개최될 예정입니다.

(C) 우리는 필히 소방관들의 처우와 근무 환경을 개선해야 합니다.
(D) 이 행진은 타인을 구하기 위해 비극적으로 목숨을 잃은 영웅들을 기릴 것입니다. 정답 (D)

**144.** 정답 (B)

**145.** 정답 (A)

**146.** 정답 (D)

## Part 7

문제 147~148번은 다음 편지를 참조하시오.

5월 10일

(147) Bob Miller
Jamestown High School Choir
8923 Charleston Blvd
Jamestown, Delaware 67830

Miller 씨께,

(147) 귀하의 합창단이 다음달 Jamestown 퍼레이드에서 공연하도록 선발되었음을 알려드리게 되어 기쁩니다. 퍼레이드는 6월 15일 오전 11시에 시작됩니다. 단원 모두 늦어도 오전 10시까지 Fulton Center 주차장에 모이도록 해 주십시오. 퍼레이드에 참여하는 모든 단체들이 정렬해야 하므로, 모든 공연자들이 늦어도 퍼레이드 시작 1시간 전에 출석하는 것이 중요합니다. (148) 퍼레이드는 Jamestown Botanical Gardens에서 출발하여 Moore Street 전 구간을 행진할 것입니다. 모든 공연자들이 Fulton Center 주차장으로 돌아올 수 있도록 셔틀버스가 제공될 것입니다. 셔틀버스는 Jamestown 시청 뒤에 위치해 있을 것입니다.

감사합니다.

Bonnie Cutler
행사 진행자

**147.** Miller 씨는 누구일 것 같은가?
(A) 퍼레이드 조직자
(B) 현지 음악 평론가
(C) 직업 가수
(D) 학교 합창단의 책임자 정답 (D)

**148.** 퍼레이드는 어디에서 시작될 것인가?
(A) 고등학교
(B) 주차장
(C) Jamestown 시청
(D) 식물원 정답 (D)

문제 149~150번은 다음 공지를 참조하시오.

(149) Wilson Windows
85 Kent Street
Tilford, MA 28191
800-555-1988
www.wilsonwindows.com

따끈따끈한 신제품!

(149) 고객님께서는 저희의 최고 고객 중 한 분이므로, 현재 저희가 취급하는 혁신적인 제품에 대해 알려드리고 싶습니다. Security Film이라고 하

는데, 이것이 있으면 어떤 창문이든 부술 수 없는 보안창으로 바뀔 수 있습니다. 이 제품은 사업체들이 놀랍도록 낮은 가격으로 보안을 증대시키도록 해 줄 것입니다. 실제로 고객님의 사업체는 지금 신형 고도 보안 창문의 10% 비용으로 기존의 창문을 Security Film으로 변환할 수 있습니다. 그러므로 Security Film이 얼마나 좋은지 와서 보세요.

(150) 저희는 현재 특가판매를 하고 있습니다. 3월 10일까지 1000피트의 Security Film을 구매하시면 설치비를 절반 가격으로 해 드립니다. 곧 뵙게 되기를 바랍니다!

**149.** Security Film에 대해 언급된 것은 무엇인가?
(A) 보안 회사에서 승인을 받았다.
(B) 고도의 보안 창문에만 적용된다.
(C) 창문의 이가 빠지는 것을 막아준다.
(D) Wilson Windows에서 구할 수 있다. 정답 (D)

**150.** 고객들은 특가판매를 통해 무엇을 얻을 수 있는가?
(A) 설치에 대한 할인
(B) 3월 10일 이전의 설치
(C) 추가로 설치할 Security Film
(D) Security Film에 대한 더 나은 가격 정답 (A)

**문제 151-152번은 다음 문자 메시지를 참조하시오.**

Richard Crane [오전 11:02]
문제가 있어요, Lisa. (151) **다음 주 금요일 저녁에 있을 Royal King's Orchestra의 공연 표를 두 매 구매했는데요, 생각하지 못한 일이 발생해서 공연에 갈 수가 없게 되었어요.** 그 공연에 갈 수 없어서 너무 아쉬울 따름이에요.

Lisa Livingstone [오전 11:03]
안됐네요. 당신이 정말 운이 없는 것 같네요. 그 공연 표들은 어떻게 하실 건가요?

Richard Crane [오전 11:05]
다음 주에 당신 친구가 외지에서 방문한다고 언급했던 것이 기억나서요. (152) **이 표들을 가지고 가서 친구하고 함께 공연을 보러 가는 것은 어때요?**

Lisa Livingstone [오전 11:08]
(152) **Richard, 참 친절하시네요.** 좋은 생각이고, 저도 Royal King's Orchestra를 너무 좋아하긴 하는데요. 금요일 저녁 계획은 이미 정해놓은 상태라서요. Scott도 Royal King's Orchestra의 엄청난 팬이에요.

Richard Crane [오전 11:09]
알아요, 저도 이미 그에게 확인해봤어요. 다음 주에 해야 할 서류작업이 산더미라고 하더라고요. 사실 제일 비싼 표를 구매했는데 이 표들은 환불이 불가해서요. 내가 할 수 있는 것이 없는 것 같아요.

Lisa Livingstone [오전 11:11]
회사 사내 전산망에 표를 판매한다는 공지를 올리는 건 어때요? 분명히 그 표를 사고 싶어하는 사람들이 있을 거예요.

Richard Crane [오전 11:12]
좋은 생각이네요. 지금 당장 해야겠어요. 당신이 언급한대로, 분명 이 표를 덥석 사고 싶어하는 사람이 있을 거예요.

Lisa Livingstone [오전 11:14]
제 말이 그 말이에요, Richard. 힘내서 한 번 해봐요! 나도 가까운 동료들에게 그 공연에 갈 수 있는지 한 번 물어볼게요.

**151.** Crane 씨의 문제점은 무엇인가?
(A) 그는 해야 할 서류작업이 너무 많다.
(B) 그는 표들을 구매할 수 있는 여력이 안 된다.

(C) 그는 휴가를 낼 수가 없다.
(D) 그는 음악 공연에 참석할 수가 없다. 정답 (D)

**152.** 오전 11시 8분에 Livingstone 씨가 "You're sweet, Richard."라고 말한 의도는 무엇인가?
(A) 그는 단 것을 좋아한다.
(B) 그가 그녀에게 아첨한다.
(C) 그는 친절하다.
(D) 그는 약간 우유부단한 성격이다. 정답 (C)

**문제 153-155번은 다음 광고를 참조하시오.**

**Mario's Pizza Place**
728 North Capital Street, Baltimore
301-555-8291

Baltimore의 명물인 Mario's Pizza Place는 50년 이상 영업해 왔습니다. 저희의 전통적인 New York 스타일 피자는 수많은 상을 받았습니다. 그러니 한 조각 드시러 오세요. 정말 마음에 드실 것입니다!

저희는 또한 아래의 메뉴도 제공합니다.
• 호기, 미트볼 샌드위치, 스테이크와 치즈 샌드위치는 모두 저희가 매일 굽는 빵으로 제공됩니다.
• 주문에 따라 제공되는 칼조네
• 40가지 품목 중에서 고를 수 있는 샐러드 바
• (153) **저희 가게에서 만든 10종의 디저트**

(154) **영업시간: 월요일~토요일 오전 10시 30분부터 오후 8시까지**
**여름 (5월~9월): 1시간 더 늦게까지 영업합니다.**

(155) **수요일은 가족의 밤입니다.** 가족들은 라지 치즈피자를 반값에 드실 수 있습니다. 각 1달러 50센트에 토핑을 추가하실 수 있습니다.

**153.** Mario's Pizza Place에 대해 무엇이라고 언급되어 있는가?
(A) 10년간 영업했다.
(B) 슈퍼마켓에서 피자를 구할 수 있다.
(C) 확장하고 있는 전국적인 체인이다.
(D) 이 레스토랑에서 디저트를 만든다. 정답 (D)

**154.** 광고에 의하면, 5월에 무슨 일이 있는가?
(A) 레스토랑에서 여름 특별상품을 제공한다.
(B) 레스토랑이 일요일에 문을 연다.
(C) 레스토랑에서 특별 메뉴를 제공한다.
(D) 레스토랑이 오후 9시에 문을 닫는다. 정답 (D)

**155.** 가족의 밤에 대해 무엇이라고 나타나 있는가?
(A) 레스토랑에서 가장 바쁜 밤이다.
(B) 평일 저녁에 열린다.
(C) 여름에만 열린다.
(D) 새로운 판촉용 제공이다. 정답 (B)

**문제 156-158번은 다음 회람을 참조하시오.**

수신: 전 직원
발신: Eugene Claire
날짜: (158) **6월 18일**
제목: 바쁜 시즌의 채용

안녕하세요?

아시다시피 우리는 여름에 대부분의 일감이 들어옵니다. 그래서 이 시기에 충분한 직원들이 있는 것이 중요합니다. 현재 우리는 여름에 예정해 둔 모든 프로젝트들을 완료하기에 직원들이 충분하지 않습니다. 지역 신문에 광고를 내기 전에, 추천할 수 있는 아는 사람이 있는지 알고 싶습니다. (156) 물론 저는 현 직원들의 확실한 추천을 받는 직원을 채용하고 싶습니다. 그러면 일을 할 수 있을 뿐만 아니라 우리 모두와 잘 맞는 사람을 채용한다는 것을 제가 알 수 있습니다.

(157) 여러분과 우리 회사 모두에 좋은 거래가 되도록, 우리 회사에 취직하는 근로자를 추천해 준 사람에게 150달러 보너스를 제공할 것입니다. (156/158) 적격인 사람을 아신다면 다음주 안에 저에게 연락 주십시오. (158) 그때까지 우리의 채용 필요를 충족시키지 못한다면, 지역 신문에 연락할 것입니다.

Eugene Claire
인사 담당 이사
Enton 여행사

**156.** 이 회람의 목적은 무엇인가?

(A) 직원 급여 인상을 발표하기 위해
(B) 이번 시즌의 건설 프로젝트를 발표하기 위해
(C) 직원들에게 채용할 사람들을 알아봐 달라고 요청하기 위해
(D) 직원들에게 보너스가 직원 효율성에 근거할 것임을 상기시키기 위해

정답 (C)

**157.** Claire 씨는 누구인가?

(A) 회사 고객
(B) 회사 임원
(C) 임시 직원
(D) 공인 회계사

정답 (B)

**158.** 회람에 의하면 Claire 씨는 6월 25일 이후 곧 무엇을 할 것 같은가?

(A) 지역 신문과 연락한다.
(B) 신규 직원이 완료한 프로젝트들을 검토한다.
(C) 직원 효율성 향상을 위해 교육을 제공한다.
(D) 직원들에게 시즌 직원의 필요성을 발표한다.

정답 (A)

문제 159~161번은 다음 홈페이지를 참조하시오.

---

### Smith Lawn and Garden

(161) 호주에 30년 이상 양질의 실외용 제품을 공급했습니다.

Smith Lawn and Garden에서 게스트로 구매하시려면 <u>여기</u>를 클릭하세요.

Smith Lawn and Garden의 온라인 쇼핑객 계정으로 등록하시려면 <u>여기</u>를 클릭하세요.

(159) Smith Lawn and Garden의 회원 가입 시 혜택:
(160) 이메일을 통한 신제품 및 세일 관련 정기 업데이트
(160) 신제품 및 단종 제품에 대한 회원 대상 할인
이 웹사이트를 통한 빠른 2단계 구매
(161) 호주 내 무료 배송 (해외 소포는 국제 배송료 대상이 됩니다.)

등록은 안전하고 쉽습니다. (160) 또한 청구서 발부 정보를 저장하실 수도 있습니다. 저희가 청구서 발부 정보를 암호화해 두므로 안전하며, 구매하실 때마다 다시 입력하지 않으셔도 됩니다. 그러니 오늘 저희 사이트에 등록하세요. (160) 등록하실 때 저희 온라인 상담 데스크에서 도움을 받으실 수도 있습니다. 1분이면 됩니다!

---

**159.** 홈페이지의 목적은 무엇인가?

(A) 온라인 쇼핑객 계정의 이점을 설명하는 것
(B) 고객에게 어떤 물품이 단종되었음을 알리는 것

(C) 잔디 및 정원 물품의 새로운 제품군을 홍보하는 것
(D) 고객에게 새로운 온라인 서비스를 알리는 것

정답 (A)

**160.** 등록의 이점으로 나타나 있지 않은 것은 무엇인가?

(A) 재고가 있는 신제품에 대한 정보
(B) 구매 도중의 온라인 도움
(C) 할인된 상품
(D) 저장된 청구서 발부 정보

정답 (B)

**161.** Smith Lawn and Garden에 대해 무엇이 암시되어 있는가?

(A) 최근에 새로운 창고를 건립했다.
(B) 20년간 영업했다.
(C) 미국에 해외 사무소를 운영한다.
(D) 국내 배송은 요금을 청구하지 않는다.

정답 (D)

문제 162~163번은 다음 기사를 참조하시오.

---

Hollywood Post
Celebrities and Entertainment

By Alliso Bank

(162) Channel 4에서 새로 시작하는 텔레비전 드라마인 City Life에서는 Wendy Smith가 인기 있는 New York 신문사의 출판 책임자인 Margie Banks 역할로 주연을 맡는다. Steven Wentworth가 감독하여 New York City에서 100% 촬영된 이 드라마는 New York City의 싱글 여성의 삶을 재미 있게 보여준다. (163) 첫 회는 9월 4일 수요일 The Greg Henderson Comedy Hour가 끝난 뒤 오후 9시에 방영된다.

---

**162.** City Life의 주인공은 누구인가?

(A) Wendy Smith
(B) Margie Banks
(C) Steven Wentworth
(D) Greg Henderson

정답 (B)

**163.** 이 기사에 의하면, 9월 4일에 무슨 일이 있을 것인가?

(A) 뉴스 방송이 제작될 것이다.
(B) 어떤 신문이 임원을 소개할 것이다.
(C) TV 시리즈가 시작될 것이다.
(D) TV 드라마가 상을 받을 것이다.

정답 (C)

문제 164~167번은 다음 편지를 참조하시오.

---

### Singapore Business Expo

5월 8일

Jaheed Gupta
9201 Hearth Place
San Diego, CA 90182

Gupta 씨께,

(165) 올해 8월 5~8일 개최될 Singapore Business Expo의 참석 건으로 연락 드립니다. 선생님께서 (164) 강연하는 것은 7일 오후로 일정을 잡았습니다.

(165) 또한 제 비서가 이번 행사가 열릴 Plaza Hotel에 선생님의 객실을 예약했음을 알려드리고 싶습니다. 저희는 모든 엑스포 행사를 위해 그곳의 Grand Ballroom을 예약했습니다. 분명 매일 행사장을 오가시는 데 문제가 없으실 것입니다.

이 호텔이 편안하고 호화로운 곳임을 알게 되실 것이라고 확신합니다.

(165) 게다가 도시가 아름다우며, City Harbor, Freedom Tower, Xialou Shopping District 같은 명소가 있습니다. 우리는 오후 일부 시간에 관광을 할 것입니다. 호텔이 시내에 있으므로, 짧은 시간에 많은 훌륭한 것들을 볼 수 있을 것입니다.

(167) 엑스포에서 연설하실 내용의 사본이 저희에게 필요함을 알려드리고 싶습니다. 행사 최소 3주 전에 저에게 제출해 주십시오. 저희 법무팀 및 홍보팀에서 선생님께서 제공하실 정보를 승인해야 하기 때문입니다. (166) 다시 뵙게 되어 정말 좋습니다. 몇 번 회의에서 마주친 적이 있지만, 제가 주최하는 곳은 아니었지요.

Zao Li
부회장, Singapore Business Association

**164.** 첫 번째 단락 두 번째 줄의 "deliver"와 의미상 가장 유사한 단어는 무엇인가?
(A) 가져오다
(B) 승인하다
(C) 발표하다
(D) 기부하다      정답 (C)

**165.** 편지에 언급되지 않은 것은 무엇인가?
(A) 교통편 세부사항
(B) 호텔의 위치
(C) 행사 장소
(D) 행사 일자      정답 (A)

**166.** Li 씨는 어떻게 Gupta 씨를 알고 있는가?
(A) 그가 받은 많은 상을 통해
(B) 출판된 작품을 통해
(C) 엑스포 신청을 통해
(D) 이전 행사의 참석을 통해      정답 (D)

**167.** [1], [2], [3] 그리고 [4]로 표기된 위치 중에서 아래 문장이 가장 적합한 곳은 어디인가?
"엑스포에서 연설하실 내용의 사본이 저희에게 필요함을 알려드리고 싶습니다."
(A) [1]
(B) [2]
(C) [3]
(D) [4]      정답 (C)

문제 168-171번은 다음 기사를 참조하시오.

(4월 2일) Winston County는 행복할 이유가 있습니다. (168/170) 2주 전 군의 공무원들이 움푹 패인 도로 문제를 처리하기 위해 도로 보수 예산을 증액하기로 투표했습니다.

(168/169) 올해 겨울은 혹독했고, 제설기와 결빙 방지 화학물질의 사용 증가로 인해 군의 도로 표면에 광범위한 문제가 생겼습니다. 그래서 군은 움푹 패인 곳들로 인한 차량 손상에 대해 많은 항의를 받았습니다.

(171) 이 문제를 처리하기 위해, 공무원들은 도로 보수를 위한 예산 증대를 요청했습니다. (170) 군은 도로 보수에 보통 연간 2백만 달러를 지출합니다. 그러나 올 겨울에 야기된 움푹 패인 곳들을 보수하기 위해 4백만 달러 이상 비용이 들 것이라고 추정되었습니다.

분명 이 예산 증액은 필요합니다. 대부분의 군 주민들이 이동시 자동차에 의존하고 있으며, 운전하지 않는 사람들은 군의 공공 버스 시스템을 이용하는데 이 또한 도로가 좋은 상태에 있어야 다닐 수 있습니다. 군의 경제는 차량에 크게 의존하고 있으므로, 이 조치는 비즈니스 활동이 평상시처럼 지속되도록 해 줄 것입니다.

**168.** Winston County는 어떤 문제를 겪고 있는가?
(A) 예산 기획에서의 오류
(B) 도로 보수 실패
(C) 도로 손상
(D) 증가한 교통량      정답 (C)

**169.** 두 번째 단락 네 번째 줄의 "extensive"와 의미상 가장 유사한 단어는 무엇인가?
(A) 충분한
(B) 바라는
(C) 주기적인
(D) 상당한      정답 (D)

**170.** 군의 도로 보수 예산에 대해 언급되지 않은 것은 무엇인가?
(A) 액수가 불충분했다.
(B) 재검토되어야 했다.
(C) 2주 전 증액되었다.
(D) 증가한 교통량에 근거했다.      정답 (D)

**171.** [1], [2], [3] 그리고 [4]로 표기된 위치 중에서 아래 문장이 가장 적합한 곳은 어디인가?
"이 문제를 처리하기 위해, 공무원들은 도로 보수를 위한 예산 증대를 요청했습니다."
(A) [1]
(B) [2]
(C) [3]
(D) [4]      정답 (B)

문제 172-175번은 다음 온라인 채팅 토론을 참조하시오.

| | |
|---|---|
| Agatha Franklin | [오후 2:10] |

(172) Campbell 씨, 2층에 있는 제 사무실의 냉방 장치가 제대로 작동하지 않는 것처럼 보여요. 제가 리모컨을 이용해서 냉방 장치를 작동시키면, 불빛은 들어오는데 시원한 바람이 나오질 않네요.

| | |
|---|---|
| Michael Campbell | [오후 2:13] |

미안해요, Franklin 씨. 하지만 모든 시설 관리 직원들이 지금 각자 맡은 바 일을 하느라 바빠요. 그래서 한동안 냉방 장치를 수리해드릴 수가 없을 것 같아요.

| | |
|---|---|
| Agatha Franklin | [오후 2:14] |

열기 때문에 제가 노력한다고 해도 업무에 집중을 할 수가 없어요. 안타깝게도 제가 할 수 있는 것이라고는 느슨하게 앉아서 최대한 많은 물을 마시는 것뿐이에요.

| | |
|---|---|
| Rene Girard | [오후 2:15] |

(174) 네, 여긴 너무 더워요. (173/174) Campbell 씨, 우리가 3층 사무실로 옮겨서 업무를 보는 것이 어떨까요?

| | |
|---|---|
| Agatha Franklin | [오후 2:16] |

더운 근무 환경에서 일하다가 건강상의 문제가 발생할까 싶어요.

| | |
|---|---|
| Michael Campbell | [오후 2:16] |

알겠습니다. 제가 인사과에 이 문제를 해결하기 위해서 연락을 해볼게요.

| | |
|---|---|
| Michael Campbell | [오후 2:18] |

좋습니다. (174/175) 부장님이 3층 사무실을 사용하라고 허락하셨어요.

| | |
|---|---|
| Rene Girard | [오후 2:18] |

(175) 고맙습니다. 이제야 제대로 일을 할 수 있겠어요.

| | |
|---|---|
| Agatha Franklin | [오후 2:19] |

좋아요, (175) 이제 마음이 좀 놓이네요. 고마워요.

| 1 | Herbal 891 | 은행잎 추출물 캡슐 100정이 들어간 병 | $12 |
|---|---|---|---|
| (179) 2 | Herbal 913 | 톱야자 캡슐 200정이 들어간 병 | $32 |

배송비: $5.00
총액: $66.00

지불방법: 7813으로 끝나는 고객님의 신용카드 계정으로 청구됨

주문 관련 질문이 있으시면 customerservice@vitaminhouse.com으로 연락 주세요.

---

수신: 〈customerservice@vitaminhouse.com〉
발신: 〈b.farmer@menno.com〉
(177) 날짜: 8월 15일
제목: 주문번호 829201

안녕하세요?

(176) 저는 최근에 귀사에서 몇 가지 제품을 전화로 주문했습니다. 저는 Frank Miller 씨의 도움을 받았습니다. (177) 어제 우편으로 주문품을 받았고, 제가 주문한 모든 물품이 들어 있었습니다. 그러나 청구서에서 한 가지 문제를 알아차렸습니다. (178/179) 제가 톱야자 캡슐을 1병 추가로 주문했다고 되어 있는데, 저는 그러지 않았습니다. 제 신용카드에도 이 추가 1병이 청구되었습니다.

(179) 이 문제를 빨리 해결해줄 수 있기를 바랍니다. 저는 추가 1병을 주문하지 않았고, 추가 1병을 받지도 않았으나, 이 건이 청구되었습니다. 추가 1병에 대해 저에게 청구된 수량에 대해 제 계정으로 입금해 주시기 바랍니다.

(180) 이 문제가 해결되었음을 제 이메일 주소로 연락하여 확인해 주십시오.

감사합니다.

Betty Farmer

---

**172.** Franklin 씨의 문제는 무엇인가?
(A) 그녀는 운반해야 할 짐이 많다.
(B) 그녀는 처리해야 할 서류작업이 많다.
(C) 그녀는 편안하게 일을 할 수가 없다.
(D) 그녀는 적절한 급여를 지급받지 못했다. 정답 (C)

**173.** Girard 씨가 원하는 것은 무엇인가?
(A) 그의 사무실을 보수한다.
(B) 정보를 공유한다.
(C) 다른 장소로 이동한다.
(D) 누군가에 도움을 요청하고자 연락한다. 정답 (C)

**174.** Franklin 씨와 Girard 씨에 대해 유추할 수 있는 것은 무엇인가?
(A) 그들은 새로운 기계를 구매하기 원한다.
(B) 그들은 같은 사무실에서 근무한다.
(C) 그들은 대학시절부터 알고 지낸 사이이다.
(D) 그들은 최근에 채용되었다. 정답 (B)

**175.** 오후 2시 19분에 Franklin 씨가 "Great, that's a load off my mind."라고 말한 의도는 무엇인가?
(A) 그녀는 새로운 업무에 대한 걱정이 크다.
(B) 그녀는 무게를 가볍게 하기 위해 짐에서 몇몇 물건들을 치웠다.
(C) Girard 씨는 그녀의 일을 맡게 될 적절한 사람을 찾았다.
(D) Campbell 씨는 그녀의 불편함을 감소시키기 위해 적절한 조치를 취했다. 정답 (D)

**문제 176-180번은 다음 청구서와 이메일을 참조하시오.**

Vitamin House

청구서

고객명: Betty Farmer
주문번호: 829201
주문일: 8월 10일
주문 접수자: Frank Miller
배송주소: 1800 Benson Road, Saint Petersburg, FLA 39422
예상 배송일: 8월 12~14일
집 전화: (800)555-1000
사무실 전화: (800)800-9000

| 수량 | 물품 | 설명 | 가격 |
|---|---|---|---|
| 1 | Vitamin 181 | 씹어먹는 vitamin C 200정이 들어간 병 | $6 |
| 1 | Fiber 561 | 오렌지맛 섬유질 혼합 5파운드 용기 | $11 |

**176.** Miller 씨는 누구일 것 같은가?
(A) Vitamin House 사의 직원
(B) Farmer 씨의 직원 중 한 명
(C) 지역 병원의 영양사
(D) 배송사의 직원 정답 (A)

**177.** Farmer 씨는 언제 주문 상품을 받았는가?
(A) 8월 10일
(B) 8월 12일
(C) 8월 14일
(D) 8월 15일 정답 (C)

**178.** Farmer 씨는 왜 이메일을 보냈는가?
(A) 신용카드가 기한 만료되었다.
(B) 청구서 발부 오류가 있었다.
(C) 잘못된 제품을 받았다.
(D) 제품의 사용기한이 지났다. 정답 (B)

**179.** Farmer 씨는 자신의 신용카드에 얼마가 추가될 것으로 예상하는가?
(A) $6
(B) $11
(C) $12
(D) $16 정답 (D)

**180.** Vitamin House 고객 서비스는 어떻게 Farmer 씨에게 답신해야 하는가?
(A) 이메일을 발송한다.
(B) 집 전화로 연락한다.

(C) 사무실 전화로 연락한다.

(D) 우편을 통해 편지를 발송한다. 　　　　　정답 (A)

**문제 181-185번은 다음 기사와 이메일을 참조하시오.**

---

3월 23일 - (182) Prime Hotel의 소유주 Tom Stanford는 최대한 지역에서 구할 수 있는 제품과 서비스를 활용하는 것이 좋다고 생각한다. 이 호텔의 레스토랑에서 제공하는 대부분의 고기와 채소는 Virginia 농장에서 나온다. 심지어 그는 호텔의 극장무대에서 지역 공연자들의 재능을 선보인다. (181) 그리고 8월 한달 동안 이 호텔은 Virginia 주민이자 Grand Award 수상인 Edgar Stevenson의 음악을 특집으로 선보일 것이다. (183) "저는 가능하면 항상 지역 상품을 구매합니다. 지역 재능인들이 저희 호화로운 호텔에서 공연하는 것도 해야 하지 않겠어요?"라고 Stanford 씨는 말하며, Stevenson 씨가 그렇게 유명한 이유를 확인하도록 손님들을 초대한다. "지역 음악계를 계속 지켜보는 사람들이 아니라면, 저희 호텔에서 공연하는 대부분의 예술가들을 알지 못할 것입니다. 그러나 그 공연들은 항상 놀랍지요."

---

수신: Edgar Stevenson 〈edgars@topmusic.com〉
발신: Tom Stanford 〈tstanford@primehotel.com〉
날짜: 7월 6일
제목: 다가오는 공연들

Stevenson 씨께,

다음달 저희 호텔에서 귀하를 모시게 되어 정말 기쁩니다. 저는 귀하의 작품의 큰 팬이며, 지난 여러 해 동안 귀하의 공연을 여러 차례 보았습니다. (184) 현재 해외 투어 중이신 것을 알고 있지만, 저희 호텔에서의 공연에 앞서 몇 가지를 정리해야 합니다. (185) 연주곡들이 얼마나 오래 걸릴지 알려주시겠습니까? 공연 티켓과 기타 자료를 인쇄하려면 알아야 합니다. 또한 귀하의 사진이 필요합니다. 얼굴사진뿐만 아니라 공연하시는 사진도 받을 수 있다면 좋겠습니다. 다음주 안에 이 사안에 대해 연락 주시면 정말 감사하겠습니다.

Tom Stanford

---

**181.** 이 기사는 무엇을 논의하는가?

(A) 지역 사업체의 리모델링

(B) 지역 호텔 매수

(C) 다가오는 공연들

(D) 지역의 새로운 레스토랑 　　　　　정답 (C)

**182.** Stanford 씨에 대해 무엇이 언급되어 있는가?

(A) 호텔 공급품을 위해 지역 물품을 쓰는 것을 선호한다.

(B) 지역 음악 밴드의 일원이었다.

(C) 지역 음악가들 사이에서 유명하다.

(D) Virginia에 다른 사업체들을 갖고 있다. 　　　　　정답 (A)

**183.** Stanford 씨는 방문객들이 호텔에서 무엇을 하도록 초대하는가?

(A) 저녁식사 중 테이블에서 음악을 신청한다.

(B) 지역 음악계에 관여한다.

(C) 자신의 호텔에 투숙한다.

(D) 음악 공연을 관람한다. 　　　　　정답 (D)

**184.** Stevenson 씨에 대해 무엇이 암시되어 있는가?

(A) 작년에 자신의 작품으로 상을 받았다.

(B) 이제는 Virginia에 살지 않는다.

(C) 현재 Virginia 외부에 있다.

(D) 다음달에 공연을 하지 않을 수도 있다. 　　　　　정답 (C)

**185.** 이메일에 의하면, Stanford 씨는 Stevenson 씨에게서 무엇을 필요로 하는가?

(A) Stevenson 씨의 이미지들

(B) Stevenson 씨의 공연 장소

(C) Stevenson 씨의 은행 계좌번호

(D) Stevenson 씨가 연주할 노래 목록 　　　　　정답 (A)

**문제 186-190번은 다음 홈페이지들과 이메일을 참조하시오.**

---

http://www.fellashoeorthotics.com

Fella Custom Shoe Orthotics

자주 문의되는 질문들

**Fellas Custom Shoe Orthotics는 어떤 종류의 제품을 생산합니까?**

Fellas Custom Shoe Orthotics는 남성, 여성, 아동용 신발 보조기를 제작합니다. 저희 신발 보조기 대부분은 보통의 일상 용품으로 만들어졌습니다. 고객의 발에 맞도록 가열 주조할 수 있는 등록 상표가 붙은 열가소성 수지 또는 섬유유리 합성물을 통상적으로 사용합니다. 그러나 저희는 전문화된 신발 보조기도 제공합니다. (187) 예를 들면 저희의 가열 주조할 수 있는 탄소섬유 신발 보조기는 특히 육상경기용 신발에 사용되도록 개발되었습니다. 이 신발 보조기는 가볍고 내구성이 있으며 매우 단단합니다.

**누가 저희 제품을 사용합니까?**

(186) 저희는 미국 및 아시아의 여러 회사에 저희 신발 보조기를 제공합니다. 저희의 모든 제품은 간단하고 실패할 염려가 없는 과정을 통해 가열 주조될 수 있으며, 언제나 주문 제작한 딱 맞는 느낌을 드립니다.

**Fellas Custom Shoe Orthotics가 우리 회사의 공급업체가 되도록 어떻게 요청할 수 있습니까?**

회의 일정을 잡기 위해 저희 직원 중 한 명에게 연락 주십시오. (187) 저희 직원들은 무료 제품 샘플 및 계약 요건을 제공해드릴 수 있습니다.

---

http://www.fellashoeorthotics.com/personneldepartment/
personnelroaster

영업직원 명단

아시아 지역: Daisuke Tanaka / 〈d.tanaka@fellashoeorthotics.co.jp〉
호주 지역 : Devora Morgan / 〈dmorgan@fellashoeorthotics.co.au〉
서부 유럽 지역: Francois Jalabert / 〈f.jalabert@fellashoeorthotics.co.fr〉
동부 유럽 지역: Anatoly Konenko / 〈akonenko@fellashoeorthotics.co.ru〉
북미 지역: Stanley Parker / 〈s.parker@fellashoeorthotics.com〉
중미 지역: Julian Sanchez / 〈js@fellashoeorthotics.com〉
(190) **남미 지역**: Maria Jimenez / 〈m.jimenez@fellashoeorthotics.co.ar〉

---

수신: Stanley Parker 〈s.parker@fellashoeorthotics.com〉
발신: Jaime Foster 〈jaimefoster@elavie.co.ar〉
날짜: 6월 12일
제목: 귀사의 제품에 대한 관심

Parker 씨께,

(190) 저희 회사는 남미에 기반을 둔 보조기 유통업체입니다. 저희는 신발 보조기, 의수/의족, 정형외과의 등/목 보조기와 같은 의료업계를 위한 보조기를 제공합니다. 지난달 저는 Las Vegas에서 열린 US National Orthotics 무역 박람회에 참가했으며, 귀사의 부스를 몇 차례 방문했습니다. (188/189) 저는 귀사의 육상경기 신발 보조기의 품질 및 가격에 상당한 감명을 받았으며, 이를 대량 주문하려고 합니다. 귀사의 제품은 저

---

희가 현재 공급업체에서 받고 있는 고무 제품보다 훨씬 우수합니다. 저희는 한동안 더 가벼운 제품을 찾고 있었으며, 귀사의 제품 일부가 분명 딱 맞습니다.

저는 귀사의 제품 샘플을 받아보고 가능하면 계약에 들어가기 위해 귀사의 상담원 중 한 명과 이야기하고 싶습니다. 제가 귀사와 비즈니스를 시작하기 위해 이 지역에서 누구를 만나야 하는지 알려주십시오.

Jaime Foster
Elavie Orthopedic Medical Suppliers

**186.** Fellas Custom Shoe Orthotics에 대해 언급하고 있는 것은 무엇인가?
(A) 육상경기 신발만을 제작한다.
(B) 병원에만 제품을 판매한다.
(C) 대개 국내 회사들과 협업한다.
(D) 여러 나라에서 사업을 한다. 　　정답 (D)

**187.** Parker 씨에 대해 사실일 가능성이 높은 것은 무엇인가?
(A) 신발 보조기 샘플을 보낼 수 있다.
(B) 북미 및 남미 양쪽에서 일한다.
(C) Foster 씨와 몇 차례 만났다.
(D) 그의 사무실은 미국 서부해안에 기반을 두고 있다. 　　정답 (A)

**188.** Foster 씨는 자신이 구매하는 제품에 어떤 종류의 재료를 사용하기를 원할 가능성이 가장 높은가?
(A) 고무
(B) 열가소성 수지
(C) 섬유유리 합성물
(D) 탄소섬유 　　정답 (D)

**189.** 이메일 첫 번째 단락 다섯 번째 줄의 "intend"와 의미상 가장 유사한 단어는?
(A) 계획하다
(B) 보이다
(C) 요청하다
(D) 질문하다 　　정답 (A)

**190.** Foster 씨가 견본품을 받으려면 누구에게 연락을 해야 할 것 같은가?
(A) Debora Morgan
(B) Francois Jalabert
(C) Julian Sanchez
(D) Maria Jimenez 　　정답 (D)

**문제 191-195번은 다음 편지, 이메일 그리고 영수증을 참조하시오.**

Pearl Fabrics
769 Creek Road
Clayton, NC 27520

10월 18일

Nancy Granger 씨
57 Central Avenue
New York, NY 10002

Granger 씨께,

**(192) 죄송하지만 요청하신 다음 품목들은 생산이 중단되었습니다.**

제품 #00013834 (Jenny's) 면, Pink 101, 단색 (길이 12ft), 19.99달러

그 제품의 제조사인 Jenny's가 일주일 전에 생산을 중단했습니다. 해당 제품의 재고가 약간 남아 있긴 합니다만, 이를 제외하면 해당 제품을 더 구

---

할 수 없음을 알려드리게 되어 유감으로 생각합니다. 따라서 다음의 제품들을 추천해 드립니다.

제품 #00081230 (Fabricland) 면, Rose Pink, 단색 (길이 6ft), 10.99달러 혹은

제품 #00109314 (Fabricland) 면, (195) **Pink Salmon, 단색 (길이 6ft), 13.99달러** 혹은

제품 #00056918 (Inkcloth) 면, Light Pink, 단색 (길이 12ft) 11.99달러

앞서 언급한 제품과 질감이랑 색이 비슷한 제품들을 정리해봤습니다. 제품들의 차이점은 가격, 길이, 그리고 색상입니다. 화면 모니터가 색상간의 (191) **미묘한** 차이를 표현하지 못할 수 있습니다. 더 정밀한 검토를 위해 3개의 제품들의 표본을 보내드릴 수 있습니다. 질문에 도움이 되셨으면 좋겠습니다.

항상 감사합니다.

Kara Strong
고객 센터 담당자
Pearl Fabrics

---

수신: Jake Fisher 〈jakefisher84@fisherdesigns.com〉
발신: Nancy Granger 〈nancy.granger01@fisherdesigns.com〉
날짜: 10월 23일
제목: 단종된 천

안녕하세요 Fisher 씨. 안타깝게도 좋지 않은 소식을 전해드려야 할 것 같습니다. Pearl Fabrics 사의 직원에 따르면 우리가 Spring Flash 커튼을 제작할 때 주로 사용하는 천인 Pink 101이 단종되었다고 합니다. 일단 남아있는 재고는 제가 다 주문해놓았지만 Jenny's 사에서 다시 생산을 하지 않는 이상, 다른 천을 찾아보는 것 외에는 선택의 여지가 없는 것 같습니다. 거기서 대용품으로 추천하는 제품의 몇 가지 견본들을 보내줬습니다. 모두 면으로 되어 있지만, 색이나 질감에서 약간 다릅니다. (194) 게다가 Fabricland 사의 모든 천들은 Pink 101보다 더 무겁습니다.

(195) **색과 질감이 제일 비슷한 건 Pink Salmon입니다. 그러나 이 제품**을 추천하고 싶지는 않습니다. (194) 그 다음으로 비슷한 제품은 Inkcloth의 제품입니다. 색은 비슷해 보이지만 원래 사용하던 제품보다 더 가볍습니다. 이런 직물로 튼튼한 커튼을 제작할 수 있을지 확신이 서질 않습니다. (193) 만약 Fabricland의 제품을 쓰게 된다면 커튼의 가격을 인상해야 합니다. Inkcloth의 제품을 사용한다면 품질의 하락을 감내해야 합니다. 더 자세히 보실 수 있도록 내일 회의에 모든 표본들을 가져가도록 하겠습니다. 내일 뵙겠습니다.

Nancy Granger

---

거래 영수증

Pearl Fabrics
769 Creek Road
Clayton, NC 27520
(919) 319-4928

02/16 11:55

이름: Nancy Granger
요청한 제품 번호: #000000AA19317
수령인: Fisher Designs
내용물: (193) 제품 #00109314 (Fabricland) 면, Pink Salmon, 단색 (길이 6ft), $13.99
수량: 20

세금 (6%): $16.79
총: $296.59

저희와 거래해주셔서 감사합니다.

**191.** 편지의 세 번째 단락 세 번째 줄의 "subtle"와 의미상 가장 유사한 단어는 무엇인가?
- (A) 합리적인
- (B) 작은
- (C) 결정적인
- (D) 영향력 있는 　　　　　　　　　　　정답 (B)

**192.** 편지의 목적은 무엇인가?
- (A) 배달이 지연된 이유를 설명하기 위해서
- (B) 천을 판매하는 다른 상점을 추천하기 위해서
- (C) 무료 배송을 제공하는 특별한 판촉을 제안하기 위해서
- (D) 제품의 상황에 대해 전달하기 위해서 　　　정답 (D)

**193.** Fisher Designs 사에게 향후 어떤 일이 일어날 것 같은가?
- (A) Spring Flash 커튼의 가격을 올릴 것이다.
- (B) Spring Flash 커튼의 생산을 멈출 것이다.
- (C) 다른 곳에서 천 공급처를 찾을 것이다.
- (D) 스스로 천을 생산하여 공급할 것이다. 　　정답 (A)

**194.** 어느 천이 가장 가벼운가?
- (A) Pink 101
- (B) Rose Pink
- (C) Pink Salmon
- (D) Light Pink 　　　　　　　　　　　정답 (D)

**195.** Pink Salmon 제품의 문제점은 무엇일 것 같은가?
- (A) 가격이 너무 비싸다.
- (B) 너무 가볍다.
- (C) 나쁜 품질로 악명이 높다.
- (D) 합성 섬유로 제작되었다. 　　　　　　정답 (A)

문제 196-200번은 다음 웹페이지와 공지, 그리고 이메일을 참조하시오.

---

http://www.booksworld.com/category

**Books World**

| 홈 | 최근 소식 | **카테고리** | 주문 |
|---|---|---|---|

분야 베스트 셀러 도서: 요리법

1. *Behind the Kitchen*(부엌 뒤에서), Anthony Barry
식당 여는 것을 꿈꾸고 있나요? Barry 씨의 남다른 통찰력과 조언으로 요식업에서 (196) 큰 돈을 버는 법을 배우세요.

2. *Happy Table*(행복한 식탁), Karen Wilson
당신의 식탁 위 음식이 당신과 당신 가족의 건강과 행복을 결정합니다. 올바른 재료들을 선택하고 올바르게 요리하는 방법을 알려드립니다.

3. (198) *Understanding the Food Industry*(요식 업계 이해하기), Rodney Sanford
요식 업계에서 성공하기 위해서는 업계를 이해해야 합니다. 요식업에 막 뛰어든 사람들이 자주 범하는 실수를 피하는 법을 확인하세요. 음식점 운영에 관심이 있다면, 이것은 꼭 읽어야 할 책입니다.

4. *Food, Language, and Culture*(음식, 언어, 그리고 문화), Rodney Sanford
무엇이 한 국가의 음식, 언어, 그리고 문화를 결정하는 걸까요? 그리고 결과적으로 그것들이 어떻게 그 국가와 국민에게 영향을 미칠까요? 10개 이상의 언어로 번역된 Sanford 씨의 책에서 알아보세요.

---

Bloomfield 공공 도서관
6월 넷째 주의 행사

(199) 6월 20일, 월요일 – (198) 성공한 작가이자 레스토랑 대표 Rodney Sanford 씨가 그의 최신 저서에 설명된 음식점 운영 방법을 논하기 위해 우리 도서관을 방문합니다. Sanford 씨는 행사 후에 참가자들을 위해 그의 책에 사인해줄 것입니다.

6월 22일, 수요일 – (197) 보호자 동반 유치원생들과 유아들을 위한 재미 있고 함께 즐길 수 있는 음악으로 가득한 행사가 준비되어 있습니다. 여러 계절과 날씨를 주제로 한 노래가 다양한 악기로 연주됩니다. 이 신나는 음악 수업 참여를 위해 따로 신청하실 필요는 없습니다.

---

수신: 〈customerservice@bloomfieldpl.org〉
발신: Melvin Charles 〈mcharles@opmail.com〉
날짜: 6월 27일
제목: Bloomfield 공공 도서관

담당자께,

(199) 저는 최근 Bloomfield 공공 도서관에서 진행된 행사에 참석했습니다. 저는 Sanford 씨의 지식과 생각에 깊게 감명받았습니다. 그가 토론 시간에 가르쳐준 것들은 저의 사업 계획을 실행하는 것과 관련하여 정말 큰 자산이 될 것입니다.

(200) 또한, 도서 *Behind the Kitchen*이 대여 가능할 때 문자로 알림 받기를 희망합니다. 제가 빌리려 했을 때는 이미 대출된 상태였습니다. 제 휴대전화 번호는 (210) 555-3918입니다. 감사합니다.

(199) Melvin Charles

**196.** 웹 페이지의 첫 문단, 두 번째 줄의 "good"과 의미상 가장 가까운 단어는?
- (A) 쾌적한
- (B) 상당한
- (C) 후한
- (D) 진짜의 　　　　　　　　　　　　정답 (B)

**197.** Bloomfield 공공 도서관에 대해 시사된 것은?
- (A) 어린이들을 위한 행사를 연다.
- (B) 행사 등록을 위하여 회원카드가 있어야 한다.
- (C) 현재 신입직원을 채용하고 있다.
- (D) 정기적으로 운영시간이 바뀐다. 　　　정답 (A)

**198.** 어떤 책이 최근에 Bloomfield 공공 도서관에서 저자에 의해 서명되었는가?
- (A) *Behind the Kitchen*
- (B) *Happy table*
- (C) *Understanding the Food Industry*
- (D) *Food, Language, and Culture* 　　　정답 (C)

**199.** Charles 씨에 대해 맞는 것은?
- (A) 자주 Bloomfield 공공 도서관을 방문한다.
- (B) Bloomfield 공공 도서관에서 일한다.
- (C) Sanford 씨의 도서 중 하나를 구매하기 원한다.
- (D) 음식점 개업에 관심이 있다. 　　　　정답 (D)

**200.** Charles 씨는 Bloomfield 공공 도서관에 무엇을 해달라고 요청하는가?
- (A) 도서의 출간일을 알려달라고
- (B) Sanford 씨의 행사가 또 언제 있을지 알려달라고
- (C) 책이 언제 도서관으로 반납되는지 알려달라고
- (D) 그의 주소지로 새 책을 보내달라고 　　정답 (C)

**1.** 미W
(A) He's staring at a monitor.
(B) He's looking into a photocopier.
(C) He's moving printing equipment into a room.
(D) He's reading a notice on a board.

(A) 그는 모니터를 응시하고 있다.
(B) 그는 복사기 내부를 보고 있다.
(C) 그는 인쇄 장비를 방 안으로 운반하고 있다.
(D) 그는 게시판의 공지를 읽고 있다. 정답 (B)

**2.** 호M
(A) She is typing on a laptop.
(B) She is taking off her boots.
(C) She is tying her shoe.
(D) She is using a power tool.

(A) 그녀는 노트북 컴퓨터의 자판을 치고 있다.
(B) 그녀는 부츠를 벗고 있다.
(C) 그녀는 신발 끈을 묶고 있다.
(D) 그녀는 전동 공구를 사용하고 있다. 정답 (C)

**3.** 영W
(A) Some high rise buildings stand in a row on the busy street.
(B) Scaffolding has been installed on the face of a structure.
(C) Some banners are being removed from the side of a building.
(D) Earth-moving machines have been left at a construction site.

(A) 몇몇 고층 건물들이 복잡한 거리를 따라 일렬로 줄지어 서있다.
(B) 비계가 건물 앞면에 설치되어 있다.
(C) 몇몇 현수막들이 건물 측면에서 제거되고 있다.
(D) 굴착기들이 공사 현장에 남아 있다. 정답 (B)

**4.** 미M
(A) Some fruit has been stacked in cartons.
(B) Some products are being wrapped in plastic.
(C) Some plants are on display outside a shop.
(D) Some people are unloading a shipment of boxes.

(A) 과일이 상자에 담겨 쌓여 있다.
(B) 몇몇 제품들이 비닐로 포장되고 있다.
(C) 화초들이 상점 외부에 진열되어 있다.
(D) 몇몇 사람들이 선적된 상자들을 내리고 있다. 정답 (A)

**5.** 미W
(A) All of the cars are parked in a public garage.
(B) Some people are parking bicycles into a rack.
(C) A cart full of items is being wheeled through a doorway.
(D) A vehicle has stopped at a service station.

(A) 모든 자동차들이 공영 주차장에 주차되어 있다.
(B) 몇몇 사람들이 자전거 보관소에 자전거를 세우고 있다.
(C) 물건이 가득 찬 카트가 입구를 지나가고 있다.
(D) 자동차가 주유소에 정차해 있다. 정답 (D)

**6.** 영W
(A) Curtains are flapping in the wind.

(B) Some cushions are being removed from a sofa.
(C) There is an armchair around a table.
(D) The tiles on the floor are being waxed.

(A) 커튼이 바람에 펄럭이고 있다.
(B) 몇몇 쿠션들을 소파에서 치우고 있다.
(C) 테이블 주변에 팔걸이 의자가 있다.
(D) 바닥 타일에 왁스칠이 되고 있다. 정답 (C)

**7.** 미M 영W
Who's responsible for purchasing printing paper?
(A) Her secretary did.
(B) Yes, on the last page.
(C) Probably Mr. Robinson.

인쇄용지 구매를 담당하는 사람이 누구인가요?
(A) 그녀의 비서가 했어요.
(B) 네, 마지막 페이지에요.
(C) 아마도 Robinson 씨일 겁니다. 정답 (C)

**8.** 영W 미M
Where is the new company cafeteria?
(A) We had lunch together.
(B) The food was great.
(C) On the third floor.

회사의 새로운 구내식당은 어디에 있나요?
(A) 우리는 점심식사를 함께 했어요.
(B) 음식이 정말 훌륭했어요.
(C) 3층에요. 정답 (C)

**9.** 미M 미W
May I have the check, please?
(A) On May 10.
(B) You should check your eyesight.
(C) Here you are, sir.

계산서를 주시겠어요?
(A) 5월 10일에요.
(B) 시력검사를 받으셔야겠네요.
(C) 여기 있습니다, 손님. 정답 (C)

**10.** 호M 영W
Why is the corporate event being held at the local trade center?
(A) On June 3 at 10:00.
(B) Because it has a big hall.
(C) Formal attire is required.

회사 행사가 지역 무역 센터에서 열리는 이유가 뭔가요?
(A) 6월 3일 10시에요.
(B) 대형 홀이 있기 때문이에요.
(C) 정장을 입어야 합니다. 정답 (B)

**11.** 미M 미W
Could I use your calculator?
(A) Help yourself.
(B) No, it requires good math skills.
(C) To get accurate answers.

당신 계산기를 써도 될까요?

(A) 얼마든지 쓰세요.
(B) 아니오. 그건 훌륭한 수학 실력을 요구해요.
(C) 정확한 답을 얻기 위해서요.  정답 (A)

**12.** 호M 미W

Who will have the top performance results this quarter?
(A) Some blank paper and envelopes.
(B) We'll know after reviewing the sales data.
(C) It is the best show that I've ever seen.

누가 이번 분기에 가장 좋은 실적을 거둘까요?
(A) 백지와 봉투요.
(B) 매출 자료를 검토하고 나면 알게 되겠지요.
(C) 제가 지금까지 봤던 공연 중 최고예요.  정답 (B)

**13.** 영W 미M

Why were you late for the flight?
(A) I'm sorry for being late.
(B) Please check in at the airport.
(C) The road was blocked due to heavy snow.

비행기 시간에 늦은 이유가 뭐죠?
(A) 늦어서 죄송합니다.
(B) 공항에서 탑승 수속을 해주세요.
(C) 폭설로 인해 길이 막혔습니다.  정답 (C)

**14.** 미M 미W

Were you able to reserve concert tickets?
(A) There were a lot of visitors.
(B) It was an exciting music performance.
(C) No, they were already sold out.

콘서트 표를 예매할 수 있었나요?
(A) 방문객들이 많았어요.
(B) 신나는 음악 공연이었어요.
(C) 아니오, 이미 매진됐어요.  정답 (C)

**15.** 호M 미W

How did you learn about the new job opening?
(A) You can start work early next week.
(B) From a job advertisement.
(C) It's not that easy.

새로운 일자리에 대해 어떻게 알았어요?
(A) 다음주 초부터 일을 시작하시면 됩니다.
(B) 구인 광고에서요.
(C) 그리 쉽진 않아요.  정답 (B)

**16.** 미M 영W

What time does the Jangs Furniture Shop close?
(A) Some chairs and desks.
(B) Why don't you call the store?
(C) Sure, I have some free time tonight.

Jangs 가구점은 언제 문을 닫습니까?
(A) 몇몇 의자들과 책상들이요.
(B) 매장에 전화해 보지 그래요?
(C) 그럼요, 저는 오늘밤에 시간이 있어요.  정답 (B)

**17.** 영W 미M

Why don't you let me carry your bag to the hotel front desk?
(A) I'd like a room with an ocean view.

(B) No, thanks. I can manage myself.
(C) Yes, the store carries a variety of bags.

제가 가방을 호텔 안내 데스크까지 운반해 드릴까요?
(A) 바다가 보이는 방을 원해요.
(B) 감사합니다만, 사양할게요. 제가 할 수 있어요.
(C) 네, 그 상점에선 다양한 가방들을 취급해요.  정답 (B)

**18.** 미W 호M

Who should I talk to about my medical benefits?
(A) I'm on medication now.
(B) Mr. Powell in Personnel.
(C) Yes, you can take sick leave.

의료 보험 혜택과 관련해서 누구와 이야기를 해야 하나요?
(A) 저는 현재 약물 치료중이에요.
(B) 인사부의 Powell 씨요.
(C) 네, 당신은 병가를 낼 수 있어요.  정답 (B)

**19.** 미M 미W

Is Ms. Harrison in her office now?
(A) Yes, I can drop by your office.
(B) No, I'll be out of town for a week.
(C) Yes, but she's on another call.

Harrison 씨는 지금 사무실에 계신가요?
(A) 네, 당신 사무실에 들릴 수 있어요.
(B) 아니오, 저는 일주일간 출장을 갑니다.
(C) 네, 하지만 다른 전화를 받고 있습니다.  정답 (C)

**20.** 호M 미W

Is it okay if I leave the office a couple of hours early tomorrow?
(A) Would you please complete this form?
(B) Yes, he resigned for personal reasons.
(C) Sure, I reserved my plane ticket to London.

내일 두 시간 정도 일찍 퇴근해도 괜찮을까요?
(A) 이 서류 양식을 작성해 주시겠어요?
(B) 네, 그는 개인적인 이유로 사임했어요.
(C) 그럼요, London 행 항공권을 예약했어요.  정답 (A)

**21.** 호M 미M

Would you prefer a cheese or beef sandwich?
(A) For here or to go?
(B) Do you have vegetarian options?
(C) It's a nutritious and healthy meal.

치즈 샌드위치가 좋으세요, 아니면 소고기 샌드위치가 좋으세요?
(A) 여기서 드실 건가요, 아니면 포장해 가실 건가요?
(B) 채식주의 메뉴가 있나요?
(C) 그건 영양이 많고 건강에 좋은 음식이에요.  정답 (B)

**22.** 미M 영W

Weren't we supposed to have a quarterly meeting today?
(A) No, at the conference room on the second floor.
(B) It's been delayed until next Wednesday.
(C) Yes, we should meet the deadline.

오늘 분기별 회의를 열기로 하지 않았나요?
(A) 아니오, 2층에 있는 회의실에서요.
(B) 다음주 수요일로 연기되었어요.
(C) 네, 우리는 마감시한을 맞춰야 해요.  정답 (B)

**23.** [미W] [미M]

Mr. Jackson will present his new furniture designs at the meeting next week.
(A) No, he's a good speaker.
(B) I'm really looking forward to seeing them.
(C) A large selection of designs.

Jackson 씨는 그의 새로운 가구 디자인을 다음주 회의에서 선보일 겁니다.
(A) 아니오, 그는 뛰어난 연설자예요.
(B) 그 디자인에 대한 기대가 큽니다.
(C) 다양한 종류의 디자인이에요.　　　　　　정답 (B)

**24.** [호M] [미W]

Would you like to discuss the financial matter after lunch?
(A) Yes, I really enjoyed your food.
(B) I'd like to, but I have a dental appointment then.
(C) Some financial documents on your desk.

점심식사 후에 재정 문제에 대해서 논의하시겠어요?
(A) 네, 당신 음식이 정말 맛있네요.
(B) 그러고 싶습니다만, 그 때는 제가 치과 예약이 있어서요.
(C) 당신 책상 위에 있는 몇몇 재정 관련 서류들이요.　　정답 (B)

**25.** [미M] [영W]

Which airline are you taking to Manchester?
(A) Actually, I prefer an aisle seat.
(B) From 9:00 A.M. to 5:00 P.M.
(C) The express bus is far less expensive.

Manchester에 갈 때 어느 항공사를 이용할 건가요?
(A) 사실 복도 쪽 자리를 선호합니다.
(B) 오전 9시부터 오후 5시까지요.
(C) 고속 버스가 훨씬 덜 비싸요.　　　　　　정답 (C)

**26.** [호M] [미W]

I thought Ms. Parker was supposed to be transferred to the Atlanta branch.
(A) You can transfer to another train at the next station.
(B) No, it was a little over three hours.
(C) Yes, but she'll come to the Hayward branch next month.

Parker 씨가 Atlanta 지점으로 전근 가는 줄 알았어요.
(A) 다음 역에서 다른 기차로 환승하실 수 있습니다.
(B) 아니오, 세 시간이 약간 넘었어요.
(C) 네, 하지만 그녀는 다음달에 Hayward 지점으로 갑니다.　정답 (C)

**27.** [미M] [영W]

Why don't we take a ten-minute coffee break?
(A) It was a ten-minute drive.
(B) Yes, we should fix it.
(C) I have to do some paperwork.

10분 정도 커피를 마시며 쉬는 건 어떨까요?
(A) 차로 10분 거리예요.
(B) 네, 우리는 그걸 수리해야 해요.
(C) 전 서류 작업을 좀 해야 해요.　　　　　정답 (C)

**28.** [미W] [호M]

The store is much more crowded with shoppers this afternoon.
(A) Please go down the hall.
(B) There's a summer sale today.
(C) Your order will be shipped soon.

상점이 오후에 더 많은 쇼핑객들로 북적이네요.
(A) 복도를 따라 가세요.
(B) 오늘 여름 할인 행사가 있어요.
(C) 주문하신 상품은 곧 배송이 될 겁니다.　　정답 (B)

**29.** [미M] [영W]

I think Sue can help us organize the annual corporate banquet.
(A) She quit her job last Wednesday.
(B) We need some business card organizers.
(C) Some amplifiers, speakers, and a podium.

Sue가 연례 회사 연회를 준비하는 걸 도와줄 수 있을 것이라고 생각해요.
(A) 그녀는 지난주 수요일에 퇴사했어요.
(B) 우리는 명함집이 몇 개 필요해요.
(C) 몇몇 증폭기, 스피커, 그리고 연단이요.　　정답 (A)

**30.** [호M] [미W]

Should we recruit some new computer graphic designers next month?
(A) We guaranteed a fair evaluation.
(B) Oh, that's a great idea.
(C) You should submit your résumé to Personnel.

우리가 다음달에 새로운 컴퓨터 그래픽 디자이너들을 채용해야 하나요?
(A) 우리는 공정한 평가를 보장했습니다.
(B) 아, 그거 좋은 생각이네요.
(C) 이력서를 인사부에 제출하셔야 합니다.　　정답 (B)

**31.** [미M] [미W]

Our new branch office is scheduled to open next month, isn't it?
(A) No, it's very spacious.
(B) Yes, it starts at five.
(C) Which one are you referring to?

우리의 새로운 지점이 다음달에 개장할 예정이죠, 그렇지 않나요?
(A) 아니오, 그 곳은 굉장히 넓어요.
(B) 네, 5시에 시작해요.
(C) 어느 지점을 이야기하는 건가요?　　　정답 (C)

## Part 3

문제 32-34번은 다음 대화를 참조하시오. [미M] [미W]

M: (32) **I'm almost finished with the fence. Then it just needs to be painted.** Once I've nailed these final few planks of wood, you can get on with the painting. (33) **Did you pick up all the supplies we need?**

W: (33) **Yes, although I wasn't able to find any paintbrushes in the truck.** I might have left them at the store. I'm going to give the store a call to ask someone there.

M: Okay. (34) **Once we've got the brushes, we should be able to get the whole fence done this afternoon.** Painting it shouldn't take much more than a couple of hours.

-----

M: 울타리는 거의 끝났어요. 이제 페인트칠만 하면 되겠네요. 이 마지막 나무 판자들만 못으로 박으면 당신이 페인트칠을 할 수 있어요. 우리에게 필요한 물품들을 모두 가져왔나요?

W: 네, 하지만 트럭에서 페인트 붓은 찾을 수 없었어요. 상점에 두고 왔는지도 모르겠네요. 전화해서 물어볼게요.

M: 좋아요. 붓만 있으면 오늘 오후에 전체 울타리에 대한 작업을 끝낼 수

있을 겁니다. 도색 작업에 두 시간 이상은 안 걸릴 거예요.

**32.** 화자들은 무엇을 하고 있는가?
(A) 화초들을 구매한다.
(B) 울타리 작업을 한다.
(C) 차량을 수리한다.
(D) 트럭을 도색한다.　　　　　　　　　　　정답 (B)

**33.** 화자들은 무엇이 필요한가?
(A) 나무 판자
(B) 여분의 부품
(C) 페인트
(D) 붓　　　　　　　　　　　　　　　　　정답 (D)

**34.** 작업은 언제 완료되겠는가?
(A) 오늘 아침
(B) 오늘 오후
(C) 내일 아침
(D) 모레　　　　　　　　　　　　　　　　정답 (B)

**문제 35-37번은 다음 대화를 참조하시오.** 〔ⓜM〕〔ⓜW〕

M: Hi, Sally! It's Peter. (35) **I'm in the conference room and am ready for my meeting with Kate at 1:30, but she isn't here.** She isn't answering her cell phone either. Did she mention anything about arriving late?
W: Kate thought the meeting was at 2 P.M. She must still be at the dentist.
M: When is she expected back? (36) **If she doesn't return soon, I might have to reschedule the meeting.**
W: Hold on! (37) **Kate just got back. I'll let her know that you are waiting for her.** She'll be there as soon as possible.

-------------------------------------------------

M: 안녕하세요, Sally! 저는 Peter입니다. 저는 회의실에 있고 1시 30분에 Kate와 회의를 할 준비가 된 상태인데, 그녀가 이곳에 없군요. 그리고 휴대전화도 받지 않네요. 그녀가 늦게 도착한다고 말한 적이 있나요?
W: Kate는 회의가 오후 2시에 있는 걸로 알고 있던데요. 그녀는 아직 치과에 있을 거예요.
M: 그녀가 언제 돌아올 건가요? 만일 바로 오지 않는다면 회의 일정을 다시 잡아야 할 것 같네요.
W: 잠시만요! Kate가 막 도착했어요. 당신이 기다리고 있다고 말해 줄게요. 그녀가 최대한 빨리 그곳으로 갈 겁니다.

**35.** 남자에 따르면 무엇이 문제인가?
(A) 그는 일정이 중복되었다.
(B) 그는 비행기를 놓쳤다.
(C) 그는 치통을 겪고 있다.
(D) 그는 회의를 제때 시작할 수 없다.　　　정답 (D)

**36.** 남자가 원하는 것은 무엇인가?
(A) 치과를 찾는다.
(B) 발표를 한다.
(C) 회의를 연기한다.
(D) 항공권을 예매한다.　　　　　　　　　정답 (C)

**37.** 여자는 무엇을 할 것이라고 언급하는가?
(A) 내일 일찍 도착한다.
(B) Kate를 회의실로 보낸다.

(C) 회사 행사를 준비한다.
(D) 직원에게 일정 변경에 대해 알린다.　　정답 (B)

**문제 38-40번은 다음 대화를 참조하시오.** 〔영W〕〔ⓜM〕

W: Wow! Mr. Fisher, (38) **can you see all these cars at the intersection? Honestly, I wasn't expecting this much traffic.** What should we do?
M: I think we're in trouble now. (39) **If we don't make it to this meeting on time, Mr. Edward won't sign the contract.**
W: Um… if we just ride in this car, we won't get there by 2 o'clock. (40) **Why don't we leave our car in a nearby public parking lot and take the subway?** Mr. Edward's office is located on 11th Street. It's only three blocks away from here.

-------------------------------------------------

W: 와! Fisher 씨, 교차로의 이 모든 차들이 보이나요? 솔직히 이 정도로 막힐 것이란 생각은 못했어요. 어떻게 해야 할까요?
M: 참 곤란하게 됐네요. 만약 우리가 이 회의에 제시간에 도착하지 못한다면 Edward 씨는 계약서에 서명을 하지 않을 겁니다.
W: 음… 우리가 이 차에 그냥 있기만 하면 2시까지 도착할 수 없을 겁니다. 우리 차를 근처에 있는 공영 주차장에 두고 지하철을 타고 가는 건 어떨까요? Edward 씨의 사무실이 11번가에 위치하고 있어요. 여기서 고작 세 블록 떨어져 있어요.

**38.** 여자가 "Can you see all these cars at the intersection?"이라고 말할 때 여자가 의미하는 바는 무엇인가?
(A) 그녀는 자신의 발표에 대해 걱정하고 있다.
(B) 그녀는 자동차 회사에서 근무하는 것에 자부심을 느낀다.
(C) 그녀는 새로운 자동차들을 고객에게 소개하길 원한다.
(D) 그녀는 심한 교통체증에 놀랐다.　　　정답 (D)

**39.** 화자들이 Edward 씨를 만나는 이유는 무엇인가?
(A) 영업 발표를 하기 위해서
(B) 취업 제의를 하기 위해서
(C) 새로운 자동차 디자인을 논의하기 위해서
(D) 계약을 체결하기 위해서　　　　　　　정답 (D)

**40.** 여자가 제안하는 것은 무엇인가?
(A) 회의를 취소한다.
(B) 회사 차량을 검사한다.
(C) 그녀의 발표 일정을 재조정한다.
(D) 대중교통을 이용한다.　　　　　　　　정답 (D)

**문제 41-43번은 다음 대화를 참조하시오.** 〔ⓜW〕〔ⓜM〕

W: (41) **Hello. This is Lisa Franklin from the Pacific Clinic. I'm calling you back because we had a cancelation today, and I know that you really want an appointment.**
M: Thanks a lot. I'd like to see a doctor as soon as possible because I fell down some stairs, and my leg is in a lot of pain.
W: Well, I think we can fit you in today at 2 o'clock. (42/43) **I'd be happy to make a new appointment for you right now, but (43) I've just realized that it's already 1 o'clock. Will you be able to make it here on time?**
M: (43) **Sure, no problem. My friend is here, and he will drive me over right now.** Thanks again.

-------------------------------------------------

W: 안녕하세요. 저는 Pacific Clinic에서 연락 드리는 Lisa Franklin입니다. 오늘 예약 취소가 생겨서 고객님께서 꼭 예약하길 원하셨기에 연락을 드렸습니다.

M: 정말 감사드려요. 가능한 빨리 진찰을 받고 싶어서요. 왜냐하면 제가 계단에서 넘어졌는데 다리 통증이 상당히 심합니다.

W: 음, 오늘 2시에 예약을 해드리는 것이 가능합니다. 지금 예약을 해드릴 수 있긴 합니다만 벌써 1시네요. 시간 맞춰 병원에 도착하실 수 있겠어요?

M: 물론이죠. 괜찮습니다. 여기 제 친구가 있는데 저를 바로 태워다 줄 겁니다. 다시 한 번 감사드려요.

**41.** 화자들은 무엇을 논의하고 있는가?
(A) 불량품
(B) 새로운 처방전
(C) 수술
(D) 병원 예약 　　　　　　　　　　　정답 (D)

**42.** 여자는 즉시 무엇을 할 것이라고 말하는가?
(A) 의사에게 연락한다.
(B) 반품된 상품을 수령한다.
(C) 주문을 취소한다.
(D) 새로운 예약을 잡는다. 　　　　　정답 (D)

**43.** 남자는 무엇을 하기로 동의하는가?
(A) 택시를 부른다.
(B) 예약을 연기한다.
(C) 병원을 방문한다.
(D) 처방전을 발급한다. 　　　　　　정답 (C)

---

**문제 44-46번은 다음의 3자 대화를 참조하시오.** 호M 영W 미M

M1: Thank you for coming on such short notice. You know, (44) **things have been so hectic while recording some songs for our new album scheduled to be released next month.** We also need to prepare for our third official tour, which kicks off with two shows at the municipal stadiums in London and Dublin.

W: No problem. I totally understand.

M1: Good. (44) **So we definitely love the photographs you took of our band.** (45) **We'd like to put them on new T-shirts for fans and sell them during our tour in England and Ireland.**

W: Thank you for the compliment. I'm looking forward to having a mutual business relationship with you.

M2: Oh, (45) **could you create some images which would fit on fan books and tote bags, too?**

W: (46) **If you fill out a survey form and give me some information about the style of your band,** I can create and design any of the images you want after a couple of photoshoots. It usually takes a week to complete the work.

---

M1: 급하게 전갈을 드렸음에도 이렇게 찾아주셔서 감사합니다. 아시다시피, 다음달에 출시되기로 한 새로운 앨범에 수록할 몇 곡을 녹음하는 것과 관련해서 일이 바쁘게 돌아가고 있어요. 우리는 또한 London과 Dublin의 시립 경기장에서 하게 될 두 번의 공연과 함께 시작하는 세 번째 공식 순회 공연도 준비를 해야 합니다.

W: 그럼요. 저는 충분히 이해하고 있습니다.

M1: 좋습니다. 우리 밴드를 위해서 당신이 촬영해준 사진들이 정말 좋아요.

---

그 사진들을 팬들을 위해 마련한 새로운 티셔츠에 인쇄해서 영국과 아일랜드에서 순회공연을 하는 동안 이를 판매하고자 합니다.

W: 칭찬에 감사드립니다. 저도 공동 사업 관계에 대한 기대가 큽니다.

M2: 아, 그리고 팬북과 여성용 가방에 어울리는 이미지들도 새로 만들어주실 수 있나요?

W: 설문지를 작성해서 당신의 밴드 스타일에 대한 정보를 주신다면, 두 번 정도 사진 촬영을 한 후에 원하시는 그 어떤 이미지도 만들고 디자인할 수 있습니다. 대개 작업이 종료될 때까지 일주일이 걸립니다.

**44.** 남자들은 누구일 것 같은가?
(A) 녹음 엔지니어
(B) 사진작가
(C) 행사 기획자
(D) 음악가 　　　　　　　　　　　정답 (D)

**45.** 남자들은 여자에게 무엇을 요청하는가?
(A) 광고를 촬영한다.
(B) 새로운 관광 패키지를 제공한다.
(C) 앨범을 위한 곡들을 녹음한다.
(D) 상품용 이미지들을 제작한다. 　　정답 (D)

**46.** 여자가 남자들에게 요청하는 것은 무엇인가?
(A) 작성된 설문지
(B) 교용 계약서
(C) 새로운 악기
(D) 홍보 물품 　　　　　　　　　　정답 (A)

---

**문제 47-49번은 다음 대화를 참조하시오.** 미M 미W

M: Hi. This is Spencer Miller. I'm returning your call about the position I applied for last week.

W: Oh, yes, Mr. Miller. (47) **We would like you to join our team as a financial analyst for capital investment projects.**

M: Oh, thank you very much. I'm looking forward to working with you soon. (48) **When would you like me to start?**

W: We have a couple of large projects going on right now, so (49) **we want you to start working with us as soon as possible once we're done with your background check, which usually takes up to two days.** How much notice do you think you need to give your current employer?

---

M: 안녕하세요. 저는 Spencer Miller라고 합니다. 지난주에 제가 지원한 직책에 관해 연락을 주셨기에 답신 전화를 드립니다.

W: 아, 네, Miller 씨. Miller 씨를 자본 투자 프로젝트를 위한 재정 분석가로 우리 팀에 모시고 싶어서 연락을 드렸습니다.

M: 아, 감사합니다. 귀사에서 함께 일할 수 있길 고대하고 있습니다. 언제부터 일을 시작하면 될까요?

W: 현재 진행 중인 두 개의 대규모 프로젝트가 있어서, 대개 이틀 정도 걸리는 Miller 씨에 대한 신원조회가 완료되고 나면 최대한 빨리 업무를 시작해 주셨으면 합니다. 현재 근무하고 있는 회사에는 얼마 전에 퇴사를 알려줘야 합니까?

**47.** 여자는 누구일 것 같은가?
(A) 재정 분석가
(B) 투자자
(C) 프로젝트 담당 회계사
(D) 인사부장 　　　　　　　　　　정답 (D)

**48.** 남자는 무엇에 관해 문의하는가?
(A) 연봉
(B) 시작일자
(C) 휴가시간
(D) 연수 기회 　　　　　　　　　　　　　정답 (B)

**49.** 남자가 일하기에 앞서 여자는 무엇을 할 것인가?
(A) 신원 조회를 한다.
(B) 남자의 연봉을 협상한다.
(C) 직원 오리엔테이션을 진행한다.
(D) 취업 면접을 시행한다. 　　　　　　　정답 (A)

**문제 50-52번은 다음의 3자 대화를 참조하시오.** 미M 미W 영W

M: Hi, Ms. Walker. (50) **Mr. Taylor called me yesterday and said that our marketing budget has been reduced by 15%.** We may have to rethink our advertising strategy for our toothpaste.
W1: Oh, no, Mr. Lee. (51) **We changed all the logos and packaging last week.**
W2: (51) **Yes, I know.** I think we should move ahead even though our budget is tight, or our customers won't know they are the same products.
W1: But how are we going to promote our products? To solidify our brand image, coherent and sophisticated marketing methods are necessary. We need more funds than we have now.
M: That's a good point. (52) **I'll call Mr. Taylor back and see if he can reduce the budgets of some other products so that we can focus on our promotions.** I'll let you know as soon as I hear back from him.

- - - - - - - - - - - - - - - - - - - - - - - - - - - - - -

M: 안녕하세요, Walker 씨. Taylor 씨가 어제 제게 연락해서 우리의 마케팅 예산이 15% 삭감되었다고 말하더군요. 우리 치약 제품에 대한 광고 전략을 다시 생각해봐야 할지도 모르겠어요.
W1: 아, 저런, Lee 씨. 우리는 지난주에 제품의 모든 로고와 포장을 변경했어요.
W2: 네, 저도 알고 있어요. 저는 우리 예산이 적더라도 제품 홍보를 계속해야 한다고 생각해요. 그렇지 않으면 고객들이 동일한 제품이란 점을 인식하지 못할 수도 있습니다.
W1: 그런데 어떻게 홍보를 하죠? 우리 브랜드 이미지를 확고히 하기 위해서는 일관되고 치밀한 마케팅 전략은 필수입니다. 그러려면 지금보다 더 많은 예산이 필요합니다.
M: 좋은 지적입니다. 제가 Taylor 씨에게 다시 연락해서 다른 제품의 예산을 삭감하여 우리 제품의 홍보에 집중할 수 있는지 여부에 대해 알아보도록 하겠습니다. 답변을 듣자 마자 알려드릴게요.

**50.** 화자들은 어떤 문제점을 언급하고 있는가?
(A) 삭감된 예산
(B) 부정적인 의견
(C) 시장 점유율의 손실
(D) 부실한 포장 　　　　　　　　　　　정답 (A)

**51.** 여자들이 회사 제품에 대해 언급한 것은 무엇인가?
(A) 로고가 다시 디자인되었다.
(B) 매출이 하락하고 있다.
(C) 포장의 품질이 향상되었다.
(D) 판촉 행사들이 성공적이지 못했다. 　정답 (A)

**52.** 남자는 이후에 무엇을 할 것 같은가?
(A) 행사를 취소한다.
(B) 광고 회사에 연락을 취한다.
(C) 더 많은 자금 확보를 위해 노력한다.
(D) 점장과 이야기한다. 　　　　　　　정답 (C)

**문제 53-55번은 다음 대화를 참조하시오.** 영W 미M

W: Brian, do you have some free time this afternoon? I'm going to be doing some test marketing for the new skincare product, and (54) **I need your input.**
M: Sure, that's our new line in male anti-wrinkle products. Why are you doing test marketing? Aren't you sure that the products will appeal to the target customers?
W: Actually, we aren't. (53) **Apparently, some men didn't like the strong scent in the original product.** So we made some changes, and our test groups gave us positive feedback on a lower-strength scent. Now, I want to try out the product in some real-life buying situations before we release it on a national scale.
M: Fortunately, I worked on some similar projects in the first quarter. (55) **I can give you some data for reference.**

- - - - - - - - - - - - - - - - - - - - - - - - - - - - - -

W: Brian, 오늘 오후에 시간 좀 있어요? 새로운 피부 관리 제품을 위한 테스트 마케팅을 하려고 하는데 당신의 조언이 필요해요.
M: 물론이에요, 그게 남성 주름 방지용 신제품이죠. 왜 테스트 마케팅을 하려고 해요? 그 제품들이 고객층의 관심을 끌 것이라는 것을 확신하지 않나요?
W: 사실 그렇진 않아요. 듣자 하니 어떤 남자 고객들은 기존 제품의 강한 향을 좋아하지 않더라고요. 그래서 몇 가지 변화를 줬고 테스트 그룹은 덜 강한 향에 대해 긍정적인 의견을 줬어요. 전국에 그 제품이 출시되기 전에 몇몇 실제 구매 환경에서 제품을 시험적으로 시도해 보고 싶어요.
M: 다행스럽게도 제가 1분기에 몇 가지 유사한 프로젝트를 했어요. 참고하도록 당신에게 몇 가지 자료를 줄 수 있어요.

**53.** 제품의 문제점은 무엇인가?
(A) 가격이 비싸다.
(B) 고객의 마음을 사로잡는 데 실패했다.
(C) 향이 지나치게 강하다.
(D) 품질 테스트에 통과하지 못했다. 　　정답 (C)

**54.** 여자는 남자에게 무엇을 하라고 언급하는가?
(A) 품질 테스트를 취소한다.
(B) 고객 의견을 검토한다.
(C) 그녀에게 조언을 한다.
(D) 프로젝트를 운영한다. 　　　　　　정답 (C)

**55.** 남자는 제안하는 것은 무엇인가?
(A) 신제품을 개발한다.
(B) 화장품을 산다.
(C) 제품에 변화를 준다.
(D) 정보를 공유한다. 　　　　　　　　정답 (D)

M: (56) **The head of the Personnel Department, Mr. Moore, told me that his department was not very happy with the new approval procedure for obtaining office supplies.**

W: Well, I know that it can be time consuming to have supply requests approved, (57) **but it's the best way to cut down on unnecessary expenses.**

M: I understand that, but Mr. Moore said that Personnel employees need a lot of materials and that approving all the requests takes up too much time.

W: (58) **Um… maybe we can make an inventory sheet that the Personnel employees can sign when they take supplies. That would be much simpler for them, save time, and help us track who's using what.**

---

M: 인사부장인 Moore 씨가 그의 부서가 새로운 비품 구매 결재 절차가 만족스럽지 않다고 말했어요.

W: 글쎄요, 비품 요청을 승인받는 것이 시간 낭비가 될 수 있다는 것은 알지만 불필요한 비용을 줄이기 위한 최선의 방법이에요.

M: 이해합니다만 Moore 씨는 인사부 직원들이 많은 물품을 필요로 하고, 요청한 물품들이 승인되기까지 너무 많은 시간이 걸린다고 말했어요.

W: 음… 인사부 직원들이 비품을 받을 때 그들이 서명할 수 있는 물품 재고 목록을 만들 수도 있어요. 그렇게 하면 훨씬 더 간단하고, 시간도 절약하고, 누가 무엇을 사용하는지 우리가 추적하는 데도 도움이 될 겁니다.

**56.** 화자들은 무엇에 대해 논의하는가?
(A) 주문 추적 방법
(B) 영업시간 연장의 제안
(C) 새로운 재고 시스템의 도입
(D) 물품 구매에 관한 새로운 방침          정답 (D)

**57.** 여자에 따르면 결정이 내려진 이유는 무엇인가?
(A) 비용을 절감하기 위해서
(B) 시간을 절약하기 위해서
(C) 생산성을 증가시키기 위해서
(D) 새로운 법을 준수하기 위해서          정답 (A)

**58.** 여자가 제안하는 것은 무엇인가?
(A) 더 많은 사무용품을 구매한다.
(B) 배송 정책을 변경한다.
(C) 절차를 좀 더 수월하게 만든다.
(D) 온라인상에 구인 광고를 게재한다.          정답 (C)

M: Hey, Vanessa! Do you have a minute to talk?

W: You look very upset, Harry. What's going on?

M: You know, (59) **I've been working on the Motion Sportswear account.** It's too hard to satisfy that company. (59, 60) **Whenever I send a graphic design for its commercial films, someone there always wants me to revise it.** It seems like it takes forever to get anything approved. It's happened almost twenty times just this month. Can you believe it?

W: Do you know what? (60) **Motion Sportwear was my second account here.** It sounds like the company hasn't changed a bit.

M: Really? I see there's no improvement.

W: Um… here's my solution: (61) **Ask your manager, Mr. Morgan, to give the company a call.** He can help with your problem.

---

M: 안녕, Vanessa! 잠시 이야기 좀 할 수 있을까요?

W: 굉장히 화가 나있는 것 같아요, Harry. 무슨 일이에요?

M: 알다시피, 제가 Motion Sportswear 광고주하고 일을 하고 있잖아요. 그 회사는 만족시키기가 너무 어려워요. 제가 매번 광고용 그래픽 디자인을 보낼 때마다 그쪽에서 누군가 항상 수정하길 원해요. 마치 영원히 승인을 안 해줄 것처럼 보여요. 이번달에만 그런 일이 거의 20번이나 발생했어요. 믿어지나요?

W: 그거 알아요? Motion Sportswear는 제가 이 곳에서 두 번째로 일한 광고주였어요. 그 회사는 전혀 바뀐 것이 없네요.

M: 진짜요? 개선된 게 없는 것 같아 보이네요.

W: 음… 제 해결책은 이거예요. 당신 상사인 Morgan 씨에게 그 회사에게 전화를 하라고 해요. 그가 당신 문제를 해결하는 데 도움이 될 겁니다.

**59.** 화자들은 어디에서 근무할 것 같은가?
(A) 회계사무소
(B) 광고회사
(C) 게임 제작업체
(D) 백화점          정답 (B)

**60.** 여자가 "Motion Sportwear was my second account here."라고 말할 때 여자가 의미하는 바는 무엇인가?
(A) 그녀는 여러 개의 은행 계좌를 갖고 있다.
(B) 그녀는 남자의 일에 대해 알고 있다.
(C) 그녀는 더 이상 그 고객과 일하지 않는다.
(D) 그녀는 남자가 화가 난 이유를 충분히 이해한다.          정답 (D)

**61.** 여자가 남자에게 제안하는 것은 무엇인가?
(A) 다른 일을 찾는다.
(B) 그래픽 디자인을 수정한다.
(C) 신규 고객을 유치한다.
(D) 그의 상사로부터 도움을 받는다.          정답 (D)

M: (62) **Security Department. What can I do for you?**

W: Um… hi. I'm Gwyneth Patterson, the head researcher of the laboratory. I received a new access card last week. But when I used my card to try to open the laboratory's secured door this morning, (63) **error code 004 repeatedly appeared on the screen.** What's wrong with my card?

M: Don't worry. Nothing is wrong with your access card. Please visit the office at your convenience, and I'll fix it.

W: Oh, that's a relief. (64) **I'll go to the security office after lunch.** Thank you for your help.

---

M: 보안과입니다. 어떻게 도와드릴까요?

W: 음… 안녕하세요. 저는 실험실에서 근무하는 수석 연구원 Gwyneth Patterson이에요. 제가 지난주에 새로운 출입카드를 받았어요. 그런데 오늘 아침에 실험실의 보안문을 열기 위해서 제 카드를 사용했는데 화면에 오류 코드 004만 반복적으로 뜨더라고요. 제 카드에 무슨 문제가 있나요?

M: 걱정 안 하셔도 됩니다. 출입카드에는 문제가 없습니다. 편하실 때 저희 사무실을 방문해 주시면 제가 해결해 드리겠습니다.

W: 아, 다행이에요. 그럼 점심식사 후에 보안과로 가겠습니다. 도와주셔서 감사드려요.

## 일반 출입카드 오류 코드

| | |
|---|---|
| 001 | 데이터베이스 접근 제한 |
| 002 | 출입카드 손상 |
| 003 | 프린터 오작동 |
| (63) 004 | 미등록 차량 |

**62.** 남자는 누구일 것 같은가?
(A) 실험실 연구원
(B) 안내직원
(C) 보안 전문가
(D) 소프트웨어 개발자 　　　　　　　　　　　정답 (C)

**63.** 그래픽을 보시오. 여자의 카드가 아침에 제대로 작동하지 않은 이유는 무엇인가?
(A) 그녀의 카드가 손상되었다.
(B) 데이터베이스 시스템이 고장났다.
(C) 일부 보안기기에 오작동이 발생했다.
(D) 그녀의 자동차가 등록되지 않았다. 　　　정답 (D)

**64.** 여자는 무엇을 할 것이라고 언급하는가?
(A) 보안과를 방문한다.
(B) 연구 논문을 출간한다.
(C) 내일 일찍 출근한다.
(D) 새로운 출입카드를 발급한다. 　　　　　정답 (A)

**문제 65-67번은 다음 대화와 대여표를 참조하시오.** 〔미W〕〔미M〕

W: Oakland Car Rental. How can I help you?
M: Hello. (65) I'm moving my office from San Jose to Oakland this weekend, so I need to rent a pickup truck or a cargo van.
W: Oh, welcome to Oakland. We rent various vehicles according to their sizes and purposes. How much will you be transporting?
M: I am just moving a few things. I have three computers and printers, four desks and chairs, two copy machines, two couches, and a couple of cabinets. I think that's all.
W: In that case, (66) I'd recommend the smallest rental we have. It's twelve feet long and can hold up to 2,000 pounds.
M: But I want to give myself more comfort and safety while driving. (66) Maybe the one fifteen feet in length would be fine if it's available.
W: Sure, no problem. (67) What day do you want to use it? I'll prepare the rental contract and send it to you by e-mail.

------------------------------------

W: Oakland Car Rental입니다. 어떻게 도와드릴까요?
M: 안녕하세요. 저는 이번 주말에 San Jose에서 Oakland로 사무실을 이전하려고 해서 소형 트럭이나 화물 운송용 승합차를 빌려야 합니다.
W: 아, Oakland에 오시는 걸 환영합니다. 저희는 크기와 목적에 따라 다양한 차량을 제공하고 있습니다. 어느 정도 짐을 운송할 계획이신가요?
M: 몇 개만 옮기면 됩니다. 컴퓨터와 프린터 각각 세 대, 책상과 의자 각각 네 개, 복사기 두 대, 소파 2개, 그리고 서류함 2개예요. 제 생각엔 그게 다예요.
W: 그런 경우라면 저는 가장 작은 차량을 추천해 드리고 싶어요. 길이는 12피트이고 최대 2,000파운드의 무게를 수용할 수 있습니다.
M: 그런데 저는 운전을 편하고 안전하게 하고 싶네요. 15피트 길이의 차량이 대여 가능하다면 그게 좋을 것 같아요.

---

W: 물론이에요, 문제없습니다. 무슨 요일에 사용하실 건가요? 제가 임대 계약서를 작성해서 이메일로 발송해 드리겠습니다.

## OAKLAND 차량 대여표

| 소형 트럭<br>12피트 길이 | 화물 운송용 승합차<br>(66) 15피트 길이 |
|---|---|
| 일반 운송 트럭<br>18피트 길이 | 대형 운송 트럭<br>22피트 길이 |

**65.** 남자가 차량을 대여해야 하는 이유는 무엇인가?
(A) 휴가를 가기 위해서
(B) 사무실을 이전하기 위해서
(C) 집으로부터 가구를 운송하기 위해서
(D) 새로운 상점의 개장을 돕기 위해서 　　　정답 (B)

**66.** 그래픽을 보시오. 남자는 어떤 차량을 원하는가?
(A) 소형 트럭
(B) 화물 운송용 승합차
(C) 일반 운송 트럭
(D) 대형 운송 트럭 　　　　　　　　　　　정답 (B)

**67.** 여자가 남자에게 요청하는 것은 무엇인가?
(A) 그의 운전면허증
(B) 임대 계약서 사본
(C) 보증금
(C) 대여 날짜 　　　　　　　　　　　　　　정답 (D)

**문제 68-70번은 다음 대화와 극장 안내판을 참조하시오.** 〔호M〕〔영W〕

M: Jane, don't forget that tonight we will see the play that I reserved tickets for last week.
W: Sure, it begins at 7:30, right? Should we get there early?
M: I think so. The play is very popular. All the tickets are already sold out, and (69) there are no assigned seats. (68) We need to get there when the theater opens to grab good seats where the actors and actresses can easily be seen.
W: I heard the play reminds people about what is important in life. That's probably why it's so popular.
M: I agree. You know, traffic is heavy at rush hour. We should use the subway after work. (70) Don't you think we should eat something on our way to the theater?
W: (70) There's a great place for fish and chips near the theater. We can eat there.

------------------------------------

M: Jane, 제가 지난주에 예약한 연극을 오늘밤에 관람한다는 사실 잊지 마세요.
W: 물론이에요, 7시 30분에 시작하죠, 그렇죠? 극장에 일찍 도착해야 할까요?
M: 제 생각엔 그래요. 그 연극이 인기가 많거든요. 표는 이미 매진되었고 그 극장은 지정 좌석제도 아니에요. 그래서 배우들이 잘 보이는 좋은 곳에 자리를 잡으려면 극장 문 여는 시점에 도착해야 해요.
W: 그 연극이 삶에서 무엇이 중요한지 일깨워준다고 들었어요. 아마도 그

래서 그 연극이 인기가 많을 거예요.

M: 동감이에요. 알다시피 퇴근 시간이면 교통정체가 심할 겁니다. 퇴근하고 지하철을 타는 게 좋을 것 같아요. 극장으로 가는 길에 뭔가 요기를 좀 해야 하지 않을까요?

W: 극장 근처에 피시 앤 칩스를 잘하는 곳이 하나 있어요. 거기서 먹고 가도 돼요.

---

### London 46 Theater 공연

Live Once, Buried Twice
매표소 운영 시간
11:00 A.M. – 7:00 P.M.
**(68) 입장 오후 6:30**
공연 시작 오후 8:00
종연 오후 10:30
입장 마감 오후 8:20

---

**68.** 그래픽을 보시오. 화자들은 극장에 언제 도착할 계획인가?
(A) 오후 6시 30분
(B) 오후 8시
(C) 오후 8시 30분
(D) 오후 10시 30분　　　　　　　　정답 (A)

**69.** 남자가 극장에 대해 언급하는 것은 무엇인가?
(A) 다양한 공연들을 상연한다.
(B) 지정 좌석제를 실시하지 않는다.
(C) 오랜 역사와 훌륭한 전통이 있다.
(D) 한정된 수의 표를 할인가에 판매한다.　정답 (B)

**70.** 화자들은 연극을 보기 전에 무엇을 할 것 같은가?
(A) 표를 예매한다.
(B) 식사를 한다.
(C) 기념품을 구입한다.
(D) 일정을 확인한다.　　　　　　　　정답 (B)

---

## Part 4

문제 71-73번은 다음 전화 메시지를 참조하시오. 영W

Good morning. This message is for Mr. Preston. **(72) My name is Lena Stanley. I'm the human resources manager for Sloane Digital Design.** It's 10 o'clock on Monday morning right now. **(71) I just received your application for the computer graphic designer position, and I'd like to arrange an interview with you on Thursday at 3 P.M.** if possible. **(73) Please contact me at 799-9815 and let me know if this date and time are suitable.** I hope to see you then.

- - - - - - - - - - - - - - - - - - - - - - - - - - - - - - -

안녕하세요. Preston 씨를 위한 메시지입니다. 제 이름은 Lena Stanley입니다. Sloane Digital Design의 인사부장입니다. 지금은 월요일 오전 10시입니다. 컴퓨터 그래픽 디자이너 직에 대한 귀하의 지원서를 접수했으며, 가능하면 목요일 오후 3시에 면접 일정을 잡으려고 합니다. 799~9815로 연락하셔서 이 날짜와 시간이 적절한지 알려주세요. 그럼 그 때 뵐 수 있길 바랍니다.

**71.** 화자는 무엇에 관해 언급하고 있는가?
(A) 회의 안건

---

(B) 근무 일정
(C) 입사 지원서
(D) 새로운 홈페이지　　　　　　　　정답 (C)

**72.** 화자는 누구인가?
(A) 인사부장
(B) 선임 연구원
(C) 금융 분석가
(D) 컴퓨터 프로그래머　　　　　　　정답 (A)

**73.** 화자는 청자에게 무엇을 제안하는가?
(A) 직원 회의에 참석한다.
(B) 온라인으로 지원서를 작성한다.
(C) 추천서를 제공한다.
(D) 전화 연락을 한다.　　　　　　　정답 (D)

---

문제 74-76번은 다음 담화를 참조하시오. 미W

Good morning and welcome to today's meeting. **(74) I'm Lisa Stewart,** the head of Security. As you all know, **(75) every employee will be getting a new access card next week. (76) I've been asked to come in and show you how to use the security system at the main entrance of the building.** This training will be very helpful to you all. The access card and the security system are both easy to use and will really increase the security of the building. You need to use this card every time you enter or leave the building and also when you log onto the computer network. Additionally, new passwords for accessing security system will be given to each employee in 2 weeks. **(76) Now, let's proceed with the training.**

- - - - - - - - - - - - - - - - - - - - - - - - - - - - - - -

안녕하세요, 오늘 회의에 오신 것을 환영합니다. 저는 보안 팀장인 Lisa Stewart입니다. 여러분 모두 아시다시피, 모든 직원이 다음주에 새로운 접속 카드를 받게 되실 것입니다. 여러분에게 건물의 정문에 설치된 보안 시스템의 사용법을 알려주라는 요청을 받고 왔습니다. 이 교육은 여러분 모두에게 매우 유용할 것입니다. 접속 카드와 보안 시스템은 둘 다 사용하기가 쉽고 건물의 보안을 실질적으로 강화시켜 줄 것입니다. 건물을 출입할 때는 물론이고 컴퓨터 네트워크에 접속할 때도 항상 이 카드를 사용하셔야 합니다. 추가로 말씀드리면 2주 후에 보안 시스템 접속용 새 비밀번호도 직원 각각에게 제공될 예정입니다. 이제 교육을 진행하겠습니다.

**74.** 화자는 어느 부서에서 근무하는가?
(A) 마케팅부
(B) 홍보부
(C) 보안과
(D) 인사부　　　　　　　　　　　　정답 (C)

**75.** 화자에 따르면 다음주에 직원들에게 제공되는 것은 무엇인가?
(A) 새로운 비밀번호
(B) 접속 카드
(C) 주차 공간
(D) 사무실 열쇠　　　　　　　　　　정답 (B)

**76.** 화자는 이후에 무엇을 할 것인가?
(A) 기술 교육을 한다.
(B) 견본품을 나눠준다.
(C) 새 소프트웨어를 설치한다.
(D) 프로젝트를 마무리한다.　　　　　정답 (A)

**문제 77-79번은 다음 연설문을 참조하시오.** 영W

Good afternoon and (77/78) **welcome to the Animal Society's annual volunteer appreciation luncheon. (77) We want to thank you for all the hard work you've done over the past year.** Our organization wouldn't exist without you. We'd especially like to recognize those of you who worked on the adoption campaign. (79) **Your efforts on social media and at events in your neighborhood contributed to a 27% increase in the number of adoptions this year, which is the highest we've ever seen!** We hope to capitalize on that momentum as we focus on fundraising next year. But for now, let's enjoy the afternoon! Thank you once again for all that you do for us.

-----

안녕하세요, Animal Society의 연례 자원봉사 사은 오찬 행사에 오신 걸 환영합니다. 저희는 여러분이 지난 한 해 동안 애써 주신 노고에 감사드리고 싶습니다. 저희 단체는 여러분이 아니었다면 존재할 수 없었을 것입니다. 특히 동물 입양 분야에서 근무하신 여러분께서 굉장히 수고가 많았다고 말씀드리고 싶습니다. 여러분이 소셜 미디어와 지역 행사에서 기울이신 노력은 올해 동물 입양 건수가 27%나 증가하는 결과를 이끌어내는 데 큰 기여를 했는데, 이는 역대 최고의 수치입니다! 우리는 이러한 기세를 기회로 내년에 있을 기금 마련에 집중하였으면 합니다. 하지만 지금은 즐겁게 오찬을 갖도록 합시다! 다시 한 번 여러분께서 저희 단체를 위해 수고해주신 것에 감사드립니다.

**77.** 화자에 따르면 행사가 개최되는 이유는 무엇인가?
(A) 자원봉사자들에게 감사하기 위해서
(B) 기금을 모으기 위해서
(C) 입양을 널리 알리기 위해서
(D) 기념일을 축하하기 위해서 　　　　　정답 (A)

**78.** 화자는 어떤 단체에서 일할 것 같은가?
(A) 시장조사 및 컨설팅 업체
(B) 소비자 권익 보호 단체
(C) 언론 기관
(D) 동물 복지 단체 　　　　　정답 (D)

**79.** 화자가 입양 캠페인과 관련하여 언급한 내용은 무엇인가?
(A) 굉장히 성공적이었다.
(B) 많은 자원봉사자들이 필요했다.
(C) 언론에서 언급했다.
(D) 효과적이지 않았다. 　　　　　정답 (A)

**문제 80-82번은 다음 전화 메시지를 참조하시오.** 미M

Hi. My name is Sam Goldman, and (80) **I work over at Sanders Lumber.** We are having an employee appreciation night at the President Hotel, and I believe our personnel manager ordered food from your catering service. (81) **He just informed me that we'll need both vegetarian and non-vegetarian meal options and that he would like menu cards to be placed at each table.** We'll be setting up the room ourselves, so I'd like to pick up the cards this week if possible. (82) **I can head over tomorrow at lunch if that's convenient.** When you check my message, please call me back and let me know.

-----

안녕하세요. 제 이름은 Sam Goldman이라고 하는데요, Sanders Lumber에서 근무하고 있습니다. 직원 사은회를 President Hotel에서 개

최할 예정이며, 저희 인사부장님이 귀사의 출장요리를 주문한 것으로 알고 있습니다. 그는 제게 채식주의자용 식단과 일반 식단이 모두 필요하다는 것과 각 테이블마다 메뉴 카드가 놓였으면 한다고 말씀하셨습니다. 저희가 행사장을 직접 준비를 해야 해서, 가능하시면 그 메뉴 카드를 이번 주에 수령하고 싶습니다. 번거롭지 않으시면 내일 점심 때 그 곳으로 찾아가도록 하겠습니다. 제 메시지를 확인하면 답신 전화를 주셔서 제 제안이 어떤지 알려주십시오.

**80.** 화자는 어디에서 일할 것 같은가?
(A) 출장요리 업체
(B) 목재 공급 매장
(C) 인쇄 회사
(D) 행사 기획 업체 　　　　　정답 (B)

**81.** 남자가 전화한 이유는 무엇인가?
(A) 행사를 취소하기 위해서
(B) 장소를 예약하기 위해서
(C) 출장요리의 요청사항을 전달하기 위해서
(D) 위치를 확인하기 위해서 　　　　　정답 (C)

**82.** 화자는 내일 무엇을 할 것인가?
(A) 출장요리 업체를 방문한다.
(B) 의견을 정리한다.
(C) 고객의 주문을 접수한다.
(D) 요리 시연회에 참석한다. 　　　　　정답 (A)

**문제 83-85번은 회의 내용을 참조하시오.** 영W

Good afternoon, everyone. I'm pleased that you could all make it. We have an urgent matter to discuss. (83/84) **In the last quarter here, we've seen our tablet computer sales decrease sharply.** Using some more detailed market analysis, (84) **we've seen especially high losses for our more expensive products.** I don't think that any of you will be surprised by the numbers in front of you. (84) **I need everyone on deck with our restructuring plans to improve our sales.** With that in mind, (85) **I'd like to bring in Ms. Jenkins, our new sales strategist.** Please let's give her a warm welcome.

-----

안녕하세요, 여러분. 여러분 모두 회의에 참석해 주셔서 기쁩니다. 우리가 긴급하게 논의해야 할 사안이 있습니다. 지난 분기에 우리는 태블릿 컴퓨터의 매출이 급격하게 하락하는 걸 지켜봤습니다. 조금 더 자세한 시장 분석 자료를 이용하면, 가격이 비싼 제품에서의 손실이 특히 컸습니다. 여러분 앞에 놓인 수치를 보고 놀라실 분은 없을 거라는 생각이 듭니다. 저는 여러분 모두가 매출 향상을 위한 조정 계획에 함께 해주시길 바랍니다. 이를 염두에 두고 저는 새로운 영업 전략 전문가인 Jenkins 씨를 모시겠습니다. 그를 따뜻하게 환영해 주시길 바랍니다.

**83.** 화자가 언급한 문제점은 무엇인가?
(A) 청구서 문제
(B) 매출 하락
(C) 고객 불만
(D) 대량 해고의 가능성 　　　　　정답 (B)

**84.** 여자가 "I need everyone on deck with our restructuring plans to improve our sales."라고 말할 때 의미하는 바는 무엇인가?
(A) 그녀는 업무상의 실수에 실망했다.
(B) 그녀는 추천한 대로 따라야 할지 고민이다.

(C) 그녀는 청자들이 함께 하길 원한다.

(D) 그녀는 매출 증가를 위해 더욱 창의적인 아이디어가 필요하다.

정답 (C)

**85.** 화자에 따르면 Jenkins 씨는 누구인가?

(A) 시장 조사원

(B) 임원

(C) 전기 공학자

(D) 영업 전문가

정답 (D)

**문제 86-88번은 다음 담화를 참조하시오.** 回W

Travelers, we have made our final stop on the full-day tour. If you look out the trolley to your left, (86) you'll see the Twelve Oaks Performance Hall, where we'll be attending an orchestral performance at 4:00. We've arrived about thirty minutes early, so you'll have just enough time to visit some shops in the area and still get back by 3:50. There's a cultural museum at the end of this street, and next to it is Sandy's Donut Shop. Even though it's not well known, (87) Sandy's Donut Shop's ice cream is delicious. I'm sure you can enjoy some refreshing dessert there. Okay, (88) I'm going to give you your tickets now. That way, we can meet in the performance hall.

--------------------------------------------

여행객 여러분, 오늘 여행의 마지막 종착지에 도착했습니다. 여러분이 타고 계신 전차의 좌측을 보시면 우리가 관람할 4시 오케스트라 공연이 있을 Twelve Oaks 공연홀이 보이실 겁니다. 우리는 대략 30분 일찍 도착했기 때문에 이 지역의 일부 상점을 방문하고 3시 50분까지 공연장으로 돌아갈 시간은 충분합니다. 이 거리 끝에는 문화 박물관이 있고 그 옆에는 Sandy's Donut Shop이 있습니다. 아주 유명한 곳은 아니지만 Sandy's Donut Shop의 아이스크림은 맛있습니다. 그 곳에서 여러분이 맛있는 후식을 즐기실 수 있을 것이라고 확신합니다. 자, 이제 여러분께 공연표를 배부해 드리도록 하겠습니다. 그러면 우리 모두 공연홀에서 만날 수 있습니다.

**86.** 청자들은 오후 4시에 무엇을 할 것인가?

(A) 아이스크림을 먹는다.

(B) 전차에 탑승한다.

(C) 공연을 관람한다.

(D) 문화 박물관에 방문한다.

정답 (C)

**87.** 화자가 "Sandy's Donut Shop's ice cream is delicious."라고 언급한 이유는 무엇인가?

(A) 두 개의 아이스크림 브랜드를 비교하기 위해서

(B) 청자들에게 맛있는 도너츠를 먹도록 권장하기 위해서

(C) 청자들이 그 곳에 방문하도록 추천하기 위해서

(D) 상점이 널리 알려진 이유를 설명하기 위해서

정답 (C)

**88.** 화자는 이후에 무엇을 할 것 같은가?

(A) 공연을 관람한다.

(B) 예약을 한다.

(C) 기념품을 구매한다.

(D) 표를 배부한다.

정답 (D)

**문제 89-91번은 다음 교통 방송을 참조하시오.** 回M

Good afternoon, everyone. The time is now 5:30. (90) This is

Daniel Radcliffe with your local traffic update. (89) If you are coming home from work on the Ocean View Highway, take note that traffic there is backed up by about an hour due to a three-car rear-end collision. An ambulance and the fire department are on their way to the scene. So if you are not on the highway yet, try to avoid getting on. If you are taking the Richmond Bridge, traffic there is smooth with no backups or delays. Downtown traffic is bumper to bumper, but once you get past Mission Street, it will be smooth again. (91) I'll be back later with another traffic update. Stay tuned to BCBK.

--------------------------------------------

안녕하십니까, 여러분? 현재 시각은 5시 30분입니다. 저는 지역 교통 소식을 전해드리는 Daniel Radcliffe입니다. 퇴근길에 Ocean View Highway를 이용하는 분들은 3중 추돌 사고로 인해 약 한 시간 가량 지체되고 있다는 점에 유의하시기 바랍니다. 구급차와 소방차가 현장으로 출동하고 있습니다. 그러므로 아직 고속도로로 진입하지 않으신 운전자들께서는 가급적 다른 길을 이용하십시오. Richmond Bridge를 이용하시는 분들은 소통이 원활해 길이 막히거나 지체되는 곳이 없다는 점 알려드립니다. 시내는 차량이 꽉 막힌 상태이며 Mission Street를 지나면 정체가 풀리겠습니다. 저는 또 다른 교통 소식과 함께 다시 돌아오겠습니다. BCBK에 채널 고정하십시오.

**89.** 화자는 어떤 문제점을 언급하는가?

(A) 공사 지연

(B) 교통 문제

(C) 기계 결함

(D) 악천후

정답 (B)

**90.** 화자는 누구일 것 같은가?

(A) 컴퓨터 수리공

(B) 공사 감독

(C) 뉴스 보도 기자

(D) 정부 공무원

정답 (C)

**91.** 화자는 이후에 무엇을 할 것인가?

(A) 안전검사를 실시한다.

(B) 신입직원을 훈련시킨다.

(C) 새로운 소식을 전달한다.

(D) 곧 있을 행사에 관해 논의한다.

정답 (C)

**문제 92-94번은 다음 안내문을 참조하시오.** 回W

(92) Welcome to the San Francisco-Tiburon Ferry Harbor. (93) We will experience a delay in ferry service to the city today due to high winds. Because the National Weather Service has issued a high-wind advisory for the entire San Francisco Bay area, we must postpone the departure of the 8 A.M. ferry. There is no estimated time for this delay as the weather service has issued the advisory until further notice. We sincerely apologize for this delay. We are coordinating with city transportation officials to attempt to arrange alternative overland transportation. (94) We will notify you immediately when arrangements are confirmed for our passengers.

--------------------------------------------

San Francisco-Tiburon 여객선 항구에 오신 것을 환영합니다. 강풍으로 인해 시내로 가는 여객선 운항 서비스에 지연이 있겠습니다. 기상청에서 전체 San Francisco Bay 지역에 강풍 주의보를 발령한 관계로 오전 8시 여객선의 출항을 연기해야 합니다. 기상청이 추후 통지가 있을 때까

지 강풍 주의보를 발령했기 때문에 이 출항 지연이 얼마나 지속될 것인지에 대해서는 말씀드리기 어렵습니다. 출항 지연에 대해 진심으로 사과드립니다. 현재 시 교통과 공무원들과 지상으로 연결되는 대체 교통 수단을 마련하고자 조정 중에 있습니다. 준비가 되는 대로 바로 승객 여러분께 공지해 드리겠습니다.

**92.** 안내문이 방송되는 장소는 어디인가?
(A) 비행기
(B) 여객선
(C) 항구 사무실
(D) 기자 회견장     정답 (C)

**93.** 화자에 따르면 지연을 초래한 이유는 무엇인가?
(A) 기계적인 문제
(B) 대규모 선박 교통량
(C) 기상 상태
(D) 시스템 소프트웨어 오작동     정답 (C)

**94.** 청자들은 이후에 무엇을 할 것 같은가?
(A) 배를 타고 여행한다.
(B) 표를 환불한다.
(C) 안전 절차에 대해 배운다.
(D) 다음 안내방송을 기다린다.     정답 (D)

문제 95~97번은 다음 전화 메시지와 주문 양식을 참조하시오. ⓂM

Hi there. I'm calling for James McCraw, the manager at Charlie's Therapeutics. I'm following up on the weekly order you just sent us (95) **because I was surprised by the number of coffee cups you requested.** You don't usually want so many. I'm happy to correct the number to match your usual order if necessary. Call me back if that's not okay. (96) **By the way, I'll be away on vacation next week.** (97) **If anything comes up, you can call Ms. Kensington. She'll be covering my accounts while I'm gone.**

---

안녕하세요. Charlie's Therapeutics의 매니저인 James McCraw 씨에게 연락을 드립니다. 귀하가 요청하신 커피잔의 수가 놀라워서 방금 보내주신 주간 주문량을 확인해 보고자 연락을 드립니다. 보통 그렇게 많은 양을 원하시지 않잖아요. 필요하시다면 귀하의 일반적인 주문량대로 수정해드릴 수 있습니다. 만약 주문량이 올바르지 않다면 다시 연락주십시오. 그런데 제가 다음주에는 휴가를 떠납니다. 만약 무슨 일이 발생하면 Kensington 씨에게 연락을 주세요. 그녀가 제가 자리를 비우는 동안 제 업무를 대신 처리할 겁니다.

## 주문서

| 제품 | 수량 |
|---|---|
| 티셔츠 | 100 |
| 엽서 | 150 |
| (95) 커피잔 | 500 |
| 캔디 바 | 700 |

**95.** 그래픽을 보시오. 주문서에서 어떤 수량이 변경될 것인가?
(A) 100
(B) 150
(C) 500

(D) 700     정답 (C)

**96.** 화자는 다음주에 무엇을 할 것인가?
(A) 그는 새로운 음료를 출시할 것이다.
(B) 그는 사무실을 비울 것이다.
(C) 그는 새로운 직장에서 업무를 시작할 것이다.
(D) 그는 특별한 장비를 사용할 것이다.     정답 (B)

**97.** 화자는 Kensington 씨가 무엇을 할 것이라고 이야기하는가?
(A) 그녀는 전액 환불을 요청할 것이다.
(B) 그녀는 새로운 직원들을 훈련시킬 것이다.
(C) 그녀는 새로운 커피잔들을 보낼 것이다.
(D) 그녀는 남자의 일을 대신 처리할 것이다.     정답 (D)

문제 98~100번은 다음 전화 메시지와 일정표를 참조하시오. 호M

Hi. I'm calling for Mr. Wilson in Conference Room Scheduling. This is William Baker. I would like to change my room reservation. (98) **I had the Presidential Library reserved for 10:00 this morning for a meeting with some clients.** However, I realized that's not going to work because I'm serving refreshments to my clients. (99) **I noticed that my colleague, Ms. Lawrence, has a meeting at the same time, so maybe she could switch rooms with me.** Could you check with her please and confirm that I can use the room that she signed up for? I'm showing a video to my clients, so (100) **I need to tell the audio-visual group where to set up the equipment.**

---

안녕하세요. 회의실 일정 담당 부서에서 근무하는 Wilson 씨에게 연락을 드립니다. 저는 William Baker라고 합니다. 제 회의실 예약을 변경하고 싶습니다. 저는 오전 10시 고객들과의 만남을 위해 Presidential Library을 예약했습니다. 그러나 고객들에게 다과를 제공해야 하는 관계로 이 회의실이 부적절하다는 점을 알았습니다. 제 동료인 Lawrence 씨가 같은 시간에 회의가 있다는 사실을 알았는데, 아마 그녀가 저와 회의실을 바꿔줄 수 있을지도 모르겠네요. 그녀에게 확인해서 제가 그녀가 예약한 회의실을 사용할 수 있는지 여부를 확정해서 알려주시겠습니까? 고객들에게 영상도 보여주려 해서 시청각 장비 담당자들에게 어느 곳에 장비를 설치해야 하는지 알려주기도 해야 합니다.

| 10:00–12:00 시간대 | 예약자 |
|---|---|
| Presidential Library | Mr. Baker |
| (99) Convention Room | Ms. Lawrence |
| Conference Room A | Ms. Wallace |
| Conference Room B | 예약 없음 |

**98.** 화자가 방을 예약한 이유는 무엇인가?
(A) 고객들과 만나기 위해서
(B) 강연을 하기 위해서
(C) 세미나를 개최하기 위해서
(D) 발표의 사전 연습을 하기 위해서     정답 (A)

**99.** 그래픽을 보시오. 화자는 어느 방을 사용하길 원하는가?
(A) The Presidential Library
(B) The Convention Room
(C) Conference Room A

**100.** 화자는 무엇을 하길 원한다고 언급하는가?
(A) 무료 음료
(B) 유인물을 프린트하는 것
(C) 예약 일정을 재조정하는 것
(D) 영상 장비를 설치하는 것　　　　　정답 (D)

## Part 5

**101.** 유럽의 금융 기관들은 미국에서 발생한 재정상의 어려움으로 인해 중국에 투자한 자금을 회수할 것이다.　　　　　정답 (C)

**102.** 모든 부서장들은 친숙한 업무와 새로 주어지는 업무 모두 잘 수행할 것으로 기대된다.　　　　　정답 (A)

**103.** 시립 미술관은 현재 보수공사로 인해 폐쇄된 상태이며 내년 9월에 재개장할 예정이다.　　　　　정답 (A)

**104.** 거의 100개국에서 온 수천 명의 연구원들이 다음달 Stockholm에서 개최될 기후 변화에 관한 국제 학술 회의에 참여할 예정이다.　　　　　정답 (C)

**105.** 최근에 시립 대학교에 등록한 대학생 수의 증가는 임대 부동산에 대한 수요 증가로 이어졌다.　　　　　정답 (C)

**106.** 한정된 시간 동안 고객 여러분은 저희의 새롭고 강력한 노트북 컴퓨터를 무이자 대출로 계약금 없이 구매하실 수 있습니다.　　　　　정답 (D)

**107.** 미국의 해외 관광객 수는 경기 불황으로 인해 급격히 줄어서 전년 대비 12% 하락하였다.　　　　　정답 (C)

**108.** 산림청에 따르면 규정을 준수하지 않는 사람은 누구든 간에 벌금이 부과되거나 산을 다시 방문하는 것이 금지될 것이다.　　　　　정답 (C)

**109.** 이 방법은 종종 잘못 이해하거나 완전하게 이해하지 못하는 주제들을 명확하게 해주도록 도와준다.　　　　　정답 (B)

**110.** 예상하지 못한 오디오 화상 회의 시스템의 고장으로 인해 발표는 다음 주 수요일로 연기되었다.　　　　　정답 (C)

**111.** 우리 보안팀들은 발생할 수 있는 모든 상황에 즉각적으로 대처하고자 24시간 내내 근무를 선다.　　　　　정답 (A)

**112.** Alabama의 오래된 제조 공장들 중 한 곳이 한 달 간의 생산 중단 끝에 마침내 가동을 재개했다.　　　　　정답 (D)

**113.** 고도로 발전된 의료 기술은 외과의사들이 섬세한 수술을 더욱 정밀하게 하도록 도움을 줄 수 있다.　　　　　정답 (C)

**114.** 지난달 Mandoo Tech 사는 대부분의 사람들이 사용하는 컴퓨터 크기의 절반인 새로운 컴퓨터를 출시하였으며, 이는 시장에 나와 있는 가장 작은 크기의 컴퓨터이다.　　　　　정답 (B)

**115.** 새로 개선된 컨테이너 트럭들은 거의 이전 트럭들만큼이나 무겁지만 훨씬 더 튼튼하고 조종하기가 쉽다.　　　　　정답 (A)

**116.** 신선함을 유지하기 위해서는 이 양파와 토마토들을 냉장고에 넣어 화씨 36도 이하로 보관해야 한다.　　　　　정답 (D)

**117.** 제약 특허 기간이 만료되면 다른 회사들이 현재 비용의 1/4에 해당하는 비용으로 최초 약제와 동일한 약을 제조할 수 있다.　　　　　정답 (A)

**118.** 모든 영업 관련 서류를 처리하는 업무를 담당하는 사람은 영업차장인 Andrew Kim이다.　　　　　정답 (C)

**119.** 경제학자들은 국가 경제에 영향을 미치는 개인 및 사회적 경제 활동을 연구할 뿐만 아니라 향후 세계 경제의 추이를 정기적으로 예측하고자 노력한다.　　　　　정답 (A)

**120.** 11번 가에 위치하고 있는 신발 가게에서는 고객들이 선택할 수 있는 다양한 종류의 브랜드를 제공한다.　　　　　정답 (D)

**121.** 한 업계 전문가는 Zayo Auto 사의 SS Motors 사 인수는 두 회사 사이의 자동차 기술 격차를 6년에서 3년으로 좁히게 될 것이라고 말했다.　　　　　정답 (A)

**122.** 신문 보도에 따르면 우리 회사의 브랜드 가치는 전세계 120개의 다국적 기업들 중 13위를 차지했다.　　　　　정답 (B)

**123.** 이 박물관은 미국의 철도 역사를 보존하고 있는 미국 내의 가장 오래된 기관들 중 한 곳이다.　　　　　정답 (C)

**124.** 만약에 그 회사가 중국에서 이 새로운 에너지 음료를 판매했다면 아마도 그 제품들은 인기를 끌지 못했을 것이다.　　　　　정답 (C)

**125.** 산소 부족, 극한의 기후, 그리고 동상을 포함한 많은 요소들이 일부 높은 산들의 등반을 어렵게 만든다.　　　　　정답 (C)

**126.** 분할 납부를 한 고객은 그 다음달에 5달러의 연체료와 함께 남은 잔액을 지불해야 한다.　　　　　정답 (A)

**127.** 일부 사람들이 우리와 매우 다르다고 해도 우리는 그들의 문화와 지역 풍습을 존중해야 한다.　　　　　정답 (A)

**128.** 수리를 받기 위해 서비스 센터로 컴퓨터를 가지고 오는 고객들은 보통 한 시간 이내에 수리가 완료된 후 신속하게 연락을 받게 될 것이다.　　　　　정답 (B)

**129.** 불경기로 인해 대부분의 직원들은 국내 경기가 향상될 때까지 여름 휴가 가는 것을 연기할 것이다.　　　　　정답 (D)

**130.** 많은 사무직 근로자들이 업무와 반복되는 일상생활로 인해 피곤하거나 스트레스를 받을 때마다 커피 같은 카페인을 과용하는 것 같다.　　　　　정답 (C)

## Part 6

**문제 131-134번은 다음 광고를 참조하시오.**

### The East Seafood Restaurant

East Seafood Restaurant은 빠른 식사를 원하는 사람들과 아이가 있는 가족을 위한 훌륭한 선택입니다. 저희는 킹크랩 요리를 15분 안에 받으실 수 있도록 보장하며, 그렇지 않으면 고객의 식사 비용은 저희가 내겠습니다! 저희 식사는 손으로 자른 감자튀김, 건강에 좋은 샐러드 바와 다양한 청량음료를 포함합니다.

오늘 저희 레스토랑 회원으로 신청해 보세요. 방문하실 때마다 회원 카드에 도장이 찍힐 것입니다. 10번의 방문 후에는 무료 바닷가재 요리를 드실 수 있습니다. 회원은 East Seafood Restaurant 로고가 새겨진 티셔츠, 모자와 같은 Blue Ocean 상품에 대해 20퍼센트 할인 혜택을 받으실 수 있습니다. <u>또한 회원은 레스토랑이 붐빌 때 우선적으로 자리 안내를 받으실 수 있습니다.</u>

East Seafood Restaurant은 연회비로 40달러를 받습니다. 회원카드는 신용카드가 아니기 때문에 식사비를 지불하는 데 사용될 수 없음을 알아주시기 바랍니다.

**131.** 정답 (C)

**132.** 정답 (D)

**133.** (A) 또한 회원은 레스토랑이 붐빌 때 우선적으로 자리 안내를 받으실 수 있습니다.
(B) 저희 식당은 버스와 지하철을 이용하여 방문하시기 편리한 곳에 위치하고 있습니다.
(C) 저희 식당 회원 수는 상당히 증가했습니다.
(D) 연어나 참치와 같은 우수한 해산물은 심장 건강을 촉진시키는 것으로 알려져 있습니다. 정답 (A)

**134.** 정답 (A)

---

문제 135-138번은 다음 회람을 참조하시오.

**회람**

발신: North America 사 인사 및 급여 지급 부서
수신: 전 직원
날짜: 1월 8일
제목: 급여 명세서 송부 방침 변화

지난 몇 달간 급여를 은행 계좌로 직접 입금을 받는 많은 직원들의 급여 명세서는 서면 급여 명세서가 아닌 전자 급여 명세서로 대체되어 왔습니다. 여러분의 마지막 서면 급여 명세서는 인쇄되어 1월 15일에 여러분에게 송부될 것입니다. 만약 계속해서 서면 급여 명세서를 받기 원하시는 경우, 1월 중순에 발송해드릴 지시 사항을 따르시면 됩니다. 전자 급여 명세서를 송부해 드리는 것은 인사 및 급여 자가 서비스의 사용을 권장하기 위한 목적의 일환입니다.

인사 및 급여 자가 서비스를 사용함으로써 여러분은 현재와 과거의 급여 정보를 몇 초만에 쉽게 접근하실 수 있습니다. 또한 급여 명세서의 작성 및 송부와 관련된 회사 비용의 일부가 절감될 것입니다. <u>이러한 방침의 변경은 궁극적으로 직원들의 편의에 기여할 것입니다.</u> 저희는 직원들의 편의를 개선할 수 있는 방법을 모색하는 것이야말로 인사부의 최우선 업무 중 하나라고 믿고 있습니다. 감사합니다.

**135.** 정답 (D)

**136.** 정답 (D)

**137.** 정답 (B)

**138.** (A) 우리 직원들은 회사의 성공에 중요한 역할을 담당했습니다.
(B) 경영진은 요청받은 대로 모든 직원의 상여금을 인상하고자 할 의사가 있습니다.
(C) 이러한 방침의 변경은 궁극적으로 직원들의 편의에 기여할 것입니다.
(D) 직장 내 기술의 목적은 바로 직원들이 행하는 매일의 업무를 용이하게 하는 데 있습니다. 정답 (C)

---

문제 139-142번은 다음 공지를 참조하시오.

**7월 1일 월요일 시행**
**이전 공지**

7월 1일부로 Cheese Pastry Factory의 현 위치가 변경됩니다. 저희는 Hayward에 위치한 본사를 폐쇄하고 Oakland에 위치한 새로운 사무실로 이전하는 절차를 시작했습니다.

제품이나 서비스와 관련된 문의나 문제점에 관한 서신은 이제 다음 주소로 발송되어야 합니다: Cheese Pastry Factory, 110 Telegraph Lane, Oakland, California 94577.

그러나 저희 온라인 매장인 www.cpf.com과 직원 이메일 주소는 변경되지 않습니다. 유감스럽게도 저희는 아직 Oakland 전화국으로부터 새로운 전화번호와 팩스번호를 받지 못했습니다. <u>저희는 향후 48시간 내에 새로운 전화번호와 팩스번호를 회사 홈페이지에 게재할 수 있기를 바라고 있습니다.</u>

Cheese Pastry Factory를 대표하여 귀하의 양해에 감사드리며 계속해서 California 북부 지역의 최대 규모의 페이스트리 제공업체에서 구매해 주시길 바랍니다.

**139.** 정답 (D)

**140.** 정답 (D)

**141.** (A) 저희 회사는 다양한 빵과 페이스트리를 생산하는 것으로 명성이 높습니다.
(B) 귀하의 집 주소나 전화번호와 같은 개인 정보는 비밀로 유지되어야 합니다.
(C) 저희는 향후 48시간 내에 새로운 전화번호와 팩스번호를 회사 홈페이지에 게재할 수 있기를 바라고 있습니다.
(D) 다른 소셜 네트워킹 서비스들은 고객과의 중요한 소통 채널이 될 것입니다. 정답 (C)

**142.** 정답 (A)

---

문제 143-146번은 다음 편지를 참조하시오.

**OLIVER TOYS**

Ms. Rita White
909 Star Avenue
Bakersfield, CA 90232

White 씨께,

10월 26일에 작성해서 보내주신 편지에 대해 감사드립니다. 저는 교체품을 요청하시는 귀하의 편지를 수령했다는 것을 알려드리고자 답신을 씁니다. 저희는 제품들이 온전한 상태로 있다면 고객의 기대를 충족시키지 못한 제품을 항상 기꺼이 교체해 드리고 있습니다.

제품을 저희에게 반품하기 위해서는 배송 시에 받은 송장과 함께 본래 포장 상태로 발송해 주셔야 합니다. 또한 저희 홈페이지의 고객 서비스 코너에서 반품 라벨을 프린트하여 이를 반품하시고자 하는 제품에 부착해 주십시오.

저희 반품 정책은 제품을 온전한 상태로 구매일로부터 30일 이내에 반품해 주셔야 한다는 점 기억하시기 바랍니다. <u>구매하신 제품에 대해 만족하지 못하신 점 매우 죄송하게 생각합니다.</u> 하지만 귀하의 반품을 시의적절하게 처리할 수 있도록 최선을 다하겠으니 안심하셔도 됩니다.

Brian McGrigger

**143.** 정답 (B)

**144.** 정답 (C)

**145.** (A) 오랜 시간 저희 제품을 애용해 주셔서 감사합니다.
(B) 많은 불만사항들은 부실한 품질의 제품과 서비스에 기인합니다.
(C) 구매하신 제품에 대해 만족하지 못하신 점 매우 죄송하게 생각합니다.
(D) 저희는 어떤 제품이 고객을 만족시키는지 파악하고자 시장 조사를 활용하고 있습니다. 정답 (C)

**146.** 정답 (A)

## Part 7

**문제 147-148번은 다음 문자 메시지를 참조하시오.**

발신: Harry Robinson, (212) 545-6313
수신: 수요일, 6월 3일, 오후 5:30

안녕하세요, Johansson 씨.

자동차 시동을 걸다가 배터리가 방전되었어요. 그래서 제 차를 차고에서 꺼내어 11번가에 있는 자동차 수리점까지 견인하기 위해 견인차를 부를 수 밖에 없었고요. 지금은 여기서 제 차의 배터리가 교체되길 기다리고 있어요.

(147) 저는 당신이 저 대신 오늘 저녁 근무를 서줄 수 있을지 궁금해요. (148) 만약 오늘 밤 저 대신 근무를 서실 수 있다면 최대한 빨리 답장을 주세요. 물론, 대체 근무가 가능하시다면, 제가 다음 주에 있을 당신의 근무를 대신 서드릴게요. 고마워요.

**147.** Robinson 씨가 문자 메시지를 보낸 이유는 무엇인가?
(A) 그의 자동차를 수리하기 위해서
(B) 직장까지 차편을 요청하기 위해서
(C) 휴가를 떠나기 위해서
(D) 그의 저녁 근무를 대신 서줄 수 있는지 물어보기 위해서 정답 (D)

**148.** Johansson 씨가 빠르게 해달라고 요청을 받은 것은 무엇인가?
(A) Robinson 씨를 데리러 온다.
(B) 답장을 보낸다.
(C) 고객을 위한 저녁식사를 요리한다.
(D) 배터리를 충전한다. 정답 (B)

**문제 149-150번은 다음 편지를 참조하시오.**

5월 10일

Catherine Townsend 씨
8290 Sears Street
Nassau, Bahamas

Townsend 씨께,

(149) 저희 온라인 설문조사를 완료해 주셔서 감사 드리고 싶습니다. (150) 사의를 표하기 위해 저희는 고객님의 자택으로 쿠폰을 보내드렸습니다. 이 쿠폰은 다음에 저희 스파를 방문하실 때 전체 방문 금액의 20%를 할인 받는 데 사용하실 수 있을 것입니다. 쿠폰은 만기일이 없으며, 고객님 및 동반 1인의 스파 서비스에 사용하실 수 있습니다.

또한 Wilson Spa Rewards Club에 대해 알려드리고 싶습니다. 이 클

럽의 회원들은 저희 스파의 모든 서비스를 15% 할인받으실 수 있습니다. 게다가 Wilson Spa Rewards Club 회원들은 이 카드를 사용하여 Wimbledon Resort, Belington Inn, Kudhara Yoga Center, Cool Island Café에서 할인을 받으실 수 있습니다.

다시 한번 감사 드립니다. 고객님께서 다음에 방문하실 때 평소와 같은 높은 수준의 서비스를 제공해드릴 수 있기를 고대합니다.

Amy Banks 배상
Wilson Spa 사장

**149.** 이 편지는 Wilson Spa에 대해 무엇을 암시하는가?
(A) 추가적인 직원들을 채용하려 하고 있다.
(B) 고객들에게 의견을 요청한다.
(C) 사업체들을 위해 오프라인 설문조사를 한다.
(D) 최근에 추가적인 장소에 문을 열었다. 정답 (B)

**150.** 이 편지에 의하면, Townsend 씨는 다음 방문 시 무엇을 할 수 있는가?
(A) 입사 지원서를 작성함
(B) 할인 카드를 구매함
(C) 계약을 연장함
(D) 할인을 받음 정답 (D)

**문제 151-152번은 다음 문자 메시지를 참조하시오.**

MARK HARRIS [오전 11:18]
12시 30분 말고 1시에 만날 수 있을까요?

MARK HARRIS [오전 11:20]
기차에 약간의 기술적인 문제가 있는 것 같아서, 제 시간에 갈 수 없을 것 같네요.

ANTHONY CARTER [오전 11:21]
그렇군요. 괜찮습니다. (152) 식당에는 전화했나요?

MARK HARRIS [오전 11:23]
아직이요. (152) 우선 당신에게 확인을 해 보려고 했거든요. 바로 전화를 할게요.

ANTHONY CARTER [오전 11:27]
알았어요. 어떻게 됐는지 말해 주세요.

MARK HARRIS [오전 11:31]
(152) 문제가 있어요. 오후 1시에는 이용할 수 있는 테이블이 없어요. 1시 30분으로 예약을 할 수는 있는데, 너무 늦죠. 다른 곳에서 만나길 원하세요?

ANTHONY CARTER [오전 11:33]
그래요, 너무 늦어요. (151) 우리가 지난 번 만났던 식당에서 보는 것이 어떨까요? 막판 예약도 받았던 것으로 기억하는데요.

MARK HARRIS [오전 11:34]
좋은 생각이에요. 그곳에서 만나요.

**151.** Carter 씨에 대해 암시되는 것은 무엇인가?
(A) 그는 악천후로 인해 약속에 늦을 것이다.
(B) 그는 이전에 Harris 씨를 만난 적이 있다.
(C) 그는 식당 예약을 하려고 한다.
(D) 그는 주로 자가용으로 출근한다. 정답 (B)

**152.** 11시 31분에 Harris 씨가 "There's a problem."이라고 표현한 것이 의미하는 바는 무엇인가?
(A) 그는 교통체증에 걸렸다.
(B) 그는 차를 수리해야 한다.
(C) 그는 이미 점심을 먹었다.

(D) 원하는 시간에 테이블 예약을 할 수 없었다. 　　　정답 (D)

## 문제 153-155번은 다음 공지를 참조하시오.

**주차 공지**

주차장이 재포장 및 재도색되면서 마침내 모든 직원들을 위한 충분한 주차 공간이 마련되었습니다.

(153) 비상구와 하역장 주변에 있는 주차 금지 표지를 잘 지켜주시기 바랍니다. (154) 정문 근처에 있는 공간은 손님과 장애인을 위해 마련된 곳입니다. 이곳에 주차된 직원들의 차는 견인될 것입니다.

많은 직원들의 요청에 따라, (155) 회사의 경영진이 "여성 전용" 주차장을 마련했습니다. 여성직원들에게 안전하고 편안한 환경을 조성하기 위해 주차요원들도 여성이 담당하게 될 것입니다. 회사 경영진들은 이 지역에서, 어쩌면 전국에서 최초일 수도 있는 이번 조치가 전국으로 확산되기를 바라고 있습니다.

**153.** 주차가 금지된 곳은 어디인가?
(A) 정문 근처
(B) 하역장
(C) 여성 전용 주차장
(D) 장애인 전용 주차장 　　　정답 (B)

**154.** 직원이 고객용 주차장에 주차하면 어떠한 일이 발생하는가?
(A) 벌금 청구서가 발부될 것이다.
(B) 차가 견인될 것이다.
(C) 주차가 1주일간 금지될 것이다.
(D) 주차 자격이 철회될 것이다. 　　　정답 (B)

**155.** 여성 전용 주차장의 특징은 무엇인가?
(A) 1층에 위치하고 있다.
(B) 주 내에서 가장 안전한 주차장이다.
(C) 일반 대중에게도 개방될 것이다.
(D) 여성 관리인에 의해 운영될 것이다. 　　　정답 (D)

## 문제 156-157번은 다음 광고를 참조하시오.

**Southwest Air Cargo**

(156) Southwest Air Cargo는 서류, 소포, 그리고 화물을 전 세계로 운송하는 분야에서 개척자적인 항공 화물 운송회사입니다.

Southwest Air Cargo는 전 세계 경제 활동의 70%를 차지하는 시장을 영업일 기준 1~2일 안에 모두 연결합니다. 심지어 하루 24시간 내내 고객이 전화를 하면 90분 내로 운송해야 하는 물품을 수령하는 서비스도 제공하고 있습니다. (157) 이것은 정말 긴급한 화물에 대해 사전 예약이나 마감 시간 같은 것이 없다는 의미입니다. 또한 원하는 목적지까지 안전하고 확실하게 도착한다는 점을 믿어도 됩니다. 왜냐하면 화물들을 추가로 다루거나 이동시키지 않아서 사실상 이동 중에 발생하는 피해 가능성을 제거했기 때문입니다.

추가 정보나 긴급 화물 운송 요청이 필요하면 (800) 762-3787로 전화주세요.

**156.** 무엇이 광고되고 있는가?
(A) 운송 서비스
(B) 새로운 우편 시스템
(C) 여행사
(D) 상업용 항공사 　　　정답 (A)

**157.** Southwest Air Cargo에 대해 언급이 된 것은?
(A) 운송시간이 훨씬 짧다.
(B) 예약이 필요하지 않다.
(C) 운송 경비가 상대적으로 저렴하다.
(D) 철저한 정비가 정기적으로 이뤄진다. 　　　정답 (A)

## 문제 158-161번은 다음 편지를 참조하시오.

**Wonder Fresh Organic Grocery**

5월 2일

VIP 회원님께,

Wonder Fresh Organic Grocery의 최신 진행상황을 업데이트해 드리고 싶습니다. (158/160) 아마 아시겠지만 저희는 바로 옆의 건물을 매입했습니다. 현재 그 공간으로 저희 식료품점을 확장 중이며, 저희 공간에 6천 평방미터가 추가될 것입니다. 뿐만 아니라 기존 점포도 보수하고 있습니다.

또한 확장으로 인해 저희 제과점의 규모가 더 커질 것임을 알려드리고 싶습니다. 더 많은 종류의 빵, 페이스트리, 기타 제과 상품을 제공할 것입니다. (159) 저희 상점이 6월 7일 토요일까지 완전히 보수, 확장될 것으로 예상합니다. 그리고 이러한 멋진 발전을 축하하기 위해, 그 다음 토요일에 재개장 축하행사를 할 것입니다.

저희는 VIP 회원님들을 위해 많은 특가 상품 및 경품을 제공할 것입니다. (160) 뿐만 아니라 저희의 새로운 식당가에서 무료 점심식사 쿠폰을 받게 되실 것입니다. (161) 또한 저희가 이 편지에 15달러 선불 카드를 동봉했음을 확인하셨을 것입니다. 저희 상점을 지속적으로 이용해주신 것에 대한 감사를 표하기 위한 선물입니다. 6월 한달 내내 어떤 물품이든 구입하는 데 사용하실 수 있을 것입니다.

감사합니다.

Wonder Fresh Organic Grocery

**158.** 이 편지의 목적은 무엇인가?
(A) 고객에게 회원 자격이 곧 만료될 것임을 알린다.
(B) 식료품점의 공사 작업을 발표한다.
(C) 새로운 유기농 제품에 대해 광고한다.
(D) 이용할 수 있는 소매 공간에 대한 정보를 전달한다. 　　　정답 (B)

**159.** Wonder Fresh Organic Grocery는 언제 특별 행사를 개최할 것인가?
(A) 5월 2일
(B) 5월 9일
(C) 6월 7일
(D) 6월 14일 　　　정답 (D)

**160.** 이 편지에 언급되지 않은 것은 무엇인가?
(A) 상점이 더 커질 것이다.
(B) 새로운 식당가가 생길 것이다.
(C) 이용권이 제공될 것이다.
(D) 신상품이 매출을 증가시킬 것이다. 　　　정답 (D)

**161.** 이 편지에 첨부된 것은 무엇인가?
(A) 감사 인사 노트
(B) 새로운 회원 카드
(C) 할인 쿠폰
(D) 선불 카드 　　　정답 (D)

문제 162-163번은 다음 정보를 참조하시오.

---

**(162) Cheese Online Shopping Mall 배송 약관**

● 만약 여러분이 저희 온라인 쇼핑몰에서 제품을 구매하시면, 일반적으로 주문한 날로부터 이틀 안에 배송됩니다.

● 만약 여러분이 주문하고자 하는 제품들이 일시적으로 재고에서 떨어지면, 여러분에게 배송되는 데 최대 일주일이 걸릴 것입니다. 창고에 제품을 비축하는 데 대략 2일에서 3일 정도 소요된다는 점을 양해해주시길 바랍니다.

● 만약 여러분이 주문한 제품이 재고에서 떨어진 상태이고 주문이 이월되어야만 한다면, 여러분의 요청을 접수하자마자 바로 연락을 드리도록 하겠습니다.

● 저희는 소량의 비용을 받고 선물 포장도 해드립니다. 만약 선물 포장을 선택하시고자 한다면, 온라인 주문 양식지에 있는 해당 박스에 표시를 하시도록 하세요. 무료 선물 배송은 여러분의 주문액이 100달러 이상 되는 경우 제공됩니다.

● 3개 이상의 제품을 주문하시는 경우, 혹은 **(163) 최소 150달러를 구매하는 경우**, 그리고 Los Angeles 지역에 거주하는 경우 무료 배송 서비스를 제공합니다. 여러분은 저희 홈페이지인 www.speedshopping.net에서 배송 비용 및 기타 비용을 확인하실 수 있습니다.

---

**162.** 정보문의 목적은 무엇인가?
(A) 신제품을 홍보하기 위해서
(B) 회사 방침을 설명하기 위해서
(C) 주소 변경을 알리기 위해서
(D) 배송료의 인상을 발표하기 위해서   정답 (B)

**163.** 만약 고객이 150달러를 구매하면 무엇이 제공되는가?
(A) 무료 포장
(B) 경품
(C) 무료 배송
(D) 할인 쿠폰   정답 (C)

**문제 164-167번은 다음 회람을 참조하시오.**

---

**회람**

발신: Brandon McGraw
수신: 전 직원
날짜: 10월 14일
제목: Thermotex 실험실 냉동고

직원 여러분,

**(164) 여러분들 중 일부가 최근에 새로 구입한 Themotex 실험실 냉동고의 존재와 활용에 대해 모르고 있다는 사실을 알게 되었습니다.** 이 장치는 3층 생물학 실험실에 있는 BioWare 냉동고 옆에 놓여 있습니다. 이 냉동고는 영하 70도에 맞춰져 있으며, 표본 및 특정 박테리아 균주에 대한 최적의 보관소가 되고 있습니다. **(165) 고급 온도 통제 장치를 갖추고 있으며,** 이 장치는 1층 보안 부서에 연결되어 있는 경보장치도 함께 갖추고 있습니다. 만약 온도가 5도 상승하면 경보가 작동하고 보안 부서에 알려지게 됩니다. **(167) 이것은 영하 온도의 일정한 유지를 가능하게 하고 저장된 생물 표본의 온전한 상태를 보장합니다.**

냉동고의 상태를 최고로 유지하려는 노력의 일환으로 다음 사항들을 준수하기 바랍니다. 냉동고에 폭발 방지 장치가 있지만, 가연성과 휘발성이 있는 화학물질을 보관하거나 그런 종류의 화학물질을 냉동고 근처에 두는 것을 삼가하기 바랍니다. 그리고 냉동고를 (5분 이상) 장기간 열어둘 때는 보안 부서에 연락을 해서 경보가 울리게 되면 알 수 있도록 하기 바랍니다.

적어도 6개월에 한 번은 냉동고를 청소하고 점검을 하고 문제가 있을 경우 즉시 관리 부서에 연락하기 바랍니다. **(166) 점심식사 후, 직원 여러분 모두에게 이메일을 통해 냉동고 설명서를 보내드리도록 하겠습니다.**

Brandon McGraw
연구소장

---

**164.** 회람의 목적은 무엇인가?
(A) 직원들에게 새로운 구매안에 대해 전달한다.
(B) 회사 보안에 대해 주의를 준다.
(C) 연구에서의 몇몇 문제점들을 다룬다.
(D) 새로운 기계에 대한 정보를 제공한다.   정답 (D)

**165.** 회람의 내용에 따르면, Themotex 실험실 냉동고의 주목할 만한 특징은 무엇인가?
(A) 일부 생물 표현들만 저장이 가능하다.
(B) 5도 이상 온도가 오르지만 아무런 반응은 없다.
(C) 폭발력이 있고 가연성이 있는 화학물질에 민감하다.
(D) 안정적으로 온도를 유지하는 조절 장치가 있다.   정답 (D)

**166.** McGraw 씨는 오늘 오후에 무엇을 할 것 같은가?
(A) 연구자들 앞에서 발표를 한다.
(B) 기계를 수리할 기술자를 보낸다.
(C) 생물학적 견본을 냉동고에 저장한다.
(D) 이메일을 통해 안내서를 직원에게 발송한다.   정답 (D)

**167.** [1], [2], [3] 그리고 [4]로 표기된 위치 중에서 아래 문장이 가장 적합한 곳은 어디인가?
"이것은 영하 온도의 일정한 유지를 가능하게 하고, 저장된 생물 표본의 온전한 상태를 보장합니다."
(A) [1]
(B) [2]
(C) [3]
(D) [4]   정답 (B)

**문제 168-171번은 다음 광고를 참조하시오.**

---

Thompson Air Conditioning
더 저렴한 가격으로 최고를 얻으세요!

**(168) 고객님 댁의 에어컨을 교체한지 얼마나 되었나요? 10년이 넘었다면, 올 여름 고객님의 집을 준비하기 위해 새 에어컨 구매를 고려하시는 것이 좋습니다.**

**(171) 에어컨이 오래되면 효율성이 떨어집니다.** 이는 더 긴 가동시간과 더 높은 전기세를 야기합니다. 또한 에어컨이 뜨거운 여름 공기 속의 습기를 제거하지 못하기 때문에 집이 덜 쾌적한 것을 알아차릴 것입니다.

고객님 댁의 에어컨을 교체할 때가 되었다고 생각하신다면, Thompson Air Conditioning에 전화 주십시오. **(169) 저희는 20종 이상의 에어컨 모델을 구비하고 있으며, 모든 모델이 National Energy Saver에서 5점을 받은 것입니다.** 게다가 저희 에어컨은 경쟁사의 유사한 모델보다 10% 저렴합니다.

**(170) 그리고 이제 4월 한달 내내 특별 판매를 진행합니다. 저희 에어컨 중 한 대를 구매하시고 설치비 절반을 할인 받으세요. 그렇습니다! 설치비를 50% 할인 받으실 수 있습니다.** 단, 4월말 이전에 구매를 하셔야 합니다.

마지막으로, 설치하실 때 저희가 무료로 고객님 댁의 배관을 점검해 드릴 것입니다. 이는 고객님 댁의 중앙 냉난방 시스템에 청소 또는 수리가 필요한 부분을 찾아낼 수 있다는 의미입니다.

감사합니다!

---

**168.** 이 광고는 누구를 대상으로 할 것 같은가?
(A) 수리공들
(B) 주택 소유주들
(C) 건물 관리자들
(D) 에어컨 유통업체들
정답 (B)

**169.** Thompson Air Conditioning의 어떤 장점이 언급되었는가?
(A) 수리비가 저렴하다.
(B) 두 가지 모델로 나온다.
(C) 다른 에어컨보다 가동비가 더 저렴하다.
(D) 경쟁사보다 더 저렴하다.
정답 (D)

**170.** 고객은 어떻게 할인을 받을 수 있는가?
(A) 할인 코드를 사용한다.
(B) 다른 상품들을 구매한다.
(C) 광고 전단지를 제시한다.
(D) 5월 이전에 에어컨을 구매한다.
정답 (D)

**171.** [1], [2], [3] 그리고 [4]로 표기된 위치 중에서 아래 문장이 가장 적합한 곳은 어디인가?
"에어컨이 오래되면 효율성이 떨어집니다."
(A) [1]
(B) [2]
(C) [3]
(D) [4]
정답 (A)

**문제 172-175번은 다음 온라인 채팅 토론을 참조하시오.**

Sam Smith [오후 1:10]
(172) **지난 주에 소프트웨어 개발직 구인 광고를 보고 보낸 이력서가 엄청나게 많아요. 제 말을 믿으세요.** 몇 부나 접수했는지 알고 싶지 않을 겁니다.

Rose Wilson [오후 1:11]
음… 지금까지 지원서를 몇 부나 접수했는데요?

Sam Smith [오후 1:11]
대략 천 명이에요. 놀랍지요. 그렇죠? 실업 문제가 현재 심각한 사회 문제란 생각이 드네요.

Nina Park [오후 1:12]
뭐라고요? 천 명이요? (172/175) **우리는 산더미 같은 이력서와 자기 소개서에 깔리겠네요.**

Sam Smith [오후 1:13]
(175) **맞아요, 면접을 봐야 할 지원자들을 선별하는 것도 쉽지 않은 일이 될 것임에 틀림없어요.**

Sam Smith [오후 1:16]
(173) **저도 현재 소프트웨어 개발자 인력이 부족하다는 것은 알고 있어요.** 하지만 이 지원자들 중에서 약 70%는 불합격시켜야 하는데, 저는 이 부분이 참 싫어요.

Nina Park [오후 1:17]
우리가 언제 면접을 시작해야 하나요?

Sam Smith [오후 1:19]
우리 본래 계획은 이번 주에 적합한 지원자들을 선별하고, 다음 주부터 면접을 시작할 수 있도록 일을 처리하는 것이었어요.

Nina Park [오후 1:18]
하지만 저는 직원들의 인사기록을 갱신해야 하는 막중한 업무가 있어요. 이러지도 저러지도 못하고 답답하네요.

Sam Smith [오후 1:19]
사실, 회사의 감사가 곧 시작될 예정이에요. 저도 이를 준비하느라 바쁘고요.

Rose Wilson [오후 1:20]
(174) **그러면 한 주 정도 지원자 선별 작업을 연기하는 건 어때요? 어차피 우리 모두 각자의 업무들이 있어서 바쁘잖아요.**

Sam Smith [오후 1:22]
확실히, 당신 말이 맞아요. 제가 오늘 오후에 있을 회의에서 Harrison 씨에게 이 문제에 관해 이야기해볼게요.

**172.** 화자들은 어느 부서에서 근무할 것 같은가?
(A) 시설 관리
(B) 회계
(C) 인사
(D) 소프트웨어 개발
정답 (C)

**173.** 회사에 관해 언급된 것은 무엇인가?
(A) 충분한 인력이 없다.
(B) 구인 공고를 할 것이다.
(C) 새로운 곳으로 이전할 것이다.
(D) 재정 안정성이 필요하다.
정답 (A)

**174.** Wilson 씨가 제안하는 것은 무엇인가?
(A) 훌륭한 지원자들을 선별한다.
(B) 소프트웨어 개발 센터를 운영한다.
(C) 예정된 행사를 연기한다.
(D) Harrison 씨와 새로운 채용 계획을 논의한다.
정답 (C)

**175.** 오후 1시 13분에 Smith 씨가 "You can say that again."이라고 쓴 것이 의미하는 바는 무엇인가?
(A) 그는 직장동료들과 협업을 해야 할 필요가 있다.
(B) 그는 새로운 계획에서 몇 가지 문제점들을 인식하고 있다.
(C) 그는 동료 의견을 받아들인다.
(D) 그는 다른 직원에게 발언할 기회를 주길 원한다.
정답 (C)

**문제 176-180번은 다음 안내문과 양식을 참조하시오.**

CompuMax 컴퓨터 활용 워크숍

컴퓨터 초보자인가요? 새로운 직업을 위해 컴퓨터 사용 기술을 향상시키고 싶으신가요? 파일 관리 소프트웨어에 대해 배우고 싶으신가요? 최신 소프트웨어와 프로그램 사용 방법을 알고 싶으신가요? (176) **CompuMax 컴퓨터 활용 워크숍은 학생에서부터 경영진에 이르기까지 여러분 모두에게 필요한 것을 제공합니다.** 저희는 광범위한 워크숍을 (177) **제공합니다.** 이는 여러분들에게 다양한 형태로 도움이 될 수 있습니다. 저희 홈페이지 www.compumax.com의 내용을 살펴보세요. 저희의 가장 인기 많은 워크숍 일부가 아래에 열거되어 있습니다.

1. (178) **데이터베이스와 스프레드시트** – 정보를 구성하고 추적하며 기록하는 것뿐 아니라 데이터베이스와 스프레드시트를 만드는 방법을 배웁니다.
• 3월 26일 토요일 오전 9시-11시 참가비: 45달러

2. (178) **컴퓨터 사용 기초** - 컴퓨터를 최대한 활용하는 방법과 컴퓨터를 바이러스로부터 보호하는 방법을 배웁니다.
• 5월 22일 토요일 오전 9시-11시 참가비: 20달러

3. (178) **문서 작성** - 회보와 같은 전문적인 문서를 작성하는 방법과 효율적으로 문서의 포맷을 만들고 인쇄하는 방법을 배웁니다.
• 7월 7일 토요일 오전 8시30분-10시30분 참가비: 35달러

4. **(178/179) 그래픽과 프레젠테이션** – 효율적인 슬라이드 쇼 제작 방법, 그래픽과 로고 구성 방법, 디지털 사진 편집 방법과 이것들을 온라인으로 보여주는 방법을 배웁니다.
  • 9월 9일 토요일 오전 8시30분–10시30분 참가비: 50달러

---

워크숍 신청서

이름: Bob Forrest

주소: 4319 San Pedro Blvd, Los Angeles CA 92001

전화 번호: (213) 5678–8376

이메일: bforrest@quickmail.com

워크숍 번호: (179) **4**

일시: 9월 9일

하고 싶은 말: (180) **워크숍 장소를 알려주세요.** 공지에서 장소에 대해 언급된 내용을 찾을 수가 없었습니다.

---

**176.** 안내문의 목적은 무엇인가?
(A) 수업 신청을 확인한다.
(B) 일련의 워크숍을 홍보한다.
(C) 컴퓨터 소프트웨어의 할인을 공지한다.
(D) 프레젠테이션 일정을 변경한다.　　　　정답 (B)

**177.** 안내문에 따르면, 첫 번째 단락 네 번째 줄의 "deliver"와 가장 의미가 유사한 단어는 무엇인가?
(A) 전송하다
(B) 주문하다
(C) 제공하다
(D) 보내다　　　　정답 (C)

**178.** 워크숍의 주제가 아닌 것은 무엇인가?
(A) 문서 작성
(B) 데이터 구성
(C) 기본적인 컴퓨터 사용 기술
(D) 비디오와 오디오 소프트웨어　　　　정답 (D)

**179.** Bob Forrest 씨가 참석하고자 하는 워크숍의 참가비는 얼마인가?
(A) 20달러
(B) 35달러
(C) 45달러
(D) 50달러　　　　정답 (D)

**180.** Forrest 씨가 알고자 하는 것은 무엇인가?
(A) 워크숍 비용에 포함되는 것
(B) 단체 할인 가능 여부
(C) 강의 장소
(D) 강사진　　　　정답 (C)

---

**문제 181–185번은 다음 명함과 이메일을 참조하시오.**

The Institute of Fine Arts

Rose Douglass
관장

The Institute of Fine Arts
1001 North Michigan 가
(185) **Chicago,** Il 60603

---

홈페이지: www.ifa.edu
연락처: (312) 444–3800
이메일: rdouglass@ifa.edu

---

수신: Rose Douglass 〈rdouglass@ifa.edu〉
발신: Kelly Preston 〈kpreston@coolmail.com〉
날짜: 6월 3일
제목: 저와 관련된 정보

Douglass 씨께,

(182) 지난 주 Boston에서 개최된 Anderson 미술관의 50주년 기념 축하연에서 만나 뵙고 현대 미술에 관해 이야기를 나눌 수 있었던 것은 제게 큰 영광이었습니다.

(181/183) 저는 귀하가 근무하는 The Institute of Fine Arts에서 큐레이터를 물색 중이라는 말씀을 해주신 점에 진심으로 감사드립니다. 저는 제가 그 직책에 아주 적합한 지원자라고 확실히 믿습니다. 저는 현재 Atlanta에 위치한 Georgia 미술관의 작품 보관 책임자로 근무하고 있습니다. 현재 제 직무는 예술계에서 장기적인 가치를 가진 예술품들을 평가, 수집, 구성하고 보존하는 일을 하고 있습니다.

대학 시절부터 저는 미술관이 상징하는 모든 것들을 경외해왔습니다. 미술관 특유의 신비로움과 독특한 분위기야말로 제가 더욱 더 이 분야에 종사하길 바라도록 만드는 엄청난 복합적인 요인이었습니다. (183) 미술관과 예술작품에 대한 저의 사랑이야말로 귀 미술관의 큐레이터 직책에 지원하게 만드는 유일한 원동력입니다. (184) 귀하께서 축하연에서 제게 예술품의 가치와 해당 작품의 세계사적 입지를 파악할 수 있는 전문가를 찾고 있다고 말씀하셨는데 제가 바로 그러한 정확한 안목을 지니고 있는 사람이라고 확실하게 말씀드릴 수 있습니다. 그것이 바로 제가 귀하가 찾는 큐레이터에 적합한 사람임에 확신하는 이유입니다.

(185) 저는 이 직책에서 귀하와 함께 근무할 수 있는 가능성이 있다는 사실에 굉장히 기쁘며, 직접 만나 뵙고 제가 미술관에 어떻게 도움이 될 수 있는지 논의할 수 있길 바랍니다. 제가 면접 일정을 요청하기 위해 귀하의 사무실에 연락을 드리고자 하며 만약 제게 연락을 주시고자 한다면 (404) 814–4000으로 전화를 주시면 됩니다.

시간 내셔서 제 이메일을 읽어주신 배려에 감사드립니다. 저는 추후에 큐레이터 직책에 대한 제 자격요건을 논의할 수 있는 기회가 오길 기대합니다.

Kelly Preston

---

**181.** 이메일이 작성된 이유는 무엇인가?
(A) 신입 직원 채용을 건의하기 위해서
(B) 축하연 준비에 대한 도움을 받기 위해서
(C) 새로운 일자리에 지원하기 위해서
(D) 신문 기사를 위한 인터뷰를 요청하기 위해서　　　　정답 (C)

**182.** Douglass 씨에 대해 언급된 것은 무엇인가?
(A) 그녀는 이전에 Preston 씨를 만난 적이 없다.
(B) 그녀는 현재 Atlanta에 있는 미술관에서 근무한다.
(C) 그녀는 Boston에서 개최된 행사에 참석했다.
(D) 그녀는 전시회 기획과 개최에 뛰어난 재능을 보유하고 있다.　　정답 (C)

**183.** Preston 씨가 관심을 보이는 것은 무엇인가?
(A) 그녀의 최초 전시회를 개최하는 것
(B) The Institute of Fine Arts에서 근무하는 것
(C) Georgia 미술관에서 인턴으로 근무하는 것
(D) Anderson 미술관에서 몇몇 그림을 구매하는 것　　　　정답 (B)

**184.** Preston 씨가 Douglass 씨에게 완벽한 선택임을 확신하는 이유가 무엇인가?

    (A) 그녀는 진정한 예술의 가치를 파악할 수 있는 통찰력을 지니고 있다.

    (B) 그녀는 많은 순회 전시회들을 개최해왔다.

    (C) 그녀는 현대 미술작품들을 수집하고 인상주의를 연구해왔다.

    (D) 그녀는 희미해진 그림들을 이전 상태로 복원시킬 수 있다.     정답 (A)

**185.** Preston 씨는 Douglass 씨를 어느 도시에서 만나길 원하는가?

    (A) Boston

    (B) Atlanta

    (C) Chicago

    (D) Philadelphia     정답 (C)

---

문제 186-190번은 다음 안내문과 웹사이트 그리고 이메일을 참조하시오.

---

메모리 카드간에 데이터를 전송하는 방법

(190) 이 페이지에서는 단계별 설명을 통해 한 메모리 카드에서 다른 메모리 카드로 데이터를 전송하는 방법이 제공됩니다.

필요한 것:

• 두 개의 (186) **호환이 가능한** 메모리 카드(동일한 수준의 메모리 카드여야 함)

• 메모리 카드를 인식할 수 있는 컴퓨터(상업적 이용이 가능한 카드 리더/라이터 혹은 본체 내에 설치된 카드 슬롯을 통해서)

중요한 것:

• 폴더 내에 있는 파일들을 변경, 이동, 혹은 지우지 말 것

• 폴더를 원 메모리 카드에 재복사하면서 자료를 덮어쓰지 말 것

해야 할 것:

• 데이터가 저장된 카드를 카드 슬롯 혹은 카드 리더/라이터에 삽입한다.

• 메모리 카드를 컴퓨터 장비에서 찾고 카드에 접속한다.

• 데이터를 선택하고 이를 데스크탑 컴퓨터에 복사한다.

• 메모리 카드를 꺼낸다.

• 데이터를 전송하고 싶은 메모리 카드를 삽입한다.

• 메모리 카드를 컴퓨터 장비에서 찾고 카드에 접속한다.

• 데스크탑 컴퓨터에 있는 복사된 폴더를 선택하고 이를 두 번째 메모리 카드로 이동한다.

---

http://www.ponetocards.com/contact_us

성명: Eugene Daniels

이메일: eugene.daniels@mimimail.com

제목: 제 메모리 카드가 등록이 안되네요.

메시지(정확한 답변을 위해 최대한 상세하게 설명하세요):

(187) 제가 제목에서도 썼듯이, 제 메모리 카드가 제 카메라에 등록이 안 됩니다. 저는 설명서에 있는 모든 내용대로 따라서 했기 때문에 왜 그런지 이해가 안되네요. 제가 가지고 있던 원 메모리 카드가 제 사진과 음악을 담기엔 작은 8GB 용량인지라, 저는 가서 32GB 메모리 카드를 구매했어요. 새로 구매한 32GB 메모리 카드에는 모델명이 Poneto: Kamang memory card 32GB라고 적혀 있고요, 제 원 메모리 카드는 Poneto: Haru memory card 8GB라고 적혀 있어요. 저는 어떠한 변경 없이 자료를 복사하여 붙여 넣었지만 (187) 제 카메라는 계속 "메모리 카드에 문제가 있습니다: 오류 403"이라고만 합니다. 어떻게 해야 할까요?

---

수신: Eugene Daniels 〈eugene.daniels@email.com〉

발신: Poneto Support 〈noreply@poneto.net〉

날짜: 6월 8일

제목: 답신: 제 메모리 카드가 등록이 안되네요.

• 이 메시지는 고객님이 최근 제출하신 메시지를 바탕으로 Poneto Support에서 자동으로 발송되는 메시지임을 유념해 주십시오. (189) **Poneto Support에서 근무하는 직원들이 읽을 수 없으므로 이 메시지에 대한 답장은 하지 마시기 바랍니다.**

안녕하세요, Daniels 씨.

최근 저희 Poneto Support에게 메시지를 작성하여 제출해주신 점에 감사 드립니다. 저희는 고객님께서 저희에게 알려주신 내용에 대한 케이스 파일을 작성하였고, 최적의 답변을 제공하기 위해서 이 안건에 대한 평가를 시행했습니다.

안타깝게도, 고객님께서는 잘못된 계열의 메모리 카드를 사용하신 것 같습니다. Kamang과 Haru는 다른 시스템을 지원하는 다른 계열의 메모리 카드입니다. (188) **고객님의 카메라는 오직 Haru 계열의 메모리 카드만 지원하는 것으로 보입니다.** 저희가 드릴 수 있는 말씀은 Kamang 메모리 카드는 반품하시고, Haru 메모리 카드를 구매하셔야 한다는 것입니다. 여전히 문제점에 직면하시게 된다면, 주저하지 말고 저희에게 다시 연락을 주시기 바랍니다. 감사합니다.

Poneto Support Team

---

**186.** 이메일의 두 번째 단락, 두 번째 줄 "compatible"과 의미상 가장 유사한 단어는 무엇인가?

    (A) 경쟁적인

    (B) 비슷한

    (C) 복잡한

    (D) 교환할 수 있는     정답 (D)

**187.** Daniels 씨가 Poneto 사의 홈페이지에 메시지를 제출한 이유는 무엇인가?

    (A) 회사 제품에 대한 사용 후기를 제출하기 위해서

    (B) 신제품에 관한 더 많은 정보를 얻기 위해서

    (C) Poneto 사의 부실한 고객 서비스에 대한 불만을 제기하기 위해서

    (D) 제품 오작동에 대한 해결책을 요청하기 위해서     정답 (D)

**188.** Daniels 씨가 메모리 카드와 함께 카메라를 사용하려면 무엇을 해야 하는가?

    (A) 설명서의 지침을 정확하게 따라야 한다.

    (B) 오직 Haru 메모리 카드만 사용해야 한다.

    (C) Ponento 사의 수리 서비스를 받아야 한다.

    (D) 그가 보유한 Kamang 메모리 카드에 충분한 공간을 확보해야 한다.     정답 (B)

**189.** 이메일에서 언급된 것은 무엇인가?

    (A) Poneto 사는 결함이 있는 카메라와 관련하여 Daniels 씨에게 보상해 줄 것이다.

    (B) 이메일을 통해 Poneto 지원 팀 직원에게 연락할 수 없다.

    (C) Daniels 씨는 모든 자료를 분실했다.

    (D) Daniels 씨의 카메라는 오래된 이전 제품이다.     정답 (B)

**190.** Poneto 사 메모리 카드에 관해 사실이 아닌 것은 무엇인가?

    (A) 메모리 카드 사이에 데이터를 전송하는 것은 불가능하다.

    (B) 한 계열 이상의 제품이 존재한다.

    (C) 대개 다양한 용량의 제품들이 출시된다.

    (D) 데이터는 컴퓨터를 통해 사용자가 변경할 수 있다.     정답 (A)

문제 191-195번은 다음 광고와 이메일들을 참조하시오.

---

SUNHILL 여름 임대

(192) SUNHILL 아파트는 5성급 휴양지 숙박시설에서 요구되는 높은 기준을 충족시키는 편의시설과 가구를 구비하고 있으며 South Beach Vacations LLC에 의해 관리되고 있습니다. 개별적으로 바다를 바라볼 수 있는 특징, 아름다움과 고급스런 분위기, 5성급 수준의 편의시설과 서비스, 개별적인 발코니, 유명하고 조용하고 편리한 Art Deco 구역에 자리잡고 있는 위치적 장점까지 복합적으로 제공하는 South Beach 지역의 다른 아파트는 없습니다. 이 아파트는 역사적으로 유서가 깊은 South Beach Art Deco 구역의 중심부에 위치하고 있습니다. 만약 더 많은 정보가 필요하시거나 예약을 원하시면, Marsha Everton 씨의 이메일 계정인 meverton@shsl.com으로 이메일을 보내주시기 바랍니다.

SUNHILL APARTMENT
1000 Beach Drive
Miami, Florida 23711

---

수신: Maria Casares 〈mcasares@bkmail.com〉
발신: Marsha Everton 〈meverton@shsl.com.〉
제목: 예약
날짜: 5월 23일

Casares 씨께,

(192) Sunhill Summer Rentals를 또 다시 선택해 주셔서 감사합니다. (191) Miami 시 Beach Drive 1000번지에 위치한 Sunhill 아파트에 대한 고객님의 인터넷 임대 요청이 접수되었음을 확인해 드리고자 이메일을 발송합니다. 저희 상담원 중 한 명이 고객님의 예약을 검토하였고, 요청하신 날짜에 403호가 이용 가능함을 확인하였습니다. 고객님께서는 저희 아파트 403호에서 6월 8일부터 14일까지 체류하실 것입니다. 고객님의 거래번호는 72877771입니다.

제출하신 신용카드(끝자리 8891)에 872달러 40센트가 청구되었습니다. 고객님의 예약은 최종적인 것이며, 이 요금은 체류 취소를 선택하시더라도 환불되지 않음에 유의해 주십시오.

(194) 저희 상담원 중 한 명이 이달 말이 되기 전에 연락을 드려 저희 아파트에서 체류하실 때 알고 계셔야 할 새로운 지침사항을 알려드릴 것입니다.

질문이나 우려 사항이 있으시면, 저희에게 800-555-1000으로 전화 주십시오. (193) 전화 주실 때 거래번호를 질문 받게 될 것이므로 이를 미리 준비해 주십시오. 이용해 주셔서 감사 드리며, 좋은 시간 되시기를 기원합니다.

Marsha Everton
고객 서비스 매니저
Sunhill 여름 임대 사업부

---

수신: Marsha Everton 〈meverton@shsl.com〉
발신: Maria Casares 〈mcasares@bkmail.com〉
날짜: 6월 5일
제목: 답장: 예약

Everton 씨께,

6월 8일~14일 Sunhill Summer Rentals에 대한 제 예약(#72877771) 건으로 연락 드립니다. (194) 귀하의 이메일에는 제가 여름 임대와 관련된 세부사항을 연락 받게 될 것이라고 언급되어 있었습니다. 또한 지난달 말까지 연락이 있을 것이라고 했지요. 하지만 저는 귀사에서 아무런 연락도 받지 못했습니다.

(194) 제가 출발하기 전에 이 정보를 전달받을 수 있다면 대단히 감사하겠

습니다. 그러니 가능한 빨리 이 정보를 알려 주시기 바랍니다. 저는 이메일을 통해 알려주신 전화번호로 귀사에 여러 차례 (195) 연락을 시도했으나, 매번 통화가 곧장 음성사서함으로 연결되었습니다.

가능한 빨리 저에게 연락 주십시오.

감사합니다.

Maria Casares
(800) 692-9815

---

**191.** 첫 번째 이메일의 목적은 무엇인가?
(A) 더 많은 정보를 요청하기 위해
(B) 어떤 서비스에 대한 지불을 요청하기 위해
(C) 예약 문제를 나타내기 위해
(D) 예약이 되었음을 확인하기 위해 　　　정답 (D)

**192.** Casares 씨에 관해 암시되는 것은 무엇인가?
(A) 그녀는 South Beach Vacations LLC에서 근무한다.
(B) 그녀는 작년에도 Sunhill 아파트를 임대했다.
(C) 그녀는 이전에 전화 상으로 Everton 씨와 통화한 적이 있다.
(D) 그녀는 매 여름마다 휴가 차 Miami를 방문한다. 　　　정답 (B)

**193.** Casares 씨가 Sunhill Summer Rentals에 연락할 때 그들에게 제공해야 하는 것은 무엇인가?
(A) 은행 계좌 번호
(B) 거래 번호
(C) 합법적인 신분증
(D) 영수증 원본 　　　정답 (B)

**194.** Casares 씨가 Everton 씨에게 요청하는 것은 무엇인가?
(A) 개정된 거주 방침
(B) 아파트 방번호
(C) 지불 수단 안내
(D) 아파트로 가는 길 안내 　　　정답 (A)

**195.** 두 번째 이메일 두 번째 단락 두 번째 줄의 "reach"와 의미상 가장 유사한 단어는?
(A) 도착하다
(B) 연락하다
(C) 추월하다
(D) 늘어나다 　　　정답 (B)

---

문제 196-200번은 다음 보도자료들과 표를 참조하시오.

---

The Verdi Opera House

즉시 배포

Philadelphia, Pennsylvania, 3월 10일 – 이 지역에서 가장 오래된 오페라 극장인 Verdi Opera House는 봄 공연 일자를 발표했습니다. (196) 5개의 공연 중에는 Verdi Opera House에서 20년 전 데뷔했던 Philadelphia Opera Company의 공연이 포함될 것입니다.

공연 일정은 다음과 같습니다.

| 일자 | 오페라 제목 | 오페라단 |
|---|---|---|
| 3월 29일 | The Medium | The Wilson Opera Company |
| 4월 9일 | The Spring Marriage | The Philadelphia Opera Company |
| 4월 18일 | Gloriana | Opera La Fezzata |

| 5월 2일 | Carmen | The California Opera Company |
| --- | --- | --- |
| (199) **5월 12일** | (199) **La Giaconda** | (199) **Opera Cornuti** |

티켓은 140달러부터 구입 가능합니다. 티켓을 구매하시려면, 저희 온라인 매장 verdioperahouse.com/tickets를 방문해 주십시오. (198) **Verdi Opera House VIP 회원이신 분은 본인 표 값의 20% 할인 및 동반자 50% 할인 혜택을 받으실 수 있습니다. 구매 시 회원 ID 번호를 사용하시면 됩니다.**

공연에 대한 더 많은 정보를 알아보시려면, 저희 안내 데스크 800-555-8921로 연락 주십시오.

---

The Verdi Opera House
즉시 배포

Philadelphia, Pennsylvania, 3월 19일—(197) **이 지역의 최근 폭풍으로 인해 저희 건물이 상당히 훼손되었습니다.** 이로 인한 보수 작업이 완료되는 데 두 달 정도가 소요될 것이므로, 봄 일정을 상당수 변경해야 했습니다. (197) **현재, 저희는 모든 봄 공연 일정을 여름으로 재조정할 계획입니다.** (199) **Opera Cornuti의 공연을 제외하면 올 봄 저희 극장에선 공연이 없을 것입니다.** (200) **연기된 행사의 티켓을 이미 갖고 계시다면, 계속 보유하실 것을 권장합니다. 이후 공연을 관람하실 수 있는 표로 교환하실 수 있습니다.** 공연 일정 조정에 대해 더 알아보시려면, 저희 홈페이지인 www.verdioperahouse.com/news를 방문해 주십시오. 표 값의 전액 환불을 요청하시려면, 800-222-7391로 연락 주시기 바랍니다.

---

오페라 공연표

The Verdi Opera House

성함: Ms. Hannah Palmer / Verdi Opera House VIP 회원

(199) **La Giaconda**

발코니 석 / B48-5

0  36000  29145  2

**196.** 20년 전 Verdi Opera House에서 공연한 극단은 어디인가?

(A) The Wilson Opera Company

(B) The Philadelphia Opera Company

(C) Opera La Fezzata

(D) Opera Cornuti                                  정답 (B)

**197.** Verdi Opera House가 모든 행사를 올 여름으로 연기하고자 하는 이유는 무엇인가?

(A) 새로운 공연을 준비하는 데 더 많은 시간이 필요하다.

(B) 심각한 재정난을 겪고 있다.

(C) 예술 공연 시설이 파손되었다.

(D) 봄 축제에 대해 관심을 갖는 사람들이 줄었다.      정답 (C)

**198.** Palmer 씨에 관해 암시되는 것은 무엇인가?

(A) 그녀는 Verdi Opera House를 소유하고 있다.

(B) 그녀는 20% 할인 혜택을 받았다.

(C) 그녀는 구매한 표에 대한 전액 환불을 요구할 것이다.

(D) 그녀는 친구들과 함께 공연을 관람할 계획이다.      정답 (B)

**199.** Palmer 씨는 언제 공연을 볼 것인가?

(A) 4월 18일

(B) 4월 27일

(C) 5월 2일

(D) 5월 12일                                      정답 (D)

**200.** 두 번째 보도자료에 의하면, 이미 표를 구매한 사람들이 할 수 있는 것은 무엇인가?

(A) 두 장의 표로 보상판매를 받는다.

(B) 모든 예정된 오페라에 사용한다.

(C) 반납하고 일부 환불을 받는다.

(D) 향후에 다른 티켓으로 교환한다.                 정답 (D)

**1.** 미M

(A) The woman is disposing of her gloves.
(B) The woman is pouring a mixture into a pot.
(C) The woman is looking through a microscope.
(D) The woman is wearing a lab coat.

(A) 여자는 장갑을 버리고 있다.
(B) 여자는 혼합물을 용기에 붓고 있다.
(C) 여자가 현미경을 들여다보고 있다.
(D) 여자가 실험실 가운을 입고 있다.　　　　　　정답 (D)

**2.** 미W

(A) A person is watering some flowers with a hose.
(B) A person is pulling up some weeds from the ground.
(C) A person is kneeling by the wheel of a car.
(D) A person is tending to a plant in a vegetable garden.

(A) 한 사람이 호스를 이용하여 꽃에 물을 주고 있다.
(B) 한 사람이 땅에서 잡초를 뽑고 있다.
(C) 한 사람이 자동차 바퀴 옆에 무릎을 꿇고 있다.
(D) 한 사람이 텃밭에 있는 식물을 돌보고 있다.　　정답 (D)

**3.** 영W

(A) They're gazing at a painting in the art gallery.
(B) They're taking a picture of an outdoor scene.
(C) Several paintings are being exhibited outside.
(D) The staircase is lined with a display of classical prints on a wall.

(A) 그들은 화랑에 있는 그림을 보고 있다.
(B) 몇몇 그림들이 야외에서 전시되고 있다.
(C) 그들은 야외 풍경을 사진으로 찍고 있다.
(D) 계단이 고풍스런 그림이 전시된 한 벽을 따라 일렬로 뻗어있다.　　　　　　　　　　　　　　　　　정답 (A)

**4.** 호M

(A) Some water jugs are stored on a rack.
(B) Some office equipment is underneath a desk.
(C) There is a water dispenser near a door.
(D) The floor is being covered with carpeting.

(A) 몇몇 물통들이 선반에 보관되어 있다.
(B) 몇몇 사무기기가 책상 밑에 있다.
(C) 문 근처에 정수기가 있다.
(D) 바닥에 카펫이 깔리고 있다.　　　　　　　정답 (C)

**5.** 미W

(A) The intersection is deserted.
(B) Lines are being painted on a road.
(C) The road is illuminated by streetlights.
(D) The city skyline is obscured by clouds.

(A) 교차로에 인적이 없다.
(B) 차선이 도로에 그려지고 있다.
(C) 도로가 가로등에 의해 밝혀져 있다.
(D) 도시의 지평선이 구름으로 인해 흐릿하다.　　정답 (C)

**6.** 미M

(A) A man is plugging a computer into a power outlet.

(B) They are seated on stools in a waiting area.
(C) There are some cords lying on top of a desk.
(D) A piece of equipment is being packed in a crate.

(A) 한 남자가 컴퓨터의 전원 코드를 콘센트에 꽂고 있다.
(B) 그들은 대기실에 있는 등받이가 없는 의자에 앉아 있다.
(C) 책상 위에 몇몇 선들이 놓여 있다.
(D) 한 장비가 상자에 포장되고 있다.　　　　　정답 (C)

**7.** 미W 미M

Where can I find Ms. Fonda's accounting office?
(A) Last week, I guess.
(B) Lisa might know.
(C) I've found your missing bag.

Fonda 씨의 회계 사무소가 어디에 있나요?
(A) 지난주일 걸요.
(B) Lisa가 알 거예요.
(C) 당신이 잃어버린 가방을 찾았어요.　　　　정답 (B)

**8.** 호M 미W

When did you move into your new office?
(A) About two weeks ago.
(B) How about next Tuesday?
(C) It's very close to the office.

새 사무실에는 언제 이전하셨나요?
(A) 약 2주 전에요.
(B) 다음주 화요일은 어떤가요?
(C) 사무실과 굉장히 가까워요.　　　　　　　정답 (A)

**9.** 미W 미M

Who's taking over for Isabella while she's on vacation?
(A) I can't wait for my summer vacation.
(B) I haven't been informed yet.
(C) It'll take about an hour to get there.

Isabella가 휴가를 간 사이에 그녀의 업무는 누가 맡나요?
(A) 여름 휴가가 빨리 왔으면 싶네요.
(B) 아직 들은 바 없습니다.
(C) 그곳까지 가는 데 한 시간 정도 소요됩니다.　정답 (B)

**10.** 호M 미W

Are there any extra copies for the tax seminar?
(A) Yes, there was one seminar last week.
(B) I brought 100 copies of the book.
(C) Take a look on the desk over there.

세금 관련 세미나에 관한 여분의 인쇄물이 있습니까?
(A) 네, 지난주에 세미나가 하나 있었어요.
(B) 제가 그 책을 100부 가져왔어요.
(C) 저쪽에 있는 책상 위를 보세요.　　　　　정답 (C)

**11.** 호M 미M

Won't you be making a speech at the international conference next week?
(A) No, it won't take long.
(B) It'll be held at the Hamilton Hotel.
(C) Yes, but I have to cancel it.

다음주에 있을 국제 회의에서 연설하시지 않나요?
(A) 아니오, 오래 걸리지 않을 겁니다.
(B) Hamilton Hotel에서 개최될 겁니다.
(C) 네, 그런데 취소해야 합니다. 정답 (C)

**12.** 미W 미M

Why are our sales predictions so far off the mark?
(A) He's coming from far away.
(B) It's marked on the order form.
(C) You should ask the sales manager.

우리 판매 예측이 목표에서 그렇게 많이 벗어난 이유가 뭐가요?
(A) 그는 멀리서 오고 있어요.
(B) 주문서에 표시가 되어 있어요.
(C) 영업부장에게 물어보세요. 정답 (C)

**13.** 미M 영W

What's the reason for Mr. White being late for the meeting this morning?
(A) I heard that traffic held him up.
(B) To attend the meeting.
(C) Yes, he's out of the office today.

오늘 아침 회의에 White 씨가 늦은 이유가 뭐가요?
(A) 교통체증 때문이라고 들었어요.
(B) 회의에 참석하기 위해서요.
(C) 네, 그는 오늘 외근입니다. 정답 (A)

**14.** 미W 영W

Would you please fill out an application form to get a membership card?
(A) Sure, we'll exempt the shipping charge.
(B) I can't find a pen around here.
(C) The position was already filled.

회원 카드를 받으려면 신청서를 작성해 주시겠습니까?
(A) 물론이에요, 배송료를 면제해 드리겠습니다.
(B) 펜을 찾을 수가 없네요.
(C) 그 직책은 이미 충원이 되었어요. 정답 (B)

**15.** 호M 미W

Why didn't anyone tell me about the change in the date of the sales
meeting?
(A) Let's set the date for June 3.
(B) Well, I was just about to.
(C) Our sales are higher than expected.

영업 회의의 날짜가 변경된 것을 왜 아무도 제게 알려주지 않았나요?
(A) 6월 3일로 날짜를 정하죠.
(B) 음, 지금 막 하려던 참이었어요.
(C) 우리 매출이 예상보다 높아요. 정답 (B)

**16.** 호M 영W

How often does your company take inventory?
(A) Please put them in the warehouse.
(B) Two times in a row.
(C) Whenever it's necessary.

귀사에서는 재고 조사를 얼마나 자주 하시나요?
(A) 그것들을 창고에 넣어주세요.
(B) 두 번 연속으로요.

(C) 필요할 때마다 해요. 정답 (C)

**17.** 미W 미M

I don't know how to use this new computer graphic software.
(A) Several computer graphic designers.
(B) I'd like a soft drink.
(C) Neither do I.

저는 이 새로운 컴퓨터 그래픽 소프트웨어를 어떻게 사용하는지 모릅니다.
(A) 몇몇 컴퓨터 그래픽 디자이너들이요.
(B) 저는 탄산음료를 마시고 싶어요.
(C) 저도 모릅니다. 정답 (C)

**18.** 호M 미W

Will the manufacturing plant close for the upcoming national holiday?
(A) I need a round-trip ticket.
(B) Our store opens at 9:00 every day.
(C) We usually get a notice about that.

제조 공장이 다가올 공휴일에 문을 닫나요?
(A) 저는 왕복표가 필요해요.
(B) 우리 상점은 매일 9시에 개장해요.
(C) 그 점은 대개 공지를 받아요. 정답 (C)

**19.** 영W 미M

Should I send this package by regular mail or by courier?
(A) Thanks for reminding me.
(B) Whichever is more convenient.
(C) Yes, I can send them later.

이 소포를 일반 우편으로 보내야 할까요, 아니면 택배로 보내야 할까요?
(A) 상기시켜 주셔서 감사합니다.
(B) 편한 쪽으로 하세요.
(C) 네, 그것들은 제가 나중에 보낼 수 있어요. 정답 (B)

**20.** 미W 미M

Where did you get the used camera?
(A) Yes, it's digital.
(B) It was not expensive.
(C) From one of my former colleagues.

그 중고 카메라는 어디에서 구하셨나요?
(A) 네, 그건 디지털이에요.
(B) 비싸지 않았어요.
(C) 이전 직장 동료에게서요. 정답 (C)

**21.** 호M 미W

Should I send the revised contract to Ms. Jenkins?
(A) No, she has already received it.
(B) The invoices aren't complete.
(C) Yes, here's my contact number while I'm away.

Jenkins 씨에게 수정된 계약서를 보내야 하나요?
(A) 아니오, 그녀는 이미 받았어요.
(B) 송장이 아직 마무리되지 않았어요.
(C) 네, 여기 제가 없는 동안 제 연락처예요. 정답 (A)

**22.** 호M 미M

I think the company can't afford to hire more temporary workers, can it?
(A) It's temporarily out of stock.

(B) Sorry. I have no idea.

(C) We're short of staff.

회사가 더 많은 임시 직원들을 채용할 여력이 안 된다고 생각해요, 그렇죠?

(A) 일시적으로 재고가 동이 났어요.

(B) 미안합니다만, 저는 모릅니다.

(C) 우리는 직원이 부족해요. 정답 (B)

**23.** [미W] [영W]

Can you extend the deadline for the new design to next Tuesday?

(A) Yes, it's very stylish.

(B) Please ask for extension 7399 at this number.

(C) That doesn't leave you much time to complete it.

새로운 디자인의 마감시한을 다음주 화요일까지 연장해줄 수 있나요?

(A) 네, 굉장히 멋있네요.

(B) 이 번호로 연락해서 내선번호 7399로 연결해 달라고 하세요.

(C) 그렇게 해도 마무리하는 데 충분한 시간은 되지 않아요. 정답 (C)

**24.** [호M] [미W]

Would you like to join us for dinner this evening?

(A) Yes, maybe next time.

(B) Here is your bill.

(C) I'd like to, but I have other plans.

오늘 저녁에 저희와 함께 저녁식사를 하시겠어요?

(A) 네, 아마도 다음에요.

(B) 여기 계산서 있습니다.

(C) 그러고는 싶지만, 선약이 있어요. 정답 (C)

**25.** [미W] [호M]

What's being served at the farewell party for Mr. Winters?

(A) I think the food was fine.

(B) At a job fair earlier this year.

(C) Let me check on that for you.

Winters 씨를 위한 환송회에서 제공되는 음식이 뭔가요?

(A) 제 생각에 음식은 훌륭했어요.

(B) 올해 초에 있었던 취업 박람회에서요.

(C) 제가 알아봐 드릴게요. 정답 (C)

**26.** [호M] [영W]

Can you tell me where I can get tickets for the new play?

(A) It was an interesting movie.

(B) Yes, there's no late charge for that.

(C) Can you go?

새로운 연극 표를 어디에서 구매할 수 있는지 알려 주시겠어요?

(A) 재미있는 영화였어요.

(B) 네, 그 부분에 대한 연체료는 없어요.

(C) 가실 수 있어요? 정답 (C)

**27.** [미W] [미M]

Would it be better to respond to the official invitation by e-mail or by letter?

(A) Yes, I am invited to the film festival.

(B) Either would be fine.

(C) Please let me know.

공식 초청에 대한 답장을 이메일로 하는 것이 좋을까요, 아니면 편지로 하는 것이 좋을까요?

(A) 네, 저는 영화제에 초청받았어요.

(B) 어느 쪽이든 좋아요.

(C) 알려주세요. 정답 (B)

**28.** [호M] [영W]

Has Mr. McGowan already read over the market analysis report?

(A) Twenty copies were printed.

(B) Yes, I've already reported it to police.

(C) No, he's reading it now.

McGowan 씨가 시장 분석 보고서를 벌써 다 읽었습니까?

(A) 20부가 인쇄되었어요.

(B) 네, 제가 이미 경찰에 신고했어요.

(C) 아니오, 그는 지금 읽고 있는 중이에요. 정답 (C)

**29.** [미W] [호M]

Why don't we put these documents in folders before we bring them to the client?

(A) There is a stationery store nearby.

(B) Please sign it at the bottom of the page.

(C) Yes, you should stand in front of the podium.

이 서류들을 고객에게 가져가기에 앞서 서류철에 넣어두는 것이 어떨까요?

(A) 근처에 문구점이 있어요.

(B) 페이지 하단에 서명해 주세요.

(C) 네, 연단 앞에 서셔야 합니다. 정답 (A)

**30.** [호M] [영W]

These ergonomic office chairs are perfectly designed for our employees.

(A) Yes, they are new hires.

(B) Do you know how much they are?

(C) We need several designers for the project.

이 인체공학적 사무용 의자들은 우리 직원들에게 맞춰 완벽하게 디자인된 제품입니다.

(A) 네, 그들은 신입 사원이에요.

(B) 가격이 얼마인지 알고 있나요?

(C) 우리는 그 프로젝트를 위해 몇몇 디자이너들이 필요합니다. 정답 (B)

**31.** [미M] [미W]

Every employee will get a special bonus at the end of the year.

(A) Their profits dropped considerably.

(B) Will it be wired to our bank accounts?

(C) Yes, I'll pay by credit card.

모든 직원이 연말에 특별 보너스를 받게 될 겁니다.

(A) 그들의 수익이 상당히 하락했어요.

(B) 우리 은행 계좌로 입금되나요?

(C) 네, 신용카드로 계산할게요. 정답 (B)

**Part 3**

문제 32-34번은 다음 대화를 참조하시오. [호M] [영W]

M: Hello. **(32) I'd like to buy these three books and this economics magazine. How much do I owe you?**

W: That'll be $57.60, including sales tax. Do you have a bookstore membership card?

M: No. You accept most major credit cards, right? By the way, what is special about the membership card? Do I get any benefits if I have it?

W: We accept all major credit cards, cash, and personal checks. **(34) If you become a member of the bookstore, you can get 20% off regular prices. (33) Are you interested in being a member? All you have to do is fill out this application card.**

--------

M: 안녕하세요. 저는 여기 책 세 권과 이 경제잡지를 구매하고 싶은데요. 가격이 어떻게 되죠?

W: 판매세 포함해서 57달러 60센트 되겠습니다. 저희 회원카드가 있으신가요?

M: 없어요. 주요 신용카드는 다 받으시죠, 그렇죠? 그런데 회원카드의 특별한 점이 뭔가요? 그걸 가지고 있으면 제가 혜택을 받을 수 있는 건가요?

W: 저희는 주요 신용카드, 현금, 그리고 개인수표까지 모두 다 받습니다. 저희 서점의 회원이 되면 정가에서 20% 할인을 받으실 수 있습니다. 회원 가입에 관심이 있으신가요? 이 회원카드 신청서만 작성하시면 됩니다.

**32.** 대화가 이루어지는 장소는 어디인가?
(A) 서점
(B) 인쇄소
(C) 은행
(D) 도서관 　　　　　　　　정답 (A)

**33.** 남자가 회원이 되길 원한다면 무엇을 해야 하는가?
(A) 점장에게 이야기해야 한다.
(B) 신청서를 작성해야 한다.
(C) 다른 계산원을 찾아야 한다.
(D) 책 한 권을 주문해야 한다. 　　정답 (B)

**34.** 회원에 가입함으로써 남자가 받게 되는 것은 무엇인가?
(A) 쿠폰
(B) 무료 구독
(C) 가격 할인
(D) 상품권 　　　　　　　　정답 (C)

**문제 35-37번은 다음 대화를 참조하시오.** 미M 미W

M: Oh, Ms. Anderson, I'm so glad that I bumped into you here. Are you by any chance going to be in the office around 3 o'clock? Actually, I'm on my way to attend the staff meeting right now. I think I won't return to the office until after 3, so **(35) I was wondering if you would be able to sign for a package being delivered.**

W: I'll be in the office until 7 P.M. **(36) Just let me know when you expect the package to arrive.**

M: It is supposed to get here between 4 and 5 o'clock. **(37) I'll call the shipping company immediately and have it delivered to you instead of me.** They are very important documents, so losing them would create a great deal of trouble. Thank you, Ms. Anderson.

--------

M: 아, Anderson 씨, 여기서 이렇게 만나니 참 반가워요. 혹시 3시쯤에 사무실에 계실 수 있나요? 사실 제가 지금 직원 회의에 참석하러 가는 길이에요. 3시가 지나야 사무실로 복귀할 수가 있을 것 같은데, 저 대신에 소포를 수령하고 수취인 서명을 해주실 수 있을지 궁금해서요.

W: 제가 저녁 7시까지 사무실에 있을 겁니다. 소포가 언제 도착할 것인지만 알려주세요.

M: 4시에서 5시 사이에 도착하기로 되어 있어요. 제가 바로 배송회사에 연락을 해서 저 대신에 당신에게 소포가 배송되도록 할게요. 아주 중요한 서류들이라서 그 서류들을 분실하면 아주 큰 문제가 발생하게 돼요. 고마워요, Anderson 씨.

**35.** 여자가 요청 받은 것은 무엇인가?
(A) 회사 야유회에 참석한다.
(B) 소포를 수령한다.
(C) 새로운 계약서를 작성한다.
(D) 문서를 발송한다. 　　　　정답 (B)

**36.** 여자가 요청하는 정보는 무엇인가?
(A) 구체적인 시간
(B) 주문번호
(C) 견적가
(D) 배송지 　　　　　　　　정답 (A)

**37.** 남자는 이후에 무엇을 할 것인가?
(A) 협상을 재개한다.
(B) 배송을 한다.
(C) 회의 일정을 정한다.
(D) 전화를 한다. 　　　　　　정답 (D)

**문제 38-40번은 다음의 3자 대화를 참조하시오.** 호M 영W 미W

M: You know, this is usually our busiest season. But we don't have nearly as many clients as we did at this time last year. **(38) Why don't we find a way to advertise our business aggressively and nationally?**

W1: That might be a good idea. **(39) But the company is financially strapped these days, so our advertisement budget for this quarter has been reduced, too.** That's why we can't spend money on a massive advertising campaign.

M: **(40) Maybe we could do it in the form of an event like a charity fundraiser.**

W2: I think that is a low-cost event. That way, our firm would be talked about without it looking like our business is sluggish.

W1: That's a good idea. Let's bring it up in the next board meeting. Of course, we can talk more about it over lunch.

--------

M: 알다시피 지금이 일반적으로 가장 바쁜 시기예요. 하지만 고객의 수가 작년 이맘때만 못하네요. 우리 사업을 적극적으로 그리고 전국적으로 광고할 수 있는 방법을 모색하는 건 어떨까요?

W1: 그것도 좋은 생각이긴 합니다. 하지만 최근에 회사의 재정 상황이 좋지 않아서 이번 분기의 광고 예산도 역시 삭감된 상태예요. 그래서 대규모 광고에 자금을 쓸 여력이 되질 않는 겁니다.

M: 어쩌면 자선 모금 행사처럼 행사 형식의 광고를 할 수도 있습니다.

W2: 비용이 적게 드는 행사일 것이란 생각이 드네요. 그렇게 하면 우리 회사의 사업이 부진한 것처럼 보이지 않으면서도 회사의 이름이 사람들에게 많이 회자될 것 같습니다.

W1: 그건 좋은 생각이네요. 다음 이사회에서 안건으로 다뤄보도록 합시다. 물론 우리는 점심식사를 하면서 이 부분에 대해 좀 더 이야기를 나눠보도록 하지요.

**38.** 대화의 주제는 무엇인가?
(A) 더 많은 고객의 유치
(B) 연수 기획
(C) 새로운 광고 제작

(D) 경영 개선                정답 (A)

**39.** 회사의 문제점은 무엇인가?
(A) 파산 가능성
(B) 시장 점유율의 하락
(C) 고비용의 광고
(D) 악화되는 재정 상태          정답 (D)

**40.** 남자는 무엇을 제안하고 있는가?
(A) 광고 세미나에 참석한다.
(B) 다른 마케팅 전략을 사용한다.
(C) 재정 지원을 요청한다.
(D) 자선 행사를 기획한다.          정답 (D)

---

**문제 41-43번은 다음 대화를 참조하시오.** 미M 미W

M: Hello. I was told that I can get a parking permit here.
W: (41) We offer building residents a three-month parking permit for $270, a six-month permit for $490, and a one-year permit for $950.
M: Hmm, can I get a monthly parking permit? I'm a market analyst at the BK Ad Company's research center, and (42) my market research project is supposed to be completed in about two months.
W: Sure, (43) we sell monthly parking permits to nonresidents, but the rate is just the same as the daily one. The daily rate is $3.

---

M: 안녕하세요. 이 곳에서 주차권을 받을 수 있다고 들었는데요.
W: 건물 입주자에게 3개월 주차권은 270달러, 6개월 주차권은 490달러, 그리고 1년 주차권은 950달러에 판매하고 있습니다.
M: 음, 월 주차권을 구입할 수 있을까요? 저는 BK 광고사의 연구 센터에서 일하는 시장 분석가인데, 제 시장 조사 프로젝트가 약 두 달 후면 종료되거든요.
W: 물론이에요. 저희는 외부인에게도 월 주차권을 판매하고 있습니다만, 월 주차 요금은 매일 주차 요금과 동일합니다. 매일 주차 요금은 3달러입니다.

**41.** 여자는 누구일 것 같은가?
(A) 주차 관리인
(B) 마케팅 전문가
(C) 법률 고문
(D) 트럭 운전사          정답 (A)

**42.** 남자에 따르면 프로젝트는 얼마간 지속되는가?
(A) 한 달
(B) 두 달
(C) 여섯 달
(D) 일 년          정답 (B)

**43.** 여자가 주차권에 대해 언급한 내용은 무엇인가?
(A) 발급받는 데 약 일주일이 소요된다.
(B) 월 주차권은 누구에게나 판매된다.
(C) 오직 건물 거주자들만 주차권을 구입할 자격이 된다.
(D) 주차권을 발급받으려면 운전면허증을 제시해야 한다.          정답 (B)

---

**문제 44-46번은 다음 대화를 참조하시오.** 영W 호M

W: (44) The master bathroom is already looking great. I think you've done a great job. Will everything be done this week?
M: Yes, that's the plan. (45) I was going to complete the work today, but the bathroom cabinet I ordered will not be arriving until tomorrow, so I will install it on Friday along with a new mirror and a towel hanger.
W: That sounds good. (46) Can you give me a rough estimate on how much it will cost for you to work on the kitchen by Friday? I don't want to do anything fancy, but I want to replace the kitchen counter and the cupboards at a minimum.

---

W: 큰 욕실은 이미 좋아 보이는데요. 일을 아주 잘해 주신 것 같습니다. 모든 작업이 이번주에 마무리가 되는 건가요?
M: 네, 그럴 계획이에요. 원래는 오늘 모든 작업을 완료할 생각이었습니다만, 제가 주문한 욕실장이 내일이나 되어야 도착해서 욕실장을 새로운 거울과 수건걸이와 함께 금요일에 설치할 예정입니다.
W: 좋군요. 금요일까지 부엌에 대한 작업을 하는 데 소요되는 비용의 대략적인 견적을 알려주실 수 있나요? 화려하게 뭔가를 하고 싶진 않지만 최소한 부엌 조리대와 찬장은 교체하고 싶네요.

**44.** 대화의 주제는 무엇인가?
(A) 주택 보수
(B) 공사 일정
(C) 사업 대출
(D) 정기 할인 판매          정답 (A)

**45.** 남자가 오늘 작업을 마무리하지 못한 이유는 무엇인가?
(A) 몇몇 인부들이 일을 할 수가 없었다.
(B) 일부 가구가 도착하지 않았다.
(C) 그의 보수 공사 자금이 부족하다.
(D) 공급업체에서 잘못된 자재를 배송했다.          정답 (B)

**46.** 여자가 남자에게 금요일까지 해달라고 요청한 것은 무엇인가?
(A) 서류 작업을 마무리한다.
(B) 과정을 점검한다.
(C) 주방용품을 주문한다.
(D) 견적을 제출한다.          정답 (D)

---

**문제 47-49번은 다음 대화를 참조하시오.** 영W 미M

W: Mr. Ryan, (47/48) could I talk to you about the new winter coat design after your meeting?
M: (48) My meeting was delayed. Something's come up with my client.
W: Okay. Um… I reviewed your design this morning. I really liked the overall design. But the only thing I'm concerned about is that there aren't enough outside pockets.
M: Hmm… you mean, it is winter, so people walk around with their hands in their pockets, right?
W: Yes, that's what I'm talking about. I think you should add more outside pockets.
M: All right. It shouldn't be too hard to add some more pockets. (49) I'll modify the original design and e-mail it to you as soon as possible.

---

W: Ryan 씨, 회의가 끝난 후에 새로운 겨울 코트 디자인에 대해 이야기

를 나눌 수 있을까요?

M: 제 회의가 연기되었어요. 제 고객에게 무슨 일이 생긴 것 같네요.

W: 그렇군요. 음… 제가 오늘 오전에 당신 디자인을 살펴봤어요. 전반적으로 디자인이 너무 좋습니다. 그런데 제가 딱 한 가지 걱정되는 건 외부 주머니가 충분하지 않다는 거예요.

M: 흠… 그러니까 겨울이라서 사람들이 주머니에 손을 넣고 다닌다 이거죠?

W: 네, 그게 제가 말씀드리는 내용이에요. 외부 주머니를 추가해야 할 것 같아요.

W: 좋습니다. 주머니를 추가하는 건 크게 어려울 것이 없어요. 제가 디자인을 변경한 후 최대한 빨리 변경한 디자인을 이메일로 보내 드리겠습니다.

**47.** 화자들은 어떠한 산업에 종사할 것 같은가?
(A) 패션
(B) 관광
(C) 건축
(D) 출판 　　　　　　　　　　　　　　　　정답 (A)

**48.** 남자가 "My meeting was delayed."라고 말할 때 의미하는 바는 무엇인가?
(A) 그는 다음주에 휴가를 가는 것이 가능하다.
(B) 그는 자신의 프로젝트에 대해 우려하고 있다.
(C) 그는 안건에 대해 논의할 수 있는 시간적 여력이 있다.
(D) 그는 자신의 업무 일정이 바뀌어서 화가 난다. 　정답 (C)

**49.** 남자는 이후에 무엇을 할 것 같은가?
(A) 몇몇 동료들에게 연락한다.
(B) 설문지를 수거한다.
(C) 디자인을 변경한다.
(D) 정보를 판매업체에 전달한다. 　　　　　　정답 (C)

---

**문제 50-52번은 다음의 3자 대화를 참조하시오.** 미M 미W 영W

M: Hey, Jennifer. I'm talking with a customer on the phone now. (50) **He ordered 100 yellow T-shirts to be delivered to his office on Thursday. But he wants red T-shirts instead now.** What can I do?

W1: George, if he wants to change his order, just do what he wants. (51) **But I just sold and sent 100 red T-shirts to one of my customers, so we don't have any red T-shirts in stock.**

W2: Um… I seriously doubt that we can get more red T-shirts from the factory before Thursday. That's the real problem.

M: Oh, is there anything else I can do for him? It's kind of a big order, so I don't want the customer to cancel his current order just because we are short on red T-shirts.

W1: Well, we have plenty of blue and orange T-shirts in the warehouse. (52) **Why don't you advise him to change his order** to blue or orange instead of red? But if he says no, you don't have any choice but to offer him a full refund.

---

M: 안녕하세요, Jennifer. 지금 고객과 전화통화를 하고 있어요. 그가 목요일에 사무실로 노란색 티셔츠 100벌을 배송해 달라고 주문을 했어요. 그런데 이제 와서 색상을 빨간색으로 변경해 달라고 하네요. 어떻게 해야 하죠?

W1: George, 만약 그 고객이 주문 변경을 원한다면 그렇게 하도록 하세요. 하지만 제가 이미 고객 한 분에게 빨간색 티셔츠 100벌을 판매해서 발송한 상태라서 빨간색 티셔츠가 더 이상 재고에 없어요.

W2: 음… 목요일 전까지 공장에서 빨간색 티셔츠를 들여오는 것은 쉽지 않을 것 같은데요. 그게 진짜 문제네요.

M: 아, 그러면 무슨 다른 방법이 없을까요? 나름 큰 주문이기 때문에 단

---

지 빨간색 티셔츠가 부족하다는 이유만으로 그 고객의 주문 취소는 원하지 않거든요.

W1: 글쎄요. 파란색과 오렌지색 티셔츠는 재고량이 많아요. 빨간색 대신에 파란색이나 오렌지색 티셔츠로 색깔을 변경하도록 권고해보는 것은 어떨까요? 그렇지만 그 고객이 싫다고 하면 전액 환불을 해주는 것을 제외하곤 방법이 없어요.

**50.** 고객이 주문에서 변경하고자 하는 사항은 무엇인가?
(A) 수량
(B) 색상
(C) 배송 주소
(D) 배송 방법 　　　　　　　　　　　　　　정답 (B)

**51.** 한 여자가 언급하는 문제점은 무엇인가?
(A) 송장이 분실되었다.
(B) 제품이 단종되었다.
(C) 주문한 물건이 이미 배송되었다.
(D) 제품이 일시적으로 재고가 없는 상태이다. 　정답 (D)

**52.** 남자는 이후에 무엇을 할 것 같은가?
(A) 고객에게 다른 색상을 제안한다.
(B) 고객에게 전액 환불을 해준다.
(C) 서면으로 불만사항을 제기한다.
(D) 견적서를 수정한다. 　　　　　　　　　　정답 (A)

---

**문제 53-55번은 다음 대화를 참조하시오.** 미W 호M

W: Hello. This is Suite 1703. (53) **I'm calling because it looks like the air conditioner here is not working.**

M: Sorry for the inconvenience. (54) **We already know about that problem, and the facility maintenance crew is trying to figure out what happened to the central cooling system.**

W: How long will it take to fix it? (55) **Some important clients are coming to my office this afternoon.** I don't want them to have an unpleasant experience during their visit.

M: We hope the problem will be addressed by lunchtime. Thanks for your patience.

---

W: 안녕하세요. 1703호입니다. 여기 에어컨이 고장 난 것 같아서 연락을 드렸어요.

M: 불편을 끼쳐 죄송합니다. 저희가 이미 그 문제에 대해서 알고 있고, 시설 관리 직원이 중앙 냉방 시스템에 어떤 문제가 발생했는지 원인을 파악하고 있습니다.

W: 수리하는 데 얼마나 걸릴까요? 오늘 오후에 중요한 고객들이 제 사무실에 오거든요. 그 분들이 제 사무실을 방문하는 동안에 불편한 상황을 겪도록 하고 싶진 않아요.

M: 점심식사 시간까지는 문제점이 해결될 수 있길 바라고 있습니다. 양해 감사드립니다.

**53.** 여자의 문제점은 무엇인가?
(A) 그녀의 자동차가 고장이 났다.
(B) 그녀의 서류 작업이 끝나지 않았다.
(C) 그녀의 항공편이 취소되었다.
(D) 그녀의 사무실이 덥다. 　　　　　　　　정답 (D)

**54.** 남자는 누구일 것 같은가?
(A) 배관공
(B) 공항 직원

(C) 시설 관리인
(D) 자동차 정비공            정답 (C)

**55.** 여자는 오늘 오후에 무엇을 할 것인가?
(A) 회의 일정을 재조정한다.
(B) 보고서 작성을 완료한다.
(C) 고객들과 만난다.
(D) 냉방 기기를 주문한다.      정답 (C)

**문제 56-58번은 다음 대화를 참조하시오.** 호M 영W

M: Sarah, (56) **what do you think of the new logistics management software that we had installed?**
W: (56) **I'm very pleased with it.** (57) **The instructions are certainly intuitive and easy to use.** One drawback though is that it takes a lot of time to use as we have to enter all the data manually from the old system.
M: Yes, that's true. (58) **Luckily, we have a new assistant starting work next week.** I think transferring the data would be a good task for her to start with. If you can show her what needs to be done, she should be able to get all the data entered within a week or so.

--------------------------------------------------

M: Sarah, 우리가 설치한 새로운 물류 관리 소프트웨어에 대해 어떻게 생각해요?
W: 저는 매우 만족하고 있어요. 설명서가 확실히 이해하기 쉽고 사용하기도 쉬워요. 하지만 옛날 시스템에서 수동으로 모든 데이터를 입력해야 해서 사용하는 데 시간이 오래 걸린다는 것이 한 가지 문제점이에요.
M: 네, 사실이에요. 다행히 다음주부터 새 보조 직원이 일을 시작해요. 데이터 이전 작업은 보조 직원이 일을 시작할 수 있는 좋은 업무가 될 것 같아요. 당신이 그녀에게 무엇을 해야 하는지 알려주면 그녀가 약 일주일 안에 모든 데이터를 입력해 놓을 수 있을 겁니다.

**56.** 여자가 "I'm very pleased with it."이라고 언급한 이유는 무엇인가?
(A) 그녀의 새로운 컴퓨터의 성능이 매우 좋다.
(B) 그녀의 주문품이 예상보다 빨리 도착했다.
(C) 새로 설치된 프로그램이 매우 유용하다.
(D) 그녀의 회사가 매출 증가를 기록했다.   정답 (C)

**57.** 여자는 새로운 소프트웨어에 대해 무엇이라고 언급하는가?
(A) 도면을 그리기에 좋다.
(B) 가격이 적당하다.
(C) 설명서가 간단하다.
(D) 서버에서 주문을 입력하게 해 준다.   정답 (C)

**58.** 다음주에 무슨 일이 일어날 것인가?
(A) 새로운 직원이 일을 시작할 것이다.
(B) 소프트웨어 프로그램이 설치될 것이다.
(C) 특별 공연이 있을 것이다.
(D) 한 직원이 전근할 것이다.     정답 (A)

**문제 59-61번은 다음의 대화를 참조하시오.** 미M 미W

M: Thank you, Ms. Wallace. (59) **This is the receipt for the dining set you purchased.** Please keep it to show when the furniture is delivered. (60) **Which day is best for delivery?**
W: (60) **Saturday afternoon would be great.** Ah, do I have to

pay for delivery?
M: No, you don't have to. The delivery fee is included in the price. (61) **However, if you would like us to remove your old furniture, you can pay for that in advance.**
W: I'll have to call you about that. My daughter just moved, and she may take the old pieces.

--------------------------------------------------

M: 감사합니다, Wallace 씨. 이건 고객님이 구매하신 식탁 세트에 대한 영수증입니다. 잘 보관했다가 가구가 배달될 때 보여주시면 됩니다. 배달은 어느 요일이 좋으신가요?
W: 토요일 오후가 좋습니다. 아, 제가 배송료를 지불해야 하나요?
M: 아뇨, 그러실 필요가 없습니다. 배송료는 가격에 포함이 되어 있습니다. 하지만 저희가 고객님의 오래된 가구를 치워 드리길 원하시면 그 부분에 대해선 비용을 미리 지불하셔도 됩니다.
W: 그 부분은 다시 연락을 드려야겠네요. 제 딸이 막 이사를 해서 그 오래된 가구를 사용할지도 모르겠어요.

**59.** 대화는 어디에서 이루어지고 있겠는가?
(A) 은행
(B) 배송회사
(C) 식당
(D) 가구점            정답 (D)

**60.** Wallace 씨가 배달을 요청하는 날은 무슨 요일인가?
(A) 목요일
(B) 금요일
(C) 토요일
(D) 일요일            정답 (C)

**61.** Wallace 씨의 오래된 가구가 처리되길 원한다면 그녀는 무엇을 해야 하는가?
(A) 비용을 지불한다.
(B) 더 많은 인부를 채용한다.
(C) 배송 트럭을 빌린다.
(D) 지역 자선 단체에 기부한다.     정답 (A)

**문제 62-64번은 다음 다음 대화와 청구서를 참조하시오.** 호M 미W

M: (62) **Hello. This is KB Mobile Telecommunication Systems. How may I assist you?**
W: This is Vanessa Finley. I am calling about an incorrect billing. (63) **I am absolutely sure that I paid my bill on time, yet there's a late charge on my monthly statement.** Please take a look at your records and explain the discrepancy.
M: Let me check. Oh, I see. We had a problem with our server in Australia. It affected a lot of our valued customers' accounts. It appears that a mistake was made on your bill. We are pleased you noticed the discrepancy. (63) **I will subtract that charge immediately.**
W: I got it. Thank you for your help.
M: You're welcome. Ms. Finley, I can see that your mobile contract with us will expire soon. (64) **Please stay on the line so that I can tell you about some new options available to long-time customers like yourself. There are many new benefits I think you'll be interested in hearing about.**

--------------------------------------------------

M: 안녕하세요, KB Mobile Telecommunication Systems입니다. 어떻게 도와 드릴까요?
W: 저는 Vanessa Finley라고 합니다. 잘못된 청구에 대해 문의하려고 전

80

화했습니다. 저는 확실히 제때에 청구서 요금을 지불했는데 월 청구서에 연체료가 부과되었더군요. 기록을 보시고 왜 이러한 차이가 발생했는지 설명해 주세요.

M: 확인해 보겠습니다. 아, 알겠습니다. 호주에 있는 서버에 문제가 있었습니다. 그것이 저희 소중한 고객님들의 계정에 영향을 미쳤습니다. 계산서에 착오가 생긴 것 같습니다. 고객님께서 이러한 오류를 발견하셔서 다행입니다. 제가 그 연체료를 바로 빼 드리겠습니다.

W: 알겠습니다. 도움에 감사드려요.

M: 천만에요. Finley 씨, 고객님의 이동통신 사용 계약이 곧 만료될 것이라고 나와 있는데요. 고객님과 같은 장기 고객님께 제공되는 새로운 선택 사항들에 대해 알려드릴 수 있도록 끊지 말고 기다려 주십시오. 고객님께서 관심을 가지실 만한 새로운 혜택이 많이 있습니다.

## 월별 요금 청구서

고객명: Vanessa Finley

요금 내역
월별 서비스 이용료:     $28.00
**(63) 연체료**     **$4.00**
세금     $2.50

총계:     $34.00

**62.** 남자는 어떤 사업체에 종사하고 있을 것 같은가?
(A) 컴퓨터 제조업체
(B) 건설 회사
(C) 휴대전화 회사
(D) 부동산 중개업체     정답 (C)

**63.** 그래픽을 보시오. 여자의 청구서에서 얼마의 금액이 공제될 것인가?
(A) $2.50
(B) $4.00
(C) $28.00
(D) $34.00     정답 (B)

**64.** 남자가 여자에게 대기하라고 요청한 이유는 무엇인가?
(A) 예약을 확인하기 위해서
(B) 관리자에게 전화를 연결시켜 주기 위해서
(C) 새로운 휴대전화를 소개하기 위해서
(D) 그녀에게 혜택에 관한 정보를 제공하기 위해서     정답 (D)

**문제 65–67번은 다음 대화와 전단지를 참조하시오.** 영W 호M

W: Hello. (65) **I was browsing the Lucky 7 Supermarket Web site, and I found three frying pans that are on sale and I'd like to buy them.**

M: All right. (66) **Normally, our customers receive their orders in two business days, but it might take a little longer right now because of our current promotion.**

W: That's fine. But I have a question about the promotion. Since the frying pans are already marked down, can I receive the additional discount? I think my total price is good enough for the additional discount.

M: Sure. Every order we process is eligible for the promotion. The more you spend, the more you save.

W: Okay, let's see... hmm... (67) **My total price will be $110 before the additional discount is applied.**

---

M: Yes. It looks like you're going to save quite a bit of money today.

----------------------------------------

W: 안녕하세요. 제가 Lucky 7 슈퍼마켓의 홈페이지를 살펴봤는데요. 할인 중인 프라이팬이 세 개가 있어서 구입하려고 합니다.

M: 알겠습니다. 보통 저희 고객들께서는 주문품을 이틀 후에 받으시지만 현재 진행 중인 저희 판촉 행사로 인해 지금은 시간이 조금 더 걸릴 수도 있습니다.

W: 그건 괜찮아요. 그런데 판촉 행사에 대해서 질문이 있어요. 그 프라이팬들은 이미 가격이 할인됐는데 여전히 추가 할인을 받을 수 있나요? 제 구입 총액이면 추가 할인을 받기에 충분할 것 같아서요.

M: 물론입니다. 저희가 진행하는 모든 주문은 판촉 행사에 해당됩니다. 더 많이 구입할수록 더 많이 할인 받으실 수 있습니다.

W: 알겠습니다. 음… 추가 할인이 적용되기 전에 제 총액은 110달러가 되겠네요.

M: 네. 오늘 꽤 많은 금액을 절약하시게 되는 것 같네요.

## Lucky 7 슈퍼마켓
### 특별 여름 판촉 행사

| 총 구매액 | 추가 할인 |
|---|---|
| $10 – $49 | 7% |
| $50 – $99 | 15% |
| $100 – $199 | 20% |
| $200 이상 | 25% |

**65.** 여자가 하려는 것은 무엇인가?
(A) 거래를 취소한다.
(B) 전화에 답신한다.
(C) 제품에 대해 불평한다.
(D) 상품을 구입한다.     정답 (D)

**66.** 남자가 언급하는 문제점은 무엇인가?
(A) 주문이 처리될 수 없다.
(B) 한 제품이 현재 구매할 수 없다.
(C) 배송이 평소보다 늦어질 것이다.
(D) 홈페이지가 제대로 작동하지 않고 있다.     정답 (C)

**67.** 그래픽을 보시오. 여자는 할인을 얼마나 받겠는가?
(A) 7%
(B) 15%
(C) 20%
(D) 25%     정답 (C)

**문제 68–70번은 다음 대화와 열차 시간표를 참조하시오.** 미M 영W

M: Excuse me. (68) **I couldn't print my ticket from my computer,** but I paid for it online through your Web site.

W: No problem. I can print your ticket here for you. You'll just need to show me the confirmation number and some form of legal identification.

M: Sure. One moment, please. Here's my driver's license. And... you can see the confirmation number on my receipt.

W: Good. It's printing now. Okay, here's your ticket.

M: Thanks. (69) **My train's scheduled to depart at 2:30 P.M. Is it on time?**

W: Yes, it is. I see that you have some luggage there. If you need any assistance with it, (70) **we move our passengers' baggage for free.** Just speak to one of the employees wearing a green jacket, and they'll be able to help you.

---

M: 실례합니다. 제 컴퓨터에서 표를 뽑을 수가 없었는데요. 하지만 홈페이지를 통해 온라인으로 표값을 지불했습니다.
W: 문제없습니다. 제가 여기서 뽑아 드리면 됩니다. 확인 번호와 법적 신분증을 보여주시면 됩니다.
M: 그러죠. 잠시만요, 여기 제 운전 면허증입니다. 그리고… 제 영수증에 적혀 있는 확인 번호를 보실 수 있을 겁니다.
W: 좋습니다. 지금 표를 뽑는 중입니다. 네, 표 여기 있습니다.
M: 감사합니다. 제 기차가 오후 2시 30분 출발 예정인데요. 제 시간에 출발하겠죠?
W: 네, 그렇습니다. 짐이 좀 있으신 것 같네요. 도움이 필요하시면 승객분들의 짐을 무료로 옮겨 드립니다. 초록색 상의를 입은 직원 아무에게나 도움을 요청하시면 도움을 드릴 겁니다.

### Daly City 기차역 열차 시간표

| 도착지 | 도착 시간 | 현재 상태 |
|---|---|---|
| Fairfield | 오후 2:10 | 출발 중 |
| Napa Valley | 오후 2:20 | 정시 출발 |
| (69) Richmond | 오후 2:30 | 정시 출발 |

**68.** 남자가 할 수 없었던 것은 무엇인가?
(A) 기차역을 찾는 것
(B) 표를 뽑는 것
(C) 예약을 변경하는 것
(D) 신분증을 제시하는 것　　　　　　　정답 (B)

**69.** 그래픽을 보시오. 남자의 목적지는 어디인가?
(A) Daly City
(B) Fairfield
(C) Napa Valley
(D) Richmond　　　　　　　　　　　정답 (D)

**70.** 여자에 따르면 무료로 제공되는 것이 무엇인가?
(A) 좌석 업그레이드
(B) 다과
(C) 수하물 처리
(D) 무선 인터넷　　　　　　　　　　정답 (C)

## Part 4

**문제 71-73번은 다음 담화를 참조하시오.** 미M

Hello, everyone! (72) **Welcome and thank you for attending the Phyzar Pharmaceutical Company's 12th annual award banquet. (71/72) As your vice president, it's my pleasure to present the employee of the year award tonight.** This year, the award goes to David Clinton. Under Mr. Clinton's leadership, the development team has created most of our popular medicines on the market for the last ten years. (73) **Mr. Clinton has been with the Phyzar Pharmaceutical Company for our entire twelve years in business.** Mr. Clinton, please come up to the stage. Let's give him a big round of applause!

---

안녕하세요, 여러분! Phyzar 제약회사의 설립 12주년 기념 연례 시상식에 참석하신 여러분에게 환영과 감사의 말씀 전합니다. 부사장으로서 오늘밤 올해의 우수 직원상을 발표하게 된 것을 영광스럽게 생각합니다. 올해 이 상은 David Clinton 씨에게 돌아가겠습니다. Clinton 씨의 주도 하에 신약 개발팀은 지난 10년간 시장에서 인기를 끌고 있는 대부분의 약을 개발했습니다. Clinton 씨는 Phyzar 제약회사의 창립 이후 12년을 함께 해왔습니다. Clinton 씨, 무대 위로 올라와 주십시오. 우리 모두 그에게 큰 박수갈채를 보냅시다!

**71.** 담화의 목적은 무엇인가?
(A) 신제품 시연
(B) 동료 환송
(C) 직원 시상
(D) 은퇴 발표　　　　　　　　　　　정답 (C)

**72.** 청중은 누구일 것 같은가?
(A) 지점장들
(B) 해외 투자자들
(C) 직원들
(D) 의사들　　　　　　　　　　　　정답 (C)

**73.** Clinton 씨는 회사에서 얼마 동안 근무했는가?
(A) 2년
(B) 10년
(C) 12년
(D) 20년　　　　　　　　　　　　　정답 (C)

**문제 74-76번은 다음 회의 내용을 참조하시오.** 미W

Um… before finishing up this meeting, there's some good news I want to share with you. There's a college three blocks away from our office. (74) **I heard this morning that the college will have an architectural design course next month. (75) Professor Jake Wallace will teach the course. This is huge. He's one of the world's most highly respected architects.** Can you believe such a renowned architect is teaching college students in a small town? Anyway, (74/75) **this is a once-in-a-life-time opportunity.** I'd like all of you to take advantage of this opportunity by taking the course. Registration starts next week. (74/75) **Please keep in mind that many architects like us want to attend this course.** Okay, I'm done. Ah, (76) **please don't forget to keep me posted on your current projects.**

---

음… 회의를 끝내기 전에 한 가지 여러분과 공유하고 싶은 좋은 소식이 있습니다. 우리 사무실에서 세 블록 정도 떨어진 곳에 대학이 하나 있습니다. 제가 오늘 오전에 들었는데, 그 대학에서 다음달에 건축 디자인 강좌를 개설한다고 합니다. Jake Wallace 교수가 강의할 예정입니다. 이건 정말 대단한 일입니다. 그는 전세계에서 가장 존경받는 건축가들 중 한 분이거든요. 그렇게 유명한 건축가가 이 조그만 마을에서 대학생들을 지도하고 계시다니 믿어집니까? 어쨌든, 이건 정말 인생 일대의 기회입니다. 그래서 여러분이 모두 그 강좌를 수강하는 기회를 누리도록 하길 바랍니다. 등록은 다음주부터 시작합니다. 우리와 같은 많은 건축가들이 그 분의 강좌를 듣길 원한다는 사실 꼭 기억해 두시고요. 좋습니다, 저는 할 말 다 했어요. 아, 지금 맡고 있는 프로젝트에 대한 새로운 소식들을 주기적으로 제게 알려주는 것 잊지 마세요.

**74.** 청자들은 어디에서 근무하는 것 같은가?
(A) 연구소
(B) 자동차 제조업체
(C) 건축회사
(D) 의류회사 　　　　　　　　　　　정답 (C)

**75.** 화자가 "Please keep in mind that many architects like us want to attend this course."라고 말할 때 암시하는 바는 무엇인가?
(A) 그녀는 세미나실을 확장해야 할 필요가 있다.
(B) 그녀는 더 많은 사무용품을 주문하길 원한다.
(C) 청자들은 최대한 서둘러서 등록해야 한다.
(D) 청자들은 자신에 대해 자부심을 느껴야 한다. 　정답 (C)

**76.** 화자가 청자들에게 상기시키는 것은 무엇인가?
(A) 일의 진척에 따른 소식을 전달한다.
(B) 설계가 가능하도록 충분히 배운다.
(C) 원가 절감 방안을 제안한다.
(D) 건축 부지를 물색한다. 　　　　　　　정답 (A)

**문제 77-79번은 다음 안내문을 참조하시오.** ⓊⓂ

Good morning. I'm Nate Ford, the president of Lake Cream Homes and Properties. (77) **Thank you for visiting our head office today to attend this informational meeting for potential first-time home buyers.** It is widely known that Lake Cream is a great place to live. (77) **I would like you to hear about our new apartment complex in the area from Fiona McBride and Justin Walter.** First, we'll be hearing from Ms. McBride, a real estate veteran, who will be talking about the new parks and recreational facilities available to all apartment residents. (78) **Secondly, we'll be hearing from Mr. Walter, our mayor, about the local business climate.** (79) **After lunch, we'll take all of you on a tour of the area so that you can see the wonderful homes we are currently offering.** The tour will last about one hour, and then we'll return to the office around 2 o'clock.

--------------------------------------------

안녕하세요. 저는 Lake Cream Homes and Properties의 사장인 Nate Ford입니다. 최초로 주택을 구매하시고자 하는 분들에게 정보를 제공하기 위한 홍보 회의에 참석하고자 오늘 저희 본사를 방문해주신 점에 감사드립니다. Lake Cream이 살기 좋은 곳이란 사실은 널리 알려진 바 있습니다. 저희가 이 지역에 건설한 새로운 아파트 단지에 관해 Fiona McBride 씨와 Justin Walter 씨가 발표하고자 하는 내용을 경청해주시길 바랍니다. 우선 부동산 전문가인 McBride 씨가 아파트의 모든 주민들이 이용할 수 있는 새로운 공원들과 오락 시설에 관해 말씀드릴 것입니다. 이어서 시장님인 Walter 씨가 이 곳의 사업 환경에 관해 말씀드릴 것입니다. 점심식사를 마치고 난 후에는 여러분 모두를 모시고 저희가 현재 제공하고 있는 멋진 아파트들을 직접 보실 수 있도록 이 지역에 대한 견학을 시행하고자 합니다. 견학은 한 시간 정도 소요될 것이며 오후 2시쯤에 본사로 돌아올 것입니다.

**77.** 이 행사의 목적은 무엇인가?
(A) 새로운 공사 기금 마련
(B) 기업가들에 대한 시상
(C) 새로운 주거 시설에 대한 홍보
(D) 공사 완공의 축하 　　　　　　　　　정답 (C)

**78.** 시장은 무엇에 관해 발표할 것인가?
(A) 사업 환경
(B) 다가오는 공직 선거
(C) 직접 투자
(D) 새로운 부동산 시장의 흐름 　　　　　정답 (A)

**79.** 화자에 따르면 오후에는 어떤 일이 예정되어 있는가?
(A) 공청회
(B) 영업 발표
(C) 사업 오찬
(D) 새로운 주택 견학 　　　　　　　　　정답 (D)

**문제 80-82번은 다음 라디오 방송을 참조하시오.** ⓊⓂ

Good morning, listeners. You're tuned in to KCXR Radio Montana. I'm Max Davidson, and I'm here with your local news update. (80) **The Rossiter Hotel will finally unveil its newest addition this Saturday: a modern spa and sauna facility.** The Inner Glow Spa took over 18 months to construct and will be accessible to both hotel guests and non-guests. (81) **Anyone who goes to www.innerglowforever.com can print a one-time-use coupon that can be used for a 50-percent discount at the opening event on Saturday.** And some of you may be wondering how you can find time to visit the spa to enjoy its amenities. (82) **You're in luck! It will operate around the clock seven days a week! So you'll always be able to find time to pamper yourself.**

--------------------------------------------

안녕하세요, 청취자 여러분. 여러분은 지금 KCXR Radio Montana를 듣고 계십니다. 저는 Max Davidson이며 여러분께 최신 지역 뉴스를 전해 드리겠습니다. Rossiter Hotel이 마침내 이번주 토요일에 최신 시설물을 공개합니다. 바로 현대적인 스파와 사우나 시설입니다. Inner Glow Spa는 짓는 데 18개월이 걸렸으며 호텔 숙박 손님과 일반 손님 모두 이용 가능할 것입니다. www.innerglowforever.com을 방문하는 분은 누구나 토요일에 있을 개장 기념 행사에서 50퍼센트 할인을 받을 수 있는 1회용 쿠폰을 프린트하실 수 있습니다. 그리고 여러분 중에는 이 스파를 방문하고 편의 시설을 즐길 시간을 어떻게 내야 할지 궁금한 분들도 계실 것입니다. 여러분은 운이 좋으십니다! 이 시설은 하루 24시간 일주일 내내 운영됩니다! 그러므로 여러분 자신을 가꿀 시간을 언제든지 만드실 수 있을 것입니다.

**80.** 화자에 따르면 이번 주말에 무슨 일이 예정되어 있는가?
(A) 건축 공사 프로젝트가 시작될 것이다.
(B) 한 호텔이 자사의 설립을 기념할 것이다.
(C) 한 소매업체가 계절 할인을 시작할 것이다.
(D) 한 스파 시설이 영업을 위해 개장할 것이다. 　정답 (D)

**81.** 청자들은 어떻게 할인을 받을 수 있는가?
(A) 홈페이지를 방문함으로써
(B) 이메일을 보냄으로써
(C) 행사에 참석함으로써
(D) 예약함으로써 　　　　　　　　　　　정답 (A)

**82.** 화자가 "You're in luck."이라고 말할 때 무엇을 의미하는가?
(A) 시내에 많은 훌륭한 편의 시설이 있다고 생각한다.
(B) 청자들에게 기분 좋은 소식을 전할 것이다.
(C) 라디오 경연대회의 결과를 발표할 것이다.
(D) 청자들이 무료 선물을 받을 것이라고 생각한다. 　정답 (B)

Making home improvements? Come on down to Mimi Furnishers on Bailey Road. We have four floors full of fabulous furniture for every room in your house. Mimi Furnishers has been the local leader in home furnishings for over fifty years. (83) **We have the biggest selection anywhere in the area,** and (84) **we are currently offering a discount of 50% on all of our products to all customers at our store as a part of our fiftieth anniversary celebration. Can you believe it?** Don't miss this bargain offer. What's more, (85) **we'll launch our new department specializing in home appliances next month.** So don't delay. Come and join the excitement at Mimi Furnishers today!

--------

주택 개조를 하고 계신가요? Bailey Road의 Mimi Furnishers로 오세요. 주택의 모든 방을 위한 근사한 가구가 4층 가득히 전시되어 있습니다. Mimi Furnishers는 50년 넘게 이 지역의 주거용 가구업계의 선두주자였습니다. 저희는 이 지역에서 가장 다양한 제품을 보유하고 있으며, 현재 50주년 기념 행사의 일환으로 매장을 찾아 주신 모든 고객분께 저희가 판매하는 전 제품에 대해 50% 할인 혜택을 제공하고 있습니다. 놀랍지 않으신가요? 이 할인 행사를 놓치지 마세요. 그리고 또 하나, 다음달에는 가전제품 전문매장을 개장합니다. 그러니 미루지 마세요. 오늘 Mimi Furnishers로 와서 기쁨을 함께 나누시기 바랍니다!

**83.** 화자에 따르면 이 상점은 무엇으로 알려졌는가?
(A) 빠른 배송
(B) 고객 편의시설
(C) 다양한 제품
(D) 저렴한 가격 　　　　　　정답 (C)

**84.** 화자가 "Can you believe it?"이라고 말할 때 암시하는 것은 무엇인가?
(A) 그녀는 광고의 내용을 믿을 수 없다.
(B) 그녀는 상점이 제공하는 서비스에 감명을 받았다.
(C) 그녀는 이 할인 혜택이 매우 놀랍다고 생각한다.
(D) 그녀는 회사 제품들의 품질에 놀라워하고 있다. 　정답 (C)

**85.** 이 상점은 다음달에 무엇을 판매하기 시작할 것인가?
(A) 출장 연회 서비스
(B) 가전제품
(C) 주택용 가구
(D) 전문가용 제품 　　　　　　정답 (B)

(86/87) **This is going to be our last rehearsal before the theater production opens in three days.** Over the past three months, our advertising team has been promoting the play with posters and flyers, and they've also promoted it on the Internet and the radio. Thousands of people have already reserved tickets for the play, which has its opening night this Saturday. In a month's time after the final night of the play, we are going to have a celebration party at the Regent Park Hotel downtown. (88) **We are still planning the party, so I would appreciate it if someone could help with that.** Let me know if you have some free time to do that. Thanks again and good luck, everybody.

--------

이번이 3일 후에 우리의 새 연극 작품을 무대에 올리기 전 마지막 리허설이 될 것입니다. 지난 3개월 동안 광고 팀은 포스터와 전단지를 이용해 연극을 홍보해 왔고, 또한 인터넷과 라디오를 통해서도 홍보했습니다. 수천 명이 이번 토요일에 있을 초연을 관람하기 위해 이미 표를 예매했습니다. 한 달 후 마지막 밤 공연이 끝나면 시내의 Regent Park 호텔에서 축하 파티를 열 예정입니다. 아직 파티를 계획하고 있기 때문에 누군가 그것을 좀 도와주면 고맙겠습니다. 파티 계획을 도와줄 시간이 있는 사람은 알려주세요. 다시 한 번 감사드리고 모두 행운을 빕니다.

**86.** 화자는 어디에서 일하겠는가?
(A) 호텔
(B) 마케팅 회사
(C) 라디오 방송국
(D) 극단 　　　　　　정답 (D)

**87.** 화자는 3일 후에 무슨 일이 있을 것이라고 언급하는가?
(A) 연극 공연이 종료될 것이다.
(B) 파티가 열릴 것이다.
(C) 영화가 개봉될 것이다.
(D) 연극 초연이 있을 것이다. 　　　정답 (D)

**88.** 화자는 무엇과 관련하여 도움을 요청하고 있는가?
(A) 연극 홍보
(B) 포스터 배부
(C) 상점 개점 준비
(D) 파티 준비 　　　　　　정답 (D)

Hi, Ms. Bailey. (89) **This is Emily Fisher at City Printing Solutions. Your intern brought your latest order this morning,** (89/90) **but I just want to confirm the quantity.** The form he submitted requests 50,000 flyers to be printed. However, you usually only order 5,000. I know this is a rush order, so we will start printing 5,000 this afternoon. I think I will start on the rest of the flyers after I hear from you just in case. (91) **Please e-mail me at your earliest convenience.** I'll call you tomorrow morning if I haven't heard from you. Thanks!

--------

안녕하세요, Bailey 씨. 저는 City Printing Solutions의 Emily Fisher입니다. 귀사의 수습 직원이 오늘 아침에 최근에 작성된 주문서를 가지고 왔는데요, 그 주문양을 확인하고 싶어서요. 인턴 직원이 제출한 주문서에는 전단지 5만 장을 인쇄해 달라고 요청이 되어 있습니다. 하지만 당신은 보통 5천 장을 주문하셨죠. 이것이 급한 주문인 건 알고 있어서 오늘 오후에 5천 장을 인쇄할 예정이에요. 그러나 나머지 전단지는 만약을 대비해서 당신에게 확실한 말을 듣고 난 후에 인쇄하려고 생각 중입니다. 가능한 빨리 제게 이메일을 보내주세요. 만약 계속 연락을 받지 못하면 내일 오전에 당신에게 전화 드리도록 할게요. 감사합니다!

**89.** 화자는 누구일 것 같은가?
(A) 고객
(B) 수습 직원
(C) 고객 서비스 담당자
(D) 광고 전문가 　　　　　　정답 (C)

**90.** 메시지의 목적은 무엇인가?
(A) 면접을 요청하기 위해서
(B) 예약을 확인하기 위해서

(C) 특가 판매를 홍보하기 위해서
(D) 수량을 재확인하기 위해서 　　　　　　　　정답 (D)

**91.** 청자는 이후에 무엇을 할 것 같은가?
(A) 수습 직원과 이야기한다.
(B) 이메일을 보낸다.
(C) 구매 가능한 제품들을 본다.
(D) 전단지를 인쇄한다. 　　　　　　　　정답 (B)

문제 92-94번은 다음 담화를 참조하시오. 🇬🇧W

Attention, employees. I'm Vanessa Simpson, your personnel director. (92/94) **Please remember to park on the street next week as the parking garage is being repainted.** The work should be finished by the end of next week, and we will let you know if there are any delays. If you have any questions, (93) **please contact Mr. Bobby Singh, the head of Maintenance. He is in charge of the project.** You have been e-mailed a map with street parking areas. Please allow time to park and to walk to avoid tardiness.

주목해 주시기 바랍니다. 직원 여러분. 저는 여러분의 인사 담당 이사인 Vanessa Simpson입니다. 다음주에 주차장의 도색 작업이 진행되기 때문에 노상 주차를 해야 한다는 점을 기억해주시길 바랍니다. 작업은 다음 주말까지 완료될 것이며 지연되는 경우 여러분께 알려드리도록 할 것입니다. 질문이 있으시면 시설관리부장인 Bobby Singh 씨에게 연락하십시오. 그가 이 작업의 책임자입니다. 직원 여러분께 노상 주차를 할 수 있는 곳을 알려주는 지도를 이메일로 발송했습니다. 주차에 필요한 시간과 이곳까지 걸어야 하는 시간까지 고려하여 지각하는 일이 없도록 해주십시오.

**92.** 어떤 변경사항이 발표되고 있는가?
(A) 직원들은 주차장을 이용할 수 있다.
(B) 새로운 주차 관리인이 채용되었다.
(C) 노상 주차는 더 이상 허용되지 않는다.
(D) 주차장은 일시적으로 폐쇄된다. 　　　　정답 (D)

**93.** Bobby Singh 씨의 직업은 무엇인가?
(A) 공사장 인부
(B) 작업 관리자
(C) 건축가
(D) 인사 전문가 　　　　　　　　　　　정답 (B)

**94.** 이 일이 일어난 이유는 무엇인가?
(A) 어떤 곳에 새롭게 도색을 하기 위해서
(B) 더 많은 고객 주차 공간을 확보하기 위해서
(C) 주차장을 철거하기 위해서
(D) 직원들이 지각하는 것을 예방하기 위해서 　　정답 (A)

문제 95-97번은 다음 전화 메시지와 티켓을 참조하시오. 🇬🇧W

Hello, Mr. White. (95) **This is Stacy Jackson at Century 74 Cinema returning your call. You inquired about our location and ticket prices.** The theater is on the corner of Harder Street and Orchard Road. Mr. White, it is very easy to find because our building is the only square building in the area. Let me tell you about the ticket prices. On weekdays, all movie tickets cost seven dollars. (96) **On weekends, the price goes**

up to fourteen dollars, but we're currently offering a special promotion. (97) **If you come to watch a movie in the morning on Saturday or Sunday, you just need to pay eight dollars,** which means you can save six dollars. Well, you can spend the six dollars on popcorn, soda, and other foods. I appreciate your interest and hope to see you soon at Century 74 Cinema.

안녕하세요, White 씨. 저는 Century 74 Cinema에서 답신 전화를 하는 Stacy Jackson입니다. 저희 위치와 표 가격에 대해 문의하셨죠. 극장은 Harder Street와 Orchard Road의 모퉁이에 위치하고 있습니다. White 씨, 저희 극장은 이 지역에서 유일한 정사각형 건물이기 때문에 찾기가 무척 수월합니다. 표 가격에 대해서 알려드리겠습니다. 주중에는 모든 영화표 가격이 7달러입니다. 주말에는 가격이 인상되어 14달러지만 현재 특별 홍보 행사를 진행 중입니다. 토요일이나 일요일 오전에 영화를 관람하면 8달러만 지불하시면 되고, 이는 6달러를 절약하실 수 있게 된다는 것을 의미합니다. 그러면 그 6달러로 팝콘과, 탄산음료 및 다른 먹거리를 구매하실 수도 있겠지요. 관심에 감사드리며 저희 Century 74 Cinema에서 조만간 뵐 수 있길 기대합니다.

### Century 74 Cinema
### 입장권

영화: We Were Brave Soldiers
날짜: 1월 10일 (97) **토요일**
시간: (97) **오전 10:40**

Brandon White 씨

**95.** 여자가 전화하는 이유는 무엇인가?
(A) 질문에 대해 답변을 하기 위해서
(B) 주문을 확인하기 위해서
(C) 직원 복리후생 혜택에 관해 문의하기 위해서
(D) 정보를 요청하기 위해서 　　　　　　　정답 (A)

**96.** 화자가 Century 74 Cinema에 관해 언급한 것은 무엇인가?
(A) 주중에만 운영한다.
(B) 교통이 편리한 곳에 위치하고 있다.
(C) 할인 티켓을 제공하고 있다.
(D) 조만간 폐쇄된다. 　　　　　　　　　정답 (C)

**97.** 그래픽을 보시오. White 씨의 영화표는 얼마이겠는가?
(A) 6달러
(B) 7달러
(C) 8달러
(D) 14달러 　　　　　　　　　　　　　정답 (C)

문제 98-100번은 다음 지시문과 좌석배치도를 참조하시오. 🇬🇧W

Good to see you, everyone. I'm so pleased that all of you are here to watch our TV audition program *Britain Has Superstars*. (98) **I'm Megan Hunt, and I oversee all aspects of the production of this program.** Let me give you all complete instructions for it. You know, we have many performers on the show today. (99) **You should stay around the side entrance so that you don't disturb the artistic director and other performers as they make their way to and from the stage.** Um… one more thing. (100) **If you want to take pictures with some performers you like, you should move to the**

**photo shoot zone after the show.** Please be aware that taking photographs is not allowed except in the photo shoot zone. Thank you for your understanding and full cooperation in advance. Enjoy the show.

----

만나뵙게 되어 반갑습니다, 여러분. 저희 TV 오디션 프로그램인 'Britain Has Superstars'를 관람하고자 이 곳에 와주셔서 기쁩니다. 저는 Megan Hunt라고 하며 이 프로그램 제작의 전반적인 부분을 감독하고 있습니다. 여러분 모두에게 프로그램 관람에 관한 전체 주의사항을 전달하고자 합니다. 아시다시피, 오늘 저희 프로그램에는 많은 공연자들이 출연합니다. 여러분은 예술 감독과 다른 공연자들이 무대로 오고 가는 데 방해가 되지 않도록 옆문 주변에 계셔야 합니다. 음… 한 가지가 더 있습니다. 만약 여러분이 좋아하는 공연자들과 사진 촬영을 하고 싶으면, 프로그램이 끝난 후 사진 촬영 구역으로 이동하셔야 합니다. 사진 촬영 구역을 제외하고 일체의 사진 촬영이 허용되지 않는다는 점을 알아두시기 바랍니다. 여러분의 이해와 전적인 협조에 미리 감사의 말씀을 드리고자 합니다. 즐거운 관람이 되시길 바랍니다.

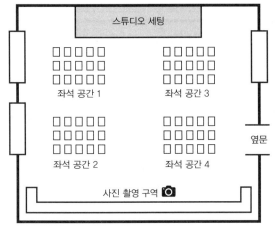

스튜디오 세팅

좌석 공간 1　　좌석 공간 3

좌석 공간 2　　좌석 공간 4

옆문

사진 촬영 구역 📷

**98.** 화자는 누구일 것 같은가?
(A) 예술 평론가
(B) 공연자
(C) 프로그램 제작자
(D) 전문 사진가　　　　정답 (C)

**99.** 그래픽을 보시오. 청자들은 어느 좌석 공간에 착석할 것 같은가?
(A) 좌석 공간 1
(B) 좌석 공간 2
(C) 좌석 공간 3
(D) 좌석 공간 4　　　　정답 (D)

**100.** 공연자들과 사진을 찍고 싶은 청자들은 어떻게 해야 하는가?
(A) 스튜디오 세팅으로 이동한다.
(B) 자신의 카메라를 가지고 온다.
(C) 사진 촬영 구역으로 간다.
(D) 지역 자선 단체에 기부한다.　　정답 (C)

---

**Part 5**

**101.** 해마다 전세계로부터 많은 관광객들이 인기 많은 관광 명소들을 구경하기 위해 Arizona를 방문한다.　　정답 (A)

**102.** Best Business Consulting 사는 해외에서 잠재 고객들을 유치하고자 항상 자사의 성공적인 프로젝트 이면에 놓인 이유들을 강조하는 소개책자들

을 발송한다.　　정답 (B)

**103.** 내 회사를 포함하여 Syracuse에 있는 몇몇 지역 기업들은 대개 자사 매출의 일부를 시립 고아원에 기부한다.　　정답 (B)

**104.** 계산원들은 대개 그들의 근무 시간 동안 서있는데, 이는 그들을 매우 피곤하게 할 수 있다.　　정답 (D)

**105.** 시장은 시가 심각한 교통 정체 문제를 겪고 있으므로 향후 10년 동안 기차, 버스, 그리고 낙후된 지하철에 집중적으로 투자할 것이라고 말했다.　　정답 (C)

**106.** 시 의회에서는 몇몇 항공 전문가들을 공항 관제 시스템을 감독하게 될 항공 기술 위원회에 임명하였다.　　정답 (B)

**107.** 모든 영업 사원들은 해외 고객들과의 약속을 지키는 데 더욱 주의를 기울여야 한다.　　정답 (B)

**108.** 허가 받지 않은 직원들은 언제나 출입제한 구역에 진입할 수 없음을 유의하십시오.　　정답 (C)

**109.** 비록 지난 3년간 경제가 호황이었지만 소득 성장률은 지속적으로 하락해 왔다.　　정답 (D)

**110.** 모든 의료 기록은 안전하게 보관될 것이며 관련이 있건 없건 제삼자에게는 기록이 제공되지 않을 것이다.　　정답 (B)

**111.** 회사는 새로운 요트에 대한 수요가 저조하여 구조조정의 일환으로 회사 인력의 10%를 감축하기로 결정했다.　　정답 (B)

**112.** 이 도시에는 도심 지역 전역에 걸쳐 10개의 시립 공원이 있으며, 이는 대부분의 주민들이 많은 수목들 근처에서 살면서 깨끗한 공기를 마실 수 있음을 의미한다.　　정답 (C)

**113.** 그녀는 경영학 학위를 취득하자 남아프리카 공화국으로 돌아가 가족 사업인 보석 무역에 합류하였다.　　정답 (C)

**114.** 만약 복사기가 전혀 작동하지 않으면, 복사기의 플러그가 꽂혀 있는지, 그리고 전원 스위치가 'ON' 상태로 켜져 있는지 여부를 확인하세요.　정답 (D)

**115.** 편의점에서 점심 도시락을 구매할 때마다 고객들은 제조일, 제조업체, 그리고 유통기간과 같은 세부사항을 항상 확인하는 것이 권장된다.　정답 (D)

**116.** 개정된 법에 따라 모든 손님은 모든 주류 제품을 구매할 시 특별 주 판매세를 지불해야 한다.　　정답 (A)

**117.** 주문한 제품이 10월까지 배송되지 못한다면 회사는 그 주문을 취소하고 다른 공급업체를 물색해야만 할 것이다.　　정답 (C)

**118.** 설문조사 결과는 New York의 자동차 보험 비용이 미국 내 다른 도시들보다 상당히 비싸다는 점을 보여줬다.　　정답 (D)

**119.** 요청하신 대로 저희 회사는 귀하에게 가격 목록과 함께 최신 제품 안내 책자를 택배로 보내 드립니다.　　정답 (C)

**120.** 많은 회사들과는 달리 저희 회사는 최신 현대 장비를 구비하고 있어서, 저희 귀하의 주문품을 배송할 때마다 제품의 우수한 품질이 보장됩니다.　　정답 (C)

**121.** 동남아 국가들이 경제 성장을 이루기 위해서는 건전한 경제개발 계획을 수립하고 해외 직접 투자와 무역에 우호적인 국내 환경을 조성하는 것이 필요하다. 정답 (A)

**122.** 지난주에 기록적인 홍수로 인해 피해를 입은 북동부 지역 주민들은 비가 잦아들자 피해를 복구하기 위해 박차를 가했다. 정답 (D)

**123.** 고객이 다음달에 우리 회사를 방문하여 이사진과 만날 때쯤이면 수석 건축가는 새로운 사무실 건물의 설계를 다 마무리했을 것이다. 정답 (D)

**124.** 수습 기간이 완료되면 인턴 직원들 중 일부는 정직원으로 채용될 것이고 회사는 그들에게 상당한 급여와 추가 복리후생 혜택을 제공할 것이다. 정답 (B)

**125.** 대형 다국적 기업들 중 한 곳인 BK 전자는 현재 20개국 출신의 15,000명 이상의 직원들을 보유하고 있다. 정답 (B)

**126.** Ryan 영화사는 국내 최고의 영화 제작사의 모든 회계 업무를 담당할 경력 있는 회계사를 구하고 있다. 정답 (A)

**127.** 일부 사람들은 원자력 발전소가 안전하고 지속적이며 저렴한 청정 에너지의 원천을 제공한다고 믿고 있다. 정답 (D)

**128.** 경매는 구매자와 판매자에게 흥미진진하면서도 동시에 효과적인 방법임을 증명하고 있다. 정답 (D)

**129.** 눈을 보호하기 위한 보안경을 착용하지 않은 연구원들은 화학 실험실에 대한 입실이 허용되지 않는다. 정답 (B)

**130.** 예약한 날에 방문하지 못하면 다른 진료 예약일이 논의될 수 있도록 병원 접수 직원에게 알려야 한다. 정답 (B)

## Part 6

문제 131~134번은 다음 회람을 참조하시오.

---

**회 람**

수신: 전 직원
발신: 부사장 Joseph C. Smith

Randy Jones 씨가 다른 기회를 추구하고자 Red Jet 항공사 사장직에서 즉시 사임하겠다는 의사를 제게 밝혔습니다. Randy는 우리나라의 대표적인 지역 항공사의 성장과 앞으로 나아가야 할 방향을 결정하는 데 중요한 역할을 했습니다. 수년간의 특별한 기여와 강력한 지도력에 감사를 드립니다. 그가 나아가는 길이 잘 되기를 바랍니다.

오늘부로 Fred Martin 씨가 Red Jet 항공사의 사장직을 맡게 될 것입니다. Fred는 새로운 사장이 되어 항공사의 기획, 운영, 재정 부분에 관한 폭넓은 경험과 지도력을 보일 것입니다. 그는 과거에 고객 관리 부장, 전략 및 사업 개발 담당 전무, 그리고 경영 기획 담당 이사를 역임했습니다. 그는 우리 항공사가 열정과 전문성을 겸비할 수 있게 할 것이며, 저는 그가 여러분의 성원에 힘입어 우리 회사를 새로운 차원의 우수한 항공사로 이끌어줄 것이라고 믿습니다. 우리 항공사가 계속 힘차게 날개짓을 할 수 있도록 노력해주신 여러분께 감사드립니다.

---

**131.** 정답 (B)

**132.** 정답 (C)

**133.** (A) 그 다음에 그는 38세의 나이에 최연소 최고경영자가 되었습니다.
(B) 새로운 최고경영자가 어떻게 우리 회사를 이끌어 나갈지 기다려 봅시다.
(C) 전 최고경영자는 뛰어난 항공기를 만드는 데 혁신적인 아이디어를 사용했습니다.
(D) 수년간의 특별한 기여와 강력한 지도력에 감사를 드립니다. 정답 (D)

**134.** 정답 (B)

문제 135~138번은 다음 이메일을 참조하시오.

---

수신: Sheldon King 〈kingsh@hoi.com〉
발신: Linda Hamilton 〈lh@cosmopolitangazette.com〉
날짜: 8월 1일
제목: 새로운 홈페이지에 관해

King 씨께,

귀하는 Cosmopolitan Gazette의 소중한 구독자이시므로 곧 출시되는 저희의 흥미진진한 새로운 홈페이지 cosmopolitangazette.com에 대해 직접 알려드리고 싶습니다.

8월 12일 월요일부터 최신 뉴스를 이 홈페이지에서 누리실 수 있을 것입니다. 인쇄판 신문은 인쇄 매체 전용 콘텐츠를 계속 제공할 것이지만, 또한 홈페이지도 대화형 십자말풀이와 포럼과 같은 인터넷의 힘을 활용하는 고유한 콘텐츠를 보유하게 됩니다. 이것은 독자들이 신문과 홈페이지를 모두 동일한 수준으로 즐기시는 것이 가능하다는 것을 의미한다고 확신합니다.

홈페이지의 주요 부분은 일반 대중에게 공개될 것이지만, 귀하와 독자분들은 구독자 전용의 고급 콘텐츠를 찾아보실 수 있는 특별 구독자 공간에 접근하실 수 있을 것입니다. Cosmopolitan Gazette를 지속적으로 애용해주신 점에 감사드립니다.

Linda Hamilton

---

**135.** 정답 (D)

**136.** 정답 (A)

**137.** 정답 (B)

**138.** (A) 주의해야 할 10가지의 가장 일반적인 홈페이지 오류와 문제점들이 있습니다.
(B) Cosmopolitan Gazette를 지속적으로 애용해주신 점에 감사드립니다.
(C) 갑작스러운 변화로 인해 초래될지도 모를 모든 문제점들에 대해 미리 사과를 드립니다.
(D) 구독자들에게 여러분이 그들의 성원에 얼마나 감사하는지 깊이 있고 시의적절한 감사 이메일을 통해 말씀해 주십시오. 정답 (B)

문제 139~142번은 다음 편지를 참조하시오.

---

Kane 씨께,

열정, 헌신, 업계의 전문적 지식.

이들이 바로 제 원동력의 원천이며, 이들은 또한 제가 업무에 반영하는 특징이기도 합니다. 저는 제가 하는 일에 열정적입니다. 새로운 시장을 개척할 때 저는 항상 밑바닥에서부터 시작합니다. 그 누구도 제게 3천만 달러 가치의 브랜드를 가져다가 4천만 달러 가치의 브랜드로 성장시키라고 한 적은 없었습니다. 대신에 그들은 새로운 브랜드와 새로운 시장을 주고 제가 성공시키는 것을 지켜볼 뿐이었습니다.

---

저는 최선을 다하고자 헌신합니다. 저는 업무를 우선시하고 고객 서비스에 담긴 진심을 믿는 소위 "소매를 걷어 올리고" 일하는 부류의 사람입니다. 저는 업계와 관련해 깊은 전문 지식을 갖고 있습니다. 이 분야에서 15년이 넘게 일했기 때문에, 저는 제조업체, 소매업체, 그리고 대형 할인점에서 소규모 자영업체에 이르기까지 크고 작은 모든 매장들의 대표들과 잘 알고 있으며 존중 받고 있습니다.

제 열정, 헌신 그리고 업계의 전문 지식의 더 많은 부분을 공유할 수 있는 기회를 갖고 싶습니다. 답장 기대하고 있겠습니다.

Mina Weston

**139.**                                            정답 (C)

**140.**                                            정답 (B)

**141.** (A) 저는 어려운 상황에 대처하는 법을 알고 있습니다.
        (B) 저는 업계와 관련해 깊이 있는 전문 지식을 갖고 있습니다.
        (C) 저는 이 회사에 오래 근무해왔습니다.
        (D) 제 경험을 기반으로 귀하에게 좋은 조언을 드릴 수 있습니다.  정답 (B)

**142.**                                            정답 (C)

---

문제 143-146번은 다음 편지를 참조하시오.

Murphy 씨께:

Manchester 대기 질 워크숍에 참석해 주셔서 감사합니다. 워크숍이 유익하고 가치가 있다고 생각하셨기를 바랍니다. 저희의 주된 목표는 대기 질과 기타 환경 문제에 대한 이해를 높이고 교실 수업을 지원할 수 있는 자료를 소개하고 제공하는 것이었습니다.

워크숍에서 많은 주제들이 다루어졌으며 발표자들은 여러분과 자신의 전문 지식을 공유하는 역할을 훌륭하게 해냈습니다. 발표자에게 문의사항이 있는 경우 첨부한 발표자 연락처 정보를 참조하시기 바랍니다.

귀하의 열정은 우리의 시간을 생산적이고 재미있게 만드는 데 도움을 주었습니다. 평가에 대한 귀하의 의견과 제안에 감사드리며, 향후 워크숍이 더욱 성공적이 될 수 있도록 각 의견에 대한 검토가 이루어질 것을 약속드립니다.

다시 한번 대기 질 워크숍에 참여해 주셔서 감사합니다. 향후에 이 교육을 다른 사람들에게 추천해 주시기 바랍니다. 행운이 가득하시길 바랍니다.

Isabella Choi
회장
Manchester 대기 질 협회

**143.**                                            정답 (B)

**144.**                                            정답 (D)

**145.** (A) 우리는 또한 환경오염으로부터 초래되는 문제점들을 겪어왔습니다.
        (B) 환경에 관한 새로운 워크숍은 11월 11-13일에 개최될 예정입니다.
        (C) 귀하의 열정은 우리의 시간을 생산적이고 재미있게 만드는 데 도움을 주었습니다.
        (D) 연구 결과 자동차 배기가스가 대기의 질을 악화시키는 주된 요소임이 밝혀졌습니다.  정답 (C)

**146.**                                            정답 (A)

---

## Part 7

문제 147-148번은 다음 다음 편지를 참조하시오.

Fairway Car Insurance
899 Potomac Avenue
Nelsonville, MD 77181

**(148) 2월 28일**

Theodore Houston
Re: 고객 계정 #091182

Houston 씨께,

**(147) 고객님의 새 주소로 계정 정보를 업데이트해 주셔서 감사합니다. 또한 모든 서신을 종이 문서 형태로 새 우편주소 899 Filmore Street, Milton, MD 77172로 배송 받을 것을 선택하셨습니다.**

이달 마지막 날짜에 계정 변경을 하셔서, 월 청구서가 이미 기존 주소로 발송되었음에 유의해 주십시오. **(148) 청구서 발송팀에 이번 달 내역서를 다시 요청했으며, 앞으로 이틀 안에 새 주소에서 내역서를 받아보실 수 있을 것입니다.** 그 사이에 이번 달 청구서를 조회하고 싶으시면, fairway.com의 온라인 고객 계정에서 조회하실 수 있습니다. 고객님 보험증권의 이 기능에 접근하고 싶으시면 고객 계정 번호와 비밀번호만 입력하시면 됩니다.

감사합니다, Houston 씨.

Amy Raymond
고객서비스 상담원

**147.** 이 편지는 무엇에 관한 것인가?
        (A) 보험에 대한 질문
        (B) 새로운 보험증권의 가입
        (C) 우편주소의 변경
        (D) 모든 보험증권에 추가된 새로운 특징  정답 (C)

**148.** Raymond 씨는 Houston 씨에게 무엇이라고 말하는가?
        (A) 그의 2월 청구서가 곧 도착할 것이다.
        (B) 모든 보험증권 정보를 온라인에서 받아야 한다.
        (C) 청구서를 잘못된 부서로 보냈다.
        (D) 새로운 내역서를 받기 위해 서식을 작성해야 할 것이다.  정답 (A)

---

문제 149-150번은 다음 공지를 참조하시오.

ASIAN AIRWAYS
Hungda 가 250번지 Wai Kee 산업빌딩 1F - 7F
Kwun Tong 구, Hong Kong

항공 노선 예약이 초과 됐을 때에는 드문 경우로 승객이 예약 확인을 했더라도 비행기에 좌석이 없을 수 있습니다. 비행기 예약이 초과되면, 항공사 직원이 먼저 항공사가 선택한 보상을 받는 대신에 예약을 기꺼이 포기할 지원자가 있는지 알아볼 때까지는 누구도 좌석이 취소되지 않을 것입니다. **(149) 만약 지원자가 충분하지 않다면 항공사는 자사의 특별 탑승 우선순위에 따라 다른 사람들의 탑승을 취소하게 됩니다.**

보상 체계에서, **(150) 초과예약 때문에 탑승이 취소된 승객은 이뤄지지 않은 비행에 대한 탑승권 비용을 수수료 없이 변제 받고 가급적 빠른 시기에 최종 목적지를 변경하거나, 승객 편의에 따라 훗날 일정을 재조정하는 것 가운데에서 하나를 선택할 수 있는 권리가 주어집니다.** 승객은 또한 항공사의 최저 금전 보상에 따라 즉시 금전적인 보상을 받을 권리가 주어집니다. 어떤 경우든지 이 보상은 최종 목적지까지 가는 항공료를 초과할 수 없습니다.

**149.** 중복 예약의 경우, 탑승이 취소될 것 같은 사람은 누구인가?
(A) 항공권을 늦게 예약한 사람
(B) 수하물 수속을 하지 않은 사람
(C) 예약을 확인하지 않은 사람
(D) 낮은 우선 탑승 순위를 지닌 사람  　　　　　정답 (D)

**150.** 미 탑승객을 위한 보상이 아닌 것은 무엇인가?
(A) 추가 항공 마일리지 제공
(B) 향후 일정 조정
(C) 수수료 없이 항공료 환불
(D) 지연에 대한 추가 보상  　　　　　　　　　정답 (A)

### 문제 151-152번은 다음 문자 메시지를 참조하시오.

DAVID JOHNSON 　　　　　　　　　　　[오전 7:17]
주간 일정을 제 이메일로 보내줄 수 있어요? 제가 찾지 못하겠네요.

DAVID JOHNSON 　　　　　　　　　　　[오전 7:19]
그리고, 전기 기술자가 오늘 언제 오는지 확인해줄 수 있어요? 저는 오후 2시인 줄 알았는데 Richard는 오후 3시라고 하네요.

SARAH MOORE 　　　　　　　　　　　　[오전 7:21]
물론이죠. 확실하게 하려고 해서 묻는 건데요, 이번 주 일정을 원하시는 건가요, 아니면 다음 주 일정을 원하시는 건가요?

DAVID JOHNSON 　　　　　　　　　　　[오전 7:25]
다음 주 일정표를 주세요. (151) **이번 주 일정표는 한 부 가지고 있어요.**

SARAH MOORE 　　　　　　　　　　　　[오전 7:27]
네. 바로 보내드릴게요.

DAVID JOHNSON 　　　　　　　　　　　[오전 7:57]
빠른 처리 고마워요. 당신이 보낸 이메일을 받았어요. (152) **전기 기술자와 연락은 되었나요?**

SARAH MOORE 　　　　　　　　　　　　[오전 7:58]
(152) **지금 막 통화를 했어요. 오후 3시쯤 방문할 거라고 하네요.**

DAVID JOHNSON 　　　　　　　　　　　[오전 8:00]
(152) **알았어요. 분명히 오후 2시라고 생각했었는데요. 명확하게 해줘서 고마워요.**

**151.** Johnson 씨에 관해 언급된 것은 무엇인가?
(A) 그는 오늘 고객과 만날 것이다.
(B) 그는 숙련된 전기 기술자이다.
(C) 그는 현재 근무 일정표를 보유하고 있다.
(D) 그는 오후 3시에 Moore 씨의 사무실을 방문할 것이다  　정답 (C)

**152.** 오전 8:00에 Johnson 씨가 "Thanks for clarifying."이라고 말한 의미는 무엇인가?
(A) Moore 씨가 Johnson 씨에게 정확한 파일들을 보냈다.
(B) Moore 씨는 전기 기술자에게 변경된 예약에 관해 설명했다.
(C) Moore 씨가 Johnson 씨의 질문에 대해 명확하게 답변을 해줬다.
(D) Moore 씨는 Johnson 씨가 서류 작업을 좀 더 정확하게 할 수 있도록 도와줬다.  　　　　　　　　　　　　　　　정답 (C)

### 문제 153-155번은 다음 정보를 참조하시오.

Speedo
배송과 반품

(153) **저희는 해외 모든 주소로 유명 브랜드 화장품을 배송해 드립니다.**

(154) **무료 배송, 익일 배송, 2일 배송은 미국 본토 목적지에만 적용됩니다.** 해외 고객님들은 특급 배송(5일~7일)을 이용하실 수 있습니다. 더 상세한 정보는 고객 서비스 부서로 연락 주십시오. 해외 주문 시에는 관세가 부과될 수 있으며, 이는 고객님의 책임임을 유의해 주십시오.

(155) **물품이 사용되지 않았고 원래의 포장으로 반송된다면, 구매 후 30일 내에 반품하실 수 있습니다. 건강과 안전 및 화장품의 특성으로 인해, 결함이 있는 경우가 아니라면 개봉한 제품은 반품하실 수 없습니다.** 전화나 온라인으로 주문하신 제품도 저희 매장 어디서든 반품하실 수 있으며, 제공된 반송주소로 우편으로 보내주셔도 됩니다. 반품 시 배송비는 고객님 부담이며, 제품에 결함이 있는 경우 배송비를 환불해 드립니다.

**153.** Speedo 사는 무엇을 하는가?
(A) 모든 물품을 무료로 배송한다.
(B) 포장재를 생산한다.
(C) 건강관리 제품을 제공한다.
(D) 화장품을 판매한다.  　　　　　　　　　　정답 (D)

**154.** 어떠한 배송 방식이 언급되지 않았는가?
(A) 무료 배송
(B) 당일 배송
(C) 익일 배송
(D) 2일 배송  　　　　　　　　　　　　　　　정답 (B)

**155.** Speedo 사의 반품 정책에 대해 언급된 것은 무엇인가?
(A) 반품은 우편을 통해 무료로 배송이 가능하다.
(B) 고객들이 반품하고자 하는 제품은 매장으로 가져와야만 한다.
(C) 훼손되지 않은 제품은 개봉되지 않았을 경우에만 반품될 수 있다.
(D) 화장품은 건강 및 안전 상의 이유로 반품할 수 없다.  　정답 (C)

### 문제 156-157번은 다음 메시지를 참조하시오.

메시지 대상자: Gilbert Porter 씨
메시지 수신일 및 시간: 11월 23일 화요일 오후 3시 30분
연락자: Jane Keller 씨
회사: Anderson 회계법인
연락처: (510) 882-3845

수신 메시지 내용:

(156) **Keller 씨가 내일 있을 당신과의 회의를 다음 주 수요일 오전 11시로 연기하고자 전화했습니다.** 그녀는 회의를 연기하는 것이 당신을 곤란하게 하는지 알고 싶어 합니다. 그녀가 퇴근하기 전에 연락을 하여 회의를 연기해도 되는지 여부를 알려주셨으면 합니다. (157) **그리고 그녀는 당신이 사무실을 방문하기 전에 지난 5년간의 재무제표를 팩스로 발송해 줄 것을 상기시켜 달라고 제게 부탁했습니다.**

메시지 수신자: Lee Thompson

**156.** Keller 씨가 Porter 씨에게 연락한 이유는 무엇인가?
(A) 내일 회의를 취소하기 위해서
(B) 최근에 한 주문을 확인하기 위해서
(C) 새로운 회의 일자를 정하기 위해서
(D) 서류작업을 요청하기 위해서  　　　　　　　정답 (C)

**157.** Porter 씨가 요청 받은 것은 무엇인가?
(A) 시간을 엄수한다.
(B) 회사 행사를 준비한다.
(C) 몇몇 서류들을 확인한다.
(D) 재무 자료를 발송한다. .  　　　　　　　　　정답 (D)

> ### Franconia Daily News
>
> (161) 5월 16일 토요일－(159) Franconia의 Cynthia Barber 시장은 어제 시가 8번가부터 Garner 가에 이르는 구역의 Main 가를 확장하는 공사의 자금을 제공할 것이라고 발표했다. (158) 확장된 Main 가는 지난 10년 간 이 지역에 존재한 교통 문제를 개선할 뿐만 아니라 Main 가에 위치한 사업체들이 더 많은 고객들을 유치할 수 있도록 할 것이다.
>
> (160) 이 공사는 몇 년간 반대에 부딪혔다. 그러나 점차 증가하는 문제들은 주민들에게 변화를 불러 왔으며 결국 시 의회는 주민 대다수가 이 공사를 지지한다는 결론에 도달하게 되었다.
>
> Barber 시장은 이 공사가 다음달 초 이전에 시작될 것이라고 말했다. 프로젝트의 잠정 완료 시기는 내년 12월이다. (159) 이 공사로 인해 Main 가를 비롯해 8번가, 9번가, Garner 가, Brown 대로의 일부가 오랜 기간 동안 폐쇄될 것으로 예상된다.

**158.** 도로공사가 필요한 이유는 무엇인가?
(A) Franconia 시에 교통 문제가 있다.
(B) Main 가 주변 사업들이 손해를 보고 있다.
(C) 도로가 여름에 비로 인해 자주 침수된다.
(D) 위험한 도로 상태로 인해 자주 사고가 난다.  정답 (A)

**159.** 내년의 대부분의 시간 동안 어떠한 도로가 공사 중일 것 같은가?
(A) Main 가
(B) 8번 가
(C) Garner 가
(D) Brown 대로  정답 (A)

**160.** 두 번째 단락 세 번째 줄의 "warranted"와 의미상 가장 유사한 단어는 무엇인가?
(A) 반대했다
(B) 명확하게 했다
(C) 정당화했다
(D) 과장했다  정답 (C)

**161.** [1], [2], [3] 그리고 [4]로 표기된 위치 중에서 아래 문장이 가장 적합한 곳은 어디인가?
"프로젝트의 잠정 완료 시기는 내년 12월이다."
(A) [1]
(B) [2]
(C) [3]
(D) [4]  정답 (C)

> (162) Securecar.com은 여러분의 차량을 위한 새로운 Safe2U 실시간 보안 경보 시스템을 안내하고자 합니다. Safe2U가 있으면 하루 24시간, 주 7일, 1년 365일 차량의 보안상태를 아실 수 있습니다.
>
> Safe2U는 모든 자동차에 사용 가능합니다. 이동식 데이터통신 시스템을 보유한 신형 차량 소유주들에게 Safe2U 가입은 인터넷에 접속하여 등록을 하는 것이 전부일 정도로 쉽습니다. (163) 구형 모델 소유주 분들은 전국 곳곳에 위치한 저희 서비스 센터 중 한 곳으로 차량을 갖고 와서 Safe2U 하드웨어 모듈을 설치하셔야 합니다.
>
> Safe2U 시스템은 차량에 어떠한 일이 발생할 때 알려드리는 프로그램을 사용합니다. 누군가 차 문을 열려고 하고 있나요? 누가 창문을 깨뜨렸나요? 누군가 운전대 잠금 장치를 풀려고 하고 있나요? 그렇다면 이런 일이 발생하는 순간 Safe2U 시스템이 알려드릴 것입니다.
>
> 또한 Safe2U 시스템은 차량이 도난 당한 경우 차량 추적에도 사용할 수 있음을 알게 되어 기쁘실 것입니다. 그리고 자동차에 열쇠를 놓고 내리신 경우 차 문을 열어드릴 수도 있습니다!
>
> 비쌀 것 같다고요? 그렇지 않습니다! (164) 서비스 이용료는 한 달에 9달러입니다.

**162.** 이 정보는 누구를 위한 것인가?
(A) 주택 구매자
(B) 자동차 판매업자
(C) 보안 전문가
(D) 자동차 소유주  정답 (D)

**163.** securecar.com에 대해 언급된 것은 무엇인가?
(A) 전국에 지점이 있다.
(B) 차량 안전 장비를 생산한다.
(C) 최근에 경쟁사 중 한 곳과 합병이 되었다.
(D) 새로운 서비스는 기존 고객들에게만 제공한다.  정답 (A)

**164.** [1], [2], [3] 그리고 [4]로 표기된 위치 중에서 아래 문장이 가장 적합한 곳은 어디인가?
"서비스 이용료는 한 달에 9달러입니다."
(A) [1]
(B) [2]
(C) [3]
(D) [4]  정답 (D)

> ### Merrifield Professional Center의
> ### 모든 입주자 분들께 알립니다
>
> 6월 21일
>
> (165) 다음 달 초부터 Merrifield Professional Center는 재활용 프로그램을 시작할 것입니다. 종이, 캔, 플라스틱 용기의 재활용을 수반하는 이 프로그램은 환경을 보존하고 입주자들의 비용을 줄이는 것이 목표입니다. 이 계획은 건물의 각 사무실에 재활용 쓰레기통을 설치하는 것입니다. 입주자 분들께서 물품을 분리하여 적절한 쓰레기통에 넣으실 것을 권장합니다. 매주 A1 Recycling Company가 재활용품을 수거하러 올 것입니다. (166) 그 이후 A1 사는 재활용품을 재활용센터에 판매하고 우리에게 그 수익의 일부를 지불할 것입니다. 우리 건물에게 발생하는 수익금은 월 관리비 인하의 형태로 입주자 분들께 제공될 것입니다.
>
> 재활용 쓰레기통은 그 안에 어떠한 종류의 물품들을 두어야 하는지 표시가 될 것입니다. (167) 그러나 어떠한 물품이 재활용이 가능한지 여부에 확신이 서지 않는다면 A1 직원 Alfred Morris 씨에게 555-1212, 내선번호 728로 연락 주십시오.
>
> 만약 이 프로그램에 관한 질문이 있으시면 Cynthia Moore 씨에게 555-1000, 내선번호 378로 연락 주십시오.
>
> 건물 관리팀
> Merrifield Professional Center

**165.** 이 공지의 목적은 무엇인가?
(A) 제품을 홍보한다.
(B) 새 프로그램을 발표한다.
(C) 회의 일자를 알린다.
(D) 통조림 제품의 기부를 요청한다.  정답 (B)

**166.** 건물 관리팀은 월 관리비를 어떻게 줄일 계획인가?

(A) 인건비를 삭감한다.

(B) 주차비를 인상하여 청구한다.

(C) 재활용품을 판매한다.

(D) 에너지 효율성이 좋은 새로운 전구를 사용한다.　　　정답 (C)

**167.** 공지에서 Morris 씨에게 연락해야 할 이유로 언급된 것은 무엇인가?

(A) 어떠한 물품들을 새로운 쓰레기통에 버릴 수 있는지 알아보기 위해

(B) 인상된 임대료에 대한 세부사항을 요청하기 위해

(C) 새로운 프로젝트를 위한 자료를 요청하기 위해

(D) 보안에 대한 우려를 알리기 위해　　　정답 (A)

**문제 168-171번은 다음 이메일을 참조하시오.**

수신: 〈carlj@nmail.com〉

발신: 〈jcook@asaelectronics.com〉

날짜: 8월 3일

제목: 공장 품질보증서

Jahini 씨께,

최근 고객님의 ASA 전자 제품 구매 건으로 저희에게 연락 주셔서 감사합니다. (168/170) 저희가 판매하는 모든 제품은 공장 품질보증서로 보장됩니다. 여기 품질보증서의 세부사항이 있습니다:

· (169) 기본 공장 품질보증서는 24개월간 제품을 보장합니다.

· 품질보증 기간 중 제품에 문제가 생기면, 기계를 교환 또는 무상수리해 드릴 것입니다.

· (170) 공장 품질보증 기간 만료 후 6개월간 월 25달러로 품질보증을 연장하실 수 있습니다.

· (170) 품질보증 기간의 수리는 ASA 전자에서 처리되어야 합니다. ASA 전자를 통하지 않은 수리는 제품의 품질보증서를 자동으로 무효화할 것입니다.

· (171) 모든 제품은 ASA 전자로 반송되기 전에 품질보증에 대해 사전에 승인을 받아야 합니다. 저희 고객 서비스 부서에 품질보증 문제에 대한 간략한 설명을 보내 주십시오. 해당 영업일 안에 연락을 받으실 것입니다.

품질보증서에 관해 더 많은 정보가 필요하시거나 제가 도와드릴 다른 일이 있다면, 저에게 연락 주십시오.

John Cook 배상

제품 지원팀

ASA 전자

전화: 800-555-6817

팩스: 800-555-6889

**168.** 이 이메일의 목적은 무엇인가?

(A) 수리된 품목의 요금을 상세히 제시한다.

(B) 고객에게 품질보증 정보를 제공한다.

(C) 고객에게 품질 보증된 물품을 반품하는 방법에 관해 알려준다.

(D) 최근 제품 구매에 대한 청구서 발부 세부사항을 전달한다.　　　정답 (B)

**169.** ASA 전자에서 제공받는 제품에 대해 언급한 것은 무엇인가?

(A) 2년 품질보증서와 함께 판매된다.

(B) 연간 50달러로 품질보증을 받을 수 있다.

(C) 고객이 만족하지 않을 경우 반품할 수 있다.

(D) 제품의 수명이 다할 때까지 무료 수리를 받을 수 있다.　　　정답 (A)

**170.** 이메일에서 언급되지 않은 것은 무엇인가?

(A) ASA 전자가 제공하는 모든 제품들은 품질보증서가 있다.

(B) ASA 전자는 자사에서 판매하는 모든 제품을 생산한다.

(C) 품질 보증서는 추가 비용을 지불하여 연장될 수 있다.

(D) 품질 보증된 제품은 ASA 전자에서 수리되어야 한다.　　　정답 (B)

**171.** 제품에 수리가 필요할 경우 고객은 무엇을 해야 하는가?

(A) 지역 전자제품 수리점으로 가져간다.

(B) 고객 서비스 부서에 연락한다.

(C) 제품을 원래 포장에 넣어 반품한다.

(D) 영수증 사본과 함께 품질 보증을 청구한다.　　　정답 (B)

**문제 172-175번은 다음 온라인 채팅 토론을 참조하시오.**

David Faraday　　　　　　　　　　[오후 2:10]

Charlotte, 새 카메라 디자인 작업은 어떻게 되어가요? 당신의 팀이 이 작업에 몇 달간 긴 시간을 투입한 것으로 알고 있어요.

Charlotte McGowan　　　　　　　　[오후 2:13]

분명히 그랬죠. 우리는 자전거 손잡이에 안전하게 고정시킬 수 있는 카메라 디자인을 만들어냈어요.

Rita Hamilton　　　　　　　　　　[오후 2:14]

멋지네요! 저도 자전거를 타는데, 저도 그런 것을 분명히 좋아해요.

Charlotte McGowan　　　　　　　　[오후 2:15]

고객들이 심지어 빠른 속도로 자전거를 타는 동안에도 사진을 찍을 수 있게 해 주지요. 이 혁신적인 제품을 통해 우리가 다른 경쟁사들을 능가할 것이라고 생각해요.

David Faraday　　　　　　　　　　[오후 2:17]

이 제품은 수천만 미국인들의 인기를 얻으며 시장을 휩쓸 거예요.

Charlotte McGowan　　　　　　　　[오후 2:18]

그러길 바래요. (172) 알다시피, 이런 부류의 제품을 디자인하는 것은 일반적으로 무척 힘이 들거든요. 이런 제품은 두 가지 기능을 합쳐야 한다는 점이 한 가지 이유이기도 하고요.

David Faraday　　　　　　　　　　[오후 2:21]

(175) 마침내 해냈잖아요. 언제 출시 준비가 될 것으로 예상하나요?

Charlotte McGowan　　　　　　　　[오후 2:25]

첫 번째 단계는 시제품 사용 집단들을 운영하는 것이지요. (174) 다음 주에 시제품을 사용해 보도록 몇몇 소비자들을 초청했어요. 그들의 의견을 바탕으로 디자인에 필요한 수정을 할 거예요. 그리고 나서 4/4분기에 본격적인 생산에 들어갈 수 있기를 바래요.

David Faraday　　　　　　　　　　[오후 2:27]

우리는 시장의 주요 업체들 중에서 제일 큰 수익을 얻게 될 것이라 생각해요. (173) 저와 우리 영업사원들이 꼭 그렇게 되도록 할 거예요.

Charlotte McGowan　　　　　　　　[오후 2:31]

듣던 중 반가운 소리네요. 저는 올해 말에 우리가 훌륭한 실적으로 인해 특별 상여금을 분명히 받게 될 것이라고 믿어요.

**172.** McGowan 씨의 디자인 프로젝트에 관해 유추할 수 있는 것은 무엇인가?

(A) 몇몇 멋진 디자인들이 창작되었다.

(B) 자금부족으로 지연되고 있다.

(C) 일정보다 앞서서 완료되었다.

(D) 고된 작업이었다.　　　정답 (D)

**173.** Faraday 씨는 어떠한 종류의 일을 하는가?

(A) 그는 제품 디자인 서비스를 제공한다.

(B) 그는 고객을 위한 광고 영상을 제작한다.

(C) 그는 다양한 종류의 자전거를 개발한다.

(D) 그는 영업망을 통해 제품을 판매한다.　　　정답 (D)

**174.** 다음 주에는 어떠한 일이 발생할 것인가?

    (A) 몇몇 디자이너들이 채용될 것이다.

    (B) 신제품이 시험될 것이다.

    (C) 회사에서 시즌 할인 판매를 실시할 것이다.

    (D) 광고가 시행될 것이다.             정답 (B)

**175.** 오후 2시 21분에 Faraday 씨가 "You finally made it."이라고 쓴 것이 의미하는 바는 무엇인가?

    (A) McGowan 씨가 유명한 디자인 전시회를 준비했다.

    (B) McGowan 씨는 새롭고 혁신적인 카메라를 제작했다.

    (C) McGowan 씨는 중요한 계약을 마무리했다.

    (D) McGowan 씨는 그녀의 프로젝트를 성공적으로 끝냈다.    정답 (D)

**문제 176-180번은 다음 이메일들을 참조하시오.**

---

수신: Natalia Dormer 〈nd@ghj.com〉

발신: Elly Spears 〈spears@ca.com〉

날짜: 11월 11일 목요일 오후 5시 15분

제목: Cosmopolitan Style

Dormer 씨께,

저희를 만나기 위해 저희 사무실에 와 주셔서 감사합니다. 저희는 귀하의 아이디어에 깊은 감명을 받았으며, 귀하를 채용하는 데 관심이 있습니다. 아시다시피 이 직책은 아주 경쟁이 심합니다. (176) **자격이 있는 여러 지원자들이 저희와 면접을 보았으나, 채용 마지막 절차에 귀하를 포함한 몇 분만을 선정했습니다.**

(177/178) **이미 언급했듯이 새로운 컴퓨터 그래픽 디자이너는 화장품을 생산하는 몇몇 회사들을 위한 광고 제작팀의 일원이 될 것입니다. 이 팀은 John Williams 씨가 이끌고 있으며, 그는 매출 향상을 위한 귀하의 아이디어를 듣고 싶어합니다.**

(176/179) **11월 18일 목요일 오후 1시에 다시 와 주셨으면 하며, 이 날짜가 어려우면 11월 23일 같은 시간에 오셨으면 합니다.** 이 날짜들 중 시간이 되시는 때가 있으면 제 비서 Simpson 씨에게 연락하여 오실 수 있음을 확인해 주십시오. 다시 만나기를 고대합니다.

Elly Spears 드림

인사 담당 이사

---

수신: Elly Spears 〈spears@ca.com〉

(180) **발신: Natalia Dormer 〈nd@ghj.com〉**

날짜: 11월 11일 목요일 오후 9시 12분

제목: 답장: Cosmopolitan Style

Spears 씨께,

(180) **컴퓨터 그래픽 디자이너 직책에 관해 저에게 연락 주셔서 감사합니다.** 저는 여전히 이 직책에 관심이 있으며, 저의 광고 경력 및 귀사의 광고 방향에 대한 제 아이디어를 말씀드릴 수 있는 기회를 주시면 감사하겠습니다. (179) **유감스럽게도 저는 11월 18일에 Seattle 광고 회의에서 발표를 하기로 이미 약속이 되어 있으나, 23일에는 분명 시간이 됩니다.**

뿐만 아니라, 요구하신 추천서 관련하여 제 상사인 Brian Stone 씨에게 저를 위한 추천서를 발급해주도록 요청하였습니다. 그가 곧 연락을 드릴 것입니다. 저는 다음 면접에 제 작업 샘플을 가지고 가겠습니다.

감사합니다.

Natalia Dormer

---

**176.** 첫 번째 이메일의 목적은 무엇인가?

    (A) 서류를 요청하는 것

    (B) 입사 면접 일정을 잡는 것

    (C) 광고 아이디어를 요청하는 것

    (D) 작업 프로젝트를 배정하는 것         정답 (B)

**177.** Spears 씨는 어떠한 업체에서 근무할 것 같은가?

    (A) 잡지사

    (B) 컴퓨터 그래픽 소프트웨어 개발업체

    (C) 인력회사

    (D) 광고대행사            정답 (D)

**178.** 첫 번째 이메일에 의하면, Williams 씨는 무슨 업무를 하는가?

    (A) 소매업체들과의 계약을 처리한다.

    (B) 회사 대변인으로 일한다.

    (C) 화장품을 광고하는 팀을 관리한다.

    (D) 소프트웨어 프로그램을 개발하는 엔지니어 그룹을 총괄한다.  정답 (C)

**179.** Dormer 씨는 언제 Spears 씨와 만날 것인가?

    (A) 11월 11일

    (B) 11월 18일

    (C) 11월 23일

    (D) 11월 25일            정답 (C)

**180.** Cosmopolitan Style 사의 직원이 아닌 사람은 누구인가?

    (A) Spears 씨

    (B) Williams 씨

    (C) Simpson 씨

    (D) Dormer 씨            정답 (D)

**문제 181-185번은 다음 광고와 이메일을 참조하시오.**

---

**Island Creek Books**

160 Elm Drive, (181) **Sacramento**, CA

**(181) 6월 4일 일요일 책 사인회!**

Jerry Miller, Sharon Woodman, Maria Jimenez, Cindy Sanders 작가를 만나세요.

(181) **6월 4일 일요일 Island Creek Books는 베스트셀러 작가 네 분을 초청할 것입니다.** 이 작가분들의 최신작을 구입하실 수 있으며, 저자들의 친필사인을 받으실 수 있습니다. 책 사인뿐만 아니라, 각 작가들이 공개 토론회를 열고 대중과 질의응답 시간을 가질 것입니다. (182) **Island Creek Café는 커피, 페이스트리, 샌드위치 등 다과를 제공할 것입니다.**

(182) **이 행사는 저희 서점에서 개최하는 네 번째 동종의 행사가 될 것이며, 언제나와 마찬가지로 무료로 대중에게 개방됩니다.** 오셔서 작가분들과 함께 즐거운 하루 보내시기 바랍니다.

| 초청 작가 | |
|---|---|
| (183) **Miller 씨** | 오전 11시 |
| (183) **Woodman 씨** | 오후 12시 30분 |
| Jimenez 씨 | 오후 2시 |
| Sanders 씨 | 오후 3시 30분 |

---

수신: 〈woodman@1writer.net〉

발신: 〈bjackson@islandcreekbooks.com〉

날짜: 6월 1일
제목: 일요일 일정

Woodman 씨께,

(184) 메시지 보내 주셔서 감사합니다. (183) 메시지를 받은 뒤 저는 시간대 변경과 관련하여 Miller 씨에게 연락했습니다. 그는 기꺼이 작가님과 시간대를 바꿔주겠다고 했습니다.

(185) 작가님이 National Writer's Guild Novel of the Year Award 수상을 위해 Los Angeles로 이동해야 해서 시간대를 앞당기셔야 하는 점을 이해합니다. 저희 행사에 참여하고 시상식을 위해 Los Angeles로 이동하느라 작가님이 시간에 쫓기실 것을 알고 있으며, 저희 책 사인회 참석 약속을 지켜 주셔서 진심으로 감사 드립니다.

Brenda Jackson

**181.** 광고에 의하면, 6월 4일 Sacramento에서 무슨 일이 있을 것인가?
(A) 상점이 재고정리 행사를 열 것이다.
(B) 서점이 개점 행사를 할 것이다.
(C) 몇몇 작가들이 대중을 위해 책에 사인해 줄 것이다.
(D) 작가들이 새 책을 출시할 것이다.                    정답 (C)

**182.** 이 행사에 대해 암시되지 않은 것은 무엇인가?
(A) 참석자들을 위해 다과를 제공할 것이다.
(B) 무료로 참석할 수 있을 것이다.
(C) 작가들에게 상을 줄 것이다.
(D) 전에도 열린 적이 있다.                          정답 (C)

**183.** Miller 씨는 언제 발표할 가능성이 가장 높은가?
(A) 오전 11시
(B) 오후 12시 30분
(C) 오후 2시
(D) 오후 3시 30분                                  정답 (B)

**184.** Jackson 씨가 이메일을 발송한 이유는 무엇인가?
(A) 지불 세부사항을 논의한다.
(B) 작가에게 상에 대해 알린다.
(C) 요청에 답변을 한다.
(D) 회의를 계획한다.                                정답 (C)

**185.** Los Angeles에서 어떠한 일이 발생할 것 같은가?
(A) 작가가 작품에 대한 인정을 받을 것이다.
(B) 작가가 발표를 할 것이다.
(C) 작가가 자신의 집을 지을 것이다.
(D) 작가가 은퇴할 것이다.                           정답 (A)

**문제 186-190번은 다음 이메일들과 영수증을 참조하시오.**

수신: ⟨bwilson@csu.edu⟩
발신: ⟨pturner6@csu.edu⟩
날짜: 4월 7일
제목: 최근 구매

Wilson 박사님께,

최근 야전 연구 장비 구매에 대해 알려드리기 위해 메일을 보냅니다. 제가 급하게 장비가 필요해서 개인 신용카드로 구매를 할 수밖에 없었습니다. (186) 연구비로 비용을 돌려 받을 수 있도록 해 주시겠어요? 영수증 원본을 첨부합니다. (188) 다행히 10%의 할인을 받아 생각보다 저렴한 가격에 장비들을 구매했습니다.

(187) 도시의 여러 곳에서 토양 샘플 수집을 위해 장비를 사용할 예정입니다. 이미 16개의 토양 샘플을 수집해서 각각의 샘플에 대한 분석을 끝냈습니다. 그에 대한 데이터는 다음 달에 제출할 저의 논문에 포함될 것입니다.

도움과 지도에 진심으로 감사 드립니다.

Patrick Turner

---

수신: ⟨pturner6@csu.edu⟩
발신: ⟨customerservice@greenproducts.net⟩
날짜: 4월 3일
제목 355829 주문에 대한 영수증

Patrick Turner 씨,

최근에 Green Products에서 구입을 해 주셔서 감사 드립니다. 고객님의 주문(#355829)의 상세 내역이 담긴 영수증을 첨부합니다. 고객님의 상품들은 영업일 기준 7~14일 내로 배송되는데, (190) 긴급 배송을 위한 추가비용을 내면 영업일 기준 4일 안에 배송됩니다.

(189) 반품은 물건 수령일 기준으로 30일 안에 해야 합니다. 반품 자격을 갖추려면 제품상태가 수령할 때와 같은 상태이고, 원래 포장상태도 유지해야 합니다. 배송비는 포함되지 않습니다. 저희가 제품을 수령하면 지불했던 방식대로 환불을 해 드립니다.

고객님께 다시 도움을 드릴 수 있길 바랍니다.

Kate Fonda
고객 관리 담당
Green Products

---

Green Products

장비 영수증
주문번호: 355829

세부 내역

| | |
|---|---|
| 신속한 토양 테스트 세트<br>제품 번호 1000459 | $34.00 |
| 작은 용기 (20개)<br>제품 번호 1003294 | $10.00 |
| 삽<br>제품 번호 120024 | $8.00 |
| 수분계<br>제품 번호 19001 | $22.00 |
| (190) 긴급 배송 | $8.50 |
| (188) 정기 고객 할인 10% | $8.25 |
| 합계 | $74.25 |

Green Products에서 쇼핑을 해 주셔서 감사합니다.

**186.** Turner 씨가 Wilson 박사에게 요청한 것은 무엇인가?
(A) 구매자에게 야전 장비를 돌려주라는 것
(B) 자신의 논문을 위해 야전 장비를 구입해 달라는 것
(C) 수집된 토양 샘플을 분석해 달라는 것
(D) 연구비로 보상받을 수 있게 해 달라는 것           정답 (D)

**187.** Turner 씨가 수집하고자 하는 것은 무엇인가?
(A) 대기 중 습도
(B) 토양 샘플
(C) 실험 정보
(D) 제품 영수증                                    정답 (B)

**188.** Turner 씨에 대해 암시되는 것은 무엇인가?
- (A) 그는 전원에 넓은 농장을 소유하고 있다.
- (B) 그는 대학시절부터 Wilson 박사와 알고 지냈다.
- (C) 그는 이전에 Green Products에서 물품을 구입한 적이 있다.
- (D) 그는 농업 교육 분야에서 뛰어난 명성을 지니고 있다.     정답 (C)

**189.** 제품을 반품하기 위한 조건은 무엇인가?
- (A) 상점을 직접 방문한다.
- (B) 영수증 원본을 발송한다.
- (C) 사전에 반품할 제품을 통보한다.
- (D) 일정 기간 내에 제품을 반품한다.     정답 (D)

**190.** Turner 씨의 주문에 대해 가장 사실에 가까운 것은 무엇인가?
- (A) 자신이 쓴 비용에 대한 환급을 받을 수 없다.
- (B) 자신의 주문이 과잉청구 되었다.
- (C) 주문한 상품이 영업일 기준 4일 안에 도착할 것이다.
- (D) Turner 씨가 원하는 일부 상품 재고가 없다.     정답 (C)

**문제 191-195번은 다음 편지와 이메일, 그리고 공지를 참조하시오.**

---

Predictive Analytics Business Conference
2233 Bainbridge 가
Philadelphia PA 19119

2월 3일

Mason 씨에게,

저는 귀하가 예측 분석 경영 회의에 참석하여 발표하시도록 초청장을 (191) **드리게** 되어 영광으로 생각합니다. 회의는 3월 10일부터 18일까지 Pennsylvania 주에 위치한 Philadelphia 시에서 개최될 예정입니다. 귀하는 아래와 같은 내용을 발표하도록 예정되어 있습니다.

     수익 모델링 & 예측 보전
     3월 11일, 수요일 오전 10시-11시 45분
     Madison Hills Hotel 회의실 481호
     발표자: Triotex Enterprise 사의 Frances Mason 씨

회의실은 의자, 테이블, 방송 시스템, 스크린, 영사기 그리고 컴퓨터들이 구비되어 있습니다. 더 큰 모임을 위한 여분의 의자와 테이블 역시 사용이 가능합니다. (192) **귀하가 다른 추가적인 시청각 장비가 필요하다면 직접 이를 준비하셔야 합니다.** 만약 시청각 장비를 임대해야 하거나 혹은 이 문제에 관한 다른 추가 질문이 있으시면, 저희 미디어 담당 기술자인 Richard Lee 씨에게 783-324-9325로 연락하시기 바랍니다.

참석에 감사 드립니다. 도움이 필요하시다면 Kylie Turner 씨에게 kturner @pab.org 혹은 783-109-9546으로 연락을 주십시오.

Anna Rodriguez
Predictive Analytics Business Conference

---

수신: Carl Hawkins ⟨carlhawkins130@ triotex.com⟩
발신: Frances Mason ⟨francesmason.14@bkmail.com⟩
날짜: 2월 6일
제목: 일정 변경?

안녕하세요, Hawkins 씨.

저는 최근에 Predictive Analytics Business Conference에서 발표해 달라는 요청을 받았습니다. 저는 이 회의가 예측 분석학과 관련하여 북미 지역에서 가장 저명한 회의 중 하나이기 때문에 발표하게 되어 영광으로 생각합니다. (193) **그런데 작은 문제가 있습니다; 저는 이 회의가 열리는 동**

일한 주간에 회사의 주간 예측 회의에서 발표해야 합니다. 저는 회의에 참석하기 위해서 한 주를 모두 사용하는 것이 가능할 것이라고 여겼는데, 회사 회의에 대해서 완전히 잊고 있었습니다. (194/195) **상당히 미안한 질문이지만 제가 18일에 발표를 해도 괜찮겠습니까?** 저는 이번 회의에 참석하는 것이 저와 Triotex 사를 위해 정말 좋은 기회라고 생각하고 있습니다.

Frances Mason

---

Predictive Analytics Business Conference
공지

(194/195) **저희는 여러분께 "Revenue Modeling & Predictive Maintenance" 강좌가 강연자의 사정으로 인해 3월 18일 수요일로 연기되었음을 알리게 되어 죄송하게 생각합니다.** (195) **대신, 저희는 Carl Hawkins 씨의 "What exactly is Predictive Analytics?"란 제목의 강연을 제공해드릴 예정입니다.** 이 강연은 예측 분석을 자세하게 설명하고 청중에게 다음 강좌에 대해 준비할 수 있도록 해드릴 것입니다. 여러분의 협조에 감사를 드립니다.

---

**191.** 편지의 첫 번째 단락 첫 번째 줄의 "extend"와 의미상 가장 유사한 단어는 무엇인가?
- (A) 개발하다
- (B) 확장하다
- (C) 제공하다
- (D) 늘리다     정답 (C)

**192.** Predictive Analytics Business Conference에 관해 언급된 것은 무엇인가?
- (A) 회의는 오직 하루만 개최될 것이다.
- (B) 참석자들은 회의가 개최되는 동안 무료 주차를 제공받는다.
- (C) 발표자는 그들이 추가하고자 하는 시청각 장비를 가지고 와야 한다.
- (D) 강연자는 발표 장비가 필요한 경우 신청서를 작성해야 한다.     정답 (C)

**193.** 이메일에 따르면 Mason 씨의 문제점은 무엇인가?
- (A) 그는 일정상의 문제가 있다.
- (B) 그는 다음 발표를 준비하는 데 실패했다.
- (C) 그는 강연에 대한 적절한 장비가 부족하다.
- (D) 그의 휴가 신청은 거절되었다.     정답 (A)

**194.** Hawkins 씨에 관해 유추할 수 있는 것은 무엇인가?
- (A) 그는 자신의 발표를 연기할 것이다.
- (B) 그는 회사의 회의를 주재할 것이다.
- (C) 그는 Mason 씨가 처리한 일에 만족했다.
- (D) 그는 3월 18일에 발표하기로 되어 있다.     정답 (D)

**195.** 3월 11일에는 어떠한 일이 발생할 것 같은가?
- (A) Mason 씨가 발표를 할 것이다.
- (B) 회의가 끝날 것이다.
- (C) Hawkins 씨의 강연이 열릴 것이다.
- (D) 새로운 장비가 회의실에 설치될 것이다.     정답 (C)

**문제 196-200번은 다음 편지와 일정표, 그리고 이메일을 참조하시오.**

---

3월 2일

Emma Petrie
Mallory Terrace 3007번지
Ottawa, ON K1A 1L1

Petrie 씨께,

귀하께서 저희 Futurecom Plasticware 주식회사의 영업 팀장 직책을 맡으실 분으로 선정되었다는 사실을 알려 드리게 되어 기쁘게 생각합니다. 4월 1일에, 귀하께서는 우리 회사의 Mulberry 지점에서 근무하는 25명의 경험 많은 영업직원들로 구성된 팀을 이끌 책임을 (196) **맡으시게** 될 것입니다. 귀하와 귀하의 팀원들은 기존의 고객 및 잠재 고객들을 대상으로 우리 회사의 휴대 전화 케이스 및 액세서리 제품들을 판매하게 됩니다.

첫 정식 근무일에 앞서, 귀하께서는 반드시 직원 오리엔테이션에 참석하셔야 합니다. 이 오리엔테이션은 3월 28일에 Mulberry 지점에서 열릴 가능성이 큽니다. 하지만 하루 일찍 개최할 수 있는 가능성도 약간 있습니다. (197) **하루 앞당기기로 결정할 경우, 멀베리 지점을 그날 이용할 수 없을 것이기 때문에 Hexford 지점을 이용할 것입니다.** 귀하께서는 앞으로 며칠 안에 최종 확정된 상세 정보를 알려 드릴 것이며, 오리엔테이션 일정표도 즉시 발송될 것입니다.

Pamela Kane
인사부장
Futurecom Plasticware 주식회사

---

### Futurecom Plasticware 주식회사

직원 오리엔테이션 일정
(197) Hexford 지점 301호

| 시간 | 교육 내용 | 연설자/강사 |
|---|---|---|
| 9:15–9:45 | 환영 연설 및 오리엔테이션 소개 | Aaron Myles |
| 9:45–10:45 | (200) Futurecom Plasticware 주식회사: 철학 및 연혁 | Tracey Dugan |
| 10:45–12:15 | (198) 혁신적인 제품 디자인 및 회사만의 강점 | Greg Parker |
| 1:30–2:45 | (198) 기존 및 잠재 구매자들과의 의사 소통 | Jane Lewis |
| 2:45–4:15 | 시간 및 효율성을 최대화하기 위한 전략 | Emily Hong |
| 4:15–5:30 | 앞으로의 프로젝트, 개발 사항 및 (198) 목표 | Luke Thewlis |

오리엔테이션 참가자들은 문의사항이 있을 경우에 운영부장인 Kim Christie 씨에게 k_christie@futurecom.net 또는 555-2134로 연락하시기 바랍니다.

---

수신: Kim Christie 〈k_christie@futurecom.net〉
발신: Emma Petrie 〈e_petrie@futurecom.net〉
날짜: 4월 1일
제목: 최근의 오리엔테이션

Christie 씨께,

저는 Mulberry 지사의 신임 영업 팀장이며, 최근에 직원 오리엔테이션에 참석했습니다. 괜찮으시다면 두 가지 일에 대해 저를 도와주셨으면 합니다. 우선, (199) **제가 치과 예약 때문에 Myles 씨 연설의 시작 부분을 놓치게 되어서** 이 연설이 시작될 때 배부된 유인물이 있었는지 궁금합니다. 만일 그렇다면, 아직도 사본을 받아볼 수 있는지요? 또한, 약간 창피한 문제가 하나 있습니다. (200) **회사의 설립에 관해 연설하셨던 팀장님께서 이번 주에 점심 식사를 위해 만날 것을 제안하셨습니다.** 문제는 제가 그분의 성함이 기억나지 않는다는 것이며, 아직 그 일정에 관해 들은 바가 없습니다. 그 팀장님의 성함과 내선번호를 제게 좀 알려 주시겠습니까? 대단히 감사합니다.

Emma Petrie

---

**196.** 편지에서, 1번째 단락의 2번째 줄에 있는 단어 "assume"과 의미가 가장 유사한 것은?
(A) 문의하다
(B) 맡다
(C) 추정하다
(D) 인상하다 　　　　　　　　정답 (B)

**197.** 직원 오리엔테이션에 관해 사실일 가능성이 큰 것은 무엇인가?
(A) 두 곳의 다른 장소에서 열렸다.
(B) 90분 길이의 점심 식사 시간이 포함되었다.
(C) 3월 27일에 열렸다.
(D) 25명의 사람들이 참석했다. 　　　　정답 (C)

**198.** 직원 오리엔테이션에서 다뤄진 주제가 아닌 것은 무엇인가?
(A) 제품들의 디자인 특징
(B) 고객들과의 교류
(C) 광고 전략
(D) 미래의 목표 　　　　　　　　정답 (C)

**199.** 이메일에 따르면 Petrie 씨의 문제점은 무엇인가?
(A) 그녀는 발표 연습을 하지 못했다.
(B) 그녀는 Christie 씨와 친하지 않았다.
(C) 그녀는 예정보다 늦게 일을 시작했다.
(D) 그녀는 Myles 씨 연설의 시작 부분을 놓쳤다. 　정답 (D)

**200.** 어느 오리엔테이션 강사가 Petrie 씨를 점심 식사에 초대했을 가능성이 큰가?
(A) Tracey Dugan
(B) Greg Parker
(C) Jane Lewis
(D) Emily Hong 　　　　　　　　정답 (A)

**1.** 미M

(A) The man is sweeping the floor.
(B) The man is wiping off a table.
(C) The man is folding an apron.
(D) The man is hanging a tool on a hook.

(A) 남자가 바닥을 쓸고 있다.
(B) 남자가 테이블을 닦고 있다.
(C) 남자가 앞치마를 접고 있다.
(D) 남자가 고리에 도구를 걸고 있다.　　　　　정답 (A)

**2.** 호M

(A) They are kneeling to look at a product.
(B) They are constructing a brick walkway.
(C) They are setting traffic cones on a road.
(D) They're moving some bricks into a warehouse.

(A) 그들은 제품을 보기 위해 무릎을 꿇고 있다.
(B) 그들은 벽돌로 된 보도를 만들고 있다.
(C) 그들은 원뿔형 도로 표지를 도로 위에 놓고 있다.
(D) 그들은 벽돌을 창고로 옮기고 있다.　　　　　정답 (B)

**3.** 미M

(A) She's reaching for an item on a shelf.
(B) She's looking at an item in her bag.
(C) She's browsing through some clothes on a rack.
(D) She's waiting in line at a register.

(A) 그녀는 선반에 놓인 상품을 향해 팔을 뻗고 있다.
(B) 그녀는 가방 속에 있는 물건을 보고 있다.
(C) 그녀는 옷걸이에 걸린 옷을 구경하고 있다.
(D) 그녀는 계산대에 줄을 서서 기다리고 있다.　　　정답 (C)

**4.** 호M

(A) The woman is viewing a statue outside.
(B) A path is shaded by an umbrella.
(C) Rows of potted plants are hanging in a greenhouse.
(D) A floppy hat is shielding the woman's face from sunlight.

(A) 여자는 야외에 있는 조각상을 보고 있다.
(B) 오솔길이 파라솔에 의해 그늘져 있다.
(C) 화분에 담긴 화초들이 온실 속에 여러 줄로 매달려 있다.
(D) 챙이 넓은 모자가 햇볕으로부터 여자의 얼굴을 가리고 있다.　정답 (D)

**5.** 영W

(A) A dock is crowded with tourists.
(B) A boat has been docked under a canopy.
(C) A storm is tossing a boat on the water.
(D) Some boats are tied to a dock with some ropes.

(A) 부두는 관광객들로 붐비고 있다.
(B) 배 한 척이 차양 밑에 정박해 있다.
(C) 폭풍이 물 위에서 배를 흔들고 있다.
(D) 몇몇 배들이 부두에 밧줄로 묶여 있다.　　　　정답 (B)

**6.** 미W

(A) Some photocopiers are being installed in an office.
(B) Some paper trays have been left open.
(C) Some cabinet drawers are full of stationery supplies.
(D) Some boxes have been stacked on both sides of a copy machine.

(A) 몇몇 복사기들이 사무실에 설치되고 있다.
(B) 몇몇 종이함들이 열려 있다.
(C) 몇몇 캐비닛 서랍이 문구용품으로 가득 차 있다.
(D) 몇몇 상자들이 복사기 양 옆에 쌓여 있다.　　　정답 (D)

## Part 2

**7.** 미M 영W

When will the road maintenance be completed?
(A) It will increase our maintenance costs.
(B) Not for another month.
(C) Since the beginning of April.

도로 보수공사는 언제 완공되나요?
(A) 그건 우리의 유지 비용을 증가시킬 거예요.
(B) 한 달은 지나야 될 거예요.
(C) 4월 초부터요.　　　　　　　　　　　정답 (B)

**8.** 호M 미W

Where can we reserve our tickets for the movie?
(A) About 9:00 P.M.
(B) I don't think I can go.
(C) This seat is taken.

우리 영화 관람권을 어디에서 예약할 수 있을까요?
(A) 대략 오후 9시예요.
(B) 저는 영화를 보러 못 갈 것 같아요.
(C) 이 자리는 주인이 있어요.　　　　　　　정답 (B)

**9.** 미M 영W

How often do I need to replace these batteries?
(A) Actually, they are rechargeable.
(B) Yes, it's very convenient.
(C) It is one of the best places around here.

이 건전지를 얼마나 자주 교체해야 할까요?
(A) 사실 그건 충전용 건전지예요.
(B) 네, 매우 편리해요.
(C) 이 근처에서 제일 좋은 장소 중 한 곳이에요.　정답 (A)

**10.** 호M 영W

Did you see the dinner menu?
(A) No, it's too expensive.
(B) I want a table for four.
(C) I think it's reasonably priced.

저녁 메뉴를 보셨나요?
(A) 아니오, 너무 비싸네요.
(B) 4명이 앉을 테이블을 원합니다.
(C) 가격이 적절하다고 생각해요.　　　　　　정답 (C)

**11.** 미M 미W

Who has been hired as the treasurer?
(A) The hiring plan was canceled last week.
(B) She's very tired.
(C) To earn a higher education.

회계 담당자로 채용된 사람이 누구인가요?
(A) 채용 계획은 지난주에 취소되었어요.

(B) 그녀는 무척 피곤해요.
(C) 고등교육을 받기 위해서요. 정답 (A)

**12.** 영W 미M
What's the fastest way to get to the Hayward Commercial Center?
(A) Near city hall.
(B) Bella would know.
(C) It's a 20-minute drive.

Hayward Commercial Center까지 가는 가장 빠른 길은 뭔가요?
(A) 시청 근처예요.
(B) Bella가 알 겁니다.
(C) 차로 20분 걸려요. 정답 (B)

**13.** 호M 미W
How long should I keep the quarterly report?
(A) It's 100 pages long.
(B) In the company data archives.
(C) Only a week, I think.

분기별 보고서를 얼마 동안 보관해야 하나요?
(A) 100페이지 분량이에요.
(B) 회사 기록 보관소예요.
(C) 일주일이면 될 거예요. 정답 (C)

**14.** 미M 영W
Are you driving or taking a bus to New York?
(A) It's energy efficient.
(B) Do the buses run on Sundays?
(C) Every fifteen minutes.

New York까지 운전해서 갈 건가요, 아니면 버스를 타고 갈 건가요?
(A) 그게 에너지 효율성이 좋아요.
(B) 일요일에도 버스가 운행하나요?
(C) 15분마다요. 정답 (B)

**15.** 호M 미W
May I use your digital camera to shoot some pictures in my office?
(A) Sure, but I need it in two hours.
(B) To take quality photographs.
(C) No sugar or cream. Thanks.

제 사무실에서 사진을 찍는 데 당신의 디지털 카메라를 사용해도 될까요?
(A) 그럼요, 하지만 저도 두 시간 후에 필요해요.
(B) 좋은 사진을 찍기 위해서요.
(C) 설탕이나 크림은 넣지 마세요. 고마워요. 정답 (A)

**16.** 미M 영W
I think our company should use environmentally friendly products.
(A) Good working conditions.
(B) We'll resume production soon.
(C) Won't they be expensive?

저는 우리 회사가 친환경 제품을 사용해야 한다고 생각합니다.
(A) 좋은 근무 환경이요.
(B) 우리는 곧 생산을 재개할 겁니다.
(C) 그건 비싸지 않나요? 정답 (C)

**17.** 영W 미M
Where can I register for the seminar on investment opportunities?

(A) The due date has been delayed.
(B) Several new investors.
(C) You should register online.

투자 기회에 관한 세미나 등록은 어디서 할 수 있나요?
(A) 만기일이 연기되었어요.
(B) 몇몇 새로운 투자자들이요.
(C) 온라인으로 등록하셔야 합니다. 정답 (C)

**18.** 호M 미W
You should rewrite the annual report, shouldn't you?
(A) Once a year.
(B) Yes, I'll do that tomorrow.
(C) The annual sale ended yesterday.

연간 보고서를 다시 작성하셔야 하죠, 그렇지 않나요?
(A) 1년에 한 번이요.
(B) 네, 내일 하려구요.
(C) 연례 할인 행사가 어제 끝났어요. 정답 (B)

**19.** 미M 영W
Does Mr. McDonald have any experience in tax accounting?
(A) Please call me a taxi.
(B) Yes, he wants to open a bank account.
(C) We're searching for someone with a background in software development.

McDonald 씨가 세무 회계 분야에 경험이 있나요?
(A) 택시를 불러주세요.
(B) 네, 그는 은행 계좌를 개설하길 원해요.
(C) 우리는 소프트웨어 개발 분야의 경력자를 찾고 있어요. 정답 (C)

**20.** 미W 호M
Ms. Miller came to work very early this morning.
(A) I think she has a lot to get through.
(B) Sorry. I can't drive you to work today.
(C) Let's take the bus.

Miller 씨는 오늘 아침에 굉장히 일찍 출근했어요.
(A) 그녀가 할 일이 무척 많은 것 같아요.
(B) 미안합니다. 오늘은 직장까지 차로 모셔다 드리질 못하겠네요.
(C) 버스를 탑시다. 정답 (A)

**21.** 미M 영W
Have you finished drafting the new business proposal, or do you need more time to complete it?
(A) I'm almost done with it.
(B) Yes, it's still working.
(C) A new clock on the wall.

신규 사업 제안서 작성을 마무리했나요, 아니면 완성하는 데 시간이 더 필요한가요?
(A) 거의 다 했습니다.
(B) 네, 그건 여전히 작동 중이에요.
(C) 벽에 있는 새로운 시계예요. 정답 (A)

**22.** 영W 미M
When are we expected to discuss the marketing issues?
(A) Almost two weeks ago.
(B) We have several items on the agenda to address.
(C) When the marketing analysis report comes in.

마케팅 관련 사안들을 언제 논의할 것으로 예상되나요?
(A) 거의 2주 전에요.
(B) 우리는 다뤄야 할 몇 가지 안건들이 있어요.
(C) 마케팅 분석 보고서가 오면요.　　　　　　정답 (C)

**23.** 호M 미W

What is the fax number for Sugar Business Consulting?
(A) 310 Sunset Boulevard.
(B) I'll have to look it up.
(C) Almost $200 this year.

Sugar Business Consulting 사의 팩스 번호는 어떻게 되나요?
(A) Sunset 대로 310번지예요.
(B) 찾아봐야 합니다.
(C) 올해는 거의 200달러예요.　　　　　　정답 (B)

**24.** 미M 영W

The photocopier is out of order again, isn't it?
(A) Yes, I've already ordered them.
(B) Twenty dollars per copy.
(C) I used it just now.

복사기가 다시 고장이 났죠, 그렇지 않나요?
(A) 네, 이미 그것들을 주문했어요.
(B) 권 당 20달러예요.
(C) 제가 방금 사용했는데요.　　　　　　정답 (C)

**25.** 미W 호M

Would you like me to show you where the Human Resources Department is?
(A) I received a map from the receptionist.
(B) Yes, I want to watch the show.
(C) We should hire ten more employees.

인사과가 어디 있는지 제가 안내해 드릴까요?
(A) 안내 직원에게서 지도를 받았어요.
(B) 네, 그 공연을 관람하고 싶어요.
(C) 우리는 10명의 직원을 더 채용해야 합니다.　　　정답 (A)

**26.** 미M 영W

Hasn't the technician finished repairing our data storage system yet?
(A) Yes, they contain some data.
(B) Much more expensive than expected.
(C) He needs more time to complete the work.

기술자가 우리 자료 저장 시스템에 대한 수리를 끝내지 않았나요?
(A) 네, 거기에는 자료가 들어 있어요.
(B) 예상보다 훨씬 더 비싸요.
(C) 그가 작업을 마무리하려면 시간이 더 필요해요.　정답 (C)

**27.** 미W 미M

Which restaurant should I take the client to?
(A) He signed a big contract.
(B) Actually, I'm new to this city.
(C) A dinner table for three.

어느 식당으로 고객을 모시고 가면 될까요?
(A) 그는 큰 계약에 서명했어요.
(B) 사실 저는 이 도시에 온지 얼마 안됐어요.
(C) 세 명이 저녁식사를 할 수 있는 테이블이요.　정답 (B)

**28.** 호M 미W

Where can I find the spring jackets your department store carries?
(A) I don't know who lost it.
(B) Please check the price tag.
(C) We haven't stocked the new inventory yet.

이 백화점에서 판매하는 봄 재킷은 어디에서 찾을 수 있을까요?
(A) 누가 그것을 분실했는지 모르겠어요.
(B) 가격표를 확인해 보세요.
(C) 아직 신상품이 입고되지 못했어요.　　　정답 (C)

**29.** 미M 영W

I haven't purchased my plane ticket to San Francisco yet.
(A) What time will you arrive at the airport?
(B) I think it will be expensive to buy now.
(C) More space for carry-on luggage.

San Francisco 행 항공권을 아직 구입하지 못했어요.
(A) 공항에 몇 시에 도착할 건가요?
(B) 지금 구매하기엔 가격이 비싸다고 생각해요.
(C) 수하물을 위한 더 많은 공간이요.　　　정답 (B)

**30.** 호M 미W

The vice president is leaving on an urgent business trip this afternoon.
(A) Is Mr. Parker still living in Boston?
(B) Then I'll reschedule his meeting for some other day.
(C) There is some on the bottom shelf.

부사장님이 오늘 오후에 긴급한 출장을 떠나게 되었어요.
(A) Parker 씨는 여전히 Boston에 살고 있나요?
(B) 그러면 그의 회의 일정을 다른 날로 재조정해야겠네요.
(C) 하단 선반에 약간 있습니다.　　　정답 (B)

**31.** 영W 미M

Wasn't the elevator supposed to be repaired before the lunch break?
(A) The Facilities Management Department.
(B) That has been postponed until next Tuesday.
(C) Since then, it has broken down.

승강기가 점심시간이 되기 전에 수리되기로 한 것 아니었나요?
(A) 시설관리 부서예요.
(B) 그게 다음주 화요일로 연기되었어요.
(C) 그때 이후로 고장이 났어요.　　　정답 (B)

## Part 3

문제 32-34번은 다음 대화를 참조하시오. 미W 호M

W: Hey, Steven. (32) **Someone sent an e-mail to ask if we sell Alpha staplers. I don't think we stock that brand anymore, right?**

M: Oh, we do. We sell Alpha staplers and staples, but we're temporarily sold out now.

W: (33) **Then I should reply to the customer after lunch.** Do you know when we will get some more?

M: I have to double-check the order book, (34) **but I think we'll get some next Monday.**

W: 안녕하세요, Steven. 우리가 Alpha 스테이플러를 판매하는지 이메일로 문의한 분이 있어요. 우리가 그 상표 제품은 더 이상 갖고 있지 않은 걸로 알고 있는데요, 맞죠?

M: 아, 있어요. Alpha 스테이플러와 철심까지 모두 판매하지만 지금은 일시적으로 품절된 상태예요.

W: 그러면 제가 점심식사 후에 손님에게 답장을 해야겠네요. 상품들이 언제 입고되는지 알아요?

M: 제가 주문장을 다시 한 번 확인해봐야 합니다만, 다음주 월요일에 제품이 입고되는 걸로 알고 있어요.

**32.** 화자들은 무엇에 대해 논의하는가?
(A) 사무용품
(B) 지연된 주문
(C) 분실된 서류
(D) 재고 조사　　　　　　　　　　　　　정답 (A)

**33.** 여자는 오늘 오후에 무엇을 할 것인가?
(A) 비품을 주문한다.
(B) 판매업체에 연락한다.
(C) 서류 양식을 작성한다.
(D) 이메일을 보낸다.　　　　　　　　　　정답 (D)

**34.** 남자에 따르면 다음주 월요일에는 어떤 일이 발생할 것 같은가?
(A) 주문이 이루어질 것이다.
(B) 사무용품이 도착할 것이다.
(C) 무료 점심식사가 제공될 것이다.
(D) 생산이 재개될 것이다.　　　　　　　정답 (B)

**문제 35-37번은 다음 대화를 참조하시오.** 호M 미W

M: Hello there! I'm calling about the one-bedroom apartment for rent on Collins Road you advertised in the *Cupertino Chronicle*. (35) I'd like to know if it is still available and if so, when I can move in.

W: I think you can move into the apartment on November 1. It is fully furnished and located on the corner of Lake Forest, so it's cozy and has beautiful scenery. (36) In addition, there are several types of public transportation near the apartment complex. Are you able to come to see it tomorrow?

M: Sure, no problem. I'm enjoying a weeklong vacation now, so I'm free all day tomorrow.

W: Then (37) why don't you come by the apartment management office at 1 o'clock and take a look around the apartment? I'm sure you'll like it here.

- - - - - - - - - - - - - - - - - - - - - - - - - - - - - -

M: 안녕하세요! Cupertino Chronicle에 광고한 Collins Road에 위치한 방 하나짜리 아파트 임대에 대해 문의하고자 연락 드립니다. 그 아파트가 여전히 임대 가능한지, 혹 그렇다면 언제 입주가 가능할지 알고 싶습니다.

W: 11월 1일에 입주하시는 것이 가능합니다. 이 아파트는 모든 가구를 완비하고 있고 Forest 호수에 인접해 있어서 아주 편안하고 아름다운 풍경을 지니고 있습니다. 게다가 아파트 단지 근처에 다양한 대중교통편을 갖추고 있습니다. 내일 아파트를 보러 오실 수 있나요?

M: 물론이에요, 문제없어요. 제가 지금 일주일간 휴가를 보내고 있기 때문에 내일 하루 종일 시간이 됩니다.

W: 그러면 내일 아파트 관리 사무실로 1시까지 방문해서 아파트를 한 번 둘러보시는 것은 어때요? 분명히 좋아하실 겁니다.

**35.** 남자는 아파트에 대해 무엇을 알고 싶어 하는가?
(A) 월세
(B) 위치
(C) 임대 가능성
(D) 대중교통 접근성　　　　　　　　　　정답 (C)

**36.** 여자가 아파트에 대해 언급한 내용은 무엇인가?
(A) 그의 직장 근처에 있다.
(B) 현재 입주한 사람이 있다.
(C) 교통이 편리하다.
(D) 고급 가구가 구비되어 있다.　　　　정답 (C)

**37.** 화자들은 언제 만날 것 같은가?
(A) 오후 1시
(B) 오후 2시
(C) 오후 3시
(D) 오후 4시　　　　　　　　　　　　　정답 (A)

**문제 38-40번은 다음 대화를 참조하시오.** 영W 미M

W: Hello, My name is Sandra Heard, and I'm in Room 401. (38) The radiator in here has made the room quite warm suddenly. And I don't know how to lower the temperature.

M: Oh, that is inconvenient. I'm sorry, but Mr. Wilson is the only one who does maintenance, and he's off tonight. (39) I can put you in a different room though. Let me see. Yes, we have a balcony suite. Don't worry. We won't charge you extra.

W: That would be nice. Could I ask you a favor? I'm running out to dinner now and won't be back until late. (40) Could you have someone move my bags to the new room?

- - - - - - - - - - - - - - - - - - - - - - - - - - - - - -

W: 안녕하세요, 제 이름은 Sandra Heard인데 401호에 묵고 있어요. 여기 있는 라디에이터가 갑작스럽게 더워져서요. 그런데 온도를 어떻게 낮춰야 하는지 모르겠네요.

M: 아, 불편하시겠네요. 죄송합니다만 Wilson 씨가 시설관리를 담당하는 유일한 사람인데 그가 오늘밤에 비번입니다. 대신 다른 방으로 잡아드릴게요. 어디 보자. 네, 발코니가 있는 스위트 룸이 하나 있어요. 걱정하지 마십시오. 추가 비용을 청구하지 않을 겁니다.

W: 좋네요. 부탁 하나 드려도 될까요? 제가 지금 저녁식사를 하러 나가는 길인데요, 좀 늦게 들어올 것 같아요. 직원을 통해 제 가방들을 새 방으로 옮기도록 해주실 수 있나요?

**38.** 여자가 남자에게 전화하는 이유는 무엇인가?
(A) 사라진 물건에 관해 묻기 위해서
(B) 최근의 구매에 관해 논의하기 위해서
(C) 기기의 문제점에 대해 알리기 위해서
(D) 회의 일정을 재조정하기 위해서　　　정답 (C)

**39.** 남자는 여자에게 무엇을 제공하는가?
(A) 수리비 할인
(B) 다른 스위트 룸
(C) 임시 통행증
(D) 무료 배송　　　　　　　　　　　　　정답 (B)

**40.** 여자가 남자에게 요청하는 것은 무엇인가?
(A) 그녀의 짐을 옮기도록 한다.
(B) 가격을 논의한다.
(C) 장비를 수리한다.

> M1: Welcome to the Star Fitness Center. How can I help you?
>
> W: Good morning, I'm Kate Johnson. I work at the accounting firm across the street. **(41) I'm here to inquire about your corporate fitness programs.**
>
> M1: The center manager can help you on the matter. David, this lady wants to talk about our corporate fitness programs.
>
> M2: That's great. We provide a variety of corporate fitness programs taught by certified fitness professionals.
>
> W: That's good to know. **(42) How long do the classes usually last?** I'm concerned about the length of the classes because I can only work out during lunchtime.
>
> M2: We offer both 25-minute and 50-minute classes. **(43) If you need more information, I can give you some pamphlets.**

---

M1: Star Fitness Center에 오신 걸 환영합니다. 어떻게 도와드릴까요?

W: 안녕하세요, 저는 Kate Johnson이라고 합니다. 길 건너편에 위치한 회계사무소에서 근무하고 있어요. 기업 운동 프로그램에 관해 문의하고자 방문했어요.

M1: 그 부분에 대해선 센터장님이 도움을 주실 겁니다. David, 이 여자분이 기업 운동 프로그램에 대해 이야기하길 원하세요.

M2: 좋습니다. 저희는 자격을 보유한 운동 전문가들이 지도하는 다양한 기업 운동 프로그램을 제공하고 있습니다.

W: 듣던 중 반가운 소리네요. 대개 수업 시간은 얼마나 되나요? 저는 점심식사 시간만 운동하는 것이 가능해서 수업의 길이에 관심이 있어요.

M1: 25분 수업과 50분 수업을 모두 제공하고 있습니다. 더 많은 정보가 필요하시면 안내책자를 드리도록 할게요.

**41.** 여자는 무엇에 대해 알고 싶어하는가?
(A) 컴퓨터 교육
(B) 탄력 근무 시간
(C) 무료 셔틀 버스 서비스
(D) 운동 수업      정답 (D)

**42.** 여자는 무엇에 관해 관심을 가지고 있는가?
(A) 공간 요구 사항
(B) 건강 보험 프로그램
(C) 시간 제한
(D) 강사의 자격      정답 (C)

**43.** David은 여자에게 무엇을 제공하는가?
(A) 안내책자
(B) 다과
(C) 그의 휴대전화 번호
(D) 무료 라커      정답 (A)

> W: Good morning, Mr. Grant. Are the rooms ready for the guests to arrive?
>
> M: Yes, Ms. Waterhouse. **(44) I've checked all of them,** and the interns are just putting on the finishing touches. People should start arriving in about thirty minutes, and the conference is scheduled to begin at 10:00.

> W: Great. Thank you. **(45) I put all of the binders in the conference room. Please have the interns arrange them before the lunch meeting.** Oh, did you get a chance to order the food?
>
> M: Yes, I did. **(46) I'll call to give the restaurant a final head count after the first meeting starts.**

---

W: 안녕하세요, Grant 씨. 도착하는 손님들을 위한 방은 다 준비가 된 상태인가요?

M: 네, Waterhouse 씨. 제가 모든 방을 확인했고, 수습사원들이 최종적으로 방 정리를 하고 있습니다. 손님들은 대략 30분 후에 도착하기 시작할 예정이며 회의는 10시에 시작합니다.

W: 좋네요, 감사드려요. 제가 모든 서류철을 회의실에 가져다 두었어요. 수습사원들이 오찬 회의 전에 그 서류철들을 배치하도록 해주세요. 아, 혹시 음식은 주문하셨나요?

M: 네, 했습니다. 첫 회의가 시작한 후 제가 식당에 연락을 해서 최종적인 손님의 수를 알려주려고 합니다.

**44.** 남자는 무엇을 준비하고 있는가?
(A) 회의
(B) 수습직원 오리엔테이션
(C) 취업 면접
(D) 원격 회의      정답 (A)

**45.** 수습직원들은 점심 전에 무엇을 해야 하는가?
(A) 자료를 배치한다.
(B) 특별 손님들을 맞이한다.
(C) 오리엔테이션에 참석한다.
(D) 점심식사를 주문한다.      정답 (A)

**46.** Grant 씨는 회의가 시작된 후에 무엇을 할 것인가?
(A) 휴식을 취한다.
(B) 서류철을 구매한다.
(C) 다른 행사를 준비한다.
(D) 음식 주문을 확인한다.      정답 (D)

> W: Good afternoon, **(47) I'm Jinhye Kim, and I'm here for my second interview with Sally Murphy at 2 o'clock.**
>
> M1: Oh, hi, Ms. Kim. I'm her secretary, Tom Moore. Nice to meet you. **(48) I'm afraid Ms. Murphy is not in the office at the moment. She went to the conference room on the seventh floor after she received a sudden call to attend a board meeting.** But she will probably be back in 15 minutes or so. Would you mind waiting for a moment?
>
> W: Not at all. Do you happen to know where I can sit and relax over some coffee while waiting for Ms. Murphy?
>
> M2: Ms. Kim? I'm Brian Porter. I can show you to the guest lounge. Please follow me, Ms. Kim.
>
> M1: You can have some coffee and snacks there. **(49) I've got your cell phone number here on your résumé. I'll call you as soon as Ms. Murphy returns to her office.**

---

W: 안녕하세요, 저는 김진혜라고 하고, 오늘 Sally Murphy 씨와 오후 2시로 예정된 2차 면접을 보러 왔습니다.

M1: 아, 안녕하세요, Kim 씨. 저는 그녀의 비서 Tom Moore라고 합니다. 만나서 반갑습니다. 죄송하지만 Murphy 씨가 지금 사무실에 안 계십니다.

(D) 저녁식사 장소를 추천해준다.      정답 (A)

이사회에서 긴급 회의 소집 연락을 받고 7층 회의실로 가셨습니다. 하지만 15분 정도면 돌아오실 겁니다. 잠시만 기다리고 계시겠어요?

W: 물론입니다. 혹시 Murphy 씨를 기다리는 동안 잠시 앉아서 커피 한 잔 할 수 있는 곳을 알고 계신가요?

M2: Kim 씨? 저는 Brian Porter라고 합니다. 제가 고객 휴게실로 안내해 드리겠습니다. 따라오세요, Kim 씨.

M1: 거기로 가시면 커피와 간식을 드실 수가 있어요. 여기 이력서에 휴대폰 번호가 나와 있네요. Murphy 씨가 사무실로 돌아오시면 바로 연락을 드리도록 하겠습니다.

**47.** 여자는 누구일 것 같은가?
(A) 인사 담당 이사
(B) 비서
(C) 커피숍 주인
(D) 면접 대상자　　　　　　　　　　　정답 (D)

**48.** Sally Murphy 씨가 현재 사무실을 비운 이유는 무엇인가?
(A) 그녀는 외근하고 있다.
(B) 그녀는 회의에 참석하고 있다.
(C) 그녀는 늦은 점심식사를 하고 있다.
(D) 그녀는 다른 지원자들의 면접을 보고 있다.　　정답 (B)

**49.** Moore 씨가 여자에게 제안하는 것은 무엇인가?
(A) 수리공을 보낸다.
(B) 그녀에게 연락을 한다.
(C) 발표를 한다.
(D) 다과를 제공한다.　　　　　　　　　정답 (B)

문제 50-52번은 다음 대화를 참조하시오. [미W] [미M]

W: Hi, Carl. (50) **Did you see the schedule for next month's fitness classes? You are scheduled to teach the two classes you requested.** I hope the times work out for you.

M: Oh, wow. Thanks! Hmm… I see two classes are back to back with no break.

W: Yes, is that a problem?

M: Well, (51) **the aerobics class is scheduled to start right after my weightlifting class. This means I will only have five minutes to put away the exercise equipment and to get ready for the next class. That is going to be pretty hard.**

W: Oh, I see. That makes sense. (52) **Why don't I just change the starting time of your aerobics class?** Let's have it start 15 minutes later.

--------

W: 안녕하세요, Carl. 다음달 운동 수업 일정을 봤어요? 당신이 요청했던 두 과정을 지도하기로 일정이 잡혀 있어요. 수업 시간에 문제가 없길 바래요.

M: 와, 감사합니다! 음… 두 과정의 수업이 휴식 시간이 없이 연강이네요.

W: 네, 그게 문제가 될까요?

M: 글쎄요, 웨이트 수업이 끝난 직후에 에어로빅 수업이 시작하네요. 이건 운동 장비를 치우고 다음 수업 준비를 할 수 있는 시간이 고작 5분밖에 안 된다는 걸 뜻하거든요. 이건 정말 힘들 것 같네요.

W: 아, 알겠어요. 일리가 있네요. 제가 에어로빅 수업의 시작 시간을 변경해 드리는 건 어떨까요? 15분 뒤에 시작하는 걸로 하지요.

**50.** 화자들은 어디에서 근무할 것 같은가?
(A) 헬스 클럽
(B) 스포츠용품 판매점
(C) 제조 공장

---

(D) 지역 대학　　　　　　　　　　　　정답 (A)

**51.** 남자가 "That is going to be pretty hard."라고 말할 때 암시하는 바는 무엇인가?
(A) 그는 자원봉사를 요청한다.
(B) 그는 한 직원의 이름을 알고자 한다.
(C) 그는 일이 거의 실현 가능하지 않다고 생각한다.
(D) 그는 지원자의 자격 요건에 관심을 갖고 있다.　정답 (C)

**52.** 여자는 무엇을 하겠다고 제안하는가?
(A) 재고를 확인한다.
(B) 업무 공간을 청소한다.
(C) 문의사항에 답변을 한다.
(D) 일정을 변경한다.　　　　　　　　　정답 (D)

문제 53-55번은 다음 대화를 참조하시오. [미W] [미M]

W: Good morning, Mr. Walker. (53/54) **Do you have the medical record file for the first appointment this morning?** I think the name is Rhonda Morgan.

M: Yes, it's on your desk. The files for all of your appointments today are there. Hers should be the first one.

W: Oh, that's so helpful. Thanks a lot.

M: No problem. Ah, (55) **the painters are going to be working in the hospital archives today, so I already got every hard copy file out before they start.** They told me it'll take about two days for the paint to completely dry. I think we should not use the archives for the next three days.

--------

W: 안녕하세요, Walker 씨. 오늘 오전에 있는 첫 번째 예약 손님의 진찰 기록부가 있나요? 그 환자 이름은 Rhonda Morgan이에요.

M: 네, 당신 책상 위에 있어요. 오늘 예약 손님들의 모든 자료는 그 곳에 두었어요. 그녀의 자료가 첫 번째 자료일 겁니다.

W: 아, 큰 도움을 주셨네요. 감사해요.

M: 천만에요. 아, 페인트칠 하는 분들이 오늘 병원 기록 보관소를 작업할 거라서, 그 분들이 작업하기 전에 제가 모든 서류 자료들을 밖으로 꺼내 놨습니다. 페인트가 완전히 마르는 데 2일 정도 걸릴 것이라고 하네요. 앞으로 3일 정도는 자료실을 사용하면 안 될 것 같아요.

**53.** 여자는 어떤 업종에서 근무하는가?
(A) 세탁소
(B) 서점
(C) 페인트 업체
(D) 병원　　　　　　　　　　　　　　정답 (D)

**54.** 여자는 남자에게 무엇을 요청하는가?
(A) 특정 파일
(B) 서류철의 가격
(C) 추적 번호
(D) 환자의 이름　　　　　　　　　　　정답 (A)

**55.** 남자가 모든 서류 자료를 꺼내 놓은 이유는 무엇인가?
(A) 오늘 예약이 많다.
(B) 컴퓨터실을 이용할 수가 없다.
(C) 일부 직원들이 자료를 백업할 것이다.
(D) 곧 보수작업이 시작될 것이다.　　　정답 (D)

**문제 56-58번은 다음 대화를 참조하시오.** 미W 미M

W: Hello. This is Mina Jackson, the building manager. I just received your text message about a problem in your office.

M: Thank you for calling back so quickly. **(56) There's a damp patch on the ceiling in my office, and it seems to be getting bigger.**

W: **(56) Actually, the maintenance team is currently repairing a leaky sink in the restaurant above your office.** This problem should be resolved soon. So you don't have to worry about that.

M: Oh, I see. **(57) Do you think the maintenance workers could take a look at my ceiling after they finish the repairs?** I just want to make sure that this hasn't caused any structural damage to my office.

W: No problem. **(58) I'll send them down to check your ceiling. Is there anything else I can do for you?**

M: **(58) That's all.** Thank you for your concern.

--------------------------------------

W: 안녕하세요. 저는 건물 관리인 Mina Jackson입니다. 사무실에 발생한 문제점에 대한 당신의 문자 메시지를 방금 받았어요.

M: 이렇게 빨리 연락 주셔서 감사합니다. 제 사무실 천장에 젖은 부분이 있는데, 그 부분이 점점 확장되는 것 같아요.

W: 사실 저희 시설 관리팀이 현재 그 사무실 위층에 있는 식당에서 물이 새고 있는 싱크대를 수리하고 있습니다. 그 문제는 곧 해결될 겁니다. 그러니 걱정하지 않으셔도 됩니다.

M: 아, 알겠습니다. 수리가 마무리된 후에 시설 관리팀 직원들이 제 사무실 천장도 한 번 봐주실 수 있을까요? 이 일이 제 사무실에 구조적인 문제를 일으키지 않았는지 확실히 하고 싶어서요.

W: 물론이에요. 제가 그들을 보내서 당신 사무실의 천장도 살펴보도록 할게요. 제가 도와드릴 만한 또 다른 일이 있을까요?

M: 그게 전부예요. 걱정해 주셔서 감사드립니다.

**56.** 화자들은 어떤 문제에 대해 이야기하고 있는가?
(A) 파손된 사무실
(B) 새로운 레스토랑
(C) 건물 보수 공사 계획
(D) 배관 문제　　　　　　　　　　정답 (D)

**57.** 남자가 여자에게 원하는 것은 무엇인가?
(A) 오래된 부엌 싱크대를 교체한다.
(B) 전액 환불한다.
(C) 새로운 사무실로 이사한다.
(D) 천장을 검사한다.　　　　　　　정답 (D)

**58.** 남자가 "That's all."이라고 말할 때 의미하는 바는 무엇인가?
(A) 그는 자신이 원하는 사무실을 선택했다.
(B) 그는 이미 자신이 가지고 있는 모든 것을 줬다.
(C) 그는 다른 원하는 것이 없다.
(D) 그는 파손된 기계를 자신이 직접 수리했다.　정답 (C)

**문제 59-61번은 다음 대화를 참조하시오.** 미M 영W

M: Rachel, **(59) have you finalized the training budget for next year?** The deadline is this Friday. We can't afford to miss it.

W: **(60) I'm almost done, but I'm still waiting for Matt Salinger in Human Resources to confirm some numbers.**

He's working on a training program for new employees. I can't submit the budget report until he checks all of the numbers.

M: **(61) Let me talk to Frank Marshall, who Matt reports to,** to see if he can expedite the process since Matt is caught up with some other work. Frank can sort out his priorities for him, and then, hopefully, we can nail down those numbers quickly.

--------------------------------------

M: Rachel, 내년 연수 예산을 마무리했나요? 마감시한이 이번주 금요일이에요. 마감시한을 넘겨선 안 될 텐데요.

W: 거의 다 했는데 인사과의 Matt Salinger 씨가 몇 가지 수치를 확인해주길 기다리고 있어요. 그가 신입직원들을 위한 연수 프로그램에 대한 작업을 하고 있거든요. 그의 수치 확인 없이는 예산 보고서를 제출할 수가 없어요.

M: 제가 Matt의 상사인 Frank Marshall 씨에게 이야기해서 Matt가 다른 업무를 처리해야 하니 지금 하고 있는 일을 그가 신속히 처리해줄 수 있는지 여부에 대해서 물어볼게요. Frank가 그를 위해서 우선적으로 처리해야할 업무를 분류해 주고 나면 아마도 우리가 그 수치들을 빠르게 확정할 수 있을 것이라고 봐요.

**59.** 대화의 주제는 무엇인가?
(A) 시장 자료를 분석하는 것
(B) 발표하는 것
(C) 회의 일정을 잡는 것
(D) 시간에 맞춰 예산안을 제출하는 것　정답 (D)

**60.** 여자가 언급하는 내용은 무엇인가?
(A) 그녀는 오늘밤 늦게까지 일한다.
(B) 그녀의 보고서가 아직 마무리되지 않았다.
(C) 그녀는 금요일에 연수를 받을 것이다.
(D) 그녀의 보고서는 마케팅 활동에 대한 것이다.　정답 (B)

**61.** Frank Marshall은 누구일 것 같은가?
(A) Rachel의 전 고용주
(B) Matt의 부하 직원
(C) Rachel의 부서장
(D) Matt의 직속 상사　　　　　　　정답 (D)

**문제 62-64번은 다음 대화와 메뉴를 참조하시오.** 호M 영W

M: Hello! Welcome to the Farm Bistro. Are you ready to order, or do you need some more time to decide what to eat?

W: Well, **(62) one of my colleagues recommended this place to me since your restaurant serves good vegetarian dishes. (63) Actually, she recommended the watermelon salad, but I can't find it on the menu.**

M: **(63) We only have that in the summer.** Our menu usually changes depending on the availability of ingredients during each season.

W: That's good to know. Hmm... What would you recommend then?

M: **(64) I think the potato salad would be great for you.** Our chefs make it every day, and most customers love it. It can also help you stay healthy during these cold days.

W: Um... **(64) Okay. I think I'll try it.** Thank you for your recommendation. Ah... **(64) Please get me a glass of lemonade first.**

--------------------------------------

M: 안녕하세요! Farm Bistro에 오신 걸 환영합니다. 주문할 준비가 되셨나

요, 아니면 주문하기 위한 시간이 더 필요하신가요?

W: 음, 제 동료 한 사람이 이 레스토랑에서 훌륭한 채식주의자 식단을 제공한다고 제게 추천을 해주더군요. 사실 그녀는 수박 샐러드를 추천했는데 메뉴판에서는 찾을 수가 없네요.

M: 수박 샐러드는 여름에만 제공합니다. 저희 메뉴는 대개 제철 재료의 가용성에 따라 바뀝니다.

W: 알겠습니다. 음… 그러면 무엇을 추천해주실 수 있나요?

M: 감자 샐러드가 고객님께 적절할 것으로 생각됩니다. 저희 요리사들이 감자 샐러드를 매일 만드는데 대부분의 손님들이 감자 샐러드를 좋아하세요. 또한 감자 샐러드는 요즘처럼 쌀쌀할 때 건강을 유지할 수 있도록 도움을 주는 음식입니다.

W: 음… 좋아요. 감자 샐러드를 한 번 먹어볼게요. 추천에 감사드려요. 아… 먼저 레모네이드 한 잔 주세요.

---

## Farm Bistro
### 오늘 점심 메뉴!

---

#### 음료

탄산음료 – $1.00
커피 – $1.50
(64) 레모네이드 – $2.00
녹차 – $2.50

---

#### 주 요리

사과 샐러드 – $5.00
(64) 감자 샐러드 – $6.00
참치 샌드위치 – $8.00

---

**62.** 여자의 동료가 Farm Bistro를 추천한 이유는 무엇인가?
(A) 명성이 높다.
(B) 교통이 좋은 곳에 위치하고 있다.
(C) 훌륭한 채식주의자 식단을 보유하고 있다.
(D) 하루 특정 시간대에 저렴한 가격으로 제공한다.　　정답 (C)

**63.** 남자가 수박 샐러드에 관해 언급한 것은 무엇인가?
(A) 여름에만 제공된다.
(B) 새로 개발된 메뉴이다.
(C) 주방장 특선 요리 중 하나이다.
(D) 오직 전채로만 제공된다.　　정답 (A)

**64.** 그래픽을 보시오. 여자의 식사 비용은 얼마인가?
(A) $5.00
(B) $6.00
(C) $7.00
(D) $8.00　　정답 (D)

**문제 65–67번은 다음 대화와 목록을 참조하시오.** Ⓜ Ⓦ

M: Hello. I'm looking for an Internet provider. I'd like to find out about your service plans.

W: Certainly. We offer the best prices in the area. As you can see from this chart, the longer the contract, the lower the cost.

M: **(65) What if I want to cancel the contract ahead of the agreed-upon date?**

W: **(65) We would charge you a penalty according to our policy.**

---

M: Um… Actually, **(66/67) I'm going to transfer overseas in about half a year, so I need a six-month plan.** But I want the lowest possible price.

W: All right. We can do that for you. Would you like to sign a contract right now?

M: No problem. Let's do that.

---

M: 안녕하세요. 저는 인터넷 공급 업체를 찾고 있습니다. 귀사의 인터넷 서비스 요금제에 대해 알고 싶습니다.

W: 알겠습니다. 저희는 이 지역에서 가장 저렴한 가격을 제공합니다. 이 표에서 알 수 있듯이 계약 기간이 길어질수록 이용 요금은 낮아집니다.

M: 만약 제가 약정된 날짜 이전에 계약을 취소하길 원하면요?

W: 저희 회사 정책에 따라 위약금을 청구하게 됩니다.

M: 음… 사실 저는 약 6개월 후에 해외로 전근을 갈 예정이라서 6개월만 인터넷 서비스가 필요합니다. 하지만 가능한 최저 가격을 원해요.

W: 괜찮습니다. 그렇게 해드릴 수 있습니다. 지금 계약서에 서명하시겠습니까?

M: 물론입니다. 그렇게 하죠.

---

| 인터넷 서비스 요금제 | 서비스 요금 |
|---|---|
| 분기 요금제 | $21.00 |
| (67) 6개월 요금제 | $30.00 |
| 1년 요금제 | $38.00 |
| 2년 요금제 | $65.00 |

**65.** 추가 비용이 부과되는 때는 언제인가?
(A) 고객이 새로운 지역으로 이사할 때
(B) 계약이 일찍 해지될 때
(C) 월 사용료 지불이 연체될 때
(D) 새로운 선택사항이 원래 요금제에 추가될 때　　정답 (B)

**66.** 남자에 따르면 6개월 후에 어떠한 일이 발생하는가?
(A) 그는 출장을 간다.
(B) 계약이 갱신된다.
(C) 그는 해외로 간다.
(D) 새로운 인터넷 시스템이 개발된다.　　정답 (C)

**67.** 그래픽을 보시오. 남자는 그의 서비스 비용으로 얼마를 지불할 것 같은가?
(A) $21
(B) $30
(C) $38
(D) $65　　정답 (B)

**문제 68–70번은 다음 대화와 일정표를 참조하시오.** Ⓦ Ⓜ

W: Hi, George. **(68) I hear the condominium renovations are moving along pretty well.** Are there any problems that you can foresee?

M: It is an old house, but it doesn't have any major structural problems. Since we started working, a lot of progress has been made.

W: Sounds good. I want to put this property on the market in the beginning of May. Actually, it's the most appropriate time to sell a house. Could you get this work done by then?

M: I need to check my calendar. Hmm. Let me see. **(69) We just completed the floor installation. We start painting next week.** Yes, I'm confident we will be done by the end of April.

W: That's fantastic, George. (70) **Could you send me a rough estimate of your total expenses?** I need it for potential buyers' questions even before the renovations are complete. I need to come up with a price for the house.

---

W: 안녕하세요, George. 콘도미니엄 보수 공사가 꽤 잘 진행되고 있다고 들었어요. 예상되는 문제가 있나요?

M: 집이 오래됐긴 합니다만 큰 구조적인 문제는 없어요. 우리가 공사를 시작한 이후로 많은 진전이 있었습니다.

W: 좋아요. 저는 이 콘도미니엄을 5월 초에 매각하고 싶어요. 사실 그 때가 집을 팔 수 있는 최적의 시기죠. 그 때까지 작업을 마무리해주실 수 있나요?

M: 제가 일정을 확인해 볼게요. 음. 어디 보자. 우리가 막 바닥재 설치를 완료했어요. 다음주에는 페인트칠을 할 겁니다. 네, 4월 말까지는 작업이 다 끝날 것이라고 확신합니다.

W: 정말 좋습니다, George. 전체 공사비의 견적을 보내주시겠어요? 보수 공사가 완료되기 전에라도 집을 구매하고자 하는 잠재 고객들을 위해 필요해요. 집의 매매가를 생각해야 하거든요.

## 보수 공사 일정

| | |
|---|---|
| 1주차 | 전기 배선 |
| 2주차 | 바닥재 설치 |
| (69) 3주차 | 내부 도색 |
| 4주차 | 외부 도색 |

**68.** 남자의 직업은 무엇일 것 같은가?
(A) 공사 관리자
(B) 창고 직원
(C) 철물점 주인
(D) 건축가 　　　　　　　　　　　　　정답 (A)

**69.** 그래픽을 보시오. 다음주에 몇 주차 보수공사가 시작되는가?
(A) 1주차
(B) 2주차
(C) 3주차
(D) 4주차 　　　　　　　　　　　　　정답 (C)

**70.** 남자에게 요청되는 것은 무엇인가?
(A) 비용 목록을 보낸다.
(B) 새로운 홈페이지를 디자인한다.
(C) 초청장을 작성한다.
(D) 여자 대신 다음주에 근무한다. 　　　정답 (A)

## Part 4

문제 71-73번은 다음 전화 메시지를 참조하시오. 미W

Hello, Mr. Baker. This is Jenna Williams from AT&C, your Internet service provider. (71/72) **I'm calling to let you know that your Internet connection will be shut down on Monday and Tuesday due to regular maintenance work.** (73) **Of course, you and your employees will be able to access our wireless Internet service, but there will be some problems with its speed.** I'm really sorry for the inconvenience this may cause you and your staff. We will restore your Internet connection as

---

soon as possible. If you have any questions, please call me at 420-0909. Thank you for your cooperation in advance.

---

안녕하세요, Baker 씨. 저는 고객님의 인터넷 서비스 제공업체인 AT&C의 Jenna Williams라고 합니다. 월요일과 화요일에 정기 보수 작업으로 인해 인터넷 연결이 차단될 것임을 알려 드리고자 연락을 드렸습니다. 물론 고객님과 고객님의 직원들은 저희 무선 인터넷 서비스에 접속하실 수 있습니다만, 속도에 문제가 있을 것입니다. 이로 인해 고객님과 고객님의 직원들에게 불편함을 드리게 된 점 죄송하게 생각합니다. 최대한 빨리 인터넷을 복구시키도록 하겠습니다. 궁금한 점이 있으시면 420-0909로 연락 주십시오. 고객님의 협조에 미리 감사의 말씀을 전합니다.

**71.** 여자가 전화한 이유는 무엇인가?
(A) 정보를 전달하기 위해서
(B) 계약을 종료하기 위해서
(C) 예약을 확인하기 위해서
(D) 새로운 무선 인터넷을 광고하기 위해서 　정답 (A)

**72.** 화자에 따르면 작업에 소요되는 시간은 얼마나 되는가?
(A) 1일
(B) 2일
(C) 3일
(D) 일주일 　　　　　　　　　　　　　정답 (B)

**73.** 무선 네트워크와 관련된 문제점은 무엇인가?
(A) 조만간 차단될 것이다.
(B) 속도가 느리다.
(C) 복잡한 장비가 필요하다.
(D) 사용료가 여전히 비싸다. 　　　　　정답 (B)

문제 74-76번은 다음 담화를 참조하시오. 영W

Hello. This is Lisa Fredrick, the accounting manager. (74) **I'd like to inform you that there has been a change in the way travel reimbursements will be handled.** (75) **Management has asked for reports detailing the types of expenditures made while traveling for work.** So our current forms are no longer sufficient. (76) **Now, before you travel, you must log your trip in on an online form. The business travel expenses you'd like to be reimbursed must be entered into the intranet system no later than five days after you return.** In addition, they must be accompanied by uploaded images of your original receipts. Thank you for your understanding and cooperation in advance.

---

안녕하세요. 저는 회계부장인 Lisa Fredrick입니다. 여러분께 출장비용 처리 방식에 대한 변경 사항을 알려드리고자 합니다. 경영진에서는 업무로 인한 출장 동안 소요되는 비용을 종류별로 자세하게 밝히는 보고서를 요청해 왔습니다. 따라서 현재 서류 양식만으로는 불충분하게 되었습니다. 이제는 출장에 앞서 온라인 서류 양식에 여러분의 출장을 입력해야 합니다. 환급을 받고자 하는 출장 비용은 출장에서 복귀한 후 늦어도 5일 이내에 사내 전산망 시스템에 입력해야 합니다. 아울러 비용과 함께 필히 영수증 원본들에 대한 이미지 파일이 첨부되어야만 합니다. 여러분의 이해와 협조에 미리 감사의 말씀을 전합니다.

**74.** 담화의 주제는 무엇인가?
(A) 출장 예산
(B) 인터넷 접속

(C) 회사의 새로운 방침
(D) 회사 이전                                                    정답 (C)

**75.** 화자에 따르면 회사는 무엇을 알고 싶어 하는가?
(A) 주문 현황
(B) 새로운 출장 방침
(C) 비용에 관한 상세한 정보
(D) 회계 기준                                                    정답 (C)

**76.** 화자가 청자들에게 요청하는 것은 무엇인가?
(A) 그들의 자료 정확성을 향상시킨다.
(B) 관련 정보를 시스템에 입력한다.
(C) 회사 행사에 일찍 도착한다.
(D) 휴가 여행의 영수증을 보관한다.                              정답 (B)

---

문제 77-79번은 다음 담화를 참조하시오. 미M

(77) **If you haven't noticed, we are in the process of expanding the parking lots and improving the parking payment system.** By this time next month, all employees will be assigned a parking permit and a permanent parking space. Each permit will contain a photo of the employee and a description of their vehicle. (78) **But here's the thing.** (78/79) **Please make sure everyone in your department completes the appropriate forms by Friday.** We'll have permits made and distributed about a week before the new lots open. Any late forms will result in delays.

- - - - - - - - - - - - - - - - - - - - - - - - - - - - - -

만약 여러분이 모르고 계셨다면 우리가 현재 주차장을 확장하고 주차 요금 지불 시스템을 개선하는 과정에 있다는 것을 알아 두십시오. 다음달 이 때쯤이면 모든 직원들에게 주차 허가증과 계속해서 사용할 수 있는 주차 공간이 할당될 것입니다. 주차 허가증에는 직원의 사진과 차량에 대한 내용이 포함될 것입니다. 하지만 중요한 건 이겁니다. 여러분의 부서에 있는 모든 직원들이 금요일까지 해당 서류를 작성할 수 있도록 해주십시오. 새로운 주차장이 개장되기에 앞서 대략 일주일 전에 주차 허가증이 제작되어 배포되도록 할 것입니다. 서류를 늦게 제출하면 그만큼 주차 허가증을 발급받는 것이 지연될 것입니다.

**77.** 화자는 무엇에 관해 논의하고 있는가?
(A) 새로운 주차 관리자
(B) 효과적인 급여 지급 체계
(C) 개선된 주차 시설
(D) 많은 서류 작업                                              정답 (C)

**78.** 화자가 "But here's the thing."이라고 말할 때 의미하는 바는 무엇인가?
(A) 그는 고려해야 할 사항을 소개할 것이다.
(B) 그는 논란이 되는 문제점을 지적할 것이다.
(C) 그는 회사의 부실한 서비스에 대해 불만을 제기할 것이다.
(D) 그는 사람들이 가지고 싶어 하는 것을 보여줄 것이다.          정답 (A)

**79.** 청자들이 이번주 후반까지 하도록 요청 받는 것은 무엇인가?
(A) 새로운 허가증을 수령한다.
(B) 새로운 은행 계좌를 개설한다.
(C) 서류를 작성한다.
(D) 보험 증서를 제출할 준비를 한다.                             정답 (C)

---

문제 80-82번은 다음 전화 메시지를 참조하시오. 미W

Hello. I'm calling to leave a message for Mr. Ryan. (80) **This is Lisa Wick from Marlowe's Carpet and Flooring.** We were scheduled to deliver and install some carpeting in your store early tomorrow morning, (81) **but during the thunderstorm this morning, a telephone pole and an electric transformer came down, and they are blocking the road from our factory.** We simply can't move our trucks until the pole and the transformer are cleared. I'm sorry for the inconvenience; I hope it doesn't affect your business. (82) **Please call me when you get this message** and we can reschedule a time convenient for you. (82) **You know my cell phone number.** Thank you.

- - - - - - - - - - - - - - - - - - - - - - - - - - - - - -

안녕하세요. Ryan 씨를 위한 메시지를 남기고 있습니다. 저는 Marlowe's Carpet and Flooring의 Lisa Wick입니다. 저희가 내일 오전 일찍 귀하의 상점에 카펫을 배송하고 설치할 예정이었지만, 오늘 아침에 뇌우가 일어났을 때 전신주가 넘어지고 전기 변압기가 떨어져서 공장에서 나가는 도로를 막았습니다. 전신주와 변압기가 치워질 때까지는 저희 트럭을 움직일 수가 없게 됐습니다. 불편을 끼쳐 드려 죄송합니다. 이 일이 고객님의 사업에 영향을 미치지 않기를 바랍니다. 이 메시지를 받고 제게 연락을 주시면 귀하에게 편한 시간을 다시 잡아드리겠습니다. 제 휴대전화 번호 아시죠. 감사합니다.

**80.** 화자는 어느 업체에서 근무하는가?
(A) 전자회사
(B) 인터넷 서비스 제공업체
(C) 카펫 제조회사
(D) 운송회사                                                    정답 (C)

**81.** 여자가 "They are blocking the road from our factory."라고 말할 때 의미하는 바는 무엇인가?
(A) 그녀는 공장을 가동시킬 수가 없다.
(B) 그녀는 다른 길로 우회할 것이다.
(C) 그녀는 트럭을 수리해야 한다.
(D) 그녀는 제때 주문품을 배송할 수가 없다.                      정답 (D)

**82.** 화자가 청자에게 제안하는 것은 무엇인가?
(A) 주문을 취소한다.
(B) 그녀의 휴대전화로 연락한다.
(C) 늦은 배송에 따른 비용을 지불한다.
(D) 두 제품의 가격을 비교한다.                                  정답 (B)

---

문제 83-85번은 다음 전화 메시지를 참조하시오. 영W

Hi. This is Phoebe Kates at Baybrook Medical calling for Mr. Foster. (83/84) **I want to confirm your appointment for physical therapy at 3 P.M. on June 3.** (84) **The therapy can be strenuous, so please be sure to wear comfortable clothes and to eat a solid lunch.** If you have any questions about what the appointment will entail, don't hesitate to call us during regular business hours. Before you visit, (85) **could you call your medical insurance company and have someone there fax us your latest information?** That needs to be updated before you begin treatment. Thank you and have a nice day.

- - - - - - - - - - - - - - - - - - - - - - - - - - - - - -

안녕하세요. 저는 Baybrook 병원의 Phoebe Kates라고 하며 Foster 씨에게 연락을 드립니다. 6월 3일 오후 3시로 예정되어 있는 물리치료 예약을 확인하고자 합니다. 물리치료는 힘이 많이 드니 편한 복장으로 점심식사를 든든히 하고 내원해 주시길 당부드립니다. 예약과 관련된 질문이 있다면 주저하지 마시고 업무 시간에 저희에게 연락을 주십시오. 내원하기 전에 의료보험 회사에 연락을 해서 귀하의 최근 의료보험 관련 정보를 저희에게 팩스로 보내주도록 처리해주실 수 있겠습니까? 치료를 시작하기 전에 귀하의 관련 정보를 갱신하는 데 필요합니다. 감사합니다. 좋은 하루 되세요.

**83.** 화자가 전화한 이유는 무엇인가?
(A) 그녀의 주소록을 갱신하기 위해서
(B) 예약을 확인하기 위해서
(C) 보험에 가입하기 위해서
(D) 주문 내역을 변경하기 위해서        정답 (B)

**84.** Foster 씨는 6월 3일에 무엇을 해야 하는가?
(A) 점심을 잘 먹는다.
(B) 그의 예약을 확인한다.
(C) 보험 정보를 갱신한다.
(D) 몇몇 서류를 작성한다.        정답 (A)

**85.** 화자가 청자에게 요청하는 것은 무엇인가?
(A) 규칙적으로 운동한다.
(B) 이전 병력을 확인한다.
(C) 팩스 번호를 알려준다.
(D) 그의 보험 정보를 발송한다.        정답 (D)

---

문제 86-88번은 다음 광고를 참조하시오. [M][W]

(86) The Fitness Center of Stockton is a 60,000-square-foot medically integrated facility that features state-of-the-art equipment along with a staff of degreed health professionals. We provide all the education and support you'll need to make a lasting commitment to your health. (87) With more than 120 machines, you are certain to find something that suits your needs. That's why we are the top fitness center in the Stockton city area. The Fitness Center of Stockton is also conveniently located near Stockton Bart Station. Anyone who signs up for a one-year membership will save 25% off the regular price. (88) We'll work to enhance your healthy lifestyle for today and the future. You won't be disappointed at all.

---

Fitness Center of Stockton은 6만 평방 피트의 크기의 의료 통합 시설로 최첨단 장비 뿐만 아니라 학위를 보유한 보건 전문가들이 있습니다. 저희는 여러분이 꾸준히 건강을 유지하기 위해 필요한 모든 교육과 지원을 제공합니다. 120개가 넘는 기계를 보유하고 있어서 여러분의 필요에 맞는 장비를 확실히 찾으실 수 있습니다. 그것이 바로 저희가 Stockton 시 지역에서 가장 우수한 헬스클럽인 이유입니다. Fitness Center of Stockton은 또한 Stockton Bart 역 근처에 위치하여 교통 접근성이 좋습니다. 1년 회원권을 등록하면 정가의 25% 할인 혜택을 받으시게 됩니다. 현재와 미래에 여러분의 건강한 삶을 향상시켜 드리고자 노력할 것입니다. 절대 실망하지 않으실 겁니다.

**86.** 화자는 어떤 업종에서 근무하는가?
(A) 병원
(B) 부동산 중개업체
(C) 헬스 클럽

(D) 케이블 TV 회사        정답 (C)

**87.** 화자에 따르면 이 업체는 무엇으로 유명한가?
(A) 혁신적인 제품
(B) 전문 의사
(C) 적절한 가격
(D) 다양한 장비        정답 (D)

**88.** 화자가 "You won't be disappointed at all."이라고 말할 때 의미하는 바는 무엇인가?
(A) 신제품의 품질이 좋다.
(B) 사람들은 고수익에 만족하고 있다.
(C) 고객들은 건강한 삶을 살 것이다.
(D) 몇몇 문제점들은 재발하지 않을 것이다.        정답 (C)

---

문제 89-91번은 다음 담화를 참조하시오. [M]

Good evening and thank you for making time in your busy schedules for this extra board meeting. (89/90) Now, I'd like to introduce the newest board member, Daniel Stevens. (90) Mr. Stevens has been the international sales director for Beagle Heavy Industries here in Atlanta for the last 10 years. He will be the vice president after Ms. Campbell leaves next month. We are very lucky to have Mr. Stevens as the vice president, and we expect he will be a tremendous asset (91) as we expand into three new foreign markets next year. Mr. Stevens will also be leading the aggressive advertising campaign for our new line of products. Now, here is Mr. Stevens. Let's give him a big round of applause.

---

안녕하십니까, 바쁜 일정에도 불구하고 시간을 내어 추가 소집된 이사회에 참석해주신 점에 감사드립니다. 이제 새롭게 이사회의 일원이 된 Daniel Stevens 씨를 소개하고자 합니다. Stevens 씨는 이 곳 Atlanta에 있는 Beagle Heavy Industries에서 최근 10년간 해외영업 담당 이사로 근무해왔습니다. 그는 다음달에 Campbell 씨가 퇴사한 후 부사장 직을 맡게 될 것입니다. Stevens 씨를 부사장으로 모시게 되어 행운이며 내년에 세 곳의 새로운 해외시장으로 사업을 확장하게 되면서 그가 큰 도움이 될 것이라고 기대하고 있습니다. Stevens 씨는 또한 우리 신제품을 위한 적극적인 광고 캠페인을 이끌게 될 것입니다. 자, Stevens 씨입니다. 그에게 큰 박수 갈채를 보내주시기 바랍니다.

**89.** 담화의 목적은 무엇인가?
(A) 채용 계획을 발표하기 위해서
(B) 부서장들에게 회의 일정을 상기시키기 위해서
(C) 새로운 이사회의 일원을 소개하기 위해서
(D) 새로운 사업 확장 계획의 개요를 전달하기 위해서        정답 (C)

**90.** Daniel Stevens 씨는 어떤 분야의 경험을 보유하고 있는가?
(A) 마케팅
(B) 홍보
(C) 해외영업
(D) 인사        정답 (C)

**91.** 화자에 따르면 회사는 내년에 무엇을 할 것인가?
(A) 더 많은 직원들을 채용할 것이다.
(B) 새로운 공장을 건설할 것이다.
(C) 해외시장을 개척할 것이다.
(D) 적극적인 광고를 시작할 것이다.        정답 (C)

Good morning, everyone. (92/93) **I'd like to remind you all that the new tablet computers have arrived, and the technical support team is conducting a performance test on the new computerized shipping system now.** You should bring the tablets with you on every delivery just like you do with your clipboards. Every delivery should be logged into the application program, and there should also be an electronic signature from the customer and a timestamp from you. (94) **The tablets will be ready to use on Sunday, so please be sure to read the instruction manual thoroughly before then.** Any questions should be directed to your supervisor. Thank you and have a good day.

안녕하세요, 여러분. 새로운 태블릿 컴퓨터들이 도착해서 현재 기술지원팀이 새롭게 전산화된 배송 시스템에 대한 성능 테스트 중임을 알려드리고자 합니다. 이 태블릿은 매번 배송할 때마다 여러분의 클립보드처럼 가지고 다니셔야 합니다. 모든 배송은 응용 프로그램에 접속이 이루어져야 하며, 또한 고객으로부터 전자서명을 받고 여러분이 발송 날짜 및 시간을 기록해야 합니다. 이 태블릿은 일요일부터 사용할 준비가 될 것이므로 그 이전에 필히 사용 설명서를 꼼꼼하게 읽으셔야만 합니다. 질문이 있으면 여러분의 상사에게 해주시면 되겠습니다. 감사드리고 좋은 하루 되십시오.

**92.** 화자는 무엇에 관해 언급하는가?
(A) 새로운 안전 시스템
(B) 경영 연수 프로그램
(C) 수정된 배송 경로
(D) 새로운 기술의 채택 　　　　　정답 (D)

**93.** 화자는 어디에서 근무할 것 같은가?
(A) 이삿짐 회사
(B) 소프트웨어 개발 회사
(C) 택배 회사
(D) 컴퓨터 제조 공장 　　　　　정답 (C)

**94.** 청자들은 일요일 전에 무엇을 해야 하는가?
(A) 사용 설명서를 읽는다.
(B) 책을 구매한다.
(C) 소프트웨어를 설치한다.
(D) 일부 장비를 반납한다. 　　　　　정답 (A)

May I have your attention, please? (95) **Due to a severe storm coming ashore, all of our ferry operations have been suspended.** However, the storm is quickly moving off the coast, and (96) **we expect to resume operations for the last departure of the day.** When we announce the boarding call in a little while, we will be opening the upper deck of the ferry to accommodate all the extra passengers. (97) **Because of the strong winds from the river, you may feel very cold up there, so we highly recommend that you wear a jacket.** We apologize for any inconvenience caused. Thank you for your understanding and cooperation.

주목해 주시겠습니까? 해변에 상륙한 강한 폭풍으로 인해 저희 모든 여객선 운항이 중단된 상태입니다. 하지만 폭풍이 빠르게 해변을 벗어나고 있으므

로 마지막 여객선 출발이 재개될 것으로 예상되고 있습니다. 조금 있다가 탑승 안내방송을 할 때 추가 승객들을 모두 탑승시키기 위해서 여객선 상단 갑판 문을 개방할 것입니다. 강바람이 강한 탓에 상단 갑판에서 추위를 느끼실 수도 있으니 재킷 착용을 적극 권장합니다. 불편을 끼쳐드린 점 사과드립니다. 여러분의 이해와 협조에 감사드립니다.

### Richmond Island 여객선 시간표

| 출발 시각 | 도착 시각 |
|---|---|
| 오전 8:30 | 오전 9:00 |
| 오전 10:00 | 오전 10:30 |
| 오후 7:00 | 오후 7:30 |
| (96) 오후 9:30 | 오후 10:00 |

**95.** 운항 중단을 초래한 것은 무엇인가?
(A) 기술적인 문제
(B) 승무원 부족
(C) 악천후
(D) 탑승 과정상의 문제 　　　　　정답 (C)

**96.** 그래픽을 보시오. 여객선은 언제 출발할 것인가?
(A) 오전 8시 30분
(B) 오전 10시
(C) 오후 7시
(D) 오후 9시 30분 　　　　　정답 (D)

**97.** 화자가 청자들에게 권고하는 것은 무엇인가?
(A) 두꺼운 옷을 입는다.
(B) 휴가를 간다.
(C) 나중에 출근한다.
(D) 영수증을 보관한다. 　　　　　정답 (A)

(98) **You are invited to the biggest sale at Zendar's Furniture!** Located behind the Destin Shopping Mall, Zendar's Furniture has been producing quality furniture for 20 years. (98) **To celebrate the 20th anniversary of our store, we will be offering all of our furniture**—that's right; all of it—at discounted prices for a whole week. (99) **Bring a copy of an anniversary pamphlet to receive an extra $20 discount on your purchase as well!** The schedule of this historical sale event is written on the anniversary pamphlets. From modern to classic furniture, we have it all. (100) **Due to a simple publishing mistake, the pamphlet indicates that glass furniture is on sale on Tuesday, but it's actually been mixed up with marble furniture. Please note that the two dates have been switched.**

Zendar's Furniture의 가장 큰 할인 행사에 초대합니다! Destin Shopping Mall 뒤에 위치한 Zendar's Furniture는 20년간 품질 좋은 가구를 생산해왔습니다. 저희 매장의 개장 20주년을 맞이하여 모든 가구, 그렇습니다, 말 그대로 모든 가구를 일주일 동안 할인가에 제공해 드립니다. 기념일 안내 팜플렛을 가지고 오시면 구매한 제품의 할인가에서 20달러를

추가 할인해 드립니다! 이 역대급 할인 행사의 일정은 기념일 팜플렛에 나와 있습니다. 현대식 가구에서 고전 기구에 이르기까지 저희는 모든 것을 구비하고 있습니다. 단순한 인쇄상의 실수로, 팜플렛에는 유리 가구에 대한 할인이 화요일로 예정되어 있다고 소개하고 있지만 대리석 가구에 대한 할인 일정과 뒤바뀌어 있습니다. 두 상품의 할인 날짜가 뒤바뀌어 있다는 점에 유의해 주시기 바랍니다.

## 주간 할인 프로그램

| 가구 종류 | 날짜 |
|---|---|
| 목재 가구 | 2월 21일 |
| (100) 유리 가구 | 2월 22일 |
| (100) 대리석 가구 | 2월 23일 |
| 철재 가구 | 2월 24일 |

**98.** 광고 중인 것은 무엇인가?
(A) 상업용 부동산
(B) 상점 이전
(C) 기념일 할인 행사
(D) 특별 회원가 　　　　　　　　정답 (C)

**99.** 청자들이 요청 받는 것은 무엇인가?
(A) 할인 일정을 확인하기 위해 상점에 연락한다.
(B) 쿠폰을 수령하기 위해 특정한 날에만 방문한다.
(C) 신분증을 가지고 온다.
(D) 추가 할인을 위해 안내책자를 제시한다. 　정답 (D)

**100.** 그래픽을 보시오. 대리석 가구에 대한 할인 행사는 언제인가?
(A) 2월 21일
(B) 2월 22일
(C) 2월 23일
(D) 2월 24일 　　　　　　　　정답 (B)

## Part 5

**101.** 올해 수상자는 Alabama에 있는 제조 공장에 대한 견학과 엄청난 상품을 받게 될 것이다. 　　　　　정답 (D)

**102.** 수익금의 일부는 노숙자와 배고픈 New York 사람들을 돕기 위해 지역 자선 단체에 기부될 것이다. 　　　　정답 (D)

**103.** Ruby & Kabi 가구는 지난 5년간 고객들에게 다양한 종류의 DIY 조립 형태의 가구를 제공해왔다. 　　　　정답 (D)

**104.** 새로운 London 지사 사무실에서 걸어갈 수 있는 거리에 뛰어나면서 독특한 몇몇 레스토랑들이 위치해 있다. 　　정답 (A)

**105.** 연간 상여금의 액수는 회사의 수익성에 따라 해마다 달라진다. 　정답 (B)

**106.** 폭풍과 우박이 떨어지는 악천후에도 불구하고 대부분의 부서장들이 어제 회의에 참석했다. 　　　　　정답 (D)

**107.** 몇몇 고객들은 Ryan 사가 제조한 신제품의 전반적인 품질에 실망했다. 　　　　　　정답 (B)

**108.** 중앙은행의 통화정책 위원회는 기준 금리를 변경하지 않기로 투표를 통해 만장일치로 결정했다. 　　　정답 (B)

**109.** 회사의 브랜드 이미지를 강화시키는 것은 유럽 시장에서 매출을 향상시킬 수 있는 가장 효과적인 방법들 중 하나이다. 　정답 (B)

**110.** 많은 요청으로 인해 수정된 시장 분석 보고서의 제출 마감시한은 1월 10일로 연장되었다. 　　　　정답 (D)

**111.** 새로운 세제 제품은 우리 연구진에 의해 철저하게 시험되었기 때문에 고객들이 사용하기에 완벽할 정도로 안전하다. 　정답 (B)

**112.** 정부는 감세가 경제를 다시 활성화시키고 현재의 불경기로부터 벗어나는 데 도움을 줄 것이라고 굳게 믿고 있다. 　정답 (B)

**113.** 조립 라인에서 근무하는 대부분의 직원들은 회사가 그들에게 고용보장과 의료보험 혜택을 약속한 후에 마침내 공장 이전 계획에 서명하였다. 　　　　정답 (C)

**114.** 이 적립 포인트는 Maxie 백화점에서 할인된 가격의 식사와 상품들로 교환할 수 있다. 　　　　정답 (B)

**115.** 이 가스전은 우리 회사가 최초로 상업적 가치를 지닌 천연 가스를 개발한 곳이다. 　　　　　정답 (D)

**116.** Komi International 사의 투자는 국내 금융계에서 유일한 대규모의 해외 직접 투자이다. 　　　　정답 (D)

**117.** 귀하의 이용에 감사하여 귀하가 온라인 혹은 매장에서 물건을 구매할 때 사용하실 수 있는 20% 할인 쿠폰을 제공하고자 합니다. 　정답 (D)

**118.** 타인을 배려하셔서 극장 내에서 다른 관객들과 무대에 있는 배우들에게 불편함을 초래할 수 있는 행동은 하지 않도록 해주십시오. 　정답 (D)

**119.** 지난 분기에 우리의 새로운 차종들이 출시된 이후 엄청난 인기를 끌어왔다. 　　　　　정답 (B)

**120.** 첨부된 것은 귀하의 특정한 척추 통증에 대한 철저한 진단에 필요한 정보를 제공하기 위해 제작된 설문지입니다. 　정답 (B)

**121.** 유명한 일부 기상학자들은 지구 기후변화 문제의 약 25%에 해당하는 책임은 산림 파괴에 있다고 말했다. 　정답 (B)

**122.** 한 국제 보건 기구에 의해 발표된 최근 보고서에 따르면, 지역과 국가별로 변이한 다양한 감기 바이러스들이 존재한다. 　정답 (C)

**123.** 만약 KBG Electronics 사의 순이익이 사장과 이사회의 기대치를 초과하면 직원들은 상당한 금액의 상여금을 받게 될 것이다. 　정답 (A)

**124.** 이 새로운 방법은 도서관의 규모와 복잡함을 상당히 줄여줄 뿐만 아니라 도서들과 참고자료들을 관리하기 위해 요구되는 사서들의 수도 감소시킬 것이다. 　　　　정답 (D)

**125.** 건축 자재의 모든 파손은 파손이 발생한 지 24시간 이내에 공사 관리자에게 곧바로 보고되어야 한다. 　　　정답 (B)

**126.** 독립적으로 일하는 것을 선호하는 직원들도 있고 동료들과 함께 일할 때 더 잘하는 직원들도 있다. 　　　정답 (C)

**127.** 가장 중요한 문제는 우리 회사가 한국 시장으로 얼마나 빨리 진출할 수 있는지 여부이다. 정답 (B)

**128.** Winters 씨는 관리직을 제안 받았지만 더 많은 돈을 벌 수 있는 곳을 찾기 때문에 이를 거절했다. 정답 (C)

**129.** GE Technology 사는 새로운 컴퓨터 소프트웨어가 대부분의 컴퓨터 운영 시스템들과 호환이 가능하다고 주장하지만 일부 고객들은 그렇지 않다고 말한다. 정답 (C)

**130.** 곧 있을 국제 비즈니스 회의의 모든 참석자들은 Top 호텔이나 President 호텔 중 더 쾌적하고 편리한 곳에서 숙박할 수 있다. 정답 (D)

## Part 6

**문제 131-134번은 다음 편지를 참조하시오.**

Hwang 씨께,

이 편지는 제가 현 직책에서 사임할 것임을 뜻하는 공식 통지로 받아주시길 바랍니다. 2주 전 통지가 표준 규정임은 알고 있습니다. 하지만 가능하다면 회사와의 고용 계약을 가능한 빨리 해지해 주시면 감사하겠습니다. 만약 제 후임자를 교육시키거나 업무 인수인계가 용이하도록 하기 위해 도움을 드릴 수 있다면 기꺼이 그렇게 하겠습니다.

지난 7년간 전문적이고 개인적인 발전을 이룰 수 있도록 제게 제공해주신 기회들에 대해 고마움을 표현하고 싶습니다. 저는 회사에서 즐겁게 근무했으며 재직하는 동안 지원해 주신 점에 감사드립니다. 제 마지막 근무 종료 일자와 관련된 답변을 듣길 기대합니다.

James Taylor
해외 영업부장

**131.** (A) 2주 전 통지가 표준 규정임은 알고 있습니다.
(B) 일부 직원들은 심하게 비난을 받고 결국 해고를 당했습니다.
(C) 귀하는 더 깊은 지식과 논리적인 사고 능력을 갖추게 될 것입니다.
(D) 저는 무역이 평화와 번영에 도움이 된다고 주장해왔습니다. 정답 (A)

**132.** 정답 (C)

**133.** 정답 (B)

**134.** 정답 (D)

**문제 135-138번은 다음 편지를 참조하시오.**

Winston 씨께:

저는 2월 1일에 Union City 통신사로부터 요금 징수 통고장을 수령했습니다. 편지에는 11월 16일부터 12월 15일까지의 미납금이 납부되지 않았다는 내용이 게재되어 있습니다. 이 편지는 아울러 제가 즉각적으로 조치를 취하지 않으면 휴대전화 서비스가 중단될 것임을 밝히고 있습니다. 그러나 저는 미납된 요금은 1월 10일에 납부했음을 두 번째로 알려드리고자 합니다.

저는 1월 18일에 이 문제와 관련하여 귀사의 직원으로부터 전화를 받았으며, 그에게 귀사로 미납액 46.92달러에 대한 수표를 발송했음을 알렸습니다. 안타깝게도 그의 이름을 기록해놓진 않았습니다. 저는 귀사가 이 문제를 제대로 처리하지 않음에 불쾌함을 느낍니다. 또한 그 때 보낸 수표의 사본을 여기에 동봉합니다.

이 문제가 이번에 최종적으로 처리되길 희망합니다.

John Kensington
(510) 692-3355
첨부: 수표 사본

**135.** 정답 (C)

**136.** 정답 (D)

**137.** 정답 (B)

**138.** (A) 이 판결은 다른 소송들을 초래할 것으로 예상되고 있습니다.
(B) 회사에서는 다음 달부터 월별 요금을 인하하기로 결정했습니다.
(C) 우리 시는 대형 휴대전화 서비스 제공업체들에 의해 충분한 서비스를 제공받고 있습니다.
(D) 이 문제가 이번에 최종적으로 처리되길 희망합니다. 정답 (D)

**문제 139-142번은 다음 이메일을 참조하시오.**

수신: Elizabeth Giles ⟨eg@eventspace.com⟩
발신: Robert Shaw ⟨rshaw@alphabusiness.com⟩
날짜: 10월 26일
제목: 컴퓨터 일일 수업

Giles 씨께,

회사에서 11월 10일 토요일에 컴퓨터 일일 수업을 열 예정입니다. 안타깝게도 본사에서 너무 많은 인원을 등록한 관계로 좀 더 넓은 공간을 찾아야 합니다.

저희는 적어도 16개의 전원 콘센트와 컴퓨터 장비를 설치할 수 있는 여러 개의 긴 테이블이 있는 대형 회의실이 필요합니다. 또한 50명 정도의 인원이 먹을 수 있는 점심 뷔페도 필요합니다.

저희와 유사한 수업으로 귀사의 시설을 이용해 본 다른 회사들로부터 많은 추천을 받았습니다. 그래서 귀사의 시설과 직원들이 최고라는 것도 알게 되었습니다. 이용 가능 여부와 가격을 논의하기 위해 저에게 편하신 시간에 전화해 주시기 바랍니다.

감사합니다.

Robert Shaw
인사부장
(610) 837-2454 / 내선번호 119

**139.** 정답 (D)

**140.** 정답 (D)

**141.** 정답 (A)

**142.** (A) 무엇이든 보수를 해야 할 필요가 있으면 저희에게 알려주세요.
(B) 학교 교육에 대한 공공 투자에 감사하고 있습니다.
(C) 이용 가능 여부와 가격을 논의하기 위해 저에게 편하신 시간에 전화해 주시기 바랍니다.
(D) 컴퓨터의 속도가 갈수록 빨라진다는 것은 더 이상 놀라운 일이 아닙니다. 정답 (C)

문제 143-146번은 다음 웹페이지를 참조하시오.

http:www.westerndairyguild.org

매년 Western Dairy Guild(서부 지역 낙농조합, WDG)는 낙농업의 발전을 위해 유제품을 위한 대규모 무역 박람회를 개최하고 낙농 기술과 과학에 관한 교육 포럼들을 실시하고 있습니다. 오늘날 대부분의 낙농가들이 최첨단 기술을 활용하는 덕분에 미국의 낙농업은 빠르게 성장하고 있습니다. 미국 서부 지역에서 생산되는 유가공 제품들은 그 품질을 국내와 해외에서 모두 인정받고 있습니다.

세계적으로 유명한 요리사들의 대부분도 오랫동안 이 지역에서 생산되는 유제품을 사용해왔습니다. 미국 내에서 가장 유명한 유제품 행사 중 하나인 State Milk Quality Contest가 다음달에 WDG에 의해 개최됩니다. 전 세계의 우유 생산업자들이 이곳으로 와서 경쟁을 펼치게 됩니다. Paul Edwards 씨가 작년의 우승자였습니다. 그의 소에서 생산한 우유가 100점 만점에 97.4점이란 최고점을 받았습니다.

**143.** 정답 (A)

**144.** 정답 (C)

**145.** (A) 여러분은 호텔 홈페이지를 통해 직접 숙박을 예약할 수 있습니다.
(B) 전 세계의 우유 생산업자들이 이곳으로 와서 경쟁을 펼치게 됩니다.
(C) 자동화 기술은 농장들이 유제품을 생산하는 방식에 변화를 주고 있습니다.
(D) 많은 행사들이 방문객들의 이목을 사로잡기 위해 개최될 것입니다.
정답 (B)

**146.** 정답 (D)

## Part 7

문제 147-148번은 다음 공지를 참조하시오.

공지

6월 2일부터 6월 14일까지 내부 개조 작업으로 인해 구내가 폐쇄됨을 모든 Good Times Café 고객님들께 알려드립니다. 고객님들께 더욱 더 유쾌한 분위기를 제공하기 위해 모든 층을 새롭게 단장하고, (147) **다양한 종류의 잡지책과 소설책을 커피와 함께 즐길 수 있는 소규모 도서관을 1층에 추가할 예정입니다.**

새롭게 단장된 Good Times Café를 기념하기 위해 (148) **6월 15일 모든 고객님들께** Good Times Café **머그컵을 나누어 줄 예정입니다.** 뿐만 아니라, 재개장일에 모든 음료수를 할인 가격으로 제공할 예정입니다.

고객님의 편의를 도모하여 일주일 내내 영업합니다: 평일은 오전 10시에서 오후 11시까지, 주말은 오전 10시에서 오후 12시까지 영업합니다.

언제나, 고객님들의 이용에 감사 드리며 고객님들을 다시 보는 그날을 고대하겠습니다.

**147.** 매장에 대해 언급된 내용은 무엇인가?
(A) 추가로 층을 만들 것이다.
(B) 독서 장소가 생길 것이다.
(C) 영업 시간을 변경할 것이다.
(D) 새로운 메뉴를 만들 것이다.
정답 (B)

**148.** 6월 15일에 고객들은 무엇을 무상으로 받는가?
(A) 머그컵
(B) 잡지

(C) 디저트
(D) 커피
정답 (A)

문제 149-150번은 다음 광고를 참조하시오.

Moab Forrest 통나무집

저희 Moab Forrest 국립 공원 서비스는 Moab Forrest 국립공원 내에 25개의 아름다운 통나무집을 건축하겠다는 계획을 발표하게 되어 기쁩니다. 작업은 약 2주 후에 시작될 예정입니다. 계획대로 진행된다면, 한 달 이내에 부지 정리와 구조적인 주요 기초 작업을 위한 준비가 될 것으로 기대합니다. 막대한 업무로 보이나, 저희는 여름철이 시작되기 전에 모든 것을 완료시키기 위해 필사적으로 애쓰고 있습니다. (150) **새 통나무집은 올 6월까지 완공될 것입니다.**

(150) **이용 가능한 객실은 두 종류입니다:** 기본 객실은 두 개의 층으로 되어 있고 5명까지 수용 가능합니다: 단체 객실은 세 개의 층으로 되어 있고 10명까지 수용 가능합니다. 두 종류의 객실 모두 냉난방 장치가 되어있고, 욕조를 포함한 현대식 화장실이 구비되어 있습니다. (149) **또한 주방에는 냉장고와 전자레인지, 세탁기와 가스레인지 등 모든 종류의 주방 기기들이 갖추어져 있습니다.**

(150) **Moab Forrest 통나무집은 아름다운 Pleasant 호수 옆에 접근이 용이하게 위치하게 될 것입니다.** 도시의 열기를 피해 국립공원에서 낚시와 수영, 수상 스포츠를 즐기고자 하는 사람이라면 누구에게나 최적의 장소입니다. 통나무집의 사전 예약을 원하신다면, Moab Forrest 국립 공원 서비스의 직원에게 오늘 연락하세요.

(150) **6월 4일부터 대부분의 객실이 이용 가능합니다.** 자세한 내용은 555-6892로 문의하세요.

**149.** 통나무집에 관해 언급된 내용은 무엇인가?
(A) 공사는 2주 전에 시작되었다.
(B) 주방 기기들이 포함되어 있다.
(C) 침실이 매우 넓다.
(D) 많은 인원을 수용할 수는 없다.
정답 (B)

**150.** 광고에 언급된 정보가 아닌 것은 무엇인가?
(A) 통나무집의 첫 개장 일자
(B) 이용 가능한 통나무집의 종류
(C) 통나무집 사용료
(D) 통나무집의 위치
정답 (C)

문제 151-152번은 다음 문자 메시지를 참조하시오.

Jennifer Longman [오전 11:13]
한 공무원이 오늘 이른 아침에 새로운 식품 위생 허가증을 가지고 왔어요. 이전하고 동일하게 계산대 뒤에 있는 벽에 부착하면 될까요?

Michael Western [오전 11:14]
아니오. (152) 시 의회에서 2주 전에 새로 개정된 식품 위생 법안을 통과시켰다는 소식 못 들었어요?

Jennifer Longman [오전 11:15]
(152) 아니오, 전혀 못 들었어요. 제게도 좀 알려줄 수 있나요?

Michael Western [오전 11:18]
(151) 개정된 새로운 식품 위생법은 식품 위생 허가증이 모든 고객들이 볼 수 있도록 정문에서 한 걸음 이내에 있는 곳에 부착해야 한다고 규정하고 있어요.

Jennifer Longman           [오전 11:19]

그러면, 제가 허가증을 상점 정문 옆에 부착하면 될까요?

Michael Western           [오전 11:20]

**(151) 우리 고객들의 대부분이 상점의 정문을 통과하잖아요. 그 지점이 제일 좋은 위치 같네요.**

Jennifer Longman           [오전 11:21]

하지만 기존의 식품 위생 허가증이 금요일에 만기될 때까지 며칠 더 남아 있어서요. 이번 주 금요일에 폐장하고 나면 부착해야겠어요.

**151.** Western 씨는 Longman 씨에게 무엇을 하도록 요청하는가?

(A) 판매를 알리는 표지를 부착한다.

(B) 짐을 계산대 근처에 둔다.

(C) 행사를 위한 음식을 준비한다.

(D) 서류를 새로운 곳에 부착한다.     정답 (D)

**152.** 오전 11시 15분에 Longman 씨가 "Why don't you fill me in?"이라고 쓴 것이 의미하는 바는 무엇인가?

(A) 그녀는 Western 씨와 함께 점심식사를 하길 원한다.

(B) 그녀는 Western 씨를 도와줄 시간적 여력이 된다.

(C) 그녀는 Western 씨의 말에 감명을 받았다.

(D) 그녀는 Western 씨로부터 정보를 전달받아야 할 필요가 있다.     정답 (D)

문제 153-155번은 다음 정보를 참조하시오.

저하된 의욕과 건강 문제, 일에 갖는 불만, 그리고 직원 이직률은 종종 직장 스트레스의 첫 징후가 된다. 그러나 때때로 전혀 단서가 나타나지 않기도 한데, 특히 직원들이 일자리를 잃을까 두려워한다면 더욱 그렇다. (153) 분명하고 널리 알려진 징후가 없다는 것이 직장 스트레스에 관한 우려를 떨쳐내거나 예방 프로그램의 중요성을 경시하는 타당한 이유가 되지는 못한다.

(153) 문제를 파악하라. 부서장들, 근로자 대표들, 그리고 직원들 사이의 그룹 토론은 풍부한 정보원을 제공할 것이다. 작은 회사에서는 이런 토론이 스트레스 문제들을 철저히 밝혀내고 치료하기 위해 필요한 전부일 수도 있다. 좀 더 큰 조직에서는 그런 토론이 많은 직원들로부터 스트레스를 주는 작업환경에 관한 자료를 모으는 정식 조사를 기획하는 데 이용될 수도 있다.

(153) 조정 정책을 고안하고 시행하라. (154) 작은 회사에서는, 직장 스트레스 문제를 파악하는 데 도움이 되는 비공식적 논의는 또한 직장 스트레스 예방을 위한 효과적인 아이디어들을 창출할 수 있다. 대규모 회사에서는, 좀 더 공식적인 과정이 필요할 수도 있다. 종종 첫 번째 단계에서 얻을 수 있는 자료와 외부 전문가와의 상담 결과의 분석을 토대로 직장 스트레스 예방의 추천 해결책을 개발하도록 하나의 팀에 지시할 수 있다.

(153) 조정 정책을 평가하라. 평가는 조정 과정에서 필수적이다. (155) 평가는 조정 정책이 원하는 효과를 만들어 냈는지, 그리고 정책 방향에 있어서 변화가 필요한지 결정하기 위해 필요하다. 평가는 작업환경, 인지된 스트레스의 정도, 건강 문제, 만족도 등에 관해 직원들이 제공한 정보를 포함해, 정책의 문제 확인 단계에서 수집된 정보들에 초점을 맞춰야 한다.

**153.** 이 정보문의 주제는 무엇인가?

(A) 직장 스트레스는 무엇인가?

(B) 직장 스트레스와 건강과의 관계

(C) 직장 스트레스를 예방하는 단계

(D) 직장 스트레스가 생산성에 미치는 영향     정답 (C)

**154.** 중소 회사에서는 비공식 논의가 어떤 목적으로 이용될 수 있는가?

(A) 일부 위험한 정신질환의 치료

(B) 노사의 단결

(C) 직장 스트레스를 초래하는 근무 환경의 확인

(D) 직장 스트레스를 예방할 수 있는 해결책의 파악     정답 (D)

**155.** 정보에 따르면, 평가에 의해 결정되는 것은 무엇인가?

(A) 조정 정책의 실제 효과

(B) 최고의 생산성을 얻기 위한 방법

(C) 직원들의 건강 상태

(D) 추후에 직장 스트레스가 발생할 가능성     정답 (A)

문제 156-157번은 다음 공지를 참조하시오.

공지

저희는 항상 환경 친화적 운영으로 환경 보호와 보존에 힘써왔습니다. 모든 객실에 에너지와 물 절약형 장비를 설치하고, 쓰레기의 양을 줄이고, 발생한 쓰레기들은 재활용하며, 여러 환경 보호 기술들을 전 직원이 행해야 하는 직무에 포함시켰습니다-(156/157) 이런 조치들이 기존 숙박시설과 환경을 책임지는 저희 숙박시설과의 차이를 만들어냅니다. (156) 물 절약에 도움이 되고자 저희 고객님들께 아래와 같은 사항을 제안하고자 합니다:

● 양치를 하는 동안, 얼굴에 비누칠을 하거나 면도를 하는 동안에 수도꼭지를 잠근다.

● 세면대 바닥에 채워진 소량의 물로 면도기를 헹군다.

● 샤워하면서 몸을 적실 때만 수도를 틀고, 비누칠을 할 때는 수도꼭지를 잠근다: 그리고 헹굴 때 다시 수도를 튼다. 머리를 감을 때도 같은 방법으로 한다.

● 샤워는 5분으로 제한하고, 목욕할 때 욕조는 10인치 가량만 채운다.

● 불필요하게 변기 물을 내리지 않는다. 휴지와 다른 쓰레기를 쓰레기통에 버린다.

**156.** 이 공지는 무엇에 관한 것인가?

(A) 물을 절약하는 방법

(B) 새로 채택된 환경 보존 방법

(C) 수질 오염을 예방하는 방법

(D) 환경 보호 방침     정답 (A)

**157.** 이 공지는 어디에서 볼 수 있을 것 같은가?

(A) 여행 잡지

(B) 아파트 로비

(C) 호텔 객실

(D) 열차     정답 (C)

문제 158-161번은 다음 기사를 참조하시오.

*Daily Fresh가 새로운 비누를 출시하다*

Los Angeles – KB 산업 주식회사의 자회사인 Daily Fresh는 손 전용 액상비누 시장에 진출할 것이라고 발표했다. (158) 신제품인 Flow 'n' Fresh는 3월 15일 California 전역에서 판매에 들어갈 것이다. 나머지 주에서는 5월 21일부터 Flow 'n' Fresh의 판매를 시작할 것이다.

(161) Flow 'n' Fresh의 출시와 함께 텔레비전, 출판 매체 및 인터넷을 통한 광고전이 펼쳐질 것이다. 텔레비전 광고와 인터넷 광고는 2월 25일 California에서 시작된다. 출판 매체를 통한 광고는 5월 1일에 시작될 것이다.

Daily Fresh는 California에서 가장 오래된 비누 제조업체로 이번 액상 비누의 출시는 기존의 고형 비누 판매가 하락한 이후에 이루어진 것이다. (160) 결과적으로, 이 회사의 가장 오래되고 제일 판매가 많은 비누인

Fresh Day의 매출액은 지난 2년간 30퍼센트 하락하였다. (159) 액상 비누 시장으로의 진출은 Daily Fresh가 비누 시장에서 다시 선두를 차지하고자 하는 희망에서 이루어진 것이다.

앞으로 12개월 동안 Daily Fresh는 멜론, 딸기, 올리브와 꿀 향이 나는 네 개의 액상 비누를 출시할 것이다. 그 다음 12개월 동안에는 레몬, 라벤더와 장미 향의 세 개 제품을 시장에 더 선보일 것이다.

Las Vegas, San Diego, Rochester에서 실시한 초기 시장 조사는 Flow 'n' Fresh가 전국의 소비자들을 사로잡을 것임을 보여준다.

**158.** Flow 'n' Fresh가 언제 전국적으로 판매될 것인가?
(A) 2월 25일
(B) 3월 15일
(C) 5월 1일
(D) 5월 21일 　　　　　　　　　　　　　정답 (D)

**159.** Daily Fresh가 액상 비누 시장에 진출하려는 이유는 무엇인가?
(A) California 주에서 회사의 위상을 높이기 위해서
(B) 현재 상품의 판매를 증가시키기 위해서
(C) 시장에서의 선두 자리를 재확립하기 위해서
(D) 여러 나라에서 신규 매장을 개장하기 위해서 　　정답 (C)

**160.** 최근 Daily Fresh 사에 발생한 일은 무엇인가?
(A) 회사가 시장 점유율을 증가시켰다.
(B) 회사는 그 어느 때보다도 성장했다.
(C) 회사는 신선한 유기농 제품을 개발했다.
(D) 회사는 급격한 매출 하락을 겪었다. 　　　　　정답 (D)

**161.** [1], [2], [3] 그리고 [4]로 표시된 곳 중에, 아래 문장이 들어가기에 가장 적절한 곳은?
"Flow 'n' Fresh의 출시와 함께 텔레비전, 출판 매체 및 인터넷을 통한 광고전이 펼쳐질 것이다."
(A) [1]
(B) [2]
(C) [3]
(D) [4] 　　　　　　　　　　　　　　　정답 (B)

문제 162-163번은 다음 회람을 참조하시오.

---

회람

수신: 전 직원

발신: Jill Larson, 인사 담당 이사

(162) 직원들은 합당한 사유가 있으면 병가를 낼 수 있습니다. 주 20시간 이상 근무하는 모든 정규직원은 유급병가를 낼 수 있고 고용일로부터 병가시간이 누적되기 시작합니다. 연장 휴가(6일 이상)를 얻으려면 진단서가 필요합니다. 진단서를 제출하지 않으면 정기휴가, 보상 휴가 혹은 무급휴가로 재조정됩니다. 직원들은 가능하면 휴가 2주 전에 결근계를 작성해서 제출해야 합니다.

(163) 병가수당을 받을 수 있는 자격이 되는 정규직원들은 부서장의 사전 결재를 얻은 경우 정기 검진 목적으로 아직 쓰지 않은 병가를 사용할 수 있습니다. 유급 병가는 3개월 이상 근무해야만 가능합니다.

여러분의 이해와 전적인 협조에 미리 감사의 말씀 전합니다.

Jill Larson
인사 담당 이사

---

**162.** 회람은 무엇에 관한 것인가?
(A) 병가 신청 안내
(B) 병가일수
(C) 병가 기간 연장
(D) 병가를 내기 위한 요구조건 　　　　　　　정답 (A)

**163.** 정기검진을 받기 위해 사용하지 않은 병가를 내고자 하는 직원들에게 필요한 것은 무엇인가?
(A) 의사의 서명
(B) 상사의 승인
(C) 결근계
(D) 의료 보험증 　　　　　　　　　　　　정답 (B)

문제 164-167번은 다음 광고를 참조하시오.

---

Sky Cycles: 우리의 열정, 우리의 자전거!

(164) 통근자 여러분, 끝없는 교통정체나 초만원인 요금이 비싼 열차에 지치셨나요? 자전거로 어디든 다녔던 행복한 나날을 기억하시나요? 다시 해보는 게 어때요?

지금이 자전거로 복귀하기에 딱 좋은 때입니다. 6월 내내 저희 매장의 모든 자전거를 25%까지 할인해 드립니다. (165) 게다가 액세서리는 30%까지, 사이클링복은 35%까지 할인해 드립니다. 게다가 헬멧과 반사경 등 안전장비는 50%까지 할인해 드립니다!

그리고 잊지 마세요, (166) Sky Cycles는 지방정부와 협력하여 여러분이 자전거를 구매하실 때 지방정부로부터 다양한 재정지원을 제공받으실 수 있도록 하고 있습니다.

(167) Sky Cycles는 자전거 타기를 통한 더 나은 삶을 목표로 10년 전에 창립되었습니다. 저희는 산악자전거와 도로용 자전거부터, 매일 편안한 출퇴근길을 갈망하는 사람들에게 이상적인 통근용 자전거에 이르기까지 모든 종류의 자전거를 취급합니다.

---

**164.** 자전거 타기의 어떠한 장점이 광고를 통해 암시되고 있는가?
(A) 통근자의 건강에 유익하다.
(B) 여름에 운전보다 낫다.
(C) 다른 운송수단보다 저렴하다.
(D) 사람들이 보다 여유 있게 느끼도록 도와준다. 　정답 (C)

**165.** 의류에는 어떠한 할인율이 제공되는가?
(A) 25%
(B) 30%
(C) 35%
(D) 50% 　　　　　　　　　　　　　　　정답 (C)

**166.** Sky Cycles에 대해 무엇이 언급되는가?
(A) 최근에 사업을 시작했다.
(B) 정부와 협업한다.
(C) 통근용 자전거 전문이다.
(D) 환경보호를 우선시한다. 　　　　　　　정답 (B)

**167.** [1], [2], [3] 그리고 [4]로 표시된 곳 중에, 아래 문장이 들어가기에 가장 적절한 곳은?
"Sky Cycles는 자전거 타기를 통한 더 나은 삶을 목표로 10년 전에 창립되었습니다."
(A) [1]
(B) [2]
(C) [3]
(D) [4] 　　　　　　　　　　　　　　　정답 (D)

문제 168-171번은 다음 편지를 참조하시오.

Carmichael 씨에게,

(168/170) 지난 1년 반 동안 제 집과 관련하여 겪었던 모든 일에 귀하가 주신 도움에 감사드립니다. 귀하의 도움, 지식, 노력과 지원이 없었더라면 절대로 주택을 매각하지 못했을 것입니다.

귀하의 부하 직원인 Robin Jenkins 씨는 몇 년 전 제가 주택을 구입할 때 인내심 있게 도움을 주셨습니다. 그 때 저희는 적절한 주택을 찾기까지 3, 4개월 동안 여러 주택들을 둘러봐야 했습니다. 제가 구매하고자 하는 주택을 결정했을 때 그는 전문적인 방법으로 거래가 무사히 성사될 수 있도록 노력했습니다. (169) 새로운 직장 때문에 Boston을 떠나 Sacramento로 떠나게 되었을 때도 저는 주택을 매각하기 위해 즉시 귀사를 선택했습니다. 불행히도 주택을 매각하는 과정에서 사소한 어려움을 겪게 되었지요. 세입자였던 Ailey Taylor 씨가 두 달 동안 임대료를 지불하지 않았던 것이었습니다. (171) 저는 그녀에게 임대 계약서의 내용대로 이사 갈 것을 요구했지만 그녀는 그것을 거절했습니다. 그러나 그 일은 귀사에게는 문제가 아니더군요. 제게는 큰 문제였지만 귀하의 직원에게는 사소한 것이었고, 그 문제에 냉철하게 대응하여 쉽게 해결해 버렸습니다. 저는 안도할 수 있었습니다. 제 주택이 잘 처리되었으니 말입니다.

다른 사람들과 제 첫 주택을 어떻게 구매하고 매각했는지 이야기할 기회가 있을 때마다 저는 Imperial 부동산이 없었다면 그 일을 처리할 수 없었을 것이라고 이야기하는 것을 빠뜨리지 않습니다. 부동산 중개업자를 그렇게 많이 신뢰하고 있다는 것이 이상하게 생각될지 모르겠지만 이는 모두 사실입니다.

제가 귀사를 위해 할 수 있는 일이 있으면 저에게 알려주시기 바랍니다.

David Ferguson

**168.** 편지의 목적은 무엇인가?
(A) 부동산 매물을 소개하기 위해서
(B) 법적 조언을 구하기 위해서
(C) 헌신적인 서비스에 대한 고마움을 표현하기 위해서
(D) 부동산 중개업자에게 이사를 통보하기 위해서　　　정답 (C)

**169.** Ferguson 씨가 주택을 다시 매각한 이유는 무엇인가?
(A) 그는 급전이 필요했다.
(B) 그는 좀 더 큰 집으로 이사하길 원했다.
(C) 그는 일을 하러 다른 도시로 가야만 했다.
(D) 그는 주택 융자 할부금을 체납했다.　　　정답 (C)

**170.** Morris Carmichael 씨는 누구일 것 같은가?
(A) 변호사
(B) 부동산 중개업자
(C) 건축가
(D) 부동산 소유주　　　정답 (B)

**171.** Ferguson 씨가 Taylor 씨에게 요청한 것은 무엇인가?
(A) 과중한 세금을 피하기 위해 그 주택을 매각할 것
(B) 계약서의 일부 항목의 내용을 수정할 것
(C) 그 주택에서 즉시 퇴거할 것
(D) 법적 소송이 없이 그녀의 문제점을 해결할 것　　　정답 (C)

문제 172-175번은 다음 온라인 채팅 토론을 참조하시오.

Linda Steadman　　　　　　　　　　　　　　　[오후 1:20]
(172) Samantha, 우리 내일 기념행사 준비가 다 되었나요? (172/173) 고객은 우리가 오전 9시 30분부터 준비하길 원하시더라고요. 교통 정체

를 고려하면, 최소한 8시에는 출발해야 할 것 같아요.

Samantha Fox　　　　　　　　　　　　　　　[오후 1:22]
문제가 하나 있어요. (172) 오전 8시 이전에 시장에서 유기농 채소를 구매해서 가져갈 수 없을 것 같아요.

Linda Steadman　　　　　　　　　　　　　　　[오후 1:23]
뭐라고요? (173) 그러면 우리가 9시 30분까지 그 곳에 도착할 수가 없어요. 어쩌죠? 고객에게 연락해서 지연이 조금 발생할 수도 있겠다고 말씀 드렸나요?

Samantha Fox　　　　　　　　　　　　　　　[오후 1:25]
아직요. Brandon이 지금 그 문제를 해결하려고 애쓰고 있어요. Brandon이 한 농장주와 전화 통화를 하며 우리에게 필요한 유기농 채소를 구매할 수 있을지 알아보고 있어요.

Brandon Grant　　　　　　　　　　　　　　　[오후 1:28]
좋은 소식이 있어요. 내일 오전 7시 30분에 Holiday 농장에서 우리가 필요한 유기농 채소를 구매할 수 있게 되었어요.

Samantha Fox　　　　　　　　　　　　　　　[오후 1:29]
좋아요. (174) 그럼 제가 고객에게 연락해서 내일 행사에 대한 준비가 다 되었다고 말씀을 드릴게요.

Brandon Grant　　　　　　　　　　　　　　　[오후 1:30]
고객이 행사를 언제 시작하길 원하셨죠?

Samantha Fox　　　　　　　　　　　　　　　[오후 1:31]
고객은 11시에 행사를 시작하길 원하고 있어요. 우리가 가서 준비를 하고 음식을 데우는 데 필요한 시간은 충분해요.

Linda Steadman　　　　　　　　　　　　　　　[오후 1:33]
알겠지만, 고객에게 요청하신 모든 음식들을 두려면 꽤 많은 공간이 필요할 것 같은데요.

Brandon Grant　　　　　　　　　　　　　　　[오후 1:33]
행사 장소가 큰 무도장 같은 곳이에요. 상당히 커요. 그 점은 걱정 안 해도 됩니다.

Linda Steadman　　　　　　　　　　　　　　　[오후 1:34]
좋아요. (175) 우리가 모든 상황을 적절하게 통제하고 있는 것처럼 보이네요. 내일 행사는 순조롭게 진행될 것이라 확신해요. 이제 좀 쉬어도 될 것 같아요.

**172.** 화자들은 어디에서 근무할 것 같은가?
(A) 출장 요리 회사
(B) 보건소
(C) 지역 농장
(D) 식당　　　정답 (A)

**173.** 화자들은 행사 장소에 언제 도착할 것인가?
(A) 오전 7시 30분
(B) 오전 8시
(C) 오전 9시 30분
(D) 오전 11시　　　정답 (C)

**174.** Fox 씨는 이후에 무엇을 할 것 같은가?
(A) 유기농 식품을 주문한다.
(B) 고객과 연락을 취한다.
(C) 그녀의 발표를 준비한다.
(D) 지역 농장에 이메일을 발송한다.　　　정답 (B)

**175.** 오후 1시 34분에, Steadman 씨가 "Now, I think we can all relax."라고 쓴 것이 의미하는 바는 무엇인가?
(A) 그녀는 기념식 후에 피곤함을 느끼고 있다.

(B) 그녀는 그들이 행사에 잘 대비한 상태라고 생각한다.

(C) 그녀는 고객이 만족하길 바라고 있다.

(D) 그녀는 짧은 휴식을 제안하고 있다. 　　　　정답 (B)

---

**문제 176-180번은 다음 일정과 이메일을 참조하시오.**

<table>
<tr><td colspan="4" align="center">BELLE BOOKS</td></tr>
<tr><td colspan="4" align="center">(176) 경영학의 2월을 위한 북 토크!</td></tr>
<tr><th>일요일 저녁 7시</th><th>행사 진행자</th><th>저자</th><th>최신 저서</th></tr>
<tr><td>2월 2일</td><td>Charles Winters</td><td>Margaret Michaels</td><td>Risk to Gain</td></tr>
<tr><td>2월 9일</td><td>Deborah Stokes</td><td>Ashley Dedham</td><td>Modern Investment Strategies</td></tr>
<tr><td>(179) 2월 16일</td><td>Thomas Racine</td><td>Stanley Mills</td><td>The Psychology of Business Gurus</td></tr>
<tr><td>(179) 2월 23일*</td><td>Amy Kane</td><td></td><td></td></tr>
</table>

*2월 23일에 인근의 Mason College에서 동창회 행사가 있을 것입니다. 그때 주차가 제한될 가능성이 있으니 미리 계획해 주십시오.

---

수신: Thomas Racine 〈tracine@loneowl.com〉

발신: Charles Winters 〈cw@bellebooks.com〉

(176) 날짜: 1월 10일

제목: 북 토크 일자

안녕하세요 Thomas.

(178) 비즈니스에 대해 세계적으로 찬사를 받은 몇 권의 책을 집필한 저자인 Robin Baker와 북 토크를 개최할 멋진 기회에 대해 제가 방금 알게 되었습니다. 그는 2월 13일부터 16일까지 우리 시에 올 것이며, 현재 2월 16일 일요일에 시간이 됩니다. 다음달 북 토크의 현재 일정은 그날 저녁 Stanley Mills 씨가 강연하기로 되어 있지요. 그러나 저는 Mills 씨를 개인적으로 압니다. 그리고 그가 근처에 살며, 다음달 마지막 북 토크로 일정을 변경하는 것에 반대하지 않을 것 같다는 점도 알고 있습니다. 현재 마지막 날 일정에 사람이 없으니 이렇게 하면 우리의 일이 잘 풀릴 것입니다.

(177) Mills 씨에게 연락하여 그의 북 토크 일정을 나중으로 변경해도 괜찮은지 알아봐 주겠어요? 그리고 나서 Baker 씨에게 연락하여 16일에 초청하고 싶다고 알려 주세요. (179) 마지막으로 Amy Kane 씨에게 그녀가 행사 진행을 담당하는 날에 Mills 씨가 (180) 출연할 것이라고 알려주세요.

감사합니다.

Charles Winters

**176.** Belle Books에 대해 암시된 것은 무엇인가?

(A) 투자에 관한 책만 판매한다.

(B) 비즈니스 책에 대해 특가를 제공한다.

(C) 다음달에 정기적인 행사를 개최할 것이다.

(D) 지역 대학의 캠퍼스에 위치해 있다. 　　　　정답 (C)

**177.** 이메일이 발송된 이유는 무엇인가?

(A) 작가에 대한 더 많은 정보를 요청하기 위해

(B) 직원에게 북 토크를 주최할 것을 요청하기 위해

(C) 계획 변경에 도움을 받기 위해

(D) 출간 비용에 대해 문의하기 위해 　　　　정답 (C)

**178.** Baker 씨에 대해 무엇이라고 나타나 있는가?

(A) 이미 Belle Books에 다녀갔다.

(B) 방문 일정을 변경해야 할 것이다.

---

(C) 다른 나라에 알려져 있다.

(D) 임금인상을 요청하고 있다. 　　　　정답 (C)

**179.** Winters 씨는 2월 23일에 어떤 책을 특집으로 다루고 싶어하는가?

(A) *Risk to Gain*

(B) *Modern Investment Strategies*

(C) *The Psychology of Business Gurus*

(D) *Buy and Sell Houses Now* 　　　　정답 (C)

**180.** 이메일 두 번째 단락 세 번째 줄의 "appearing"과 의미상 가장 유사한 단어는?

(A) 앉다

(B) 참여하다

(C) 나타나다

(D) 멀리 사라지다 　　　　정답 (B)

---

**문제 181-185번은 다음 보고서와 이메일을 참조하시오.**

<table>
<tr><td colspan="2" align="center">(181) 출장 경비 보고서</td></tr>
<tr><td colspan="2">직원: Sophia Jones / 서명: Sophia Jones<br>출장 기간 종료일: 8월 15일</td></tr>
<tr><td colspan="2" align="center">(181) 환급 비용 발생 내역</td></tr>
<tr><th>항목</th><th>비용</th></tr>
<tr><td>숙박</td><td>$798.67</td></tr>
<tr><td>식사</td><td>$224.58</td></tr>
<tr><td>항공료</td><td>$985.74</td></tr>
<tr><td>2일간의 렌트카</td><td>$176.00</td></tr>
<tr><td>주차</td><td>$18.00</td></tr>
<tr><td>택시비(봉사료 포함)</td><td>$42.00</td></tr>
<tr><td>세금</td><td>$84.03</td></tr>
<tr><td>총계</td><td>$2,329.02</td></tr>
</table>

모든 영수증은 보고서 이면에 첨부되어 있습니다.

---

수신: Sophia Jones 〈sjones@bellecorporation.com〉

발신: Charlotte Miller 〈cmiller@bellecorporation.com〉

날짜: 8월 20일

제목: 환급

Jones 씨에게,

저는 어제 귀하의 출장 경비 보고서를 받았고 당신의 보고서와 첨부한 영수증 원본들을 꼼꼼하게 살펴봤습니다. 그런데 우리가 처리해야 할 한 가지 문제점이 있더군요.

(182/183) 안타깝게도 귀하가 3일간 체류한 숙박료가 회사의 출장 경비 지침 사항을 초과하고 있습니다. 숙박료와 관련된 기준 환급액이 1박에 200 달러임을 고려할 때, 귀하의 숙박료 798.67달러는 최대 허용 금액에서 198.67달러 초과한 상태이며 이는 귀하에 의해 지불되어야만 합니다.

그러나 회사는 (185) 국제 비즈니스 컨벤션으로 인해 Boston 지역의 호텔 비가 갑자기 증가한 점과 이사진에서 컨벤션에 참석할 것을 늦게 결정하여, 귀하가 숙박료가 비싼 호텔 외에 다른 선택의 여지가 없었다는 점을 충분히 인식하고 있습니다. (184) 따라서 귀하가 숙박료의 전액 환급을 원하시면, RBSAE 서류양식을 작성해주실 것을 요청하고자 합니다. 해당 서류양식은 우리 회사의 공식 홈페이지인 www.bellacorporation.com/forms에서 내려 받는 것이 가능합니다.

이 서류를 8월 29일 목요일까지 제출해주시면 귀하의 보고서에 기재된 환급 총액이 다음 달 급여에 포함될 것입니다.

협조에 감사드립니다.

Charlotte Miller
회계 부장

**181.** 보고서가 발송된 이유는 무엇인가?
(A) 환급의 승인
(B) 출장비 환급 요청
(C) 출장 예산 요청
(D) 근무 과정과 관련된 주요 정보 제공 　　　　　정답 (B)

**182.** 최대 허용 금액을 초과한 비용은 무엇인가?
(A) 숙박
(B) 식사
(C) 주차
(D) 교통 　　　　　정답 (A)

**183.** Jones 씨가 호텔에서 숙박한 기간은 며칠인가?
(A) 2일
(B) 3일
(C) 4일
(D) 5일 　　　　　정답 (B)

**184.** Jones 씨가 전액 환급을 받기 위해 해야 할 일은 무엇인가?
(A) 그녀의 재직 증명서를 제출한다.
(B) 회의에 필요한 몇몇 파일들을 내려 받는다.
(C) 영수증 원본을 보고서에 첨부한다.
(D) 추가 환급을 위한 서류를 작성한다. 　　　정답 (D)

**185.** Jones 씨의 출장과 관련하여 유추할 수 있는 것은 무엇인가?
(A) 그녀는 자동차를 대여하지 않았다.
(B) 그녀는 저렴한 호텔에 투숙했다.
(C) 회의는 보스턴에서 개최되었다.
(D) 일부 영수증이 분실되었다. 　　　　　정답 (C)

문제 186-190번은 다음 전단지와 편지, 그리고 주차권을 참조하시오.

Shakespeare 팬들에게:
Royal 극단이 San Francisco로 옵니다!

Royal 극단이 William Shakespeare의 고전극
〈베니스의 상인〉을 공연합니다.

장소: 샌프란시스코 다운타운 극장
일시: 10월 12일 일요일 오후 7시
　　　10월 18일 토요일 오후 7시
　　　10월 24일 금요일 오후 7시
　　　10월 26일 일요일 오후 7시
표 가격: 성인 75달러 / 16세 미만 어린이 25달러

사전 예약은 저희 홈페이지인 www.sfdtheater.com을 방문하셔서 표 예매 링크를 클릭하시면 됩니다. (186) **표 가격을 지불하시려면, 개인수표를 저희 샌프란시스코 다운타운 극장으로 발송해주시거나 저희 홈페이지에서 신용 카드로 인터넷 예약 지불을 선택하시면 됩니다.**

표는 공연 시간 두 시간 전에 저희 매표소를 통해 구매하실 수도 있습니다만 그 시간에 좌석이 남아있을 것이란 (187) **보장**은 해드리지 못합니다. (186) **매표소를 통해 구매되는 표는 필히 현금으로 계산하셔야 합니다.** 감사합니다.

세부적인 정보를 원하시면 575-4331로 연락하시거나 cs@sfdtheater.com 을 통해 고객 서비스 부서로 이메일을 보내주십시오.

San Francisco Downtown 극장
Orchard 대로 2301번지
San Francisco, CA 94105

10월 3일

West 씨에게,

조만간 있을 Royal 극단의 공연을 소개해 드리게 되어 무척이나 기쁘게 생각합니다. 10월 12일과 18일 San Francisco downtown 극장에서 〈베니스의 상인〉을 무대에 올리게 되었습니다.

공연 세부사항은 아래와 같습니다:

일시: 10월 12일 일요일 오후 7시
　　　10월 18일 토요일 오후 7시
　　　10월 24일 금요일 오후 7시
　　　10월 26일 일요일 오후 7시
장소: 샌프란시스코 다운타운 극장
표 가격: 성인 75달러 / 16세 미만 어린이 25달러
비고: 5세 미만 어린이는 입장을 불허합니다.

〈베니스의 상인〉은 William Shakespeare의 작품으로 항상 널리 사랑 받는 연극이지만 (189) **무대에서의 공연을 관람하기가 어렵습니다.** 귀하께서 〈베니스의 상인〉 공연을 관람하시길 바라는 마음으로 정중히 초청하오며 공연 표를 구입해주시길 당부드립니다. (188) **항상 그러하듯, 우수 고객님들에겐 무료 주차와 저녁식사가 제공됩니다.**

공연에 참석하여 자리를 빛내주시기 바랍니다. 아주 아름다운 저녁이 될 것이라 확신합니다. 초청을 고려해주신 점, 앞선 감사의 말씀을 전합니다.

William Baker
최고 경영자
San Francisco Downtown 극장

SAN FRANCISCO DOWNTOWN 극장

(188) **우수 고객용 주차권**

(190) **10월 18일 토요일**
입차: 오후 6시 18분
출차: 오후 9시 40분

(188) **주차비: $0**

**186.** 결제수단으로 언급된 것이 아닌 것은 무엇인가?
(A) 신용카드
(B) 우편환
(C) 개인수표
(D) 현금 　　　　　정답 (B)

**187.** 전단지 세 번째 단락 첫 번째 줄의 "guarantee"과 의미상 가장 유사한 단어는?
(A) 보증하다
(B) 유지하다
(C) 보장하다
(D) 예약하다 　　　　　정답 (C)

**188.** West 씨에 대해 암시되는 것은 무엇인가?
(A) 그녀는 전에 극장에서 다른 연극들을 관람한 적이 있다.
(B) 그녀는 이미 신용카드로 결제했다.

(C) 그녀는 공연 당일 저녁에 표를 수령할 것이다.

(D) 그녀는 혼자서 공연을 관람하러 갈 것이다.     정답 (A)

**189.** 편지에 따르면, 〈베니스의 상인〉에 대해 언급된 것은 무엇인가?

(A) 팬들 사이에서 인기가 없다.

(B) 많은 비평가들의 호평을 받았다.

(C) 자주 공연되지 않는다.

(D) 현대적 형태로 각색되었다.     정답 (C)

**190.** West 씨는 언제 공연을 봤겠는가?

(A) 10월 12일

(B) 10월 18일

(C) 10월 24일

(D) 10월 26일     정답 (B)

**문제 191-195번은 다음 이메일들과 일정표를 참조하시오.**

---

수신: Kris Livingstone 〈klivingstone@rantzen.com〉

발신: Brenda Fabian 〈bfian@rantzen.com〉

날짜: 8월 29일

제목: London 출장

첨부: 열차 일정표

요청하신대로, 9월 5일 Glasgow 발 London 행 기차의 세부사항을 보냅니다. 보시다시피, 일반 열차보다 대략 30분 일찍 도착하는 급행열차를 이용하실 수 있습니다. 결정하시면 알려주세요. 예약해 드리겠습니다.

**(191) Debbie Gibson 씨를 위한 티켓 예약도 원하신다고 말씀하셨죠? 그 분도 당신과 같은 열차표를 원하십니까?**

Brenda Fabian

인사과

---

### 열차 일정표

**9월 5일**

| 열차 번호 | (191) 78(급행) | 23(일반) | 77(급행) | 24(일반) |
|---|---|---|---|---|
| 출발 Glasgow | 오전 7:24 | 오전 7:30 | 오전 7:54 | 오전 8:01 |
| 도착 London | (191) 오후 1:13 | 오후 1:55 | 오후 1:43 | 오후 2:26 |

**9월 7일**

| 열차 번호 | 81(급행) | 33(일반) | 82(급행) | 32(일반) |
|---|---|---|---|---|
| 출발 Glasgow | (193) 오후 1:35 | 오후 1:55 | 오후 2:10 | 오후 2:45 |
| 도착 London | 오후 7:27 | 오후 8:00 | 오후 7:58 | 오후 8:52 |

---

수신: Brenda Fabian 〈bfian@rantzen.com〉

발신: Kris Livingstone 〈klivingstone@rantzen.com〉

날짜: 8월 30일

제목: 회신: London 출장

안녕하세요? Brenda.

여행을 계획하기 위해 당신이 들인 수고에 감사를 드립니다. 저는 Manchester 지점에서 온 지점장님을 만나 마지막으로 발표를 검토할 수 있도록 **(192) 오후 1:30 전에** London에 도착해야 합니다. **(193) 돌아오는 기차는 말씀하신 것 중에 가장 이른 시간에 출발하는 기차를 예약해 주시겠**

---

습니까?

Gibson 씨는 제가 떠난 다음날인 9월 6일, London으로 떠날 계획입니다. 하지만 저희는 9월 7일 같은 시간에 함께 돌아올 것입니다. Gibson 씨를 위해 Glasgow로 돌아오는 표를 예약해 주실 수 있습니까?

**(194/195) 또한, Manchester의 동료들이 어떤 호텔에 머물지 Manchester 지점으로 연락해서 알아보실 수 있을까요? (195) 저희는 영업기술에 관한 발표를 함께 해야 하기 때문에 같은 호텔에 예약하여 같이 일하고자 합니다.**

다시 한 번 감사의 말씀 전합니다.

Kris Livingstone

---

**191.** Livingstone 씨에게 요청되는 것은 무엇인가?

(A) Gibson 씨에게 연락한다.

(B) 표를 예매한다.

(C) 서류를 작성한다.

(D) 추가 정보를 제공한다.     정답 (D)

**192.** Livingstone 씨가 원하는 London 행 열차번호는 몇 번일 것 같은가?

(A) 78

(B) 23

(C) 77

(D) 24     정답 (A)

**193.** Livingstone 씨가 London 발 Glasgow 행 열차에 탑승하길 원하는 시간은 언제일 것 같은가?

(A) 오후 1:35

(B) 오후 1:55

(C) 오후 2:10

(D) 오후 2:45     정답 (A)

**194.** Livingstone 씨가 Fabian 씨에게 요청하는 것은 무엇인가?

(A) Gibson 씨에게 연락을 하여 동의를 얻을 것

(B) 그와 회의에 동행할 것

(C) 호텔 예약을 취소할 것

(D) Manchester 사무실과 연락을 취할 것     정답 (D)

**195.** Livingstone 씨에 대해 암시하고 있는 것은 무엇인가?

(A) 그는 9월 6일 Glasgow로 돌아갈 것이다.

(B) 그는 Gibson 씨와 London으로 갈 것이다.

(C) 그는 호텔방을 이미 예약했다.

(D) 그는 Manchester의 동료들과 함께 일할 것이다.     정답 (D)

**문제 196-200번은 다음 안내문과 이메일, 그리고 공지를 참조하시오.**

---

### 신입사원을 위한 정기 워크숍

**(196) 우리 회사에서는 다음 달에 입사한지 6개월 미만의 신입사원들을 대상으로 하는 정기 워크숍을 개최할 예정입니다. 참석은 필수입니다.**

날짜: 1월 15일~17일 오후 6시~9시 (퇴근 이후)

**(197) 장소: New York 시에 위치한 King 호텔 – 2층 회의실**

이 워크숍들은 회사 신입사원들에게 최신 연수를 제공하고자 기획이 되었습니다. **(200) 워크숍 기간 동안, 각 직원은 타 부서에 있는 직원들뿐만 아니라 중역들과 친분을 쌓을 수 있는 기회를 갖게 될 것입니다.** 신입사원들은 또한 회사의 신제품에 대한 지식과 올해의 새로운 판매 전략 및 매출 목표에 관해 교육받을 것입니다.

**(196) 건강 문제나 개인적인 사유로 워크숍에 참석하지 못하는 신입사원은 인사부장인 Juliet Hwang 씨에게 행사에 불참하게 됨을 필히 전달하고**

---

그녀로부터 허가를 받아야 합니다.

감사합니다. 그리고 여러분 모두를 그 곳에서 뵐 수 있길 바랍니다.

George Winston
최고 경영자
Yellow Chip 사

---

수신: George Winston 〈gwinston@yellowchip.com〉
발신: Juliet Hwang 〈jhwang@yellowchip.com〉
날짜: 1월 10일
제목: 회신: 다가올 워크숍

Winston 씨께,

**(198) 제게 다음주 워크숍에 불참하게 되는 신입사원들의 명단을 제출해줄 것을 요청하셨죠. 여기 명단이 있습니다.**

Jane Parker

Jane Parker 씨에 관해서 말씀드리면, 제가 그녀에게 신입사원을 위한 워크숍에 불참할 수 있는 허가서를 발급했습니다. **(199) 그녀의 불참 사유는 그녀의 아버님의 별세이며, 이로 인해 그녀는 고향인 Missouri로 가서 가족 장례식에 참석해야만 합니다.** 저희는 이미 그녀의 아버님 별세에 대해 조의를 전했으며 **(200) 회계 이사인 James Brown 씨가 장례식에 참석할 계획입니다.**

Juliet Hwang
인사부장

---

부고
Robert Parker 씨를 기리며

Joplin에 거주하는 노령의 Robert Parker 씨는 전신 쇠약으로 인해 토요일 이른 오전에 사망하였으며 그의 죽음은 지역 사회에 많은 슬픔을 불러오고 있다.

**(200) 장례식은 Robert Parker 씨 자택에서 그의 딸 Jane Parker 씨와 함께, 성 요한 교회의 예배와 함께 1월 17일 오전에 진행될 것이며** 성 요한 교회 공동묘지에 매장될 것이다.

---

**196.** 신입사원을 위한 정기 워크숍에 관해 언급된 것은 무엇인가?
(A) 회사에서는 적절한 숙박을 보장한다.
(B) 모든 직원은 필히 참석해야 한다.
(C) 적절한 사유가 없으면 어떠한 신입사원도 불참할 수 없다.
(D) 다양한 능력 개발 프로그램을 제공한다. 정답 (C)

**197.** Yellow Chip 사에 관해 암시되는 것은 무엇인가?
(A) New York 시에 위치하고 있다.
(B) 전문 장례 서비스를 제공한다.
(C) 1년에 두 차례씩 정기 워크숍을 개최한다.
(D) 지난 몇 년간 신입사원을 채용하지 않았다. 정답 (A)

**198.** Hwang 씨가 이메일을 보낸 이유는 무엇인가?
(A) Missouri 방문 일정을 잡기 위해서
(B) 워크숍에서 나온 주장을 반박하기 위해서
(C) Parker 씨 가족에게 조의를 표하기 위해서
(D) 불참자의 이름을 전달하기 위해서 정답 (D)

**199.** Jane Parker 씨에 관해 유추할 수 있는 것은 무엇인가?
(A) 그녀는 Missouri로 출장을 간다.
(B) 그녀는 회사 행사에서 발표를 한다.
(C) 그녀는 입사한 지 6개월 미만이다.

(D) 그녀는 최근 많은 워크숍에 참석했다. 정답 (C)

**200.** 1월 17일에는 어떠한 일이 발생할 것 같은가?
(A) 신제품이 출시된다.
(B) 회사 행사가 시작된다.
(C) 한 중역이 워크숍에 불참한다.
(D) 몇몇 직원들이 다른 나라를 방문한다. 정답 (C)

자신의 정답 개수를 기준으로 본인의 점수를 개략적으로 환산해 볼 수 있는 자료입니다.
정확한 계산법이 아닌 추정치임을 참고하시기 바랍니다.

| Listening Comprehension | | Reading Comprehension | |
|---|---|---|---|
| 정답 개수 | 환산점수 | 정답 개수 | 환산점수 |
| 96-100 | 470-495 | 96-100 | 470-495 |
| 91-95 | 440-470 | 91-95 | 450-470 |
| 86-90 | 410-440 | 86-90 | 420-450 |
| 81-85 | 370-410 | 81-85 | 380-420 |
| 76-80 | 340-370 | 76-80 | 350-380 |
| 71-75 | 310-340 | 71-75 | 330-350 |
| 66-70 | 280-310 | 66-70 | 300-330 |
| 61-65 | 250-280 | 61-65 | 270-300 |
| 56-60 | 230-250 | 56-60 | 240-270 |
| 51-55 | 200-230 | 51-55 | 210-240 |
| 46-50 | 170-200 | 46-50 | 190-210 |
| 41-45 | 150-170 | 41-45 | 170-190 |
| 36-40 | 120-150 | 36-40 | 140-170 |
| 31-35 | 90-120 | 31-35 | 110-140 |
| 26-30 | 70-90 | 26-30 | 90-110 |
| 21-25 | 40-70 | 21-25 | 70-90 |
| 16-20 | 30-40 | 16-20 | 50-70 |
| 11-15 | 10-30 | 11-15 | 30-50 |
| 6-10 | 5-10 | 6-10 | 10-30 |
| 1-5 | 5 | 1-5 | 0 |
| 0 | 5 | 0 | 0 |

# Actual Test 06

## LISTENING (Part I ~ IV)

| NO. | ANSWER | NO. | ANSWER | NO. | ANSWER | NO. | ANSWER | NO. | ANSWER |
|---|---|---|---|---|---|---|---|---|---|
| 1 | a b c d | 21 | a b c d | 41 | a b c d | 61 | a b c d | 81 | a b c d |
| 2 | a b c d | 22 | a b c d | 42 | a b c d | 62 | a b c d | 82 | a b c d |
| 3 | a b c d | 23 | a b c d | 43 | a b c d | 63 | a b c d | 83 | a b c d |
| 4 | a b c | 24 | a b c d | 44 | a b c d | 64 | a b c d | 84 | a b c d |
| 5 | a b c | 25 | a b c d | 45 | a b c d | 65 | a b c d | 85 | a b c d |
| 6 | a b c d | 26 | a b c d | 46 | a b c d | 66 | a b c d | 86 | a b c d |
| 7 | a b c | 27 | a b c d | 47 | a b c d | 67 | a b c d | 87 | a b c d |
| 8 | a b c | 28 | a b c d | 48 | a b c d | 68 | a b c d | 88 | a b c d |
| 9 | a b c | 29 | a b c d | 49 | a b c d | 69 | a b c d | 89 | a b c d |
| 10 | a b c | 30 | a b c d | 50 | a b c d | 70 | a b c d | 90 | a b c d |
| 11 | a b c | 31 | a b c d | 51 | a b c d | 71 | a b c d | 91 | a b c d |
| 12 | a b c | 32 | a b c d | 52 | a b c d | 72 | a b c d | 92 | a b c d |
| 13 | a b c | 33 | a b c d | 53 | a b c d | 73 | a b c d | 93 | a b c d |
| 14 | a b c | 34 | a b c d | 54 | a b c d | 74 | a b c d | 94 | a b c d |
| 15 | a b c | 35 | a b c d | 55 | a b c d | 75 | a b c d | 95 | a b c d |
| 16 | a b c | 36 | a b c d | 56 | a b c d | 76 | a b c d | 96 | a b c d |
| 17 | a b c | 37 | a b c d | 57 | a b c d | 77 | a b c d | 97 | a b c d |
| 18 | a b c | 38 | a b c d | 58 | a b c d | 78 | a b c d | 98 | a b c d |
| 19 | a b c | 39 | a b c d | 59 | a b c d | 79 | a b c d | 99 | a b c d |
| 20 | a b c | 40 | a b c d | 60 | a b c d | 80 | a b c d | 100 | a b c d |

## READING (Part V ~ VII)

| NO. | ANSWER | NO. | ANSWER | NO. | ANSWER | NO. | ANSWER | NO. | ANSWER |
|---|---|---|---|---|---|---|---|---|---|
| 101 | a b c d | 121 | a b c d | 141 | a b c d | 161 | a b c d | 181 | a b c d |
| 102 | a b c d | 122 | a b c d | 142 | a b c d | 162 | a b c d | 182 | a b c d |
| 103 | a b c d | 123 | a b c d | 143 | a b c d | 163 | a b c d | 183 | a b c d |
| 104 | a b c d | 124 | a b c d | 144 | a b c d | 164 | a b c d | 184 | a b c d |
| 105 | a b c d | 125 | a b c d | 145 | a b c d | 165 | a b c d | 185 | a b c d |
| 106 | a b c d | 126 | a b c d | 146 | a b c d | 166 | a b c d | 186 | a b c d |
| 107 | a b c d | 127 | a b c d | 147 | a b c d | 167 | a b c d | 187 | a b c d |
| 108 | a b c d | 128 | a b c d | 148 | a b c d | 168 | a b c d | 188 | a b c d |
| 109 | a b c d | 129 | a b c d | 149 | a b c d | 169 | a b c d | 189 | a b c d |
| 110 | a b c d | 130 | a b c d | 150 | a b c d | 170 | a b c d | 190 | a b c d |
| 111 | a b c d | 131 | a b c d | 151 | a b c d | 171 | a b c d | 191 | a b c d |
| 112 | a b c d | 132 | a b c d | 152 | a b c d | 172 | a b c d | 192 | a b c d |
| 113 | a b c d | 133 | a b c d | 153 | a b c d | 173 | a b c d | 193 | a b c d |
| 114 | a b c d | 134 | a b c d | 154 | a b c d | 174 | a b c d | 194 | a b c d |
| 115 | a b c d | 135 | a b c d | 155 | a b c d | 175 | a b c d | 195 | a b c d |
| 116 | a b c d | 136 | a b c d | 156 | a b c d | 176 | a b c d | 196 | a b c d |
| 117 | a b c d | 137 | a b c d | 157 | a b c d | 177 | a b c d | 197 | a b c d |
| 118 | a b c d | 138 | a b c d | 158 | a b c d | 178 | a b c d | 198 | a b c d |
| 119 | a b c d | 139 | a b c d | 159 | a b c d | 179 | a b c d | 199 | a b c d |
| 120 | a b c d | 140 | a b c d | 160 | a b c d | 180 | a b c d | 200 | a b c d |

# Actual Test 07

## LISTENING (Part I ~ IV)

| NO. | ANSWER | NO. | ANSWER | NO. | ANSWER | NO. | ANSWER |
|---|---|---|---|---|---|---|---|
| | A B C D | | A B C D | | A B C D | | A B C D |
| 1 | a b c d | 21 | a b c d | 41 | a b c d | 61 | a b c d |
| 2 | a b c d | 22 | a b c d | 42 | a b c d | 62 | a b c d |
| 3 | a b c d | 23 | a b c d | 43 | a b c d | 63 | a b c d |
| 4 | a b c d | 24 | a b c d | 44 | a b c d | 64 | a b c d |
| 5 | a b c d | 25 | a b c d | 45 | a b c d | 65 | a b c d |
| 6 | a b c d | 26 | a b c d | 46 | a b c d | 66 | a b c d |
| 7 | a b c d | 27 | a b c d | 47 | a b c d | 67 | a b c d |
| 8 | a b c | 28 | a b c d | 48 | a b c d | 68 | a b c d |
| 9 | a b c | 29 | a b c d | 49 | a b c d | 69 | a b c d |
| 10 | a b c | 30 | a b c d | 50 | a b c d | 70 | a b c d |
| 11 | a b c | 31 | a b c d | 51 | a b c d | 71 | a b c d |
| 12 | a b c | 32 | a b c d | 52 | a b c d | 72 | a b c d |
| 13 | a b c | 33 | a b c d | 53 | a b c d | 73 | a b c d |
| 14 | a b c | 34 | a b c d | 54 | a b c d | 74 | a b c d |
| 15 | a b c | 35 | a b c d | 55 | a b c d | 75 | a b c d |
| 16 | a b c | 36 | a b c d | 56 | a b c d | 76 | a b c d |
| 17 | a b c | 37 | a b c d | 57 | a b c d | 77 | a b c d |
| 18 | a b c | 38 | a b c d | 58 | a b c d | 78 | a b c d |
| 19 | a b c | 39 | a b c d | 59 | a b c d | 79 | a b c d |
| 20 | a b c | 40 | a b c d | 60 | a b c d | 80 | a b c d |

(81–100 continued)

| NO. | ANSWER |
|---|---|
| | A B C D |
| 81 | a b c d |
| 82 | a b c d |
| 83 | a b c d |
| 84 | a b c d |
| 85 | a b c d |
| 86 | a b c d |
| 87 | a b c d |
| 88 | a b c d |
| 89 | a b c d |
| 90 | a b c d |
| 91 | a b c d |
| 92 | a b c d |
| 93 | a b c d |
| 94 | a b c d |
| 95 | a b c d |
| 96 | a b c d |
| 97 | a b c d |
| 98 | a b c d |
| 99 | a b c d |
| 100 | a b c d |

## READING (Part V ~ VII)

| NO. | ANSWER | NO. | ANSWER | NO. | ANSWER | NO. | ANSWER | NO. | ANSWER |
|---|---|---|---|---|---|---|---|---|---|
| | A B C D | | A B C D | | A B C D | | A B C D | | A B C D |
| 101 | a b c d | 121 | a b c d | 141 | a b c d | 161 | a b c d | 181 | a b c d |
| 102 | a b c d | 122 | a b c d | 142 | a b c d | 162 | a b c d | 182 | a b c d |
| 103 | a b c d | 123 | a b c d | 143 | a b c d | 163 | a b c d | 183 | a b c d |
| 104 | a b c d | 124 | a b c d | 144 | a b c d | 164 | a b c d | 184 | a b c d |
| 105 | a b c d | 125 | a b c d | 145 | a b c d | 165 | a b c d | 185 | a b c d |
| 106 | a b c d | 126 | a b c d | 146 | a b c d | 166 | a b c d | 186 | a b c d |
| 107 | a b c d | 127 | a b c d | 147 | a b c d | 167 | a b c d | 187 | a b c d |
| 108 | a b c d | 128 | a b c d | 148 | a b c d | 168 | a b c d | 188 | a b c d |
| 109 | a b c d | 129 | a b c d | 149 | a b c d | 169 | a b c d | 189 | a b c d |
| 110 | a b c d | 130 | a b c d | 150 | a b c d | 170 | a b c d | 190 | a b c d |
| 111 | a b c d | 131 | a b c d | 151 | a b c d | 171 | a b c d | 191 | a b c d |
| 112 | a b c d | 132 | a b c d | 152 | a b c d | 172 | a b c d | 192 | a b c d |
| 113 | a b c d | 133 | a b c d | 153 | a b c d | 173 | a b c d | 193 | a b c d |
| 114 | a b c d | 134 | a b c d | 154 | a b c d | 174 | a b c d | 194 | a b c d |
| 115 | a b c d | 135 | a b c d | 155 | a b c d | 175 | a b c d | 195 | a b c d |
| 116 | a b c d | 136 | a b c d | 156 | a b c d | 176 | a b c d | 196 | a b c d |
| 117 | a b c d | 137 | a b c d | 157 | a b c d | 177 | a b c d | 197 | a b c d |
| 118 | a b c d | 138 | a b c d | 158 | a b c d | 178 | a b c d | 198 | a b c d |
| 119 | a b c d | 139 | a b c d | 159 | a b c d | 179 | a b c d | 199 | a b c d |
| 120 | a b c d | 140 | a b c d | 160 | a b c d | 180 | a b c d | 200 | a b c d |

# Actual Test 08

## LISTENING (Part I ~ IV)

| NO. | ANSWER | NO. | ANSWER | NO. | ANSWER | NO. | ANSWER | NO. | ANSWER |
|-----|--------|-----|--------|-----|--------|-----|--------|-----|--------|
| 1 | a b c d | 21 | a b c | 41 | a b c d | 61 | a b c d | 81 | a b c d |
| 2 | a b c d | 22 | a b c | 42 | a b c d | 62 | a b c d | 82 | a b c d |
| 3 | a b c d | 23 | a b c | 43 | a b c d | 63 | a b c d | 83 | a b c d |
| 4 | a b c d | 24 | a b c | 44 | a b c d | 64 | a b c d | 84 | a b c d |
| 5 | a b c d | 25 | a b c | 45 | a b c d | 65 | a b c d | 85 | a b c d |
| 6 | a b c d | 26 | a b c | 46 | a b c d | 66 | a b c d | 86 | a b c d |
| 7 | a b c d | 27 | a b c | 47 | a b c d | 67 | a b c d | 87 | a b c d |
| 8 | a b c d | 28 | a b c | 48 | a b c d | 68 | a b c d | 88 | a b c d |
| 9 | a b c d | 29 | a b c | 49 | a b c d | 69 | a b c d | 89 | a b c d |
| 10 | a b c d | 30 | a b c d | 50 | a b c d | 70 | a b c d | 90 | a b c d |
| 11 | a b c d | 31 | a b c d | 51 | a b c d | 71 | a b c d | 91 | a b c d |
| 12 | a b c d | 32 | a b c d | 52 | a b c d | 72 | a b c d | 92 | a b c d |
| 13 | a b c d | 33 | a b c d | 53 | a b c d | 73 | a b c d | 93 | a b c d |
| 14 | a b c d | 34 | a b c d | 54 | a b c d | 74 | a b c d | 94 | a b c d |
| 15 | a b c d | 35 | a b c d | 55 | a b c d | 75 | a b c d | 95 | a b c d |
| 16 | a b c d | 36 | a b c d | 56 | a b c d | 76 | a b c d | 96 | a b c d |
| 17 | a b c d | 37 | a b c d | 57 | a b c d | 77 | a b c d | 97 | a b c d |
| 18 | a b c d | 38 | a b c d | 58 | a b c d | 78 | a b c d | 98 | a b c d |
| 19 | a b c d | 39 | a b c d | 59 | a b c d | 79 | a b c d | 99 | a b c d |
| 20 | a b c d | 40 | a b c d | 60 | a b c d | 80 | a b c d | 100 | a b c d |

## READING (Part V ~ VII)

| NO. | ANSWER | NO. | ANSWER | NO. | ANSWER | NO. | ANSWER | NO. | ANSWER |
|-----|--------|-----|--------|-----|--------|-----|--------|-----|--------|
| 101 | a b c d | 121 | a b c d | 141 | a b c d | 161 | a b c d | 181 | a b c d |
| 102 | a b c d | 122 | a b c d | 142 | a b c d | 162 | a b c d | 182 | a b c d |
| 103 | a b c d | 123 | a b c d | 143 | a b c d | 163 | a b c d | 183 | a b c d |
| 104 | a b c d | 124 | a b c d | 144 | a b c d | 164 | a b c d | 184 | a b c d |
| 105 | a b c d | 125 | a b c d | 145 | a b c d | 165 | a b c d | 185 | a b c d |
| 106 | a b c d | 126 | a b c d | 146 | a b c d | 166 | a b c d | 186 | a b c d |
| 107 | a b c d | 127 | a b c d | 147 | a b c d | 167 | a b c d | 187 | a b c d |
| 108 | a b c d | 128 | a b c d | 148 | a b c d | 168 | a b c d | 188 | a b c d |
| 109 | a b c d | 129 | a b c d | 149 | a b c d | 169 | a b c d | 189 | a b c d |
| 110 | a b c d | 130 | a b c d | 150 | a b c d | 170 | a b c d | 190 | a b c d |
| 111 | a b c d | 131 | a b c d | 151 | a b c d | 171 | a b c d | 191 | a b c d |
| 112 | a b c d | 132 | a b c d | 152 | a b c d | 172 | a b c d | 192 | a b c d |
| 113 | a b c d | 133 | a b c d | 153 | a b c d | 173 | a b c d | 193 | a b c d |
| 114 | a b c d | 134 | a b c d | 154 | a b c d | 174 | a b c d | 194 | a b c d |
| 115 | a b c d | 135 | a b c d | 155 | a b c d | 175 | a b c d | 195 | a b c d |
| 116 | a b c d | 136 | a b c d | 156 | a b c d | 176 | a b c d | 196 | a b c d |
| 117 | a b c d | 137 | a b c d | 157 | a b c d | 177 | a b c d | 197 | a b c d |
| 118 | a b c d | 138 | a b c d | 158 | a b c d | 178 | a b c d | 198 | a b c d |
| 119 | a b c d | 139 | a b c d | 159 | a b c d | 179 | a b c d | 199 | a b c d |
| 120 | a b c d | 140 | a b c d | 160 | a b c d | 180 | a b c d | 200 | a b c d |

# Actual Test 09

## LISTENING (Part I ~ IV)

| NO. | ANSWER | NO. | ANSWER | NO. | ANSWER | NO. | ANSWER | NO. | ANSWER |
|---|---|---|---|---|---|---|---|---|---|
| | A B C D | | A B C D | | A B C D | | A B C D | | A B C D |
| 1 | ⓐ ⓑ ⓒ | 21 | ⓐ ⓑ ⓒ ⓓ | 41 | ⓐ ⓑ ⓒ ⓓ | 61 | ⓐ ⓑ ⓒ ⓓ | 81 | ⓐ ⓑ ⓒ ⓓ |
| 2 | ⓐ ⓑ ⓒ | 22 | ⓐ ⓑ ⓒ ⓓ | 42 | ⓐ ⓑ ⓒ ⓓ | 62 | ⓐ ⓑ ⓒ ⓓ | 82 | ⓐ ⓑ ⓒ ⓓ |
| 3 | ⓐ ⓑ ⓒ | 23 | ⓐ ⓑ ⓒ ⓓ | 43 | ⓐ ⓑ ⓒ ⓓ | 63 | ⓐ ⓑ ⓒ ⓓ | 83 | ⓐ ⓑ ⓒ ⓓ |
| 4 | ⓐ ⓑ ⓒ | 24 | ⓐ ⓑ ⓒ ⓓ | 44 | ⓐ ⓑ ⓒ ⓓ | 64 | ⓐ ⓑ ⓒ ⓓ | 84 | ⓐ ⓑ ⓒ ⓓ |
| 5 | ⓐ ⓑ ⓒ | 25 | ⓐ ⓑ ⓒ ⓓ | 45 | ⓐ ⓑ ⓒ ⓓ | 65 | ⓐ ⓑ ⓒ ⓓ | 85 | ⓐ ⓑ ⓒ ⓓ |
| 6 | ⓐ ⓑ ⓒ | 26 | ⓐ ⓑ ⓒ ⓓ | 46 | ⓐ ⓑ ⓒ ⓓ | 66 | ⓐ ⓑ ⓒ ⓓ | 86 | ⓐ ⓑ ⓒ ⓓ |
| 7 | ⓐ ⓑ ⓒ | 27 | ⓐ ⓑ ⓒ | 47 | ⓐ ⓑ ⓒ ⓓ | 67 | ⓐ ⓑ ⓒ ⓓ | 87 | ⓐ ⓑ ⓒ ⓓ |
| 8 | ⓐ ⓑ ⓒ | 28 | ⓐ ⓑ ⓒ | 48 | ⓐ ⓑ ⓒ ⓓ | 68 | ⓐ ⓑ ⓒ ⓓ | 88 | ⓐ ⓑ ⓒ ⓓ |
| 9 | ⓐ ⓑ ⓒ | 29 | ⓐ ⓑ ⓒ | 49 | ⓐ ⓑ ⓒ ⓓ | 69 | ⓐ ⓑ ⓒ ⓓ | 89 | ⓐ ⓑ ⓒ ⓓ |
| 10 | ⓐ ⓑ ⓒ | 30 | ⓐ ⓑ ⓒ | 50 | ⓐ ⓑ ⓒ ⓓ | 70 | ⓐ ⓑ ⓒ ⓓ | 90 | ⓐ ⓑ ⓒ ⓓ |
| 11 | ⓐ ⓑ ⓒ | 31 | ⓐ ⓑ ⓒ | 51 | ⓐ ⓑ ⓒ ⓓ | 71 | ⓐ ⓑ ⓒ ⓓ | 91 | ⓐ ⓑ ⓒ ⓓ |
| 12 | ⓐ ⓑ ⓒ | 32 | ⓐ ⓑ ⓒ | 52 | ⓐ ⓑ ⓒ ⓓ | 72 | ⓐ ⓑ ⓒ ⓓ | 92 | ⓐ ⓑ ⓒ ⓓ |
| 13 | ⓐ ⓑ ⓒ | 33 | ⓐ ⓑ ⓒ | 53 | ⓐ ⓑ ⓒ ⓓ | 73 | ⓐ ⓑ ⓒ ⓓ | 93 | ⓐ ⓑ ⓒ ⓓ |
| 14 | ⓐ ⓑ ⓒ | 34 | ⓐ ⓑ ⓒ | 54 | ⓐ ⓑ ⓒ ⓓ | 74 | ⓐ ⓑ ⓒ ⓓ | 94 | ⓐ ⓑ ⓒ ⓓ |
| 15 | ⓐ ⓑ ⓒ | 35 | ⓐ ⓑ ⓒ | 55 | ⓐ ⓑ ⓒ ⓓ | 75 | ⓐ ⓑ ⓒ ⓓ | 95 | ⓐ ⓑ ⓒ ⓓ |
| 16 | ⓐ ⓑ ⓒ | 36 | ⓐ ⓑ ⓒ | 56 | ⓐ ⓑ ⓒ ⓓ | 76 | ⓐ ⓑ ⓒ ⓓ | 96 | ⓐ ⓑ ⓒ ⓓ |
| 17 | ⓐ ⓑ ⓒ | 37 | ⓐ ⓑ ⓒ | 57 | ⓐ ⓑ ⓒ ⓓ | 77 | ⓐ ⓑ ⓒ ⓓ | 97 | ⓐ ⓑ ⓒ ⓓ |
| 18 | ⓐ ⓑ ⓒ | 38 | ⓐ ⓑ ⓒ | 58 | ⓐ ⓑ ⓒ ⓓ | 78 | ⓐ ⓑ ⓒ ⓓ | 98 | ⓐ ⓑ ⓒ ⓓ |
| 19 | ⓐ ⓑ ⓒ | 39 | ⓐ ⓑ ⓒ | 59 | ⓐ ⓑ ⓒ ⓓ | 79 | ⓐ ⓑ ⓒ ⓓ | 99 | ⓐ ⓑ ⓒ ⓓ |
| 20 | ⓐ ⓑ ⓒ | 40 | ⓐ ⓑ ⓒ | 60 | ⓐ ⓑ ⓒ ⓓ | 80 | ⓐ ⓑ ⓒ ⓓ | 100 | ⓐ ⓑ ⓒ ⓓ |

## READING (Part V ~ VII)

| NO. | ANSWER | NO. | ANSWER | NO. | ANSWER | NO. | ANSWER | NO. | ANSWER |
|---|---|---|---|---|---|---|---|---|---|
| | A B C D | | A B C D | | A B C D | | A B C D | | A B C D |
| 101 | ⓐ ⓑ ⓒ ⓓ | 121 | ⓐ ⓑ ⓒ ⓓ | 141 | ⓐ ⓑ ⓒ ⓓ | 161 | ⓐ ⓑ ⓒ ⓓ | 181 | ⓐ ⓑ ⓒ ⓓ |
| 102 | ⓐ ⓑ ⓒ ⓓ | 122 | ⓐ ⓑ ⓒ ⓓ | 142 | ⓐ ⓑ ⓒ ⓓ | 162 | ⓐ ⓑ ⓒ ⓓ | 182 | ⓐ ⓑ ⓒ ⓓ |
| 103 | ⓐ ⓑ ⓒ ⓓ | 123 | ⓐ ⓑ ⓒ ⓓ | 143 | ⓐ ⓑ ⓒ ⓓ | 163 | ⓐ ⓑ ⓒ ⓓ | 183 | ⓐ ⓑ ⓒ ⓓ |
| 104 | ⓐ ⓑ ⓒ ⓓ | 124 | ⓐ ⓑ ⓒ ⓓ | 144 | ⓐ ⓑ ⓒ ⓓ | 164 | ⓐ ⓑ ⓒ ⓓ | 184 | ⓐ ⓑ ⓒ ⓓ |
| 105 | ⓐ ⓑ ⓒ ⓓ | 125 | ⓐ ⓑ ⓒ ⓓ | 145 | ⓐ ⓑ ⓒ ⓓ | 165 | ⓐ ⓑ ⓒ ⓓ | 185 | ⓐ ⓑ ⓒ ⓓ |
| 106 | ⓐ ⓑ ⓒ ⓓ | 126 | ⓐ ⓑ ⓒ ⓓ | 146 | ⓐ ⓑ ⓒ ⓓ | 166 | ⓐ ⓑ ⓒ ⓓ | 186 | ⓐ ⓑ ⓒ ⓓ |
| 107 | ⓐ ⓑ ⓒ ⓓ | 127 | ⓐ ⓑ ⓒ ⓓ | 147 | ⓐ ⓑ ⓒ ⓓ | 167 | ⓐ ⓑ ⓒ ⓓ | 187 | ⓐ ⓑ ⓒ ⓓ |
| 108 | ⓐ ⓑ ⓒ ⓓ | 128 | ⓐ ⓑ ⓒ ⓓ | 148 | ⓐ ⓑ ⓒ ⓓ | 168 | ⓐ ⓑ ⓒ ⓓ | 188 | ⓐ ⓑ ⓒ ⓓ |
| 109 | ⓐ ⓑ ⓒ ⓓ | 129 | ⓐ ⓑ ⓒ ⓓ | 149 | ⓐ ⓑ ⓒ ⓓ | 169 | ⓐ ⓑ ⓒ ⓓ | 189 | ⓐ ⓑ ⓒ ⓓ |
| 110 | ⓐ ⓑ ⓒ ⓓ | 130 | ⓐ ⓑ ⓒ ⓓ | 150 | ⓐ ⓑ ⓒ ⓓ | 170 | ⓐ ⓑ ⓒ ⓓ | 190 | ⓐ ⓑ ⓒ ⓓ |
| 111 | ⓐ ⓑ ⓒ ⓓ | 131 | ⓐ ⓑ ⓒ ⓓ | 151 | ⓐ ⓑ ⓒ ⓓ | 171 | ⓐ ⓑ ⓒ ⓓ | 191 | ⓐ ⓑ ⓒ ⓓ |
| 112 | ⓐ ⓑ ⓒ ⓓ | 132 | ⓐ ⓑ ⓒ ⓓ | 152 | ⓐ ⓑ ⓒ ⓓ | 172 | ⓐ ⓑ ⓒ ⓓ | 192 | ⓐ ⓑ ⓒ ⓓ |
| 113 | ⓐ ⓑ ⓒ ⓓ | 133 | ⓐ ⓑ ⓒ ⓓ | 153 | ⓐ ⓑ ⓒ ⓓ | 173 | ⓐ ⓑ ⓒ ⓓ | 193 | ⓐ ⓑ ⓒ ⓓ |
| 114 | ⓐ ⓑ ⓒ ⓓ | 134 | ⓐ ⓑ ⓒ ⓓ | 154 | ⓐ ⓑ ⓒ ⓓ | 174 | ⓐ ⓑ ⓒ ⓓ | 194 | ⓐ ⓑ ⓒ ⓓ |
| 115 | ⓐ ⓑ ⓒ ⓓ | 135 | ⓐ ⓑ ⓒ ⓓ | 155 | ⓐ ⓑ ⓒ ⓓ | 175 | ⓐ ⓑ ⓒ ⓓ | 195 | ⓐ ⓑ ⓒ ⓓ |
| 116 | ⓐ ⓑ ⓒ ⓓ | 136 | ⓐ ⓑ ⓒ ⓓ | 156 | ⓐ ⓑ ⓒ ⓓ | 176 | ⓐ ⓑ ⓒ ⓓ | 196 | ⓐ ⓑ ⓒ ⓓ |
| 117 | ⓐ ⓑ ⓒ ⓓ | 137 | ⓐ ⓑ ⓒ ⓓ | 157 | ⓐ ⓑ ⓒ ⓓ | 177 | ⓐ ⓑ ⓒ ⓓ | 197 | ⓐ ⓑ ⓒ ⓓ |
| 118 | ⓐ ⓑ ⓒ ⓓ | 138 | ⓐ ⓑ ⓒ ⓓ | 158 | ⓐ ⓑ ⓒ ⓓ | 178 | ⓐ ⓑ ⓒ ⓓ | 198 | ⓐ ⓑ ⓒ ⓓ |
| 119 | ⓐ ⓑ ⓒ ⓓ | 139 | ⓐ ⓑ ⓒ ⓓ | 159 | ⓐ ⓑ ⓒ ⓓ | 179 | ⓐ ⓑ ⓒ ⓓ | 199 | ⓐ ⓑ ⓒ ⓓ |
| 120 | ⓐ ⓑ ⓒ ⓓ | 140 | ⓐ ⓑ ⓒ ⓓ | 160 | ⓐ ⓑ ⓒ ⓓ | 180 | ⓐ ⓑ ⓒ ⓓ | 200 | ⓐ ⓑ ⓒ ⓓ |

# Actual Test 10

## LISTENING (Part I ~ IV)

| NO. | ANSWER | NO. | ANSWER | NO. | ANSWER | NO. | ANSWER | NO. | ANSWER |
|---|---|---|---|---|---|---|---|---|---|
| | A B C D | | A B C D | | A B C D | | A B C D | | A B C D |
| 1 | a b c d | 21 | a b c d | 41 | a b c d | 61 | a b c d | 81 | a b c d |
| 2 | a b c d | 22 | a b c d | 42 | a b c d | 62 | a b c d | 82 | a b c d |
| 3 | a b c d | 23 | a b c d | 43 | a b c d | 63 | a b c d | 83 | a b c d |
| 4 | a b c d | 24 | a b c d | 44 | a b c d | 64 | a b c d | 84 | a b c d |
| 5 | a b c d | 25 | a b c d | 45 | a b c d | 65 | a b c d | 85 | a b c d |
| 6 | a b c d | 26 | a b c d | 46 | a b c d | 66 | a b c d | 86 | a b c d |
| 7 | a b c d | 27 | a b c d | 47 | a b c d | 67 | a b c d | 87 | a b c d |
| 8 | a b c d | 28 | a b c d | 48 | a b c d | 68 | a b c d | 88 | a b c d |
| 9 | a b c d | 29 | a b c d | 49 | a b c d | 69 | a b c d | 89 | a b c d |
| 10 | a b c d | 30 | a b c d | 50 | a b c d | 70 | a b c d | 90 | a b c d |
| 11 | a b c d | 31 | a b c d | 51 | a b c d | 71 | a b c d | 91 | a b c d |
| 12 | a b c d | 32 | a b c d | 52 | a b c d | 72 | a b c d | 92 | a b c d |
| 13 | a b c d | 33 | a b c d | 53 | a b c d | 73 | a b c d | 93 | a b c d |
| 14 | a b c d | 34 | a b c d | 54 | a b c d | 74 | a b c d | 94 | a b c d |
| 15 | a b c d | 35 | a b c d | 55 | a b c d | 75 | a b c d | 95 | a b c d |
| 16 | a b c d | 36 | a b c d | 56 | a b c d | 76 | a b c d | 96 | a b c d |
| 17 | a b c d | 37 | a b c d | 57 | a b c d | 77 | a b c d | 97 | a b c d |
| 18 | a b c d | 38 | a b c d | 58 | a b c d | 78 | a b c d | 98 | a b c d |
| 19 | a b c d | 39 | a b c d | 59 | a b c d | 79 | a b c d | 99 | a b c d |
| 20 | a b c d | 40 | a b c d | 60 | a b c d | 80 | a b c d | 100 | a b c d |

## READING (Part V ~ VII)

| NO. | ANSWER | NO. | ANSWER | NO. | ANSWER | NO. | ANSWER | NO. | ANSWER |
|---|---|---|---|---|---|---|---|---|---|
| | A B C D | | A B C D | | A B C D | | A B C D | | A B C D |
| 101 | a b c d | 121 | a b c d | 141 | a b c d | 161 | a b c d | 181 | a b c d |
| 102 | a b c d | 122 | a b c d | 142 | a b c d | 162 | a b c d | 182 | a b c d |
| 103 | a b c d | 123 | a b c d | 143 | a b c d | 163 | a b c d | 183 | a b c d |
| 104 | a b c d | 124 | a b c d | 144 | a b c d | 164 | a b c d | 184 | a b c d |
| 105 | a b c d | 125 | a b c d | 145 | a b c d | 165 | a b c d | 185 | a b c d |
| 106 | a b c d | 126 | a b c d | 146 | a b c d | 166 | a b c d | 186 | a b c d |
| 107 | a b c d | 127 | a b c d | 147 | a b c d | 167 | a b c d | 187 | a b c d |
| 108 | a b c d | 128 | a b c d | 148 | a b c d | 168 | a b c d | 188 | a b c d |
| 109 | a b c d | 129 | a b c d | 149 | a b c d | 169 | a b c d | 189 | a b c d |
| 110 | a b c d | 130 | a b c d | 150 | a b c d | 170 | a b c d | 190 | a b c d |
| 111 | a b c d | 131 | a b c d | 151 | a b c d | 171 | a b c d | 191 | a b c d |
| 112 | a b c d | 132 | a b c d | 152 | a b c d | 172 | a b c d | 192 | a b c d |
| 113 | a b c d | 133 | a b c d | 153 | a b c d | 173 | a b c d | 193 | a b c d |
| 114 | a b c d | 134 | a b c d | 154 | a b c d | 174 | a b c d | 194 | a b c d |
| 115 | a b c d | 135 | a b c d | 155 | a b c d | 175 | a b c d | 195 | a b c d |
| 116 | a b c d | 136 | a b c d | 156 | a b c d | 176 | a b c d | 196 | a b c d |
| 117 | a b c d | 137 | a b c d | 157 | a b c d | 177 | a b c d | 197 | a b c d |
| 118 | a b c d | 138 | a b c d | 158 | a b c d | 178 | a b c d | 198 | a b c d |
| 119 | a b c d | 139 | a b c d | 159 | a b c d | 179 | a b c d | 199 | a b c d |
| 120 | a b c d | 140 | a b c d | 160 | a b c d | 180 | a b c d | 200 | a b c d |

# 토익 실전서는 이 책 한 권이면 충분합니다!

**시나공 혼자서 끝내는 토익**
## 950 실전 모의고사
고경희, 이관우 지음 | 728쪽 | 22,000원

---

## ········ 900은 기본, 만점까지 가능한 12회분, 2400제 수록! ········

**❶ 최신 경향을 반영한 12회분, 2400제 수록!**
최근 출제 경향을 완벽하게 반영한 2400제를 수록했습니다.

**❷ 친절한 해설집 온라인 무료 다운로드!**
필요한 문제만 간편하게 확인할 수 있게 해설집을 PDF로 제공합니다.

**❸ 만점 대비용 '독학용 복습 노트' 제공!**
저자들의 강의 노하우가 담긴 '만점 훈련용' 독학용 학습노트를 제공합니다.

> **LC** 저자의 수업 방식을 그대로 가져온 소리 통암기 훈련 및 MP3 제공
> **RC** 고득점을 좌우하는 어휘 문제를 통해 고난도 어휘 학습

**❹ 실전용, 복습용, 1.2배속, 고사장 소음버전 MP3 무료 다운로드!**
www.gilbut.co.kr에서 무료로 다운로드 하세요.

---

| 권장하는 점수대 | 400 | 500 | 600 | 700 | 800 | 900 |
|---|---|---|---|---|---|---|

| 이 책의 난이도 | 쉬움 | 비슷함 | 어려움 |
|---|---|---|---|